Simplified Pronunciation Symbols

(See the Introduction for detailed explanation)

Symbol	Example	as in
a A	FAD, ASK	f**a**d, **a**sk
ā Ā	FĀD	f**a**de
ah AH	BAH-thuhr, KAHT;	b**o**ther, c**o**t;
	FAH-thuhr, AHSK	f**a**ther, **a**sk
aw AW	KAWT, LAW	c**au**ght, l**aw**
b B	BID	**b**id
ch CH	CHIP	**ch**ip
d D	DID	**d**i**d**
e E	FED	f**e**d
ē Ē	BĒD	b**ea**d
f F	FIT	**f**it
g G	GET	**g**et
ḡ Ḡ	ah-ME-ḡō	Span. **amigo** (*Anglicized alternative* g)
h H	HED	**h**ead
hl HL	hlah-NEHL-ē	Welsh **Llanelli** (*Anglicized alternative* l *or* thl)
hw HW	HWET, HWICH	**wh**et, **wh**ich
i I	BID	b**i**d
ī Ī	BĪ, RĪD, LĪ	b**uy**, r**i**de, l**ie**
j J	JET	**j**et
k K	KIK, KUK	**k**i**ck**, **c**oo**k**
kh KH	BAHKH, IKH, LAHKH	Ger. **Bach**, i**ch**, Scottish **loch**.
l L	LEG, MID-l	**l**eg, midd**le**
m M	MEN	**m**en
n N	NET, KIT-n	**n**et, kitte**n**
ng NG	RING, RINGK	ri**ng**, ri**n**k
ō Ō	KŌT	c**oa**t
oi OI	BOI, KOIN	b**oy**, c**oi**n
o͞o O͞O	MO͞OD	m**oo**d
ow OW	OWT, NOW	**ou**t, n**ow**
p P	PIN, LIP	**p**in, li**p**
r R	RED, KAHRD	**r**ed, ca**r**d
s S	SIT	**s**it
t T	TŌ, SIT-ing	**t**oe, sit**t**ing
th TH	THIN	**th**in
th TH	THIS	**th**is
u U	GUD, PUT, PUR	g**oo**d, p**u**t, p**oo**r
ue UE	RUE, FUE-luhn;	Fr. **rue**, Ger. **fühlen**;
	FUEL-uhn	Ger. **füllen**
uh UH	buh-NAN-uh, BUHD	b**a**n**a**n**a**, b**u**d
uhr UHR	BET-uhr, BUHRD	bett**er**, b**ir**d
uh(r) UH(R)	BUH(R)F,	*Anglicization of* Fr. **boeuf**, Ger. **Hölle**.
	HUH(R)L-uh	
	FUH(R),	*Anglicization of* Fr. **feu**, Ger. **Höhle**.
	HUH(R)-luh	
v V	VET	**v**et
v V	ahv-LAHR	Span. **hablar** (*Anglicized alternative* b *or* v)
w W	WET, WICH	**w**et, **w**itch
y Y	YES	**y**es
z Z	ZIP	**z**ip
zh ZH	MEZH-uhr	mea**s**ure

Pronouncing Dictionary

of

Proper Names

Pronunciations for more than 23,000 Proper Names,
Selected for Currency, Frequency, or Difficulty of Pronunciation

*Including Place Names; Given Names; Names of Famous
Individuals; Cultural, Literary, and Historical Names;
Mythological Names; Names of Peoples and Tribes; Company
Names and Product Names; with Pronunciations Transcribed into
the International Phonetic Alphabet and a Simplified Phonetic
Respelling; and Including an Explanatory Introduction*

Editor:

John K. Bollard

Associate Editors:

Frank R. Abate and **Katherine M. Isaacs**

Omnigraph
Penobscot Building • Det

Editorial Staff

John K. Bollard, *Editor*

Frank R. Abate and Katherine M. Isaacs, *Associate Editors*

Rima McKinzey, *Contributing Editor*

Elaine Chasse, Jennifer Feola, Terri Finkeldey, Elizabeth Jewell,
Jane Wozniak, *Editorial Assistants*

Design Consultant: John F. Kallio

Computer Consultant: Stephen Bladey

Data Processing and Typesetting: Weimer Graphics, Inc.

Indianapolis, Ind.

Omnigraphics, Inc.

Eric F. Berger, *Vice President, Production*

Laurie Lanzen Harris, *Vice President, Editorial Director*

Peter E. Ruffner, *Vice President, Administration*

James A. Sellgren, *Vice President, Operations & Finance*

Frederick G. Ruffner, Jr., *Publisher*

Copyright © 1993 Omnigraphics, Inc.

Library of Congress Cataloging-in-Publication Data

Pronouncing dictionary of proper names : pronunciations for more than 23,000 proper names,
selected for currency, frequency, or difficulty of pronunciation / edited by John K. Bollard :
associate editors, Frank R. Abate and Katherine M. Isaacs.
    p.   cm.
    "Including place names; given names; names of famous individuals; cultural, literary, and
historical names; mythological names; names of peoples and tribes; company names and product
names; with pronunciations transcribed into the International Phonetic Alphabet and a
simplified phonetic respelling and including an explanatory introduction."
    ISBN 1-55888-311-8 (lib. bdg. : alk. paper)
    1. English language--Pronunciation--Dictionaries. 2. Names--Pronunciation.   I. Bollard,
John K.
PE1137.P82 1993   93-608
423'.1--dc20   CIP

Printed in the United States of America

Contents

Contents

Preface

In this world of instantaneous global communication, where national and international affairs are matters of daily concern and discussion, we find that our knowledge of geography, of well-known personages, and of other peoples and cultures can no longer be confined to the familiar. As a result, especially in the realm of names and proper nouns, we are often confronted with an uncertainty about pronunciation. How is a name to be pronounced, particularly if we have never heard it spoken aloud or if we are not sure of what we heard? English spelling is notorious for being only an approximate, often ambiguous indication of pronunciation, and proper names are particularly troublesome in this regard. Couple this with the need to talk about people, places, things, and ideas from around the world and it would seem that to sound well informed we ought to know not only English, but the rules for pronouncing more than a few other languages as well.

This *Pronouncing Dictionary of Proper Names* is designed to lessen this uncertainty by indicating acceptable pronunciations for a wide range of names that may not easily be found in other reference sources. Pronunciations appear both in a respelling system that should be "user-friendly" to the non-specialist, and in a version of the International Phonetic Alphabet (IPA), widely employed by linguists and other specialists.

The pronunciations shown in the *Pronouncing Dictionary of Proper Names* reflect the major variations in American dialects, and to the best of our ability we have represented the local or personal pronunciations used by those who live in a particular place or who themselves bear a particular name. We have drawn on a wide range of current reference books, studies of pronunciation in English and other languages, and on the actual pronunciations of those familiar with the person, place, or subject in question. Thus, we are confident that the users of the *Pronouncing Dictionary of Proper Names* will find it a reliable guide to the pronunciation of more than 23,000 names. Both common and unusual names may be found here, making this dictionary useful to native English speakers as well as to those who have learned or are learning English as a second or additional language.

I have enjoyed working with Frank Abate and Katherine Isaacs of Omnigraphics, who selected the bulk of the names for inclusion and who spent many hours refining the conception, layout, and design of this dictionary. A considerable debt of gratitude is also owed to Rima McKinzey, who read through and corrected the pronunciations with great skill and dispatch and made many valuable suggestions. Further improvements were made through an innovation used, we believe, for the first time in the preparation of any dictionary—pronunciations were actually "proof-listened." Through facilities made available by AT & T Bell Laboratories of Murray Hill, New Jersey, all pronunciations were actually *heard* using speech-synthesis technology. We are particularly grateful to Ken Church and Richard Sproat of Bell Labs for making the necessary arrangements.

Thanks also go to Dick Doll, Chuck Lacy, and the staff of Weimer Graphics, Inc. of Indianapolis, Ind., who, besides typesetting, developed the programming that automatically generated drafts of the simplified respellings used in this dictionary from formal IPA transcriptions (for further details, consult the **Introduction**). Their work transformed a collection of raw data into the pages you see here, and they accepted with graceful equanimity all the quirks, complexities, and problems we presented them with. Many friends and colleagues tolerated my frequent requests for information about pronunciations in their fields of knowledge or about places they have lived in or visited. Craig Davis of Smith College has freely shared his knowledge, linguistic expertise, and time in discussions of many names in a number of areas. Special thanks in this regard go to Dennis Hudson, also of Smith College, whose interests and understanding are wide-ranging and who has made both freely available to me; his contribution to this book is not limited to advice on the terminology of those world religions in which he is recognized as expert.

Finally, while living with any writer is trying, living with a lexicographer—who may seem more interested in words and isolated names rather than whole sentences or coherent ideas—must be doubly so. For her contribution to this book, for her patience, for her understanding of me if not always of my often obscure queries, and for her encouragement, mere thanks seem woefully inadequate, but they are offered here to my wife, Margaret Lloyd, as small recompense.

May 1993

John K. Bollard
Florence, Massachusetts

Introduction

The Pronouncing Dictionary of Proper Names (*PDPN*) provides pronunciations for some 23,000 names that are frequently encountered in speech and reading. Entries are briefly identified and current English pronunciations are shown both in a simplified phonetic respelling and in a formal transcription. In many cases alternative or variant pronunciations that may be considered as acceptable variants are also shown.

For foreign names not as widely known in English, it is assumed that the English-speaking users of this book will be interested in approximating the pronunciation of the language of origin, without being required to learn the intricacies of pronunciation for many different languages. The pronunciations given for such names enable the reader to do just this. Careful use of the transcriptions should result in an intelligent, acceptable English pronunciation of the name in question.

Selection Criteria

With the universe of proper names numbering in the many millions, clearly some criteria are needed to select the most useful entries and maintain a convenient size.

Frequency and Currency

Certain classes of items considered of primary interest for their frequency or currency are covered in depth. These include:

Countries of the world (and terms for inhabitants)
National capitals and other important cities
Principal landmarks
U.S. states, state capitals, and important cities
Common given names and surnames
Principal religions of the world
Principal languages of the world
Principal ethnic groups of the world

Names "Difficult to Pronounce"

For many of the entries in *PDPN*, inclusion was on the grounds of difficulty. The spelling of a name, even a fairly common American English name, is not always a clear indication of how it is pronounced. Certain names, those of foreign origin to a native speaker of English, perhaps many names to someone learning English, may be problematic. This is true especially when a name that one wishes to say has been encountered only in writing. Some of the more unusual or foreign-sounding names may cause difficulty or uncertainty even after one has heard them. *PDPN* provides a handy resource in such instances, providing a fully acceptable pronunciation—in an easy to use form—for thousands of troublesome names.

Categories of Names Covered

The following categories of names are covered in *PDPN*. In selecting individual entries for these categories, emphasis was on the criteria noted above—frequency, currency, and variation or troublesomeness of pronunciation for many speakers of English:

Given Names and Surnames: about 3,000 of the most common given names (including their non-English forms), and some 1,000 commonly encountered surnames

Geographic Names: historically and culturally significant cities, regions, provinces, states; noted buildings, streets, neighborhoods, stadiums; historical and cultural sites of importance

Geographical Features: mountains and mountain ranges, valleys, oceans and seas, rivers, lakes, deserts, etc.

People: famous and infamous individuals, both living and dead, particularly those whose names may be considered "difficult to pronounce"

Nature and the Environment: breeds of animals (dogs, cats, horses, etc.); major taxonomic groups (Arthropods, Echinoderms, etc.); names of dinosaurs; natural phenomena

History: peoples, cultures, tribes; dynasties and royal houses, kings, rulers

Politics and Current Affairs: national legislative bodies; parties and factions; news agencies and services; newspapers and magazines

Literature: authors and their works; settings, both fictional and real; literary characters

Religion: sects and denominations; sacred books (including books of the Bible); founders, prophets; popes; shrines and holy places

Philosophy: schools; philosophers; "-ologies & -isms"

Culture and the Arts: museums and works of art; musical works; groups, orchestras, ensembles; concert halls; holidays around the world; art/musical/cultural festivals; awards

Company and Product Names: especially if "difficult to pronounce"

Popular Culture: celebrities, products, and designers, especially if "difficult to pronounce"

Food and Drink: wines and spirits; brands of beer; famous dishes

Science and Technology: chemical elements; subatomic particles; units of measure; theories; "-ologies & -isms"; eponymic phrases, as for apparatus (e.g., Petri dish); aircraft; pronounced computer acronyms; computer languages; satellites; stars, planets, constellations, astronomical features and phenomena.

Cross References and Variant Spellings

Many names, especially foreign place names, appear in various forms, depending for instance on the source language and the manner in which the name has been anglicized, as in **Kraków/Cracow**. Some places, entities, and a number of people, too, have more than one name; **Beijing/Peiping/Peking**, **Cambodian/Khmer**, and *Kareem* **Abdul-Jabbar**/*Lew* **Alcindor** are familiar examples. Two types of cross reference are used to direct the reader to alternative names and variant spellings of names.

Cross references for alternative names are given in square brackets following the boldface headword:

Beijing [Peiping, Peking]
   city, China
Peiping [Beijing]
   city, China
Peking [Beijing]
   city, China

In some cases the cross reference is given only at the less common form, directing the reader to a more common or more fully anglicized form:

Makkah [Mecca]
   city, Saudi Arabia
Mecca
   city, Saudi Arabia, center of Islam

Square-bracketed cross-references always lead to entries with a different pronunciation. Many names, however, have variant spellings which represent the same pronunciation. Such variants are given at the main entry, separated by commas:

Betsey, Betsy
   pers. name

Sometimes only a part of the name is shown in order to indicate a spelling variation:

Tchaikovsky, Tsch-
   Peter Ilyich, *Russian composer*

If spelling variants do not fall in close alphabetical proximity, the variant spelling will be entered at its own place with a cross reference to the main entry given in the entry identification:

Tschaikovsky
   See **Tchaikovsky**

Entry Identifications

Each entry has brief entry identification on the line below. These identifications are intentionally very concise, and are meant only to specify the name being pronounced, not to define the name in detail.

Some abbreviated identifications are used, especially *pl. name*, for particularly common place (geographic) names. The identification *pers. name* is used for personal names, that is, both given names and surnames of people. For many non-English given names, the identification states the foreign language in which the name is so pronounced. Entries for surnames may also specify in the identification a particular individual (by given name) who has that surname. Entries for some unusual given names specify in the identification the surname of the individual who uses the given name being pronounced. The identification *pert. to* is used to refer not only to the adjectival forms of proper names, but also to indicate "demonyms" (names that are used for residents or inhabitants), or other relationships.

References to states of the United States use the standard two-letter postal abbreviations.

Variant Pronunciations

The pronunciations given in this book may be considered acceptable in American English, as judged by the editors. Where there are two or more pronunciations for a given entry, a more common pronunciation is given first, if that may be confidently determined. However, the widespread variation in the speech of American and other English speakers makes it difficult to assess the relative frequency of common, acceptable variants. In many cases pronunciation differences between two or more widely used dialects (for example, the dialects of the north-central U.S., eastern New England, the upper and lower South, and the Southwest—each spoken by millions of Americans) require the representation of two or more equally acceptable variants. A classic example is the name **Mary**.

In cases of foreign names, transcriptions that represent the pronunciation of the language of origin are given first, followed by anglicized versions, as at **Bach**. In cases where the first pronunciation shown for a non-English name differs markedly from or is not as common as other anglicized pronunciations, the subsequent anglicized variant or variants are preceded by a dollar sign, [$], to indicate that they are common U.S. pronunciations:

Cortés

Hernán *or* Hernando; *Spanish conquistador*	kawr-TĀS, [$] kawr-TEZ, KAWR-tez	kɔːrˈteːs, [$] kɔːʳtez, ˈkɔːʳˌtez

A number of names are pronounced significantly differently in the U.S. and Britain. In these cases a U.S. pronunciation is given first and the British version or versions are preceded by a pound sign, [£]:

Davies

family name	DĀ-vēz, [£] DĀ-vis	ˈdeːviːz, [£] ˈdeːvis

Two Pronunciation Systems

The *Pronouncing Dictionary of Proper Names* shows pronunciations in two different systems. A simplified pronunciation system, based on familiar conventions of English spelling, is shown in the middle (second) column of the text. The second system employs the alphabet of the International Phonetic Association (IPA), widely used by linguists and found in several standard dictionaries. Considerable attention has been given to making these systems comparable and compatible. Both show the same basic information, though the IPA provides more phonetic detail for those who are interested.

In the body of the book the two pronunciation respellings or transcriptions are shown in side-by-side columns. In the explanation of each system that follows, pairs of uprights | . . . | set off the simplified respellings; slash marks or virgules / . . . / enclose IPA transcriptions.

Simplified Pronunciation System

The simplified pronunciation system uses ordinary letters or combinations of letters to represent sounds. Diacritical marks and unusual symbols or combinations of letters are kept to a minimum; only a macron and an underline are used. As will be familiar to many from traditional practice, the macron |⁻| is used above vowels to represent the "long" vowels *e, i, o,* and *oo* (as in *beat, bite, boat,* and *boot*). Of course, as with any system, it will help to spend a few minutes learning the conventions used to represent sounds in *PDPN*. The simplified symbols are explained below.

Pronunciation Key

For quick reference, a summarized key to the simplified pronunciation system appears at the bottom of every text page in *PDPN*. The key indicates with an example word the sound represented by each of the simplified symbols. A fuller form of the key also appears on the inside front and back covers of *PDPN* and is also given below.

Stress

In simplified respellings, heavily stressed syllables are indicated by full-size capital letters: **Daisy** |DĀ-zē|, **Decatur** |di-KĀT-uhr|, **Arness** |ahr-NES|. Entries with one syllable are shown as stressed, that is, in all uppercase symbols. Though by its very nature stress is relative, any syllable spoken without context, as in a dictionary citation form, must be given some degree of stress. Thus, an isolated utterance of the name *Smith* is closer in sound to the first (stressed) syllable of *smithy* than to the second (unstressed) syllable of the phrase *blacksmith shop*. Thus, to show the pronunciation of *smithy* as |SMITH-ē| but *Smith* as |smith| would be both phonetically inconsistent and possibly confusing; hence the entry **Smith** |SMITH|.

Secondary, or lighter, stress is shown in small capital letters: **Stonehenge** |STŌN-HENJ|, **Alamo** |AL-uh-MŌ|.

In accordance with international usage, no stress is shown for languages such as Korean and Japanese, which have relatively equal stress on each syllable. Though French dictionaries generally show no stress, pronunciations of French names in *PDPN* are shown with stress indicated in the simplified version. This is in accord with the general impression of French pronunciation on the native English speaker's ear. No stress is shown in the corresponding IPA transcription of French names.

Simplified Pronunciation Symbols

The following lists, arranged more or less "alphabetically," include all of the symbols used in the simplified system. The list of English vowels and consonants is followed by a list of some non-English sounds. It is helpful to think of these characters as just symbols and not as letters of the alphabet. While a single letter of the alphabet may represent several different sounds in ordinary English spelling (for example, *a* in *act, ape, all, above; g* in *go, gin, beige*), each simplified pronunciation symbol has just the single sound value indicated below.

Symbol	Example	as in
a A	FAD, ASK	**fad, ask** } Some speakers use I ah I in *ask.*
ā Ā	FĀD	**fade**
ah AH	FAH-**th**uhr, AHSK	**father, ask** ⎱ Many U.S. speakers do not
	BAH-**th**uhr, KAHT	**bother, cot** ⎰ rhyme *father* and *bother;* see the IPA chart.
aw AW	KAWT, LAW	**caught, law** } Many U.S. speakers use I ah I in these words, rhyming *caught* with *cot.*
b B	BID	**bid**
ch CH	CHIP	**chip**
d D	DID	**did**
e E	FED	**fed**
ē Ē	BĒD	**bead**
f F	FIT	**fit**
g G	GET	**get**
h H	HED	**head**
hw HW	HWET, HWICH	**whet, which** } Many U.S. and British speakers pronounce these the same as *wet* and *witch.*
i I	BID	**bid**
ī Ī	BĪ, RĪD, LĪ	**buy, ride, lie**
j J	JET	**jet**
k K	KIK, KUK	**kick, cook**
l L	LEG, MID-l	**leg, middle**
m M	MEN	**men**
n N	NET, KIT-n	**net, kitten**
ng NG	RING, RINGK	**ring, rink**
ō Ō	KŌT	**coat**
oi OI	BOI, KOIN	**boy, coin**
o͞o O͞O	MO͞OD	**mood**
ow OW	OWT, NOW	**out, now**
p P	PIN, LIP	**pin, lip**
r R	RED, KAHRD	**red, card**
s S	SIT	**sit**
t T	TŌ, SIT-ing	**toe, sitting**
th TH	THIN	**thin**
th TH	THIS	**this**
u U	GUD, PUT, PUR	**good, put, poor**
uh UH	buh-NAN-uh, BUHD	**banana, bud**
uhr UHR	BET-uhr, BUHRD	**better, bird**
v V	VET	**vet**
w W	WET, WICH	**wet, witch**
y Y	YES	**yes**
z Z	ZIP	**zip**
zh ZH	MEZH-uhr	**measure**

Simplified Vowel Symbols

Most of the traditional "short" vowel sounds are represented by single letters. (There is no plain "o" symbol, as explained in the section on | ah | below.)

| a | as in *bat.*
| e | as in *bed.*
| i | as in *bid.*
| u | as in *good, put, full.*

The traditional "long" vowels are represented by single characters with macrons or by double characters.

| ā | as in *bake.*
| ē | as in *bead.*
| ī | as in *bide, lie.*
| ō | as in *boat.*
| o͞o | as in *food.* (The macron is used here to avoid confusion with the *oo* in *look.*)

A few additional vowel sounds are represented by double characters:

| ah | as in *father* and *bother.* The combination | ah | is used, rather than | o | because: (1) It avoids the misleading use of different symbols for the same sound. For example, for most Americans *Mach* rhymes with *mock*; hence | MAHK | for both, not | MAHK | for one and | MOK | for the other, as in some dictionaries. (2) It conforms to actual phonetic fact—for most U.S. speakers this is an unrounded vowel, that is, it is pronounced without a rounding of the lips associated with the letter "o". (3) It is more consistent with the spelling and pronunciation of a high percentage of names in *PDPN*, especially non-English names.

Most U.S. speakers rhyme the stressed vowels of *father* and *bother.* For those who do not rhyme these vowels, the distinction is shown in the IPA transcriptions. For example, the simplified respellings for these words would be | FAH<u>TH</u>-uhr | and | BAH<u>TH</u>-uhr |, whereas the IPA transcriptions would be /ˈfɑˈðəʳ/ (= /ˈfɑðəʳ, ˈfɑːðəʳ/) versus /ˈbɑðəʳ/, thus allowing for both rhyming and non-rhyming pronunciations. In any case, users of this book are simply recommended to use the sound suggested by the simplified respelling that is natural to their own speech and no confusion should occur.

| aw | as in *law* and *bought.* Many speakers in the U.S. do not rhyme *cot* and *caught*; we represent their differing pronunciations as | KAHT | and | KAWT |. But a great number of U.S. speakers (in eastern New England, western Pennsylvania, and increasingly elsewhere, particularly in the midwest, west, and southwest) do not distinguish between | ah | and | aw |. That is, they regularly rhyme such pairs as *cot—caught, collar—caller, hock—hawk, wok—walk,* and *stocking—stalking.* Such speakers will quite naturally interpret both | ah | and | aw | as the single sound they normally use.

| uh, UH | as in *banana* and *bud.* This symbol is used to represent the most frequent vowel sound in English, sometimes called the "neutral vowel." It is the vowel of the unstressed syllables in such words as <u>A</u>mer<u>i</u>c<u>a</u>, b<u>a</u>nan<u>a</u>, cab<u>i</u>net, nati<u>on</u>, comput<u>ed</u>, and b<u>e</u>liev<u>a</u>ble. In such unstressed syllables in the actual speech of many Americans this sound may vary from the vowel | uh | usually heard at the end of *sofa* to an

unstressed version of the I i I sound in *sit,* as often heard in the last syllable of *habit.* In some dictionaries the symbol /ə/, called "schwa," pronounced I SHWAH I, is used to represent this sound.

In stressed syllables I UH I represents the sound of the vowel of *bud* and *glove.* In most U.S. speech the quality of this stressed vowel is much the same as it is in unstressed positions, thus the simplified system uses the same symbol to represent this vowel in both situations.

I uhr, UHR I represents a vowel-consonant combination that has a vowel similar to I uh I and I UH I, but the presence of I r I changes the vowel sound to that heard in *sister, bird, work,* and *hurry.*

Familiar combinations are also used to show diphthongs:

I oi I as in *boy.*
I ow I as in *now.*

Simplified Consonant Symbols

The following characters represent the familiar and usual English sounds of the corresponding letter of the alphabet: I b, d, f, h, m, n, p, s, t, v, z I.

The remaining consonant symbols may be described as follows:

I ch I as in *chip.* (This is actually a combination of two sounds: I t I + I sh I.)

I g I as in *get, game* (never as in *gem*). See I j I.

I hw I as in *whet, which* when pronounced differently than *wet, witch.* Many U.S. and British speakers do not have I hw I in their speech; such speakers pronounce both *wet* and *whet* as I WET I.

I j I as in *jet, gem.* (This is actually a combination of two sounds: I d I + I zh I.)

I l I as in *leg, miller,* and *middle.*

In Polish there are two distinct I l I sounds. The simplified system represents both of these as I l I. Polish names spelled with an ordinary *l* are pronounced with the tongue-tip I l I heard in English *lily;* Polish names spelled with the slant-crossed *ł* (called barred l) are pronounced with an I l I produced farther back on the tongue, as in some pronunciations of English *pool.* The latter sound may be approximated in Polish names by using a I w I, as in **Czesław** I CHES-lahf I or I CHES-wahf I, and **Wałesa** I vah-LE^n-suh I or I vah-WE^n-suh I. This Polish back *l* is represented as /ł/ in IPA.

I ng I as in *ring, rink.* This is actually a single sound, not two; compare *singer* I SING-uhr I and *finger* I FING-guhr I.

I r I as in *red, card.* The pronunciation of speakers who do not pronounce I r I before another consonant or a pause is not represented in the simplified respellings, though it is indicated in the IPA transcriptions. See /^{r}/ in the IPA section below. In French and Portuguese, I r I is frequently made with the uvula, at the back of the mouth. In many other languages it is trilled or is pronounced by tapping the tip of the tongue just once behind the teeth, as it is in Spanish and in many British and Scots dialects. To indicate the tapped I r I, as opposed to the usual U.S. retroflex I r I, some American cartoonists spell the British pronunciation of *very* as "veddy."

This is similar to the voiced tap of the tongue heard in both *ladder* and *latter* in most U.S. dialects.

I sh I as in *show*. This is actually a single sound, not two.

I th I as in *thin*. This is actually a single sound, not two. It is an "unvoiced" *th,* that is, the *th* sound is made without vibration of the vocal cords.

I th I as in *this*. This is actually a single sound, not two. It is a "voiced" *th,* that is, the *th* sound is made with vibration of the vocal cords. Note the use of the underline to indicate voicing, as distinct from unvoiced I th I without the underline.

I w I as in *wet*. When shown without a vowel symbol preceding it in the same syllable, this symbol represents consonantal *w*. There is no consonantal I w I in the simplified symbols I aw I and I ow I.

I y I as in *yes*. Always represents the consonant *y*, never a vowel sound as in the *y* at the end of *city*.

I zh I as in *measure*. This is actually a single sound, not two.

Some Non-English Vowels and Consonants

Special symbols or combinations of symbols, some with macrons or underlining, are used to indicate several sounds that are present in foreign names, though not commonly used in English.

Simplified	Examples	
ḡ Ḡ	ah-ME-ḡō	Span. **amigo**; *Anglicized alternative:* I g I.
hl HL	hlah-NEHL-ē	Welsh **Llanelli**; *Anglicized alternative:* I l I *or* I thl I.
kh KH	BAHKH, IKH, LAHKH	Ger. **Bach**, **ich**, Scottish **loch**.
n	BAWⁿ	*after a nasalized vowel, as in* Fr. **bon**; *Anglicized alternative:* I n I.
ue UE	rue, FUE-luhn FUEL-uhn	Fr. **rue**, Ger. **fühlen**. Ger. **füllen**.
uh(r) UH(R)	BUH(R)F, HUH(R)L-uh	*Anglicization of* Fr. **boeuf**, Ger. **Hölle**.
	FUH(R), HUH(R)-luh	*Anglicization of* Fr. **feu**, Ger. **Höhle**.
v V	ahv-LAHR	Span. **hablar**; *Anglicized alternative:* I b I or I v I.

Non-English Sounds

l ḡ l as in Spanish *amigo*. This consonant is pronounced much like l g l, except that the flow of air is never completely stopped as it is with English l g l. It is similar to l kh l but with vibration of the vocal cords. In most English contexts l g l is an acceptable alternative.

l hl l as in Welsh *Llanelli*. This is a voiceless *l* produced by placing the tongue in the position for l l l and simply blowing air past the side of the tongue; the l l l of English *clean* is very similar. Many English speakers substitute either a regular English l l l or the combination l thl l; thus *Llanelli* l hlah-NEHL-ē l could be anglicized as l thlah-NETH-lē l or l la-NEL-ē l

l kh l as in Ger. *Bach, ich,* Scots *loch.* In German there are two distinct phonemes (sounds that differentiate words) in *Bach* and *ich,* but the distinction is not usually maintained in English. In *PDPN* the difference is indicated only in the IPA transcriptions. These consonants are pronounced much like the l k l in *book* and *beak,* except that the flow of air is never completely stopped as it is with l k l. In most English contexts l k l is an acceptable alternative; when spelled *H* or *Ch* at the beginning of a word, as in *Hanukkah* or *Chanukah,* l h l is an acceptable alternative.

l ⁿ l as in French *bon* or *Mont Blanc.* The raised *n* does not itself stand for a sound; rather it indicates that the preceding vowel (or occasionally diphthong) is nasalized—that is, pronounced with the nasal passages open.

l ue, UE l The vowel shown as /yː/ in IPA, represented by the *ue* of French *rue* and the *üh* of German *fühlen,* is shown as l ue, UE l in the simplified system. It can be approximated in English by pronouncing the *ee* of *feel* while keeping the lips fully rounded as in the vowel sound of *fool.*

The vowel shown as /y/ in IPA, represented by the *ü* of German *füllen,* is also shown as l ue, UE l in the simplified system. It can be approximated by pronouncing the *i* of *fill* while keeping the lips somewhat rounded as in the vowel sound of *full.*

Some common anglicizations of these sounds are l ē l, l i l, l u l, l yo͞o l, and l yu l.

l uh(r), UH(R) l The vowel shown as /œ/ in IPA, as in French *boeuf,* German *Hölle,* is similar to the vowel of English *bird,* without the l r l sound. In the simplified respellings it is anglicized to l uh(r), UH(R) l. It can be more closely approximated by pronouncing the *e* of *bed* with the lips somewhat rounded as in *bought.*

The vowel shown as /œː/ in IPA, as in French *feu,* German *Höhle,* is similar to the sound above and is similarly anglicized. It can be approximated by pronouncing the *ay* of *hay* while keeping the lips fully rounded as in the vowel sound of *hoe.*

l v̱ l as in Spanish *hablar* is produced with the two lips, rather than with the upper teeth and lower lip as in English l v l. In most English contexts either a l b l or a l v l is an acceptable alternative.

Pronunciations in the
International Phonetic Alphabet (IPA)

In 1888 the International Phonetic Association (IPA) was formed and its members devised a phonetic alphabet for representing the pronunciation of any language. The basic principles for this alphabet are that each symbol stands for only one sound, each sound is represented by only one symbol, and the symbols are based on the shapes of characters in the Roman alphabet (insofar as is possible). The transcriptions appearing in the third column in the text of *PDPN* employ a version of the IPA alphabet that is familiar to many linguists. In this introduction, IPA transcriptions are enclosed in slant lines / . . . /; square brackets [. . .] are occasionally used to discuss a degree of phonetic or dialectal variation implied by the IPA symbols as they are used in *PDPN*.

While the basic pronunciation information provided by both the simplified and IPA systems is compatible, the IPA transcriptions show more phonetic detail and dialectal variation than is possible in the simplified versions. These differences are outlined below, as are the particular conventions of IPA transcriptions used in *PDPN*.

The IPA transcriptions in *PDPN* are *broadly phonemic;* that is, each symbol represents a sound that is a phoneme (a meaningfully significant unit of sound) in some or all dialects of English. By the very nature of a wide-ranging dictionary of names, it is also necessary to include a few symbols to represent sounds not commonly found as phonemes in English words or names but that are phonemes in other languages. These have been kept to a minimum, and anglicized equivalents are either shown explicitly in both IPA and simplified columns, or the IPA symbols may be rendered as anglicizations in the simplified respelling column.

Regional or Dialectal Variation

In the IPA transcriptions in *PDPN*, variation in the regional or dialectal use or distribution of phonemes is explicitly shown, for there is no single variety of speech in the U.S. that is standard for the whole country. For example, **Quincy** is pronounced /ˈkwin(t)siˑ/ in some parts of the U.S. and /ˈkwinziˑ/ in others; **Gary** is pronounced /ˈgæriˑ/ by some speakers and /ˈgeriˑ/ by others. In such cases, variant pronunciations are shown in *PDPN*. However, regional or dialectal differences in the actual *sound* of each phoneme usually remain implicit. A native speaker of English using *PDPN* will interpret each symbol in phonetic accord with his or her natural speech, depending on the context. For example, the pronunciation of the phoneme /i/ in *bid* varies regionally in American English. Millions of speakers, especially in the northern half of the U.S., pronounce *bid* as a simple monophthong: /ˈbid/. But millions of other speakers, especially in the southeastern states, pronounce *bid* as a single syllable with a diphthongal glide: [ˈbiəd]. The IPA transcription for *bid* in *PDPN* would be /ˈbid/, which users will naturally and automatically interpret appropriately for their own dialects. Non-native speakers of English, of course, will approximate the pronunciation of whatever variety of English they have learned or are learning to use.

Such phonetic differences are part of what gives our language the rich variety and range of character that it enjoys. *Any* transcription can only be a partial representation of the living sounds of the language. Even though *PDPN* does not explicitly represent variation at this level of narrow phonetic detail, users still will be able to reproduce pronunciations that are both widely acceptable and consistent with their own natural speech.

Stress in IPA Transcriptions

In IPA, primary stress is indicated by a raised mark and secondary stress by a lowered one: **Daisy** /ˈdeːziˌ/, **Decatur** /diˈkeːt̮əʳ/, **Alamo** /ˈæləˌmoː/, **Stonehenge** /ˈstoːnˌhendʒ/. Single syllable entries are generally transcribed with primary stress on the understanding that, though stress is relative, the utterance of an isolated form without the context of running speech requires a degree of stress comparable to that of a relatively stressed syllable in context, as in *Smith* /ˈsmiθ/ and *smithy* /ˈsmiθiˌ/. In accord with international practice, no stress is shown in those languages, such as French, Japanese, and Korean, which have relatively level stress or stress that is variable according to context in a sentence.

Vowels in IPA Transcriptions

The following discussion of vowels will outline briefly the phonetic production of vowel sounds and will note the significance of any relevant IPA diacritic marks used with them.

IPA	Example	as in
æ	ˈfæd, ˈæsk	f<u>a</u>d, <u>a</u>sk
ɑ	ˈbɑðəʳ, ˈkɑt, ˈfɑðəʳ	b<u>o</u>ther, c<u>o</u>t, f<u>a</u>ther
ɑː	ˈfɑːðəʳ, ˈɑːsk	f<u>a</u>ther, <u>a</u>sk
ɑi	ˈbɑi, ˈrɑid	b<u>uy</u>, r<u>i</u>de
ɑu	ˈbɑu, ˈnɑu	b<u>ough</u>, n<u>ow</u>
e	ˈfed	f<u>e</u>d
eː	ˈfeːd	f<u>ade</u>
i	ˈbid	b<u>i</u>d
iː	ˈbiːd	b<u>ea</u>d
oː	ˈkoːt	c<u>oa</u>t
ɔː	ˈkɔːt, ˈlɔː	c<u>au</u>ght, l<u>aw</u>
ɔi	ˈbɔi, ˈkɔin	b<u>oy</u>, c<u>oin</u>
u	ˈgud, ˈput, puʳ	g<u>oo</u>d, p<u>u</u>t, p<u>oor</u>
uː	ˈmuːd, ˈmjuːzik	m<u>oo</u>d, m<u>u</u>sic
ə	bəˈnænə, ˈbəd	b<u>a</u>nana, b<u>u</u>d
əʳ	ˈbəʳd, ˈbət̮əʳ	b<u>ir</u>d, butt<u>er</u>

IPA Vowel Symbols

A vowel is produced when sound generated by the vocal cords passes through the mouth without significant obstruction. The sound of a particular vowel is determined by a number of factors, among the more important of which are the shape of the mouth cavity and the position of the tongue and lips. The height of the tongue within the central mouth area plays a major role in the differing pronunciation of vowels. Thus, the vowels are usually classified as low, mid, or high, and as front, central, or back, according to the position of the highest part of the tongue when the vowel is sounded.

For example, in the high front vowel of *beat* the tongue is raised close to the upper front of the mouth cavity. For the low front vowel of *bat* the mouth is open wider and the tongue lowered; for *bought* the tongue is low and moved farther toward the back of the mouth. In English the back vowels are generally accompanied by some degree of lip-rounding. Thus, a doctor asks a patient to say "Ah" in order to examine the patient's throat, for in pronouncing that low central vowel the mouth is open wide, the tongue is lowered, and the lips are unrounded.

This can be elucidated by the use of a diagram. **Diagram 1** represents a schematic vertical cross-section of the central mouth cavity. The front of the mouth is toward the left of the diagram; the back is toward the right. (For ease of reference, the diagram is divided accordingly and the resulting boxes are numbered from 1 to 9.)

For the present discussion, the vowels of American English are classified into two broad categories: simple vowels, as in *bit, bet, bat, pot, put,* and *but,* and augmented

Diagram 1: The Vowel Chart

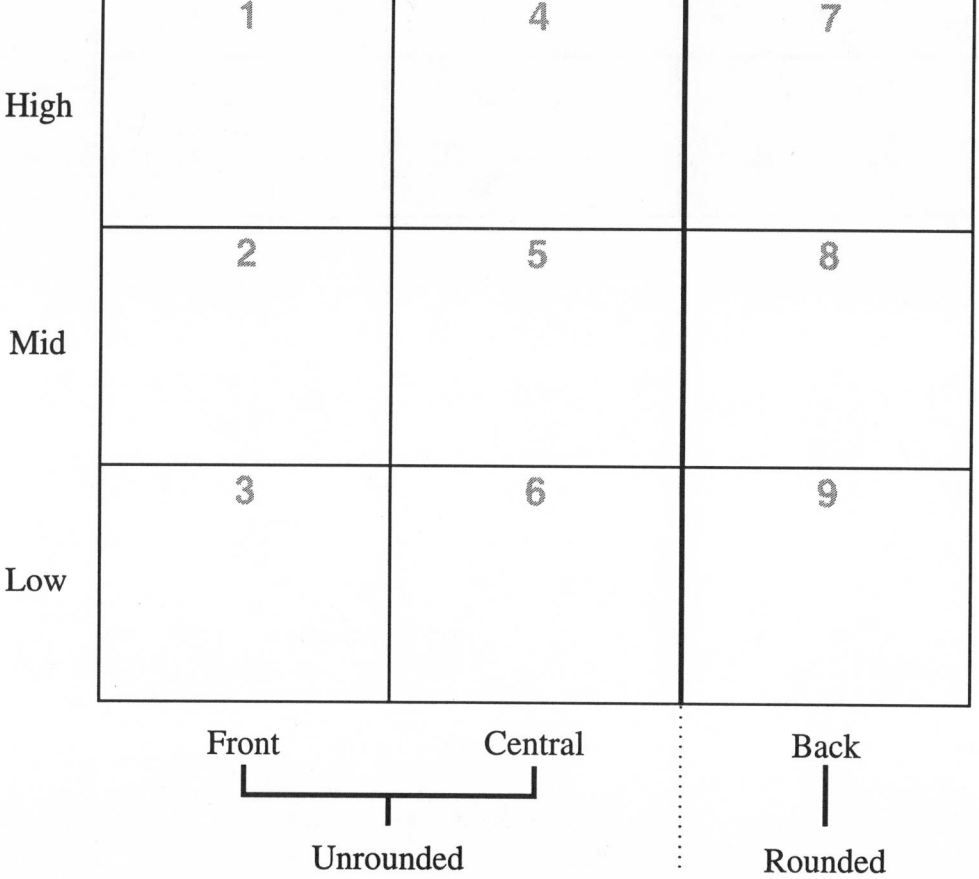

vowels, as in *beat, bait, bought, boat, boot,* and *bird.* These two categories are discussed below.

Simple Vowels

The simple vowels, traditionally called "short vowels," are sometimes called *lax vowels* because the muscle of the tongue is relatively relaxed when they are spoken. They are also called *checked vowels* because, with the exception of /ə/, they do not usually occur at the end of a word or syllable. That is, checked vowels are almost always followed by a consonant, as in *bit, bet, bat, hot,* and *put.* **Diagram 2** shows the relative positions of the simple vowels.

1. /i/ as in *bit.*

2. /e/ as in *bet.* The symbol /ẽ/ with the tilde indicating nasalization is used to represent the nasalized vowel heard in French *vin* /ˈvẽ/; to American ears this vowel might sound closer to the vowel of *bat,* as in [ˈvæ̃], but since in *PDPN* this vowel occurs most frequently in French names, the symbol /ẽ/ is used to accord with French practice.

Diagram 2: The Simple Vowels

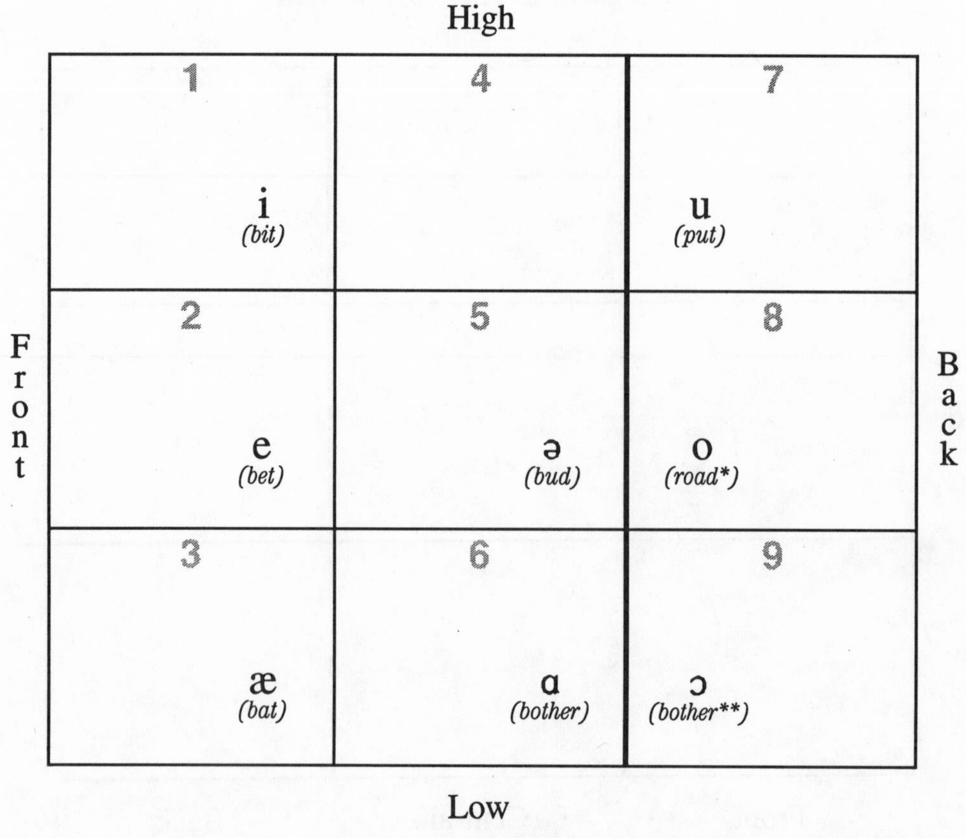

High

1	4	7
i *(bit)*		u *(put)*
2	5	8
e *(bet)*	ə *(bud)*	o *(road*)*
3	6	9
æ *(bat)*	ɑ *(bother)*	ɔ *(bother**)*

F
r
o
n
t   B
a
c
k

Low

*   eastern New England (in certain names)
** British

3. /æ/ as in *bat.*

4. The high central vowel, represented in IPA by [ɨ], is not phonemic in English; that is, it does not contrast with other vowel sounds to make different English words. Nor is it necessary to show a distinction in *PDPN* for languages in which [ɨ] may be phonemic, for the distinction would be lost on English speakers, who regularly and quite adequately anglicize and interpret it as /i/ or /ə/. Therefore, no high central vowel symbol is used in *PDPN.*

5. /ə/ as in *but* and the second vowel of *sofa.* Some transcribers use /ʌ/ to represent the mid-central stressed vowel and reserve /ə/ for the so-called "neutral" vowel in unstressed positions. However, in most American speech the quality of the mid-central vowel does not vary significantly as a result of stress alone and the single symbol /ə/ is sufficient. Thus, in *PDPN* /ə/ is used to represent the mid-central vowel in both stressed and unstressed syllables. Because of its frequency in unstressed syllables, the vowel /ə/ is the most common vowel in American English. The actual phonetic realization of unstressed /ə/ varies considerably depending both on dialect and on the sounds it occurs in conjunction with. For example, the final vowel of *pages* may range from [ə] to [i], though a transcription in *PDPN* would show only /ˈpeːdʒəz/.

6. /ɑ/ as in *hot, cod.* Those speakers, particularly in eastern New England and southern Britain, who have a low, back, somewhat rounded vowel [ɔ] for these words will automatically interpret the symbol /ɑ/ as [ɔ] in accordance with their own speech; see /ɔ/ below. The symbol /ɑ/ also represents the sound of *â* in French *château* and of *a* in Spanish *hablar.*

　　The symbol /ɑ̃/ with the tilde indicating nasalization is used to represent the nasalized vowel heard in French *blanc* /blɑ̃/.

7. /u/ as in *put, good.*

8. /o/ is phonemic American English only in the older speech of New England, where it distinguishes *road* /ˈrod/ from *rode* /ˈroːd/. Even in New England this distinction is rapidly disappearing, and it is reflected in *PDPN* transcriptions only occasionally (as at the entry for **Holyoke**) in names where it is fairly common locally, but even there only in free variation with /oː/.

9. /ɔ/ as in eastern New England or British *pot, cod, bother.* This rounded low back vowel occurs as a phoneme in some English dialects, resulting in distinct vowels in *cart* /ˈkɑːt/ and *cot* /ˈkɔt/. The great majority of U.S. speakers, however, have only one vowel, /ɑ/, in these words *cart* /ˈkɑrt/ and *cot* /ˈkɑt/; hence /ɔ/ is not used in *PDPN.* Speakers with the rounded [ɔ] in their speech will interpret /ɑ/ as [ɔ] where appropriate for their dialect—usually where it is spelled with an *o.* However, the phonemic vowel contrast in such pairs as *cart—cot, heart—hot,* and *father—bother* for such speakers is, indeed, represented in *PDPN* as explained below in the discussions of /ɑː/ and /r/. Some other languages do contrast /ɔ/ and /ɔː/ phonemically, but since most U.S. speakers do not have such a contrast /ɔː/ is used throughout *PDPN;* see /ɔː/ below.

　　The symbol /ɔ̃/ with the tilde indicating nasalization is used to represent the nasalized vowel heard in French *bon* /bɔ̃/.

Augmented Vowels

The augmented vowels, many of which are traditionally called "long vowels," may be thought of as similar to the corresponding simple vowels with the addition of one or more features. This augmentation is indicated by the use of a special colon /ː/ in conjunction with a simple vowel symbol. In general, the augmented vowels are produced with the tongue more tense than for the simple vowels. Hence the augmented vowels are often referred to as *tense vowels.* They may also be referred to as *free vowels,* because they occur at the end of words or syllables, as in *play, see,* and *blue.* Another common feature in English is some degree of diphthongization or movement of the tongue from one position to another. Also, the augmented front vowels are usually produced farther forward in the mouth than the corresponding simple vowels. The back vowels are usually pronounced farther back, with the addition of greater lip-rounding.

NOTE: In *PDPN* the half-colon /ˑ/ is used to indicate that in some speech a simple vowel is heard and in other speech the corresponding augmented vowel is heard. It might be thought of as the shorthand equivalent of an IPA colon in parenthesis. Thus, transcriptions such as /ˈsiti̭ˑ/ for *city* (=/ˈsiti̭(ː)/) indicate that some speakers say /ˈsiti̭ː/ and others say /ˈsiti̭/.

Diagram 3 adds the augmented vowels to the schematic outline of simple vowels. This shows the relative positions of the augmented vowels both to each other and to the simple vowels.

The augmented vowels in English are often diphthongal; that is, the vowel begins with the mouth and tongue in one position and ends after a change in their position. When it occurs, this movement begins at or near the position for the corresponding simple vowel and moves upward and toward the front or back as indicated in **Diagram 3.** For instance the vowel of *late* /leɪt/ is actually [ei] in most (but not all) U.S. speech, beginning at the position of /e/ and moving toward /i/ or even /iː/. This diphthongization is shown in square brackets in the explanations below. In many other languages the augmented vowels are true monophthongs, articulated at a higher and/or more tense position than the corresponding simple vowel.

1. /iː/ as in *beat.*

2. /eː/ as in *bait.* Often pronounced in English as [ei], in other languages as monophthongal [eː].

3. /æː/ as in *cab* or *can* ("to preserve") in dialects that distinguish the two senses of *can* in "Let's can [ˈkæːn] what we can [ˈkæn]." This vowel is often realized as [æə] or [æi]. /æː/ is not used in *PDPN* because its phonemic status is uncertain and limited in its geographic distribution and even there restricted to a very few items (and perhaps then only in careful speech), such as *can* "to preserve" vs. *can* "to be able" and *halve* vs. *have.* In most U.S. speech [æː] occurs as a positional variant of /æ/ in certain phonetic contexts—most notably before nasals, as in *man* and *ham.*

4. The high central augmented vowel, represented in IPA by /ɨː/, is not phonemic in English and is, therefore, not used in *PDPN*; see the note on the simple vowel 4 /ɨ/ above.

5. /ɝː/ as in *bird.* The presence of *r* after a vowel and before a consonant or pause has the effect of constricting the tongue (drawing it back or lowering it and bending back the tongue tip), thus affecting the quality of the preceding vowel. In dialects in which preconsonantal or prepausal *r* is not pronounced as /r/, the mid-central vowel

Diagram 3: The Augmented & Simple Vowels

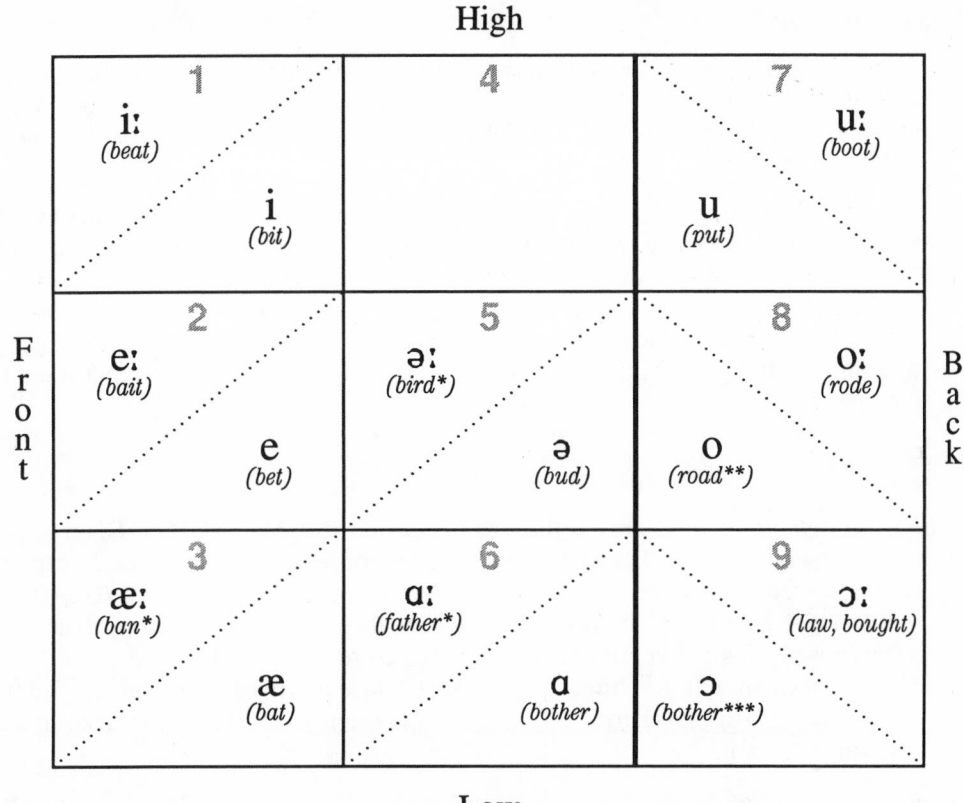

High

1 iː *(beat)* — i *(bit)*	**4**	**7** uː *(boot)* — u *(put)*
2 eː *(bait)* — e *(bet)*	**5** əː *(bird*)* — ə *(bud)*	**8** oː *(rode)* — o *(road**)*
3 æː *(ban*)* — æ *(bat)*	**6** ɑː *(father*)* — ɑ *(bother)*	**9** ɔː *(law, bought)* — ɔ *(bother***)*

Front ... Back

Low

*   in some dialects
**   eastern New England (in certain names)
***   British

of *bird* /ˈbəːd/ is distinct from the vowel of *bud* /ˈbəd/; in comparison with the latter, the vowel of *bird* /ˈbəːd/ is raised and/or lengthened in duration, as well as affected by the shift in the position and tenseness of the tongue. The pronunciation of those who do pronounce this *r* may be represented simply as /ˈbərd/. In *PDPN* a transcription such as /ˈbəᵊrd/ for *Byrd* indicates that many speakers pronounce /ˈbərd/, and many others pronounce /ˈbəːd/; see /ʳ/ below.

In some New York City speech and in parts of the southeastern U.S., /əː/ may be diphthongized in the direction of /i/, resulting in [əi]. Those who do not use this diphthongized vowel often comment on it or satirize it as *boid* or *Boyd* for *bird,* though only for a very small and diminishing number of New Yorkers is *bird* actually realized as /ˈbɔid/; other New Yorkers will differentiate *Boyd* /ˈbɔid/ and *bird* [ˈbəid] = /ˈbəːd/. In the southeastern U.S. *Boyd* and *bird* are always distinct.

6. /ɑ/ as in *father* in the speech of those who do not rhyme it with *bother* and in *ask* in the speech of those who use a vowel distinct from that in *black*. This is also the vowel of French *patte*. The vowel /ɑː/ is also to be understood as the alternative to

/ɑr/ for those speakers who do not pronounce preconsonantal or prepausal *r*. Thus /ˈpɑʳk/ for *park* indicates that some speakers say /ˈpɑrk/ and others say /ˈpɑːk/; see /ʳ/ below.

7. /uː/ as in *boot*.

8. /oː/ as in *slow, coat*. Usually pronounced as diphthongal [ou] in U.S. speech. In educated southern British speech /oː/ is often realized as [əu]. In other languages /oː/ is usually monophthongal [oː], i.e., a rounded mid back vowel that does not move in the direction of /u/.

9. /ɔː/ as in *bought, caught, caller* in the speech of those who do not rhyme these with *cot* and *collar*. The growing number of U.S. speakers in eastern New England, western Pennsylvania, the midwest, west, and southwest who *do* rhyme such pairs as *cot—caught* and *collar—caller* will interpret /ɔː/ as their own appropriate variety of /ɑ/. In some dialects, such as in the southeastern U.S., /ɔː/ is often diphthongal [ou]; in some northeastern dialects it is often strongly rounded and sometimes diphthongized as [ɔːə].

Diphthongs

1. /ɑi/ as in *sigh, night, buy*. This diphthong begins in the area of box 6 in **Diagram 4** and moves toward or into that of box 1. In some southeastern U.S. speech, especially before voiced consonants such as /d/ or /z/ in contrast to unvoiced /t/ or /s/, the diphthongal movement is minimal or even absent, though in compensation the onset vowel [ɑ] is either lengthened or raised to /ɑː/ or both lengthened and raised. Thus, in such speech *tide* /ˈtɑid/ (= [ˈtɑˑd,ˈtɑːd]) does not rhyme with either *Tod* /ˈtɑd/ or *Tad* /ˈtæd/. This southern version of /ɑi/ is often parodied or satirized by those who do not use it.

2. /ɑu/ as in *now, house, out*. This diphthong begins in the area of box 6 in **Diagram 4** and moves toward or into that of box 7. In some dialects, such as parts of Canada and the upper midwestern U.S., and parts of Virginia, when it occurs before voiceless consonants such as /s/ or /t/ (e.g. in *house* and *out*), this diphthong is realized as [əu], which others may interpret as /oː/. The symbol /ɑũ/ with the tilde indicating nasalization is used to represent the nasalized diphthong in Portuguese *são* /ˈsɑũ/.

3. /ɔi/ as in *boy, coin*. This diphthong begins in the area of box 9 in **Diagram 4** and moves toward or into that of box 1. In dialects or utterances where the diphthongal movement does not actually reach the position of /i/ in box 1, this diphthong may be realized as [ɔə] or [ɔːə].

Diagram 4: The Diphthongs

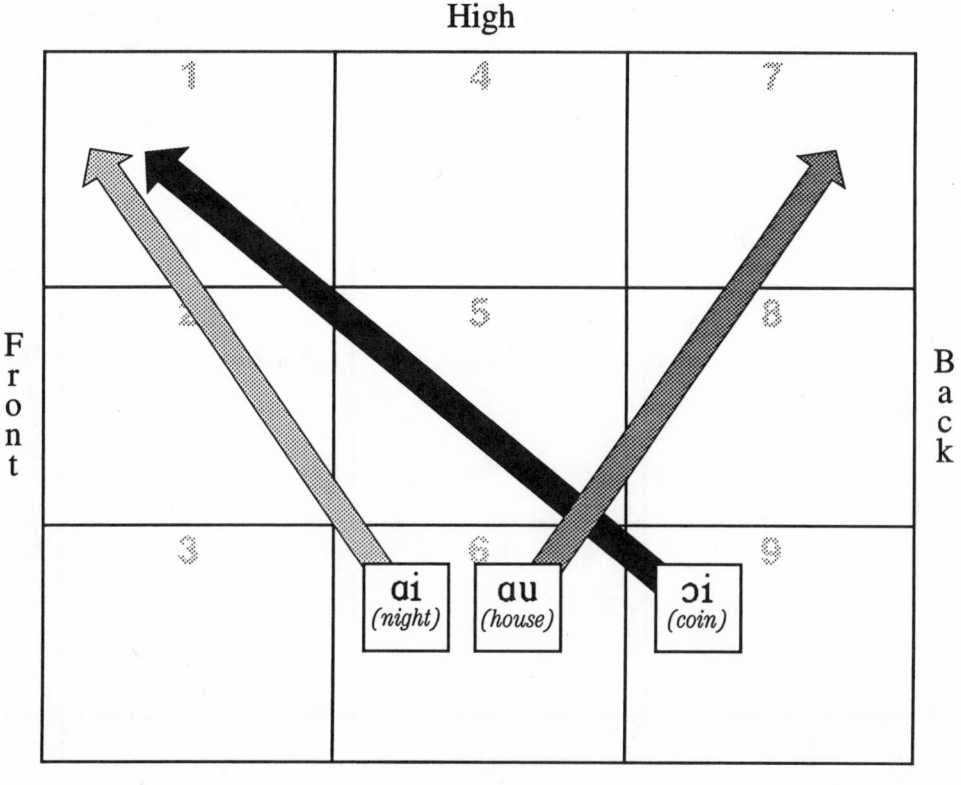

High

Low

Four Non-English Vowels

As shown in **Diagram 5** below, the non-English vowels used in *PDPN* are front rounded vowels, i.e., vowels pronounced in approximately the same position as the corresponding unrounded English vowels, but accompanied by lip rounding. The simple front rounded vowels are accompanied by slight lip rounding; the augmented front rounded vowels are accompanied by rather more, tense lip rounding.

1. /yː/ as in German *fühlen,* French *rue.* A high, tense front vowel, fully rounded.

2. /y/ as in German *füllen.* A high, lax front vowel, somewhat rounded.

3. /œː/ as in German *Höhle,* French *feu.* A mid, tense front vowel, fully rounded.

4. /œ/ as in German *Hölle,* French *boeuf.* A mid, lax front vowel, somewhat rounded. The symbol /œ̃/ with the tilde indicating nasalization is used to represent the nasalized vowel in French *un* / œ̃/.

Diagram 5: Non-English Front Rounded Vowels

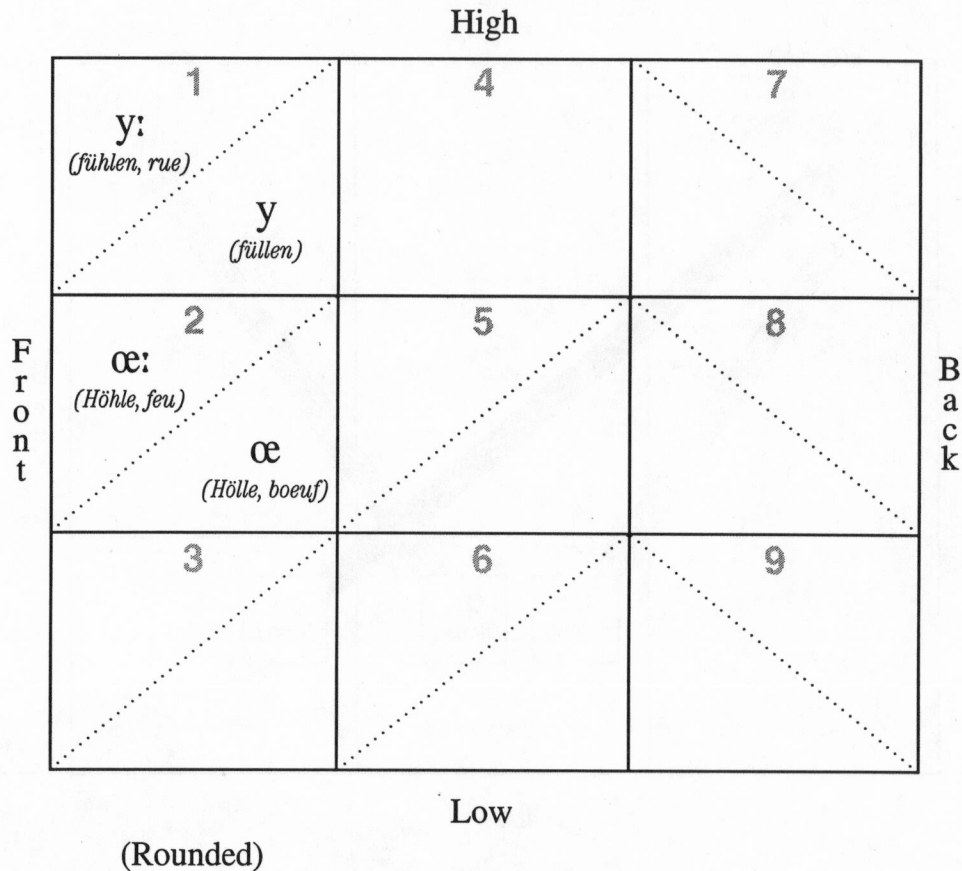

German: fühlen, füllen, Höhle, Hölle
French: rue, feu, boeuf

Consonants in IPA Transcription

In contrast to vowels, a consonant is produced when the flow of air is partly or fully obstructed at some point in the throat or mouth or by the tongue or lips. The particular nature of a consonant is determined by the place in which the flow of air is obstructed and by the presence or absence of voicing from the vocal cords.

Following is a table of the IPA consonant symbols used in *PDPN*. The table is followed by a few notes on sounds which deserve some commentary in their English contexts and on sounds that are not English consonant phonemes. Consonants not discussed in the notes should be easily understood from the examples given in the table itself.

IPA Consonant Symbols

IPA	Example	as in
b	'bid	**bid**
β	aβ'lar	Spanish **hablar**
ç	'iç	German **ich**
d	'dɪd	**did**
dʒ	'dʒɛt	**jet**
ð	'ðɪs	**this**
f	'fɪt	**fit**
g	'gɛt	**get**
ɣ	a'miːɣoː	Spanish **amigo**
h	'hɛd	**head**
hw	'hwɛt	**whet**
j	'jɛs	**yes**
k	'keːk	**cake**
l	'lɛg	**leg**
ļ	'mɪdļ	**middle**
ł	'tʃɛslaːf	Polish **Czesław**
ḷ	ḷa'nɛḷiˑ	Welsh **Llanelli**
m	'mɛn	**men**
m̦	'oːpm̦	some pronunciations of **open**
n	'nɛt	**net**
ņ	'kɪtņ	**kitten**
ŋ	'rɪŋ, 'rɪŋk	**ring, rink**
ɲ	'diːɲ	French **digne**
p	'pɪn	**pin**
r	'rɛd, 'mɛriˑ	**red, merry**
ʳ (raised r)	'kaʳd, = 'kard, 'kaːd	**card**
ṛ	'ṛanðə	Welsh **Rhondda**
s	'sɪt	**sit**
ʃ	'ʃoː	**show**
t	'toː, 'toːt	**toe, tote**
ţ	'sɪţɪŋ, 'hiːţəd	most U. S. pronunciations of **sitting, heated**
tʃ	'tʃɪp	**chip**
θ	'θɪŋk	**think**
v	'vɛt	**vet**
w	'wɛt	**wet**
x	'lax, 'bax	Scottish **loch**, German **Bach**
ɥ	lɥiː	French **lui**
z	'zɪp	**zip**
ʒ	'vɪʒən, 'beːʒ	**vision, beige**
ʘ	'ʘxũ	**!Kung** (an implosive click)
ʖ	'ʖɔːsaː	**Xhosa** (an implosive click)

IPA Consonant Symbols

/ß/ as in Spanish *hablar*. This represents a voiced bilabial fricative. It is a fricative sound like /v/, but it is pronounced with the two lips like /b/, rather than with the upper teeth and lower lip. In most contexts where it occurs, /b/ and /v/ are acceptable alternatives in English.

/ç/ as in German *ich*. In some languages the palatal fricative /ç/, heard in German *ich*, contrasts phonemically with the velar fricative /x/, heard in German *Bach*. English speakers, who generally have neither sound as a significant feature of their speech, may find it difficult to distinguish between the two. In general, this is not a problem; /ç/ usually occurs before or after front vowels and English speakers will produce the appropriate sound automatically in such positions, because the tongue is moved forward to produce the neighboring vowel. In contrast, /x/ usually occurs before or after central or back vowels in which the tongue is positioned farther back.

For both /ç/ and /x/ the sound /k/ is an acceptable anglicization in the middle and at the end of words, as in *Joachim* and *loch;* /h/ is an acceptable variant at the beginning of words, as in *chutzpah* and *Chanukah.*

/dʒ/ as in *judge*. Many linguists interpret the consonants of *judge* as a combination of /d/ + /ʒ/, giving /'dʒədʒ/. This is the method adopted in *PDPN*. Other linguists interpret these as single fricative consonants, represented by the single symbol /ǰ/.

/ɣ/ as in Spanish *amigo*. This symbol represents a voiced fricative that is pronounced like /x/ but with the addition of voicing. In English, /g/ is an acceptable alternative.

/hw/ as in *whet*. In *PDPN* the pronunciation of *whet* is indicated as /'hwet/ when it is pronounced differently than *wet* /'wet/. Some linguists analyze the sound preceding the vowel in *whet* as a single consonant, represented as /ʍ/.

/l/ as in *leg, pool*. See /l̩, m̩, n̩/ and /ł/ below.

/l̩, m̩, n̩/ as in *middle, open,* and *kitten*. The mark /ˌ/ under /l, m, n/ indicates that the consonant so marked is syllabic; that is, the consonant alone forms the nucleus of a syllable with no vowel. Thus, for *buttoning* the transcription /'bətn̩iŋ/ represents a three-syllable pronunciation /'bət-n̩-iŋ/, while /'bətniŋ/ represents a two syllable pronunciation /'bət-niŋ/. The incidence of syllabic consonants varies somewhat in English dialects and at different stylistic levels; the usual alternatives are /əl, əm, ən/. Syllabic /m̩/ is heard much less frequently than /l̩/ and /n̩/; it occurs most frequently between two bilabial consonants in casual speech, as in *an open boat* /ən 'oːpm̩ 'boːt/ in contrast with *an open eye* /ən 'oːpən 'ɑi/ or *an open sea* /ən 'oːpən 'siː/.

/l̥/ as in Welsh *Llanelli*. This is a voiceless *l* produced by placing the tongue in the position for /l/ and simply blowing air past the side of the tongue; the /l/ of English *clean* is very similar. Many English speakers substitute either a regular English /l/ or the combination /θl/; thus *Llanelli* /l̥ɑ'neḷiˑ/ could be anglicized as /θlɑ'neθliˑ/ or /lɑ'neliˑ/

/ł/ as in Polish *Czesław, Wałesa*. In English the /l/ of *leg* and the /l/ of *pool* are actually pronounced in different parts of the mouth. The /l/ of *pool* is farther back than that of *leg*. But these variants of /l/ belong to the same English phoneme and need only one symbol because there are no English words distinguished solely by such a difference. In Polish, on the other hand, these two variations of /l/ are phonemic. In *PDPN* the symbol /ł/ is used to represent the sound represented in the Polish spelling by an *l* with a slanted bar through it. This Polish phoneme is similar to the /l/ of English *pool,* and it may be approximated either with /l/ or with the phonetically similar /w/.

/m/ as in *men, home.* See also /l̩, m̩, n̩/ above.

/n/ as in *none.* See also /l̩, m̩, n̩/ above.

/ŋ/ as in *ring, singer, sink, finger.* Note that this is a single sound and that in words such as *ring, singer,* and *sink* there is no following /g/ sound. In some other words, such as *finger, longer,* and *stronger,* the /ŋ/ is followed by /g/ in most English dialects. Compare *singer* /'siŋər/ and *finger* /'fiŋgər/.

/ɲ/ as in French *digne.* This is a palatal nasal consonant pronounced farther back on the tongue than /n/. In French it is frequently represented by *gn.*

/r/ as in *red, merry.* Most consonants are produced in a particular way in one particular part of the mouth. However, the consonant represented by /r/ may be pronounced in different ways in different languages and in different dialects and varieties of English. In U.S. English /r/ is most frequently pronounced with the tongue in a retroflex position, with the tip of the tongue turned up or back. In some varieties of American and British English, and in other languages, such as Spanish, /r/ may be a trill or a single tap of the tongue tip on the alveolar ridge behind the teeth. This is similar to the sound heard for *dd* in *ladder* and for *tt* in *latter* in most U.S. dialects; see the note on /t/ below. To indicate a British pronunciation which uses this tapped /r/, as opposed to the retroflex or trilled /r/, some American cartoonists spell "very" as "veddy."

/ʳ/ the raised *r,* as in *card.* In most U.S. speech /r/ before another consonant or a pause is pronounced with the tongue in a retroflex position as outlined in the previous section. However, in some U.S. speech (primarily in eastern New England, the New York metropolitan area, and the southeastern states) and in educated southern British speech, an *r* in the spelling is not pronounced /r/ when it occurs before another consonant (as in *card, burn,* or *Can you hear me?),* or before a pause (as in *Who took my car?).* This feature is often referred to as *r*-dropping, though the *r* is not always completely dropped. In many cases *r* may be realized as a lengthening of the preceding vowel (e.g. *arms* may be homophonous with *alms* /'ɑːmz/), or as a diphthongization by the addition of an unstressed, non-syllabic /ə/ to the preceding vowel (e.g. *hire Lear* may sound similar to *Hialeah*). The raised /ʳ/ in *PDPN* indicates that some speakers pronounce a consonantal /r/ while others augment the preceding vowel by lengthening or diphthongizing it, or (especially after unstressed syllables) by simply dropping the /r/ altogether.

Some "*r*-dropping" dialects pronounce a word-final /r/ when the next word begins with a vowel, as in *your apple,* and others do not. This is known as a "linking *r*"; it occurs consistently in southern British speech, frequently in the *r*-dropping speech of eastern New England, and often in that of New York City, though it is less common in other *r*-dropping American English. A related development is the occurrence of an "intrusive *r*" between a word ending in /ə/ or /ɔː/ (and occasionally /ɑ/) and another word beginning in a vowel, but where there is no *r* in the spelling, as in the phrase *law and order,* which may be pronounced /ˌlɔːrənˈbːdə/ by British and some American *r*-droppers. This intrusive *r* occasions much comment from those who do not use it, but it is simply an extended application of the rule for linking *r*. Intrusive *r* is most frequent among British and eastern New England *r*-droppers.

This is the feature that accounts for /r/ the heard at the end of the word *Cuba* as often remarked on in the speech of President John F. Kennedy. Intrusive *r* is not shown in *PDPN* or, indeed, in most general dictionaries.

The following examples illustrate the types of variation implied by the raised /ʳ/; in these examples the raised dot ['] is used to indicate a lengthening or prolongation of the vowel without diphthongization.

beard	/ˈbiʳd/	=	[ˈbird]	*or*	[ˈbiəd, ˈbiˑd]
bear	/ˈbæʳ, ˈbeʳ/	=	[ˈbær, ˈber]	*or*	[ˈbæə, ˈbæˑ, ˈbeə, ˈbeˑ]
bird	/ˈbəʳd/	=	[ˈbərd]	*or*	[ˈbəːd]
bard	/ˈbɑʳd/	=	[ˈbɑrd]	*or*	[ˈbɑːd]
bored	/ˈboːʳd, ˈbɔːʳd/	=	[ˈboːrd, ˈbɔːrd]	*or*	[ˈboːəd, ˈbɔːəd, ˈbɔːd]
moored	/ˈmuʳd/	=	[ˈmurd]	*or*	[ˈmuəd, ˈmuˑd]
better	/ˈbeṭəʳ/	=	[ˈbeṭər]	*or*	[ˈbeṭə]

NOTE: In *PDPN* these distinctions are indicated in the IPA transcriptions with raised r but are not reflected in the simplified respellings.

/ɾ̥/ as in Welsh *Rhondda*. This is actually an unvoiced /r/, though some linguists may interpret it as /hr/. In Welsh it is usually a voiceless tapped or trilled /r/. A plain voiced /r/ is an acceptable English equivalent, as is /hr/.

/t/ as in *tight, kitten*.

/ṭ/ as in *sitting*. As with most consonants, the sound of /t/ varies according to its position in the word. For instance, the plosive /t/ in *team* is aspirated or released, whereas in *meet* the /t/ is stopped but often not aspirated or released. In most U.S. speech a /t/ between vowels is pronounced as a voiced tap of the tongue. This voiced /ṭ/ does not usually occur at the beginning of a stressed syllable, as in *potato* /pəˈteːtoː/, though in some New England speech one may indeed hear /bəˈṭeːṭə/. In *PDPN* the voiced /t/ is indicated as /ṭ/ in positions where U.S. speakers commonly use it, with the understanding that in some dialects—and especially in British and other non-American varieties of English—intervocalic /t/ is usually the voiceless and aspirated stop /t/ rather than a voiced tap.

/tʃ/ as in *church*. Many linguists interpret the sounds spelled with *ch* in *church* as a combination of /t/ + /ʃ/, giving /ˈtʃərtʃ/. This is the method adopted in *PDPN*. Other linguists interpret these as single fricative consonants, represented by the single symbol /č/.

/x/ as in Scottish *loch*, German *Bach*. See also /ç/ above. For both /ç/ and /x/ the sound /k/ is an acceptable anglicization in the middle and at the end of words, as in *Joachim* and *loch;* /h/ is an acceptable variant at the beginning of words, as in *chutzpah* and *Chanukah*.

/ɥ/ as in French *lui*. This sound, actually a rounded /j/, is difficult for native English speakers to reproduce; it may be approximated by pronouncing /w/. Note, however, that in French *lui* /lɥiː/ is distinct from *Louis* /lwiː/.

/ʇ/, /ʖ/ as in *!Kung* and *Xhosa* respectively. These represent sounds used in some African languages that are clicks or implosive consonants. The first is similar to the palatal sound made to imitate a popping cork; the second is similar to the sound English speakers make on the side of the tongue to gee up a horse.

Diacritics Used in IPA transcriptions

IPA	Example	as in	Explanation
/ˈ/	/ˈæpəl/	**apple**	primary stress
/ˌ/	/ˈæpəlˌsɔːs/	**applesauce**	secondary stress
/ː/	/ˈniːt/	**neat**	an augmented vowel
/ˑ/	/ˈhæpiˑ/	**happy**	variation between simple and augmented vowels
/˜/	/bɔ̃/	French **bon**	nasalization of a vowel
/ˬ/	/ˈsi̬tiŋ, ˈhiːṯəd/	**sitting, heated**	voicing of a usually unvoiced consonant
/˳/	/l̥ɑˈnel̥iˑ/	Welsh **Llanelli**	the voiceless equivalent of a voiced consonant
/ˌ/	/ˈkitn̩/	**kitten**	a syllabic consonant
/ˬ/	/məˈt̡ildə/	Russian **Mathilde**	a palatalized consonant

Note on palatalization: In some languages, such as Russian and Irish Gaelic, a consonant is sometimes palatalized, that is, pronounced with the tongue touching or moving toward the palate, adding a /j/-like sound to the consonant. This palatalization is indicated by the addition of a hook to the bottom right of the character, e.g. /ɽ, t̡, ʐ, m̡ / in Russian *Lavrenti* /ləvˈɽentij/, Kuzmich /kuːʐˈm̡iːtʃ/. In *PDPN* palatalization is shown only in the IPA transcriptions and not in the simplified respellings.

Abbreviations

States of the United States are identified with the standard two-letter postal abbreviations.

cent.	century	*pert.*	pertaining
co.	company	*pl.*	plural
corp.	corporation	*pl. name*	place name
dept.	department	*prov.*	province
E	East	*S*	South
lang.	language	*sg.*	singular
mtn.	mountain	*tdmk*	trademark
mts.	mountains	*US*	United States
N	North	*W*	West
pers. name	personal name		

Simplified Pronunciation Symbols

Symbol	Example	as in
a A	FAD, ASK	fad, ask
ā Ā	FĀD	fade
ah AH	BAH-thuhr, KAHT;	bother, cot;
	FAH-thuhr, AHSK	father, ask
aw AW	KAWT, LAW	caught, law
b B	BID	bid
ch CH	CHIP	chip
d D	DID	did
e E	FED	fed
ē Ē	BĒD	bead
f F	FIT	fit
g G	GET	get
ğ Ğ	ah-ME-ğō	Span. amigo (*Anglicized alternative* g)
h H	HED	head
hl HL	hlah-NEHL-ē	Welsh Llanelli (*Anglicized alternative* l *or* thl)
hw HW	HWET, HWICH	whet, which
i I	BID	bid
ī Ī	BĪ, RĪD, LĪ	buy, ride, lie
j J	JET	jet
k K	KIK, KUK	kick, cook
kh KH	BAHKH, IKH, LAHKH	Ger. Bach, ich, Scottish loch.
l L	LEG, MID-l	leg, middle
m M	MEN	men
n N	NET, KIT-n	net, kitten
ng NG	RING, RINGK	ring, rink
ō Ō	KŌT	coat
oi OI	BOI, KOIN	boy, coin
oo OO	MOOD	mood
ow OW	OWT, NOW	out, now
p P	PIN, LIP	pin, lip
r R	RED, KAHRD	red, card
s S	SIT	sit
t T	TŌ, SIT-ing	toe, sitting
th TH	THIN	thin
th TH	THIS	this
u U	GUD, PUT, PUR	good, put, poor
ue UE	RUE, FUE-luhn;	Fr. rue, Ger. fühlen;
	FUEL-uhn	Ger. füllen
uh UH	buh-NAN-uh, BUHD	banana, bud
uhr UHR	BET-uhr, BUHRD	better, bird
uh(r) UH(R)	BUH(R)F,	*Anglicization of* Fr. boeuf, Ger. Hölle.
	HUH(R)L-uh	
	FUH(R),	*Anglicization of* Fr. feu, Ger. Höhle.
	HUH(R)-luh	
v V	VET	vet
v V	ahv-LAHR	Span. hablar (*Anglicized alternative* b *or* v)
w W	WET, WICH	wet, witch
y Y	YES	yes
z Z	ZIP	zip
zh ZH	MEZH-uhr	measure

International Phonetic Alphabet Symbols

IPA Symbol	Example	as in
English Consonants		
b	'bid	**bid**
d	'did	**did**
dʒ	'dʒet	**jet**
ð	'ðis	**this**
f	'fit	**fit**
g	'get	**get**
h	'hed	**head**
hw	'hwet	**whet**
j	'jes	**yes**
k	'keːk	**cake**
l	'leg	**leg**
ḷ	'midḷ	**middle**
m	'men	**men**
m̩	'oːpm̩	**open** (some pronunciations)
n	'net	**net**
ṇ	'kitṇ	**kitten**
ŋ	'riŋ, 'riŋk	**ring, rink**
p	'pin	**pin**
r	'red, 'meriˑ	**red, merry**
ʳ (raised r)	'kaʳd (= 'kard, 'kaːd)	**card**
s	'sit	**sit**
ʃ	'ʃoː	**show**
t	'toː, 'toːt	**toe, tote**
ṭ	'siṭiṇ, 'hiːṭəd	**sitting, heated** (most U.S. pronunciations)
tʃ	'tʃip	**chip**
θ	'θiŋk	**think**
v	'vet	**vet**
w	'wet	**wet**
z	'zip	**zip**
ʒ	'viʒən, 'beːʒ	**vision, beige**

IPA Symbol	Example	as in
English Vowels		
ə	bə'nænə, 'bəd	**banana, bud**
əʳ	'bəʳd, 'bəṭəʳ	**bird, butter**
æ	'fæd, 'æsk	**fad, ask**
ɑ	'baðəʳ, 'kɑt, 'faðəʳ	**bother, cot, father**
ɑː	'fɑːðəʳ, 'ɑːsk	**father, ask**
ai	'bai, 'raid	**buy, ride**
au	'bau, 'nau	**bough, now**
e	'fed	**fed**
eː	'feːd	**fade**
i	'bid	**bid**
iː	'biːd	**bead**
oː	'koːt	**coat**
ɔː	'kɔːt, 'lɔː	**caught, law**
ɔi	'bɔi, 'kɔin	**boy, coin**
u	'gud, 'put, puʳ	**good, put, poor**
uː	'muːd, 'mjuːzik	**mood, music**

IPA Symbol	Example	as in
Non-English Vowels		
œ	'hœlə, bœf	German **Hölle**, French **boeuf**
œː	'hœːlə, fœː	German **Höhle**, French **feu**
y	'fylən	German **füllen**
yː	'fyːlən, ryː	German **fühlen**, French **rue**

IPA Symbol	Example	as in
Non-English Consonants		
β	aβ'lar	Spanish **hablar**
ç	'iç	German **ich**
ɣ	a'miːɣoː	Spanish **amigo**
ł	'tʃesłaːf	Polish **Czesław**
ḷ	ḷa'neḷiˑ	Welsh **Llanelli**
ɲ	'diːɲ	French **digne**
r̥	'r̥anðə	Welsh **Rhondda**
x	'lax, 'bax	Scottish **loch**, German **Bach**
ɥ	lɥiː	French **lui**
ʗ	'ʗxũ	**!Kung** (an implosive click)
ʖ	'ʖhɔːsaː	**Xhosa** (an implosive click)

Diacritics used in IPA transcriptions

IPA Symbol	Example	as in	Explanation
'	'æpəl	**apple**	primary stress
ˌ	'æpəlˌsɔːs	**applesauce**	secondary stress
ː	'niːt	**neat**	an augmented vowel
ˑ	'hæpiˑ	**happy**	variation between simple and augmented vowels
~	bɔ̃	French **bon**	nasalization of a vowel
ˬ	'siṭiṇ, 'hiːṭəd	**sitting, heated**	voicing of a usually unvoiced consonant
˳	ḷa'neḷiˑ	Welsh **Llanelli**	the voiceless equivalent of a voiced consonant
ˌ	'kitṇ	**kitten**	a syllabic consonant
ˌ	mə'ṭildə	Russian **Mathilde**	a palatalized consonant

A

AAA
  American Automobile Assoc.   TRIP-uhl Ā; Ā-Ā-Ā   ˌtripəl 'eːˌ ˌeːˌeː'eː

AAAS
  American Assoc. for the   TRIP-uhl Ā ES   ˌtripəl ˌeː 'es
    Advancement of Science

Aachen
  city, Germany   AH<u>KH</u>-uhn   'ɑxən

Aage
  pers. name   AW-guh   'ɔːgə

Aalborg, Ålborg
  port, Denmark   AWL-BAWRG   'ɔlˌbɔːʳg

Aalsmeer
  commune, Netherlands   AHLS-MER   'ɑlsˌmeʳ

Aalto
  Alvar, *Finnish designer*   AHL-tō   'ɑltoː

Aare
  river, Switzerland   AHR-uh   'ɑrə

Aaron
  1. pers. name   AR-uhn, ER-uhn   'ærən, 'erən
  2. Danish, German   AHR-AWN   'ɑrˌɔːn
  3. French   ah-RAWⁿ   ɑrɔ̃

Aart
  pers. name, Dutch   AHRT   'ɑːʳt

Aass
  Norwegian beer   AHS   'ɑs

Abaco
  island, British Virgin Islands   AB-uh-KŌ   'æbəˌkoː

Ābādān
  port, Iran   AHB-uh-DAHN, AB-uh-DAN   ˌɑbə'dɑn, ˌæbə'dæn

Abaddon
  destroying angel   uh-BAD-n   ə'bædn̩

Abadía
  pers. name, Spanish   ah<u>v</u>-ah-<u>TH</u>Ḗ-ah   ɑβɑ'ðiːɑ

Abas
  Perseus's great-grandfather   AB-uhs   'æbəs

Abate
  family name   uh-BAHT-ē, uh-BĀT   ə'bɑṭiˑ, ə'beːt

Abba
  1. Swedish rock group; pers. name   AB-uh   'æbə
  2. Hebrew title   AHB-bah   'ɑːbbɑ

Abbado
  Claudio, *Italian conductor*   uh-BAHD-ō, ahb-BAHD-ō   ə'bɑdoː, ab'bɑdoː

Abbasid
  Islamic dynasty   AB-uh-sid, uh-BAS-id   'æbəsid, ə'bæsid

Abbeville
  1. US pl. name; US publisher   AB-ē-VIL   'æbi',vil
  2. commune, France   ahb-VĔL, ah-buh-VĔL   ɑːbviːl, ɑːbəviːl

Abdallah
  1. pers. name   ab-DAL-uh   æb'dælə
  2. Arabic, Persian   AHB-dah-LAH   ˌɑːbdɑːˈlɑː

Abdel
  pers. name, Arabic   uhb-DUL   əb'dul

Abdias
  Old Testament book   ab-DĪ-uhs   æb'daiəs

Abdul
  1. pers. name; Paula, *US pop*   ab-DOOL, AB-dul   æb'duːl, 'æbdul
    entertainer
  2. Arabic   uhb-DUL   əb'dul

Abdul Aziz, King
  airport, Jeddah, Saudi Arabia   KING ahb-DOOL ah-ZĒZ   ˌkiŋ ab,duːl a'ziːz

Abdul-Jabbar
  Kareem, *US basketball player*   ab-DOOL-juh-BAHR   æb,duˈldʒəˈbɑʳ

Abdullah
  1. pers. name   ab-DUHL-uh   æb'dələ
  2. Arabic, Persian   AHB-dul-AH   ˌɑːbdul'ɑː

Abdus
  pers. name, Punjabi   ahb-DUS   ab'dus

Abe
  1. pers. name   ĀB   'eːb
  2. lang., Ivory Coast   AHB-ā   'abeː

Abednego
  Biblical name   uh-BED-ni-gō   ə'bednigoː

Abel
  1. pers. name   Ā-buhl   'eːbəl
  2. Danish, Dutch, Norwegian   AHB-uhl   'aːbəl
  3. French   ah-BEL   aːbel

Abelam
  Papuan people, New Guinea   uh-BEL-uhm   ə'beləm

Abelard
  Peter, *French philosopher*   AB-uh-LAHRD   'æbə,lɑʳd

Abelardo
  pers. name, Spanish   ahv-ā-LAHR-t͟hō   aβeː'larðoː

Abelian
  mathematics system   uh-BĒ-lē-uhn, uh-BĒL-yuhn   ə'biːliːən, ə'biːljən

Abelson
  Philip Hauge, *US physical chemist*   Ā-buhl-suhn   'eːbəlsən

Abenaki [Abnaki]
  N. American people   AB-uh-NAHK-ē, AB-uh-NAK-ē,   ˌæbə'naki', ˌæbə'næki',
     AHB-uh-NAHK-ē   ˌabə'naki'

Abercrombie, -by
  pers. name   AB-uhr-KRAHM-bē, -KRUHM-bē   'æbəʳ,krɑmbi', -,krəmbi'

Aberdeen
  1. seaport, Scotland   AB-uhr-DĒN   ˌæbəʳ'diːn
  2. US pl. name   AB-uhr-DĒN   'æbəʳ,diːn

Aberdonian
  pert. to Aberdeen   AB-uhr-DŌ-nē-uhn,   ˌæbəʳ'doːniːən,
     AB-uhr-DŌN-yuhn   ˌæbəʳ'doːnjən

Key (col. 2):   a: fad   ā: fade   ah: father   ar: Mary   aw: law   e: fed   ē: feed   er: merry   i: hid   ī: hide   ō: coat   ōō: boot
oi: boy   ow: now   u: put   uh: above   uhr: bird   ch: chop   ng: ring   sh: show   th: thick   t͟h: this   zh: measure

Abergavenny
  1. borough, Wales   AB-uhr-guh-VEN-ē   ˌæbəˈᵍgəˈveniˑ
  2. British title & family name   AB-uhr-guh-VEN-ē, AB-uhr-GEN-ē   ˌæbəˈᵍgəˈveniˑ, ˌæbəˈᵍgeniˑ

Aberystwyth
  town, Wales   AB-uh-RIS-TWITH,   ˌæbəˈrisˌtwiθ, ˌæbəˈrəsˌtwiθ
     AB-uh-RUHS-TWITH

Abidjan
  seaport, Ivory Coast   AB-i-JAHN   ˌæbiˈdʒɑn

Abidjanaise, L'
  see L'Abidjanaise

Abiel
  pers. name   AHB-ē-uhl, Ā-bē-uhl, uh-BĪ-uhl   ˈabiːəl, ˈeːbiːəl, əˈbɑiəl

Abigail
  pers. name   AB-uh-GĀL   ˈæbəˌgeːl

Abijah
  pers. name   uh-BĪ-juh   əˈbɑidʒə

Abilene
  1. city, TX   AB-uh-LĒN   ˈæbəˌliːn
  2. region, Syria   AB-uh-LĒ-nē   ˌæbəˈliːniˑ

Abílio
  pers. name   ah-BĒL-yo͞o   ɑːˈbiːljuː

Abimelech
  Biblical name   uh-BIM-uh-LEK   əˈbiməˌlek

Abingdon
  town, England   AB-ing-duhn   ˈæbiŋdən

Abinoam
  Biblical name   uh-BIN-uh-wuhm, uh-BIN-uh-WAM   əˈbinəwəm, əˈbinəˌwæm

Abipón
  S. American people   AB-uh-PAHN, AB-uh-PAHN,   ˈæbəˌpan, ˌæbəˈpan,
     AB-uh-PÔN   ˌæbəˈpoːn

Abitibi
  lake, Canada   AB-uh-TIB-ē   ˌæbəˈtibiˑ

Abkhaz
  lang., people, Georgia   ahb-KAHZ, ahb-KAHS   abˈkaz, abˈkas

Abnaki [Abenaki]
  N. American people   ab-NAHK-ē, ab-NAK-ē, ahb-NAHK-ē   æbˈnɑkiˑ, æbˈnækiˑ, abˈnɑkiˑ

Abner
  pers. name   AB-nuhr   ˈæbnəʳ

Abolhassan
  pers. name, Arabic (A. Bani-Sadr)   AHB-uhl-<u>kh</u>ah-SAHN,   ˌabəlxaˈsan, Ⓢ ˌabəlhaˈsan
     Ⓢ AHB-uhl-hah-SAHN

Abraham
  1. pers. name   Ā-bruh-HAM   ˈeːbrəˌhæm
  2. Danish, Norwegian   AH-brah-HAHM   ˈaːbraˌhaːm
  3. French   ah-brah-AHM   aːbraːˈɑːm
  4. German   AHB-rah-HAHM   ˈabraˌham
  5. Spanish   ah<u>v</u>-RAHN, ah<u>v</u>-rah-AHN   aβˈran, aβraˈan
  6. Swedish   AHB-rah-HAHM   ˈabraːˌham

Abrahán
  pers. name   ah<u>v</u>-RAHN, ah<u>v</u>-rah-AHN   aβˈran, aβraˈan

Abram
  1. pers. name   Ā-bruhm   ˈeːbrəm
  2. Russian   uh-BRAHM   əˈbraːm

Foreign Sounds: ue: *Fr.* **rue**, *Ger.* f**ü**llen   uh(r): *Fr.* b**oeuf**, *Ger.* H**ö**hle   <u>kh</u>: *Ger.* i**ch**, *Scot.* lo**ch**   g̃: *Sp.* ami**g**o   <u>v</u>: *Sp.* ha**b**lar
hl: *Welsh* **Ll**anelli.   CAPITALS: primary stress.   SMALL CAPS: secondary stress.   Ⓢ: U.S. pron.   Ⓛ: British pron.

Abrams
Talber, *US aviator, explorer*	Ā-bruhmz	'eɪbrəmz

Abruzzi
region, Italy	ah-BRŌŌT-sē, uh-BRŌŌT-sē	ɑ'bruːtsiˑ, ə'bruːtsiˑ

Absalom
pers. name	AB-suh-luhm	'æbsələm

absinthe
liquor	AB-sinth	'æbsinθ

Absolut
vodka brand	AHP-sō-LŌŌT	ˌɑpsoː'luːt

Abu
1. pers. name, Arabic	ah-BŌŌ	ɑ'buː
2. Persian	AHB-ōō	'ɑːbuː

Abu Dhabi
state & town, United Arab Emirates	AHB-ōō T͟HAHB-ē, AHB-ōō DAHB-ē	ˌɑbuː 'ðabiˑ, ˌɑbuː 'dabiˑ

Abu Simbel
site, Egypt	AHB-ōō SIM-buhl	ˌɑbuː 'simbəl

Abū Żabī [Abu Dhabi]
state & town, United Arab Emirates	AHB-ōō T͟HAHB-ē	ˌɑbuː 'ðabiˑ

Abydos
town, Egypt	uh-BĪD-uhs	ə'baɪdəs

Abyssinia [Ethiopia]
country, Africa	AB-uh-SIN-ē-uh, AB-uh-SIN-yuh	ˌæbə'siniːə, ˌæbə'sinjə

Abzug
Bella, *US politician*	AB-zug	'æbzug

Academus
legendary Attic hero	AK-uh-DĒ-muhs, AK-uh-DĀ-muhs	ˌækə'diːməs, ˌækə'deːməs

Acadia
National Park, *ME; region, Canada*	uh-KĀD-ē-uh	ə'keːdiːə

Acadian
pert. to Acadia; *French-Canadian exile*	uh-KĀD-ē-uhn	ə'keːdiːən

Acadie
French form of Acadia	ah-kah-DĒ	ɑːkɑːdiː

Acapulco
town, Mexico	AHK-uh-PUL-kō, AK-, -PŌŌL-kō	ˌɑkə'pulkoː, ˌæk-, -'puːlkoː

Acapulco de Juárez
town, Mexico	ahk-uh-PŌŌL-kō t͟hā K͟HWAHR-es	ɑkə'puːlkoː ðeː 'xwɑres

Acarnania
dept, Greece	AK-uhr-NĀ-nē-uh	ˌækəʳ'neːniːə

Acastus
Argonaut	uh-KAS-tuhs	ə'kæstəs

Accipiter
hawk genus	ak-SIP-uht-uhr	æk'sipəʈəʳ

Accomack
county, VA	AK-uh-MAK	'ækəˌmæk

Accra
seaport, Ghana	uh-KRAH	ə'krɑ

Aceldama
potter's field	uh-SEL-duh-muh	ə'seldəmə

Acestes
host of Aeneas in Sicily	uh-SES-tēz	ə'sestiːz

Key (col. 2): a: fad ā: fade ah: father ar: Mary aw: law e: fed ē: feed er: merry i: hid ī: hide ō: coat ōō: boot
oi: boy ow: now u: put uh: above uhr: bird ch: chop ng: ring sh: show th: thick t͟h: this zh: measure

Achaea [Achaia]
   dept, Greece   uh-KĒ-uh   əˈkiːə

Achaean League
   ancient Greek alliance   uh-KĒ-uhn   əˈkiːən

Achaemenid
   Persian dynasty   uh-KĒ-muh-nid   əˈkiːmənid

Achaemenides
   companion of Odysseus   AK-uh-MEN-uh-DĒZ   ˌækəˈmenəˌdiːz

Achaia [Achaea]
   region, ancient Greece   uh-KĪ-uh, uh-KĀ-uh   əˈkaiə, əˈkeːə

Achates
   1. friend of Aeneas; pers. name   uh-KĀT-ēz   əˈkeːţiːz
   2. Swedish   ah-KAHT-uhs   ɑːˈkɑţəs

Achebe
   Chinua, *Nigerian writer*   ah-CHĀ-bā   aˈtʃeːbeː

Achelous
   Boeotian river god   AK-uh-LŌ-uhs   ˌækəˈloːəs

Achernar
   star   AK-uhr-NAHR, Ā-kuhr-NAHR   ˈækəʳˌnɑʳ, ˈeːkəʳˌnɑʳ

Acheron
   river in Hades   AK-uh-RAHN, AK-uh-ruhn   ˈækəˌran, ˈækərən

Acheson
   Dean, *US statesman*   ACH-uh-suhn   ˈætʃəsən

Achille
   1. pers. name, French   ah-SHĒL   ɑːʃiːl
   2. Italian   ah-KĒL-lā   aˈkiːlleː

Achille Lauro
   hijacked Italian cruise ship   ah-KĒL-lā LOWR-ō   aˈkiːlleː ˈlauroː

Achilles
   1. Homeric hero; pers. name   uh-KIL-ēz   əˈkiliːz
   2. German   ah-KHIL-uhs   aˈçiləs

Achinese
   see Atjehnese

Achiote
   plant   AHK-ē-ŌT-ē   ˌakiːˈoːţiˑ

Achitophel
   Biblical name   uh-KIT-uh-FEL   əˈkiţəˌfel

Achmed
   pers. name   AHKH-med, ahkh-MET   ˈaxmed, axˈmet

Acholi [Akoli]
   lang., people, Uganda, Sudan   uh-KŌ-lē, uh-CHŌ-lē   əˈkoːliˑ, əˈtʃoːliˑ

Acis
   lover of Galatea   Ā-suhs   ˈeːsəs

Acisclo
   pers. name, Spanish   ah-THĒS-klō, ah-SĒS-klō   aˈθiːskloː, aˈsiːskloː

Acislo
   pers. name, Spanish   ah-THĒ-slō, ah-SĒ-slō   aˈθiːsloː, aˈsiːsloː

Ackerman
   Bettye Louise, *US actress*   AK-uhr-muhn   ˈækəʳmən

Acoma
   N. American people   AHK-uh-MAW, AK-uh-MAW   ˈakəˌmɔː, ˈækəˌmɔː

Aconcagua
   Mount, *Argentina*   AHK-uhn-KAHG̃-wah,   ˌakənˈkaɣwa,
        Ⓢ AK-uhn-KAHG-wuh, AHK-   Ⓢ ˌækənˈkagwə, ˌak-

Foreign Sounds: ue: *Fr.* **rue**, *Ger.* **füllen**   uh(r): *Fr.* **boeuf**, *Ger.* **Höhle**   kh: *Ger.* **ich**, *Scot.* **loch**   g̃: *Sp.* **amigo**   v: *Sp.* **hablar**
hl: *Welsh* **Llanelli**.   CAPITALS: primary stress.   SMALL CAPS: secondary stress.   Ⓢ: U.S. pron.   Ⓔ: British pron.

Aconite
　plant　　　　　　　　　　　AK-uh-NĪT　　　　　　　　　'ækə,naɪt
Açores, Ilhas dos [Azores]
　island archipelago, Portugal　IL-yuhz duz uh-SAWR-ish,　'iljəz duz ə'sɔːriʃ, ə'sɔːris
　　　　　　　　　　　　　　uh-SAWR-is
Acre
　1. state, Brazil　　　　　　AHK-ruh, AH-krah　　　　'akrə, 'akrɑ
　2. town, district, Israel　　AHK-uhr, Ā-kuhr　　　　'akəʳ, 'eːkəʳ
Acrisius
　grandfather of Perseus　　uh-KRISH-(ē-)uhs　　　　ə'kriʃ(iː)əs
Acropolis
　Athenian citadel　　　　　uh-KRAHP-uh-luhs　　　　ə'krɑpələs
Actaeon
　mythical Greek hunter　　ak-TĒ-uhn　　　　　　　æk'tiːən
actinium
　element　　　　　　　　　ak-TIN-ē-uhm　　　　　æk'tiniːəm
Actium
　promontory, battlesite, Greece　AK-shē-uhm, AK-tē-uhm　'ækʃiːəm, 'æktiːəm
Acuff
　Roy, *US country singer*　　Ā-KUHF　　　　　　　　'eɪ,kəf
Acura
　car make　　　　　　　　AK-yuh-ruh　　　　　　'ækjərə
Acushnet
　US golf equipment co.　　uh-KUSH-nuht, -NET　　　ə'kuʃnət, -,net
Ada
　1. programming lang.; pers. name　ĀD-uh　　　　　　　'eːdə
　2. French　　　　　　　　ah-DAH　　　　　　　　ɑːdɑː
　3. Italian　　　　　　　　AH-dah　　　　　　　　'ɑdɑ
Adad-nirari
　name, Assyrian kings　　uh-DAHD-nuh-RAHR-ē, -nē-RAHR-ē　ə,dɑdnə'rɑriˑ, -niˑ'rɑriˑ
Adah
　wife of Lamech; pers. name　ĀD-uh　　　　　　　　'eːdə
Adair
　county, IA, KY, MO, OK; pers.　uh-DAR, uh-DER　　　　ə'dæʳ, ə'deʳ
　name
Adak
　Alaskan island　　　　　Ā-DAK　　　　　　　　'eɪ,dæk
Adalbert
　1. pers. name, Danish　　AHD-ahl-BERT　　　　　'ɑːdɑːl,bert
　2. German　　　　　　　AHD-ahl-BERT　　　　　'ɑdɑl,beʳt
Adam
　1. pers. name　　　　　AD-uhm　　　　　　　'ædəm
　2. Danish, Polish, Serbo-Croatian　AHD-ahm　　　　　　'ɑːdɑːm
　3. Dutch　　　　　　　AHD-ahm　　　　　　'ɑːdɑm
　4. French　　　　　　　ah-DAHⁿ　　　　　　　ɑːdã
　5. German　　　　　　AHD-ahm　　　　　　'ɑdɑm
　6. Russian　　　　　　uh-DAHM　　　　　　ə'dɑːm
　7. Swedish　　　　　　AH-dahm　　　　　　'ɑdɑːm
Adams
　John, *2nd US president;* John　AD-uhmz　　　　　　'ædəmz
　Quincy, *6th US president*
Adán
　pers. name, Spanish　　ah-THAHN　　　　　　a'ðan
Adar
　Jewish month　　　　　ah-DAHR, AHD-AHR　　a'dɑʳ, 'ad,aʳ

Key (col. 2):　a: fad　ā: fade　ah: father　ar: Mary　aw: law　e: fed　ē: feed　er: merry　i: hid　ī: hide　ō: coat　ōō: boot
oi: boy　ow: now　u: put　uh: above　uhr: bird　ch: chop　ng: ring　sh: show　th: thick　th̲: this　zh: measure

Adar Sheni [Veadar]
Jewish month   ah-DAHR shā-NĒ, SHĀ-nē   ɑ,dɑʳ ʃeːˈniː, ˈʃeːniˑ

Addams
Jane, US social worker (Nobel   AD-uhmz   ˈædəmz
l931)

Addington
pers. name   AD-ing-tuhn   ˈædiŋtən

Addis Ababa
city, Ethiopia   AD-uhs AB-uh-buh   ˌædəs ˈæbəbə

Addison
Joseph, English author; pers.   AD-uh-suhn   ˈædəsən
name

Adela
1. pers. name   AD-l-uh, uh-DĀ-luh, uh-DEL-uh   ˈædlə, əˈdeːlə, əˈdelə
2. Spanish   ah-THĀ-lah   ɑˈðeːlɑ

Adelaide
1. port, Australia; pers. name   AD-l-ĀD   ˈædlˌeːd
2. Italian   AHD-ā-LAH-ē-dā   ˌɑdeːˈlaiːdeː

Adélaïde
pers. name, French   ah-dā-lah-ĒD   ɑːdeːlɑːiːd

Adelbert
1. pers. name   AD-l-buhrt, uh-DEL-   ˈædlbəʳt, əˈdel-
2. German   AHD-uhl-BERT   ˈɑdəlˌbeʳt

Adele
1. pers. name   uh-DEL   əˈdel
2. German   ah-DĀ-luh   ɑˈdeːlə

Adèle
1. pers. name   uh-DEL   əˈdel
2. French   ah-DEL   ɑːdel

Adeline
1. pers. name   AD-l-ĪN, -ĒN, -uhn   ˈædlˌain, -ˌiːn, -ən
2. Danish   AHD-uh-LĒ-nuh   ˌɑːdəˈliːnə

Adelphi
University, NY   uh-DEL-FĪ   əˈdelˌfai

Aden
seaport, gulf, Yemen   AHD-n, ĀD-n, AD-n   ˈɑdn̩, ˈeːdn̩, ˈædn̩

Adenauer
Konrad, German statesman   AHD-n-OW(-uh)r, AD-n-OW(-uh)r   ˈɑdn̩,au(ə)ʳ, ˈædn̩,au(ə)ʳ

Adeodato
pers. name   AHD-Ā-ō-DAH-tō   ˌɑd,eːoːˈdɑtoː

Adeodatus
Christian saint; pope   ĀD-ē-AHD-uht-uhs   ˌeːdiːˈɑdəțəs

Adherbal
Numidian ally of Rome   ad-HUHR-buhl   ædˈhəʳbəl

Adhola
lang., people, Uganda, Kenya   uh-DŌ-luh   əˈdoːlə

Adidas
tdmk, athletic wear   uh-DĒD-uhs   əˈdiːdəs

Adige
river, Italy   AHD-uh-JĀ   ˈɑdə,dʒeː

Adirondack
mtn. range, NY   AD-uh-RAHN-DAK   ˌædəˈrɑn,dæk

Adlai
pers. name   AD-lā, -lē, -LĪ   ˈædleː, -liˑ, -ˌlɑi

Foreign Sounds: ue: *Fr.* **rue**, *Ger.* f**ü**llen   uh(r): *Fr.* b**oeu**f, *Ger.* H**öh**le   <u>kh</u>: *Ger.* i**ch**, *Scot.* lo**ch**   g̃: *Sp.* ami**g**o   v: *Sp.* ha**b**lar
hl: *Welsh* L**l**anelli.   CAPITALS: primary stress.   SMALL CAPS: secondary stress.   Ⓢ: U.S. pron.   Ⓑ: British pron.

Adler

pers. name	AD-luhr	'ædlər

Admete

Samian legendary heroine	ad-MĔT-ē	æd'miːt̬i'

Admetus

Argonaut	ad-MĔT-uhs	æd'miːt̬əs

Adolf

1. pers. name	AD-AHLF, ĀD-AHLF, -AWLF; uh-DAHLF, uh-DAWLF	'æd,ɑlf, 'eːd,ɑlf, -,ɔːlf; ə'dɑlf, ə'dɔːlf
2. Czech, Danish	AH-DAWLF	'ɑː,dɔːlf
3. Dutch, German, Norwegian, Polish, Swedish	AHD-AWLF	'ɑd,ɔːlf
4. Russian	uh-DAWLF	ə'dɔːl̩f

Adolfo

1. pers. name, Italian	ah-DAWL-fō	ɑ'dɔːlfoː
2. Spanish	ah<u>th</u>-AWL-fō	ɑð'ɔːlfoː

Adolph

1. pers. name	AD-AHLF, ĀD-AHLF, -AWLF; uh-DAHLF, uh-DAWLF	'æd,ɑlf, 'eːd,ɑlf, -,ɔːlf; ə'dɑlf, ə'dɔːlf
2. Danish, German	AHD-AWLF	'ɑd,ɔːlf

Adolphe

1. pers. name	AD-AHLF, ĀD-AHLF, -AWLF; uh-DAHLF, uh-DAWLF	'æd,ɑlf, 'eːd,ɑlf, -,ɔːlf; ə'dɑlf, ə'dɔːlf
2. French	ah-DAWLF	ɑːdɔːlf

Adolpho

pers. name, Portuguese	ah-<u>TH</u>AWL-fo͞o	ɑː'ðɔːlfuː

Adolphus

king of Germany, pers. name	uh-DAWL-fuhs, -DAHL-fuhs	ə'dɔːlfəs, -'dɑlfəs

Adonai

Hebrew title for God	AD-uh-NĪ, AHD-uh-NOI	,ædə'nɑi, ,ɑdə'nɔi

Adonais

elegy on Keats by Shelley	AD-n-Ā-uhs, AD-uh-NĀ-uhs	,ædn̩'eːəs, ,ædə'neːəs

Adonijah

pers. name	AD-uh-NĪ-juh, AD-n-Ī-juh	,ædə'nɑidʒə, ,ædn̩'ɑidʒə

Adonis

handsome youth of Greek myth	uh-DAHN-uhs, uh-DŌ-nuhs	ə'dɑnəs, ə'doːnəs

Adrastus

Argive king	uh-DRAS-tuhs	ə'dræstəs

Adriaan, Adriaen

pers. name, Dutch	AH-drē-AHN	'ɑːdriː,ɑːn

Adrian

1. E. D., English physiologist (Nobel 1932); pers. name	Ā-drē-uhn	'eːdriːən
2. Dutch	AH-drē-AHN	'ɑːdriː,ɑn
3. German	AHD-rē-AHN	'ɑdriː,ɑn

Adriani

John, *US physician*	Ā-drē-AHN-ē, Ā-drē-AN-ē	,eːdriː'ɑni', ,eːdriː'æni'

Adriano

1. pers. name, Italian	AHD-rē-AHN-ō	,ɑdriː'ɑnoː
2. Spanish	ah-<u>thr</u>ē-AHN-ō	ɑðriː'ɑnoː

Adriatic

Sea, *Mediterranean*	Ā-drē-AT-ik	,eːdriː'æt̬ik

Adrienne

1. pers. name	Ā-drē-EN, -uhn; Ā-drē-EN	'eːdriː,en, -ən; ,eːdriː'en
2. French	ah-drē-EN	ɑːdriːen

Key (col. 2):   a: fad   ā: fade   ah: father   ar: Mary   aw: law   e: fed   ē: feed   er: merry   i: hid   ī: hide   ō: coat   o͞o: boot
oi: boy   ow: now   u: put   uh: above   uhr: bird   ch: chop   ng: ring   sh: show   th: thick   <u>th</u>: this   zh: measure

Adventism
  religion AD-vent-IZ-uhm, uhd-VENT-IZ-uhm 'ædvɛnt͵izəm, əd'vent͵izəm
Adyĝhe, Adygei
  lang., Europe UH-DŌŌG-yuh, Ⓢ AHD-uh-GÃ, ͵ə'duːgjəi, Ⓢ 'adə͵geː,
    AHD-uh-GÃ ͵adə'geː
Adyukru
  lang., Ivory Coast uh-DYŌŌ-krōō ə'djuːkruː
Aeacus
  ruler of Myrmidons Ē-uh-kuhs 'iːəkəs
Aeaea
  island home of Circe in the ē-Ē-uh iː'iːə
    Odyssey
Aechmagoras
  beloved of Heracles ēk-MAG-uh-ruhs, ek- iːk'mægərəs, ek-
Aedon
  woman transformed into Ē-DAHN, ā-ĒD-n 'iː͵dɑn, eː'iːdn̩
    nightingale
Aeetes
  father of Medea ē-Ē-TĒZ, ē-ĒT-ēz iː'iː͵tiːz, iː'iːʈiːz
Aegaeon
  hundred-headed giant ē-JĒ-uhn, ē-JĒ-AHN i'dʒiːən, i'dʒiː͵ɑn
Aegean
  Sea, Mediterranean i-JĒ-uhn, ē-JĒ-uhn i'dʒiːən, iː'dʒiːən
Aegestes
  son of Aegesta ē-JES-TĒZ i'dʒes͵tiːz
Aegeus
  father of Theseus ē-JĒ-uhs, Ē-JŌŌS i'dʒiːəs, 'iː͵dʒuːs
Aegidius
  pers. name e-GĒD-yus, e-GĒD-ē-us, i-JID-ē-uhs e'giːdjus, e'giːdiːus,
    i'dʒidiːəs
Aegina
  Greek island i-JĪ-nuh i'dʒɑinə
Aegir
  Scandinavian sea god Ã-GIR ͵'eː͵giʳ
Aegisthus
  lover of Clytemnestra ē-JIS-thuhs i'dʒisθəs
Aegospotami
  ancient battlesite, Thrace Ē-guh-SPAHT-uh-MĪ ͵iːgə'spɑʈə͵mɑi
Aegyptus
  ruler of Egypt ē-JIP-tuhs i'dʒiptəs
Aelfric
  English abbot AL-frik, AL-frich 'ælfrik, 'ælfritʃ
Aelius
  pers. name Ē-lē-uhs 'iːliːəs
Aelius Aristides
  Greek rhetorician Ē-lē-uhs AR-uh-STĪD-ĒZ 'iːliːəs ͵ærə'stɑid͵iːz
Aemilianus
  pers. name i-MIL-ē-Ā-nuhs i͵m(iliː'eːnəs
Aemilius
  pers. name i-MIL-ē-uhs, -MIL-yuhs i'miliːəs, -'miljəs
Aeneas
  Trojan hero; ancestor of Romans i-NĒ-uhs, Ⓔ ē-NĒ-uhs i'niːəs, Ⓔ iː'niːəs
Aeneid
  epic, Vergil i-NĒ-uhd, Ⓔ Ē-nē-uhd i'niːəd, Ⓔ 'iːniːəd

Foreign Sounds: ue: *Fr.* **rue**, *Ger.* **füllen** uh(r): *Fr.* **boeuf**, *Ger.* **Höhle** kh: *Ger.* **ich**, *Scot.* **loch** ĝ: *Sp.* **amigo** v: *Sp.* **hablar**
hl: *Welsh* **Llanelli**. CAPITALS: primary stress. SMALL CAPS: secondary stress. Ⓢ: U.S. pron. Ⓔ: British pron.

Aeolia
  island of Aeolus   ē-Ō-lē-uh, ā-Ō-lē-uh   iː'oːliːə, eː'oːliːə
Aeolian
  musical mode; ancient Greek people   ē-Ō-lē-uhn, ā-Ō-lē-uhn   iː'oːliːən, eː'oːliːən
Aeolic
  Aeolian   ē-AHL-ik   iː'alik
Aeolis
  coastal region, Asia Minor   Ē-uh-luhs   'iːələs
Aeolus
  Greek god of wind   Ē-uh-luhs   'iːələs
Aepytus
  son of Merope   ē-PĒT-uhs   i'piːʈəs
Aer Lingus
  Irish airline   AR-LING-guhs, ER-   ˌæʳ'liŋɡəs, ˌeʳ-
Aeroflot
  Russian airline   AR-uh-FLAWT, ER-, -FLŌT   'ærəˌflɔːt, 'er-, -ˌfloːt
Aeromexico
  Mexican airline   Ī-rō-MĀ-hi-kō   ˌairoː'meˑhikoː
Aerope
  mother of Agamemnon and Menelaus   ā-ER-uh-pē, IR-uh-pē   eː'erəpiˑ, 'irəpiˑ
Aerospatiale
  French aircraft co.   ah-ā-raw-spahs-YAHL   aːeːrɔːspaːsjaːl
Aeschines
  Athenian orator   ES-ki-NĒZ, Ⓔ Ē-ski-   'eskiˌniːz, Ⓔ 'iːski-
Aeschylus
  Greek tragedian   ES-kuh-luhs, Ⓔ Ē-skuh-   'eskələs, Ⓔ 'iːskə-
Aesculapian
  pert. to Aesculapius   ES-k(y)uh-LĀ-pē-uhn, Ⓔ ĒS-   ˌesk(j)ə'leːpiːən, Ⓔ ˌiːs-
Aesculapius [Asclepius]
  Greek god of medicine   ES-k(y)uh-LĀ-pē-uhs, Ⓔ ĒS-   ˌesk(j)ə'leːpiːəs, Ⓔ ˌiːs-
Æsir
  Scandinavian gods   Ā-ZIR, Ā-SIR   'eːˌziʳ, 'eːˌsiʳ
Aeson
  father of Jason   Ē-suhn   'iːsən
Aesop
  Greek fablist   Ē-SAHP, Ē-suhp   'iːˌsɑp, 'iːsəp
Aesopian
  pert. to Aesop   ē-SŌ-pē-uhn, ē-SAHP-ē-uhn   iː'soːpiːən, iː'sɑpiːən
Aethalides
  Argonaut   ē-THAL-uh-DĒZ   i'θæləˌdiːz
Aether
  personification of the upper sky   Ē-thuhr   'iːθəʳ
Aethra
  mother of Theseus   Ē-thruh   'iːθrə
Aetna
  1. US insurance co.   ET-nuh   'etnə
  2. see Etna
Aetolia
  dept, Greece   ē-TŌL-yuh, ē-TŌ-lē-uh   iː'toːljə, iː'toːliːə
Aetolian League
  ancient Greek alliance   ē-TŌ-lē-uhn   iː'toːliːən
Aetolus
  son of Endymion   ē-TŌ-luhs, ĒT-l-uhs   iː'toːləs, 'iːtʲəs

Key (col. 2):   a: fad   ā: fade   ah: father   ar: Mary   aw: law   e: fed   ē: feed   er: merry   i: hid   ī: hide   ō: coat   ōō: boot
oi: boy   ow: now   u: put   uh: above   uhr: bird   ch: chop   ng: ring   sh: show   th: thick   th̲: this   zh: measure

Afar [Danakil]
  lang., people, E. Africa   AH-FAHR   'ɑˌfɑʳ

Afars and Issas
  former name for Djibouti   AHF-AHRZ uhn(d) ē-SAHZ   'afˌaʳz ən(d) iː'saz

Affenpinscher
  dog breed   AF-uhn-PIN-chuhr   'æfənˌpintʃəʳ

Affligem Tripel
  Belgian beer   AHF-liḡ-uhm TRIP-uhl   'ɑfliɣəm 'tripəl

Afghan
  resident of Afghanistan; lang.   AF-GAN   'æfˌgæn

Afghanistan
  republic, Asia   af-GAN-uh-STAN   æf'gænəˌstæn

AFL-CIO
  labor organization   Ā-EF-EL-SĒ-Ī-Ō   ˌeːˌef'elˌsiːˌai'oː

Afra
  pers. name   AF-ruh   'æfrə

Afrânio
  pers. name, Portuguese   uh-FRAHN-yōō, ah-   ə'frɑːnjuː, ɑː-

Africa
  continent   AF-ri-kuh   'æfrikə

African
  pert. to Africa   AF-ri-kuhn   'æfrikən

Africanus
  pers. name   AF-ri-KĀ-nuhs   ˌæfri'keːnəs

Afrikaans
  lang., S. Africa   AF-ri-KAHN(T)S, AF-ri-KAHNZ   ˌæfri'kɑn(t)s, ˌæfri'kɑnz

Afrikander, Africander
  cattle   AF-ri-KAN-duhr   ˌæfri'kændəʳ

Afrikaner
  speaker of Afrikaans   AF-ri-KAHN-uhr   ˌæfri'kɑnəʳ

Afro-
  a combining form meaning   AF-rō   'æfroː
  African

AFSCME
  American Federation of State,   AF-skmē   'æfskmiˑ
  County, and Municipal
  Employees

Afusare
  lang., Nigeria   AF-yōō-SAHR-ē   ˌæfju'sariˑ

Agag
  Amelekite king   Ā-GAG   'eːˌgæg

Aga Khan
  head of Shi'ism   AHG-uh KHAHN, KAHN   ˌagə 'xan, 'kan

Agamedes
  legendary architect   AG-uh-MĒ-DĒZ   ˌægə'miːˌdiːz

Agamemnon
  leader of Greeks against Trojans   AG-uh-MEM-NAHN,   ˌægə'memˌnan,
                                    AG-uh-MEM-nuhn   ˌægə'memnən

Agaña
  town, Guam   uh-GAHN-yuh   ə'ganjə

Agapetus, Agapitus
  papal name   AG-uh-PĒT-uhs   ˌægə'piːṭəs

Foreign Sounds: ue: *Fr.* **rue**, *Ger.* **füllen**   uh(r): *Fr.* **boeuf**, *Ger.* **Höhle**   kh: *Ger.* **ich**, *Scot.* **loch**   ḡ: *Sp.* **amigo**   v: *Sp.* **hablar**
hl: *Welsh* **Llanelli**.   CAPITALS: primary stress.   SMALL CAPS: secondary stress.   ⑤: U.S. pron.   ⑫: British pron.

Agar
1. lang., Sudan, Ethiopia	AH-GAHR	'ɑˌgɑʳ
2. Biblical name	Ā-GAHR	'eːˌgɑʳ
3. seaweed derivative	AHG-uhr	'ɑgəʳ

Agassi
Andre, *US tennis player*	AG-uh-sē	'ægəsiˑ

Agassiz
Louis, *US naturalist; lake, Canada*	AG-uh-sē	'ægəsiˑ

Agatha
pers. name	AG-uh-thuh	'ægəθə

Agathe
1. pers. name, French	ah-GAHT	ɑːgɑːt
2. German	ah-GAH-tuh	ɑ'gɑtə

Agatho
pope	AG-uh-THŌ	'ægəˌθoː

Agathocles
tyrant of Syracuse	uh-GATH-uh-KLĒZ	ə'gæθəˌkliːz

Agathon
1. Greek poet, playwright	AG-uh-THAHN	'ægəˌθɑn
2. pers. name, French	ah-gah-TAWⁿ	ɑːgɑːtɔ̃

Agave
daughter of Cadmus	uh-GAHV-ē	ə'gɑviˑ

Agdistis
hermaphrodite in Greek myth	ag-DIS-tuhs	æg'distəs

Agee
James, *US writer*	Ā-jē	'eːdʒiˑ

Agenor
1. father of Europa, Cadmus, Phoenix, Cilix	uh-GEN-AWR, uh-GĀ-NAWR	ə'genˌɔːʳ, ə'geːˌnɔːʳ
2. pers. name, German	ah-GĀ-NAWR	ɑ'geːˌnɔːʳ

Agénor
pers. name, French	ah-zhā-NAWR	ɑːʒeːnɔːr

Ageratum
plant	AJ-uh-RĀT-uhm	ˌædʒə'reːʈəm

Agesilaus
name, Spartan kings	uh-JES-uh-LĀ-uhs	əˌdʒesə'leːəs

Agfa
tdmk for photographic film	AG-fuh	'ægfə

Aggada, the [Haggadah]
part of Jewish Talmud	uh-GAHD-uh, uh-GAWD-uh, ah-; ahg-uh-DAH	ə'gɑdə, ə'gɔːdə, ɑ-; ɑgə'dɑ

Aggeus
Old Testament book	a-GĒ-uhs	æ'giːəs

Aggies
Texas A&M team	AG-ēz	'ægiˑz

Agincourt
village, France, battle site, 1415	AJ-uhn-KAWR(T), AZH-	'ædʒənˌkɔːʳ(t), 'æʒ-

Agis
Spartan king	Ā-juhs	'eːdʒəs

Aglaia
one of the Graces	uh-GLĪ-uh, uh-GLĀ-uh	ə'glaiə, ə'gleːə

Key (col. 2):   a: fad   ā: fade   ah: father   ar: Mary   aw: law   e: fed   ē: feed   er: merry   i: hid   ī: hide   ō: coat   o͞o: boot
oi: boy   ow: now   u: put   uh: above   uhr: bird   ch: chop   ng: ring   sh: show   th: thick   t̲h̲: this   zh: measure

Agnes
1. pers. name	AG-nuhs	'ægnəs
2. German	AHG-nes	'agnes
3. Norwegian	AHNG-nuhs	'aŋnəs

Agnès
pers. name, French	ahn-YES	aːnjes

Agnew
Spiro T., *US politician*	AG-N(Y)ŌO	'æg‚n(j)uː

Agnoetism
early Christian sect	AG-nō-ĒT-IZ-uhm, AG-nō-ĒT-IZ-uhm	‚ægnoː'iːt‚izəm, 'ægnoː‚iːt‚izəm

Agnolo
pers. name	AHN-yō-lō	'anjoːloː

Agnon
S. Y., *Israeli author (Nobel 1966)*	AG-NAHN, AHG-NAHN	'æg‚nan, 'ag‚nan

Agnus Dei
Christian symbol ("Lamb of God"); section of the Mass	AHG-NUS DĀ(-ē), AHG-NŌOS, AHN-YŌOS, AG-nuhs	‚ag‚nus 'deː(iː), ‚ag‚nuːs, ‚an‚juːs, ‚ægnəs

Agonistes
see Samson Agonistes

Agostinho
pers. name, Portuguese	uh-gŌOsh-TĒN-yōo, AH-gŌOs-	əguːʃ'tiːnjuː, ‚aːguːs-

Agostino
pers. name, Italian	AHG-ō-STĒ-nō	‚agoː'stiːnoː

Agra
city, India, site of Taj Mahal	AHG-ruh	'agrə

Agricola
pers. name	uh-GRIK-uh-luh	ə'grikələ

Ağrı Dağı [Ararat]
mtn., Turkey	AHĞ-rē dah-ĞĒ	‚aɣriː da'ɣiː

Agrigenetics
US corp.	AG-ruh-juh-NET-iks, AG-rē-	‚ægrədʒə'neţiks, ‚ægri'-

Agrigento
town, prov, Italy	AHG-ri-JEN-tō	‚agri'dʒentoː

Agrippa
1. Marcus Vipsanius, *Roman statesman; pers. name*	uh-GRIP-uh	ə'gripə
2. French	ah-grē(p)-PAH	aːgriː(p)paː

Agrippina
Roman pers. name	AG-ruh-PĒ-nuh, AG-ruh-PĪ-nuh	‚ægrə'piːnə, ‚ægrə'painə

Agronsky
Martin, *TV commentator*	uh-GRAHN-skē	ə'granskiˑ

Agua Caliente Band
N. American people	AHG-wuh kahl-YEN-tā	'agwə kal'jenteː

Aguacatec
lang., Guatemala	uh-GWAH-kuh-TEK	ə'gwakə‚tek

Aguascalientes
city, state, Mexico	ahğ-wah-skahl-YEN-tās	aɣwaskal'jenteːs

Aguecheek
Sir Andrew, *character in* Twelfth Night, *Shakespeare*	Ā-gyŌO-CHĒK	'eːgjuˑ‚tʃiːk

Aguila
Spanish beer	ah-GĒ-lah	a'giːla

Agulhas
cape, southern tip of Africa	uh-GUHL-uhs	ə'gələs

Foreign Sounds: ue: *Fr.* **rue**, *Ger.* **füllen** uh(r): *Fr.* **boeuf**, *Ger.* **Höhle** kh: *Ger.* i**ch**, *Scot.* lo**ch** ğ: *Sp.* ami**go** v: *Sp.* ha**b**lar hl: *Welsh* **Ll**anelli. CAPITALS: primary stress. SMALL CAPS: secondary stress. ⓢ: U.S. pron. ⓑ: British pron.

Agustín
  pers. name .... ah-gōōs-TĒN .... aguːsˈtiːn
Ahab
  king of Israel; character in Moby
  Dick, *H. Melville* .... Ā-HAB .... ˈeːˌhæb
Ahasuerus [Xerxes]
  King of Persia .... Ā-HAZ-yōō-IR-uhs, Ā-HAZ-yōō-ER-uhs ... ˌeːˌhæzjuːˈirəs, ˌeːˌhæzjuːˈerəs
Ahaz
  King of Judah .... Ā-HAZ .... ˈeːˌhæz
Ahenobarbus
  Roman cognomen .... uh-HĒ-nuh-BAHR-buhs, uh-HEN-uh-, ... əˌhiːnəˈbɑˤbəs, əˌhenə-,
                                                 uh-HĀ-nuh- .... əˌheːnə-
Aherne
  pers. name .... uh-HUHRN, Ā-HUHRN .... əˈhəˤn, ˈeːˌhəˤn
Ahithopel
  Hebrew counselor of King David .... uh-HITH-uh-FEL .... əˈhiθəˌfel
Ahmad
  pers. name, Arabic .... AHM-ahd, AHM-ad .... ˈɑmɑd, ˈɑmæd
Ahmadabad
  city, state, India .... AHM-uhd-uh-BAHD .... ˈɑmədəˌbɑd
Ahmed
  1. pers. name .... AHM-uhd .... ˈɑməd
  2. Albanian .... ah<u>kh</u>-MED .... ɑxˈmed
  3. Arabic .... AHM-ed .... ˈɑmed
  4. Turkish .... ah-MET .... ɑˈmet
Ahmet
  pers. name, Turkish .... ah-MET .... ɑˈmet
Ahmose
  Egyptian pharaoh .... AHM-ŌS .... ˈɑmˌoːs
Ahuntsic
  College, CT .... uh-HUHN(T)-sik .... əˈhən(t)sik
Ahura Mazda
  Zoroastrian god .... uh-HUR-uh MAHZ-duh, AH-HUR-uh ... əˈhurə ˈmɑzdə, ˈɑˌhurə
Ahvenanmaa [Åland]
  Finnish islands, Baltic Sea .... AH<u>KH</u>-vuh-nahn-MAH .... ˈɑxvənɑnˌmɑ
Aiaru
  Babylonian month .... Ī-AHR-ōō .... aiˈɑruː
Aïda
  opera, Verdi .... Ī-ĒD-uh .... aiˈiːdə
Aidan
  pers. name .... ĀD-n .... ˈeːdn̩
AIDS
  Acquired Immune Deficiency .... ĀDZ .... ˈeːdz
  Syndrome
Aiello
  Danny, *US entertainer* .... Ī-(Y)EL-ō .... aiˈ(j)eloː
Aiken
  Howard H., *scientist; county, city,* ... Ā-kuhn .... ˈeːkən
  SC; *Technical College,* SC; *pers.*
  name
Aikins
  Claude, *US actor* .... Ā-kuhnz .... ˈeːkənz
Aileen
  pers. name .... Ī-LĒN .... aiˈliːn

---

Key (col. 2): a: fad ā: fade ah: father ar: Mary aw: law e: fed ē: feed er: merry i: hid ī: hide ō: coat ōō: boot
oi: boy ow: now u: put uh: above uhr: bird ch: chop ng: ring sh: show th: thick <u>th</u>: this zh: measure

Ailey
　Alvin, Jr., *US dancer,* 　　Ā-lē 　　　　　　　'eːliˑ
　　choreographer
Aimé, Aimee, Aimée
　1. pers. name 　　　　ā-MĀ, em-Ā 　　　eːˈmeː, emˈeː
　2. French 　　　　　　em-Ā 　　　　　　emeː
Aino
　1. lang., people, Japan 　Ī-nō 　　　　　　　'aɪnoː
　2. pers. name, Finnish 　Ī-naw 　　　　　　　'aɪnɔː
Ainsworth
　city, IA, NE 　　　　　ĀNZ-WUHRTH 　　　'eːnz͵wəʳθ
Aintree
　town, England; site of Grand 　ĀN-trē 　　　　　'eːntriˑ
　　National steeplechase
Ainu [Aino]
　lang., people, Japan 　　Ī-nōō 　　　　　　　'aɪnuː
Aire
　1. river, England 　　　AR, ER 　　　　　　'æʳ, 'eʳ
　2. river, France 　　　ER, ⑤ AR 　　　　er, ⑤ 'æʳ, 'eʳ
Airedale
　dog breed 　　　　　　AR-DĀL, ER-DĀL 　'æʳ͵deːl, 'eʳ͵deːl
Aisha
　pers. name 　　　　　Ā-shuh, Ī-shuh, ah-Ē-shuh 　'eːʃə, 'aɪʃə, aˈiːʃə
Aisne
　river, dept, France 　　EN, ⑤ ĀN 　　　　en, ⑤ 'eːn
Aitken, Aitkin
　pers. name 　　　　　ĀT-kuhn, Ā-kuhn 　'eːtkən, 'eːkən
Aitkin
　county, MN 　　　　　Ā-kuhn 　　　　　　'eːkən
Aius Locutius
　a divine voice 　　　　Ā-(y)uhs lō-KYŌŌ-shuhs 　'eː(j)əs loːˈkjuːʃəs
Aiwa
　audio equipment co. 　　Ī-wuh, Ā-wuh 　　　'aɪwə, 'eːwə
Aix-en-Provence
　city, France 　　　　　ĀK-SAHⁿ-prō-VAHⁿS 　͵eˑk͵sãproːˈvãs
Aix-la-Chapelle
　city, Germany 　　　　ĀK-slah-shuh-PEL 　͵eˑkslaʃəˈpel
Aix-les-Bains
　town, France 　　　　āk-slā-BEⁿ 　　　　eˑksleːˈbẽ
Ajaccio
　seaport, Corsica 　　　ah-YAHCH-ō, ah-ZHAHK-syō 　aˈjatʃoː, aːʒaːksjoː
Ajax
　the Great, *son of Telamon;* the 　Ā-JAKS 　　　　'eː͵dʒæks
　　Lesser, *leader of Locrians*
　　against Trojans
Ajmān
　town, state, United Arab Emirates 　aj-MAHN, aj-MAN 　ædʒˈmɑn, ædʒˈmæn
Akaba
　see 'Aqaba
Akai
　audio equipment co. 　　uh-KĪ, AK-Ī 　　　əˈkaɪ, 'æk͵aɪ
Akan [Twi]
　lang., Ghana, Ivory Coast 　AHK-AHN 　　　　'ak͵an
Akbar
　emperor of India 　　　AK-buhr, AK-BAHR 　'ækbəʳ, 'æk͵baʳ

Foreign Sounds: ue: *Fr.* **rue,** *Ger.* **füllen** uh(r): *Fr.* **boeuf,** *Ger.* **Höhle** kh: *Ger.* **ich,** *Scot.* **loch** ḡ: *Sp.* **amigo** v: *Sp.* **hablar**
hl: *Welsh* **Llanelli.** CAPITALS: primary stress. SMALL CAPS: secondary stress. ⑤: U.S. pron. Ⓔ: British pron.

Ak-Chin
  Indian reservation, US   ak-CHIN   æk'tʃin
Aker
  Egyptian earth god   AK-uhr, Ā-kuhr, AHK-uhr   'ækəʳ, 'eːkəʳ, 'akəʳ
Akhnaton
  Egyptian pharaoh   ahk-NAHT-n   ak'natṇ
Akihito
  Japanese emperor   ah-kē-hē-tō   akiːhiːtoː
Akim
  1. pers. name, Polish   AH-kēm   'aːkiːm
  2. Russian   UHK-YĒM   ˌək'jiːm
Akita
  port, Japan; dog breed   uh-KĒT-uh, ah-KĒT-uh   ə'kiːṭə, a'kiːṭə
Akitsune
  pers. name, Japanese   ah-kēt-sun-e   akiːtsune
Akkad
  ancient Asian region   AHK-AHD, AK-AD   'ak,ad, 'æk,æd
Akkadian
  ancient lang.   uh-KAD-ē-uhn, ak-AD-ē-uhn, uh-KĀD-ē-uhn   ə'kædiːən, æk'ædiːən, ə'keːdiːən
Akoli [Acholi]
  lang., people, Uganda, Sudan   uh-KŌ-lē   ə'koːliˑ
Akron
  city, OH   AK-ruhn   'ækrən
Aksel
  pers. name   AHK-SEL   'aːk,sel
Akvavit
  liquor   AHK-wuh-VĒT, AHK-vah-VĒT   ˌakwə'viːt, 'akva'viːt
Akyab [Sittwe]
  town, Burma   ak-YAB   æk'jæb
Al
  pers. name   AL   'æl
Alabama
  state, US   AL-uh-BAM-uh   ˌælə'bæmə
Alabama-Coushatta
  Indian reservation, US   AL-uh-BAM-uh-ku-SHAHT-uh   ˌælə'bæməku'ʃaṭə
Alabaman
  pert. to Alabama   AL-uh-BAM-uhn   ˌælə'bæmən
Alabamian
  pert. to Alabama   AL-uh-BAM-ē-uhn   ˌælə'bæmiːən
Alacaluf
  S. American people   AL-uh-kuh-LOOF, AL-uh-kuh-LOOF   ˌæləkə'luːf, 'æləkəˌluːf
Alachua
  county, FL   uh-LAHCH-uh-WĀ, uh-LACH-uh-WĀ, -uh-wuh   ə'latʃəˌweː, ə'lætʃəˌweː, -əwə
Aladdin
  hero, Arabian Nights   uh-LAD-n   ə'lædṇ
Alain
  1. pers. name   AL-uhn   'ælən
  2. French   ah-LEⁿ   aːlẽ
Alamance
  stream, county, NC   AL-uh-MAN(T)S   'æləˌmæn(t)s
Alameda
  city, county, CA   AL-uh-MĒD-uh   ˌælə'miːdə

Key (col. 2):   a: fad ā: fade ah: father ar: **M**a**ry** aw: l**aw** e: f**e**d ē: f**ee**d er: m**erry** i: h**i**d ī: h**i**de ō: c**oa**t ōō: b**oo**t
oi: b**oy** ow: n**ow** u: p**u**t uh: **a**bove uhr: b**ir**d ch: **ch**op ng: ri**ng** sh: **sh**ow th: **th**ick <u>th</u>: **this** zh: mea**s**ure

Alamein
  see El Alamein
Alamo
  mission, San Antonio, TX AL-uh-MŌ 'ælə,moː
Alamogordo
  county, dam, NM AL-uh-muh-GAWR-dō ,æləmə'gɔːʳdoː
Alamosa
  county, city, CO AL-uh-MŌ-suh, AL-uh-MOO-suh ,ælə'moːsə, ,ælə'muːsə
Alan
  pers. name AL-uhn 'ælən
Alana
  pers. name uh-LAHN-uh, uh-LAN-uh ə'lɑnə, ə'lænə
Åland [Ahvenanmaa]
  Finnish islands, Baltic Sea AW-luhnd 'ɔːlənd
Al-Anon
  US organization AL-uh-NAHN 'ælə,nɑn
Alaouite, Alawite Druze
  people, Syria AL-uh-WĒT DROOZ, AL-uh-WĒT 'ælə,wiːt 'druːz, ,ælə'wiːt
Alar
  tdmk for a pesticide AL-AHR 'æl,ɑʳ
Alaric
  1. pers. name AL-uh-rik 'ælərik
  2. French ah-lah-RĒK ɑːlɑːriːk
Alasdair
  pers. name AL-uh-stuhr 'æləstəʳ
Alaska
  state, US uh-LAS-kuh ə'læskə
Alaskan malamute
  dog breed uh-LAS-kuhn MAL-uh-MYOOT ə,læskən 'mælə,mjuːt
al-Assad
  Hafez, *president, Syria* AHL-uh-SAHD, Ⓢ AL-uh-SAD ,ɑːlə'saːd, Ⓢ ,ælə'sæd
Alastair
  pers. name AL-uh-STAR, -STER; AL-uh-stuhr 'ælə,stæʳ, -,steʳ; 'æləstəʳ
Alba
  pers. name AHL-bah 'ɑlbɑ
Albacete
  prov, Spain ahl-vah-SÄ-tä ɑlβɑ'seːteː
Alban
  1. pers. name AWL-buhn, AL- 'ɔːlbən, 'æl-
  2. French ahl-BAHⁿ ɑːlbã
  3. German ahl-BAHN, AHL-BAHN ɑl'bɑn, 'ɑl,bɑn
Albani
  Danish beer AHL-bah-nē 'ɑːlbɑːniˑ
Albania
  republic, Europe al-BĀ-nē-uh, awl-, -nyuh æl'beːniːə, ɔːl-, -njə
Albanian
  lang., Albania al-BĀ-nē-uhn, awl-, -nyuhn æl'beːniːən, ɔːl-, -njən
Alban League
  ancient Latin confederation AL-buhn, AWL- 'ælbən, 'ɔːl-
Albano
  lake, Italy al-BAHN-ō, ahl- æl'bɑnoː, ɑl-
Albany
  1. city, county, NY; river, Canada AWL-buh-nē 'ɔːlbəniˑ
  2. city, Australia AL-buh-nē 'ælbəniˑ
  3. city, GA awl-BE-nē ɔːl'beniˑ

Foreign Sounds: ue: *Fr.* **rue**, *Ger.* **füllen** uh(r): *Fr.* **boeuf**, *Ger.* **Höhle** <u>kh</u>: *Ger.* **ich**, *Scot.* **loch** g̱: *Sp.* **amigo** <u>v</u>: *Sp.* **hablar** hl: *Welsh* **Llanelli**. CAPITALS: primary stress. SMALL CAPS: secondary stress. Ⓢ: U.S. pron. Ⓛ: British pron.

Albatross
  sea bird | AL-buh-TRAWS, -TRAHS | 'ælbə,trɔːs, -,trɑs

Albee
  Edward, *US writer* | AWL-bē, AL-bē | 'ɔːlbiˑ, 'ælbiˑ

Albemarle
  George Monck, Duke of, *English general; county, VA; town, sound, college, NC* | AL-buh-MAHRL | 'ælbə,mɑ^rl

Alberghetti
  Anna Maria, *US entertainer* | AL-buhr-GET-ē | ,ælbə^r'geṭiˑ

Alberic
  pers. name | AL-buh-rik | 'ælbərik

Alberich
  king of the dwarves in Teutonic myth; pers. name | AHL-buh-RI<u>KH</u> | 'ɑlbə,riç

Albericus
  pers. name | AL-buh-RĪ-kuhs | ,ælbə'rɑikəs

Albert
  1. *pers. name* | AL-buhrt | 'ælbə^rt
  2. *Danish, Finnish, Hungarian* | AHL-BERT | 'ɑːl,bert
  3. *Dutch* | AHL-BERT | 'ɑl,bert
  4. *French* | ahl-BER | ɑːlber
  5. *German* | AHL-BERT | 'ɑl,be^rt
  6. *Norwegian* | AHL-buhrt, AHL-BERT | 'ɑlbərt, 'ɑl,bert
  7. *Swedish* | AHL-buhrt | 'ɑːlbərt

Alberta
  province, Canada; pers. name | al-BUHRT-uh | æl'bə^rtə

Alberto
  1. *pers. name, Italian* | ahl-BER-tō | al'bertoː
  2. *Portuguese* | ahl-BER-tōō | al'bertuː
  3. *Spanish* | ahl-<u>V</u>ER-tō | al'ßertoː

Albertus
  1. *pers. name* | al-BUHRT-uhs | æl'bə^rṭəs
  2. *Dutch* | ahl-BER-tues | al'bertys

Albertus Magnus
  German philosopher, saint; college, CT | al-BUHRT-uhs MAG-nuhs | æl'bə^rṭəs 'mægnəs

Albertville
  1. *city, AL* | AL-buhrt-VIL | 'ælbə^rt,vil
  2. *village, France* | ahl-ber-VĒL, Ⓢ AL-buhr-VIL | ɑːlberviːl, Ⓢ 'ælbə^r,vil

Albigenses
  medieval Christian sect | AL-buh-JEN-SĒZ | ,ælbə'dʒen,siːz

Albigensian
  pert. to Albigenses | AL-buh-JEN-sē-uhn | ,ælbə'dʒensiːən

Albigensianism
  tenets of the Albigenses | AL-buh-JEN-sē-uh-NIZ-uhm | ,ælbə'dʒensiːə,nizəm

Albinus
  Roman cognomen | al-BĪ-nuhs | æl'bɑinəs

Albion
  ancient name of Gt. Britain; US pl. name; College, MI; *pers. name* | AL-bē-uhn | 'ælbiːən

Alborán Basin
  Mediterranean Sea | AL-buh-RAHN | ,ælbə'rɑn

Key (col. 2):   a: fad ā: fade ah: father ar: **Mary** aw: **law** e: fed ē: feed er: **merry** i: hid ī: hide ō: coat ōō: boot
oi: **boy** ow: **now** u: **put** uh: **above** uhr: **bird** ch: **chop** ng: **ring** sh: **show** th: **thick** <u>th</u>: **this** zh: **measure**

Ålborg
  see Aalborg
Albrecht
  1. pers. name, Danish   AHL-BRE<u>KH</u>T   'aːl,breçt
  2. German   AHL-BRE<u>KH</u>T   'al,breçt
Albuquerque
  city, NM   AL-buh-KUHR-kē, AL-byuh-KUHR-kē   'ælbə,kəʳkiˑ, 'ælbjə,kəʳkiˑ
Alcaeus
  Greek poet   al-SĒ-uhs   æl'siːəs
Alcan
  highway, Alaska-Canada   AL-KAN   'æl,kæn
Alcántara
  commune, Spain   ahl-KAHNT-uh-ruh, al-KANT-uh-ruh   al'kɑnṭərə, æl'kænṭərə
Alcatraz
  island, prison, San Francisco Bay   AL-kuh-TRAZ   'ælkə,træz
Alcazar
  Moorish palace   AL-kuh-ZAHR, al-KAZ-uhr   ,ælkə'zɑʳ, æl'kæzəʳ
Alceste
  opera, Gluck   al-SEST   æl'sest
Alcestis
  tragedy, Euripides   al-SES-tuhs   æl'sestəs
Alcibiades
  Athenian leader   AL-suh-BĪ-uhd-ēz   ,ælsə'baiədiːz
Alcide
  1. pers. name, French   ahl-SĒD   aːlsiːd
  2. Italian   ahl-SĒ-dā   al'siːdeː
Alcides
  pers. name, Spanish   ahl-SĒ-<u>th</u>ās, ahl-THĒ-<u>th</u>ās   al'siːðeːs, al'θiːðeːs
Alcindor
  Lew, *former name of* Kareem   al-SIN-duhr   æl'sindəʳ
    Abdul-Jabbar
Alcinoüs
  king of Phaeacia, host to   al-SIN-uh-wuhs   æl'sinəwəs
    Odysseus, Jason, and Medea
Alcmaeon
  son of Amphiaraus   alk-MĒ-uhn   ælk'miːən
Alcmene
  wife of Amphitryon, mother of   alk-MĒ-nē   ælk'miːniˑ
    Heracles
Alcoa
  city, TN; US aluminum co.   al-KŌ-uh   æl'koːə
Alcorn
  county, MS   AWL-KAWRN   'ɔːl,kɔːʳn
Alcott
  Louisa May, *US writer;* Bronson,   AWL-kuht, AL-kuht, AWL-KAHT,   'ɔːlkət, 'ælkət, 'ɔːl,kɑt,
    US educator, philosopher   AL-KAHT   'æl,kɑt
Alcuin
  English scholar   AL-kwuhn   'ælkwən
Alcyone
  wife of Ceyx; star in Pleiades   al-SĪ-uh-nē   æl'saiəniˑ
Alcyoneus
  giant defeated by Hercules   al-SĪ-uh-NĒ-uhs, al-SĪ-uh-NOOS   æl,saiə'niːəs, æl'saiə,nuːs
Alda
  Alan, *US actor, writer, director*   AWL-duh   'ɔːldə

Foreign Sounds: ue: *Fr.* **rue**, *Ger.* **füllen**   uh(r): *Fr.* **boeuf**, *Ger.* **Höhle**   <u>kh</u>: *Ger.* i**ch**, *Scot.* lo**ch**   ḡ: *Sp.* ami**g**o   v̱: *Sp.* ha**b**lar
hl: *Welsh* **Ll**anelli.   CAPITALS: primary stress.   SMALL CAPS: secondary stress.   Ⓢ: U.S. pron.   Ⓑ: British pron.

Aldebaran
   star   al-DEB-uh-ruhn   æl'debərən

Alder
   Kurt, *German chemist (Nobel*   AHL-duhr   'ɑldəʳ
   1950)

Alderney
   Channel Island   AWL-duhr-nē   'ɔːldəʳniˑ

Aldershot
   borough, Hampshire, England   AWL-duhr-SHAHT   'ɔːldəʳˌʃɑt

Alderson Broaddus
   College, WV   AWL-duhr-suhn BRAWD-uhs   'ɔːldəʳsən 'brɔːdəs

Aldine
   print types by A. Manutius   AWL-DĪN, AWL-DĒN   'ɔːlˌdain, 'ɔːlˌdiːn

Aldo
   pers. name   AHL-dō   'ɑldoː

Aldous
   pers. name (A. Huxley)   AWL-duhs   'ɔːldəs

Aldredge
   Theoni, *Greek costume designer*   AWL-drij   'ɔːldridʒ

Aldrin
   Edwin E. 'Buzz', *US astronaut*   AWL-druhn   'ɔːldrən

Aldwinckle
   village, England   AH-nik-uhl   'ɑːnikəl

Alec, Aleck
   pers. name   AL-uhk   'ælək

Alecost
   herb   ĀL-KAHST   'eːlˌkɑst

Alecto
   see Allecto

Aleichem
   Shalom, *pseudonym of* Sholem   uh-LĀ-kuhm, uh-LĀ-<u>kh</u>uhm   ə'leːkəm, ə'leːxəm
   Rabinowitz, *US author*

Aleixandre
   Vicente, *Spanish poet (Nobel*   ahl-ek-SAHN-dre   alek'sɑndre
   1977)

Alejandro
   pers. name, Spanish   ahl-ā-<u>KH</u>AHN-drō   aleː'xɑndroː

Alejo
   pers. name, Portuguese   ahl-Ā-zhoo̅   al'eːʒuː

Alekhine, Alekhin
   Alexander, *Russian chess master*   UHL-YŌ<u>KH</u>-yin   ˌəl'joːxjin

Aleksander
   pers. name, Polish   AH-lek-SAHN-der   ˌɑːlek'sɑːnder

Aleksandr
   pers. name, Russian   UHL-yik-SAHN-duhr   ˌəljik'sɑːndər

Aleksandra
   pers. name, Russian   UHL-yik-SAHN-druh   ˌəljik'sɑːndrə

Aleksey
   pers. name, Russian   UHL-yik-SYĀ(-ē)   ˌəljik'sjeː(iː)

Alekseyevich
   pers. name, Russian   UHL-yik-SYĀ(-yiv)-yich   ˌəljik'sjeː(jiv)jitʃ

Alekseyevna
   pers. name, Russian   UHL-yik-SYĀ(-yuh)v-nuh   ˌəljik'sjeː(jə)vnə

Key (col. 2):   a: fad   ā: fade   ah: father   ar: Mary   aw: law   e: fed   ē: feed   er: merry   i: hid   ī: hide   ō: coat   o̅o̅: boot
oi: boy   ow: now   u: put   uh: above   uhr: bird   ch: chop   ng: ring   sh: show   th: thick   <u>th</u>: this   zh: measure

Alemán
  Miguel, *president, Mexico;* Mateo,   ahl-ā-MAHN   aleː'man
    Spanish writer
Alemanni
  Germanic tribes   AL-uh-MAN-ē   ˌælə'mæniˑ
Alemannic
  German dialect   AL-uh-MAN-ik   ˌælə'mænik
Alençon
  city, France   ah-lah^n-SAW^n aːlãsɔ̃
Aleppo
  city, Syria   uh-LEP-ō   ə'lepoː
Alessandro
  pers. name   AH-lās-SAHN-drō   ˌaleːs'sandroː
Aletsch
  glacier, Switzerland   AHL-ich   'alitʃ
Aleut
  N. American people   AL-ē-O͞OT, AL-ē-O͞OT, uh-LO͞OT   ˌæliː'uːt, 'æliːˌuːt, ə'luːt
Aleutians
  island chain, AK   uh-LO͞O-shuhnz   ə'luːʃənz
Alex
  pers. name   AL-uhks   'æləks
Alexa
  pers. name   uh-LEK-suh   ə'leksə
Alexander
  1. pers. name   AL-ig-ZAN-duhr, EL-, ⓔ ZAHN-duhr   ˌælig'zændə^r, ˌel-, ⓔ
          -'zaːndə^r
  2. Dutch   AH-lek-SAHN-duhr   ˌaːlek'sandər
  3. Finnish, Polish   AH-lek-SAHN-der   ˌaːlek'saːnder
  4. German   AHL-ek-SAHN-duhr   ˌalek'sandə^r
  5. Norwegian   AHL-uhk-SAHN-duhr   ˌalək'sandər
  6. Russian   uhl-yik-SAHN-duhr   əljik'saːndər
  7. Swedish   AH-luhk-SAHN-duhr   ˌaːlək'saːndər
Alexandra
  1. pers. name   AL-ig-ZAN-druh, EL-, ⓔ -ZAHN-   ˌælig'zændrə, ˌel-, ⓔ -'zaːn-
  2. Danish   AH-lek-SAHN-druh   ˌaːlek'saːndrə
Alexandre
  1. pers. name   AL-ig-ZAN-duhr, EL-, ⓔ -ZAHN-   ˌælig'zændə^r, ˌel-, ⓔ -'zaːn-
  2. French   ah-lek-SAH^{n}DR, -SAH^n-druh   aːleksãdr, -sãdrə
Alexandretta
  former name of Gulf of   AL-ig-zan-DRET-uh, EL-, ⓔ   ˌæligzæn'dretə, ˌel-, ⓔ
    Iskenderun   -zahn-DRET-uh   -zaːn'dretə
Alexandria
  Egyptian seaport; US pl. name   AL-ig-ZAN-drē-uh, EL-   ˌælig'zændriːə, ˌel-
Alexei, Alexey
  1. pers. name   uh-LEK-sā   ə'lekseː
  2. Russian   UHL-yiks-YĀ(-ē)   ˌəljiks'jeː(iː)
Alexis
  1. pers. name   uh-LEK-suhs   ə'leksəs
  2. Finnish   AH-LEK-sis   'aːˌleksis
Alfa
  Dutch beer   AHL-fuh   'alfə
Alfalfa
  character in Little Rascals   al-FAL-fuh   æl'fælfə
Alfa Romeo
  tdmk for a car   AL-fuh ruh-MĀ-ō   ˌælfə rə'meːoː

Foreign Sounds: ue: *Fr.* rue, *Ger.* füllen   uh(r): *Fr.* boeuf, *Ger.* Höhle   kh: *Ger.* ich, *Scot.* loch   ḡ: *Sp.* amigo   v: *Sp.* hablar
hl: *Welsh* Llanelli.   CAPITALS: primary stress.   SMALL CAPS: secondary stress.   Ⓢ: U.S. pron.   ⓔ: British pron.

Al Fatah
  Palestinian group   AHL fah-TAH, fuh-TAH, FAH-TAH, AL   ‚aːl faˈta, fəˈta, ˈfa‚ta, ‚æl

Alfonse
  pers. name   AL-FAHNS, -FAHNZ; AL-FAHNS, -FAHNZ   ˈæl‚fans, -‚fanz; ælˈfans, -ˈfanz

Alfonsin
  Raul R., *president, Argentina*   ahl-fawn-SĒN   alfɔːnˈsiːn

Alfonso
  1. pers. name   al-FAHN-sō, -zō   ælˈfansoː, -zoː
  2. German   ahl-FAWN-zō   alˈfɔːnzoː
  3. Italian, Spanish   ahl-FAWN-sō   alˈfɔːnsoː

Alfred
  1. pers. name   AL-fruhd, AL-fuhrd   ˈælfrəd, ˈælfəʳd
  2. Dutch   AHL-FRET   ˈal‚fret
  3. Finnish, Swedish   AHL-FRED   ˈaːl‚fred
  4. French   ahl-FRED   aːlfred
  5. German   AHL-FRĀT   ˈal‚freːt
  6. Norwegian   AHL-FRED   ˈal‚fred
  7. Polish   AHL-FRET   ˈaːl‚fret

Alfreda
  pers. name   al-FRĒD-uh   ælˈfriːdə

Alfredo
  1. pers. name, Italian   ahl-FRĀ-dō   alˈfreːdoː
  2. Spanish   ahl-FRĀ-thō   alˈfreːðoː

Alfvén
  Hannes Olof, *Swedish physicist (Nobel 1970)*   al(f)-VĀN, AL(F)-VEN   æl(f)ˈveːn, ‚æl(f)ˈven

Alger
  Horatio, *writer*   AL-juhr   ˈældʒəʳ

Algeria
  republic, Africa   al-JIR-ē-uh   ælˈdʒiriːə

Algerian
  pert. to Algeria *or* Algiers   al-JIR-ē-uhn   ælˈdʒiriːən

Algernon
  1. pers. name   AL-juhr-nuhn, -NAHN   ˈældʒəʳnən, -‚nan
  2. French   ahl-zher-NAWⁿ   aːlʒernɔ̃

Algiers
  city, Algeria   al-JIRZ   ælˈdʒiʳz

ALGOL
  programming lang.   AL-GAWL, AL-GAHL   ˈæl‚gɔːl, ˈæl‚gal

Algol
  binary star   AL-GAWL, AL-GAHL   ˈæl‚gɔːl, ˈæl‚gal

Algoma
  University, *Canada*   al-GŌ-muh   ælˈgoːmə

Algonkin [Algonquin]
  N. American people   al-GAHNG-kuhn   ælˈgaŋkən

Algonquin
  N. American people   al-GAHN-kwuhn, al-GAHNG-kwuhn   ælˈgankwən, ælˈgaŋkwən

Alhambra
  1. city, CA   al-HAM-bruh   ælˈhæmbrə
  2. Moorish palace, Granada, Spain   ahl-AHM-brah, Ⓢ al-HAM-bruh, al-HAHM-bruh   alˈambra, Ⓢ ælˈhæmbrə, ælˈhambrə

Key (col. 2):   a: fad   ā: fade   ah: father   ar: Mary   aw: law   e: fed   ē: feed   er: merry   i: hid   ī: hide   ō: coat   o͞o: boot
oi: boy   ow: now   u: put   uh: above   uhr: bird   ch: chop   ng: ring   sh: show   th: thick   t͟h: this   zh: measure

Ali

1. Muhammad, *US boxer; pers.*   ah-LĒ; AL-ē, AHL-ē   ɑ'liː; 'æliˑ, 'ɑliˑ
    name
2. *Arabic*   ah-LĒ, a-LĒ   ɑː'liː, æ'liː
3. *Persian*   ah-LĒ   ɑː'liː
4. *Turkish*   ah-LĒ   ɑ'liː

Alianza Republicana Nacionalista
[Arena]

   political party, El Salvador   ahl-ē-AHN-sah rä-poō-blē-KAHN-ah   ɑliː'ɑnsɑ reːpuːbliː'kɑnɑ
     nah-sē-ō-nah-LĒ-stah   nɑsiːoːnɑ'liːstɑ

Ali Baba

   hero, Arabian Nights   AL-ē BAHB-uh   ˌæliː 'bɑbə

Alicante

   town, prov, Spain   ahl-ē-KAHN-tä, ⓢ AL-i-KANT-ē   ɑliː'kɑnteː, ⓢ ˌæli'kænti

Alice

1. *pers. name*   AL-uhs   'æləs
2. *French*   ah-LĒS   ɑːliːs
3. *German*   ah-LĒ-suh   ɑ'liːsə
4. *Italian*   ah-LĒ-chā   ɑ'liːtʃeː

Alicia

1. *pers. name*   uh-LISH(-ē)-uh, uh-LĒ-shuh   ə'liʃ(iː)ə, ə'liːʃə
2. *Italian*   ah-LĒ-chah   ɑ'liːtʃa
3. *Spanish*   ah-LĒS-yah, ah-LĒTH-yah   ɑ'liːsja, ɑ'liːθja

Al-'id al-Kabir

   Islamic festival   ahl-ID AHL-kahb-IR   ɑl'id ˌɑlkɑb'ir

Alison

   pers. name   AL-uh-suhn   'æləsən

Alistair

   pers. name   AL-uh-STAR, AL-uh-STER,   'æləˌstæ^r, 'æləˌste^r, 'æləstə^r
     AL-uh-stuhr

Alitalia

   Italian airline   AL-i-TAL-yuh, AL-i-TAL-ē-uh   ˌæli'tæljə, ˌæli'tæliːə

Alka-Seltzer

   tdmk for an over-the-counter   AL-kuh-SELT-suhr   'ælkəˌseltsə^r
    medicine

Allah

   Islamic name for God   AHL-uh, AL-uh, AHL-AH, ah-LAH   'ɑlə, 'ælə, 'ɑlˌɑ, ɑ'lɑ

Allahabad

   city, district, India   AL-uh-huh-BAD, -BAHD   'æləhəˌbæd, -ˌbɑd

Allais

   Maurice, *French economist,*   ah-LE   ɑːle
    engineer (Nobel 1988)

Allamakee

   county, IA   AL-uh-muh-KĒ   ˌæləmə'kiː

Allan

   pers. name   AL-uhn   'ælən

Allardice, -dyce

   pers. name   AL-uhr-DĪS   'ælə^{r}ˌdɑis

All-Bran

   tdmk for a brand of cereal   AWL-BRAN   'ɔːlˌbræn

Allecto, Alecto

   one of the Greek Furies   uh-LEK-tō   ə'lektoː

Allegan

   county, city, MI   AL-i-guhn   'æligən

Foreign Sounds: **ue**: *Fr.* **rue**, *Ger.* f**ü**llen **uh(r)**: *Fr.* b**oeu**f, *Ger.* H**öh**le **kh**: *Ger.* i**ch**, *Scot.* lo**ch** **g̃**: *Sp.* ami**g**o **v**: *Sp.* ha**b**lar
hl: *Welsh* **Ll**anelli. CAPITALS: primary stress. SMALL CAPS: secondary stress. ⓢ: U.S. pron. ⓛ: British pron.

Allegheny
county, PA; river, mts., US　　　AL-uh-GĀ-nē, AL-uh-GEN-ē　　　ˌæləˈgeːniˈ, ˌæləˈgeniˈ

Allegri
pers. name (A. A. Correggio)　　uh-LEG-rē, uh-LĀ-grē　　　əˈlegriˈ, əˈleːgriˈ

Allegro, L'
see L'Allegro

Allemande
dance　　　　　AL-uh-MAND, AL-uh-MAND　　　ˈæləˌmænd, ˌæləˈmænd

Allen
pers. name　　　　AL-uhn　　　ˈælən

Allende Gossens
Salvador, president, Chile　　ah-YEN-dā GAW-sens　　aˈjendeː ˈgɔːsens

Allentown
city, PA　　　　AL-uhn-TOWN　　　ˈælənˌtɑun

Allergan
US personal products co.　　AL-uhr-GAN　　　ˈæləʳˌgæn

Allhallows Eve
Oct. 31　　　　awl-HAL-ōz　　　ɔːlˈhæloːz

Allie, Ally
pers. name　　　AL-ē　　　ˈæliˈ

Allison
pers. name　　　AL-uh-suhn　　　ˈæləsən

Allium
genus of onions and garlic　　AL-ē-uhm　　　ˈæliːəm

Allora
town, Australia　　AL-uh-ruh　　　ˈælərə

Allosaurus
dinosaur　　　AL-uh-SAWR-uhs　　　ˌæləˈsɔːrəs

Allsop, Allsopp
pers. name　　　AWL-SAHP　　　ˈɔːlˌsɑp

All Souls
college, Oxford Univ.　　AWL SŌLZ　　　ˌɔːl ˈsoːlz

Allvar
pers. name, Swedish　　AHL-VAHR　　　ˈɑːlˌvɑːʳ

Alma
1. Crimean river; US pl. name;　　AL-muh　　　ˈælmə
pers. name
2. German　　　AHL-mah　　　ˈɑlmɑ

Alma-Ata
city, Kazakhstan　　AL-muh-uh-TAH　　　ˌælmə-əˈtɑ

Almadén
tdmk for wine　　AL-muh-DEN, AL-muh-DEN　　　ˌælməˈden, ˈælməˌden

Almagest
Ptolemaic work on astronomy　　AL-muh-JEST　　　ˈælməˌdʒest

Alma-Tadema
Sir Lawrence, British painter　　AL-muh-TAD-uh-muh　　　ˈælməˈtædəmə

Almería
province, town, Spain　　AHL-mā-RĒ-uh　　　ˌɑlmeːˈriːə

Al Mina
Syria, site of ancient trading post　　ahl MĒ-nuh, al　　　ɑːl ˈmiːnə, æl

Alnu
people　　　AL-N(Y)OO　　　ˈælˌn(j)uː

Alnwick
castle, England　　AN-ik　　　ˈænik

Key (col. 2):　a: fad　ā: fade　ah: father　ar: Mary　aw: law　e: fed　ē: feed　er: merry　i: hid　ī: hide　ō: coat　ōō: boot
oi: boy　ow: now　u: put　uh: above　uhr: bird　ch: chop　ng: ring　sh: show　th: thick　th̲: this　zh: measure

Aloadae
 sons of Poseidon   al-Ō-uh-dē, AL-uh-WĀD-ē   æl'oːədiˑ, ˌælə'weːdiˑ

Aloha
 Stadium, *Honolulu, HI; Hawaiian*   uh-LŌ-HAH   ə'loːˌhɑ
  greeting

Alois
 1. pers. name   uh-LOIS   ə'lɔis
 2. Czech   AH-LOIS   'ɑːˌlɔis
 3. German   AHL-ō-ÊS, AHL-OIS   'aloːˌiːs, 'alˌɔis

Aloisius
 1. pers. name   AL-uh-WISH-uhs   ˌælə'wiʃəs
 2. German   AHL-ō-ÊZ-yus, -Ê-zē-us   ˌaloˑ'iːzjus, -'iːziˑus

Aloïsius
 pers. name, French   ah-lō-ēz-YUES   ɑːloˑiːzjyːs

Alonso
 1. pers. name   uh-LAHN-zō   ə'lɑnzoː
 2. Italian, Spanish   ah-LAWN-sō   a'lɔːnsoː

Alonzo
 pers. name   uh-LAHN-zō   ə'lɑnzoː

Aloys
 1. pers. name, French   ah-law-ÊS   ɑːlɔːiːs
 2. German   AHL-aw-ues, AHL-OIS   'alɔːys, 'alˌɔis

Aloyse
 pers. name, French   ah-law-ÊZ   ɑːlɔːiːz

Aloysius
 pers. name   AL-uh-WISH-uhs   ˌælə'wiʃəs

Alpena
 city, county, MI   al-PÊ-nuh   æl'piːnə

Alpenziger
 cheese   AL-puhn-ZÊ-guhr   'ælpənˌziːgəʳ

Alpert
 Herb, *US musician*   AL-puhrt   'ælpəʳt

Alpes Bernoises [Bernese Alps]
 mtn. range, Switzerland   ahl-puh bern-WAHZ   ɑːlpə bernwaːz

Alpes Cottiennes [Cottian Alps]
 Alpine mtn. range   ahl-puh kaw-TYEN   ɑːlpə kɔːtjen

Alpes-de-Haute-Provence
 dept., France   ahlpuh duh ōt pruh-VAHⁿS   ɑːlpə də oːt prəvɑ̃s

Alpes de Savoie [Savoy Alps]
 Alpine mtn. range   ahl-puh duh sahv-WAH   ɑːlpə də saːvwaː

Alpes du Dauphiné [Dauphiné Alps]
 Alpine mtn. range   ahl-puh due dō-fē-NĀ   ɑːlpə dyː doːfiːneː

Alpes Graies [Graian Alps]
 Alpine mtn. range   ahl-puh GRĀ   ɑːlpə greː

Alpes-Maritimes
 Alpine mtn. range   ahl-puh-mah-rē-TÊM   ɑːlpəmɑːriːtiːm

Alpha Boötes [Arcturus]
 star   AL-fuh bō-ŌT-ēz   ˌælfə boː'oːʧiːz

Alpha Centauri
 triple star   AL-fuh sen-TAWR-ē   ˌælfə sen'tɔːriˑ

Alpheus
 Greek river god   al-FÊ-uhs   æl'fiːəs

Foreign Sounds: ue: *Fr.* **rue**, *Ger.* **füllen** uh(r): *Fr.* **boeuf**, *Ger.* **Höhle** <u>kh</u>: *Ger.* **ich**, *Scot.* **loch** g̅: *Sp.* **amigo** <u>v</u>: *Sp.* **hablar**
hl: *Welsh* **Llanelli**. CAPITALS: primary stress. SMALL CAPS: secondary stress. Ⓢ: U.S. pron. Ⓒ: British pron.

Alphonse
   1. pers. name   AL-FAHNS, -FAHNZ; al-FAHNS,   'æl₁fɑns, -₁fɑnz; æl'fɑns,
                               -FAHNZ   -'fɑnz
   2. French   ahl-FAWⁿS, ahl-FAWⁿ-suh   ɑːlfɔ̃s, ɑːlfɔ̃sə

Alphonso
   pers. name   al-FAHN-sō, al-FAHN-zō   æl'fɑnsoː, æl'fɑnzoː

Alpi Liguri [Ligurian Alps]
   Alpine mtn. range   AHL-pē LĒ-gur-ē   ₁ɑlpiː 'liːguriː

Alpine
   county, CA; town, TX; pert. to the   AL-PĪN   'æl₁pɑin
     Alps

Alpi Pennine [Pennine Alps]
   Alpine mtn. range   AHL-pē pān-NĒ-nā   ₁ɑlpiː peːn'niːneː

Alpi Reti [Rhaetian Alps]
   Alpine mtn. range   AHL-pē RĀ-tē   ₁ɑlpiː 'reːtiː

Alps
   mtn. range, Europe   ALPS   'ælps

Alpujarras, Alpuxaras, Las
   mountainous region, Spain   lahs ahl-poo-<u>KH</u>AHR-uhs   lɑs ɑlpuː'xɑrəs

Alsace
   province, France   al-SAS, al-SĀS   æl'sæs, æl'seːs

Alsacienne
   quiche with onions   ahl-sahs-YEN   ɑːlsɑːsjen

al-Sadat
   Anwar, *see* Sadat, al-

Alsatian
   European people; dog breed   al-SĀ-shuhn   æl'seːʃən

Alsop
   pers. name   AWL-SAHP   'ɔːl₁sɑp

Alston
   pers. name   AWL-stuhn   'ɔːlstən

Altadena
   city, CA   AL-tuh-DĒ-nuh   ₁æltə'diːnə

Altai
   lang., Russia; mts., Asia   AL-TĪ   'æl₁tɑi

Altaic
   lang. family   al-TĀ-ik   æl'teːik

Altair
   star   al-TĪR, al-TAR   æl'tɑiʳ, æl'tæʳ

Altai Shan
   mtn. range, Asia   AL-TĪ SHAHN   'æl₁tɑi 'ʃɑn

Altamira
   caverns, Spain   AHL-tuh-MIR-uh, AL-tuh-MIR-uh   ₁ɑltə'mirə, ₁æltə'mirə

Altamont
   city, IL, OR, TN   AL-tuh-MAHNT   'æltə₁mɑnt

Altbairisch
   German beer   ahlt-BĪ-rish   ɑlt'bɑiriʃ

Altdorfer
   Albrecht, *German artist*   AHLT-DAWR-fuhr   'ɑlt₁dɔːʳfəʳ

Altenmünster
   German beer   AHL-tuhn-MUEN-stuhr   'ɑltən₁myːnstəʳ

Althaea
   mother of Meleager   al-THĒ-uh   æl'θiːə

Althea
   pers. name   al-THĒ-uh   æl'θiːə

Key (col. 2):   a: **fad**   ā: **fade**   ah: **father**   ar: **Mary**   aw: **law**   e: **fed**   ē: **feed**   er: **merry**   i: **hid**   ī: **hide**   ō: **coat**   o͞o: **boot**
oi: **boy**   ow: **now**   u: **put**   uh: **above**   uhr: **bird**   ch: **chop**   ng: **ring**   sh: **show**   th: **thick**   <u>th</u>: **this**   zh: **measure**

Althing
  ancient Icelandic legislative body   AWL-THING, AHL-THING   'ɔːl,θiŋ, 'ɑl,θiŋ

Althorp
  town, England   AWL-truhp, AWL-THAWRP   'ɔːltrəp, 'ɔːl,θɔːʳp

Altman
  Sidney, *US biologist (Nobel 1989)*   AWLT-muhn   'ɔːltmən

Alto Adige
  Italy, former admin. district   AHL-tō AHD-uh-jā   ˌɑltoː 'ɑdədʒeː

Altoona
  town, PA   al-TŌŌ-nuh   æl'tuːnə

Altrincham
  town, England   AWL-tring-uhm   'ɔːltriŋəm

Altun Shan
  mtn. range, China   AHL-TUN SHAHN, ⑤ AL-tuhn   'ɑl'tun 'ʃɑn, ⑤ 'æltən

Alturas Rancheria
  Indian reservation, US   al-TUR-uhs RAN-chuh-RĒ-uh   æl'turəs ˌræntʃə'riːə

aluminium
  British variant of aluminum   AL-yuh-MIN-ē-uhm   ˌæljə'miniːəm

aluminum
  element   uh-LŌŌ-muh-nuhm   ə'luːmənəm

Alur
  lang., people, Uganda, Zaire,   AH-LUR, ah-LUR   'ɑˌluʳ, ɑ'luʳ
  Sudan

Alured
  pers. name   AL-yuh-RED   'æljəˌred

Alva
  1. pers. name   AL-vuh   'ælvə
  2. Spanish   AHL-v̠ah   'ɑlβa

Alvar
  pers. name, Finnish   AHL-VAHR   'ɑːlˌvɑːʳ

Álvares
  pers. name, Portuguese   AHL-vuh-rish, AHL-vahr-is   'ɑlvəriʃ, 'ɑlvɑːris

Alvarez
  Luis W., *US physicist (Nobel 1968)*   AL-vuh-REZ   'ælvəˌrez

Álvarez
  pers. name, Spanish   AHL-vahr-ās, -āth   'ɑlvareːs, -eːθ

Alvaro
  pers. name, Spanish   ahl-V̠AHR-ō   ɑl'βaroː

Alvernia
  College, *PA*   al-VUHR-nē-uh   æl'vəʳniːə

Alverno
  College, *WI*   al-VUHR-nō   æl'vəʳnoː

Alvin
  pers. name   AL-vuhn   'ælvən

Alyattes
  Lydian king   AL-ē-AT-ēz   ˌæliː'æ̠iːz

Alyssum
  plant   uh-LIS-uhm   ə'lisəm

Alzado
  Lyle, *US football player*   al-ZĀD-ō   æl'zeːdoː

Alzheimer's
  disease of progressive dementia   AHLTS-HĪ-muhrz   'ɑlts,hɑiməʳz

Amadeo
  1. Italian   AHM-ah-DĀ-ō   ˌɑmɑ'deːoː
  2. Spanish   ahm-ah-T̠HĀ-ō   ɑmɑ'ðeːoː

Foreign Sounds: ue: *Fr.* **rue**, *Ger.* **füllen**   uh(r): *Fr.* **boeuf**, *Ger.* **Höhle**   k̠h: *Ger.* i**ch**, *Scot.* lo**ch**   ḡ: *Sp.* ami**g**o   v̠: *Sp.* ha**b**lar
hl: *Welsh* **Ll**anelli.   CAPITALS: primary stress.   SMALL CAPS: secondary stress.   ⑤: U.S. pron.   ⓛ: British pron.

Amadeus
1. pers. name	AM-uh-DĒ-uhs, AHM-, -DĀ-uhs	ˌæməˈdiːəs, ˌam-, -ˈdeːəs
2. German	AH-mah-DĀ-us	ˌamaˈdeːus
3. Swedish	AH-mah-DĀ-uhs	ˌamɑːˈdeːəs

Amadis
1. pers. name	AM-uhd-uhs	ˈæmədəs
2. French	ah-mah-DĒS	ɑːmɑːdiːs

Amado
pers. name	ah-MAH<u>TH</u>-ō	aˈmaðoː

Amador
county, CA	AM-uh-DAWR	ˈæməˌdɔːʳ

Amahuaca
S. American people	AHM-uh-WAHK-uh, AM-	ˌaməˈwakə, ˌæm-

Amalekites
ancient Middle Eastern people	AM-uh-LEK-ĪTS, uh-MAL-uh-KĪTS	ˈæməˌlekˌaits, əˈmæləˌkaits

Amalfi
town, Italy	uh-MAHL-fē	əˈmalfiˑ

Amalthea
nurse of the infant Zeus; satellite of Jupiter	AM-uhl-THĒ-uh, uh-mal-THĒ-uh	ˌæməlˈθiːə, əmælˈθiːə

Aman
Folk Ensemble, dance co., CA	AH-MAHN, uh-MAHN	ˈɑˌman, əˈman

Amana
city; IA; tdmk for an appliance brand	uh-MAN-uh	əˈmænə

Amanda
1. pers. name	uh-MAN-duh	əˈmændə
2. German	ah-MAHN-duh	aˈmandə

Amandine
pers. name, French	ah-mah[n]-DĒN	ɑːmãdiːn

Amaranth
plant	AM-uh-RANTH	ˈæməˌrænθ

Amaretto di Saronno
liqueur brand	AM-uh-RET-ō dē suh-RAWN-ō, AHM-	ˌæməˈretoː diˑ səˈrɔːnoː, ˌam-

Amarillo
city, TX	AM-uh-RIL-ō, AM-uh-RIL-uh	ˌæməˈriloː, ˌæməˈrilə

Amarit
Thai beer	AHM-uh-rit	ˈamərit

Amaryllis
pers. name	AM-uh-RIL-uhs	ˌæməˈriləs

Amasis
Egyptian king	uh-MĀ-suhs	əˈmeːsəs

Amata
wife of Latinus in Virgil's Aeneid	uh-MAHT-uh	əˈmatə

Amati
Italian family of violin makers	ah-MAHT-ē, uh-MAHT-ē	aˈmatiˑ, əˈmatiˑ

Amaury
1. pers. name	uh-MAWR-ē, AM-uhr-ē, Ā-muhr-ē	əˈmɔːriˑ, ˈæməriˑ, ˈeːməriˑ
2. French	ah-maw-RĒ	ɑːmɔːriː

Amazon
river, S. America; female warrior	AM-uh-ZAHN, AM-uh-zuhn	ˈæməˌzan, ˈæməzən

Amba
lang., people, Africa	AHM-buh, AM-buh	ˈambə, ˈæmbə

Amber
pers. name	AM-buhr	ˈæmbəʳ

Key (col. 2):   a: fad ā: fade ah: father ar: Mary aw: law e: fed ē: feed er: merry i: hid ī: hide ō: coat ōō: boot
oi: boy   ow: now u: put uh: above uhr: bird ch: chop ng: ring sh: show th: thick <u>th</u>: this zh: measure

Ambo [Avamba]
   lang., people, Angola, Namibia   AHM-bō, AM-bō   'amboː, 'æmboː

Amboina
   island, district, town, Indonesia   am-BOI-nuh   æm'bɔinə

Amboise
   commune, France   ahⁿ-BWAHZ   ãbwɑːz

Ambon
   island, district, port, Moluccas   AM-BAHN   'æm,bɑn

Ambrogio
   pers. name   ahm-BRŌ-jō   ɑm'broːdʒoː

Ambrose
   1. pers. name   AM-BRŌZ, -BRŌS   'æm,broːz, -,broːs
   2. Dutch   AHM-BRŌS   'ɑm,broːs

Ambrosian
   pert. to Ambrose   am-BRŌ-zhuhn, am-BRŌ-zē-uhn   æm'broːʒən, æm'broːziːən

Ambrosius
   1. pers. name   am-BRŌ-zhuhs, am-BRŌ-zē-uhs   æm'broːʒəs, æm'broːziːəs
   2. Dutch   ahm-BRŌ-sē-ues   ɑm'broːsiːys
   3. German   ahm-BRŌZ-yus, ahm-BRŌ-zē-us   ɑm'broːzjus, ɑm'broːziːus

Amdahl
   US computer co.   AM-DAHL, AHM-DAHL   'æm,dɑl, 'ɑm,dɑl

Ameche
   Don, *US entertainer;* Alan, *US football player*   uh-MĒ-chē   ə'miːtʃiˑ

Amedeo
   pers. name, Italian   AHM-ā-DE-ō   ˌameːˈdeoː

Amelia
   1. pers. name   uh-MĒL-yuh   ə'miːljə
   2. Italian   ah-MEL-yah   ɑ'meljɑ
   3. Spanish   ah-MĀL-yah   ɑ'meːljɑ

Amen [Amon]
   Egyptian god of the air   AHM-uhn, Ā-muhn   'ɑmən, 'eːmən

Amenhotep
   king of Egypt   AHM-uhn-HŌ-TEP   ˌɑmən'hoː,tep

Amenophis
   name, Egyptian pharaohs   AHM-uh-NŌ-fuhs   ˌɑmə'noːfəs

Amen-Ra
   Egyptian sun god   AHM-uhn-RAH   ˌɑmən'rɑ

Amerasian
   Asian American   AM-uh-RĀ-zhuhn, AM-uh-RĀ-shuhn   ˌæmə'reːʒən, ˌæmə'reːʃən

America
   Western Hemisphere, esp. US   uh-MER-uh-kuh, uh-MUHR-uh-kuh, uh-MAR-uh-kuh   ə'merəkə, ə'mərəkə, ə'mærəkə

American
   pert. to America   uh-MER-uh-kuhn, uh-MUHR-uh-kuhn, uh-MAR-uh-kuhn   ə'merəkən, ə'mərəkən, ə'mærəkən

Americana
   things pert. to America   uh-MER-uh-KAHN-uh, uh-MER-uh-KAN-uh   əˌmerə'kɑnə, əˌmerə'kænə

American Cyanamid
   US biotechnology co.   sī-AN-uh-muhd   sai'ænəməd

Foreign Sounds: ue: *Fr.* **rue**, *Ger.* f**ü**llen uh(r): *Fr.* b**oeuf**, *Ger.* H**ö**hle <u>kh</u>: *Ger.* i**ch**, *Scot.* lo**ch** ḡ: *Sp.* ami**g**o <u>v</u>: *Sp.* ha**b**lar
hl: *Welsh* **Ll**anelli. CAPITALS: primary stress. SMALL CAPS: secondary stress. ⑤: U.S. pron. Ⓛ: British pron.

Americanism		
American English usage	uh-MER-uh-kuh-NIZ-uhm, uh-MUHR-uh-kuh-NIZ-uhm, uh-MAR-uh-kuh-NIZ-uhm	ə'merəkə,nizəm, ə'mərəkə,nizəm, ə'mærəkə,nizəm
americium		
element	AM-uh-RISH-ē-uhm, AM-uh-RIS-ē-uhm	,æmə'riʃiːəm, ,æmə'risiːəm
Américo		
pers. name	ah-MĀ-rē-kō	ɑ'meːriːkoː
Americus		
1. pers. name	uh-MER-i-kuhs	ə'merikəs
2. Dutch	ah-MĀ-rē-kuhs	ɑː'meːriːkəs
Amerigo		
pers. name, Italian	AHM-ā-RĒ-gō, [$] uh-MER-uh-GŌ	,ɑmeː'riːgoː, [$] ə'merə,goː
Amerind		
American Indian people or lang.	AM-uh-RIND	'æmə,rind
Amerindian		
pert. to American Indians	AM-uh-RIN-dē-uhn	,æmə'rindiːən
Amharic		
lang., Ethiopia	am-HAR-ik, ahm-HAHR-ik	æm'hærik, ɑm'hɑrik
Amharinya [Amharic]		
lang., Ethiopia	AM-huh-RĒN-yuh	,æmhə'riːnjə
Amherst		
town, MA, NY, Canada; county, VA; peninsula, district, Burma	AM-uhrst, AM-HUHRST	'æmə^{r}st, 'æm,hə^{r}st
Amhrán na bhFiann		
Irish natl. anthem	AHV-rawn nah VĒ-uhn	'ɑvrɔːn nɑ 'viːən
Ami		
pers. name	ah-MĒ	ɑːmiː
Amidism		
Buddhist sect	AM-uhd-IZ-uhm	'æməd,izəm
Amiens		
town, France	ahm-YE^{n}	ɑːmjẽ
Amilcare		
pers. name, Italian	ah-MĒL-KAHR-ā	ɑ'miːl,kɑreː
Amin		
Idi, *ruler, Uganda*	ah-MĒN	ɑ'miːn
Amintore		
pers. name, Italian	ah-MĒN-TAWR-ā	ɑ'miːn,tɔːreː
Amiri		
pers. name	ah-MIR-ē	ɑ'miriˑ
Amish		
Christian sect	AHM-ish, AM-ish, Ā-mish	'ɑmiʃ, 'æmiʃ, 'eːmiʃ
Amite		
county, MS	ā-MĒT	eː'miːt
Amity		
pers. name	AM-uht-ē	'æməţiˑ
Amityville		
town, NY	AM-uht-ē-VIL	'æməţiˑ,vil
Amman		
city, Jordan	ah-MAHN, uh-MAHN, uh-MAN	ɑ'mɑn, ə'mɑn, ə'mæn
Ammenemes		
name, Egyptian pharaohs	AHM-uh-NĀ-mēz, AM-uh-NĒ-mēz	,ɑmə'neːmiːz, ,æmə'niːmiːz
Ammianus Marcellinus		
Roman historian	AM-ē-Ā-nuhs MAHR-suh-LĪ-nuhs	,æmiː'eːnəs ,mɑ^{r}sə'lɑinəs

Key (col. 2): a: **fad** ā: **fade** ah: **father** ar: **Mary** aw: **law** e: **fed** ē: **feed** er: **merry** i: **hid** ī: **hide** ō: **coat** o͞o: **boot** oi: **boy** ow: **now** u: **put** uh: **above** uhr: **bird** ch: **chop** ng: **ring** sh: **show** th: **thick** t͟h: **this** zh: **measure**

Ammon
Field, *ballpark, Pittsburgh, PA*   AM-uhn   'æmən

Ammon [Amon]
Egyptian god of the air   AHM-uhn, AM-uhn   'amən, 'æmən

Ammonite
ancient Semitic people, lang.   AM-uh-NĪT   'æmə,nait

Amoco
American Oil Co.   AM-uh-KŌ   'æmə,koː

Amon
Egyptian god of the air   AHM-uhn, AM-uhn, Ā-muhn   'amən, 'æmən, 'eːmən

Amon-Re
Egyptian sun god   AHM-uhn-RĀ, AM-uhn-RĀ, Ā-muhn-RĀ   ,amən're:, ,æmən're:, ,e:mən're:

Amontillado
wine   ah-MAHN-tē-YAHTH-ō, ⑤ uh-MAHN-tuh-LAHD-ō   a,mantiː'jaðoː, ⑤ ə,mantə'ladoː

Amorites
Mesopotamian desert people   AM-uh-RĪTS   'æmə,raits

Amory
pers. name   Ā-muh-rē   'eːmariˑ

Amos
1. *Old Testament book; pers. name*   Ā-muhs   'eːməs
2. *Czech*   AH-maws   'amɔːs

Amoy [Xiamen]
city, China   ah-MOI   a'mɔi

Ampére
André-Marie, *French physicist*   ahⁿ-PER   ãper

Amphiaraus
legendary Greek seer & Argonaut   AM-fē-uh-RĀ-uhs   ,æmfiːə're:əs

Amphictyon
legendary king of Athens   am-FIK-tē-AHN, am-FIK-tē-uhn   æm'fiktiː,an, æm'fiktiːən

Amphion
son of Zeus and Antiope   am-FĪ-uhn, AM-fē-uhn   æm'faiən, 'æmfiːən

Amphipolis
ancient Macedonian city   am-FIP-uh-luhs   æm'fipələs

Amphitrite
queen of the sea, wife of Poseidon   AM-fuh-TRĪT-ē   ,æmfə'traiţiˑ

Amphitryon
husband of Alcmene & stepfather to Heracles   am-FI-trē-uhn, -trē-AHN   æm'fitriːən, -triː,an

Amritsar
city, district, India   UHM-RIT-suhr, ahm-RIT-suhr   ,əm'ritsəʳ, am'ritsəʳ

Amstel
Dutch beer   AHM-stuhl   'amstəl

Amsterdam
city, Netherlands; US pl. name   AM-stuhr-DAM   'æmstəʳ,dæm

Amtrak
US railroad   AM-TRAK   'æm,træk

Amuesha
lang., people, Peru   ahm-WĀ-shuh   am'we:ʃə

Amun [Amon]
Egyptian god of the air   AHM-uhn, AM-uhn, Ā-muhn   'amən, 'æmən, 'eːmən

Amundsen
Roald, *Norwegian explorer*   AHM-uhn-suhn   'amənsən

Foreign Sounds: ue: *Fr.* **rue**, *Ger.* **füllen**   uh(r): *Fr.* **boeuf**, *Ger.* **Höhle**   kh: *Ger.* **ich**, *Scot.* **loch**   ǥ: *Sp.* ami**g**o   v: *Sp.* ha**b**lar
hl: *Welsh* **Ll**anelli.   CAPITALS: primary stress.   SMALL CAPS: secondary stress.   ⑤: U.S. pron.   ⑫: British pron.

Amur
  river, Asia   ah-MUR   ɑˈmuʳ

Amuzgo
  lang., people, Mexico   ah-MOOS-gō, uh-MOOZ-gō   ɑˈmuːsgoː, əˈmuːzgoː

Amway
  trademark for housewares   AM-WĀ   ˈæmˌweː

Amy
  pers. name   Ā-mē   ˈeːmiˑ

Amymone
  daughter of Danaus and Europa   AM-Ī-MŌ-nē   ˌæmˌaiˈmoːniˑ

Amyraldism
  Christian sect   AM-uh-RAL-DIZ-uhm   ˌæməˈrælˌdizəm

Anabaptism
  Christian sect   AN-uh-BAP-TIZ-uhm   ˌænəˈbæpˌtizəm

Anabaptist
  believer in Anabaptism   AN-uh-BAP-tuhst   ˌænəˈbæptəst

Anacin
  pain reliever, tdmk   AN-uh-suhn   ˈænəsən

Anacletus
  pope   AN-uh-KLĒT-uhs   ˌænəˈkliːʈəs

Anaconda
  city, MT; S. American snake   AN-uh-KAHN-duh   ˌænəˈkɑndə

Anacreon
  Greek writer   uh-NAK-rē-uhn, -rē-AHN   əˈnækriːən, -riːˌɑn

Anaheim
  city, CA   AN-uh-HĪM   ˈænəˌhaim

Anaïs
  pers. name (A. Nin)   uh-NĪ-uhs, uh-NĀ-uhs   əˈnaiəs, əˈneːəs

Ananias
  Biblical name   AN-uh-NĪ-uhs   ˌænəˈnaiəs

Ananke
  Greek goddess of necessity;   uh-NANG-kē, uh-NAN-KĒ   əˈnæŋkiˑ, əˈnænˌkiː
    satellite of Jupiter

Anasazi
  N. American people   AHN-uh-SAHZ-ē   ˌɑnəˈsɑziˑ

Anastas
  pers. name, Russian   uh-NUHS-TAHS   əˌnəsˈtɑːs

Anastasia
  1. pers. name   AN-uh-STĀ-zh(ē-)uh, -sh(ē-)uh   ˌænəˈsteːʒ(iː)ə, -ʃ(iː)ə
  2. German   AHN-ah-STAHZ-yuh, -STAHZ-ē-uh   ˌɑnɑˈstazjə, -ˈstaziːə

Anastasio
  1. pers. name, Italian   AHN-ahs-TAHZ-yō   ˌɑnɑsˈtazjoː
  2. Spanish   ahn-ahs-TAHS-yō   ɑnɑsˈtasjoː

Anastasius
  1. pers. name   AN-uh-STĀ-zh(ē-)uhs, -sh(ē-)uhs   ˌænəˈsteːʒ(iː)əs, -ʃ(iː)əs
  2. German   AHN-ah-STAHZ-yus, -STAHZ-ē-us   ˌɑnɑˈstazjus, -ˈstaziːus

Anat
  1. Egyptian goddess of war   AHN-uht   ˈɑnət
  2. pers. name   uh-NAHT   əˈnɑt

Anatol
  pers. name, Russian   uh-NUH-TAWL   əˌnəˈtɔːl

Anatole
  1. pers. name   AN-uh-TŌL, -TAWL   ˈænəˌtoːl, -ˌtɔːl
  2. French   ah-nah-TAWL   ɑːnɑːtɔːl

Key (col. 2):   a: fad   ā: fade   ah: father   ar: Mary   aw: law   e: fed   ē: feed   er: merry   i: hid   ī: hide   ō: coat   ōō: boot
oi: boy   ow: now   u: put   uh: above   uhr: bird   ch: chop   ng: ring   sh: show   th: thick   th: this   zh: measure

Anatoli, Anatoly		
pers. name, Russian	uh-NUH-TAWL-yi, [$] AN-uh-TŌ-lē	əˌnəˈtɔːljij, [$] ˌænəˈtoːliˑ
Anatolia		
region, Turkey	AN-uh-TŌ-lē-uh, AN-uh-TŌL-yuh	ˌænəˈtoːliːə, ˌænəˈtoːljə
Anatolian		
lang. family	AN-uh-TŌ-lē-uhn, AN-uh-TŌL-yuhn	ˌænəˈtoːliːən, ˌænəˈtoːljən
Anatosaurus		
dinosaur	uh-NAT-uh-SAWR-uhs, AN-AT-uh-SAWR-uhs	əˌnætəˈsɔːrəs, ˌænˌætəˈsɔːrəs
Anaxagoras		
Greek philosopher	AN-AK-SAG-uh-ruhs	ˌænˌækˈsægərəs
Anaximander		
Greek philosopher	uh-NAK-suh-MAN-duhr, uh-NAK-suh-MAN-duhr	əˈnæksəˌmændə^{r}, əˌnæksəˈmændə^{r}
Anaximenes		
Greek philosopher	AN-ak-SIM-uh-NĒZ	ˌænækˈsiməˌniːz
Anchises		
father of Aeneas	an-KĪ-zēz, ang-KĪ-zēz	ænˈkɑiziːz, æŋˈkɑiziːz
Ancilla Domini		
College, *IN*	an-SIL-uh DAHM-uh-nē	ænˌsilə ˈdɑməniˑ
Ancona		
city, Italy	ahng-KŌ-nuh, ang-KŌ-nuh	ɑŋˈkoːnə, æŋˈkoːnə
Ancyra		
ancient name of Ankara	an-SĪ-ruh	ænˈsɑirə
Andalucía		
region, Spain	ahn-duh-lo͞o-SĒ-uh, ahn-duh-lo͞o-THĒ-uh	ɑndəluːˈsiːə, ɑndəluːˈθiːə
Andalusia		
city, AL	AN-duh-LO͞O-zhuh, AN-duh-LO͞O-zhē-uh	ˌændəˈluːʒə, ˌændəˈluːʒiːə
Andaman		
islands, sea, Asia	AN-duh-muhn, AN-duh-MAN	ˈændəmən, ˈændəˌmæn
Andean		
pert. to Andes Mts.	an-DĒ-uhn, AN-dē-uhn	ænˈdiːən, ˈændiːən
Anders		
1. Danish	AHN-uhrs	ˈɑːnərs
2. Swedish	AHN-duhrs	ˈɑːndərs
Andersen		
1. pers. name	AN-duhr-suhn	ˈændə^{r}sən
2. Hans Christian, Danish author	AHN-uhr-suhn; [$] AN-duhr-suhn	ˈɑːnərsən; [$] ˈændə^{r}sən
Anderson		
C. D., *US physicist (Nobel 1936);* Philip W., *US physicist (Nobel 1977); pers. name*	AN-duhr-suhn	ˈændə^{r}sən
Andes		
mtn. range, S. America	AN-dēz	ˈændiːz
Andhra Pradesh		
state, India	AHN-druh pruh-DĀSH, pruh-DESH	ˌɑndrə prəˈdeːʃ, prəˈdeʃ
Ando		
pers. name, Japanese	ahn-dō	ɑndoː
Andoni		
lang., Nigeria	an-DŌ-nē	ænˈdoːniˑ
Andorra		
principality, Europe	an-DAWR-uh, an-DAHR-uh	ænˈdɔːrə, ænˈdɑrə

Foreign Sounds: ue: *Fr.* **rue**, *Ger.* **füllen** uh(r): *Fr.* **boeuf**, *Ger.* **Höhle** kh: *Ger.* **ich**, *Scot.* **loch** g̃: *Sp.* ami**g**o v̲: *Sp.* ha**b**lar hl: *Welsh* **Llanelli**. CAPITALS: primary stress. SMALL CAPS: secondary stress. [$]: U.S. pron. [£]: British pron.

Andorran
  pert. to Andorra　　　　　　　an-DAWR-uhn, an-DAHR-ụhn　　　　æn'dɔːrən, æn'dɑrən

Andover
  town, MA; town, Canada;　　　AN-DŌ-vuhr, AN-duh-vuhr　　　'æn,doːvəˢ, 'ændəvəˢ
  borough, England

André
  1. pers. name　　　　　　　　AHN-drā　　　　　　　　　　　　'andreː
  2. French　　　　　　　　　　ahⁿ-DRĀ　　　　　　　　　　　ãdreː
  3. Swedish　　　　　　　　　ahn-DRĀ　　　　　　　　　　　ɑːn'dreː

Andre
  pers. name; wine brand　　　　AHN-drā　　　　　　　　　　　'andreː

Andrea
  1. pers. name　　　　　　　　AN-drē-uh, AHN-　　　　　　　'ændriːə, 'an-
  2. Italian　　　　　　　　　　ahn-DRE-ah　　　　　　　　　an'dreɑ

Andrea del Sarto
  see Sarto, del

Andrea Doria
  ship, sunk 1956　　　　　　　AN-drē-uh DŌR-ē-uh, DAWR-ē-uh　,ændriːə 'doːriːə, 'dɔːriːə

Andreas
  1. pers. name　　　　　　　　AN-drē-uhs, AN-drā-uhs;　　　'ændriːəs, 'ændreːəs;
  　　　　　　　　　　　　　　an-DRĀ-uhs　　　　　　　　　æn'dreːəs
  2. Danish　　　　　　　　　　ahn-DRI-ahs　　　　　　　　　ɑːn'driɑːs
  3. Dutch, German, Norwegian　　ahn-DRĀ-ahs　　　　　　　　　an'dreɑs
  4. Latin　　　　　　　　　　AN-drē-uhs, an-DRĒ-uhs　　　'ændriːəs, æn'driːəs
  5. Mod. Greek　　　　　　　ahn-THRE-ahs　　　　　　　　an'ðreas
  6. Swedish　　　　　　　　　ahn-DRĀ-ahs　　　　　　　　　ɑːn'dreːɑːs

Andreevich, Andreyevich
  pers. name, Russian　　　　　UHN-DRĀ(-yiv)-YICH　　　　　,ən'dreː(jiv),jitʃ

Andrei, Andrey
  pers. name, Russian　　　　　UHN-DRĀ(-ē), Ⓢ AHN-DRĀ　　,ən'dreː(iː), Ⓢ 'an,dreː

Andress
  Ursula, *US actress*　　　　　AN-druhs　　　　　　　　　　'ændrəs

Andretti
  Mario, *US race car driver*　　an-DRET-ē, ahn-DRET-ē　　　æn'dreţiˑ, an'dreţiˑ

Andrew
  pers. name　　　　　　　　　AN-dr͞oo　　　　　　　　　　'ændruː

Andrić
  Ivo, *Serbo-Croatian author (Nobel*　AHN-drich, AHN-drēch　　　'ɑːndritʃ, 'ɑːndriːtʃ
  1961)

Andries
  pers. name, Dutch　　　　　　AHN-drēs　　　　　　　　　　'andriːs

Andrija
  pers. name, Serbo-Croatian　　ahn-DRĒ-yah　　　　　　　　ɑːn'driːjaː

Androcles
  fabled Roman slave who helped a　AN-druh-KLĒZ　　　　　　　'ændrə,kliːz
  lion

Androgeos
  son of Minos and Pasiphae　　an-DRAHJ-ē-uhs　　　　　　æn'drɑdʒiːəs

Andromache
  wife of Hector in Greek legend　an-DRAHM-uh-kē　　　　　　æn'drɑməkiˑ

Andromeda
  wife of Perseus in Greek legend;　an-DRAHM-uhd-uh　　　　　æn'drɑmədə
  constellation & galaxy

Key (col. 2):　a: fad　ā: fade　ah: father　ar: Mary　aw: law　e: fed　ē: feed　er: merry　i: hid　ī: hide　ō: coat　o͞o: boot
oi: boy　ow: now　u: put　uh: above　uhr: bird　ch: chop　ng: ring　sh: show　th: thick　th: this　zh: measure

Andronicus
  1. name, Eastern Roman   AN-druh-NĪ-kuhs, an-DRAHN-i-kuhs   ˌændrəˈnɑikəs, ænˈdrɑnikəs
  emperors
  2. see Titus Andronicus
Andropov
  Yuri, *president, USSR*   ahn-DRAW-puhf, ⑤ an-DRŌ-PAWF   ɑnˈdrɔːpəf, ⑤ ænˈdrɔːˌpɔːf
Andros
  1. island, Bahamas   AN-druhs   ˈændrəs
  2. island, Greece   AHN-DRAWS, AN-druhs   ˈɑnˌdrɔːs, ˈændrəs
Androscoggin
  river, county, ME   AN-druh-SKAHG-uhn   ˌændrəˈskɑgən
Andrzej
  pers. name, Polish   AHN-jā   ˈɑːndʒeː
Andvari, Andwari
  Scandinavian mythological dwarf   ahnd-VAHR-ē   ɑndˈvɑriˑ
Andy
  pers. name   AN-dē   ˈændiˑ
Aneurin
  ancient Welsh poet; pers. name   uh-NĪ-ruhn   əˈnɑirən
Anfinsen
  Christian B., *US biochemist (Nobel*   AN-fuhn-suhn   ˈænfənsən
  1972)
Angami
  lang., people, India, Burma   an-GAHM-ē   ænˈgɑmiˑ
Angara
  river, Russia   AHNG-guh-RAH   ˌɑːŋgəˈrɑː
Angaran
  continental shield, Asia   ahng-GAR-uhn   ɑŋˈgærən
Angas
  lang., Nigeria   AHNG-guhs   ˈɑŋgəs
Angel
  pers. name   ĀN-juhl   ˈeːndʒəl
Ángel, Angel
  pers. name, Spanish   AHNG-khāl, ĀN-juhl, AHN-hel   ˈɑnçeːl, ˈeːndʒəl, ˈɑnhel
Angela
  1. pers. name   AN-juh-luh   ˈændʒələ
  2. Italian   ahn-JĀ-lah   ɑnˈdʒeːlɑ
Angel Falls [Churún Merú]
  waterfall, Venezuela   ĀN-juhl   ˈeːndʒəl
Angelica
  1. pers. name   an-JEL-i-kuh   ænˈdʒelikə
  2. German   ahng-GĀ-lē-kah   ɑŋˈgeːliːkɑ
  3. Italian   ahn-JEL-ē-kah   ɑnˈdʒeliːkɑ
Angelico
  1. Fra, Italian painter   ahn-JEL-i-kō   ɑnˈdʒelikoː
  2. pers. name   an-JEL-ē-kō, ahn-   ænˈdʒeliːkoː, ɑn-
Angelina
  river, county, TX; pers. name   AN-juh-LĒ-nuh   ˌændʒəˈliːnə
Angelino
  resident of Los Angeles   AN-juh-LĒ-nō   ˌændʒəˈliːnoː
Angélique
  pers. name   ahⁿ-zhā-LĒK   ãʒeːliːk

Foreign Sounds: ue: *Fr.* **rue**, *Ger.* **f**ü**llen**   uh(r): *Fr.* **b**oeuf, *Ger.* H**öh**le   kh: *Ger.* i**ch**, *Scot.* lo**ch**   g: *Sp.* ami**g**o   v: *Sp.* ha**b**lar
hl: *Welsh* L**l**anelli.   CAPITALS: primary stress.   SMALL CAPS: secondary stress.   ⑤: U.S. pron.   ⓛ: British pron.

Angell

Sir Norman, *English author,* ĀN-juhl　　　　　　　　'eɪndʒəl
politician (Nobel 1933); Roger,
US baseball writer

Angelo

1. State University, *TX; pers.*　AN-juh-lō　　　　　　'ændʒəloː
name

2. German, Italian　　　　　　ahn-JÃ-lō　　　　　　ɑn'dʒeːloː

Angelou

Maya, *US writer*　　　　　　AHN-juh-LŌO, AHN-zhuh-LŌO,　'ɑndʒə,luː, 'ɑnʒə,luː,
　　　　　　　　　　　　　　AHN-juh-LŌ *(her own pron.)*　'ɑndʒə,loː *(her own*
　　　　　　　　　　　　　　　　　　　　　　　　　　pron.)

Angelus

prayer　　　　　　　　　　AN-juh-luhs　　　　　'ændʒələs

Angers

city, France　　　　　　　ahⁿ-ZHÃ　　　　　　ãʒeː

Angevin

pert. to Anjou　　　　　　AN-juh-vuhn　　　　'ændʒəvən

Angie

pers. name　　　　　　　AN-jē　　　　　　　'ændʒiˑ

Angkor Wat

Khmer temple, Cambodia　AHNG-kuhr WAHT, AHNG-KAWR　'aŋkəʳ 'wat, 'aŋ,kɔːʳ 'wat
　　　　　　　　　　　　　WAHT

Angles

European people　　　　ANG-guhlz　　　　　'æŋgəlz

Anglesey

island, former county, Wales　ANG-guhl-sē　　　'æŋgəlsiˑ

Anglia

Latin for England　　　　ANG-glē-uh　　　　'æŋgliːə

Anglican

pert. to Church of England　ANG-gli-kuhn　　'æŋglikən

Anglicanism

Christian denomination　ANG-gli-kuh-NIZ-uhm　'æŋglikə,nizəm

Anglo

pert. to England; *non-Hispanic*　ANG-glō　　'æŋgloː

Anglo-American

English and American　　ANG-glō-uh-MER-uh-kuhn,　,æŋgloːə'merəkən,
　　　　　　　　　　　　　-uh-MUHR-uh-kuhn,　　-ə'mərəkən, -ə'mærəkən
　　　　　　　　　　　　　-uh-MAR-uh-kuhn

Anglo-Catholic

high church Anglican　　ANG-glō-KATH-(uh-)lik　,æŋgloː'kæθ(ə)lik

Anglo-Indian

pert. to India *and* England *or*　ANG-glō-IN-dē-uhn　,æŋgloː'indiːən
English

Anglo-Irish

pert. to Ireland *and* England *or*　ANG-glō-Ī-rish　,æŋgloː'airiʃ
English

Anglophile

admirer of England　　　ANG-gluh-FĪL　　　'æŋglə,fail

Anglophilia

admiration for England　ANG-gluh-FIL-ē-uh　,æŋglə'filiːə

Anglophobe

one who dislikes England　ANG-gluh-FŌB　　'æŋglə,foːb

Anglophobia

dislike of England　　　ANG-gluh-FŌB-ē-uh　,æŋglə'foːbiːə

Key (col. 2): a: fad ā: fade ah: father ar: Mary aw: law e: fed ē: feed er: merry i: hid ī: hide ō: coat ōō: boot
oi: boy　ow: now　u: put　uh: above　uhr: bird　ch: chop　ng: ring　sh: show　th: thick　th̲: this　zh: measure

Anglophone
  English-speaking   ANG-gluh-FŌN   'æŋglə,foːn

Anglo-Saxon
  European lang. (Old English)   ANG-glō-SAK-suhn   ,æŋgloː'sæksən

Angola
  republic, Africa   ang-GŌ-luh, an-   æŋ'goːlə, æn-

Angolan
  pert. to Angola   ang-GŌ-luhn, an-   æŋ'goːlən, æn-

Angora
  former name of Ankara; *breed of*   ang-GŌR-uh, an-GŌR-uh, -GAWR-uh   æŋ'goːrə, æn'goːrə, -'goːrə
  cat, goat, or rabbit

Angostura
  former name of Ciudad Bolivar,   ANG-guh-ST(Y)UR-uh   ,æŋgə'st(j)urə
  Venezuela; aromatic bark used
  in bitters

Ångström
  Anders Jonas, *Swedish scientist*   AWNG-struhm, ⑤ ANG-struhm   'ɔːŋstrəm, ⑤ 'æŋstrəm

Anguilla
  island, West Indies   ang-GWIL-uh, an-   æŋ'gwilə, æn-

Angus
  pers. name   ANG-guhs   'æŋgəs

Anhalt
  state, Germany   AHN-HAHLT   'ɑn,hɑlt

Anheuser-Busch
  US beer co.   AN-HĪ-zuhr-BUSH   ,æn,hɑizər'buʃ

anhinga
  bird   an-HING-guh   æn'hiŋgə

Anhui, Anhwei
  province, China   AHN-(H)WĀ   'ɑn'(h)weː

Anhur
  Egyptian sun god   AHN-HUR   'ɑn,hur

Anhwei
  see Anhui

ANI
  automatic number identification   AN-ē, Ā-EN-Ī   'æni', ,eː,en'ɑi

ani
  bird   ah-NĒ   ɑ'niː

Anicetus
  pope   AN-i-SĒT-uhs   ,æni'siːţəs

Anita
  1. pers. name   uh-NĒT-uh   ə'niːţə
  2. Danish, German, Spanish   ah-NĒ-tah   ɑ'niːtɑ

Anjelica
  pers. name (A. Huston)   an-JEL-i-kuh   æn'dʒelikə

Anjou
  province, France; town, Canada   ahⁿ-ZHŌŌ; ⑤ AHN-JŌŌ, ahn-ZHŌŌ,   ɑ̃ʒuː; ⑤ 'ɑn,dʒuː, ɑn'ʒuː,
            AN-JŌŌ   'æn,dʒuː

Ankara
  city, province, Turkey   AHNG-kuh-ruh, ANG-kuh-ruh   'ɑŋkərə, 'æŋkərə

Ankwe
  lang., Nigeria   AHNG-kwā   'ɑŋkweˑ

Ankylosaurus
  dinosaur   AN-kuh-luh-SAWR-ē-uh   ,æŋkələ'sɔːriːə

Ann
  pers. name   AN   'æn

Foreign Sounds: ue: *Fr.* **rue**, *Ger.* f**ü**llen   uh(r): *Fr.* b**oeu**f, *Ger.* H**ö**hle   <u>kh</u>: *Ger.* i**ch**, *Scot.* lo**ch**   g̱: *Sp.* ami**g**o   <u>v</u>: *Sp.* ha**b**lar
hl: *Welsh* **Ll**anelli.   CAPITALS: primary stress.   SMALL CAPS: secondary stress.   ⑤: U.S. pron.   ⓛ: British pron.

Anna
1. pers. name	AN-uh	'ænə
2. Dutch	AHN-ah	'ɑnɑː
3. French	ahn-NAH	ɑːnnɑː
4. German	AHN-ah	'ɑnɑ
5. Italian, Latvian	AHN-nah	'ɑnnɑ
6. Polish, Swedish	AHN-nah	'ɑːnnɑː
7. Russian	AHN-nuh	'ɑːnnə

Annabella
pers. name	AN-uh-BEL-uh	ˌænə'belə

Anna Karénina
novel, L. Tolstoy	AHN-uh kuh-REN-uh-nuh	'ɑnə kə'renənə

Annamarie, Anna-Marie
pers. name	AN-uh-muh-RĒ	ˌænəmə'riː

Anna Perenna
Roman goddess	AN-uh puh-REN-uh	ˌænə pə'renə

Annapolis
city, MD	uh-NAP-(uh-)luhs	ə'næp(ə)ləs

Annapurna
mtn. range, Nepal	AN-uh-PUR-nuh	ˌænə'purnə

Ann Arbor
city, MI	an AHR-buhr	æn 'ɑʳbəʳ

Anne
1. pers. name	AN	'æn
2. French	AHN	ɑn, ɑːn
3. Swedish	AHN	'ɑːn
4. German	AHN-uh	'ɑnə

Anne Arundel
county, MD	AN uh-RUHN-dl, *locally* AN uh-RUHN-l, AN uh-RAN-l	ˌæn ə'rəndļ, *locally* ˌæn ə'rənļ, ˌæn ə'rænļ

Annelida
worm phylum	uh-NEL-uhd-uh	ə'nelədə

Annemarie
1. pers. name	AN-muh-RĒ	ˌænmə'riː
2. German	AHN-uh-mah-RĒ	ˌɑnəmɑ'riː

Annenberg
Walter, *founder* TV Guide *magazine, US ambassador to England*	AN-uhn-BUHRG	'ænənˌbəʳg

Annette
1. Islands Reserve, Indian reservation, US	a-NET, uh-NET	æ'net, ə'net
2. pers. name	uh-NET	ə'net
3. French	ah-NET	ɑːnet
4. German	ah-NET-uh	ɑ'neţə

Annibale
pers. name, Italian	AHN-nē-BAH-lä	ˌɑnniː'bɑleː

Annie
pers. name	AN-ē	'æniˑ

Anno
Japanese writer, illustrator	ahn-nō	ɑnnoː

Anno Domini
'in the year of the Lord'	AN-ō DAHM-uh-nē, DAHM-uh-NĪ	ˌænoː 'dɑməniˑ, 'dɑməˌnɑi

Annunzio
pers. name, Italian	ahn-NOONT-sē-ō	ɑn'nuːntsiːoː

Key (col. 2): a: fad ā: fade ah: father ar: Mary aw: law e: fed ē: feed er: merry i: hid ī: hide ō: coat o͞o: boot
oi: boy ow: now u: put uh: above uhr: bird ch: chop ng: ring sh: show th: thick t̲h̲: this zh: measure

Anoka
    county, MN   uh-NŌ-kuh   əˈnoːkə

Anoka-Ramsey
    Community College, *MN*   uh-NŌ-kuh-RAM-zē   əˈnoːkəˈræmziˑ

Anouilh
    Jean, *French author*   ah-N$\overline{OO}$, $ a-N$\overline{OO}$-ē   ɑːnuːj, $ æˈnuːiˑ

Anpu [Anubis]
    Egyptian god of the dead   AHN-P$\overline{OO}$ ˈɑnˌpuː

Anqet [Anuket]
    Egyptian goddess   AHNG-kuht   ˈɑŋkət

Anschluss
    political union of Austria,   AHN-SHLUS   ˈɑnˌʃlus
    Germany

Anse, L'
    see L'Anse

Ansel
    pers. name   AN-suhl   ˈænsəl

Anselm
    1. Christian saint, philosopher;   AN-SELM   ˈænˌselm
    pers. name
    2. German   AHN-ZELM   ˈɑnˌzelm
    3. Swedish   AHN-selm, AHN-suhlm   ˈɑːnselm, ˈɑːnsəlm

ANSI
    American National Standards   AN-zē, AN(T)-sē   ˈænziˑ, ˈæn(t)siˑ
    Institute

Antaeus
    1. Libyan giant in Greek myth   an-TĒ-uhs, an-TĀ-uhs   ænˈtiːəs, ænˈteːəs
    2. US literary magazine   an-TĀ-uhs   ænˈteːəs

Antalcidas
    King's Peace of, *Spartan-Persian*   an-TAL-suh-duhs   ænˈtælsədəs
    pact

Antananarivo
    city, Madagascar   AHN-tuh-NAHN-uh-RĒ-vō,   ˌɑntəˌnɑnəˈriːvoː, ˌæntəˌnæn-
     AN-tuh-NAN-

Antarctica
    continent   ant-AHRK-ti-kuh, ant-AHRT-i-kuh   æntˈɑʳktikə, æntˈɑʳtikə

Antares
    star   an-TAR-ēZ   ænˈtærˌiːz

Antenor
    adviser to Priam   an-TEN-uhr, an-TEN-AWR,   ænˈtenəʳ, ænˈtenˌɔːʳ,
     an-TĒ-nawr   ænˈtiːnɔːʳ

Anterus
    pope   ANT-uh-ruhs   ˈæntərəs

Anthony
    1. pers. name   AN-thuh-nē, £ AN-tuh-nē   ˈænθəniˑ, £ ˈæntəniˑ
    2. Dutch   ahn-TŌ-nē   ɑnˈtoːniː

Antibes
    city, French Riviera   ahⁿ-TĒB   ãtiːb

Antichrist
    antagonist of Christ   ANT-ē-KRĪST, AN-TĪ-KRĪST   ˈæntiˌkrɑist, ˈænˌtaiˌkrɑist

Anticleia
    wife of Laertes, mother of   ANT-i-KLĒ-uh, ANT-i-KLĀ-uh   ˌæntiˈkliːə, ˌæntiˈkleːə
    Odysseus

Anticosti
    island, Canada   ANT-i-KAWS-tē   ˌæntiˈkɔːstiˑ

Foreign Sounds: ue: *Fr.* **rue**, *Ger.* **füllen**   uh(r): *Fr.* **boeuf**, *Ger.* **Höhle**   kh: *Ger.* **ich**, *Scot.* **loch**   g̃: *Sp.* amigo   v: *Sp.* hablar
hl: *Welsh* **Llanelli**.   CAPITALS: primary stress.   SMALL CAPS: secondary stress. $: U.S. pron.   £: British pron.

Antietam
  village, creek, battle site, MD   an-TĒT-uhm   æn'tiːʈəm

Antigone
  daughter of Oedipus; play,   an-TIG-uh-nē   æn'tigəniˑ
   Sophocles

Antigonus Doson
  Macedonian regent   an-TIG-uh-nuhs DŌ-SAHN   æn'tigənəs 'doːˌsɑn

Antigonus Gonatas
  Macedonian king   an-TIG-uh-nuhs GAHN-uht-uhs   æn'tigənəs 'gɑnəʈəs

Antigua
  1. island, Caribbean   an-TĒ-gwuh, an-TIG-wuh   æn'tiːgwə, æn'tigwə
  2. city, Guatemala   ahn-TĒǦ-wah; ⑤ an-TĒ-gwuh,   ɑn'tiːɣwɑ; ⑤ æn'tiːgwə,
         an-TIG-wuh   æn'tigwə

Antigua and Barbuda
  island nation, Caribbean   an-TĒ-gwuh uhn(d) bahr-B͞OO-duh,   æn'tiːgwə ən(d) bɑʳ'buːdə,
         an-TIG-wuh   æn'tigwə

Antiguan
  pert. to Antigua   an-TĒ-gwuhn, an-TIG-wuhn   æn'tiːgwən, æn'tigwən

Antillean
  pert. to Antilles   an-TIL-ē-uhn   æn'tiliːən

Antilles
  islands, West Indies   an-TIL-ēz   æn'tiliːz

Antillian
  College, *Puerto Rico*   an-TIL-ē-uhn   æn'tiliːən

Antilochus
  son of Nestor   an-TIL-uh-kuhs   æn'tiləkəs

antimony
  element   ANT-uh-MŌ-nē   'æntəˌmoːniˑ

Antinous
  suitor of Penelope   an-TIN-uh-wuhs   æn'tinəwəs

Antioch
  ancient Syrian city; city, CA;   ANT-ē-AHK   'æntiːˌɑk
   university, OH

Antiochus
  son of Heracles; ancient Syrian   an-TĪ-uh-kuhs   æn'taiəkəs
   kings

Antiope
  mother of Amphion and Zethus;   an-TĪ-uh-pē   æn'taiəpiˑ
   queen of the Amazons

Antipas
  epithet, Herod   ANT-uh-PAS, ANT-uh-puhs   'æntəˌpæs, 'æntəpəs

Antipater
  Macedonian general   an-TIP-uht-uhr   æn'tipəʈəʳ

Antipodes
  Australia and New Zealand   an-TIP-uhd-ĒZ   æn'tipədˌiːz

Antisthenes
  Greek philosopher   an-TIS-thuh-NĒZ   æn'tisθəˌniːz

Antlia
  constellation   ANT-lē-uh   'æntliːə

Antoine
  1. pers. name   AN-TWAHN, an-TWAHN   'ænˌtwɑn, æn'twɑn
  2. French   ahⁿ-TWAHN   ɑ̃twɑːn

Antoinette
  1. pers. name   AN-twuh-NET, AN-tuh-NET   ˌæntwə'net, ˌæntə'net
  2. French   ahⁿ-twah-NET   ɑ̃twɑːnet

Key (col. 2):   a: fad   ā: fade   ah: father   ar: Mary   aw: law   e: fed   ē: feed   er: merry   i: hid   ī: hide   ō: coat   o͞o: boot
oi: boy   ow: now   u: put   uh: above   uhr: bird   ch: chop   ng: ring   sh: show   th: thick   <u>th</u>: this   zh: measure

Antón
    pers. name, Spanish   ahn-TAWN   ɑn'tɔːn

Anton
    1. pers. name   AN-TAHN, AN-TŌN, ANT-n   'æn,tɑn, 'æn,tɔːn, 'æntn̩
    2. Czech, Swedish   AHN-TAWN   'ɑːn,tɔːn
    3. Dutch, Estonian, Norwegian,   AHN-TAWN   'ɑn,tɔːn
        Polish
    4. German   AHN-TŌN   'ɑːn,tɔːn
    5. Italian   ahn-TAWN   ɑn'tɔːn
    6. Russian   UHN-TAWN   ˌən'tɔːn

Antoni
    pers. name   ahn-TAW-nē   ɑːn'tɔːniː

Antonia
    1. pers. name   an-TŌ-nē-uh, an-TŌN-yuh   æn'tɔːniːə, æn'tɔːnjə
    2. French   ahⁿ-tawn-YAH   ɑ̃tɔːnjɑː
    3. Italian   ahn-TAWN-yah   ɑn'tɔːnjɑ
    4. Spanish   ahn-TŌN-yah   ɑn'tɔːnjɑ

Antonie
    pers. name, German   ahn-TŌN-yuh, ahn-TŌ-nē-uh   ɑn'tɔːnjə, ɑn'tɔːniːə

Antonin
    pers. name, French   ahⁿ-taw-NEⁿ   ɑ̃tɔːnẽ

Antonín
    pers. name, Czech   AHN-tawn-YĒN   'ɑntɔːnˌjiːn

Antonines
    Roman imperial family   AN-tuh-NĪNZ   'æntəˌnɑinz

Antoninus
    pers. name   AN-tuh-NĪ-nuhs   ˌæntə'nɑinəs

Antoninus Pius
    Roman emperor   AN-tuh-NĪ-nuhs PĪ-uhs   ˌæntə'nɑinəs 'pɑiəs

Antonio
    1. pers. name   an-TŌ-nē-ō, an-TŌN-yō   æn'tɔːniːˌoː, æn'tɔːnjoː
    2. French   ahⁿ-tawn-YŌ   ɑ̃tɔːnjoː
    3. German   ahn-TŌN-yō, ahn-TŌ-nē-ō   ɑn'tɔːnjoː, ɑn'tɔːniːˌoː
    4. Italian   ahn-TAWN-yō   ɑn'tɔːnjoː
    5. Portuguese   ahⁿ(n)-TAWN-yo͞o   ɑ̃(n)'tɔːnjuː
    6. Spanish   ahn-TŌN-yō   ɑn'tɔːnjoː

Antônio
    pers. name, Portuguese   ahⁿ(n)-TAWN-yo͞o   ɑ̃(n)'tɔːnjuː

Antonioni
    Michelangelo, *Italian film director*   AN-TŌ-nē-Ō-nē   ˌæn,tɔːniː'oːniˑ

Antonius
    1. pers. name   an-TŌ-nē-uhs, an-TŌN-yuhs   æn'tɔːniːəs, æn'tɔːnjəs
    2. Dutch   ahn-TŌ-nē-ues   ɑn'tɔːniːys

Antony
    1. Mark, *Roman general; pers.*   AN-tuh-nē   'æntəniˑ
        name
    2. Dutch   ahn-TŌ-nē   ɑn'tɔːniː
    3. French   ahⁿ-taw-NĒ   ɑ̃tɔːniː

Antrim
    city, N. Ireland; county, MI   AN-truhm   'æntrəm

Antwerp
    city, Belgium   ANT-WUHRP, AN-TWUHRP   'ænt,wəʳp, 'æn,twəʳp

Antwerpen [Anvers]
    province, Belgium   AHNT-VER-puh(n)   'ɑnt,verpə(n)

Foreign Sounds: ue: *Fr.* **rue**, *Ger.* **füllen**   uh(r): *Fr.* **boeuf**, *Ger.* **Höhle**   kh: *Ger.* **ich**, *Scot.* **loch**   g̃: *Sp.* **amigo**   v: *Sp.* **hablar**
hl: *Welsh* **Llanelli**.   CAPITALS: primary stress.   SMALL CAPS: secondary stress.   Ⓢ: U.S. pron.   Ⓛ: British pron.

Anubis
  Egyptian god of the dead   uh-N(Y)OO-buhs   ə'n(j)uːbəs

Anuket
  Egyptian goddess   AHN-(y)oo-kuht   'an(j)uːkət

Anukis [Anuket]
  Egyptian goddess   AHN-(y)oo-kuhs   'an(j)uːkəs

Anvers [Antwerpen]
  province, Belgium   ahⁿ-VER(S)   ãver(s)

Anwar
  pers. name (A. Sadat)   AHN-WAHR   'an,waʳ

Anyi
  lang., Ghana, Ivory Coast   AHN-yē   'anjiˑ

Anzac
  Australian & New Zealand armed   AN-ZAK   'æn,zæk
    forces, WW2

Anzio
  town, Italy   AN-zē-ō   'ænziːoː

ANZUS
  treaty between Australia, New   AN-zuhs   'ænzəs
    Zealand, US

Ao
  lang., Burma   OW   'au

Aoudad
  wild sheep breed   OW-DAD, AH-u-DAD   'au,dæd, 'ɑ-u,dæd

Apache
  N. American people   uh-PACH-ē   ə'pætʃiˑ

Apalachee
  N. American people   AP-uh-LACH-ē   ˌæpə'lætʃiˑ

Apalachicola
  river, bay, city, FL   AP-uh-LACH-i-KŌ-luh   ˌæpə,lætʃi'koːlə

Aparri
  port, Philippines   uh-PAHR-ē   ə'pɑriˑ

Apatosaurus
  dinosaur (Brontosaurus)   AP-uht-uh-SAWR-uhs,   ˌæpəţə'sɔːrəs, ˌeːpæţə'sɔːrəs
    Ā-PAT-uh-SAWR-uhs

Apennines
  mtn. range, Italy   AP-uh-NĪNZ   'æpə,nɑinz

Apgar score
  rating of infant health   AP-GAHR   'æp,gɑʳ

ap Gwilym
  see Dafydd ap Gwilym

Aphra
  pers. name   AF-ruh   'æfrə

Aphrodite
  Greek goddess of love   AF-ruh-DĪT-ē   ˌæfrə'daiţiˑ

Aphrodite Terra
  highland on planet Venus   AF-ruh-DĪT-ē TER-uh   ˌæfrə'daiţiˑ 'terə

Apia
  city, Samoa   uh-PĒ-uh, ah-PĒ-uh   ə'piːə, ɑ'piːə

Apis
  Egyptian god; mythical Greek   Ā-puhs   'eːpəs
    king

Apocalypse
  New Testament book   uh-PAHK-uh-LIPS   ə'pɑkə,lips

Key (col. 2):   a: fad   ā: fade   ah: father   ar: Mary   aw: law   e: fed   ē: feed   er: merry   i: hid   ī: hide   ō: coat   ōō: boot
oi: boy   ow: now   u: put   uh: above   uhr: bird   ch: chop   ng: ring   sh: show   th: thick   th̲: this   zh·: measure

Apocrypha
  non-canonical books of the Bible   uh-PAHK-ruh-fuh   ə'pɑkrəfə
Apollinaire
  Guillaume, *French poet*   ah-paw-lē-NER   ɑːpɔːliːner
Apollinarianism
  beliefs of Bishop Apollinaris   uh-PAHL-uh-NAR-ē-uh-NIZ-uhm   ə,pɑlə'næriːə,nizəm
Apollinaris
  Syrian prelate; Wilhelm, *French*   uh-PAHL-uh-NAR-uhs   ə,pɑlə'nærəs
  poet, aka G. Apollinaire
Apollo
  Greek god of prophecy and music   uh-PAHL-ō   ə'pɑlɔː
Apollonius
  1. pers. name   AP-uh-LŌ-nē-uhs   ,æpə'lɔːniːəs
  2. German   AHP-ō-LŌN-yus, AHP-ō-LŌ-nē-uhs   ,ɑpoː'lɔːnjus, ,ɑpoː'lɔːniːəs
Apollonius Rhodius
  Greek epic poet   AP-uh-LŌ-nē-uhs RŌD-ē-uhs   ,æpə'lɔːniːəs 'rɔːdiːəs
Apollyon
  angel of the bottomless pit   uh-PAHL-yuhn, uh-PAHL-ē-uhn   ə'pɑljən, ə'pɑliːən
Apophis
  Egyptian snake-demon   AP-uh-fuhs   'æpəfəs
Apostles' Creed
  Christian prayer   uh-PAHS-uhlz KRĒD   ə,pɑsəlz 'kriːd
Appalachia
  region, eastern US   AP-uh-LÃ-ch(ē-)uh,   ,æpə'leːtʃ(iː)ə, ,æpə'lætʃ(iː)ə
     AP-uh-LACH(-ē)-uh *(usual local*   *(usual local pron.),*
     pron.), AP-uh-LÃ-sh(ē-)uh   ,æpə'leːʃ(iː)ə
Appalachian
  mtn. range, US   AP-uh-LÃ-ch(ē-)uhn,   ,æpə'leːtʃ(iː)ən,
     AP-uh-LACH(-ē)-uhn,   ,æpə'lætʃ(iː)ən,
     AP-uh-LÃ-sh(ē-)uhn   ,æpə'leːʃ(iː)ən
Appaloosa
  horse   AP-uh-LOO-suh   ,æpə'luːsə
Appanoose
  county, IA   AP-uh-NOOS   'æpə,nuːs
Appassionata, The
  sonata, Beethoven   uh-PASH-uh-NAHT-uh   ə,pæʃə'nɑtə
Appenines
  mtn. range, Italy   AP-uh-NĪNZ   'æpə,nɑinz
Appennino [Appenines]
  mtn. range, Italy   AHP-pen-NĒ-nō   ,ɑppen'niːnoː
Appenzell
  canton, Switzerland   AHP-uhn(t)-SEL, ⓢ AP-uhn-ZEL   'ɑpən(t),sel, ⓢ 'æpən,zel
Appian Way [Via Appia]
  ancient Roman road   AP-ē-uhn WĀ   ,æpiːən 'weː
Appius
  pers. name   AP-ē-uhs   'æpiːəs
Appius Claudius
  Roman patrician name   AP-ē-uhs KLAWD-ē-uhs   'æpiːəs 'klɔːdiːəs
Appleton
  Sir Edward V., *English physicist*   AP-uhl-tuhn, AP-uhlt-n   'æpəltən, 'æpəltṇ
  (Nobel 1947)
Appollonia
  US actress, singer   AP-uh-LŌ-nē-uh, -LŌN-yuh   ,æpə'lɔːniːə, -'lɔːnjə
Appollonius
  Greek mathematician   AP-uh-LŌ-nē-uhs   ,æpoː'lɔːniːəs

Foreign Sounds: ue: *Fr.* **rue**, *Ger.* **füllen**   uh(r): *Fr.* **boeuf**, *Ger.* **Höhle**   <u>kh</u>: *Ger.* i**ch**, *Scot.* lo**ch**   ḡ: *Sp.* ami**g**o   <u>v</u>: *Sp.* ha**b**lar
hl: *Welsh* **Ll**anelli.   CAPITALS: primary stress.   SMALL CAPS: secondary stress.   ⓢ: U.S. pron.   ⓔ: British pron.

Appomattox
  river, county, town (site of Civil   AP-uh-MAT-iks   ˌæpə'mæt̮iks
   War surrender),VA

Apries
  Egyptian king   AP-rē-ÊZ   'æpriːˌiːz

April
  month; pers. name   Ā-pruhl   'eːprəl

Apteryx
  bird genus   AP-tuh-riks   'æptəriks

Apthorp
  pers. name   AP-THAWRP   'æpˌθɔːʳp

Apuleius
  Lucius, *N. African philosopher,*   AP-yuh-LÊ-(y)uhs   ˌæpjə'liː(j)əs
   author

Apulia
  prov, Italy   uh-P(Y)OOL-yuh   ə'p(j)uːljə

Apus
  constellation   Ā-puhs   'eːpəs

'Aqaba
  Gulf of, *Red Sea*   AHK-uh-buh, AK-uh-buh   'akəbə, 'ækəbə

'Aqaba, Akaba
  seaport, Jordan   AHK-uh-buh, AK-uh-buh   'akəbə, 'ækəbə

Aquarian
  pert. to Aquarius   uh-KWAR-ē-uhn, uh-KWER-ē-uhn   ə'kwæriːən, ə'kweriːən

Aquarids
  meteor shower   uh-KWAR-idz, uh-KWER-idz   ə'kwæridz, ə'kweridz

Aquarius
  constellation, sign of the zodiac   uh-KWAR-ē-uhs, uh-KWER-ē-uhs   ə'kwæriːəs, ə'kweriːəs

Aquascutum
  retail apparel firm   ak-wuh-SKYOOT-uhm, ahk-   ækwə'skjuːt̮əm, ak-

Aquavit
  Scandinavian liquor   AHK-wuh-VĒT   'akwəˌviːt

Aqua Vitae
  alcoholic drink   AK-wuh VĪT-ē, VĒT-ē, VĒT-ī   ˌækwə 'vait̮iˌ, 'viːt̮iˌ, 'viːt̮ˌai

Aquila
  constellation   AK-wuh-luh   'ækwələ

Aquilegia [Columbine]
  plant   AK-wuh-LÊ-j(ē-)uh   ˌækwə'liːdʒ(iː)ə

Aquinas
  St. Thomas, *Italian philosopher*   uh-KWĪ-nuhs   ə'kwainəs

Aquino
  Corazon & Benigno, *Philippine*   ah-KÊ-nō, Ⓢ uh-KÊ-nō   a'kiːnoː, Ⓢ ə'kiːnoː
   leaders

Aquitaine
  region, France   AK-wuh-TĀN   'ækwəˌteːn

Aquitania
  Latin for Aquitaine   AK-wuh-TĀ-nē-uh, -TĀN-yuh   ˌækwə'teːniːə, -'teːnjə

Ara
  constellation   AR-uh, ER-uh   'ærə, 'erə

Arabia
  peninsula, Asia   uh-RĀ-bē-uh   ə'reːbiːə

Arabic
  lang., N Africa, Middle East,   AR-uh-bik   'ærəbik
   Arabian Peninsula

Key (col. 2):   a: fad   ā: fade   ah: father   ar: Mary   aw: law   e: fed   ē: feed   er: merry   i: hid   ī: hide   ō: coat   ōo: boot
oi: boy   ow: now   u: put   uh: above   uhr: bird   ch: chop   ng: ring   sh: show   th: thick   th̲: this   zh: measure

Araby
  literary term for Arabia; story, J. Joyce   AR-uh-bē   'ærəbi·

Arachne
  mythological weaver changed into a spider   uh-RAK-nē   ə'rækni·

Arafat
  Yasir, PLO leader   AR-uh-FAT   'ærə‚fæt

Arafura
  sea, Australia   AR-uh-FUR-uh   ‚ærə'furə

Aragón, Aragon
  river, ancient kingdom, Spain   ahr-ah-ĜAWN; Ⓢ AR-uh-GAHN, AR-uh-guhn   aᵣa'yɔːn; Ⓢ 'ærə‚gɑn, 'ærəgən

Arahsamnu
  Babylonian month   AHR-ah<u>kh</u>-SAHM-no͞o   ‚ɑrɑx'sɑmnuː

Arāk
  city, Iran   uh-RAHK   ə'rɑk

Aral
  inland sea, Asia   AR-uhl   'ærəl

Aralskoye More [Aral]
  inland sea, Asia   uh-RAL-skuh-yuh MAWR-(y)uh   ə‚rælskəjə 'mɔːr(j)ə

Aram
  pers. name, Armenian   ahr-AHM   ɑr'ɑm

Aramaeans
  ancient Semitic people   AR-uh-MĀ-uhnz, AR-uh-MĒ-uhnz   ‚ærə'meːənz, ‚ærə'miːənz

Aramaic
  ancient Semitic lang.   AR-uh-MĀ-ik   ‚ærə'meːik

Aramis
  1. character in The Three Musketeers, *A. Dumas*   ah-rah-MĒS, Ⓢ AR-uh-muhs, AR-uh-MĒS   ɑːrɑːmiːs, Ⓢ 'ærəməs, ‚ærə'miːs
  2. cologne brand   AR-uh-muhs, ER-uh-muhs   'ærəməs, 'erəməs

Aran
  Irish island   AR-uhn   'ærən

Aransas
  county, TX   uh-RAN-suhs   ə'rænsəs

Arantxa
  pers. name (A. Sánchez Vicario)   ah-RAHNT-sah, Ⓢ ah-RAHN-chuh   ɑ'rɑntsɑ, Ⓢ ɑ'rɑntʃə

Arapaho
  N. American people   uh-RAP-uh-HŌ   ə'ræpə‚hoː

Arapahoe
  county, CO   uh-RAP-uh-HŌ   ə'ræpə‚hoː

Arapesh
  lang., people, New Guinea   AHR-uh-PESH   'ɑrə‚peʃ

Arara
  S. American people   uh-RAHR-uh   ə'rɑrə

Ararat [Ağrı Dağı]
  mtn.,Turkey   AR-uh-RAT   'ærə‚ræt

Aratus
  Greek general   uh-RĀT-uhs   ə'reːʈəs

Araucanian
  lang., people, S. America   uh-ROW-KAHN-ē-uhn, AR-aw-KĀ-nē-uhn   ə‚rɑu'kɑniːən, ‚ærɔː'keːniːən

Araukan [Araucanian]
  lang., people, S. America   uh-ROW-kuhn   ə'rɑukən

Foreign Sounds: ue: *Fr.* **rue**, *Ger.* füllen   uh(r): *Fr.* **boeuf**, *Ger.* Höhle   <u>kh</u>: *Ger.* i**ch**, *Scot.* lo**ch**   ĝ: *Sp.* ami**g**o   v: *Sp.* ha**b**lar   hl: *Welsh* L**l**anelli.   CAPITALS: primary stress.   SMALL CAPS: secondary stress.   Ⓢ: U.S. pron.   Ⓑ: British pron.

Arausio
  ancient name of Orange, *France*　　uh-RAW-zhē-ō　　　　　　ə'rɔːʒiːˌɔː
Arawak
  S. American people　　　　　　AR-uh-WAHK, AR-uh-WAK　　'ærəˌwɑk, 'ærəˌwæk
Arbat
  district, Moscow　　　　　　ahr-BAHT　　　　　　　　　aʳ'bɑt
Arber
  Werner, *Swiss microbiologist*　　AHR-buhr　　　　　　　'aʳbəʳ
  (Nobel 1978)
Arbitron
  media ratings　　　　　　　AHR-buh-TRAHN　　　　　'aʳbəˌtrɑn
Arborvitae
  plant　　　　　　　　　AHR-buhr-VĪT-ē　　　　　ˌaʳbəʳ'vaiţiˑ
Arbour
  Bernie, Stadium, *Hamilton,*　　AHR-buhr　　　　　　　'aʳbəʳ
  Ontario
Arbroath
  port, Scotland　　　　　　ahr-BRŌTH　　　　　　aʳ'broːθ
Arbuthnot
  pers. name　　　　　　ahr-BUHTH-nuht, AHR-buhth-NAHT　　aʳ'bəθnət, 'aʳbəθˌnɑt
Arbutus
  town, MD　　　　　　ahr-BYŌŌT-uhs　　　　　aʳ'bjuːţəs
Arcadia
  1. city, CA, FL; ancient country,　ahr-KĀD-ē-uh　　　　　aʳ'keːdiːə
  Greece
  2. region, Greece　　　　AHR-kuh-<u>TH</u>Ē-uh　　　　ˌarkə'ðiːə
Arcadian
  pert. to Arcadia　　　　ahr-KĀD-ē-uhn　　　　aʳ'keːdiːən
Arcady
  ancient name for Arcadia, *Greece*　AHR-kuhd-ē　　　　　'aʳkədiˑ
Arcaro
  George 'Eddie', *US jockey*　　ahr-KAR-ō, ahr-KER-ō　　aʳ'kæroː, aʳ'keroː
Arcas
  son of Zeus and Callisto　　AHR-kuhs　　　　　　'aʳkəs
Arc de Triomphe
  monument, Paris, France　　ahrk duh trē-AWⁿF　　aːrk də triːɔ̃f
Arce
  Manuel José, *Salvadoran*　　AHR-sā　　　　　　'aʳseː
  politician
Archaeopteryx
  prehistoric bird　　　　AHR-kē-AHP-tuh-riks　　ˌaʳkiː'aptəriks
Archaeozoic
  see Archeozoic
Archangel [Arkhangelsk]
  city, Russia　　　　　AHR-KĀN-juhl　　　　'aʳˌkeːndʒəl
Archbold
  Stadium, *Syracuse, NY*　　AHRCH-BŌLD, AHRCH-BAWLD　　'aʳtʃˌboːld, 'aʳtʃˌbɔːld
Archelaus
  ethnarch of Judea　　　AHR-kuh-LĀ-uhs　　　ˌaʳkə'leːəs
Archeozoic, Archaeozoic
  geologic period　　　　AHR-kē-uh-ZŌ-ik　　ˌaʳkiːə'zoːik
Archerd
  Army, *entertainment columnist*　AHR-chuhrd　　　　'aʳtʃəʳd
Archibald
  pers. name　　　　　AHR-chuh-BAWLD, -buhld　　'aʳtʃəˌbɔːld, -bəld

Key (col. 2):　a: fad　ā: fade　ah: father　ar: Mary　aw: law　e: fed　ē: feed　er: merry　i: hid　ī: hide　ō: coat　ōō: boot
oi: boy　ow: now　u: put　uh: above　uhr: bird　ch: chop　ng: ring　sh: show　th: thick　<u>th</u>: this　zh: measure

Archidamus
  name, Spartan kings   AHR-kuh-DĀ-muhs   ˌɑʳkə'deːməs
Archie
  pers. name   AHR-chē   'ɑʳtʃiˑ
Archilochus
  Greek poet   ahr-KIL-uh-kuhs   ɑʳˈkiləkəs
Archimède
  pers. name, French   ahr-shē-MED   ɑːrʃiːmed
Archimedean screw
  water-raising device   AHR-kuh-MĒD-ē-uhn SKRO͞O   ˌɑʳkə'miːdiːən 'skruː
Archimedes
  Greek scientist; pers. name   AHR-kuh-MĒD-ēz   ˌɑʳkə'miːdiːz
Archipenko
  Alexsandr, *Ukrainian-born US*   AHR-kyi-PYENG-kō,   ˌɑʳkji'pjeŋkoː,
    sculptor   Ⓢ AHR-ki-PENG-kō   Ⓢ ˌɑʳki'peŋkoː
Archosauria
  dinosaur subclass   AHR-kuh-SAWR-ē-uh   ˌɑʳkə'sɔːriːə
Archuleta
  county, CO   AHR-chuh-LET-uh   ˌɑʳtʃə'letə
Archy
  literary cockroach   AHR-chē   'ɑʳtʃiˑ
Arciniegas
  Germán, *Colombian author*   ahr-sēn-YĀ-ğahs   ɑrsiːn'jeːɣɑs
Arcite
  lover in "The Knight's Tale,"   ahr-SĒT-uh, AHR-SĪT   ɑʳ'siːțə, 'ɑʳˌsait
    Chaucer
Arctic
  pert. to polar north   AHRK-tik, AHRT-ik   'ɑʳktik, 'ɑʳtik
Arcturus [Alpha Boötes]
  star   ahrk-T(Y)UR-uhs   ɑʳk't(j)urəs
Ardashir
  name, kings of Persia   AHRD-uh-shuhr   'ɑʳdəʃəʳ
Ardèche
  river, dept., France   ahr-DESH   ɑːrdeʃ
Arden
  English forest   AHRD-n   'ɑʳdn̩
Ardennes
  region, Luxembourg & France   ahr-DEN   ɑrden, Ⓢ ɑʳ'den
Arecibo
  port, Puerto Rico   ahr-uh-SĒ-v̱ō   ɑrə'siːβoː
Arena [Alianza Republicana Nacionalista]
  political party, El Salvador   ah-RĀ-nah   ɑ'reːnɑ
Arenac
  county, MI   AR-uh-NAK   'ærəˌnæk
Areopagite
  member of the Areopagus   AR-ē-AHP-uh-JĪT, -GĪT   ˌæri'ɑpəˌdʒait, -ˌgait
Areopagitica
  treatise, J. Milton   AR-ē-uh-puh-JIT-i-kuh   ˌæriːəpə'dʒițikə
Areopagus
  hill, Athens; Athenian tribunal   AR-ē-AHP-uh-guhs   ˌæri'ɑpəgəs
Ares
  Greek god of war   AR-ĒZ, ER-ĒZ   'ærˌiːz, 'erˌiːz
Aretha
  pers. name (A. Franklin)   uh-RĒ-thuh   ə'riːθə

Foreign Sounds: ue: *Fr.* **rue**, *Ger.* f**ü**llen uh(r): *Fr.* b**oeu**f, *Ger.* H**öh**le <u>kh</u>: *Ger.* i**ch**, *Scot.* lo**ch** ğ: *Sp.* ami**g**o v̱: *Sp.* ha**b**lar
hl: *Welsh* **Ll**anelli. CAPITALS: primary stress. SMALL CAPS: secondary stress. Ⓢ: U.S. pron. Ⓑ: British pron.

Arethusa
  mythological nymph   AR-uh-TH(Y)OO-zuh   ˌærə'θ(j)uːzə

Arezzo
  prov, Italy   ah-RET-sō, uh-RET-sō   a'retsoː, ə'retsoː

Argentina
  republic, S. America   AHR-juhn-TĒ-nuh   ˌaʳdʒən'tiːnə

Argentine
  pert. to Argentina   AHR-juhn-TĒN, -TĪN   'aʳdʒən,tiːn, -ˌtain

Argentine, The
  alternate name for Argentina   AHR-juhn-TĒN, -TĪN   'aʳdʒən,tiːn, -ˌtain

Argentino
  lake, Argentina; pers. name   ahr-ḡān-TĒ-nō   arɣeːn'tiːnoː

Argive
  pert. to Argos   AHR-JĪV, AHR-GĪV   'aʳˌdʒaiv, 'aʳˌgaiv

Argo
  Jason's ship; island, Nile River,   AHR-gō   'aʳgoː
  Sudan

Argolis
  district, Greece   AHR-guh-luhs   'aʳgələs

argon
  element   AHR-GAHN   'aʳˌgan

Argonauts
  Jason's companions on the Argo   AHR-guh-NAWTS   'aʳgəˌnɔːts

Argonne
  region, forest, France   ahr-GAWN, ⓢ ahr-GAHN, AHR-GAHN   aːrgɔːn, ⓢ aʳgan, 'aʳˌgan

Argos
  city, Greece   AHR-GAWS, AHR-guhs   'aʳˌgɔːs, 'aʳgəs

Argus
  Odysseus's dog; many-eyed   AHR-guhs   'aʳgəs
  guardian of Io

Argyle, Argyll
  Scottish pl. name; knitting   ahr-GĪL, AHR-GĪL   aʳ'gail, 'aʳˌgail
  pattern; pers. name

Argyll and Bute
  district, Scotland   ahr-GĪL uhn(d) BYOOT   aʳ'gail ən(d) 'bjuːt

Ari
  lang., Ethiopia; pers. name   AHR-ē   'ariˑ

Ariadne
  daughter of Minos and Pasiphae   AR-ē-AD-nē   ˌæriː'ædniˑ

Arian
  adherent of Arianism   AR-ē-uhn, ER-ē-uhn   'æriːən, 'eriːən

Ariane
  French-built rocket   ahr-YAHN, ⓢ AHR-ē-AHN, AR-ē-AN   aːrjaːn, ⓢ ˌariː'an, ˌæriː'æn

Arianism
  Christian heresy   AR-ē-uh-NIZ-uhm, ER-   'æriːəˌnizəm, 'er-

Arias Sanchez
  Oscar, *Costa Rican politician*   AHR-ē-ahs SAHN-chās   'ariːas 'santʃeːs
  (Nobel 1987)

Ariccia
  town, Italy   ah-RĒ(T)-chah   a'riː(t)tʃa

Aricia
  former name of Ariccia   uh-RISH(-ē)-uh   ə'riʃ(iː)ə

Key (col. 2):   a: fad   ā: fade   ah: father   ar: **Mary**   aw: law   e: fed   ē: feed   er: merry   i: hid   ī: hide   ō: coat   oo: boot
oi: boy   ow: now   u: put   uh: above   uhr: bird   ch: chop   ng: ring   sh: show   th: thick   th: this   zh: measure

Ariel
spirit in The Tempest,   AR-ē-uhl, ER-   'æri:əl, 'er-
Shakespeare; satellite of
Uranus; British research
satellite

Aries
constellation, sign of the zodiac   AR-(ē-)-ĒZ, ER-   'ær(i:),i:z, 'er-

Arikara
N. American people   uh-RIK-uh-ruh   ə'rikərə

Arimathaea, Arimathea
town, ancient Palestine   AR-uh-muh-THĒ-uh, ER-   ,ærəmə'θi:ə, ,er-

Arion
semilegendary Greek poet &   uh-RĪ-uhn   ə'raiən
musician; winged horse of
Adrastus

Ariosto
Ludovico, Italian poet   AHR-ē-AHS-tō, AHR-ē-Ō-stō   ,ari:'asto:, ,ari:'o:sto:

Aristaeus
Greek mythological bee-keeper   AR-uh-STĒ-uhs, ER-   ,ærə'sti:əs, ,er-

Aristagoras
ancient Ionian revolutionary   AR-uh-STAG-uh-ruhs   ,ærə'stægərəs

Aristarchus
crater on Moon   AR-uh-STAHR-kuhs, ER-   ,ærə'sta^{r}kəs, ,er-

Aristide
1. Jean Bertrand, Haitian priest,   ah-rē-STĒD, ⑤ AR-uh-STĒD, ER-   a:ri:sti:d, ⑤ ,ærə'sti:d, ,er-
politician; pers. name, French
2. Italian   ah-RĒ-stē-dā   a'ri:sti:de:

Aristides
1. Athenian statesman; pers. name   AR-uh-STĪD-ēz   ,ærə'staidi:z
2. Spanish   ah-rē-STĒ-<u>th</u>ās   ari:'sti:ðe:s

Aristippus
Greek philosopher   AR-uh-STIP-uhs, ER-   ,ærə'stipəs, ,er-

Aristophanes
Greek comic playwright   AR-uh-STAHF-uh-NĒZ, ER-   ,ærə'stafə,ni:z, ,er-

Aristophanic
pert. to Aristophanes   uh-RIS-tuh-FAN-ik,   ə,ristə'fænik, ,ærəstə'fænik,
AR-uh-stuh-FAN-ik, ER-uh-stuh-   ,erəstə-

Aristotelian
pert. to Aristotle   AR-uh-stuh-TĒL-yuhn, -TĒ-lē-uhn   ,ærəstə'ti:ljən, -'ti:li:ən

Aristotelianism
philosophy of Aristotle   AR-uh-stuh-TĒL-yuh-NIZ-uhm,   ,ærəstə'ti:ljə,nizəm,
-TĒ-lē-uh-NIZ-uhm   -'ti:li:ə,nizəm

Aristotle
Greek philosopher   AR-uh-STAHT-l, AR-uh-STAHT-l   'ærə,statl̩, ,ærə'statl̩

Arizona
state, US   AR-uh-ZŌ-nuh   ,ærə'zo:nə

Arkadhía [Arcadia]
region, Greece   AHR-kuh-<u>TH</u>Ē-uh, AHR-kuh-DĒ-uh   ,arkə'ði:ə, ,a^{r}kə'di:ə

Arkadi, Arkady
pers. name, Russian   UHR-KAHD-yi   ,ər'ka:djij

Arkansan
person from AR   ahr-KAN-zuhn   a^r'kænzən

Foreign Sounds: ue: *Fr.* **rue**, *Ger.* **füllen**   uh(r): *Fr.* **b**oe**uf**, *Ger.* **Höhle**   <u>kh</u>: *Ger.* i**ch**, *Scot.* lo**ch**   ḡ: *Sp.* ami**g**o   v̱: *Sp.* ha**b**lar
hl: *Welsh* **Ll**anelli.   CAPITALS: primary stress.   SMALL CAPS: secondary stress.   ⑤: U.S. pron.   ⑥: British pron.

Arkansas
  1. US river — ahr-KAN-zuhs *(usual in KS, often in CO)*, AHR-kuhn-SAW *(usual elsewhere)* — ar'kænzəs *(usual in KS, often in CO)*, 'aᴿkən,sɔː *(usual elsewhere)*
  2. state, US — AHR-kuhn-SAW — 'aᴿkən,sɔː

Arkhangelsk [Archangel]
  city, Russia — ahr-KAN-GELSK — aᴿ'kæn,gelsk

Arlanda
  airport, Stockholm — AHR-LAHN-duh — 'ar,landə

Arlberg
  mtn. pass, Austria; skiing technique — AHRL-BERK, AHRL-BUHRG — 'aᴿl,beᴿk, 'aᴿl,bəᴿg

Arledge
  Roone, *US television executive* — AHR-lij — 'aᴿlidʒ

Arlen
  pers. name — AHR-luhn — 'aᴿlən

Arlene
  pers. name — ahr-LĒN, ⓔ AHR-LĒN — aᴿ'liːn, ⓔ 'aᴿ,liːn

Arles
  town, France — AHRL — aːrl

Arlin
  pers. name — AHR-luhn — 'aᴿlən

Arlington
  city, TX; town, MA; natl. cemetery, VA; pers. name — AHR-ling-tuhn — 'aᴿliŋtən

Arlo
  pers. name — AHR-lō — 'aᴿloː

Arlyn
  pers. name — AHR-luhn — 'aᴿlən

Armada
  Spanish fleet — ahr-MAHD-uh, ahr-MĀD-uh, ahr-MAD-uh — aᴿ'madə, aᴿ'meːdə, aᴿ'mædə

Armageddon
  Christian final battle — AHR-muh-GED-n — ,aᴿmə'gedn̩

Armagh
  county, Ireland — ahr-MAH, AHR-MAH — aᴿ'ma, 'aᴿ,ma

Armagnac
  district, France; brandy — ahr-mahn-YAHK, Ⓢ AHR-muhn-YAK — aːrmaːnjaːk, Ⓢ ,aᴿmən'jæk

Armand
  1. pers. name — AHR-muhnd, AHR-MAHND, ahr-MAHND — 'aᴿmənd, 'ar,mand, ar'mand
  2. French — ahr-MAHⁿ — aːrmã
  3. German — AHR-MAHNT — 'aᴿ,mant
  4. Romanian — ahr-MAHND — ar'mand

Armande
  pers. name, French — ahr-MAHⁿD — aːrmãd

Armando
  pers. name, Italian, Spanish — ahr-MAHN-dō — ar'mandoː

Armani
  Giorgio, *Italian designer* — ahr-MAHN-ē — aᴿ'maniˑ

Armatrading
  Joan, *US singer* — AHR-muh-TRĀD-ing — 'aᴿmə,treːdiŋ

Armenia
  1. republic, Asia — ahr-MĒ-nē-uh — aᴿ'miːniːə
  2. city, Colombia — ahr-MĂN-yuh — aᴿ'meːnjə

Key (col. 2): a: fad ā: fade ah: father ar: **Mary** aw: **law** e: fed ē: feed er: merry i: hid ī: hide ō: coat ōō: boot
oi: boy ow: now u: put uh: above uhr: bird ch: chop ng: ring sh: show th: thick <u>th</u>: this zh: measure

Armenian

   lang., W. Asia; pert. to Armenia   ahr-MĒ-nē-uhn, -nyuhn   ɑʳˈmiːniːən, -njən

Armentieres, Armentières

   city, France   ahr-mahⁿ-TYER, Ⓢ AHR-muhn-tē-ER,   ɑːrmãtjer, Ⓢ ˌɑʳməntiːˈeʳ,
           Ⓔ AHR-muhn-TIRZ   Ⓔ ˈɑʳmən,tiʳz

Arminianism

   teachings of J. Arminius   ahr-MIN-ē-uh-NIZ-uhm   ɑʳminiːəˌnizəm

Arminius

   Jacobus, *Dutch theologian;*   ahr-MIN-ē-uhs   ɑʳminiːəs
     Germanic hero

Armistead

   pers. name   AHR-muh-STED, -stuhd   ˈɑʳməˌsted, -stəd

Armitage

   Ballet, *dance co., NY*   AHR-muht-ij   ˈɑʳmət̮idʒ

Armstrong

   Louis, *US musician;* Neil, *US*   AHRM-STRAWNG   ˈɑʳm,strɔːŋ
     astronaut; pers. name

Army

   pers. name (A. Archerd)   AHR-mē   ˈɑʳmiˑ

Arnaud, Arnault

   pers. name, French   ahr-NŌ   ɑːrnoː

Arnaz

   Desi, *US entertainer*   ahr-NEZ   ɑʳnez

Arne

   1. Thomas, *English composer*   AHRN   ˈɑʳn

   2. pers. name   AHR-nē   ˈɑʳniˑ

   3. Czech   AHR-ne   ˈɑrne

   4. Norwegian   AHR-nuh   ˈɑrnə

Arness

   James, *US actor*   ahr-NES   ɑʳnes

Arnhem

   city, Netherlands   AHRN-HEM, AHR-nuhm   ˈɑʳn,hem, ˈɑʳnəm

Árni

   pers. name, Icelandic   OWD-nē *[sic]*   ˈɑudniː *[sic]*

arnica

   herb   AHR-ni-kuh   ˈɑʳnikə

Arno

   river, Italy; pers. name, German   AHR-nō   ˈɑʳnoː

Arnold

   1. pers. name   AHR-nuhld   ˈɑʳnəld

   2. Danish, Norwegian   AHR-nawl   ˈɑrnɔːl

   3. Dutch   AHR-NAWLT   ˈɑr,nɔːlt

   4. French   ahr-NAWLD   ɑːrnɔːld

   5. German   AHR-NAWLT   ˈɑʳ,nɔːlt

Arnoldson

   K. P., *Swedish author, politician*   AHRN-l-suhn, AHR-nuhld-suhn   ˈɑʳn̩sən, ˈɑʳnəldsən
     (*Nobel 1908*)

Aroostook

   county, ME   uh-ROOS-tuhk, uh-RUS-tuhk, -tik   əˈruːstək, əˈrustək, -tik

Arouet

   pers. name, French (F. M. A. de   ahr-WE   ɑːrwe
     Voltaire)

Arp

   1. Bill, *US humorist*   AHRP   ˈɑʳp

   2. Jan, *French artist, poet*   AHRP   ɑːrp

Foreign Sounds: ue: *Fr.* **rue**, *Ger.* f**ü**llen uh(r): *Fr.* b**oeu**f, *Ger.* H**öh**le k͟h: *Ger.* i**ch**, *Scot.* lo**ch** g̃: *Sp.* ami**g**o v̲: *Sp.* ha**b**lar
hl: *Welsh* **Ll**anelli. CAPITALS: primary stress. SMALL CAPS: secondary stress. Ⓢ: U.S. pron. Ⓔ: British pron.

Arpad

   pers. name   AHR-pad   'ɑʳpæd

Árpád

   pers. name, Hungarian   AHR-pahd   'ɑrpɑd

ARPANET

   Advanced Research Projects   AHR-puh-NET   'ɑʳpə‚net
    Agency Network, computer
    network

Arpino

   Italian town, home of Cicero ahr-PĒ-no   ɑʳ'piːno

Arpinum

   Latin form of Arpino   ahr-PĪ-nuhm   ɑʳ'pɑinəm

Arquette

   Rosanna, *US actress*   ahr-KET   ɑʳ'ket

Arras

   town, France   ah-RAHS, Ⓢ uh-RAHS, AR-uhs   ɑːrɑs, Ⓢ ə'rɑs, 'ærəs

Arrau

   Claudio, *Chilean pianist*   ahr-ROW, Ⓢ uh-ROW   ɑr'rɑu, Ⓢ ə'rɑu

Arrhenius

   S. A., *Swedish physicist, chemist* uh-RĀ-nē-uhs, uh-RĒ-nē-uhs ə'reːniːəs, ə'riːniːəs
    (Nobel 1903)

Arrow

   Kenneth J., *US economist (Nobel* AR-ō   'æroː
    1972)

arsenic

   element   AHRS-nik, AHRS-n-ik   'ɑʳsnik, 'ɑʳsn̩ik

Arsenio

   1. pers. name   ahr-SIN-ē-ō, ahr-SIN-yō, ahr-SEN- ɑʳ'siniːoː, ɑʳ'sinjoː, ɑʳ'sen-
   2. Italian   ahr-SEN-yō   ɑr'senjoː
   3. Spanish   ahr-SĂN-yō   ɑr'seːnjoː

Art

   pers. name   AHRT   'ɑʳt

Artaxerxes

   king, Persia   AHRT-uh(g)-ZUHRK-SĒZ   ‚ɑʳtə(g)'zəʳk‚siːz

Art Deco

   design style   AHR(T) dā-KŌ, DĀ-kō, DEK-ō ‚ɑʳ(t) deɪ'koː, 'deɪkoː, 'dekoː

Artemis

   Greek goddess of the moon; pers. AHRT-uh-muhs   'ɑʳt̬əməs
    name

Artemision

   ancient wonder at Ephesus   AHRT-uh-MIZH-uhn   ‚ɑʳt̬ə'miʒən

Artemisium

   cape, Euboea   AHRT-uh-MĒ-zē-uhm,   ‚ɑʳt̬ə'miːziːəm, -'miːʒ(iː)əm
                    -MĒ-zh(ē-)uhm

Artemus

   pers. name   AHRT-uh-muhs   'ɑʳt̬əməs

Arthropods

   segmented invertebrates   AHR-thruh-PAHDZ   'ɑʳθrə‚pɑdz

Key (col. 2): a: f**a**d ā: f**a**de ah: f**a**ther ar: M**ar**y aw: l**aw** e: f**e**d ē: f**ee**d er: m**er**ry i: h**i**d ī: h**i**de ō: c**oa**t o͞o: b**oo**t
oi: b**oy** ow: n**ow** u: p**u**t uh: **a**bove uhr: b**ir**d ch: **ch**op ng: ri**ng** sh: **sh**ow th: **th**ick th̲: **th**is zh: mea**s**ure

Arthur

    1. Chester A., 21st US president;   AHR-thuhr   'ɑʳθəʳ
       legendary British ruler; pers.
       name

    2. French   ahr-TUER   ɑːrtyːr

    3. German   AHR-tur   'ɑʳtur

    4. Hungarian   AHR-tur   'ɑrtur

    5. Portuguese   uhr-TO͞OR, ahr-   ər'tuːr, ɑːr-

    6. Welsh   AHR-thir   'ɑrθir

Arthurian

    pert. to King Arthur   ahr-TH(Y)UR-ē-uhn   ɑʳ'θ(j)uriːən

Artiodactyla

    hoofed animals   AHRT-ē-ō-DAK-tuh-luh   ˌɑʳt̬iːoː'dæktələ

Artis

    pers. name   AHRT-uhs   'ɑʳt̬əs

Artium Baccalaureus

    bachelor of arts, A.B. or B.A.   AHRT-ē-uhm BAK-uh-LŌR-ē-uhs,   'ɑʳt̬iːəm ˌbækə'loːriːəs,
                       -LAWR-ē-uhs   -'loːriːəs

Artium Magister

    master of arts, M.A.   AHRT-ē-uhm MAJ-uh-stuhr   'ɑʳt̬iːəm 'mædʒəstəʳ

Art Nouveau

    design style   AHR(T) no͞o-VŌ   ˌɑʳ(t) nuː'voː

Artois

    former province, France   ahr-TWAH   ɑːrtwɑː

Artur

    1. pers. name, German   AHR-tur   'ɑʳtur

    2. Polish   AHR-to͞or   'ɑːrtuːr

    3. Portuguese   uhr-TO͞OR, ahr-   ər'tuːr, ɑːr-

    4. Russian   UHR-TO͞OR   ˌər'tuːr

    5. Swedish   AHR-tuhr   'ɑːrtər

Arturi

    pers. name, Finnish   AHR-tur-ē   'ɑːʳturi·

Arturo

    1. pers. name, Italian, Spanish ahr-TO͞O-rō   ɑr'tuːroː

    2. Portuguese   uhr-TO͞O-ro͞o, ahr-   ər'tuːruː, ɑːr-

Artus

    1. pers. name, Dutch   AHR-tues   'ɑrtys

    2. French   ahr-TUES   ɑːrtys

Artzybasheff

    Mikhail, *Russian novelist*   UHRT-si-BAH-shif   ˌəʳtsi'bɑːʃif

Arua

    S. American people   AHR-uh-WAH, AHR-uh-WAH 'arəˌwa, ˌarə'wa

Aruba

    island, Caribbean   uh-RO͞O-buh   ə'ruːbə

Arumanian [Romanian]

    lang., Europe   AHR-o͞o-MÃ-nē-uhn   ˌɑruˈmeːniːən

Arundel

    borough, England   AR-uhn-duhl   'ærəndəl

ARVN

    Army, Republic of (South)   AHR-vuhn   'ɑʳvən
       Vietnam

Aryan

    Indo-European people or lang. AR-ē-uhn, ER-ē-uhn, AHR-yuhn 'æriːən, 'eriːən, 'ɑrjən

Arzawa

    ancient Luwian city   ahr-ZAH-wuh   ɑʳ'zɑwə

Foreign Sounds: ue: *Fr.* **rue**, *Ger.* füllen uh(r): *Fr.* **boeuf**, *Ger.* Höhle <u>kh</u>: *Ger.* i<u>ch</u>, *Scot.* lo<u>ch</u> ḡ: *Sp.* amigo ṿ: *Sp.* hablar
hl: *Welsh* Llanelli. CAPITALS: primary stress. SMALL CAPS: secondary stress. Ⓢ: U.S. pron. Ⓑ: British pron.

Asa
  pers. name   Ā-suh   'eːsə

asafetida, asafoetida
  plant   AS-uh-FIT-uhd-ē, AS-uh-FET-uhd-uh   ˌæsə'fițədiˑ, ˌæsə'fețədə

Asahi
  Japanese beer   ah-sah-hē   ɑsɑhiː

Asaph
  pers. name   AS-uhf, Ā-suhf   'æsəf, 'eːsəf

Asbury
  Ball Park, *Chicago, IL; pers. name* AZ-BER-ē, AZ-b(uh-)rē   'æzˌberiˑ, 'æzb(ə)riˑ

Asbury Park
  city, NJ   AZ-BER-ē PAHRK, AZ-b(uh-)rē   ˌæzˌberiˑ 'pɑʳk, ˌæzb(ə)riˑ
                        PAHRK   'pɑʳk

Ascanius [Iulus]
  son of Aeneas   as-KĀ-nē-uhs   æs'keːniːəs

Ascension
  parish, LA; island, Atlantic uh-SEN-chuhn   ə'sentʃən

Asch
  Sholem, *Polish writer*   AHSH, ASH   'ɑːʃ, 'æʃ

Ascham
  Roger, *English writer*   AS-kuhm   'æskəm

ASCII
  American Standard Code for AS-kē   'æskiˑ
    Information Interchange

Asclepius [Aesculapius]
  Greek god of medicine   as-KLĀ-pē-uhs, as-KLĒ-pē-uhs æs'kleːpiːəs, æs'kliːpiːəs

Ascot
  village, race track, England AS-kuht, AS-kaht   'æskət, 'æskɑt

Asea Brown Bovari
  multi-national power systems uh-SĀ-(y)uh BROWN bō-VER-ē ə'seː(j)ə 'brɑun boː'veriˑ
    corp.

ASEAN
  Southeast Asian treaty   AHS-ē-AHN, AS-ē-AHN, AS-ē-uhn 'ɑsiːˌɑn, 'æsiːˌɑn, 'æsiːən
    organization

Asgard
  abode of Scandinavian gods AS-GAHRD, AZ-GAHRD   'æsˌgɑʳd, 'æzˌgɑʳd

Asgeir
  pers. name, Icelandic   AHS-GĀR   'ɑsˌgeːr

Asgeirsson
  Asgeir, *Icelandic statesman* AHS-gār-SAWN   'ɑsgeːrˌsɔːn

Ashanti
  African people; region, Ghana uh-SHANT-ē, uh-SHAHNT-ē ə'ʃæntiˑ, ə'ʃɑntiˑ

Ashby
  pers. name   ASH-bē   'æʃbiˑ

Ashby-de-la-Zouch
  town, England   ASH-bē duh lah Z̄O̅O̅SH   'æʃbiˑ də lɑ 'zuːʃ

Ashdod
  town, Israel   ASH-DAHD   'æʃˌdɑd

Ashe
  Arthur, *US tennis player* ASH   'æʃ

Asher
  pers. name   ASH-uhr   'æʃəʳ

Asheville
  city, NC   ASH-vuhl, ASH-VIL   'æʃvəl, 'æʃˌvil

Key (col. 2):   a: fad ā: fade ah: father ar: Mary aw: law e: fed ē: feed er: merry i: hid ī: hide ō: coat o̅o̅: boot
oi: boy ow: now u: put uh: above uhr: bird ch: chop ng: ring sh: show th: thick <u>th</u>: this zh: measure

Ashikei		
pers. name, Japanese	ah-shē-kā	ɑʃiːkeː
Ashkenazi		
Jew of Eastern & Central Europe	ASH-kuh-NAZ-ē, AHSH-kuh-NAHZ-ē	ˌæʃkəˈnæziˑ, ˌɑʃkəˈnɑziˑ
Ashkenazim		
pl. of Ashkenazi	ASH-kuh-NAZ-uhm, AHSH-kuh-NAHZ-uhm	ˌæʃkəˈnæzəm, ˌɑʃkəˈnɑzəm
Ashkhabad		
city, Turkmenistan	ASH-kuh-BAD, ASH-kuh-BAHD	ˈæʃkəˌbæd, ˈæʃkəˌbɑd
Ashland		
US pl. name	ASH-luhnd	ˈæʃlənd
Ashleigh, Ashley, Ashlie		
pers. name	ASH-lē	ˈæʃliˑ
Ashluslay		
S. American people	AHSH-luh-SLĪ	ˌɑʃləˈslɑi
Ashmole		
Elias, *English antiquary*	ASH-MŌL	ˈæʃˌmoːl
Ashmolean		
museum, library, Oxford, England	ash-MŌ-lē-uhn, ash-MŌL-yuhn	æʃˈmoːliːən, æʃˈmoːljən
Ashrawi		
Hanan, *Palestinian spokeswoman*	ahsh-RAH-wē	ɑʃˈrɑwiˑ
Ash-Shaqra [Shaqra]		
town, Saudi Arabia	ahsh shuhk-RAH	ɑʃ ʃəkˈrɑ
Ashtabula		
county, OH	ASH-tuh-BYOO-luh	ˌæʃtəˈbjuːlə
Ashtoreth [Astarte]		
Mesopotamian goddess of love	ASH-tuh-RETH	ˈæʃtəˌreθ
Ashura		
Islamic fast day	uh-SHUR-uh	əˈʃurə
Ashurbanipal		
Assyrian king	AHSH-ur-BAHN-i-PAHL	ˌɑʃurˈbɑniˌpɑl
Ashur-nasir-pal		
name, Assyrian kings	AHSH-ur-NAHZ-uhr-PAHL	ˌɑʃu^{r}ˈnɑzə^{r}ˌpɑl
Asia		
continent; daughter of Oceanus	Ā-zhuh, Ā-shuh	ˈeːʒə, ˈeːʃə
Asiago		
Italian cheese	AHS-ē-AHG-ō	ˌɑsiːˈɑgoː
Asia Minor		
ancient region	Ā-zhuh MĪ-nuhr, Ā-shuh	ˌeːʒə ˈmɑinə^{r}, ˌeːʃə
Asian		
pert. to Asia	Ā-zhuhn, Ā-shuhn	ˈeːʒən, ˈeːʃən
Asiatic		
pert. to Asia	Ā-zhē-AT-ik, Ā-shē-, Ā-zē-	ˌeːʒiːˈæt̬ik, ˌeːʃiː-, ˌeːziː-
Asimov		
Isaac, *US author*	AZ-uh-MAWF, AZ-uh-MAWV	ˈæzəˌmɔːf, ˈæzəˌmɔːv
Askew		
pers. name	AS-kyoo	ˈæskjuː
Askin		
Leon, *US director, actor, producer, writer*	AS-kuhn	ˈæskən
Asmara		
capital of Eritrea, *Ethiopia*	ahs-MAHR-uh	ɑsˈmɑrə
Asmat		
lang., New Guinea	AHZ-MAHT, AHS-MAHT	ˈɑzˌmɑt, ˈɑsˌmɑt

Foreign Sounds: ue: *Fr.* **rue**, *Ger.* **füllen** uh(r): *Fr.* **boeuf**, *Ger.* **Höhle** kh: *Ger.* **ich**, *Scot.* **loch** g̃: *Sp.* **amigo** v: *Sp.* **hablar** hl: *Welsh* **Llanelli**. CAPITALS: primary stress. SMALL CAPS: secondary stress. Ⓢ: U.S. pron. Ⓔ: British pron.

Asmodeus
   devil   az-muh-DĒ-uhs, as-MŌD-ē-uhs; *(in*   æzmə'diːəs, æs'mɔːdiːəs; *(in*
                             Paradise Lost) AS-muh-DĒ-uhs, az-   *Paradise Lost)*
                                                        ‚æsmə'diːəs, æz-

Asnuntuck
   Community College, *CT*   uh-SNUHN-tuhk   ə'snəntək
Ašo
   lang., Burma   AHSH-ō, AHS-ō   'aʃoː, 'asoː
Asotin
   county, WA   uh-SŌT-n   ə'soːtn̩
Aspartame
   artificial sweetener   AS-puhr-TĀM, uh-SPAHR-TĀM   'æspəʳ‚teɪm, ə'spɑʳ‚teɪm
Aspasia
   Greek consort of Pericles   as-PĀ-sh(ē-)uh, as-PĀ-zh(ē-)uh   æs'peɪʃ(iː)ə, æs'peɪʒ(iː)ə
Aspen
   city, CO   AS-puhn   'æspən
Asperges
   rite of sprinkling with holy water   a-SPUHR-jēz   æ'spəʳdʒiːz
Asphodel
   plant   AS-fuh-DEL   'æsfə‚del
Aspidistra
   plant   AS-puh-DIS-truh   ‚æspə'distrə
Assad, al-
   see al-Assad
Assal
   lake, Djibouti   ah-SAHL   ɑ'sɑl
Assam
   state, India   ah-SAHM, uh-SAM, AS-AM   ɑ'sɑm, ə'sæm, 'æs‚æm
Assamese
   pert. to Assam   AS-uh-MĒZ, -MĒS   ‚æsə'miːz, -'miːs
Asser
   1. Welsh monk, tutor to Alfred the   AS-uhr   'æsəʳ
     Great
   2. T. M. C., Dutch jurist, law   AHS-uhr   'ɑsəʳ
     professor (Nobel 1911)
Assiniboin, -ne
   N. American people   uh-SIN-uh-BOIN   ə'sinə‚boin
Assiniboine
   river, mtn., Canada   uh-SIN-uh-BOIN   ə'sinə‚boin
Assisi
   commune, Italy   uh-SĒ-sē, uh-SĒ-zē   ə'siːsiˑ, ə'siːziˑ
Assouan, Assuan
   see Aswān
Assyria
   ancient Near Eastern kingdom   uh-SIR-ē-uh   ə'siriːə
Assyrian
   lang., pert. to Assyria   uh-SIR-ē-uhn   ə'siriːən
Assyriologist
   student of Assyria   uh-SIR-ē-AHL-uh-juhst   ə‚siriː'alədʒəst
Assyriology
   study of Assyria   uh-SIR-ē-AHL-uh-jē   ə‚siriː'alədʒiˑ
Asta
   pers. name   AST-uh   'æstə
Astaire
   Fred, *US dancer, actor*   uh-STAR, uh-STER   ə'stæʳ, ə'steʳ

Key (col. 2):   a: fad   ā: fade   ah: father   ar: Mary   aw: law   e: fed   ē: feed   er: merry   i: hid   ī: hide   ō: coat   o͞o: boot
oi: boy   ow: now   u: put   uh: above   uhr: bird   ch: chop   ng: ring   sh: show   th: thick   th̲: this   zh: measure

Astarte [Ashtoreth]
  Mesopotamian goddess of love   uh-STAHRT-ē, a-STAHRT-ē   ə'stɑᴴʈiˑ, æ'stɑᴴʈiˑ
astatine
  element   AS-tuh-TĒN   'æstəˌtiːn
Asti
  prov & town, Italy   AHS-tē   'ɑstiˑ
Astin
  Patty Duke, US actress   AS-tuhn   'æstən
Asti Spumante
  wine   AHS-tē spu-MAHN-tā, AS-, -MAHNT-ē   ˌɑstiˑ spu'mɑnteːˌ ˌæs-, -'mɑntiˑ
Aston
  F. W., English physicist (Nobel 1922); pers. name   AS-tuhn   'æstən
Aston Martin
  car make   AS-tuhn MAHRT-n   ˌæstən 'mɑᴴtn̩
Astor
  pers. name   AS-tuhr   'æstəᴴ
Astoria
  district, New York City   uh-STŌR-ē-uh, uh-STAWR-ē-uh, a-   ə'stoːriːə, ə'stɔːriːə, æ-
Astraea
  daughter of Zeus and Themis   as-TRĒ-uh   æs'triːə
Astrakhan
  city, Russia   AS-truh-KAN, AS-truh-kuhn   'æstrəˌkæn, 'æstrəkən
Astrid
  1. pers. name, Danish   AHS-trēth   'ɑːstriːð
  2. Swedish   AHS-trid   'ɑstrid
Astrodome
  stadium, Houston, TX   AS-truh-DŌM   'æstrəˌdoːm
Astrophel
  Sir Philip Sidney's poetic name for himself   AS-truh-FEL   'æstrəˌfel
Astroturf
  tdmk for artificial grass   AS-trō-TUHRF   'æstroːˌtəᴴf
Asturias
  Miguel Angel, Guatemalan author (Nobel 1967); region Spain   ahs-TUR-yahs; Ⓢ uh-ST(Y)UR-ē-uhs, a-   as'turjɑs; Ⓢ ə'st(j)uriːəs, æ-
Astyages
  Median king   a-STĪ-uh-JĒZ   æ'staiəˌdʒiːz
Astyanax
  son of Hector and Andromache   a-STĪ-uh-NAKS   æ'staiəˌnæks
Asu
  lang., Africa   AHS-o͞o   'ɑsuː
Asunción
  city, dept., Paraguay; pers. name, Spanish   ah-so͞on-SYŌN, -THYŌN, Ⓢ ah-SO͞ON(T)-sē-ŌN   ɑsuːn'sjoːn, -'θjoːn, Ⓢ ɑˌsuːn(t)siˑ'oːn
Asuncion
  island, Micronesia   ah-SO͞ON-sē-ŌN   ɑˌsuːnsiˑ'oːn
Aswān, Assuan
  city, dam, Egypt   a-SWAHN, ah-SWAHN   æ'swɑn, ɑ'swɑn
Aswān Dam
  dam, Egypt   a-SWAHN DAM, AS-WAHN DAM   æˌswɑn 'dæm, ˌæsˌwɑn 'dæm
Atacama
  desert, people, prov, Chile   AHT-uh-KAHM-uh, AT-   ˌɑʈə'kɑmə, ˌæʈ-

---

Foreign Sounds: ue: *Fr.* **rue,** *Ger.* füllen   uh(r): *Fr.* **boeuf,** *Ger.* Höhle   kh: *Ger.* ich, *Scot.* loch   ḡ: *Sp.* amigo   y̱: *Sp.* hablar   hl: *Welsh* Llanelli.   CAPITALS: primary stress.   SMALL CAPS: secondary stress.   Ⓢ: U.S. pron.   Ⓛ: British pron.

Atacameño
  S. American people   AHT-uh-kuh-MĀN-yō   ˌɑtəkəˈmeːnjoː

Atahualpa, Atahuallpa
  Incan king   AHT-uh-WAHL-puh   ˌɑtəˈwɑlpə

Atakapa
  N. American people   uh-TAK-uh-puh, uh-TAHK-uh-puh,   əˈtækəpə, əˈtakəpə, -ˌpɔː,
                                -PAW, -PAH   -ˌpɑ

Atalanta
  mythological heroine who raced   AT-l-ANT-uh   ˌætl̩ˈæntə
  her suitors

Atari
  US toy brand   uh-TAHR-ē   əˈtɑriˑ

Atascosa
  county, TX   AT-uh-SKŌ-suh   ˌætəˈskoːsə

Ataturk, Atatürk
  see Kemal Atatürk

Atayal [Tayal]
  Malayasian people, lang.   AHT-uh-YAHL   ˌɑtəˈjɑl

Ate
  Greek goddess of error &   AHT-ē, ĀT-ē, AH-TĀ, Ā-TĒ   ˈɑtiˑ, ˈeːtiˑ, ˈɑˌteː, ˈeːˌtiː
  foolhardiness

Aten [Aton]
  Egyptian god   AHT-n, ĀT-n   ˈɑtn̩, ˈeːtn̩

Athabasca, -ka
  lake, river, univ., Canada ATH-uh-BAS-kuh   ˌæθəˈbæskə

Athabascan
  people, lang., N. America   ATH-uh-BAS-kuhn   ˌæθəˈbæskən

Athamas
  father of Phrixus and Helle ATH-uh-muhs   ˈæθəməs

Athan
  English Christian saint   ATH-uhn   ˈæθən

Athanase
  pers. name, French   ah-tah-NAHZ   ɑːtɑːnɑːz

Athanasian
  Christian creed   ATH-uh-NĀ-zhuhn, -NĀ-shuhn   ˌæθəˈneːʒən, -ˈneːʃən

Athanasius
  Christian saint; pers. name ATH-uh-NĀ-sh(ē-)uhs, -sē-uhs,   ˌæθəˈneːʃ(iː)əs, -siːəs, -ziːəs
                                -zē-uhs

Atharva-Veda
  Hindu magic spells   uh-TAHR-vuh-VĀD-uh   əˈtɑʳvəˈveːdə

Athelstan
  English king   ATH-uhl-STAN, A<u>TH</u>-uhl-, -STAHN   ˈæθəlˌstæn, ˈæðəl-, -ˌstɑn

Athelstane
  pers. name   ATH-uhl-STĀN   ˈæθəlˌsteːn

Athena
  Greek goddess of wisdom   uh-THĒ-nuh   əˈθiːnə

Athenaeum
  gentlemen's club, London   ATH-uh-NĒ-uhm   ˌæθəˈniːəm

Athene [Athena]
  Greek goddess of wisdom   uh-THĒ-nē, uh-THĒ-nuh   əˈθiːniˑ, əˈθiːnə

Athenian
  pert. to Athens   uh-THĒ-nē-uhn   əˈθiːniːən

Athens
  city, Greece; US pl. name   ATH-uhnz   ˈæθənz

Key (col. 2): a: fad ā: fade ah: father ar: M**a**ry aw: l**a**w e: fed ē: feed er: m**e**rry i: hid ī: hide ō: coat o͞o: boot
oi: b**o**y ow: n**o**w u: put uh: **a**bove uhr: b**i**rd ch: **ch**op ng: ri**ng** sh: **sh**ow th: **th**ick <u>th</u>: **th**is zh: mea**s**ure

Athínai [Athens]		
city, Greece	ah-THĒ-nā	ɑ'θiːneː
Athol		
city, MA	ATH-AWL	'æθ,ɔːl
Atholl		
mtn. district, Scotland	ATH-uhl	'æθəl
Athos		
1. one of The Three Musketeers, *A. Dumas*	ah-TŌS, [$] ATH-ŌS, Ā-THŌS	ɑːtoːs, [$] 'æθ,oːs, 'eː,θoːs
2. mtn., Greece	ATH-AHS, Ā-THAHS	'æθ,ɑs, 'eː,θɑs
Atjehnese, Achinese		
lang., people, North Sumatra	ACH-uh-NĒZ, -NĒS	,ætʃə'niːz, -'niːs
Atkins		
Chet, *US guitarist; pers. name*	AT-kuhnz	'ætkənz
Atkinson		
pers. name	AT-kuhn-suhn	'ætkənsən
Atlanta		
city, GA	uht-LANT-uh, at-LANT-uh	ət'læntə, æt'læntə
Atlantic		
ocean	uht-LANT-ik, at-LANT-ik	ət'læntik, æt'læntik
Atlantis		
mythical island	uht-LANT-uhs, at-LANT-uhs	ət'læntəs, æt'læntəs
Atlas		
mtn. system, Africa; giant who supports the heavens	AT-luhs	'ætləs
Atlee		
pers. name	AT-lē	'ætliˑ
Atli		
Old Norse form of Atilla	AHT-lē	'ɑtliˑ
Atman		
Hindu individual soul; the universal self	AHT-muhn, AHT-MAHN	'ɑtmən, 'ɑt,mɑn
Atoka		
county, OK	uh-TŌ-kuh	ə'toːkə
Aton [Aten]		
Egyptian god	AHT-n, AH-TŌN, ĀT-n, Ā-TAHN	'ɑtn̩, 'ɑ,toːn, 'eːtn̩, 'eː,tɑn
Atreus		
father of Agamemnon and Menelaus	Ā-trē-uhs, Ā-TR͞OOS	'eːtriːəs, 'eː,truːs
Atropos		
one of the Fates	A-truh-PAHS	'ætrə,pɑs
Attala		
county, MS	uh-TAL-uh	ə'tælə
Attenborough		
Sir Richard, *British actor, director;* David, *British naturalist*	AT-n-b(uh-)ruh	'ætn̩b(ə)rə
Attica		
region, Greece; city, IN; village, prison, NY	AT-i-kuh	'æt̬ikə
Atticism		
expression from Attic Greek	AT-uh-SIZ-uhm	'æt̬ə,sizəm
Attikí [Attica]		
region, Greece	AHT-i-K(Y)Ē	,ɑt̬i'k(j)iː

Foreign Sounds: ue: *Fr.* **rue**, *Ger.* **fü**llen uh(r): *Fr.* b**oeu**f, *Ger.* H**ö**hle kh: *Ger.* i**ch**, *Scot.* lo**ch** g̃: *Sp.* ami**g**o v̲: *Sp.* ha**b**lar hl: *Welsh* **Ll**anelli. CAPITALS: primary stress. SMALL CAPS: secondary stress. [$]: U.S. pron. [£]: British pron.

Attila
  1. *king of the Huns; pers. name*   AT-l-uh, uh-TIL-uh   'ætlə, ə'tilə
  2. *Hungarian*   ah-TIL-ah   a'tila
Attis
  companion of Cybele   AT-uhs   'ætəs
Attleboro
  city, MA   AT-l-buhr-uh, -buh-ruh, -buh-rō   'ætlbər-ə, -bə-rə, -bəroː
Attu
  Alaskan island   A-t$\overline{oo}$ 'ætuː
Attucks
  Crispus, *Black American patriot*   AT-uhks   'ætəks
Atum
  Egyptian creator god   AHT-uhm   'atəm
Atuona
  village, Marquesas Islands   AHT-uh-WŌ-nuh   ‚atə'woːnə
Aube
  river, France   ŌB   oːb
Aube Nouvelle, L'
  see L'Aube Nouvelle
Auberjonois
  René, *US actor*   Ō-buhr-zhahn-WAH   ‚oːbəʳʒaŋ'wa
Auberon
  pers. name   AW-buh-ruhn, Ō-buh-ruhn, -RAHN   'oːbərən, 'oːbərən, -‚ran
Aubervilliers
  commune, France   ō-ber-vēl-YÃ   oːberviːljeː
Aubrey
  pers. name   AWB-rē   'oːbriˑ
Auburn
  US pl. name   AW-buhrn   'oːbəʳn
Aubusson
  1. Piérre d', *French soldier,*   ō-bue-SAWⁿ   oːbyːsɔ̃
     cardinal; commune, France
  2. *rug*   ō-bue-SAWⁿ, Ⓢ Ō-buh-SAHN   oːbyːsɔ̃, Ⓢ 'oːbə‚san
Aubyn
  Christian saint   AW-buhn   'oːbən
Auch
  town, France   ŌSH   oːʃ
Auchentoshan
  Scotch distillery   AW<u>KH</u>-uhn-TAW-shuhn, -TAHSH-uhn   'oːxən‚toːʃən, -‚taʃən
Auchincloss
  Louis, *US writer*   AW-kuhn-KLAHS   'oːkən‚klas
Auchinleck
  1. Sir Claude, *British field*   AW-kuhn-LEK, AW-kuhn-LEK,   ‚oːkən'lek, 'oːkən‚lek,
     marshall   ah<u>kh</u>-uhn-LEK   axən'lek
  2. *parish, Scotland*   AH<u>KH</u>-uhn-LEK, AW-kuhn-LEK,   ‚axən'lek, ‚oːkən'lek,
        AW-<u>kh</u>uhn-LEK   'oːxən‚lek
  3. *James Boswell's estate,*   AF-LEK   'æf‚lek
     Scotland
Auckland
  city, New Zealand   AW-kluhnd   'oːklənd
Aude
  river, France   ŌD   oːd
Auden
  Wystan Hugh, *English poet in US*   AWD-n   'oːdṇ

Key (col. 2):   a: fad ā: fade ah: father ar: Mary aw: law e: fed ē: feed er: merry i: hid ī: hide ō: coat $\overline{oo}$: boot
oi: boy ow: now u: put uh: above uhr: bird ch: chop ng: ring sh: show th: thick <u>th</u>: this zh: measure

Audi
    car co.   OWD-ē   'audiˑ
Audie
    pers. name   AWD-ē   'ɔːdiˑ
Audrain
    county, MO   aw-DRĀN, AW-DRĀN   ɔː'dreːn, 'ɔːˌdreːn
Audrey
    pers. name   AW-drē   'ɔːdriˑ
Audubon
    John James, US naturalist   AWD-uh-buhn, AWD-uh-BAHN   'ɔːdəbən, 'ɔːdəˌbɑn
Audubon's caracara
    hawk   AWD-uh-buhnz KAR-uh-KAR-uh,   'ɔːdəbənz ˌkærə'kærə,
                AWD-uh-BAHNZ, KAR-uh-kuh-RAH   'ɔːdəˌbɑnz, ˌkærəkə'rɑ
Auel
    Jean M., US writer   OW(-uh)l   'au(ə)l
Auerbach
    1. Berthold, German writer   OW(-uh)r-BAH<u>KH</u>, -BAHK   'au(ə)ʳˌbɑx, -ˌbɑk
    2. Red, sports personality   OW(-uh)r-BAK, -BAHK   'au(ə)ʳˌbæk, -ˌbɑk
Auge
    1. mother of Telephus in Greek   OW-gē, OW-jē, AW-jē   'augiˑ, 'audʒiˑ, 'ɔːdʒiˑ
    myth
    2. pers. name, French   ŌZH   oːʒ
Augean stables
    filthy stables cleaned by Heracles   aw-JĒ-uhn   ɔː'dʒiːən
Augeas
    owner of Augean stables   aw-JĒ-uhs   ɔː'dʒiːəs
Augier
    pers. name, French   ōzh-YĀ   oːʒjeː
Auglaize
    county, OH   aw-GLĀZ   ɔː'gleːz
Augsburg
    1. city, Germany   OWKS-BURK, Ⓢ AWGZ-BUHRG,   'auksˌbuʳk, Ⓢ 'ɔːgzˌbəʳg,
                OWGZ-BURG   'augzˌbuʳg
    2. College, MN   AWGZ-BUHRG   'ɔːgzˌbəʳg
August
    1. month; pers. name   AW-guhst   'ɔːgəst
    2. Danish, Finnish, German   OW-gust   'august
    3. Polish   OW-go͞ost   'auguːst
    4. Swedish   OW-guhst   'augəst
Augusta
    1. US pl. name; pers. name   aw-GUHST-uh, uh-   ɔː'gəstə, ə-
    2. French   aw-gue-STAH, ō-   ɔːgyːstaː, oː-
    3. German   ow-GUS-tah   au'gusta
    4. region, Sicily; pers. name,   ow-GO͞O-stah   au'guːsta
    Italian
    5. Spanish   ow-G͞O͞O-stah   au'ɣuːsta
Augustan
    pert. to Augustus   uh-GUHS-tuhn, aw-   ə'gəstən, ɔː-
Augustana
    College, IL, SD   AW-guhs-TAN-uh   ˌɔːgəs'tænə
Auguste
    1. pers. name, French   aw-GUST, ō-   ɔːgyːst, oː-
    2. German   ow-GUS-tuh   au'gustə
Augustijn
    Belgian beer   OW-ğuhs-TĪN   'auɣəsˌtain

Foreign Sounds: ue: *Fr.* **rue**, *Ger.* f**ü**llen uh(r): *Fr.* b**oeu**f, *Ger.* H**öh**le <u>kh</u>: *Ger.* i**ch**, *Scot.* lo**ch** ğ: *Sp.* ami**g**o ṿ: *Sp.* ha**b**lar
hl: *Welsh* **Ll**anelli. CAPITALS: primary stress. SMALL CAPS: secondary stress. Ⓢ: U.S. pron. Ⓔ: British pron.

Augustín
   pers. name, Spanish   ow-gōō-STĒN   auguːˈstiːn
Augustin
   1. pers. name   aw-GUHS-tuhn, uh-   ɔːˈgəstən, ə-
   2. Czech   OW-gust-YIN   ˈaugustˌjin
   3. Dutch   OW-gue-STĪN   ˈaugyːˌstain
   4. French   aw-gue-STEⁿ, ō-   ɔːgyːstẽ, oː-
   5. German   OW-gus-TĒN   ˌaugusˈtiːn
   6. Swedish   OW-guh-STĒN   ˌaugəˈstiːn
Augustine
   1. pers. name   AW-guhs-TĒN, aw-GUHS-tuhn,   ˈɔːgəsˌtiːn, ɔːˈgəstən, əˈgəstən
                 uh-GUHS-tuhn
   2. French   aw-gues-TĒN, ō-   ɔːgyːstiːn, oː-
Augustine, St.
   see St. Augustine
Augustinerbräu München
   German beer   OW-gus-TĒ-nuhr-BROI MUEN-<u>kh</u>uhn   ˌaugusˈtiːnəʳˌbrɔi ˈmynçən
Augustinians
   religious order   AW-guh-STIN-ē-uhnz   ˌɔːgəˈstiniːənz
Augusto
   1. pers. name, Italian   ow-GŌŌ-stō   auˈguːstoː
   2. Portuguese   ow-GŌŌSH-tōō, -GŌŌS-tōō   auˈguːʃtuː, -ˈguːstu
   3. Spanish   ow-GŌŌ-stō   auˈguːstoː
Augustus
   1. Roman emperor; pers. name   aw-GUHS-tuhs, uh-   ɔːˈgəstəs, ə-
   2. German   ow-GUS-tus   auˈgustus
Auld Lang Syne
   Scottish song   ŌL-(D)ANG-ZĪN, -ŌL-(D)LANG-, -SĪN   ˌɔːl,(d)æŋˈzain, ˌɔːl,(d)læŋ-, -ˌsain
Aulis
   ancient Greek city   AW-luhs, OW-luhs   ˈɔːləs, ˈauləs
Aulus
   Roman praenomen   OW-luhs, AW-luhs   ˈauləs, ˈɔːləs
Aung San Suu Kyi
   Burmese opposition leader   OWNG SAHN SŌŌ CHĒ   ˈauŋ ˈsɑn ˈsuː ˈtʃiː
Aura
   mother of Inachus   AWR-uh   ˈɔːrə
Aurangabad
   city, India   ow-RUHNG-(g)uh-BAHD   auˈrəŋ(g)əˌbad
Aurèle
   pers. name   aw-REL, ō-   ɔːrel, oː-
Aurelia
   pers. name   aw-RĒ-lē-uh   ɔːˈriːliːə
Aurelian
   Roman emperor   aw-RĒ-lē-uhn   ɔːˈriːliːən
Aureliano
   pers. name   ow-rāl-YAHN-ō   aureːlˈjanoː
Aurelio
   1. pers. name, Italian   ow-REL-yō   auˈreljoː
   2. Spanish   ow-RĀL-yō   auˈreːljoː
Aurelius
   1. pers. name   aw-RĒ-lē-uhs, aw-RĒL-yuhs   ɔːˈriːliːəs, ɔːˈriːljəs
   2. German   ow-RĀL-yus, ow-RĀ-lē-us   auˈreːljus, auˈreːliːus
Aureomycin
   tdmk for chlortetracycline   AW-rē-ō-MĪS-n   ˌɔːriːoːˈmaisn̩

Key (col. 2):   a: f**a**d   ā: f**a**de   ah: f**a**ther   ar: M**a**ry   aw: l**a**w   e: f**e**d   ē: f**ee**d   er: m**e**rry   i: h**i**d   ī: h**i**de   ō: c**oa**t   ōō: b**oo**t
oi: b**oy**   ow: n**ow**   u: p**u**t   uh: **a**bove   uhr: b**ir**d   ch: **ch**op   ng: ri**ng**   sh: **sh**ow   th: **th**ick   <u>th</u>: **th**is   zh: mea**s**ure

Auriga
   constellation   aw-RĪ-guh   ɔːˈrɑigə

Aurillac
   town, France   aw-rē-(Y)AHK   ɔːriːˈ(j)ɑːk

Aurora
   1. Roman dawn goddess; pers.   uh-RŌR-uh, aw-, -RAWR-   əˈrɔːrə, ɔː-, -ˈrɔːr-
     name
   2. German, Spanish   ow-RŌ-rah   ɑuˈrɔːrɑ

Aurora Australis
   'Southern Lights'   uh-RŌR-uh aw-STRĀ-luhs,   əˈrɔːrə ɔːˈstreːləs, əˈrɔːrə,
                       uh-RAWR-uh, ahs-TRĀ-luhs   ɑsˈtreːləs

Aurora Borealis
   'Northern Lights'   uh-RŌR-uh BŌR-ē-AL-uhs,   əˈrɔːrə ˌbɔːriːˈæləs, əˈrɔːrə,
                       uh-RAWR-uh, BAWR-, ⓔ -Ā-luhs   ˌbɔːr-, ⓔ -ˈeːləs

Aurore
   pers. name, French   aw-RAWR, ō-RAWR   ɔːrɔːr, oːrɔːr

Auschwitz [Oświęcim]
   Nazi concentration camp, Poland   OWSH-ᴠɪᴛs, OWSH-ᴡɪᴛs   ˈɑuʃˌvits, ˈɑuʃˌwits

Aushi
   lang., Africa   OW-shē   ˈɑuʃiˑ

Ausone
   French wine   ō-ZAWN   oːzɔːn

Ausonio
   pers. name   ow-ZAWN-yō   ɑuˈzɔːnjoː

Aussie
   an Australian   aw-sē, AHS-ē; ⓔ *& Austral.* AW-zē   ɔːsiˑ, ˈɑsiˑ; ⓔ *& Austral.* ˈɔːziˑ

Austen
   pers. name   AWS-tuhn   ˈɔːstən

Auster
   literary, South Wind   AW-stuhr   ˈɔːstəʳ

Austerlitz
   battle site, Czech republic;   OW-stuhr-ʟɪᴛs, AW-   ˈɑustəʳˌlits, ˈɔː-
     Frederick, *orig. surname of* Fred
     Astaire

Austin
   city, TX; pers. name   AW-stuhn   ˈɔːstən

Australasia
   portion of Oceania   AWS-truh-LĀ-zhuh, AHS-, -LĀ-shuh   ˌɔːstrəˈleːʒə, ˌɑs-, -ˈleːʃə

Australe, Mare
   see Mare Australe

Australia
   continent, nation   aw-STRĀL-yuh, ahs-TRĀL-yuh,   ɔːˈstreːljə, ɑsˈtreːljə, əˈstreːljə
                      uh-STRĀL-yuh

Australian
   pert. to Australia   aw-STRĀL-yuhn, uh-;   ɔːˈstreːljən, ə-; ɑsˈtreːljən
                      ahs-TRĀL-yuhn

Australopithecus
   genus of hominids   aw-STRĀ-lō-PITH-i-kuhs,   ɔːˌstreːloˈpiθikəs,
                      AW-struh-lō-PITH-i-kuhs   ˌɔːstrəloˈpiθikəs

Austria
   republic, Europe   AWS-trē-uh, AHS-   ˈɔːstriːə, ˈɑs-

Austrian
   pert. to Austria   AWS-trē-uhn, AHS-   ˈɔːstriːən, ˈɑs-

Austro-
   combining form for Austria   AW-strō, AW-strō   ˈɔːstroː, ˌɔːstroː

Foreign Sounds: ue: *Fr.* **rue**, *Ger.* f**ü**llen uh(r): *Fr.* b**oeu**f, *Ger.* H**öh**le <u>kh</u>: *Ger.* i**ch**, *Scot.* lo**ch** ğ: *Sp.* ami**g**o v̱: *Sp.* ha**b**lar
hl: *Welsh* **Ll**anelli. CAPITALS: primary stress. Sᴍᴀʟʟ Cᴀᴘs: secondary stress. Ⓢ: U.S. pron. Ⓔ: British pron.

Austro-Hungarian
  European empire   AW-strō-huhng-GAR-ē-uhn,   ˌɔːstroːhəŋˈgæriːən,
                                   -huhng-GER-ē-uhn   -həŋˈgeriːən

Austronesia
  region, S. Pacific   AW-struh-NĒ-zhuh, AHS-truh-,   ˌɔːstrəˈniːʒə, ˌɑstrə-, -ˈniːʃə
                                   -NĒ-shuh

Autauga
  county, AL   aw-TAW-guh   ɔːˈtɔːgə

Autolycus
  Argonaut; grandfather of Odysseus   aw-TAHL-i-kuhs   ɔːˈtɑlikəs

Automedon
  charioteer of Achilles; Greek poet aw-TAHM-uhd-uhn,   ɔːˈtamədən, ɔːˈtaməˌdɑn
                                   aw-TAHM-uh-DAHN

Autry
  Orvon Gene, US singer, actor,   AW-trē   ˈɔːtriˑ
  executive

Auvergne
  province, France   aw-VERN-yuh; Ⓢ ō-VERN(-yuh),   ɔːˈvern; Ⓢ oːˈveʳn(jə),
                                   ō-VUHRN   oːˈvəʳn

Auxerre
  town, France   ō-SER   oːser

Auxerrois
  medieval countship, France   aw-ser-WAH   ɔːserwɑː

Ava
  pers. name   Ā-vuh, AHV-uh   ˈeːvə, ˈɑvə

Avalon
  Frankie, US pop singer; Celtic AV-uh-LAHN   ˈævəˌlɑn
  island paradise

Avamba [Ambo]
  lang., people, Angola, Namibia uh-VAHM-buh   əˈvɑmbə

Avar
  lang., people, Caucasus Mts.   AH-VAHR   ˈɑˌvɑʳ

Avellino
  prov & town, Italy   AHV-el-LĒ-nō, Ⓢ AHV-uh-LĒ-nō   ˌavelˈliːnoː, Ⓢ ˌavəˈliːnoː

Ave Maria
  prayer   AHV-ā muh-RĒ-uh   ˌaveː məˈriːə

Aventine
  hill, Rome, Italy   AV-uhn-TĪN, AV-uhn-TĒN   ˈævənˌtain, ˈævənˌtiːn

Averell
  pers. name   Ā-v(uh-)ruhl   ˈeːv(ə)rəl

Averett
  College, VA   Ā-v(uh-)ruht   ˈeːv(ə)rət

Averroes
  Arab philosopher   uh-VER-uh-WĒZ, AV-uh-RŌ-ēz   əˈverəˌwiːz, ˌævəˈroːiːz

Averroism, Averrhoism
  philosophy of Averroes   uh-VER-uh-WIZ-uhm,   əˈverəˌwizəm, ˌævəˈroːˌizəm
                                   AV-uh-RŌ-IZ-uhm

Avery
  pers. name   Ā-vuh-rē, ĀV-rē   ˈeːvəriˑ, ˈeːvriˑ

Avia
  sportswear brand   Ā-vē-uh   ˈeːviːə

Avianca
  Colombian airline   ahv-yahng-kuh   aβjaŋkə

Avicenna
  Islamic philosopher   AV-uh-SEN-uh   ˌævəˈsenə

Key (col. 2): a: fad ā: fade ah: father ar: Mary aw: law e: fed ē: feed er: merry i: hid ī: hide ō: coat ōō: boot
oi: boy ow: now u: put uh: above uhr: bird ch: chop ng: ring sh: show th: thick th̲: this zh: measure

Avignon
   prov & town, France   ah-vēn-YAW[n]   ɑːviːnjɔ̃
Avila
   College, MO   AV-uḣ-luh   'ævələ
Ávila
   prov, city, Spain   AHV̱-ē-lah, Ⓢ AHV-i-luh   'aβiːla, Ⓢ 'avilə
Avis
   car rental co.   Ā-vuhs   'eːvəs
Avogadro's number
   chemical constant   AV-uh-GAHD-rōz, AHV-   ˌævə'gɑdroːz, ˌav-
Avon
   1. town, CT, MA; city, OH; brand   Ā-VAHN   'eːˌvɑn
     of cosmetics
   2. county, various rivers, England   Ā-vuhn   'eːvən
   3. village, NY; river, Devonshire,   AV-uhn   'ævən
     England
   4. loch, river, Scotland   AHN   'ɑːn
Avoyelles
   parish, LA   uh-VOI-uhlz, AV-wah-YEL   ə'vɔiəlz, ˌævwa'jel
Avraam
   pers. name, Russian   uhv-RUH-AHM   əvˌrə'ɑːm
AWACS
   surveillance system   Ā-WAKS   'eːˌwæks
Awaji
   island, Japan   ah-wahj-ē   ɑwadʒiˑ
Awa Odori
   Japanese holiday   ah-wah ō-dawr-ē   ɑwa oːdɔːriː
Awlad'Ali
   people, Africa   OW-lahd-al-Ē   'ɑuladæl'iː
AWOL
   absent without leave   Ā-WAWL   'eːˌwɔːl
Axel
   1. pers. name   AK-suhl   'æksəl
   2. Danish, Swedish   AHK-suhl   'ɑːksəl
   3. German, Norwegian   AHK-suhl   'aksəl
Axelrod
   Julius, US pharmacologist (Nobel   AK-suhl-RAHD   'æksəlˌrad
     1970)
Axl
   pers. name   AK-suhl   'æksəl
Axminster
   town, England; carpet   AK-SMIN(T)-stuhr   'ækˌsmin(t)stə[r]
Axton
   Hoyt, US singer, composer   AK-stuhn   'ækstən
Ayacucho
   department, Peru   Ī-uh-KOO-chō   ˌaiə'kuːtʃoː
Ayaida
   people, Africa   ah-YĪD-uh   ɑ'jaidə
Ayatollah
   Shiite Muslim title   Ī-uh-TŌ-luh, Ī-uh-TAHL-uh,   ˌaiə'toːlə, ˌaiə'talə, ˌaiə'tələ,
                   Ī-uh-TUHL-uh, Ī-uh-tuh-LAH   ˌaiətə'la
Ayer
   pers. name   Ā(-uh)r, ER, AR   'eː(ə)[r], 'e[r], 'æ[r]
Ayinger Altbairisch
   German beer   Ī-ing-uhr ahlt-BĪ-rish   'ai-iŋə[r] alt'bairiʃ

Ayinger Export-Weissbier
  German beer   Ī-ing-uhr ek-SPAWRT-VĪS-BIR   'ai-iŋəʳ ek,spɔːʳt'vais,biʳ
Ayinger Fest-Märzen
  German beer   Ī-ing-uhr FEST-MERT-suhn   'ai-iŋəʳ 'fest,meʳtsən
Ayinger Jahrhundert-Bier
  German beer   Ī-ing-uhr YAHR-HUN-duhrt-BIR   'ai-iŋəʳ 'jaʳ,hundəʳt,biʳ
Ayinger Maibock
  German beer   Ī-ing-uhr MĪ-BAHK   'ai-iŋəʳ 'mai,bak
Ayinger Ur-Weizen
  German beer   Ī-ing-uhr UR-VĪT-suhn   'ai-iŋəʳ 'uʳ,vaitsən
Aykroyd
  Dan, *US actor, comedian*   AK-ROID   'æk,rɔid
Aylesbury
  town, England   ĀLZ-b(uh-)rē, ĀLZ-BER-ē   'eːlzb(ə)riˑ, 'eːlz,beriˑ
Aymara
  lang., people, S. America   Ī-muh-RAH, ī-MAHR-uh   ˌaimə'ra, ai'marə
Ayn
  pers. name (A. Rand)   ĪN, ĀN   'ain, 'eːn
Ayodhya
  city, India   uh-YUHD-yuh   ə'jədjə
Ayr
  town, Australia; town, river, AR, ER   'æʳ, 'eʳ
    Scotland
Ayres
  Lew, *US actor*   ARZ, ERZ   'æʳz, 'eʳz
Ayrshire
  county, Scotland   AR-shuhr, ER-shuhr, -SHIR   'æʳʃəʳ, 'eʳʃəʳ, -ˌʃiʳ
Azalea Bowl
  stadium, Palatka, FL   uh-ZĀL-yuh BŌL   ə'zeːljə ˌboːl
Azande [Zande]
  lang., Africa   uh-ZAN-dē   ə'zændiˑ
Azariah
  Apocryphal book; pers. name   AZ-uh-RĪ-uh   ˌæzə'raiə
Azazel
  evil spirit   uh-ZĀ-zuhl   ə'zeːzəl
Azenberg
  Emanuel, *theatrical producer*   Ā-zuhn-BUHRG   'eːzən,bəʳg
Azerbaijan, Azerbaidzhan
  republic, Asia   AZ-uhr-bī-ZHAHN, -JAHN   ˌæzəʳbai'ʒan, -'dʒan
Azerbaijani
  lang., people, Asia   AZ-uhr-BĪ-JAHN-ē,   ˌæzəʳˌbai'dʒaniˑ,
                                     AZ-uhr-BĪ-ZHAHN-ē   ˌæzəʳˌbai'ʒaniˑ
Azeri [Azerbaijani]
  lang., Asia   ah-ZER-ē   a'zeriˑ
Aziz
  Tariq, *Iraqi politician*   ah-ZĒZ   a'ziːz
Azores
  islands, Atlantic   Ā-ZŌRZ, Ā-ZAWRZ, uh-ZŌRZ,   'eːˌzoːʳz, 'eːˌzɔːʳz, ə'zoːʳz,
                                     uh-ZAWRZ   ə'zɔːʳz
Azov
  sea, Europe   AZ-AWF, ĀZ-AWF, -AHV   'æz,ɔːf, 'eːz,ɔːf, -ˌav
Aztec
  N. American people   AZ-TEK   'æz,tek
Azteca [Aztec]
  N. American people   az-TĀ-kuh   æz'teːkə

Key (col. 2): a: fad ā: fade ah: father ar: Mary aw: law e: fed ē: feed er: merry i: hid ī: hide ō: coat ōō: boot
oi: boy ow: now u: put uh: above uhr: bird ch: chop ng: ring sh: show th: thick th̲: this zh: measure

Aztec-Tanoan
   ancient lang., N. America   AZ-TEK-TAHN-uh-wuhn   ˌæz,tekˈtɑnəwən
Azusa
   city, CA   uh-Z$\overline{OO}$-suh   əˈzuːsə

B

Baader-Meinhof
   German terrorist group   BAHD-uhr-M$\overline{\text{I}}$N-HAWF   ˌbɑdəʳˈmɑinˌhɔːf
Baakpe
   lang., Africa   BAHK-pā, BAK-pā   ˈbɑkpeˑ, ˈbækpeˑ
Baal
   Semitic storm god; idol   B$\overline{\text{A}}$(-uh)l, BAHL   ˈbeː(ə)l, ˈbɑl
Baalbek
   town, Lebanon   BAHL-BEK, B$\overline{\text{A}}$-uhl-BEK, BAL-BEK   ˈbɑlˌbek, ˈbeːəlˌbek, ˈbælˌbek

Baalism
   religion   B$\overline{\text{A}}$L-IZ-uhm   ˈbeːlˌizəm
Ba'al Shem-Tov [Besht]
   cognomen of Israel ben Eliezer   BAHL SHEM T$\overline{\text{O}}$V   ˈbɑl ˈʃem ˈtoːv
Babar
   elephant in books by Jean de Brunhoff   bah-BAHR, Ⓢ buh-BAHR, BAHB-AHR, B$\overline{\text{A}}$-BAHR   bɑːbɑːr, Ⓢ bəˈbɑʳ, ˈbɑbˌɑʳ, ˈbeːˌbɑʳ
Babbitt
   novel & character, S. Lewis; pers. name   BAB-uht   ˈbæbət
Babbittry
   attitude of Babbit   BAB-uh-trē   ˈbæbətriˑ
Babe
   pers. name   B$\overline{\text{A}}$B   ˈbeːb
Babel
   1. Biblical city, tower   B$\overline{\text{A}}$-buhl, BAB-uhl   ˈbeːbəl, ˈbæbəl
   2. Isaac, Russian writer   BAH-byil, Ⓢ BAB-uhl   ˈbɑːbjiḷ, Ⓢ ˈbæbəl
Babette
   pers. name   ba-BET, buh-   bæˈbet, bə-
Babilonia
   Tai, *US figure skater*   BAB-uh-L$\overline{\text{O}}$-nē-uh, -L$\overline{\text{O}}$N-yuh   ˌbæbəˈloːniːə, -ˈloːnjə
Babism
   doctrine of 19th century Iranian religious sect   BAHB-IZ-uhm   ˈbabˌizəm
Babs
   pers. name   BABZ   ˈbæbz
Babycham
   tdmk for a beverage   B$\overline{\text{A}}$-bē-SHAM   ˈbeːbiˑˌʃæm
Babylon
   ancient city, Iraq; village, NY   BAB-uh-luhn, -LAHN   ˈbæbələn, -ˌlɑn

---

Foreign Sounds: ue: *Fr.* **rue,** *Ger.* f**ü**llen   uh(r): *Fr.* b**oeu**f, *Ger.* H**öh**le   <u>kh</u>: *Ger.* i**ch**, *Scot.* lo**ch**   ḡ: *Sp.* ami**g**o   ᴠ: *Sp.* ha**b**lar   hl: *Welsh* **Ll**anelli.   CAPITALS: primary stress.   SMALL CAPS: secondary stress.   Ⓢ: U.S. pron.   Ⓔ: British pron.

Babylonia
 ancient Asian empire BAB-uh-LŌ-nē-uh, -nyuh ˌbæbə'loːniːə, -njə
Baca
 county, CO BĀ-kuh 'beːkə
Bacall
 Lauren, *US actress* buh-KAWL, buh-KAHL bə'kɔːl, bə'kɑl
Bacardi
 tdmk for rum buh-KAHRD-ē bə'kɑʳdiˑ
Baccarat
 game; glassmakers BAHK-uh-RAH, BAK-uh-RAH, ˌbɑkə'rɑ, ˌbækə'rɑ,
  BAHK-uh-RAH, BAK-uh-RAH 'bɑkəˌrɑ, 'bækəˌrɑ
Bacchae
 attendants of Bacchus BAK-ē, BAK-ī 'bækiː, 'bækˌɑi
Bacchanalia
 ancient Greek festival BAK-uh-NĀL-yuh, -NĀ-lē-uh ˌbækə'neːljə, -'neːliːə
Bacchic
 pert. to Bacchus BAK-ik 'bækik
Bacchus
 Greco-Roman god of wine; pers. BAK-uhs, BAHK-uhs 'bækəs, 'bɑkəs
  name
Bach
 family of German composers & BAH<u>KH</u>, BAHK 'bɑx, 'bɑk
  musicians
Bachama
 lang., Nigeria bah-SHAHM-uh, bah-CHAHM-uh bɑ'ʃɑmə, bɑ'tʃɑmə
Bacharach
 Burt, *US composer; former* BAK(-uh)-RAK 'bæk(ə)ˌræk
  ballpark, Atlantic City, NJ
Bacon
 Francis, *English philosopher;* BĀ-kuhn 'beːkən
  Roger, *English philosopher*
Bacone
 College, *OK* buh-KŌN bə'koːn
Baconian
 pert. to F. Bacon bā-KŌ-nē-uhn, bā-KŌN-yuhn beː'koːniːən, beː'koːnjən
Bactria
 ancient Asian country BAK-trē-uh 'bæktriːə
Bactrian camel
 Asian two-humped camel BAK-trē-uhn KAM-uhl ˌbæktriːən 'kæməl
Bad
 German place-name element BAHT, BAHD 'bɑt, 'bɑd
Badaga
 lang., people, South India buh-DAHG-uh bə'dɑgə
Bade
 lang., Nigeria BAHD-ā 'bɑdeˑ
Baden
 1. *city, Austria; former state,* BAHD-n 'bɑdn̩
  Germany
 2. *pers. name, English* BĀD-n 'beːdn̩
Baden-Baden
 city, Germany BAHD-n-BAHD-n ˌbɑdn̩'bɑdn̩
Baden-Powell
 Robert, *founder of Boy Scouts* BĀD-n-PŌ-uhl, BĀD-n-POW(-uh)l ˌbeːdn̩'poːəl, ˌbeːdn̩'pɑu(ə)l

---

Key (col. 2): a: fad ā: fade ah: father ar: Mary aw: law e: fed ē: feed er: merry i: hid ī: hide ō: coat ōō: boot
oi: boy ow: now u: put uh: above uhr: bird ch: chop ng: ring sh: show th: thick <u>th</u>: this zh: measure

Baden-Württemberg
   province, Germany   BAHD-n-VURT-uhm-BERK,   'bɑdn̩'vyᵣtəm,beᵣk,
       Ⓢ -WUHRT-uhm-BUHRG,   Ⓢ -'wəᵣtəm,bəᵣg,
       -WIRT-uhm-BUHRG   -'wiᵣtəm,bəᵣg

Badham
   John, *US film director*   BAD-uhm   'bædəm

Bad Lands
   arid region, SD, NE   BAD LAN(D)Z   'bæd ˌlæn(d)z

Baedeker
   German publisher; guidebook   BĀD-i-kuhr, BED-i-kuhr   'beːdikəᵣ, 'bedikəᵣ

Baekeland
   Leo Hendrick, *US chemist*   BAK-uh-LAHNT, Ⓢ BĀK-(uh-)luhnd   'bækə,lɑnt, Ⓢ 'beːk(ə)lənd

Baeyer
   Adolf von, *German organic*   BĀ-(y)uhr   'beː(j)əᵣ
     chemist (Nobel 1905)

Baez
   Joan, *US singer-songwriter*   BĪ-EZ, BAH-EZ, bī-EZ, BĪZ *(her own*   'bai,ez, 'bɑ,ez, bai'ez, 'baiz
     pron.)   *(her own pron.)*

Bafang
   lang., Cameroon   bah-FAHNG   bɑ'faŋ

Baffin
   bay, island, Arctic Ocean   BAF-uhn   'bæfən

Bafou
   lang., Cameroon   bah-FO͞O   bɑ'fuː

Bagehot
   Walter, *English economist*   BAJ-uht   'bædʒət

Baggins
   see Bilbo Baggins

Baghdad
   city, Iraq   BAG-DAD, bag-DAD   'bæg,dæd, bæg'dæd

Bagirmi
   lang., people, Chad   buh-GIR-mē   bə'giᵣmiˑ

Bagnold
   Enid, *English writer*   BAG-nuhld   'bægnəld

Bagobo
   lang., people, Philippine Islands   buh-GŌ-bō   bə'goːboː

Bagration
   Petr, *Russian general*   BUH-GRUH-tyi-YAWN   ˌbə,grətji'jɔːn

Baguio
   city, Philippines   BAHG̃-ē-ō   'bɑɣiːoː

Bahá'í
   religion   buh-HĪ   bə'hai

Baha'ism
   religion   bah-HAH-IZ-uhm, buh-, -HĪ-IZ-uhm   bɑ'hɑ,izəm, bə-, -'hai,izəm

Bahamas, The
   islands, Atlantic   buh-HAHM-uhz, buh-HĀ-muhz *(not*   bə'hɑməz, bə'heːməz *(not*
      used by residents)   *used by residents)*

Bahamian
   pert. to the Bahamas   buh-HĀ-mē-uhn, buh-HAHM-ē-uhn   bə'heːmiːən, bə'hɑmiːən

Bahasa Indonesian
   lang., Indonesia   buh-HAHS-uh IN-duh-NĒ-zhuhn,   bə'hɑsə ˌində'niːʒən, -'niːʃən
      -NĒ-shuhn

Bahia
   state, Brazil   bah-Ē-uh, Ⓢ buh-HĒ-uh   bɑ'iːə, Ⓢ bə'hiːə

Foreign Sounds: ue: *Fr.* **r**u**e**, *Ger.* f**ü**llen   uh(r): *Fr.* b**oeu**f, *Ger.* H**öh**le   <u>kh</u>: *Ger.* i**ch**, *Scot.* lo**ch**   g̱: *Sp.* ami**g**o   v̱: *Sp.* ha**b**lar
hl: *Welsh* L**l**anelli.   CAPITALS: primary stress.   SMALL CAPS: secondary stress.   Ⓢ: U.S. pron.   Ⓛ: British pron.

Bahnar
  lang., people, South Vietnam   buh-NAHR, BAH-NAHR, bah-NAHR   bə'nɑ^r, 'bɑˌnɑ^r, bɑ'nɑ^r
Bahrain
  island, country, Persian Gulf   bah-RĀN, bah<u>kh</u>-RĀN   bɑ'reːn, bɑx'reːn
Bahraini
  pert. to Bahrain   bah-RĀN-ē, bah<u>kh</u>-RĀN-ē   bɑ'reːniˑ, bɑx'reːniˑ
Bai, Pai
  lang., China   BĪ   'bɑi
Baiae
  ancient Roman resort   BĪ-Ē, BĀ(-Ē)   'bɑiˌiː, 'beː(ˌiː)
Baikal
  lake, Siberia   bī-KAHL, bī-KAWL, bī-KAL   bɑi'kɑl, bɑi'kɔːl, bɑi'kæl
Baika-sai
  Japanese festival   bī-kah-sī   bɑikɑsɑi
Baines
  pers. name (L. B. Johnson)   BĀNZ   'beːnz
Baio
  Scott, *US actor*   BĀ-ō   'beːoː
Baird
  Bil, *US puppeteer, author*   BARD, BERD   'bæ^rd, 'be^rd
Baisak
  Hindu New Year   VĪ-SHAHK   'βɑiˌʃɑk
Baja California
  peninsula, Mexico   BAH-hah KAL-uh-FAWRN-yuh,   'bɑhɑ ˌkælə'fɔː^rnjə,
       KAL-uh-FAWR-nē-uh   ˌkælə'fɔː^rniːə
Baja California Norte
  state, Mexico   NAWR-tā   'nɔː^rteː
Baja California Sur
  state, Mexico   SUR   'su^r
Bajer
  Fredrik, *Danish politician, author*   BĪ(-uh)r   'bɑi(ə)^r
  (Nobel 1908)
Bakelite
  tdmk for plastic   BĀ-kuh-LĪT, BĀ-KLĪT   'beːkəˌlɑit, 'beːˌklɑit
Bakerloo
  London underground line   BĀ-kuhr-LOO   ˌbeːkə^r'luː
Bakewell
  town, England   BĀK-WEL, BĀK-wuhl   'beːkˌwel, 'beːkwəl
Bakhtiari
  Iranian people   BAHK-tē-AHR-ē, bahk-TYAHR-ē   ˌbɑktiː'ɑriˑ, bɑk'tjɑriˑ
Bakke case
  US Supreme Court case   BAHK-ē, BAK-ē   'bɑkiˑ, 'bækiˑ
Bakker
  1. James, *US TV evangelist*   BĀ-kuhr   'beːkə^r
  2. Robert T., *US paleontologist*   BAHK-uhr   'bɑkə^r
Bakr
  Abu, *political leader*   BAHK-uhr   'bɑkə^r
Bakshi
  Ralph, *US film producer, director*   BAK-shē   'bækʃiˑ
Bakst
  Leon, *Russian painter/designer*   BAHKST   'bɑːkst
Baku
  city, Azerbaijan   bah-KOO   bɑ'kuː
Bakue
  lang., Liberia, Ivory Coast   buh-KOO-ā   bə'kuːeː

Key (col. 2): a: fad ā: fade ah: father ar: Mary aw: law e: fed ē: feed er: merry i: hid ī: hide ō: coat o͞o: boot
oi: boy ow: now u: put uh: above uhr: bird ch: chop ng: ring sh: show th: thick <u>th</u>: this zh: measure

Bakunin
Mikhail, *Russian anarchist* buh-KOON-yin bəˈkuːnjin

Bala
lake, Wales BAHL-uh ˈbɑlə

Balaam
Old Testament prophet BĀ-luhm ˈbeːləm

Bala-Cynwyd
1. town, Wales BAHL-uh-KUHN-wid ˌbɑləˈkənwid
2. town, PA BAL-uh-KIN-wid ˌbæləˈkinwid

Balanchine
George, *US choreographer* BAL-uhn-CHĒN, -SHĒN; ˌbælənˈtʃiːn, -ˈʃiːn;
  BAL-uhn-CHĒN, -SHĒN ˈbælən,tʃiːn, -,ʃiːn

Balanta
lang., people, Guinea-Bissau, buh-LAHNT-uh, buh-LANT-uh bəˈlɑntə, bəˈlæntə
Senegal

Balantak
lang., South Sulawesi (Celebes) BAL-uhn-TAHK ˈbælən,tɑk

Balatón
lake, Hungary BAW-luh-TŌN, BAL-uh-TAHN ˈbɔːlə,toːn, ˈbælə,tɑn

Balboa
Vasco Nuñez de, *Spanish explorer* bal-BŌ-uh bælˈboːə

Balch
Emily G., *US economist,* BAWLCH ˈbɔːltʃ
sociologist (Nobel 1946)

Baldassare
pers. name BAHL-dahs-SAHR-ā ˌbɑldɑsˈsɑreː

Baldr, Balder
Scandinavian hero-god BAWL-duhr ˈbɔːldəʳ

Balduin
pers. name BAHL-duh-WĒN ˌbɑldəˈwiːn

Baldung Grien
Hans, *artist* BAHL-dung GRĒN ˈbɑlduŋ ˈgriːn

Baldwin
pers. name BAWLD-wuhn ˈbɔːldwən

Bâle
French form of Basel, *Switzerland* BAHL bɑl

Baleares, Islas
island group, Mediterranean ĒZ-lahs bahl-ē-AHR-uhs ˈiːzlɑs bɑliːˈɑrəs

Balearic Islands [Baleares, Islas]
island group, Mediterranean BAL-ē-AR-ik ˌbæliːˈærik

Balenciaga
Cristóbal, *Spanish fashion* bahl-en-THYAHG-ah bɑlenˈθjɑɣɑ
designer

Balfour Declaration
British support for Israel BAL-fuhr, BAL-FŌR, BAL-FAWR ˈbælfəʳ, ˈbæl,foːʳ, ˈbæl,fɔːʳ

Bali
Indonesian island; lang., Africa BAHL-ē, BAL-ē ˈbɑliˑ, ˈbæliˑ

Balikpapan
port, Borneo BAHL-ik-PAHP-AHN ˌbɑlikˈpɑp,ɑn

Balinese
lang., people, Bali BAHL-uh-NĒZ, BAL-, -NĒS ˌbɑləˈniːz, ˌbæl-, -ˈniːs

Baliol
pers. name BĀL-yuhl ˈbeːljəl

Balkan
peninsula, mts., eastern Europe BAWL-kuhn ˈbɔːlkən

Foreign Sounds: ue: *Fr.* **rue**, *Ger.* **füllen** uh(r): *Fr.* **boeuf**, *Ger.* **Höhle** <u>kh</u>: *Ger.* **ich**, *Scot.* **loch** ḡ: *Sp.* amigo v: *Sp.* hablar
hl: *Welsh* **Llanelli**. CAPITALS: primary stress. SMALL CAPS: secondary stress. Ⓢ: U.S. pron. Ⓔ: British pron.

Balkans
countries on Balkan Peninsula   BAWL-kuhnz   'bɔːlkənz

Balkar [Karachay]
lang., people, Caucasus Mts.   bahl-KAHR, BAHL-KAHR   bɑl'kɑʳ, 'bɑl,kɑʳ

Balkhash
lake, Kazakhstan   bal-KASH, bahl-KAHSH   bæl'kæʃ, bɑl'kɑʃ

Ballantine
US brewery   BAL-uhn-TĪN   'bælən,tɑin

Ballarat
city, Australia   BAL-uh-RAT   'bælə,ræt

Ballater
village, Scotland   BAL-uht-uhr   'bælətəʳ

Ballesteros
Seve, Spanish golfer   bah(l)-yes-TĀ-rōs, BAHL-uh-STER-ōs   bɑ(l)jes'teːroːs, 'bɑlə,steroːs

Ballet Folklórico de México
Mexican dance troupe   bah-LĀ fōl-KLAWR-ē-kō thā MĀ-hē-kō   bɑ'leː foːl'klɔːriːkoː ðeː 'meˑhiːkoː

Ballet Russe
dance company   ba-LĀ RUS, R$\overline{OO}$S   bæ'leː 'rus, 'ruːs

Ballina
city, Australia   BAL-uh-nuh   'bælənə

Balliol
college, Oxford Univ.   BĀL-ē-uhl   'beːliːəl

Ballo in Maschera
opera, Verdi   BAHL-lō in mahs-KĀ-rah   'bɑlloː in mɑs'keːrɑ

Bally
Swiss shoe co.; game mfg. co.   bah-YĒ; Ⓢ BAL-ē, BAHL-ē   bɑːjiː; Ⓢ 'bæliˑ, 'bɑliˑ

Balmoral
castle, Scotland   bal-MAWR-uhl, bal-MAHR-uhl   bæl'mɔːrəl, bæl'mɑrəl

Balochi [Baluchi]
lang., Middle & Near East   buh-LŌ-chē   bə'loːtʃiˑ

Balor
evil Irish god   BĀ-luhr, BĀ-LAWR   'beːləʳ, 'beːˌlɔːʳ

Balranald
town, Australia   bal-RAN-ld   bæl'rænl̩d

Baltasar, Baltazar
pers. name, Spanish   bahl-tah-SAHR, -THAHR   bɑltɑ'sɑr, -'θɑr

Baltasare
pers. name, Italian   BAHL-tah-ZAHR-ā   ˌbɑltɑ'zɑreː

Balthasar
1. *pers. name*   BAL-thuh-ZAHR; bal-THĀ-zuhr, -THAZ-uhr   'bælθə,zɑʳ; bæl'θeːzəʳ, -'θæzəʳ
2. *Dutch*   BAHL-tah-SAHR   'bɑltɑːˌsɑr
3. *French*   bahl-tah-ZAHR   bɑːltɑːzɑːr
4. *German*   BAHL-tah-ZAHR   'bɑltɑ,zɑʳ

Balthazar
1. *pers. name*   BAL-thuh-ZAHR; BAL-THĀ-zuhr, -THAZ-uhr   'bælθə,zɑʳ; bæl'θeːzəʳ, -'θæzəʳ
2. *French*   bahl-tah-ZAHR   bɑːltɑːzɑːr

Baltic
Sea, N. Atlantic; region, N. Europe   BAWL-tik   'bɔːltik

Key (col. 2):   a: fad   ā: fade   ah: father   ar: Mary   aw: law   e: fed   ē: feed   er: merry   i: hid   ī: hide   ō: coat $\overline{oo}$: boot
oi: boy   ow: now   u: put   uh: above   uhr: bird   ch: chop   ng: ring   sh: show   th: thick   th̲: this   zh: measure

Baltimore
   1. city, MD   BAWL-tuh-MŌR, BAWL-tuh-MAWR,   'bɔːltə,moːʳ, 'bɔːltə,mɔːʳ,
                     (esp. by residents)   *(esp. by residents)*
                     BAWL-(uh-)muhr   'bɔːl(ə)məʳ
   2. David, US microbiologist (Nobel   BAWL-tuh-MŌR, -MAWR, -muhr   'bɔːltə,moːʳ, -,mɔːʳ, -məʳ
   1975)

Baluchi [Balochi]
   lang., Middle & Near East   buh-L͞OO-chē   bə'luːtʃiˑ

Balúchistán
   province, Pakistan   buh-L͞OO-chuh-STAHN, -STAN   bə,luːtʃə'stɑn, -'stæn

Balzac
   Honoré de, French novelist   bahl-ZAHK, Ⓢ BAWL-ZAK, BAL-ZAK   bɑːlzɑːk, Ⓢ 'bɔːl,zæk,
                                               'bæl,zæk

Bamako
   city, Mali   BAM-uh-KŌ   'bæmə,koː

Bambara
   lang., Africa   bam-BAHR-uh   bæm'bɑrə

Bamber
   pers. name   BAM-buhr   'bæmbəʳ

Bamberg
   city, Germany   BAHM-BERK, Ⓢ BAM-BUHRG   'bam,beʳk, Ⓢ 'bæm,bəʳg

Bambi
   deer, Disney character; pers. name   BAM-bē   'bæmbiˑ

Bamileke
   lang., Cameroon   BAHM-uh-LÃ-kā   ,bamə'leːkeː

Banbury
   town, England   BAN-b(uh-)rē, BAM-b(uh-)rē   'bænb(ə)riˑ, 'bæmb(ə)riˑ

Banda
   islands, sea, Pacific; lang., Africa   BAN-duh, BAHN-duh   'bændə, 'bandə

Band-Aid
   tdmk for bandages   BAN-DĀD, ban-DĀD   'bæn,deːd, bæn'deːd

Bandaranaike
   Sirimavo, Sri Lankan politician   BUHN-duh-ruh-NĪ-kuh   ,bəndərə'naikə

Bandera
   county, TX   ban-DER-uh   bæn'derə

Bandjabi
   lang., Cen. Africa   bahn-JAHB-ē   ban'dʒabiˑ

Bandoeng, Bandung
   city, Java   BAHN-DUNG, BAN-DUNG, -DUHNG   'ban,duŋ, 'bæn,duŋ, -,dəŋ

Bandundu
   prov & town, Zaire   bahn-D͞OON-d͞oo   ban'duːnduː

Baneasa
   airport, Romania   BAHN-ā-AHS-uh   ,baneː'asə

Banff
   city, former county, Scotland;   BAMF   'bæmf
   town, Canada

Bangalore
   city, India   BAHNG-guh-LŌR, -LAWR   'baŋgə,loːʳ, -,lɔːʳ

Banghāzī [Benghazi]
   city, former province, Libya   bahn-GAHZ-ē, bahng-GAHZ-ē,   ban'gaziˑ, baŋ'gaziˑ,
                     bang-GAHZ-ē, -GAZ-ē   bæŋ'gaziˑ, -'gæziˑ

Bangkok
   city, Thailand   BANG-KAHK, bang-KAHK   'bæŋ,kak, bæŋ'kak

Foreign Sounds: ue: *Fr.* **r**ue, *Ger.* f**ü**llen   uh(r): *Fr.* b**oeu**f, *Ger.* H**öh**le   <u>kh</u>: *Ger.* i**ch**, *Scot.* lo**ch**   g̃: *Sp.* ami**g**o   v: *Sp.* ha**b**lar
hl: *Welsh* **Ll**anelli.   CAPITALS: primary stress.   SMALL CAPS: secondary stress.   Ⓢ: U.S. pron.   Ⓛ: British pron.

Bangla
   lang., India — BAHNG-gluh, BANG-gluh, BUHNG-gluh — 'bɑŋglə, 'bæŋglə, 'bəŋglə

Bangladesh
   republic, Asia — BAHNG-gluh-DESH, BANG-, BUHNG-, -DĀSH — ˌbɑŋglə'deʃ, ˌbæŋ-, ˌbəŋ-, -'deːʃ

Bangladeshi
   pert. to Bangladesh — BAHNG-gluh-DESH-ē, BANG-, BUHNG-, -DĀ-shē — ˌbɑŋglə'deʃiˑ, ˌbæŋ-, ˌbəŋ-, -'deːʃiˑ

Bangor
   1. town, N. Ireland — BANG-guhr — 'bæŋgəʳ
   2. city, Wales — BANG-guhr, BANG-gawr — 'bæŋgəʳ, 'bæŋgɔːʳ
   3. city, ME, PA — BANG-GAWR, BAN-GAWR, BANG-guhr — 'bæŋˌgɔːʳ, 'bænˌgɔːʳ, 'bæŋgəʳ

Bangui
   1. city, Central African Republic — bahng-GĒ, BAHNG-GĒ — bɑŋ'giː, 'bɑŋˌgiː
   2. city, Philippines; bay, South China Sea — BAHNG-gē — 'bɑŋgiˑ

Bangweulu
   lake, Zambia — BANG-wē-OO-loo — ˌbæŋwiː'uːluː

Bani-Sadr
   Abolhassan, *former Iranian president* — BAHN-ē-SAHD-uhr — ˌbɑniˑ'sɑdəʳ

Banjermasin, Bandjarmasin
   town, Indonesia — BAN-juhr-MAHS-n, BAHN- — ˌbændʒəʳ'mɑsn̩, ˌbɑn-

Banjul
   city, Gambia — BAHN-JOOL — 'bɑnˌdʒuːl

Bankim
   pers. name, Bengali — BAWNG-kim — 'bɔːŋkim

Bann
   Irish river — BAN — 'bæn

Banna
   lang., Ethiopia — BAHN-uh, BAN-uh — 'bɑnə, 'bænə

Bannock
   N. American people — BAN-uhk, BAN-ik — 'bænək, 'bænik

Bannockburn
   village, Scotland — BAN-uhk-BUHRN, BAN-uhk-BUHRN — 'bænək,bəʳn, ˌbænək'bəʳn

Banquo
   character in Macbeth, Shakespeare — BANG-kwō, BAN-kwō — 'bæŋkwoː, 'bænkwoː

Banting
   Sir Frederick G., *Canadian physician (Nobel 1923)* — BANT-ing — 'bæntiŋ

Bantu
   lang., people, Africa — BAN-too, BAHN-too — 'bæntuː, 'bɑntuː

Banyuwangi, Banjuwangi
   port, Indonesia — BAHN-yuh-WAHNG-ē — ˌbɑnjə'wɑŋiˑ

Banzan
   pers. name, Japanese — bahn-zahn — bɑnzɑn

Bao Dai
   Vietnamese politician — BOW DĪ, BAH-ō DĪ — 'bɑu 'dɑi, 'bɑoː 'dɑi

Baptist
   1. pers. name — BAP-tuhst, BAB-tuhst — 'bæptəst, 'bæbtəst
   2. Dutch, German — bahp-TIST — bɑp'tist

Key (col. 2): a: **fad** ā: **fade** ah: **father** ar: **Mary** aw: **law** e: **fed** ē: **feed** er: **merry** i: **hid** ī: **hide** ō: **coat** ōō: **boot**
oi: **boy** ow: **now** u: **put** uh: **above** uhr: **bird** ch: **chop** ng: **ring** sh: **show** th: **thick** <u>th</u>: **this** zh: **measure**

Baptista
  1. pers. name   bap-TIS-tuh   bæp'tistə
  2. Flemish   bahp-TIS-tah   bɑp'tistɑ
  3. Portuguese   buh-TĒSH-tuh, bah-TĒ-stah   bə'tiːʃtə, bɑː'tiːstɑː

Baptiste
  pers. name, French   bah-TĒST   bɑːtiːst

Bara
  Theda, *US actress*   BAR-uh   'bærə

Barabbas
  Jewish prisoner in New Testament   buh-RAB-uhs   bə'ræbəs

Baraga
  county, MI   BAR-uh-guh   'bærəgə

Barajas
  airport, Madrid   BAHR-ah-hahs, -hah   'bɑrɑhɑs, -hɑ

Baraka
  Imamu Amiri, *US poet*   BAHR-uh-kuh, buh-RAHK-uh   'bɑrəkə, bə'rɑkə

Barambu
  lang., Sudan, Congo   buh-RAHM-bo͞o   bə'rɑmbuː

Baranof
  island, AK   BAR-uh-NAWF, BAR-uh-NAHF, buh-RAHN-uhf   'bærə,nɔːf, 'bærə,nɑf, bə'rɑnəf

Bárány
  Robert, *Austrian physician (Nobel 1914)*   BAHR-AHN-yuh   'bɑr,ɑnjə

Barat
  College, IL   buh-RAT   bə'ræt

Barbacoa
  S. American people   BAHR-buh-KŌ-uh   ,bɑrbə'koːə

Barbadian
  pert. to Barbados   bahr-BĀD-ē-uhn   bɑrbeːdiːən

Barbados
  island, West Indies   bahr-BĀD-uhs, -ōz, -ōs, -ahs   bɑrbeːdəs, -oːz, -oːs, -ɑs

Barbara
  1. pers. name   BAHR-b(uh-)ruh   'bɑrb(ə)rə
  2. German   BAHR-bahr-ah   'bɑrbɑrɑ
  3. Italian   BAHR-bahr-ah   'bɑrbɑrɑ
  4. Russian   BUHR-BAH-ruh   ,bər'bɑːrə

Barbarossa
  epithet, Frederick I, Germany   BAHR-buh-RAHS-uh   ,bɑrbə'rɑsə

Barbary
  region, West Africa   BAHR-buh-rē   'bɑrbəriˑ

Barbeau
  Adrienne, *US actress*   bahr-BŌ   bɑrboː

Barbee
  Victor, *US ballet dancer*   BAHR-bē   'bɑrbiˑ

Barbera
  Joe, *US cartoonist*   bahr-BER-uh   bɑrberə

Barbie
  Klaus, *Nazi war criminal; tdmk for a toy doll; pers. name*   BAHR-bē   'bɑrbiˑ

Barbiere di Siviglia
  opera, Rossini   bahr-BYER-ā dē si-VĒL-yah   bɑrbjereː diː si'viːljɑ

Barbirolli
  Sir John, *British conductor*   BAHR-buh-RAHL-ē   ,bɑrbə'rɑliˑ

Foreign Sounds: ue: *Fr.* **r**ue, *Ger.* f**ü**llen   uh(r): *Fr.* b**oe**uf, *Ger.* H**ö**hle   <u>kh</u>: *Ger.* i**ch**, *Scot.* lo**ch**   g̃: *Sp.* ami**g**o   <u>v</u>: *Sp.* ha**b**lar
hl: *Welsh* **Ll**anelli.   CAPITALS: primary stress.   SMALL CAPS: secondary stress.   ⓢ: U.S. pron.   ⓑ: British pron.

Barbizon
  school of painting   BAHR-buh-ZAHN   'bɑʳbə,zɑn

Barbour
  county, AL, WV   BAHR-buhr   'bɑʳbəʳ

Barbra
  pers. name   BAHR-bruh   'bɑʳbrə

Barbuda
  see Antigua and Barbuda

Barcelona
  prov & town, Spain   BAHR-thuh-LŌ-nuh,   ˌbɑʳθə'loːnə, ˌbɑʳsə'loːnə
         BAHR-suh-LŌ-nuh

Barclaycard
  tdmk for a bank card   BAHR-klē-KAHRD   'bɑʳkliˑˌkɑʳd

Barclays
  bank, United Kingdom   BAHR-klēz   'bɑʳkliˑz

Barcoo
  river, Australia   bahr-KOO   bɑʳ'kuː

Bardeen
  John, *US physicist (Nobel 1956,*   bahr-DĒN   bɑʳ'diːn
    1972)

Bardolino
  wine   BAHRD-l-Ē-nō, BAHRD-uh-LĒ-nō   ˌbɑʳdl̩'iːnoː, ˌbɑʳdə'liːnoː

Bardot
  Brigitte, *French actress*   bahr-DŌ   bɑːrdoː

Bare'e
  lang., Central Sulawesi (Celebes)   buh-RÃ-Ã   bə'reːˌeː

Barenboim
  Daniel, *US pianist, conductor*   BAR-uhn-BOIM   'bærən,bɔim

Barents Sea
  Arctic   BAR-uhn(t)s, BAHR-uhn(t)s   'bærən(t)s, 'bɑrən(t)s

Bari
  lang., people, Africa; prov & town,   BAHR-ē   'bɑriˑ
    Italy

barium
  element   BAR-ē-uhm, BER-ē-uhm   'bæriːəm, 'beriːəm

Barking and Dagenham
  industrial borough, England   BAHR-king uhn DAG-nuhm,   'bɑʳkiŋ ən 'dægnəm, 'bɔːkiŋ
         BAW-king

Barkla
  C. G., *English physicist (Nobel*   BAHR-kluh   'bɑʳklə
    1917)

Barlach
  Ernst, *artist*   BAHR-LAHKH   'bɑʳ,lɑx

Bar-le-Duc
  commune, France   bahr-luh-DUEK   bɑːrlədyːk

Barlow, Barlowe
  pocket knife; pers. name   BAHR-lō   'bɑʳloː

Barmecide feast
  incident, Arabian Nights   BAHR-muh-SĪD FĒST   ˌbɑʳmə,said 'fiːst

Barnabas
  pers. name   BAHR-nuh-buhs   'bɑʳnəbəs

Barnaby
  pers. name   BAHR-nuh-bē   'bɑʳnəbiˑ

Key (col. 2):   a: fad   ā: fade   ah: father   ar: Mary   aw: law   e: fed   ē: feed   er: merry   i: hid   ī: hide   ō: coat   ōō: boot
oi: boy   ow: now   u: put   uh: above   uhr: bird   ch: chop   ng: ring   sh: show   th: thick   th: this   zh: measure

Barnard
  Dr. Christiaan, *South African*   BAHR-nuhrd   'bɑᵣnəᵣd
    surgeon; College, *NY; pers.*
    name
Barnegat
  inlet, bay of Atlantic Ocean, NJ   BAHR-ni-GAT, BAHR-ni-guht   'bɑᵣni,gæt, 'bɑᵣnigət
Barnet
  borough, England   BAHR-nuht   'bɑᵣnət
Barney
  pers. name   BAHR-nē   'bɑᵣniˑ
Barnouw
  Erik, *US author, educator*   BAHR-NŌ   'bɑᵣ,noː
Barnstable
  county, MA   BAHRN-stuh-buhl   'bɑᵣnstəbəl
Barnstaple
  bay, borough, England   BAHRN-stuh-puhl,   'bɑᵣnstəpəl, 'bɑᵣnstəbəl
                                         BAHRN-stuh-buhl
Barnum
  P. T., *US showman*   BAHR-nuhm   'bɑᵣnəm
Barnwell
  city, county, SC   BAHRN-wuhl   'bɑᵣnwəl
Baron, Barron
  pers. name   BAR-uhn   'bærən
Barona
  Indian reservation, US   buh-RŌ-nuh   bə'roːnə
Baroque art
  elaborately ornamented style   buh-RŌK, ba-RŌK, -RAHK, -RAWK   bə'roːk, bæ'roːk, -'rɑk, -'rɔːk
Barranquilla
  city, Colombia   bahr-rahn-KĒ(L)-yuh,   barrɑn'kiː(l)jə,
                                           Ⓢ BAR-uhn-KĒ-(y)uh   Ⓢ ,bærən'kiː(j)ə
Barre
  town, MA, VT   BAR-ē   'bæriˑ
Barrett
  pers. name   BAR-uht   'bærət
Barry
  pers. name; island, Wales   BAR-ē   'bæriˑ
Barrymore
  US acting family   BAR-ē-MŌR, BAR-ē-MAWR   'bæriˑ,moːᵣ, 'bæriˑ,mɔːᵣ
Barstow
  College, *CA*   BAHR-stō   'bɑᵣstoː
Bart
  pers. name   BAHRT   'bɑᵣt
Barth
  1. Karl, *Swiss theologian*   BAHRT   'bɑᵣt
  2. John, *US author*   BAHRTH   'bɑᵣθ
Barthes
  Roland, *French critic/author*   BAHRT   bɑːrt
Barthold
  1. pers. name, Dutch   BAHR-TAWLT   'bɑr,tɔːlt
  2. German   BAHR-TAWLT   'bɑᵣ,tɔːlt
Bartholdi
  Frédéric Auguste, *French sculptor*   bahr-tawl-DĒ, Ⓢ bahr-TAWL-dē,   bɑːrtɔːldiː, Ⓢ bɑᵣ'tɔːldiˑ,
                                         bahr-TAHL-dē   bɑᵣ'tɑldiˑ
Bartholomaeus
  pers. name, Latin   bahr-TAHL-uh-MĒ-uhs, -THAHL-   bɑᵣ,tɑlə'miːəs, -,θɑl-

---

Foreign Sounds: ue: *Fr.* **rue**, *Ger.* **füllen** uh(r): *Fr.* **boeuf**, *Ger.* **Höhle** kh: *Ger.* **ich**, *Scot.* **loch** g̃: *Sp.* **amigo** v̲: *Sp.* **hablar**
hl: *Welsh* **Llanelli**. CAPITALS: primary stress. SMALL CAPS: secondary stress. Ⓢ: U.S. pron. Ⓔ: British pron.

Bartholomaus
  1. pers. name, Dutch   BAHR-TŌ-lō-MĀ-ues   ˌbɑrˌtoːloːˈmeːys
  2. German   BAHR-TŌ-lō-ME-us   ˌbɑʳˌtoːloːˈmeus
Bartholomeu
  pers. name, Portuguese   BAHR-tōō-lōō-MĀ-u   ˌbɑːrtuːluːˈmeːu
Bartholomeus
  pers. name, Dutch   BAHR-TŌ-lō-MĀ-ues   ˌbɑrˌtoːloːˈmeːys
Bartholomew
  pers. name   bahr-THAHL-uh-MYŌŌ   bɑʳˈθɑləˌmjuː
Bartleby
  story, H. Melville   BAHRT-l-bē   ˈbɑʳtļbiˑ
Bartlesville Wesleyan
  College, *OK*   BAHRT-uhlz-VIL WEZ-lē-uhn, ˈbɑʳtļz,vil ˈwezliːən,
                                    WES-lē-uhn   ˈwesliːən
Bartlett
  pers. name   BAHRT-luht   ˈbɑʳtlət
Bartók
  Bela, *Hungarian composer*   BAHR-TAHK, BAHR-TAWK   ˈbɑʳˌtɑk, ˈbɑʳˌtɔːk
Bartolomé
  pers. name, Spanish   bahr-tō-lō-MĀ   bɑrtoːloːˈmeː
Bartolomeo
  1. pers. name, Italian   BAHR-tō-lō-ME-ō   ˌbɑrtoːloːˈmeoː
  2. Spanish   bahr-tō-lō-MĀ-ō   bɑrtoːloːˈmeːoː
Bartolommeo
  pers. name, Italian   BAHR-tō-lōm-ME-ō   ˌbɑrtoːloːmˈmeoː
Barton
  Clara, *US founder of Red Cross;* BAHRT-n   ˈbɑʳtn̩
  Derek H. R., *English organic*
  chemist (Nobel 1969)
Baruch
  1. Old Testament book; pers.   buh-RŌŌK, BAHR-ŌŌK   bəˈruːk, ˈbɑrˌuːk
  name
  2. Bernard, US statesman   buh-RŌŌK   bəˈruːk
Baruj
  pers. name, Spanish   BAHR-ōōkh   ˈbɑruːx
Baryshnikov
  Mikhail, *ballet dancer*   buh-RISH-ni-kuhf,   bəˈriʃn̩ikəf, ⑤ bəˈriʃni,kɔːf,
                                    ⑤ buh-RISH-ni-KAWF, -KAWV   -ˌkɔːv
Barzun
  Jacques, *US author*   bahr-ZUHN   bɑʳˈzən
Basa
  lang., Africa   BAHS-uh   ˈbɑsə
Basant Panchami
  Hindu festival   VUHS-uhnt PUHN-chuh-mē   ˈβəsənt ˈpəntʃəmiˑ
Basari
  lang., Guinea, Senegal, Gambia buh-SAHR-ē   bəˈsariˑ
Bascomb
  pers. name   BAS-kuhm   ˈbæskəm
Basel
  city, Switzerland   BAHZ-uhl   ˈbazəl
Basenji
  dog breed   buh-SEN-jē, buh-ZEN-jē   bəˈsendʒiˑ, bəˈzendʒiˑ
Basherawa
  lang., Nigeria   buh-SHER-uh-wuh   bəˈʃerəwə

Key (col. 2):   a: fad   ā: fade   ah: father   ar: Mary   aw: law   e: fed   ē: feed   er: merry   i: hid   ī: hide   ō: coat   ōō: boot
oi: boy   ow: now   u: put   uh: above   uhr: bird   ch: chop   ng: ring   sh: show   th: thick   th̲: this   zh: measure

Bashevis
  pers. name (I. B. Singer) | buh-SHEV-uhs | bə'ʃevəs

Bashkir
  republic, Asia | bash-KIR | bæʃ'kiʳ

Bashō
  poetic name of Matsuo Munefusa, | bah-shō | baʃoː
    Japanese poet

Basie
  Count, *US bandleader* | BĀ-sē | 'beːsiˑ

Basil
  pers. name | BAZ-uhl, BĀ-zuhl | 'bæzəl, 'beːzəl

Basilius
  1. pers. name, German | bah-ZĒL-yus, bah-ZĒ-lē-us; | bə'ziːljus, bə'ziːliːus;
    | BAHZ-i-LĒ-us | ˌbazi'liːus
  2. Latin | buh-SIL-ē-uhs, buh-ZIL-ē-uhs | bə'siliːəs, bə'ziliːəs

Basingstoke
  town, England | BĀ-zing-STŌK | 'beːziŋˌstoːk

Baskerville
  John, *English typographer;* | BAS-kuhr-VIL | 'bæskəʳˌvil
    typefont

Basle
  alternate spelling for Basel, | BAHL | 'bɑl
    Switzerland

Basotho
  people, Lesotho (pl. Masotho) | bah-SŌT-ō, bah-SOOT-oo | bə'soːt̪oː, bə'suːt̪uː

Basov
  Nikolai Gennadiyevich, *Russian* | BAH-SAWF, BAHS-AWV | 'bɑːˌsɔːf, 'bɑsˌɔːv
    physicist (Nobel 1964)

Basque
  lang., people, Europe | BASK | 'bæsk

Basra
  prov & town, Iraq | BAHS-ruh, BAHZ-ruh | 'bɑsrə, 'bazrə

Basrah, Al [Basra]
  prov & town, Iraq | ahl BAHS-ruh, ahl BUHS-ruh, al | ɑːl 'bɑsrə, ɑːl 'bəsrə, æl
    BAS-ruh | 'bæsrə

Bas-Rhin
  dept, France | BAH-REⁿ | bɑrẽ

Bass
  Saul, *graphic designer, filmmaker;* | BAS | 'bæs
    tdmk for English ale; tdmk for
    shoes

Basse-Normandie
  region, France | BAHS nawr-mahⁿ-DĒ | bas nɔːrmãdiː

Bassist
  College, *OR* | BAS-uhst | 'bæsəst

Bast
  Egyptian sun goddess | BAST, BAHST | 'bæst, 'bast

Bastet [Bast]
  Egyptian sun goddess | BAS-tuht, BAHS-tuht | 'bæstət, 'bastət

Bastiano
  pers. name | bahs-TYAHN-ō | bas'tjanoː

Bastille
  French prison | bah-STĒL | baːstiːl

Bastogne
  district, Belgium | bah-STAWN-yuh, Ⓢ bas-TŌN(-yuh) | bɑːstɔːɲ, Ⓢ bæs'toːn(jə)

Foreign Sounds: ue: *Fr.* **rue**, *Ger.* **füllen**   uh(r): *Fr.* **boeuf**, *Ger.* **Höhle**   kh: *Ger.* **ich**, *Scot.* **loch**   ğ: *Sp.* **amigo**   v: *Sp.* **hablar**
hl: *Welsh* **Llanelli**.   CAPITALS: primary stress.   SMALL CAPS: secondary stress.   Ⓢ: U.S. pron.   Ⓑ: British pron.

Bastrop
  county, TX   BAS-truhp   'bæstrəp
Basutoland
  former name of Lesotho   buh-SO͞OT-ō-LAND   bə'suːt̥oː,lænd
Bataan
  prov, Philippines   buh-TAN, buh-TAHN   bə'tæn, bə'tan
Batak [Toba]
  lang., people, Sumatra   buh-TAHK, bah-TAHK   bə'tak, ba'tak
Batang
  town, Indonesia   BAH-TAHNG   'ba,taŋ
Batavia
  city, Indonesia; US pl. name   buh-TĀ-vē-uh   bə'teːviːə
Bateke
  lang., Cen. Africa   buh-TĀ-kā   bə'teːkeː
Bateman
  Jason, *actor;* Justine, *actress*   BĀT-muhn   'beːtmən
Ba'th
  political party, Iraq and Syria   BAHTH, BATH   'baˑθ, 'bæθ
Bathsheba
  consort of King David   bath-SHĒ-buh   bæθ'ʃiːbə
Batista
  1. Fulgencio, *Cuban leader*   bah-TĒ-stah, Ⓢ buh-TĒ-stuh   ba'tiːsta, Ⓢ bə'tiːstə
  2. pers. name, Portuguese   bah-TĒSH-tuh, -tah   baː'tiːʃtə, -taː
Batman
  comic-book hero   BAT-MAN   'bæt,mæn
Baton Rouge
  city, LA   BAT-n RO͞OZH   ,bætn̩ 'ruːʒ
Bats
  lang., Georgia   BAHTS, BATS   'bats, 'bæts
Batswana
  people, Botswana   baht-SWAHN-uh   bat'swanə
Batta
  lang., Cameroon   BAT-uh   'bæt̥ə
Battenberg
  town, Germany   BAHT-n-BERK, Ⓢ BAT-n-BUHRG   'batn̩,beʳk, Ⓢ 'bætn̩,bəʳg
Battersea
  English district   BAT-uhr-sē   'bætəʳsiˑ
Battista
  pers. name, Italian   baht-TĒ-stah   bat'tiːsta
Battus
  founder of Cyrene in Libya   BAT-uhs   'bæt̥əs
Baubo
  hostess of Demeter   BAW-bō   'bɔːboː
Bauchi
  state, town, Nigeria   BOW-chē   'bautʃiˑ
Baucis
  hostess of Zeus and Hermes   BAW-suhs   'bɔːsəs
Baudelaire
  Charles, *French poet*   bōd(-uh)-LER, Ⓢ bōd-LAR, bōd-LER   boːd(ə)ler, Ⓢ boːdlæʳ, boːd'leʳ
Baudouin
  king of Belgium   bō-DWEⁿ   boːdwẽ
Bauer
  Martin, *theatrical producer*   BOW(-uh)r   'bau(ə)ʳ

Key (col. 2):   a: fad   ā: fade   ah: father   ar: Mary   aw: law   e: fed   ē: feed   er: merry   i: hid   ī: hide   ō: coat   oo: boot
oi: boy   ow: now   u: put   uh: above   uhr: bird   ch: chop   ng: ring   sh: show   th: thick   th: this   zh: measure

Bauhaus
design school BOW-HOWS 'bɑu,hɑus

Baumé
Antoine, *French chemist;* bō-mā, Ⓢ bō-MĀ boːmeː, Ⓢ boː'meː
hydrometric scale

Bausch & Lomb
US optics co. BOWSH uhn(d) LAHM ˌbɑuʃ ən(d) 'lɑm

Bautista
pers. name, Spanish bow-TĒ-stah bɑu'tiːstɑ

Bavaria
prov, Germany buh-VER-ē-uh, buh-VAR-ē-uh bə'veriːə, bə'væriːə

Bavarian
Alps, *mtn. range, Germany* buh-VER-ē-uhn, buh-VAR-ē-uhn bə'veriːən, bə'væriːən

Baya
Bantu people BĪ-(y)uh 'bai(j)ə

Bayamesa, La
see La Bayamesa

Bayamo
river, city, Cuba buh-YAHM-ō bə'jɑmoː

Bayamón
river, city, Puerto Rico BĪ-uh-MŌN ˌbaiə'moːn

Bayard
pers. name BĪ-uhrd, BĀ-uhrd 'baiəʳd, 'beːəʳd

Bay de Noc
Community College, *MI* BĀ duh NAHK 'beː də 'nɑk

Bayer
tdmk, aspirin BĀ-uhr, BER 'beːəʳ, 'beʳ

Bayerische Alpen
mtn. range, Germany BĪ-uh-RISH-uh AHL-puhn 'baiə,riʃə 'ɑlpən

Bayerische Motoren Werke
German car co. (BMW) BĪ-uh-RISH-uh MŌT-uh-ruhn 'baiə,riʃə 'moːʈərən 'veʳkə
VER-kuh

Bayerische Wald
Bavarian forest BĪ-uh-RISH-uh VAHLT 'baiə,riʃə 'vɑlt

Bayern [Bavaria]
prov, Germany BĪ-uhrn 'baiəʳn

Bayern Munich
German soccer team BĪ-uhrn MYŌO-nik, MYŌO-nikh 'baiəʳn 'mjuːnik, 'mjuːnix

Bayeux Tapestry
12th c. tapestry bah-YUH(R), Ⓢ bī-(Y)ŌO, bā-(Y)ŌO bɑːjœː, Ⓢ bai'(j)uː, beː'(j)uː

Bayh
political family, IN BĪ 'bai

Baykal, Ozero [Baikal]
lake, Siberia ōz-YER-uh bī-KAHL oːz'jerə bai'kɑl

Bayonne
1. city, NJ bā-ŌN beː'oːn
2. town, France bah-YAWN, Ⓢ bā-ŌN bɑːjoːn, Ⓢ beː'oːn

Bayreuth
city, Germany; music festival bī-ROIT, BĪ-ROIT bai'rɔit, 'bai,rɔit

Beach-la-Mar [Bêche-de-Mer]
lang., Vanuatu, Solomon Islands BĒCH-luh-MAHR ˌbiːtʃlə'mɑʳ

Beaconsfield
1. district, England BEK-uhnz-FĒLD, BĒ-kuhnz-FĒLD 'bekənz,fiːld, 'biːkənz,fiːld
2. pl. name, Australia, Canada, S. BĒ-kuhnz-FĒLD 'biːkənz,fiːld
Africa

Foreign Sounds: ue: *Fr.* **rue**, *Ger.* **füllen** uh(r): *Fr.* **boeuf**, *Ger.* **Höhle** kh: *Ger.* i**ch**, *Scot.* lo**ch** ğ: *Sp.* ami**g**o v̲: *Sp.* ha**b**lar
hl: *Welsh* **Ll**anelli. CAPITALS: primary stress. SMALL CAPS: secondary stress. Ⓢ: U.S. pron. Ⓛ: British pron.

Beadle
　G. W., *US biochemical geneticist* 　BĒD-l 　'biːdl̩
　(Nobel 1958)
Beard
　Charles A., *historian* 　BĒRD 　'biʳd
Beardsley
　pers. name 　BĒRDZ-lē 　'biʳdzliˑ
Béarn
　region, France 　bā-AHRN 　beːɑːrn
Béarnaise
　egg-based sauce 　BĀ-uhr-NĀZ, BĀ-ahr-NĀZ, ber-NĀZ 　ˌbeːəʳneːz, ˌbeːɑʳneːz,
　　　　　　　　　　　　　　　　　　　　　　　　　　　beʳneːz

Beatles, the
　English rock group 　BĒT-lz 　'biːtl̩z
Beatrice
　1. pers. name 　BĒ-uh-truhs, BĒ-truhs, bē-A-truhs, 　'biːətrəs, 'biːtrəs, biːˈætrəs,
　　　　　　　　BĀ-uh-truhs 　　'beːətrəs
　2. German 　BĀ-ah-TRĒ-suh 　ˌbeːɑˈtriːsə
　3. Italian 　BĀ-ah-TRĒ-chā 　ˌbeːɑˈtriːtʃeː
　4. city, NE 　bē-A-truhs 　biːˈætrəs
Beatrix
　1. pers. name 　BĒ-uh-triks, BĒ-triks; bē-A-triks, 　'biːətriks, 'biːtriks;
　　　　　　　　BĀ-uh-triks 　　biːˈætriks, 'beːətriks
　2. German 　bā-AH-triks 　beːˈɑtriks
　3. Latin 　bē-Ā-triks 　biːˈeːtriks
Beatty
　1. Clyde, US circus owner 　BĒT-ē 　'biːt̮iˑ
　2. Ned, US actor; Warren, US 　BĂT-ē, BĒT-ē 　'beːt̮iˑ, 'biːt̮iˑ
　　actor
Beatus
　1. pers. name, German 　bā-AH-tus 　beːˈɑtus
　2. Latin 　bē-ĀT-uhs, bā-AH-tus 　biːˈeːt̮əs, beːˈɑtus
Beau
　pers. name (B. Brummell) 　BŌ 　'boː
Beauchamp
　pers. name, English 　BĒ-chuhm 　'biːtʃəm
Beauclerk
　Topham, *English dandy* 　BŌ-KLER 　'boːˌkleʳ
Beaufort
　1. county, town, NC 　BŌ-fuhrt, BŌŌ-fuhrt, BŌŌ-fuhrd 　'boːfəʳt, 'buːfəʳt, 'buːfəʳd
　2. county, city, SC 　BYŌŌ-fuhrt 　'bjuːfəʳt
　3. scale of wind force 　BŌ-fuhrt 　'boːfəʳt
　4. Sea, Arctic 　BŌ-fuhrt 　'boːfəʳt
　5. pers. name 　BŌ-fuhrt, BYŌŌ-fuhrt 　'boːfəʳt, 'bjuːfəʳt
Beaujolais
　region, wine, France 　bō-zhaw-LE, ⓈBŌ-zhuh-LĂ, -zhō-LĂ 　boːʒɔːle, Ⓢ ˌboːʒəˈleˑ, -ʒoːˈleˑ
Beaulieu
　1. parish, abbey, England 　BYŌŌ-lē 　'bjuːliˑ
　2. US winery 　bōl-YUH(R), BŌL-yŌŌ 　boːlˈjə(r), 'boːljuː
Beaumes de Venise
　wine 　BŌM duh vuh-NĒZ 　boːm də vəniːz
Beaumont
　pers. name 　BŌ-MAHNT, -muhnt 　'boːˌmɑnt, -mənt
Beaune
　wine 　BŌN 　boːn

Key (col. 2):　a: fad　ā: fade　ah: father　ar: Mary　aw: law　e: fed　ē: feed　er: merry　i: hid　ī: hide　ō: coat　ōō: boot
oi: boy　ow: now　u: put　uh: above　uhr: bird　ch: chop　ng: ring　sh: show　th: thick　th̲: this　zh: measure

Beauséjour
town, Manitoba   BŌ-SĀ-ZHUHR, BŌ-zuh-ZHUHR   ˌboːˌseːˈʒəʳ, ˈboːzəˌʒəʳ

Beauvoir
Simone de, *French writer*   bōv-WAHR   boːvwɑːr

Beaver
N. American people   BĒ-vuhr   ˈbiːvəʳ

Béchamel
white sauce   BĀ-shuh-MEL   ˌbeːʃəˈmel

Bêche-de-Mer [Beach-la-Mar, Bislama]
lang., Vanuatu, Solomon Islands   BĀSH-duh-MER   ˌbeːʃdəˈmeʳ

Bechet
Sidney, *jazz soprano saxophonist*   buh-SHĀ   bəˈʃeː

Bechtel
Group, Inc., US co.   BEK-TEL, bek-TEL   ˈbekˌtel, bekˈtel

Bechuana
Bantu people, lang.   BECH(-uh)-WAHN-uh   ˌbetʃ(ə)ˈwɑnə

Bechuanaland [Botswana]
republic, Africa   BECH(-uh)-WAHN-uh-LAND   ˌbetʃ(ə)ˈwɑnəˌlænd

Becker
Boris, *tennis player*   BEK-uhr   ˈbekəʳ

Becket
Thomas à, *English saint*   BEK-uht   ˈbekət

Beckett
Samuel, *Irish author (Nobel 1969)*   BEK-uht   ˈbekət

Beckmann
Max, *German artist*   BEK-MAHN   ˈbekˌmɑn

Becky
pers. name   BEK-ē   ˈbekiˑ

Becquerel
A. H., *French physicist (Nobel 1903)*   bek(-uh)-REL   bek(ə)rel

Bede
Anglo-Saxon scholar; pers. name   BĒD   ˈbiːd

Bedell
pers. name   buh-DEL   bəˈdel

Bedford
pers. name; pl. name   BED-fuhrd   ˈbedfəʳd

Bedfordshire
county, English   BED-fuhrd-shuhr, -SHIR   ˈbedfəʳdʃəʳ, -ˌʃiʳ

Bedivere
Arthurian hero   BED-uh-VIR   ˈbedəˌviʳ

Bedloe's Island
former name, Liberty Island, NY   BED-lōz   ˈbedloːz

Bednorz
J. Georg, *German crystallographer (Nobel 1987)*   BED-NAWRTS   ˈbedˌnɔːʳts

Bedouin
nomadic Arab   BED(-uh)-wuhn   ˈbed(ə)wən

Bedřich
pers. name, Czech   BED-rzhi<u>kh</u>, ⓢ BED-uhr-ZHI<u>KH</u>   ˈbedrʒiç, ⓢ ˈbedəʳˌʒix

Beecham
Sir Thomas, *English conductor*   BĒ-chuhm   ˈbiːtʃəm

Beecher
family of US clergy; pers. name   BĒ-chuhr   ˈbiːtʃəʳ

Beelzebub
    devil; fallen angel in Paradise   bē-EL-zuh-BUHB; BĒL-zuh-BUHB,   biː'elzə‚bəb; 'biːlzə‚bəb, 'bel-
      Lost, *Milton*   BEL-

Beerbohm
    Max, *English critic*   BIR-BŌM, BIR-buhm   'biʳ‚boːm, 'biʳbəm

Beernaert
    Auguste, *Belgian politician (Nobel*   BER-NAHRT   'beʳ‚nɑʳt
      1909)

Beersheba
    district, Israel   bir-SHĒ-buh, ber-SHĒ-buh,   biʳ'ʃiːbə, beʳ'ʃiːbə, bəʳ'ʃiːbə
                    buhr-SHĒ-buh

Beery
    Noah, *US actor*   BIR-ē   'biriˑ

Beethoven
    Ludwig van, *German composer*   BĀT-HŌ-vuhn, ⑤ BĀ-TŌ-vuhn,   'beːt‚hoːvən, ⑤ 'beː‚toːvən,
                    BĀT-ō-vuhn   'beːt‚oːvən

Beeton
    pers. name   BĒT-n   'biːtņ

Begin
    Menachem, *Israeli prime minister*   buh-GĒN, BĀ-gin   bə'giːn, 'beːgin
      (Nobel 1978)

Begley
    Ed, Jr., *US producer, actor*   BEG-lē   'begliˑ

Beguine
    dance   buh-GĒN   bə'giːn

Behan
    Brendan, *Irish writer*   BĒ-uhn   'biːən

Behar
    see Bihar

Behemoth
    legendary Biblical animal   bi-HĒ-muhth, BĒ-uh-muhth,   bi'hiːməθ, 'biːəməθ, -‚mɔːθ,
                    -MAWTH, -MAHTH   -‚mɑθ

Behistun [Bīsitūn]
    town, Iran   BĀ-his-TOON   ‚beːhis'tuːn

Behn
    Aphra, *English writer*   BEN, ⑤ BĀN   'ben, ⑤ 'beːn

Behring
    E. A. von, *German bacteriologist*   BER-ing   'beriŋ
      (Nobel 1901)

Beiden, Pete
    Field, *ballpark, Fresno, CA*   PĒT BĪD-n   'piːt 'baidņ

Beiderbecke
    Bix, *US jazz musician*   BĪD-uhr-BEK   'baidəʳ‚bek

Beijing [Peiping, Peking]
    city, China   BĀ-JING, BĀ-ZHING   'beː'dʒiŋ, 'beː'ʒiŋ

Beirut
    city, Lebanon   bā-ROOT   beː'ruːt

Beja
    lang., people, Sudan, Ethiopia   BĀ-juh   'beːdʒə

Bekaa
    valley, Lebanon   buh-KAH, bek-AH   bə'kɑ, bek'ɑ

Békésy
    Georg von, *US physiologist (Nobel*   BĀ-kuh-shē   'beːkəʃiˑ
      1961)

Key (col. 2):   a: fad ā: fade ah: father ar: **M**ary aw: law e: fed ē: feed er: merry i: hid ī: hide ō: coat oo: boot
oi: boy ow: now u: put uh: above uhr: bird ch: chop ng: ring sh: show th: thick th: this zh: measure

Bekka, The		
governorate, Lebanon	thuh be-KAH	ðə be'ka
Bel & the Dragon		
Apocryphal book	BEL	'bel
Bela		
pers. name	BEL-uh, BĀ-luh, BĒ-luh	'belə, 'beːlə, 'biːlə
Béla		
pers. name, Hungarian	BĀ-lah	'beːla
Belafonte		
Harry, *US singer*	BEL-uh-FAHNT-ē	'belə,fanti'
Belarus [Byelorussia]		
republic, E. Europe	BEL-uh-RO̅O̅S, BĀ-luh-RO̅O̅S	,belə'ruːs, ,beːlə'ruːs
Belasco		
David, *US playwright/producer*	buh-LAS-kō	bə'læskoː
Belau [Palau]		
islands, Pacific	buh-LOW	bə'lau
Belding		
pers. name	BEL-ding	'beldiŋ
Belém		
city, Brazil	be-LĀ [$] buh-LEM	be'lẽː [$] bə'lem
Belfast		
city, N. Ireland	BEL-FAST, bel-FAST	'bel,fæst, bel'fæst
Bel Geddes		
US acting family	bel GED-ēz	bel 'gediˑz
Belgian		
pert. to Belgium	BEL-juhn	'beldʒən
Belgian Malinois		
dog breed	MAL-uhn-WAH	,mælən'wa
Belgian Tervuren		
dog breed	TUHR-VYUR-uhn, ter-	,təʳ'vjurən, teʳ-
Belgium		
country, Europe	BEL-juhm	'beldʒəm
Belgrade [Beograd]		
city, Serbia	BEL-GRĀD, -GRAHD, -GRAD; bel-GRĀD, -GRAHD, -GRAD	'bel,greːd, -,grad, -,græd; bel'greːd, -'grad, -'græd
Belgravia		
district, London, England	bel-GRĀ-vē-uh	bel'greːviːə
Belial		
devil; fallen angel in Paradise Lost, *J. Milton*	BĒ-lē-uhl, BĒL-yuhl	'biːliːəl, 'biːljəl
Belinda		
pers. name	buh-LIN-duh	bə'lində
Belisarius		
general, Eastern Roman Empire	BEL-uh-SAR-ē-uhs, BEL-uh-SAHR-ē-uhs	,belə'særiːəs, ,belə'sariːəs
Belize		
country, river, city, Cen. America	buh-LĒZ	bə'liːz
Belizean		
pert. to Belize	buh-LĒ-zē-uhn	bə'liːziːən
Belkin		
Boris David, *Russian violinist*	BYEL-kyin	'bjeḻkjin
Belknap		
county, NH	BEL-NAP	'bel,næp
Bell & Howell		
US camera co.	BEL uhn(d) HOW(-uh)l	,bel ən(d) 'hau(ə)l

Foreign Sounds: ue: *Fr.* **rue**, *Ger.* **füllen** uh(r): *Fr.* **boeuf**, *Ger.* **Höhle** kh: *Ger.* **ich**, *Scot.* **loch** ḡ: *Sp.* ami**g**o v̱: *Sp.* ha**b**lar hl: *Welsh* **Llanelli**. CAPITALS: primary stress. SMALL CAPS: secondary stress. [$]: U.S. pron. [£]: British pron.

Bella

1. pers. name	BEL-uh	'belə
2. German	BEL-ah	'belɑ
3. Italian	BEL-lah	'bellɑ

Bella Coola

N. American people   BEL-uh K$\overline{OO}$-luh   ˌbelə 'kuːlə

Bellamy

Ralph, US actor; pers. name   BEL-uh-mē   'beləmiˑ

Bellarmine

College, KY   BEL-AHR-muhn, BEL-AHR-MĒN   'belˌɑʳmən, 'belˌɑʳˌmiːn

Belleau

village, France   be-LŌ   beloː

Belleek

town, Ireland; porcelain   buh-LĒK   bə'liːk

Bellerophon

Greek mythological hero   buh-LER-uh-fuhn, -FAHN   bə'lerəfən, -ˌfɑn

Belle Strasbourgeoise, La

see La Belle Strasbourgeoise

Bellevue

College, NE; hospital, New York City   BEL-vy$\overline{oo}$ 'belvjuː

Belle-Vue Kriek

Belgian beer   bel-VUH(R) KRĒK   bel'vœː 'kriːk

Belli

Melvin, US attorney   BEL-ī   'belˌai

Bellingshausen

sea, South Pacific Ocean   BEL-ingz-HOWZ-n   'beliŋzˌhauzn

Bellini

family of Italian painters; Vincenzo, Italian composer   bāl-LĒ-nē, ⑤ be-LĒ-nē, buh-   beˑl'liːniˑ, ⑤ be'liːniˑ, bə-

Bellona

Roman goddess of war   buh-LŌ-nuh   bə'loːnə

Bellow

Saul, US author (Nobel 1976)   BEL-ō   'beloː

Belmopan

town, Belize   BEL-mō-PAN   ˌbelmoː'pæn

Belo Horizonte

city, Brazil   BĀ-lō HAWR-uh-ZAHNT-ē, BEL-ō, HAHR-   'beːloː ˌhɔːrə'zɑntiˑ, 'beloː, ˌhɑr-

Beloit

College, WI; city, KS, WI   buh-LOIT   bə'loit

Belorussia

republic, Europe   BEL-o-RUHSH-uh   ˌbelo'rəʃə

Belorussian [Bielo-, Byelo-]

lang., Belorussia, Poland   BEL-ō-RUHSH-uhn   ˌbeloː'rəʃən

Bel Paese

tdmk for a soft cheese   BEL pah-Ā-zuh, pah-Ā-zē   ˌbel pɑ'eːzə, pɑ'eːziˑ

Belshazzar

king of Babylon   bel-SHAZ-uhr   bel'ʃæzəʳ

Beltane

Celtic pagan festival   BEL-TĀN, BEL-tuhn, BEL-tuh-nuh   'belˌteːn, 'beltən, 'beltənə

Beltrami

county, MN   bel-TRAM-ē   bel'træmiˑ

Beluga

sturgeon; caviar; whale   buh-L$\overline{OO}$-guh   bə'luːgə

Key (col. 2):   a: fad   ā: fade   ah: father   ar: Mary   aw: law   e: fed   ē: feed   er: merry   i: hid   ī: hide   ō: coat $\overline{oo}$: boot   oi: boy   ow: now   u: put   uh: above   uhr: bird   ch: chop   ng: ring   sh: show   th: thick   <u>th</u>: this   zh: measure

Belus
  father of Egyptus and Danaus   BEL-uhs   'beləs
Belushi
  James, John, *US entertainers*   buh-L͞O͞O-shē   bə'luːʃiˑ
Belva
  pers. name   BEL-vuh   'belvə
Belvoir
  1. castle, pl. name, England   BĒ-vuhr   'biːvəᶜ
  2. street, London, England   BEL-VWAWR   'bel‚vwɔːᶜ
  3. see Fort Belvoir
Bemba
  lang., Africa   BEM-buh   'bembə
Bemidji
  city, MN   buh-MIJ-ē   bə'midʒiˑ
Bemis
  US industrial products co.   BĒ-muhs   'biːməs
Ben
  pers. name   BEN   'ben
Bena
  lang., people, Africa   BEN-uh, BĀ-nuh   'benə, 'beːnə
Benacerraf
  Baruj, *US immunologist (Nobel*   ben-AS-uh-ruhf   ben'æsərəf
  1980)
Benadryl
  tdmk for a medication   BEN-uh-DRIL   'benə‚dril
Benalla
  city, Australia   buh-NAL-uh   bə'nælə
Benares [Varanasi]
  city, India   buh-NAHR-uhs   bə'nɑᶜəs
Benatar
  Pat, *rock singer*   BEN-uh-TAHR   'benə‚tɑᶜ
Benavente y Martínez
  Jacinto, *Spanish playwright (Nobel*   bān-ah-VĀN-tä ē mahr-TĒ-näth,   beːnɑ'veːnteː iː mɑr'tiːneːθ,
  1922)   mahr-TĒ-näs; Ⓢ BEN-uh-VENT-ē ē   mɑr'tiːneːs;
  mahr-TĒ-nuhs   Ⓢ ‚benə'ventiː iː
  mɑᶜ'tiːnəs
Benazir
  pers. name (B. Bhutto)   BEN-uh-ZIR, BEN-uh-ZIR   ‚benə'ziᶜ, 'benə‚ziᶜ
Benchley
  Peter, *US author*   BENCH-lē   'bentʃliˑ
Bendigo
  city, Australia   BEN-duh-gō   'bendəgoː
Benedetto
  pers. name   BĀ-nä-DĀT-tō   ‚beːneː'deːttoː
Benedict
  1. pers. name   BEN-uh-DIKT, Ⓔ *also* BEN-it   'benə‚dikt, Ⓔ *also* 'benit
  2. Dutch   BĀ-nuh-dikt   'beːnədikt
  3. German   BĀ-nä-dikt   'beːneːdikt
Bénédict
  pers. name, French   bā-nā-DĔKT   beːneːdiːkt
Benedictine
  monk; liqueur   BEN-uh-DIK-tuhn, -TĒN   ‚benə'diktən, -‚tiːn
Benedictus
  section of the Mass; pers. name,   BEN-i-DIK-tuhs   ‚beni'diktəs
  Latin

Foreign Sounds: ue: *Fr.* **rue**, *Ger.* **füllen** uh(r): *Fr.* **boeuf**, *Ger.* **Höhle** <u>kh</u>: *Ger.* **ich**, *Scot.* **loch** ḡ: *Sp.* ami**g**o ṿ: *Sp.* ha**b**lar
hl: *Welsh* **Llanelli**. CAPITALS: primary stress. SMALL CAPS: secondary stress. Ⓢ: U.S. pron. Ⓔ: British pron.

Benedikt
  pers. name, German   BĀ-nä-dikt   'beːneːdikt

Benelux countries
  Belgium, Luxembourg, and the   BEN-uh-LUHKS   'benə,ləks
  Netherlands

Benét
  Stephen Vincent & William Rose,   buh-NĀ   bə'neː
  US writers

Benetton
  clothing retailer   BEN-uh-TAHN, BEN-uh-tuhn   'benə,tɑn, 'benətən

Benevento
  prov & town, Italy   BEN-uh-VEN-tō   ,benə'ventoː

Benewah
  county, ID   BEN-WAH, BEN-WAW   'ben,wɑ, 'ben,wɔː

Bengal
  region, India; bay, Indian Ocean   ben-GAWL, beng-GAWL, -GAHL   ben'gɔːl, beŋ'gɔːl, -'gɑl

Bengalese
  pert. to Bengal   BENG-guh-LĒZ, BENG-guh-LĒS, BEN-   ,beŋgə'liːz, ,beŋgə'liːs, ,ben-

Bengali
  lang., people, Bangladesh, India   ben-GAW-lē, ben-GAHL-ē, beng-   ben'gɔːliˈ, ben'gɑliˈ, beŋ-

Benghazi [Banghāzī]
  city, former province, Libya   ben-GAHZ-ē, beng-GAHZ-ē, -GAZ-ē   ben'gɑziˈ, beŋ'gɑziˈ, -'gæziˈ

Bengt
  pers. name, Swedish   BENGT   'beŋt

Benguela
  region, city, Angola; Atlantic   ben-G(W)EL-uh, beng-G(W)EL-uh   ben'g(w)elə, beŋ'g(w)elə
  current

Ben Gurion
  David, *Israeli leader; airport, Tel*   BEN gur-YAWN, ⑤ ben GUR-ē-uhn   ,ben gur'jɔːn, ⑤ ben 'guriːən
  Aviv

Bénigne
  pers. name, French   bā-nēn-yuh   beːniːɲ

Benigno
  pers. name, Spanish   bā-NĒG-nō   beː'niːgnoː

Benihana
  Japanese restaurant chain   BEN-ē-HAHN-uh   ,beni'hɑnə

Benin
  country, river, city, bight, Africa   buh-NĒN, buh-NIN   bə'niːn, bə'nin

Beninese
  pert. to Benin   BEN-uh-NĒZ, -NĒS   ,benə'niːz, -'niːs

Beni Suef
  city, Egypt   BEN-ē su-ĀF   ,beniˈ su'eːf

Benito
  pers. name, Italian, Spanish   bā-NĒT-ō   beː'niːʈoː

Benito Cereno
  story, H. Melville   buh-NĒT-ō suh-RĒ-nō   bə'niːʈoː sə'riːnoː

Benjamim
  pers. name, Portuguese   BĀ-zhuh-MIⁿ, -zhah-MIⁿ   ,bẽːʒə'mĩ̃ː, -ʒɑ'mĩ̃ː

Benjamin
  1. pers. name   BEN-juh-muhn, BENJ-muhn   'bendʒəmən, 'bendʒmən
  2. Dutch   BEN-yah-muhn   'benjɑːmən
  3. French   benⁿ-zhah-MEⁿ   bẽʒɑːmẽ
  4. German   BEN-yah-mēn   'benjɑmiːn
  5. Hungarian   BEN-yah-min   'benjɑːmin

Key (col. 2):   a: fad ā: fade ah: father ar: Mary aw: law e: fed ē: feed er: merry i: hid ī: hide ō: coat o͞o: boot
oi: boy ow: now u: put uh: above uhr: bird ch: chop ng: ring sh: show th: thick th̲: this zh: measure

Benne Seed
   sesame seed   BEN-ē   'beniˑ

Bennett
   pers. name   BEN-uht   'benət

Ben Nevis
   mtn., Scotland   ben NEV-uhs   ben 'nevəs

Benno
   1. pers. name, German   BEN-ō   'benoː
   2. Russian   BEN-nuh   'bennə

Benny
   pers. name   BEN-ē   'beniˑ

Benoît
   pers. name, French   buhn-WAH   bənwaː

Benoit Samuelson
   Joan, US marathoner   buh-NOIT SAM-yuh(-wuh)l-suhn   bə'nɔit 'sæmjə(wə)lsən

Bentham
   Jeremy, English jurist, philosopher   BEN-thuhm   'benθəm

Benthamism
   philosophy of Bentham   BEN-thuh-MIZ-uhm   'benθə,mizəm

Benthamite
   adherent of Benthamism   BEN-thuh-MĪT   'benθə,mait

Bentley
   tdmk for an English car   BENT-lē   'bentliˑ

Benvenuto
   pers. name   BĀN-vā-N͞OO-tō   ,beːnveː'nuːtoː

Benz
   Karl Friedrich, German engineer   BENTS, Ⓢ BENZ   'bents, Ⓢ 'benz

Benzedrine
   tdmk for amphetamine   BEN-zuh-DRĒN   'benzə,driːn

Beograd [Belgrade]
   city, Serbia   BĀ-uh-GRAHD   'beːə,graːd

Beothuk
   N. American people   BĀ-uh-THUK   'beːə,θuk

Beowulf
   Old English poem   BĀ-uh-WULF   'beːə,wulf

Beqa'a, El [The Bekka]
   governorate, Lebanon   EL be-KAH   ,el be'ka

Berba
   lang., Benin   BUHR-buh   'bəʳbə

Berber
   lang., people, Africa   BUHR-buhr   'bəʳbəʳ

Berceuse
   lullaby   ber-SUH(R)Z   bersœːz

Berchtesgaden
   town, Bavaria   BERKH-tuhs-GAHD-n   'berxtəs,gadn̩

Berchtoldstag
   Jan. 2nd holiday, Switzerland   BERKH-TŌLT-STAHG   'berx,toːlt,stag

Berdyaev, Berdyayev
   Nicolai, Russian philosopher   byird-YAH-yif   bjird'jaːjif

Berea
   College, KY; city, OH   buh-RĒ-uh   bə'riːə

Beregovoy
   Pierre, prime minister, France   ber-uh-gōv-WAH   berəgoːvwa

---

Foreign Sounds: ue: *Fr.* **rue**, *Ger.* f**ü**llen uh(r): *Fr.* b**oeu**f, *Ger.* H**öh**le <u>kh</u>: *Ger.* i**ch**, *Scot.* lo**ch** g̃: *Sp.* ami**g**o v̱: *Sp.* ha**b**lar
hl: *Welsh* **Ll**anelli. CAPITALS: primary stress. SMALL CAPS: secondary stress. Ⓢ: U.S. pron. Ⓛ: British pron.

Berenice
  pers. name   BER-uh-NĪ-sē, -NĪ-kē, -NĒ-chā, -NĒS   ˌberə'naisiˑ, -'naikiˑ,
                                                                                      -'niːtʃeɪ, -'niːs

Berenice's Hair [Coma Berenices]
  constellation   BER-uh-NĪ-sēz HAR, HER   ˌberə'naisiˑz 'hæ^r, 'he^r
Beresford
  Bruce, *Australian film director*   BER-uhz-fuhrd, BER-uhs-fuhrd   'berəzfə^rd, 'berəsfə^rd
Berg
  Paul, *US molecular biologist*   BUHRG   'bə^rg
    (Nobel 1980)
Bergama
  town, Turkey   buhr-GAHM-uh   bə^rgɑmə
Bergamo
  prov & town, Italy   BER-guh-MŌ   'be^rgə,moː
Bergen
  1. Community College, *county, NJ*   BUHR-guhn   'bə^rgən
  2. *city, Norway*   BUHR-guhn, BER-guhn   'bə^rgən, 'be^rgən
Berger
  Richard L., *US film executive*   BUHR-guhr   'bə^rgə^r
Bergerac
  commune, France   ber-zhuh-RAHK   berʒərɑːk
Bergisch-Gladbach
  city, Germany   BER-gish-GLAHT-BAHKH   ˌbergiʃ'glɑt,bɑx
Bergius
  Friedrich, *German chemist (Nobel*   BER-gē-us   'be^rgiːus
    1931)
Bergman
  Ingmar, *Swedish film director*   BER-mahn, Ⓢ BUHRG-muhn   'bermɑːn, Ⓢ 'bə^rgmən
Bergson
  Henri, *French philosopher (Nobel*   berk-SAWⁿ, berk-SAWN,   berksɔ̃, berksɔːn,
    1927)   Ⓢ BERG-suhn   Ⓢ 'be^rgsən
Bergsonism
  philosophy of Bergson   BERG-suh-NIZ-uhm   'be^rgsə,nizəm
Bergström
  Sune K., *Swedish biochemist*   BER(Y)-STRUH(R)M,   'ber(j),strœm, Ⓢ 'bə^rg,strəm
    (Nobel 1982)   Ⓢ BUHRG-STRUHM
Bering
  Sea, *Strait, N. Pacific*   BIR-ing, BER-ing   'biriŋ, 'beriŋ
Beringer
  tdmk for a wine   BER-in-juhr   'berindʒə^r
Berisha
  Sali, *president, Albania*   buh-RISH-uh, buh-RĒ-shuh   bə'riʃə, bə'riːʃə
Berke
  pers. name (B. Breathed)   BUHRK   'bə^rk
Berkeleianism
  philosophy of G. Berkeley   BAHRK-lē-uh-NIZ-uhm, Ⓢ BUHRK-;   'bɑ^rkliːə,nizəm, Ⓢ 'bə^rk-;
                                              BAHR-KLĒ-uh-NIZ-uhm, Ⓢ BUHR-   ˌbɑ^r'kliːə,nizəm, Ⓢ ˌbə^r-
Berkeley
  1. *US pl. name*   BUHR-klē   'bə^rkliˑ
  2. *pers. name*   BUHR-klē, Ⓔ BAHR-klē   'bə^rkliˑ, Ⓔ 'bɑ^rkliˑ
  3. George, *British philosopher*   BAHR-klē, Ⓢ BUHR-klē   'bɑ^rkliˑ, Ⓢ 'bə^rkliˑ
berkelium
  element   BUHR-klē-uhm, Ⓔ *also*   'bə^rkliːəm, Ⓔ *also*
                                              buhr-KĒ-lē-uhm   bə^r'kiːliːəm

---

Key (col. 2):   a: fad   ā: fade   ah: father   ar: Mary   aw: law   e: fed   ē: feed   er: merry   i: hid   ī: hide   ō: coat   o͞o: boot
oi: boy   ow: now   u: put   uh: above   uhr: bird   ch: chop   ng: ring   sh: show   th: thick   th̲: this   zh: measure

Berkhamsted
  town, England   BUHR-kuhm-stuhd,   'bəʳkəmstəd, 'bɑʳkəmstəd,
     BAHR-kuhm-stuhd, -STED   -ˌsted

Berks [Berkshire]
  county, England   BAHRKS   'bɑʳks

Berkshire
  1. hills, county, MA   BUHRK-SHIR, BUHRK-shuhr   'bəʳkˌʃiʳ, 'bəʳkʃəʳ
  2. county, England   BAHRK-shuhr, BUHRK-shuhr, -SHIR   'bɑʳkʃəʳ, 'bəʳkʃəʳ, -ˌʃiʳ

Berle
  1. Adolf Augustus, US diplomat   BUHR-lē   'bəʳliˑ
  2. Milton, US actor, comedian   BUHRL, BUHR-uhl   'bəʳl, 'bərəl

Berlin
  1. city, Germany   ber-LĔN, Ⓢ buhr-LIN   beʳˈliːn, Ⓢ bəʳˈlin
  2. US pl. name   BUHR-luhn, BUHR-LIN   'bəʳlən, 'bəʳˌlin

Berliner Kindl Weisse
  German beer   ber-LIN-uhr KIN-dl VĪ-suh   beʳˈlinəʳ 'kindl̩ 'vaisə

Berlioz
  Hector, French composer   ber-LYŌZ, Ⓢ BER-lē-ŌZ   berljoːz, Ⓢ 'beʳliːˌoːz

Berlitz
  lang. schools   BUHR-luhts   'bəʳləts

Bermagui
  town, Australia   BUHR-muh-GYOO-ē   ˌbəʳməˈgjuːiˑ

Bermuda
  islands, Atlantic   buhr-MYOOD-uh   bəʳˈmjuːdə

Bermudan
  pert. to Bermuda   buhr-MYOOD-n   bəʳˈmjuːdn̩

Bern, Berne
  canton, city, Switzerland   BERN, BUHRN   'beʳn, 'bəʳn

Bernadette
  pers. name   BUHR-nuh-DET   ˌbəʳnəˈdet

Bernalillo
  county, NM   BUHRN-l-Ē-ō   ˌbəʳnl̩ˈiːoː

Bernard
  1. pers. name   buhr-NAHRD, BUHR-NAHRD,   bəʳˈnaʳd, 'bəʳˌnaʳd,
     BUHR-nuhrd   'bəʳnəʳd
  2. Dutch   BER-NAHRT   'berˌnɑrt
  3. French   ber-NAHR   bernaːr
  4. Polish   BER-nahrt   'bernaːrt

Bernarde
  pers. name, French   ber-NAHRD   bernaːrd

Bernardine
  Christian monastic order   BUHR-nuhr-DĒN   ˌbəʳnəʳˈdiːn

Bernardino
  1. pers. name, Italian   BĂR-nahr-DĒ-nō   ˌbeːrnɑrˈdiːnoː
  2. Portuguese   BUHR-nuhr-DĒ-noo, buhr-nahr-   ˌbərnərˈdiːnuː, bərnɑːr-
  3. Spanish   ber-nahr-THĔ-nō   bernarˈðiːnoː

Bernardo
  1. pers. name, Italian   ber-NAHR-dō   berˈnardoː
  2. Portuguese   buhr-NAHR-doo, ber-   bərˈnaːrduː, ber-
  3. Spanish   ber-NAHR-thō   berˈnarðoː

Bernardus
  1. pers. name   buhr-NAHR-duhs   bəʳˈnaʳdəs
  2. Dutch   ber-NAHR-dues   ber'nardys

Bernay
  pers. name   BER-nā, buhr-NĀ   'berneː, bəʳˈneː

Foreign Sounds: ue: *Fr.* **r**ue, *Ger.* f**ü**llen   uh(r): *Fr.* b**oeu**f, *Ger.* H**öh**le   <u>kh</u>: *Ger.* i**ch**, *Scot.* lo**ch**   ğ: *Sp.* ami**g**o   v: *Sp.* ha**b**lar
hl: *Welsh* **Ll**anelli.   CAPITALS: primary stress.   SMALL CAPS: secondary stress.   Ⓢ: U.S. pron.   Ⓛ: British pron.

Berner Alpen [Bernese Alps]
　mtn. range, Switzerland　　　BER-nuhr AHL-puhn　　　　　,beʳnər 'ɑlpən

Bernese Alps
　mtn. range, Switzerland　　　BUHR-NĒZ ALPS, BUHR-NĒS　　　,bəʳniːz 'ælps, 'bəʳniːs

Bernese Oberland [Bernese Alps]
　mtn. range, Switzerland　　　buhr-NĒZ Ō-buhr-LAHNT,　　　bəʳniːz 'oːbəʳ,lɑnt,
　　　　　　　　　　　　　　　　Ō-buhr-LAND　　　　　　　　　'oːbəʳ,lænd

Bernhard
　1. pers. name, Danish, Dutch　BERN-HAHRT　　　　　　　　'bern,hɑrt
　2. German　　　　　　　　　BERN-HAHRT　　　　　　　　'beʳn,hɑʳt

Bernhardt
　Sarah, *French actress*　　　　ber-NAHR, Ⓢ BUHRN-HAHRT　　bernɑːr, Ⓢ 'bəʳn,hart

Bernice
　pers. name　　　　　　　　buhr-NĒS, BUHR-nuhs　　　　bəʳniːs, 'bəʳnəs

Bernie
　pers. name　　　　　　　　BUHR-nē　　　　　　　　　'bəʳniˑ

Bernina
　Italian sewing machine co.　　buhr-NĒ-nuh　　　　　　　bəʳniːnə

Bernina, Piz
　peak, Switzerland　　　　　PĒTS buhr-NĒ-nuh　　　　　,piːts bəʳniːnə

Bernini
　Giovanni Lorenzo, *Italian artist*　buhr-NĒ-nē　　　　　　　bəʳniːniˑ

Bernkasteler
　German beer　　　　　　　BERN-kahs-TEL-uhr　　　　,beʳnkɑs'teləʳ

Bernoulli
　Jacques, *Swiss mathematician*　ber-noo-(Y)Ē, Ⓢ buhr-NOO-lē,　bernuː(j)iː, Ⓢ bəʳnuːliˑ,
　　　　　　　　　　　　　　　ber-NOO-ē　　　　　　　　　ber'nuːiˑ

Bernstein
　1. Carl, US journalist　　　　BUHRN-STĒN, BUHRN-STĪN　　'bəʳn,stiːn, 'bəʳn,stain
　2. Leonard, US conductor,　　BUHRN-STĪN, BUHRN-STĒN　　'bəʳn,stain, 'bəʳn,stiːn
　　composer

Berra
　Yogi, *US baseball player*　　BER-uh　　　　　　　　　'berə

Berrien
　county, GA, MI　　　　　　BER-ē-uhn　　　　　　　　'beriːən

Berrima
　town, Australia　　　　　　BER-uh-muh　　　　　　　'berəmə

Bert
　1. pers. name　　　　　　　BUHRT　　　　　　　　　'bəʳt
　2. German　　　　　　　　BERT　　　　　　　　　　'beʳt

Berta
　lang., Ethiopia, Sudan　　　BUHRT-uh　　　　　　　　'bəʳtə

Bertha
　1. pers. name　　　　　　　BUHR-thuh　　　　　　　　'bəʳθə
　2. German　　　　　　　　BER-tah　　　　　　　　　'beʳtɑ

Berthe
　pers. name, French　　　　BERT　　　　　　　　　　bert

Berthold
　1. pers. name, French　　　ber-TAWLD　　　　　　　bertɔːld
　2. German　　　　　　　　BER-TAWLT　　　　　　　'beʳ,tɔːlt

Bertie
　1. county, NC　　　　　　　buhr-TĒ, BUHR-TĒ　　　　bəʳtiː, 'bəʳ,tiː
　2. pers. name　　　　　　　BUHRT-ē　　　　　　　　'bəʳtiˑ

Bertil
　pers. name, Swedish　　　　BER-tuhl　　　　　　　　'beʳtəl

Key (col. 2):　a: fad　ā: fade　ah: father　ar: Mary　aw: law　e: fed　ē: feed　er: merry　i: hid　ī: hide　ō: coat　oo: boot
oi: boy　ow: now　u: put　uh: above　uhr: bird　ch: chop　ng: ring　sh: show　th: thick　th: this　zh: measure

Bertillon		
1. Alphonse, *French anthropologist*	ber-tē-YAW^n	bertiːjɔ̃
2. system of identification	BUHRT-l-AHN, BER-tē-YAW^n	'bə^{r}tl̩,ɑn, ,be^{r}tiː'jɔ̃
Bertinelli		
Valerie, *US actress*	BUHRT-n-EL-ē	,bə^{r}tn̩'eliˑ
Bertolt		
pers. name, German	BER-TAWLT	'be^r,tɔːlt
Bertolucci		
Bernardo, *Italian film director*	BERT-l-OO-chē	,be^{r}tl̩'uːtʃiˑ
Bertram		
pers. name	BUHR-truhm	'bə^{r}trəm
Bertrand		
1. pers. name	BUHR-truhnd	'bə^{r}trənd
2. French	ber-TRAH^n	bertrɑ̃
Berwick		
1. pers. name	BUHR-wik, Ⓔ BER-ik	'bə^{r}wik, Ⓔ 'berik
2. US pl. name	BUHR-wik	'bə^{r}wik
Berwickshire		
county, Scotland	BER-ik-shuhr, -SHIR, -SHĪR	'berikʃə^r, -,ʃi^r, -,ʃai^r
Berwick-upon-Tweed		
town, England	BER-ik-uh-pahn-TWĒD	'berikəpɑn'twiːd
Beryl		
pers. name	BER-uhl	'berəl
beryllium		
element	buh-RIL-ē-uhm	bə'riliːəm
Berzelius		
Jöns Jakob, *Swedish scientist*	buhr-ZĀ-lē-uhs, buhr-ZĒ-lē-uhs	bə^r'zeːliːəs, bə^r'ziːliːəs
Bes		
Egyptian god	BES, BĀS	'bes, 'beːs
Besançon		
town, France	buh-zah^n-SAW^n, buh-ZAN(T)-suhn	bəzɑ̃sɔ̃, bə'zæn(t)sən
Besht		
acronym of Ba'al Shem-Tov	BESHT	'beʃt
Bess		
pers. name	BES	'bes
Bessarabia		
region, Europe; former prov, Romania	BES-uh-RĀ-bē-uh	,besə'reːbiːə
Bessemer		
city, AL, MI; borough, PA; steel-making process	BES-uh-muhr	'besəmə^r
Bessie		
pers. name	BES-ē	'besiˑ
Bessmertnykh		
Alexander, *government official, USSR*	buhsh-MERT-nikh	bəʃ'me^{r}tnix
Bestia		
Roman cognomen	BES-chē-uh, BESH-chē-uh, BES-tē-uh	'bestʃiːə, 'beʃtʃiːə, 'bestiːə
Betamax		
tdmk for a videotape system	BĀT-uh-MAKS	'beːtə,mæks
Betelgeuse		
star	BET-l-JOOZ, BĒT-l-JOOZ, -JOOS	'betl̩,dʒuːz, 'biːtl̩,dʒuːz, -,dʒuːs

Bethany
　　US pl. name; town, Jordan; pers.　　BETH-uh-nē　　　　　　　　'beθəni'
　　　name
Bethe
　　Hans Albrecht, US physicist　　　　BĀT-uh　　　　　　　　　　'beːţə
　　　(Nobel 1967)
Bethel
　　division, AK; archaeological site,　　BETH-uhl　　　　　　　　　'beθəl
　　　Jordan
Bethesda
　　district, MD　　　　　　　　　　　buh-THEZ-duh　　　　　　　bə'θezdə
Bethlehem
　　town, Jordan; city, PA;　　　　　　BETH-li-HEM, BETH-lē-(h)uhm　'beθli,hem, 'beθliː(h)əm
Bethsaida
　　ancient city, possibly in Galilee　　beth-SĀ-uhd-uh　　　　　　beθ'seːədə
Bethune
　　1. Mary McLeod, US educator　　buh-TH(Y)OON　　　　　　bə'θ(j)uːn
　　2. British pers. name　　　　　　　BĒT-n　　　　　　　　　　'biːtn̩
Bethune-Cookman
　　College, FL　　　　　　　　　　　buh-TH(Y)OON-KUK-muhn　bə'θ(j)uːn'kukmən
Betje
　　pers. name　　　　　　　　　　　BECH-uh　　　　　　　　　'betʃə
Betjeman
　　Sir John, English poet　　　　　　BECH-uh-muhn　　　　　　'betʃəmən
Betsey, Betsy
　　pers. name　　　　　　　　　　　BET-sē　　　　　　　　　　'betsi'
Bette
　　pers. name　　　　　　　　　　　BET　　　　　　　　　　　'bet
Bettina
　　1. pers. name　　　　　　　　　　buh-TĒ-nuh, be-　　　　　　bə'tiːnə, be-
　　2. German　　　　　　　　　　　be-TĒ-nah　　　　　　　　be'tiːnɑ
Bettino
　　pers. name, Italian　　　　　　　bāt-TĒ-nō　　　　　　　　beːt'tiːnoː
Betty, Bettye
　　pers. name　　　　　　　　　　　BET-ē　　　　　　　　　　'beţi'
Beulah
　　pers. name　　　　　　　　　　　BYOO-luh　　　　　　　　'bjuːlə
Bevan
　　Aneurin, British politician; pers.　　BEV-uhn　　　　　　　　'bevən
　　　name
Beverley, -ly
　　pers. name　　　　　　　　　　　BEV-uhr-lē　　　　　　　　'bevərli'
Beverly Hills
　　city, CA　　　　　　　　　　　　BEV-uhr-lē HILZ　　　　　'bevərli' 'hilz
Beverwijk
　　commune, Netherlands　　　　　BĀ-vuhr-VĪK　　　　　　　'beːvər,vɑik
Bewick
　　Thomas, English artist　　　　　　BYOO-ik　　　　　　　　'bjuːik
Bexar
　　county, TX　　　　　　　　　　　BAR, BER　　　　　　　　'bær, 'ber
Bexley
　　borough, England; city, OH　　　BEKS-lē　　　　　　　　　'beksli'
Beyle [Stendhal]
　　Marie Henri, French writer　　　　BEL　　　　　　　　　　　bel

Key (col. 2):　　a: fad　ā: fade　ah: father　ar: **Mary**　aw: **law**　e: fed　ē: feed　er: **merry**　i: hid　ī: hide　ō: coat　ōō: boot
oi: **boy**　ow: **now**　u: put　uh: **above**　uhr: **bird**　ch: **chop**　ng: **ring**　sh: **show**　th: **thick**　th̲: **this**　zh: measure

Bézique, Be-
   game   buh-ZĒK   bə'ziːk

Bhadgaon
   former name of Bhaktapur, *Nepal*   BUHD-GOWN   'bəd,gaun

Bhagavad Gita
   Hindu text   BAHG-uh-VAHD GĒT-uh,   ,bagə,vad 'giːṭə, ,bəgə,vəd
                      BUHG-uh-VUHD GĒ-tuh   'giːtə

Bhaktapur
   city, Nepal   BUHK-tuh-PUR   'bəktə,puʳ

Bharat
   Sanskrit name of India   BUH-ruht   'bərət

Bhil
   people, India   BĒL   'biːl

Bhili
   lang., India   BĒ-lē   'biːliˑ

Bhimrao
   pers. name   BĒM-ROW   'biːm,rɑu

Bhojpuri
   lang., India   BAHJ-puh-rē   'badʒpəriˑ

Bhopal
   state, city, India   bō-PAHL   boː'pɑl

Bhotia
   Asian people   BŌT-ē-uh   'boːṭiːə

Bhumibol Adulyadej
   king, Thailand   POO-mē-PŌN ah-DOON-luh-DĀT *[sic]*   'puːmiː,poːn a'duːnlə,deːt
                                   [sic]

Bhután
   kingdom, Himalayas   bu-TAN, boo-TAHN   bu'tæn, buː'tɑn

Bhutanese
   pert. to Bhutan   BOOT-n-ĒZ, -ĒS   ,buːtṇ'iːz, -'iːs

Bhutia [Murmi]
   lang., India (Sikkim), Nepal   BOOT-ē-uh   'buːṭiːə

Bhutto
   Benazir Ali, *Pakistani politician*   BOO-tō   'buːtoː

Biafra
   former region, Nigeria; Bight of,   bē-AF-ruh, bē-AHF-ruh, bī-AF-ruh   biː'æfrə, biː'ɑfrə, bai'æfrə
     bay, Africa

Białystok
   city, Poland   bē-AHL-ē-STAWK   biː'aɫiˑ,stɔk

Bianca
   1. pers. name   bē-AHNG-kuh, -ANG-kuh   biː'ɑŋkə, -'æŋkə
   2. Italian   BYAHNG-kah   'bjaŋkɑ

Biarritz
   commune, France   byah-RĒTS, Ⓢ BĒ-uh-RITS,   bjɑːriːts, Ⓢ ,biːə'rits,
                    BĒ-uh-RITS   'biːə,rits

Bible
   Christian holy book   BĪ-buhl   'baibəl

Bibliothecarius
   antipope   BIB-lē-ō-te-KAR-ē-uhs, -KER-   ,bibliːoːte'kæriːəs, -'ker-

Bibliothèque nationale
   library, Paris   bē-blē-aw-TEK nahs-yaw-NAHL   biːbliːoːtek naːsjoːnaːl

Bic
   tdmk for pens, cigarette lighters   BIK   'bik

Bicester
   town, England   BIS-tuhr   'bistəʳ

Foreign Sounds: ue: *Fr.* **rue**, *Ger.* **füllen**   uh(r): *Fr.* **boeuf**, *Ger.* **Höhle**   kh: *Ger.* **ich**, *Scot.* **loch**   ḡ: *Sp.* **amigo**   v̱: *Sp.* **hablar**
hl: *Welsh* **Llanelli**.   CAPITALS: primary stress.   SMALL CAPS: secondary stress.   Ⓢ: U.S. pron.   Ⓛ: British pron.

Bichon frise
dog breed   bē-SHAWⁿ frē-ZĀ   biː‚ʃɔ̃ friːˈzeː

Biddeford
town, ME   BID-uh-fuhrd   ˈbidəfəʳd

Biddulph
town, England   BID-UHLF, BID-l   ˈbid‚əlf, ˈbidl̩

Bideford
town, England   BID-uh-fuhrd   ˈbidəfəʳd

Biden
Joseph R., Jr., US politician   BĪD-n   ˈbaidn̩

Bieckert
Argentinian beer   BĒ-kuhrt   ˈbiːkəʳt

Biederman
Charles Joseph, US artist   BĒD-uhr-muhn   ˈbiːdəʳmən

Biedermeier
style of furnishings   BĒD-uhr-MĪ(-uh)r   ˈbiːdəʳ‚mai(ə)ʳ

Bielorussian [Belo-, Byelo-]
lang., Belorussia, Poland   bē-EL-ō-RUHSH-uhn, BYEL-ō-   biː‚eloˈrəʃən, ‚bjeloː-

Bienaimé
pers. name, French   byeⁿ-ne-MĀ   bjẽnemeː

Bien Hoa
province, Vietnam   byen hō-uh   bjen hoːə

Bienvenu
pers. name, French   byeⁿv(-uh)-NUE   bjẽv(ə)nyː

Bienville
1. parish, LA   bē-EN-vuhl, bē-EN-VIL   biːˈenvəl, biːˈen‚vil
2. lake, Canada   bē-EN-VIL, byahⁿ-VIL   biːˈen‚vil, bjãvil

Bierstadt
Albert, artist   BIR-STAT, BIR-SHTAHT   ˈbiʳ‚stæt, ˈbiʳ‚ʃtat

Bigelow
US carpet co.   BIG-uh-LŌ   ˈbigə‚loː

Big Foot [Sasquatch]
legendary manlike creature   BIG FUT   ˈbig ‚fut

Bihać
town, Bosna-Hercegovina   BĒ-HAHCH   ˈbiː‚hatʃ

Bihar, Behar
state, India   bi-HAHR   biˈhaʳ

Bihari
lang., India, Nepal   bē-HAHR-ē   biˈhariˑ

Bikaner
state, city, India   BIK-uh-NER, BĒ-kuh-NER, -NIR   ‚bikəˈneʳ, ‚biːkəˈneʳ, -ˈniʳ

Bikel
Theodore, US entertainer   bi-KEL   biˈkel

Bikini
atoll, Marshall Islands   buh-KĒ-nē   bəˈkiːniˑ

Biko
Stephen, S. African activist   BĒ-kō   ˈbiːkoː

Bikol
lang., people, Philippine Islands   bē-KŌL   biːˈkoːl

Bilaan
lang., people, Philippine Islands   bē-LAH-AHN, bē-LAHN   biːˈla‚an, biːˈlan

Bilbao
city, Spain   bil-V̲AH-ō, ⑤ bil-BOW, bil-BĀ-ō   bilˈβaoː, ⑤ bilˈbau, bilˈbeːoː

Key (col. 2):   a: fad   ā: fade   ah: father   ar: Mary   aw: law   e: fed   ē: feed   er: merry   i: hid   ī: hide   ō: coat   o͞o: boot
oi: boy   ow: now   u: put   uh: above   uhr: bird   ch: chop   ng: ring   sh: show   th: thick   th̲: this   zh: measure

Bilbo Baggins
   character in The Hobbit, *J. R. R.*   BIL-bō BAG-inz   'bilbo: 'bæginz
   Tolkien
Bildad
   Biblical name   BIL-DAD   'bil,dæd
Bilin
   lang., Ethiopia   buh-LĒN   bə'li:n
Bill
   pers. name   BIL   'bil
Billie
   pers. name   BIL-ē   'bili·
Billingsgate
   London fish market   BIL-ingz-GĀT   'biliŋz,ge:t
Billy
   pers. name   BIL-ē   'bili·
Biloxi
   town, MS; N. American people   buh-LUHK-sē, buh-LAHK-sē   bə'ləksi·, bə'laksi·
Bimini
   islands, British Virgin Islands   BIM-uh-nē   'biməni·
Biminis
   pl. form of Bimini   BIM-uh-nēz   'biməni·z
Binet
   1. Alfred, French psychologist   bē-NE, Ⓢ buh-NĀ   bi:ne, Ⓢ bə'ne:
   2. intelligence test   buh-NĀ   bə'ne:
Bing
   pers. name; cherries   BING   'biŋ
Bingen
   city, Germany   BING-uhn   'biŋən
Binghamton
   city, NY   BING-uhm-tuhn   'biŋəmtən
Bing Yin
   Chinese year (Tiger)   BING YIN   'biŋ 'jin
Bini [Edo]
   lang., people, Nigeria   buh-NĒ   bə'ni:
Binnig
   Gerd, German physicist (Nobel   BIN-i<u>kh</u>   'biniç
   1986)
Biographia Literaria
   prose work, Coleridge   BĪ-uh-GRAF-ē-uh LIT-uh-RAR-ē-uh   ,baiə'græfi:ə ,litə'ræri:ə
Bioko
   island, Equatorial Guinea   bē-Ō-kō   bi:'o:ko:
Biola
   University, CA   bī-Ō-luh   bai'o:lə
Bion
   Greek pastoral poet   BĪ-AHN   'bai,an
BIOS
   basic input-output system   BĪ-AHS, BĪ-ŌS   'bai,as, 'bai,o:s
Bios Copper
   Belgian beer   BĒ-ahs KAHP-uhr, BĪ-ahs   'bi:as 'kapəʳ, 'baias
Birgit
   pers. name, Swedish   BIR-yit   'biʳjit
Birgitta
   pers. name, Swedish   bir-GIT-uh   biʳ'git̪ə

Foreign Sounds: ue: *Fr.* **rue**, *Ger.* f**ü**llen uh(r): *Fr.* b**oeu**f, *Ger.* H**öh**le <u>kh</u>: *Ger.* i**ch**, *Scot.* lo**ch** ḡ: *Sp.* ami**g**o v̄: *Sp.* ha**b**lar
hl: *Welsh* **Ll**anelli. CAPITALS: primary stress. SMALL CAPS: secondary stress. Ⓢ: U.S. pron. Ⓔ: British pron.

Birmingham		
1. city, AL	BUHR-ming-HAM	'bə^{r}miŋˌhæm
2. city, England	BUHR-ming-uhm, BRUHM-uh-juhm	'bə^{r}miŋəm, 'brəmədʒəm
Birnam Wood		
former forest, Scotland	BUHR-nuhm WUD	'bə^{r}nəm 'wud
Birobidzhan		
city, admin. div., Russia	BIR-ō-buh-JAHN	ˌbiroːbə'dʒɑn
Bisaya [Sebuano]		
lang., people, Philippine Islands	buh-SĪ-(y)uh	bə'sɑi(j)ə
Biscay		
bay of Atlantic, W France & N Spain; prov, Spain	BIS-kā	'biskeː
Biscayne		
bay, FL; car model	bis-KĀN, BIS-KĀN	bis'keːn, 'bisˌkeːn
Bisho		
town, S. Africa	BĒ-shō	'biːʃoː
Bishop		
Elizabeth, *US poet;* J. Michael, *US microbiologist (Nobel 1989)*	BISH-uhp	'biʃəp
Bīsitūn [Behistun]		
town, Iran	BĒ-suh-TOO͞N	ˌbiːsə'tuːn
Bislama [Bêche-de-Mer]		
lang., Vanuatu, Solomon Islands	BĒ-sluh-MAH	ˌbiːslə'mɑˑ
Bismarck		
1. Otto von, *German statesman*	BIS-MAHRK, Ⓢ BIZ-MAHRK	'bisˌmɑ^{r}k, Ⓢ 'bizˌmɑ^{r}k
2. city, ND; archipelago, sea, Pacific	BIZ-MAHRK	'bizˌmɑ^{r}k
bismuth		
element	BIZ-muhth	'bizməθ
Bissau		
seaport, Guinea-Bissau	bis-OW, bis-OW^n	bis'ɑu, bis'ɑũ
Bisset		
Jacqueline, *US entertainer*	BIS-uht	'bisət
Bisu [Bes]		
Egyptian god	BIS-o͞o	'bisuː
Bitburg		
town, Germany	BIT-BURK, Ⓢ BIT-BUHRG	'bitˌburk, Ⓢ 'bitˌbə^{r}g
Bitburger		
German beer	BIT-BUR-guhr, Ⓢ BIT-BUHR-guhr	'bitˌbu^{r}gə^r, Ⓢ 'bitˌbə^{r}gə^r
Bithynia		
ancient state, Asia Minor	buh-THIN-ē-uh	bə'θiniːə
Bitlis		
prov, Turkey	bit-LĒS	bit'liːs
Bix		
pers. name (B. Biederbecke)	BIKS	'biks
Bizerte		
port, Tunisia	buh-ZERT-ē, bi-ZERT	bə'ze^{r}ṭiˑ, bi'ze^{r}t
Bizet		
Georges, *French composer*	bē-ZE, Ⓢ bē-ZĀ	biːze, Ⓢ biː'zeː
Bjarni		
pers. name	BYAHD-nē	'bjɑdniː
Bjørn, Björn		
pers. name	BYUHRN	'bjœːrn

Key (col. 2): a: **fad** ā: **fade** ah: **father** ar: **Mary** aw: **law** e: **fed** ē: **feed** er: **merry** i: **hid** ī: **hide** ō: **coat** o͞o: **boot** oi: **boy** ow: **now** u: **put** uh: **above** uhr: **bird** ch: **chop** ng: **ring** sh: **show** th: **thick** t͟h: **this** zh: **measure**

Bjørnson

Bjørnstjerne, *Norwegian author* BYUHRN-suhn 'bjœːrnsən
(*Nobel 1903*)

Bjørnstjerne

pers. name, Norwegian BYUHRN-STYER-nuh 'bjœːrn,stjernə

Black

James, *British pharmacologist* BLAK 'blæk
(*Nobel 1988*); Sea, *Europe,*
Asia; various rivers, US

Blackett

P. M. S., *British physicist (Nobel* BLAK-uht 'blækət
1948)

Blackfeet

pl. of Blackfoot BLAK-FĒT 'blæk,fiːt

Blackfoot

N. American people BLAK-FUT 'blæk,fut

Blackfriars

district, 16th-century theater, blak-FRĪ-uhrz, BLAK-FRĪ-uhrz blæk'fraiəᵣz, 'blæk,fraiəᵣz
London, England

Black Maria

patrol wagon BLAK muh-RĪ-uh ,blæk mə'raiə

Blackpool

town, Lancashire BLAK-PŌŌL 'blæk,puːl

Blair

pers. name BLAR, BLER 'blæᵣ, 'bleᵣ

Blaise

1. pers. name BLĀZ 'bleːz
2. French BLEZ blez

Blakeney

Sir Percival, *hero of* The Scarlet BLĀK-nē 'bleːkniˑ
Pimpernel

Blanc

1. Louis, French historian BLAHⁿ blɑ̃
2. Mel, US cartoon voice BLANGK 'blæŋk
3. Cape, Africa BLAHⁿ, Ⓢ BLANGK blɑ̃, Ⓢ 'blæŋk

Blanc, Mont

see Mont Blanc

Blanc fumé

wine BLAHⁿ fue-MÃ blɑ̃ fyːmeː

Blanchard

James J., *US politician* BLAN-chuhrd 'blæntʃəᵣd

Blanche

1. pers. name BLANCH 'blæntʃ
2. French BLAHⁿSH blɑ̃ʃ

Blarney

town, Ireland BLAHR-nē 'blɑᵣniˑ

Blasco-Ibáñez

Vincente, *Spanish novelist* BLAHS-kō-ē-VAHN-yäth, 'blaskoːiː'βanjeːθ, -iː'βanjeːs
-ē-VAHN-yäs

Blaupunkt

German audio co. BLOW-PUNG(K)T 'blau,puŋ(k)t

Blavatsky

Madame Helena, *founder of* bluh-VAT-skē, bluh-VAHT-skē blə'vætskiˑ, blə'vɑtskiˑ
Theosophy

Foreign Sounds: ue: *Fr.* **rue**, *Ger.* füllen   uh(r): *Fr.* **boeuf**, *Ger.* **Höhle**   k̲h̲: *Ger.* i**ch**, *Scot.* lo**ch**   ğ: *Sp.* amiğo   v̲: *Sp.* haḇlar
hl: *Welsh* **Ll**anelli.   CAPITALS: primary stress.   SMALL CAPS: secondary stress.   Ⓢ: U.S. pron.   Ⓒ: British pron.

Bleecker
　　street, New York City; stadium,　BLĒ-kuhr　　　　　　'bliːkəʳ
　　Albany, NY
Blenheim
　　town, palace, England; borough,　BLEN-uhm　　　　　　'blenəm
　　New Zealand; English/French
　　form of Blindheim
Blériot
　　Louis, *French aviator/inventor*　blār-YŌ, ⑤ BLER-ē-ō　 bleːrjoː, ⑤ 'bleriːˌoː
Bleu cheese
　　cheese　　　　　　　　BLUH(R), BLOO　　　'blœː, 'bluː
Blindheim [Blenheim]
　　village, Germany　　　　BLINT-HĪM　　　　　　'blint,haim
Blitz Weinhard
　　beer　　　　　　　　　BLITS VĪN-HAHRT, WĪN-HAHRT　'blits 'vain,haʳt, 'wain,haʳt
Bloch
　　1. Felix, *US physicist (Nobel 1952)*　BLAHK　　　　　　'blak
　　2. Konrad E., *US biochemist*　BLAHK, BLAWK, BLAW<u>KH</u>　'blak, 'blɔːk, 'blɔːx
　　(Nobel 1964)
Bloembergen
　　Nicolaas, *US physicist (Nobel*　BLOOM-BUHR-guhn　　'bluːm,bəʳgən
　　1981)
Bloemfontein
　　city, South Africa　　　BLOOM-FAHN-TEN　　'bluːm,fan,ten
Blois
　　city, France　　　　　BLWAH, ⑤ bluh-WAH　blwaː, ⑤ blə'wa
Blood
　　N. American people　　BLUHD　　　　　　　'bləd
Bloom
　　pers. name　　　　　BLOOM　　　　　　　'bluːm
Bloomfield
　　US pl. name; pers. name　BLOOM-FĒLD　　　　'bluːm,fiːld
Bloomingdales
　　US department store　　BLOO-ming-DĀLZ　　'bluːmiŋ,deːlz
Bloomington
　　city, IN　　　　　　BLOO-ming-tuhn　　'bluːmiŋtən
Bloomsbury
　　district, London　　　BLOOMZ-b(uh-)rē　　'bluːmzb(ə)riˑ
Blount
　　county, AL, TN; pers. name　BLUHNT　　　　　　'blənt
Blücher
　　Gebhard von, *Prussian militarist*　BLUE-<u>kh</u>uhr, ⑤ BLOO-kuhr　'blyːxəʳ, ⑤ 'bluːkəʳ
Bluebeard
　　fairy tale character　　BLOO-BĒRD　　　　'bluːˌbiʳd
Blumberg
　　Baruch Samuel, *US biochemist*　BLUHM-BUHRG, BLOOM-BUHRG　'bləm,bəʳg, 'bluːm,bəʳg
　　(Nobel 1976)
Blyth
　　1. Edward, *English naturalist*　BLĪ, BLĪ<u>TH</u>, BLĪ<u>TH</u>　'blai, 'blaiθ, 'blaið
　　2. borough, England　　BLĪ<u>TH</u>　　　　　　'blaið
Blythe
　　pers. name　　　　　BLĪ<u>TH</u>　　　　　　'blaið
Blyton
　　Enid, *British author*　　BLĪT-n　　　　　　'blaitṇ

Key (col. 2):　a: fad　ā: fade　ah: father　ar: Mary　aw: law　e: fed　ē: feed　er: merry　i: hid　ī: hide　ō: coat　ōo: boot
oi: boy　ow: now　u: put　uh: above　uhr: bird　ch: chop　ng: ring　sh: show　th: thick　th: this　zh: measure

BMW		
German car marque	BĒ-em-DUHB-uh(l-)yo͞o	ˌbiːemˈdəbə(l)juˑ
B'nai B'rith		
international Jewish organization	buh-NĀ BRITH	bəˌneː ˈbriθ
Bo		
1. pers. name	BŌ	ˈboː
2. Swedish	BO͞O	ˈbuː
Boabdil		
Spanish name of Muhammad XI, sultan of Granada	bō-ahv̲-DĒL	boːaβˈdiːl
Boadicea [Boudicca]		
ancient British queen	BŌ-uhd-uh-SĒ-uh	ˌboːədəˈsiːə
Boal		
town, Spain	BWAHL	ˈbwɑl
Boas		
Franz, *US anthropologist*	BŌ-AZ	ˈboːˌæz
Boaz		
Biblical name	BŌ-AZ	ˈboːˌæz
Bob		
pers. name	BAHB	ˈbɑb
Bobby		
pers. name	BAHB-ē	ˈbɑbiˑ
Bobko		
Karol J., *US astronaut, shuttle pilot*	BAHB-kō	ˈbɑbkoː
Bobo		
lang., Mali, Burkina Faso	BŌ-bō	ˈboːboː
Bobst		
Elmer Holmes, Library, *New York City*	BAHBST, BAHPST	ˈbɑbst, ˈbɑpst
Boca Raton		
town, FL	BŌ-kuh-ruh-TŌN	ˌboːkərəˈtoːn
Boccaccio		
1. Giovanni, *medieval Italian author*	bōk-KAHT-chō, [$] buh-KAHCH-(ē-)ō	boːkˈkɑttʃoː, [$] bəˈkɑtʃ(iː)oː
2. pers. name; game	buh-KAHCH-(ē-)ō	bəˈkɑtʃ(iː)oː
Boche		
disparaging term for a German soldier	BAWSH, BAHSH	ˈbɔːʃ, ˈbɑʃ
Bodensee		
lake, Swiss Alps	BŌD-n-ZĀ	ˈboːdn̩ˌzeː
Bodhisattva		
Buddhist holy one	BŌD-uh-SUHT-vuh, -SAHT-vuh	ˌboːdəˈsətvə, -ˈsɑtvə
Bodhran		
Irish drum	BAWR-uhn, BAWT̲H̲-ruhn	ˈbɔːrən, ˈbɔːðrən
Bodie		
island, NC	BAHD-ē	ˈbɑdiː
Bodleian		
library, Oxford Univ., England	bahd-LĒ-uhn, BAHD-lē-uhn	bɑdˈliːən, ˈbɑdliːən
Bodo		
lang., people, India	BŌD-ō	ˈboːdoː
Bodoni		
type style	buh-DŌ-nē, bō-DŌ-nē	bəˈdoːniˑ, boːˈdoːniˑ
Boehm		
Richard Wood, *US ambassador*	BŌM	ˈboːm

Boeing
  US aerospace co.   BŌ-ing   'boːiŋ

Boeotia
  prov, Greece   bē-Ō-shuh   biːˈoːʃə

Boeotian
  pert. to Boeotia   bē-Ō-sh(ē-)uhn   biːˈoːʃ(iː)ən

Boer
  War, S. Africa   BŌR, BAWR, BUR   'boːr, 'bɔːr, 'bur

Boerne
  city, TX   BUHR-nē   'bərniˑ

Boethius
  medieval philosopher   bō-Ē-thē-uhs   boːˈiːθiːəs

Boeuf Bourguignon
  stew with wine   buh(r)f bur-gē-NYAWⁿ, BẼF bur-gēn-YAWⁿ   bœf burgiːɲɔ̃, ˌbiːf buʳgiˑn'jɔ̃

Bogalusa
  city, LA   BŌ-guh-LOO-suh   ˌboːgəˈluːsə

Bogart
  Humphrey, *US actor*   BŌ-GAHRT   'boːˌgaʳt

Bogdan
  1. pers. name, Bulgarian, Polish   BAWG-DAHN   'bɔːgˌdaːn
  2. Romanian   bawg-DAHN   bɔːgˈdɑn
  3. Russian   BUHG-DAHN   ˌbəgˈdaːn

Boggabilla
  town, Australia   BAHG-uh-BIL-uh   ˌbagəˈbilə

Boghaz-Koy
  Hittite ruins, Turkey   BŌ-(G)AHZ-KOI   ˌboːˌ(g)ɑzˈkɔi

Bognor Regis
  town, England   BAHG-nuhr RĒ-juhs   ˌbagnəʳ 'riːdʒəs

Bogotá
  river, city, Colombia   BŌ-guh-TAW, -TAH   ˌboːgəˈtɔː, -ˈtɑ

Bogota
  city, NJ   buh-GŌT-uh   bəˈgoːʈə

Bogumil
  pers. name, German   BŌ-gum-ĒL   'boːgum,iːl

Bogumił
  pers. name, Polish   baw-GOO-mēl   bɔːˈguːmiːɫ

Bohai
  see Po Hai

Bohan
  Marc, *French fashion designer*   baw-AHⁿ   bɔːɑ̃

Bohème, La
  opera, Puccini   LAH bō-EM   ˌlɑ boːˈem

Bohemia
  prov, Czech republic   bō-HĒ-mē-uh   boːˈhiːmiːə

Bohol
  island, strait, Philippines   bō-HAWL   boːˈhɔːl

Bohr
  Aage N., *Danish physicist (Nobel 1975); his father* Niels H. D., *Danish physicist (Nobel 1922)*   BŌR, BAWR   'boːr, 'bɔːr

Bohun, de
  Anglo-Norman family in Welsh Marches   duh BOON   də 'buːn

Key (col. 2):   a: fad   ā: fade   ah: father   ar: Mary   aw: law   e: fed   ē: feed   er: merry   i: hid   ī: hide   ō: coat   oo: boot
oi: boy   ow: now   u: put   uh: above   uhr: bird   ch: chop   ng: ring   sh: show   th: thick   th: this   zh: measure

Bohuslav
  pers. name   BAW-hus-lahf   'bɔːhuslɑːf

Boipatong
  township, South Africa   BOI-puh-TAWNG, BOI-puh-TAWNG   ˌbɔipə'tɔːŋ, 'bɔipəˌtɔːŋ

Bois de Boulogne
  park, Paris, France   bwah duh b‾oo-LAWN-yuh, ⑤ BWAH duh b‾oo-LŌN, b‾oo-LOIN   bwɑː də buːlɔːŋ, ⑤ 'bwɑ də buː'loːn, buː'lɔin

Bois de Vincennes
  park, Vincennes, France   bwahd ve^n-SEN   bwɑːd ṽɛsen

Boise
  county, ID   BOI-sē *(local pron.)*, BOI-zē   'bɔisiˑ *(local pron.)*, 'bɔiziˑ

Bojaxhiu [Mother Teresa]
  Agnes Gonxha, *Albanian religious (Nobel 1979)*   bō-yah<u>kh</u>-Y‾OO   boːjɑx'juː

Bokaro
  city, Bihar, India   bō-KAHR-ō   boː'kɑroː

Bokhara
  1. rug   b‾oo-<u>KH</u>AHR-uh, bō-KAHR-uh   buː'xɑrə, boː'kɑrə
  2. see Bukhara

Bokmål [Dano-Norwegian]
  literary Norwegian   B‾OOK-MAWL, ⑤ BUK-MAWL, -MAHL   'buːkˌmɔːl, ⑤ 'bukˌmɔːl, -ˌmɑl

Bolero
  dance   buh-LER-ō   bə'leroː

Boleslav
  Bohemian ruler; pers. name   BŌ-luh-SLAHF   'boːləˌslɑf

Bolesław
  Polish ruler; pers. name   baw-LES-lahf   bɔː'leslɑːf

Boleyn
  Anne, *wife of Henry VIII, mother of Elizabeth I*   bu-LIN, BUL-uhn   bu'lin, 'bulən

Bolger
  Ray, *US actor*   BŌL-juhr   'boːldʒəʳ

Bolingbroke
  Henry of, *King Henry IV*   ⓔ BAHL-ing-BRUK, BUL-ing-BRUK, ⑤ BŌ-ling-BRUK, -BRŌK   ⓔ 'bɑliŋˌbruk, 'buliŋˌbruk, ⑤ 'boːliŋˌbruk, -ˌbroːk

Bolinger
  Dwight, *US linguist*   BAHL-uhn-juhr   'bɑləndʒəʳ

Bolívar
  Simón, *S. American leader; S. American pl. name*   bō-LḔ-<u>v</u>ahr, ⑤ buh-LḔ-VAHR, BAHL-uh-vuhr   boː'liːβɑr, ⑤ bə'liːˌvɑʳ, 'bɑləvəʳ

Bolivar
  US pl. name; pers. name   BAHL-uh-vuhr   'bɑləvəʳ

Bolivia
  republic, S. America   buh-LIV-ē-uh   bə'liviːə

Bolivian
  pert. to Bolivia   buh-LIV-ē-uhn   bə'liviːən

Böll
  Heinrich, *German author (Nobel 1972)*   BUH(R)L   'bœːl

Bolla
  tdmk for Italian wine   BŌ-luh   'boːlə

Bollard
  John K., *US lexicographer*   BAHL-uhrd, ⓔ BAHL-AHRD   'bɑləʳd, ⓔ 'bɑlˌɑʳd

---

Foreign Sounds: ue: *Fr.* **r**ue, *Ger.* f**ü**llen   uh(r): *Fr.* b**oeu**f, *Ger.* H**öh**le   <u>kh</u>: *Ger.* i**ch**, *Scot.* lo**ch**   ḡ: *Sp.* ami**g**o   <u>v</u>: *Sp.* ha**b**lar   hl: *Welsh* **Ll**anelli.   CAPITALS: primary stress.   SMALL CAPS: secondary stress.   ⑤: U.S. pron.   ⓔ: British pron.

Bologna
 prov & town, Italy · buh-LŌN-yuh, buh-LŌ-nuh · bə'loːnjə, bə'loːnə
Bolognese
 1. pert. to Bologna, Italy · BŌ-luhn-(Y)ĒZ, BŌ-luhn-(Y)ĒS · ˌboːlən'(j)iːz, ˌboːlən'(j)iːs
 2. pasta sauce · BŌ-luhn-(Y)ĒZ, BŌ-luhn-(Y)ĒS, BŌ-luhn-YĀZ · ˌboːlən'(j)iːz, ˌboːlən'(j)iːs, ˌboːlən'jeːz
Bolshevik
 communist · BŌL-shuh-vik, BAWL-, BAHL- · 'boːlʃəvik, 'boːl-, 'bɑl-
Bolshevism
 doctrines of Bolsheviks · BŌL-shuh-VIZ-uhm, BAWL-, BAHL- · 'boːlʃəˌvizəm, 'boːl-, 'bɑl-
Bolshevist
 follower of Bolsheviks · BŌL-shuh-vuhst, BAWL-, BAHL- · 'boːlʃəvəst, 'boːl-, 'bɑl-
Bolshoi
 ballet, Moscow · BŌL-SHOI, BAWL-SHOI · 'boːlˌʃɔi, 'boːlˌʃɔi
Bolt Beranek and Newman
 US high-technology co. · BŌLT buh-RAN-ik uhn(d) N(Y)OO-muhn · 'boːlt bə'rænik ən(d) 'n(j)uːmən
Bolzano
 Bernhard, *Austrian theologian* · bawlt-SAHN-ō · boːlt'sɑnoː
Bombay
 city, India · bahm-BĀ · bɑm'beː
Bon
 Buddhist festival · BAHN · 'bɑn
Bona Dea
 Roman divinity · BŌ-nuh DĀ-uh · ˌboːnə 'deːə
Bonaire
 island, Netherlands Antilles · buh-NAR, buh-NER · bə'nær, bə'nerʳ
Bonamy
 pers. name · BAHN-uh-mē · 'bɑnəmiˑ
Bonaparte [Buonaparte]
 Corsican family, incl. Napoléon · baw-nah-PAHRT, $ BŌ-nuh-PAHRT · boːnɑːpart, $ 'boːnəˌpɑʳt
Bonaventura
 1. pers. name, German · BŌ-nah-ven-TOO-rah · ˌboːnaven'tuːra
 2. Italian · BAW-nahv-en-TOO-rah · ˌbɔːnahven'tuːra
Bonaventure
 1. pers. name · BAHN-uh-VEN-chuhr, BAHN-uh-VEN- · ˌbanə'ventʃəʳ, 'banəˌven-
 2. French · baw-nah-vahⁿ-TUER · boːnaːvãtyːr
Bondi
 beach, Australia · BAHN-DĪ, bahn-DĪ · 'banˌdai, ban'dai
Bone [Boni]
 gulf, Indonesia · BŌ-nē · 'boːniˑ
Bonheur
 Rosa, *French painter* · baw-NUHR · boːnœr
Bon Homme
 county, SD · BAHN-uhm · 'banəm
Boni [Bone]
 gulf, Indonesia · BŌ-nē · 'boːniˑ
Boniface
 pers. name · BAHN-uh-fuhs, -FĀS · 'banəfəs, -ˌfeːs
Bonifacius
 1. pers. name · BAHN-uh-FĀ-sh(ē-)uhs · ˌbanə'feːʃ(iː)əs
 2. German · BŌ-nē-FAHTS-yus, -FAHT-sē-us · ˌboːniˑ'fatsjus, -'fatsiːus
Bonin
 Islands, *Pacific* · BŌ-nuhn · 'boːnən

Key (col. 2): a: fad ā: fade ah: father ar: Mary aw: law e: fed ē: feed er: merry i: hid ī: hide ō: coat ōō: boot oi: boy ow: now u: put uh: above uhr: bird ch: chop ng: ring sh: show th: thick t̲h̲: this zh: measure

Bonior
   David, *US politician*   BAHN-yuhr   'banjəʳ

Bonjour Tristesse
   novel, Françoise Sagan   bawⁿ-ZHOOR trēs-TES   bɔ̃ʒuˑr triːstes

Bon Jovi
   rock group   bahn JŌ-vē   ban 'dʒoːviˑ

Bonn
   former capital, W. Germany   BAHN, BAWN   'ban, 'bɔːn

Bonnard
   Pierre, *French artist*   baw-NAHR   bɔːnaːr

Bonneville
   1. Benjamin, *American explorer;*   BAHN-uh-VIL   'banə,vil
     county, ID
   2. US car model   BAHN-uh-VIL, BAHN-ē-VIL   'banə,vil, 'baniˑ,vil

Bonnezeaux
   French wine   bawn-ZŌ   bɔːnzoː

Bonnie, Bonny
   pers. name   BAHN-ē   'baniˑ

Bono
   Sonny, *US entertainer, politician;*   BŌ-nō   'boːnoː
     Irish rock singer

Bontok
   lang., people, Philippine Islands   bahn-TAHK   ban'tak

Bonynge
   Richard, *Austrian conductor*   BAHN-ing   'baniŋ

Boogie-woogie
   musical style   BUG-ē-WUG-ē, BOO-gē-WOO-gē   ,bugiˑ'wugiˑ, ,buːgiˑ'wuːgiˑ

Booker
   pers. name   BUK-uhr   'bukəʳ

Boole
   George, *English mathematician*   BOOL   'buːl

Boolean
   pert. to G. Boole; *algebra*   BOO-lē-uhn   'buːliːən

Boorman
   John, *British film producer,*   BUR-muhn, BAWR-muhn   'buʳmən, 'bɔːʳmən
     director

Boorstin
   Daniel J., *US author*   BUR-stuhn, BAWR-stuhn   'buʳstən, 'bɔːʳstən

Boötes
   constellation   bō-ŌT-ēz   boːˈoːţiːz

Bop
   local name for Bophuthatswana   BAHP   'bap

Bophuthatswana
   Black enclaves, South Africa   BŌ-poo-taht-SWAHN-uh   ,boːpuːtat'swanə

Bora-Bora
   island, French Polynesia   BŌR-uh-BŌR-uh, BAWR-uh-BAWR-uh   ,boːrə'boːrə, ,bɔːrə'bɔːrə

Borach
   Fanny, *orig. name of* Fanny Brice   BŌR-uhk, BAWR-uhk   'boːrək, 'bɔːrək

Borah
   William E., *US political leader*   BŌR-uh, BAWR-uh   'boːrə, 'bɔːrə

Borchert
   Field, *ballpark, Milwaukee, WI*   BAWR-chuhrt   'bɔːʳtʃəʳt

Bordeaux
   city, France; wine   bawr-DŌ   bɔːʳ'doː

Foreign Sounds: ue: *Fr.* **rue**, *Ger.* **füllen**   uh(r): *Fr.* **boeuf**, *Ger.* **Höhle**   <u>kh</u>: *Ger.* **ich**, *Scot.* **loch**   ḡ: *Sp.* **amigo**   ṿ: *Sp.* **hablar**
hl: *Welsh* **Llanelli**.   CAPITALS: primary stress.   SMALL CAPS: secondary stress.   Ⓢ: U.S. pron.   Ⓑ: British pron.

Bordelaise
  brown sauce   BAWRD-l-ĀZ   ˌbɔːʳdl̩ˈeɪz

Bordet
  Jules, Belgian bacteriologist   bawr-DĀ   bɔːrdeː
  (Nobel 1919)

Boreades
  children of the North Wind   BŌR-ē-AD-ēz, BAWR-ē-AD-ēz   ˌbɔːriːˈædiːz, ˌbɔːriːˈædiːz

Boreal owl
  bird   BŌR-ē-uhl OWL, BAWR-   ˈbɔːriːəl ˈaul, ˈbɔːr-

Boreas
  Greek god of the North Wind   BŌR-ē-uhs, BAWR-ē-uhs   ˈbɔːriːəs, ˈbɔːriːəs

Borg
  Bjorn, Swedish tennis player   BAWR-yuh, Ⓢ BAWRG   ˈbɔːrj, Ⓢ ˈbɔːʳg

Borge
  Victor, US comedian, pianist   BAWR-guh   ˈbɔːʳgə

Borges
  Jorge Luis, Argentinian author   BAWR-ğās, Ⓢ BAWR-HĀS   ˈbɔːrɣeːs, Ⓢ ˈbɔːʳˌheːs

Borghese, Galleria
  picture gallery, Rome, Italy   GAHL-uh-RĒ-uh bawr-GĀ-zā   ˌgalǝˈriːǝ bɔːʳˈgeːzeː

Borgia
  Italian family   BAWR-jah, BAWR-juh, BAWR-zhuh   ˈbɔːʳdʒɑ, ˈbɔːʳdʒǝ, ˈbɔːʳʒǝ

Borglum
  Gutzon, US sculptor   BAWR-gluhm   ˈbɔːʳgləm

Borgnine
  Ernest, US actor   BAWRG-NĪN   ˈbɔːʳgˌnain

Borgoña
  red Iberian wine   bawr-GŌN-yuh   bɔːʳˈgoːnjǝ

Boris
  1. pers. name   BŌR-uhs, BAWR-uhs, BAHR-uhs   ˈbɔːrǝs, ˈbɔːrǝs, ˈbarǝs
  2. Bulgarian   BAWR-ēs, baw-RĒS   ˈbɔːriːs, bɔːˈriːs
  3. Russian   BUHR-YĒS   ˌbǝrˈjiːs

Boris Godunov
  Mussorgsky opera   BŌR-uhs GŌD-n-AWF, BAWR-uhs,   ˌbɔːrǝs ˈgoːdn̩ˌɔːf, ˌbɔːrǝs,
           GAWD-n-AWF, guh-dōō-NAWF   ˈgoːdn̩ˌɔːf, gǝduːˈnɔːf

Borisoglebsk
  city, Russia   buh-RIS-uh-GLEPSK   bǝˌrisǝˈglepsk

Borlaug
  Norman E., US agricultural   BAWR-LAWG   ˈbɔːʳˌlɔːg
  scientist (Nobel 1970)

Born
  Max, German physicist (Nobel   BAWRN   ˈbɔːʳn
  1954)

Borneo
  island, Asia   BAWR-nē-ō   ˈbɔːʳniːoː

Bornholm
  island, Denmark   BAWRN-HŌ(L)M   ˈbɔːʳnˌhoː(l)m

Borodin
  Aleksandr, Russian composer,   buh-RUHD-YĒN, Ⓢ BAWR-uh-DĒN   bǝˌrǝdˈjiːn, Ⓢ ˌbɔːrǝˈdiːn
  chemist

boron
  element   BŌR-AHN, BAWR-AHN   ˈbɔːrˌɑn, ˈbɔːrˌɑn

Bororo
  S. American people   BŌR-uh-RŌ   ˌbɔːrǝˈroː

Borscht Belt
  Jewish resorts, Catskill Mts., NY   BAWRSHT BELT   ˈbɔːʳʃt ˌbelt

---

Key (col. 2):   a: fad   ā: fade   ah: father   ar: Mary   aw: law   e: fed   ē: feed   er: merry   i: hid   ī: hide   ō: coat   ōō: boot
oi: boy   ow: now   u: put   uh: above   uhr: bird   ch: chop   ng: ring   sh: show   th: thick   <u>th</u>: this   zh: measure

Borzoi		
dog; publisher's imprint	BAWR-ZOI	'bɔːʳˌzɔi
Bosch		
1. Carl, *German chemist (Nobel 1931)*	BAWSH, BAHSH	'bɔːʃ, 'bɑʃ
2. Hieronymus, *Dutch painter*	BAWS, [$] BAHSH, BAWSH	'bɔːs, [$] 'bɑʃ, 'bɔːʃ
3. manufacturing co.	BAHSH, BAWSH	'bɑʃ, 'bɔːʃ
Bosco		
Philip Michael, *US actor*	BAHS-kō	'bɑskoː
Bose		
1. Satyendranath, *Indian scientist*	BŌS, BAWS, BAWSH, BŌZ	'boːs, 'bɔs, 'bɔːʃ, 'boːz
2. US audio co.	BŌZ	'boːz
Bosley		
Tom, *US actor; pers. name*	BAHZ-lē	'bɑzliˑ
Bosna-Hercegovina		
republic, E Europe	BAHS-nuh-HERT-suh-GŌ-vē-nuh, -GŌ-vuh-nuh	'bɑsnə'heʳtsəˌgoːviːnə, -ˌgoːvənə
Bosnia and Herzegovina		
republic, E Europe	BAHZ-nē-uh uhn(d) HERT-suh-gō-VĒ-nuh, HERT-suh-GŌ-vuh-nuh, HUHRT-	'bɑzniːə ən(d) ˌheʳtsəgoː'viːnə, ˌheʳtsə'goːvənə, ˌhəʳt-
Bosporus		
strait, Turkey	BAHS-p(uh-)ruhs	'bɑsp(ə)rəs
Bosque		
county, TX	BAHS-kē	'bɑskiˑ
Bosque Redondo		
Indian reservation, US	BAHSK ri-DAHN-dō	'bɑsk ri'dɑndoː
Bosse		
Field, *ballpark, Evansville, IL*	BAWS, BAHS	'bɔːs, 'bɑs
Bossier		
parish, LA	BŌ-zhuhr	'boːʒəʳ
Boston		
city, MA; mts., AR; borough, England	BAW-stuhn	'bɔːstən
Boston Camerata		
chamber orchestra and chorus, MA	BAW-stuhn KAHM-uh-RAHT-uh	ˌbɔːstən ˌkɑmə'rɑt̬ə
Bostwick		
Barry, *US actor*	BAHS-twik	'bɑstwik
Boswell		
pers. name	BAHZ-WEL, -wuhl	'bɑzˌwel, -wəl
Bosworth Field		
English battlefield	BAHZ-wuhrth FĒLD	ˌbɑzwəʳθ 'fiːld
Botany Bay		
inlet, former penal colony, Australia	BAHT-n-ē BĀ, BAHT-nē	'bɑtn̩iˑ 'beː, 'bɑtniˑ
Botetourt		
county, VA	BAHT-uh-TAHT, BŌT-uh-TAWRT	'bɑt̬əˌtɑt, 'boːt̬əˌtɔːʳt
Botha		
P. W., *S. African political leader*	BU-uh-tah, [$] BŌT-uh	'buətɑː, [$] 'boːt̬ə
Bothe		
Walther, *German physicist (Nobel 1954)*	BŌT-uh	'boːt̬ə
Bothnia		
gulf, Baltic Sea	BAHTH-nē-uh	'bɑθniːə

Foreign Sounds: ue: *Fr.* **rue**, *Ger.* **füllen** uh(r): *Fr.* **boeuf**, *Ger.* **Höhle** kh: *Ger.* **ich**, *Scot.* **loch** ḡ: *Sp.* **amigo** v̲: *Sp.* **hablar** hl: *Welsh* **Llanelli**. CAPITALS: primary stress. SMALL CAPS: secondary stress. [$]: U.S. pron. [£]: British pron.

Botswana
  republic, Africa   baht-SWAHN-uh   bɑt'swɑnə

Botticelli
  Sandro, *Italian artist; game*   BAHT-uh-CHEL-ē   ˌbɑtə'tʃeliˑ

Botticino
  Italian wine   BAHT-uh-CHĒ-nō   ˌbɑtə'tʃiːnoˑ

Bottineau
  county, ND   BAHT-n-Ō, BAHT-uh-NŌ   ˌbɑtn̩'oˑ, ˌbɑtə'noˑ

Boubou
  bird   BOO-BOO   'buˑˌbuˑ

Boucher
  François, *French painter*   boo-SHĀ   buˑʃeˑ

Bouches-du-Rhône
  dept, France   boosh-(uh-)due-RŌN   buˑʃ(ə)dyːroːn

Boudicca [Boadicea]
  ancient British queen   boo-DIK-uh   buˑ'dikə

Bougainville
  island, Pacific   BOO-guhn-VIL, BŌ-guhn-, BUG-uhn-   'buːgən,vil, 'boːgən-, 'bugən-

Bougainvillea
  plant   BOO-guhn-VIL-yuh, BŌ-, BUG-uhn-, -VĒ-(y)uh   ˌbuːgən'viljə, ˌboː-, ˌbugən-, -'viː(j)ə

Bouguereau
  Adolphe-William, *French painter*   boo-GRŌ, boo-guh-RŌ   buːgroˑ, buːgəroˑ

Boulanger
  Nadia, *French music teacher/ conductor*   boo-lahⁿ-ZHĀ   buːlɑ̃ʒeˑ

Boulder
  city, CO   BŌL-duhr   'boːldəʳ

Boule
  ancient Athenian council   BOO-lē, boo-LĀ   'buːliˑ, buː'leˑ

Bouleuterion
  ancient Athenian council building   BOO-L(Y)OO-TIR-ē-AHN   ˌbuːˌl(j)uː'tiriːˌɑn

Boulez
  Pierre, *French composer, conductor*   boo-LEZ   buːlez

Boulogne
  seaport, France   boo-LAWN-yuh, Ⓢ boo-LŌN, boo-LOIN   buːlɔːɲ, Ⓢ buːˈloːn, buːˈlɔin

Boulogne-sur-Mer
  seaport, France   boo-lawn-yuh-suer-MER   buːlɔːɲsyːrmer

Boult
  Sir Adrian, *English conductor*   BŌLT   'boːlt

Boumédienne
  Mohammed, *Algerian politician*   boo-mād-YEN   buːmeːdjen

Boun Pimay
  Laotian festival   BŌN pim-Ī   'boːn pim'ai

Bourbon
  1. county, KA, KY; alcoholic beverage   BUHR-buhn   'bəʳbən
  2. French royal family   boor-BAWⁿ   buˑrbõ

Bourbonnais
  prov, France   boor-baw-NE, Ⓢ BUR-buh-NĀ   buːrboːne, Ⓢ ˌbuʳbə'neˑ

Key (col. 2):   a: fad   ā: fade   ah: father   ar: Mary   aw: law   e: fed   ē: feed   er: merry   i: hid   ī: hide   ō: coat   ōō: boot
oi: boy   ow: now   u: put   uh: above   uhr: bird   ch: chop   ng: ring   sh: show   th: thick   <u>th</u>: this   zh: measure

Bourgeois		
Léon, *French politician (Nobel 1920)*	bur-ZHWAH	burʒwɑː
Bourgogne [Burgundy]		
former kingdom, region, France	bo͞or-GAWN-yuh	buːrgɔːɲ
Bourgueil		
French wine	bur-GUH(R)-yuh, Ⓢ bawr-GĪ, bur-	burgœj, Ⓢ bɔːʳ'gɑi, buʳ-
Bourguiba		
Habib, *president, Tunisia*	bur-GĒ-buh	buʳ'giːbə
Bourj Barajneh		
Palestinian refugee camp, Beirut	BURZH buh-RAHZH-nuh	'buʳʒ bə'rɑʒnə
Bournemouth		
town, England	BAWRN-muhth, BURN-muhth	'bɔːʳnməθ, 'buʳnməθ
Bourse		
European stock exchange	BURS, BŌRS, BAWRS	'buʳs, 'boːʳs, 'bɔːʳs
Boutros		
pers. name (B. Boutros-Ghali)	BO͞O-trōs, BO͞O-truhs	'buːtroːs, 'buːtrəs
Boutros-Ghali		
Boutros, *UN Secretary General*	BO͞O-trōs-ḠAHL-ē, Ⓢ BO͞O-trōs-GAHL-ē, BO͞O-truhs-	ˌbuːtroːs'ɣɑliˑ, Ⓢ ˌbuːtroːs'gɑliˑ, ˌbuːtrəs-
Bouvet		
Norwegian island, Atlantic	BO͞O-vā	'buːveː
Bouvier		
family name	BO͞O-vē-Ā, bo͞ov-YĀ	'buːviːˌeː, buːv'jeː
Bouvier des Flandres		
dog breed	BO͞O-vē-Ā duh FLAN-duhrz, FLAH^{n}DR	ˌbuːviː'eː də 'flændəʳz, 'flɑ̃dr
Bovary		
Madame, *character, G. Flaubert*	bō-vah-RĒ, Ⓢ BŌ-v(uh-)rē	boːvɑːriː, Ⓢ 'boːv(ə)riˑ
Bovet		
Daniel, *Italian pharmacologist (Nobel 1957)*	bō-VĀ	boː'veː
Bowdoin		
College, *ME*	BŌD-n	'boːdn̩
Bowery		
district, New York City	BOW-(uh-)rē	'bɑu(ə)riˑ
Bowie		
1. Jim, *American soldier & pioneer; knife*	BO͞O-ē, BŌ-ē	'buːiˑ, 'boːiˑ
2. David, *British rock musician*	BŌ-ē	'boːiˑ
Bowral		
town, Australia	BOW-ruhl	'bɑurəl
Bowyer		
pers. name	BŌ-yuhr, BOI-(y)uhr	'boːjəʳ, 'bɔi(j)əʳ
Box Butte		
county, NE	BAHKS-BYO͞OT	'bɑksˌbjuːt
Boxer		
dog breed	BAHK-suhr	'bɑksəʳ
Boyacá		
dept, Colombia	boi-yuh-KAH	bɔijə'kɑ
Boyanup		
town, Australia	BOI-(y)uh-NUHP	'bɔi(j)əˌnəp
Boyd		
pers. name	BOID	'bɔid

Foreign Sounds: ue: *Fr.* **rue**, *Ger.* **fü**llen uh(r): *Fr.* b**oeu**f, *Ger.* H**ö**hle kh: *Ger.* i**ch**, *Scot.* lo**ch** ḡ: *Sp.* ami**g**o v̱: *Sp.* ha**b**lar hl: *Welsh* **Ll**anelli. CAPITALS: primary stress. SMALL CAPS: secondary stress. Ⓢ: U.S. pron. [£]: British pron.

Boyd Orr		
John, *Scottish nutritionist (Nobel 1949)*	BOID AWR	'bɔid 'ɔː^{r}
Boylan		
John Patrick, *US record producer, songwriter*	BOI-luhn	'bɔilən
Boyne		
Irish river, battle site	BOIN	'bɔin
Boynton		
pers. name	BOINT-n	'bɔintn̩
Boz		
pen name of C. Dickens	BAHZ, BŌZ *(Dickens' pronunc.)*	'bɑz, 'boːz *(Dickens' pronunc.)*
Bozcaada		
Turkish island, Aegean	BŌZ-jah-DAH	ˌboːzdʒɑ'dɑ
Brabançonne, La		
see La Brabançonne		
Brabant		
former duchy of Netherlands; prov, Belgium	bruh-BANT, bruh-BAHNT	brə'bænt, brə'bɑnt
Brabantio		
character in Othello, *Shakespeare*	bruh-BANT-ē-ō, bruh-BAN(T)-shē-ō	brə'bæntiːoː, brə'bæn(t)ʃiːoː
Brachiosaurus		
dinosaur	BRAK-ē-uh-SAWR-uhs	ˌbrækiːə'sɔːrəs
Bracknell		
Lady, *character in* The Importance of Being Earnest, *O. Wilde*	BRAK-nl, BRAK-nuhl	'bræknl̩, 'bræknəl
Bradbury		
Ray, *US author*	BRAD-BER-ē, BRAD-b(uh-)rē	'brædˌberiˑ, 'brædb(ə)riˑ
Bradenton		
city, FL	BRĀD-n-tuhn	'breːdn̩tən
Bradford		
city, PA; pers. name	BRAD-fuhrd	'brædfə^{r}d
Bradley		
pers. name	BRAD-lē	'brædliˑ
Braemar		
village, Scotland	brā-MAHR	breː'mɑ^{r}
Braga		
prov & town, Portugal	BRAHG-uh	'brɑːgə
Bragança		
prov & town, Portugal; city, Brazil	bruh-GAH^{n}N-suh	brə'gɑ̃nsə
Bragg		
Sir William H. *& his son* Sir W. Lawrence, *English physicists (Nobel 1915)*	BRAG	'bræg
Brahe		
Tycho, *Danish astronomer*	BRAH-huh, [S] BRAH(-hē)	'brɑːhə, [S] 'brɑ(hiː)
Brahma		
1. Hindu universal soul; Hindu god, member of supreme triad	BRAHM-uh	'brɑmə
2. breed of cattle and fowl	BRĀ-muh, BRAHM-uh, BRAM-uh	'breːmə, 'brɑmə, 'bræmə
Brahman, -min		
1. high caste Hindu	BRAHM-uhn	'brɑmən
2. breed of cattle and fowl	BRĀ-muhn, BRAHM-uhn, BRAM-uhn	'breːmən, 'brɑmən, 'bræmən

Key (col. 2): a: **fad** ā: **fade** ah: **father** ar: **Mary** aw: **law** e: **fed** ē: **feed** er: **merry** i: **hid** ī: **hide** ō: **coat** o͞o: **boot** oi: **boy** ow: **now** u: **put** uh: **above** uhr: **bird** ch: **chop** ng: **ring** sh: **show** th: **thick** t͟h: **this** zh: **measure**

Brahmanic
  pert. to Brahman Hindus   bruh-MAHN-ik, bruh-MAN-ik   brə'mɑnik, brə'mænik

Brahmanism
  religion   BRAHM-uh-NIZ-uhm, BRAH-muh-   'brɑmə,nizəm, 'brɑːmə-

Brahmaputra
  river, Tibet, China   BRAHM-uh-P(Y)O͞O-truh   ˌbrɑmə'p(j)uːtrə

Brahmin
  high caste Hindu; upper-class New   BRAHM-uhn, BRAH-muhn   'brɑmən, 'brɑːmən
    Englander

Brahmoism
  Hindu doctrine   BRAHM-uh-WIZ-uhm,   'brɑmə,wizəm,
     BRAH-muh-WIZ-uhm   'brɑːmə,wizəm

Brahms
  Johannes, *German composer*   BRAHMS, Ⓢ BRAHMZ   'brɑms, Ⓢ 'brɑmz

Brahui
  lang., people, Pakistan   brah-HO͞O-ē   brɑ'huːiˑ

Braille
  Louis, *French teacher of the blind;*   BRAH-yuh, Ⓢ BRĀL   brɑj, Ⓢ 'breːl
    system of writing for the blind

Brainerd
  Community College, *MN*   BRĀ-nuhrd   'breːnəʳd

Braintree
  town, MA   BRĀN-trē   'breːntriː

Bramwell
  pers. name   BRAM-wuhl, -WEL   'bræmwəl, -,wel

Branagan
  Laura, *US singer*   BRAN-uh-guhn   'brænəgən

Brancacci
  chapel, Italy   brahn-KAHT-chē   brɑn'kattʃiˑ

Branchus
  founder of the oracle at Didymas   BRANG-kuhs   'bræŋkəs

Brancusi
  Constantin, *Romanian sculptor*   BRAHN-ko͞osh, Ⓢ bran-KO͞O-sē   'brɑnkuːʃ, Ⓢ bræn'kuːsiˑ

Brandeis
  University, *MA*   BRAN-DĪS   'bræn,dɑis

Brandenburg
  city, Germany   BRAHN-duhn-BURK,   'brɑndən,buʳk,
     Ⓢ BRAN-duhn-BUHRG   Ⓢ 'brændən,bəʳg

Brandi
  pers. name   BRAN-dē   'brændiˑ

Brando
  Marlon, *US actor*   BRAN-dō   'brændoː

Brandon
  pers. name   BRAN-duhn   'brændən

Brandt
  Willy, *W. German chancellor*   BRAHNT, BRANT   'brɑnt, 'brænt
    (Nobel 1971)

Brandy
  alcoholic beverage; pers. name   BRAN-dē   'brændiˑ

Branford
  pers. name   BRAN-fuhrd   'brænfəʳd

Braniff
  US airline   BRAN-uhf   'brænəf

Foreign Sounds: ue: *Fr.* **rue**, *Ger.* **füllen**   uh(r): *Fr.* **boeuf**, *Ger.* **Höhle**   <u>kh</u>: *Ger.* **ich**, *Scot.* **loch**   ḡ: *Sp.* **amigo**   ṿ: *Sp.* **hablar**
hl: *Welsh* **Llanelli**.   CAPITALS: primary stress.   SMALL CAPS: secondary stress.   Ⓢ: U.S. pron.   Ⓛ: British pron.

Branting
   Karl Hjalmar, *Swedish statesman*   BRAHNT-ing, ⑤ BRANT-ing   'brɑːntiŋ, ⑤ 'bræntiŋ
   (Nobel 1921)

Branwen
   pers. name   BRAN-wuhn, BRAHN-, -WEN   'brænwən, 'brɑːn-, -ˌwen

Braque
   Georges, *French painter*   BRAHK   brɑːk

Brasenose
   college, Oxford Univ.   BRĀZ-NŌZ   'breɪz,noːz

Brasidas
   Spartan general   BRAS-uhd-uhs   'bræsədəs

Brasilia
   capital city, Brazil   bruh-ZIL-yuh, bruh-ZĒL-yuh   brə'ziljə, brə'ziːljə

Brasseurs Biere de Paris
   French beer   brah-SUHR BYER-uh duh pah-RĒ   brɑːsœr bjerə də pɑːriː

Brassin de Garde Saint Leonard
   French beer   brah-SEⁿ duh GAHRD seⁿ lā-aw-NAHR   brɑːsẽ də gɑːrd sẽ leːɔːnɑːr

Bratislava
   capital, Slovakia   BRAHT-uh-SLAHV-uh, BRAT-   ˌbrɑtə'slavə, ˌbræt̮-

Bratsk
   city, Russia   BRAHTSK   'brɑːtsk

Brattain
   Walter, *US physicist (Nobel 1956)*   BRAT-n   'brætn̩

Brattleboro
   town, VT   BRAT-l-BUHR-uh, BRAT-l-BUH-ruh   'brætl̩,bər-ə, 'brætl̩,bə-rə

Braun
   1. C. F., *German physicist (Nobel 1909);* Wernher von, *US engineer*   BROWN, ⑤ BRAWN   'braun, ⑤ 'brɔːn
   2. housewares co.   BRAWN   'brɔːn

Brauneberg
   German wine   BROWN-uh-BERK   'braunə,beʳk

Braunschweig
   prov & town, Germany   BROWN-SHFĪK, ⑤ BROWN-SHWĪG   'braun,ʃfaik, ⑤ 'braun,ʃwaig

Braverman
   Charles Dell, *US film producer, director*   BRĀ-vuhr-muhn   'breɪvəʳmən

Brazil
   republic, S. America   bruh-ZIL   brə'zil

Brazilian
   pert. to Brazil   bruh-ZIL-yuhn   brə'ziljən

Brazoria
   county, TX   bruh-ZŌR-ē-uh, bruh-ZAWR-ē-uh   brə'zoːriə, brə'zɔːriə

Brazos
   river, county, TX   BRAZ-uhs   'bræzəs

Brazosport
   College, *TX*   BRAZ-uh-SPAWRT   'bræzə,spɔːʳt

Brazzaville
   city, Congo   BRAZ-uh-VIL, BRAHZ-uh-VĒL   'bræzə,vil, 'brɑzə,viːl

Bream
   Julian, *British guitarist*   BRĒM   'briːm

Breathalyser
   tdmk for an alcohol tester   BRETH-uh-LĪ-zuhr   'breθə,laizəʳ

Key (col. 2): a: fad ā: fade ah: father ar: Mary aw: law e: fed ē: feed er: merry i: hid ī: hide ō: coat ōō: boot
oi: boy ow: now u: put uh: above uhr: bird ch: chop ng: ring sh: show th: thick th: this zh: measure

Breathed
   Berke, *US cartoonist*   BRETH-uhd   'breθəd

Breathitt
   county, KY   BRETH-uht   'breθət

Brébeuf
   Jean de, *French explorer*   brä-BUH(R)F   breːbœf

Brecht
   Bertolt, *German playwright/poet*   BREKHT, BREKT   'breçt, 'brekt

Breckinridge
   John C., *US vice president*   BREK-uhn-RIJ   'brekən‚ridʒ

Brecknockshire
   former county, Wales   BREK-nuhk-shuhr, BREK-NAHK-,   'breknəkʃəʳ, 'brek‚nɑk-,
                                -SHIR   -‚ʃiʳ

Breda
   city, Netherlands   brä-DAH   breːˈdɑ

Bremen
   1. city, GA, IN   BREM-uhn   'bremən
   2. city, state, Germany   BRĀ-muhn, Ⓢ BREM-uhn,   'breːmən, Ⓢ 'bremən,

Bremerhaven
   seaport, Germany   BRĀ-muhr-HAHF-uhn,   'breːməʳ‚hafən,
                        Ⓢ BREM-uhr-HAHV-uhn   Ⓢ 'breməʳ‚havən

Brenau
   College, GA   BREN-OW   'bren‚ɑu

Brenda
   pers. name   BREN-duh   'brendə

Brendan
   pers. name   BREN-duhn   'brendən

Bren gun
   submachine gun   BREN GUHN   'bren ‚gən

Brennan
   William Joseph, Jr., *US Supreme* BREN-uhn   'brenən
      Court justice

Brenner
   mtn. pass, Tirol Alps   BREN-uhr PAS   'brenəʳ 'pæs

Brent
   borough, England   BRENT   'brent

Brenton
   pers. name   BRENT-n   'brentṇ

Brescia
   1. College, KY   BRESH-uh   'breʃə
   2. prov & town, Italy   BRĀ-shuh, BRESH-uh   'breːʃə, 'breʃə

Breslau [Wrocław]
   city , Poland   BRES-LOW   'bres‚lɑu

Brest
   port, France   BREST   brest

Brest-Litovsk
   city, Belorussia   BREST-luh-TAWFSK   ‚brestlə'tɔːfsk

Bret, Brett
   pers. name   BRET   'bret

Bretagne [Brittany]
   prov, France   bruh-TAHN-yuh   brətɑːɲ

Breton
   Celtic people, lang., Brittany   BRET-n   'bretṇ

Foreign Sounds: ue: *Fr.* **rue**, *Ger.* **füllen**   uh(r): *Fr.* **boeuf**, *Ger.* **Höhle**   <u>kh</u>: *Ger.* i**ch**, *Scot.* lo**ch**   g̃: *Sp.* ami**g**o   <u>v</u>: *Sp.* ha**b**lar
hl: *Welsh* **Ll**anelli.   CAPITALS: primary stress.   SMALL CAPS: secondary stress.   Ⓢ: U.S. pron.   Ⓛ: British pron.

Breuer
   Marcel, *US architect, furniture*   BROI(-uh)r   'brɔi(ə)ʳ
      designer
Breughel
   see Brueghel
Brevard
   county, FL; town, college, NC   bruh-VAHRD   brə'vɑʳd
Brewarrina
   town, Australia   bruh-WAHR-uh-nuh   brə'wɑrənə
Brewster
   pers. name   BROO-stuhr   'bruːstəʳ
Brezhnev
   Leonid, *president, USSR*   BREZH-nyuhf, BREZH-NEF   'breʒnjəf, 'breʒ,nef
Brian
   1. pers. name   BRĪ-uhn   'brɑiən
   2. Irish Gaelic   BRĒ-uhn   'briːən
Brian Boru
   Irish king   BRĒ-uhn buh-ROO, BRĪ-uhn   ,briːən bə'ruː, ,brɑiən
Briand
   Aristide, *French statesman (Nobel*   brē-AHⁿ   briːɑ̃
      1926)
Briard
   dog breed   brē-AHR(D)   briː'ɑʳ(d)
Briareus
   hundred-armed monster in Greek   brē-AR-ē-uhs, brī-   briː'æriːəs, brɑi-
      mythology
Brice
   Fanny, *US entertainer; pers. name*   BRĪS   'brɑis
Bridalveil
   waterfall, Yosemite National Park   BRĪD-l-VĀL   'brɑidl̩,veːl
Brideshead
   estate in E. Waugh novels   BRĪDZ-HED   'brɑidz,hed
Bridgeport
   city, AL, CT   BRIJ-PŌRT, BRIJ-PAWRT   'bridʒ,poːʳt, 'bridʒ,pɔːʳt
Bridget
   pers. name   BRIJ-uht   'bridʒət
Bridgetown
   city, Barbados; town, Canada   BRIJ-TOWN   'bridʒ,tɑun
Bridgman
   P. W., *US physicist (Nobel 1946)*   BRIJ-muhn   'bridʒmən
Bridlington
   town, England   BRID-ling-tuhn, *(locally)*   'bridliŋtən, *(locally)*
       BUHR-ling-tuhn, BAW-ling-tuhn   'bəʳliŋtən, 'bɔːliŋtən
Bridport
   town, England   BRID-PAWRT   'brid,pɔːʳt
Brie
   region, France; cheese   BRĒ   'briː
Brienz
   lake, Switzerland   brē-EN(T)S   briː'en(t)s
Brienzer See [Brienz]
   lake, Switzerland   brē-EN(T)-suhr ZĀ   briː'en(t)səʳ ,zeː
Brigadoon
   Lerner & Loewe musical   BRIG-uh-DOON   ,brigə'duːn
Brighton
   town, England   BRĪT-n   'brɑitn̩

Key (col. 2):   a: fad   ā: fade   ah: father   ar: Mary   aw: law   e: fed   ē: feed   er: merry   i: hid   ī: hide   ō: coat   ōō: boot
oi: boy   ow: now   u: put   uh: above   uhr: bird   ch: chop   ng: ring   sh: show   th: thick   <u>th</u>: this   zh: measure

Brigid
  pers. name — BRIJ-uhd — 'brɪdʒəd
Brigitta
  1. pers. name, Italian — brē-JĔT-tah — briːˈdʒiːttɑ
  2. Swedish — bri-GĔ-tah — briˈgiːtɑː
Brigitte
  1. pers. name — BRIJ-uht, BRIZH-uht, bruh-ZHĔT — 'brɪdʒət, 'brɪʒət, brəˈʒiːt
  2. French — brē-ZHĔT — briːʒiːt
Brill
  E.J., Dutch publishing co. — BRIL — 'brɪl
Brillo
  tdmk for a cleaning pad — BRIL-ō — 'brɪloː
Brindisi
  prov & town, Italy — BRIN-duh-zē, BRĔN-duh-zē — 'brɪndəziˑ, 'briːndəziˑ
Brinell number/test/hardness
  measurements for metals & alloys — bruh-NEL — brəˈnel
Brinkley
  David, *US news commentator* — BRING-klē — 'brɪŋkliˑ
Brinley
  pers. name — BRIN-lē — 'brɪnliˑ
Brinsley
  pers. name — BRINZ-lē — 'brɪnzliˑ
Brisa Cerveza Ligera
  Mexican beer — BRĔ-sah ser-VĂ-sah lē-<u>KH</u>ER-ah — 'briːsɑ serˈveːsɑ liːˈxerɑ
Brisbane
  city, Australia — BRIZ-buhn, BRIZ-BĂN — 'brɪzbən, 'briz,beːn
Brisco-Hooks
  Valerie, *US Olympic track and field athlete* — BRIS-kō-HUKS — ˌbriskoːˈhuks
Briseis
  favorite slave of Achilles — bruh-SĂ-uhs — brəˈseːəs
Brises
  father of Briseis — BRĪ-sēz — 'brɑisiːz
Bristol
  city, England — BRIST-l — 'brɪstl̩
Bristol-Myers Squibb
  US pharmaceutical co. — BRIST-l-MĪ(-uh)r(z) SKWIB — ˌbrɪstl̩,mɑi(ə)ʳ(z) 'skwib
Britain
  kingdom, Europe — BRIT-n — 'brɪtn̩
Britannia
  literary term for Great Britain — bruh-TAN-yuh, bruh-TAN-ē-uh — brəˈtænjə, brəˈtæniːə
Britannic
  pert. to Britain — bruh-TAN-ik — brəˈtænik
Briticism
  British English usage — BRIT-uh-SIZ-uhm, BRIT-uh-SHIZ-uhm — 'brɪtə,sizəm, 'brɪtə,ʃizəm
British
  pert. to Britain — BRIT-ish — 'brɪtɪʃ
British Columbia
  province, Canada — BRIT-ish kuh-LUHM-bē-uh — ˌbrɪtɪʃ kəˈləmbiːə
Britisher
  person from Britain — BRIT-uh-shuhr — 'brɪtəʃəʳ
Britomartis
  Cretan goddess — BRIT-uh-MAHRT-uhs — ˌbrɪtəˈmɑʳtəs
Briton
  inhabitant of Britain — BRIT-n — 'brɪtn̩

Brittanica *encyclopedia*	bri-TAN-i-kuh	bri'tænikə
Brittany [Bretagne] *prov, France; pers. name*	BRIT-n-ē, BRIT-nē	'britn̩iˑ, 'britniˑ
Brixham *town, England*	BRIK-suhm	'briksəm
Brno *city, Czech republic*	BUHR-nō	'bəʳnoː
Brobdingnag *fictional land created by Jonathan Swift*	BRAHB-ding-NAG, BRAHB-dig-NAG	'brɑbdiŋˌnæg, 'brɑbdigˌnæg
Brobdingnagian *inhabitant of* Brobdingnag	BRAHB-ding-NAG-ē-uhn, BRAHB-dig-NAG-ē-uhn	ˌbrɑbdiŋ'nægiːən, ˌbrɑbdig'nægiːən
Broca Pierre Paul, *French surgeon*	braw-KAH, $ brō-KAH	brɔːkɑː, $ broː'kɑ
Broca's area *speech center of brain*	brō-KAHZ	broː'kɑz
Broccoli Albert Romolo, *US film producer*	BRAHK-(uh-)lē	'brɑk(ə)liˑ
Brock Karena Diane, *ballerina*	BRAHK	'brɑk
Brodie *pers. name*	BRŌD-ē	'broːdiˑ
Brodsky Joseph, *Russian-born US poet (Nobel 1987)*	BRAWT-ski; $ BRAHT-skē, BRAHD-skē	'brɔːtskʲij; $ 'brɑtskiˑ, 'brɑdskiˑ
Broederbond *Afrikaner group*	BRO͞OD-uhr-BAWNT, $ BRO͞OD-uhr-BAHNT, -BAHND	'bruːdəʳˌbɔːnt, $ 'bruˑdəʳˌbɑnt, -ˌbɑnd
Broglie, de Louis, *French physicist (Nobel 1929)*	duh BRAW-yuh, duh BROI	də brɔːj, də brɔi
Brokaw Tom, *US broadcast journalist*	BRŌ-KAW	'broːˌkɔː
Broke Arthur, *English poet;* Sir Philip, *English naval officer*	BRUK	'bruk
Brolin James, *US actor*	BRŌ-luhn	'broːlən
Brolio *Italian wine*	BRŌL-yō	'broːljoː
bromine *element*	BRŌ-MĒN	'broːˌmiːn
Bromley *borough, England*	BRUHM-lē, BRAHM-lē	'brəmliˑ, 'brɑmliˑ
Bronislaw *pers. name*	brahn-Ē-slahf, BRAHN-uhs-LAHF	brɑn'iːslaf, 'brɑnəsˌlaf
Bronisław *pers. name, Polish*	braw-NĒ-slahf	brɔː'niːsłaːf
Bronowski Jacob, *British mathematician*	bruh-NAWF-skē, bruh-NAHF-skē	brə'nɔːfskiˑ, brə'nɑfskiˑ
Bronstein Arthur J., *US phonetician; pers. name*	BRAHN-STĒN	'brɑnˌstiːn

Key (col. 2): a: **fad** ā: **fade** ah: **father** ar: **Mary** aw: **law** e: **fed** ē: **feed** er: **merry** i: **hid** ī: **hide** ō: **coat** o͞o: **boot** oi: **boy** ow: **now** u: **put** uh: **above** uhr: **bird** ch: **chop** ng: **ring** sh: **show** th: **thick** t͟h: **this** zh: **measure**

Brontë
  family of English authors   BRAHNT-ē, BRAHN-tā   'brɑnti', 'brɑnteː

Brontosaurus
  dinosaur (Apatosaurus)   BRAHNT-uh-SAWR-uhs   ˌbrɑntə'sɔːrəs

Bronwen
  pers. name   BRAHN-wuhn, -WEN   'brɑnwən, -ˌwen

Bronwyn
  pers. name   BRAHN-wuhn   'brɑnwən

Bronx
  river, NY; borough, New York City   BRAHNGKS   'brɑŋks

Brook, Brooke
  pers. name   BRUK   'bruk

Brooklyn
  borough, New York City   BRUK-luhn   'bruklən

Brooks
  Van Wyck, historian; pers. name   BRUKS   'bruks

Broome
  county, NY   BROOM, BRUM   'bruːm, 'brum

Brothers Karamazov, The
  novel, Dostoyevsky   KAR-uh-MAHD-zawf   ˌkærə'mɑdˌzɔf

Brougham
  1. Henry Peter, English statesman   BRUM, BROO(-uh)m, BRŌ(-uh)m, BRAWM   'brum, 'bruː(ə)m, 'broː(ə)m, 'brɔm
  2. carriage or automoblie   BROO(-uh)m, BRŌ(-uh)m, BRAWM   'bruː(ə)m, 'broː(ə)m, 'brɔm

Brouilly
  wine region, France   broo-YĒ   bruːjiː

Broward
  county, FL   BROW-uhrd   'brauəʳd

Brower
  David Ross, US conservationist   BROW(-uh)r   'brau(ə)ʳ

Brown
  pers. name   BROWN   'brɑun

Browne
  Sir Thomas, English author   BROWN   'brɑun

Brownie
  fictional elf; pers. name   BROW-nē   'brɑuni'

Browning
  Robert & Elizabeth Barrett, English poets; pers. name   BROW-ning   'brɑuniŋ

Broz [Tito]
  Josip, Yugoslav statesman   BRAWZ, BRŌZ   'brɔːz, 'broːz

Brubeck
  Dave, US jazz musician   BROO-BEK   'bruːˌbek

Bruce
  pers. name   BROOS   'bruːs

Bruckner
  Anton, Austrian composer/organist   BRUK-nuhr   'bruknəʳ

Brueghel, Bruegel, Breughel
  family of Flemish painters   BRUH(R)-ğuhl, Ⓢ BROI-guhl   'brœːɣəl, Ⓢ 'brɔigəl

Bruges
  town, Belgium   BRUEZH, BROOZH   'bryːʒ, 'bruːʒ

Brugge [Bruges]
  town, Belgium   BRUEG-uh   'bryːgə

Brugh na Boinne
  prehistoric burial site, Ireland   BROO nuh BOIN   ˌbruː nə 'boin

---

Foreign Sounds: ue: *Fr.* **rue**, *Ger.* f**ü**llen uh(r): *Fr.* b**oeu**f, *Ger.* H**ö**hle <u>kh</u>: *Ger.* i**ch**, *Scot.* lo**ch** ğ: *Sp.* ami**g**o v̲: *Sp.* ha**b**lar
hl: *Welsh* L**l**anelli.   CAPITALS: primary stress. SMALL CAPS: secondary stress. Ⓢ: U.S. pron. Ⓛ: British pron.

Bruichladdich
  Scotch whiskey   BROO̅-ich-LAD-ē   ˌbruːitʃˈlædiˑ

Brule
  county, SD   BROO̅L, BROO̅-lē   ˈbruːl, ˈbruːliˑ

Brumaire
  month, French Revolutionary   brue-MER   bryːmer
    calendar

Brummell
  George Bryan (Beau), English   BRUHM-uhl   ˈbrəməl
    dandy

Brundisium
  ancient name of Brindisi   BRUHN-DIZH(-ē)-uhm   ˌbrənˈdiʒ(iː)əm

Brunei
  river, sultanate, Borneo   bru-NĪ, BROO̅-NĪ   bruˈnai, ˈbruːˌnai

Bruneian
  pert. to Brunei   bru-NĪ-uhn, BROO̅-NĪ-uhn   bruˈnaiən, ˈbruːˌnaiən

Brunei Darussalam
  official name for Brunei   bru-NĪ DAHR-uh-suh-LAHM   bruˈnai ˌdarəsəˈlam

Brunelleschi
  Filippo, Florentine architect   BROO̅N-l-ES-kē   ˌbruːnl̩ˈeskiˑ

Brunhild
  German legendary heroine   BROO̅N-HILT   ˈbruːn̩ˌhilt

Brunhilde, Brunnhilde
  German legendary heroine   broo̅n-HIL-duh   bruˈn̩ˈhildə

Brünnhilde
  German form of Brunhilde   bruen-HIL-duh, Ⓢ broo̅n-HIL-duh   bryːnˈhildə, Ⓢ bruˈn̩ˈhildə

Bruno
  1. pers. name   BROO̅-nō   ˈbruːnoː
  2. French   brue-NÔ   brynoː
  3. German, Italian, Swedish   BROO̅-nō   ˈbruːnoː
  4. Lithuanian   BRUN-aw   ˈbrunɔː

Brunswick
  city, GA, OH; prov & town,   BRUHNZ-wik   ˈbrənzwik
    Germany

Brussel [Brussels]
  city, Belgium   BRUES-uhl   ˈbrysəl

Brussels
  city, Belgium   BRUHS-uhlz   ˈbrəsəlz

Brussels griffon
  dog breed   BRUHS-uhlz GRIF-uhn   ˈbrəsəlz ˈgrifən

Brut
  1. cologne brand; English or   BROO̅T   ˈbruːt
    French Arthurian chronicle
  2. Welsh chronicle   BRUED, BRID, Ⓢ BRIT   ˈbryd, ˈbrid, Ⓢ ˈbrit

Brutus
  pers. name   BROO̅T-uhs   ˈbruːtʃəs

Bruxelles [Brussels]
  city, Belgium   brue-SEL   bryːsel

Bryan
  William Jennings, US lawyer,   BRĪ-uhn   ˈbraiən
    politician; pers. name

Bryansk
  city, Russia   brē-AHN(T)SK   briːˈɑn(t)sk

Bryant
  pers. name   BRĪ-uhnt   ˈbraiənt

Key (col. 2):   a: fad   ā: fade   ah: father   ar: Mary   aw: law   e: fed   ē: feed   er: merry   i: hid   ī: hide   ō: coat   o̅o̅: boot
oi: boy   ow: now   u: put   uh: above   uhr: bird   ch: chop   ng: ring   sh: show   th: thick   th̲: this   zh: measure

Brylcreem
   tdmk for a hair product   BRIL-KRÊM   'bril,kriːm

Bryn
   pers. name   BRIN   'brin

Brynhild
   Valkyrie in Scandinavian legend   BRIN-HILD   'brin,hild

Brynley
   pers. name   BRIN-lē   'brinliˑ

Bryn Mawr
   College, town, PA   BRIN MAWR, BRIN MAHR   ,brin 'mɔːʳ, ,brin 'maʳ

Brynmawr
   town, Wales   brin-MOWR, Ⓢ brin-MOW(-uh)r   brin'maur, Ⓢ brin'mau(ə)ʳ

Brynner
   Yul, US actor   BRIN-uhr   'brinəʳ

Brythonic
   branch of Celtic langs   brith-AHN-ik   briθ'ɑnik

Brzezinski
   Zbigniew, US statesman   bruh-ZHIN-skē, bruh-ZIN-skē, buhr-   brə'ʒinskiˑ, brə'zinskiˑ, bəʳ-

B'Shevat
   Jewish holiday   buh-shuh-VAHT, buhsh-VAHT   bəʃə'vat, bəʃ'vat

Bual
   Portuguese wine grape   BWAHL   'bwɑl

Buart Nark, Buat Nak
   Buddhist holy day   BWAHT NAHK, buh-WAHT NAHK   'bwɑˑt 'nɑk, bə'wɑˑt 'nɑk

Buber
   Martin, philosopher   B͞OO-buhr   'buːbəʳ

Bucaramanga
   city, Colombia   B͞OO-kuh-ruh-MAHNG-guh   ,buːkərə'mɑŋgə

Bucephalus
   horse of Alexander the Great   by͞oo-SEF-uh-luhs   bjuː'sefələs

Buchan
   John, Scottish author   BUH<u>KH</u>-uhn, BUHK-uhn   'bəxən, 'bəkən

Buchanan
   1. James, 15th US president;   by͞oo-KAN-uhn, byuh-   bjuˑ'kænən, bjə-
     James M., US economist (Nobel
     1986)
   2. US pl. name   by͞oo-KAN-uhn, buh-, byuh-   bjuˑ'kænən, bə-, bjə-

Bucharest
   city, Romania   B(Y)͞OO-kuh-REST   'b(j)uːkə,rest

Buchenwald
   Nazi concentration camp,   B͞OO-<u>kh</u>uhn-VAHLT,   'buːxən,valt,
     Germany   Ⓢ B͞OO-kuhn-WAWLD   Ⓢ 'buːkən,wɔːld

Buchmanism
   principles of Moral Rearmament   BUHK-muh-NIZ-uhm   'bəkmə,nizəm

Buchmanite
   one who believes in Buchmanism   BUHK-muh-NĪT   'bəkmə,nait

Buchner
   Eduard, German chemist (Nobel   B͞OOK-nuhr, BUK-nuhr   'buːknəʳ, 'buknəʳ
     1907)

Buchwald
   Art, US columnist   BUHK-WAWLD, BUK-WAWLD   'bək,wɔːld, 'buk,wɔːld

Buck
   Pearl S., US author (Nobel 1938)   BUHK   'bək

Foreign Sounds: **ue**: *Fr.* **rue**, *Ger.* f**ü**llen **uh(r)**: *Fr.* b**oeu**f, *Ger.* H**öh**le <u>kh</u>: *Ger.* i**ch**, *Scot.* lo**ch** **g̅**: *Sp.* ami**g**o **v̲**: *Sp.* ha**b**lar
hl: *Welsh* **Ll**anelli. CAPITALS: primary stress. SMALL CAPS: secondary stress. Ⓢ: U.S. pron. Ⓑ: British pron.

Buckingham
1. *borough, palace, England;*   BUHK-ing-uhm, BUHK-ing-HAM   'bəkiŋəm, 'bəkiŋˌhæm
   county, VA
2. Lindsey, *US rock musician*   BUHK-ing-HAM   'bəkiŋˌhæm

Buckinghamshire
county, England   BUHK-ing-uhm-shuhr,   'bəkiŋəmʃəʳ, 'bəkiŋəmˌʃiʳ
                                   BUHK-ing-uhm-SHIR

Buckley
William F., Jr., *US columnist,*   BUHK-lē   'bəkliˑ
editor, commentator

Buckminster
pers. name   BUHK-MIN(T)-stuhr   'bəkˌmin(t)stəʳ

Buckner
Bill, *US baseball player*   BUHK-nuhr   'bəknəʳ

Bucovina, Bukovina
region, Eastern/Central Europe   BOO-kuh-VĒ-nuh   ˌbuːkə'viːnə

Bucyrus
city, OH   byu-SĪ-ruhs   bju'sɑirəs

Bud
pers. name   BUHD   'bəd

Budapest
city, Hungary   BOOD-uh-PEST, BOOD-uh-PESHT, 'buːdəˌpest, 'buːdəˌpeʃt,
                                   BYOOD-   'bjuːd-

Buddha
founder of Buddhism   BUD-uh, BOOD-uh   'budə, 'buːdə

Buddha Visakha
Buddhist holiday   BUD-uh VISH-uh-kuh, BOOD-uh 'budə 'βiʃəkə, 'buːdə

Buddhism
religion   BOOD-IZ-uhm, BUD-IZ-uhm   'buːdˌizəm, 'budˌizəm

Buddleia
plant   BUHD-lē-uh   'bədliːə

Buddy
pers. name   BUHD-ē   'bədiˑ

Budé
French publisher   bue-DĀ   byːdeː

Buduma
lang., people, Chad   buh-DOO-muh   bə'duːmə

Budweiser
US beer   BUHD-WĪ-zuhr   'bədˌwɑizəʳ

Buel, Buell
pers. name   BYOOL, BYOO-uhl   'bjuːl, 'bjuːəl

Buena
borough, NJ   BYOO-nuh   'bjuːnə

Buena Park
city, CA   BYOO-nuh PAHRK   ˌbjuːnə 'pɑʳk

Buenaventura
city, Colombia   bwā-nah-vān-TYOO-rah,   bweːnɑβeːn'tjuːrɑ,
                                   Ⓢ BWEN-uh-ven-T(Y)UR-uh,   Ⓢ ˌbwenəven't(j)urə,
                                   BWĀ-nuh-   ˌbweːnə-

Buena Vista
1. *college, county, IA; lake, mtn.,* BYOO-nuh VIS-tuh   ˌbjuːnə 'vistə
   CA; city, GA, VA
2. *mtn., Costa Rica; island,*   BWĀ-nuh VĒS-tuh   ˌbweːnə 'viːstə
   Pacific

Key (col. 2):   a: fad   ā: fade   ah: father   ar: **M**ary   aw: law   e: fed   ē: feed   er: merry   i: hid   ī: hide   ō: coat   oo: boot
oi: boy   ow: now   u: put   uh: above   uhr: bird   ch: chop   ng: ring   sh: show   th: thick   th̲: this   zh: measure

Buena Vista Rancheria
   Indian reservation, US   BWĀ-nuh VIS-tuh RAN-chuh-RĒ-uh   ˌbweːnə ˈvistə ˌræntʃəˈriːə

Buenos Aires
   prov & city, Argentina   BWĀ-nuhs AR-ēz, ER-ēz, ĪR-ēz;   ˌbweːnəs ˈæriːz, ˈeriːz, ˈairiːz;
                            BŌ-nuhs   ˌboːnəs

Bufadora, La
   port, Mexico   lah boo-fah-<u>TH</u>Ō-rah   lɑ buːfɑˈðoːrɑ

Buffalo
   US pl. name   BUHF-uh-LŌ   ˈbəfəˌloː

Buffkins
   Archie Lee, *US performing arts*   BUHF-kuhnz   ˈbəfkənz
    administrator

Bug
   river, Poland   BOOG, Ⓢ BUHG   ˈbuːg, Ⓢ ˈbəg

Buganda
   native kingdom, Uganda   b(y)oo-GAHN-duh   b(j)uːˈgandə

Bugatti
   Italian car co.   bu-GAHT-ē   buˈgaṭiˑ

Buginese
   lang., people, South Sulawesi   BUHG-uh-NĒZ, -NĒS   ˌbəgəˈniːz, -ˈniːs
    (Celebes)

Bugloss
   plant   BYOO-GLAHS, BYOO-GLAWS   ˈbjuːˌglas, ˈbjuːˌgloːs

Buhl
   city, ID   BYOOL   ˈbjuːl

Buick
   US car co.   BYOO-ik   ˈbjuːik

Buidhe
   pers. name, Irish   BOO-uh(-<u>th</u>uh)   ˈbuːə(ðə)

Buisson
   F. É., *French educator (Nobel*   bwē-SAWⁿ   bwiːsɔ̃
    1927)

Buitenzorg
   city, Indonesia   BĪT-n-ZAWRG   ˈbaitn̩ˌzɔːʳg

Bujumbura
   city, Burundi   BOO-juhm-BUR-uh   ˌbuːdʒəmˈburə

Bukhara, Bokhara
   city, Uzbekistan   boo-KHAHR-uh   buːˈxɑrə

Bukharin
   Nikolai, *Russian political leader*   boo-KAHR-yin   buːˈkɑrjin

Bukidnon
   lang., people, Philippine Islands   boo-KID-NAHN   buːˈkidˌnɑn

Bukovina
   see Bucovina

Bulahdelah
   town, Australia   BUL-uh-DĒ-luh   ˌbuləˈdiːlə

Bulbul
   bird   BUL-BUL   ˈbulˌbul

Bulgakov
   Mikhail, *writer*   bool-GAH-kuhf   buːlˈgɑːkəf

Bulganin
   Nikolai A., *Premier, USSR*   buhl-GAHN-yēn, Ⓢ bul-GAN-uhn   bəlˈgɑːnjiˑn, Ⓢ bulˈgænən

Bulgar
   Bulgarian   BUHL-GAHR, BUHL-guhr   ˈbəlˌgɑʳ, ˈbəlgəʳ

Foreign Sounds: ue: *Fr.* **rue**, *Ger.* f**ü**llen   uh(r): *Fr.* b**oeu**f, *Ger.* H**öh**le   <u>kh</u>: *Ger.* i**ch**, *Scot.* lo**ch**   g̅: *Sp.* ami**g**o   v̲: *Sp.* ha**b**lar
hl: *Welsh* L**l**anelli.   CAPITALS: primary stress.   SMALL CAPS: secondary stress.   Ⓢ: U.S. pron.   Ⓔ: British pron.

Bulgaria
  republic, Europe   buhl-GAR-ē-uh, bul-, -GER-   bəl'gæriːə, bul-, -'ger-

Bulgarian
  lang., Bulgaria; pert. to Bulgaria   BUHL-GAR-ē-uhn, bul-, -GER-   ,bəl'gæriːən, bul-, -'ger-

Bull
  1. John, *personification of*   BUL   'bul
    England
  2. Olaf, *Norwegian poet;* Ole,   BOOL   'buːl
    Norwegian violinist

Bulli
  town, Australia   BUL-ī   'bul,ɑi

Bull Moose
  member of Progressive Party   bul MOOS   bul 'muːs

Bulloch
  county, GA   BUL-uhk   'bulək

Bullock
  county, AL   BUL-uhk   'bulək

Bulova
  tdmk for watches and clocks   BUL-uh-vuh   'buləvə

Bulu
  lang., people, Africa   BOO-loo   'buːluː

Bulwer-Lytton
  Edward, *English novelist*   BUL-wuhr-LIT-n   ,bulwəʳ'litn̩

Buna
  village, New Guinea   BOO-nuh   'buːnə

Bunche
  Ralph, *US diplomat (Nobel 1950)*   BUHNCH   'bəntʃ

Buncombe
  county, NC   BUHNG-kuhm   'bəŋkəm

Bund
  pro-Nazi organization in US   BUNT, BUND, BUHND   'bunt, 'bund, 'bənd

Bundesbank
  German bank   BUN-duhs-BAHNGK, -BANGK   'bundəs,baŋk, -,bæŋk

Bundesliga
  German soccer league   BUN-duhs-LĒ-guh   'bundəs,liːgə

Bundesrat
  German upper house of   BUN-duhs-RAHT   'bundəs,rat
    Parliament

Bundestag
  German lower house of   BUN-duh-STAHG   'bundə,stag
    Parliament

Bundesversammlung
  Austrian federal assembly   BUN-duhs-fer-ZAHM-lung   ,bundəsfer'zamluŋ

Bundeswehr
  armed forces, W. Germany   BUN-duhs-VER   'bundəs,veʳ

Bundt
  type of cake pan   BUHNT   'bənt

Bunin
  I. A., *Russian author (Nobel 1933)*   BOON-yuhn, BOON-YĒN   'buːnjən, 'buːn,jiːn

Bunnahabhain
  distillery, Scotland   BUHN-uh-HAHV-uhn   ,bənə'havən

Bunraku
  Japanese puppet theater   bun-rahk-oo   bunrakuː

Buñuel
  Luis, *Spanish film director*   bun-WEL   bun'wel

Key (col. 2):   a: fad ā: fade ah: father ar: Mary aw: law e: fed ē: feed er: merry i: hid ī: hide ō: coat oo: boot
oi: boy ow: now u: put uh: above uhr: bird ch: chop ng: ring sh: show th: thick th̲: this zh: measure

Bunyan
    John, *English writer;* Paul, *US*   BUHN-yuhn   ˈbənjən
      legendary woodsman

Bunyanesque
    pert. to Bunyan   BUHN-yuh-NESK   ˌbənjəˈnesk

Buonaparte
    Italian form of Bonaparte   BWAW-nah-PAHR-tä,   ˌbwɔːnɑˈpɑrteː,
               Ⓢ BŌ-nuh-PAHRT   Ⓢ ˈboːnəˌpɑʳt

Burbank
    city, CA   BUHR-BANGK   ˈbəʳˌbæŋk

Burberry
    English clothing co.   BUHR-buh-rē, BUHR-buhr-ē,   ˈbəʳbə-riˈ, ˈbəʳbər-iˈ,
               Ⓢ BUHR-BER-ē   Ⓢ ˈbəʳˌberiˈ

Burdett
    pers. name   buhr-DET   bəʳˈdet

Burdock
    plant   BUHRD-uhk   ˈbəʳdək

Bureau
    county, IL   BYOOR-ō, BYUR-ō   ˈbjuːroː, ˈbjuroː

Burger
    Warren Earl, *US Supreme Court*   BUHR-guhr   ˈbəʳgəʳ
      justice

Burgerbräu
    German beer   BUR-guhr-BROI   ˈbuʳgəʳˌbrɔi

Burgess
    Anthony, *British writer; pers.*   BUHR-juhs   ˈbəʳdʒəs
      name

Burghardt
    pers. name   BUHRG-HAHRT   ˈbəʳgˌhɑʳt

Burghoff
    Gary, *US actor*   BUHR-GAWF, BUHR-GAHF   ˈbəʳˌgɔːf, ˈbəʳˌgaf

Burgos
    city, Spain; cheese   BUR-ḡōs, BUR-GŌS   ˈburɣoːs, ˈbuʳˌgoːs

Burgoyne
    John, *British general*   BUHR-GOIN, buhr-GOIN   ˈbəʳˌgɔin, bəʳˈgɔin

Burgundian
    pert. to Burgundy   buhr-GUHN-dē-uhn   bəʳˈgəndiːən

Burgundy
    region, France; wine   BUHR-guhn-dē   ˈbəʳgəndiˈ

Burkina Faso
    republic, Africa   bur-KĒ-nuh FAHS-ō   buʳˈkiːnə ˈfɑsoː

Burl
    pers. name   BUHRL   ˈbəʳl

Burleigh
    county, ND   BUHR-lē   ˈbəʳliˈ

Burley
    city, ID   BUHR-lē   ˈbəʳliˈ

Burlingame
    city, CA   BUHR-luhn-GĀM   ˈbəʳlənˌgeːm

Burma [Myanmar]
    republic, Asia   BUHR-muh   ˈbəʳmə

Burmese
    lang., Burma   BUHR-MĒZ, -MĒS   ˌbəʳˈmiːz, -ˈmiːs

Foreign Sounds: ue: *Fr.* rue, *Ger.* füllen   uh(r): *Fr.* boeuf, *Ger.* Höhle   <u>kh</u>: *Ger.* i<u>ch</u>, *Scot.* lo<u>ch</u>   ḡ: *Sp.* ami<u>g</u>o   <u>v</u>: *Sp.* ha<u>b</u>lar
hl: *Welsh* Llanelli.   CAPITALS: primary stress.   SMALL CAPS: secondary stress.   Ⓢ: U.S. pron.   Ⓣ: British pron.

Burnet
  Sir Macfarlane, *Australian*   buhr-NET, BUHR-nuht   bəʳnet, 'bəʳnət
    virologist (Nobel 1960)

Burnett
  Carol, *US actress, comedienne*   BUHR-NET   ˌbəʳnet

Burnham
  pers. name   BUHRN-uhm   'bəʳnəm

Burnham-on-Sea
  town, England   BUHR-nuhm-ahn-SĒ, -awn-SĒ   ˌbəʳnəmanˈsiː, -ɔːnˈsiː

Burns
  George, *US comedian; pers. name*   BUHRNZ   'bəʳnz

Burrhus
  pers. name (B. F. Skinner)   BUHR-uhs, BUH-ruhs   'bər-əs, 'bə-rəs

Burroughs
  Edgar Rice, *US writer;* William S.,   BUHR-ōz, BUH-rōz, BUHR-uhz,   'bər-oːz, 'bə-roːz, 'bər-əz,
    US writer   BUH-ruhz   'bə-rəz

Burroughs Wellcome
  British pharmaceutical co.   BUH-rōz WEL-kuhm, BUHR-ōz,   'bə-roːz 'welkəm, 'bər-oːz,
     BUH-ruhz, BUHR-uhz   'bə-rəz, 'bər-əz

Bursa
  prov & town, Turkey   bur-SAH   buʳsa

Burstyn
  Ellen, *US actress*   BUHR-stuhn   'bəʳstən

Burt
  pers. name   BUHRT   'bəʳt

Burton
  pers. name   BUHRT-n   'bəʳtn̩

Burundi
  republic, Africa   buh-ROON-dē   bə'ruːndiˑ

Burundian
  pert. to Burundi   buh-ROON-dē-uhn   bə'ruːndiːən

Burushaski
  lang., India, Pakistan   BUR-uh-SHAHS-kē   ˌburə'ʃaskiˑ

Buryat
  lang., people, Russia   bur-YAHT, BUR-ē-AHT   buʳjat, 'buriːˌat

Bury St. Edmunds
  town, England   BER-ē suhnt ED-muhn(d)z, sānt   ˌberiː sənt 'edmən(d)z, seːnt

Buscaglia
  Leo, *US physician*   buh-SKAL-ē-uh   bə'skæliːə

Busch
  US beer; stadium, St. Louis, MO   BUSH   'buʃ

Busey
  Gary, *US actor, musician*   BYOO-zē, BYOO-sē   'bjuːziˑ, 'bjuːsiˑ

Bush
  George, *41st US president*   BUSH   'buʃ

Bushido
  code of samurai   bush-(i-)dō, Ⓢ BUSH-i-DŌ,   buʃ(i)doː, Ⓢ 'buʃiˌdoː,
     BOO-shi-DŌ   'buːʃiˌdoː

Bushman [San]
  lang., people, Angola   BUSH-muhn   'buʃmən

Busiris
  mythical king of Egypt   byoo-SĪ-ruhs   bju'saɪrəs

Busoni
  Ferruccio, *Italian pianist,*   b(y)oo-ZŌ-nē   b(j)u'zoːniˑ
    composer

Key (col. 2): a: fad ā: fade ah: father ar: Mary aw: law e: fed ē: feed er: merry i: hid ī: hide ō: coat o͞o: boot
oi: boy ow: now u: put uh: above uhr: bird ch: chop ng: ring sh: show th: thick th̲: this zh: measure

Busuanga
  island, Philippines   bōō-SWAHNG-uh   buːˈswɑŋə

Butch
  pers. name   BUCH   ˈbutʃ

Butenandt
  Adolf, *German biochemist (Nobel 1939)*   BŌŌT-n-AHNT   ˈbuːtn̩ˌɑnt

Buteo
  hawk genus   BYŌŌT-ē-ō   ˈbjuːţiːˌoː

Butes
  son of Boreas   BYŌŌT-ēz   ˈbjuːţiːz

Buthelezi
  Mangosuthu, *S. African leader*   BŌŌT-l-Ā-zē, BŌŌ-tuh-LĀ-zē   ˌbuːtlˈeːziˑ, ˌbuːtəˈleːziˑ

Butler
  Nicholas Murray, *US educator (Nobel 1931);* Samuel, *English poet*   BUHT-luhr   ˈbətləʳ

Buto [Edjo]
  Egyptian guardian goddess   B(Y)ŌŌT-ō   ˈb(j)uːţoː

Butte
  city, MT; county, CA, ID, SD   BYŌŌT   ˈbjuːt

Buxtehude
  Dietrich, *Danish composer*   BUKS-duh-HŌŌ-thuh, *Ger.* BUK-stuh-HŌŌD-uh, Ⓢ BUK-stuh-HŌŌD-uh   ˌbuksdəˈhuːðə, *Ger.* ˌbukstəˈhuːdə, Ⓢ ˈbukstəˌhuːdə

Buyi [Puyi]
  lang., China   BŌŌ-YĒ   ˈbuːˈjiː

Buys Ballot
  Christoph, *Dutch meteorologist*   BUH(R)IS buh-LAWT   ˈbœis bəˈlɔːt

Buys Ballot's law
  air pressure principle   BĪS buh-LAHTS LAW, BĪZ   ˌbais bəˌlɑts ˈlɔː, ˌbaiz

Buzyges
  mythical inventor of the yoke   byōō-ZĪ-jēz   bjuˈzaidʒiːz

Buzz
  pers. name   BUHZ   ˈbəz

Buzzards Bay
  inlet, town, MA   BUHZ-uhrdz BĀ   ˌbəzəʳdz ˈbeː

BVD
  brand of underwear   BĒ-vē-DĒ   ˌbiːviːˈdiː

Byblis
  daughter of Miletus   BIB-luhs   ˈbibləs

Byblos
  ancient Phoenician seaport   BIB-luhs   ˈbibləs

Bydgoszcz
  prov & town, Poland   BID-GAWSH(CH)   ˈbidˌgɔːʃ(tʃ)

Byelorussia [Belarus]
  republic, E. Europe   BYEL-ō-RUHSH-uh, bē-EL-ō-   ˌbjeloːˈrəʃə, biːˌeloː-

Byelorussian [Belo-, Bielo-]
  lang., Belorussia, Poland   bē-EL-ō-RUHSH-uhn, BYEL-ō-   biːˌeloːˈrəʃən, ˌbjeloː-

Byerly Turk
  racehorse   BĪ(-uh)r-lē TUHRK   ˈbai(ə)ʳliˑ ˈtəʳk

Byng
  Julian H.G., *English general*   BING   ˈbiŋ

Foreign Sounds: ue: *Fr.* **rue**, *Ger.* **fü**llen   uh(r): *Fr.* **bœuf**, *Ger.* **Hö**hle   <u>kh</u>: *Ger.* i**ch**, *Scot.* lo**ch**   ğ: *Sp.* ami**g**o   <u>v</u>: *Sp.* ha**b**lar
hl: *Welsh* **Ll**anelli.   CAPITALS: primary stress.   SMALL CAPS: secondary stress.   Ⓢ: U.S. pron.   Ⓛ: British pron.

Byrd
  Richard E., *US explorer;* Robert   BUHRD   'bəʳd
    C., *US fiddler;* William, *English*
    composer; pers. name

Byrne
  David, *US musician, composer*   BUHRN   'bəʳn

Byron
  George Gordon, Lord, *English*   BĪ-ruhn   'bairən
    poet; pers. name

Byronic
  pert. to Lord Byron   bī-RAHN-ik   bai'ranik

Bysshe
  pers. name (P. B. Shelley)   BISH   'biʃ

Byzantine Empire
  Eastern Roman Empire   BIZ-n-TĒN, buh-ZAN-, BĪZ-n-;   'bizn̩,tiːn, bə'zæn-, 'baizn̩-;
         BIZ-n-TĪN   'bizn̩,tain

Byzantinism
  political doctrine   buh-ZAN-tuh-NIZ-uhm,   bə'zæntə,nizəm,
         -ZANT-n-IZ-uhm   -'zæntn̩,izəm

Byzantium
  ancient name for Istanbul   buh-ZAN-sh(ē-)uhm, -ZANT-ē-uhm   bə'zænʃ(iː)əm, -'zæntiːəm

Byzas
  founder of Byzantium   BĪ-zuhs, BĒ-zuhs   'baizəs, 'biːzəs

C

Caan
  James, *US actor, director*   KAHN   'kɑn

Cab
  pers. name (C. Calloway)   KAB   'kæb

Cabarrus
  county, NC   kuh-BAR-uhs, kuh-BER-uhs   kə'bærəs, kə'berəs

Cabazon Band
  N. American people   KAB-uh-ZŌN, KAB-uh-ZŌN   'kæbə,zoːn, ,kæbə'zoːn

Cabell
  county, WV; pers. name   KAB-uhl   'kæbəl

Cabernet
  wine variety   KAB-uhr-NĀ, -NE   ,kæbəʳneː, -'ne

Cabiri, Cabeiri
  mysterious Greek divinities   kuh-BIR-ē   kə'biriˑ

Cabot
  notable American family; pers.   KAB-uht   'kæbət
    name

Cabral
  Pedro, *Portuguese navigator*   kuh-BRAHL   kə'brɑl

Key (col. 2):   a: fad   ā: fade   ah: father   ar: Mary   aw: law   e: fed   ē: feed   er: merry   i: hid   ī: hide   ō: coat   ōō: boot
oi: boy   ow: now   u: put   uh: above   uhr: bird   ch: chop   ng: ring   sh: show   th: thick   th̲: this   zh: measure

Cabrillo
  College, *CA*   kuh-BRĔ-(y)ō   kəˈbriː(j)oː
Cabrini
  Frances X. (Mother), *US nun;*   kuh-BRĔ-nē, ka-   kəˈbriːniˈ, kæ-
     College, *PA*
Caca
  pre-Roman goddess of the hearth   KĀ-kuh, KAHK-uh   ˈkeːkə, ˈkɑkə
Cacao
  plant   kuh-KOW, kuh-KĀ-ō   kəˈkau, kəˈkeːoː
Caccia
  cape, Italy   KAHCH-uh   ˈkatʃə
Cáceres
  prov & town, Spain   KAHTH-uh-räs, KAHS-uh-räs   ˈkaθəreːs, ˈkasəreːs
Cachalote
  South American bird   KASH-uh-LŌT   ˈkæʃəˌloːt
Cacharel
  perfume   KASH-uh-REL   ˌkæʃəˈrel
Cache
  river, AR; county, UT   KASH   ˈkæʃ
Caciocavallo
  Italian cheese   KAH-chō-kuh-VAHL-ō   ˌkatʃoːkəˈvaloː
Cacique
  Native American chief or political   kuh-SĒK   kəˈsiːk
     boss in the Hispanic Americas
Cacus
  pre-Roman fire god   KĀ-kuhs   ˈkeːkəs
Cadbury
  British candy co.   KAD-b(uh-)rē, Ⓢ KAD-BER-ē   ˈkædb(ə)riˈ, Ⓢ ˈkædˌberiˈ
CAD-CAM
  computer design system   KAD-KAM   ˈkædˌkæm
Caddo
  N. American people; parish, LA;   KAD-ō   ˈkædoː
     county, OK
Caddom
  N. American people   KAD-uhm   ˈkædəm
Cadillac
  1. city, MI; US car make   KAD-l-AK   ˈkædlˌæk
  2. Antoine de La Mothe, Sieur de,   kah-dē-YAHK, Ⓢ KAD-l-AK   kaːdiˈjaːk, Ⓢ ˈkædlˌæk
     French colonialist
Cadiz
  1. city, KY   KĀD-iz   ˈkeːdiz
  2. village, OH   KAD-iz   ˈkædiz
  3. city, Philippines   KAHD-ēs   ˈkɑdiːs
Cádiz, Cadiz
  prov & town, Spain   KAH-thēth, KAH-thēs, Ⓢ kuh-DIZ,   ˈkaðiːθ, ˈkaðiːs, Ⓢ kəˈdiz,
                  KĀD-iz, KAHD-iz, KAD-iz   ˈkeːdiz, ˈkɑdiz, ˈkædiz
Cadmean
  pert. to Cadmus   KAD-mē-uhn   ˈkædmiːən
cadmium
  element   KAD-mē-uhm   ˈkædmiːəm
Cadmus
  mythical founder of Thebes; pers.   KAD-muhs   ˈkædməs
     name
Cadogan
  pers. name   kuh-DUHG-uhn   kəˈdəgən

Foreign Sounds: ue: *Fr.* **rue**, *Ger.* **füllen**   uh(r): *Fr.* **boeuf**, *Ger.* **Höhle**   <u>kh</u>: *Ger.* i**ch**, *Scot.* lo**ch**   ḡ: *Sp.* ami**g**o   <u>v</u>: *Sp.* ha**b**lar
hl: *Welsh* **Llanelli**.   CAPITALS: primary stress.   SMALL CAPS: secondary stress.   Ⓢ: U.S. pron.   Ⓛ: British pron.

Cadwallader
  pers. name   kad-WAHL-uhd-uhr, kuhd-   kæd'wɑlədəʳ, kəd-

Caecilius
  Roman name   suh-SIL-ē-uhs, kī-KIL-ē-uhs   sə'siliːəs, kɑi'kiliːəs

Caeculus
  founder of Praeneste   SĒ-kyuh-luhs   'siːkjələs

Caecus
  Roman cognomen   SĒ-kuhs, KĪ-kuhs   'siːkəs, 'kɑikəs

Caedmon
  Anglo-Saxon poet   KAD-muhn   'kædmən

Caedmonian
  pert. to Caedmon   kad-MŌ-nē-uhn   kæd'moːniːən

Caelian
  hill, Rome, Italy   SĒ-lē-uhn   'siːliːən

Caelius
  Roman name   SĒ-lē-uhs, KĪ-lē-uhs   'siːliːəs, 'kɑiliːəs

Caelum
  constellation   SĒ-luhm   'siːləm

Caelus
  personification of the sky   SĒ-luhs, KĪ-luhs   'siːləs, 'kɑiləs

Caen
  city, France   KAHⁿ, Ⓢ KAHN   kɑ̃, Ⓢ 'kɑn

Caerdydd [Cardiff]
  city, Wales   kīr-DĒTH   kɑir'diːð

Caerleon
  district, Wales   kahr-LĒ-uhn   ˌkɑʳliːən

Caernarfon, -von
  town, Wales   kahr-NAHR-vuhn, kuhr-NAHR-vuhn   kɑʳ'nɑʳvən, kəʳ'nɑʳvən

Caernarvonshire
  former county, Wales   kuhr-NAHR-vuhn-shuhr, kahr-, -SHIR   kəʳ'nɑʳvənʃəʳ, kɑʳ-, -ˌʃiʳ

Caerphilly
  town, Wales; cheese   kīr-FIL-ē   kɑiʳ'filiˑ

Caesar
  Julius, *Roman general &*   SĒ-zuhr   'siːzəʳ
    statesman; pers. name

Caesarea
  ancient city, Middle East   SĒ-zuh-RĒ-uh, SES-uh-RĒ-uh,   ˌsiːzə'riːə, ˌsesə'riːə, ˌsezə'riːə
     SEZ-uh-RĒ-uh

Caesarean
  pert. to Caesar; *surgical birth*   si-ZAR-ē-uhn, si-ZER-ē-uhn   si'zæriːən, si'zeriːən

Cagliari
  prov & town, Italy   KAHL-yuh-rē   'kɑljəriˑ

Cahenslyism
  Catholic ethnic-group plan   kuh-HENZ-lē-IZ-uhm, -HENS-   kə'henzliːˌizəm, -'hens-

Cahil Dehe Band
  N. American people   kuh-HĒL DĀ-hā   kə'hiːl 'deːheː

Cahn
  Sammy, *US lyric songwriter*   KAHN   'kɑn

Cahors
  town, France   kah-AWR   kaɔːr

Cahto
  N. American people   KAHT-ō   'katoː

Cahuilla
  N. American people   kuh-WĒ-uh   kə'wiːə

Key (col. 2):   a: fad   ā: fade   ah: father   ar: Mary   aw: law   e: fed   ē: feed   er: merry   i: hid   ī: hide   ō: coat   o͞o: boot
oi: boy   ow: now   u: put   uh: above   uhr: bird   ch: chop   ng: ring   sh: show   th: thick   th̲: this   zh: measure

Caiaphas
    Biblical name   KĪ-uh-fuhs   'kaɪəfəs

Caicos
    islands, Bahamas   KĀ-kuhs, KĪ-kōs   'keːkəs, 'kaɪkoːs

Caingang
    S. American people   KĪN-GANG   'kaɪn,gæŋ

Cainism
    Gnostic heresy   KĀ-NIZ-uhm   'keː,nizəm

Cairngorm
    mtn. & mtn. range, Scotland   KARN-GAWRM, KERN-GAWRM   'kæ^{r}n,gɔː^{r}m, 'ke^{r}n,gɔː^{r}m

Cairns
    seaport, Australia   KARNZ, KERNZ   'kæ^{r}nz, 'ke^{r}nz

Cairo
    1. city, Egypt   KĪ-rō   'kaɪroː
    2. city, GA, IL   KER-ō, KĀ-rō   'keroː, 'keːroː

Cair Paravel
    fictional castle, C.S. Lewis   KĪR PAR-uh-VEL   ,kaɪ^r ,pærə'vel

Caithness
    district, Scotland   KĀTH-nes, KĀTH-nuhs, kāth-NES   'keːθnes, 'keːθnəs, keːθ'nes

Caitlin
    pers. name   KĀT-luhn   'keːtlən

Caius
    1. pers. name   KĀ-uhs, KĪ-uhs   'keːəs, 'kaɪəs
    2. Gonville and Caius College,   KĒZ   'kiːz
      Cambridge University

Cajun
    French Catholic from Arcadia, in   KĀ-juhn   'keːdʒən
      LA

Cakchiquel
    lang.. Cen. America   KAHK-chi-KEL, KAHK-chi-KEL   ,kaktʃi'kel, 'kaktʃi,kel

Calabria
    region, Italy   kuh-LĀ-brē-uh, kuh-LAHB-rē-uh   kə'leːbriːə, kə'labriːə

Caladium
    plant   kuh-LĀD-ē-uhm   kə'leːdiːəm

Calais
    1. seaport, France   kah-LE, Ⓢ ka-LĀ, KAL-ā   ka'le, Ⓢ kæ'leː, 'kæleː
    2. city, ME   KAL-uhs   'kæləs

Calamus
    plant   KAL-uh-muhs   'kæləməs

Calaveras
    river, county, CA; warbler   KAL-uh-VER-uhs   ,kælə'verəs

Calcasieu
    river, parish, LA   KAL-kuh-SHOO   'kælkə,ʃuː

Calceolaria
    plant   KAL-sē-uh-LAR-ē-uh   ,kælsiːə'læriːə

Calchas
    Greek seer during Trojan War   KAL-kuhs   'kælkəs

calcium
    element   KAL-sē-uhm   'kælsiːəm

Calcutta
    city, India   kal-KUHT-uh   kæl'kətə

Caldecott
    children's book award for   KAWL-duh-KAHT   'kɔːldə,kat
      illustrators

Foreign Sounds: ue: *Fr.* **rue**, *Ger.* füllen   uh(r): *Fr.* **boeuf**, *Ger.* Höhle   <u>kh</u>: *Ger.* **ich**, *Scot.* loch   ğ: *Sp.* amigo   v̦: *Sp.* hablar   hl: *Welsh* Llanelli.   CAPITALS: primary stress.   SMALL CAPS: secondary stress.   Ⓢ: U.S. pron.   Ⓛ: British pron.

Caldus
  Roman cognomen   KAWL-duhs   'kɔːldəs
Caleb
  pers. name   KĀ-luhb   'keːləb
Caledonia
  ancient name for Scotland; US pl. name   KAL-uh-DŌN-yuh, KAL-uh-DŌ-nē-uh   ˌkælə'doːnjə, ˌkælə'doːniːə
Caledonian
  pert. to Caledonia   KAL-uh-DŌN-yuhn, KAL-uh-DŌ-nē-uhn   ˌkælə'doːnjən, ˌkælə'doːniːən
Calendula
  plant   kuh-LEN-juh-luh   kə'lendʒələ
Calfee Park
  Pulaski, VA   KAF-ē   'kæfiˑ
Calgary
  city, Canada   KAL-guh-rē   'kælgəriˑ
Calgon
  US cleaning products co.   KAL-GAHN, KAL-guhn   'kælˌgɑn, 'kælgən
Calhoun
  John C., US politician; US pl. name; pers. name   kal-HOON, KAL-HOON, kuh-HOON   kæl'huːn, 'kælˌhuːn, kə'huːn
Cali
  city, Colombia   KAHL-ē   'kɑliˑ
Caliari [Veronese]
  Paolo, Venetian painter   kahl-YAHR-ē   kal'jariˑ
Caliban
  slave in The Tempest, *Shakespeare*   KAL-uh-BAN   'kæləˌbæn
Calicut
  city, India   KAL-i-kuht   'kælikət
California
  state, US; gulf, Mexico   KAL-uh-FAWRN-yuh   ˌkælə'fɔːʳnjə
Californio
  resident of California   KAL-uh-FAWRN-yō   ˌkælə'fɔːʳnjoː
californium
  element   KAL-uh-FAWR-nē-uhm   ˌkælə'fɔːʳniːəm
Caligula
  Roman emperor   kuh-LIG-yuh-luh   kə'ligjələ
Calixto
  pers. name   kah-LĒ(K)S-tō   kɑ'liː(k)stoː
Calixtus
  pope   kuh-LIK-stuhs   kə'likstəs
Calla
  plant   KAL-uh   'kælə
Callao
  prov & town, Peru   kuh-YAH-ō, kuh-YOW   kə'jaoː, kə'jau
Calley
  William L., Jr., US officer at My Lai   KA-lē   'kæliˑ
Callias
  Peace of, Athenian-Persian pact   KAL-ē-uhs   'kæliːəs
Callimachus
  Greek poet   kuh-LIM-uh-kuhs   kə'liməkəs

Key (col. 2): a: fad ā: fade ah: father ar: Mary aw: law e: fed ē: feed er: merry i: hid ī: hide ō: coat o͞o: boot oi: boy ow: now u: put uh: above uhr: bird ch: chop ng: ring sh: show th: thick t͟h: this zh: measure

Calliope
  1. muse of epic poetry;   kuh-LĪ-uh-pē   kə'laiəpiˑ
    hummingbird
  2. street, New Orleans   KAL-ē-ŌP   'kæliˑˌoːp
Callirhoe
  mother of Geryon and Echidna   kuh-LIR-uh-wē   kə'lirəwiˑ
Callisto
  nymph loved by Zeus; satellite of   kuh-LIS-tō   kə'listoː
    Jupiter
Callistus
  pope   kuh-LIS-tuhs   kə'listəs
Callot
  Jacques, *French painter/engraver*   kah-LŌ   kaːloː
Calloway
  Cab, *US jazz singer*   KAL-uh-WĀ   'kæləˌweː
Caloosahatchee
  National Wildlife Refuge, *river, FL*   kuh-LOO-suh-HACH-ē   kəˌluːsə'hætʃiˑ
Caloris
  basin on Mercury   kuh-LŌR-uhs, -LAWR-   kə'loːrəs, -'loːr-
Calotrope
  plant   KAL-uh-TRŌP   'kæləˌtroːp
Calphalon
  tdmk for cookware   KAL-fuh-LAHN   'kælfəˌlɑn
Calpurnia
  Julius Caesar's wife   kal-PUHR-nē-uh   kæl'pəʳniːə
Calpurnius
  pers. name, Latin   kal-PUHR-nē-uhs   kæl'pəʳniːəs
Calumet
  river, lake, harbor, Chicago, IL;   KAL-yuh-MET, KAL-yuh-muht   'kæljəˌmet, 'kæljəmət
    county, WI; industrial area, IN,
    IL
Calumet City
  city, IL   KAL-yuh-MET SIT-ē, KAL-yuh-muht   ˌkæljəˌmet 'siṭiˑ, ˌkæljəmət
Calumet Farm
  horse-breeding farm, KY   KAL-yuh-MET FAHRM, KAL-yuh-muht   ˌkæljəˌmet 'faʳm, ˌkæljəmət
Calusa
  N. American people   kuh-LOO-suh   kə'luːsə
Calvados
  dept, France; apple brandy   kahl-vah-DŌS, ⑤ KAL-vuh-DŌS,   kaːlvaːdoːs, ⑤ ˌkælvə'doːs,
                          -DAWS, -DAHS   -'doːs, -'dɑs
Calvary [Golgotha]
  site of Christ's crucifixion   KAL-v(uh-)rē   'kælv(ə)riˑ
Calvert
  pers. name   KAL-vuhrt   'kælvəʳt
Calvin
  John, *French theologian;* Melvin,   KAL-vuhn   'kælvən
    US chemist (Nobel 1961); pers.
    name
Calvinism
  religion   KAL-vuh-NIZ-uhm   'kælvəˌnizəm
Calvinist
  one who adheres to Calvinism   KAL-vuh-nuhst   'kælvənəst
Calvino
  Italo, *writer*   kahl-VĒ-nō, kal-VĒ-nō   kɑl'viːnoː, kæl'viːnoː

Foreign Sounds: ue: *Fr.* **rue,** *Ger.* **füllen**   uh(r): *Fr.* **boeuf,** *Ger.* **Höhle**   <u>kh</u>: *Ger.* **ich,** *Scot.* **loch**   ğ: *Sp.* **amigo**   <u>v</u>: *Sp.* **hablar**   hl: *Welsh* **Llanelli.**   CAPITALS: primary stress.   SMALL CAPS: secondary stress.   ⑤: U.S. pron.   ⑫: British pron.

Calvo
  Paul MacDonald, *US governor,*   KAL-vō   ˈkælvoː
    Guam

Calvus
  Roman cognomen   KAL-vuhs   ˈkælvəs

Calydon
  ancient city, Greece   KAL-uh-DAHN, KAL-uhd-n   ˈkæləˌdɑn, ˈkælədn̩

Calypso
  lover of Odysseus; style of West   kuh-LIP-sō   kəˈlipsoː
    Indian music

Cam
  river, Cambridgeshire, England KAM   ˈkæm

Camacan
  S. American people   KAHM-uh-KAHN   ˌkɑməˈkɑn

Camagüey
  prov & town, Cuba   KAHM-uh-GWĀ, KAM-uh-GWĀ ˌkɑməˈgweː, ˌkæməˈgweː

Camaldolites
  religious order   kuh-MAL-duh-LĪTS   kəˈmældəˌlaits

Camarasaurus
  dinosaur   KAM-uh-ruh-SAWR-uhs   ˌkæmərəˈsɔːrəs

Camargue, La
  island, Rhone river, France   lah kah-MAHRG   laː kɑːmɑːrg

Camas
  county, ID; city, WA   KAM-uhs   ˈkæməs

Cambodia [Kampuchea]
  republic, SE Asia   kam-BŌD-ē-uh   kæmˈboːdiːə

Cambodian [Khmer]
  lang., people, Indochina   kam-BŌD-ē-uhn   kæmˈboːdiːən

Cambrai
  city, France   kahⁿ-BRE   kãbre

Cambria
  county, PA; Latin & poetic name KAM-brē-uh   ˈkæmbriːə
    for Wales

Cambria Heights
  Queens, New York City   KĀM-brē-uh HĪTS   ˌkeːmbriːə ˈhaits

Cambrian
  mtn. range, Wales; geologic period KAM-brē-uhn, KĀM-brē-uhn ˈkæmbriːən, ˈkeːmbriːən

Cambridge
  city, MA; city, university, England KĀM-brij   ˈkeːmbridʒ

Cambridgeshire
  county, England   KĀM-brij-shuhr, -SHIR   ˈkeːmbridʒʃəʳ, -ˌʃiʳ

Cambyses
  Persian king   kam-BĪ-SĒZ   kæmˈbaiˌsiːz

Camden
  city, NJ, ME; borough, England KAM-duhn   ˈkæmdən

Camelia
  pers. name   kuh-MĒL-yuh   kəˈmiːljə

Camellia
  flower   kuh-MĒL-yuh   kəˈmiːljə

Camelopardalis
  constellation   kuh-MEL-uh-PAHRD-l-uhs,   kəˌmeləˈpɑʳdləs, ˌkæməloː-
                             KAM-uh-lō-

Camelot
  site of King Arthur's court   KAM-uh-LAHT   ˈkæməˌlɑt

Key (col. 2): a: fad ā: fade ah: father ar: Mary aw: law e: fed ē: feed er: merry i: hid ī: hide ō: coat ōō: boot
oi: boy ow: now u: put uh: above uhr: bird ch: chop ng: ring sh: show th: thick th: this zh: measure

Camembert
  village, France; cheese   kah-mem-BER, ⑤ KAM-uhm-BER   kɑːmember, ⑤ 'kæməm,beʳ

Camenae
  prophetic nymphs of Roman   kuh-MĒ-nē   kə'miːniˑ
    springs

Camerata Bern
  chamber orchestra, Switzerland   KAHM-uh-RAHT-uh BERN   ˌkɑmə'rɑtə 'beʳn

Cameron
  univ., OK; pl. name, US; pers.   KAM-(uh-)ruhn   'kæm(ə)rən
    name

Cameroon
  republic, Africa   KAM-uh-R͞OON   ˌkæmə'ruːn

Cameroonian
  pert. to Cameroon   KAM-uh-R͞OO-nē-uhn   ˌkæmə'ruːniːən

Camilla
  1. female warrior who fought   kuh-MIL-uh   kə'milə
    Aeneas; pers. name
  2. Italian   kah-MĒL-lah   kɑ'miːllɑ
  3. Norwegian   kah-MIL-lah   kɑ'millɑ

Camille
  1. pers. name   kuh-MĒL   kə'miːl
  2. French   kah-MĒ   kɑːmiːj

Camillo
  1. pers. name, German   kah-MIL-ō   kɑ'miloː
  2. Italian   kah-MĒL-lō   kɑ'miːlloː
  3. Portuguese   kuh-MĒ-l͞oo, kah-   kə'miːluː, kɑː-

Camillus
  Roman cognomen   kuh-MIL-uhs   kə'miləs

Camorra
  Italian secret society   kuh-MAWR-uh   kə'mɔːrə

Camp
  pers. name   KAMP   'kæmp

Campa
  S. American people   KAHM-puh   'kɑmpə

Campanella
  Roy, *US baseball executive*   KAM-puh-NEL-uh   ˌkæmpə'nelə

Campania
  region, Italy   kahm-PAHN-yuh, kam-PĂN-yuh,   kɑm'pɑnjə, kæm'peːnjə,
     kam-PĀ-nē-uh   kæm'peːniːə

Campari
  tdmk for an alcoholic drink   kahm-PAHR-ē   kɑm'pɑʳiˑ

Campbell
  US pl. name; pers. name   KAM-buhl, *also* KAM-uhl   'kæmbəl, *also* 'kæməl

Campeche
  state, city, Mexico; bay, Gulf of   kahm-PĀ-chä, ⑤ kam-PĒ-chē   kɑm'peːtʃeː, ⑤ kæm'piːtʃiː
    Mexico

Campion
  Thomas, *English poet & composer*   KAM-pē-uhn, KAM-pyuhn   'kæmpiːən, 'kæmpjən

Camptosaurus
  dinosaur   KAM(P)-tuh-SAWR-uhs   ˌkæm(p)tə'sɔːrəs

Camp Verde
  Indian reservation, US   kamp VUHRD-ē, VERD-ē   kæmp 'vəʳdiˑ, 'veʳdiˑ

Cam Ranh Bay
  military base, Vietnam   KAM rahn BĀ   ˌkæm rɑn 'beː

Foreign Sounds: ue: *Fr.* **rue**, *Ger.* f**ü**llen   uh(r): *Fr.* b**oeu**f, *Ger.* H**öh**le   <u>kh</u>: *Ger.* i**ch**, *Scot.* lo**ch**   ḡ: *Sp.* ami**g**o   <u>v</u>: *Sp.* ha**b**lar
hl: *Welsh* L**l**anelli.   CAPITALS: primary stress.   SMALL CAPS: secondary stress.   ⑤: U.S. pron.   ⓛ: British pron.

Camrose Lutheran
  College, *Canada*   KAM-RŌZ LŌŌ-th(uh-)ruhn   'kæm,roːz 'luːθ(ə)rən
Camus
  Albert, *French author (Nobel*   kah-MUE, ⑤ ka-MŌŌ   kaːmyː, ⑤ kæ'muː
  1957)
Cana
  Biblical town   KĀ-nuh   'keːnə
Canaan
  Biblical name, Palestine   KĀ-nuhn   'keːnən
Canaanites
  ancient Palestinian people   KĀ-nuh-NĪTS   'keːnə,naits
Canace
  daughter of Aeolus and Aenarete   KAN-uh-sē   'kænəsiˑ
Cañada
  College, *CA*   kuhn-YAHD-uh, kan-   kən'jadə, kæn-
Canada
  country, N. America   KAN-uhd-uh, kah-nah-DAH   'kænədə, kaːnaːdaː
Canadian
  pert. to Canada   kuh-NĀD-ē-uhn   kə'neːdiːən
Çanakkale Boğazı [Dardanelles]
  strait, Turkey   CHAHN-uh-kuh-LĀ bō-ĞAHZ-ē   ˌtʃanəkə'leː boːˈɣaziˑ
Cañar
  Ecuador   kuhn-YAHR   kən'jaʳ
Canarias, Islas [Canary Islands]
  islands, Atlantic   ĒZ-lahs kuh-NAHR-ē-ahs   'iːzlas kə'nariːas
Canaries [Canary Islands]
  islands, Atlantic   kuh-NER-ēz   kə'neriˑz
Canary Islands
  islands, Atlantic   kuh-NER-ē Ī-luhn(d)z   kəˌneriˑ 'ɑilən(d)z
Canaveral
  cape, FL   kuh-NAV-(uh-)ruhl   kə'næv(ə)rəl
Canberra
  city, Australia   KAN-b(uh-)ruh, ⑤ KAN-BER-uh   'kænb(ə)rə, ⑤ 'kæn,berə
Canby
  city, MN, OR   KAN-bē   'kænbiˑ
Cancer
  constellation, sign of the zodiac KAN-suhr   'kænsəʳ
Cancún
  city, Mexico   kan-KŌŌN   kæn'kuːn
Candice
  pers. name   KAN-duhs   'kændəs
Candida
  play, G.B. Shaw   kan-DĒD-uh   kæn'diːdə
Candide
  novel, Voltaire   kahⁿ-DĒD, ⑤ kan-DĒD   kɑ̃diːd, ⑤ kæn'diːd
Candlemas
  Christian holy day (Feb. 2)   KAN-dl-muhs   'kændl̩məs
Canea
  town, Greece   kuh-NĒ-uh   kə'niːə
Canens
  personification of song   KĀ-nuhnz   'keːnənz
Canes Venatici
  constellation   KĀ-NĒZ vuh-NĀT-uh-SĪ   'keːˌniːz vəˈneːt̬ə,sai

---

Key (col. 2):   a: fad   ā: fade   ah: father   ar: Mary   aw: law   e: fed   ē: feed   er: merry   i: hid   ī: hide   ō: coat   ōō: boot
oi: boy   ow: now   u: put   uh: above   uhr: bird   ch: chop   ng: ring   sh: show   th: thick   <u>th</u>: this   zh: measure

Canetti
  Elias, *Bulgarian author (Nobel*   kuh-NET-ē   kə'neṭi·
  1981)
Caniff
  Milton, *US cartoonist*   kuh-NIF   kə'nif
Canisius
  College, *NY*   kuh-NISH-(ē-)uhs   kə'niʃ(iː)əs
Canis Major
  constellation   KĀ-nuhs MĀ-juhr   ˌkeːnəs 'meːdʒəʳ
Canis Minor
  constellation   KĀ-nuhs MĪ-nuhr   ˌkeːnəs 'mɑinəʳ
Canna
  plant   KAN-uh   'kænə
Cannae
  Italy, site of Hannibal's victory   KAN-ē   'kæniː
Cannanore
  city, islands, India   KAN-uh-NŌR, KAN-uh-NAWR   'kænəˌnoːʳ, 'kænəˌnɔːʳ
Cannes
  town, France; film festival   KAHN, ⑤ KAN   kɑːn, ⑤ 'kæn
Cañon
  wren   KAN-yuhn   'kænjən
Canoncito
  Indian reservation, US   KAN-yuhn-SĒT-ō   ˌkænjən'siːṭoː
Canopus
  steersman of the Argo; star   kuh-NŌ-puhs   kə'noːpəs
Canossa
  village, Italy   kuh-NAHS-uh   kə'nɑsə
Canowindra
  town, Australia   kuh-NOWN-druh   kə'nɑundrə
Canseco
  Jose, *US baseball player*   kuhn-SĀ-kō, kan-SĀ-kō   kən'seːkoː, kæn'seːkoː
Cantab
  abbreviation for Cantabrigian   KAN-TAB   'kænˌtæb
Cantabria
  region, Spain   kahn-TAHV̱-rē-ah   kɑn'taβriːɑ
Cantabrigia
  Latin form of Cambridge   KANT-uh-BRIJ-(ē-)uh   ˌkæntə'bridʒ(iː)ə
Cantabrigian
  student at or graduate of   KANT-uh-BRIJ-ē-uhn   ˌkæntə'bridʒiːən
  Cambridge Univ.
cantata
  choral composition   kuhn-TAHT-uh   kən'tɑṭə
Cantenac-Margaux
  French wine   kahⁿt-NAHK-mahr-GŌ   kɑ̃tnɑːkmɑːrgoː
Canterbury
  town, England   KANT-uhr-b(uh-)rē,   'kæntəʳb(ə)ri·, 'kæntəʳˌberi·
                                        KANT-uhr-BER-ē
Canticle of Canticles
  Old Testament book   KANT-i-kuhl(z)   'kæntikəl(z)
Cantinflas
  Mexican entertainer   KAN-tuhn-FLAHS   'kæntənˌflɑs
Canton
  town, MA; city, OH; atoll, Pacific KANT-n   'kæntn̩
Canton [Guangzhou]
  city, China   KAN-TAHN, kan-TAHN   'kænˌtɑn, kæn'tɑn

Foreign Sounds: ue: *Fr.* **rue**, *Ger.* **füllen**   uh(r): *Fr.* **boeuf**, *Ger.* **Höhle**   k̲h̲: *Ger.* **ich**, *Scot.* **loch**   g̱: *Sp.* **amigo**   v̱: *Sp.* **hablar**
hl: *Welsh* **Llanelli**.   CAPITALS: primary stress.   SMALL CAPS: secondary stress.   ⑤: U.S. pron.   ⓣ: British pron.

Cantonese		
lang., China; pert. to Canton, *China*	KANT-n-ĒZ, -ĒS	ˌkæntn̩ˈiːz, -ˈiːs
Canuck		
slang for French Canadian	kuh-NUHK	kəˈnək
Canucks		
Vancouver, B.C., hockey team	kuh-NUHKS	kəˈnəks
Canute, Cnut		
early king of England, Denmark, Norway	kuh-N(Y)O͞OT	kəˈn(j)uːt
Canyon de Chelly		
National Monument, *AZ*	KAN-yuhn duh SHĀ-lē	ˈkænjən də ˈʃeːliˑ
Caodaism		
East Asian religion	kow-DĪ-IZ-uhm	kɑuˈdɑiˌizəm
Caol Ila		
Scotch whiskey distillery	KLĒ-luh	ˈkliːlə
Capaneus		
one of the Seven against Thebes	KAP-uh-NĒ-uhs	ˌkæpəˈniːəs
Cap-de-Mourlin		
French wine	kahp-duh-mur-LE^{n}	kɑːpdəmurlɛ̃
Cape Cod		
peninsula, MA	kāp KAHD	keːp ˈkɑd
Cape Girardeau		
county, city, MO	KĀP juh-RAHRD-ō	ˌkeːp dʒəˈrɑʳdoː
Čapek		
Karel, *Czech playwright*	CHAH-pek	ˈtʃɑːpek
Capella		
star	kuh-PEL-uh	kəˈpelə
Capercaillie		
bird (fowl)	KAP-uhr-KAL-(y)ē	ˌkæpəʳˈkæl(j)iˑ
Capernaum		
Biblical town	kuh-PUHR-nē-uhm	kəˈpəʳniːəm
Capetian		
French royal dynasty	kuh-PĒ-shuhn	kəˈpiːʃən
Capetown		
city, S. Africa	KĀP-TOWN	ˈkeːpˌtɑun
Cape Verde		
islands, Atlantic	KĀP VUHRD	ˌkeːp ˈvəʳd
Cape Verdean		
pert. to Cape Verde	KĀP VUHRD-ē-uhn	ˌkeːp ˈvəʳdiːən
Capezio		
shoe mfr.	kuh-PĒ-zē-ō	kəˈpiːziːoː
Capilano		
Stadium, *Vancouver, Canada*	KAP-uh-LAHN-ō, -LAN-ō	ˌkæpəˈlɑnoː, -ˈlænoː
Capistrano		
mission, CA, site of swallows' return	KAP-uh-STRAHN-ō	ˌkæpəˈstrɑnoː
Capitan Grande		
Indian reservation, US	KAP-uh-TAN GRAND(-ē)	ˈkæpəˌtæn ˈgrænd(iˑ)
Capitoline		
hill, Rome, Italy	KAP-uht-l-ĪN, Ⓔ kuh-PIT-l-ĪN	ˈkæpətl̩ˌɑin, Ⓔ kəˈpitl̩ˌɑin
Capodimonte		
Italian town; ceramic ware	KAHP-ō-dē-MAHN-TĀ	ˌkɑpoːdiˑˈmɑnˌteː
Capo Ferrato		
Sardinian wine	KAHP-ō fer-AH-tō	ˌkɑpoː ferˈɑtoː

Key (col. 2): a: **fad** ā: **fade** ah: **father** ar: **Mary** aw: **law** e: **fed** ē: **feed** er: **merry** i: **hid** ī: **hide** ō: **coat** o͞o: **boot** oi: **boy** ow: **now** u: **put** uh: **above** uhr: **bird** ch: **chop** ng: **ring** sh: **show** th: **thick** t͟h: **this** zh: **measure**

Capone
  Al 'Scarface', *US gangster* — kuh-PŌN — kə'pɔːn

Caporetto
  Italian form of Kobarid — KAP-uh-RET-ō — ˌkæpə'reţɔː

Capote
  Truman, *US author* — kuh-PŌT-ē — kə'pɔːţiˑ

Capote Ute
  N. American people — kuh-PŌT-ē YOŌT — kə'pɔːţiˑ 'juːt

Cappadocia
  region, Turkey — KAP-uh-DŌ-sh(ē-)uh — ˌkæpə'dɔːʃ(iː)ə

Capra
  Frank, *US film producer, director* — KAP-ruh — 'kæprə

Capreae
  Latin form of Capri — KAP-rē-Ē — 'kæpriːˌiː

Capri
  island, Italy — ka-PRĒ, kuh-PRĒ, KAHP-rē, KAP-rē — kæ'priː, kə'priː, 'kɑpriˑ, 'kæpriˑ

Capricorn
  constellation, sign of the zodiac — KAP-ri-KAWRN — 'kæpriˌkɔːᵣn

Capricornus
  constellation — KAP-ri-KAWR-nuhs — ˌkæpri'kɔːᵣnəs

Capshaw
  Kate, *US actress* — KAP-SHAW — 'kæpˌʃɔː

Capua
  town, Italy — KAP-yuh-wuh — 'kæpjəwə

Capucci
  shoe mfr. — kah-POŌT-chē, kuh-POŌ-chē — kɑ'puːttʃiˑ, kə'puːtʃiˑ

Capuchins
  religious order — KAP-(y)uh-shuhnz, kuh-PYOŌ-shuhnz — 'kæp(j)əʃənz, kə'pjuːʃənz

Capucine
  French entertainer — kah-pue-SĒN — kɑːpyːsiːn

Capulet
  Juliet's family in Romeo & Juliet — KAP-yuh-luht — 'kæpjələt

Caracalla
  Roman emperor — KAR-uh-KAL-uh — ˌkærə'kælə

Caracara
  bird — KAR-uh-KAR-uh, KAR-uh-kuh-RAH — ˌkærə'kærə, ˌkærəkə'rɑ

Caracas
  city, Venezuela — kuh-RAK-uhs, kuh-RAHK-uhs — kə'rækəs, kə'rɑkəs

Caracul
  sheep breed — KAR-uh-kuhl — 'kærəkəl

Caradoc
  1. pers. name — kuh-RAHD-awg, -uhk — kə'rɑdɔːg, -ək
  2. Welsh — kah-RAH-dawg — kɑːˈrɑːdɔːg

Caravaggio
  Michelangelo da, *Italian painter* — KAR-uh-VAHJ-ō, KAR-uh-VAHZH-ō, -VAHJ-ē-ō, -VAHZH-ē-ō — ˌkærə'vɑdʒɔː, ˌkærə'vɑʒɔː, -'vɑdʒiːˌɔː, -'vɑʒiːˌɔː

Caravanche [Karawanken]
  Alpine mtn. range — KAH-re-VAHNG-kā — ˌkɑre'vɑŋkeː

Carbo
  Roman cognomen — KAHR-bō — 'kɑᵣbɔː

carbon
  element — KAHR-buhn — 'kɑᵣbən

Carbonari
　European secret political party　　KAHR-buh-NAHR-ē　　　　,kaʳbə'nari·

Carbonnieux
　French wine　　kahr-bawn-YUH(R)　　　　kaːrbɔːnjœː

Carcassonne
　city, France　　kahr-kah-SAWN, ⑤ kahr-kuh-SAWN,　　kaːrkaːsɔːn, ⑤ kaʳkə'sɔːn,
　　　　-SŌN　　　　-'soːn

Carchemish
　ancient Hittite capital, Turkey　　KAHR-kuh-MISH, kahr-KĒ-mish　　'kaʳkə,miʃ, kaʳ'kiːmiʃ

Cardamom
　mtn. range, Thailand; spice　　KAHRD-uh-muhm, KAHRD-uh-MAHM　　'kaʳdəməm, 'kaʳdə,mam

Cárdenas
　Lázaro, *president, Mexico*　　KAHR-T̲H̲Ā-nahs, ⑤ KAHRD-n-AHS　　'kaʳ,ðeːnas, ⑤ 'kaʳdn̩,as

Cardiff [Caerdydd]
　city, Wales　　KAHR-duhf　　　　'kaʳdəf

Cardiganshire
　former county, Wales　　KAHRD-uh-guhn-shuhr, -SHIR, -SHĪR　　'kaʳdəgənʃəʳ, -,ʃiʳ, -,ʃaiʳ

Cardin
　Pierre, *French fashion designer*　　kahr-DEⁿ, ⑤ kahr-DAN, kahr-DAⁿ　　kaːrdẽ, ⑤ kaʳ'dæn, kaʳ'dæ̃

Cardinale
　Claudia, *Italian entertainer*　　KAHRD-n-AHL-ā　　　　,kaʳdn̩'aleː

Cardinal Stritch
　College, *WI*　　KAHRD-n-uhl STRICH, KAHRD-nuhl　　'kaʳdn̩əl 'stritʃ, 'kaʳdnəl

Carducci
　Giosuè, *Italian poet (Nobel 1906)*　　kahr-DŌŌT-chē; ⑤ kahr-DŌŌ-chē　　kar'duːttʃiː, ⑤ kaʳ'duːtʃi·

Carew
　pers. name　　kuh-RŌŌ　　　　kə'ruː

Carey
　pers. name　　KAR-ē, KER-ē　　　　'kæri·, 'keri·

Caria
　ancient district, Asia Minor　　KAR-ē-uh, KER-ē-uh　　'kæriːə, 'keriːə

Carib
　S. & Cen. American people　　KAR-uhb　　　　'kærəb

Caribbean
　sea　　KAR-uh-BĒ-uhn, kuh-RIB-ē-uhn　　,kærə'biːən, kə'ribiːən

Caribou
　N. American people　　KAR-uh-BŌŌ　　　　'kærə,buː

Carignan
　wine grape variety　　kahr-ēn-YAHⁿ　　　　kaːriːnjã

Carineña
　Spanish wine　　KAHR-ē-NĂN-yuh　　　　,kari:'neːnjə

Carinthia
　state, Austria　　kuh-RIN-thē-uh　　　　kə'rinθiːə

Carioca
　dance　　KAR-ē-Ō-kuh　　　　,kæri:'oːkə

Caririi
　S. American people　　KAR-uh-RĒ　　　　,kærə'riː

Carl
　1. pers. name　　KAHRL, KAHR-uhl　　　　'kaʳl, 'karəl
　2. Danish, Norwegian, Swedish　　KAHRL　　　　'karl
　3. Finnish　　KAHRL　　　　'kaːrl
　4. German　　KAHRL　　　　'kaʳl

Carla
　pers. name　　KAHR-luh　　　　'kaʳlə

Key (col. 2):　a: fad　ā: fade　ah: father　ar: Mary　aw: law　e: fed　ē: feed　er: merry　i: hid　ī: hide　ō: coat　ōō: boot
oi: boy　ow: now　u: put　uh: above　uhr: bird　ch: chop　ng: ring　sh: show　th: thick　t̲h̲: this　zh: measure

Carleton
   College, *MN; pers. name*   KAHRL-tuhn, KAHRLT-n   ˈkɑʳltən, ˈkɑʳltn̩

Carlin
   George, *US comedian*   KAHR-luhn   ˈkɑʳlən

Carlisle
   John, *US politician; pl. name;*   kahr-LĪL, KAHR-LĪL, kuhr-LĪL   kɑʳˈlail, ˈkɑʳˌlail, kəʳˈlail
   pers. name

Carlo
   1. pers. name   KAHR-lō   ˈkɑʳloː
   2. Italian   KAHR-lō   ˈkarloː
   3. Swedish   KAHR-lō   ˈkaːrloː

Carlo Rossi
   wine   KAHR-lō RAWS-ē   ˌkɑʳloː ˈrɔːsiˑ

Carlos
   1. pers. name   KAHR-lōs, KAHR-luhs   ˈkɑʳloːs, ˈkɑʳləs
   2. German   KAHR-LAWS   ˈkɑʳˌlɔːs
   3. Portuguese   KAHR-lōōsh, -lōōs   ˈkaːrluːʃ, -luːs
   4. Spanish   KAHR-lōs   ˈkarloːs

Carlota
   pers. name, Spanish   kahr-LŌ-tah   karˈloːta

Carlotta
   1. pers. name   kahr-LAHT-uh   kɑʳˈlɑtə
   2. Italian   kahr-LAWT-tah   karˈlɔːtta

Carlovingian [Carolingian]
   Frankish dynasty of Charlemagne   KAHR-luh-VINJ-(ē-)uhn   ˌkɑʳləˈvindʒ(iː)ən

Carlsbad
   city, CA, NM; caverns, NM   KAHRLZ-BAD, KAHR-uhlz-BAD   ˈkɑʳlz,bæd, ˈkarəlz,bæd

Carlsberg
   Danish beer   KAHRLS-BERG̃, Ⓢ KAHRLZ-BUHRG   ˈkarls,berɣ, Ⓢ ˈkɑʳlz,bəʳg

Carlstadt
   borough, NJ   KAHRL-STAT   ˈkɑʳl,stæt

Carlton
   pers. name   KAHRL-tuhn, KAHRLT-n   ˈkɑʳltən, ˈkɑʳltn̩

Carly
   pers. name   KAHR-lē   ˈkɑʳliˑ

Carlyle
   city, IL   kahr-LĪL, KAHR-LĪL   kɑʳˈlail, ˈkɑʳˌlail

Carmarthenshire
   former county, Wales   kuhr-MAHR-thuhn-shuhr, kahr-,   kəʳˈmɑʳðənʃəʳ, kɑʳ-, -ˌʃiʳ
       -SHIR

Carme
   satellite of Jupiter   KAHR-mā   ˈkɑʳmeː

Carmel
   1. city, CA   kahr-MEL   kɑʳˈmel
   2. town, IN, NY; Mount, Israel   KAHR-muhl   ˈkɑʳməl

Carmela
   pers. name   kahr-MEL-uh   kɑʳˈmelə

Carmelites
   religious order   KAHR-muh-LĪTS   ˈkɑʳməˌlaits

Carmen
   pers. name   KAHR-muhn   ˈkɑʳmən

Carmenta
   Roman nymph, mother of   kahr-MEN-tuh   kɑʳˈmentə
   Evander

Foreign Sounds: ue: *Fr.* **rue**, *Ger.* füllen   uh(r): *Fr.* **boeuf**, *Ger.* Höhle   kh: *Ger.* i**ch**, *Scot.* lo**ch**   g̃: *Sp.* ami**g**o   v: *Sp.* ha**b**lar
hl: *Welsh* **Ll**anelli.   CAPITALS: primary stress.   SMALL CAPS: secondary stress.   Ⓢ: U.S. pron.   Ⓛ: British pron.

Carmichael

    1. Hoagy, *US songwriter*   KAHR-MĪ-kuhl, kahr-MĪ-kuhl   'kaͬ,maikəl, kɑͬ'maikəl

    2. community, CA   KAHR-MĪ-kuhl   'kaͬ,maikəl

Carmina Burana

    collection of medieval songs;   KAHR-MĒ-nuh b(y)u-RAHN-uh,   ,kaͬ,miːnə b(j)u'ranə,

    choral work, Orff   kahr-muh-nuh   kaͬmənə

Carmona

    commune, Spain   kahr-MŌ-nuh   kaͬ'moːnə

Carna

    virgin huntress in Greek myth   KAHR-nuh   'kaͬnə

Carnac

    commune, France (megalithic site) KAHR-NAK   'kaͬ,næk

Carnarvon

    fishing port, Western Australia   kahr-NAHR-vuhn, kuhr-NAHR-vuhn kaͬ'naͬvən, kəͬ'naͬvən

Carnauba

    palm   kahr-NAW-buh, kahr-NOW-buh,   kaͬ'nɔːbə, kaͬ'naubə,

                            KAHR-nah-OO-buh   ,kaͬna'uːbə

Carnaval-Souvenir de Chicoutimi

    Quebec festival   kahr-nah-VAHL-soov(-uh)-NIR duh   kaːrnaːvaːlsuːv(ə)nir də

                            shē-koo-tē-MĒ   ʃiːkuːtiːmiː

Carnegie

    Andrew, *US industrialist; concert* KAHR-nuh-gē, kahr-NEG-ē   'kaͬnəgiˑ, kaͬ'negiˑ

    hall, New York City; pers. name

Carnegie-Mellon

    univ., Pittsburgh, PA   KAHR-nuh-gē-MEL-uhn,   ,kaͬnəgiˑ'melən,

                            kahr-NEG-ē-MEL-uhn   kaͬ,negiˑ'melən

Carnelian

    chalcedony   kahr-NEL-yuhn   kaͬ'niːljən

Carner

    Joanne Gunderson, *US golfer*   KAHR-nuhr   'kaͬnəͬ

Carnes

    Kim, *rock singer*   KAHRNZ   'kaͬnz

Carney

    Art, *US actor*   KAHR-nē   'kaͬniˑ

Carnic

    Alps, *Alpine mtn. range*   KAHR-nik   'kaͬnik

Carnivora

    meat-eaters   kahr-NIV-uh-ruh   kaͬ'nivərə

Carnosauria

    dinosaur infraorder   KAHR-nuh-SAWR-ē-uh   ,kaͬnə'sɔːriːə

Carol, Carole

    pers. name   KAR-uhl, KER-uhl   'kærəl, 'kerəl

Carolina

    1. early American colony   KAR-uh-LĪ-nuh   ,kærə'lainə

    2. city, Puerto Rico   KAHR-uh-LĒ-nuh, KAR-uh-LĒ-nuh   ,karə'liːnə, ,kærə'liːnə

Caroline

    1. archipelago, Pacific; pers. name KAR-uh-LĪN, KAR-uh-luhn, KER-   'kærə,lain, 'kærələn, 'ker-

    2. French   kah-raw-LĒN   kaͬɔːliːn

    3. county, MD, VA   KAR-uh-LĪN, KER-   'kærə,lain, 'ker-

Carolingian

    Frankish dynasty of Charlemagne KAR-uh-LIN-j(ē-)uhn   ,kærə'lindʒ(iː)ən

Carolinian

    pert. to the Carolinas *or*   KAR-uh-LIN-ē-uhn,   ,kærə'liniːən, ,kærə'liːnjən

    Carolingian   KAR-uh-LĒN-yuhn

Key (col. 2): a: fad ā: fade ah: father ar: Mary aw: law e: fed ē: feed er: merry i: hid ī: hide ō: coat oo: boot
oi: boy ow: now u: put uh: above uhr: bird ch: chop ng: ring sh: show th: thick th: this zh: measure

Carolus
   1. pers. name, French   kah-raw-LUES   kɑːrɔːlyːs
   2. Latin   KAR-uh-luhs   'kærələs
Carolus Magnus
   Latin form of Charlemagne   KAR-uh-luhs MAG-nuhs   'kærələs 'mægnəs
Carolyn
   pers. name   KAR-uh-luhn   'kærələn
Caron
   Leslie, *entertainer*   kuh-RŌN   kə'roːn
Carotene
   pigment   KAR-uh-TĒN   'kærə,tiːn
Carpaccio
   Vittore, *Italian painter*   kahr-PAHCH-ō, kahr-PAHCH-ē-ō   kɑrʳ'pɑtʃoː, kɑrʳ'patʃiː,oː
Carpathian
   mtn. range, Europe   kahr-PĀ-thē-uhn   kɑrʳ'peːθiːən
Carpatho-Ukraine
   region in Ukraine   KAHR-puh-thō-yoo-KRĀN   'kɑrʳpəθoːjuʳkreːn
Carpentaria
   Gulf of, *inlet, Australia*   KAHR-puhn-TER-ē-uh, -TAR-ē-uh   ˌkɑrʳpən'teriːə, -'tæriːə
Carracci
   Annibale, *Italian painter*   kahr-RAHCH-ē   kɑr'rɑtʃiˑ
Carradine
   David, Keith & John, *US actors*   KAR-uh-DĒN, KER-uh-DĒN   'kærə,diːn, 'kerə,diːn
Carrageen
   seaweed   KAR-uh-GĒN   'kærə,giːn
Carrara
   commune, Italy   kuh-RAHR-uh   kə'rɑrə
Carrefour
   French retailer   kahr-FOOR, Ⓢ kahr-FŌR, kahr-FAWR   kɑːrfuːr, Ⓢ kɑrʳfoːʳ, kɑrʳfɔːʳ
Carrel
   Alexis, *French surgeon, biologist*   kah-REL, Ⓢ kuh-REL, KAR-uhl   kɑːrel, Ⓢ kə'rel, 'kærəl
   (Nobel 1912)
Carrera
   Barbara, *actress*   kuh-RER-uh   kə'rerə
Carreras
   Jose, *Spanish tenor*   kahr-RER-ahs   kɑr'reras
Carrhae
   site of Roman defeat, 53 B.C.   KAR-ē, KER-ē   'kæriˑ, 'keriˑ
Carrie
   pers. name   KAR-ē, KER-ē   'kæriˑ, 'keriˑ
Carrier
   N. American people   KAR-ē-uhr, KER-ē-uhr   'kæriːəʳ, 'keriːəʳ
Carroll
   Lewis, *pseudonym of* C. L.   KAR-uhl, KER-uhl   'kærəl, 'kerəl
   Dodgson, *English writer; pers.*
   name
Carruades de Château Lafite
   wine   kahr-WAHD duh shah-TŌ lah-FĒT   kɑːrwɑːd də ʃatoː lɑːfiːt
Carruth
   Gorton, *US author*   kuh-ROOTH   kə'ruːθ
Carruthers
   pers. name   kuh-RUH<u>TH</u>-uhrz   kə'rəðəʳz
Carson
   pers. name   KAHR-suhn   'kɑrʳsən

Foreign Sounds: ue: *Fr.* **rue**, *Ger.* **füllen**   uh(r): *Fr.* **boeuf**, *Ger.* **Höhle**   <u>kh</u>: *Ger.* **ich**, *Scot.* **loch**   ğ: *Sp.* **amigo**   v: *Sp.* **hablar**
hl: *Welsh* **Llanelli**.   CAPITALS: primary stress.   SMALL CAPS: secondary stress.   Ⓢ: U.S. pron.   Ⓛ: British pron.

Carta Blanca
  Mexican beer   KAHR-tah BLAHNG-kah   'kɑrtɑ 'blɑŋkɑ

Cartagena
  city, Spain, Colombia   kahr-tah-GĀ-nah,   kɑrtɑ'yeːnɑ, Ⓢ ˌkɑrt̬ə'geːnə,
           Ⓢ KAHRT-uh-GĀ-nuh, -JĒ-nuh,   -'dʒiːnə, -'heːnə
           -HĀ-nuh

Carter
  Jimmy, 39th US president; pers.   KAHRT-uhr   'kɑrt̬ər
    name

Carteret
  1. borough, NJ; county, NC   KAHRT-uh-RET   ˌkɑrt̬ə'ret
  2. village, France   kahr-TRE, kahr-tuh-RE,   kɑːrtre, kɑrtəre, Ⓢ ˌkɑrt̬ə'reː
           Ⓢ KAHRT-uh-RĀ

Cartesian
  pert. to Descartes   kahr-TĒ-zhuhn, Ⓔ kahr-TĒ-zē-uhn   kɑr'tiːʒən, Ⓔ kɑr'tiːziːən

Cartesianism
  philosophy of Descartes   kahr-TĒ-zhuh-NIZ-uhm   kɑr'tiːʒə,nizəm

Carthage
  ancient African city; US pl. name KAHR-thij   'kɑrθidʒ

Carthaginian
  pert. to Carthage   KAHR-thuh-JIN-ē-uhn   ˌkɑrθə'dʒiniːən

Carthusians
  religious order   kahr-TH(Y)O͞O-zhuhnz   kɑr'θ(j)uːʒənz

Cartier
  1. jewelry retailer; pers. name KAHRT-ē-Ā, kahr-TYĀ   'kɑrt̬iːˌeː, kɑr'tjeː
  2. French   kahr-TYĀ   kɑːrtjeː

Cartier-Bresson
  Henri, *French photographer* kahr-tyā-brā-SAWⁿ   kɑːrtjeːbreːsɔ̃

Cartland
  Barbara, *British author*   KAHRT-luhnd   'kɑrtlənd

Caruso
  Enrico, *Italian tenor*   kuh-RO͞O-sō, kuh-RO͞O-zō   kə'ruːsoː, kə'ruːzoː

Carvalho
  pers. name, Portuguese kuhr-VAHL-yo͞o   kər'valjuː

Casablanca
  seaport, Morocco; movie KAS-uh-BLANG-kuh, KAZ-;   ˌkæsə'blæŋkə, ˌkæz-;
           KAHS-uh-BLAHNG-kuh, KAHZ-   ˌkɑsə'blɑŋkə, ˌkɑz-

Casa Grande
  National Monument, *AZ*   KAHS-uh GRAHN-dē, GRAHN-dä 'kɑsə 'grɑndiː, 'grɑndeː

Casals
  Pablo, *Spanish cellist/composer* kuh-SAHLZ   kə'salz

Casanova
  Francesco, *Italian artist;* Giovanni KAS-uh-NŌ-vuh, KAZ-uh-NŌ-vuh ˌkæsə'noːvə, ˌkæzə'noːvə
    Giacomo, *Italian adventurer &*
    sensualist

Cäsar
  pers. name, German   TSEZ-AHR   'tsez,ɑr

Casaubon
  The Rev. Edward, *character in* kuh-SAW-buhn   kə'sɔːbən
    George Eliot's Middlemarch

Casbah
  see Kasbah

Cascais
  fishing port, Portugal   kahsh-KĪSH   kaʃ'kaiʃ

Key (col. 2): a: fad ā: fade ah: father ar: Mary aw: law e: fed ē: feed er: merry i: hid ī: hide ō: coat o͞o: boot
oi: boy ow: now u: put uh: above uhr: bird ch: chop ng: ring sh: show th: thick tẖ: this zh: measure

Casey
   pers. name   KĀ-sē   'keːsiˑ

Cashmere
   see Kashmir

Casimir
   1. pers. name   KAZ-uh-MIR   'kæzə‚mi^r
   2. French   kah-zē-MĒR   kɑːziːmiːr

Casino
   town, Australia   kuh-SĒ-nō   kə'siːnoː

Casio
   electronics co.   KAS-ē-ō   'kæsiː‚oː

Caspar
   1. comic book ghost; pers. name   KAS-puhr   'kæspə^r
   2. Danish   KAHS-PAHR   'kɑːs‚pɑr
   3. Dutch, Norwegian   KAHS-PAHR   'kɑs‚pɑr
   4. German   KAHS-PAHR   'kɑs‚pɑ^r

Casper
   city, WY; pers. name   KAS-puhr   'kæspə^r

Caspian
   inland sea, Europe & Asia;   KAS-pē-uhn   'kæspiːən
     character, C.S. Lewis

Cass
   county, IN; pers. name   KAS   'kæs

Cassaba [Cassava]
   edible root   kuh-SAHB-uh   kə'sɑbə

Cassandra
   Trojan prophetess; pers. name   kuh-SAN-druh   kə'sændrə

Cassatt
   Mary, US painter   kuh-SAT   kə'sæt

Cassava
   edible root   kuh-SAHV-uh   kə'sɑvə

Cassavetes
   John, US actor   KAS-uh-VET-ēz, KAS-uh-VĒT-ēz   ‚kæsə'veʈiːz, ‚kæsə'viːʈiːz

Cassell
   reference book publisher   KAS-uhl   'kæsəl

Cassia
   1. county, ID   KASH-(ē-)uh   'kæʃ(iː)ə
   2. spice   KASH-uh   'kæʃə

Cassidy
   Fred, US lexicographer   KAS-uhd-ē   'kæsədiˑ

Cassin
   René, French jurist, statesman   kah-SE^n kɑːsẽ
     (Nobel 1968)

Cassini
   Oleg, US fashion designer   kuh-SĒ-nē   kə'siːniˑ

Cassiopeia
   mother of Andromeda;   KAS-ē-uh-PĒ-(y)uh   ‚kæsiːə'piː(j)ə
     constellation

Cassiphone
   daughter of Odysseus and Circe   kuh-SIF-uh-nē   kə'sifəniˑ

Cassis
   French wine   ka-SĒ   kæ'siː

Cassius
   pers. name   KASH-(ē-)uhs, KAS-ē-uhs   'kæʃ(iː)əs, 'kæsiːəs

---

Foreign Sounds: ue: *Fr.* **rue**, *Ger.* f**ü**llen   uh(r): *Fr.* b**oeu**f, *Ger.* H**ö**hle   <u>kh</u>: *Ger.* i**ch**, *Scot.* lo**ch**   ḡ: *Sp.* ami**g**o   ṿ: *Sp.* ha**b**lar
hl: *Welsh* **Ll**anelli.   CAPITALS: primary stress.   SMALL CAPS: secondary stress.   Ⓢ: U.S. pron.   Ⓑ: British pron.

Cassowary
   Australian bird   KAS-uh-WER-ē   'kæsə,weri·

Cassubian [Kashubian]
   lang., Europe   kas-YŌŌ-bē-uhn, kash-ŌŌ-bē-uhn   kæs'juːbiːən, kæʃ'uːbiːən

Castalia
   town, OH   kas-TĂ-lē-uh   kæs'teːliːə

Castel Gandolfo
   site of papal palace   KAS-TEL gahn-DAHL-fō, KAHS-TEL,   ‚kæs,tel gɑn'dɑlfoː, ‚kas,tel,
                           gahn-DAWL-fō   gɑn'dɔːlfoː

Castiglione
   Conte Baldassare, Italian   KAHS-tēl-YŌ-nä   ‚kastiːl'joːneː
    diplomat & writer

Castile
   region, NY; region, Spain   ka-STĔL   kæ'stiːl
    [Castilla]

Castilian
   Spanish dialect   kas-TIL-yuhn   kæs'tiljən

Castilla [Castile]
   region, Spain   kah-STĒ(L)-yah   kɑ'stiː(l)ja

Castilla-La Mancha
   region, Spain   kah-STĒ(L)-yah-lah-MAHN-chuh   kɑ'stiː(l)jalɑ'mantʃə

Castilla-León
   region, Spain   kah-STĒ(L)-yah-lā-ŌN   kɑ'stiː(l)jaleː'oːn

Castor
   twin of Pollux in Greek myth; star   KAS-tuhr   'kæstəʳ
    Alpha Geminorum

Castries
   capital, St. Lucia   ka-STRĒ, KAHS-TRĒS   kæ'striː, 'kas,triːs

Castro
   Fidel, president, Cuba   KAS-trō   'kæstroː

Castrol
   motor oil brand   KAS-TRŌL, KAS-TRAHL   'kæs,troːl, 'kæs,tral

Castruccio
   pers. name   kahs-TRŌŌT-chō   kas'truːttʃoː

Caswell
   county, NC   KAZ-wuhl, KAZ-WEL   'kæzwəl, 'kæz,wel

Catahoula
   lake, parish, LA   KAT-uh-HŌŌ-luh   ‚kæʈə'huːlə

Catalan
   lang., Spain   KAT-l-uhn, KAT-l-AN, KAT-l-AN   'kæʈl̩ən, 'kæʈl̩,æn, ‚kæʈl̩'æn

Çatal Huyuk
   Neolithic site, central Turkey   CHAHT-l HŌŌ-yuk   'tʃatl̩ 'huːjuk

Catalonia
   region, Spain   KAT-l-ŌN-yuh, KAT-l-Ō-nē-uh   ‚kæʈl̩'oːnjə, ‚kæʈl̩'oːniːə

Catalonian [Catalan]
   lang., Spain   KAT-l-Ō-nē-uhn   ‚kæʈl̩'oːniːən

Catalpa
   tree genus   kuh-TAL-puh, kuh-TAH(L)-puh,   kə'tælpə, kə'tɑ(l)pə,
               kuh-TAW(L)-puh, -buh   kə'tɔː(l)pə, -bə

Cataluña, -lunya [Catalonia]
   region, Spain   KAHT-uh-LŌŌN-yuh, KAT-l-ŌŌN-yuh   ‚kaʈə'luːnjə, ‚kæʈl̩'uːnjə

Catania
   prov & town, Italy   kuh-TAHN-yuh, kuh-TĂN-yuh   kə'tanjə, kə'teːnjə

Key (col. 2):   a: fad   ā: fade   ah: father   ar: Mary   aw: law   e: fed   ē: feed   er: merry   i: hid   ī: hide   ō: coat   ōō: boot
oi: boy   ow: now   u: put   uh: above   uhr: bird   ch: chop   ng: ring   sh: show   th: thick   th̲: this   zh: measure

Catawba		
river, US; N. American people; college, NC; grape variety	kuh-TAW-buh, kuh-TAHB-uh	kə'tɔːbə, kə'tɑbə
Caterham and Warlingham		
town, England	KĀT-uh-ruhm uhn(d) WAWR-ling-uhm	'keːṭərəm ən(d) 'wɔːʳliŋəm
Caterina		
pers. name, Italian	KAH-tā-RĒ-nah	ˌkɑteː'riːnɑ
Cates		
pers. name	KĀTS	'keːts
Cathar		
medieval Christian sect	KATH-AHR	'kæθˌɑʳ
Catharine		
pers. name	KATH-(uh-)ruhn	'kæθ(ə)rən
Catharism		
religion	KATH-uh-RIZ-uhm, KATH-AHR-IZ-uhm	'kæθəˌrizəm, 'kæθˌɑrˌizəm
Cathay		
literary term for China	kuh-THĀ, ka-THĀ	kə'θeː, kæ'θeː
Cather		
Willa, *US author*	KATH-uhr	'kæðəʳ
Catherine		
1. pers. name	KATH-(uh-)ruhn	'kæθ(ə)rən
2. French	kah-tuh-RĒN, kah-TRĒN	kɑːtəriːn, kɑːtriːn
Cathleen ni Houlihan		
play, W. B. Yeats	kath-LĒN nē HOO-luh-HAN	kæθ'liːn niˑ 'huːləˌhæn
Catholic		
Christian religion	KATH-(uh-)lik	'kæθ(ə)lik
Catholicism		
Christian religion	kuh-THAHL-uh-SIZ-uhm	kə'θɑləˌsizəm
Cathrine		
pers. name	KATH-ruhn	'kæθrən
Cath's		
nickname of St. Catherine' s College, *Cambridge Univ.*	KATS	'kæts
Cathy		
pers. name	KATH-ē	'kæθiˑ
Catiline		
Roman conspirator	KAT-l-ĪN	'kætḷˌɑin
Cato		
M. Porcius, *Roman statesman*	KĀT-ō	'keːṭoː
Catoosa		
county, GA	kuh-TOO-suh	kə'tuːsə
Catreus		
son of Minos and Pasiphae	KA-trē-uhs, KA-TROOS	'kætriːəs, 'kæˌtruːs
Catrin		
pers. name	KA-truhn	'kætrən
Catrina		
pers. name	kuh-TRĒ-nuh	kə'triːnə
Catrine		
pers. name	KA-TRĒN	'kæˌtriːn
Catron		
county, NM	kuh-TRAHN	kə'trɑn
Catskill		
mtn. range, village, NY	KAT-SKIL	'kætˌskil

Foreign Sounds: ue: *Fr.* **rue**, *Ger.* **füllen** uh(r): *Fr.* **boeuf**, *Ger.* **Höhle** kh: *Ger.* **ich**, *Scot.* **loch** g̃: *Sp.* **amigo** v̲: *Sp.* **hablar** hl: *Welsh* **Llanelli**. CAPITALS: primary stress. SMALL CAPS: secondary stress. [$]: U.S. pron. [£]: British pron.

Cattaraugus
   county, Indian reservation, NY   KAT-uh-RAW-guhs,   'kæṭə,rɔːgəs, ˌkæṭə'rɔːgəs
                               KAT-uh-RAW-guhs

Cattegat
   see Kattegat

Catton
   Bruce, *US historian*   KAT-n   'kætn̩

Catulle
   pers. name, French   kah-TUEL   kɑːtyːl

Catullus
   Roman poet   kuh-TUHL-uhs   kə'tələs

Caucasia [Caucasus]
   region, mtn. range, between   kaw-KĀ-zhuh, kaw-KĀ-shuh   kɔː'keːʒə, kɔː'keːʃə
      Europe and Asia

Caucasian
   pert. to Caucasus; *Indo-European*   kaw-KĀ-zhuhn, kaw-KAZH-uhn, Ⓔ   kɔː'keːʒən, kɔː'kæʒən, Ⓔ
      race   kaw-KĀ-zē-uhn   kɔ'keːziːən

Caucasus
   region, mtn. range, between   KAW-kuh-suhs   'kɔːkəsəs
      Europe and Asia

Caunus
   son of Miletus   KAW-nuhs   'kɔːnəs

Cauthen
   Steve, *US-born jockey*   KAW-thuhn, KAHTH-uhn   'kɔːθən, 'kɑθən

Cauvery
   waterfall, river, India   KAW-vuh-rē   'kɔːvəriˑ

Cavalleria Rusticana
   opera, Mascagni   KAV-uh-luh-RĒ-uh RUS-ti-KAHN-uh   ˌkævələ'riːə ˌrusti'kɑnə

Cavatina
   simple melody   KAV-uh-TĒ-nuh, KAHV-uh-TĒ-nuh   ˌkævə'tiːnə, ˌkɑvə'tiːnə

Cavell
   Edith, *English nurse, WW1*   KAV-uhl, kuh-VEL   'kævəl, kə'vel

Cavendish
   William, *British prime minister*   KAV-uhn-dish   'kævəndiʃ

Cavett
   Dick, *US talk show host*   KAV-uht   'kævət

Cavite
   prov, port, Philippines   kuh-VĒT-ē   kə'viːṭiˑ

Cawdor
   parish, Scotland   KAWD-uhr   'kɔːdəʳ

Cawley
   Evonne Goolagong, *Australian*   KAW-lē   'kɔːliˑ
      tennis player

Caxton
   William, *English printer*   KAK-stuhn   'kækstən

Cayapa
   S. American people   kuh-YAHP-uh, kī-AHP-uh   kə'japə, kai'apə

Cayapo
   S. American people   KAH-yuh-PŌ, KĪ-uh-PŌ   ˌkajə'poː, ˌkaiə'poː

Cayenne
   city, French Guiana; spice   kī-EN, kā-EN   kai'en, keː'en

Cay Lobos
   island, British Virgin Islands   KĒ LŌ-bōs, KĀ, LŌ-bōz, LŌ-buhs   ˌkiː 'loːboːs, 'keː, 'loːboːz,
                                                        'loːbəs

---

Cayman

islands, West Indies | kā-MAN, *attributively (as in "C. Islands")* KĀ-muhn | keː'mæn, *attributively (as in "C. Islands")* 'keːmən

Caymus

winery, CA | KĀ-muhs | 'keːməs

Cayo Verde

lime liqueur | KĪ-ō VERD-ē, VUHRD-ē | ˌkɑioː 'veʳdiˑ, 'vəʳdiˑ

Cay Sal

island, British Virgin Islands | KĒ SAL, KĀ | 'kiː 'sæl, 'keː

Cayuga

lake, county, NY; N. American people | kuh-YOO-guh, KYOO-guh, kā-(Y)OO-guh | kə'juːgə, 'kjuːgə, keː'(j)uːgə

Cayuse

N. American people | KĪ-(Y)OOS, kī-(Y)OOS | 'kɑiˌ(j)uːs, kɑi'(j)uːs

Cazenovia

village, NY (birthplace of Hiawatha) | KAZ-uh-NŌ-vē-uh | ˌkæzə'noːviːə

CD-ROM

compact disk-read-only memory | SĒ-dē-RAHM | ˌsiːdiːˈrɑm

Ceausescu

Nicolae, *former president, Romania* | chow-SHESH-koo | tʃɑu'ʃeʃkuː

Cebu

island & seaport, Philippines | sā-BOO | seː'buː

Cebuano

see Sebuano

Cech

Thomas R., *US biochemist (Nobel 1989)* | CHEKH, CHEK | 'tʃex, 'tʃek

Cecil

1. E. A. R., *English statesman (Nobel 1937)* | SES-uhl, SIS-uhl | 'sesəl, 'sisəl
2. *pers. name* | SĒ-suhl, Ⓛ SES-uhl, SIS-uhl | 'siːsəl, Ⓛ 'sesəl, 'sisəl
3. *county, MD* | SIS-uhl, SĒ-suhl | 'sisəl, 'siːsəl

Cecile

pers. name | suh-SĒL, Ⓛ SES-ĒL, SES-uhl, SIS-uhl | sə'siːl, Ⓛ 'ses,iːl, 'sesəl, 'sisəl

Cécile

1. *pers. name, French* | sā-SĒL | seːsiːl
2. *Canadian French* | sā-SIL | seːsil

Cecilia

pers. name | suh-SIL-ē-uh, suh-SIL-yuh, suh-SĒL-yuh | sə'siliːə, sə'siljə, sə'siːljə

Cecillo Village

Indian reservation, US | suh-SĒ(L)-yō | sə'siː(l)joː

Cecily

pers. name | SIS-(uh-)lē, SES-(uh-)lē | 'sis(ə)liˑ, 'ses(ə)liˑ

Cecrops

mythical king of Attica | SEK-RAHPS | 'sekˌrɑps

Cedalion

instructor of Hephaestus | si-DĀ-lē-uhn | si'deːliːən

Čedomilj

pers. name | CHED-aw-MĒL | 'tʃedɔːˌmiːḷ

Cedric

pers. name | SED-rik, SĒ-drik | 'sedrik, 'siːdrik

Foreign Sounds: ue: *Fr.* **rue**, *Ger.* **füllen** uh(r): *Fr.* **boeuf**, *Ger.* **Höhle** kh: *Ger.* **ich**, *Scot.* **loch** g̠: *Sp.* **amigo** v̠: *Sp.* **hablar** hl: *Welsh* **Llanelli**. CAPITALS: primary stress. SMALL CAPS: secondary stress. Ⓢ: U.S. pron. Ⓛ: British pron.

Cegelec
    French electric power co.   sej-el-EK   sedʒelek

Ceilidh
    Trail, *Cape Breton Island, Nova*   KĀ-lē   'keːliˑ
        Scotia; Irish & Scottish evening
        of musical entertainment

Ceiriog
    pers. name, Welsh   KER-yawg   'kerjɔːg

Cela
    Camilo José, *Spanish author*   thā-LAH, sā-LAH   θeːˈla, seːˈla
        (Nobel 1989)

Celandine
    plant   SEL-uhn-DĪN, SEL-uhn-DĒN   'selən,dain, 'selən,diːn

Celanese
    tdmk for a synthetic fiber   SEL-uh-NĒZ, SEL-uh-NĒZ   ,selə'niːz, 'selə,niːz

Celebes [Sulawesi]
    island, sea, Indonesia   SEL-uh-BĒZ, suh-LĒ-bez   'selə,biːz, sə'liːbiːz

Celebrator Doppelbock
    German beer   CHĀ-lā-BRAH-TAWR DAHP-uhl-BAHK   ,tʃeːleːˈbraˌtɔʳ 'dapəl,bak

Celest, Celeste
    pers. name   suh-LEST   sə'lest

Céleste
    pers. name, French   sā-LEST   seːlest

Celestine
    pope   SEL-uh-STĪN; suh-LES-tin, -TĪN   'selə,stain; sə'lestin, -,tain

Celeus
    king of Eleusis   SĒ-lē-uhs, SĒL-YOOS   'siːliːəs, 'siːljuːs

Celia
    pers. name   SĒL-yuh   'siːljə

Cellini
    Benvenuto, *Florentine artist;*   chuh-LĒ-nē   tʃəˈliːniˑ
        jewelers

Cello
    musical instrument   CHEL-ō   'tʃeloˑ

Celluloid
    tdmk for a thermoplastic   SEL-yuh-LOID   'seljə,lɔid

Celsius
    Anders, *Swedish astronomer;*   SEL-sē-uhs, SEL-shuhs   'selsiːəs, 'selʃəs
        temperature scale

Celtic
    lang. family   KEL-tik, SEL-tik   'keltik, 'seltik

Celtics
    basketball team, Boston; soccer   SEL-tiks   'seltiks
        team, Scotland

Celtic Sea
    sea, Atlantic Ocean   KEL-tik SĒ, SEL-tik   ,keltik 'siː, ,seltik

Celts
    people, Europe   KELTS, SELTS   'kelts, 'selts

Celtus
    son of Heracles and Celtine   SEL-tuhs   'seltəs

Cemal
    pers. name, Turkish   ke-MAHL   ke'mal

Cenci, The
    tragedy, P. B. Shelley   CHEN-chē   'tʃentʃiˑ

Key (col. 2):   a: fad ā: fade ah: father ar: Mary aw: law e: fed ē: feed er: merry i: hid ī: hide ō: coat ōō: boot
oi: boy ow: now u: put uh: above uhr: bird ch: chop ng: ring sh: show th: thick th: this zh: measure

Cenis, Mont		
Alpine pass	mawⁿ SNĒ, mawⁿ suh-NĒ	mɔ̃ sniː, mɔ̃ səniː
Cenozoic		
geologic era	SĒ-nuh-ZŌ-ik, SEN-uh-	ˌsiːnə'zoːik, ˌsenə-
Centaur		
mythical creature; constellation	SEN-TAWR	'senˌtɔːʳ
Centaurus		
constellation	sen-TAWR-uhs	sen'tɔːrəs
Centel		
US telephone co.	SEN-TEL, sen-TEL	'senˌtel, sen'tel
Centex		
US construction co.	SEN-TEKS	'senˌteks
Centre		
1. county, PA; town, AL	SENT-uhr	'sentəʳ
2. region, France	SAHⁿTR	sɑ̃tr
Centre Pompidou		
city, France	sahⁿ-truh pawⁿ-pē-DOO	sɑ̃trə pɔ̃piːduː
Centuriate assembly		
Roman legislative body	sen-T(Y)UR-ē-uht uh-SEM-blē	sen't(j)uriːət ə'sembliˑ
Cephalonia		
region, Greece	SEF-uh-LŌN-yuh, -LŌ-nē-uh	ˌsefə'loːnjə, -'loːniːə
Cephalus		
husband of Procris	SEF-uh-luhs	'sefələs
Cepheids		
type of variable star	SĒ-fē-uhdz, SEF-ē-uhdz	'siːfiːədz, 'sefiːədz
Cepheus		
Argonaut, husband of Cassiopeia; constellation	SĒ-FYOOS, SĒ-fē-uhs	'siːˌfjuːs, 'siːfiːəs
Ceram, Seram		
island, Indonesia; sea, Pacific	SĀ-RAHM	'seːˌrɑm
Ceramus		
mythical inventor of pottery	suh-RAM-uhs	sə'ræməs
Ceratopsia		
dinosaur suborder	SER-uh-TAHP-sē-uh	ˌserə'tɑpsiːə
Ceratosaurus		
dinosaur	SER-uht-ō-SAWR-uhs	ˌserətoː'sɔːrəs
Cerberus		
3-headed dog of Hades	SUHR-b(uh-)ruhs	'səʳb(ə)rəs
Cercopes		
mythical dwarves who robbed Heracles	suhr-KŌ-pēz	səʳ'koːpiːz
Cerenkov		
see Cherenkov		
Cerenkov effect, Che-		
light emission caused by a charged particle	chuh-RENG-kawf, -kuhf	tʃə'reŋkɔːf, -kəf
Ceres		
1. Roman harvest goddess; asteroid	SIR-ēz	'siriːz
2. Danish beer	SE-rās	'sereːs
Cerf		
Bennett, US publisher	SUHRF	'səʳf
Cerigo [Cythera]		
Mediterranean island	CHER-i-GŌ	'tʃeriˌgoː

Foreign Sounds: ue: *Fr.* **ru**e, *Ger.* f**ü**llen uh(r): *Fr.* b**oeu**f, *Ger.* H**öh**le kh: *Ger.* i**ch**, *Scot.* lo**ch** g̱: *Sp.* ami**g**o v̱: *Sp.* ha**b**lar hl: *Welsh* **Ll**anelli. CAPITALS: primary stress. SMALL CAPS: secondary stress. Ⓢ: U.S. pron. Ⓛ: British pron.

cerium
   element — SIR-ē-uhm — 'siriːəm

CERN
   acronym, European particle physics laboratory — SUHRN — 'səᵣn

Cerritos
   city, College, *CA* — suh-RĒT-uhs — sə'riːţəs

Cerro Coso
   Community College, *CA* — SER-ō KŌ-sō — 'seroː 'koːsoː

Cerro de Punta
   see Punta, Cerro de

Cerro Gordo
   county, IA — SER-uh GAWRD-ō — ˌserə 'gɔːᵣdoː

Cerulean warbler
   bird — suh-R͞OO-lē-uhn WAWR-bluhr — sə'ruːliːən 'wɔːᵣbləᵣ

Cervantes Saavedra
   Miguel de, *Spanish novelist* — ther-V̲A̲HN-tās sah-ah-V̲A̲T̲H̲-rah, ⑤ suhr-VAN-tēz — θer'βanteːs sɑ-ɑ'βeːðrɑ, ⑤ səᵣ'væntiːz
    SAH(-uh)-V̲A̲-druh, ser-VAHN-TĀS — ˌsa(ə)'veːdrɑ, seᵣ'van,teːs

Cervin, Mont [Matterhorn]
   mtn. range, Switzerland, Italy — mawⁿ ser-VEⁿ — mɔ̃ servẽ

Cervino, Monte [Matterhorn]
   mtn. range, Switzerland, Italy — MŌN-tā cher-VĒ-nō — ˌmoːnteː tʃer'viːnoː

Césaire
   pers. name, French — sā-ZER — seːzer

Cesar
   pers. name, Spanish — SĀ-sahr, THĀ-sahr, ⑤ SĀ-zahr — 'seːsɑᵣ, 'θeːsɑᵣ, ⑤ 'seːzɑᵣ

César
   1. pers. name, French — sā-ZAHR — seːzɑːr
   2. Spanish — SĀ-sahr, THĀ- — 'seːsɑr, 'θeː-

Cesare
   pers. name, Italian — CHĀ-zahr-ā — 'tʃeːzareː

Cesareo
   pers. name, Spanish — sā-SAHR-ā-ō, thā- — seː'sareːoː, θeː-

cesium
   element — SĒ-zē-uhm — 'siːziːəm

Cessna
   US aircraft co. — SES-nuh — 'sesnə

Cetacea
   order of whales & porpoises — sē-TĀ-sh(ē-)uh — siː'teːʃ(iː)ə

Ceto
   mother of the Graeae — SĒT-ō — 'siːţoː

Cetus
   constellation — SĒT-uhs — 'siːţəs

Ceuta
   Spanish military station, port, Morocco — THĀ-͞OOT-uh, SĀ-͞OOT-uh — 'θeːˌuːţə, 'seːˌuːţə

Cévennes
   mtn. range, France — sā-VEN — seːven

Ceylon [Sri Lanka]
   island, state, Indian Ocean — si-LAHN, sā-LAHN — si'lan, seː'lan

Ceyx
   friend of Heracles — SĒ-iks — 'siːiks

Cézanne
   Paul, *French painter* — sā-ZAHN — seːzɑːn

Key (col. 2): a: fad ā: fade ah: father ar: Mary aw: law e: fed ē: feed er: merry i: hid ī: hide ō: coat ͞oo: boot oi: boy ow: now u: put uh: above uhr: bird ch: chop ng: ring sh: show th: thick th̲: this zh: measure

Chablis		
wine	shuh-BLĒ, shah-, sha-	ʃə'bliː, ʃa-, ʃæ-
Chabot		
College, *CA*	shuh-BŌ	ʃə'boː
Cha-cha		
dance	CHAH-CHAH	'tʃa,tʃa
Chachalaca		
S. & Cen. American bird	CHAH-chuh-LAHK-uh	ˌtʃatʃə'lakə
Chaco		
region, central S. America	CHAHK-ō	'tʃakoː
Chaconne		
dance	shah-KAWN, shah-KAHN,	ʃa'kɔːn, ʃa'kan, ʃa'kən, ʃæ-
	shah-KUHN, sha-	
Chad		
country, Africa; pers. name	CHAD	'tʃæd
Chadian		
pert. to Chad	CHAD-ē-uhn	'tʃædiːən
Chadron		
State College, *NE*	SHAD-ruhn	'ʃædrən
Chadwick		
Sir James, *English physicist*	CHAD-wik	'tʃædwik
(Nobel 1935)		
Chaeronea		
ancient city, Greece	KER-uh-NĒ-uh, KIR-	ˌkerə'niːə, ˌkir-
Chafee		
John H., *US politician*	CHĀ-fē	'tʃeːfiˑ
Chaffey		
College, *CA*	CHAF-ē	'tʃæfiˑ
Chaffinch		
songbird	CHAF-inch	'tʃæfintʃ
Chagall		
Marc, *Russian painter in France*	shah-GAHL	ʃaːgaːl
Chagres		
river, Panama	CHAHG-ruhs, CHAG-ruhs	'tʃagrəs, 'tʃægrəs
Chagrin		
river, OH	shuh-GRIN, SHUG-ruhn, SHAG-ruhn	ʃə'grin, 'ʃugrən, 'ʃægrən
Chahar		
prov, Mongolia	CHAH-HAHR	'tʃa'haˑr
Chaim		
1. pers. name, Hebrew	khī-(Y)IM, KH<u>Ī</u>-(y)im	xai'(j)im, 'xai(j)im
2. Yiddish	KH<u>Ī</u>-(y)im	'xai(j)im
Chain		
E. B., *British biochemist (Nobel*	CHĀN	'tʃeːn
1945)		
Chalcedon		
ancient city, Asia Minor	KAL-suh-DAHN, kal-SĒD-n	'kælsəˌdan, kæl'siːdn̩
Chalcedony		
quartz	kal-SED-n-ē, chal-SED-n-ē;	kæl'sedniˑ, tʃæl'sedniˑ;
	KAL-suh-DŌ-nē, CHAL-suh-DŌ-nē	'kælsəˌdoːniˑ, 'tʃælsəˌdoːniˑ
Chalcidice		
peninsula, Greece	chal-SID-uh-sē	tʃæl'sidəsiˑ
Chalciope		
second wife of Aegeus	kal-SĪ-uh-pē	kæl'saiəpiˑ
Chalcis		
city, Greece	KAL-suhs, KAL-kuhs	'kælsəs, 'kælkəs

Foreign Sounds: ue: *Fr.* **rue**, *Ger.* füllen uh(r): *Fr.* **boeuf**, *Ger.* Höhle kh: *Ger.* i**ch**, *Scot.* lo**ch** g̶: *Sp.* ami**g**o v̲: *Sp.* ha**b**lar
hl: *Welsh* **Ll**anelli. CAPITALS: primary stress. SMALL CAPS: secondary stress. ⑤: U.S. pron. ⑥: British pron.

Chalcodon
   father of Chalciope and Elephenor　　KAL-kuh-DAHN　　　　　'kælkə,dɑn

Chalcolithic Age
   latter Neolithic period, Near East　　KAL-kuh-LITH-ik　　　　,kælkə'liθik

Chalcopyrite
   mineral　　KAL-kuh-PĪ-RĪT　　　　,kælkə'pai,rɑit

Chaldea, Chaldaea
   region of Babylonia　　kal-DĒ-uh　　　　kæl'diːə

Chaldean
   pert. to Chaldea　　kal-DĒ-uhn　　　　kæl'diːən

Chaldee [Chaldean]
   pert. to Chaldea　　kal-DĒ　　　　kæl'diː

Chaliapin
   Fëdor, *Russian opera star*　　shuhl-YAHP-yin　　　　ʃəl'jaːpjin

Chalma
   Mexico　　CHAHL-mah　　　　'tʃalmɑ

Chalmers
   pers. name　　CHAL-muhrz, CHAHL-　　　　'tʃælməᵣz, 'tʃɑl-

Cham
   lang., people, Indochina　　CHAHM　　　　'tʃam

Chamaeleon, Chameleon
   constellation　　kuh-MĒL-yuhn, kuh-MĒ-lē-uhn　　　　kə'miːljən, kə'miːliːən

Chamberlain
   Sir Austen, *British statesman*　　CHĀM-buhr-luhn　　　　'tʃeːmbəᵣlən
   (Nobel 1925) & his brother
   Neville, *British statesman;*
   Owen, *US physicist (Nobel*
   1959)

Chambéry
   city, France　　shahⁿ-bā-RĒ　　　　ʃɑ̃beːriː

Chamois
   antelope; fabric　　SHAM-ē, sham-WAH　　　　'ʃæmiˑ, ʃæm'wɑ

Chamonix
   mtn. valley, France　　shah-maw-NĒ　　　　ʃɑːmɔːniː

Chamorro
   Violetta, *Nicaraguan politician;*　　chuh-MAWR-ō　　　　tʃə'mɔːroː
   lang., people, Guam

Champagne
   region, France　　shahⁿ-PAHN-yuh, ⑤ sham-PĀN　　　　ʃɑ̃paːɲ, ⑤ ʃæm'peːn

Champagne-Ardenne
   region, France　　shahⁿ-pahn-yahr-DEN　　　　ʃɑ̃paːnjaːrden

Champaign
   county, IL, OH; city, IL　　sham-PĀN　　　　ʃæm'peːn

Champigny
   French wine　　shahⁿ-pēn-YĒ　　　　ʃɑ̃piːnjiː

Champlain
   lake, NY, VT, & Quebec　　sham-PLĀN　　　　ʃæm'pleːn

Champollion
   Jean-François, *French*　　shah-pawl-YAWⁿ　　　　ʃɑːpɔːljɔ̃
   Egyptologist

Champs Élysées
   boulevard, Paris, France　　SHAHⁿZ ā-lē-ZĀ　　　　ʃɑ̃z eːliːzeː

Chancellor
   John William, *US news*　　CHAN(T)-s(uh-)luhr　　　　'tʃæn(t)s(ə)ləᵣ
   correspondent

Key (col. 2):　a: fad　â: fade　ah: father　ar: Mary　aw: law　e: fed　ē: feed　er: merry　i: hid　ī: hide　ō: coat　ōō: boot
oi: boy　ow: now　u: put　uh: above　uhr: bird　ch: chop　ng: ring　sh: show　th: thick　th̲: this　zh: measure

Chandigarh
   city, India   CHUHN-dē-guhr   'tʃəndiːgəʳ
Chandra
   1. pers. name, Bengali   CHAWN-draw   'tʃɔːndrɔː
   2. Sanskrit   CHUHN-druh   'tʃəndrə
Chandragupta
   1st emperor of India   CHUHN-druh-GUP-tuh   ˌtʃəndrə'guptə
Chandrasekhar
   Subrahmanyan, *US astrophysicist*   CHUHN-druh-SĀ-kuhr   ˌtʃəndrə'seːkəʳ
   (Nobel 1983)
Chandrasekhara
   pers. name, Bengali   CHUHN-druh-SHĀ-kuh-ruh   ˌtʃəndrə'ʃeːkərə
Chanel
   fragrance   shuh-NEL   ʃə'nel
Chanell
   pers. name   shuh-NEL   ʃə'nel
Changan [Xian]
   city, China   CHAHNG-AHN   'tʃaŋ'an
Changchun, Ch'ang-ch'ung
   city, China   CHAHNG-CHUN   'tʃaŋ'tʃun
Changi
   airport, Singapore   JAHNG-GĒ   'dʒaŋ'giː
Chang Jiang [Yangtze]
   river, China   CHAHNG jē-AHNG   'tʃaŋ dʒiː'aŋ
Changsha, Ch'ang-sha
   city, China   CHAHNG-SHAH   'tʃaŋ'ʃa
Chang Tso-lin
   see Zhang Zuolin
Chantal
   town, Haiti   shahⁿ-TAHL, Ⓢ shahn-TAHL   ʃɑ̃taːl, Ⓢ ʃan'tal
Chant de Railliemant
   national anthem, Cameroon   SHAHⁿ duh rī-yē-MAHⁿT   ʃɑ̃ də raijiːmɑ̃t
Chanticleer
   rooster; US vocal ensemble   CHANT-i-KLIR, SHANT-i-KLIR   ˌtʃænti'kliʳ, ˌʃænti'kliʳ
Chantilly
   1. town, France   shahⁿ-tē-YĒ   ʃɑ̃tiːjiː
   2. village, VA   shan-TIL-ē   ʃæn'tiliˑ
Chanukah
   Jewish holiday   K̲HAHN-uh-kuh, HAHN-uh-kuh   'xanəkə, 'hanəkə
Chao
   pers. name   CHOW   'tʃau
Chao Phraya
   river, Thailand   chow PRĪ-uh   tʃau 'praiə
Chaos
   void preceding the Greek gods;   KĀ-AHS   'keːˌas
   computer network protocol
Chapellet
   California wine   SHAP-uh-LĀ   ˌʃæpə'leː
Chaplin
   Charlie, *US actor*   CHAP-luhn   'tʃæplən
Chappaquiddick
   island, MA   CHAP-uh-KWID-ik   ˌtʃæpə'kwidik
Chapultepec
   fortress, park, Mexico City   chuh-PŌŌL-tuh-PEK   tʃə'puːltəˌpek

---

Foreign Sounds: ue: *Fr.* **rue**, *Ger.* **füllen** uh(r): *Fr.* **boeuf**, *Ger.* **Höhle** k̲h: *Ger.* **ich**, *Scot.* **loch** g̲: *Sp.* **amigo** v̲: *Sp.* **hablar** hl: *Welsh* **Llanelli**. CAPITALS: primary stress. SMALL CAPS: secondary stress. Ⓢ: U.S. pron. Ⓛ: British pron.

Charcot
Jean M., *French scientist*   shahr-KŌ   ʃɑːrkoː

Chardin
Jean, *French traveler*   shahr-DEⁿ   ʃɑːrdẽ

Chardonnay
wine   SHAHRD-n-Ā, SHAHR-duh-NĀ, SHAHRD-n-Ā   ˌʃɑʳdn̩ˈeː, ˌʃɑʳdəˈneː, ˈʃɑʳdn̩ˌeː

Charente
river, dept, France   shah-RAHⁿT   ʃɑːrãt

Chargoggagoggman-chaugagogg-chaubunagungamaug [Chaubunagungamaug]
lake, MA   chahr-GAHG-uh-GAHG-man-CHAW-guh-GAHG-chaw-BUHN-uh-GUHNG-guh-MAWG   tʃɑʳˈgagəˌgagmæn ˈtʃɔːgəˌgagtʃɔː ˌbənəˈgəŋgəˌmɔːg

Chari, Shari
river, Africa   SHAHR-ē   ˈʃariˑ

Chariclo
mother of Tiresias   KAR-i-KLŌ   ˈkæriˌkloː

Charing Cross
district, London   CHAR-ing KRAWS, CHER-ing   ˌtʃæriŋ ˈkrɔːs, ˌtʃeriŋ

Charis
singular of Charites   KAR-uhs   ˈkærəs

Charisse
Cyd, *US actress*   shuh-RĒS   ʃəˈriːs

Charites
Roman goddesses of beauty   KAR-uht-ēz   ˈkærət̬iːz

Chariton
county, MO; river, US   SHAR-uht-n   ˈʃærətn̩

Charlemagne
1. *Frankish king; pers. name*   SHAHR-luh-MĀN   ˈʃɑʳləˌmeːn
2. *French*   shahr-luh-MAHN-yuh   ʃɑːrləmaːɲ

Charles
1. *pers. name*   CHAHRLZ   ˈtʃɑʳlz
2. *Dutch*   SHAHRL   ˈʃɑrl
3. *French*   SHAHRL   ʃɑːrl

Charles de Gaulle [Roissy]
airport, Paris   SHAHRL duh GŌL   ʃɑːrl də goːl

Charleston
city, county, SC   CHAHRL-stuhn, CHAHRLZ-tuhn   ˈtʃɑʳlstən, ˈtʃɑʳlztən

Charlevoix
county, MI   SHAHR-luh-VOI   ˈʃɑʳləˌvoi

Charley, Charlie
pers. name   CHAHR-lē   ˈtʃɑʳliˑ

Charlotte
1. *city, MI*   shahr-LAHT, SHAHR-luht   ʃɑʳˈlat, ˈʃɑʳlət
2. *city, NC; county, FL, VA; pers. name*   SHAHR-luht   ˈʃɑʳlət
3. *French*   shahr-LAWT   ʃɑːrlɔːt
4. *German*   shahr-LAW-tuh   ʃɑʳˈlɔːtə
5. *Swedish*   shahr-LAWT   ʃɑːrˈlɔːt

Charlotte Amalie
city, US Virgin Islands   SHAHR-luht uh-MAHL-yuh   ˈʃɑʳlət əˈmaljə

Key (col. 2):   a: fad   ā: fade   ah: father   ar: Mary   aw: law   e: fed   ē: feed   er: merry   i: hid   ī: hide   ō: coat   ōō: boot   oi: boy   ow: now   u: put   uh: above   uhr: bird   ch: chop   ng: ring   sh: show   th: thick   th̲: this   zh: measure

Charlton		
pers. name	CHAHRLT-n, CHAHRL-tuhn	'tʃɑ^{r}ltn̩, 'tʃɑ^{r}ltən
Charmat		
sparkling wine production method	shahr-MAH	ʃɑːrmɑː
Charmides		
dialogue of Plato	KAHR-muh-DĒZ	'kɑ^{r}mə,diːz
Charo		
US entertainer	CHAHR-ō, CHAR-ō, CHER-ō	'tʃɑroː, 'tʃæroː, 'tʃeroː
Charolais		
breed of cattle	SHAR-uh-LĀ	,ʃærə'leː
Charon		
ferryman of Hades; satellite of Pluto	KAR-uhn, KER-uhn	'kærən, 'kerən
Charro Days		
Mexican border fiesta	CHAHR-ō	'tʃɑroː
Charrúa		
S. American people	chuh-R͞OO-uh	tʃə'ruːə
Chartism		
political movement	CHAHRT-IZ-uhm	'tʃɑ^{r}t̬,izəm
Chartres		
city, France	SHAHRTR, [S] SHAHRT, SHAHR-truh	ʃɑːrtr, [S] 'ʃɑ^{r}t, 'ʃɑ^{r}trə
Chartreuse		
French liqueur	shahr-TRUH(R)Z, [S] shahr-TR͞OOZ, -TR͞OOS	ʃɑːrtrœːz, [S] ʃɑ^{r}'truːz, -'truːs
Charybdis		
personified whirlpool off Sicily	kuh-RIB-duhs, shuh-, chuh-	kə'ribdəs, ʃə-, tʃə-
Chasid		
see Hasid		
Chassagne-Montrachet		
French wine	shah-SAHN-yuh-maw^{n}-rah-SHE	ʃɑːsɑːɲmɔ̃rɑːʃe
Chassahowitzka		
National Wildlife Refuge, *FL*	CHAS-uh-HOW-(w)uht-skuh	,tʃæsə'hau(w)ətskə
Chateaubriand		
François, *French statesman & author*	shah-tō-brē-AH^{n}	ʃɑːtoːbriːɑ̃
Château-Chalon		
wine	shah-TŌ-shah-LAW^{n}	ʃatoːʃɑːlɔ̃
Chateau Chevalier		
wine	sha-TŌ SHEV-uh-LIR, shuh-val-YĀ	ʃæ'toː ,ʃevə'li^{r}, ʃəvæl'jeː
Château-Couhins		
wine	shah-TŌ-ko͞o-E^{n}S	ʃatoːkuːẽs
Chateauguay, Chât-		
town, Canada; river, US & Canada	SHAT-uh-GĀ, [S] SHAT-uh-gē, SHAT-uh-GĀ	,ʃæt̬ə'geː, [S] 'ʃæt̬əgiˑ, 'ʃæt̬ə,geː
Château-Haut-Brion		
wine	shah-TŌ-ō-brē-AW^{n}	ʃatoːoːbriːɔ̃
Château-Lafite		
wine	shah-TŌ-lah-FĒT	ʃatoːlɑːfiːt
Château-Latour		
wine	shah-TŌ-lah-T͞OOR	ʃatoːlɑːtuːr
Chateau Leonay		
wine	sha-TŌ LĒ-uh-NĀ, -NĪ	ʃæ'toː ,liːə'neː, -'nai
Château-Margaux		
wine	shah-TŌ-mahr-GŌ	ʃatoːmɑːrgoː

Foreign Sounds: ue: *Fr.* **rue**, *Ger.* **füllen** uh(r): *Fr.* **boeuf**, *Ger.* **Höhle** kh: *Ger.* **ich**, *Scot.* **loch** g̱: *Sp.* ami**g**o v̱: *Sp.* ha**b**lar hl: *Welsh* **Llanelli**. CAPITALS: primary stress. SMALL CAPS: secondary stress. [S]: U.S. pron. [E]: British pron.

Chateau Montelena
   wine   sha-TÕ MAHNT-l-Ã-nuh   ʃæˈtoː ˌmɑntlˈeːnə

Château-Mouton-Rothschild
   wine   shah-TÕ-mōō-TAWⁿ-rawt-SHÊLD   ʃɑtoːmuːtõrɔːtʃiːld

Châteauneuf-du-Pape
   wine   shah-tō-NUH(R)F-due-PAHP   ʃɑtoːnœfdyːpɑːp

Chateau St. Jean
   winery, CA   sha-TÕ sänt JÊN   ʃæˈtoː seːnt ˈdʒiːn

Chateau Souverain
   winery, CA   sha-TÕ SŌŌ-vuh-REN, SŌŌ-vuh-RÃN   ʃæˈtoː ˌsuːvəˈren, ˈsuːvəˌreːn

Chateau Yaldara
   wine   sha-TÕ YAL-duh-ruh   ʃæˈtoː ˈjældərə

Chatham
   College, PA, county, GA, NC; city,   CHAT-uhm   ˈtʃæʈəm
     Canada; borough, England;
     islands, New Zealand

Chatino
   lang., people, Mexico   chuh-TÊ-nō   tʃəˈtiːnoː

Chattahoochee
   river, US; county, GA   CHAT-uh-HŌŌ-chē   ˌtʃæʈəˈhuːtʃiˈ

Chattanooga
   city, TN   CHAT-uh-NŌŌ-guh, CHAT-n-ŌŌ-guh,   ˌtʃæʈəˈnuːgə, ˌtʃæʈn̩ˈuːgə,
                             CHAT-uh-NU-guh   ˌtʃæʈəˈnugə

Chatterjee, Chatterji
   Bankim Chandra, Indian novelist   CHAT-uhr-jē   ˈtʃæʈəʳdʒiˈ

Chatterley
   Connie, character in Lady   CHAT-uhr-lē   ˈtʃæʈəʳliˈ
     Chatterley's Lover, *D.H.*
     Lawrence

Chattooga
   county, GA   chuh-TŌŌ-guh   tʃəˈtuːgə

Chaubunagungamaug
[Chargoggagoggman-
chaugagoggchau-
bunagungamaug]
   lake, MA   chaw-BUHN-uh-GUHNG-guh-MAWG   tʃɔː,bənəˈgəngə,mɔːg

Chaucer
   Geoffrey, English poet   CHAW-suhr   ˈtʃɔːsəʳ

Chaucerian
   pert. to Chaucer   chaw-SIR-ē-uhn, chaw-SER-ē-uhn   tʃɔːˈsiriːən, tʃɔːˈseriːən

Chaudet
   Denis-Antoine, French sculptor   shaw-DE   ʃɔːde

Chaulmoogra
   tree   chawl-MŌŌ-gruh   tʃɔːlˈmuːgrə

Chauncey
   pers. name   CHAWN-sē, CHAHN-   ˈtʃɔːnsiˈ, ˈtʃɑn-

Chautauqua
   county, KA, NY; lake, town, NY;   shuh-TAWK-wuh   ʃəˈtɔːkwə
     National Wildlife Refuge, *IL*

Chaves
   1. county, NM   CHAV-uhs, SHAV-uhs   ˈtʃævəs, ˈʃævəs
   2. commune, Portugal   SHAHV-ēsh   ˈʃɑːviːʃ

Chavez
   Cesar, US union official   SHAHV-EZ, CHAH-VEZ   ˈʃav,ez, ˈtʃɑ,vez

---

Key (col. 2):   a: fad ā: fade ah: father ar: Mary aw: law e: fed ē: feed er: merry i: hid ī: hide ō: coat ōō: boot
oi: boy ow: now u: put uh: above uhr: bird ch: chop ng: ring sh: show th: thick th: this zh: measure

Chavin
    S. American people   chuh-VĒN   tʃəˈviːn

Chayefsky
    Paddy, *US author*   chī-EF-skē, chī-EV-skē   tʃaiˈefskiˑ, tʃaiˈevskiˑ

Chayim
    1. pers. name, Hebrew   k<u>h</u>ī-(Y)IM, K<u>H</u>Ī-(y)im   xaiˈ(j)im, ˈxai(j)im
    2. Yiddish   K<u>H</u>Ī-(y)im   ˈxai(j)im

Chaz
    perfume brand   CHAZ   ˈtʃæz

Che
    pers. name, Spanish   CHĀ   ˈtʃeː

Cheatham
    county, TN   CHĒT-uhm   ˈtʃiːtəm

Cheboksary
    city, Russia   CHEB-ahk-SAHR-yi, -SAHR-ē   ˌtʃebakˈsaːrjij, -ˈsariˑ

Cheboygan
    river, county, city, MI   shi-BOI-guhn   ʃiˈbɔigən

Chechen
    lang., people, Georgia and   chuh-CHEN   tʃəˈtʃen
      Kazakhstan

Cheddar
    town, England; cheese   CHED-uhr   ˈtʃedər

Chehalis
    N. American people   chuh-HĀ-luhs   tʃəˈheːləs

Cheju
    island, S. Korea   chā-jo͞o   tʃeːdʒuː

Cheka
    secret police, USSR   CHEK-uh   ˈtʃekə

Chekhov
    Anton, *Russian writer*   CHE<u>KH</u>-uhf, Ⓢ CHEK-AWF,   ˈtʃexəf, Ⓢ ˈtʃekˌɔːf, ˈtʃekˌɔːv
      CHEK-AWV

Chekiang
    see Zhejiang

Chekov
    Pavel, *character, Star Trek*   CHEK-AWF, CHEK-AWV   ˈtʃekˌɔːf, ˈtʃekˌɔːv

Chelan
    county, WA   shuh-LAN   ʃəˈlæn

Chelone
    girl changed into a tortoise   kē-LŌ-nē   kiːˈloːniˑ

Chelsea
    city, MA; London borough; pers.   CHEL-sē   ˈtʃelsiˑ
      name

Cheltenham
    city, England; type font   CHELT-n-uhm   ˈtʃeltn̩əm

Chelyabinsk
    city, Russia   chel-YAH-buhn(t)sk   tʃelˈjaːbən(t)sk

Chemehuevi
    N. American people   CHEM-uh-WĀ-vē   ˌtʃeməˈweːviˑ

Chemin-de-fer
    game   shuh-MAN-duh-FER   ʃəˌmændəˈferʳ

Chemnitz [Karl Marx Stadt]
    city, Germany   <u>KH</u>EM-nits   ˈçemnits

Chemung
    river, US; county, NY   shi-MUHNG   ʃiˈməŋ

Foreign Sounds: **ue**: *Fr.* **rue**, *Ger.* f**ü**llen   **uh**(r): *Fr.* b**oeu**f, *Ger.* H**ö**hle   <u>kh</u>: *Ger.* i**ch**, *Scot.* lo**ch**   ḡ: *Sp.* ami**g**o   <u>v</u>: *Sp.* ha**b**lar
hl: *Welsh* **Ll**anelli.   CAPITALS: primary stress.   SMALL CAPS: secondary stress.   Ⓢ: U.S. pron.   Ⓛ: British pron.

Chenango
river, county, NY — shuh-NANG-gō — ʃəˈnæŋgoː

Chen-chiang
see Zhejiang

Cheney
Richard B., *US politician;* — CHĀ-nē — ˈtʃeːniˑ
Stadium, *Tacoma, WA*

Chengchow
see Zhengzhou

Chengdu, Ch'ung-tu
city, China — CHUHNG-D$\overline{\text{OO}}$ — ˈtʃəŋˈduː

Chénier
André, *French poet* — shān-YĀ — ʃeːnjeː

Chenin Blanc
wine — shuh-ne^{n}-BLAH^{n}, Ⓢ SHEN-in — ʃənẽblã, Ⓢ ˌʃenin ˈblaŋk
BLAHNGK

Chennault
Claire, *US militarist* — shuh-NAWLT — ʃəˈnɔːlt

Cheops [Khufu]
Egyptian pharoah — KĒ-AHPS — ˈkiːˌɑps

Cher
1. US entertainer — SHER — ˈʃe^{r}
2. river, dept, France — SHER — ʃer

Cherbourg
seaport, France — sher-B$\overline{\text{OO}}$R, Ⓢ SHER-BUR(G), — ʃerbuːr, Ⓢ ˈʃe^{r}ˌbu^{r}(g),
SHUHR-BUR(G) — ˈʃə^{r}ˌbu^{r}(g)

Cheremis [Mari]
lang., people, Russia — CHER-uh-MIS, CHER-uh-MĒS — ˌtʃerəˈmis, ˌtʃerəˈmiːs

Cherenkov, Ce-
Pavel Alekseevich, *Russian* — chir-yin-KAWF, Ⓢ chuh-RENG-kawf, — tʃirjinˈkɔːf, Ⓢ tʃəˈreŋkɔːf,
physicist (Nobel 1958) — -kuhf — -kəf

Cherenkov effect
see Cerenkov effect

Cherepovets
city, Russia — chi-ri-PUH-VYETS, — tʃiriˌpəˈvjets,
Ⓢ CHER-uh-puh-VETS — Ⓢ ˌtʃerəpəˈvets

Cherie, Chérie
pers. name — shuh-RĒ, sher-Ē, SHER-ē — ʃəˈriː, ʃerˈiː, ˈʃeriˑ

Cheri-Suisse
Swiss liqueur — shā-RĒ-SWĒS — ʃeːriːswiːs

Cherna [Crna]
river, Macedonia — CHER-nuh — ˈtʃe^{r}nə

Chernenko
Konstantin, *gen. secy. USSR* — chern-YENG-kō — tʃe^{r}nˈjeŋkoː

Chernobyl
city, Ukraine — chir-NŌ-bil, Ⓢ chuhr-NŌ-buhl — tʃirˈnoːbil̩, Ⓢ tʃə^{r}noːbəl

Cherokee
N. American people — CHER-uh-kē — ˈtʃerəkiˑ

Chersonese, The
any of several European & Asian — KUHR-suh-NĒZ, -NĒS; — ˈkə^{r}sə,niːz, -,niːs; ˌkə^{r}sə'niːz,
peninsulas — KUHR-suh-NĒZ, -NĒS — -ˈniːs

Cherubim
order of angels — CHER-(y)uh-BIM — ˈtʃer(j)ə,bim

Cherwell
river, district, Oxfordshire — CHAHR-wuhl — ˈtʃɑ^{r}wəl

Key (col. 2):   a: fad   ā: fade   ah: father   ar: Mary   aw: law   e: fed   ē: feed   er: merry   i: hid   ī: hide   ō: coat $\overline{\text{oo}}$: boot
oi: boy   ow: now   u: put   uh: above   uhr: bird   ch: chop   ng: ring   sh: show   th: thick   th̲: this   zh: measure

Cheryl
    pers. name   SHER-uhl   'ʃerəl

Chesapeake Bay
    inlet, Atlantic Ocean   CHES-uh-PĒK BĀ   'tʃesə,piːk 'beː

Chesebrough-Pond's
    US cosmetics co.   CHĒZ-bruh-PAHN(D)Z   ,tʃiːzbrə'pɑn(d)z

Cheshire
    county, England; cheese; cat   CHESH-uhr, CHESH-ɪR   'tʃeʃərˢ, 'tʃeʃˌiˢ

Chessline Park
    Philadelphia, PA   CHES-LĪN   'tʃes,lɑin

Chester
    pl. name, US & England; pers.   CHES-tuhr   'tʃestəˢ
      name

Chet
    pers. name   CHET   'tʃet

Chetnik
    member, Serbian nationalist   chet-NĒK   tʃet'niːk
      group

Cheval Blanc
    wine   shuh-vahl BLAHⁿ   ʃəvɑːl blɑ̃

Chevalier
    Maurice, French-born entertainer   sh(uh-)vahl-YĀ, Ⓢ shuh-VAL-yā   ʃ(ə)vɑːljeː, Ⓢ ʃə'væljeː

Chevaliers du Tastevin
    French wine order   sh(uh-)vahl-YĀ due tahs-tuh-VEⁿ   ʃ(ə)vɑːljeː dyː tɑːstəvẽ

Cheviot
    1. county, OH   SHIV-ē-uht, SHEV-ē-uht   'ʃiviːət, 'ʃeviːət
    2. range of hills, English-Scottish   CHĒ-vē-uht *(local pron.)*,   'tʃiːviːət *(local pron.)*,
      border   CHEV-ē-uht, CHIV-ē-uht,   'tʃeviːət, 'tʃiviːət,
                          Ⓢ SHEV-ē-uht   Ⓢ 'ʃeviːət

Chevrolet
    US car make   SHEV-ruh-LĀ   ,ʃevrə'leː

Chevy
    1. nickname for Chevrolet   SHEV-ē   'ʃeviˑ
    2. pers. name   CHEV-ē   'tʃeviˑ

Chevy Chase
    urban district, MD; US comedian   CHEV-ē CHĀS   'tʃeviˑ 'tʃeːs

Chewa [Nyanja]
    lang., people, Africa   CHĀ-wah   'tʃeːwɑ

Cheyenne
    N. American people; city, WY   shī-AN, shī-EN   ʃɑi'æn, ʃɑi'en

Cheyney
    town, PA   CHĀ-nē   'tʃeːniˑ

Chiang Kai-shek
    Chinese leader; airport, Taipei   jē-AHNG KĪ-SHEK, Ⓢ CHANG   dʒiː'ɑŋ 'kɑi'ʃek, Ⓢ ,tʃæŋ
                          kī-SHEK   kɑi'ʃek

Chianti
    wine   kē-AHNT-ē, kē-ANT-ē   kiː'ɑntiˑ, kiː'æntiˑ

Chiapas
    state, Mexico   chē-AHP-uhs   tʃiː'ɑpəs

Chiari
    commune, Italy   kē-AHR-ē   kiː'ɑriˑ

Chiat-Day
    US advertising co.   SHĪ-uht-DĀ   ,ʃɑiət'deː

Chibcha
    S. American people   CHIB-chah   'tʃibtʃɑ

Foreign Sounds: ue: *Fr.* **rue**, *Ger.* **füllen**   uh(r): *Fr.* **boeuf**, *Ger.* **Höhle**   <u>kh</u>: *Ger.* **ich**, *Scot.* **loch**   g̃: *Sp.* **amigo**   <u>v</u>: *Sp.* **hablar**
hl: *Welsh* **Llanelli**.   CAPITALS: primary stress.   SMALL CAPS: secondary stress.   Ⓢ: U.S. pron.   Ⓛ: British pron.

Chic
   French beer   SHĒK   ʃiːk

Chicago
   city, IL   shuh-KAHG-ō, shuh-KAW-gō, chuh-   ʃəˈkagoː, ʃəˈkɔːgoː, tʃə-

Chicana
   Mexican-American (fem.)   chi-KAHN-uh, shi-KAHN-uh   tʃiˈkanə, ʃiˈkanə

Chicano
   Mexican-American (masc.)   chi-KAHN-ō, shi-KAHN-ō   tʃiˈkanoː, ʃiˈkanoː

Ch'i-ch'i-ha-erh
   see Qiqihar

Chichén Itzá
   village, archaeological site,   chi-CHEN ēt-SAH   tʃi,tʃen iˈtˈsɑ
     Mexico

Chichester
   town, England   CHICH-uh-stuhr   ˈtʃitʃəstəʳ

Chichewa
   lang., SE Africa   CHĒ-chuh-WAW   ˈtʃiːtʃə,wɔː

Chichibu
   city, Japan   chē-chē-bo͞o   tʃiːtʃiːbuː

Chick
   pers. name   CHIK   ˈtʃik

Chickadee
   songbird   CHIK-uh-dē   ˈtʃikədiː

Chickasaw
   N. American people   CHIK-uh-SAW   ˈtʃikə,sɔː

Chico
   city, CA; rivers, Argentina,   CHĒ-kō   ˈtʃiːkoː
     Phillipines; pers. name

Chicopee
   town, MA   CHIK-uh-pē   ˈtʃikəpiˑ

Chicot
   county, AR   SHĒ-kō   ˈʃiːkoː

Chicxulub
   town, Mexico   chē(k)-so͞o-LO͞OB   tʃiː(k)suːˈluːb

Chihli [Po Hai]
   gulf, Yellow Sea   JIR-LĒ, CHĒ-LĒ   ˈdʒirˈliː, ˈtʃiːˈliː

Chihuahua
   state, city, Mexico; dog   chuh-WAH-wah, shuh-, -wuh   tʃəˈwɑwɑ, ʃə-, -wə

Chilcotin
   N. American people   chil-KŌT-n   tʃilˈkoːtn̩

Childe
   pers. name (C. Hassam)   CHĪLD   ˈtʃaild

Chile
   republic, S. America   CHĒ-lā, CHIL-ē   ˈtʃiːleː, ˈtʃiliˑ

Chilean
   pert. to Chile   CHIL-ē-uhn, chuh-LĀ-uhn   ˈtʃiliːən, tʃəˈleːən

Chili
   town, NY   CHĪ-LĪ   ˈtʃai,lai

Chilkat, -cat
   N. American people   CHIL-KAT   ˈtʃil,kæt

Chillagoe
   town, Australia   CHIL-uh-gō   ˈtʃiləgoː

Chillicothe
   US pl. name   CHIL-uh-KAHTH-ē, CHIL-uh-KAW-thē   ˌtʃiləˈkaθiˑ, ˌtʃiləˈkɔːθiˑ

Key (col. 2):   a: fad   ā: fade   ah: father   ar: **M**ary   aw: **law**   e: fed   ē: feed   er: **merry**   i: hid   ī: hide   ō: coat   o͞o: boot
oi: **boy**   ow: **now**   u: put   uh: **above**   uhr: **bird**   ch: **chop**   ng: **ring**   sh: **show**   th: **thick**   <u>th</u>: **this**   zh: measure

Chillon
   castle, Switzerland   shē-YAWⁿ, Ⓢ shil-AHN, SHIL-AHN,   ʃiːjɔ̃, Ⓢ ʃilˈɑn, ˈʃilˌɑn, ˈʃilən
                            SHIL-uhn

Chiltern Hills
   hill range, England   CHIL-tuhrn HILZ   ˈtʃiltəʳn ˈhilz

Chimaera, Chimera
   monster in Greek mythology   kī-MIR-uh, kuh-MIR-uh   kaiˈmirə, kəˈmirə

Chimay
   Belgian beer   chē-MĪ   tʃiːˈmai

Chimborazo
   mtn., Ecuador   CHIM-buh-RAHZ-ō, SHIM-   ˌtʃimbəˈrɑzoː, ˌʃim-

Chimu
   S. American people   chē-MOO   tʃiːˈmuː

Chin
   hills, people, Burma; pers. name   CHIN   ˈtʃin

China
   republic, Asia   CHĪ-nuh   ˈtʃainə

Chi-nan
   see Jinan

Chinantec
   lang., people, Mexico   CHIN-uhn-TEK   ˈtʃinənˌtek

Chinatown
   urban district designator   CHĪ-nuh-TOWN   ˈtʃainəˌtaun

Chincoteague
   town, VA; bay, MD, VA   SHING-kuh-TĒG, CHING-kuh-TĒG;   ʃiŋkəˈtiːg, ˌtʃiŋkəˈtiːg;
                      SHING-kuh-TĒG, CHING-kuh-TĒG   ˈʃiŋkəˈtiːg, ˈtʃiŋkəˈtiːg

Chindwin
   river, Burma   CHIN-DWIN   ˈtʃinˈdwin

Chinese
   lang., people, Asia   chī-NĒZ, -NĒS   tʃaiˈniːz, -ˈniːs

Ching Hai
   see Tsing Hai

Chinghai
   see Qinghai

Chingpaw
   lang., people, Burma, South   CHING-PAW   ˈtʃiŋˌpɔː
      China

Ching Sen
   Chinese ceremony   CHING SUHN   ˈtʃiŋ ˈsən

Chinh
   Truong, *president, Vietnam*   CHIN   ˈtʃin

Chinkiang [Zhenjiang]
   city, China   JIN-yē-AHNG   ˈdʒinjiːˈɑŋ

Chino
   city, CA   CHĒ-nō   ˈtʃiːnoː

Chinook
   N. American people   shuh-NUK, chuh-NUK, -NOOK   ʃəˈnuk, tʃəˈnuk, -ˈnuːk

Chinua
   pers. name (C. Achebe)   CHIN-yuh-wuh   ˈtʃinjəwə

Chios
   island, Greece   KĒ-AHS, KĪ-AHS   ˈkiːˌɑs, ˈkaiˌɑs

Chipewyan
   N. American people   CHIP-uh-WĪ-uhn   ˌtʃipəˈwaiən

Chipola
   river, US, college, FL   chuh-PŌ-luh   tʃəˈpoːlə

Foreign Sounds: ue: *Fr.* **rue**, *Ger.* f**ü**llen uh(r): *Fr.* b**oeu**f, *Ger.* H**öh**le <u>kh</u>: *Ger.* i**ch**, *Scot.* lo**ch** ğ: *Sp.* ami**g**o <u>v</u>: *Sp.* ha**b**lar
hl: *Welsh* **Ll**anelli. CAPITALS: primary stress. SMALL CAPS: secondary stress. Ⓢ: U.S. pron. Ⓛ: British pron.

Chippendale
furniture style ... CHIP-uhn-DĀL ... 'tʃipən,deɪl

Chippewa [Ojibwa]
N. American people ... CHIP-uh-WAW, -WAH, -WĀ, -wuh ... 'tʃipə,wɔː, -,wɑ, -,weː, -wə

Chiquita
tdmk for bananas ... chi-KĒT-uh ... tʃi'kiːtə

Chi Rho
Christian symbol ... KĪ RŌ, KĒ RŌ ... 'kɑi 'roː, 'kiː 'roː

Chiricahua
N. American people ... CHIR-e-KAH-wuh ... ,tʃire'kɑwə

Chirico
Giorgio de, *Italian painter* ... KĒ-ri-KŌ, KIR-i-KŌ ... 'kiːri,koː, 'kiri,koː

Chiriguano
S. American people ... CHIR-uh-GWAHN-ō ... ,tʃiᵣə'gwɑnoː

Chiron
Centaur who reared Achilles and Jason ... KĪ-ruhn ... 'kɑirən

Chiroptera
order of bats ... kī-RAHP-tuh-ruh ... kɑi'rɑptərə

Chisago
county, MN ... shi-SAW-gō ... ʃi'sɔːgoː

Chisholm
cattle trail ... CHIZ-uhm ... 'tʃizəm

Chita
pers. name (C. Rivera) ... CHĒT-uh ... 'tʃiːtə

Chitimacha
N. American people ... CHIT-uh-MAHSH-uh ... ,tʃitə'mɑʃə

Chitradurga
town, India ... CHIT-ruh-DUHR-guh ... ,tʃitrə'dəᵣgə

Chittagong
region, Bangladesh ... CHIT-uh-GAHNG, CHIT-uh-GAWNG ... 'tʃitə,gɑŋ, 'tʃitə,gɔːŋ

Chivas Regal
Scotch liquor ... SHIV-uhs RĒ-guhl ... ,ʃivəs 'riːgəl

Chloe, Chloë
pers. name ... KLŌ-ē ... 'kloːiˑ

chlorine
element ... KLŌR-ĒN, KLAWR-ĒN ... 'kloːr,iːn, 'klɔːr,iːn

Chloris
Greek flower goddess ... KLŌR-uhs, KLAWR-uhs ... 'kloːrəs, 'klɔːrəs

Chlotilde
1. pers. name, French ... klaw-TĒLD ... klɔːtiːld
2. German ... klō-TIL-duh ... kloː'tildə

Choate
US prep school ... CHŌT ... 'tʃoːt

Chocó
S. American people ... chuh-KŌ ... tʃə'koː

Choctaw
N. American people ... CHAHK-taw ... 'tʃɑktɔː

Choiseul
Solomon Islands ... shwah-ZUH(R)L ... ʃwazœl

Chokwe
see Ciokwe

Chol
lang., people, Mexico ... CHŌL ... 'tʃoːl

Key (col. 2): a: fad ā: fade ah: father ar: Mary aw: law e: fed ē: feed er: merry i: hid ī: hide ō: coat o͞o: boot
oi: boy ow: now u: put uh: above uhr: bird ch: chop ng: ring sh: show th: thick t͟h: this zh: measure

Chŏllanam		
prov, Korea	chuhl-lah-nahm	tʃəllanam
Chŏllapuk		
prov, Korea	chuhl-lah-puk	tʃəllapuk
Cholmondeley		
town, England; British family name	CHUHM-lē	'tʃəmliˑ
Chomsky		
Noam, *US linguist*	CHAHM(P)-skē	'tʃam(p)skiˑ
Chomskyan		
pert. to Chomsky	CHAHM(P)-skē-uhn	'tʃam(p)skiːən
Chondokyo		
religion	chahn-DŌK-yō	tʃan'doːkjoː
Chongjin		
prov, N. Korea	chuhng-jēn	tʃəŋdʒiːn
Chongqing, Chungking		
town, China	CHUHNG-KING	'tʃəŋ'kiŋ
Chono		
S. American people	CHŌ-nō	'tʃoːnoː
Chontal		
lang., people, Mexico	chawn-TAHL	tʃɔːn'tal
Choosuk		
Korean festival	cho͞o-suk	tʃuːsuk
Cho Oyu		
Mount, *Himalayas*	CHŌ ō-YO͞O	ˌtʃoː oː'juː
Chopin		
1. Frédéric, *Polish composer, pianist*	*Polish* KHAWP-yin, *French* shaw-PE^{n}, [$] SHŌ-PAN, SHŌ-PA^{n}	*Polish* 'xɔːpjin, *French* ʃɔːpẽ, [$] 'ʃoːˌpæn, 'ʃoːˌpæ̃
2. Katherine, *US writer*	SHŌ-PAN, shō-PAN, SHŌ-puhn	'ʃoːˌpæn, ʃoː'pæn, 'ʃoːpən
Chortí		
lang., people, Guatemala, Honduras	CHAWRT-ē	'tʃɔːʳtiˑ
Choteau		
city, MT	SHŌ-tō	'ʃoːtoː
Chou En-Lai, Jou Enlai, Zhou Enlai		
premier, China	JŌ EN-LĪ	'dʒoː 'en'lai
Chough		
type of crow	CHUHF	'tʃəf
Chouteau		
county, MT	SHŌ-tō	'ʃoːtoː
Chowan		
river, county, NC	chuh-WAHN	tʃə'wan
Chow chow		
dog	CHOW CHOW	'tʃau ˌtʃau
Choxo-no-Sekku		
Chrysanthemum Day *(Sept. 9), Japan*	chōk-sō-nō-sek-ko͞o	tʃoːksoːnoːsekkuː
Choybalsan		
city, Mongolia	CHOI-bahl-SAHN	ˌtʃɔibal'san
Chremonidean War		
Athens-Sparta conflict	KRĒ-muh-NID-ē-uhn	ˌkriːmə'nidiːən
Chrétien		
pers. name, French	krā-TYE^{n}, [$] krā-TYEN	kreːtjẽ, [$] kreː'tjen
Chris		
pers. name	KRIS	'kris

Foreign Sounds: ue: *Fr.* **rue**, *Ger.* **fü**llen uh(r): *Fr.* b**oeu**f, *Ger.* H**ö**hle kh: *Ger.* i**ch**, *Scot.* lo**ch** g̃: *Sp.* ami**g**o v̲: *Sp.* ha**b**lar hl: *Welsh* **Ll**anelli. CAPITALS: primary stress. SMALL CAPS: secondary stress. [$]: U.S. pron. [£]: British pron.

Chrissie, Chrissy
   pers. name   KRIS-ē   'krisi·

Christ
   see Jesus Christ

Christabel
   poem, Coleridge; pers. name   KRIS-tuh-BEL, -buhl   'kristə,bel, -bəl

Christadelphianism
   Christian sect   KRIS-tuh-DEL-fē-uh-NIZ-uhm   ,kristə'delfiːə,nizəm

Christ Church
   college, Oxford Univ.   KRĪS(T) CHUHRCH   'krɑis(t) ,tʃəʳtʃ

Christchurch
   city, New Zealand   KRĪS(T)-CHUHRCH   'krɑis(t),tʃəʳtʃ

Christen
   1. pers. name, Danish   KRIS-tuhn   'kristən
   2. Norwegian   KRIS-tn   'kristn̩

Christendom
   the Christian world   KRIS-n-duhm   'krisn̩dəm

Christiaan
   pers. name, Dutch   KRIS-tē-AHN   'kristiː,ɑːn

Christian
   1. pert. to Christianity; *pers. name*   KRIS-chuhn, KRISH-   'kristʃən, 'kriʃ-
   2. Danish   KRĒ-styahn   'kriːstjɑːn
   3. Dutch   KRIS-tē-AHN   'kristiː,ɑn
   4. French   krē-STYAHⁿ   kriːstjã
   5. German   KRIS-tyahn, -tē-AHN   'kristjɑn, -tiː,ɑn
   6. Norwegian   KRIS-tyahn   'kristjɑn
   7. Swedish   KRIS-tē-ahn, KRISH-ahn   'kristiːɑːn, 'kriʃɑːn

Christiana
   pers. name, German   kris-TYAHN-ah, -tē-AHN-ah   kris'tjɑnɑ, -tiː'ɑnɑ

Christianity
   religion   KRIS-chē-AN-uht-ē, KRISH-chē-,   ,kristʃiː'ænəti·, ,kriʃtʃiː-,
                       KRIS-tē-   ,kristiː-

Christie
   pers. name   KRIS-tē   'kristi·

Christina
   pers. name   kris-TĒ-nuh   kris'tiːnə

Christine
   1. pers. name   kris-TĒN, KRIS-TĒN   kris'tiːn, 'kris,tiːn
   2. French   krē-STĒN   kriːstiːn
   3. German   kris-TĒ-nuh   kris'tiːnə
   4. Swedish   kri-STĒN   kri'stiːn

Christmas
   1. Christian holiday; island,   KRIS-muhs   'krisməs
     Indian Ocean; island, Pacific,
     see Kiritimati Atoll

Christmastide
   Christmas season   KRIS-muh-STĪD   'krismə,stɑid

Christmastime
   Christmas season   KRIS-muh-STĪM   'krismə,stɑim

Christobel
   pers. name   KRIS-tuh-BEL   'kristə,bel

Christofer
   pers. name, Norwegian, Swedish   kris-TAW-fuhr   kris'tɔːfər

Christoff
   pers. name, German   KRIS-TAWF   'kris,tɔːf

Key (col. 2): a: fad ā: fade ah: father ar: **M**ary aw: law e: fed ē: feed er: merry i: hid ī: hide ō: coat o͞o: boot
oi: **b**oy ow: now u: put uh: above uhr: bird ch: chop ng: ring sh: show th: thick t͟h: this zh: measure

Christoffer
　　pers. name, Swedish　　　kris-TAWF-fuhr　　　　　kris'tɔːffər
Christoph
　　1. pers. name, Dutch, German,　KRIS-TAWF　　　　　　'kris,tɔːf
　　　Swedish
　　2. Hungarian　　　　　　KRIS-tawf　　　　　　　'kristɔːf
Christophe
　　pers. name, French　　　　krē-STAWF　　　　　　kriːstɔːf
Christopher
　　1. pers. name　　　　　　KRIS-tuh-fuhr　　　　　'kristəfəʳ
　　2. Swedish　　　　　　　kris-TAW-fuhr　　　　　kris'tɔːfər
Christovão
　　pers. name, Portuguese　　KRĒSH-tōō-VOWⁿ, KRĒS-　,kriːʃtuː'vaũ, ,kriːs-
Christ's College
　　college, Cambridge Univ.　　KRĪS(TS) KAHL-ij　　　'kraɪs(ts) ,kalidʒ
Christy
　　pers. name　　　　　　　KRIS-tē　　　　　　　'kristiˑ
chromium
　　element　　　　　　　　KRŌ-mē-uhm　　　　　'kroːmiːəm
Chrysaor
　　son of Poseidon and Medusa　krī-SĀ-AWR　　　　　kraɪ'seːˌɔːʳ
Chryseis
　　Trojan woman given to　　krī-SĒ-uhs, krī-SĀ-uhs　kraɪ'siːəs, kraɪ'seːəs
　　　Agamemnon in Iliad
Chryses
　　father of Chryseis　　　　KRĪ-sēz　　　　　　　'kraɪsiːz
Chrysippus
　　son of Pelops and Axioche　krī-SIP-uhs　　　　　kraɪ'sipəs
Chrysler
　　US car mfr.; building, New York　KRĪ-sluhr　　　　　'kraɪsləʳ
　　　City
Chrysopelia
　　tree nymph in Arcadia　　KRĪ-suh-PĒ-lē-uh, -PĒL-yuh　,kraɪsə'piːliːə, -'piːljə
Chrysostom
　　John, Christian saint　　KRIS-uhs-tuhm, kris-AHS-tuhm　'krisəstəm, kris'astəm
Chrystal
　　pers. name　　　　　　　KRIS-tl　　　　　　　'kristl̩
Chūbu
　　region, Honshu Island, Japan　choo-boo　　　　　　tʃuːbuː
Chuck
　　pers. name　　　　　　　CHUHK　　　　　　　'tʃək
Chugach
　　National Forest, AK　　　CHOO-gach　　　　　　'tʃuːgætʃ
Chūgoku
　　region, Honshu Island, Japan　choo-gō-koo　　　　　tʃuːgoːkuː
Chuj
　　lang., people, Guatemala　CHOO(KH), CHOO-ē　　'tʃuː(x), 'tʃuːiˑ
Chukchi
　　Sea, part of Arctic ocean; lang.,　CHUHK-chē, CHUK-chē　'tʃəktʃiˑ, 'tʃuktʃiˑ
　　　Russia
Chula Vista
　　city, CA　　　　　　　CHOO-luh VIS-tuh　　,tʃuːlə 'vistə
Chumash
　　N. American people　　　CHOO-mash　　　　　'tʃuːmæʃ

Chung
  pers. name   CHUNG, CHUHNG   'tʃuŋ, 'tʃəŋ
Ch'ungch'ŏngnam
  prov., S. Korea   chung-chahng-nahm   tʃuŋtʃaŋnam
Ch'ungch'ŏngpuk
  prov., S. Korea   chung-chahng-puk   tʃuŋtʃaŋpuk
Chung-chia [Puyi]
  lang., people, China   JUNG-JAH, JUNG-jē-AH   'dʒuŋ'dʒa, 'dʒuŋdʒiː'a
Chungking
  see Chongqing
Ch'ung-tu
  see Chengdu
Chung Yeung
  Chinese festival   JUNG yuh-UNG   'dʒuŋ jə'uŋ
Chur
  town, Switzerland   KUR   'kuʳ
Churchill
  Sir Winston L. S., *British*   CHUHR-CHIL, Ⓢ *also* CHUHRCH-HIL   'tʃəʳ,tʃil, Ⓢ *also* 'tʃəʳtʃ,hil
    statesman, author (Nobel 1953);
    college, Cambridge Univ.; pl.
    name
Churún Merú [Angel Falls]
  waterfall, Venezuela   chu-RŌŌN mā-RŌŌ   tʃu'ruːn meː'ruː
Chust
  see Khust
Chuvash
  lang., people, Russia   CHŌŌ-VAHSH, chu-VAHSH   'tʃuː,vaʃ, tʃu'vaʃ
Chuzzlewit
  Martin, *character in* Martin   CHUHZ-uhl-WIT   'tʃəzəl,wit
    Chuzzlewit, *C. Dickens*
Ciao!
  shoe co.; Italian greeting   CHOW   'tʃau
Ciardi
  John, *US poet*   CHAHRD-ē   'tʃaʳdiˑ
Ciba-Geigy
  pharmaceutical co.   SĒB-uh-GĪ-gē   ,siːbə'gaigiˑ
Cibber
  Colley, *English poet, actor*   SIB-uhr   'sibəʳ
Cibola
  Stadium, *McCook, NE*   SĒ-buh-luh   'siːbələ
Ciboney
  Cuban people   SĒ-buh-NĀ   ,siːbə'neː
Ciccone
  Madonna Louise, *original name of*   chi-KŌ-nē   tʃi'koːniˑ
    Madonna, *US entertainer*
Cicely
  fictional town, AK; pers. name   SIS-(uh-)lē   'sis(ə)liˑ
Cicero
  Roman orator & statesman; town,   SIS-uh-RŌ   'sisə,roː
    IL
Cicéron
  pers. name, French   sē-sā-RAWⁿ   siːseːrɔ̃
Ciceronian
  pert. to Cicero   SIS-uh-RŌ-nē-uhn, SIS-uh-RŌN-yuhn ,sisə'roːniːən, ,sisə'roːnjən

---

Key (col. 2): a: f**a**d â: f**a**de ah: f**a**ther ar: M**a**ry aw: l**a**w e: f**e**d ē: f**ee**d er: m**e**rry i: h**i**d ī: h**i**de ō: c**oa**t ōō: b**oo**t
oi: b**oy** ow: n**ow** u: p**u**t uh: **a**bove uhr: b**i**rd ch: **ch**op ng: ri**ng** sh: **sh**ow th: **th**ick th: **th**is zh: mea**s**ure

Cicily
    pers. name   SIS-(uh-)lē   'sis(ə)li·

Cicones
    allies of the Trojans   si-KŌ-NĒZ   si'koː,niːz

Cid, El
    cognomen of Rodrigo Diaz de Vivar   el THĒ<u>TH</u>, Ⓢ el SID   el 'θiːð, Ⓢ el 'sid

Cienfuegos
    port, Cuba   sē-en-FWĀ-ḡōs   siːen'fweːyoːs

Cilicia
    ancient country, Asia Minor   suh-LISH-(ē-)uh   sə'liʃ(iː)ə

Cilix
    founder of Cilicia   SIL-iks   'siliks

Cillas
    charioteer of Pelops   SIL-uhs   'siləs

Cimabue
    Giovanni, *Italian painter*   CHĒ-muh-B̄O̅O̅-ä   ˌtʃiːmə'buːeː

Cimarron
    US river; county, OK; city, KS   SIM-uh-RŌN, SIM-uh-RAHN, SIM-uh-ruhn   'simə,roːn, 'simə,rɑn, 'simərən

Cimbri
    Germanic or Celtic people   SIM-BRĪ, KIM-brē   'sim,brɑi, 'kimbri·

Cimmerians
    mythical people dwelling in darkness   suh-MER-ē-uhnz   sə'meriːənz

Cimon
    Athenian leader   SĪ-muhn   'sɑimən

Cinchona
    plant   sing-KŌ-nuh, sin-CHŌ-nuh   siŋ'koːnə, sin'tʃoːnə

Cincinnati
    city, OH   SIN-suh-NAT-ē, SIN-suh-NAT-uh   ˌsinsə'næti·, ˌsinsə'nætə

Cincinnatian
    pert. to Cincinnati   SIN-suh-NAT-ē-uhn   ˌsinsə'nætiːən

Cincinnatus
    Roman general; pers. name   SIN-suh-NAT-uhs   ˌsinsə'nætəs

Cinco de Mayo
    May 5th holiday, Mexico   SING-kō <u>th</u>ä MĪ-ō   'siŋkoː ðeː 'mɑioː

Cinderella
    fairy tale character   SIN-duh-REL-uh   ˌsində'relə

Cindy
    pers. name   SIN-dē   'sindi·

Cinerama
    tdmk for a movie process   SIN-uh-RAM-uh, SIN-uh-RAHM-uh   ˌsinə'ræmə, ˌsinə'rɑmə

Cinna
    Roman leader   SIN-uh   'sinə

Cinnabar
    mineral   SIN-uh-BAHR   'sinə,bɑʳ

Cinnamon
    spice   SIN-uh-muhn   'sinəmən

Cinquefoil
    plant   SINGK-FOIL, SANGK-FOIL   'siŋk,fɔil, 'sæŋk,fɔil

Cinque Ports
    port association, England   SINGK PŌRTS, PAWRTS   'siŋk ,poːʳts, ,pɔːʳts

Cinqueterre
    coastal region, Italy   CHING-kwuh-TER-ä   ˌtʃiŋkwə'tereː

Foreign Sounds: ue: *Fr.* **rue**, *Ger.* **füllen**   uh(r): *Fr.* **boeuf**, *Ger.* **Höhle**   <u>kh</u>: *Ger.* **ich**, *Scot.* **loch**   ḡ: *Sp.* **amigo**   <u>v</u>: *Sp.* **hablar**
hl: *Welsh* **Llanelli**.   CAPITALS: primary stress.   SMALL CAPS: secondary stress.   Ⓢ: U.S. pron.   Ⓛ: British pron.

Cinyras
　first king of Cyprus　　　SIN-uh-ruhs　　　'sinərəs
Cinzano
　wine　　　chin-ZAHN-ō　　　tʃin'zɑnoː
Ciokwe, Chokwe
　lang., Africa　　　CHAWK-wä　　　'tʃɔːkweː
Circassian
　lang., SE Europe　　　suhr-KASH-uhn　　　səʳkæʃən
Circe
　sorceress in Odyssey　　　SUHR-sē　　　'səʳsiˑ
Circinus
　constellation　　　SUHRS-n-uhs　　　'səʳsɳəs
Cirencester
　town, England　　　SĪ-ruhn-SES-tuhr, SIS-it-uhr　　　'sairən,sestəʳ, 'sisitəʳ
Cisalpine Gaul
　Roman province　　　sis-AL-PĪN GAWL　　　sis'æl,pɑin 'gɔːl
Cisco
　Junior College, *TX*　　　SIS-kō　　　'siskoː
Ciskei
　Black enclave, South Africa　　　SIS-KĪ　　　'sis,kɑi
Cisneros
　Sandra, *US novelist*　　　sis-NER-ōs　　　sis'neroːs
Cissie
　pers. name　　　SIS-ē　　　'sisiˑ
Cistercians
　religious order　　　sis-TUHR-shuhnz　　　sis'təʳʃənz
Citadel, The
　military college, SC　　　SIT-uhd-l, SIT-uh-DEL　　　'siṭədl̩, 'siṭə,del
Cithaeron
　king of Plataea　　　suh-THIR-AHN, suh-THĒ-RAHN　　　sə'θir,ɑn, sə'θiː,rɑn
Citibank
　US bank　　　SIT-ē-BANGK　　　'siṭiˑ,bæŋk
Citicorp
　US financial co.　　　SIT-ē-KAWRP　　　'siṭiˑ,kɔːʳp
Citium
　ancient city, Cyprus　　　SISH-(ē-)uhm　　　'siʃ(iː)əm
Citlaltépetl [Orizaba]
　mtn., city, Mexico　　　sēt-LAHL-TĀ-PET-l　　　siːt,lɑl'teː,petl̩
Citroën
　French car co.　　　sē-traw-EN　　　siːtrɔːen
Citron
　fruit　　　SI-truhn　　　'sitrən
Città Vecchia
　city, Malta　　　chi-TAH VEK-yah　　　tʃi'tɑ 'vekjɑ
Ciudad de México
　city, Mexico　　　syoo-THAH(TH) thuh MĀ-hē-kō　　　sjuː'ðɑ(ð) ðə 'meˑhiːkoː
Ciudad Real
　prov & town, Spain　　　syoo-THAH(TH) rä-AHL　　　sjuː'ðɑ(ð) reː'al
Ciudad Trujillo
　city, Dominican Republic　　　syoo-THAH(TH) troo-KHĒ(L)-yō　　　sjuː'ðɑ(ð) truˑ'çiː(l)joː
Clackamas
　river, county, OR　　　KLAK-uh-muhs　　　'klækəməs
Claflin
　College, *SC*　　　KLAF-luhn　　　'klæflən

Key (col. 2): a: fad ä: fade ah: father ar: **M**ary aw: **l**aw e: fed ē: feed er: **m**erry i: hid ī: hide ō: coat o͞o: boot
oi: **b**oy ow: **n**ow u: **p**ut uh: **a**bove uhr: **b**ird ch: **ch**op ng: ri**ng** sh: **sh**ow th: **th**ick th̲: **th**is zh: mea**s**ure

Claiborne
   1. Liz, *US fashion designer*   KLĀ-BAWRN   'kleɪˌbɔːʳn
   2. pers. name   KLĀ-buhrn, KLĀ-BAWRN   'kleɪbəʳn, 'kleɪˌbɔːʳn

Clair, Claire
   1. pers. name   KLAR, KLER   'klæʳ, 'kleʳ
   2. French   KLER   kler
   3. German   KLER   'kleʳ

Clairette
   wine grape   kler-ET   kler'et

Clairol
   hair-products brand   KLAR-AWL, KLER-AWL   'klærˌɔːl, 'klerˌɔːl

Clallam
   county, WA   KLAL-uhm   'klæləm

Clallam, Klallam
   N. American people   KLAL-uhm   'klæləm

Clara
   1. pers. name   KLAR-uh   'klærə
   2. French   klah-RAH   klɑːrɑː
   3. German, Spanish   KLAHR-ah   'klɑrɑ

Clare
   pers. name   KLAR, KLER   'klæʳ, 'kleʳ

Clare Hall
   college, Cambridge Univ.   KLER HAWL, Ⓢ *also* KLAR   'kleʳ ˌhɔːl, Ⓢ *also* 'klæʳ

Clarence
   1. pers. name   KLAR-uhns   'klærəns
   2. French   klah-RAHⁿS   klɑːrãs

Clarendon
   county, SC; city, AR, TX; Oxford printing press   KLAR-uhn-duhn   'klærəndən

Claret
   red wine   KLAR-uht   'klærət

Claretian
   religious order   kluh-RĒ-shuhn   klə'riːʃən

Clarice
   pers. name   KLAR-uhs, KLER-uhs   'klærəs, 'klerəs

Clarinet
   musical instrument   KLAR-uh-NET, KLAR-uh-NET   ˌklærə'net, 'klærəˌnet

Clarissa
   pers. name   kluh-RIS-uh   klə'risə

Clark
   Petula, *British actress; pers. name*   KLAHRK   'klɑʳk

Clarke
   pers. name   KLAHRK   'klɑʳk

Clarkson
   pers. name   KLAHRK-suhn   'klɑʳksən

Clatsop
   county, Community College, *OR*   KLAT-suhp   'klætsəp

Claud
   pers. name   KLAWD   'klɔːd

Claude
   1. Albert, *Belgian biologist (Nobel 1974)*   KLŌD   kloːd
   2. pers. name   KLAWD   'klɔːd
   3. French   KLŌD   kloːd

Foreign Sounds: ue: *Fr.* **rue**, *Ger.* f**ü**llen   uh(r): *Fr.* b**œu**f, *Ger.* H**öh**le   kh: *Ger.* i**ch**, *Scot.* lo**ch**   g̃: *Sp.* ami**g**o   v̄: *Sp.* ha**b**lar hl: *Welsh* **Ll**anelli.   CAPITALS: primary stress.   SMALL CAPS: secondary stress.   Ⓢ: U.S. pron.   Ⓛ: British pron.

Claudette
   pers. name   klaw-DET   klɔ'det

Claudia
   pers. name   KLAWD-ē-uh   'klɔːdiːə

Claudian
   pert. to Claudius   KLAWD-ē-uhn   'klɔːdiːən

Claudine
   pers. name   klō-DĒN   kloːdiːn

Claudio
   1. pers. name, Italian   KLOWD-yō   'klaudjoː
   2. Spanish   KLOW<u>TH</u>-yō   'klauðjoː

Cláudio
   pers. name, Portuguese   KLOW<u>TH</u>-yoō   'klauðjuː

Claudius
   1. Roman emperor; pers. name   KLAWD-ē-uhs   'klɔːdiːəs
   2. German   KLOWD-yus, KLOW-dē-us   'klaudjus, 'klaudiːus

Claudius Gothicus
   Roman emperor   KLAWD-ē-uhs GAHTH-i-kuhs   'klɔːdiːəs 'gaθikəs

Claus
   pers. name, Dutch, Norwegian   KLOWS   'klaus

Clausewitz
   Karl von, *Prussian militarist*   KLOW-zuh-VITS   'klauzə,vits

Clavell
   James, *US writer*   kluh-VEL   klə'vel

Claxton
   pers. name   KLAK-stuhn   'klækstən

Clayburgh
   Jill, *US actress*   KLĀ-BUHRG   'kleɪ,bəʳg

Clayton
   pers. name   KLĀT-n   'kleɪtn̩

Cleanthes
   Greek philosopher   klē-AN-THĒZ   kliː'æn,θiːz

Clearasil
   tdmk for a skin care product   KLIR-uh-SIL   'klirə,sil

Cleary
   Beverly Atlee, *US author*   KLIR-ē   'kliriˑ

Cleburne
   county, AL, AR; city, TX   KLĒ-buhrn   'kliːbəʳn

Cleese
   John, *British actor*   KLĒZ   'kliːz

Cleisthenes
   tyrant of Sicyon; Athenian   KLĪS-thuh-NĒZ   'klaisθə,niːz
    statesman

Clem
   pers. name   KLEM   'klem

Clematis
   plant   KLEM-uht-uhs, kli-MAT-uhs,   'klemətəs, kli'mætəs,
                        kli-MAHT-uhs   kli'matəs

Clémence
   pers. name, French   klā-MAHⁿS   kleːmãs

Clemence
   pers. name   KLEM-uhns   'kleməns

Clemenceau
   Georges, *political leader*   klā-mahⁿ-SŌ, ⓢ KLEM-uhn-SŌ   kleːmãsoː, ⓢ ,klemən'soː

Key (col. 2):   a: fad ā: fade ah: father ar: Mary aw: law e: fed ē: feed er: merry i: hid ī: hide ō: coat o͞o: boot
oi: boy   ow: now   u: put   uh: above   uhr: bird   ch: chop   ng: ring   sh: show   th: thick   <u>th</u>: this   zh: measure

Clemens
   1. Samuel, *US author, aka* Mark   KLEM-uhnz   'klemənz
      Twain; *pers. name*
   2. German   KLĀ-mens   'kleːmens
   3. Latin   KLEM-uhnz, KLĒ-muhnz   'klemənz, 'kliːmənz
Clement
   pers. name   KLEM-uhnt   'klemənt
Clément
   pers. name, French   klā-MAHⁿ   kleːmã
Clemente
   1. Roberto, *US baseball player*   kluh-MENT-ē   klə'mentiˑ
   2. pers. name, Italian   klā-MEN-tā   kleː'menteː
   3. Spanish   klā-MĀN-tā   kleː'meːnteː
Clémentine
   pers. name, French   klā-mahⁿ-TĒN   kleːmãtiːn
Clementine
   pers. name   KLEM-uhn-TĪN   'klemən,tain
Cleo
   pers. name   KLĒ-ō   'kliːoː
Cleomenes
   name, Spartan kings   klē-AHM-uh-NĒZ   kliː'amə,niːz
Cleon
   Athenian general & politician   KLĒ-AHN   'kliː,an
Cleone
   Athenian general   klē-Ō-nē   kliː'oːniˑ
Cleopatra
   Egyptian queen   KLĒ-uh-PA-truh, -PĀ-truh, -PAH-truh   ,kliːə'pætrə, -'peːtrə, -'patrə
Clerc-Milon-Mondon
   wine   KLER-mē-LAWⁿ-mawⁿ-DAWⁿ   klermiːlɔ̃mɔ̃dɔ̃
Clerihew
   quatrain rhyming aabb; pers.   KLER-i-HYŌŌ   'kleri,hjuː
     name
Clerkes of Oxenford
   choral ensemble, England   KLAHRKS uhv AHK-suhn-fuhrd,   'klaʳks əv 'aksənfəʳd,
                                       AHK-suhn-FAWRD   'aksən,fɔːʳd
Clermont
   Fulton's steamboat   KLER-MAHNT   'kleʳ,mant
Clermont-Ferrand
   city, France   kler-mawⁿ-fuh-RAHⁿ   klermɔ̃fərã
Clete
   nurse to Penthesilea   KLĒT-ē   'kliːṭiˑ
Clevedon
   town, England   KLĒV-duhn   'kliːvdən
Cleveland
   Grover, *22d & 24th US president;*   KLĒV-luhnd   'kliːvlənd
    city, OH; county, AR, NC, OK;
    county, England; pers. name
Cliburn
   Van, *US pianist*   KLĪ-buhrn   'klaibəʳn
Clichy
   suburb of Paris, France   klē-SHĒ   kliːʃiː
Clicquot
   champagne   klē-KŌ   kliːkoː
Cliff
   pers. name   KLIF   'klif

Clifford
   pers. name   KLIF-uhrd   'klifəᶦd

Clifton
   pers. name   KLIF-tuhn   'kliftən

Clinelish
   Scotch whisky   KLĬN-LĒSH   'klain,liːʃ

Clinique
   skincare products   kluh-NĒK   klə'niːk

Clio
   1. muse of history   KLĪ-ō, KLĒ-ō   'klaioː, 'kliːoː
   2. street, New Orleans; advertising   KLĒ-ō   'kliːoː
      award

Clive
   pers. name   KLĪV   'klaiv

Clodius
   pers. name   KLŌD-ē-uhs   'kloːdiːəs

Cloncurry
   town, Australia   klahn-KUH-rē   klɑn'kəriˑ

Clootie
   the Devil   KLŌŌT-ē   'kluːʈiˑ

Cloris
   pers. name   KLŌR-uhs, KLAWR-uhs   'kloːrəs, 'klɔːrəs

Clos de Bèze
   wine   KLŌ duh BEZ   kloː də bez

Clos de Tart
   wine   KLŌ duh TAHR   kloː də tɑr

Clos de Vougeot
   wine   KLŌ duh vōō-ZHŌ   kloː də vuːʒoː

Clos du Bois
   winery, CA   KLŌ duh BWAH   ˌkloː də 'bwɑ

Clos du Roi
   wine   KLŌ duer WAH   kloː dyːr wɑː

Clos Fourtet
   wine   KLŌ fur-TE   kloː furte

Clotho
   one of the Fates   KLŌ-thō   'kloːθoː

Clotilde
   1. pers. name, French   klaw-TĒLD   klɔːtiːld
   2. Italian   klō-TĒL-dā   kloː'tiːldeː

Clough
   pers. name   KLUHF, KLŌ   'kləf, 'kloː

Clouseau
   fictional French police inspector   klōō-ZŌ   kluːzoː

Clovis
   pers. name   klaw-VĒS, KLŌ-vis   klɔːviːs, 'kloːvis

Cluj
   county, Romania   KLŌŌZH   'kluːʒ

Clumber
   spaniel   KLUHM-buhr   'kləmbəᶦ

Cluny
   commune, abbey, France; lace   klue-NĒ, Ⓢ klōō-NĒ   klyːniː, Ⓢ kluː'niː

Clwyd
   river, county, Wales   KLŌŌ-id, Ⓢ KLŌŌ-ēd   'kluˑid, Ⓢ 'kluːiˑd

Clwydian
   pert. to Clwyd   klōō-ID-ē-uhn   kluː'idiːən

Key (col. 2):   a: fad   ā: fade   ah: father   ar: **M**ary   aw: **law**   e: fed   ē: feed   er: **m**erry   i: hid   ī: hide   ō: coat   ōō: boot
oi: **boy**   ow: **now**   u: put   uh: **above**   uhr: **b**ird   ch: **chop**   ng: ri**ng**   sh: **show**   th: **th**ick   <u>th</u>: **this**   zh: measure

Clyde
   river, Scotland; pers. name   KLĪD   'klɑid

Clydesdale
   horse breed   KLĪDZ-DĀL   'klɑidz,deːl

Clymene
   mother of Atlas, Prometheus,   KLIM-uh-nē   'kliməniˑ
   Epimetheus

Clymenus
   founder of the Olympic Games   KLIM-uh-nuhs   'klimənəs

Clytemnestra
   wife of Agamemnon   KLĪT-uhm-NES-truh, ⓔ   ˌklɑiţəm'nestrə, ⓔ
                  KLĪ-tuhm-NĒ-struh   ˌklɑitəm'niːstrə

CMOS
   complementary metal oxide   SĒ-MAHS   'siːˌmɑs
   silicon semiconductor

Cnaeus, Cneius
   Roman praenomen   NĒ-uhs   'niːəs

Cnidus
   ancient Greek city   NĪD-uhs, kuh-NĪD-uhs   'nɑidəs, kə'nɑidəs

Cnossus
   ancient Cretan city   NAHS-uhs   'nɑsəs

Cnut
   see Canute

Coahoma
   county, MS   kō-HŌ-muh   koˈhoːmə

Coahuila
   state, Mexico   KŌ-uh-WĒ-luh   ˌkoːə'wiːlə

Coahuiltec
   N. American people   KŌ-uh-WĒL-TEK   ˌkoːə'wiːlˌtek

Coase
   Ronald H., *British-born US*   KŌS   'koːs
   economist

Coatlicue
   Mayan earth goddess   kō-AHT-li-KWĀ, kō-AT-li-KWĀ   koːˈɑtliˌkweː, koːˈætliˌkweː

cobalt
   element   KŌ-BAWLT, KŌ-buhlt   'koːˌbɔːlt, 'koːbəlt

Cobar
   town, Australia   KŌ-BAHR   'koːˌbɑʳ

COBE
   Cosmic Background Explorer   KŌ-bē   'koːbiˑ

Coblenz
   see Koblenz

COBOL
   programming lang.   KŌ-BAWL, KŌ-BAHL   'koːˌbɔːl, 'koːˌbɑl

Coburn
   James, *US actor*   KŌ-buhrn   'koːbəʳn

Coca-Cola
   soft drink brand & co.   kō-kuh-KŌ-luh, *in rapid speech*   ˌkoːkə'koːlə, *in rapid speech*
                  kō-KŌ-luh   koːˈkoːlə

Cocama
   see Kokama

Cochabamba
   dept, Bolivia   KŌ-chuh-BAHM-buh   ˌkoːtʃə'bɑmbə

Cochimi
   N. American people   KŌ-chuh-MĒ   ˌkoːtʃə'miː

Foreign Sounds: ue: *Fr.* **rue**, *Ger.* f**ü**llen   uh(r): *Fr.* b**oeu**f, *Ger.* H**öh**le   <u>kh</u>: *Ger.* i**ch**, *Scot.* lo**ch**   g̱: *Sp.* ami**g**o   <u>v</u>: *Sp.* ha**b**lar
hl: *Welsh* **Ll**anelli.   CAPITALS: primary stress.   SMALL CAPS: secondary stress.   Ⓢ: U.S. pron.   ⓔ: British pron.

Cochin
seaport, India   kō-CHIN   koːˈtʃin
Cochise
1. Apache leader   kō-CHĒS   koːˈtʃiːs
2. county, AZ   kuh-CHĒS, kō-CHĒS   kəˈtʃiːs, koːˈtʃiːs
Cochiti
N. American people   kō-CHĒT-ē   koːˈtʃiːʈiˑ
Cochoa
song bird   kuh-CHŌ-uh   kəˈtʃoːə
Cockaigne, Cockayne
Land of, *fabled land of luxury*   kah-KĀN   kaˈkeːn
Cockburn
British family name   KŌ-buhrn   ˈkoːbəˈn
Cockcroft
Sir John D., *British physicist*   KAHK-(K)RAWFT   ˈkak,(k)rɔːft
(*Nobel 1951*)
Cockney
person from east end of London,   KAHK-nē   ˈkakniˑ
England
Coconino
county, AZ   KŌ-kuh-NĒ-nō   ˌkoːkəˈniːnoː
Cocopah
N. American people   KŌ-kuh-PAH, KŌ-kuh-PAH   ˈkoːkə,pɑ, ˌkoːkəˈpɑ
Cocos Islands
atolls, Indian Ocean   KŌ-kuhs   ˈkoːkəs
Cocteau
Jean, *Frenchwriter*   kawk-TŌ, Ⓢ kahk-TŌ   kɔːktoː, Ⓢ kakˈtoː
Codex Juris Canonici
Roman Catholic Church law   KŌD-EKS JUR-uhs KAN-uh-NĪ-sē,   ˈkoːd,eks ˈdʒurəs
                                                 YUR-uhs, KAN-uh-NĒ-sē   ˌkænəˈnaisiˑ, ˈjurəs,
                                                                                                 ˌkænəˈniːsiˑ
Codington
county, SD   KAHD-ing-tuhn   ˈkadiŋtən
Codrus
son of Melanthus; king of Athens   KAHD-ruhs   ˈkadrəs
Cody
William "Buffalo Bill", *US scout,*   KŌD-ē   ˈkoːdiˑ
entertainer
Coelenterates
marine invertebrates   sē-LENT-uh-RĀTS, suh-   siːˈlentəˌreːts, sə-
Coeliris
dinosaur   SĒ-luh-ruhs   ˈsiːlərəs
Coelophysis
dinosaur   sē-LŌ-fuh-zuhs, sē-LAHF-uh-zuhs,   siːˈloːfəzəs, siːˈlafəzəs, -səs;
                                                 -suhs; SĒ-luh-FĪ-suhs   ˌsiːləˈfaisəs
Coelurosauria
dinosaur infraorder   SĒL-yuh-rō-SAWR-ē-uh   ˌsiːljəroːˈsɔːriːə
Coelus
Roman name for Uranus   SĒ-luhs   ˈsiːləs
Coetzee
S. African family name   kōōt-SI-uh, kōōt-SĒ   kuːtˈsiə, kuːtˈsiː
Coeur d'Alene
river, city, lake, ID; N. American   KAWRD-l-ĀN   ˌkɔːˈdl̩ˈeːn
people

Key (col. 2): a: fad ā: fade ah: father ar: **Mary** aw: **law** e: fed ē: feed er: merry i: hid ī: hide ō: coat o͞o: boot
oi: boy ow: now u: put uh: above uhr: bird ch: chop ng: ring sh: show th: thick t͟h: this zh: measure

Coeur de Lion

   Richard I of England,   kuhr duh LYAWⁿ, Ⓢ KUHR duh   kœr də ljɔ̃, Ⓢ ˌkəʳ də ˈlɑiən,
   "lionhearted"   LĪ-uhn, LĒ-uhn   ˈliːən

Coeus

   son of Uranus and Gaia   SĒ-uhs   ˈsiːəs

Coffee

   county, AL, GA, TN   KAW-fē, KAHF-ē   ˈkɔːfiˑ, ˈkɑfiˑ

Coggan

   Frederick Donald, archbishop of   KAHG-uhn   ˈkɑgən
     Canterbury

Cognac

   brandy   KŌN-YAK, KAWN-YAK, KAHN-YAK   ˈkoːnˌjæk, ˈkɔːnˌjæk,
                                              ˈkɑnˌjæk

Cohan

   George M., composer   KŌ-HAN   ˈkoːˌhæn

Cohen

   Stanley, US biochemist (Nobel   KŌ-uhn   ˈkoːən
     1986)

Cohn

   Sam, US film and theatrical agent   KŌN   ˈkoːn

Cohoes

   city, NY   kuh-HŌZ   kəˈhoːz

Cohosh

   herb   KŌ-HAHSH   ˈkoːˌhɑʃ

Coimbra

   district, Portugal   ku-IM-bruh, kō-IM-bruh   kuˈimbrə, koːˈimbrə

Cointreau

   liqueur   kweⁿ-TRŌ   kwẽˈtroː

Cointrin

   airport, Geneva   kweⁿ-TREⁿ   kwẽtrẽ

Coke

   British family name   KUK, KŌOK, KŌK   ˈkuk, ˈkuːk, ˈkoːk

Colbert

   1. Claudette, US actress   kawl-BER, KŌL-BER   kɔːlˈbeʳ, ˈkoːlˌbeʳ
   2. county, AL   KAHL-buhrt   ˈkɑlbəʳt

Colby

   College, ME; city, KS, WI; cheese   KŌL-bē   ˈkoːlbiˑ

Colchester

   1. town, CT, VT; county, Nova   KŌL-CHES-tuhr, KŌL-chuh-stuhr   ˈkoːlˌtʃestəʳ, ˈkoːltʃəstəʳ
     Scotia, Canada
   2. town, England   KŌL-chuh-stuhr   ˈkoːltʃəstəʳ

Colchicum

   plant   KAHL-chi-kuhm, KAHL-ki-kuhm   ˈkaltʃikəm, ˈkalkikəm

Colchis

   ancient country, Asia   KAHL-kuhs   ˈkalkəs

Coldstream Guards

   British royal regiment   KŌL(D)-STRĒM GAHRDZ   ˌkoːl(d)ˌstriːm ˈgɑʳdz

Cole

   pers. name   KŌL   ˈkoːl

Coleridge

   Samuel Taylor, English poet   KŌL-rij, KŌ-luh-rij   ˈkoːlridʒ, ˈkoːləridʒ

Colet

   John, English educator   KAHL-uht   ˈkalət

Foreign Sounds: ue: *Fr.* **rue**, *Ger.* **füllen**   uh(r): *Fr.* **boeuf**, *Ger.* **Höhle**   <u>kh</u>: *Ger.* **ich**, *Scot.* **loch**   g̶: *Sp.* **amigo**   v̶: *Sp.* **hablar**
hl: *Welsh* **Llanelli**.   CAPITALS: primary stress.   SMALL CAPS: secondary stress.   Ⓢ: U.S. pron.   Ⓛ: British pron.

Colette
  1. pers. name   kuh-LET   kə'let
  2. French   kaw-LET   kɔːlet
  3. Sidonie, *French writer*   kaw-LET, ⑤ kuh-LET, kahl-ET   kɔːlet, ⑤ kə'let, kɑl'et
Coleus
  plant   KŌ-lē-uhs   'koːliːəs
Colgate
  University, *NY*   KŌL-GĀT   'koːl,geːt
Colima
  state, Mexico   kuh-LĒ-muh   kə'liːmə
Colima warbler
  songbird   kuh-LĒ-muh WAWR-bluhr   kə'liːmə 'wɔːʳbləʳ
Colin
  1. pers. name   KAHL-uhn, KŌ-luhn   'kalən, 'koːlən
  2. French   kaw-LEⁿ   kɔːlẽ
  3. German   KŌ-lin, -lēn   'koːlin, -liːn
Collarenebri
  town, Australia   KAHL-uh-REN-uh-BRĪ   ,kalə'renə,brɑi
Colleen
  pers. name   kahl-ĒN   kal'iːn
College Misericordia
  college, PA   KAHL-ij MIZ-uh-ri-KAWR-dē-uh,   'kalidʒ ,mizəri'kɔːʳdiːə,
                                           MIZ-ER-i-KAWR-dē-uh   ,miz,eri'kɔːʳdiːə
Colleton
  county, SC   KAHL-uht-n   'kalətn̩
Colley
  pers. name (C. Cibber)   KAHL-ē   'kaliˑ
Colli Albani
  Italian wine   KAHL-ē ahl-BAHN-ē   'kaliː al'baniˑ
Colli Piacentini
  Italian wine   KAHL-ē PYAH-chen-TĒ-nē   'kaliː ,pjɑtʃen'tiːniˑ
Cologne [Köln]
  city, Germany   kuh-LŌN   kə'loːn
Colombia
  republic, S. America   kuh-LUHM-bē-uh, kuh-LŌM-bē-uh   kə'ləmbiːə, kə'loːmbiːə
Colombian
  pert. to Colombia   kuh-LUHM-bē-uhn, kuh-LŌM-bē-uhn   kə'ləmbiːən, kə'loːmbiːən
Colombo
  city, Sri Lanka   kuh-LUHM-bō   kə'ləmboː
Colón
  Cristóbal, *Spanish name for*   kuh-LŌN   kə'loːn
    Christopher Columbus; *prov,*
    city, Panama; town, Argentina;
    town, Cuba
Colonus
  Sophoclean setting   kuh-LŌ-nuhs   kə'loːnəs
Colorado
  1. river, state, & desert, US   KAHL-uh-RAD-ō, KAHL-uh-RAHD-ō   ,kalə'rædoː, ,kalə'radoː
  2. river, Argentina; S. American   KAHL-uh-RAHD-ō   ,kalə'radoː
    people
Colosseum
  ampitheater, Rome   KAHL-uh-SĒ-uhm   ,kalə'siːəm
Colossians
  New Testament book   kuh-LAHSH-(ē-)uhnz,   kə'laʃ(iː)ənz, kə'lasiːənz
                                           kuh-LAHS-ē-uhnz

Key (col. 2):   a: fad ā: fade ah: father ar: Mary aw: law e: fed ē: feed er: merry i: hid ī: hide ō: coat ōō: boot
oi: boy   ow: now   u: put   uh: above   uhr: bird   ch: chop   ng: ring   sh: show   th: thick   th̲: this   zh: measure

Colossus of Rhodes
  ancient wonder   kuh-LAHS-uhs uhv RŌDZ   kə'lɑsəs əv 'roːdz

Colquhoun
  Patrick, *Scottish merchant, police*   kuh-HŌŌN   kə'huːn
    reformer

Colquitt
  county, GA   KAHL-kwit   'kɑlkwit

Colton
  city, CA   KÔLT-n   'koːltn̩

Coltrane
  John, *US jazz musician*   kōl-TRĀN, KŌL-TRĀN   koːl'treːn, 'koːl,treːn

Columba
  constellation   kuh-LUHM-buh   kə'ləmbə

Columbia
  river, US & Canada; District of,   kuh-LUHM-bē-uh   kə'ləmbiːə
    US; University, NY

Columbiana
  county, OH   kuh-LUHM-bē-AN-uh   kə,ləmbiː'ænə

Columbine [Aquilegia]
  plant   KAHL-uhm-BĪN   'kɑləm,bain

columbium
  element   kuh-LUHM-bē-uhm   kə'ləmbiːəm

Columbus
  Christopher, *Italian-born Spanish*   kuh-LUHM-buhs   kə'ləmbəs
    explorer; city, OH; pers. name

Colusa
  county, CA   kuh-LŌŌ-suh   kə'luːsə

Colusa Rancheria
  Indian reservation, US   kuh-LŌŌ-suh RAN-chuh-RĒ-uh   kə'luːsə ,ræntʃə'riːə

Coma Berenices [Berenice's Hair]
  constellation   KŌ-muh BER-uh-NĪ-sēz   'koːmə ,berə'naisiːz

Comal
  county, TX   kuh-MAHL   kə'mɑl

Comanche
  N. American people; county, KS,   kuh-MAN-chē   kə'mæntʃiˑ
    OK, TX

Comaneci
  Nadia, *Romanian gymnast*   KŌ-muh-NĂCH, KŌ-muh-NĒCH   ,koːmə'neːtʃ, ,koːmə'niːtʃ

Comecon
  Eastern bloc trade group   KAHM-i-KAHN   'kɑmi,kɑn

Comédie Française
  French national theater   kaw-mā-DĒ frahⁿ-SEZ   kɔːmeːdiˑ frãsez

Comenius
  John Amos, *Moravian bishop*   kuh-MĀ-nē-uhs, kuh-MĒ-nē-uhs   kə'meːniːəs, kə'miːniːəs

COMEX
  commodities exchange   KAHM-EKS, KAHM-iks   'kɑm,eks, 'kɑmiks

Comfrey
  plant   KUHM(P)-frē   'kəm(p)friˑ

Comines, Commines, Commynes
  Philippe de, *French politician*   kaw-MĒN   kɔːmiːn

Cominform
  Communist organization   KAHM-uhn-FŌRM,   'kɑmən,foːʳm,
                   KAHM-uhn-FAWRM   'kɑmən,fɔːʳm

Comintern
  Communist organization   KAHM-uhn-TUHRN   'kɑmən,təʳn

Foreign Sounds: **ue**: *Fr.* **rue**, *Ger.* **füllen** **uh(r)**: *Fr.* **bœuf**, *Ger.* **Höhle** **kh**: *Ger.* **ich**, *Scot.* **loch** **ḡ**: *Sp.* **amigo** **v̄**: *Sp.* **hablar**
hl: *Welsh* **Llanelli.** CAPITALS: primary stress. SMALL CAPS: secondary stress. ⑤: U.S. pron. ⑪: British pron.

Comiskey
  Park, *ballpark, Chicago, IL*   kuh-MIS-kē   kə'miski·

Comitia centuriata
  Roman legislative assembly   kō-MISH-(ē-)uh SEN-T(Y)UR-ē-ĀT-uh,   koː'miʃ(iː)ə ˌsen,t(j)uriː'eːţə,
       -AHT-uh   -'aţə

Comitia curiata
  early Roman legislative assembly   kō-MISH-(ē-)uh KYUR-ē-ĀT-uh,   koː'miʃ(iː)ə ˌkjuriː'eːţə, -'aţə
       -AHT-uh

Comitia tributa
  Roman legislative assembly   kō-MISH-(ē-)uh trī-BYŌŌT-uh   koː'miʃ(iː)ə traɪ'bjuːţə

Commager
  Henry Steele, *US historian*   KAHM-i-juhr   'kamidʒəʳ

Commedia dell' Arte
  early Italian comedy   kuh-MĀD-ē-uh DEL AHRT-ē,   kə'meːdiːə ˌdel 'aʳţi·,
       kuh-MED-ē-uh   kə'mediːə

Commercy
  commune, France; small cupcakes   kaw-mer-SĒ, Ⓢ KAHM-uhr-SĒ   koːmersiː, Ⓢ ˌkaməʳsiː

Commines
  see Comines

Commodus
  Roman emperor   KAHM-uhd-uhs   'kamədəs

Commynes
  see Comines

Como
  prov & lake, Italy   KŌ-mō   'koːmoː

Comoran
  pert. to or inhabitant of Comoros   KAHM-uh-ruhn, kuh-MAWR-uhn   'kamərən, kə'mɔːrən

Comoros
  islands   KAHM-uh-RŌZ, -RŌS; kuh-MAWR-ōz,   'kaməˌroːz, -ˌroːs;
       -ōs   kə'mɔːroːz, -oːs

Compadre
  Stadium, *Chandler, AZ*   kuhm-PAH-drā   kəm'padreː

Compaq
  US computer co.   KAHM-PAK   'kamˌpæk

Compiègne
  city, France   kawⁿ-PYEN   kɔ̃pjen

Compsognathus
  dinosaur   kahmp-SAHG-nuh-thuhs   kamp'sagnəθəs

Compton
  A. H., *US physicist (Nobel 1927)*   KAHM(P)-tuhn   'kam(p)tən

Comte
  Auguste, *French philosopher*   KAWⁿT   kɔ̃t

Comtism
  philosophy of Comte   KAHM-TIZ-uhm, KAWⁿ(N)-TIZ-uhm   'kamˌtizəm, 'kɔ̃(n)ˌtizəm

Comus
  Roman god of mirth; masque, J.   KŌ-muhs   'koːməs
    Milton

ConAgra
  US farm products co.   KAHN-AG-ruh, kahn-AG-ruh   'kanˌægrə, kan'ægrə

Conakry, Konakri
  city, Guinea   KAHN-uh-krē   'kanəkri·

Conan
  1. pers. name   KAWN-uhn, KŌ-nuhn   'kɔːnən, 'koːnən
  2. the Barbarian, film character   KŌ-NAN, KŌ-nuhn   'koːˌnæn, 'koːnən

---

Key (col. 2):   a: fad   ā: fade   ah: father   ar: Mary   aw: law   e: fed   ē: feed   er: merry   i: hid   ī: hide   ō: coat   ōō: boot
oi: boy   ow: now   u: put   uh: above   uhr: bird   ch: chop   ng: ring   sh: show   th: thick   th̲: this   zh: measure

Concepción
  city, Chile; dept., Paraguay; pers.   kawn-seps-YAWN,   kɔːnseps'jɔːn, kɔːnθep'θjɔːn
  name   kawn-thep-THYAWN

Concepcion
  David Ismael, *US baseball player*   kuhn-SEP-sē-ŌN   kən,sepsiː'oːn

Concepción, La
  see La Concepción

Concertgebouw
  orchestra, Netherlands   kawn-SERT-ḡuh-BOW,   kɔːn'seᶜtɣə,bau,
              ⑨ kuhn-SERT-guh-BOW,   ⑨ kən'seᶜtgə,bau,
              kuhn-SUHRT-   kən'səᶜt-

Concertina
  musical instrument   KAHN-suhr-TĒ-nuh   ,kansəᶜtiːnə

Concertino
  short concerto   KAHN-chuhr-TĒ-nō   ,kantʃəᶜtiːnoː

Concho
  river, county, TX   KAHN-chō   'kantʃoː

Conchobor
  legendary Irish king   KAHNG-khuh-vuhr, KAHNG-khuhr,   'kaŋxəvər, 'kaŋxər,
              ⑨ KAHNG-kuh-vuhr   ⑨ 'kaŋkəvəᶜ

Concilium plebus tributum
  Roman plebeian assembly   kuhn-SIL-ē-uhm PLĀ-buhs   kən'siliːəm 'pleːbəs
              tri-BYOOT-uhm, PLĒ-buhs   tri'bjuːʈəm, 'pliːbəs

Concord
  1. river, town, MA, city, CA, NH;   KAHNG-kuhrd, KAHN-, -KAWRD   'kaŋkəᶜd, 'kan-, -,kɔːᶜd
  grape
  2. city, NC   KAHN-KAWRD, KAHNG-KAWRD   'kan,kɔːᶜd, 'kaŋ,kɔːᶜd

Concorde
  supersonic passenger plane   KAHNG-KAWRD, KAHN-KAWRD   'kaŋ,kɔːᶜd, 'kan,kɔːᶜd

Condé Nast
  publishing co.   KAHN-dā NAST, KAHN-dē   ,kandeː 'næst, ,kandiˑ

Condobolin
  town, Australia   kuhn-DŌ-bluhn   kən'doːblən

Condoleezza
  pers. name   KAHN-duh-LĒ-zuh   'kandə,liːzə

Condor
  vulture   KAHN-duhr, KAHN-DAWR   'kandəᶜ, 'kan,dɔːᶜ

Conecuh
  river, county, AL   kuh-NĀ-kuh   kə'neːkə

Conejos
  county, CO   kuh-NĀ-uhs, kuh-NĀ-huhs   kə'neːəs, kə'neːhəs

Conestoga [Susquehanna]
  N. American people   KAHN-uh-STŌ-guh   ,kanə'stoːgə

Coney Island
  resort, NY   KŌ-nē Ī-luhnd   'koːniˑ 'ailənd

Confucian
  pert. to Confucius   kuhn-FYOO-shuhn   kən'fjuːʃən

Confucianism
  doctrines of Confucius   kuhn-FYOO-shuh-NIZ-uhm   kən'fjuːʃə,nizəm

Confucius
  Chinese philosopher   kuhn-FYOO-shuhs   kən'fjuːʃəs

Conga
  dance; drum   KAHNG-guh   'kaŋgə

Congo [Zaire]
  river, republic, Africe   KAHNG-gō   'kaŋgoː

Foreign Sounds: ue: *Fr.* **rue**, *Ger.* **füllen**   uh(r): *Fr.* **boeuf**, *Ger.* **Höhle**   kh: *Ger.* **ich**, *Scot.* **loch**   ḡ: *Sp.* **amigo**   v: *Sp.* **hablar**
hl: *Welsh* **Llanelli**.   CAPITALS: primary stress.   SMALL CAPS: secondary stress.   ⑨: U.S. pron.   ⑫: British pron.

Congolese
  pert. to the Congo | KAHNG-guh-LĒZ, -LĒS | ˌkaŋɡə'liːz, -'liːs

Congregational
  Christian church | KAHNG-gri-GĀ-shuhn-l, | ˌkaŋɡri'ɡeːʃənl,
  | KAHNG-gri-GĀSH-nuhl | ˌkaŋɡri'ɡeːʃnəl

Congregationalism
  system of church governance | KAHNG-gri-GĀ-shuhn-l-ɪz-uhm, | ˌkaŋɡri'ɡeːʃənlˌizəm,
  | KAHNG-gri-GĀSH-nuh-LIZ-uhm | ˌkaŋɡri'ɡeːʃnəˌlizəm

Congreve
  William, *English dramatist* | KAHN-GRĒV, KAHNG-GRĒV | 'kanˌɡriːv, 'kaŋˌɡriːv

Coniston Water
  lake, England | KAHN-uh-stuhn WAWT-uhr, | 'kanəstən ˌwɔːṭəʳ, 'waṭəʳ
  | WAHT-uhr |

Connacht, Connaught
  prov, Irish Republic | KAHN-AWT, kuh-NAWT | 'kanˌɔːt, kə'nɔːt

Connecticut
  river, state, US | kuh-NET-i-kuht | kə'neṭikət

Connemara
  region, Irish Republic | KAHN-uh-MAHR-uh, | ˌkanə'mɑrə, ˌkanə'mærə
  | KAHN-uh-MAR-uh |

Connery
  Sean, *British actor* | KAHN-uh-rē | 'kanəriˑ

Connie
  pers. name | KAHN-ē | 'kaniˑ

Conniff
  Ray, *US conductor, composer* | KAHN-if | 'kanif

CONOCO
  oil co. | KAHN-uh-KŌ | 'kanəˌkoː

Conon
  pope | KŌ-NAHN, KŌ-nuhn | 'koːˌnɑn, 'koːnən

Conor
  pers. name | KAHN-uhr | 'kanəʳ

Conquian
  game | KAHNG-kē-uhn | 'kaŋkiːən

Conrad
  1. pers. name | KAHN-RAD, -ruhd | 'kanˌræd, -rəd
  2. Danish | KAWN-RAH__TH__ | 'kɔːnˌrɑð
  3. Dutch, German | KAWN-RAHT | 'kɔːnˌrɑt

Conrad Grebel
  College, *Canada* | KAHN-RAD GRĀ-buhl | 'kanˌræd 'ɡreːbəl

Conrail, ConRail
  US rail freight carrier | KAHN-RĀL | 'kanˌreːl

Conroy
  pers. name | KAHN-ROI | 'kanˌrɔi

Consentes
  the twelve major Roman deities | kuhn-SEN-tēz | kən'sentiːz

Considine
  Bob, *US journalist* | KAHN-suh-DĪN | 'kansəˌdain

Consilium
  Roman imperial cabinet | kuhn-SIL-ē-uhm | kən'siliːəm

Constable
  John, *English painter* | KAHN-stuh-buhl | 'kanstəbəl

Key (col. 2):   a: fad ā: fade ah: father ar: Mary aw: law e: fed ē: feed er: merry i: hid ī: hide ō: coat o͞o: boot
oi: boy   ow: now   u: put   uh: above   uhr: bird   ch: chop   ng: ring   sh: show   th: thick   th̲: this   zh: measure

Constance
    1. lake, Swiss Alps; pers. name   KAHN-stuhn(t)s   'kɑnstən(t)s
    2. French   kawⁿ-STAHⁿS   kɔ̃stɑ̃s
    3. see Konstanz
Constantin
    1. pers. name   KAHN-stuhn-TIN   'kɑnstən,tin
    2. French   kawⁿ-stahⁿ-TEⁿ   kɔ̃stɑ̃tẽ
    3. German, Romanian   KAWN-stahn-TĒN   ˌkɔːnstɑn'tiːn
Constantine
    1. Roman emperor; pers. name   KAHN-stuhn-TĒN, -TĪN   'kɑnstən,tiːn, -ˌtain
    2. town, Algeria   KAHN-stuhn-TĒN   'kɑnstən,tiːn
Constantinople
    former name of Istanbul   KAHN-STANT-n-Ō-puhl   ˌkɑnˌstæntn̩'oːpəl
Constantius
    name, Roman emperors   kahn-STAN-chē-uhs, -STAN-shē-uhs   kɑn'stæntʃiːəs, -'stænʃiːəs
Consus
    Roman harvest god   KAHN-suhs   'kɑnsəs
Contac
    tdmk for a cold medicine   KAHN-TAK   'kɑn,tæk
Contadina
    food co.   KAHNT-uh-DĒ-nuh   ˌkɑntə'diːnə
Contadora
    C. American political process   kōn-tah-DAWR-ah,   koːntɑ'dɔːrɑ, ˌkɑntə'dɔːrə
                 KAHNT-uh-DAWR-uh
Contadora, Isla
    island, Panama   ĒZ-lah kōn-tah-DAWR-ah   'iːzlɑ koːntɑ'dɔːrɑ
Conte
    Silvio, *US politician*   KAHNT-ē   'kɑntiˑ
Contra
    anti-Sandinista group   KAHN-truh, KŌN-truh   'kɑntrə, 'koːntrə
Contra Costa
    county, CA   KAHN-truh KAHS-tuh, KAW-stuh   ˌkɑntrə 'kɑstə, 'kɔːstə
Conure
    parrot   KAHN-yuhr   'kɑnjəʳ
Conway
    English form of Conwy; *pers.*   KAHN-WĀ   'kɑn,weː
      name
Conwy
    town, Wales   KAHN-wē   'kɑnwiˑ
Cooder
    Ry, *US guitarist, recording artist*   KŌOD-uhr   'kuːdəʳ
Cooke
    Alistair, *Anglo-American journalist*   KUK   'kuk
Coolabah
    Australian tree   KŌO-luh-BAH   'kuːlə,bɑː
Coolangatta
    town, Australia   KŌOL-uhn-GAT-uh   ˌkuːlən'gætə
Coolgardie
    town, Australia   kōol-GAHRD-ē   ku'lgɑʳdiˑ
Coolidge
    Calvin, *30th US president*   KŌO-lij   'kuːlidʒ
Coonabarabran
    town, Australia   KŌO-nuh-BAR-uh-BRAN, KUN-uh-   ˌkuːnə'bærə,bræn, ˌkunə-
Coonamble
    town, Australia   kōo-NAM-buhl   kuˈnæmbəl

Foreign Sounds: ue: *Fr.* **rue,** *Ger.* füllen   uh(r): *Fr.* **boeuf,** *Ger.* Höhle   <u>kh</u>: *Ger.* i<u>ch</u>, *Scot.* lo<u>ch</u>   ḡ: *Sp.* ami**g**o   v̱: *Sp.* ha**b**lar
hl: *Welsh* **Ll**anelli.   CAPITALS: primary stress.   SMALL CAPS: secondary stress.   Ⓢ: U.S. pron.   Ⓑ: British pron.

Coonatto
  Australia   k͞oo-NAT-ō   kuˈnætoː

Cooper
  James Fenimore, *US writer;* Leon   K͞OO-puhr, KUP-uhr   ˈkuːpəʳ, ˈkupəʳ
  N., *US physicist (Nobel 1972)*

Coorg [Kodagu]
  lang., people, India   KURG   ˈkuʳg

Coors
  US beer   KURZ   ˈkuʳz

Coos
  1. county, OR; N. American   K͞OOS   ˈkuːs
  people
  2. county, NH   kō-AHS, KŌ-ahs   koːˈɑs, ˈkoːɑs

Coosa
  river, county, AL   K͞OO-suh   ˈkuːsə

Cootamundra
  town, Australia   K͞OOT-uh-MUHN-druh   ˌkuːʈəˈməndrə

Copacabana
  beach, Rio de Janeiro, Brazil   KŌ-puh-kuh-BAN-uh   ˌkoːpəkəˈbænə

Copenhagen [København]
  city, Denmark   KŌ-puhn-HAHG-uhn,   ˌkoːpənˈhagən,
         KŌ-puhn-HĀ-guhn   ˈkoːpənˌheːgən

Copernicus [Kopernik, Koppernigk]
  Nicolaus, *Polish astronomer*   kuh-PUHR-ni-kuhs,   kəˈpəʳnikəs, koːˈpəʳnikəs
         kō-PUHR-ni-kuhs

Copiah
  county, MS   kuh-PĪ-uh   kəˈpaiə

Copiah-Lincoln
  Junior College, MS   kuh-PĪ-uh-LING-kuhn   kəˈpaiəˈliŋkən

Copland
  Aaron, *US composer*   KŌP-luhnd   ˈkoːplənd

Copley
  John Singleton, *US painter;*   KAHP-lē   ˈkɑpliˑ
  square, Boston, MA

Coppélia
  ballet, Delibes   kō-pāl-YAH   koːpeːljɑː

copper
  element   KAHP-uhr   ˈkɑpəʳ

Copperfield
  David, *Dickens character;* David,   KAHP-uhr-FĒLD   ˈkɑpəʳˌfiːld
  US magician

Coppin
  State College, MD   KAHP-uhn   ˈkɑpən

Coppola
  Francis Ford, *US film director*   KAHP-uh-luh   ˈkɑpələ

Copt
  member of Coptic *church*   KAHPT   ˈkɑpt

Coptic
  Afro-Asiatic lang.; Christian sect.   KAHP-tik   ˈkɑptik

Coquilles St. Jacques
  scallop dish   kaw-KĒ seⁿ ZHAHK, Ⓢ kō-KĒL sa(n)   kɔkiːj sẽ ʒɑːk, Ⓢ koːˈkiːl
         ZHAHK   sæ(n) ˈʒɑk

Cora
  pers. name   KŌR-uh, KAWR-uh   ˈkoːrə, ˈkɔːrə

Key (col. 2):   a: fad   ā: fade   ah: father   ar: Mary   aw: law   e: fed   ē: feed   er: merry   i: hid   ī: hide   ō: coat   o͞o: boot
oi: boy   ow: now   u: put   uh: above   uhr: bird   ch: chop   ng: ring   sh: show   th: thick   <u>th</u>: this   zh: measure

Coral
  Sea, *South Pacific*   KAWR-uhl SĒ, KAHR-uhl   ˌkɔːrəl ˈsiː, ˌkɑrəl

Corazon
  pers. name, Spanish   KAWR-uh-ZŌN   ˌkɔːrəˈzoːn

Corbières
  district, France; wine   kawr-BYER   kɔːrbjer

Corbulo
  Roman general & conspirator   KAWR-byuh-LŌ   ˈkɔːʳbjəˌloː

Corbusier, Le
  pseudonym of J. C. Jeanneret,   luh kawr-buez-YÃ   lə kɔːrbyːzjeː
    Swiss architect

Corcoran
  School of Art, Washington, D. C.   KAWR-kuh-ruhn   ˈkɔːʳkərən

Corcyra
  ancient name of Corfu   kawr-SĪ-ruh   kɔːʳˈsɑirə

Cordelia
  youngest daughter in King Lear,   kawr-DĚL-yuh, kawr-DĒ-lē-uh   kɔːʳˈdiːljə, kɔːʳˈdiːliːə
    Shakespeare

Cordell
  pers. name   kawr-DEL   kɔːʳˈdel

Cordero
  Angel, *US jockey*   kawr-DER-ō   kɔːʳˈderoː

Cordial Médoc
  wine   kawrd-YAHL mā-DAWK   kɔːrdjɑːl meːdɔːk

Cordillera Central
  mtn. range, Andes   KAWRD-l-(Y)ER-uh SEN-TRAHL,   ˌkɔːʳdlˈ(j)erə ˌsenˈtral,
     KAWRD-ē-ER-uh   ˌkɔːʳdiːˈerə

Cordillera Mérida
  mtn. range, Venezuela   KAWRD-l-(Y)ER-uh MER-uhd-uh,   ˌkɔːʳdlˈ(j)erə ˈmerədə,
     KAWRD-ē-ER-uh   ˌkɔːʳdiːˈerə

Córdoba, Cordova
  pl. name, Argentina, Colombia,   KAWR-dō-v̲ah; Ⓢ KAWR-duh-buh,   ˈkɔːrdoːβa; Ⓢ ˈkɔːʳdəbə,
    Mexico, Spain   KAWR-duh-vuh   ˈkɔːʳdəvə

Cordon Bleu
  1. attributive, used of excellent   kawr-DAWⁿ BLUH(R)   kɔːrdõ blœː
    cooking (esp. French)
  2. African songbird   KAWRD-n BLOO   ˌkɔːʳdn̩ ˈbluː

Cordova
  see Córdoba

CORE
  Congress of Racial Equality   KŌR, KAWR   ˈkoːʳ, ˈkɔːʳ

Corea
  Chick, *jazz musician*   kuh-RĒ-uh   kəˈriːə

Coreopsis
  plant   KAWR-ē-AHP-suhs   ˌkɔːriːˈɑpsəs

Corey
  Elias James, *US chemist (Nobel*   KŌR-ē, KAWR-ē   ˈkoːriˈ, ˈkɔːriˈ
    1990); pers. name

Corfam
  tdmk for a synthetic leather   KAWR-FAM   ˈkɔːʳˌfæm

Corfu
  island, Greece   kawr-FOO, KŌR-f(y)oo   kɔːʳˈfuː, ˈkoːʳf(j)uː

Corgi
  dog breed   KAWR-gē   ˈkɔːʳgiˈ

Foreign Sounds: ue: *Fr.* **rue**, *Ger.* **füllen**   uh(r): *Fr.* **boeuf**, *Ger.* **Höhle**   k̲h: *Ger.* **ich**, *Scot.* **loch**   g̃: *Sp.* **amigo**   v̲: *Sp.* **hablar**
hl: *Welsh* **Llanelli**.   CAPITALS: primary stress.   SMALL CAPS: secondary stress.   Ⓢ: U.S. pron.   Ⓑ: British pron.

Cori
   Carl F. & *his wife* Gerty, *US*   KÔR-ē, KAWR-ē   'kɔːriˑ, 'kɔːriˑ
     biochemists (Nobel 1947)

Corinna
   pers. name   kuh-RIN-uh, -RĒ-nuh   kə'rinə, -'riːnə

Corinne
   pers. name   kuh-RIN, -RĒN   kə'rin, -'riːn

Corinnus
   legendary Trojan poet   kawr-IN-uhs   kɔːr'inəs

Corinth
   city, Greece   KAWR-inth, KAHR-   'kɔːrinθ, 'kɑr-

Corinthian
   architectural order   kuh-RIN-thē-uhn   kə'rinθiːən

Corinthians
   New Testament book   kuh-RIN-thē-uhnz   kə'rinθiːənz

Corinthus
   king of Corinth   kuh-RIN-thuhs   kə'rinθəs

Coriolanus
   play, Shakespeare   KÔR-ē-uh-LĀ-nuhs,   ˌkɔːrⁱiːə'leːnəs, ˌkɔːriːə'leːnəs
                      KAWR-ē-uh-LĀ-nuhs

Coriolis effect
   phenomenon   KÔR-ē-Ō-luhs, KÔR-ē-uh-LĒS, KAWR-   ˌkɔːriˑ'oːləs, ˌkɔːriːə'liːs, ˌkɔːr-

Cork
   county, borough, Eire   KAWRK   'kɔːʳk

Corliss
   pers. name (C. Lamont)   KAWR-luhs   'kɔːʳləs

Cormack
   Allan MacLeod, *South*   KAWR-muhk   'kɔːʳmək
     African-born US physicist
     (Nobel 1979)

Corneille
   Pierre, *French writer; pers. name*   kawr-NE, ⑤ kawr-NĀ(L)   kɔːrnej, ⑤ kɔːʳneː(l)

Cornel
   pers. name (C. Wilde)   kawr-NEL   kɔːʳ'nel

Cornelia
   pers. name   kawr-NĒL-yuh, -NĒ-lē-uh   kɔːʳ'niːljə, -'niːliːə

Cornelis
   pers. name, Dutch   kawr-NĀ-luhs   kɔːʳ'neːləs

Cornelius
   pers. name   kawr-NĒL-yuhs, -NĒ-lē-uhs   kɔːʳ'niːljəs, -'niːliːəs

Cornell
   University, *NY*   kawr-NEL   kɔːʳ'nel

Cornforth
   John Warcup, *Australian-born*   KAWRN-fuhrth, -FŌRTH, -FAWRTH   'kɔːʳnfəʳθ, -ˌfoːʳθ, -ˌfɔːʳθ
     British chemist (Nobel 1975)

Cornish
   Celtic lang.   KAWR-nish   'kɔːʳniʃ

Cornwall
   former county, England; pers.   KAWRN-WAWL, KAWRN-wuhl   'kɔːʳn,wɔːl, 'kɔːʳnwəl
     name

Cornwallis
   Charles, *British general*   kawrn-WAHL-uhs   kɔːʳn'wɑləs

Corona
   Puerto Rican beer   kō-rō-NAH, ⑤ kuh-RŌ-nuh   koːroː'nɑ, ⑤ kə'roːnə

Key (col. 2):   a: f**a**d   ā: f**a**de   ah: f**a**ther   ar: M**a**ry   aw: l**a**w   e: f**e**d   ē: f**ee**d   er: m**e**rry   i: h**i**d   ī: h**i**de   ō: c**oa**t   ōō: b**oo**t
oi: b**oy**   ow: n**ow**   u: p**u**t   uh: **a**bove   uhr: b**ir**d   ch: **ch**op   ng: ri**ng**   sh: **sh**ow   th: **th**ick   th: **th**is   zh: mea**s**ure

Corona Australis
   constellation   kuh-RŌ-nuh aw-STRĂ-luhs,   kə'roːnə ɔː'streːləs, ɑs'treːləs
                     ahs-TRĂ-luhs

Corona Borealis
   constellation   kuh-RŌ-nuh BŌR-ē-AL-uhs, BAWR-   kə'roːnə ˌboːriː'æləs, ˌbɔːr-

Coronides
   daughters of Orion   kuh-RAHN-uhd-ēz   kə'rɑnədiːz

Coronis
   mother of Asclepius by Apollo   kuh-RŌ-nuhs   kə'roːnəs

Coronus
   Argonaut   kuh-RŌ-nuhs   kə'roːnəs

Corot
   Jean Baptiste Camille, *French*   kaw-RŌ   kɔːroː
   painter

Corowa
   town, Australia   KAHR-uh-wuh, KAWR-uh-wuh   'kɑrəwə, 'kɔːrəwə

Corpus Christi
   city, TX; Christian festival   KAWR-puhs KRIST-ē   ˌkɔːʳpəs 'kristiˑ

Correggio
   Antonio Allegri, *Italian painter*   kuh-REJ-ō, kuh-REJ-ē-ō   kə'redʒoː, kə'redʒiːˌoː

Corregidor
   island, Philippines   kuh-REG-uh-DAWR   kə'regəˌdɔːʳ

Corriedale
   sheep breed   KAWR-ē-DĀL   'kɔːriˑˌdeːl

Corrientes
   prov & town, Argentina   kawr-rē-EN-tās   kɔːrriː'enteːs

Corrigan
   Mairead, *Irish peace activist*   KAWR-i-guhn   'kɔːrigən
   (Nobel 1976)

Corse [Corsica]
   Mediterranean island   KAWRS   kɔːrs

Corsica
   Mediterranean island   KAWR-si-kuh   'kɔːʳsikə

Corsican
   pert. to Corsica   KAWR-si-kuhn   'kɔːʳsikən

Cortaillod
   wine   kawr-tī-YŌ   kɔːrtaijoː

Cortes
   parliament in Spain & Portugal   KAWR-TES, KAWR-TEZ   'kɔːʳˌtes, 'kɔːʳˌtez

Cortés
   1. Hernán *or* Hernando, *Spanish*   kawr-TĀS, Ⓢ kawr-TEZ, KAWR-TEZ   kɔːr'teːs, Ⓢ kɔːʳ'tez, 'kɔːʳˌtez
   conquistador
   2. region, Honduras   kawr-TĀS   kɔːr'teːs

Cortese
   wine   kawr-TĀ-zā   kɔːʳ'teːzeː

Cortina d'Ampezzo
   village, ski resort, Italy   kawr-TĒ-nuh dahm-PET-sō   kɔːʳ'tiːnə dɑm'petsoː

Cortina Rancheria
   Indian reservation, US   kawr-TĒ-nuh RAN-chuh-RĒ-uh   kɔːʳ'tiːnə ˌræntʃə'riːə

Coruña, La
   see La Coruña

Corvallis
   city, OR   kawr-VAL-uhs   kɔːʳ'væləs

Corvina
   wine   kawr-VĒ-nuh   kɔːʳ'viːnə

Foreign Sounds: ue: *Fr.* rue, *Ger.* füllen uh(r): *Fr.* boeuf, *Ger.* Höhle <u>kh</u>: *Ger.* ich, *Scot.* loch ğ: *Sp.* amigo v̶: *Sp.* hablar
hl: *Welsh* Llanelli. CAPITALS: primary stress. SMALL CAPS: secondary stress. Ⓢ: U.S. pron. Ⓔ: British pron.

Corvo
   tdmk for an Italian wine   KAWR-vō   'kɔːʳvoː

Corvus
   constellation   KAWR-vuhs   'kɔːʳvəs

Cory
   pers. name   KŌR-ē, KAWR-ē   'koːriˑ, 'kɔːriˑ

Corydon
   pers. name   KŌR-uh-duhn, KAWR-uh-duhn,   'koːrədən, 'kɔːrədən, -ˌdɑn
                             -DAHN

Cos
   see Kós

Cosa Nostra
   organized crime group   KŌ-suh NŌ-struh, KŌ-zuh   ˌkoːsə 'noːstrə, ˌkoːzə

Cos d'Estournel
   wine   kaws des-tur-NEL   kɔːs desturnel

Cosell
   Howard, *US sportscaster*   kō-SEL   koː'sel

Coshocton
   county, OH   kuh-SHAHK-tuhn   kə'ʃɑktən

Cosi fan tutte
   opera, Mozart   kō-SĒ FAHN T͞OŌT-tä, T͞OŌT-ē   koːˌsiː ˌfɑn 'tuːtteː, 'tuːʈiˑ

Cosima
   pers. name, German   KŌ-zē-mah   'koːziːmɑ

Cosimo
   pers. name, Italian   KAW-zē-mō   'kɔːziːmoː

Cosmo
   1. nickname for Cosmopolitan   KAHZ-mō   'kɑzmoː
     magazine; pers. name
   2. Italian   KAWZ-mō   'kɔːzmoː

Cosmos
   1. the universe; PBS television   KAHZ-muhs, KAHZ-MŌS,   'kɑzməs, 'kazˌmoːs,
    series   KAHZ-MAHS   'kaz ˌmas
   2. flower   KAHZ-muhs, KAHZ-muhz   'kɑzməs, 'kɑzməz

Cossack
   elite corps of Russian horsemen   KAHS-AK, KAHS-uhk   'kasˌæk, 'kasək

Costa Blanca
   resort, Spain   KŌ-stuh BLAHNG-kuh   ˌkoːstə 'blɑŋkə

Costa Brava
   resort, Spain   KŌ-stuh BRAHV-uh   ˌkoːstə 'brɑvə

Costa de Almeria
   resort, Spain   KŌ-stuh thā AHL-mä-RĒ-uh   ˌkoːstə ðeː ˌalmeː'riːə

Costa de la Luz
   resort, Spain   KŌ-stuh thā lah L͞OŌS   ˌkoːstə ðeː lɑ 'luːs

Costa del Azahar
   resort, Spain   KŌ-stuh thel AHZ-ah-KHAHR   ˌkoːstə ðel ˌɑzɑ'xɑr

Costa de Lisboa
   region, Portugal   KŌ-stuh dā lēzh-VŌ-uh   ˌkoːstə deː liːʒ'voːə

Costa del Sol
   region, Spain   KŌS-tah thel SŌL   'koːstɑ ðel 'soːl

Costa de Prata
   region, Portugal   KŌ-stuh dā PRAHT-uh   ˌkoːstə deː 'prɑːʈə

Costa do Algarve
   region, Portugal   KŌ-stuh dō ahl-AHR-vä   ˌkoːstə doː al'ɑːʳveː

Costa Dorada
   resort, Spain   KŌ-stuh dō-RAHTH-uh   ˌkoːstə doː'rɑðə

Key (col. 2):   a: fad ā: fade ah: father ar: Mary aw: law e: fed ē: feed er: merry i: hid ī: hide ō: coat o͞o: boot
oi: boy ow: now u: put uh: above uhr: bird ch: chop ng: ring sh: show th: thick th: this zh: measure

Costa do Sol
   region, Portugal   KŌ-stuh dō SŌL   ˌkɔːstə doː ˈsoːl

Costa Dourada
   region, Portugal   KŌ-stuh DŌ-o͞o-RAHD-uh   ˌkɔːstə ˈdoːuːˌraːdə

Costa Mesa
   city, CA   KŌ-stuh MĀ-suh, KAHS-tuh   ˌkɔːstə ˈmeːsə, ˌkɑstə

Costa Rica
   republic, S. America   KAHS-tuh RĒ-kuh, KAWS-tuh, KŌS-tuh   ˌkɑstə ˈriːkə, ˌkɔːstə, ˌkoːstə

Costa Rican
   pert. to Costa Rica   KAHS-tuh RĒ-kuhn, KAWS-tuh, KŌS-tuh   ˌkɑstə ˈriːkən, ˌkɔːstə, ˌkoːstə

Costa Verde
   region, Portugal   KŌ-stuh VERD-uh   ˌkɔːstə ˈverdə

Costello
   Elvis, *British musician, songwriter;* kahs-TEL-ō   kasˈteloː
     Lou, *US actor*

Costilla
   county, CO   kahs-TĒ-uh   kasˈtiːə

Cosumnes River
   College, *CA*   kuh-SUHM-nuhs RIV-uhr   kəˈsəmnəs ˈrivəʳ

Côte, La
   region, France   lah KŌT   lɑː koːt

Côte Blonde
   region, France   kōt BLAWⁿD   koːt blɔ̃d

Côte Brune
   region, France   kōt BRUEN   koːt bryːn

Côte Chalonnaise
   region, France   kōt shah-law-NEZ   koːt ʃaːlɔːnez

Côte d'Azur
   French Riviera   kōt dah-ZUER, Ⓢ KŌT duh-ZUR   koːt daːzyːr, Ⓢ ˌkoːt dəˈzuʳ

Côte de Beaune
   region, France; wine   kōt duh BŌN   koːt də boːn

Côte de Beaune Villages
   wine   kōt duh BŌN vē-LAHZH   koːt də boːn viːlaːʒ

Côte de Bourg
   region, France   kōt duh BO͞OR   koːt də buːr

Côte de Brouilly
   region, France   kōt duh bro͞o-YĒ   koːt də bruːjiː

Côte de Nuits
   region, France   kōt duh NWĒ, Ⓢ KŌT duhn WĒ   koːt də nɥiː, Ⓢ ˌkoːt dən ˈwiː

Côte des Blancs
   region, France   kōt duh BLAHⁿ   koːt də blɑ̃

Côte d'Ivoire [Ivory Coast]
   republic, Africa   KŌT dēv-WAHR   ˌkoːt diːvˈwaʳ

Côte d'Or
   region, French   kōt DAWR   koːt dɔːr

Côte Rôtie
   region, France   kōt raw-TĒ, rō-TĒ   koːt rɔːtiː, roːtiː

Côtes de Castillon
   region, France   kōt duh kah-stē-YAWⁿ   koːt də kaːstiːjɔ̃

Côtes de Provence
   region, France   kōt duh praw-VAHⁿS   koːt də prɔːvɑ̃s

Côtes-du-Nord
   dept, France   kōt-due-NAWR   koːtdyːnɔːr

Foreign Sounds: ue: *Fr.* **rue**, *Ger.* **füllen**   uh(r): *Fr.* **boeuf**, *Ger.* **Höhle**   <u>kh</u>: *Ger.* i**ch**, *Scot.* lo**ch**   g̶: *Sp.* ami**g**o   v: *Sp.* ha**b**lar
hl: *Welsh* **Ll**anelli.   CAPITALS: primary stress.   SMALL CAPS: secondary stress.   Ⓢ: U.S. pron.   Ⓛ: British pron.

Côtes du Rhône
  region, France   kōt due RŌN   koːt dyː roːn
Cotinga
  South American bird   kō-TING-guh, kuh-   koː'tiŋgə, kə-
Cotonou
  port, Africa   KŌT-n-OO   ˌkoːtn̩'uː
Cotopaxi
  volcano, prov., Ecuador   KŌT-uh-PAHK-sē, -PAK-sē   ˌkoːṭə'pɑksiˑ, -'pæksiˑ
Cotswolds
  hills, England   KAHT-swuhldz, KAHT-SWŌLDZ   'kɑtswəldz, 'kɑtˌswoːldz
Cotta
  Roman cognomen   KAHT-uh   'kɑṭə
Cottbus
  county, Germany   KAHT-bus   'kɑtbus
Cottey
  College, *MO*   KAHT-ē   'kɑṭiˑ
Cottian
  Alps, *Alpine mtn. range*   KAHT-ē-uhn   'kɑṭiːən
Cotton
  pers. name   KAHT-n   'kɑtn̩
Coucal
  type of cuckoo   KOO-kuhl   'kuːkəl
Coué
  Emile, *French psychotherapist*   KWĀ   kweː
Coues's
  flycatcher   KOWZ   'kɑuz
Cougar
  pers. name   KOO-guhr, KOO-GAHR   'kuːgəʳ, 'kuːˌgɑʳ
Coulomb
  Charles Augustin de, *French*   koo-LAWⁿ, Ⓢ KOO-LAHM, KOO-LŌM,   kuːlɔ̃, Ⓢ 'kuːˌlɑm, 'kuːˌloːm,
    physicist   koo-LŌM   kuː'loːm
Count
  title; pers. name (C. Basie)   KOWNT   'kɑunt
Courant
  newspaper, Hartford, CT   KUHR-uhnt, KUH-ruhnt   'kər-ənt, 'kə-rənt
Courbet
  Gustave, *French painter*   kur-BE   kurbe
Cournand
  A. F., *US physician (Nobel 1956)*   kur-NAHⁿ   kuʳ'nɑ̃
Courtenay
  pers. name   KŌRT-nē, KAWRT-nē, -n-ā   'koːʳtniˑ, 'kɔːʳtniˑ, -ṇeː
Courteney, Courtney
  pers. name   KŌRT-nē, KAWRT-nē   'koːʳtniˑ, 'kɔːʳtniˑ
Courvoisier
  cognac   KURV-WAHZ-YĀ   ˌkuʳvˌwɑz'jeː
Coushatta
  N. American people   ku-SHAHT-uh   ku'ʃɑṭə
Cousteau
  Jacques, *undersea explorer*   koo-STŌ   kuːstoː
Cousy
  Bob, *US sports personality*   KOO-zē   'kuːziˑ
Coutet
  wine   ku-TE, Ⓢ koo-TĀ   kute, Ⓢ kuː'teː
Covarrubias
  Miguel, *Mexican artist*   kō-yahr-ROOB-yahs   koːβarˈruːbjɑs

Key (col. 2): a: fad ā: fade ah: father ar: Mary aw: law e: fed ē: feed er: merry i: hid ī: hide ō: coat ōō: boot oi: boy ow: now u: put uh: above uhr: bird ch: chop ng: ring sh: show th: thick th: this zh: measure

Coveleski
 Stanley, *Regional Stadium, South* STAN-lē KŌ-vuh-LES-kē 'stænli' ˌkoːvə'leski'
 Bend, IN
Covent Garden
 district, London KUHV-uhnt GAHRD-n ˌkəvənt 'gɑˡdn̩
Coventry
 1. city, England KAHV-uhn-trē, KUHV-uhn-trē 'kɑvəntri', 'kəvəntri'
 2. town, CT, RI KUHV-uhn-trē, KAHV-uhn-trē 'kəvəntri', 'kɑvəntri'
Covina
 city, CA kō-VĒ-nuh koː'viːnə
Covington
 US pl. name KUHV-ing-tuhn 'kəviŋtən
Cowdrey
 pers. name KOW-drē, KOW-drā 'kaudri', 'kaudreː
Coweta
 county, GA kuh-WĒT-uh kə'wiːtə
Cowley Fathers
 religious order KOW-lē, KOO͞-lē 'kauli', 'kuːli'
Cowlitz
 county, WA KOW-luhts 'kauləts
Cowper
 1. William, English poet KOO͞-puhr, KUP-uhr, KOW-puhr 'kuːpəˡ, 'kupəˡ, 'kaupəˡ
 2. pers. name KOW-puhr, KOO͞-puhr 'kaupəˡ, 'kuːpəˡ
Coxsackie
 village, NY kuk-SAHK-ē, kahk-SAK-ē kuk'sɑki', kɑk'sæki'
Cozumel, Isla
 island, Caribbean ĒZ-lah KŌ-zuh-MEL 'iːzlɑ ˌkoːzə'mel
Cracow
 see Kraków
Craig
 pers. name KRĀG, KREG 'kreːg, 'kreg
Craighead
 county, AR KRĀG-HED 'kreːgˌhed
Craigie
 William, *Scottish linguist* KRĀ-gē 'kreːgi'
Cram
 Donald J., *US chemist (Nobel* KRAM 'kræm
 1987)
Cranbrook
 city, British Columbia, Canada KRAN-BRUK, KRAM-BRUK 'krænˌbruk, 'kræmˌbruk
Crangi
 airport, Singapore KRAHNG-gē, KRANG-gē 'krɑŋgi', 'kræŋgi'
Cranmer
 Thomas, *Protestant archbishop* KRAN-muhr 'krænməˡ
Crassus
 Roman general KRAS-uhs 'kræsəs
Crater
 constellation KRĀT-uhr 'kreːtəˡ
Cratylus
 dialogue of Plato KRAT-l-uhs 'krætl̩əs
Craveri's murrelet
 sea bird kruh-VER-ēz MUHR-luht krə'veriːz 'məˡlət
Crayola
 tdmk for crayons krā-Ō-luh kreː'oːlə

Foreign Sounds: **ue**: *Fr.* **rue**, *Ger.* **füllen**   **uh(r)**: *Fr.* **boeuf**, *Ger.* **Höhle**   kh: *Ger.* **ich**, *Scot.* **loch**   ḡ: *Sp.* amigo   v̲: *Sp.* hablar
hl: *Welsh* **Llanelli**.   CAPITALS: primary stress.   SMALL CAPS: secondary stress.   (§): U.S. pron.   (£): British pron.

Crécy
   village, France   krā-SĒ   kreːsiː

Crécy, potage
   cream of carrot soup   pō-TAHZH krā-SĒ   poːˈtɑˑʒ kreːˈsiː

Credit Lyonnais
   French bank   krā-DĒ lyaw-NE   kreːdiː ljɔːne

Cree
   N. American people   KRĒ   ˈkriː

Creek
   N. American people   KRĒK   ˈkriːk

Creighton
   1. family name   KRĀT-n, ⓔ KRĪT-n   ˈkreːtn̩, ⓔ ˈkraitn̩
   2. University, *NE*   KRĀT-n   ˈkreːtn̩

Creme Chantilly
   sweetened whipped cream   krem shahⁿ-tē-YĒ   krem ʃɑ̃tiːjiː

Crème de Menthe
   liqueur   KREM duh MEN(T)TH, KRĒM, MINT   ˌkrem də ˈmen(t)θ, ˌkriːm, ˈmint

Cremer
   Sir William R., *English pacifist*   KRĒ-muhr   ˈkriːməʳ
   (Nobel 1903)

Cremona
   prov, city, Italy   kruh-MŌ-nuh   krəˈmoːnə

Creole
   lang., Haiti   KRĒ-ŌL   ˈkriːˌoːl

Creon
   king of Corinth, host to Jason and   KRĒ-AHN   ˈkriːˌɑn
    Medea; king of Thebes

Crépy
   region, France   krā-PĒ   kreːpiː

Cres
   early king of Crete   KRES   ˈkres

Cresphontes
   king of Messenia   kres-FAHN-TĒZ   kresˈfɑnˌtiːz

Crespigny
   street, London   kres-PĒ-nē   kresˈpiːniˑ

Crespin
   Régine, *opera star*   kres-PEⁿ   krespẽ

Cressida [Criseyde]
   legendary lover in Shakespeare's   KRES-uhd-uh   ˈkresədə
    Troilus & Cressida

Cresson
   Edith, *French prime minister*   krā-SAWⁿ   kreˈsɔ̃

Cressy
   English form of Crécy   KRES-ē   ˈkresiˑ

Cresta Blanca
   wine   KRES-tuh BLANG-kuh, BLAHNG-kuh   ˌkrestə ˈblæŋkə, ˈblɑŋkə

Creswick
   pers. name   KREZ-ik   ˈkrezik

Cretaceous
   geologic period   kri-TĀ-shuhs, krē-   kriˈteːʃəs, kriː-

Cretan
   pert. to Crete   KRĒT-n   ˈkriːtn̩

Crete
   island, Greece   KRĒT   ˈkriːt

Key (col. 2): a: fad ā: fade ah: father ar: Mary aw: law e: fed ē: feed er: merry i: hid ī: hide ō: coat ōō: boot
oi: boy ow: now u: put uh: above uhr: bird ch: chop ng: ring sh: show th: thick th̲: this zh: measure

Creus, Cabo
  cape, Spain | KAH<u>V</u>-ō krä-$\overline{OO}$S | ˌkaβoː kreːˈuːs

Creusa
  wife of Aeneas; mother of Ion by | krē-(Y)$\overline{OO}$-suh, krä-(Y)$\overline{OO}$-suh | kriːˈ(j)uːsə, kreːˈ(j)uːsə
    Apollo

Creuse
  region, France | KRUH(R)Z | krœːz

Creutzfeldt-Jakob
  brain disorder | KROITS-felt-YAHK-ōb | ˌkrɔitsfeltˈjakoːb

Crichton
  James, *Scottish prodigy;* Michael, | KRĪT-n | ˈkraitn̩
    US writer

Crick
  F. H. C., *English molecular* | KRIK | ˈkrik
    biologist (Nobel 1962)

Crimea
  peninsula, Ukraine | krī-MĒ-uh, kruh-MĒ-uh | kraiˈmiːə, krəˈmiːə

Crimean
  pert. to Crimea | krī-MĒ-uhn | kraiˈmiːən

Criolo
  lang., W. Africa | krē-Ō-lō | kriːˈoːloː

Crioulo
  lang., W. Africa | krē-Ō-lō, krē-$\overline{OO}$-lō | kriːˈoːloː, kriːˈuːloː

Crisco
  tdmk for shortening | KRIS-kō | ˈkriskoː

Criseyde [Cressida]
  legendary lover in Chaucer's | kruh-SĀD-uh | krəˈseːdə
    Troilus & Criseyde

Crisium, Mare
  see Mare Crisium

Crispian
  pers. name | KRIS-pē-uhn | ˈkrispiːən

Crispin
  pers. name | KRIS-puhn | ˈkrispən

Crispus
  pers. name | KRIS-puhs | ˈkrispəs

Crist
  Judith, *US film, drama critic* | KRIST | ˈkrist

Cristal
  Portuguese beer | krē-STAHL | kriːˈstɑl

Cristina
  pers. name, Italian | krē-STĒ-nah | kriːˈstiːnɑ

Cristóbal
  town, Panama; pers. name, | krē-STŌ-<u>v</u>ahl, Ⓢ kris-TŌ-buhl | kriːˈstoːβɑl, Ⓢ krisˈtoːbəl
    Spanish

Cristoforo
  pers. name | krē-STAW-fō-rō | kriːˈstɔːfoːroː

Critheis
  mother of Homer | kri-THĀ-uhs | kriˈθeːəs

Critias
  Athenian despot; dialogue of Plato | KRISH-(ē-)uhs, KRIT-ē-uhs | ˈkriʃ(iː)əs, ˈkriṭiːəs

Crito
  dialogue of Plato | KRĪT-ō | ˈkraitoː

Crittenden
  county, AR | KRIT-n-duhn | ˈkritn̩dən

Foreign Sounds: ue: *Fr.* ru**e**, *Ger.* f**ü**llen uh(r): *Fr.* b**œu**f, *Ger.* H**öh**le <u>kh</u>: *Ger.* i**ch**, *Scot.* lo**ch** g̱: *Sp.* ami**g**o <u>v</u>: *Sp.* ha**b**lar
hl: *Welsh* **Ll**anelli. CAPITALS: primary stress. SMALL CAPS: secondary stress. Ⓢ: U.S. pron. Ⓛ: British pron.

Crna [Cherna]		
river, Macedonia	TSUHR-nuh, SUHR-nuh	'tsərnə, 'sərnə
Crna Gora [Montenegro]		
republic, E. Europe (former kingdom)	TSUHR-nuh GŌR-uh, SUHR-nuh, GAWR-uh	ˌtsərnə 'goːɾə, ˌsərnə, 'gɔːrə
Croat [Croatian]		
inhabitant of Croatia	KRŌT, KRŌ-AT, KRŌ-AHT	'kroːt, 'kroːˌæt, 'kroːˌɑt
Croatia [Hrvatska]		
republic, E. Europe	krō-Ā-sh(ē-)uh	kroː'eːʃ(iː)ə
Croatian [Croat]		
inhabitant of or pert. to Croatia	krō-Ā-shuhn	kroː'eːʃən
Croce		
1. Benedetto, *Italian historian*	KRŌ-chā	'kroːtʃeː
2. Jim, *US singer*	KRŌ-chē	'kroːtʃiˑ
Crockett		
Davy, *US frontiersman*	KRAHK-uht	'krɑkət
Crocodylia		
reptilian order	KRAHK-uh-DIL-ē-uh	ˌkrɑkə'diliːə
Croesus		
Lydian king of legendary wealth	KRĒ-suhs	'kriːsəs
Crohn's disease		
bowel disorder	KRŌNZ duh-ZĒZ	'kroːnz dəˌziːz
Croix de Guerre		
French military award	krwah duh GER, [S] K(R)WAH duh GER	krwɑː də ger, [S] ˌk(r)wɑ də 'ge^{r}
Cro-Magnon		
early homo sapiens	krō-MAG-nuhn, krō-MAN-yuhn	kroː'mægnən, kroː'mænjən
Crommelin's		
comet	KRAHM-uh-linz	'krɑməlinz
Cromwell		
1. Oliver *& his son* Richard, *English statesmen*	KRAHM-WEL, KRUHM-WEL, KRAHM-wuhl, KRUHM-wuhl	'krɑmˌwel, 'krəmˌwel, 'krɑmwəl, 'krəmwəl
2. town, CT; town, New Zealand	KRAHM-WEL, KRAHM-wuhl	'krɑmˌwel, 'krɑmwəl
Cronin		
James W., *US physicist (Nobel 1980)*	KRŌ-nuhn	'kroːnən
Cronkite		
Walter, *US journalist*	KRAHNG-KĪT, KRAHN-	'krɑŋˌkait, 'krɑn-
Cronus		
Greek god, father of Zeus	KRŌ-nuhs	'kroːnəs
Crosby		
Bing, *US entertainer*	KRAWZ-bē	'krɔːzbiˑ
Crotalaria		
plant	KRŌT-l-AR-ē-uh	ˌkroːtḷ'æriːə
Croteau		
Gary, *hockey player*	kruh-TŌ	krə'toː
Croton		
1. river, NY	KRŌT-n	'kroːtṇ
2. founder of Crotona	KRŌT-n, KRŌ-TAHN	'kroːtṇ, 'kroːˌtɑn
Crotona		
Greek colony in Italy	kruh-TŌ-nuh	krə'toːnə
Croton-on-Hudson		
village, NY	KRŌT-n-AHN-HUHD-suhn, -AWN-	ˌkroːtṇˌɑn'hədsən, -ˌɔːn-
Crotus		
foster-brother of the Muses	KRŌT-uhs	'kroːt̬əs

Key (col. 2): a: **fad** ā: **fade** ah: **father** ar: **Mary** aw: **law** e: **fed** ē: **feed** er: **merry** i: **hid** ī: **hide** ō: **coat** o͞o: **boot** oi: **boy** ow: **now** u: **put** uh: **above** uhr: **bird** ch: **chop** ng: **ring** sh: **show** th: **thick** t͟h: **this** zh: **measure**

Crow		
N. American people	KRŌ	ˈkroː
Crowe		
1. Adm. William James, Jr., *former Chair, US Joint Chiefs of Staff*	KROW	ˈkrau
2. Catherine, *English novelist;* Sir Joseph Archer, *English critic*	KRŌ	ˈkroː
Crowell		
Thomas Y., *US publisher*	KRŌ-uhl	ˈkroːəl
Crowfoot		
pers. name	KRŌ-FUT	ˈkroːˌfut
Croydon		
borough, England	KROID-n	ˈkrɔidn̩
Cruickshank		
Andrew, *Scottish actor*	KRUK-SHANGK	ˈkrukˌʃæŋk
Cruikshank		
George, *English illustrator*	KRUK-SHANGK	ˈkrukˌʃæŋk
Crusoe, Robinson		
see Robinson Crusoe		
Crux		
constellation	KRUHKS	ˈkrəks
Cruz		
pers. name	KRO͞OZ	ˈkruːz
Crystal		
pers. name	KRIS-tl	ˈkristl̩
Csongrád		
county, city, Hungary	CHAWN-GRAHD	ˈtʃɔːnˌgrad
Ctesias		
Greek explorer	TĒ-zē-uhs	ˈtiːziːəs
Ctesiphon		
ancient city, Iraq	TES-uh-FAHN, TĒ-suh-FAHN	ˈtesəˌfan, ˈtiːsəˌfan
Ctimene		
sister of Odysseus	TIM-uh-nē	ˈtimənɪˑ
Cua		
lang., South Vietnam	KWAH	ˈkwa
Cuanza, Kwanza		
river, Africa	KWAHN-zuh	ˈkwanzə
Cuba		
island, West Indies	KYO͞O-buh	ˈkjuːbə
Cuba Libre		
cocktail	K(Y)O͞O-buh LĒ-bruh	ˈk(j)uːbə ˈliːbrə
Cuban		
pert. to or from Cuba	KYO͞O-buhn	ˈkjuːbən
Cucamonga		
city, CA	KO͞O-kuh-MAHNG-guh	ˌkuːkəˈmaŋgə
Cuchulainn		
legendary Irish hero	ku-KHUL-uhn, [$] kuh-HUL-uhn, kuh-HO͞O-luhn	kuˈxulən, [$] kəˈhulən, kəˈhuːlən
Cuenca		
city, Ecuador	KWENG-kuh	ˈkweŋkə
Cuernavaca		
town, Mexico	kwer-nah-VAHK-ah, [$] KWER-nuh-VAHK-uh, -VAK-uh	kwernaˈβaka, [$] ˌkweʳnəˈvakə, -ˈvækə
Cuervo Gold		
brand of tequila	KWER-vō GŌLD	ˌkweʳvoː ˈgoːld

Foreign Sounds: ue: *Fr.* **rue**, *Ger.* **füllen** uh(r): *Fr.* **boeuf**, *Ger.* **Höhle** kh: *Ger.* **ich**, *Scot.* **loch** g̃: *Sp.* **amigo** v̲: *Sp.* **hablar** hl: *Welsh* **Llanelli**. CAPITALS: primary stress. SMALL CAPS: secondary stress. [$]: U.S. pron. [£]: British pron.

Cuesta
  College, *CA*   KWĂS-tuh, KWES-tuh   'kweːstə, 'kwestə
Cugat
  Xavier, *US bandleader*   K͞OO-GAHT   'kuːˌgɑt
Cuicatec
  lang., people, Mexico   KWĒ-kuh-TEK   'kwiːkə,tek
Cuisinart
  food processor   KWĒ-zuh-NAHRT, KWĒ-zuh-NAHRT   'kwiːzəˌnɑʳt, ˌkwiːzə'nɑʳt
Cukor
  George, *US film director*   K͞OO-KAWR   'kuːˌkɔːʳ
Culiacán
  river, city, Mexico   K͞O͞OL-yuh-KAHN   ˌkuːljə'kɑn
Cullman
  county, AL   KUHL-muhn   'kəlmən
Culver
  town, IN   KUHL-vuhr   'kəlvəʳ
Culver City
  city, CA   KUHL-vuhr SIT-ē   ˌkəlvəʳ 'sitiˑ
Culver-Stockton
  College, *MO*   KUHL-vuhr-STAHK-tuhn   'kəlvəʳˌstɑktən
Culzean
  bay, Scotland   kuh-LĂN *[sic]*   kə'leːn *[sic]*
Cumae
  ancient city, Italy   KY͞OO-mē   'kjuːmiˑ
Cumaean
  pert. to Cumae   KY͞OO-mē-uhn, ky͞oo-MĂ-uhn   'kjuːmiːən, kjuˑ'meɪən
Cumaná
  city, Venezuela   k͞oo-mah-NAH   kuːmɑ'nɑ
Cumberland
  former county, England   KUHM-buhr-luhnd   'kəmbəʳlənd
Cumbria
  ancient Celtic kingdom; county,   KUHM-brē-uh   'kəmbriːə
  England
Cumin
  spice   KUHM-uhn, KY͞OO-muhn   'kəmən, 'kjuːmən
Cuna
  Central American people   K͞OO-nuh   'kuːnə
Cunard
  British steamship co.   k(y)u-NAHRD   k(j)u'nɑʳd
Cunctator
  agnomen of Q. Fabius Maximus   KUHNGK-TĀT-uhr, KUNGK-TĀT-uhr 'kəŋk,teːʈəʳ, 'kuŋk,teːʈəʳ
Cunha, da
  Tristão, *Portuguese explorer*   duh K͞OON-yuh   də 'kuːnjə
Cunnamulla
  town, Australia   KUHN-uh-MUHL-uh   ˌkənə'mələ
CUNY
  City University of New York   KY͞OO-nē   'kjuːniˑ
Cuomo
  Mario, *US politician*   KWŌ-mō   'kwoːmoː
Cupertino
  city, CA   K(Y)͞OO-puhr-TĒ-nō   ˌk(j)uːpəʳ'tiːnoː
Cupid
  Roman god of love   KY͞OO-puhd   'kjuːpəd
Cupido
  Belgian beer   k͞oo-PĒ-dō   kuː'piːdoː

Key (col. 2):   a: fad ā: fade ah: father ar: Mary aw: law e: fed ē: feed er: merry i: hid ī: hide ō: coat o͞o: boot
oi: boy   ow: now   u: put   uh: above   uhr: bird   ch: chop   ng: ring   sh: show   th: thick   th̲: this   zh: measure

Cuprinol
  tdmk for a wood preservative K(Y)OO-pruh-NAWL 'k(j)uːprə,nɔːl
Curaçao
  island, Netherlands Antilles; K(Y)UR-uh-SŌ, -SOW ,k(j)urə'soː, -'sɑu
  liqueur
Curassow
  South & Central American bird K(Y)UHR-uh-SŌ 'k(j)ərə,soː
Curetes
  attendants of the goddess Rhea; kyu-RĒT-ēz kju'riːtiːz
  guardians of Zeus on Crete
Curia
  ancient senate house, Rome KYUR-ē-uh 'kjuriːə
Curiae
  early Roman political-social KYUR-ē-Ē, -ē-Ī 'kjuriː,iː, -iː,ai
  divisions
Curiate
  early Roman assembly KYUR-ē-uht 'kjuriːət
Curie
  Marie S., French physicist (Nobel kue-RĒ, ⑤ kyu-RĒ, KYUR-ē kyːriː, ⑤ kju'riː, 'kjuri·
  1903, 1911); her husband
  Pierre, French physicist (Nobel
  1903)
Curitiba
  city, Brazil KUR-uh-TĒ-buh ,kurə'tiːbə
curium
  element KYUR-ē-uhm 'kjuriːəm
Curran
  pers. name KUHR-uhn, KUH-ruhn 'kər-ən, 'kə-rən
Currituck
  county, NC KUHR-uh-TUHK, KUHR-uh-TUHK 'kərə,tək, ,kərə'tək
Cursus Honorum
  Roman political career path KUR-suhs ahn-AWR-uhm, KUHR- 'kuʳsəs ɑn'ɔːrəm, 'kəʳ-
Curt
  1. pers. name KUHRT 'kəʳt
  2. German KURT 'kuʳt
Curtis
  pers. name KUHRT-uhs 'kəʳtəs
Curtius
  1. Ernst, German historian KURT-sē-uhs 'kuʳtsiːəs
  2. early Roman hero KUHR-sh(ē-)uhs 'kəʳʃ(iː)əs
Curzon
  pers. name KUHR-zuhn 'kəʳzən
Cush
  see Kush
Cushitic
  Afro-Asiatic lang. group ku-SHIT-ik, kOO-SHIT-ik ku'ʃitik, kuː'ʃitik
Cutex
  tdmk for nail care products KYOO-TEKS 'kjuː,teks
Cuthbert
  pers. name KUHTH-buhrt 'kəθbəʳt
Cutty Sark
  ship; Scotch brand KUHT-ē SAHRK, ⑥ KUHT-ē SAHRK 'kəti· ,sɑʳk, ⑥ ,kəti· 'sɑʳk
Cuvaison
  winery, CA KOO-vā-SAHN ,kuːveˑ'sɑn

Foreign Sounds: **ue**: *Fr.* **rue**, *Ger.* **füllen** **uh(r)**: *Fr.* **boeuf**, *Ger.* **Höhle** **kh**: *Ger.* **ich**, *Scot.* **loch** **g̃**: *Sp.* **amigo** **v**: *Sp.* **hablar**
hl: *Welsh* **Llanelli**. CAPITALS: primary stress. SMALL CAPS: secondary stress. ⑤: U.S. pron. ⑥: British pron.

Cuyahoga
 river, county, OH   KĪ-uh-HŌ-guh, kuh-HŌ-guh,   ˌkaiəˈhɔːgə, kəˈhɔːgə,
                                    -HAW-guh, -HAHG-uh   -ˈhɔːgə, -ˈhagə

Cuyapaipe Band
 N. American people   KĪ-uh-PĪ-pā   ˌkaiəˈpaipeː

Cuzco
 city, beer, Peru   KOO-skō   ˈkuːskoː

Cwmbran
 town, Wales   koom-BRAHN   kuˈmˈbran

Cybele
 Phrygian earth goddess   SIB-uh-lē   ˈsibəliˑ

Cyclades
 Aegean islands   SIK-luh-DĒZ   ˈsikləˌdiːz

Cycladic [Cyclades]
 Islands, *Aegean sea*   si-KLAD-ik, -KLĀD-   siˈklædik, -ˈkleːd-

Cyclamen
 flower   SĪ-kluh-muhn, SIK-luh-muhn   ˈsaikləmən, ˈsikləmən

Cyclopean
 pert. to Cyclops   SĪ-kluh-PĒ-uhn, sī-KLŌ-pē-uhn,   ˌsaikləˈpiːən, saiˈklɔːpiːən,
                                  sī-KLAHP-ē-uhn   saiˈklapiːən

Cyclopes
 pl. of Cyclops   sī-KLŌ-pēz   saiˈklɔːpiːz

Cyclops
 one-eyed giant in Greek   SĪ-KLAHPS   ˈsaiˌklaps
 mythology; play, Euripides

Cycnus
 son of Ares, killed by Heracles; SIK-nuhs   ˈsiknəs
 son of Poseidon, strangled by
 Achilles

Cyd
 pers. name (C. Charisse)   SID   ˈsid

Cygnet
 baby swan   SIG-nuht   ˈsignət

Cygnus
 constellation   SIG-nuhs   ˈsignəs

Cylon
 Athenian tyrant   SĪ-LAHN   ˈsaiˌlan

Cymbeline
 play, Shakespeare   SIM-buh-LĒN   ˈsimbəˌliːn

Cymraeg [Welsh]
 lang., Wales   kuhm-RĪG   kəmˈraig

Cymric
 pert. to British Celts, *esp.* Welsh   KUHM-rik   ˈkəmrik

Cymru [Wales]
 principality, Gt. Britain   KUHM-rē   ˈkəmriˑ

Cymry [Welsh]
 people, Wales   KUHM-rē   ˈkəmriˑ

Cynar
 wine   CHĒ-nahr   ˈtʃiːnarʳ

Cyndi
 pers. name   SIN-dē   ˈsindiˑ

Cynewulf
 Anglo-Saxon poet   KIN-uh-WULF, KUN-uh-WULF   ˈkinəˌwulf, ˈkunəˌwulf

Cynthia
 pers. name   SIN-thē-uh   ˈsinθiːə

Key (col. 2):   a: **fad** ā: **fade** ah: **father** ar: **Mary** aw: **law** e: **fed** ē: **feed** er: **merry** i: **hid** ī: **hide** ō: **coat** ōō: **boot**
oi: **boy** ow: **now** u: **put** uh: **above** uhr: **bird** ch: **chop** ng: **ring** sh: **show** th: **thick** th̲: **this** zh: **measure**

Cyparissus
    son of Telephus, became a cypress   SIP-uh-RIS-uhs   ˌsipəˈrisəs
    tree

Cyprian
    1. pers. name   SIP-rē-uhn   ˈsipriːən
    2. Polish   TSIP-ryahn   ˈtsiprjaːn

Cypriano
    pers. name   thē-prē-AH-nō, sē-   θiːpriːˈanoː, siː-

Cyprien
    pers. name, French   sē-prē-Eⁿ   siːpriːẽ

Cypriot
    pert. to Cyprus   SIP-rē-uht   ˈsipriːət

Cyprjan
    pers. name, Polish   TSIP-ryahn, ⑤ SIP-rē-uhn   ˈtsiprjaːn, ⑤ ˈsipriːən

Cyprus
    Mediterranean island   SĪ-pruhs   ˈsaiprəs

Cypselus
    tyrant of Corinth, one of the Seven   SIP-suh-luhs   ˈsipsələs
    Sages

Cyrano de Bergerac
    Savinien de, *French soldier,*   sē-rah-NŌ duh ber-zhuh-RAHK,   siːraːnoː də berʒəraːk,
    satirist   ⑤ SIR-uh-NŌ duh BER-zhuh-RAK,   ⑤ ˈsirəˌnoː də ˈberʒəˌræk,
              BUHR-zhuh-RAK   ˈbəʳʒəˌræk

Cyrenaica
    region, Libya   SIR-uh-NĀ-uh-kuh, SĪ-ruh-   ˌsirəˈneːəkə, ˌsairə-

Cyrenaicism
    ancient philosophical school   SIR-uh-NĀ-uh-SIZ-uhm, SĪ-ruh-   ˌsirəˈneːəˌsizəm, ˌsairə-

Cyrenaics
    followers of Aristippus of Cyrene   SIR-uh-NĀ-iks, SĪ-ruh-NĀ-iks   ˌsirəˈneːiks, ˌsairəˈneːiks

Cyrene
    nymph loved by Apollo; ancient   sī-RĒ-nē   saiˈriːniˑ
    African city

Cyrenian
    pert. to Cyrene   sī-RĒ-nē-uhn   saiˈriːniːən

Cyril
    pers. name   SIR-uhl   ˈsirəl

Cyrillianism
    Christian heresy   suh-RIL-ē-uh-NIZ-uhm   səˈriliːəˌnizəm

Cyrillic
    pert. to Cyril; *Russian alphabet*   suh-RIL-ik   səˈrilik

Cyrus
    1. Persian king; pers. name   SĪ-ruhs   ˈsairəs
    2. French   sē-RUES   siːryːs

Cythera [Cerigo]
    Mediterranean island   suh-THIR-uh   səˈθirə

Cytherea
    name for Aphrodite   SITH-uh-RĒ-uh   ˌsiθəˈriːə

Cytissorus
    grandson of King Athamas of Alos   suh-TIS-uh-ruhs   səˈtisərəs

Cyzicus
    king of the Doliones; killed by   SIZ-i-kuhs   ˈsizikəs
    Jason

Czardas
    dance   CHAHR-DAHSH, CHAHR-DASH   ˈtʃaʳˌdaʃ, ˈtʃaʳˌdæʃ

Foreign Sounds: ue: *Fr.* **rue,** *Ger.* **füllen**   uh(r): *Fr.* **boeuf,** *Ger.* **Höhle**   kh: *Ger.* **ich,** *Scot.* **loch**   ğ: *Sp.* **amigo**   v: *Sp.* **hablar**
hl: *Welsh* **Llanelli.**   CAPITALS: primary stress.   SMALL CAPS: secondary stress.   ⑤: U.S. pron.   ⑥: British pron.

Częstochowa
  city, Poland   CHEⁿ-stuh-<u>KHŌ</u>-vah,   ˌtʃɛ̃stə'xoːvaː,
                                     ⑤ CHEN-stuh-KŌ-vuh   ⑤ ˌtʃɛnstə'koːvə
Czech
  lang., people, republic, Europe   CHEK   'tʃek
Czechoslovak
  inhabitant of or pert. to   CHEK-uh-SLŌ-VAHK, -VAK   ˌtʃekə'sloːˌvak, -ˌvæk
    Czechoslovakia
Czechoslovakia
  republic, Europe   CHEK-uh-sluh-VAHK-ē-uh, -VAK-ē-uh   ˌtʃekəslə'vakiːə, -'vækiːə
Czeladz
  commune, Poland   CHEL-AHJ   'tʃel,aːdʒ
Czerny
  Karl, Austrian pianist/composer   CHER-nē   'tʃeʳniˑ
Czesław
  pers. name, Polish   CHES-lahf   'tʃeslaːf

D

DAB
  German beer   DĀ-AH-BĀ, DAHP   ˌdeːˌa'beː, 'dap
Dabney
  pers. name   DAB-nē   'dæbniˑ
Dacca, Dhaka
  city, Bangladesh   DAHK-uh, DAK-uh   'dakə, 'dækə
Dachau
  Nazi concentration camp,   DA<u>HKH</u>-ow, ⑤ DA<u>HK</u>-OW   'daxau, ⑤ 'dak,au
    Germany
Daché
  Lilly, US milliner   da-SHĀ   dæ'ʃeː
Dachshund
  dog breed   DAHKS-HUNT, -HUND; DAHK-suhnt,   'daks,hunt, -,hund;
                                       -suhnd   'daksənt, -sənd
Dacia
  ancient kingdom, Roman province   DĀ-sh(ē-)uh   'deːʃ(iː)ə
Dacian
  pert. to Dacia   DĀ-sh(ē-)uhn, DĀ-sē-uhn   'deːʃ(iː)ən, 'deːsiːən
Dacron
  tdmk for polyester fiber   DĀ-KRAHN, DAK-RAHN   'deːˌkran, 'dækˌran
Dactyls
  companions to Rhea or Cybele   DAK-tuhlz   'dæktl̩z
Dad
  informal for father   DAD   'dæd
Dada
  wife of Samon   DĀD-uh, DAD-uh   'deːdə, 'dædə

Key (col. 2): a: fad ā: fade ah: father ar: Mary aw: law e: fed ē: feed er: merry i: hid ī: hide ō: coat ōō: boot
oi: boy ow: now u: put uh: above uhr: bird ch: chop ng: ring sh: show th: thick <u>th</u>: this zh: measure

Dada [Dadaism]
  artistic movement   DAHD-ah   'dɑdɑ
Dadaism [Dada]
  artistic movement   DAHD-ah-ɪz-uhm   'dɑdɑ,izəm
Daddah
  Moktar, *Mauritanian statesman* DAHD-ah   'dɑdɑ
Daddy
  informal for father   DAD-ē   'dædiˑ
Daedalion
  father of Chione   duh-DĀ-lē-uhn   də'deːliˑən
Daedalus
  legendary builder of labyrinth DED-l-uhs, DĒD-l-uhs   'dedləs, 'diːdləs
Daemen
  College, *NY*   DĀ-muhn   'deːmən
Daewoo
  South Korean manufacturing co. dā-(w)o͞o   deː(w)uː
Daffin Park
  Savannah, *GA*   DAF-uhn   'dæfən
Dafydd
  pers. name, Welsh   DAHV-i<u>th</u>   'davið
Dafydd ap Gwilym
  Welsh poet   DAHV-i<u>th</u> ahp GWIL-im   'davið ɑp 'gwilim
Dag
  pers. name, Swedish   DAHG   'dɑg
da Gama, Vasco
  see Vasco da Gama
Dagbani
  lang., people, Ghana, Togo   dahg-BAHN-ē   dɑg'bɑniˑ
Daghur, Dagur
  lang., people, Manchuria   dah-GUR   dɑ'guʳ
Dagmar
  1. pers. name   DAG-MAHR   'dæg,mɑʳ
  2. Danish   DAHG-mahr   'dɑːgmɑr
Dagobert
  1. pers. name, French   dah-gaw-BER   dɑːgɔːber
  2. German   DAHG-ō-BERT   'dɑgoː,beʳt
Dagomba
  lang., Ghana   duh-GAHM-buh   də'gɑmbə
Daguerre
  Louis Jacques Mandé, *French*   dah-GER, Ⓢ duh-GER   dɑːger, Ⓢ də'geʳ
  inventor
Dagur
  see Daghur
Dagwood
  comic strip figure; large sandwich DAG-WUD   'dæg,wud
Dahl
  Roald, *British writer*   DAHL   'dɑˑl
Dahlia
  plant   DAL-yuh, DAHL-yuh, Ⓔ DĀL-yuh   'dæljə, 'dɑljə, Ⓔ 'deːljə
Dahlonega
  city, GA   duh-LAHN-uh-guh   də'lɑnəgə
Dahomey
  republic, Africa   duh-HŌ-mē, dah-   də'hoːmiˑ, dɑ-
Daihatsu
  Japanese car co.   dī-HAHT-so͞o   dɑi'hɑtsuː

Foreign Sounds: ue: *Fr.* **rue**, *Ger.* **füllen** uh(r): *Fr.* **boeuf**, *Ger.* **Höhle** <u>kh</u>: *Ger.* **ich**, *Scot.* **loch** ḡ: *Sp.* **amigo** ᵛ: *Sp.* **hablar** hl: *Welsh* **Llanelli**. CAPITALS: primary stress. SMALL CAPS: secondary stress. Ⓢ: U.S. pron. Ⓔ: British pron.

Dai Ichi Kangyo
  Japanese bank   dī ē-chē kahng-(g)yō   dɑi iːtʃiː kaŋ(g)joː

Dáil Eireann
  legislature, Ireland   DOIL ER-(y)uhn   'dɔil 'er(j)ən

Daimler
  Gottlieb, *German engineer*   DĪM-luhr, Ⓢ DĂM-luhr   'daimlərᵣ, Ⓢ 'deːmləᵣ

Dai Nippon
  Japanese printing co.   dī nip-ahn   dɑi nipɑn

Daiquiri
  1. alcoholic drink   DĪ-kuh-rē, DAK(-uh)-rē   'daikəriˑ, 'dæk(ə)riˑ
  2. commune, Cuba   DĪ-kuh-RĒ   ˌdaikə'riː

Dairen [Dalian]
  city, China   DĪ-RUHN, DĪ-REN   'dai'rən, 'dai'ren

Daisy
  pers. name   DĀ-zē   'deːziˑ

Daiwa
  Japanese bank   dī-wah   daiwɑ

Dakar
  city, Senegal   duh-KAHR, DAK-ᴀʜʀ   də'kɑᵣ, 'dæk͵ɑᵣ

Dakota, Dakotah
  N. American people   duh-KŌT-uh   də'koːtə

Dakotan
  pert. to Dakota   duh-KŌT-n   də'koːtn̩

Daladier
  Edouard, *French statesman*   dah-lahd-YĂ   daːlaːdjeː

Dalai Lama
  Tibetan spiritual leader   DAHL-ī LAHM-uh   'dal͵ai 'lamə

Dalandzadgad
  provincial capital, Mongolia   DAHL-ahn-JAHD-ɢᴀʜᴅ   ˌdalan'dʒad͵gad

Dale
  pers. name   DĀL   'deːl

Dalén
  Nils Gustaf, *Swedish inventor*   duh-LĂN   də'leːn
  (Nobel 1912)

Dalgliesh
  Adam, *fictional police inspector, P.*   dal-GLĒSH, dahl-GLĒSH   dæl'gliːʃ, dal'gliːʃ
  D. James

Dalhousie
  town, Canada   dal-HOW-zē   dæl'hauziˑ

Dali
  Salvador, *Spanish artist*   DAHL-ē, dah-LĒ *(his own pron.)*   'daliˑ, da'liː *(his own pron.)*

Dalian, Dalien [Dairen]
  city, China   DAH-lē-EN   'daliˑ'en

Dallas
  city, TX   DAL-uhs   'dæləs

Dalles, The
  city, OR   ṯhuh DALZ   ðə 'dælz

Dalmatia
  coastal region, Croatia   dal-MĀ-sh(ē-)uh   dæl'meːʃ(iː)ə

Dalmatian
  dog breed   dal-MĀ-shuhn   dæl'meːʃən

Dalmaticus
  Roman cognomen   dal-MAT-i-kuhs   dæl'mæt̬ikəs

Daltry
  Roger, *British rock singer*   DAWL-trē, DAHL-trē   'dɔːltriˑ, 'daltriˑ

Key (col. 2):   a: fad   ā: fade   ah: father   ar: Mary   aw: law   e: fed   ē: feed   er: merry   i: hid   ī: hide   ō: coat   ōō: boot
oi: boy   ow: now   u: put   uh: above   uhr: bird   ch: chop   ng: ring   sh: show   th: thick   ṯh: this   zh: measure

Daly
   Tyne, *US actress;* Tim, *US actor*   DĀ-lē   'deːliˑ

Dalziel
   James Henry, *British newspaper*   DAL-zēl, dē-EL   'dælziːl, diː'el
   owner

Dam
   Henrik, *Danish biochemist (Nobel*   DAHM   'dɑm
   1943)

Damaschke
   E.C. "Dutch," Field, *ballpark,*   duh-MAS-kē   də'mæskiˑ
   Oneonta, NY

Damascus
   capital, Syria   duh-MAS-kuhs   də'mæskəs

Dámaso
   pers. name   DAH-mah-sō, THAH-   'dɑmɑsoː, 'ða-

Damasus
   pope   DAM-uh-suhs   'dæməsəs

D'Amato
   Alfonse, *US politician*   duh-MAHT-ō   də'mɑt̬oː

D'Amboise
   Jacques, *US ballet dancer*   dahm-BWAHZ   dɑm'bwɑz

Damián
   pers. name, Spanish   dahm-YAHN, thahm-   dɑm'jɑn, ðɑm-

Damian
   1. pers. name   DĂM-yuhn, DĀ-mē-uhn   'deːmjən, 'deːmiːən
   2. German   dahm-YAHN, DAHM-ē-AHN   dɑm'jɑn, ˌdɑmiː'ɑn

Damiano
   pers. name, Italian   dahm-YAHN-ō   dɑm'jɑnoː

Damião
   pers. name, Portuguese   duhm-YOW[n], thuhm-, dahm-,   dəm'jaũ, ðəm-, dɑːm-,
                      thahm-   ðɑːm-

Damien
   1. pers. name   DĀ-mē-uhn   'deːmiːən
   2. French   dahm-YE[n]   dɑːmjẽ

Damietta
   city, Egypt   DAM-ē-ET-uh   ˌdæmiː'et̬ə

Damm
   Spanish beer   DAHM   'dɑm

Damocles
   legendary figure (sword of D.)   DAM-uh-KLĒZ   'dæməˌkliːz

Damon
   pers. name   DĀ-muhn   'deːmən

Damone
   Vic, *US entertainer*   duh-MŌN   də'moːn

Damson
   fruit   DAM-zuhn   'dæmzən

Dan
   1. river, VA; Biblical village; pers.   DAN   'dæn
   name
   2. lang., people, Liberia, Ivory   DAN, DAHN   'dæn, 'dɑn
   Coast

Dana
   pers. name   DĀ-nuh   'deːnə

Danae, Danaë
   mother of Perseus   DAN-uh-Ē, DĀ-nuh-Ē   'dænəˌiː, 'deːnəˌiː

Foreign Sounds: ue: *Fr.* **rue**, *Ger.* füllen uh(r): *Fr.* b**oeuf**, *Ger.* H**öh**le kh: *Ger.* i**ch**, *Scot.* lo**ch** ḡ: *Sp.* ami**g**o ṿ: *Sp.* ha**b**lar
hl: *Welsh* **Ll**anelli. CAPITALS: primary stress. SMALL CAPS: secondary stress. Ⓢ: U.S. pron. Ⓔ: British pron.

Danaid

daughter of Danaus; Monarch butterfly — DAN-ē-ID, DAN-ā-ID — 'dæniː,id, 'dæneː,id

Danaides, Danaïdes

daughters of Danaus; family of butterflies — duh-NĀ-uhd-ēZ — də'neːəd,iːz

Danakil [Afar]

lang., people, desert, Ethiopia, Djibouti — DAN-uh-KIL, DAN-uh-KĒL — 'dænə,kil, 'dænə,kiːl

Da Nang

seaport, Vietnam — DAH NAHNG, Ⓢ duh-NANG — 'dɑ 'nɑŋ, Ⓢ də'næŋ

Danaus

ruler of Argos, brother of Aegyptus — DAN-ē-uhs, DAN-ā-UHS — 'dæniːəs, 'dæneː,əs

Danbury

city, CT, NC — DAN-BER-ē, DAN-b(uh-)rē — 'dæn,beriˑ, 'dænb(ə)riˑ

Danceteller

dance co., PA — DAN(T)S-TEL-uhr — 'dæn(t)s,telə^r

Dandenong

Ranges, mtn., Australia — DAN-duh-NAHNG, DAN-duh-NAWNG — 'dændə,nɑŋ, 'dændə,nɔːŋ

Dandie Dinmont

terrier breed — DAN-dē DIN-MAHNT — 'dændi 'din,mɑnt

Dane

inhabitant of Denmark; pers. name — DĀN — 'deːn

Danegeld

ancient tax, England — DĀN-GELD — 'deːn,geld

Danelaw, Danelagh

English laws — DĀN-LAW — 'deːn,lɔː

Danforth

pers. name — DAN-FAWRTH — 'dæn,fɔː^rθ

Dániel

pers. name, Hungarian — DAH-nē-el — 'dɑːniːel

Daniel

1. Old Testament book; pers. name — DAN-yuhl — 'dænjəl

2. Dutch — DAH-nē-EL — 'dɑːniː,el

3. French — dahn-YEL — dɑːnjel

4. German — DAHN-yel, DAHN-ē-el — 'dɑnjel, 'dɑniːel

5. Spanish — thahn-YEL, dahn- — ðɑn'jel, dɑn-

6. Swedish — DAH-nē-el — 'dɑniːel

Daniele

pers. name, Italian — dahn-YEL-e — dɑn'jele

Danielle

pers. name — dan-YEL — dæn'jel

Daniello

pers. name, Italian — dahn-YEL-lō — dɑn'jelloː

Danilova

Alexandra, Russian ballet dancer — duh-NĒ-luh-vuh — də'niːləvə

Danish

lang., people, Europe — DĀ-nish — 'deːniʃ

D'Annunzio

Gabriele, Italian writer — dah-NOONT-sē-ō — dɑ'nuːntsiːoː

Danny

pers. name — DAN-ē — 'dæniˑ

Key (col. 2):   a: fad   ā: fade   ah: father   ar: Mary   aw: law   e: fed   ē: feed   er: merry   i: hid   ī: hide   ō: coat   o͞o: boot
oi: boy   ow: now   u: put   uh: above   uhr: bird   ch: chop   ng: ring   sh: show   th: thick   th̲: this   zh: measure

Dano-Norwegian [Bokmål]
literary Norwegian　　　　　DĀ-nō-nawr-WĒ-juhn　　　　　ˌdeːnoːnɔːrˈwiːdʒən

Dante
pers. name　　　　　DAHN-TĀ, DAN-TĀ, DANT-ē,　　　　　ˈdɑnˌteː, ˈdænˌteː, ˈdænti·,
　　　　　DAHNT-ē　　　　　ˈdɑnti·

Dante Alighieri
Italian poet　　　　　DAHN-TĀ AL-uhg-YER-ē, DAN-TĀ,　　　　　ˈdɑnˌteː ˌæləgˈjeri·, ˈdænˌteː,
　　　　　DANT-ē, DAHNT-ē　　　　　ˈdænti·, ˈdɑnti·

Dantean
pert. to Dante Alighieri　　　　　DANT-ē-uhn, DAHNT-ē-uhn,　　　　　ˈdæntiːən, ˈdɑntiːən,
　　　　　dan-TĒ-uhn, dahn-TĒ-uhn　　　　　dænˈtiːən, dɑnˈtiːən

Dantesque
pert. to Dante Alighieri　　　　　dan-TESK, dahn-TESK　　　　　dænˈtesk, dɑnˈtesk

Danton
Georges, *French revolutionary*　　　　　dahⁿ-TAWⁿ　　　　　dãtɔ̃

Danube
river, Europe　　　　　DAN-yoōb　　　　　ˈdænjuˑb

Danubian
pert. to the Danube　　　　　dan-YOO-bē-uhn, duhn-YOO-bē-uhn　　　　　dænˈjuːbiːən, dənˈjuːbiːən

Danvers
city, MA　　　　　DAN-vuhrz　　　　　ˈdænvəʳz

Danya
pers. name (D. Krupske)　　　　　DAN-yuh, DAHN-yuh　　　　　ˈdænjə, ˈdɑnjə

Danzig [Gdańsk]
city, Poland　　　　　DAHNT-sig, DANT-sig　　　　　ˈdɑntsig, ˈdæntsig

Daphne
nymph loved by Apollo; pers.　　　　　DAF-nē　　　　　ˈdæfni·
name

Daphnis
beautiful son of Hermes　　　　　DAF-nuhs　　　　　ˈdæfnəs

Daphnis and Chloë
novel, Longus　　　　　DAF-nuhs uhn(d) KLŌ-ē　　　　　ˈdæfnəs ən(d) ˈkloːi·

Daphnis et Chloé
ballet, Ravel　　　　　dahf-NĒS ā klaw-Ā　　　　　dɑːfniːs eː klɔːeː

Darcy, D'Arcy
pers. name　　　　　DAHR-sē　　　　　ˈdɑʳsi·

Dardanelles [Çanakkale Boğazı,
Hellespont]
strait, Turkey　　　　　DAHRD-n-ELZ　　　　　ˌdɑʳdn̩ˈelz

Dardanus
Trojan ancestor　　　　　DAHRD-n-uhs　　　　　ˈdɑʳdn̩əs

Dardic
lang. family　　　　　DAHRD-ik　　　　　ˈdɑʳdik

Dar es Salaam
city, Tanzania　　　　　DAHR ES suh-LAHM　　　　　ˌdɑr ˌes səˈlɑm

Darién
Spanish colony, isthmus, Panama　　　　　dahr-YEN　　　　　dɑrˈjen

Darien
city, CT; city, GA; village, IL　　　　　DAR-ē-EN, DER-ē-EN　　　　　ˌdæriːˈen, ˌderiːˈen

Darin
Bobby, James, *US entertainers*　　　　　DAR-uhn, DER-uhn　　　　　ˈdærən, ˈderən

Darius
1. *name, Persian kings; pers.*　　　　　duh-RĪ-uhs　　　　　dəˈraiəs
name
2. *French*　　　　　dahr-YUES　　　　　dɑːrjyːs

Foreign Sounds:　ue: *Fr.* **rue**, *Ger.* **füllen**　uh(r): *Fr.* **boeuf**, *Ger.* **Höhle**　kh: *Ger.* **ich**, *Scot.* **loch**　ğ: *Sp.* **amigo**　v̠: *Sp.* **hablar**
hl: *Welsh* **Llanelli**.　CAPITALS: primary stress.　SMALL CAPS: secondary stress.　Ⓢ: U.S. pron.　Ⓑ: British pron.

Darjeeling, Darjiling
  district, India; tea   dahr-JĒ-ling   dɑʳdʒiːliŋ

Darlene
  pers. name   dahr-LĒN   dɑʳliːn

Darley Arabian
  horse   DAHR-lē uh-RĀ-bē-uhn   'dɑʳliˑ ə'reːbiːən

Darlington
  county, town, SC; borough,   DAHR-ling-tuhn   'dɑʳliŋtən
    England; pers. name

Darmstadt
  prov & town, Germany   DAHRM-SHTAHT, ⑤ DAHRM-STAT   'dɑʳm,ʃtɑt, ⑤ 'dɑʳm,stæt

Darrell
  pers. name   DAR-uhl, DER-uhl   'dærəl, 'derəl

Darren
  pers. name   DAR-uhn, DER-uhn   'dærən, 'derən

Darryl
  pers. name   DAR-uhl, DER-uhl   'dærəl, 'derəl

D'Artagnan
  character in The Three   dahr-tahn-YAHⁿ, ⑤ dahr-TAN-yuhn   dɑːrtɑːnjã, ⑤ dɑʳtænjən
    Musketeers, *A. Dumas*

Darth Vader
  Star Wars villain   DAHRTH VĀD-uhr   ˌdɑʳθ 'veːdəʳ

Dartmoor
  natl. park, prison, England   DAHRT-MUR, -MŌR, -MAWR   'dɑʳt,muʳ, -ˌmoːʳ, -ˌmɔːʳ

Dartmouth
  borough, England; town, Nova   DAHRT-muhth   'dɑʳtməθ
    Scotia; college, NH

Darwin
  Charles, *Brit. scientist; pl. name;*   DAHR-wuhn   'dɑʳwən
    college, Cambridge Univ.

Darwinian
  pert. to Charles Darwin   dahr-WIN-ē-uhn   dɑʳwiniːən

Darwinism
  origin of species theory   DAHR-wuh-NIZ-uhm   'dɑʳwə,nizəm

Dasain
  Nepalese festival   DAH-SHĪN   'dɑ,ʃain

Dashiell
  pers. name   duh-SHĒL *(pron. of D. Hammett)*,   də'ʃiːl *(pron. of D.*
    DASH-uhl   *Hammett)*, 'dæʃəl

da Silva
  1. pers. name   duh SIL-vuh   də 'silvə
  2. Portuguese   t͟huh SIL-vuh, duh; t͟hah SIL-vah,   ðə 'silvə, də; ðɑː 'silvɑː, dɑː
    dah

Dassault
  French aircraft co.   dah-SŌ   dɑːsoː

Dassin
  Jules, *US director*   DAS-uhn   'dæsən

Datong, Ta-t'ung
  city, China   DAH-TUNG   'dɑ'tuŋ

Datsun
  Japanese car make   DAHT-suhn, DAT-suhn   'dɑtsən, 'dætsən

Daumier
  Honoré, *French artist*   dōm-YĀ   doːm'jeː

Daunus
  brother of Iapyx and Peucetius   DAW-nuhs   'dɔːnəs

Key (col. 2):   a: fad   ā: fade   ah: father   ar: Mary   aw: law   e: fed   ē: feed   er: merry   i: hid   ī: hide   ō: coat   o͞o: boot
oi: boy   ow: now   u: put   uh: above   uhr: bird   ch: chop   ng: ring   sh: show   th: thick   t͟h: this   zh: measure

Dauphin
 1. county, PA; river, Canada   DAW-fuhn   'dɔːfən
 2. title, French prince   dō-FE[n]   doːfẽ

Dauphiné
 prov, France; Alps, *Alpine mtn.*   dō-fē-NÃ   doːfiˈneː
 range

Dauphinoise
 cookery preparation   dō-fēn-WAHZ   doːfiːnwɑːz

Dausset
 Jean, *French immunologist (Nobel*   dō-SE   doːse
 1980)

Davallia
 plant   duh-VAL-yuh   dəˈvæljə

Davao
 seaport, Philippines   DAHV-ow, dah-VOW   'dɑvˌau, dɑˈvɑu

Dave
 pers. name   DĀV   'deːv

D'Avenant
 Sir William, *British poet laureate*   DAV-(uh-)nuhnt   'dæv(ə)nənt

Davenport
 city, Iowa   DAV-uhn-PAWRT, DAV-m-PAWRT   'dævənˌpɔːᵊt, 'dævm̩ˌpɔːᵊt

David
 1. pers. name   DĀ-vuhd   'deːvəd
 2. Dutch   DAH-vuht   'dɑːvət
 3. French   dah-VĒD   dɑːviːd
 4. German   DAHV-ēt, DAHF-ēt, -it   'dɑviːt, 'dɑfiːt, -it
 5. Hebrew   dahv-ĒD, DAW-vuhd   dɑvˈiːd, 'dɔːvəd
 6. Italian   DAHV-ēd   'dɑviːd
 7. Russian   DUHV-YĒD   ˌdəvˈjiːd

David Lipscomb
 College, *TN*   DĀ-vuhd LIP-skuhm   'deːvəd 'lipskəm

Davies
 family name   DĀ-vēz, Ⓔ DĀ-vis   'deːviːz, Ⓔ 'deːvis

da Vinci
 see Leonardo da Vinci

Davis
 family name   DĀ-vis   'deːvis

Davison
 pers. name   DĀ-vuh-suhn   'deːvəsən

Davisson
 C. J., *US physicist (Nobel 1937)*   DĀ-vuh-suhn   'deːvəsən

Davos
 Swiss resort   dah-VŌS   dɑˈvoːs

Davy
 pers. name   DĀ-vē   'deːviˑ

Dawes
 Charles G., *US vice president*   DAWZ   'dɔːz
 (Nobel 1925)

Dawn
 pers. name   DAWN, DAHN   'dɔːn, 'dɑn

Dayak [Dyak]
 people, lang., Sarawak & Borneo   DĪ-AK   'dɑiˌæk

Dayan
 Moshe, *Israeli leader*   dī-AHN, dah-YAHN   dɑiˈɑn, dɑˈjɑn

Foreign Sounds: ue: *Fr.* **rue**, *Ger.* **füllen**   uh(r): *Fr.* **boeuf**, *Ger.* **Höhle**   <u>kh</u>: *Ger.* **ich**, *Scot.* **loch**   ḡ: *Sp.* amigo   <u>v</u>: *Sp.* ha**bl**ar
hl: *Welsh* **Llanelli**.   CAPITALS: primary stress.   SMALL CAPS: secondary stress.   Ⓢ: U.S. pron.   Ⓔ: British pron.

Dayna
  pers. name   DĀ-nuh   'deɪnə

Dayton
  city, OH   DĀT-n   'deɪtn̩

Daytona Beach
  town, FL   dā-TŌ-nuh BĒCH   deɪ,toːnə 'biːtʃ

Da Yunhe
  canal, China   DAH YUN-HUH   'dɑ 'jun'hə

Dayyan
  pers. name   dī-(Y)AHN   daɪ'(j)ɑn

Dazu
  town, China   DAHD-ZOO, DAH-ZOO   'dɑd'zuː, 'dɑ'zuː

Deaf Smith
  county, TX   DEF SMITH, DĒF   ,def 'smiθ, ,diːf

Dean, Deane
  pers. name   DĒN   'diːn

DeAndre
  pers. name   dē-AN-drā, dē-AHN-drā   diː'ændreɪ, diː'ɑndreɪ

Dearborn
  county, IN; city, MI   DIR-BAWRN, DIR-buhrn   'diʳ,bɔːʳn, 'diʳbəʳn

Deauville
  resort, France   dō-VĒL, ⑤ DŌ-VIL   doːviːl, ⑤ 'doː,vil

De Baca
  county, NM   dē BAHK-uh   diː 'bɑkə

DeBakey
  Michael Ellis, *US cardiovascular*   duh-BĀ-kē   də'beɪkiˑ
    surgeon

de Balzac
  see Balzac

DeBeers
  S. African diamond mining co.   duh-BIRZ   də'biʳz

Deborah
  pers. name   DEB-(uh-)ruh   'deb(ə)rə

Debrecen
  city, Hungary   DEB-ruht-SEN   'debrət,sen

Debrett
  British publisher, peerage   duh-BRET   də'bret

Debreu
  Gerard, *French-born US*   duh-BROO   də'bruː
    economist (Nobel 1983)

Debussy
  Claude, *French composer*   duh-bue-SĒ, ⑤ DEB-yuh-SĒ,   dəbyːsiː, ⑤ ,debjə'siː,
                  DĀ-byuh-SĒ   ,deɪbjə'siː

Debye
  P. J. W., *Dutch-born US physicist*   duh-BĪ   də'baɪ
    (Nobel 1936)

DEC
  US computer co.   DEK   'dek

Decalogue
  the Ten Commandments   DEK-uh-LAWG, DEK-uh-LAHG   'dekə,lɔːg, 'dekə,lag

Decameron
  Boccaccio work   duh-KAM-uh-ruhn, -RAHN   də'kæmərən, -,rɑn

Decatur
  Stephen, *US naval officer; pl.*   di-KĀT-uhr   di'keɪţəʳ
    name, US

Key (col. 2):   a: fad   ā: fade   ah: father   ar: Mary   aw: law   e: fed   ē: feed   er: merry   i: hid   ī: hide   ō: coat   ōō: boot
oi: boy   ow: now   u: put   uh: above   uhr: bird   ch: chop   ng: ring   sh: show   th: thick   th̲: this   zh: measure

Decca
   US record co.   DEK-uh   'dekə

Deccan, Dekkan
   southern Indian peninsula   DEK-uhn, DEK-AN   'dekən, 'dek,æn

December
   month   di-SEM-buhr   di'sembəʳ

Decimus
   pers. name   DES-uh-muhs·   'desəməs

Decius
   Roman emperor; pers. name   DĒ-sh(ē-)uhs   'diːʃ(iː)əs

DeConcini
   Dennis, *US politician*   DĒ-kuhn-SĒ-nē   ˌdiːkən'siːniˑ

Dedeaux
   Field, *ballpark, Los Angeles, CA*   DĀ-DŌ   'deɪˌdoː

Dedham
   town, MA   DED-uhm   'dedəm

Deems
   pers. name (D. Taylor)   DĒMZ   'diːmz

Deepavali
   Hindu festival   DĒ-PAHV-uh-lē   'diːˌpavəliˑ

Def Leppard
   rock group   def LEP-uhrd   def 'lepəʳd

Defoe
   Daniel, *English writer*   di-FŌ   di'foː

Deforest, DeForest
   pers. name   di-FAWR-uhst, di-FAHR-uhst   di'fɔːrəst, di'furəst

Degas
   Edgar, *French artist*   duh-GAH, Ⓢ dā-GAH   dəgɑ, Ⓢ də'gɑ, deɪ'gɑ

de Gaulle
   Charles, *president, France*   duh GŌL, Ⓢ di GŌL, di GAWL   də goːl, Ⓢ di 'goːl, di 'gɔːl

De Havilland
   Geoffrey, *English aircraft*   duh HAV-uh-luhnd   də 'hævələnd
    designer; Olivia, *US actress*

Dehmelt
   Hans G., *German-born US*   DĀ-MELT, DĀ-muhlt   'deɪˌmelt, 'deɪməlt
    physicist (Nobel 1989)

Deianeira, Deianira
   wife of Hercules   DĀ-uh-NĪ-ruh, DĒ-uh-NĪ-ruh, -nē-ruh   ˌdeɪə'nɑirə, ˌdiːə'nɑirə, -niːrə

Deil
   the Devil   DĒL   'diːl

Deimos
   satellite of Mars   DĀ-mōs, DĀ-muhs   'deɪmoːs, 'deɪməs

Deinodon
   dinosaur   DĪ-nuh-DAHN   'dɑinəˌdɑn

Deiphobus
   son of Priam and Hecuba   DĀ-uh-FŌ-buhs   ˌdeɪə'foːbəs

Deiphontes
   husband of Hyrnetho   DĒ-uh-FAHN-TĒZ   ˌdiːə'fɑnˌtiːz

Deira
   ancient British kingdom   DĀ-ruh   'deɪrə

Deirdre
   pers. name   DIR-druh, DIR-drē   'diʳdrə, 'diʳdriˑ

Deir-el-Bahri
   Egyptian site, near Thebes   DER-al-BAHR-ē   'deræl'bɑriˑ

Foreign Sounds: ue: *Fr.* **rue**, *Ger.* **füllen** uh(r): *Fr.* **boeuf**, *Ger.* **Höhle** <u>kh</u>: *Ger.* i<u>ch</u>, *Scot.* lo<u>ch</u> ḡ: *Sp.* ami**g**o <u>v</u>: *Sp.* ha**b**lar
hl: *Welsh* **Ll**anelli. CAPITALS: primary stress. SMALL CAPS: secondary stress. Ⓢ: U.S. pron. Ⓣ: British pron.

Deisenhofer
　Johann, *German biochemist* | DĪ-zuhn-HŌ-fuhr | 'daɪzən,hoːfə^r
　(Nobel 1988)

De Kalb
　pl. name, US; college, GA | di KALB, *esp. southeastern US* di KAB | di 'kælb, *esp. southeastern US* di 'kæb

De Klerk
　F. W., *S. African politician* | duh KLERK, di KLUHRK | də 'kle^rk, di 'klə^rk

De Koninck
　Belgian beer | duh KAW-ningk | də 'kɔːniŋk

de Kooning
　Willem, *US painter* | duh KOO-ning | də 'kuːniŋ

DeKuyper
　brand of schnapps | di-KĪ-puhr | di'kaɪpə^r

Delacroix
　Eugène, *French painter* | duh-lah-KRWAH, Ⓢ DEL-uh-K(R)WAH | dəlaːkrwaː, Ⓢ ,delə'k(r)wa

de la Garza
　E(kika), *US politician* | DEL uh GAHR-zuh | ,del ə 'garzə

de la Madrid Hurtado
　Miguel, *president, Mexico* | dā lah mah-<u>TH</u>RĒ<u>TH</u> ōor-TAH-<u>th</u>ō | deː la ma'ðriːð uːr'taðoː

De la Mare
　Walter, *English writer* | DEL-uh-MAR, DEL-uh-MER | ,delə'mæ^r, ,delə'me^r

de la Mer
　pers. name | DEL-uh-muhr, DEL-uh-MIR | 'deləmə^r, 'delə,mi^r

Delamere
　pers. name | DEL-uh-MIR | 'delə,mi^r

Delano
　pers. name | DEL-uh-NŌ | 'delə,noː

de la Renta
　Oscar, *fashion designer* | duh luh RAHⁿ(N)-tuh, DĒ, REN-tuh | də lə 'rã(n)tə, ,diː, 'rentə

De Laurentis
　Dino, *film producer* | dā law-REN-tis, Ⓢ duh luh-RENT-uhs, DĒ | deː lɔː'rentis, Ⓢ də lə'rentəs, ,diː

Delaware
　river, state, US; N. American people [Lenni-Lenape] | DEL-uh-WAR, -WER, -wuhr | 'delə,wær, -,we^r, -wə^r

Delbrück
　Max, *German-born US biologist (Nobel l969)* | DEL-BRUEK, DEL-BRUK | 'del,bryk, 'del,bruk

Deledda
　Grazia, *Italian author (Nobel 1926)* | dā-LED-dah, Ⓢ duh-LED-uh | deː'ledda, Ⓢ də'ledə

Delft
　city, Netherlands | DELFT | 'delft

Delhi
　1. city, India | DEL-ē | 'deliˑ
　2. town, LA, NY, OH, Ontario | DEL-HĪ | 'del,haɪ

Delia
　pers. name | DĒ-lē-uh, DĒL-yuh | 'diːliːə, 'diːljə

Delian League
　Athenian alliance | DĒ-lē-uhn | 'diːliːən

Delibes
　Léo, *French composer* | duh-LĒB | də'liːb

Key (col. 2):　a: fad　ā: fade　ah: father　ar: Mary　aw: law　e: fed　ē: feed　er: merry　i: hid　ī: hide　ō: coat　ōo: boot
oi: boy　ow: now　u: put　uh: above　uhr: bird　ch: chop　ng: ring　sh: show　th: thick　<u>th</u>: this　zh: measure

Delilah
  Biblical name   di-LĪ-luh   di'lailə
Delius
  Frederick, *English composer*   DĒ-lē-uhs, DĒL-yuhs   'diːliːəs, 'diːljəs
Dell
  pers. name   DEL   'del
Della
  pers. name (D. Reese)   DEL-uh   'delə
della Robbia
  family of Italian artists   DEL-uh RŌ-bē-uh, DEL-uh RAHB-ē-uh   ˌdelə 'roːbiːə, ˌdelə 'rɑbiːə
Dell'Olio
  Louis, *US fashion designer*   del-Ō-lē-ō   del'oːliːoː
Delmarva
  Peninsula, *east coast, US*   del-MAHR-vuh   del'mɑʳvə
Delmonico
  steak cut   del-MAHN-i-kō   delˌmɑnikoː
Del Monte
  US food processing co.   del MAHNT-ē   del 'mɑntiˑ
Del Norte
  county, CA; city, CO   del NŌRT-ā, del NAWRT-ā   del 'noːʳteː, del 'nɔːʳteː
Delorimier
  Downs, *Montreal, Canada*   duh-LAWR-uhm-YĀ   dəˌlɔːrəm'jeː
Delos
  Aegean island   DĒ-LAHS, DEL-ōs   'diːˌlɑs, 'deloːs
De Los Angeles
  Victoria, *Spanish opera star*   dā laws AHNG-hel-ās   deː lɔːs 'ɑɲheleːs
De Lourdes
  College, *IL*   duh LURD(Z)   də 'luʳd(z)
Delphi
  ancient Greek city, site of oracle   DEL-FĪ   'delˌfai
Delphian
  pert. to Delphi   DEL-fē-uhn, DELF-yuhn   'delfiːən, 'delfjən
Delphic
  pert. to Delphi   DEL-fik   'delfik
Delphinium
  plant   del-FIN-ē-uhm   del'finiːəm
Delphinus
  constellation   del-FĪ-nuhs   del'fainəs
Delphus
  hero of Delphi   DEL-fuhs   'delfəs
del Sarto
  see Sarto, del
DeLuise
  Dom, *US actor*   DEL-uh-WĒZ   ˌdelə'wiːz
De Man
  Paul, *Belgian-born literary critic*   duh-MAHN   dəmɑn
de Maupassant
  see Maupassant
Demavend
  mtn., Iran   DEM-uh-VEND   'deməˌvend
Demerara
  raw sugar   DEM-uh-RER-uh, DEM-uh-RAHR-uh   ˌdemə'rerə, ˌdemə'rɑrə
Demerol
  tdmk for a sedative   DEM-uh-RAWL, -RŌL   'deməˌrɔːl, -ˌroːl

---

Demeter
  Greek earth and fertility goddess   di-MĒT-uhr   di'miːʈəʳ

Demetrios
  pers. name, Mod. Greek   the̱-MĒ-tre̱-AWS   ði:'miːtriː,ɔːs

Demetrius
  pers. name   duh-MĒ-tre̱-uhs   də'miːtriːəs

Demetrius Poliorcetes
  Macedonian king   duh-MĒ-tre̱-uhs PAHL-e̱-awr-SĒT-e̱z   də'miːtriːəs ˌpaliːɔːʳ'siːʈiːz

Demi
  pers. name (D. Moore)   duh-MĒ, DEM-e̱   də'miː, 'demiˑ

de Mille
  Cecil B., *US movie producer*   duh MIL   də 'mil

Demiphon
  king of Eleonte   DEM-uh-FAHN   'deməˌfɑn

Democrat
  member of Democratic party   DEM-uh-KRAT   'deməˌkræt

Democratic
  US political party   DEM-uh-KRAT-ik   ˌdemə'kræʈik

Democritus
  Greek philosopher   di-MAHK-ruht-uhs   di'makrəʈəs

Demodice
  aunt of Phrixus   duh-MAHD-uh-se̱   də'madəsiˑ

Demodocus
  Homeric bard   de̱-MAHD-uh-kuhs   di'madəkəs

Demophon
  son of Theseus   DEM-uh-FAHN   'deməˌfɑn

Demopolis
  city, AL   dem-AH-puh-luhs   dem'apələs

Demosthenes
  Athenian orator   di-MAHS-thuh-NĒZ   di'masθəˌniːz

Dempsey
  Jack, *US boxer*   DEM(P)-se̱   'dem(p)siˑ

Denali [McKinley]
  mtn., National Park and Preserve, *AK*   duh-NAHL-e̱   də'naliˑ

Denbigh
  town, Wales   DEN-be̱   'denbiˑ

Denbighshire [Clwyd]
  former county, Wales   DEN-be̱-shuhr, -SHIR   'denbiˑʃəʳ, -ˌʃiʳ

Dendritis
  name used by Helen in Rhodes   den-DRĪT-uhs, den-DRĒT-uhs   den'draiʈəs, den'driːʈəs

Dene, Déné
  Canadian Indian people   DEN-e̱, DEN-ā   'deniˑ, 'denˌeː

Deneb
  star   DEN-EB, DEN-uhb   'denˌeb, 'denəb

Deneuve
  Catherine, *French actress*   duh-NUH(R)V   dənœːv

Deng Xiaoping, Teng Hsiao-p'ing
  Chinese leader   DUHNG SHOW-PING   'dəŋ 'ʃau'piŋ

Denikin
  Anton, *Russian militarist*   dyin-YĒK-yin   djin'jiːkjin

Deniliquin
  town, Australia   duh-NIL-i-kwuhn   də'nilikwən

De Niro
  Robert, *US actor*   duh NIR-ō   də 'nirɔː

Key (col. 2): a: fad ā: fade ah: father ar: Mary aw: law e: fed ē: feed er: merry i: hid ī: hide ō: coat o͞o: boot
oi: boy ow: now u: put uh: above uhr: bird ch: chop ng: ring sh: show th: thick <u>th</u>: this zh: measure

Denis		
1. pers. name	DEN-uhs	'denəs
2. Dutch	duh-NĒS	də'ni:s
3. French	duh-NĒ	dəni:
4. Russian	din-YĒS	dj̩in'ji:s
Denise		
1. pers. name	duh-NĒS, -NĒZ	də'ni:s, -'ni:z
2. French	duh-NĒZ	dəni:z
Denison		
city, IA, TX; univ., OH	DEN-uh-suhn	'denəsən
Denizli		
prov & town, Turkey	DEN-uhz-LĒ	ˌdenəz'li:
Denmark		
kingdom, Europe	DEN-MAHRK	'denˌmɑʳk
Dennie, Denny		
pers. name	DEN-ē	'deniˑ
Dennis		
pers. name	DEN-uhs	'denəs
Denny's		
US restaurant chain	DEN-ēz	'deni:z
Denpasar		
city, Indonesia	duhn-PAHS-AHR	dən'pɑsˌɑʳ
Denver		
city, CO; pers. name	DEN-vuhr	'denvəʳ
Denys		
pers. name, French	duh-NĒ	dəni:
Déodat		
pers. name, French	dā-aw-DAH(T)	deːɔːdɑː(t)
De Palma		
Brian Russel, *US film writer, director*	duh PAHL-muh, duh PAWL-muh	də 'pɑlmə, də 'pɔːlmə
Depardieu		
Gerard, *French actor*	dā-pahr-DYUH(R)	deːpɑːrdjœː
DePauw		
University, *IN*	duh-PAW	də'pɔː
Depeche Mode		
rock group	duh-PESH MŌD	də'peʃ 'moːd
Depo-Provera		
tdmk for a progesterone drug	DEP-ō-pruh-VER-uh, -VIR-uh	ˌdepoːprə'verə, -'virə
De Quincey		
Thomas, *English essayist*	duh KWIN(T)-sē	də 'kwin(t)siˑ
DeQuindre		
Park, *stadium, Detroit, MI*	di-KIN-druh	di'kindrə
Derby		
1. city, CT, KS; town, VT	DUHR-bē	'dəʳbiˑ
2. city, horse race, England	DAHR-bē	'dɑʳbiˑ
Derby Line		
village, VT	DUHR-bē LĪN	ˌdəʳbiˑ 'lɑin
Derbyshire		
county, England	DAHR-bē-shuhr, -SHIR	'dɑʳbiˑʃəʳ, -ˌʃiʳ
Derdriu		
legendary Irish heroine	DER-droo	'derdru:
Derek		
pers. name	DER-ik	'derik

Foreign Sounds: ue: *Fr.* **rue**, *Ger.* **fü**llen uh(r): *Fr.* b**oeu**f, *Ger.* H**ö**hle kh: *Ger.* i**ch**, *Scot.* lo**ch** g̃: *Sp.* ami**g**o v: *Sp.* ha**b**lar hl: *Welsh* **Ll**anelli. CAPITALS: primary stress. SMALL CAPS: secondary stress. [$]: U.S. pron. [£]: British pron.

Deringer
  Henry, *US gunsmith*   DER-uhn-juhr   'derəndʒəʳ
Dermoptera
  colugos or flying lemurs   DUHR-MAHP-tuh-ruh   ˌdəʳˈmɑptərə
Dermot
  pers. name   DUHR-muht   'dəʳmət
Deroyce
  pers. name (F. D. Etheredge)   duh-ROIS   də'rɔis
Derrick
  pers. name   DER-ik   'derik
Derrida
  Jacques, *French literary critic*   der-ē-DAH, Ⓢ duhr-ē-DAH   deriːdɑ, Ⓢ dəriːˈdɑ
Derry
  town, Ireland   DER-ē   'deriˑ
Dershowitz
  Alan, *US lawyer, writer*   DUHR-shuh-WITS   'dəʳʃəˌwits
Der Spiegel
  German newspaper   der SHPĒ-guhl   deʳ ˈʃpiːgəl
Derwent
  river, England   DUHR-wuhnt   'dəʳwənt
Derwent Water
  lake, England   DUHR-wuhnt WAWT-uhr, WAHT-uhr   'dəʳwənt ˌwɔːtəʳ, ˌwɑtəʳ
de Sales
  St. Francis, *French ecclesiastic*   duh SAHL, Ⓢ duh SAHL(Z), duh   də sɑːl, Ⓢ də 'sɑl(z), də 'seːlz
                                              SĀLZ
Descartes
  René, *French philosopher*   dā-KAHRT   deːkɑːrt, Ⓢ deːˈkɑʳt
Deschutes
  river, county, OR   di-SHO͞OTS   di'ʃuːts
Desdemona
  wife of Othello   DEZ-duh-MŌ-nuh   ˌdezdə'moːnə
Deseret News
  Salt Lake City newspaper   DEZ-uh-RET N(Y)O͞OZ   ˌdezə'ret 'n(j)uːz
Desha
  county, AR   duh-SHĀ   də'ʃeː
Desi
  pers. name (D. Arnaz)   DEZ-ē   'deziˑ
De Sica
  Vittorio, *Italian director*   di SĒ-kuh   di 'siːkə
Desiderius
  1. pers. name, German   DĀ-zē-DĀR-yus, -DĀ-rē-us   ˌdeːziːˈdeːrjus, -'deːriːus
  2. Latin   DES-i-DIR-ē-uhs   ˌdesi'diriːəs
Désiré, Désirée
  pers. name, French   dā-zē-RĀ   deːziːreː
Des Moines
  river, city, IA   di-MOIN   di'mɔin
Desmond
  pers. name   DEZ-muhnd   'dezmənd
de Soto
  Hernando, *Spanish explorer*   duh SŌT-ō   də 'soːtoː
Des Plaines
  river, city, IL   des PLĀNZ   des 'pleːnz
Dessalinienne, La
  see La Dessalinienne

Key (col. 2):   a: fad   ā: fade   ah: father   ar: Mary   aw: law   e: fed   ē: feed   er: merry   i: hid   ī: hide   ō: coat   ōō: boot
oi: boy   ow: now   u: put   uh: above   uhr: bird   ch: chop   ng: ring   sh: show   th: thick   <u>th</u>: this   zh: measure

Dessau
   city, Germany   DES-ow   'des,au

de Stijl
   Dutch school of art   duh STĪL   də 'staɪl

d'Estournelles de Constant
   Paul, *French diplomat (Nobel 1909)*   dā-tur-NEL duh kaw^n-STAH^n deːturnel də kɔ̃stɑ̃

Detlev
   1. pers. name   DET-luhf   'detləf
   2. German   DET-lef   'detlef

de Tocqueville
   see Tocqueville, de

Detroit
   city, MI; river, US & Canada   di-TROIT, DĒ-TROIT   di'trɔit, 'diː,trɔit

Dettifoss
   waterfall, Iceland   DET-ē-FAWS   'detiˑfɔːs

Deucalion
   son of Prometheus, husband of Pyrrha   d(y)o͞o-KĀL-yuhn   d(j)uːˈkeːljən

Deuel
   county, NE, SD   D(Y)O͞O-uhl   'd(j)uːəl

Deukmejian
   George, *governor, CA*   d(y)o͞ok-MĀ-j(ē-)uhn   d(j)uːkˈmeːdʒ(iː)ən

Deus
   Latin for 'God'   DĀ-us, DĒ-uhs   'deːus, 'diːəs

Deusdedit
   pope   DĒ-uhs-DED-uht, -DĒD-uht   ˌdiːəs'dedət, -'diːdət

Deuteronomy
   Old Testament book   D(Y)O͞OT-uh-RAHN-uh-mē   ˌd(j)uːtə'rɑnəmiˑ

Deutsch
   German (lang.)   DOICH   'dɔitʃ

Deutsche Mark
   German currency   DOICH(-uh)-MAHRK, DOICH(-uh)-MAHRK   ˌdɔitʃ(ə)'mɑ^{r}k, 'dɔitʃ(ə),mɑ^{r}k

Deutschland
   Germany   DOICH-LAHNT, Ⓢ DOICH-luhnd, DOICH-LAND   'dɔitʃ,lant, Ⓢ 'dɔitʃlənd, 'dɔitʃ,lænd

Deutschland über Alles
   German anthem   DOICH-lahnt ue-buhr AHL-uhs   'dɔitʃlaːnt yːbər 'ɑːləs

De Valera
   Eamon, *Irish political leader*   DEV-uh-LER-uh, DEV-uh-LIR-uh   ˌdevə'lerə, ˌdevə'lirə

Devanagari
   Sanskrit script   DĀ-vuh-NAHG-uh-rē   ˌdeːvə'nɑgəriˑ

Devane
   William, *US actor*   duh-VĀN   də'veːn

Devault
   Memorial Stadium, *Bristol, VA*   duh-VŌ   də'voː

Deventer
   city, Netherlands   DĀ-vuhn-tuhr   'deːvəntə^r

Devereaux Meadow
   Raleigh, NC   DEV-uh-RŌ MED-ō, MED-uh   'devə,roː 'medoː, 'medə

Devereux
   English family, earls of Essex   DEV-uh-RO͞OKS, -RŌO, -REKS, -ruh, -RŌ   'devə,ruːks, -,ruː, -,reks, -rə, -,roː

Foreign Sounds: ue: *Fr.* **rue**, *Ger.* **füllen**   uh(r): *Fr.* **boeuf**, *Ger.* **Höhle**   kh: *Ger.* i**ch**, *Scot.* lo**ch**   g̃: *Sp.* ami**g**o   v̲: *Sp.* ha**b**lar hl: *Welsh* **Ll**anelli.   CAPITALS: primary stress.   SMALL CAPS: secondary stress.   Ⓢ: U.S. pron.   Ⓔ: British pron.

Devito
Danny Michael, *US actor*   duh-VĒT-ō   də'viːt̯oː

Devon
1. *former county, England; river,*   DEV-uhn   'devən
   Scotland
2. *river, Nottinghamshire,*   DĒ-vuhn   'diːvən
   England
3. *pers. name*   DEV-uhn, di-VAHN *(D. White)*   'devən, di'vɑn *(D. White)*

Devonian
geologic period   di-VŌ-nē-uhn   di'voːniːən

Devonshire
county, England   DEV-uhn-shuhr, -SHIR   'devənʃəʳ, -‚ʃiʳ

De Voto
Bernard A., *US historian*   di VŌT-ō   di 'voːt̯oː

De Vries
Peter, *US writer*   di VRĒS   di 'vriːs

DeVries
Dr. William C., *US surgeon*   duh-VRĒS, duh-VRĒZ   də'vriːs, də'vriːz

de Waart
Edo, *Dutch conductor*   duh VAHRT   də 'vɑːʳt

Dewar's
Scotch whiskey   D(Y)OO-uhrz, DURZ   'd(j)uːəʳz, 'duʳz

Dewey
John, *US educator;* Melvil, *US*   D(Y)OO-ē   'd(j)uːiˑ
   librarian; Thomas, *US*
   politician; pers. name

Dewhurst
Colleen, *Canadian actress*   D(Y)OO-HUHRST   'd(j)uː‚həʳst

Dexedrine
tdmk for an appetite suppressant   DEK-suh-DRĒN, -DRIN   'deksə‚driːn, -‚drin

Dexter
pers. name   DEKS-tuhr   'dekstəʳ

Dezhnev
cape, Russia   dezh-NYAWF, desh-NYAWF   deʒ'njɔːf, deʃ'njɔːf

Dezhneva, Mys [Dezhnev]
cape, Russia   MIS dezh-NYAW-vuh,   'mis deʒ'njɔːvə, deʃ'njɔːvə
   desh-NYAW-vuh

Dhahran
city, Saudi Arabia   dah-RAHN, DAH-huh-RAHN   da'rɑn, ‚dahə'rɑn

Dhaka
see Dacca

Dharma Bums, The
novel, Jack Kerouac   thuh DAHR-muh BUHMZ   ðə 'dɑʳmə 'bəmz

Dhaulagiri
mtn., Nepal   DOW-luh-GIR-ē   ‚daulə'giriˑ

Dhelfoi [Delphi]
village, Greece   thel-FĒ   ðel'fiː

Dhu'l-Hijja
Islamic month   dool-HI-yah   duːl'hija

Dhu'l-Qa'dah
Islamic month   dool-KAH-dah   duːl'kadɑ

Diablo
Stadium, *Tempe, AZ*   dē-AB-lō, dī-AB-lō   diː'æbloː, dai'æbloː

Diablo Valley
College, *CA*   dē-AB-lō, dī-AB-lō   diː'æbloː, dai'æbloː

Key (col. 2):   a: fad   ā: fade   ah: father   ar: Mary   aw: law   e: fed   ē: feed   er: merry   i: hid   ī: hide   ō: coat   oo: boot
oi: boy   ow: now   u: put   uh: above   uhr: bird   ch: chop   ng: ring   sh: show   th: thick   th: this   zh: measure

Diaghilev
  Sergei Pavlovich, *Russian ballet*   DYAHG-yil-yif, Ⓢ dē-AHG-uh-LEF   'djɑːgjiljif, Ⓢ diː'ɑgə,lef
    producer

Diaguita
  S. American people   DĒ-uh-GĒT-uh   ,diːə'giːt̪ə

Dialo
  lang., Senegal   dē-AL-ō   diː'æloː

Diamantina
  river, Australia   DĪ-uh-muhn-TĒ-nuh   ,dɑiəmən'tiːnə

Diana
  Roman moon goddess and virgin   dī-AN-uh   dɑi'ænə
    huntress; pers. name

Diane
  pers. name   dī-AN, dē-AN   dɑi'æn, diː'æn

Dianetics
  movement founded by L. Ron   DĪ-uh-NET-iks   ,dɑiə'net̪iks
    Hubbard

Dianthus
  plant   dī-AN(T)-thuhs   dɑi'æn(t)θəs

Diarmaid, Diarmid
  1. pers. name   DUHR-muhd, DUHR-muht   'dəʳməd, 'dəʳmət
  2. Irish Gaelic   DYUHR-mit   'djərmit

Dias
  Bartholomeu, *Portuguese*   DĒ-AHSH   'diː,ɑːʃ
    navigator

Diaspora
  dispersal of people from their   dī-AS-p(uh-)ruh   dɑi'æsp(ə)rə
    homeland

Diaz
  1. pers. name   DĒ-ahs   'diːɑs
  2. Portuguese   DĒ-uhsh   'diːəʃ
  3. Spanish   DĒ-ahs, DĒ-ahth   'diːɑs, 'diːɑθ

Diaz de Vivar
  Rodrigo, *Spanish hero, aka* El Cid   DĒ-ahth <u>th</u>ā vē-VAHR   'diːɑθ ðeː βiː'βɑr

Dick
  pers. name   DIK   'dik

Dickcissel
  songbird   dik-SIS-uhl, DIK-SIS-uhl   dik'sisəl, 'dik,sisəl

Dickens
  Charles, *English novelist*   DIK-uhnz   'dikənz

Dickensian
  pert. to Dickens   di-KEN-zē-uhn   di'kenziːən

Dictys
  protector of Danae and Perseus   DIK-tuhs   'diktəs

Diderik
  pers. name, Dutch   DĒ-duh-RIK   'diːdə,rik

Diderot
  Denis, *French philosopher*   dē-DRŌ, Ⓢ DĒD-uh-RŌ   diːdroː, Ⓢ 'diːdə,roː

Didion
  Joan, *US writer*   DID-ē-uhn   'didiːən

Dido
  queen of Carthage   DĪD-ō   'dɑidoː

Didrikson
  pers. name (B. D. Zaharias)   DĒ-drik-suhn   'diːdriksən

Foreign Sounds: **ue**: *Fr.* **rue**, *Ger.* **füllen**   **uh(r)**: *Fr.* **boeuf**, *Ger.* **Höhle**   **<u>kh</u>**: *Ger.* **ich**, *Scot.* **loch**   **ğ**: *Sp.* ami**g**o   **v̱**: *Sp.* ha**b**lar
hl: *Welsh* **Ll**anelli.   CAPITALS: primary stress.   SMALL CAPS: secondary stress.   Ⓢ: U.S. pron.   Ⓛ: British pron.

Diederich
  pers. name, German DĒ-duh-RIKH 'diːdə,riç

Diedrich
  pers. name DĒ-drik 'diːdrik

Diefenbaker
  John, *Canadian statesman* DĒ-fuhn-BĀ-kuhr 'diːfən,beːkəʳ

Dieffenbachia
  plant DĒ-fuhn-BAK-ē-uh, ,diːfən'bækiːə, ,diːfən'bakiːə
    DĒ-fuhn-BAHK-ē-uh

Die Fledermaus
  operetta, J. Strauss dē FLĀD-uhr-MOWS diː 'fleːdəʳ,maus

Diego
  pers. name, Spanish DYĀ-ḡō, THYĀ-, Ⓢ dē-Ā-gō 'djeːɣoː, 'ðjeː-, Ⓢ diː'eːgoː

Diego Garcia
  island, Indian Ocean dē-Ā-gō gahr-SĒ-uh diː,eːgoː gaʳ'siːə

Diegueño
  N. American people DĒ-uh-GĀN-yō ,diːə'geːnjoː

Diekirch
  town, beer, Luxembourg DĒ-KIRKH, DĒ-KIRK 'diː,kiʳx, 'diː,kiʳk

Diels
  Otto, *German chemist (Nobel 1950)* DĒLS, DĒLZ 'diːls, 'diːlz

Diem
  see Ngo Dinh Diem

Dien Bien Phu
  Vietnam DYEN BYEN FŌŌ ,djen ,bjen 'fuː

Dieppe
  seaport, France DYEP, Ⓢ dē-EP djep, Ⓢ diː'ep

Diesel
  Rudolf, *German engineer* DĒ-zuhl 'diːzəl

Dies Irae
  Latin hymn DĒ-ās IR-ā, DĒ-āz, Ē-RĀ, IR-Ī, Ē-RĪ ,diːeːs 'ireː, ,diːeːz, 'iː,reː, 'ir,ai, 'iː,rai

Diest
  town, Belgium DĒST 'diːst

Die Stem van Suid-Afrika
  national anthem, South Africa dē SHTĀM fahn suid-AHF-rē-kuh diː 'ʃteːm faːn syid'aːfriːkə

Diet
  legislature (e.g. Japanese parliament) DĪ-uht 'daiət

Dieter
  pers. name DĒT-uhr 'diːʈəʳ

Dietrich
  1. *pers. name, French* dē-TRĒK diːtriːk
  2. *German* DĒ-trikh 'diːtriç

Die Walküre
  opera, R. Wagner DĒ vahl-KUE-ruh ,diː val'kyːrə

Dihevi
  lang., Maldives duh-HĀ-vē də'heːviˑ

Dijon
  city, France; mustard dē-ZHAWⁿ; dē-ZHAHN diː3ɔ̃; diː'3an

Dijonnaise
  mustard sauce dē-zhaw-NEZ diː3ɔːnez

Dillingham
  division, AK DIL-ing-HAM 'dilin,hæm

Key (col. 2): a: fad ā: fade ah: father ar: Mary aw: law e: fed ē: feed er: merry i: hid ī: hide ō: coat ōō: boot oi: boy ow: now u: put uh: above uhr: bird ch: chop ng: ring sh: show th: thick th: this zh: measure

Dillon
   pers. name — DIL-uhn — 'dilən

DiMaggio
   Joe, US baseball player — duh-MAJ-ē-ō, duh-MAJ-ō — də'mædʒiːˌoː, də'mædʒoː

Dimashq [Damascus]
   city, Syria — di-MAHSHK — di'maʃk

Dimitri
   1. pers. name — duh-MḖ-trē — də'miːtriˑ
   2. Mod. Greek — the̱-MḖ-trē — ðiː'miːtriː
   3. Russian — dim-YḖ-tri — d̡im'jiːtrij

Dimitrie
   pers. name, Romanian — di-MḖ-tri-(y)e — di'miːtri(j)e

Dimitrije
   pers. name, Serbo-Croatian — dē-MḖ-trē-ye — diː'miːtriːje

Dimitry
   1. pers. name, Romanian — di-MḖ-tri — di'miːtri
   2. Russian — dim-YḖ-tri — d̡im'jiːtrij

Dimoetes
   brother of Troezen — DĪ-muh-WḖT-ēz — ˌdaiməˈwiːt̡iːz

Dina
   pers. name — DḖ-nuh, DĪ-nuh — 'diːnə, 'dainə

Dinah
   pers. name — DĪ-nuh — 'dainə

Dinant
   resort, Belgium — dē-NAH^n — diːnã

Dinara Planina [Dinaric Alps]
   Alpine mtn. range — DḖ-nuh-rah plah-NḖ-nuh — 'diːnəra pla'niːnə

Dinaric
   Alps, Alpine mtn. range — duh-NAR-ik — də'nærik

Dinesen
   Isak, Danish writer — DḖ-nuh-suhn, DIN-uh-suhn — 'diːnəsən, 'dinəsən

Dingell
   John D., US politician — DING-guhl — 'diŋgəl

Ding Mao
   Chinese year (Hare) — DING MOW — 'diŋ 'mau

Dinka
   people, Africa — DING-kuh — 'diŋkə

Dinkelacker
   German beer — DING-kuh-LAHK-uhr — 'diŋkəˌlakə^r

Dinkelacker Weizenkrone
   German beer — DING-kuh-LAHK-uhr VĪT-suhn-KRŌ-nuh — 'diŋkəˌlakə^r 'vaitsənˌkroːnə

Dino
   pers. name — DḖ-nō — 'diːnoː

Dinwiddie
   county, VA — DIN-WID-ē, din-WID-ē — 'dinˌwidiˑ, din'widiˑ

Dio Cassius
   Roman historian — DĪ-ō KASH-(ē-)uhs, KAS-ē-uhs — ˌdaioː 'kæʃ(iː)əs, 'kæsiːəs

Dio Chrysostom
   Greek rhetorician — DĪ-Ō kris-AHS-tuhm — 'daiˌoː kris'astəm

Diocletian
   Roman emperor — DĪ-uh-KLḖ-shuhn — ˌdaiə'kliːʃən

Diodorus Siculus
   Greek historian — DĪ-uh-DAWR-uh(s) SIK-yuh-luhs — ˌdaiəˌdɔːrə(s) 'sikjələs

---

Foreign Sounds: **ue**: *Fr.* **rue**, *Ger.* **füllen** **uh(r)**: *Fr.* **boeuf**, *Ger.* **Höhle** <u>kh</u>: *Ger.* **ich**, *Scot.* **loch** ğ: *Sp.* **amigo** **y**: *Sp.* **hablar** **hl**: *Welsh* **Llanelli**. CAPITALS: primary stress. SMALL CAPS: secondary stress. Ⓢ: U.S. pron. Ⓛ: British pron.

Diogenes
  Greek philosopher   dī-AHJ-uh-NĒZ   dai'adʒə,niːz
Diomede
  islands, Bering Strait; English   DĪ-uh-MĒD   'daiə,miːd
  form of Diomedes
Diomedes
  name of two Greek heroes   DĪ-uh-MĒD-ēz   ,daiə'miːdiːz
Dion
  Laconian king; pers. name   DĒ-AHN, DĪ-AHN, -uhn   'diː,an, 'dai,an, -ən
Dione
  mother of Aphrodite; mother of   dī-Ō-nē, dē-Ō-nē   dai'oːniˑ, diː'oːniˑ
  Niobe & Pelops; satellite of
  Saturn
Dionisio
  1. pers. name, Italian   DĒ-ō-NĒZ-yō   ,diːoːˈniːzjoː
  2. Spanish   dyō-NĒS-yō, <u>th</u>yō-   djoːˈniːsjoː, ðjoː-
Dionne
  pers. name   dē-AHN   diːˈan
Dionysia
  festival of Dionysus   DĪ-uh-NISH-uh, -NIZ-ē-uh, -NIS-ē-uh   ,daiəˈniʃə, -ˈniziːə, -ˈnisiːə
Dionysiac
  pert. to Dionysia   DĪ-uh-NISH-ē-AK, -NIZ-ē-AK,   ,daiəˈniʃiː,æk, -ˈniziː,æk,
                                                    -NIS-ē-AK   -ˈnisiː,æk
Dionysian
  pert. to Dionysus   DĪ-uh-NISH-uhn, -NĪ-sē-uhn,   ,daiəˈniʃən, -ˈnaisiːən,
                                                    -NIZ-ē-uhn   -ˈniziːən
Dionysios
  pers. name, Mod. Greek   <u>th</u>yawn-YĒS-yaws   ðjoːnˈjiːsjoːs
Dionysius
  tyrants of Syracuse; pers. name   DĪ-uh-NISH-(ē-)uhs, -NIS-ē-uhs,   ,daiəˈniʃ(iː)əs, -ˈnisiːəs,
                                                    -NĪ-sē-uhs   -ˈnaisiːəs
Dionysus
  Greek god of wine   DĪ-uh-NĪ-suhs, DĪ-uh-NĒ-suhs   ,daiəˈnaisəs, ,daiəˈniːsəs
Dior
  Christian, fashion designer   dē-AWR, DĒ-AWR   diːˈɔːr, 'diː,ɔːr
Dioscorus
  pope   dī-AHS-kuh-ruhs   dai'askərəs
Dioscuri
  the twins Castor and Pollux   DĪ-uhs-KYUR-Ī, dī-AHS-kyuh-RĪ   ,daiəsˈkjur,ai, dai'askjə,rai
Diosdado
  pers. name, Spanish   dē-ōs-<u>THAHTH</u>-ō   diːoːsˈðaðoː
Dioula
  lang., Ivory Coast   dē-Ō-luh, dē-OO-luh   diːˈoːlə, diːˈuːlə
Diplodocus
  dinosaur   duh-PLAHD-uh-kuhs   də'pladəkəs
Dirac
  P. A. M., British physicist (Nobel   di-RAK   di'ræk
  1933)
Directoire
  French Directory   dē-rek-TWAHR   diːrektwaːr
Dirk
  1. pers. name   DUHRK   'dərk
  2. Dutch   DIRK   'dirk
Dis [Orcus]
  Roman god of the Underworld   DIS   'dis

Key (col. 2):   a: fad ā: fade ah: father ar: Mary aw: law e: fed ē: feed er: merry i: hid ī: hide ō: coat ōō: boot
oi: boy   ow: now   u: put   uh: above   uhr: bird   ch: chop   ng: ring   sh: show   th: thick   <u>th</u>: this   zh: measure

Disch-Falk
   Field, *ballpark, Austin, TX*   DISH-FAW(L)K   'dɪʃ'fɔː(l)k
Dísir
   Scandinavian goddesses of battle   DIS-ɪR   'dɪs,iʳ
   and fate
Disney
   Walt, *US cartoon pioneer*   DIZ-nē   'dɪzni·
Dis Pater
   Roman Father of Riches, ruler of   DIS PĀT-uhr, PAHT-uhr   ,dɪs 'peːʈəʳ, 'pɑʈəʳ
   the Underworld
Disraeli
   Benjamin, *English statesman*   diz-RÃ-lē   diz'reːli·
District of Columbia
   see Columbia
Dives
   Roman god of riches   DĪ-vēz   'dɑiviːz
Divinitatis Baccalaureus
   bachelor of divinity, D.B.   duh-VIN-uh-TÃT-uhs   də,vinə'teːʈəs ,bækə'loːriːəs,
        BAK-uh-LÕR-ē-uhs, -LAWR-ē-uhs   -'lɔːriːəs
Divinitatis Doctor
   doctor of divinity, D.D.   duh-VIN-uh-TÃT-uhs DAHK-TAWR   də,vinə'teːʈəs 'dɑk,tɔːʳ
Divinyls
   rock group   di-VĪ-nlz   di'vɑinl̩z
Diwali
   Hindu festival   DIV-AHL-ē   'div,ɑli·
Dixie
   nickname for the southeastern US;   DIK-sē   'diksi·
   pers. name
Dixieland
   nickname for the southeastern US   DIK-sē-LAND   'diksi·,lænd
Djakarta, Jakarta
   city, Indonesia   juh-KAHRT-uh   dʒə'kaʳʈə
Django
   pers. name   JANG-gō   'dʒæŋgoː
Djawa
   see Java
Djerma
   African people   dē-ER-muh, DYER-muh   diː'eʳmə, 'djeʳmə
Djhowtey [Thoth]
   Egyptian god of wisdom   JÕ-tā   'dʒoːteː
Djibouti, Jibuti
   republic, Africa   juh-BŌŌT-ē   dʒə'buːʈi·
Djilas
   Milovan, *Yugoslav politician*   JĒ-lahs   'dʒiːlɑs
Djoser
   Egyptian king   ZHŌ-suhr, ZÕ-suhr   'ʒoːsəʳ, 'zoːsəʳ
Dmitri
   pers. name   di-MĒ-trē   di'miːtriː
Dmitry
   pers. name, Russian   DMĒ-tri   'dmiːtrij
Dnepr [Dnieper]
   river, Europe   duhn-YEPR   dən'jepr
Dnepropetrovsk
   city, Ukraine   duhn-YEP-rō-pyuh-TRAWFSK,   dən,jeproːpjə'trɔːfsk,
        NEP-rō-puh-TRAWFSK   ,neproːpə'trɔːfsk

Foreign Sounds: ue: *Fr.* **rue**, *Ger.* **füllen**   uh(r): *Fr.* **b**oeuf, *Ger.* **Höhle**   kh: *Ger.* i**ch**, *Scot.* lo**ch**   g̃: *Sp.* ami**g**o   v̲: *Sp.* ha**b**lar
hl: *Welsh* **Ll**anelli.   CAPITALS: primary stress.   SMALL CAPS: secondary stress.   Ⓢ: U.S. pron.   Ⓛ: British pron.

Dnestr [Dniester]
   river, Ukraine   duh-NYESTR   də'njestr

Dnieper [Dnepr]
   river, Europe   NĒ-puhr, duh-NĒ-puhr   'niːpəʳ, də'niːpəʳ

Dniester [Dnestr]
   river, Ukraine   NĒ-stuhr, duh-NĒ-stuhr   'niːstəʳ, də'niːstəʳ

Doberman Pinscher
   dog breed   DŌ-buhr-muhn PIN-chuhr   ,doːbəʳmən 'pintʃəʳ

Dobie
   pers. name   DŌ-bē   'doːbiˑ

Dobrynin
   Anatoly, *Russian diplomat*   duh-BRIN-yin   də'brinjin

Doc
   short for doctor; pers. name   DAHK   'dak

Docetism
   early Christian doctrine   dō-SĒT-IZ-uhm, DŌ-suh-TIZ-uhm   doː'siːt,izəm, 'doːsə,tizəm

Doctorow
   E. L., *US writer*   DAHK-tuh-RŌ   'daktə,roː

Doctor Zhivago
   novel by Boris Pasternak   DAHK-tuhr zhuh-VAHG-ō   'daktər ʒə'vagoː

Dodecanese
   island group, Greece   dō-DEK-uh-NĒZ, -NĒS   doː'dekə,niːz, -,niːs

Dodgson
   Charles, *English writer, aka* Lewis   DAHJ-suhn, DAHD-suhn   'dadʒsən, 'dadsən
   Carroll

Dodie
   pers. name   DŌD-ē   'doːdiˑ

Dodoma
   city, Tanzania   DŌD-uh-muh, -MAH   'doːdəmə, -,ma

Dodona
   ancient town, Greece   duh-DŌ-nuh, dō-   də'doːnə, doː-

Dogon
   lang., people, Mali, Burkina Faso DŌ-GAHN   'doː,gan

Dogrib
   N. American people   DAW-GRIB, DAHG-RIB   'dɔː,grib, 'dag,rib

Doha
   city, Qatar   DŌ-huh   'doːhə

Doheny
   Edward L., Memorial Library, *Los*   duh-HĒ-nē   də'hiːniˑ
   Angeles, CA

Doherty
   Joseph, *Irish nationalist*   DAW(-uh)rt-ē, DAH(-uh)rt-ē,   'dɔː(ə)ʳʈiˑ, 'da(ə)ʳʈiˑ, 'dɔːʳəʈiˑ
                                    DAWR-uht-ē

Dohnányi
   Ernő, *Hungarian composer*   daw(<u>kh</u>)-NAHN-yē, dahk-NAHN-yē dɔː(x)'naːnjiˑ, dak'nanjiˑ

Dohnanyi, von
   Christoph, *German conductor;* FAWN daw<u>kh</u>-NAHN-yē   ,fɔːn dɔːx'nanjiˑ
   Ernst, *German composer*

Doisy
   E. A., *US biochemist (Nobel 1943)* DOI-zē   'dɔiziˑ

Dolby
   tdmk for an audio recording   DŌL-bē, DAHL-bē   'doːlbiˑ, 'dalbiˑ
   system

Dolius
   gardener for Odysseus   DŌ-lē-uhs, DŌL-yuhs   'doːliːəs, 'doːljəs

---

Key (col. 2):   a: fad ā: fade ah: father ar: Mary aw: law e: fed ē: feed er: merry i: hid ī: hide ō: coat ōō: boot
oi: boy ow: now u: put uh: above uhr: bird ch: chop ng: ring sh: show th: thick <u>th</u>: this zh: measure

Dolly
  pers. name — DAHL-ē — 'dɑli·

Dolomites
  Alpine mtn. range — DŌ-luh-MĪTS, DAHL-uh-MĪTS — 'doːlə,maits, 'dɑlə,maits

Dolomitiche, Alpi [Dolomites]
  Alpine mtn. range — AHL-pē DŌ-luh-mē-TĒ-kä — 'ɑlpiː ,doːləmiˈtiːkeː

Dolomiti [Dolomites]
  Alpine mtn. range — DŌ-luh-MĒ-tē — ,doːləˈmiːtiː

Dolon
  Trojan killed by Diomedes — DŌ-luhn, DŌ-LAHN — 'doːlən, 'doː,lan

Dolores
  pers. name — duh-LŌR-uhs, duh-LAWR-uhs — də'loːrəs, də'lɔːrəs

Dom
  pers. name — DAHM — 'dɑm

Domagk
  Gerhard, *German bacteriologist,* — DŌ-MAHK — 'doː,mɑk
    pathologist (Nobel 1939)

Domain Chandon
  winery, CA — dō-MÄN shan-DAHN, duh-MÄN, — doː,meːn ʃænˈdɑn, də,meːn,
    shan-DAWN — ʃænˈdɔːn

Domenici
  Pete V., *US politician* — duh-MEN-uh-chē, DAHM-uh-NĒ-chē — də'menətʃi·, ,dɑmə'niːtʃi·

Domenico
  1. pers. name — duh-MEN-i-kō — də'menikoː
  2. Italian — dō-MÄ-nē-kō — doːˈmeːniːkoː

Domesday Book, Doomsday Book
  11th c. survey of English land — DŌŌMZ-DĀ, DŌMZ-DĀ — 'duːmz,deː, 'doːmz,deː

Domfürsten
  German beer — DAWM-FUR-stuhn — 'dɔːm,fyʳstən

Dómhnall
  pers. name, Irish — T͟HUV-nuhl, T͟HUN-uhl, DAHN-uhl — 'ðuvnəl, 'ðunəl, 'danəl

Dominate
  term for Late Roman Empire — DAHM-uh-NĀT — 'dɑmə,neːt

Domingo
  1. Placido, Mexican tenor — duh-MING-gō, dō- — də'miŋgoː, doː-
  2. pers. name, Portuguese — dōō-MI(NG)-gōō, t͟hōō- — duːˈmĩː(ŋ)guː, ðuː-
  3. Spanish — dō-MING-gō, t͟hō- — doːˈmiŋgoː, ðoː-

Domingos
  pers. name, Portuguese — du-MĒ(NG)-gōōsh, t͟hōō-, -gōōs — duˈmiː(ŋ)guːʃ, ðuː-, -guːs

Dominic
  pers. name — DAHM-uh-nik — 'dɑmənik

Dominica
  island, West Indies — DAHM-uh-NĒ-kuh, duh-MIN-uh-kuh — ,dɑmə'niːkə, də'minəkə

Dominican
  pert. to Dominica *or* Dominican — DAHM-uh-NĒ-kuhn, — ,dɑmə'niːkən, də'minəkən
    Republic — duh-MIN-uh-kuhn

Dominican Republic
  republic, West Indies — duh-MIN-uh-kuhn — də'minəkən

Dominicus
  1. pers. name — duh-MIN-i-kuhs — də'minikəs
  2. German — dō-MĒ-nē-kus — doːˈmiːniːkus

Dominique
  pers. name, French — daw-mē-NĒK — dɔːmiːniːk

Dominus
  Latin for 'Lord'   DAHM-i-nuhs, DAHM-i-NUS,   'dɑminəs, 'dɑmi‚nus,
                                DŌ-mi-NŌŌS   'do:mi‚nu:s

Domitian
  Roman emperor   duh-MISH-uhn   də'miʃən

Domitius
  Roman name   duh-MISH-(ē-)uhs   də'miʃ(i:)əs

Dom Pérignon
  French monk; champagne   dawⁿ pā-rēn-YAWⁿ, Ⓢ DAHM   dɔ̃ pe:ri:njɔ̃, Ⓢ ‚dam
                                PER-uhn-YAWN   ‚perən'jɔ:n

Domrémy
  brandy   dawⁿ-rā-MĒ   dɔ̃re:mi:

Don
  river, Russia; river, Yorkshire;   DAHN   'dɑn
    river, Scotland; pers. name

Dona Ana
  county, NM   DŌN-yuh AN-uh   ‚do:njə 'ænə

Donagh
  pers. name, Irish   T̲H̲UHN-uh, DUHN-uh   'ðənə, 'dənə

Donal
  pers. name   T̲H̲ŌŌ-nuhl, DAHN-uhl   'ðu:nəl, 'dɑnəl

Donald
  pers. name   DAHN-ld   'dɑnḷd

Donatello
  Donato, *Italian sculptor*   DAHN-uh-TEL-ō   ‚dɑnə'telo:

Donatism
  Christian heresy   DAHN-uh-TIZ-uhm, DŌ-nuh-   'dɑnə‚tizəm, 'do:nə-

Donato
  pers. name, Italian   dō-NAH-tō   do:'nɑto:

Donatus
  pers. name   do-NAH-tus   do'nɑtus

Donau [Danube]
  river, Europe   DŌ-NOW   'do:‚nau

Donegal
  city, Irish Republic   DAHN-i-GAWL, DUHN-i-GAWL   ‚dɑni'gɔ:l, ‚dəni'gɔ:l

Donets
  river, Russia and Ukraine   duh-NETS, duh-NYETS   də'nets, də'njets

Donetsk
  city, Ukraine   duh-NETSK, duh-NYETSK   də'netsk, də'njetsk

Don Giovanni
  opera, Mozart   DAHN JŌ-VAHN-nē, DAHN   ‚dɑn dʒo:'vɑnni:, ‚dɑn
                          jē-uh-VAHN-ē   dʒi:ə'vɑni'

Dongting Hu, Tung-t'ing Hu
  lake, China   DUNG-TING HŌŌ   'duŋ'tiŋ 'hu:

Doniphan
  county, KA   DAHN-uh-fuhn   'dɑnəfən

Donizetti
  Gaetano, *Italian composer*   DŌN-uh(d)-ZET-ē,   ‚do:nə(d)'zeti', ‚dɑnə(d)'zeti'
                          DAHN-uh(d)-ZET-ē

Don Juan
  legendary Spanish lover   dahn (H)WAHN; *in Byron's poem*   dɑn '(h)wɑn; *in Byron's*
                          dahn JŌŌ-uhn   *poem* dɑn 'dʒu:ən

Donleavy
  J. P., *US writer*   dahn-LĒ-vē, DUHN-; DAHN-LĒ-vē,   dɑn'li:vi', ‚dən-; 'dɑn‚li:vi',
                          DUHN-   'dən-

Key (col. 2):   a: fad â: fade ah: father ar: Mary aw: law e: fed ē: feed er: merry i: hid ī: hide ō: coat ōō: boot
oi: boy ow: now u: put uh: above uhr: bird ch: chop ng: ring sh: show th: thick t̲h̲: this zh: measure

Donna
  pers. name DAHN-uh 'dɑnə
Donnall
  pers. name DAHN-l 'dɑnļ
Donne
  John, *English poet* DUHN 'dən
Donnelly, R.R.
  US printing co. DAHN-l-ē 'dɑnļiˑ
Donny
  pers. name DAHN-ē 'dɑniˑ
Donnybrook
  suburb, Dublin, Ireland DAHN-ē-BRUK 'dɑniˑ,bruk
Donovan
  Scottish rock singer; pers. name DAHN-uh-vuhn 'dɑnəvən
Don Pasquale
  opera, Donizetti DAWN pahs-KWAHL-ā, DAHN ˌdɔːn pɑsˈkwɑleː, ˌdɑn
Don Quixote
  novel, Cervantes dahng kē-<u>KH</u>Ō-tā, ⑤ DAHNG dɑŋ kiːˈxoːteː, ⑤ ˌdɑŋ
    kē-HŌT-ē, DAHN, kē-HŌ-TĀ; ⓔ kiːˈhoːtiˑ, ˌdɑn, kiːˈhoːˌteː,
    dahng KWIK-suht, dahn ⓔ dɑŋ ˈkwiksət, dɑn
Donus
  pope DŌ-nuhs 'doːnəs
Doomsday Book
  see Domesday Book
Doonesbury
  Trudeau comic strip DO͞ONZ-BER-ē, DO͞ONZ-b(uh-)rē 'duːnz,beriˑ, 'duːnzb(ə)riˑ
Door
  county, WI DŌR, DAWR 'doːʳ, 'dɔːʳ
Doppelgänger
  ghostly double DAW-puhl-GENG-uhr, 'dɔːpəl,geŋəʳ, 'dəbəl,gæŋəʳ
    DUHB-uhl-GANG-uhr
Doppler effect
  change in frequency relative to DAHP-luhr 'dɑpləʳ
    speed
Dora
  pers. name DŌR-uh, DAWR-uh 'doːrə, 'dɔːrə
Dorado
  constellation duh-RAHD-ō də'rɑdoː
Dorcas
  pers. name DAWR-kuhs 'dɔːʳkəs
Dorchester
  borough, England; county, MD, DAWR-chuh-stuhr, DAWR-CHES-tuhr 'dɔːʳtʃəstəʳ, 'dɔːʳ,tʃestəʳ
    SC
Dordogne
  dept., France dawr-DAWN-yuh dɔːrdɔːɲ
Dordrecht
  city, Netherlands DAWR-DRE<u>KH</u>T 'dɔːʳ,drext
Dordt
  College, *IA* DAWRT 'dɔːʳt
Doré
  Gustave, *French illustrator* daw-RĀ dɔːreː
Doreen
  pers. name daw-RĒN, duh-; DŌR-ēn, DAWR- dɔː'riːn, də-; 'doːriːn, 'dɔːr-
Doria
  Andrea, *Italian political leader* DAWR-yah, ⑤ DŌR-ē-uh, DAWR-ē-uh 'dɔːrjɑ, ⑤ 'doːriːə, 'dɔːriːə

Foreign Sounds: **ue**: *Fr.* **rue**, *Ger.* f**ü**llen **uh**(r): *Fr.* b**oeu**f, *Ger.* H**öh**le <u>kh</u>: *Ger.* i**ch**, *Scot.* lo**ch** g̅: *Sp.* ami**g**o v̲: *Sp.* ha**b**lar
hl: *Welsh* L**l**anelli. CAPITALS: primary stress. SMALL CAPS: secondary stress. ⑤: U.S. pron. ⓔ: British pron.

Dorian
  musical mode; pers. name — DŌR-ē-uhn, DAWR-ē-uhn — 'dɔːriːən, 'dɔːriːən
Dorians
  ancient invaders of Greece — DŌR-ē-uhnz, DAWR- — 'dɔːriːənz, 'dɔːr-
Doric order
  architectural order — DAWR-ik, DAHR-ik — 'dɔːrik, 'dɑrik
Doris
  mother of Nereids; pers. name — DAWR-uhs, DAHR-uhs — 'dɔːrəs, 'dɑrəs
Dorothea
  pers. name — DAWR-uh-THĒ-uh, DAHR- — ,dɔːrə'θiːə, ,dɑr-
Dorothée
  pers. name, French — daw-raw-TÃ — dɔːrɔːteː
Dorothy
  pers. name — DAWR-uh-thē, DAHR- — 'dɔːrəθiˑ, 'dɑr-
Dorrigo
  town, Australia — DAHR-i-gō, DAWR-i-gō — 'dɑrigoː, 'dɔːrigoː
Dorset
  county, England — DAWR-suht — 'dɔːʳsət
Dort
  city, Netherlands — DAWRT — 'dɔːʳt
Dortmund
  city, Germany — DAWRT-MUNT, ⑤ DAWRT-muhnd — 'dɔːʳt,munt, ⑤ 'dɔːʳtmənd
Dortmunder-Actien Alt
  German beer — DAWRT-MUN-duhr-AHK-tē-uhn AHLT — 'dɔːʳt,mundəʳ,aktiːən 'alt
Dortmunder Kronen
  German beer — DAWRT-MUN-duhr KRŌ-nuhn — 'dɔːʳt,mundəʳ 'kroːnən
Dorus
  mythical ancestor of the Dorians — DŌR-uhs, DAWR-uhs — 'doːrəs, 'dɔːrəs
Dorval
  airport, Montreal — dawr-VAHL — dɔːr'vɑˑl
DOS
  disk operating system (computer software) — DAHS — 'dɑs
Dos Equis (XX)
  Mexican beer — dōs EK-ēs — doːs 'ekiːs
Dos Passos
  John, US novelist — duhs PAS-uhs — dəs 'pæsəs
Dostoyevsky
  Feodor, Russian author — duhs-TUH-YĀF-ski, ⑤ DAHS-tuh-YEF-skē, DAHS-tuh-YEV-skē — dəs,tə'jeːfskij, ⑤ ,dɑstə'jefskiˑ, ,dɑstə'jevskiˑ
Dothan
  city, AL — DŌ-thuhn — 'doːθən
Dottie
  pers. name — DAHT-ē — 'dɑţiˑ
Douai, Douay
  city, France — DWE, du-Ā — dwe, du'eː
Douala
  city, Cameroon — du-AHL-uh — du'ɑlə
Douay Bible
  English translation of Vulgate — doo-Ā, DOO-Ā — du'ˑeː, 'duːˌeː
Doubleday
  Abner, reputed US inventor of baseball — DUHB-uhl-DĀ — 'dəbəlˌdeː

Key (col. 2):   a: fad   ā: fade   ah: father   ar: Mary   aw: law   e: fed   ē: feed   er: merry   i: hid   ī: hide   ō: coat   o͞o: boot
oi: boy   ow: now   u: put   uh: above   uhr: bird   ch: chop   ng: ring   sh: show   th: thick   <u>th</u>: this   zh: measure

Doubs		
river, France	DO͞O	'duː
Doug		
pers. name	DUHG	'dəg
Dougal		
pers. name	DO͞O-guhl	'duːgəl
Douglas		
pers. name, pl. name	DUHG-luhs	'dəgləs
Douglas-Home		
Alexander, *British statesman*	DUHG-luhs-HYO͞OM, [$] *also* DUHG-luhs-YO͞OM	ˌdəgləs'hjuːm, [$] *also* ˌdəgləs'juːm
Doukhobors, Dukhobors		
Russian religious sect	DO͞O-kuh-BAWRZ	'duːkəˌbɔː^{r}z
Dover		
DE, NH, NJ, OH; city, England	DŌ-vuhr	'doːvə^{r}
Dow		
lake, Africa; US chemical co.	DOW	'dɑu
Dow-Jones		
US financial publisher	DOW-JŌNZ	ˌdɑu'dʒoːnz
Dowland		
John, *English lutenist, composer*	DOW-luhnd, DŌ-luhnd	'dɑulənd, 'doːlənd
Downing		
college, Cambridge Univ.	DOWN-ing	'dɑuniŋ
D'Oyly Carte		
English light opera company	DOI-lē KAHRT	ˌdɔiliˑ 'kɑ^{r}t
Draco		
Athenian lawgiver; constellation	DRĀ-kō	'dreːkoː
Draconian		
pert. to Draco	drā-KŌ-nē-uhn, druh-KŌ-nē-uhn	dreː'koːniːən, drə'koːniːən
Draconids		
meteor shower	druh-KAHN-idz, druh-KŌ-nidz	drə'kɑnidz, drə'koːnidz
Dracula		
novel, Bram Stoker	DRAK-yuh-luh	'drækjələ
Drakensberg [Quathlamba]		
mtn. range, S. Africa	DRAHK-uhnz-BUHRG	'drɑkənzˌbə^{r}g
Dramamine		
tdmk for a motion-sickness remedy	DRAM-uh-MĒN, DRAM-uh-min	'dræməˌmiːn, 'dræməmin
Drambuie		
liqueur	dram-B(Y)O͞O-ē	dræm'b(j)uːiˑ
Drammen		
port, Norway	DRAHM-uhn	'drɑmən
Drava		
river, Europe	DRAHV-uh	'drɑvə
Dravidian		
lang. family, India	druh-VID-ē-uhn	drə'vidiːən
Dravidic		
pert. to Dravidian	druh-VID-ik	drə'vidik
Dred		
pers. name	DRED	'dred
Dreher		
Italian beer	DRĀ-(h)uhr	'dreː(h)ə^{r}
Dreiser		
Theodore, *US author*	DRĪ-zuhr	'drɑizə^{r}

Dresden
  city, Germany   DREZ-duhn   'drezdən
Drew
  pers. name   DR$\overline{OO}$ 'druː
Drexel
  University, *PA*   DREK-suhl   'dreksəl
Dreyfus
  Alfred, *French army officer*   dre-FUES, Ⓢ DRĪ-fuhs, DRĀ-fuhs   drefyːs, Ⓢ 'draifəs, 'dreːfəs
Dreyfuss
  Richard Stephan, *US actor*   DRĪ-fuhs   'draifəs
Drogheda
  port, Republic of Ireland   DROI-uhd-uh, DRAW-uhd-uh, DROID-uh   'drɔiədə, 'drɔːədə, 'drɔidə
Druid
  one of a pre-Christian Celtic learned class   DR$\overline{OO}$-uhd, DR$\overline{OO}$-id   'druːəd, 'druːid
Druidism
  beliefs & tenets of the Druids   DR$\overline{OO}$-uhd-ɪz-uhm   'druːəd,izəm
Drury Lane
  English theatre   DRUR-ē LĀN   'druri 'leːn
Drusilla
  pers. name   dru-SIL-uh   dru'silə
Drusus
  Roman cognomen   DR$\overline{OO}$-suhs   'druːsəs
Druze
  religion   DR$\overline{OO}$Z   'druːz
Dryas
  son of Ares   DRĪ-uhs   'draiəs
Dryden
  John, *English poet*   DRĪD-n   'draidn̩
Dryer
  Fred, *US actor, football player*   DRĪ(-uh)r   'drai(ə)ʳ
Dryope
  companion to the Hamadryad nymphs   DRĪ-uh-pē   'draiəpiˑ
Dryops
  father of Dryope   DRĪ-AHPS   'drai,aps
Drysdale
  pers. name   DRĪZ-DĀL   'draiz,deːl
Dry Tortugas
  islands, FL   DRĪ tawr-T$\overline{OO}$-guhz   ,drai tɔːʳ'tuːgəz
Duala
  lang., people, Africa   d(y)$\overline{oo}$-AHL-uh   d(j)uː'alə
Duane
  pers. name   DWĀN, duh-WĀN   'dweːn, də'weːn
Duarte
  1. pers. name, Portuguese   DWAHR-tuh, <u>TH</u>WAHR-, -tā   'dwaːrtə, 'ðwaːr-, -teː
  2. Spanish   DWAHR-tā   'dwarteː
Dubai, Dubayy
  city, United Arab Emirates   duh-BĪ, d$\overline{oo}$-BĪ   də'bai, du'ʳbai
Dubbo
  city, Australia   DUHB-ō   'dəboː
Dubcek
  Alexander, *Czech politician*   D$\overline{OO}$B-CHEK   'duːb,tʃek

---

Key (col. 2):   a: fa**d**   ā: fa**de**   ah: f**a**ther   ar: M**ar**y   aw: l**aw**   e: f**e**d   ē: f**ee**d   er: m**er**ry   i: h**i**d   ī: h**i**de   ō: c**oa**t $\overline{oo}$: b**oo**t
oi: b**oy**   ow: n**ow**   u: p**u**t   uh: **a**bove   uhr: b**ir**d   ch: **ch**op   ng: ri**ng**   sh: **sh**ow   th: **th**ick   <u>th</u>: **th**is   zh: mea**s**ure

Dublin		
Ireland	DUHB-lin	'dəblin
Dubliner		
resident of Dublin	DUHB-luh-nuhr	'dəblənəʳ
Duboeuf, Georges		
wine shipper	ZHAWRZH due-BUH(R)F	ʒɔːrʒ dybœf
Du Bois		
William Edward Burghardt, US educator	d(y)o͞o BOIS	d(j)uˑ 'bɔis
Dubois		
county, IN	du-BOIS, DO͞O-BOIS	du'bɔis, 'duːˌbɔis
Dubonnet		
aperitif	D(Y)O͞O-buh-NĀ	ˌd(j)uːbə'neː
DuBose		
pers. name	d(y)o͞o-BŌZ	d(j)uː'boːz
Dubrovnik		
city, Croatia	DO͞O-BRAWV-nik, du-BRAWV-nik	'duːˌbrɔːvnik, du'brɔːvnik
Dubuffet		
Jean, French artist	due-bue-FE	dyːbyːfe
Dubuque		
city, Iowa	duh-BYO͞OK	də'bjuːk
Ducati		
Italian motorcycle co.	d(y)o͞o-KAHT-ē	d(j)uː'kɑtiˑ
Duchamp		
Marcel, French painter	due-SHAHⁿ	dyːʃɑ̃
Duchesne		
river, county, UT	du-SHĀN	du'ʃeːn
Duchin		
Peter, US entertainer	DO͞O-chuhn	'duːtʃən
Ducommun		
Elie, Swiss journalist (Nobel 1902)	due-kaw-MUHⁿ	dyːkɔmœ̃ː
Dudevant		
Amandine, married name of George Sand	dued(-uh)-VAHⁿ	dyːd(ə)vɑ̃
Dudley		
pers. name	DUHD-lē	'dədliˑ
Duesenberg		
US automobile	DO͞O-zuhn-BUHRG	'duːzənˌbəʳg
Duesseldorf		
airport, Düsseldorf	DUES-uhl-DAWRF, Ⓢ D(Y)O͞OS-uhl-DAWRF	'dysəlˌdɔːʳf, Ⓢ 'd(j)uːsəlˌdɔːʳf
Dufy		
Raoul, French artist	due-FĒ	dyːfiː
Duisburg		
city, Germany	D(Y)O͞OS-BURG, D(Y)O͞OZ-BURG, -BUHRG	'd(j)uːsˌbuʳg, 'd(j)uːzˌbuʳg, -ˌbəʳg
Dukakis		
Michael S., US politician	do͞o-KAHK-uhs	du'kɑkəs
Dukas		
Paul, French composer	due-KAHS	dyːkɑːs
Duke		
title; pers. name	D(Y)O͞OK	'd(j)uːk
Dukeries, The		
region of Nottinghamshire, England	<u>th</u>uh D(Y)O͞O-kuh-rēz	ðə 'd(j)uːkəriˑz

---

Dukhobors
  see Doukhobors

Dulbecco
  Renato, *Italian-born US*   DUHL-BEK-ō   ˌdəl'bekoː
    molecular biologist (Nobel
    1975)

Dulcinea
  beloved of Don Quixote   DUHL-suh-NĒ-uh, DUHL-suh-NĀ-uh   ˌdəlsə'niːə, ˌdəlsə'neːə

Dullea
  Keir, *US entertainer*   duh-LĀ   də'leː

Dulles
  John Foster, *US statesman*   DUHL-uhs   'dələs

Duluth
  city, MN   duh-LŌŌTH   də'luːθ

Duma
  Russian council   DŌŌ-muh, DŌŌ-MAH   'duːmə, 'duːˌma

Dumas
  1. *pers. name*   d(y)ōō-MAH, D(Y)ŌŌ-MAH   d(j)uː'ma, 'd(j)uːˌma
  2. *French*   due-MAH   dyːma

Du Maurier
  Dame Daphne, *English author*   d(y)u-MAWR-ē-Ā, d(y)u-MAHR-ē-Ā   d(j)u'mɔːriːˌeː, d(j)u'mariːˌeː

Dumbo
  Disney animated character   DUHM-bō   'dəmboː

Dum Dum
  city, India   DUHM DUHM   'dəm ˌdəm

Dumfries and Galloway
  region, Scotland   DUHM-FRĒS uhn(d) GAL-uh-WĀ   ˌdəm'friːs ən(d) 'gæləˌweː

Dunant
  J. H., *Swiss philanthropist (Nobel*   due-NAH[n]   dyːnã
    1901)

Dunaway
  Faye, *US actress*   DUHN-uh-WĀ   'dənəˌweː

Dunbar
  John, *Scottish poet*   DUHN-BAHR, DUHM-BAHR   'dənˌba[r], 'dəmˌba[r]

Duncan
  pers. name   DUHNG-kuhn   'dəŋkən

Dunciad
  poem, A. Pope   DUHN-sē-AD   'dənsiːˌæd

Dundalk
  1. *seaport, Ireland*   DUHN-DAWK, DUHN-DAWLK   ˌdən'dɔːk, ˌdən'dɔːlk
  2. *city, MD*   DUHN-DAWK   'dənˌdɔːk

Dundee
  city, Scotland   DUHN-DĒ   ˌdən'diː

Dunedin
  city, FL; city, New Zealand   DUH-NĒD-n   ˌdə'niːdn̩

Dungeness
  National Wildlife Refuge, WA;   DUHN-juh-NES, DUHNJ-NES,   ˌdəndʒə'nes, ˌdəndʒ'nes,
    headland, England   DUHN-juh-NES   'dəndʒəˌnes

Dungog
  town, Australia   duhn-GAHG, duhn-GAWG   dən'gag, dən'gɔːg

Dunhill
  tobacco products co.   DUHN-HIL   'dənˌhil

Dunkerque, Dunkirk
  seaport, France   duh[n]-KERK, Ⓢ DUHN-KUHRK,   dœ̃kerk, Ⓢ 'dənˌkə[r]k,
             DUHN-KUHRK   ˌdən'kə[r]k

Key (col. 2):   a: fad   ā: fade   ah: father   ar: Mary   aw: law   e: fed   ē: feed   er: merry   i: hid   ī: hide   ō: coat   ōō: boot
oi: boy   ow: now   u: put   uh: above   uhr: bird   ch: chop   ng: ring   sh: show   th: thick   th̲: this   zh: measure

Dunkirk
   city, IN, NY   DUHN-KUHRK   'dən,kəʳk

Dun Laoghaire [Dunleary]
   port of Dublin, Ireland   DO͞ON LER-uh, DUHN LER-uh, DUHN   ,duːn 'lerə, ,dən 'lerə, ,dən
                              LIR-ē   'liriˑ

Dunleary [Dun Laoghaire]
   port of Dublin, Ireland   DUHN-LIR-ē   ,dən'liriˑ

Dunlop
   1. tire co.   DUHN-LAHP   'dən,lɑp
   2. British family name   DUHN-LAHP   ,dən'lɑp

Dunnachie
   pers. name   DUHN-uh-<u>kh</u>ē, -kē   'dənəçiˑ, -kiˑ

Dunsinane
   1. fortified hill, Scotland   DUHN-SIN-uhn   ,dən'sinən
   2. in Macbeth, *Shakespeare*   DUHN-suh-NĀN, DUHN-suh-NĀN   ,dənsə'neːn, 'dənsə,neːn

Duns Scotus
   John, *Scottish philosopher*   DUHN SKŌT-uhs   ,dən 'skoːʈəs

Dunstan
   pers. name   DUHN-stuhn   'dənstən

Du Page
   College, *county, IL*   d(y)o͞o PĀJ   d(j)uː 'peːdʒ

Dupin
   Amandine, *maiden name of A.*   due-PEⁿ   dyːpẽ
      Dudevant (pseudonym George
      Sand); Chevalier Auguste,
      fictional detective of E. A. Poe

Duplin
   county, NC   D(Y)O͞O-pluhn   'd(j)uːplən

Du Pont, Dupont
   US chemical co.; Pierre Samuel IV,   d(y)o͞o-PAHNT, D(Y)O͞O-PAHNT   d(j)uˑ'pɑnt, 'd(j)uː,pɑnt
      US politician

duPont de Nemours
   E. I., *US chemical co. founder*   d(y)o͞o-PAHNT dā nā-MAWRZ   d(j)uˑ,pɑnt deː neː'mɔːʳz

Dupree
   J. J. M. M. W. G., *character in*   d(y)u-PRĒ   d(j)u'priː
      Milne poem

Duquesne
   University, *PA*   d(y)u-KĀN   d(j)u'keːn

Duracell
   tdmk for batteries   D(Y)UR-uh-SEL   'd(j)urə,sel

Dura-Europus
   ancient Seleucid city   D(Y)UR-uh-yu-RŌ-puhs   ,d(j)urəju'roːpəs

Duran Duran
   rock group   d(y)u-RAN d(y)u-RAN   d(j)u'ræn d(j)u'ræn

Durango
   state, Mexico   d(y)u-RANG-gō   d(j)u'ræŋgoː

Durant
   Will *and* Ariel, *US historians*   d(y)u-RANT   d(j)u'rænt

Duras
   French dukedom   due-RAHS   dyːrɑːs

Durban
   seaport, South Africa   DUHR-buhn   'dəʳbən

Durenberger
   David Ferdinand, *US politician*   D(Y)UR-uhn-BUHR-guhr   'd(j)urən,bəʳgəʳ

Dürer
  Albrecht, *German painter/*   DUER-uhr, ⑤ D(Y)UR-uhr   'dyːrə^r, ⑤ 'd(j)urə^r
  engraver

Durga Puja
  Indian festival   DUR-guh POO-juh   'durgə 'puːdʒə

Durham
  US pl. name; city, county,   DUHR-uhm, DUH-ruhm, DUR-uhm   'dər-əm, 'də-rəm, 'durəm
  England

Durian
  tasty, foul-smelling fruit   D(Y)UR-ē-uhn, D(Y)UR-ē-AHN   'd(j)uriːən, 'd(j)uriːˌɑn

Dürkheim
  1. Emile, *French sociologist*   duer-KEM   dyːrkem
  2. town, Germany   DURK-HĪM, ⑤ DIRK-HĪM, DUHRK-   'dy^rk,haim, ⑤ 'di^rk,haim,
                                                'də^rk-

Durning
  Charles, *US actor*   DUHR-ning   'də^rniŋ

Durocher
  Leo, *US baseball player, manager*   duh-RŌ-shuhr   də'roːʃə^r

Durrell
  Lawrence, Gerald, *English authors*   DUH-ruhl, DUR-uhl, DUHR-uhl   'də-rəl, 'durəl, 'dər-əl

Dürrenmatt
  Friedrich, *Swiss writer*   DUER-uhn-MAHT   'dyrənˌmɑt

Dur-Sharrukin
  ancient Assyrian city   DUR-shah-ROO-kuhn   ˌdu^rʃa'ruːkən

Duse
  Eleanora, *Italian actress*   DOO-zā   'duːzeː

Dushanbe
  city, Tadzhikistan   d(y)oo-SHAHM-buh,   d(j)uː'ʃambə,
         ⑤ d(y)oo-SHAHM-bā   ⑤ d(j)uː'ʃambeː

Dussault
  Nancy, *US entertainer*   D(Y)OO-SAWLT   'd(j)uːˌsɔlt

Dussehra
  Indian festival   DUHS-uh-ruh   'dəsərə

Düsseldorf
  city, Germany   DUES-uhl-DAWRF,   'dysəlˌdɔː^rf,
         ⑤ D(Y)OO-suhl-DAWRF   ⑤ 'd(j)uːsəlˌdɔː^rf

Dustin
  pers. name   DUHS-tuhn   'dəstən

Dutchess
  county, NY   DUHCH-uhs   'dətʃəs

Dutch [Netherlandic]
  lang., Netherlands, Belgium,   DUHCH   'dətʃ
  Suriname, Antilles

Dutoit
  Charles, *Swiss conductor*   due-TWAH, ⑤ duh-TWAH   dyːtwɑː, ⑤ də'twa

Dutra
  Eurico, *president, Brazil*   DOO-trah   'duːtrɑ

Du'uzu
  Babylonian month   du-OO-zoo   du'uːzuː

Duval
  county, FL, TX   doo-VAWL, duh-VAWL, -VAL   duː'vɔːl, də'vɔːl, -'væl

Duvalier
  Jean-Claude, *dictator, Haiti*   due-vahl-YĀ, ⑤ d(y)u-VAL-yā   dyːvɑːljeː, ⑤ d(j)u'væljeː

Duvall
  Robert, *US actor*   d(y)u-VAWL, d(y)u-VAL   d(j)u'vɔːl, d(j)u'væl

---

Key (col. 2):   a: fad   ā: fade   ah: father   ar: Mary   aw: law   e: fed   ē: feed   er: merry   i: hid   ī: hide   ō: coat   oo: boot
oi: boy   ow: now   u: put   uh: above   uhr: bird   ch: chop   ng: ring   sh: show   th: thick   <u>th</u>: this   zh: measure

Duve
    Christian de, *Belgian chemist,*   D$\overline{OO}$-vuh   'duːvə
    biologist (Nobel 1974)
Du Vigneaud
    Vincent, *US biochemist (Nobel*   d(y)$\overline{oo}$ V$\hat{E}$N-yō   d(j)uː 'viːnjoː
    1955)
Dvina
    river, gulf, Belorussia, Latvia,   DVY$\bar{E}$-nah, Ⓢ duh-V$\bar{E}$-nuh   'dvjiːnaː, Ⓢ də'viːnə
    Russia
Dvinsk
    city, Latvia   DVYINSK, Ⓢ duh-VINSK   'dvjiṇsk, Ⓢ də'vinsk
Dvorak
    1. Antonin, *Bohemian composer*   (duh-)-VAWR-ZHAHK   (də)'vɔːr,ʒɑk
    2. US pers. name; keyboard layout   (duh-)-VAWR-AK, (duh-)-VAWR-ZHAK   (də)'vɔːr,æk, (də)'vɔːr,ʒæk
Dwayne
    pers. name   DW$\bar{A}$N, duh-W$\bar{A}$N   'dweːn, də'weːn
Dwight
    pers. name   DW$\bar{I}$T, duh-W$\bar{I}$T   'dwait, də'wait
Dyak [Dayak]
    people, lang., Sarawak & Borneo   D$\bar{I}$-AK   'dai,æk
Dyckman Oval
    New York City site   D$\bar{I}$K-muhn $\bar{O}$-vuhl   'daikmən 'oːvəl
Dyersburg
    State Jr. College, *TN*   D$\bar{I}$(-uh)rz-BUHRG   'dai(ə)ʳz,bəʳg
Dyfed
    county, ancient kingdom, Wales   DUHV-ed, DUHV-id   'dəved, 'dəvid
Dylan
    1. pers. name   DIL-uhn   'dilən
    2. Welsh   DUHL-ahn, -uhn   'dəlɑːn, -ən
Dymo
    tdmk for a labeling machine   D$\bar{I}$-mō   'daimoː
D'Youville
    College, *NY*   DY$\overline{OO}$-VIL, DY$\overline{OO}$-vuhl   'djuː,vil, 'djuːvəl
Dysart
    Richard, *US actor*   D$\bar{I}$-SAHRT   'dai,sɑʳt
dysprosium
    element   dis-PR$\bar{O}$-zē-uhm,   dis'proːziːəm, dis'proːʒ(iː)əm
                     dis-PR$\bar{O}$-zh(ē-)uhm
Dyula
    lang., people, Ivory Coast,   dē-$\overline{OO}$-luh, DY$\overline{OO}$-luh   diːˈuːlə, 'djuːlə
    Burkina Faso, Ghana
Dzhugashvili
    Iosif, *orig. name of* Joseph Stalin   j$\overline{oo}$-guhsh-VY$\bar{E}$L-yē   dʒuːɡəʃ'vjiːlji'
Dzindza
    lang., Africa   (D)ZIN-(d)zuh   '(d)zin(d)zə
Dzongkha
    lang., Bhutan   DZAWNG-kuh   'dzɔːŋkə

Foreign Sounds: **ue:** *Fr.* **rue,** *Ger.* **füllen**   **uh(r):** *Fr.* **boeuf,** *Ger.* **Höhle**   <u>kh</u>: *Ger.* i**ch**, *Scot.* lo**ch**   ğ: *Sp.* ami**g**o   <u>v</u>: *Sp.* ha**b**lar
hl: *Welsh* **Llanelli.**   CAPITALS: primary stress.   SMALL CAPS: secondary stress.   Ⓢ: U.S. pron.   Ⓛ: British pron.

E

E. coli
  bacteria Escherichia coli　　　　Ē KŌ-LĪ　　　　　　　　　　　　ˌiː 'koːˌlai

Eadweard
  pers. name　　　　　　　　　ED-wuhrd　　　　　　　　　　　'edwəʳd

Eagleton
  Thomas Francis, *US politician*　Ē-guhl-tuhn　　　　　　　　　'iːgəltən

Ealing
  borough, England　　　　　Ē-ling　　　　　　　　　　　　'iːliŋ

Eames
  pers. name　　　　　　　　　ĀMZ, ĒMZ　　　　　　　　　　'eːmz, 'iːmz

Eamon, Eamonn
  pers. name　　　　　　　　　Ā-muhn　　　　　　　　　　　　'eːmən

Eannatum
  Sumerian king　　　　　　Ē-uh-NĀT-uhm, Ā-uh-NAHT-uhm　　ˌiːə'neːʈəm, ˌeːə'nɑʈəm

Earhart
  Amelia, *US aviator*　　　　ER-HAHRT, IR-HAHRT　　　　　'eʳˌhaʳt, 'iʳˌhaʳt

Earl, Earle
  pers. name　　　　　　　　　UHRL, UHR-uhl　　　　　　　　'əʳl, 'ərəl

Early
  Jubal, *American militarist*　UHR-lē　　　　　　　　　　　　'əʳliˑ

Earnest
  pers. name　　　　　　　　　UHR-nuhst　　　　　　　　　　'əʳnəst

Earp
  Wyatt, *US law officer*　　　UHRP　　　　　　　　　　　　　'əʳp

Eartha
  pers. name　　　　　　　　　UHR-thuh　　　　　　　　　　'əʳθə

Earvin
  pers. name　　　　　　　　　UHR-vin　　　　　　　　　　　'əʳvin

Eastcheap
  street, market area, London　ĒS(T)-CHĒP　　　　　　　　　'iːs(t)ˌtʃiːp

Eastern Nazarene
  College, *MA*　　　　　　Ē-stuhrn NAZ-uh-RĒN, NAZ-uh-RĒN　　'iːstəʳn ˌnæzə'riːn, 'næzəˌriːn

East Feliciana
  parish, LA　　　　　　ĒST fuh-LISH-ē-AN-uh　　　　　ˌiːst fəˌliʃiˑ'ænə

Easton
  Sheena, *pop singer*　　　Ē-stuhn　　　　　　　　　　　'iːstən

East Sussex
  county, England　　　　ēs(t) SUHS-iks　　　　　　　　iːs(t) 'səsiks

Eau Claire
  city, county, WI　　　　ō KLAR, ō KLER　　　　　　　oː 'klæʳ, oː 'kleʳ

Ebbets
  Field, *ballpark, Brooklyn, NY*　EB-uhts　　　　　　　　　'ebəts

Key (col. 2):　a: fad　ā: fade　ah: father　ar: Mary　aw: law　e: fed　ē: feed　er: merry　i: hid　ī: hide　ō: coat　ōō: boot
oi: boy　ow: now　u: put　uh: above　uhr: bird　ch: chop　ng: ring　sh: show　th: thick　th: this　zh: measure

Ebbw Vale
  town, Wales   EB-o͞o VĀL   ˌebuː ˈveɪl
EBCDIC
  extended binary coded decimal   EP-suh-DIK, EB-suh-DIK   ˈepsəˌdik, ˈebsəˌdik
    interchange code
Ebel
  jewelers   ā-BEL, Ā-buhl   eːˈbel, ˈeɪbəl
Eben
  pers. name   EB-uhn   ˈebən
Ebenezer
  1. pers. name   EB-uh-NĒ-zuhr   ˌebəˈniːzəʳ
  2. French   ā-bā-nā-ZER   eːbeːneːzer
Eberhard, -hardt
  pers. name, German   Ā-buhr-HAHRT   ˈeɪbəʳˌhaʳt
Eberhart
  Richard, US poet   EB-uhr-HAHRT   ˈebəʳˌhaʳt
Ebert
  Roger Joseph, US film critic   Ē-buhrt   ˈiːbəʳt
Ebionism
  Gnostic heresy   Ē-bē-uh-NIZ-uhm, EB-   ˈiːbiːəˌnizəm, ˈeb-
Ebony
  magazine; pers. name   EB-uh-nē   ˈebəniˑ
Eboracum
  Latin name for York, England   i-BAWR-uh-kuhm, i-BAHR-uh-kuhm,   iˈbɔːrəkəm, iˈbɑrəkəm,
     Ē-buh-RAHK-uhm   ˌiːbəˈrɑkəm
Ebro
  river, Spain   Ā-v̲rō   ˈeɪβroː
Écarté
  game   Ā-kahr-TĀ   ˌeɪkɑʳˈteɪ
Ecbatana
  capital city of Median dynasty   ek-BAT-n-uh   ekˈbætn̩ə
Ecce Homo
  depiction of Christ crowned with   EK-ā HŌ-mō, EK-ē   ˌekeˑ ˈhoːmoːˌ ˌekiˑ
    thorns
Eccles
  Sir John Carew, Australian   EK-uhlz   ˈekəlz
    neurophysiologist (Nobel 1963)
Ecclesia
  Athenian assembly   i-KLĀ-zh(ē-)uh, i-KLĒ-, -ZĒ-uh   iˈkleːʒ(iː)ə, iˈkliː-, -ziːə
Ecclesiastes
  Old Testament book   ik-LĒ-zē-AS-tēz, ek-   ikˌliːziˈæstiːz, ek-
Ecclesiasticus
  Old Testament book   ik-LĒ-zē-AS-ti-kuhs, ek-   ikˌliːziˈæstikəs, ek-
Echegaray y Eizaguirre
  José, Spanish dramatist,   ā-chā-ḡah-RĪ ē ā-thah-ḠWIR-ā,   eːtʃeːɣaˈrai iˑ eːθaˈɣwireːˌ
    mathematician (Nobel 1904)   ā-sah-ḠWIR-ā   eːsaˈɣwireː
Echidna
  half-female, half-serpent monster   i-KID-nuh   iˈkidnə
    in Greek mythology; spiny
    anteater
Echinoderms
  marine invertebrates   i-KĪ-nuh-DUHRMZ   iˈkainəˌdəʳmz
Echlin
  US motor vehicle parts co.   EK-luhn   ˈeklən

Foreign Sounds: ue: *Fr.* **rue**, *Ger.* **füllen**   uh(r): *Fr.* **boeuf**, *Ger.* **Höhle**   <u>kh</u>: *Ger.* i**ch**, *Scot.* lo**ch**   ḡ: *Sp.* ami**g**o   v̲: *Sp.* ha**b**lar
hl: *Welsh* **Ll**anelli.   CAPITALS: primary stress.   SMALL CAPS: secondary stress.   Ⓢ: U.S. pron.   Ⓔ: British pron.

Echo

  nymph rejected by Narcissus   EK-ō   'ekoː

Echuca

  town, Australia   uh-CHŌŌ-kuh   ə'tʃuːkə

Eck, Rusty

  Stadium, *Wichita, KS*   RUHS-tē EK   'rəsti· 'ek

Eckerd

  College, *FL*   EK-uhrd   'ekəʳd

Eckhard

  pers. name, German   EK-HAHRT   'ek‚haʳt

Eckstine

  Billy (William Clarence), *US singer*   EK-STĪN   'ek‚stɑin

Ecorse

  city, MI   Ē-KAWRS   'iː‚kɔːʳs

Ector

  pers. name   EK-tuhr   'ektəʳ

Ecuador

  republic, S. America   EK-wuh-DAWR, EK-wuh-DAWR   'ekwə‚dɔːʳ, ‚ekwə'dɔːʳ

Ecuadorean

  pert. to Ecuador   EK-wuh-DAWR-ē-uhn   ‚ekwə'dɔːriːən

Ed

  pers. name   ED   'ed

Edam

  town, Netherlands; cheese   ĒD-uhm, Ē-DAM   'iːdəm, 'iː‚dæm

Edda

  Icelandic saga   ED-uh   'edə

Eddie, Eddy

  pers. name   ED-ē   'edi·

Edelman

  Gerald M., *US biochemist (Nobel 1972);* Marian Wright, *children's rights activist*   ED-l-muhn   'edl̩mən

Eden

  paradise; US pl. name   ĒD-n   'iːdn̩

Edentata

  toothless mammals   Ē-DEN-TAHT-uh, Ē-DEN-TĂT-uh   ‚iː‚den'tɑțə, ‚iː‚den'teːțə

Eder

  German river   ĀD-uhr   'eːdəʳ

Ederle

  Gertrude, *sports personality*   ED-uhr-lē   'edəʳli·

Edgar

  pers. name   ED-guhr   'edgəʳ

Edgard

  pers. name, French   ed-GAHR   edgɑːr

Edgerton

  Harold E. "Doc", *US scientist, inventor*   EJ-uhr-tuhn   'edʒəʳtən

Edie

  pers. name   ĒD-ē   'iːdi·

Edina

  city, MN, MO   i-DĪ-nuh   i'dɑinə

Edinboro

  University, *PA*   ED-uhn-BUHR-uh   'edən‚bərə

Edinburg

  city, TX; town, IN   ED-n-BUHRG   'edn̩‚bəʳg

Key (col. 2):   a: fad   ā: fade   ah: father   ar: Mary   aw: law   e: fed   ē: feed   er: merry   i: hid   ī: hide   ō: coat   ōō: boot
oi: boy   ow: now   u: put   uh: above   uhr: bird   ch: chop   ng: ring   sh: show   th: thick   <u>th</u>: this   zh: measure

Edinburgh
   city, Scotland   ED-n-BUHR-uh, ED-n-BUH-ruh,   'edn̩ˌbər-ə, 'edn̩ˌbə-rə,
                       ED-n-b(uh-)ruh   'edn̩b(ə)rə
Edison
   Thomas, *US inventor*   ED-uh-suhn   'edəsən
Edith
   1. pers. name   Ē̄D-uhth   'iːdəθ
   2. French   ā-DĒT   eːdiːt
   3. German   Ā-dit   'eːdit
Edjo [Buto]
   Egyptian guardian goddess   EJ-ō   'edʒoː
Edmond
   1. pers. name   ED-muhnd   'edmənd
   2. French   ed-MAW^n edmɔ̃
Edmonton
   city, Alberta, Canada   ED-muhn-tuhn   'edməntən
Edmund
   1. pers. name   ED-muhnd   'edmənd
   2. German   ET-MUNT   'etˌmunt
Edna
   pers. name   ED-nuh   'ednə
Edo
   1. former name, Tokyo   ed-ō   edoː
   2. pers. name, Dutch   Ā-dō   'eːdoː
Edoardo
   pers. name, Italian   Ā-dō-AHR-dō   ˌeːdoː'ardoː
Edo [Bini]
   lang., people, Nigeria   ED-ō   'edoː
Édouard
   pers. name, French   ā-DWAHR   eːdwaːr
Edsel
   car make; pers. name   ED-suhl   'edsəl
Eduard
   1. pers. name, Czech   ED-u-ahrt   'eduaːrt
   2. Dutch   Ā-due-ahrt   'eːdyːart
   3. German   Ā-dōō-ahrt   'eːduːa^{r}t
   4. Russian   id-ōō-AHRT   iduː'aːrt
   5. Danish   ID-vahrd   'idvɑrd
Eduardo
   1. pers. name, Italian   ād-WAHR-dō   eːd'wardoː
   2. Portuguese   ēth-WAHR-dōō   iːð'waːrduː
   3. Spanish   ā-THWAHR-thō   eː'ðwardoː
Eduskunta
   Finnish parliament   ED-us-KUN-tah   'edusˌkuntɑ
Edvard
   1. pers. name, Danish   ID-VAHRD   'idˌvard
   2. Czech   ED-vahrt   'edvaːrt
   3. Norwegian   ED-VAHRT, ĀD-   'edˌvart, 'eːd-
   4. Swedish   ĀD-VAHRD   'eːdˌvaːrd
Edward
   1. pers. name   ED-wuhrd   'edwə^{r}d
   2. Danish   ID-VAHRD   'idˌvard
   3. German   ET-VAHRT   'etˌva^{r}t
   4. Polish   ED-VAHRT   'edˌvaːrt

Foreign Sounds: ue: *Fr.* **rue**, *Ger.* **füllen**   uh(r): *Fr.* **boeuf**, *Ger.* **Höhle**   <u>kh</u>: *Ger.* i**ch**, *Scot.* lo**ch**   ğ: *Sp.* ami**g**o   v: *Sp.* ha**b**lar
hl: *Welsh* **Ll**anelli.   CAPITALS: primary stress.   SMALL CAPS: secondary stress.   Ⓢ: U.S. pron.   Ⓑ: British pron.

Edwardian
   pert. to Edward VII of England   ed-WAWRD-ē-uhn, ed-WAHRD-ē-uhn   ed'wɔːʳdiːən, ed'waʳdiːən
Edwards
   Jonathan, *US clergyman;* Sir O.   ED-wuhrdz   'edwəʳdz
   M., *Welsh scholar; pers. name*
Edwin
   1. pers. name   ED-wuhn   'edwən
   2. German   ET-VĒN   'et,viːn
Edwina
   pers. name   ed-WĒ-nuh, -WIN-uh   ed'wiːnə, -'winə
Eemil
   pers. name, Finnish   EM-il   'emil
Eero
   pers. name, Finnish   ER-ō   'eroː
Eeyore
   character in Winnie the Pooh,   Ē-AWR   'iː,ɔːʳ
   Milne
Efes [Ephesus]
   ancient Ionian city, Asia Minor   EF-uhs   'efəs
Efi Deild
   Icelandic legislative body   EP-ē DĀLD *[sic]*   'epiː 'deːld *[sic]*
Efik
   lang., people, Nigeria   EF-ik   'efik
Efim
   pers. name   yi-FĒM   ji'fiːm
Efrem
   pers. name   EF-ruhm   'efrəm
Egas Moniz
   António, *Portuguese neurologist*   Ā-gahs mō-NĒZ   'eːgaːs moː'niːz
   (Nobel 1949)
Egbert
   pers. name   EG-buhrt   'egbəʳt
Eger
   German river   EG-er   'egeʳ
Egeria
   advisor to Numa Pompilius;   ē-JIR-ē-uh   i'dʒiriːə
   Roman goddess of springs
Egger
   Austrian beer   EG-uhr   'egəʳ
Eggleton
   Arthur C., *Canadian politician*   EG-uhl-tuhn   'egəltən
Eglantine
   bush   EG-luhn-TĪN, EG-luhn-TĒN   'eglən,tain, 'eglən,tiːn
Egmont
   1. Beethoven overture; pers. name   EG-MAHNT   'eg,mant
   2. German   EG-MAWNT   'eg,mɔːnt
Egon
   pers. name, Dutch   Ā-GAWN   'eː,gɔːn
Egri Bikavér
   wine   EG-rē BIK-uh-vuhr   'egriː 'bikəvəʳ
Egypt
   republic, Africa   Ē-juhpt, Ē-jipt   'iːdʒəpt, 'iːdʒipt
Egyptian
   pert. to Egypt   i-JIP-shuhn   i'dʒipʃən

Key (col. 2):   a: fad   ā: fade   ah: father   ar: Mary   aw: law   e: fed   ē: feed   er: merry   i: hid   ī: hide   ō: coat   o͞o: boot
oi: boy   ow: now   u: put   uh: above   uhr: bird   ch: chop   ng: ring   sh: show   th: thick   t͟h: this   zh: measure

Egyptology
  study of Egyptian antiquities   Ē-juhp-TAHL-uh-jē   ‚iːdʒəpˈtɑlədʒiˑ

Ehrenburg
  Ilya G., Russian writer   Ā-rin-BO͞ORKH, ⑤ ER-uhn-BURG, -BURK   ˈeːrin‚buːʳx, ⑤ ˈerən‚buʳg, -‚buʳk

Ehrlich
  Paul, German chemist, bacteriologist (Nobel 1908)   ER-li<u>kh</u>, ⑤ ER-lik   ˈeʳliç, ⑤ ˈeʳlik

Ehrlichman
  John Daniel, US author, former presidential assistant   ER-lik-muhn, UHR-lik-muhn   ˈeʳlikmən, ˈəʳlikmən

Eichmann
  Adolf, Nazi official   Ī<u>KH</u>-MAHN, ⑤ Ī<u>K</u>-muhn   ˈaiç‚man, ⑤ ˈaikmən

Eiffel Tower
  Paris, France   Ī-fuhl   ˈaifəl

Eigen
  Manfred, German chemist (Nobel 1967)   Ī-guhn   ˈaigən

Eiger
  mtn. range, Switzerland   Ī-guhr   ˈaigəʳ

Eigg
  island, Scotland   EG, ĀG   ˈeg, ˈeːg

Eijkman
  Christian, Dutch physician, pathologist (Nobel 1929)   ĀK-MAHN; ⑤ ĪK-muhn, ĀK-muhn   ˈeːk‚man; ⑤ ˈaikmən, ˈeːkmən

Eikenberry
  Jill, actress   Ī-kuhn-BER-ē   ˈaikən‚beriˑ

Eiki
  pers. name, Japanese   ā-kē   eːkiˑ

Eikonoklastes
  treatise, J. Milton   Ī-KAHN-uh-KLAS-tēz   ‚ai‚kanəˈklæstiːz

Eilat
  port, Israel   ā-LAHT   eːˈlɑt

Eileen
  pers. name   ī-LĒN, Ī-LĒN, Ā-LĒN   aiˈliːn, ˈai‚liːn, ˈeː‚liːn

Eilhard, -hardt
  pers. name, German   ĪL-HAHRT   ˈail‚haʳt

Einar
  1. pers. name, Danish   Ī-NAHR   ˈai‚nar
  2. Icelandic   Ā-NAHR   ˈeː‚nar
  3. Swedish   Ā-NAHR   ˈeː‚naːr

Einbecker Ur-Bock
  German beer   ĪN-BEK-uhr UR-BAHK   ˈain‚bekəʳ ˈuʳ‚bak

Eindhoven
  city, Netherlands   ĪNT-HŌ-vuhn, ĀNT-HŌ-vuhn   ˈaint‚hoːvən, ˈeːnt‚hoːvən

Einer
  pers. name   Ā-nuhr   ˈeːnər

Einstein
  Albert, German-born US physicist (Nobel 1921)   ĪN-STĪN, ĪN-SHTĪN   ˈain‚stain, ˈain‚ʃtain

einsteinium
  element   ĪN-STĪ-nē-uhm, īn-STĪ-nē-uhm   ˈain‚stainiːəm, ainˈstainiːəm

Einthoven
  Willem, Dutch physiologist (Nobel 1924)   ĀNT-HŌ-vuhn, ĪNT-HŌ-vuhn   ˈeːnt‚hoːvən, ˈaint‚hoːvən

---

Foreign Sounds: ue: *Fr.* **rue**, *Ger.* **füllen**   uh(r): *Fr.* **boeuf**, *Ger.* **Höhle**   <u>kh</u>: *Ger.* i**ch**, *Scot.* lo**ch**   ḡ: *Sp.* ami**g**o   <u>v</u>: *Sp.* ha**b**lar
hl: *Welsh* **Ll**anelli.   CAPITALS: primary stress.   SMALL CAPS: secondary stress.   ⑤: U.S. pron.   ⓩ: British pron.

Eire [Ireland]
　republic, Europe　　　　　　　　　AR-uh, ER-uh, Ī-ruh　　　　　　　'ærə, 'erə, 'airə
EISA
　extended industry standard　　　　Ā-suh　　　　　　　　　　　　　'eːsə
　　architecture
Eisaku
　pers. name, Japanese　　　　　　ā-sah-ko͞o　　　　　　　　　　　eːsakuː
Eisenhower
　Dwight D., 34th US president　　　ĪZ-n-HOW(-uh)r　　　　　　　　'aizn̩,hau(ə)ʳ
Eisteddfod
　Welsh arts festival　　　　　　　ī-STE*TH*-vuhd, -vawd　　　　ai'steðvəd, -vɔːd
Eisteddfodau
　pl. of Eisteddfod　　　　　　　　Ī-STE*TH*-VAWD-ī　　　　　　,ai,steð'vɔːd,ai
Ekoi
　lang., people, Cameroon, Nigeria　Ā-KOI　　　　　　　　　　　　'eː,kɔi
Ektachrome
　tdmk for a color film　　　　　　EK-tuh-KRŌM　　　　　　　　'ektə,kroːm
Eku Bavaria
　German beer　　　　　　　　　　Ā-ko͞o buh-VAHR-ē-uh　　　　'eːkuː bə'variːə
Eku Edelbock
　German beer　　　　　　　　　　Ā-ko͞o ĀD-l-BAHK　　　　　　'eːkuː 'eːdl̩,bak
Eku Hefe-Weizen
　German beer　　　　　　　　　　Ā-ko͞o HĀ-fuh-VĪT-suhn　　　'eːkuː 'heːfə,vaitsən
Eku Jubiläumsbier
　German beer　　　　　　　　　　Ā-ko͞o YO͞O-bil-OIMS-BIR　　'eːkuː 'juːbil,ɔims,biʳ
Eku Kulminator Urtyp Hell 28
　German beer　　　　　　　　　　Ā-ko͞o KUL-min-AH-TAWR UR-TUEP　'eːkuː 'kulmin,a,tɔʳ 'ur,tyːp
　　　　　　　　　　　　　　　　　HEL A*HKH*-tunt-SVAHNT-si*kh*　　'hel ,axtunt'svantsiç
Eku Weizen
　German beer　　　　　　　　　　Ā-ko͞o VĪT-suhn　　　　　　　'eːkuː 'vaitsən
Ela
　highest note; Guido's note　　　　ā-LAH　　　　　　　　　　　　eː'lɑ
Elagabalus
　Roman emperor　　　　　　　　　EL-uh-GAB-uh-luhs　　　　　　,elə'gæbələs
Elaine
　pers. name　　　　　　　　　　i-LĀN　　　　　　　　　　　　i'leːn
El Al
　Israeli airline co.　　　　　　　el AL, el AHL　　　　　　　　el 'æl, el 'ɑːl
El Alamein
　village, Egypt　　　　　　　　　EL AL-uh-MĀN　　　　　　　,el ,ælə'meːn
Elam
　ancient Near Eastern kingdom　　Ē-luhm　　　　　　　　　　　'iːləm
El-Amarna
　ancient Egyptian city　　　　　　EL-uh-MAHR-nuh　　　　　　,elə'mɑʳnə
Elamite
　lang., native of Elam　　　　　　Ē-luh-MĪT　　　　　　　　　'iːlə,mait
Elara
　satellite of Jupiter　　　　　　　uh-LAR-uh, uh-LER-uh, uh-LAHR-uh　ə'lærə, ə'lerə, ə'lɑrə
Elath
　ancient name of 'Aqaba; seaport,　Ā-LAHT, Ē-LATH　　　　　　'eː,lɑt, 'iː,læθ
　　Israel
Elba
　island, Mediterranean　　　　　　EL-buh　　　　　　　　　　　'elbə
Elbe
　river, Europe　　　　　　　　　EL-buh, ELB　　　　　　　　'elbə, 'elb

Key (col. 2):　a: fad　ā: fade　ah: father　ar: **M**ary　aw: law　e: fed　ē: feed　er: merry　i: hid　ī: hide　ō: coat　o͞o: boot
oi: boy　ow: now　u: put　uh: above　uhr: bird　ch: chop　ng: ring　sh: show　th: thick　th: this　zh: measure

Elberfeld
   city, Germany   EL-buhr-FELT   'elbər̩‚felt

Elbrus
   mtn., mtn. range, Caucasus Mts.   el-BRŌŌZ   el'bruːz

Elburz
   mtn. range, Iran   el-BURZ   el'buʳz

El Cajon
   city, CA   EL kuh-HŌN   ‚el kə'hoːn

El Camino
   College, CA   EL kuh-MĒ-nō   ‚el kə'miːnoː

Eldon
   pers. name   EL-duhn   'eldən

El Dorado
   1. city, AR, KS   EL duh-RĀD-ō   ‚el də'reːdoː
   2. county, CA   EL duh-RAHD-ō   ‚el də'rɑdoː
   3. city of gold   EL duh-RAHD-ō, EL duh-RĀD-ō   ‚el də'rɑdoː, ‚el də'reːdoː

Eldorado
   city, IL, TX   EL-duh-RĀD-ō   ‚eldə'reːdoː

El Dorado Springs
   city, NV   EL duh-RĀD-ō SPRINGZ   ‚el də‚reːdoː 'spriŋz

Eldridge
   pers. name   EL-drij   'eldridʒ

Elea
   ancient town, Italy   Ē-lē-uh   'iːliːə

Eleanor
   pers. name   EL-uh-nuhr, -NAWR, -NŌR   'elənəʳ, -‚nɔːʳ, -‚noːʳ

Eleanora
   pers. name, Italian   el-ā-uh-NŌR-uh   eleːə'noːrə

Eleaticism
   beliefs of the Eleatics   EL-ē-AT-uh-SIZ-uhm   ‚eliː'æʈə‚sizəm

Eleatics
   school of Greek philosophers   EL-ē-AT-iks   ‚eliː'æʈiks

Eleazar
   pers. name   EL-ē-Ā-zuhr   ‚eliː'eːzəʳ

Eleázar
   pers. name, Spanish   ā-lā-AH-sahr, -thahr   eːleː'ɑsɑr, -θɑr

Electra
   daughter of Agamemnon   uh-LEK-truh, ē-LEK-truh   ə'lektrə, i'lektrə

Electrolux
   tdmk for a vacuum cleaner   i-LEK-truh-LUHKS   i'lektrə‚ləks

Elen
   1. pers. name   EL-uhn   'elən
   2. Welsh   EL-en   'elen

Elena
   1. pers. name   EL-uh-nuh, i-LĀ-nuh, i-LĒ-nuh   'elənə, i'leːnə, i'liːnə
   2. German   Ā-lā-nah   'eːleːna
   3. Italian   EL-ā-NAH   'eleː‚na
   4. Romanian   e-LEN-ah   e'lena

Eleonora
   1. pers. name   EL-uh-NAWR-uh, -NŌR-uh   ‚elə'nɔːrə, -'noːrə
   2. Italian   Ā-lā-ō-NAWR-ah   ‚eːleːoː'nɔːrɑ

Eleonore
   pers. name, German   Ā-lā-ō-NŌ-ruh   ‚eːleːoː'noːrə

Éleonore
   pers. name, French   ā-lā-aw-NAWR   eːleːɔːnɔːr

Foreign Sounds: ue: *Fr.* **rue**, *Ger.* **füllen** uh(r): *Fr.* **boeuf**, *Ger.* **Höhle** <u>kh</u>: *Ger.* i<u>ch</u>, *Scot.* lo<u>ch</u> ḡ: *Sp.* ami**g**o <u>v</u>: *Sp.* ha**b**lar
hl: *Welsh* **Ll**anelli. CAPITALS: primary stress. SMALL CAPS: secondary stress. Ⓢ: U.S. pron. Ⓛ: British pron.

Eleusinian
  pert. to Eleusis   EL-yu-SIN-ē-uhn   ˌelju'siniːən
Eleusis [Elevsis]
  ancient Greek city   i-LŌŌ-suhs   i'luːsəs
Eleuthera
  island, Bahamas   i-LŌŌ-thuh-ruh   i'luːθərə
Eleutherios
  pers. name, Mod. Greek   EL-YEF-THER-yaws   ˌelˌjef'θerjɔːs
Eleutherius
  pope   EL-yuh-THIR-ē-uhs   ˌeljə'θiriːəs
Elevsis [Eleusis]
  town, Greece   EL-uhf-SĒS   ˌeləf'siːs
Elgar
  Sir Edward, *English composer*   EL-GAHR, EL-guhr   'elˌgɑ͏ʳ, 'elgəʳ
Elgin
  1. city, IL; US pers. name   EL-juhn   'eldʒən
  2. city, TX   EL-guhn   'elgən
  3. Marbles, Parthenon frieze;   EL-gin, EL-guhn   'elgin, 'elgən
     town, Scotland; British pers.
     name
El Greco
  see Greco, El
Eli
  1. pers. name   Ē-LĪ   'iːˌlai
  2. Welsh   Ā-lē   'eːliˑ
Elia
  1. pen name of Charles Lamb   Ē-lē-uh, ĒL-yuh   'iːliːə, 'iːljə
  2. pers. name (E. Kazan)   i-LĪ-uh   i'laiə
Elias
  1. pers. name   i-LĪ-uhs   i'laiəs
  2. Finnish   EL-YAHS   'elˌjɑːs
  3. German   ā-LĒ-ahs   eːˈliːɑs
  4. Swedish   el-Ē-ahs   el'iːɑːs
Elías
  pers. name, Spanish   ā-LĒ-ahs   eːˈliːɑs
Elie
  pers. name   Ē-lē   'iːliˑ
Élie
  pers. name, French   ā-LĒ   eːliː
Eliezer
  see Israel ben Eliezer
Elihu
  pers. name   EL-uh-HYŌŌ, i-LĪ-HYŌŌ   'eləˌhjuː, i'laiˌhjuː
Elijah
  Hebrew prophet; pers. name   i-LĪ-juh   i'laidʒə
Elinor
  pers. name   EL-uh-nuhr, -NAWR   'elənəʳ, -ˌnɔːʳ
Elion
  Gertrude B., *US chemist (Nobel*   EL-ē-uhn   'eliːən
     1988)
Eliot
  George (*pseudonym of* Mary Ann   EL-ē-uht, EL-yuht   'eliːət, 'eljət
     Evans), *English novelist;* T. S.
     US-born British poet (Nobel
     1948); pers. name

Key (col. 2): a: fad ā: fade ah: father ar: Mary aw: law e: fed ē: feed er: merry i: hid ī: hide ō: coat ōō: boot
oi: boy ow: now u: put uh: above uhr: bird ch: chop ng: ring sh: show th: thick th: this zh: measure

Eliotic
   "of Eliot" (esp. T. S. Eliot), adj.   EL-ē-AHT-ik   ,eli:'ɑʈik

Eliphalet
   pers. name   i-LIF-uh-luht, -LET   i'lifələt, -,let

Elis [Ilía]
   dept, Greece   Ē-luhs   'i:ləs

Elisabeth
   1. pers. name   i-LIZ-uh-buhth   i'lizəbəθ
   2. German   ā-LĒ-zah-BET   e:'li:za,bet
   3. Swedish   el-Ē-sah-BET   el'i:sa:,bet

Élisabeth
   pers. name, French   ā-lē-zah-BET   e:li:za:bet

Elisha
   pers. name   i-LĪ-shuh   i'laiʃə

Elisir d'Amore
   opera, Donizetti   Ā-lē-ZIR dah-MŌ-rā   ,e:li:'ziʳ da'mo:re:

Elixir Végétale
   Carthusian tonic   ā-lēk-SĒR vä-zhā-TAHL   e:li:ksi:r ve:ʒe:ta:l

Eliza
   1. pers. name   i-LĪ-zuh   i'laizə
   2. Polish   ā-LĒ-zah   e:'li:za:

Elizabeth
   1. pers. name   i-LIZ-uh-buhth   i'lizəbəθ
   2. Dutch   ā-LĒ-zah-BET   e:'li:za:,bet

Elizaveta
   pers. name, Russian   yuhl-YĒ-zah-VE-tah   jəl,ji:za:'veta:

Elke
   pers. name, German   EL-kuh   'elkə

Elkin
   town, NC; pers. name   EL-kuhn   'elkən

Elko
   county, NV; Indian reservation,   EL-kō   'elko:
     US

Ella
   pers. name   EL-uh   'elə

Ellás [Greece]
   country, Europe   e-LAHS   e'las

Ellen
   1. pers. name   EL-uhn   'elən
   2. Swedish   EL-luhn   'ellən

Ellery
   pers. name   EL-uh-rē   'eləri·

Ellesmere
   island, Canada; lake, port,   ELZ-MIR   'elz,miʳ
     England; lake, New Zealand;
     Chaucer manuscript

Ellesse
   US footwear co.   EL-ES-Ā   ,el,es'e:

Ellice
   island group, Pacific Ocean   EL-uhs   'eləs

Ellis
   Albert, *US psychologist, author,*   EL-uhs   'eləs
     educator; Havelock, *English*
     physician; island, NY; pers.
     name

Foreign Sounds: ue: *Fr.* **rue**, *Ger.* **füllen** uh(r): *Fr.* **boeuf**, *Ger.* **Höhle** <u>kh</u>: *Ger.* **ich**, *Scot.* **loch** ğ: *Sp.* **amigo** v̲: *Sp.* **hablar**
hl: *Welsh* **Llanelli**. CAPITALS: primary stress. SMALL CAPS: secondary stress. Ⓢ: U.S. pron. Ⓛ: British pron.

Ellison
 Harlan Jay, *US author;* Ralph, *US*   EL-uh-suhn   'eləsən
  author
Elman
 Mischa, *US violinist*   EL-muhn   'elmən
Elmer
 pers. name   EL-muhr   'elməʳ
Elmira
 city, NY   el-MĪ-ruh   el'mairə
Elmo
 Christian saint; pers. name   EL-mō   'elmoː
Elmore
 county, AL, ID   EL-MŌR, EL-MAWR   'el,moːʳ, 'el,mɔːʳ
El Niño
 current, Pacific Ocean   el NĒN-yō   el 'niːnjoː
Elohim
 Hebrew name for God   EL-ō-HĒM, el-Ō-HIM   ,eloː'hiːm, el'oː,him
Elohistic
 referring to God as Elohim   EL-uh-HIS-tik   ,elə'histik
Elon College
 town, college, NC   Ē-LAHN KAHL-ij   'iː,lɑn 'kɑlidʒ
El Paso
 city, TX   el PAS-ō   el 'pæsoː
Elpenor
 companion of Odysseus   el-PĒ-NAWR   el'piː,nɔːʳ
Elroy
 pers. name   EL-ROI   'el,rɔi
Elsa
 1. pers. name   EL-suh   'elsə
 2. French   el-SAH   elsɑː
 3. German   EL-zah   'elzɑ
 4. Swedish   EL-sah   'elsɑː
El Salvador
 country, Cen. America   el sahl-vah-<u>TH</u>AWR, Ⓢ el   el salvɑ'ðɔːr, Ⓢ el
          SAL-vuh-DAWR   'sælvə,dɔːʳ
Elsevier
 Dutch publishing co.   EL-suh-VIR   ,elsə'viʳ
Elsie
 pers. name   EL-sē   'elsiˑ
Elsinore
 city, lake, CA; seaport, Denmark   EL-suh-NŌR, -NAWR   'elsə,noːʳ, -,nɔːʳ
  (*setting for* Hamlet,
  Shakespeare) [Helsingør]
Elspeth
 pers. name   EL-SPETH, EL-spuhth   'el,speθ, 'elspəθ
Elton
 pers. name   ELT-n   'eltn̩
Éluard
 Paul, *pseudonym of* Eugène   āl-WAHR, Ⓢ Ā-luh-WAHR   eːlɥɑːr, Ⓢ ,eːlə'waʳ
  Grindel, *French poet*
Elul
 Jewish month   el-O͞OL, EL-ul   el'uːl, 'elul
Elvira
 pers. name   el-VĪ-ruh, -VIR-uh   el'vairə, -'virə

Key (col. 2):   a: fad   ā: fade   ah: father   ar: Mary   aw: law   e: fed   ē: feed   er: merry   i: hid   ī: hide   ō: coat   o͞o: boot
oi: boy   ow: now   u: put   uh: above   uhr: bird   ch: chop   ng: ring   sh: show   th: thick   <u>th</u>: this   zh: measure

Elvis
    pers. name   EL-vuhs, EL-vis   'elvəs, 'elvis

Elway
    John, *US football player*   EL-WĀ   'el,weɪ

Elwood
    pers. name   EL-wud   'elwud

Ely
    pers. name; pl. name   Ē-lē   'iːliˑ

Elyria
    city, OH   i-LIR-ē-uh   i'liriːə

Elysée
    palace, Paris, France   ā-lē-ZĀ   eːliːzeː

Elysian Fields
    Greek mythological realm of dead;   i-LIZH-uhn FĒL(D)Z, i-LĒ-zhuhn   i'liʒən 'fiːl(d)z, i'liːʒən
    ballpark, Hoboken, NJ; street,
    New Orleans

Elysium
    Elysian Fields   i-LIZH-uhm, i-LIZ-ē-uhm   i'liʒəm, i'liziːəm

Elytis
    Odysseus, *Greek poet (Nobel*   EL-ē-TĒS   'eliː,tiːs
    1979)

Emanuel
    1. pers. name   i-MAN-yuh(-wuh)l   i'mænjə(wə)l
    2. Czech   EM-AH-nuh-WEL   'em,ɑːnə,wel
    3. Danish   i-MAH-nuh-wuhl   i'mɑːnəwəl
    4. Dutch   ā-MAH-nue-EL   eː'mɑːnyː,el
    5. Finnish   e-MAH-nuh-WEL   e'mɑːnə,wel
    6. French   ā-mah-NWEL   eːmɑːnɥel
    7. German   ā-MAHN-o͞o-EL   eː'mɑnuː,el
    8. Swedish   e-MAH-nuh-wuhl   e'mɑnəwəl

Emanuele
    pers. name, Italian   Ā-mahn-WEL-e   ,eːmɑn'wele

Embo
    lang., Africa   EM-bō   'emboː

Embry-Riddle
    Aeronautical University, *FL*   EM-brē-RID-l   'embri'ridl̩

Emerich
    1. pers. name   EM-uh-rik   'emərik
    2. German   Ā-muh-RIKH   'eːmə,riç

Emerson
    Ralph Waldo, *US writer; pers.*   EM-uhr-suhn   'eməʳsən
    name

Emil
    1. pers. name   Ē-muhl, Ā-muhl, EM-uhl   'iːməl, 'eːməl, 'eməl
    2. Czech, Finnish, Hungarian   EM-il   'emil
    3. Danish   i-MĒL   i'miːl
    4. German   Ā-mēl   'eːmiːl
    5. Polish   EM-ēl   'emiːl
    6. Swedish   Ā-mil   'eːmil

Émil
    pers. name, French   ā-MĒL   eːmiːl

Emile
    pers. name   ā-MĒL, Ā-muhl   eː'miːl, 'eːməl

Foreign Sounds: ue: *Fr.* **rue**, *Ger.* **füllen**   uh(r): *Fr.* **boeuf**, *Ger.* **Höhle**   kh: *Ger.* **ich**, *Scot.* **loch**   ǥ: *Sp.* **amigo**   v̠: *Sp.* **hablar**
hl: *Welsh* **Llanelli.**   CAPITALS: primary stress.   SMALL CAPS: secondary stress.   Ⓢ: U.S. pron.   Ⓔ: British pron.

Émile
1. pers. name, Dutch	ā-MĒL	eː'miːl
2. French	ā-MĒL	eːmiːl

Emilia
1. pers. name	uh-MIL-ē-uh, -MIL-yuh	ə'miliːə, -'miljə
2. Spanish	ā-MĒL-yah	eː'miːlja

Emiliano
pers. name, Spanish	ā-mēl-YAHN-ō	eːmiːl'janoː

Emilia-Romagna
province, Italy	ā-MĒL-yuh-rō-MAHN-yuh	eː'miːljəroː'manjə

Emilio
pers. name, Italian, Spanish	ā-MĒL-yō	eː'miːljoː

Emily
pers. name	EM-uh-lē	'eməliˑ

Emirian
inhabitant of United Arab Emirates	i-MIR-ē-uhn	i'miriːən

Emlyn
pers. name	EM-luhn	'emlən

Emma
1. pers. name	EM-uh	'emə
2. Dutch	EM-ah	'emaː
3. French	em-MAH	emmaː
4. German	EM-ah	'emɑ
5. Italian	EM-mah	'emmɑ

Emmanuel
1. pers. name; college, GA, MA, Cambridge Univ.	i-MAN-yuh(-wuh)l	i'mænjə(wə)l
2. French	ā-mahn-WEL, em-ahn-	eːmaːnɥel, emaːn-
3. German	e-MAHN-ō̄ō-EL	e'manuˌel
4. Mod. Greek	EM-ahn-WEL	ˌeman'wel

Emmanuele
pers. name, Italian	ĀM-mahn-WEL-ā	ˌeːmmaːn'weleː

Emmaus
town, Palestine; borough, PA	e-MÃ-uhs	e'meːəs

Emmeline
pers. name	EM-uh-LĪN, EM-uh-LĒN	'eməˌlain, 'eməˌliːn

Emmentaler
original Swiss cheese	EM-uhn-TAHL-uhr	'emənˌtaləʳ

Emmet, Emmett
pers. name	EM-uht	'emət

Emmie
pers. name	EM-ē	'emiˑ

Emmy
television award; pers. name	EM-ē	'emiˑ

Emory
pers. name	EM-uh-rē	'eməriˑ

Empedocles
Greek philosopher	em-PED-uh-KLĒZ	em'pedəˌkliːz

Emporia
city, KS, VA	em-PŌR-ē-uh, em-PAWR-ē-uh	em'poːriːə, em'pɔːriːə

Empusa
cannibalistic she-monster in Greek myth	em-PYŌO-suh, em-PYŌO-zuh	em'pjuːsə, em'pjuːzə

Key (col. 2):   a: fad ā: fade ah: father ar: **Mary** aw: law e: fed ē: feed er: **merry** i: hid ī: hide ō: coat ōō: boot
oi: **boy** ow: **now** u: put uh: above uhr: bird ch: **chop** ng: **ring** sh: **show** th: **thick** th̲: **this** zh: measure

Ems
   river, Germany   EM(P)S, EMZ   'em(p)s, 'emz

Enberg
   Dick, *US sportscaster*   EN-BUHRG   'en,bəᵣg

Enceladus
   satellite of Saturn   en-SEL-uhd-uhs   en'selədəs

Encke's
   comet   ENG-kuhz   'eŋkəz

Encratism
   early Christian asceticism   ENG-kruh-TIZ-uhm, EN-   'eŋkrə,tizəm, 'en-

Enders
   J. F., *US microbiologist (Nobel 1954)*   END-uhrz   'endəᵣz

Endicott
   College, *MA*   EN-di-kuht, EN-di-KAHT   'endikət, 'endi,kɑt

Endor
   town, Israel   EN-DAWR   'en,dɔːᵣ

Endymion
   shepherd loved by Selene in Greek mythology; poem, Keats; pers. name   en-DIM-ē-uhn   en'dimiːən

Enesco
   Georges, *French form of* Gheorge Enescu   ā-nes-KÔ, Ⓢ uh-NES-kō   eːneskoː, Ⓢ ə'neskoː

Enescu
   Gheorghe, *Romanian composer/ conductor*   uh-NES-ko͞o   ə'neskuː

Enewetak
   atoll, Pacific   EN-uh-WĒ-TAHK, e-NĒ-wuh-TAHK   ,enə'wiː,tɑk, e'niːwə,tɑk

Enfant, L'
   see L'Enfant

Enfield
   town, CT, NH, NC; borough, England   EN-FĒLD   'en,fiːld

Engelbert
   1. pers. name   ENG-guhl-buhrt   'eŋgəlbəᵣt
   2. Finnish   ENG-el-BERT   'eŋel,bert
   3. German   ENG-uhl-BERT   'eŋəl,beᵣt

Engels
   Friedrich, *German political theorist*   ENG-uhls, ENG-(g)uhlz   'eŋəls, 'eŋ(g)əlz

England
   kingdom, Gt. Britain   ING-gluhnd, ING-luhnd   'iŋglənd, 'iŋlənd

Engle, L'
   see L'Engle

English
   lang., Europe, N. America   ING-glish, ING-lish   'iŋgliʃ, 'iŋliʃ

English Channel [La Manche]
   strait between England & France   ING-glish CHAN-l, ING-lish   ,iŋgliʃ 'tʃænl̩, ,iŋliʃ

Enguerrand
   pers. name, French   ahⁿ-guh-RAHⁿ   ãgərã

ENIAC
   vacuum-tube computer   Ē-nē-AK, EN-ē-AK   'iːniː,æk, 'eniː,æk

---

Foreign Sounds: ue: *Fr.* **rue**, *Ger.* füllen   uh(r): *Fr.* **boeuf**, *Ger.* **Höhle**   kh: *Ger.* i**ch**, *Scot.* lo**ch**   ğ: *Sp.* ami**g**o   v̲: *Sp.* ha**b**lar   hl: *Welsh* **Ll**anelli.   CAPITALS: primary stress.   SMALL CAPS: secondary stress.   Ⓢ: U.S. pron.   Ⓑ: British pron.

Enid
   1. city, OK; pers. name   Ē-nuhd   'iːnəd
   2. Welsh   EN-id   'enid
Enlil
   supreme Sumerian god   EN-LIL   'en,lil
Enna
   Sicilian city   EN-uh   'enə
Ennius
   Roman poet   EN-ē-uhs   'eniːəs
Eno
   Brian, British composer, musician Ē-nō   'iːnoː
Enoch
   pers. name   Ē-nuhk, Ē-nik, Ē-NAHK   'iːnək, 'iːnik, 'iː,nɑk
Enos
   Seth's son; pers. name   Ē-nuhs   'iːnəs
Enrico
   pers. name, Italian   en-RĒ-kō   en'riːkoː
Enrique
   pers. name, Spanish   ān-RĒ-kā   eˑn'riːkeː
Enriquez
   Rene, US actor   en-RĒ-kez   en'riːkez
Ensenada
   city, Mexico; town, Argentina en-se-NAH<u>TH</u>-ah,   ense'naðα, ⑤ ,en(t)se'nɑdə
                       ⑤ EN(T)-se-NAHD-uh
Ensi
   title of Sumerian city governor EN-sē   'ensiˑ
Entebbe
   town, Uganda   en-TEB-uh, en-TEB-ē   en'tebə, en'tebiˑ
Entre-Deux-Mers
   wine   ahⁿ-truh-duh(r)-MER   âtrədœːmer
Enyo
   Greek goddess of war   en-Ē-ō, en-Ī-ō   en'iːoː, en'aioː
Eocene
   geologic epoch   Ē-uh-SĒN   'iːə,siːn
Eoin
   pers. name, Irish   YŌ(-uh)n, Ō-uhn   'joː(ə)n, 'oːən
Eolian
   pert. to rock or sand carried by ē-Ō-lē-uhn   iː'oːliːən
     wind
Eolithic
   geologic period   Ē-uh-LITH-ik   ,iːə'liθik
Eolus
   mtn., CO   ē-Ō-luhs   iː'oːləs
Eos
   Greek dawn goddess   Ē-AHS   'iː,as
Epaminondas
   Theban general   i-PAM-uh-NAHN-duhs   i,pæmə'nɑndəs
Epcot
   Disneyworld attraction   EP-KAHT   'ep,kat
Epeius
   builder of the Trojan horse   e-PĀ-(y)uhs   e'peː(j)əs
Épernay
   wine   ā-per-NE   eːperne
Ephesians
   New Testament book   i-FĒ-zhuhnz   i'fiːʒənz

Key (col. 2):   a: fad ā: fade ah: father ar: Mary aw: law e: fed ē: feed er: merry i: hid ī: hide ō: coat o͞o: boot
oi: boy ow: now u: put uh: above uhr: bird ch: chop ng: ring sh: show th: thick <u>th</u>: this zh: measure

Ephesus [Efes]
  ancient Ionian city, Asia Minor   EF-uh-suhs   'efəsəs
Ephialtes
  Athenian statesman   EF-ē-AL-TĒZ   ˌefiːˈæl,tiːz
Ephor
  Spartan official   Ē-fuhr, Ē-FAWR   'iːfərᵣ, 'iːˌfɔːrᵣ
Ephraim
  pers. name   Ē-frā-uhm, -frē-uhm; EF-ruhm   'iːfreːəm, -friːəm; 'efrəm
Ephron
  Nora *and* Delia, *US writers*   EF-ruhn   'efrən
Epictetus
  Greek philosopher; Greek potter &   EP-ik-TĒT-uhs   ˌepikˈtiːtəs
  painter
Epicureanism
  philosophy of Epicurus   EP-i-kyu-RĒ-uh-NIZ-uhm,   ˌepikjuˈriːəˌnizəm,
        EP-i-KYUR-ē-uh-NIZ-uhm   ˌepiˈkjuriːəˌnizəm
Epicurus
  Greek philosopher   EP-i-KYUR-uhs   ˌepiˈkjurəs
Epidaurus
  ancient Greek seaport   EP-uh-DAWR-uhs   ˌepəˈdɔːrəs
Epigoni
  sons of Seven against Thebes   i-PIG-uh-NĪ, i-PIG-uh-nē   iˈpigəˌnai, iˈpigəniˑ
Epimetheus
  brother of Atlas & Prometheus;   EP-uh-MĒ-thē-uhs   ˌepəˈmiːθiːəs
  satellite of Saturn
Epinomis
  dialogue of Plato   EP-uh-NŌ-muhs   ˌepəˈnoːməs
Epione
  wife of Asclepius   uh-PĪ-uh-nē   əˈpaiəniˑ
Epiphany
  Christian season   i-PIF-uh-nē   iˈpifəniˑ
Epirus [Ipiros]
  region, Greece   i-PĪ-ruhs   iˈpairəs
Episcopalianism
  religion   i-PIS-kuh-PĀ-lē-uh-NIZ-uhm   iˌpiskəˈpeːliːəˌnizəm
Epithalamion
  bridal poem, E. Spenser   EP-uh-thuh-LĀ-mē-uhn   ˌepəθəˈleːmiːən
Epopeus
  king of Sicyon and Corinth   i-PŌ-pē-uhs   iˈpoːpiːəs
EPROM
  computer memory chip   Ē-PRAHM   'iːˌpram
Epsom
  town, England   EP-suhm   'epsəm
Epson
  computer co.   EP-suhn   'epsən
Epstein-Barr
  mononucleosis virus   EP-STĪN-BAHR   ˌepˌstainˈbarᵣ
Equator
  great circle at latitude 0°   i-KWĀT-uhr, Ē-KWĀT-uhr   iˈkweːtərᵣ, 'iːˌkweːtərᵣ
Equatorial Guinea
  republic, Africa   Ē-kwuh-TŌR-ē-uhl GIN-ē, EK-wuh-,   ˌiːkwəˌtoːriːəl 'giniˑ, ˌekwə-,
        -TAWR-ē-uhl   -ˌtoːriːəl
Equatorial Guinean
  pert. to Equatorial Guinea   Ē-kwuh-TŌR-ē-uhl GIN-ē-uhn,   ˌiːkwəˌtoːriːəl 'giniːən,
        EK-wuh-, -TAWR-ē-uhl   ˌekwə-, -ˌtoːriːəl

Foreign Sounds: ue: *Fr.* **rue**, *Ger.* füllen uh(r): *Fr.* **boeuf**, *Ger.* Höhle <u>kh</u>: *Ger.* i**ch**, *Scot.* lo**ch** ḡ: *Sp.* ami**g**o <u>v</u>: *Sp.* ha**b**lar
hl: *Welsh* **Ll**anelli. CAPITALS: primary stress. SMALL CAPS: secondary stress. ⓈⰁ: U.S. pron. ⓌⰁ: British pron.

Equites
   Roman social class   EK-wuh-TĀS, EK-wuh-TĒZ   'ekwə,teːs, 'ekwə,tiːz

Equuleus
   constellation   e-KW‾OO‾-lē-uhs   e'kwuːliːəs

Er
   myth, Plato's Republic   ER, UHR   'eʳ, 'əʳ

Erasistratus
   Greek physician   ER-uh-SIS-truht-uhs   ,erə'sistrəţəs

Érasme
   pers. name, French   ā-RAHSM   eːraːsm

Erasmo
   pers. name, Italian   ā-RAHZ-mō   eː'razmoː

Erasmus
   1. pers. name   i-RAZ-muhs   i'ræzməs
   2. Danish   i-RAHS-mus   i'rasmus
   3. German   ā-RAHS-mus   eː'rasmus

Erastus
   pers. name   i-RAS-tuhs   i'ræstəs

Erath
   county, TX   Ē-RATH   'iː,ræθ

Erato
   1. muse of lyric poetry   ER-uh-TŌ   'erə,toː
   2. street, New Orleans   i-RAHT-ō, i-RAT-ō   i'raţoː, i'ræţoː

Eratosthenes
   Greek scientist   ER-uh-TAHS-thuh-NĒZ   ,erə'tasθə,niːz

Erawan
   oil & gas field, Gulf of Thailand   ER-uh-WAHN, ER-uh-WAHN   'erə,wan, ,erə'wan

erbium
   element   UHR-bē-uhm   'əʳbiːəm

Erda
   Norse earth goddess   ERD-uh   'eʳdə

Erdenet
   city, Mongolia   ERD-n-ET   ,eʳdn̩'et

Erebus
   personification of the infernal   ER-uh-buhs   'erəbəs
     shades in Greek mythology;
     James Ross's ship; volcano,
     Antarctica

Erechtheum
   temple, Athens   ER-uhk-THĒ-uhm, ER-EK-   ,erək'θiːəm, ,er,ek-

Erechtheus
   king of Athens   uh-REK-thē-uhs, uh-REK-TH(Y)‾OO‾S   ə'rekθiːəs, ə'rek,θ(j)uːs

Eretria
   ancient Greek city   e-RĒ-trē-uh   e'riːtriːə

Erewhon
   utopian work, S. Butler   ER-uh-(H)WAHN   'erə,(h)wan

Erfurt
   city, Germany   ER-FURT, ER-fuhrt   'eʳ,fuʳt, 'eʳfəʳt

Erginus
   king of the Minyans; Argonaut   er-JĪ-nuhs   eʳ'dʒainəs

Erhard
   Ludwig, *German politician; pers.*   ER-HAHRT, ĀR-HAHRT   'eʳ,haʳt, 'eːʳ,haʳt
    name

Key (col. 2):   a: fad   ā: fade   ah: father   ar: Mary   aw: law   e: fed   ē: feed   er: merry   i: hid   ī: hide   ō: coat   ‾oo‾: boot
oi: boy   ow: now   u: put   uh: above   uhr: bird   ch: chop   ng: ring   sh: show   th: thick   <u>th</u>: this   zh: measure

Eric
  1. pers. name   ER-ik   'erik
  2. Danish   IR-ēk   'iriːk
  3. Norwegian   Ā-rēk   'eːriːk
  4. Swedish   Ā-rik   'eːrik

Erica
  pers. name   ER-i-kuh   'erikə

Erich
  pers. name, German   Ā-ri<u>kh</u>   'eːriç

Erichthonius
  king of Athens   ER-ik-THŌ-nē-uhs   ˌerik'θoːniːəs

Ericsson
  Leif, *Norse explorer*   ER-ik-suhn   'eriksən

Eridanus
  legendary river into which   i-RID-n-uhs   i'ridn̩əs
    Phaethon fell; constellation

Eridu
  Sumerian seaport   ER-uh-D͞OO   'erəˌduː

Erie
  lake; city, PA; canal, NY; county,   IR-ē   'iriˑ
    NY, OH, PA; North American
    people

Erigone
  mother of Staphylus; daughter of   i-RIG-uh-nē   i'rigəniˑ
    Aegisthus and Clytemnestra

Erik
  1. pers. name   ER-ik   'erik
  2. Danish   IR-ēk   'iriːk
  3. French   ā-RĒK   eːriːk
  4. German, Swedish   Ā-rik   'eːrik
  5. Norwegian   Ā-rēk   'eːriːk

Erika
  1. pers. name   ER-i-kuh   'erikə
  2. German   Ā-rē-KAH   'eːriːˌkɑ

Erin
  Ireland; pers. name   AR-uhn, ER-uhn   'ærən, 'erən

Erinyes
  the Eumenides or Furies   i-RIN-ē-ĒZ   i'riniːˌiːz

Erinys
  singular of Erinyes   i-RIN-uhs, i-RĪ-nuhs   i'rinəs, i'rainəs

Eriphyle
  sister of Adrastus & wife of   ER-uh-FĪ-lē   ˌerə'failiˑ
    Amphiaraus

Eris
  Greek goddess, personification of   ER-uhs, IR-uhs   'erəs, 'irəs
    strife

Eritrea
  region, Ethiopia   ER-uh-TRĒ-uh, ER-uh-TRĀ-uh   ˌerə'triːə, ˌerə'treːə

Erlander
  Tage, *Swedish statesman*   er-LAHN-duhr   eʳ'lɑndəʳ

Erlanger
  Joseph, *US physiologist (Nobel*   UHR-LANG-uhr   'əʳˌlæŋəʳ
    1944)

Erlau
  Hungarian commune   ER-LOW   'eʳˌlɑu

Foreign Sounds: ue: *Fr.* **rue**, *Ger.* **füllen**   uh(r): *Fr.* **boeuf**, *Ger.* **Höhle**   <u>kh</u>: *Ger.* **ich**, *Scot.* **loch**   ğ: *Sp.* **amigo**   <u>v</u>: *Sp.* **hablar**
hl: *Welsh* **Llanelli.**   CAPITALS: primary stress.   SMALL CAPS: secondary stress.   Ⓢ: U.S. pron.   Ⓑ: British pron.

Erle
   pers. name   UHRL, UHR-uhl   'əˤl, 'ərəl

Ermitage
   wine   er-mē-TAHZH   ermiːtɑːʒ

Ernani
   opera, Verdi   er-NAHN-ē   eˤnɑniˑ

Ernest
   1. pers. name   UHR-nuhst   'əˤnəst
   2. French   er-NEST   ernest
   3. German   er-NEST   eˤnest
   4. Swedish   ER-nuhst   'ernəst

Ernestine
   1. pers. name   UHR-nuh-STĒN   'əˤnə,stiːn
   2. German   ER-nes-TĒ-nuh   ,eˤnes'tiːnə
   3. French   er-nes-TĔN   ernestiːn

Ernesto
   1. pers. name, Italian   ār-NES-tō   eːr'nestoː
   2. Portuguese   ēr-NESH-too, -NES-too   iːr'neʃtuː, -'nestuː
   3. Spanish   er-NĀ-stō   er'neːstoː

Ernie
   pers. name   UHR-nē   'əˤniˑ

Ernő
   pers. name, Hungarian   ER-nuh(r)   'ernœː

Ernst
   1. Richard R., Swiss chemist   ERNST   'eˤnst
   2. pers. name   UHRNST, ERNST   'əˤnst, 'eˤnst
   3. Dutch, Norwegian, Swedish   ERNST   'ernst
   4. German   ERNST   'eˤnst

Eroica
   Beethoven's 3rd symphony   i-RŌ-ik-uh, e-RŌ-ik-uh   i'roːikə, e'roːikə

Eros
   Greek god of love; asteroid 433   ER-AHS, IR-AHS   'er,ɑs, 'ir,ɑs

Erroll
   pers. name   ER-uhl   'erəl

Erse
   Gaelic   UHRS   'əˤs

Érsekújvár [Nové Zámky]
   town, Slovakia   ER-SHEK-OOI-VAHR   ,eˤ,ʃek'uːi,vɑˤ

Erskine
   College & Seminary, *SC; pers. name*   UHR-skuhn   'əˤskən

Erté
   costume designer   er-TĀ, ER-TĀ   eˤ'teː, 'eˤ,teː

Ēr'tra [Eritrea]
   region, Ethiopia   ER-truh   'ertrə

Erving
   Julius Winfield, *US basketball player*   UHR-ving   'əˤviŋ

Erwin
   1. pers. name   UHR-wuhn   'əˤwən
   2. German   ER-vēn   'eˤviːn

Erymanthus
   son of Apollo   ER-uh-MAN-thuhs   ,erə'mænθəs

Key (col. 2):   a: fad   ā: fade   ah: father   ar: Mary   aw: law   e: fed   ē: feed   er: merry   i: hid   ī: hide   ō: coat   oo: boot
oi: boy   ow: now   u: put   uh: above   uhr: bird   ch: chop   ng: ring   sh: show   th: thick   th: this   zh: measure

Erysichthon
   Thessalian autophage punished by   ER-uh-SIK-THAHN   ˌerə'sikˌθɑn
     Demeter

Erysimum
   plant   ir-IS-uh-muhm   ir'isəməm

Eryx
   son of Aphrodite   ER-iks   'eriks

Erzquell Edelbräu
   German beer   ERTS-KVEL ĀD-l-BROI   'eᴿtsˌkvel 'eːdl̩ˌbrɔi

Esaias
   1. pers. name, Dutch   ā-SAH-YAHS, -SĪ-(Y)AHS   eː'saːˌjɑs, -'sɑiˌ(j)ɑs
   2. Swedish   e-SĪ-ahs   e'saiɑːs

Esaki
   Leo, *Japanese physicist (Nobel*   es-ah-kē   esɑkiˑ
    1973)

Esala Perahera
   Sri Lankan festival   ES-uh-luh PER-uh-HER-uh   'esələ 'perəˌherə

Esarhaddon
   Assyrian king   Ē-SAHR-HAD-n   ˌiːˌsɑᴿ'hædn̩

Esau
   Biblical name   Ē-SAW   'iːˌsɔː

Escambia
   river, US; county, AL, FL   e-SKAM-bē-uh   e'skæmbiːə

Eschenbach
   Christoph, *German pianist,*   ESH-uhn-BAH<u>KH</u>   'eʃənˌbɑx
    conductor

Escoffier
   Auguste, *French chef*   es-kawf-YĀ   eskɔːfjeː

Escondido
   city, CA   ES-kuhn-DĒD-ō   ˌeskən'diːdoː

Escorial
   building outside Madrid, Spain   es-kōr-YAHL, ⑤ es-KAWR-ē-uhl   eskoːr'jɑl, ⑤ es'kɔːriːəl

ESDI
   enhanced small device interface   ES-dē   'esdiˑ

Esdraelon
   plain, Israel   EZ-druh-Ē-luhn   ˌezdrə'iːlən

Esdras
   Old Testament book, pers. name   EZ-druhs   'ezdrəs

Esfahān
   prov & town, Iran   ES-fuh-HAHN   ˌesfə'hɑn

Eshkol
   Levi, *Israeli politician*   esh-KAWL   eʃ'kɔl

Eshowe
   village, S. Africa   ESH-uh-WĀ   'eʃəˌweː

Eskimo
   N. American & Siberian peoples   ES-kuh-MŌ   'eskəˌmoː

Esmeralda
   county, NV; pers. name   EZ-muh-RAL-duh   ˌezmə'rældə

Espérance
   1. pers. name, French   es-pā-RAHⁿS   espeːrãs
   2. German   ES-pā-RAHNS   ˌespeː'rans

Esperantist
   advocate of Esperanto   ES-puh-RAHNT-uhst,   ˌespə'rantəst, ˌespə'ræntəst
                 ES-puh-RANT-uhst

Foreign Sounds: ue: *Fr.* **r**ue, *Ger.* f**ü**llen   uh(r): *Fr.* b**oeu**f, *Ger.* H**öh**le   <u>kh</u>: *Ger.* i**ch**, *Scot.* lo**ch**   g̶: *Sp.* ami**g**o   v̶: *Sp.* ha**b**lar
hl: *Welsh* **Ll**anelli.   CAPITALS: primary stress.   SMALL CAPS: secondary stress.   ⑤: U.S. pron.   Ⓛ: British pron.

Esperanto
   artificial lang.   ES-puh-RAHN-tō, ES-puh-RANT-ō   ˌespə'rantoː, ˌespə'ræntoː
Espirito Santo
   island, state, Brazil   uh-SPIR-uh-T͞OO SAHN-too   ə'spirəˌtuː 'santuː
Espíritu Santo
   state, Vanuatu; island off Baja   uh-SPIR-uh-T͞OO SAHN-tō   ə'spirəˌtuː 'santoː
     California
Esposito
   Phil, Tony, ice hockey players ES-puh-ZĒT-ō   ˌespə'ziːţoː
Esquiline
   hill, Rome, Italy   ES-kwuh-LĪN, ES-kwuh-luhn   'eskwəˌlɑin, 'eskwələn
Esquipulas
   town, Guatemala   ES-ki-P͞OO-luhs   ˌeski'puːləs
Esquivel
   Adolfo Pérez, Argentine human ā-skē-VEL   eːskiː'βel
     rights activist (Nobel 1980)
Essaouira [Mogador]
   city, Morocco   ES-uh-WIR-uh   ˌesə'wirə
Essen
   city, Germany   ES-n   'esn̩
Essene
   Jewish ascetic sect   i-SĒN, ES-ĒN   i'siːn, 'esˌiːn
Essequibo
   river, county, Guyana   ES-uh-KWĒ-bō   ˌesə'kwiːboː
Essex
   pl. name, US, England   ES-iks   'esiks
Esso
   tdmk for oil products   ES-ō   'esoː
Est! Est!! Est!!!
   wine   EST EST EST   ˌest ˌest 'est
Este
   city, Italy   ES-tā   'esteː
Esteban
   pers. name, Spanish   ā-STĀ-vahn   eː'steːβan
Estée Lauder
   cosmetics   EST-Ā LAWD-uhr   ˌestˌeː 'lɔːdəʳ
Estefan
   Gloria, US rock singer   es-TEF-uhn, es-TEF-AHN   es'tefən, es'tefˌan
Estella
   pers. name   uh-STEL-uh, es-TEL-uh   ə'stelə, es'telə
Estelle
   pers. name   es-TEL, ES-tl, uh-STEL   es'tel, 'estl̩, ə'stel
Estes
   1. pers. name   ES-tuhs   'estəs
   2. park, CO   ES-tēz, ES-tuhs   'estiːz, 'estəs
Estevanico
   US explorer   ES-tuh-VAHN-i-kō   ˌestə'vanikoː
Esther
   Old Testament book; pers. name ES-tuhr   'estəʳ
Estonia
   Baltic republic   e-STŌ-nē-uh, e-STŌN-yuh   e'stoːniːə, e'stoːnjə
Estonian
   pert. to Estonia   es-TŌ-nē-uhn, -nyuhn   es'toːniːən, -njən
Estoril
   town, Portugal   ĒSH-tuh-RIL   ˌiːʃtə'ril

Key (col. 2): a: fad ā: fade ah: father ar: Mary aw: law e: fed ē: feed er: merry i: hid ī: hide ō: coat o͞o: boot
oi: boy ow: now u: put uh: above uhr: bird ch: chop ng: ring sh: show th: thick th̲: this zh: measure

Estragon
   herb   ES-truh-GAHN   'estrə,gɑn
Estremadura
   former prov, Portugal   ES-truh-muh-DUR-uh   ,estrəmə'durə
Estremadura, Extremadura
   region, Spain   es-trä-mah-<u>TH</u>UR-ah,   estreːmɑ'ðurɑ,
       Ⓢ E(K)S-truh-muh-DUR-uh   Ⓢ ,e(k)strəmə'durə
ETA
   Basque separatist movement   ET-uh   'eţə
Étaples
   commune, France   ä-TAHPL   eːtɑːpl
Eteocles
   son of Oedipus; brother of   i-TĒ-uh-KLĒZ   i'tiːə,kliːz
       Polynices
Ethan
   pers. name   Ē-thuhn   'iːθən
Ethel
   pers. name   ETH-uhl   'eθəl
Ethelbert
   pers. name   ETH-uhl-BUHRT   'eθəl,bəʳt
Ethelred
   English king   ETH-uhl-RED   'eθəl,red
Etheredge
   Forest Deroyce, *US politician*   ETH-(uh-)rij   'eθ(ə)ridʒ
Ethiop
   person from Ethiopia   Ē-thē-ŌP   'iːθiː,oːp
Ethiopia [Abyssinia]
   country, Africa   Ē-thē-Ō-pē-uh   ,iːθiː'oːpiːə
Ethiopian
   pert. to Ethiopia   Ē-thē-Ō-pē-uhn   ,iːθiː'oːpiːən
Ethiopic
   pert. to Ethiopia   Ē-thē-Ō-pik   ,iːθiː'oːpik
Étienne
   pers. name, French   ä-TYEN   eːtjen
Etna, Aetna
   Mount, *volcano, Sicily*   ET-nuh   'etnə
Étoile
   wine   ä-TWAHL   eː'twɑːl
Eton
   1. British school   ĒT-n   'iːtn
   2. lang., Africa   ĒT-n, Ē-TAHN, ē-TŌN   'iːtn̩, 'iː,tɑn, iː'toːn
Etonian
   pert. to Eton   ē-TŌ-nē-uhn   iː'toːniːən
Etowah
   river, GA; county, AL; town, TN   ET-uh-WAW, ĒT-ē-WAW, -WAH   'eţə,wɔː, 'iːţiˈ,wɔː, -,wɑ
Etruria
   region of ancient Italy   i-TRUR-ē-uh   i'truriːə
Etrurian
   pert. to Etruria   i-TRUR-ē-uhn   i'truriːən
Etruscan
   ancient lang.; native of or pert. to   i-TRUHS-kuhn   i'trəskən
       Etruria
Ettie, Etty
   pers. name   ET-ē   'eţiˈ

Foreign Sounds: ue: *Fr.* **rue**, *Ger.* **fü**llen   uh(r): *Fr.* b**oeuf**, *Ger.* H**öh**le   <u>kh</u>: *Ger.* i**ch**, *Scot.* lo**ch**   ğ: *Sp.* ami**g**o   v̱: *Sp.* ha**b**lar
hl: *Welsh* **Ll**anelli.   CAPITALS: primary stress.   SMALL CAPS: secondary stress.   Ⓢ: U.S. pron.   Ⓛ: British pron.

Eubanks
   Bob, *US TV entertainer*   YŌŌ-BANGKS   'juːˌbæŋks
Euboea
   island, Greece   yu-BĒ-uh   ju'biːə
Eubouleus
   legendary swineherd   yŌŌ-BŌŌ-lē-uhs   juˈbuːliːəs
Eucharist
   Holy Communion   YŌŌ-kuh-ruhst, YŌŌ-kruhst   'juːkərəst, 'juːkrəst
Euchre
   game   YŌŌ-kuhr   'juːkəʳ
Eucken
   R. C., *German philosopher (Nobel*   OI-kuhn   'ɔikən
     1908)
Euclid
   Greek mathematician; city, OH   YŌŌ-kluhd   'juːkləd
Euclidean
   pert. to Euclid   yu-KLID-ē-uhn   ju'klidiːən
Euclides
   pers. name, Portuguese   āu-KLĒ-dāsh, -dās   eːuˈkliːdeːʃ, -deːs
Eudes
   pers. name, French   UH(R)D   œːd
Eudora
   pers. name   yŌŌ-DŌR-uh, DAWR-uh   juːˈdoːrə, -'dɔːrə
Eudoxus
   Greek explorer; Greek astronomer,   yu-DAHK-suhs   ju'dɑksəs
    mathematician
Eugen
   pers. name, German   oi-GĀN   ɔi'geːn
Eugene
   city, OR; pers. name   yŌŌ-JĒN, YŌŌ-JĒN   juːˈdʒiːn, 'juːˌdʒiːn
Eugène
   pers. name, French   uh(r)-ZHEN   œːʒen
Eugene Onegin
   opera, Tchaikovsky   yu-JĒN awn-YĀ-guhn   ju'dʒiːn ɔːn'jeːgən
Eugenia
   pers. name   yŌŌ-JĒ-nē-uh, yŌŌ-JĒN-yuh   ju'dʒiːniːə, ju'dʒiːnjə
Eugenie
   pers. name, German   oi-GĀ-nē-uh, oi-GĀN-yuh   ɔi'geːniːə, ɔi'geːnjə
Eugénie
   pers. name, French   uh(r)-zhā-NĒ   œːʒeːniː
Eugenio
   1. *pers. name, Italian*   āu-JEN-yō   eːu'dʒenjoː
   2. *Spanish*   āu-<u>KH</u>ĀN-yō   eːu'çeːnjoː
Eugénio
   pers. name, Portuguese   āu-ZHĀN-yŌŌ   eːu'ʒeːnjuː
Eulalie
   pers. name   YŌŌ-luh-lē   'juːləliˑ
Eulalius
   antipope   yu-LĀ-lē-uhs, yu-LĀL-yuhs   ju'leːliːəs, ju'leːljəs
Euler
   Ulf von, *Swedish physiologist*   OI-luhr   'ɔiləʳ
    (Nobel 1970)
Euler-Chelpin
   Hans von, *German-born Swedish*   OI-luhr-KEL-puhn   ˌɔiləʳ'kelpən
    chemist (Nobel 1929)

Key (col. 2):   a: fad ā: fade ah: father ar: Mary aw: law e: fed ē: feed er: merry i: hid ī: hide ō: coat ōō: boot
oi: boy   ow: now   u: put   uh: above   uhr: bird   ch: chop   ng: ring   sh: show   th: thick   <u>th</u>: this   zh: measure

Euler Landpils
  German beer   OI-luhr LAHNT-ᴘɪʟs   ˈɔiləʳ ˈlɑnt͵pils

Euless, John
  Park, ballpark, Fresno, CA   JAHN YOO-luhs   ˈdʒɑn ˈjuːləs

Eumaeus
  swineherd of Odysseus   yoo-MĀ-uhs   juˈmeːəs

Eumenides
  the Greek Furies or Erinyes;   yu-MEN-uh-ᴅĒᴢ   juˈmenə͵diːz
    tragedy, Aeschylus

Eumolpus
  founder of Eleusian mysteries   yoo-MAWL-puhs, yoo-MAHL-puhs   juˈmɔːlpəs, juˈmɑlpəs

Euneus
  son of Jason and Hypsipyle   YOO-nē-uhs   ˈjuːniːəs

Eunice
  1. pers. name   YOO-nuhs   ˈjuːnəs
  2. Latin   yu-NĪ-sē   juˈnaisiˑ

Eunomus
  cup-bearer killed by Heracles   yoo-NŌ-muhs   juˈnoːməs

Euparkeria
  dinosaur   YOO-pahr-KER-ē-uh,   juːpɑʳkeriːə, juːpɑʳkiriːə
     YOO-pahr-KIR-ē-uh

Eupatrids
  Athenian aristocracy   yoo-PA-truhdz, YOO-puh-ᴛʀɪᴅᴢ   juːˈpætrədz, ˈjuːpə͵tridz

Euphemus
  Argonaut, son of Poseidon and   yoo-FĒ-muhs   juˈfiːməs
    Europa

Euphonia
  songbird   yoo-FŌ-nē-uh   juˈfoːniːə

Euphorbia
  plant   yoo-FAWR-bē-uh   juˈfɔːʳbiːə

Euphrates
  river, Asia   yoo-FRĀT-ēz   juˈfreːʈiːz

Euphrosyne
  pers. name   yu-FRAHS-n-ē, yu-FRAHZ-uh-nē   juˈfrɑsn̩iˑ, juˈfrɑzəniˑ

Euphues
  character, J. Lyly   YOO-fyuh-ᴡĒᴢ   ˈjuːfjə͵wiːz

Eurailpass
  European train discount fare   YUR-ĀL-ᴘᴀs, -ᴘᴀʜs   ˈjur͵eːl͵pæs, -͵pɑːs

Eurasia
  Europe & Asia   yu-RĀ-zhuh, yu-RĀ-shuh   juˈreːʒə, juˈreːʃə

Euratom
  European nuclear regulating   yur-AT-uhm   jurˈæʈəm
    organization

Eurico
  pers. name, Portuguese   āu-RĒ-koo   eːuˈriːkuː

Euripides
  Greek tragedian   yu-RIP-uh-ᴅĒᴢ   juˈripə͵diːz

Euro-
  combining form   YUR-ō, ʏᴜʀ-ō   ˈjuroː, juroː

Euroa
  town, Australia   yu-RŌ-uh   juˈroːə

Euroclydon
  a wind   yu-RAHK-luh-ᴅAHN   juˈrɑklə͵dɑn

Foreign Sounds: **ue:** *Fr.* r**ue**, *Ger.* f**ü**llen   **uh(r):** *Fr.* b**oeu**f, *Ger.* H**öh**le   <u>kh</u>: *Ger.* i**ch**, *Scot.* lo**ch**   **g̶:** *Sp.* ami**g**o   **v̠:** *Sp.* ha**b**lar
hl: *Welsh* **Ll**anelli.   CAPITALS: primary stress.   Sᴍᴀʟʟ Cᴀᴘs: secondary stress.   Ⓢ: U.S. pron.   Ⓑ: British pron.

Eurodollar
   US dollar credited to European   YUR-ō-DAHL-uhr, YUR-ō-DAHL-uhr   ˈjuroːˌdɑləʳ, ˌjuroːˈdɑləʳ
   bank

Europa
   mother of Minos by Zeus; satellite   yu-RŌ-puh   juˈroːpə
   of Jupiter

Europe
   continent   YUR-uhp   ˈjurəp

European
   pert. to Europe   YUR-uh-PĒ-uhn   jurəˈpiːən

europium
   element   yu-RŌ-pē-uhm   juˈroːpiːəm

Europort
   port, Netherlands   YUR-uh-PAWRT, YUR-ō-PAWRT   ˈjurəˌpɔːʳt, ˈjuroːˌpɔːʳt

Eurus
   the south-east or east wind in   YUR-uhs   ˈjurəs
   Roman mythology

Euryale
   Gorgon   yu-RĪ-uh-lē   juˈraiəliˑ

Eurycleia
   nurse of Odysseus   YUR-i-KLĀ-(y)uh, YUR-i-KLĒ-uh   juriˈkleː(j)ə, juriˈkliːə

Eurydice
   wife of Orpheus in Greek myth   yu-RID-uh-sē   juˈridəsiˑ

Eurylochus
   companion of Odysseus   yu-RIL-uh-kuhs   juˈriləkəs

Eurymachus
   suitor of Penelope   yu-RIM-uh-kuhs   juˈriməkəs

Eurymedon
   father of Prometheus; charioteer of   yu-RIM-uh-DAHN   juˈriməˌdɑn
   Agamemnon

Eurynome
   mother of the Graces   yu-RIN-uh-mē   juˈrinəmiˑ

Eurypylus
   king of Cyrene   yu-RIP-uh-luhs   juˈripələs

Eurysaces
   son of Telamon Ajax   yu-RIS-uh-KĒZ   juˈrisəˌkiːz

Eurystheus
   king who gave Heracles the Twelve   yu-RIS-thē-uhs, yu-RIS-THOOS   juˈrisθiːəs, juˈrisˌθuːs
   Labors

Eurythmics
   rock group   yu-RITH-miks   juˈriðmiks

Eurytus
   mythical archer   YUR-uht-uhs   ˈjurətəs

Eusden
   Laurence, *British poet laureate*   YOOZ-duhn   ˈjuːzdən

Eusebio
   1. pers. name, Italian   āu-ZEB-yō   eːuˈzebjoː
   2. Spanish   āu-SĀ̲V-yō   eːuˈseːβjoː

Eusebius
   1. pope; Christian historian; pers.   yoo-SĒB-ē-uhs   juːˈsiːbiːəs
   name
   2. German   oi-ZĀB-yus, oi-ZĀ-bē-us   ɔiˈzeːbjus, ɔiˈzeːbiːus

Eustace
   pers. name   YOO-stuhs   ˈjuːstəs

Key (col. 2):   a: fad   ā: fade   ah: father   ar: Mary   aw: law   e: fed   ē: feed   er: merry   i: hid   ī: hide   ō: coat   ōō: boot
oi: boy   ow: now   u: put   uh: above   uhr: bird   ch: chop   ng: ring   sh: show   th: thick   th̲: this   zh: measure

Eustachian tube
  auditory canal — yu-STĀ-sh(ē-)uhn, yu-STĀ-kē-uhn — juˈsteːʃ(iː)ən, juˈsteːkiːən

Euterpe
  1. muse of the flute — yu-TUHR-pē — juˈtəʳpiˑ
  2. street, New Orleans — YŌŌ-TUHRP, YŌŌ-truhp — ˈjuːˌtəʳp, ˈjuːtrəp

Euthydemus
  king of Bactria; dialogue of Plato — YŌŌ-thuh-DĒ-muhs, YŌŌ-THID-uh-muhs — juːθəˈdiːməs, juːˈθidəməs

Euthymus
  mythical hero of Temesa — YŌŌ-thuh-muhs — ˈjuːθəməs

Euthyphro
  dialogue of Plato — YŌŌ-thuh-FRŌ — ˈjuːθəˌfroː

Eutychian
  pope — yu-TIK-ē-uhn — juˈtikiːən

Euxine [Black Sea]
  Sea, Europe, Asia — YŌŌK-suhn, YŌŌK-SĪN — ˈjuːksən, ˈjuːkˌsain

Eva
  1. pers. name — Ē-vuh, Ā-vuh — ˈiːvə, ˈeːvə
  2. German — Ā-vah, Ā-fah — ˈeːva, ˈeːfɑ
  3. Norwegian — Ā-vah — ˈeːvɑ

Evadne
  mother of Iamus by Apollo — i-VAD-nē — iˈvædniˑ

Evan
  pers. name — EV-uhn — ˈevən

Evander
  mythical founder of Pallantium — i-VAN-duhr — iˈvændəʳ

Evangel
  College, MO — i-VAN-juhl — iˈvændʒəl

Evangeline
  pers. name — i-VAN-juh-LĒN, -LĪN, -luhn — iˈvændʒəˌliːn, -ˌlain, -lən

Evans
  Dame Edith, English actress; Mary Ann, *original name of* George Eliot — EV-uhnz — ˈevənz

Evanston
  city, IL — EV-uhn-stuhn — ˈevənstən

Evansville
  city, IN — EV-uhnz-VIL — ˈevənzˌvil

Evaristus
  pope — EV-uh-RIS-tuhs — ˌevəˈristəs

Eve
  pers. name — ĒV — ˈiːv

Evel
  pers. name (E. Knievel) — Ē-vuhl — ˈiːvəl

Evelyn
  pers. name — EV-(uh-)luhn, Ⓔ ĒV-lin, EV-lin — ˈev(ə)lən, Ⓔ ˈiːvlin, ˈevlin

Evenki
  lang., people, Siberia, China — uh-VENG-kē — əˈveŋkiˑ

Even [Lamut]
  lang., East Siberia — Ā-vuhn, Ē-vuhn — ˈeːvən, ˈiːvən

Evenus
  father of Marpessa — i-VĒ-nuhs — iˈviːnəs

Everest
  mtn., Himalayas — EV-(uh-)ruhst — ˈev(ə)rəst

Foreign Sounds: ue: *Fr.* rue, *Ger.* füllen   uh(r): *Fr.* boeuf, *Ger.* Höhle   kh: *Ger.* ich, *Scot.* loch   g̃: *Sp.* amigo   v̱: *Sp.* hablar   hl: *Welsh* Llanelli.   CAPITALS: primary stress.   SMALL CAPS: secondary stress.   Ⓢ: U.S. pron.   Ⓔ: British pron.

Everett
  pers. name   EV-(uh-)ruht   'ev(ə)rət

Everglades, The
  swamp, FL   EV-uhr-GLĀDZ   'evə^{r}ˌgleːdz

Everly
  Don & Phil, *US singers,*   EV-uhr-lē   'evə^{r}liː
  songwriters

Evers
  Medger, *US civil rights activist*   EV-uhrz   'evə^{r}z

Evert
  Christine Marie (Chris), *US tennis*   EV-uhrt   'evə^{r}t
  player

Everyman
  morality play   EV-rē-MAN   'evriːˌmæn

Evesham
  town, England   ĒV-shuhm   'iːvʃəm

Evgeni
  pers. name, Russian   yiv-GĀN-yē   jiv'geːnjiː

Evgenios
  pers. name, Mod. Greek   ev-YĀN-yaws   ev'jeːnjɔːs

Evian
  mineral water   ā-VYAH^n, Ⓢ EV-ē-uhn   eːvjã, Ⓢ 'eviːən

Evind
  pers. name, Finnish   Ā-vind   'eːvind

Evita
  1. pers. name   ā-VĒT-uh, uh-VĒT-uh   eˈ'viːţə, ə'viːţə
  2. Spanish   ā-V̲Ē-tah   eːˈβiːta

Evonne
  pers. name   ē-VAHN   iˈ'vɑn

Évvoia [Euboea]
  island, Greece   EV-yah   'evja

Ewald
  pers. name, German   Ā-VAHLT   'eːˌvalt

Ewan
  pers. name   YOO-uhn   'juːən

Ewe
  lang., people, Africa   Ā-WĀ, Ā-VĀ   'eːˌweː, 'eːˌveː

Ewell
  pers. name   YOO-uhl   'juːəl

Ewen
  pers. name   YOO-uhn   'juːən

Ewok
  alien race in Star Wars   Ē-WAHK   'iːˌwɑk

Excalibur
  King Arthur's sword   ek-SKAL-uh-buhr   ek'skæləbə^r

Exe
  river, England   EKS   'eks

Exeter
  US pl. name; town, England;   EK-suht-uhr   'eksətə^r
  college, Oxford Univ.

Ex-lax
  tdmk for a laxative   EK-SLAKS   'ekˌslæks

Exmoor
  English moorland   EK-SMUR, EK-SMAWR   'ekˌsmu^r, 'ekˌsmɔ^r

---

Key (col. 2):   a: fad   ā: fade   ah: father   ar: Mary   aw: law   e: fed   ē: feed   er: merry   i: hid   ī: hide   ō: coat   ōō: boot
oi: boy   ow: now   u: put   uh: above   uhr: bird   ch: chop   ng: ring   sh: show   th: thick   th: this   zh: measure

Exmouth
  town, England — EK-smuhth, EK-SMOWTH — 'eksməθ, 'ek,smɑuθ
Exocet
  anti-ship missile — EK-suh-SET, EK-sō-SET — 'eksə,set, 'eksoː,set
Exodus
  Old Testament book — EK-suhd-uhs, EG-zuhd-uhs — 'eksədəs, 'egzədəs
Expos
  Montreal baseball team — EK-SPŌZ — 'ek,spoːz
Extremadura
  see Estremadura
Exuma and Cays
  island group, Bahamas — ik-SOO-muh uhn(d) KĒZ, — ik'suːmə ən(d) 'kiːz,
  ig-ZOO-muh, KĀZ — ig'zuːmə, 'keːz
Exxon
  US oil co. — EK-SAHN — 'ek,sɑn
Exxon Valdez
  former name, US tanker — EK-SAHN val-DĒZ — 'ek,sɑn væl'diːz
Eydie
  pers. name (E. Gorme) — ĒD-ē — 'iːdiˑ
Eyre
  salt lake, Australia — AR, ER — 'ær, 'er
Eyvind
  pers. name, Norwegian, Swedish — Ā-vin — 'eːvin
Ezechiel
  pers. name, German — āt-SĀKH-yel, -SEKH-ē-uhl — eːt'seːçjel, -'seçiːəl
Ezechiel, Ezekiel
  Old Testament book; pers. name — i-ZĒK-yuhl, i-ZĒ-kē-uhl — i'ziːkjəl, i'ziːkiːəl
Ezio
  pers. name, Italian — ETS-yō — 'etsjoː
Ezra
  Old Testament book; pers. name — EZ-ruh — 'ezrə

F

Faber
  pers. name — FĀ-buhr — 'feːbər
Fabergé
  Peter Carl, *Russian jeweler;* — fah-ber-ZHĀ, ⓢ FAB-uhr-ZHĀ, — fɑːberʒeː, ⓢ ,fæbərˈʒeː,
  decorative egg; perfume co. — FAB-uhr-ZHĀ — 'fæbər,ʒeː
Fabian
  pope; pers. name — FĀ-bē-uhn — 'feːbiːən
Fabianism
  theories of the Fabian society — FĀ-bē-uh-NIZ-uhm — 'feːbiːə,nizəm
Fabio
  pers. name — FAHB-yō — 'fɑbjoː

Foreign Sounds: ue: *Fr.* **rue**, *Ger.* füllen uh(r): *Fr.* **boeuf**, *Ger.* Höhle <u>kh</u>: *Ger.* i<u>ch</u>, *Scot.* lo<u>ch</u> ğ: *Sp.* ami**g**o v: *Sp.* ha**b**lar
hl: *Welsh* **Ll**anelli. CAPITALS: primary stress. SMALL CAPS: secondary stress. ⓢ: U.S. pron. Ⓛ: British pron.

Fabiola
  queen, Belgium   FAB-ē-Ō-luh   ˌfæbiːˈoːlə
Fabius
  1. Laurent, Prime minister of   fahb-YUES   faːbjys
    France
  2. Roman cognomen   FĀ-bē-uhs   ˈfeːbiːəs
Fabricius
  1. pers. name, German   fah-BRĒT-sē-us   faˈbriːtsiːus
  2. Latin   fuh-BRISH(-ē)-uhs   fəˈbriʃ(iː)əs
Fabrizio
  pers. name, Italian   fahb-RĒTS-yō   fabˈriːtsjoː
Faeroe, Faroe
  Islands, *Atlantic*   FAR-ō, FER-ō   ˈfæroː, ˈferoː
Faeroese, Faroese
  lang., people, Faeroe Islands   FAR-uh-WĒZ, -WĒS   ˌfærəˈwiːz, -ˈwiːs
Fafnir
  dragon in Scandinavian myth   FAHF-NIR   ˈfafˌniʳ
Fagin
  character in Oliver Twist, *C.*   FĀ-guhn   ˈfeːgən
    Dickens
Fahd
  King, Saudi Arabia   FAHD   ˈfad
Fahd ibn Abdul Aziz al Saud
  Saudi Arabian politician   FAHD IB-uhn ahb-DŌŌL ah-ZĒZ ahl   ˈfad ˌibən abˈduːl aˈziːz aːl
     sah-ŌŌD   saˈuːd
Fahrenheit
  temperature scale   FAR-uhn-HĪT   ˈfærənˌhait
Fairbanks
  Douglas, *US actor; city, AK*   FAR-BANGKS, FER-BANGKS   ˈfæʳˌbæŋks, ˈfeʳˌbæŋks
Fairleigh Dickinson
  University, *NJ*   FAR-lē DIK-uhn-suhn, FER-lē   ˈfæʳliˑ ˈdikənsən, ˈfeʳliˑ
Faisal
  Saudi Arabian dynasty   FĪ-suhl   ˈfaisəl
Faisalabad
  city, Pakistan   FĪ-SAHL-uh-BAHD, FĪ-SAL-uh-BAD   ˌfaiˌsaləˈbad, ˌfaiˌsæləˈbæd
Faith
  pers. name   FĀTH   ˈfeːθ
Faiyum
  prov, Egypt   fā-(Y)ŌŌM, fī-(Y)ŌŌM   feːˈ(j)uːm, faiˈ(j)uːm
Falange, Ph-
  party of Spain's Franco   FĀ-LANJ   ˈfeːˌlændʒ
Falangist, Ph-
  member of Spanish fascist   fuh-LAN-juhst, FĀ-LAN-juhst   fəˈlændʒəst, ˈfeːˌlændʒəst
    political party
Falasha
  Ethiopian people   fuh-LAHSH-uh   fəˈlaʃə
Falcon
  hawk genus   FAL-kuhn, FAW(L)-kuhn   ˈfælkən, ˈfɔː(l)kən
Falernian
  ancient Italian wine   fuh-LUHR-nē-uhn   fəˈləʳniːən
Falerno
  Italian wine   fah-LER-nō   faˈlernoː
Faliscan
  ancient Italian people   fuh-LIS-kuhn   fəˈliskən

Key (col. 2):   a: fad   ā: fade   ah: father   ar: Mary   aw: law   e: fed   ē: feed   er: merry   i: hid   ī: hide   ō: coat   ōō: boot
oi: boy   ow: now   u: put   uh: above   uhr: bird   ch: chop   ng: ring   sh: show   th: thick   <u>th</u>: this   zh: measure

Falk
   Peter, *US actor*   FAW(L)K   'fɔː(l)k
Falkland [Malvinas, Islas]
   Islands, *Atlantic*   FAW(L)K-luhnd   'fɔː(l)klənd
Falla
   Manuel de, *Spanish composer*   FAH-yuh, FĪ-uh   'fajə, 'faiə
Fallas de San Jose
   Spanish festival   FAH-yahs <u>th</u>ā sahn hō-ZĀ   'fajas ðeː san hoː'zeː
Fallon
   county, MT; pers. name   FAL-uhn   'fælən
Fall River
   town, MA   FAWL RIV-uhr   ˌfɔːl 'rivəʳ
Falmouth
   city, MA; borough, England   FAL-muhth   'fælməθ
Falstaff
   Shakespearean character   FAWL-STAF, FAWL-STAHF   'fɔːlˌstæf, 'fɔːlˌstaːf
Falwell
   Jerry, *US TV evangelist*   FAWL-WEL, FAWL-wuhl   'fɔːlˌwel, 'fɔːlwəl
Fames
   allegorical figure of hunger   FAM-ēz, FAHM-ēz   'fæmiːz, 'famiːz
Faneuil Hall
   historic building, Boston, MA   FAN-yuhl, FAN-l, *locally sometimes* THAN-l   'fænjəl, 'fænl, *locally sometimes* 'θænl
Fanfani
   Amintore, *Italian statesman*   fahn-FAHN-ē   fan'faniˑ
Fang
   lang., Africa   FANG, FAHNG   'fæŋ, 'faŋ
Fang Lizhi
   Chinese dissident, physicist   FAHNG LĒ-JĒ   'faŋ 'liː'dʒiː
Fang Yi
   Chinese dissident   FAHNG YĒ   'faŋ 'jiː
Fannie, Fanny
   pers. name   FAN-ē   'fæniˑ
Fannius
   Roman name   FAN-ē-uhs   'fæniːəs
Fantin-Latour
   Ignace Henri, *French painter*   fahⁿ-TEⁿ-lah-TOOR   fãtɛ̃laːtuːr
Faraday
   Michael, *English physicist*   FAR-uh-DĀ, FER-uh-DĀ   'færəˌdeː, 'ferəˌdeː
Farah
   1. river, prov, town, Afghanistan   fuh-RAH   fə'ra
   2. US apparel co.   FAR-uh, FER-uh   'færə, 'ferə
Farallon Islands
   National Wildlife Refuge, CA   FAR-uh-LAHN, FER-   'færəˌlan, 'fer-
Farben, I.G.
   German corp.   Ē GĀ FAHR-buhn   ˌiː ˌgeː 'faʳbən
Farentino
   James, *US actor*   FAR-uhn-TĒ-nō   ˌfærən'tiːnoː
Fargo
   city, ND   FAHR-gō   'faʳgoː
Faribault
   county, MN   FAR-uh-BŌ   'færəˌboː
Farigoule [Romains]
   Louis Henri, *French writer*   fah-rē-GOOL   faːriːguːl

Foreign Sounds: ue: *Fr.* **rue**, *Ger.* **füllen**   uh(r): *Fr.* **boeuf**, *Ger.* **Höhle**   <u>kh</u>: *Ger.* **ich**, *Scot.* **loch**   ḡ: *Sp.* **amigo**   ᵥ: *Sp.* **hablar** hl: *Welsh* **Llanelli**.   CAPITALS: primary stress.   SMALL CAPS: secondary stress.   Ⓢ: U.S. pron.   Ⓔ: British pron.

Farley
   Walter Lorimer, *US author*   FAHR-lē   'fɑʳliˑ

Farmer
   Philip Jose, *US author*   FAHR-muhr   'fɑʳməʳ

Farnese Palace
   Rome, *Italy*   fahr-NĀ-zā   fɑʳneˑzeˑ

Faroe
   see Faeroe

Faroese
   see Faeroese

Farouk
   king, Egypt   fuh-R͞OOK   fə'ruːk

Farquharson
   Scottish family name   FAHR-kuhr-suhn, Ⓢ *also*   'fɑʳkəʳsən, Ⓢ *also*
                                FAHR-kwuhr-suhn   'fɑʳkwəʳsən

Farragut
   David, *militarist*   FAR-uh-guht   'færəgət

Farrah
   pers. name (F. Fawcett)   FAR-uh, FER-uh   'færə, 'ferə

Farrakhan
   Rev. Louis, *US political activist* FAR-uh-KAN, FAHR-uh-KAHN   'færəˌkæn, 'fɑrəˌkɑn

Farrow
   Mia Villiers, *US actress*   FAR-ō   'færoˑ

Farsi
   lang., Middle East   FAHR-sē   'fɑʳsiˑ

Fasching
   Austrian & German festival   FAHSH-ing   'fɑʃiŋ

Fascisti
   members of the Italian Fascist fah-SHĒ-stē, fa-SHIS-tē   fɑ'ʃiːstiˑ, fæ'ʃistiˑ
   party

Fashoda [Kodok]
   village, Sudan   fuh-SHŌD-uh   fə'ʃoːdə

Fasnacht
   Austrian & German festival   FAHS-NAH<u>KH</u>T   'fɑsˌnɑxt

Fasnet
   Austrian & German festival   FAHS-nuht   'fɑsnət

Fassbinder
   Rainer Werner, *German film*   FAHS-BIN-duhr   'fɑsˌbindəʳ
   director

Fastelavn
   Danish festival   FAHST-l-ahv(-uh)n   'fɑstˌlɑv(ə)n

Fátima
   town, Portugal; pers. name   FAT-uh-muh   'fæṱəmə

Fatum
   god of destiny   FAHT-uhm   'fɑṱəm

Faulkner
   William, *US author (Nobel 1949)* FAWK-nuhr   'fɔːknəʳ

Faulknerian
   pert. to Faulkner   fawk-NIR-ē-uhn, fawk-NER-ē-uhn   fɔk'niriːən, fɔk'neriːən

Fauna
   woodland goddess, sister and wife FAW-nuh   'fɔːnə
   of Faunus (Roman god)

Fauntleroy
   Little Lord, *Burnett novel*   FAHNT-luh-ROI, FAWNT-luh-ROI   'fɑntləˌrɔi, 'fɔːntləˌrɔi

---

Key (col. 2):   a: fad ā: fade ah: father ar: Mary aw: law e: fed ē: feed er: merry i: hid ī: hide ō: coat o͞o: boot
oi: boy ow: now u: put uh: above uhr: bird ch: chop ng: ring sh: show th: thick th̲: this zh: measure

Faunus
   king of Latium; Roman woodland   FAW-nuhs   'fɔːnəs
     god
Fauquier
   county, VA   faw-KIR, FAW-KIR   fɔːˈkiʳ, ˈfɔːˌkiʳ
Faure
   Elie, *French art historian*   FAWR   fɔːr
Fauré
   Gabriel, *French composer*   faw-RĀ, fō-RĀ   fɔːreː, foːreː
Faust
   legendary German magician   FOWST   'faust
Faustinus
   companion of Evander   faw-STĪ-nuhs   fɔːˈstainəs
Faustulus
   shepherd, guardian of Romulus   FAWS-chuh-luhs   'fɔːstʃələs
    and Remus
Faustus
   1. legendary German magician;   FAWS-tuhs, FOWS-tuhs   'fɔːstəs, 'faustəs
    pers. name
   2. Latin   FAWS-tuhs   'fɔːstəs
Fauve
   group of French artists   FŌV   foːv
Fauvism
   art movement   FŌ-VIZ-uhm   'foːˌvizəm
Faversham
   town, England   FAV-uhr-shuhm   'fævəʳʃəm
Fawayid
   people, Africa   FAH-wī-(Y)ID   ˌfawai'(j)id
Fawcett
   Farrah Leni, *US actress*   FAW-suht   'fɔːsət
Fawkes
   Guy, *English traitor*   FAWKS   'fɔːks
Fay, Faye
   pers. name   FĀ   'feː
Fayette
   US pl. name   fā-ET, FĀ-uht   feːˈet, 'feːət
Fayetteville
   city, AR   FĀ-uht-vuhl, FĀ-uht-VIL   'feːətvəl, 'feːətˌvil
Fayoum
   province, Egypt   fah-YŌŌM, fī-ŌŌM   faˈjuːm, faiˈuːm
Feargus
   pers. name   FUHR-guhs   'fəʳgəs
Featherstonehaugh
   town, England; British family   FETH-uhr-stuhn-HAW, FAN-SHAW,   'feðəʳstən,hɔː, 'fæn,ʃɔː,
    name   FEST-uhn-HAW, FĒ-suhn-HĀ,   'festən,hɔː, 'fiːsən,heː,
                       FIR-stuhn-HAW   'fiʳstən,hɔː
Febris
   goddess of fever   FĒ-bruhs   'fiːbrəs
February
   month   FEB-yuh-WER-ē, FEB-uh-WER-ē,   'febjə,weriˑ, 'febə,weriˑ,
                    FEB-ruh-WER-ē   'febrə,weriˑ
Februus
   Etruscan god of the Underworld   FEB-ruh-wuhs, FĒ-bruh-wuhs   'febrəwəs, 'fiːbrəwəs
Fecunditatis, Mare
   see Mare Fecunditatis

Foreign Sounds: **ue**: *Fr.* **rue**, *Ger.* f**ü**llen   **uh(r)**: *Fr.* b**oeu**f, *Ger.* H**ö**hle   <u>kh</u>: *Ger.* i**ch**, *Scot.* lo**ch**   g̃: *Sp.* ami**g**o   <u>v</u>: *Sp.* ha**b**lar
hl: *Welsh* **Ll**anelli.   CAPITALS: primary stress.   SMALL CAPS: secondary stress.   ⑤: U.S. pron.   ⑥: British pron.

Federico
  1. pers. name, Italian   FĀ-dä-RḖ-kō   ˌfeːdeːˈriːkoː
  2. Spanish   fä-<u>th</u>ä-RḖ-kō, fä-dä-   feːðeːˈriːkoː, feːdeː-
Fedor
  pers. name, German   FĀ-DŌR, FĀ-DAWR   ˈfeːˌdoːʳ, ˈfeːˌdɔːʳ
Fëdor, Fedor
  pers. name, Russian   FYAW-DAWR   ˈfjɔːˌdoːr
Feiffer
  Jules, *US cartoonist, writer*   FĪ-fuhr   ˈfaifəʳ
Feinstein
  Diane, *US politician*   FĪN-STĪN   ˈfainˌstain
Feldberg
  mtn., Germany   FELT-BERK   ˈfeltˌbeʳk
Felice
  1. pers. name   fuh-LḖS   fəˈliːs
  2. Italian   fä-LḖ-CHĀ   feːˈliːˌtʃeː
Felicia
  1. pers. name   fuh-LISH-(ē-)uh, fuh-LIS-ē-uh   fəˈliʃ(iː)ə, fəˈlisiːə
  2. Spanish   fä-LḖS-yah, fä-LḖTH-yah   feːˈliːsja, feːˈliːθja
Felician
  College, *IL*   fuh-LISH-(ē-)uhn, fuh-LḖ-sh(ē-)uhn   fəˈliʃ(iː)ən, fəˈliːʃ(iː)ən
Feliciano
  Jose, *rock musician*   fä-LḖ-sē-AHN-ō, fuh-LISH-ē-AHN-ō   feːˌliːsiˈanoː, fəˌliʃiˈanoː
Felim
  pers. name   FĀ-lim   ˈfeːlim
Felinfoel
  Welsh beer   VEL-uhn-VOIL   ˌveIənˈvɔil
Felipe
  pers. name   fä-LḖ-pä   feːˈliːpeː
Felis
  former constellation   FḖ-luhs   ˈfiːləs
Felix
  1. pers. name   FḖ-liks   ˈfiːliks
  2. Dutch, German   FĀ-liks   ˈfeːliks
Félix, Felix
  pers. name, Russian   FYĀL-yiks   ˈfjeːljiks
Fellini
  Federico, *Italian film director*   fuh-LḖ-nē   fəˈliːniˑ
Feltsman
  Vladimir, *Russian pianist*   FELT-smuhn   ˈfeltsmən
Fénelon
  François, *French prelate, writer*   fän-LAWⁿ   feːnlɔ̃
Fenian
  Irish revolutionary movement   FḖ-nē-uhn   ˈfiːniːən
Fenimore
  pers. name, (J. F. Cooper)   FEN-uh-MŌR, FEN-uh-MAWR   ˈfenəˌmoːr, ˈfenəˌmɔːʳ
Fens, The
  district, England   <u>th</u>uh FENZ   ðə ˈfenz
Fenway
  Park, *ballpark, Boston, MA*   FEN-wä   ˈfenweː
Feodor
  1. pers. name, German   FĀ-ō-DŌR, -DAWR   ˈfeːoːˌdoːʳ, -ˌdɔːʳ
  2. Russian   fyi-AW-duhr   fjiˈɔːdər
Féraud
  Louis, *French designer*   fä-RŌ   feːroː

Key (col. 2):   a: **fad**   ā: **fade**   ah: **father**   ar: **Mary**   aw: **law**   e: **fed**   ē: **feed**   er: **merry**   i: **hid**   ī: **hide**   ō: **coat**   o͞o: **boot**
oi: **boy**   ow: **now**   u: **put**   uh: **above**   uhr: **bird**   ch: **chop**   ng: **ring**   sh: **show**   th: **thick**   <u>th</u>: **this**   zh: **measure**

Ferde
   pers. name (F. Grofé)   FUHRD-ē   'fə^{r}di·

Fer-de-lance
   snake   FERD-l-AN(T)S, FERD-l-AHN(T)S   ˌfe^{r}dļ'æn(t)s, ˌfe^{r}dļ'ɑn(t)s

Ferdinand
   1. pers. name   FUHRD-n-AND   'fə^{r}dņˌænd
   2. Danish   FER-di-NAHN   'ferdiˌnɑːn
   3. Dutch   FER-dē-NAHNT   'ferdiːˌnɑnt
   4. French   fer-dē-NAH^n ferdiːnɑ̃
   5. German   FER-dē-NAHNT   'fe^{r}diːˌnɑnt

Ferenc, Ferencz
   pers. name, Hungarian   FER-en(t)s   'feren(t)s

Ferengi
   Star Trek villains   fuh-RENG-gē, fuh-REN-gē   fə'reŋgi·, fə'rengi·

Fergie
   nickname, Duchess of York   FUHR-gē   'fə^{r}gi·

Fergus
   pers. name   FUHR-guhs   'fə^{r}gəs

Fergus Falls
   Community College, *MN*   FUHR-guhs FAWLZ   'fə^{r}gəs 'fɔːlz

Ferguson
   Ma*y*nard, *Canadian trumpet*   FUHR-guh-suhn   'fə^{r}gəsən
   player

Ferhat
   pers. name   fer-HAHT   fer'hɑt

Feria de San Fermin
   Spanish holiday, 2nd week of July   FER-ē-ah <u>th</u>ā SAHN fer-MĒN   'feriːɑ ðeː ˌsɑn fer'miːn

Fermat
   Pierre de, *French scientist*   fer-MAH   fermɑː

Fermi
   Enrico, *Italian-born US physicist*   FER-mē   'fe^{r}mi·
   (Nobel 1938)

fermium
   element   FER-mē-uhm, FUHR-mē-uhm   'fe^{r}miːəm, 'fə^{r}miːəm

Fernam
   pers. name, Portuguese   fuhr-NOW^n, fer-NOW^n fər'naũ, fer'naũ

Fernandes
   pers. name, Portuguese   fuhr-NAH^n-dish, fer-NAH^n-dis   fər'nɑ̃ː(n)diʃ, fer'nɑ̃ː(n)dis

Fernandez
   1. pers. name   fuhr-NAN-DEZ   fə^r'nænˌdez
   2. Portuguese   fuhr-NAH^n-dish, fer-NAH^n-dis   fər'nɑ̃ː(n)diʃ, fer'nɑ̃ː(n)dis

Fernández
   pers. name, Spanish   fer-NAHN-dāth, -dās   fer'nɑndeːθ, -deːs

Fernando
   1. pers. name   fuhr-NAN-dō   fə^r'nændoː
   2. Italian   fer-NAHN-dō   fer'nandoː
   3. Portuguese   fuhr-NAH^n-doo, fer-   fər'nɑ̃ː(n)duː, fer-

Fernão
   pers. name, Portuguese   fuhr-NOW^n, fer-   fər'naũ, fer-

Fernet Branca
   Italian bitters   fer-NET BRAHNG-kuh   ferˌnet 'brɑŋkə

Feronia
   Roman goddess of spring   fi-RŌ-nē-uh   fi'roːniːə

Ferragamo
   pers. name, Italian   FER-uh-GAHM-ō   ˌferə'gamoː

Ferrante & Teicher
  dual pianists   fuh-RANT-ē uhn(d) TĪ-kuhr   fə'rænti· ən(d) 'taikə^r

Ferrara
  prov & town, Italy   fuh-RAHR-uh   fə'rɑrə

Ferrari
  Italian car   fuh-RAHR-ē   fə'rɑri·

Ferraris
  Galileo, *Italian scientist*   fär-RAHR-ēs, ⑤ fer-AHR-uhs   feːr'rɑriːs, ⑤ fer'ɑrəs

Ferraro
  Geraldine, *US politician*   fuh-RAHR-ō   fə'rɑroː

Ferrer
  Jose Vicente, *Puerto Rican actor,*   fuh-RER   fə're^r
    producer, director

Ferrigno
  Lou, *actor, bodybuilder*   fuh-RIG-nō   fə'rignoː

Ferris wheel
  amusement ride   FER-uhs (H)WĒL   'ferəs ˌ(h)wiːl

Ferruccio
  pers. name, Italian   fär-ROOT-chō, ⑤ fuh-ROO-ch(ē-)ō   feːr'ruːttʃoː, ⑤ fə'ruːtʃ(iː)oː

Ferrum
  College, *VA*   FER-uhm   'ferəm

Fès [Fez]
  city, Morocco   FES   'fes

Fess
  pers. name   FES   'fes

Festa de Colete Encarnado
  Portuguese festival   FES-tah dä KŌ-lä-tä   'festa deː 'koːleːteː
     EN-kahr-NAHD-oo   ˌenkɑr'naduː

Festival du Voyageur
  Manitoban festival   fes-tē-VAHL due vwah-yah-ZHUHR   festiːvaːl dy vwaːjaːʒœːr

Festus
  pers. name   fes-tuhs   festəs

Fête de la Madeleine, La
  see La Fête de la Madeleine

Fetzer
  winery, CA   FET-suhr   'fetsə^r

Feuerheerd Wearne
  Port wine   FOI-uhr-HERT VER-nuh   'fɔiə^rˌhe^rt 've^rnə

Feynman
  Richard Phillips, *US physicist*   FĪN-muhn   'fɑinmən
    (Nobel 1965)

Fez [Fès]
  city, Morocco   FEZ   'fez

Fianna Fail
  Irish political party   FĒ-uh-nuh FOIL   'fiːənə 'fɔil

Fiat
  Italian car co.   FĒ-AHT, FĒ-AT   'fiːˌat, 'fiːˌæt

Fibiger
  Johannes, *Danish pathologist*   FĒ-bē-guhr   'fiːbiːgə^r
    (Nobel 1926)

FICA
  Social Security tax act   FĪ-kuh   'faikə

Fichte
  J.G., *German philosopher*   FI<u>KH</u>-tuh   'fiçtə

Key (col. 2):   a: fad   ā: fade   ah: father   ar: Mary   aw: law   e: fed   ē: feed   er: merry   i: hid   ī: hide   ō: coat   oo: boot
oi: boy   ow: now   u: put   uh: above   uhr: bird   ch: chop   ng: ring   sh: show   th: thick   <u>th</u>: this   zh: measure

Fichteanism
  philosophy of Fichte   FIK-tē-uh-NIZ-uhm,   'fiktiːə,nizəm, 'fiçtiːə,nizəm
                      FI<u>KH</u>-tē-uh-NIZ-uhm

Fidel
  1. pers. name   fi-DEL   fi'del
  2. Spanish   fē-<u>THEL</u>   fiː'ðel

Fidelio
  pers. name   fē-DĀL-yō, fē-DĀ-lē-ō   fiː'deːljoː, fiː'deːliːoː

Fides
  personification of good faith   FĒD-ās   'fiːdeːs

Fido
  canine name   FĪD-ō   'faidoː

Fiedler
  Arthur, *US conductor*   FĒD-luhr   'fiːdləʳ

Fielding
  Henry, *English author; pers. name*   FĒL-ding   'fiːldiŋ

Fiesole
  commune, Italy   fē-Ā-zuh-LĀ   fiː'eːzə,leː

Fiesta del Arbol
  Arbor Day (March 26), Spain   fē-ES-tah <u>th</u>el ahr-<u>V</u>ŌL   fiː'esta ðel ar'ßoːl

Fiesta de la Vendimia
  Spanish grape festival   fē-EST-ah <u>th</u>ā lah ven-DĒ-mē-ah   fiː'esta ðeː la ven'diːmiːa

Fifi
  pers. name   FĒ-fē, FĒ-FĒ   'fiːfiˑ, 'fiːˌfiː

Figaro
  Marriage of, *opera, Mozart*   FIG-uh-RŌ   'figə,roː

Fiji
  islands, Pacific; fraternity   FĒ-jē   'fiːdʒiˑ
    nickname

Fijian
  lang., Fiji   FĒ-jē-uhn   'fiːdʒiːən

Filbert
  nut   FIL-buhrt   'filbəʳt

Filé
  sassafras   fuh-LĀ, fē-LĀ, FĒ-LĀ   fə'leː, fiː'leː, 'fiːˌleː

Filene's
  US department store chain   fī-LĒNZ, FĪ-LĒNZ   fai'liːnz, 'faiˌliːnz

Filioque clause
  clause, Nicene Creed   FĒ-lē-Ō-kwē KLAWZ, FĒ-lē-Ō-KWĀ   ˌfiːliː'oːkwiˑ ˌklɔːz,
                                                     ˌfiːliː'oːˌkweː

Filipina
  female native of the Philippines   FIL-uh-PĒ-nuh   ˌfilə'piːnə

Filipino
  male native of the Philippines   FIL-uh-PĒ-nō   ˌfilə'piːnoː

Filippino
  pers. name, Italian   fē-lēp-PĒ-nō, Ⓢ FIL-uh-PĒ-nō   fiːliːp'piːnoː, Ⓢ ˌfilə'piːnoː

Filippo
  pers. name, Italian   fē-LĒP-pō, Ⓢ fuh-LĒP-ō   fiː'liːppoː, Ⓢ fə'liːpoː

Fillmore
  Millard, *13th US president*   FIL-MŌR, FIL-MAWR   'filˌmoːʳ, 'filˌmɔːʳ

Filofax
  tdmk for an organizer   FĪ-lō-FAKS, FĪ-luh-FAKS   'failoːˌfæks, 'failəˌfæks

FINA
  US petroleum and natural gas co.   FĒ-nuh   'fiːnə

Foreign Sounds: ue: *Fr.* **rue**, *Ger.* **füllen**   uh(r): *Fr.* **boeuf**, *Ger.* **Höhle**   <u>kh</u>: *Ger.* i**ch**, *Scot.* lo**ch**   ğ: *Sp.* ami**g**o   <u>v</u>: *Sp.* ha**b**lar
hl: *Welsh* **Ll**anelli.   CAPITALS: primary stress.   SMALL CAPS: secondary stress.   Ⓢ: U.S. pron.   Ⓛ: British pron.

Findlay
  city, OH   FIN-(d)lē   'fin(d)liˑ
Fine Gael
  political party, Ireland   FĒ-nuh GĀL   'fiːnə 'geːl
Fingal
  pers. name   FING-guhl, FIN-guhl   'fiŋgəl, 'fingəl
Finistère
  dept., France   fē-nē-STER   fiːniːster
Finisterre
  cape, Spain   fē-ni-STER   fiːni'ster
Finlandia
  symphony, Sibelius   fin-LAN-dē-uh   fin'lændiːə
Finland [Suomi]
  republic, Europe   FIN-luhnd   'finlənd
Finn
  European people; mythological   FIN   'fin
  Irish hero
Finnair
  airline of Finland   FIN-AR, FIN-ER   'fin,ærʳ, 'fin,eʳ
Finnbogadottir
  Vigdis, *president, Iceland*   FIN-BŌ-guh-DAW-TIR   ,fin,boːgə'dɔː,tiʳ
Finnegan's Wake
  novel, Joyce   FIN-uh-guhnz WĀK   ,finəgənz 'weːk
Finney
  Albert, *British actor;* Ross Lee,   FIN-ē   'finiˑ
  US composer
Finnish
  lang., Finland, Sweden, Russia   FIN-ish   'finiʃ
Finno-Ugrian
  pert. to Finns and Ugrians   FIN-ō-(Y)OO-grē-uhn   ,finoː'(j)uːgriːən
Finno-Ugric
  lang. family   FIN-ō-(Y)OO-grik   ,finoː'(j)uːgrik
Finsen
  N. R., *Danish physician (Nobel*   FIN-suhn   'finsən
  1903)
Finsteraarhorn
  mtn., Switzerland   FIN(T)-stuhr-AHR-HAWRN   ,fin(t)stəʳ'aʳ,hɔːʳn
Fiona
  pers. name   fē-Ō-nuh, fī-Ō-nuh   fiː'oːnə, fai'oːnə
Fionnula
  pers. name (F. M. Flanagan)   fē-ŌN-yuh-luh   fiː'oːnjələ
Fior d'Alpi
  Italian liqueur   fyawr DAHL-pē   fjɔːr 'dɑlpiˑ
Fiorello
  1. pers. name   FĒ-uh-REL-ō   ,fiːə'reloː
  2. Italian   fyō-REL-lō   fjoː'relloː
Fiore Sardo
  Italian cheese   fē-ŌR-ā SAHR-dō, FYŌR-ā   fiː,oːreː 'saʳdoː, ,fjoːreː
Firenze [Florence]
  prov & town, Italy   fē-RENT-sā   fiː'rentseː
Fiscalini
  Field, *ballpark, San Bernardino,*   FIS-kuh-LĒ-nē   ,fiskə'liːniˑ
  CA

Key (col. 2):   a: **fad**   ā: **fade**   ah: **father**   ar: **Mary**   aw: **law**   e: **fed**   ē: **feed**   er: **merry**   i: **hid**   ī: **hide**   ō: **coat**   ōō: **boot**
oi: **boy**   ow: **now**   u: **put**   uh: **above**   uhr: **bird**   ch: **chop**   ng: **ring**   sh: **show**   th: **thick**   <u>th</u>: **this**   zh: **measure**

Fischer		
Emil, *German chemist (Nobel 1902);* Ernst Otto, *German inorganic chemist (Nobel 1973);* Hans, *German chemist (Nobel 1930)*	FISH-uhr	'fɪʃəʳ
Fischer-Dieskau		
Dietrich, *German baritone/ conductor*	FISH-uhr-DĒ-SKOW	ˌfɪʃəʳ'diːˌskau
Fitch		
Val L., *US physicist (Nobel 1980)*	FICH	'fɪtʃ
Fitchburg		
city, MA	FICH-BUHRG	'fɪtʃˌbəʳg
Fitzgerald		
pers. name	fits-JER-uhld	fɪts'dʒerəld
Fitzwater		
Max Marlin, *US government official*	FIT-SWAWT-uhr	'fɪtˌswɔːt̬əʳ
Fitzwilliam		
college, Cambridge Univ.	fit-SWIL-yuhm	fɪt'swɪljəm
Fiume		
city, Croatia [Rijeka]*; former province, Italy*	FYŌŌ-mā	'fjuːmeː
Fiumicino		
airport, Rome	FYŌŌ-mi-CHĒ-nō	ˌfjuːmi'tʃiːnoː
Fix		
Greek beer	FĒKS	'fiːks
Flaccus		
Roman cognomen	FLAK-uhs	'flækəs
Flacianism		
beliefs of Matthias Flacius Illyricus	FLĀ-sh(ē-)uh-NIZ-uhm	'fleːʃ(iː)əˌnɪzəm
Flageolet		
small flute	FLAJ-ē-uh-LET, FLAJ-ē-uh-LĀ	ˌflædʒiːə'let, ˌflædʒiːə'leː
Flagey-Echézeaux		
French wine	flah-ZHE-ā-shā-ZŌ	flɑːʒe-eːʃeːzoː
Flagler		
county, FL	FLAG-luhr	'flægləʳ
Flagstad		
Kirsten, *Norwegian opera star*	FLAHG-STAH, [$] FLAG-STAD	'flɑgˌstɑ, [$] 'flægˌstæd
Flagstaff		
city, AZ	FLAG-STAF	'flægˌstæf
Flambeau		
river, WI	flam-BŌ	flæm'boː
Flamenco		
dance	fluh-MENG-kō	flə'meŋkoː
Flaminian Way [Via Flamina]		
ancient Roman road	fluh-MIN-ē-uhn WĀ	fləˌmɪniːən 'weː
Flamininus		
Titus Quinctius, *Roman general*	FLAM-uh-NĪ-nuhs	ˌflæmə'naɪnəs
Flaminius		
Gaius, *Roman general*	fluh-MIN-ē-uhs	flə'mɪniːəs
Flammarion		
Camille, *French scientist*	flah-mahr-YAW^{n}	flɑːmɑːrjɔ̃

Foreign Sounds: ue: *Fr.* **rue**, *Ger.* **fü**llen uh(r): *Fr.* **boeu**f, *Ger.* **Höh**le kh: *Ger.* i**ch**, *Scot.* lo**ch** ğ: *Sp.* ami**g**o v: *Sp.* ha**b**lar hl: *Welsh* **Ll**anelli. CAPITALS: primary stress. SMALL CAPS: secondary stress. [$]: U.S. pron. [£]: British pron.

Flanagan
  Fionnula Manon, *Irish actress*   FLAN-uh-guhn   ˈflænəgən

Flanders
  region, Belgium   FLAN-duhrz   ˈflændəʳz

Flandreau
  city, SD; Indian reservation, US   FLAN-drōō   ˈflændruː

Flathead
  N. American people   FLAT-HED   ˈflæt,hed

Flaubert
  Gustave, *French author*   flō-BER   floːber

Flavel
  pers. name   fluh-VEL, FLĀ-vuhl   fləˈvel, ˈfleːvəl

Flavia
  pers. name   FLĀ-vē-uh   ˈfleːviːə

Flavian
  Roman imperial dynasty   FLĀ-vē-uhn   ˈfleːviːən

Flavius
  pers. name   FLĀ-vē-uhs   ˈfleːviːəs

Fleming
  Sir Alexander, *Scottish*   FLEM-ing   ˈflemiŋ
    bacteriologist (Nobel 1945)

Flemish
  lang., W. Europe; pert. to Flanders   FLEM-ish   ˈflemiʃ

Fletcher
  pers. name   FLECH-uhr   ˈfletʃəʳ

Fleur-de-lis
  French symbol   FLUHRD-l-Ē, FLURD-l-Ē   ˌfləʳdlˈiː, ˌfluʳdlˈiː

Fleurie
  French wine   fluhr-Ē   flœriː

Fleurs-de-lis
  plural of fleur-de-lis   FLUHRD-l-Ē(Z), FLURD-l-Ē(Z)   ˌfləʳdlˈiː(z), ˌfluʳdlˈiː(z)

Flexner
  Stuart, *US lexicographer*   FLEK-snuhr   ˈfleksnəʳ

Fliegende Holländer, der
  opera, Wagner   der FLĒ-guhn-duh HAW-LEN-duhr   deʳ ˈfliːgəndə ˈhɔː,lendəʳ

Flin Flon
  town, Canada   FLIN FLAHN   ˈflin ˌflɑn

Flintshire
  former county, Wales   FLINT-shuhr, -SHIR   ˈflintʃəʳ, -ˌʃiʳ

Flo
  pers. name   FLŌ   ˈfloː

Flora
  Roman flower goddess; pers name   FLŌR-uh, FLAWR-uh   ˈfloːrə, ˈflɔːrə

Floréal
  month, French Revolutionary   flaw-rā-AHL   floːreːɑːl
    calendar

Florence
  1. prov & town, Italy [Firenze]; *US*   FLAWR-uhn(t)s, FLAHR-uhn(t)s   ˈflɔːrən(t)s, ˈflɑrən(t)s
    pl. name; pers. name
  2. French   flaw-RAHⁿS   flɔːrãs

Florens
  1. pers. name, German   FLŌR-ens   ˈfloːrens
  2. Latin   FLŌR-enz   ˈfloːrenz

Key (col. 2): a: fad ā: fade ah: father ar: Mary aw: law e: fed ē: feed er: merry i: hid ī: hide ō: coat ōō: boot
oi: boy ow: now u: put uh: above uhr: bird ch: chop ng: ring sh: show th: thick th̲: this zh: measure

Florentine
 pert. to Florence; *served with*   FLAWR-uhn-TĒN, FLAWR-uhn-TĪN,   'flɔːrən,tiːn, 'flɔːrən,tain,
  spinach   FLAHR-uhn-   'flɑrən-

Florenz
 pers. name (F. Ziegfeld)   FLAWR-uhn(t)s, FLAHR-uhn(t)s   'flɔːrən(t)s, 'flɑrən(t)s

Flores
 island, Azores; island, sea,   FLŌR-uhs, FLAWR-uhs   'floːrəs, 'flɔːrəs
  Indonesia

Florey
 Sir Howard W., *Australian-born*   FLŌR-ē, FLAWR-ē   'floːri', 'flɔːri'
  British pathologist (Nobel 1945)

Florian
 1. pers. name   FLŌR-ē-uhn   'floːriːən
 2. German   FLŌR-yahn, FLŌR-ē-ahn   'floːʳjɑn, 'floːriːɑn

Florida
 1. state, US   FLAWR-uhd-uh, FLAHR-uhd-uh,   'flɔːrədə, 'flɑrədə, 'floːrədə
              FLŌR-uhd-uh
 2. pl. name, S America; mtns.,   flaw-RĒ-duh   flɔː'riːdə
  NM

Floridian
 pert. to Florida   fluh-RID-ē-uhn, flaw-RID-ē-uhn,   flə'ridiːən, flɔː'ridiːən,
              flah-RID-ē-uhn   flɑ'ridiːən

Florio
 James, *US politician;* John,   FLAWR-ē-ō, FLŌR-ē-ō   'flɔːriː,oː, 'floːriː,oː
  English lexicographer

Florsheim
 US shoe store chain   FLAWR-SHĪM   'flɔːʳ,ʃaim

Flory
 Paul J., *US physical chemist*   FLŌR-ē, FLAWR-ē   'floːri', 'flɔːri'
  (Nobel 1974)

Floyd
 pers. name   FLOID   'flɔid

Fluellen
 character in Henry V, *Shakespeare*   flo͞o-EL-uhn   fluː'elən

Fluor
 US engineering co.   FLUR   'fluʳ

fluorine
 element   FLUR-ĒN, FLU-uh-RĒN, FLŌR-ĒN,   'flur,iːn, 'fluə,riːn, 'floːr,iːn,
              FLAWR-ĒN   'flɔːr,iːn

Fluvanna
 county, VA   flo͞o-VAN-uh   fluː'vænə

Flynt
 Larry Claxton, *US publisher*   FLINT   'flint

FNMA
 Federal National Mortgage   FAN-ē-MĀ   ,fæni'meː
  Association

Foch
 1. Ferdinand, *French militarist*   FAWSH   fɔːʃ
 2. Nina, *US actress*   FŌSH   'foːʃ

Fodor
 Eugene, *travel author*   FŌD-uhr   'foːdəʳ

Fogelberg
 Dan, *US recording artist*   FŌ-guhl-BUHRG   'foːgəl,bəʳg

Foreign Sounds: ue: *Fr.* **rue**, *Ger.* **füllen**   uh(r): *Fr.* **boeuf**, *Ger.* **Höhle**   <u>kh</u>: *Ger.* i**ch**, *Scot.* lo**ch**   ğ: *Sp.* ami**g**o   v̲: *Sp.* ha**b**lar
hl: *Welsh* **Ll**anelli.   CAPITALS: primary stress.   SMALL CAPS: secondary stress.   Ⓢ: U.S. pron.   Ⓔ: British pron.

Fogerty
  John, *rock singer, guitarist,*　　　　FŌ-guhrt-ē　　　　　　　　'foːgəʳʈiˑ
    songwriter

Fogg
  pers. name　　　　　　　　　　　FAWG, FAHG　　　　　　　'fɔːg, 'fag

Foggia
  prov & town, Italy　　　　　　　FAWD-jah, Ⓢ FAW-juh　　　'fɔːddʒɑ, Ⓢ 'fɔːdʒə

Fohism
  Chinese Buddhism　　　　　　　FŌ-ɪZ-uhm　　　　　　　　'foː,izəm

Foix
  prov & town, France　　　　　　FWAH　　　　　　　　　　fwɑː

Fokine
  Michel, *US choreographer*　　　　FAWK-yin, faw-KĒN　　　　'fɔːkjin, fɔː'kiːn

Fokis [Phocis]
  ancient district, dept., Greece　　fō-KĒS　　　　　　　　　　foː'kiːs

Fokker
  Anthony, *Dutch aircraft designer*　FAHK-uhr, FŌ-kuhr　　　　'fakəʳ, 'foːkəʳ

Folger
  Shakespearean Library,　　　　　FŌL-juhr　　　　　　　　　'foːldʒəʳ
    Washington, D. C.; pers. name

Folies Bergére
  music hall, Paris, French　　　　faw-LĒ ber-ZHER　　　　　fɔːliˑ berʒer

Folkes
  pers. name　　　　　　　　　　　FŌLKS, FŌKS　　　　　　　'foːlks, 'foːks

Folkestone
  resort, England　　　　　　　　FŌK-stuhn　　　　　　　　　'foːkstən

Folsom
  city, prison, CA; village, NM　　FŌL-suhm　　　　　　　　　'foːlsəm

Fomalhaut
  star　　　　　　　　　　　　　FŌ-muhl-HAWT, FŌ-muh-LAWT,　'foːməl,hɔːt, 'foːmə,lɔːt,
　　　　　　　　　　　　　　　　　FŌ-muh-LŌ, FŌ-muhl-HŌT　　　'foːmə,loː, 'foːməl,hoːt

Fon
  lang., W. Africa　　　　　　　FAHN, FAWN　　　　　　　'fan, 'fɔːn

Fonda
  US acting family　　　　　　　FAHN-duh　　　　　　　　　'fandə

Fond Du Lac
  city, county, WI; Indian　　　　FAHN-dl-AK, FAHN-juh-LAK　'fandl̩,æk, 'fandʒə,læk
    reservation, US

Fons
  Roman god of springs　　　　　FAHNZ, FŌNZ　　　　　　　'fanz, 'foːnz

Fonseca
  Gulf of, *Cen. America*　　　　　fahn-SĀ-kuh　　　　　　　　fan'seːkə

Fontaine
  1. Jean de la, *French writer*　　　fawⁿ-TEN　　　　　　　　　fɔ̃ten
  2. Joan, *US actress*　　　　　　　fahn-TĀN　　　　　　　　　fan'teːn

Fontaine, La
  see La Fontaine

Fontainebleau
  palace, city, France　　　　　　fawⁿ-ten-BLŌ, Ⓢ FAHNT-n-BLŌ　fɔ̃tenbloː, Ⓢ 'fantn̩,bloː

Fontbonne
  College, *MO*　　　　　　　　　fahnt-BAHN, FAHNT-BAHN　　fant'ban, 'fant,ban

Fonteyn
  Dame Margot, *English ballet*　　fahn-TĀN, FAHN-TĀN　　　　fan'teːn, 'fan,teːn
    dancer

Key (col. 2):　a: fad　ā: fade　ah: father　ar: Mary　aw: law　e: fed　ē: feed　er: merry　i: hid　ī: hide　ō: coat　ōō: boot
oi: boy　ow: now　u: put　uh: above　uhr: bird　ch: chop　ng: ring　sh: show　th: thick　th: this　zh: measure

Fontina
   Italian cheese   fahn-TĒ-nuh   fɑnˈtiːnə

Fonzie
   TV sitcom character   FAHN-zē   ˈfɑnziˈ

Foote
   pers. name   FUT   ˈfut

Forbes
   Field, ballpark, Pittsburgh, PA; US   FAWRBZ   ˈfɔːʳbz
      publishing family

Ford
   Gerald R., 38th US president;   FAWRD   ˈfɔːʳd
      Henry, US industrialist; pers.
      name

Fordham
   University, NY   FAWRD-uhm   ˈfɔːʳdəm

Fordyce
   pers. name   FAWR-DĪS   ˈfɔːʳˌdɑis

Forest
   pers. name   FAWR-uhst, FAHR-uhst   ˈfɔːrəst, ˈfɑrəst

Forester
   pers. name   FAWR-uhs-tuhr, FAHR-   ˈfɔːrəstəʳ, ˈfɑr-

Forman
   Milos, Czech film director   FAWR-muhn   ˈfɔːʳmən

Formica
   tdmk for plastic sheeting   fawr-MĪ-kuh   fɔːʳˈmaikə

Formosa
   prov, Argentina; former name of fawr-MŌ-suh   fɔːʳˈmoːsə
      Taiwan

Formosus
   pope   fawr-MŌ-suhs   fɔːʳˈmoːsəs

Fornax
   Roman goddess of the bread oven; FAWR-NAKS   ˈfɔːʳˌnæks
      constellation

Forrest
   pers. name   FAWR-uhst, FAHR-uhst   ˈfɔːrəst, ˈfɑrəst

Fors
   Roman god of chance   FAWRS, FAWRZ   ˈfɔːʳs, ˈfɔːʳz

Forssmann
   Werner, German physician (Nobel FAWR-SMAHN   ˈfɔːʳˌsmɑn
      1956)

Forster
   pers. name   FAWR-stuhr   ˈfɔːʳstəʳ

Forsyth
   county, GA, NC   FAWR-SĪTH, fawr-SĪTH   ˈfɔːʳˌsɑiθ, fɔːʳˈsɑiθ

Forsythe
   John, US actor   FAWR-SĪTH, fawr-SĪTH   ˈfɔːʳˌsɑiθ, fɔːʳˈsɑiθ

Fortaleza
   city, Brazil   FAWRT-l-Ā-zuh   ˌfɔːʳtl̩ˈeːzə

Fort Belknap
   Indian reservation, US   FŌRT BEL-NAP, FAWRT   ˌfoːʳt ˈbelˌnæp, ˌfɔːʳt

Fort Belvoir
   military post, VA   fōrt BEL-VAWR, FAWRT   foːʳt ˈbelˌvɔːʳ, ˌfɔːʳt

Fort Berthold
   Indian reservation, US   FŌRT BUHR-TŌLD, FAWRT ˌfoːʳt ˈbəʳˌtoːld, ˌfɔːʳt

---

Foreign Sounds: ue: *Fr.* **rue,** *Ger.* **füllen** uh(r): *Fr.* **boeuf,** *Ger.* **Höhle** kh: *Ger.* **ich,** *Scot.* **loch** g̃: *Sp.* amigo v: *Sp.* ha**b**lar
hl: *Welsh* **Llanelli.** CAPITALS: primary stress. SMALL CAPS: secondary stress. ⑤: U.S. pron. ⑭: British pron.

Fort Bidwell
  Indian reservation, US   FŌRT BID-WEL, FAWRT, BID-wuhl   ˌfoːʳt ˈbidˌwel, ˌfɔːʳt, ˈbidwəl

Fort-de-France
  town, Caribbean   FAWR-duh-FRAHⁿS   ˌfɔːʳdəˈfrãs

Forth
  river, Scotland; programming   FŌRTH, FAWRTH   ˈfoːʳθ, ˈfɔːʳθ
  lang.

Fortinbras
  character in Hamlet, *Shakespeare*   FAWRT-n-BRAS   ˈfɔːʳtn̩ˌbræs

Fort Lauderdale
  city, FL   FŌRT LAWD-uhr-DĀL, FAWRT   ˌfoːʳt ˈlɔːdəʳˌdeːl, ˌfɔːʳt

Fort McDermitt
  Indian reservation, US   FŌRT muhk-DUHR-muht, FAWRT   ˌfoːʳt məkˈdəʳmət, ˌfɔːʳt

Fort McDowell
  Indian reservation, US   FŌRT muhk-DOW(-uh)l, FAWRT   ˌfoːʳt məkˈdau(ə)l, ˌfɔːʳt

Fortnum & Mason
  exclusive retailer, London   FAWRT-nuhm uhn(d) MĀ-suhn   ˈfɔːʳtnəm ən(d) ˈmeːsən

Fort Qu'Appelle
  town, Saskatchewan, Canada   FŌRT kwah-PEL, FAWRT   ˌfoːʳt kwaˈpel, ˌfɔːʳt

FORTRAN
  programming lang.   FAWR-TRAN   ˈfɔːʳˌtræn

Fort Steilacoom
  Community College, *WA*   FŌRT STĪ-luh-KOŌM, FAWRT   ˌfoːʳt ˈstailəˌkuːm, ˌfɔːʳt

Fort Ticonderoga
  fort, NY   FŌRT TĪ-KAHN-duh-RŌ-guh, FAWRT   ˌfoːʳt ˌtaiˌkandəˈroːgə, ˌfɔːʳt

Fort Totten
  Indian reservation, US   FŌRT TAHT-n, FAWRT   ˌfoːʳt ˈtatn̩, ˌfɔːʳt

Fortuna
  city, CA; Roman goddess of   fawr-T(Y)OŌ-nuh, fawr-CHOŌ-nuh   fɔːʳt(j)uːnə, fɔːʳtʃuːnə
  fortune

Fort Yuma
  Indian reservation, US   FŌRT YOŌ-muh, FAWRT   ˌfoːʳt ˈjuːmə, ˌfɔːʳt

Forum Romanum
  center of ancient Rome   FŌR-uhm rō-MAHN-uhm, FAWR-uhm   ˈfoːrəm roːˈmanəm, ˈfɔːrəm

Forza del Destino
  opera, Verdi   FAWRT-sah del des-TĒ-nō   ˈfɔːʳtsa del desˈtiːnoː

Fosbury
  Dick, *high jump champion*   FAHZ-BER-ē   ˈfazˌberiˑ

Fosse
  1. Bob, *US director*   FAW-sē, FAHS-ē   ˈfɔːsiˑ, ˈfasiˑ
  2. pers. name   FAWS, FAHS, FAW-sē, FAHS-ē   ˈfɔːs, ˈfas, ˈfɔːsiˑ, ˈfasiˑ

Fossum
  Field, *ballpark, Aberdeen, SD*   FAHS-uhm   ˈfasəm

Fotomat
  US film processing co.   FŌT-uh-MAT   ˈfoːʈəˌmæt

Foucault
  Jean, *French physicist;* Michel,   foō-KŌ   fuːkoː
  French philosopher

Fouché
  Joseph, *French politician*   foō-SHĀ   fuːʃeː

Fourier
  Jean-Baptiste, *French*   foōr-YĀ   fuːrjeː
  mathematician

Key (col. 2): a: fad ā: fade ah: father ar: **Mary** aw: **law** e: fed ē: feed er: **merry** i: hid ī: hide ō: coat oō: boot
oi: **boy** ow: **now** u: put uh: **above** uhr: **bird** ch: **chop** ng: **ring** sh: **show** th: **thick** <u>th</u>: **this** zh: measure

Fournier
    Charles, *French socialist*   fo͞orn-YĀ   fuːrnjeː
Fou-shan
    see Fushun
Fowkes
    Robert, *US linguist*   FOWKS   'fauks
Fowler
    Henry, *English lexicographer;*   FOW-luhr   'faulə^r
    William A., *US physicist (Nobel*
    1983)
Fowles
    John, *British author*   FOWLZ   'faulz
Fox
    N. American people; pers. name   FAHKS   'faks
Foyt
    A.J., *US race car driver*   FOIT   'fɔit
Fra Angelico
    Italian painter; liqueur   FRAH an-JEL-i-kō   ˌfra æn'dʒelikoː
Fra Diavolo
    Italian brigand   FRAH dē-AHV-uh-LŌ   ˌfra diː'avəˌloː
Fra Filippo Lippi
    see Lippi
Fragonard
    Jean-Honoré, *French artist*   frah-gaw-NAHR   fraːgoːnaːr
Framingham
    town, MA   FRĀ-ming-HAM   'freːmiŋˌhæm
Frampton
    Peter, *British rock musician*   FRAM(P)-tuhn   'fræm(p)tən
Fran
    pers. name   FRAN   'fræn
Françaix
    Jean, *French composer*   frahⁿ-SE   frãse
France
    1. *country, Europe; pers. name*   FRANS, FRAHNS, FRAHⁿS   'fræns, 'fraːns, frãs
    2. Anatole *(pseudonym of* J.-A. F.   FRAHⁿS, Ⓢ FRANS   frãs, Ⓢ 'fræns
    Thibault*), French author (Nobel*
    1921)
Frances
    pers. name   FRAN-suhs   'frænsəs
Francesca
    1. *pers. name*   fran-CHES-kuh   fræn'tʃeskə
    2. *Italian*   frahn-CHÄS-kah   fran'tʃeːska
Francescatti
    Zino, *French violinist*   FRAHN-ches-KAHT-ē   ˌfrantʃes'kaṭiˑ
Francesco
    pers. name   frahn-CHÄS-kō   fran'tʃeːskoː
Franche-Comté
    prov, France   frahⁿsh-kawⁿ-TĀ   frãʃkɔ̃teː
Francis
    1. *pers. name*   FRAN-suhs   'frænsəs
    2. *Dutch*   FRAHN-suhs   'fransəs
    3. *French*   frahⁿ-SĒS   frãsiːs
    4. *German*   FRAHNT-sis   'frantsis
    5. *Norwegian*   FRAHN-sis   'fransis

Foreign Sounds: ue: *Fr.* **rue,** *Ger.* **füllen**   uh(r): *Fr.* **bœuf,** *Ger.* **Höhle**   <u>kh</u>: *Ger.* i**ch,** *Scot.* lo**ch**   g̃: *Sp.* ami**g**o   ᵥ: *Sp.* ha**b**lar
hl: *Welsh* **Llanelli.**   CAPITALS: primary stress.   SMALL CAPS: secondary stress.   Ⓢ: U.S. pron.   Ⓔ: British pron.

Franciscans
  religious order   fran-SIS-kuhnz   fræn'siskənz

Francisco
  1. pers. name   fran-SIS-kō   fræn'siskoː
  2. Portuguese   frahⁿ-SĒSH-kōō, -SĒS-kōō   frãː'siːʃkuː, -'siːsku
  3. Spanish   frahn-SĒS-kō, -THĒS-kō   fran'siːskoː, -'θiːskoː

Franciscus
  James, *US actor*   fran-SIS-kuhs   fræn'siskəs

francium
  element   FRAN-sē-uhm   'frænsiːəm

Franck
  1. César Auguste, *Belgian*   FRAHⁿK, Ⓢ FRAHNGK   frãk, Ⓢ 'fraŋk
  composer
  2. James, *German-born US*   FRAHNGK   'fraŋk
  physicist (Nobel 1925)

Franco
  1. Francisco, *Spanish dictator;*   FRAHNG-kō, Ⓢ FRANG-kō   'fraŋkoː, Ⓢ 'fræŋkoː
  pers. name
  2. Italian   FRAHNG-kō   'fraŋkoː

François
  pers. name   frahⁿ-SWAH   frãswaː

Françoise
  pers. name   frahⁿ-SWAHZ   frãswaːz

Franconia
  town, NH; district, Germany   frang-KŌ-nē-uh, frang-KŌN-yuh   fræŋ'koːniːə, fræŋ'koːnjə

Franconian Forest [Frankenwald]
  mtn. range, Germany   frang-KŌ-nē-uhn FAWR-uhst, FAHR-uhst   fræŋ'koːniːən 'foːrəst, 'farəst

Francophile
  lover of things French   FRANG-kuh-FĪL   'fræŋkə,fail

Francophobe
  hater of things French   FRANG-kuh-FŌB   'fræŋkə,foːb

Frangipani
  flowering tree   FRAN-juh-PAN-ē, FRAN-juh-PAHN-ē   ,frændʒə'pæniː, ,frændʒə'paniˑ

Franglais
  mixture of French & English   frahng-GLĀ   fraŋ'gleː

Frank
  1. pers. name   FRANGK   'fræŋk
  2. French   FRAHⁿK   frãk

Frankenheimer
  John, *entertainer*   FRANG-kuhn-HĪ-muhr   'fræŋkən,haiməʳ

Frankenmuth
  city, MI; beer   FRANG-kuhn-MŌŌTH   'fræŋkən,muːθ

Frankenstein
  character in gothic novel by M.   FRANG-kuhn-STĪN   'fræŋkən,stain
  Shelley

Frankenwald [Franconian Forest]
  mtn. range, Germany   FRAHNG-kuhn-VAHLT   'fraŋkən,valt

Frankfort
  US pl. name   FRANGK-fuhrt   'fræŋkfəʳt

Frankfurt
  city, Germany   FRAHNGK-FURT, Ⓢ FRANGK-fuhrt   'fraŋk,fuʳt, Ⓢ 'fræŋkfəʳt

Frankfurt/Main
  airport, Frankfurt   FRAHNGK-FURT-MĪN   'fraŋk,fuʳt'main

Key (col. 2):   a: fad   ā: fade   ah: father   ar: Mary   aw: law   e: fed   ē: feed   er: merry   i: hid   ī: hide   ō: coat   ōō: boot
oi: boy   ow: now   u: put   uh: above   uhr: bird   ch: chop   ng: ring   sh: show   th: thick   <u>th</u>: this   zh: measure

Frankie
  pers. name FRANG-kē 'fræŋki·
Franklin, -lyn
  pers. name FRANGK-luhn 'fræŋklən
Frans
  1. pers. name, Danish, Dutch FRAHNS 'frɑns
  2. Finnish, Swedish FRAHNS 'frɑːns
Franz
  1. pers. name FRANS, FRANZ, FRAHNS 'fræns, 'frænz, 'frɑns
  2. French FRAHⁿS frɑ̃s
Franzia
  wine FRAHN(T)-sē-uh, FRAN(T)-sē-uh 'frɑn(t)siːə, 'fræn(t)siːə
Franzikus
  German beer FRAHN(T)-si-kus 'frɑn(t)sikus
Franz Josef Land
  Arctic archipelago frahn(t)s YŌ-zuhf LAHNT; FRAN(T)S JŌ-zuhf LAND, JŌ-suhf frɑn(t)s 'joːzəf ˌlɑnt; fræn(t)s 'dʒoːzəf ˌlænd, 'dʒoːsəf
Frascati
  wine frahs-KAHT-ē frɑs'kɑt̬i·
Fraser
  River, Canada FRĀ-zuhr, FRĀ-zhuhr 'freɪzəʳ, 'freɪʒəʳ
Frau
  Mrs., in German FROW 'frɑu
Frauen
  pl. of Frau FROW-uhn 'frɑuən
Fräulein
  Miss, in German FROI-LĪN 'frɔiˌlɑin
Frazier
  June, singer-songwriter; Joe, *US prize fighter* FRĀ-zhuhr 'freɪʒəʳ
Fred
  pers. name FRED 'fred
Freda
  pers. name FRĒD-uh, FRED-uh 'friːdə, 'fredə
Freddy
  pers. name FRED-ē 'fredi·
Frederic
  1. pers. name FRED(-uh)-rik 'fred(ə)rik
  2. Norwegian FRED-rik 'fredrik
Frédéric
  pers. name, French frā-dā-RĒK freːdeːriːk
Frederica
  pers. name, German FRĀ-dā-RĒ-kah ˌfreɪdeːˈriːkɑ
Frederici Honores
  former constellation FRED-uh-RĒ-kē (h)ahn-ŌR-ĒZ, (h)ahn-ŌR-uhs ˌfredə'riːki· (h)ɑn'oːrˌiːz, (h)ɑn'oːrəs
Frédérick
  French frā-dā-RĒK freːdeːriːk
Frederick
  1. pers. name FRED(-uh)-rik 'fred(ə)rik
  2. Danish FRIT͟H-rik 'friðrik
Frederico
  pers. name, Italian FRĀ-dā-RĒ-kō ˌfreɪdeːˈriːkoː
Fredericton
  city, New Brunswick, Canada FRED-(uh-)rik-tuhn 'fred(ə)riktən

---

Foreign Sounds: **ue**: *Fr.* **rue**, *Ger.* **füllen** **uh(r)**: *Fr.* **boeuf**, *Ger.* **Höhle** **kh**: *Ger.* **ich**, *Scot.* **loch** **g̃**: *Sp.* **amigo** **v̧**: *Sp.* **hablar** **hl**: *Welsh* **Llanelli**. CAPITALS: primary stress. SMALL CAPS: secondary stress. ⑤: U.S. pron. ⑭: British pron.

Frederika
1. pers. name, Danish	fri<u>th</u>-RĒ-kah	friðˈriːkɑː
2. Swedish	FRĀ-duh-RĒ-kah	ˌfreːdəˈriːkɑ

Fredonia
city, KS; village, college, NY	frē-DŌ-nē-uh, frē-DŌN-yuh	friˈdoːniːə, friˈdoːnjə

Fredric
1. pers. name	FRED-rik	ˈfredrik
2. Swedish	FRĀ-drik	ˈfreːdrik

Fredrica
pers. name	fred-RĒ-kuh	fredˈriːkə

Fredrik
1. pers. name, Danish	FRI<u>TH</u>-rik	ˈfriðrik
2. Dutch	FRĀ-druhk	ˈfreːdrək
3. Finnish, Swedish	FRĀ-drik	ˈfreːdrik
4. Norwegian	FRED-rik	ˈfredrik

Freeman
pers. name	FRĒ-muhn	ˈfriːmən

Freemont
pers. name	FRĒ-MAHNT	ˈfriːˌmɑnt

Freeport
US pl. name; town, Bahamas	FRĒ-PŌRT, FRĒ-PAWRT	ˈfriːˌpoːʳt, ˈfriːˌpɔːʳt

Freer
art gallery, Washington, DC	FRIR	ˈfriʳ

Freesia
flower	FRĒ-zh(ē-)uh, FRĒ-zē-uh	ˈfriːʒ(iː)ə, ˈfriːziːə

Freetown
town, Sierra Leone	FRĒ-TOWN	ˈfriːˌtɑun

Frege
Gottlob, *German logician*	FREG-uh, FRĀ-guh	ˈfregə, ˈfreːgə

Freiburg
city, Germany	FRĪ-BURK	ˈfraiˌbuʳk

Fremantle
city, Australia	frē-MAN-tl	friˈmæntl̩

Fremont
city, CA; pers. name	FRĒ-MAHNT	ˈfriːˌmɑnt

French
lang., W. Europe	FRENCH	ˈfrentʃ

French Guiana
French overseas dept., S. America	FRENCH gē-AN-uh, gē-AHN-uh, gī-AN-uh	ˌfrentʃ giːˈænə, giːˈɑnə, gaiˈænə

French Guianese
pert. to French Guiana	GĪ-uh-NĒZ, GĒ-uh-, -NĒS	ˌgaiəˈniːz, ˌgiːə-, -ˈniːs

Frenchman
man from France	FRENCH-muhn	ˈfrentʃmən

Freon
tdmk for fluorocarbon	FRĒ-AHN	ˈfriːˌɑn

Fresnel
Augustin Jean, *French physicist; pers. name*	frā-NEL, fre-NEL	freːnel, frenel

Fresnel lens
focusing device	FREZ-nuhl, fruh-NEL, frā-NEL	ˈfreznəl, frəˈnel, freːˈnel

Fresno
city, county, CA	FREZ-nō	ˈfreznoː

Freud
Sigmund, *Austrian psychoanalyst*	FROID	ˈfrɔid

Key (col. 2):   a: fad ā: fade ah: father ar: Mary aw: law e: fed ē: feed er: merry i: hid ī: hide ō: coat o͞o: boot
oi: boy ow: now u: put uh: above uhr: bird ch: chop ng: ring sh: show th: thick <u>th</u>: this zh: measure

Freudian
    pert. to Freud   FROID-ē-uhn   ˈfrɔidiːən
Frey
    1. Scandinavian weather god   FRĀ   ˈfreː
    2. pers. name   FRĪ   ˈfrɑi
Freya
    pers. name   FRĀ-uh   ˈfreːə
Freyja
    Scandinavian fertility goddess   FRĀ-uh   ˈfreːə
Freyr [Frey]
    Scandinavian weather god   FRĀR, FRER, FRĀ   ˈfreːʳ, ˈfreʳ, ˈfreː
Fribourg
    city, Switzerland   frē-BUR   friːbur
Friday
    day of the week   FRĪD-ē, FRĪD-ā   ˈfrɑidiˑ, ˈfrɑideː
Frideric
    pers. name (G. F. Handel)   FRĒD-rik   ˈfriːdrik
Fridtjof
    pers. name, Norwegian   FRICH-AWF   ˈfritʃˌɔːf
Fried
    A. H., *Austrian pacifist, publicist*   FRĒT, FRĒD   ˈfriːt, ˈfriːd
    (Nobel 1911)
Frieda
    1. pers. name   FRĒD-uh   ˈfriːdə
    2. German   FRĒ-dah   ˈfriːdɑ
Friedan
    Betty, *US feminist*   fri-DAN, frē-DAN   friˈdæn, friːˈdæn
Friedman
    Jerome I., *US physicist (Nobel*   FRĒD-muhn   ˈfriːdmən
    1990); Milton, *US economist*
    (Nobel 1976)
Friedrich
    1. pers. name   FRĒ-drik   ˈfriːdrik
    2. German   FRĒ-drikh   ˈfriːdriç
Friedrichshafen
    town, Germany   FRĒ-driks-HAHF-uhn   ˌfriːdriksˈhɑfən
Fries
    pers. name   FRĒS   ˈfriːs
Friesche Eilanden [Frisian Islands]
    islands, North Sea   FRĒ-suh Ī-LAHN-duhn   ˌfriːsə ˈɑiˌlɑndən
Friese-Greene
    William, *English inventor*   FRĒZ-GRĒN   ˈfriːzˈgriːn
Friesian
    cattle   FRĒ-zhuhn   ˈfriːʒən
Friesland
    province, Netherlands   FRĒS-LAHNT   ˈfriːsˌlɑnt
Frietchie
    Barbara, *Civil War heroine*   FRICH-ē   ˈfritʃiˑ
Frigga [Frigg]
    Scandinavian fertility goddess   FRIG-uh   ˈfrigə
Frigg [Frigga]
    Scandinavian fertility goddess   FRIG   ˈfrig
Frigidaire
    tdmk for a refrigerator   FRIJ-uh-DAR, FRIJ-uh-DER,   ˌfridʒəˈdæʳ, ˌfridʒəˈdeʳ,
         FRIJ-uh-DAR, FRIJ-uh-DER   ˈfridʒəˌdæʳ, ˈfridʒəˌdeʳ

Foreign Sounds: ue: *Fr.* **rue**, *Ger.* **füllen**   uh(r): *Fr.* **boeuf**, *Ger.* **Höhle**   <u>kh</u>: *Ger.* **ich**, *Scot.* **loch**   g̃: *Sp.* **amigo** v̰: *Sp.* **hablar**
hl: *Welsh* **Llanelli**.   CAPITALS: primary stress.   SMALL CAPS: secondary stress.   Ⓢ: U.S. pron.   Ⓛ: British pron.

Frigo
   cheese — FRĒ-gō — ˈfriːgoː

Frigoris, Mare
   see Mare Frigoris

Frimaire
   month, French Revolutionary — frē-MER — friːmer
    calendar

Friml
   Rudolf, *US composer* — FRIM-uhl — ˈfriməl

Frio
   river, county, TX — FRĒ-ō — ˈfriːoː

Frisbee
   tdmk for flying disk — FRIZ-bē — ˈfrizbiˑ

Frisch
   Karl von, *Austrian zoologist (Nobel* — FRISH — ˈfriʃ
    1973); Ragnar, *Norwegian*
    economist (Nobel 1969)

Frisch's
   US restaurant chain — FRISH-uhz — ˈfriʃəz

Frisian
   lang., Netherlands, Germany; — FRIZH-uhn, FRĒ-zhuhn — ˈfriʒən, ˈfriːʒən
    Islands, *North Sea*

Frito-Lay
   US snack foods co. — FRĒT-ō-LĀ, FRĒT-ō-LĀ — ˈfriːʈoːˌleː, ˌfriːʈoːˈleː

Frits
   pers. name, Dutch — FRITS — ˈfrits

Fritz
   pers. name — FRITS — ˈfrits

Friulian
   lang., people, North Italy — frē-OO-lē-uhn — friːˈuːliːən

Frobisher
   Sir Martin, *English mariner* — FRŌ-buh-shuhr — ˈfroːbəʃəʳ

Froebel
   Friedrich, *German educator* — FRUH(R)-buhl — ˈfrœːbəl

Frohman
   pers. name — FRŌ-muhn — ˈfroːmən

Froissart
   Jean, *French poet* — frwah-SAHR, Ⓢ f(r)wah-SAHR — frwaːsaːr, Ⓢ f(r)waˈsaʳ

Frome
   1. Lynette "Squeaky", *US* — FRŌM — ˈfroːm
    attempted assassin
   2. town, river, England — FROOM — ˈfruːm

Fromm
   Erich, *US psychoanalyst* — FRŌM, FRAHM — ˈfroːm, ˈfrɑm

Fronsac
   French wine — frawⁿ-SAHK — frɔ̃saːk

Frontenac
   Louis de, *political leader* — frawⁿ-tuh-NAHK — frɔ̃tənaːk

Frontignac
   wine grape variety — frawⁿ-tēn-YAHK — frɔ̃tiːnjaːk

Frontignan
   commune, France — frawⁿ-tēn-YAHⁿ — frɔ̃tiːnjɑ̃

Front National
   political party, France — FRAWⁿ nahs-yaw-NAHL — frɔ̃ naːsjɔːnaːl

---

Key (col. 2):   a: fad   ā: fade   ah: father   ar: Mary   aw: law   e: fed   ē: feed   er: merry   i: hid   ī: hide   ō: coat   oo: boot
oi: boy   ow: now   u: put   uh: above   uhr: bird   ch: chop   ng: ring   sh: show   th: thick   th: this   zh: measure

Fructidor
   month, French Revolutionary   fruek-tē-DAWR   fryːktiːdɔːr
   calendar
Fructuoso
   pers. name   frōōk-TWŌ-sȯ   fruːk'twoːsoː
Fruehauf
   US truck-trailer co.   FRŌŌ-HAWF, FRŌŌ-HAHF   'fruːˌhɔːf, 'fruːˌhaf
Frydenlund
   Norwegian beer   FRUED-n-LUND   'fryːdn̩ˌlund
FSLIC
   Federal Savings and Loan   FIZ-lik, EF-es-EL-ī-SĒ   'fɪzlik, ˌefesˌelɑi'siː
   Insurance Corporation
Fthiótis
   see Phthiotis
Fuegian
   pert. to Tierra del Fuego   fyu-Ē-jē-uhn, fyu-Ā-gē-uhn   fjuˈiːdʒiːən, fjuˈeːgiːən
Fuentes
   Carlos, *Mexican novelist &*   FWEN-tās   'fwenteːs
   playwright
Fugue
   musical composition   FYŌŌG   'fjuːg
Führer, der
   title, A. Hitler   der FUER-uhr; ⑤ der FYUR-uhr,   derʳ 'fyːrəʳ; ⑤ derʳ 'fjurəʳ,
      duhr, FIR-uhr   dəʳ, 'firəʳ
Fujayrah, Al
   emirate, town, United Arab   ahl fuh-JĪ-ruh, al   ɑːl fəˈdʒɑirə, æl
   Emirates
Fuji [Fujiyama]
   Mount, *sacred mtn., Japan*   FŌŌ-jē, FYŌŌ-jē   'fuːdʒiˑ, 'fjuːdʒiˑ
Fujian [Fukien]
   province, China   FŌŌ-jē-AHN   'fuːdʒiːˈɑn
Fujica
   Japanese camera co.   FŌŌ-ji-kuh   'fuːdʒikə
Fuji Hakone Izu
   park, Japan   fōō-jē hah-kō-nā ē-zōō   fuːdʒiː hakoːneː iːzuː
Fujimori
   Alberto, *president, Peru*   fu-khē-MAWR-ē, ⑤ FŌŌ-jē-MȎR-ē,   fuxiː'mɔːriˑ,
      -MAWR-ē   ⑤ ˌfuːdʒiˈmɔːriˑ, -'mɔːriˑ
Fuji-san [Fuji]
   sacred mtn., Japan   fōō-jē-sahn   fuːdʒiːsɑn
Fujitsu
   Japanese corp.   fōō-jit-sōō   fuːdʒitsuː
Fujiyama [Fuji]
   sacred mtn., Japan   fōō-jē-ahm-ah,   fuːdʒiːɑmɑ,
      ⑤ FŌŌ-jē-(Y)AHM-uh, FYŌŌ-   ⑤ ˌfuːdʒiːˈ(j)amə, ˌfjuː-
Fukien [Fujian]
   province, China   FŌŌ-KYEN, FŌŌ-kē-EN   'fuːˈkjen, 'fuːkiːˈen
Fukui
   Kenichi, *Japanese chemist (Nobel*   fu-ku-ē   fukuiˑ
   1981)
Fukuoka
   city, Japan   fōō-kōō-ō-kah   fuːkuːoːka
Fula
   African people   FŌŌ-luh   'fuːlə

Foreign Sounds: ue: *Fr.* rue, *Ger.* füllen   uh(r): *Fr.* bœuf, *Ger.* Höhle   kh: *Ger.* ich, *Scot.* loch   g̱: *Sp.* amigo   v̱: *Sp.* hablar
hl: *Welsh* Llanelli.   CAPITALS: primary stress.   SMALL CAPS: secondary stress.   ⑤: U.S. pron.   ⑪: British pron.

Fula
  lang., Africa   F$\overline{OO}$-LAHR   'fuː,lɑ^r

Fulani [Ful, Fulfulde]
  lang., people, Africa   F$\overline{OO}$-LAHN-ē, f$\overline{oo}$-LAHN-ē   'fuː,lɑniˑ, fuː'lɑniˑ

Fulbright
  James, *US politician; scholarship*   FUL-BRĪT   'ful,brɑit

Ful [Fulani]
  lang., people, Africa   F$\overline{OO}$L, FUL   'fuːl, 'ful

Fulfulde [Fulani]
  lang., people, West Africa   ful-FUL-dē   ful'fuldiˑ

Fulgencio
  pers. name   ful-G$\overline{A}$N-thyō, -syō   ful'ɣeːnθjoː, -sjoː

Fulmar
  bird   FUL-muhr   'fulmə^r

Fulvia
  wife of Mark Antony   FUL-vē-uh   'fulviːə

Fulvius
  pers. name, Latin   FUHL-vē-uhs, FUL-   'fəlviːəs, 'ful-

Fulvius Flaccus
  Roman popular leader   FUHL-vē-uhs FLAK-uhs, FUL-   'fəlviːəs 'flækəs, 'ful-

Fulvus
  pers. name   FUHL-vuhs, FUL-vuhs   'fəlvəs, 'fulvəs

Funafuti
  atoll, Tuvalu   F(Y)$\overline{OO}$-nuh-F(Y)$\overline{OO}$T-ē   ,f(j)uːnə'f(j)uːṭiˑ

Funchal
  port, Madeira   f$\overline{oo}$n-SHAHL, fuhn-SHAHL   fuːn'ʃal, fən'ʃal

Fundy
  Bay of, *Atlantic inlet, Canada*   FUHN-dē   'fəndiˑ

Funicello
  Annette, *US entertainer*   F$\overline{OO}$-nuh-CHEL-ō   ,fuːnə'tʃeloː

Fuquay-Varina
  town, NC   F(Y)$\overline{OO}$-KW$\overline{A}$-vuh-RĪ-nuh   'f(j)uː,kweːvə'rɑinə

Fur
  lang., Sudan, Chad   FUR, FUHR   'fu^r, 'fə^r

Furies
  Roman demons of the Underworld   FYUR-ēz   'fjuriˑz

Furius
  Roman name   FYUR-ē-uhs   'fjuriːəs

Furman
  University, *SC*   FUHR-muhn   'fə^{r}mən

Furnas
  county, NE   FUHR-nuhs   'fə^{r}nəs

Furness
  Betty, *US journalist*   FUHR-NES   ,fə^{r}nes

Furnivall
  Frederick James, *Englist*   FUHR-nuh-vuhl   'fə^{r}nəvəl
    philologist

Fürstenberg
  German beer   FUR-stuhn-BERK   'fy^{r}stən,berk

Furth
  George, *US actor, playwright*   FUHRTH   'fə^{r}θ

Furtwängler
  Wilhelm, *German conductor*   FURT-VENG-(g)luhr   'fu^{r}t,veŋ(g)lə^r

Fushun, Fou-shan
  city, China   F$\overline{OO}$-SHUN   'fuːʃun

Key (col. 2):   a: fad   ā: fade   ah: father   ar: Mary   aw: law   e: fed   ē: feed   er: merry   i: hid   ī: hide   ō: coat $\overline{oo}$: boot
oi: boy   ow: now   u: put   uh: above   uhr: bird   ch: chop   ng: ring   sh: show   th: thick   th: this   zh: measure

Futuna
 islands, Pacific   f$\overline{oo}$-T$\overline{OO}$-nuh   fuˈtuːnə
Futunan
 pert. to Futuna   f$\overline{oo}$-T$\overline{OO}$-nuhn   fuˈtuːnən
Futura
 type font   f(y)$\overline{oo}$-T(Y)UR-uh, f(y)$\overline{oo}$-CHUR-uh   f(j)uːˈt(j)urə, f(j)uːˈtʃurə
Fuzhou
 city, China   F$\overline{OO}$-J$\overline{O}$ ˈfuːˈdʒɔː
Fyodor
 pers. name, Russian   FYAWD-uhr   ˈfjɔːdər

G

Gã, Ga
 lang., people, Ghana, Togo, Benin   GAH   ˈgɑ
Ga-Adangbe
 lang., W. Africa   GAH-ah-DAHNG-bā   ˈgɑɑˈdaŋbeː
Gabès
 town, oasis, gulf, Tunisia   GAHB-uhs, GAHB-ES   ˈgabəs, ˈgab‚es
Gabon
 republic, Africa   ga-BAW^n gæˈbõ
Gabonese
 pert. to Gabon   GAB-uh-NĒZ, -NĒS   ‚gæbəˈniːz, -ˈniːs
Gabor
 1. Dennis, Hungarian-born British physicist (Nobel 1971)   GAHB-AWR, guh-BAWR   ˈgab‚ɔː^r, gəˈbɔː^r
 2. Eva, Zsa Zsa, US entertainers   guh-BAWR   gəˈbɔː^r
Gábor
 pers. name, Hungarian   GAH-bawr   ˈgɑːbɔː^r
Gaboriau
 Emile, French novelist   gah-bawr-Y$\overline{O}$ gɑːbɔːrjoː
Gaborone
 city, Botswana   GAHB-uh-R$\overline{O}$-nē   ‚gabəˈroːniː
Gabriel
 1. pers. name   G$\overline{A}$-brē-uhl   ˈgeːbriːəl
 2. Dutch   GAHB-rē-el   ˈgɑːbriːel
 3. French   gah-brē-EL   gɑːbriːel
 4. German   GAHB-rē-el   ˈgɑbriːel
 5. Norwegian, Swedish   GAHB-rē-uhl   ˈgɑbriːəl
 6. Polish   GAHB-ryel, Ⓢ GAHB-rē-el   ˈgɑːbrjel, Ⓢ ˈgɑːbriːel
 7. Portuguese   guh-brē-EL, gah-   gəbriːˈel, gɑː-
 8. Spanish   gah$\underline{v}$-rē-EL   gɑβriːˈel
Gabriela
 1. pers. name, Polish   gahb-rē-$\overline{A}$-lah   gɑːbriːˈeːlɑː
 2. Spanish   gah$\underline{v}$-rē-$\overline{A}$-lah   gɑβriːˈeːlɑ

Foreign Sounds: ue: *Fr.* **rue**, *Ger.* **füllen** uh(r): *Fr.* **b**oeuf, *Ger.* **Höhle** <u>kh</u>: *Ger.* **ich**, *Scot.* **loch** ǥ: *Sp.* amigo <u>v</u>: *Sp.* hablar
hl: *Welsh* **Llanelli**. CAPITALS: primary stress. SMALL CAPS: secondary stress. Ⓢ: U.S. pron. Ⓑ: British pron.

Gabriele
  1. pers. name, German   GAHB-rē-Ā-luh   ˌgabriːˈeːlə
  2. Italian   GAHB-rē-EL-ā   ˌgabriːˈeleː
Gabrielino
  N. American people   GĀ-brē-uh-LĒ-nō   ˌgeːbriːəˈliːnoː
Gabriella
  pers. name   GAB-rē-EL-uh, GĀ-brē-EL-uh   ˌgæbriːˈelə, ˌgeːbriːˈelə
Gabrielle
  pers. name   GAHB-rē-EL, GAB-   ˌgabriːˈel, ˌgæb-
Gabrilowitsch
  Ossip, *Russian pianist*   guhv-ril-AWV-YICH,   gəvrilˈɔːvˌjitʃ,
                                     Ⓢ GAHB-ruh-LŌ-vich   Ⓢ ˌgabrəˈloːvitʃ
Gabrjel
  pers. name, Polish   GAHB-ryel, Ⓢ GAHB-rē-el   ˈgaːbrjel, Ⓢ ˈgaːbriːel
Gabrjela, -ryela
  pers. name, Polish   GAHB-RYEL-ah, Ⓢ GAHB-rē-EL-ah   ˌgaːbˈrjelaː, Ⓢ ˌgaːbriːˈelaː
Gadarene
  pert. to biblical Gadara   GAD-uh-RĒN, GAD-uh-RĒN   ˈgædəˌriːn, ˌgædəˈriːn
Gaddafi
  see Qadhafi
Gaddang
  lang., people, Philippine Islands GAHD-AHNG, gah-DAHNG   ˈgadˌaŋ, gaˈdaŋ
Gadhafi
  see Qadhafi
gadolinium
  element   GAD-l-IN-ē-uhm   ˌgædlˈiniːəm
Gadsden
  city, AL; county FL   GADZ-duhn   ˈgædzdən
Gadwall
  duck   GAD-WAWL   ˈgædˌwɔl
Gaea [Gaia]
  Greek earth goddess   JĒ-uh   ˈdʒiːə
Gael
  Celtic inhabitant of Ireland,   GĀL   ˈgeːl
  Scotland, or the Isle of Man
Gaelic
  lang., Ireland, Scotland, Isle of GĀ-lik   ˈgeːlik
  Man
Gaelic Mod
  Scots festival   GĀ-lik MAHD   ˈgeːlik ˈmad
Gaétan
  pers. name, French   gah-ā-TAH ͫ   gaːeːtã
Gaetana
  pers. name, Italian   GAH-ā-TAHN-ah   ˌgaeːˈtana
Gaetano
  pers. name, Italian   GAH-ā-TAHN-ō   ˌgaeːˈtanoː
Gaffar
  pers. name, Arabic   GAHF-AHR   ˈgafˌaʳ
Gagarin
  Yuri, *cosmonaut, USSR*   guh-GAHR-yin, Ⓢ guh-GAHR-uhn   gəˈgaːrjin, Ⓢ gəˈgarən
Gagliano
  Marco da, *Italian priest/composer* gahl-YAH-nō   galˈjanoː
Gahan
  pers. name   GĀ-uhn   ˈgeːən

Gaia [Gaea]
the Earth, esp. personified as a Greek goddess — GĪ-(y)uh — 'gɑi(j)ə

Gail
pers. name — GĀL — 'geːl

Gaillardia
flower — guh-LAHRD-ē-uh — gə'lɑˢdiːə

Gainesville
city, FL — GĀNZ-vil, GĀNZ-vuhl — 'geːnz,vil, 'geːnzvəl

Gainsborough
Thomas, English painter — GĀNZ-BUH-ruh, GĀNZ-BUHR-uh, GĀNZ-b(uh-)ruh — 'geːnz,bə-rə, 'geːnz,bər-ə, 'geːnzb(ə)rə

Gairdner
1. lake, South Australia — GARD-nuhr, GERD-nuhr — 'gæˢdnəˢ, 'geˢdnəˢ
2. pers. name — GARD-nuhr, GERD-nuhr, GAHRD-nuhr — 'gæˢdnəˢ, 'geˢdnəˢ, 'gɑˢdnəˢ

Gaithersburg
town, MD — GĀ-thuhrz-BUHRG — 'geːθəˢz,bəˢg

Gaius
Roman praenomen — GĀ-(y)uhs, GĪ-uhs — 'geː(j)əs, 'gaiəs

Gajdusek
Daniel Carleton, US virologist (Nobel 1976) — GĪ-duh-SHEK — 'gaidə,ʃek

Galahad
Arthurian hero — GAL-uh-HAD — 'gælə,hæd

Galanos
James, US fashion designer — guh-LAHN-ōs — gə'lɑnoːs

Galápagos
Pacific islands, Equador — guh-LAHP-uh-guhs, guh-LAP-uh-guhs — gə'lɑpəgəs, gə'læpəgəs

Galatea
daughter of Nereus, lover of Acis; mother of Leucippus — GAL-uh-TĒ-uh, GAL-uh-TĀ-uh — ˌgælə'tiːə, ˌgælə'teːə

Galates
son of Heracles — GAL-uht-ēz — 'gælətiːz

Galatia
ancient country, Asia Minor — guh-LĀ-sh(ē-)uh — gə'leːʃ(iː)ə

Galatians
New Testament book — guh-LĀ-shuhnz — gə'leːʃənz

Galax
county, VA — GĀ-LAKS — 'geː,læks

Galba
Roman emperor — GAL-buh, GAWL-buh — 'gælbə, 'gɔːlbə

Galbraith
pers. name — GAL-BRĀTH — 'gæl,breːθ

Gale
US publishing co.; pers. name — GĀL — 'geːl

Galen
Greek physician — GĀ-luhn — 'geːlən

Galeotes
son of Apollo and Themisto — GAL-ē-ŌT-ēz — ˌgæliː'oːtiːz

Galerius
Roman emperor — guh-LIR-ē-uhs — gə'liriːəs

Galiceño
horse — GAL-uh-SĀN-yō — ˌgælə'seːnjoː

Foreign Sounds: ue: *Fr.* **rue**, *Ger.* **füllen** uh(r): *Fr.* **boeuf**, *Ger.* **Höhle** <u>kh</u>: *Ger.* **ich**, *Scot.* **loch** g: *Sp.* **amigo** v: *Sp.* **hablar** hl: *Welsh* **Llanelli**. CAPITALS: primary stress. SMALL CAPS: secondary stress. Ⓢ: U.S. pron. Ⓑ: British pron.

Galicia
   region, Spain   guh-LISH-(ē-)uh   gə'liʃ(iː)ə

Galician
   lang., Spain   guh-LISH-uhn   gə'liʃən

Galileans
   satellites of Jupiter   GAL-uh-LĒ-uhnz, -LĀ-uhnz   ,gælə'liːənz, -'leːənz

Galilee [Tiberias]
   region, Israel; Sea of, *lake, Israel*   GAL-uh-LĒ, GAL-uh-LĒ   'gælə,liː, ,gælə'liː

Galilei
   Galileo, *Italian scientist*   gal-uh-LĀ-Ē   gælə'leː,iː

Galileo
   1. pers. name   gal-uh-LĒ-ō, -LĀ-ō   gælə'liːoː, -'leːoː
   2. Italian   GAHL-ē-LE-ō   ,gali:'leo:

Galinthias
   friend of Alcmene   guh-LIN-thē-uhs   gə'linθiːəs

Galla [Oromo]
   lang., people, Ethiopia, Kenya   GAL-uh, GAHL-uh   'gælə, 'galə

Gallacian
   lang., Spain   guh-LĀTH-ē-uhn, guh-LĀ-shuhn   gə'leːθiːən, gə'leːʃən

Gallatin
   Albert, *US politician; US pl. name*   GAL-uht-n   'gælətn̩

Gallaudet
   College, *Washington, DC*   GAL-uh-DET, GAW-luh-DET   ,gælə'det, ,gɔːlə'det

Gallegos
   river, Argentina   gah(l)-YĀ-ḡuhs   ga(l)'jeːɣəs

Galleria Borghese
   see Borghese, Galleria

Gallia
   county, OH; ancient name of   GAL-ē-uh   'gæliːə
     France

Galliano
   Italian liqueur   gahl-YAHN-ō, GAHL-ē-AHN-ō   gal'janoː, ,gali:'anoː

Gallic
   pert. to Gaul *or* France   GAL-ik   'gælik

Gallicanism
   anti-papal movement   GAL-i-kuh-NIZ-uhm   'gælikə,nizəm

Gallicism
   French idiom or expression   GAL-uh-SIZ-uhm   'gælə,sizəm

Gallienus
   Roman emperor   GAL-ē-Ē-nuhs, GAL-ē-Ā-nuhs   ,gæli:'iːnəs, ,gæli:'eːnəs

Gallinule
   marsh bird   GAL-uh-N(Y)OŌL   'gælə,n(j)uːl

Gallipoli
   port, Italy; port, Turkey   guh-LIP-uh-lē   gə'lipəliˑ

Gallipolis
   city, OH   GAL-uh-puh-LĒS   ,gæləpə'liːs

gallium
   element   GAL-ē-uhm   'gæliːəm

Gallo
   US wine co.   GAL-ō   'gæloː

Galloway
   region, Scotland   GAL-uh-WĀ   'gælə,weː

Gallup
   George, *US pollster*   GAL-uhp   'gæləp

Key (col. 2):   a: fad ā: fade ah: father ar: Mary aw: law e: fed ē: feed er: merry i: hid ī: hide ō: coat o͞o: boot
oi: boy ow: now u: put uh: above uhr: bird ch: chop ng: ring sh: show th: thick t̲h̲: this zh: measure

Galop		
dance	GAL-uhp, ga-LŌ	'gæləp, gæ'loː
Galsworthy		
John, *English author (Nobel 1932)*	GAWLZ-WUHR-<u>th</u>ē	'gɔːlz,wəʳ<u>ð</u>iˑ
Galton		
Sir Francis, *English scientist*	GAWLT-n	'gɔːltn̩
Galungan		
Balinese New Year	guh-LUNG-(g)uhn	gə'luŋ(g)ən
Galuppi		
Baldassare, *Italian composer*	gah-L͞OOP-pē	gɑ'luːppiˑ
Galvani		
Luigi, *Italian physiologist*	gahl-VAHN-ē, gal-VAHN-ē	gɑl'vɑniˑ, gæl'vɑniˑ
Galveston		
1. *city, TX*	GAL-vuhs-tuhn	'gælvəstən
2. *town, IN*	gal-VES-tuhn	gæl'vestən
Galway		
James, *Irish flutist; city, Irish* *Republic*	GAWL-WĀ	'gɔːl,weː
Gamal		
pers. name, Arabic	guh-MAHL	gə'mɑl
Gamaliel		
pers. name	guh-MÃ-lē-uhl, guh-MÃL-yuhl	gə'meːliːəl, gə'meːljəl
Gamarra		
Agustín, *president, Peru*	gah-MAHR-rah	gɑ'mɑrrɑ
Gambetta		
Léon-Michel, *French statesman*	gahⁿ-bā-TAH	gãbeːtɑː
Gambia, The		
republic, river, Africa	<u>th</u>uh GAM-bē-uh, GAHM-	ðə 'gæmbiːə, 'gɑm-
Gambian		
pert. to the Gambia	GAM-bē-uhn, GAHM-	'gæmbiːən, 'gɑm-
Gambrinus		
mythical Flemish king	gam-BRĪ-nuhs	gæm'brɑinəs
Gan		
lang., China	GAHN, GAN	'gɑn, 'gæn
Gananoque		
resort, Ontario, Canada	GAN-uh-NAHK-wē, -wā	ˌgænə'nɑkwiˑ, -weː
Ganda		
lang., people, Africa	GAN-duh, GAHN-duh	'gændə, 'gɑndə
Gander		
river, town, Canada	GAN-duhr	'gændəʳ
Gandhara		
ancient region, India	guhn-DAHR-uh	gən'dɑrə
Gandhi		
Indira, *Indian prime minister;* Mohandas K., *Indian leader;* Rajiv, *Indian prime minister*	GAHN-dē, GAN-dē	'gɑndiˑ, 'gændiˑ
Gandolf		
Raymond, *US media* *correspondent*	GAN-DAWLF, GAN-DAHLF	'gæn,dɔːlf, 'gæn,dɑlf
Ganesh Chaturthi		
Indian festival	guh-NESH chuh-TUR-tē	gə'neʃ tʃə'tuʳtiˑ
Ganga [Ganges]		
river, India; pers. name	GUHNG-guh	'gəŋgə
Ganges		
river, India	GAN-JĒZ	'gæn,dʒiːz

Foreign Sounds: ue: *Fr.* **rue**, *Ger.* **füllen** uh(r): *Fr.* **boeuf**, *Ger.* **Höhle** <u>kh</u>: *Ger.* **ich**, *Scot.* **loch** g̃: *Sp.* amigo v̲: *Sp.* **hablar** hl: *Welsh* **Llanelli**. CAPITALS: primary stress. SMALL CAPS: secondary stress. $: U.S. pron. £: British pron.

Gani
　pers. name　　　　　　　GAHN-ē　　　　　　　　　'gɑni·

Gannet
　bird　　　　　　　　　　GAN-uht　　　　　　　　　'gænət

Gannett
　1. US publishing co.　　GAN-uht, guh-NET　　　　'gænət, gə'net
　2. pers. name　　　　　GAN-uht　　　　　　　　　'gænət

Gannon
　University, *PA*　　　　　GAN-uhn　　　　　　　　　'gænən

Gansu, Kansu
　prov, China　　　　　　GAHN-SO͞O, ⑤ GAN-SO͞O, KAN-SO͞O　　'gɑn'suː, ⑤ 'gæn'suː, 'kæn'suː

Ganymede
　cup-bearer to the Greek gods;　GAN-ē-MĒD　　　　'gæni·ˌmiːd
　　satellite of Jupiter

Garagiola
　Joe, *sports personality*　GAR-uh-JŌ-luh, GAR-uh-jē-Ō-luh　　ˌgærə'dʒoːlə, ˌgærədʒiː'oːlə

Garamond
　Claude, *French type designer*　gah-rah-MAWⁿ　　gɑːrɑːmɔ̃

Garand
　John, *US inventor*　　　guh-RAND, GAR-uhnd　　gə'rænd, 'gærənd

Garcia
　1. pers. name　　　　　gahr-SĒ-uh　　　　　　　gɑʳ'siːə
　2. Portuguese　　　　　guhr-SĒ-uh, gahr-SĒ-uh　gər'siːə, gɑːr'siːə

García
　Spanish　　　　　　　　gahr-SĒ-ah, gahr-THĒ-ah　gɑr'siːɑ, gɑr'θiːɑ

García Lorca
　Federico, *Spanish poet*　gahr-THĒ-ah LAWR-kah, gahr-SĒ-uh　gɑr'θiːɑ 'lɔːrkɑ, gɑr'siːə

García Márquez
　Gabriel, *Colombian author (Nobel*　gahr-SĒ-uh MAHR-KĀS　gɑʳ'siːə 'mɑʳˌkeːs
　　1982)

Garcia Robles
　Alfonso, *Mexican diplomat (Nobel*　gahr-SĒ-uh RŌ-<u>v</u>lās　gɑʳ'siːə 'roːβleːs
　　1982)

Garda, Lago di
　lake, Italy　　　　　　LAHG-ō dē GAHRD-ah,　　'lagoː diː 'gɑʳda, ⑤ 'gɑʳdə
　　　　　　　　　　　　⑤ GAHRD-uh

Gardena
　city, CA　　　　　　　gahr-DĒ-nuh　　　　　　　gɑʳ'diːnə

Gardenia
　Vincent, *Italian actor*　gahr-DĒN-yuh　　　　　　gɑʳ'diːnjə

Gardiner
　pers. name　　　　　　GAHRD-nuhr, GAHRD-n-uhr　'gɑʳdnəʳ, 'gɑʳdn̩ʳ

Gareth
　pers. name　　　　　　GAR-uhth, GER-uhth　　　'gærəθ, 'gerəθ

Garfield
　James A., *20th US president;*　GAHR-FĒLD　　　　　'gɑʳˌfiːld
　　comic strip cat; pers. name

Gargantua
　novel, Rabelais　　　　gahr-GAN-chuh-wuh　　　　gɑʳ'gæntʃəwə

Garhwali
　lang., India　　　　　　guhr-WAHL-ē　　　　　　gəʳ'wɑli·

Garibaldi
　Giuseppi, *Italian nationalist*　GAH-rē-BAHL-dē,　　ˌgariː'baldi·, ⑤ ˌgærə'bɔːldi·
　　leader　　　　　　　⑤ GAR-uh-BAWL-dē

Key (col. 2):　a: fad　ā: fade　ah: father　ar: **Mary**　aw: **law**　e: fed　ē: feed　er: **merry**　i: hid　ī: hide　ō: coat　o͞o: boot
oi: **boy**　ow: **now**　u: put　uh: above　uhr: b**i**rd　ch: **chop**　ng: ri**ng**　sh: **show**　th: **thick**　<u>th</u>: **this**　zh: measure

Garland
  Judy, *US entertainer; pers. name*   GAHR-luhnd   'gɑ^rlənd

Garo
  lang., people, India   GAHR-ō   'gɑroː

Garonne
  river, France   gah-RAWN, Ⓢ guh-RAHN, guh-RÔN   gɑːrɔːn, Ⓢ gə'rɑn, gə'roːn

Garret, Garrett
  pers. name   GAR-uht   'gærət

Garrick
  David, *English actor; pers. name*   GAR-ik   'gærik

Garrison
  pers. name   GAR-uh-suhn   'gærəsən

Garry
  pers. name   GAR-ē, GER-ē   'gæriˑ, 'geriˑ

Garth
  pers. name   GAHRTH   'gɑ^rθ

Garvey
  Steven, *US baseball player*   GAHR-vē   'gɑ^rviˑ

Gary
  city, IN; pers. name   GAR-ē, GER-ē   'gæriˑ, 'geriˑ

Gasão
  pers. name   guh-SOWⁿ, gah-   gə'sɑũ, gɑː-

Gascogne [Gascony]
  prov, France   gahs-KAWN-yuh   gɑːskɔɲ

Gascon
  native of Gascony, France   gahs-KAWⁿ, GAS-kuhn   gɑːskɔ̃, 'gæskən

Gasconade
  county, MO   GAS-kuh-NĀD   ˌgæskə'neːd

Gascony
  prov, France   GAS-kuh-nē   'gæskəniˑ

Gaspar
  1. pers. name   GAS-puhr   'gæspə^r
  2. Latin   GAS-pahr   'gæspɑ^r
  3. Portuguese   guhsh-PAHR, gahs-PAHR   gəʃ'pɑː^r, gɑːs'pɑː^r
  4. Spanish   gahs-PAHR   gɑs'pɑr

Gaspard
  pers. name, French   gahs-PAHR   gɑːspɑːr

Gasparo
  pers. name, Italian   gahs-PAHR-ō   gɑs'pɑroː

Gaspé
  peninsula, Canada   ga-SPĀ   gæ'speː

Gasperi, De
  Alcide, *political leader*   duh gah-spā-RĒ   də gɑːspeːriˑ

Gassendi
  crater on Moon   guh-SEN-dē   gə'sendiˑ

Gasser
  H. S., *US physiologist (Nobel 1944)*   GAS-uhr   'gæsə^r

Gassers
  Park, *former ballpark, Shreveport, LA*   GAS-uhrz   'gæsə^rz

Gastineau
  Marcus D., *US football player*   GAS-tuh-NŌ   ˌgæstə'noː

Foreign Sounds: ue: *Fr.* **rue**, *Ger.* **füllen**   uh(r): *Fr.* **boeuf**, *Ger.* **Höhle**   <u>kh</u>: *Ger.* i**ch**, *Scot.* lo**ch**   g̃: *Sp.* ami**g**o   v: *Sp.* ha**b**lar
hl: *Welsh* **Ll**anelli.   CAPITALS: primary stress.   SMALL CAPS: secondary stress.   Ⓢ: U.S. pron.   Ⓛ: British pron.

Gaston		
1. county, NC; pers. name	GAS-tuhn	'gæstən
2. French	gah-STAW^n	gɑːstɔ̃
Gastonia		
city, NC	gas-TŌ-nē-uh, gas-TŌN-yuh	gæs'toːniːə, gæs'toːnjə
Gately		
George, *US cartoonist*	GĀT-lē	'geːtliˑ
Gath		
city, Palestine	GATH	'gæθ
Gatling		
machine gun	GAT-ling	'gætliŋ
Gatsby		
Jay, *character in* The Great Gatsby, *Fitzgerald*	GATS-bē	'gætsbiˑ
Gatun		
lake, Panama	guh-T͞OO͞N	gə'tuːn
Gatwick		
airport, England	GAT-wik	'gætwik
GATX		
General American Transportation, US service co.	JĒ-Ā-TĒ-EKS	ˌdʒiːˌeːˌtiː'eks
Gaudí y Cornet		
Antonio, *Spanish architect*	gow-TH̲Ē ē kōr-NĀT	gɑu'ðiː iː koːr'neːt
Gaugamela		
ancient Assyrian village	GAW-guh-MĒ-luh	ˌgɔːgə'miːlə
Gauguin		
Paul, *French painter*	gō-GE^n	goːgɛ̃
Gaul		
Roman province	GAWL	'gɔːl
Gaulle, de		
see de Gaulle		
Gaullism		
de Gaulle movement	GŌ-LIZ-uhm, GAW-LIZ-uhm	'goːˌlizəm, 'gɔːˌlizəm
Gauloise		
tdmk for French cigarette	gōl-WAHZ	goːlwɑːz
Gaumata		
ancient Persian revolutionary	gō-MAHT-uh	goː'mɑt̬ə
Gauss		
Carl Friedrich, *German mathematician*	GOWS	'gɑus
Gaussian curve		
bell curve	GOW-sē-uhn, GOW-shuhn	'gɑusiːən, 'gɑuʃən
Gautama		
see Siddhartha Gautama		
Gautier		
1. Dick, *US actor*	gō-TYĀ	goː'tjeː
2. Léon, *French literary scholar*	gō-TYĀ	goːtjeː
Gavarnie		
waterfall, France	gahv-ahr-NĒ, [$] GAV-uhr-NĒ	gɑːvɑːrniː, [$] ˌgævəʳ'niː
Gavilan		
College, *CA*	GAV-uh-LAN, -luhn	'gævəˌlæn, -lən
Gavin		
pers. name	GAV-uhn	'gævən
Gavriil		
pers. name, Russian	guhv-ri-ĒL	gəvri'iːl

Key (col. 2): a: f**a**d ā: f**a**de ah: f**a**ther ar: M**a**ry aw: l**aw** e: f**e**d ē: f**ee**d er: m**e**rry i: h**i**d ī: h**i**de ō: c**oa**t o͞o: b**oo**t oi: b**oy** ow: n**ow** u: p**u**t uh: **a**bove uhr: b**ir**d ch: **ch**op ng: ri**ng** sh: **sh**ow th: **th**ick th̲: **th**is zh: mea**s**ure

Gavrilo
    pers. name, Serbo-Croatian   GAHV-rē-law   'gɑːvriːlɔː
Gawain
    a Knight of the Round Table   guh-WĀN, GAH-WĀN, GOW-uhn   gə'weːn, 'gɑ,weːn, 'gɑuən
Gawin
    pers. name   GOW-uhn, GAH-wuhn   'gɑuən, 'gɑwən
Gayle
    Crystal, *US singer*   GĀL   'geːl
Gaylord
    pers. name   GĀ-LAWRD   'geː,lɔːʳd
Gay-Lussac
    Joseph, *French scientist*   ge-lue-SAHK, Ⓢ GĀ-luh-SAK   gelyːsɑːk, Ⓢ ,geːlə'sæk
Gaynor
    Mitzi, *US actress*   GĀ-nuhr   'geːnəʳ
Gayo
    lang., people, North Sumatra   GĪ-ō, GAH-yō   'gɑiɔː, 'gɑjɔː
Gaza
    strip of land, town, Mediterranean   GAHZ-uh, GAZ-uh   'gɑzə, 'gæzə
Gazzara
    Ben, *US actor*   guh-ZAHR-uh, guh-ZAR-uh   gə'zɑrə, gə'zærə
Gbari
    lang., people, Nigeria   guh-BAHR-ē   gə'bɑriˑ
Gbaya
    lang., Africa   guh-BĪ-uh, guh-BAH-yuh   gə'bɑiə, gə'bɑjə
Gdańsk [Danzig]
    city, Poland   guh-DAHN(T)SK, guh-DAN(T)SK   gə'dɑːn(t)sk, gə'dæn(t)sk
Gdynia
    port, Poland   guh-DIN-ē-uh   gə'diniːə
Gê
    S. American people   ZHĀ   'ʒeː
Geauga
    county, OH   jē-AWG-uh   dʒiː'ɔːgə
Gebel-Williams
    Gunther, *German animal trainer*   GĀ-buhl-WIL-yuhmz   'geːbəl'wiljəmz
Gebhard
    pers. name, German   GEP-HAHRT   'gep,hɑʳt
Geb [Keb, Seb]
    Egyptian earth god   GEB   'geb
Gedda [Jedda]
    city, Saudi Arabia   JED-uh   'dʒedə
Gedjensen
    Samuel, *US politician*   GĀD-n-suhn   'geːdn̩sən
Geelong
    city, Australia   jē-LAHNG, jē-LAWNG   dʒiˑ'lɑŋ, dʒiˑ'lɔːŋ
Gehenna
    valley of Hinom, Israel   guh-HEN-uh   gə'henə
Gehrig
    Lou, *US baseball player*   GER-ig   'gerig
Geiger
    Hans, *German physicist; counter,*   GĪ-guhr   'gɑigəʳ
    radiation detector
Geisel
    Theodore Seuss, *US author, aka*   GĪ-zuhl   'gɑizəl
    Dr. Seuss

Foreign Sounds: ue: *Fr.* **rue**, *Ger.* **füllen**   uh(r): *Fr.* **boeuf**, *Ger.* **Höhle**   <u>kh</u>: *Ger.* **ich**, *Scot.* **loch**   g̃: *Sp.* **amigo**   v̲: *Sp.* **hablar**
hl: *Welsh* **Llanelli.**   CAPITALS: primary stress.   SMALL CAPS: secondary stress.   Ⓢ: U.S. pron.   Ⓛ: British pron.

Geissler
  Johann, *German glassblower*   GĪ-sluhr   'gaɪslə^r

Ge-Kayapo
  lang., S. America   ZHĀ-KĪ-uh-PŌ, ZHĀ-KĪ-uh-PŌ   'ʒeːˌkaɪə'poː, 'ʒeːˈkaɪəˌpoː

Gelasius
  pope   juh-LĀ-shē-uhs, -zh(ē-)uhs, -zē-uhs   dʒə'leːʃiːəs, -ʒ(iː)əs, -ziːəs

Gelbart
  Larry, *US TV producer*   GEL-BAHRT   'gelˌbɑ^rt

Gelderland
  prov, Netherlands   GEL-duhr-LAND   'geldə^rˌlænd

Geldof
  Bob, *British rock promoter*   GEL-DAHF, GEL-DAWF   'gelˌdɑf, 'gelˌdɔːf

Geller
  Uri, *US psychic*   GEL-uhr   'gelə^r

Gell-Mann
  Murray, *US physicist (Nobel 1969)* GEL-MAHN   'gelˌmɑn

Gemara
  commentary on Jewish Mishna   guh-MAHR-uh, guh-MAWR-uh,   gə'mɑrə, gə'mɔːrə, gəmɑr'ɑ
                                      guh-mahr-AH

Gemayel
  Amin, *president, Lebanon*   juh-MĪ-uhl   dʒə'maɪəl

Gemini
  constellation, sign of the zodiac JEM-uh-nē, JEM-uh-NĪ, GEM-uh-NĒ   'dʒeməniˑ, 'dʒeməˌnaɪ,
                                                                                   'geməˌniː

Geminids
  meteor shower   JEM-uh-nidz   'dʒemənidz

Gemma
  pers. name   JEM-uh   'dʒemə

Gena
  pers. name   JĒ-nuh   'dʒiːnə

Gene
  pers. name   JĒN   'dʒiːn

Genesee
  river; county, MI, NY; US beer   JEN-uh-SĒ   ˌdʒenə'siː

Geneseo
  College, *NY*   JEN-uh-SĒ-ō   ˌdʒenə'siːoː

Genesis
  Old Testament book   JEN-uh-suhs   'dʒenəsəs

Genet
  Jean, *French author*   zhuh-NE, Ⓢ zhuh-NĀ   ʒəne, Ⓢ ʒə'neː

Geneva
  city, lake, Switzerland; US pl.   juh-NĒ-vuh   dʒə'niːvə
  name

Genevanism
  Calvinism   juh-NĒ-vuh-NIZ-uhm   dʒə'niːvəˌnizəm

Genève [Geneva]
  city, Switzerland   zhuh-NEV, zhuh-NĀV   ʒə'nev, ʒə'neːv

Genever
  Dutch gin   JEN-uh-vuhr   'dʒenəvə^r

Genevieve
  pers. name   JEN-uh-VĒV   'dʒenəˌviːv

Geneviève
  pers. name, French   zhuhn-VYEV   ʒənvjev

Genghis Khan [Temujin]
  Mongol leader   JENG-guhs KAHN, GENG-guhs   ˌdʒeŋgəs 'kan, ˌgeŋgəs

---

Key (col. 2):   a: fad ā: fade ah: father ar: Mary aw: law e: fed ē: feed er: merry i: hid ī: hide ō: coat o͞o: boot
oi: boy   ow: now   u: put   uh: above   uhr: bird   ch: chop   ng: ring   sh: show   th: thick   <u>th</u>: this   zh: measure

Genii
    Roman personification of being;   JĒ-nē-ī   'dʒiːniːˌɑi
    Manes

Genna
    Vince, Stadium, *Bend, OR*   VINS JEN-uh   'vins 'dʒenə

Gennadi
    pers. name, Russian   gyuh-NAHD-yē   gjə'nɑːdjiˑ

Gennadiyevich
    patronym, Russian   gyuh-NAHD-yiv-ʏɪᴄʜ   gjə'nɑːdjivˌjitʃ

Gennes
    Pierre-Gilles de, *French physicist*   ZHEN   ʒen

Genoa
    prov & town, Italy   JEN-uh-wuh   'dʒenəwə

Genoese
    pert. to Genoa   ᴊᴇɴ-uh-WĒZ, ᴊᴇɴ-uh-WĒS   ˌdʒenə'wiːz, ˌdʒenə'wiːs

Génoise
    Italian-style cake   zhen-WAHZ   ʒen'wɑːz

Genova [Genoa]
    prov & town, Italy   JEN-uh-vuh   'dʒenəvə

GenRad
    US software systems co.   JEN-ʀᴀᴅ   'dʒenˌræd

Genscher
    Hans Dietrich, *German politician*   GEN-shuhr, GEN-chuhr   'genʃəʳ, 'gentʃəʳ

Genshi-Sai
    First Beginning holiday (Jan. 3),   gen-shē-sī   genʃiːsɑi
    Japan

Gent
    see Ghent

Gentile
    1. Giovanni, *Italian educator*   jān-TĒ-lā   dʒeːn'tiːleː
    2. non-Jew   JEN-tīl   'dʒentɑil

Gentoo
    a Hindu   JEN-too   'dʒentuː

Geoffrey
    pers. name   JEF-rē   'dʒefriˑ

Geoffroi
    pers. name, French   zhaw-FRWAH   ʒɔːfrwɑ

Geoghegan
    family name   GĀ-guhn, guh-HĀ-guhn   'geːgən, gə'heːgən

Georg
    1. pers. name, Danish   gi-AWR(Ḡ)   gi'ɔːr(ɣ)
    2. Finnish   YE-ᴀᴡʀɢ   'jeˌɔːrg
    3. German   gā-AWRᴋʜ   geː'ɔʳx
    4. Norwegian   GĀ-ᴀᴡʀɢ   'geːˌɔːrg
    5. Swedish   YĀ-awr(-yuh)   'jeːɔːrj

George
    1. pers. name   JAWRJ   'dʒɔːʳdʒ
    2. French   ZHAWRZH   ʒɔːrʒ
    3. German   ZHAWRSH   'ʒɔʳʃ
    4. Romanian   ZHURZH, YAWR-ye   'ʒurʒ, 'jɔːrje
    5. Dutch   ZHAWR-zhuh   'ʒɔːrʒə

Georges
    pers. name, French   ZHAWRZH   ʒɔːrʒ

Foreign Sounds: ue: *Fr.* **rue**, *Ger.* **fü**llen   uh(r): *Fr.* **boeuf**, *Ger.* **Höhle**   kh: *Ger.* **ich**, *Scot.* **loch**   ḡ: *Sp.* a**m**igo   v: *Sp.* ha**b**lar
hl: *Welsh* **Ll**anelli.   CAPITALS: primary stress.   SMALL CAPS: secondary stress.   Ⓢ: U.S. pron.   Ⓛ: British pron.

Georgetown
   city, Guyana; pl. name, US;   JAWRJ-TOWN   'dʒɔːˈdʒ,taun
     University, *Washington, D. C.*
Georgette
   pers. name   jawr-JET   dʒɔːˈˈdʒet
Georgi
   1. pers. name, Bulgarian   gā-AWR-gē   geˈɔːrgiː
   2. Russian   gyi-AWRG-yi   gjiˈɔːrgjij
Georgia
   state, US; republic, Caucasus   JAWR-juh   'dʒɔːˈdʒə
    Mts.; pers. name
Georgian
   pert. to Georgia *or* King George   JAWR-juhn   'dʒɔːˈdʒən
Georgiana
   pers. name   JAWR-jē-AN-uh, jawr-JAN-uh   ,dʒɔːˈdʒiːˈænə, dʒɔːˈˈdʒænə
Georgie
   pers. name   JAWR-jē   'dʒɔːˈdʒiˈ
Georgina
   pers. name   jawr-JĒ-nuh   dʒɔːˈˈdʒiːnə
Georgios
   pers. name, Mod. Greek   ye-AWR-yi-AWS   jeˈɔːrjiˌɔːs
Georgius
   1. pers. name, Latin   JAWR-j(ē-)uhs, jē-AWR-   'dʒɔːˈdʒ(iː)əs, dʒiːˈɔːr-
   2. Swedish   ye-AWR-yi-uhs   jeˈɔːrjiəs
Georgy
   pers. name, Russian   gyi-AWRG-yi   gjiˈɔːrgjij
Gephardt
   Richard Andrew, *US politician*   GEP-HAHRT   'gep,haˈt
Geraert
   pers. name, Dutch   GĀ-RAHRT   'geː,raːrt
Geraint
   Arthurian hero; pers. name, Welsh GER-ĪNT   'ger,aint
Gerald
   1. pers. name   JER-uhld   'dʒerəld
   2. French   zhā-RAHLD   ʒeːraːld
Geraldine
   pers. name   JER-uhl-DĒN   'dʒerəl,diːn
Geraldo
   pers. name (G. Rivera)   huh-RAHL-dō, huh-RAWL-dō həˈraldoː, həˈrɔːldoː
Gérard
   pers. name, French   zhā-RAHR   ʒeːraːr
Gerard
   1. pers. name   juh-RAHRD   dʒəˈraˈd
   2. Dutch   GĀ-RAHRT   'geː,raːrt
   3. German   GĀ-RAHRT   'geː,raˈt
Gerardus
   1. pers. name, Dutch   gā-RAHR-dues   geːˈrardys
   2. Latin   juh-RAHR-duhs   dʒəˈraˈdəs
Gerasimov
   Gennadi, *Russian diplomat*   ger-AHS-yē-MAWF   gerˈaːsjiˌmɔːf
Gerber
   US baby food co.   GUHR-buhr   'gəˈbəˈ

Key (col. 2): a: fad ā: fade ah: father ar: Mary aw: law e: fed ē: feed er: merry i: hid ī: hide ō: coat ōō: boot
oi: boy   ow: now   u: put   uh: above   uhr: bird   ch: chop   ng: ring   sh: show   th: thick   th: this   zh: measure

Gerd

  1. Frey's wife in Scandinavian   GERD, GER<u>TH</u>   'geᶠd, 'gerð
    mythology

  2. pers. name, German   GERT   'geᶠt

Gere

  Richard, *US actor*   GIR   'giᶠ

Gerhard

  1. pers. name, Dutch   GĀ-RAHRT   'geː,rɑrt

  2. German   GĀR-HAHRT   'geːr,hɑᶠt

  3. Norwegian   GER-HAHRT   'ger,hɑrt

  4. Swedish   YĀR-HAHRD   'jeːr,hɑːrd

Gerhardt

  pers. name   GER-HAHRT   'ger,hɑᶠt

Gerhart

  pers. name, German   GĀR-HAHRT   'geːr,hɑᶠt

Geri

  Odin's wolf   GER-ē   'geriˑ

Germain

  pers. name, French   zher-MEⁿ   ʒermẽ

Germaine

  1. pers. name   juhr-MĀN   dʒəᶠmeːn

  2. French   zher-MEⁿ   ʒermẽ

German

  lang., people, Europe   JUHR-muhn   'dʒəᶠmən

Germán

  pers. name, Spanish   <u>kh</u>er-MAHN   çer'man

Germani

  ancient German tribe   juhr-MAN-ē, juhr-MAHN-ē,   dʒəᶠ'mæniˑ, dʒəᶠ'mɑniˑ,
                           ger-MAHN-ē   geᶠ'maniˑ

Germanic

  lang. family   juhr-MAN-ik   dʒəᶠ'mænik

Germanicus

  Roman general   juhr-MAN-i-kuhs   dʒəᶠ'mænikəs

germanium

  element   juhr-MĀ-nē-uhm   dʒəᶠ'meːniːəm

Germanna

  Community College, *VA*   juhr-MAN-uh   dʒəᶠ'mænə

Germany

  republic, Europe   JUHR-muh-nē   'dʒəᶠməniˑ

Germinal

  month, French Revolutionary   zher-mē-NAHL   ʒermiːnɑːl
    calendar

Gérôme

  pers. name, French   zhā-RAWM   ʒeːrɔːm

Geronimo

  1. Apache leader; pers. name   juh-RAHN-uh-MŌ   dʒə'rɑnə,moː

  2. Italian   jā-RAW-nē-mō   dʒeː'rɔːniːmoː

Gerónimo

  pers. name, Spanish   <u>kh</u>ā-RŌ-nē-mō   çeː'roːniːmoː

Gerousia

  Spartan council   juh-ROO-zh(ē-)uh   dʒə'ruːʒ(iː)ə

Gerry

  pers. name   GER-ē   'geriˑ

Gershwin

  George, Ira, *US musicians*   GUHRSH-wuhn   'gəᶠʃwən

Foreign Sounds: ue: *Fr.* **rue**, *Ger.* **füllen**   uh(r): *Fr.* **boeuf**, *Ger.* **Höhle**   <u>kh</u>: *Ger.* **ich**, *Scot.* **loch**   ḡ: *Sp.* **amigo**   <u>v</u>: *Sp.* **hablar**
hl: *Welsh* **Llanelli.**   CAPITALS: primary stress.   SMALL CAPS: secondary stress.   Ⓢ: U.S. pron.   Ⓔ: British pron.

Gersoppa [Jog Falls]
  waterfall, India   juhr-SAHP-uh   dʒəʳˈsɑpə
Gertrud
  1. pers. name, Danish   GER-tru<u>th</u>   ˈgertruð
  2. German   GER-TROOT   ˈgeʳˌtruːt
Gertrude
  pers. name   GUHR-TROOD   ˈgəʳˌtruːd
Gertrudis
  pers. name, Spanish   kher-TROO-thēs   çerˈtruːðiːs
Gerty
  1. pers. name   GUHRT-ē   ˈgəʳt̬iˈ
  2. Czech   GERT-ē   ˈgert̬iˈ
Gervais
  pers. name, French   zher-VE   ʒerve
Gervase
  pers. name   juhr-VĀS, -VĀZ; JUHR-VĀS, -VĀZ   dʒəʳˈveɪs, -ˈveɪz; ˈdʒəʳˌveɪs,
                                                                           -ˌveɪz

Geryon
  three-headed giant   JER-ē-uhn, JER-ē-AHN   ˈdʒeriːən, ˈdʒeriːˌɑn
Gerzean culture
  prehistoric Egyptian culture   GER-zē-uhn, GUHR-   ˈgeʳziːən, ˈgəʳ-
Gestalt
  psychology, therapy   guh-SHTAWLT, guh-STAWLT   gəˈʃtɔːlt, gəˈstɔːlt
Gestapo
  German secret police, WWII   guh-STAHP-ō   gəˈstɑpoː
Gethsemane
  garden outside Jerusalem   geth-SEM-uh-nē   geθˈseməniˈ
Getty
  J. Paul, US industrialist   GET-ē   ˈget̬iˈ
Gettysburg
  town, PA   GET-ēz-BUHRG   ˈget̬iˈzˌbəʳg
Getz
  Stan, US saxophonist   GETS   ˈgets
Gewürztraminer
  German wine   guh-VURT-STRAM-uh-nuhr,   gəˈvuʳtˌstræmənəʳ,
                                    -STRAHM-uh-nuhr, -struh-MĒ-nuhr   -ˌstramənəʳ, -strəˌmiːnəʳ
Geysir
  geyser, Iceland   GĪ-zuhr   ˈgaizəʳ
Géza
  pers. name, Hungarian   GĀ-zah   ˈgeːzɑ
Gezira, Al
  region, Sudan   AHL juh-ZIR-uh, AL   ˌɑːl dʒəˈzirə, ˌæl
Ghana
  republic, Africa   GAHN-uh, GAN-uh   ˈgɑnə, ˈgænə
Ghanaian
  pert. to Ghana   gah-NĀ-(y)uhn, ga-, -NĪ-uhn   gɑˈneɪ(j)ən, gæ-, -ˈnaiən
Ghats
  mtn. system, India   GAWTS   ˈgɔːts
Gheber
  Ghebre, Iranian Zoroastrian   GĀ-buhr   ˈgeːbəʳ
Ghebre
  pers. name (G. Gheber)   GĀ-bruh   ˈgeːbrə
Gheeraert
  pers. name, Dutch   ǦĀ-RAHRT   ˈɣeːˌrɑːrt

Key (col. 2):   a: f**a**d   ā: f**a**de   ah: f**a**ther   ar: M**a**ry   aw: l**aw**   e: f**e**d   ē: f**ee**d   er: m**e**rry   i: h**i**d   ī: h**i**de   ō: c**oa**t   oo: b**oo**t
oi: b**oy**   ow: n**ow**   u: p**u**t   uh: **a**bove   uhr: b**i**rd   ch: **ch**op   ng: ri**ng**   sh: **sh**ow   th: **th**ick   <u>th</u>: **th**is   zh: mea**s**ure

Gheerardt
    pers. name, Dutch   ḠĀ-RAHRT   'ɣeːˌrɑrt

Ghent, Gent
    city, Belgium   GENT   'gent

Gheorghe
    pers. name, Romanian   GYAWR-ge   'gjɔːrge

Gheorghiu-Dej
    Gheorghe, *Romanian statesman*   GYAWR-gyo͞o-DĂ   'gjɔːʳgjuː'deː

Ghia
    Italian car designer   GĒ-uh   'giːə

Ghibelline
    Italian political party   GIB-uh-LĒN, GIB-uh-LĬN   'gibəˌliːn, 'gibəˌlain

Ghiberti
    Lorenzo, *Florentine sculptor*   gē-BERT-ē   giː'beʳʈiˑ

Ghirardelli
    square, San Francisco, CA   GIR-ahr-DEL-ē   ˌgirɑʳ'deliˑ

Ghirlandajo
    Domenico, *Italian painter*   GIR-luhn-DAH-yo͞, GIR-luhn-DĪ-ō   ˌgiʳlən'dajoː, ˌgiʳlən'daioː

Ghislain
    pers. name, French   gē-LEⁿ   giːlẽ

Giacinto
    pers. name, Italian   jah-CHĒN-tō   dʒɑ'tʃiːntoː

Giacobinids
    meteor shower   juh-KŌ-buh-nidz, ja-   dʒə'koːbənidz, dʒæ-

Giacomo
    pers. name, Italian   JAHK-ō-mō   'dʒɑkoːmoː

Giacopo
    pers. name, Italian   JAHK-ō-pō   'dʒɑkoːpoː

Giaever
    Ivar, *Norwegian-born US physicist*   YĂ-vuhr   'jeːvəʳ
    (Nobel 1973)

Giamatti
    A. Bartlett, *US educator, baseball*   j(ē-)uh-MAHT-ē   dʒ(iː)ə'mɑʈiˑ
    commissioner

Giambattista
    pers. name, Italian   JAHM-baht-TĒS-tah   ˌdʒɑmbɑt'tiːstɑ

Gian
    pers. name, Italian   JAHN   'dʒɑn

Gianni
    pers. name, Italian   JAHN-nē   'dʒɑnniː

Giano
    pers. name, Italian   JAHN-ō   'dʒɑnoː

Giants
    US sports teams; children of Gaia   JĪ-uhnts   'dʒaiənts

Giaour, The
    verse tale, Byron   JOWR   'dʒauʳ

Giauque
    W. F., *Canadian-born US chemist*   jē-ŌK   dʒiː'oːk
    (Nobel 1949)

Gibbon
    Edward, *English historian*   GIB-uhn   'gibən

Gibeon
    town, Palestine   GIB-ē-uhn   'gibiːən

Gibraltar
    strait, rock, town, Spain   juh-BRAWL-tuhr   dʒə'brɔːltəʳ

Foreign Sounds: ue: *Fr.* **rue**, *Ger.* **füllen**   uh(r): *Fr.* **boeuf**, *Ger.* **Höhle**   <u>kh</u>: *Ger.* **ich**, *Scot.* **loch**   ḡ: *Sp.* **amigo**   ṿ: *Sp.* **hablar**
hl: *Welsh* **Llanelli**.   CAPITALS: primary stress.   SMALL CAPS: secondary stress.   Ⓢ: U.S. pron.   Ⓛ: British pron.

Gibraltarian
  one from Gibraltar   juh-BRAWL-TER-ē-uhn, JIB-RAWL-,   dʒə,brɔːl'teriːən, ,dʒib,rɔːl-,
                         -TAR-ē-uhn   -'tæriːən

Gibran
  Kahlil, *Syrian poet, author*   juh-BRAHN   dʒə'brɑn

Gide
  André, *French author (Nobel*   ZHĒD   ʒiːd
    1947)

Gideon
  1. pers. name   GID-ē-uhn   'gidiːən
  2. German   GĒ-dā-AWN   'giːdeɪ,ɔːn

Gielgud
  Sir Arthur John, *British actor*   GĒL-GUD   'giːl,gud

Giessbach
  waterfall, Switz.   GĒS-BAHKH, GĒS-BAHK   'giːs,bɑx, 'giːs,bɑk

Giessen
  prov & town,Germany   GĒ-suhn   'giːsən

GIGO
  garbage in, garbage out   GĪ-GŌ, GĒ-GŌ   'gɑi,goː, 'giː,goː

Gil
  1. pers. name   GIL   'gil
  2. Portuguese   ZHIL   'ʒil
  3. Spanish   KHĒL   'çiːl

Gila
  river, US; county, AZ   HĒ-luh   'hiːlə

Gila Bend
  Indian reservation, US   HĒ-luh BEND   'hiːlə 'bend

Gila monster
  venomous lizard   HĒ-luh MAHN(T)-stuhr   'hiːlə ,mɑn(t)stəʳ

Gilbert
  1. Walter, *US molecular biologist*   GIL-buhrt   'gilbəʳt
    (Nobel 1980); Sir William S.,
    English poet; pers. name
  2. French   zhēl-BER   ʒiːlber

Gilbert [Kiribati]
  islands, Pacific   GIL-buhrt   'gilbəʳt

Gilbertese
  lang., people, Kiribati   GIL-buhrt-ĒZ, -ĒS   ,gilbəʳt̪'iːz, -'iːs

Gilbertus
  pers. name, Latin   gil-BUHRT-uhs   gil'bəʳt̪əs

Gilbey's
  tdmk for gin   GIL-bēz   'gilbi˙z

Gilboa
  Mount, *Israel*   gil-BŌ-uh   gil'boːə

Gilchrist
  pers. name   GIL-krist   'gilkrist

Gilda
  pers. name   GIL-duh   'gildə

Gildersleeve
  family name   GIL-duhr-SLĒV   'gildəʳ,sliːv

Gilead
  biblical mtn.   GIL-ē-uhd   'giliːəd

Giles
  county, VA; pers. name   JĪLZ   'dʒɑilz

Key (col. 2):   a: fad   ā: fade   ah: father   ar: Mary   aw: law   e: fed   ē: feed   er: merry   i: hid   ī: hide   ō: coat   o͞o: boot
oi: boy   ow: now   u: put   uh: above   uhr: bird   ch: chop   ng: ring   sh: show   th: thick   <u>th</u>: this   zh: measure

Gilgamesh
   Sumerian epic hero   GIL-guh-MESH   'gilgə,meʃ

Gilles
   1. pers. name, Dutch   ḠIL-uhs   'ɣiləs
   2. French   ZHĒL   ʒiːl

Gillespie
   pers. name   guh-LES-pē   gə'lespiˑ

Gillette
   Anita, *US actress;* King Camp, *US*   juh-LET   dʒə'let
      razor magnate; William, *US*
      actor

Gilliam
   Terry, *US animator, film director*   GIL-ē-uhm   'giliːəm

Gillian
   pers. name   JIL-ē-uhn, JIL-yuhn   'dʒiliːən, 'dʒiljən

Gillies
   pers. name   GIL-uhs, -uhz, -ēz   'giləs, -əz, -iːz

Gillyflower
   flower   GIL-ē-FLOW(-uh)r   'giliːˌflɑu(ə)ʳ

Gilmore
   Artis, *US basketball player*   GIL-MŌR, GIL-MAWR   'gil,moːʳ, 'gil,mɔːʳ

Gilyak [Nivkh]
   lang., people, Russia   gil-YAHK, gil-YAK   gil'jɑk, gil'jæk

Gimbel
   Jacob & Isaac, *US merchants;*   GIM-buhl   'gimbəl
      Norman, *US lyricist, TV*
      producer

Gimlet
   alcoholic drink   GIM-luht   'gimlət

Gimson
   A.C., *British phonetician*   GIM(P)-suhn   'gim(p)sən

Gina
   pers. name   JĒ-nuh   'dʒiːnə

Gingold
   Hermione, *entertainer*   GING-GŌLD   'giŋ,goːld

Gingrich
   Newt, *US politician*   GING-grich, GING-rich   'giŋgritʃ, 'giŋritʃ

Ginn & Co.
   US publisher   GIN   'gin

Ginnie, Ginny
   pers. name   JIN-ē   'dʒiniˑ

Gino
   pers. name   JĒ-nō   'dʒiːnoː

Ginsberg
   Allen, *US poet*   GINZ-BUHRG   'ginz,bəʳg

Ginza
   district, Japan   gin-zah   ginzɑ

Gioacchino
   pers. name, Italian   JŌ-uh-KĒ-nō   ,dʒoːə'kiːnoː

Gioconda, La
   opera, Ponchielli; da Vinci   LAH jō-KAHN-duh   ,la dʒoː'kɑndə
      painting (Mona Lisa)

Gion Matsuri
   Japanese festival   gyawn maht-sur-ē   gjɔːn mɑtsuriˑ

Foreign Sounds: **ue:** *Fr.* **rue,** *Ger.* **füllen**   **uh(r):** *Fr.* **boeuf,** *Ger.* **Höhle**   **kh:** *Ger.* **ich,** *Scot.* **loch**   **ḡ:** *Sp.* **amigo**   **v̱:** *Sp.* **hablar**
hl: *Welsh* **Llanelli.**   CAPITALS: primary stress.   SMALL CAPS: secondary stress.   ⓢ: U.S. pron.   ⓑ: British pron.

Giordano
  pers. name, Italian jawr-DAHN-ō dʒɔːr'danoː

Giorgio
  pers. name, Italian JŌR-jō, JAWR-jō 'dʒɔːrdʒɔː, 'dʒɔːrdʒoː

Giörgio
  pers. name, Hungarian DYUHRD-yō 'djœrdjoː

Giorgione
  Italian painter jawr-JŌ-nā dʒɔːʳ'dʒoːneː

Giorgios
  pers. name, Greek YAWR-yaws 'jɔːrjɔːs

Giosuè
  pers. name, Italian jōz-WE dʒoːz'we

Giotto
  Italian painter JAWT-tō, ⑤ JAWT-ō, jē-AHT-ō 'dʒɔːttoː, ⑤ 'dʒɔːțoː, dʒiː'ațoː

Giovanni
  pers. name, Italian jō-VAHN-nē dʒoː'vanniː

Gipsy
  pers. name JIP-sē 'dʒipsiˑ

Giraf
  Danish beer GĒ-RAHF 'giːˌraːf

Girard
  US pl. name juh-RAHRD dʒə'raʳd

Giraud
  pers. name, French zhē-RŌ ʒiːroː

Giraudoux
  Jean, *French writer* zhē-rō-DOO ʒiːroːduː

Girja
  pers. name, Hindi GIR-jah 'girdʒa

Girò di Cagliari
  Sardinian wine zhē-RŌ dē kahl-YAHR-ē ʒiˈroː diː kalˈjariː

Girolamo
  pers. name, Italian jē-RAW-lahm-ō dʒiːˈrɔːlamoː

Gironde
  French wine region zhē-RAWⁿD ʒiːrɔ̃d

Girondist
  member, French political party juh-RAHN-duhst, zhi-RAHN-duhst dʒəˈrandəst, ʒiˈrandəst

Girton
  college, Cambridge Univ. GUHRT-n 'gəʳtn̩

Gisborne
  town, New Zealand GIZ-buhrn 'gizbəʳn

Giscard d'Estaing
  Valéry, *president, France* zhis-KAHR des-TEⁿ ʒiskaːr destẽ

Giselle
  1. *pers. name* juh-ZEL, zhi-ZEL dʒəˈzel, ʒiˈzel
  2. *French* zhē-ZEL ʒiːzel

Gish
  Lillian, *US actress* GISH 'giʃ

Gitano
  US sportswear co. gi-TAHN-ō giˈtanoː

Giucciardini
  Francesco, *Italian historian* JOOT-chahr-DĒ-nē ˌdʒuːttʃarˈdiːniː

Giuliano
  pers. name, Italian jool-YAHN-ō dʒuːlˈjanoː

Key (col. 2): a: fad ā: fade ah: father ar: Mary aw: law e: fed ē: feed er: merry i: hid ī: hide ō: coat oo: boot
oi: boy ow: now u: put uh: above uhr: bird ch: chop ng: ring sh: show th: thick th: this zh: measure

Giulietta
   1. pers. name — JOO-lē-ET-uh — ,dʒuːliˈeţə
   2. Italian — jōol-YET-tah — dʒuːlˈjettɑ
Giulio
   pers. name, Italian — JOOL-yō — ˈdʒuːljoː
Giuseppe
   pers. name, Italian — jōo-ZEP-pā — dʒuːˈzeppeː
Givenchy
   Hubert de, *French fashion* — zhē-vahⁿ-SHĒ — ʒiːvɑ̃ʃiː
     designer
Givry
   French wine — zhē-VRĒ — ʒiːvriː
Giza
   site of Egyptian pyramids — GĒ-zuh — ˈgiːzə
Gîza, El
   city, Egypt — el GĒ-zuh — el ˈgiːzə
Gjellerup
   K. A., *Danish author (Nobel 1917)* — GIL-lā-RŌŌP, Ⓢ GEL-uh-RUP — ˈgilleːˌruːp, Ⓢ ˈgeləˌrup
Gladstone
   pers. name — GLAD-STŌN, Ⓔ GLAD-stuhn — ˈglædˌstoːn, Ⓔ ˈglædstən
Gladys
   pers. name — GLAD-uhs — ˈglædəs
Glamis
   village, Scotland, scene of murder — GLAHMZ, Ⓢ GLAHM-uhs, GLAM-uhs — ˈglɑːmz, Ⓢ ˈglɑməs, ˈglæməs
     in Macbeth, *Shakespeare*
Glamorgan, Mid
   see Mid Glamorgan
Glamorgan, South
   see South Glamorgan
Glamorgan, West
   see West Glamorgan
Glamorganshire
   former county, Wales — gluh-MAWR-guhn-shuhr, -SHIR — gləˈmɔːʳgənʃəʳ, -ˌʃiʳ
Glarner
   Swiss beer — GLAHR-nuhr — ˈglɑʳnəʳ
Glarus
   canton, Switzerland — GLAHR-uhs — ˈglɑrəs
Glaser
   D. A., *US physicist (Nobel 1960)* — GLĀ-zuhr — ˈgleːzəʳ
Glasgow
   city, Scotland; pers. name — GLAS-kō, -gō; GLAZ-gō; Ⓔ — ˈglæskoː, -goː; ˈglæzgoː; Ⓔ
     GLAHZ-gō, GLAHS-gō — ˈglɑːzgoː, ˈglɑːsgoː
Glashow
   Sheldon L., *US physicist (Nobel* — GLASH-ō — ˈglæʃoː
     1979)
Glasnost
   Soviet policy of candor — GLAHS-nuhst, GLAHS-NAWST, — ˈglɑsnəst, ˈglɑsˌnɔːst,
     GLAHZ-NŌST — ˈglazˌnoːst
Glassboro
   State College, *NJ* — GLAS-b(uh-)ruh, GLAS-BUHR-ō — ˈglæsb(ə)rə, ˈglæsˌbəroː
Glastonbury
   1. town, CT — GLAS-(t)uhn-BER-ē — ˈglæs(t)ənˌberiˈ
   2. borough, England — GLAS-tuhn-b(uh-)rē, GLAHS- — ˈglæstənb(ə)riˈ, ˈglɑːs-

---

Foreign Sounds: ue: *Fr.* **rue**, *Ger.* **füllen**   uh(r): *Fr.* **boeuf**, *Ger.* **Höhle**   kh: *Ger.* i**ch**, *Scot.* lo**ch**   ḡ: *Sp.* ami**g**o   v: *Sp.* ha**b**lar
hl: *Welsh* **Ll**anelli.   CAPITALS: primary stress.   SMALL CAPS: secondary stress.   Ⓢ: U.S. pron.   Ⓔ: British pron.

Glaswegian
  inhabitant of Glasgow   glas-WĒ-juhn, Ⓔ glahz-WĒ-juhn,   glæs'wiːdʒən, Ⓔ
                                   glaz-, glahs-, glas-   glɑːz'wiːdʒən, glæz-,
                                                                        glɑːs-, glæs-
Glauce
  daughter of King Creon; Creusa GLAW-sē   'glɔːsiˑ
Glaucia
  Caius Servilius, *Roman popular* GLAW-sh(ē-)uh   'glɔːʃ(iː)ə
    leader; mother of Scamander in
    Greek mythology
Glaucus
  Lycian commander in Trojan   GLAW-kuhs   'glɔːkəs
    War; son of Minos and
    Pasiphae; son of Sisyphus; sea
    god who courted Scylla
Glaxo
  British pharmaceutical co.   GLAK-sō   'glæksoː
Glazunoff
  Alexander K., *Russian composer* GLAHZ-u-NAWF, Ⓢ GLAZ-uh-NAWF,   ˌglɑːzu'nɔːf, Ⓢ 'glæzəˌnɔːf,
                                    -NAWV   -ˌnɔːv
Gleb
  pers. name, Russian   GLĀP·   'ɡl̩eːp
Glemp
  Józef, *Polish cardinal*   GLEMP   'glemp
Glen, Glenn
  pers. name   GLEN   'glen
Glenallachie
  Scotch whiskey   glen-AL-uh-kē, -k͟hē   glen'æləkiˑ, -xiˑ
Glenda
  pers. name   GLEN-duh   'glendə
Glendower [Glyndwr]
  Owen, *Welsh rebel*   glen-DOW(-uh)r   glen'dau(ə)ʳ
Glenfiddich
  Scotch whiskey   glen-FID-ik, -ik͟h, -ich   glen'fidik, -ix, -itʃ
Glengarry
  valley, Scotland; county, Ontario, glen-GAR-ē   glen'gæriˑ
    Canada
Glenlivet, The
  Scotch whiskey   t͟huh glen-LIV-uht   ðə glen'livət
Glenmorangie
  Scotch whisky   glen-MAHR-in-jē, -MAWR-   glen'marindʒiˑ, -'mɔːr-
Glen of Imaal
  dog breed   GLEN uhv i-MAHL   'glen əv i'mɑl
Gless
  Sharon, *US actress*   GLES   'gles
Glimmerglass
  Opera, *NY*   GLIM-uhr-GLAS, -GLAHS   'gliməʳˌglæs, -ˌglɑːs
Glinka
  Mikhail Ivanovitch, *Russian*   GLĒN-kuh, Ⓢ GLING-kuh   'ɡl̩iːnkə, Ⓢ 'gliŋkə
    composer
Glockenspiel
  musical instrument   GLAHK-uhn-SHPĒL, GLAHK-uhn-SPĒL   'glakənˌʃpiːl, 'glakənˌspiːl
Gloria
  pers. name   GLŌR-ē-uh, GLAWR-ē-uh   'glɔːriːə, 'glɔːriːə

Key (col. 2):   a: f**a**d   ā: f**a**de   ah: f**a**ther   ar: **Ma**ry   aw: l**a**w   e: f**e**d   ē: f**ee**d   er: **me**rry   i: h**i**d   ī: h**i**de   ō: c**oa**t   o͞o: b**oo**t
oi: b**oy**   ow: n**ow**   u: p**u**t   uh: **a**bove   uhr: b**i**rd   ch: **ch**op   ng: ri**ng**   sh: **sh**ow   th: **th**ick   t͟h: **th**is   zh: mea**s**ure

Gloucester
    US pl. name; city, England   GLAHS-tuhr, GLAW-stuhr   'glɑstəʳ, 'glɔːstəʳ

Gloucestershire
    county, England   GLAHS-tuhr-shuhr,   'glɑstəʳʃəʳ, 'glɔːstəʳʃəʳ, -‚ʃiʳ
        GLAWS-tuhr-shuhr, -SHIR

Glover
    pers. name   GLUHV-uhr   'glʌvəʳ

Gluck
    Alma, *US soprano*   GLUK   'gluk

Gluyas
    pers. name   GLOO̅-yuhs   'gluːjəs

Glyn
    pers. name   GLIN   'glin

Glyndebourne
    town, festival, England   GLĪN(D)-BAWRN, GLĬM-BAWRN   'glain(d)‚bɔːʳn, 'glaim‚bɔːʳn

Glyndwr [Glendower]
    Owain, *Welsh leader*   glin-DUR   glin'dur

Glynis
    pers. name   GLIN-uhs   'glinəs

Gnadenhutten
    village, former mission, OH   juh-NĀD-n-HUHT-n   dʒə'neːdn̩‚hətn̩

Gnaeus, Gneius
    Roman praenomen   NĒ-uhs   'niːəs

GNMA
    Government National Mortgage   JIN-ē-MĀ   ‚dʒini'ˈmeː
        Association

Gnostic
    adherent of Gnosticism   NAHS-tik   'nɑstik

Gnosticism
    beliefs of early Christian mystical   NAHS-tuh-SIZ-uhm   'nɑstə‚sizəm
        cult

Goa
    state, India; city, Philippines   GŌ-uh   'goːə

Goa, Daman and Diu
    former territory, India   GŌ-uh duh-MAN uhn(d) DĒ-oo̅   'goːə də'mæn ən(d) 'diːuː

Goajiro
    S. American people   GŌ-uh-HĒ-rō   ‚goːə'hiːroː

Gobat
    C. A., *Swiss politician,*   gō-BAH   goː'bɑ
        philanthropist (Nobel 1902)

Gobelin
    French family of tapestry makers   gaw-BLEⁿ   gɔːblẽ

Gobi
    desert, Asia   GŌ-bē   'goːbiˑ

Gobind
    pers. name (H. G. Khorana)   GŌ-BIND   'goː‚bind

Godard
    Jean Luc, *French film director*   gaw-DAHR   gɔːdɑːr

Godavari
    river, India   guh-DAHV-uh-rē   gə'davəriˑ

Goddard
    Robert, *US physicist; college, VT*   GAHD-uhrd   'gɑdəʳd

Godefroi, -froy
    pers. name, French   gawd-FRWAH   gɔːdfrwa

Foreign Sounds: ue: *Fr.* **rue**, *Ger.* **füllen** uh(r): *Fr.* **bœuf**, *Ger.* **Höhle** <u>kh</u>: *Ger.* i**ch**, *Scot.* lo**ch** g̶: *Sp.* ami**g**o v̶: *Sp.* ha**b**lar
hl: *Welsh* **Ll**anelli. CAPITALS: primary stress. SMALL CAPS: secondary stress. Ⓢ: U.S. pron. Ⓔ: British pron.

Godel, Gödel
  Kurt, US mathematician   GŌD-l, GUH(R)D-l   'goːdl̩, 'gœːdl̩

Goderich
  town, Ontario   GAHD-rich   'gɑdritʃ

Godfrey
  pers. name   GAHD-frē   'gɑdfriˑ

Godiva
  Lady, wife of Leofric, earl of   guh-DĪ-vuh   gə'dɑivə
    Mercia

Godiva Chocolatier
  US gourmet candy co.   guh-DĪ-vuh SHAW-kuh-LAH-TYĀ   gə'dɑivə ˌʃɔːkəˌla'tjeː

Godolphin Barb
  racehorse   guh-DAHL-fuhn BAHRB,   gə'dɑlfən 'bɑʳb, gə'dɔːlfən
     guh-DAWL-fuhn

Godot
  character in Waiting for Godot, *S.*   guh-DŌ   gə'doː
    Beckett

Godoy
  pers. name   gō-THOI   goː'ðɔi

Godunov
  Boris, Russian czar   guh-dōō-NAWF, Ⓢ GŌD-n-AWF,   gəduː'nɔːf, Ⓢ 'goːdn̩ˌɔːf,
     GAWD-n-AWF   'goːdn̩ˌɔːf

Godwin
  pers. name   GAHD-wuhn   'gɑdwən

Godzilla
  movie monster   gahd-ZIL-uh   gɑd'zilə

Goebbels
  Paul Joseph, Nazi propagandist   GUH(R)B-uhls, Ⓢ GUHR-buhlz   'gœbəls, Ⓢ 'gəʳbəlz

Goeppert
  pers. name, German   GUH(R)P-uhrt   'gœpəʳt

Goering, Göring
  Hermann Wilhelm, Nazi leader   GUH(R)-ring, Ⓢ GER-ing, GUHR-ing   'gœːriŋ, Ⓢ 'geriŋ, 'gəriŋ

Goethals
  George, US engineer   GŌ-thuhlz   'goːθəlz

Goethe
  1. Johann Wolfgang von, German   GUH(R)-tuh   'gœːtə
    poet
  2. street, Chicago, IL   GŌ-ĒTH, gō-Ē-thē   'goːˌiːθ, goː'iːθiˑ

Goetz
  1. Hermann, German composer   GUH(R)TS   'gœts
  2. Bernhard, New York City   GETS   'gets
    subway assailant

Gog
  Biblical name   GAHG, GAWG   'gɑg, 'gɔːg

Gogebic
  lake, county, MI; iron range, MI,   gō-GĒ-bik   goː'giːbik
    WI

Gogh, Van
  see Van Gogh

Gogmagogs
  hills near Cambridge, England   GAHG-muh-GAHGZ   ˌgɑgmə'gɑgz

Gogo
  lang., people, Africa   GŌ-gō   'goːgoː

Gogol
  Nikolai, Russian writer   GAW-guhl, GŌ-GAWL   'gɔːgəl, 'goːˌgɔːl

---

Key (col. 2):   a: fad   ā: fade   ah: father   ar: Mary   aw: law   e: fed   ē: feed   er: merry   i: hid   ī: hide   ō: coat   ōō: boot
oi: boy   ow: now   u: put   uh: above   uhr: bird   ch: chop   ng: ring   sh: show   th: thick   t͟h: this   zh: measure

Goidelic
   sub-branch of Celtic langs.   goi-DEL-ik, goi-DĒ-lik   gɔi'delik, gɔi'diːlik

Gola
   lang., people, Liberia, Sierra   GŌ-luh   'goːlə
   Leone

Golan Heights
   hilly region, Syria, annexed by   GŌ-LAHN HĪTS, GŌ-luhn   ˌgoː,lɑn 'haits, ˌgoːlən
   Israel

Golconda
   town, IL; ruined city, India   gahl-KAHN-duh   gɑl'kɑndə

gold
   element   GŌLD   'goːld

Golda
   pers. name   GŌL-duh   'goːldə

Goldberg
   Leonard, *US film and TV*   GŌL(D)-BUHRG   'goːl(d),bəᵊg
   producer

Goldblum
   Jeff, *US actor*   GŌL(D)-BLO͞OM   'goːl(d),bluːm

Goldey Beacom
   College, *DE*   GŌL-dē BĒ-kuhm   'goːldiˑ 'biːkəm

Gold Fassl
   Austrian beer   GAWLT FAHS-uhl   'gɔːlt 'fɑsəl

Goldie
   pers. name   GŌL-dē   'goːldiˑ

Goldilocks
   fairy tale character   GŌL-dē-LAHKS   'goːldiˑˌlɑks

Golding
   William, *English author (Nobel*   GŌL-ding   'goːldiŋ
   1983)

Goldoni
   Carlo, *Italian playwright*   gōl-DŌ-nē   goːl'doːniˑ

Goldstein
   Joseph L., *US molecular*   GŌL(D)-STĪN   'goːl(d)ˌstain
   geneticist (Nobel 1985)

Goldsworthy
   pers. name   GŌL(D)Z-WUHR-<u>th</u>ē   'goːl(d)zˌwəᵊðiˑ

Goldwyn
   Samuel John, Jr., *US film*   GŌL-dwuhn   'goːldwən
   producer

Golgi
   Camillo, *Italian physician (Nobel*   GAWL-jē   'gɔːldʒiː
   1906)

Golgotha [Calvary]
   site of Christ's crucifixion   GAHL-guh-thuh, gahl-GAHTH-uh   'gɑlgəθə, gɑl'gɑθə

Goliad
   county, TX   GŌ-lē-AD   'goːliːˌæd

Goliath
   Biblical giant   guh-LĪ-uhth   gə'laiəθ

Golo
   Bantu people   GŌ-lō   'goːloː

Gombei
   pers. name   GŌM-bā   'goːmbeː

Gomes
   pers. name, Portuguese   GŌ-mish, GŌ-mis   'goːmiʃ, 'goːmis

---

Foreign Sounds: ue: *Fr.* **rue**, *Ger.* **füllen** uh(r): *Fr.* **boeuf**, *Ger.* **Höhle** <u>kh</u>: *Ger.* **ich**, *Scot.* **loch** ğ: *Sp.* **amigo** v̠: *Sp.* **hablar**
hl: *Welsh* **Llanelli**. CAPITALS: primary stress. SMALL CAPS: secondary stress. Ⓢ: U.S. pron. Ⓛ: British pron.

Gómez
   pers. name, Spanish   GŌ-mās, GŌ-māth   'goːmeːs, 'goːmeːθ

Gomorrah
   Biblical city   guh-MÔR-uh, guh-MAWR-uh   gə'moːrə, gə'mɔːrə

Gompers
   Samuel, *US labor leader*   GAHM-puhrz   'gampəʳz

Gonçalo
   pers. name, Portuguese   gawnⁿ-SAH-loo   gõ'saːluː

Goncharov
   Ivan, *Russian novelist*   guhn-CHUH-RAWF   gən,tʃə'rɔːf

Gond
   aboriginal people of India   GAHND   'gand

Gondi
   lang., India   GAHN-dē   'gandiˑ

Gondwanaland
   Mesozoic supercontinent   gahn-DWAHN-uh-LAND   gan'dwanə,lænd

Goneril
   character in King Lear,   GAHN-uh-RIL, GAHN-uh-ruhl   'ganə,ril, 'ganərəl
     Shakespeare

Gongola
   state, Nigeria   gahng-GŌ-luh   gaŋ'goːlə

Gongorism
   deliberate literary obscurity   GAHNG-guh-RIZ-uhm,   'gaŋgə,rizəm, 'gaŋgə,rizəm
                                  GAHN-guh-RIZ-uhm

Gonville and Caius
   college, Cambridge Univ.   GAHN-VIL uhn(d) KĒZ, GAHN-vuhl   'gan,vil ən(d) 'kiːz, 'ganvəl

Gonxha
   pers. name (A. G. Bojaxhiu)   gōn-KHAH   goːn'xa

Gonzaga
   University, *WA*   guhn-ZAHG-uh   gən'zagə

Gonzales
   1. city, county, TX; town, LA   guhn-ZAL-uhs, guhn-ZAHL-uhs   gən'zæləs, gən'zaləs
   2. pers. name, Dutch   ğawn-ZAHL-uhs   ɣɔːn'zaləs
   3. Spanish   gawn-SAHL-ās, gawn-THAHL-ās   gɔːn'saleːs, gɔːn'θaleːs

González
   pers. name, Spanish   gawn-SAHL-ās, gawn-THAHL-āth   gɔːn'saleːs, gɔːn'θaleːθ

Goodall
   Jane, *US zoologist; pers. name*   GUD-AWL   'gud,ɔːl

Gooden
   Dwight, *US baseball player*   GUD-n   'gudn̩

Goodenough
   island, Pacific   GUD-n-UHF   'gudn̩,əf

Goodhue
   pers. name   GUD-(h)yoo   'gud(h)juː

Goodson
   Mark, *US TV producer*   GUD-suhn   'gudsən

Goolagong
   Evonne, *Australian tennis player*   GOO-luh-GAWNG   'guːlə,gɔːŋ

Goold
   pers. name   GOOLD   'guːld

Goondiwindi
   town, Australia   GUHN-duh-WIN-dē   ,gəndə'windiˑ

Gopal
   1. pers. name, Bengali   gō-PAWL(-aw)   goː'pɔːl(ɔː)
   2. Marathi   gō-PAHL(-uh)   goː'pal(ə)

Key (col. 2):   a: **fad**   ā: **fade**   ah: **father**   ar: **Mary**   aw: **law**   e: **fed**   ē: **feed**   er: **merry**   i: **hid**   ī: **hide**   ō: **coat**   oo: **boot**
oi: **boy**   ow: **now**   u: **put**   uh: **above**   uhr: **bird**   ch: **chop**   ng: **ring**   sh: **show**   th: **thick**   th: **this**   zh: **measure**

Gorbachev		
Mikhail S., *political leader, USSR (Nobel 1990)*	GAWR-buh-CHAWF, GAWR-buh-CHAWV, GAWR-buh-CHAWF	'gɔːʳbəˌtʃɔːf, 'gɔːʳbəˌtʃɔːv, ˌgɔːʳbə'tʃɔːf
Gordian knot		
knot cut by Alexander the Great	GAWRD-ē-uhn NAHT	ˌgɔːʳdiːən 'nɑt
Gordias		
Phrygian peasant who became king, maker of the Gordian knot	GAWRD-ē-uhs	'gɔːʳdiːəs
Gordimer		
Nadine, *South African author*	GAWRD-uh-muhr	'gɔːʳdəməʳ
Gordium		
ancient Phrygian city	GAWR-dē-uhm	'gɔːʳdiːəm
Gordon		
pers. name	GAWRD-n	'gɔːʳdn̩
Gore		
Albert, Jr., *US vice-president; pers. name*	GŌR, GAWR	'goːʳ, 'gɔːʳ
Gorgas		
William C., *US physician*	GAWR-guhs	'gɔːʳgəs
Gorgias		
dialogue of Plato	GAWR-jē-uhs	'gɔːʳdʒiːəs
Gorgones		
Greek deities	gawr-GŌ-nēz	gɔːʳ'goːniːz
Gorgons		
snake-haired sisters: Stheno, Euryale, and Medusa	GAWR-guhnz	'gɔːʳgənz
Gorgonzola		
cheese	GAWR-guhn-ZŌ-luh	ˌgɔːʳgən'zoːlə
Gorham		
town, NH; crystal; pers. name	GŌR-uhm, GAWR-uhm	'goːrəm, 'gɔːrəm
Gorkiy, Gorki, Gorky		
city, Russia	GAWR-kē	'gɔːʳkiˑ
Gorme		
Eydie, *US entertainer*	gawr-MĀ	gɔːʳ'meː
Gorno-Badakhshan		
region, Tadzhikistan	GAWR-nō-BAHD-uhkh-SHAHN	ˌgɔːʳnoːˌbɑdəx'ʃɑn
Goronwy		
pers. name, Welsh	gaw-RAWN-wē, (\$) guh-RAHN-wē	gɔː'rɔːnwiː, (\$) gə'rɑnwiˑ
Gorton		
pers. name (G. Carruth)	GAWRT-n	'gɔːʳtn̩
Goshen		
biblical land, ancient Egypt; US pl. name	GŌ-shuhn	'goːʃən
Goshute, Gosiute		
N. American people	GŌ-SHOOT	'goːˌʃuːt
Gosplan		
Soviet planning organization	GAWS-PLAHN	'gɔːsˌplɑn
Gossage		
Richard Michael (Goose), *US baseball player*	GAHS-ij	'gɑsidʒ
Gösser		
Austrian beer	GUH(R)S-uhr	'gœsəʳ

Foreign Sounds: ue: *Fr.* **rue**, *Ger.* **fü**llen uh(r): *Fr.* **boeuf**, *Ger.* **Hö**hle kh: *Ger.* **ich**, *Scot.* lo**ch** g̃: *Sp.* ami**g**o v: *Sp.* ha**b**lar hl: *Welsh* **Ll**anelli. CAPITALS: primary stress. SMALL CAPS: secondary stress. (\$): U.S. pron. (£): British pron.

Gösser Stiftsbräu
　Austrian beer   GUH(R)S-uhr STIFTS-BROI   'gœsə^r 'stifts,brɔi

Göteborg [Gothenburg]
　city, Sweden   YUH(R)-tuh-BAWR(-yuh)   'jœːtə,bɔːr(jə)

Gotham
　1. nickname for New York City   GAHTH-uhm   'gɑθəm
　2. town, England   GŌT-uhm, GAHT-uhm   'goːʈəm, 'gɑʈəm

Gothenburg
　city, NE   GAHTH-uhn-BUHRG   'gɑθən,bə^rg

Gothenburg [Göteborg]
　city, Sweden   GAHTH-uhn-BUHRG,　GAHT-uhn-BUHRG   'gɑθən,bə^rg, 'gɑtən,bə^rg

Gothic
　ancient lang., Europe; style of　*architecture, music, literature*   GAHTH-ik   'gɑθik

Goths
　Teutonic tribe   GAHTHS   'gɑθs

Gotland
　island, county, Sweden   GAHT-LAND, GAHT-luhnd   'gɑt,lænd, 'gɑtlənd

Götterdämmerung
　opera, R. Wagner   GUH(R)T-uhr-DEM-uh-RUNG   ,gœtə^r'demə,ruŋ

Gottfried
　1. pers. name, German   GAWT-FRĒT   'gɔːt,friːt
　2. Swedish   GAWT-FRĒD   'gɔːt,friːd

Gotthold
　pers. name, German   GAWT-HAWLT   'gɔːt,hɔːlt

Göttingen
　town, Germany   GUH(R)T-ing-uhn   'gœtiŋən

Gottlieb
　1. pers. name   GAHT-LĒB   'gɑt,liːb
　2. Finnish, Swedish   GAWT-LĒB   'gɔːt,liːb
　3. German   GAWT-LĒP   'gɔːt,liːp

Gottlob
　pers. name, German   GAWT-LŌP   'gɔːt,loːp

Gottschalk
　Louis, *US composer*   GAHCH-AWK, GAHT-SHAWK   'gɑtʃ,ɔːk, 'gɑt,ʃɔːk

Gottschalks
　US department store chain   GAHCH-AWKS, GAHT-SHAWKS   'gɑtʃ,ɔːks, 'gɑt,ʃɔːks

Goucher
　College, *MD*   GOW-chuhr   'gautʃə^r

Gouda
　city, Netherlands; cheese   ḠOWD-uh, ⑤ G͞O͞OD-uh, GOWD-uh,　HOWD-uh   'ɣaudə, ⑤ 'guːdə, 'gaudə,　'haudə

Gouden Carolus
　Belgian beer   G͞O͞OD-n KAHR-ō-lus   'guːdn̩ 'karoːlus

Gough
　square, London; pers. name   GAWF   'gɔːf

Gould
　pers. name   G͞O͞OLD   'guːld

Goulet
　Robert, *entertainer*   g͞o͞o-LĀ   guː'leː

Gounod
　Charles François, *French*　*composer*   g͞o͞o-NŌ   guːnoː

Key (col. 2):   a: fad   ā: fade   ah: father   ar: Mary   aw: law   e: fed   ē: feed   er: merry   i: hid   ī: hide   ō: coat   o͞o: boot
oi: boy   ow: now   u: put   uh: above   uhr: bird   ch: chop   ng: ring   sh: show   th: thick   <u>th</u>: this   zh: measure

Gouverneur		
pers. name	GUHV-uh-NUR, GUV-uh-NUR, -NUHR	ˌgəvəˈnu^r, ˌguvəˈnu^r, -ˈnə^r
Govier		
pers. name	gō-VIR, guh-VIR	goːˈvi^r, gəˈvi^r
Govind		
pers. name, Punjabi	gō-VIND	goːˈvind
Govinda		
pers. name, Sanskrit	gō-VIN-duh	goːˈvində
Gowdy		
Curt, *US sportscaster*	GOWD-ē	ˈgɑudiˑ
Gowen		
pers. name	GOW-uhn	ˈgɑuən
Gower		
John, *English poet*	GOW(-uh)r, GŌ(-uh)r, GAWR	ˈgɑu(ə)^r, ˈgoː(ə)^r, ˈgɔː^r
Goya		
Francisco, *Spanish painter*	GOI-(y)uh	ˈgɔi(j)ə
Gozo		
island, Mediterranean	GAWT-sō	ˈgɔːtsoː
Graafian follicle		
ovum sac	GRAF-ē-uhn, [£] GRAH-fē-uhn	ˈgræfiːən, [£] ˈgrɑːfiːən
Gracchi		
Roman reformers	GRAK-ī	ˈgrækˌɑi
Gracchus		
Roman political family	GRAK-uhs	ˈgrækəs
Grace		
pers. name	GRĀS	ˈgreːs
Graceland		
Elvis Presley's home	GRĀ-SLAND, GRĀ-sluhnd	ˈgreːˌslænd, ˈgreːslənd
Graces		
Roman goddesses	GRĀ-suhz	ˈgreːsəz
Gracey, Gracie		
pers. name	GRĀ-sē	ˈgreːsiˑ
Graco		
US industrial equipment co.	GRĀ-kō	ˈgreːkoː
Grady		
pers. name	GRĀD-ē	ˈgreːdiˑ
Graeme		
pers. name	GRĀ-uhm, GRĀM	ˈgreːəm, ˈgreːm
Graf		
Steffi, *German tennis player*	GRAHF, [$] GRAF	ˈgrɑːf, [$] ˈgræf
Graham		
pers. name	GRĀ-uhm, GRAM	ˈgreːəm, ˈgræm
Graiae		
sisters of the Gorgons	GRĀ-Ē, GRĀ-Ī	ˈgreːˌiː, ˈgreːˌɑi
Graian Alps		
Alpine mtn. range	GRĀ-(y)uhn ALPS, GRĪ-(y)uhn	ˈgreː(j)ən ˈælps, ˈgrɑi(j)ən
Graig		
pers. name	GRĀG, GREG	ˈgreːg, ˈgreg
Grail		
legendary chalice	GRĀL	ˈgreːl
Grainger		
Percy, *US composer*	GRĀN-juhr	ˈgreːndʒə^r
Grainne		
legendary Irish heroine	GROIN-yuh	ˈgrɔinjə

Gramercy
Park, *New York City*   GRAM-uhr-sē   'græməᶜsi·

Grammy
grandmother; music award   GRAM-ē   'græmi·

Grampian
hills, region, Scotland   GRAM-pē-uhn   'græmpiːən

Granada
prov, city, Spain; dept., city,   grah-NAH<u>TH</u>-ah, Ⓢ gruh-NAHD-uh   grɑ'naða, Ⓢ grə'nadə
Nicaragua

Granados
Enrique, *Spanish composer*   grah-NAH<u>TH</u>-ōs, Ⓢ gruh-NAHD-ōs   grɑ'naðoːs, Ⓢ grə'nadoːs

Grana Padano
Italian cheese   GRAHN-uh pah-DAHN-ō   ˌgranə pa'danoː

Granatelli
Andy, *auto racing sponsor*   GRAN-uh-TEL-ē   ˌgrænə'teli·

Gran Chaco
region, S. America   grahn CHAHK-ō   gran 'tʃakoː

Grand Cayman
island, Caribbean   gran(d) KĀ-MAN, KĀ-muhn, kā-MAN   græn(d) 'keːˌmæn, 'keːmən, keː'mæn

Grand Comore
island, Mozambique Channel   GRAN(D) kuh-MAWR   ˌgræn(d) kə'mɔːᶜ

Grand Coulee
valley, city, WA   gran(d) KOO-lē   græn(d) 'kuːli·

Grande Champagne
wine   GRAHⁿD shahⁿ-PAHN-yuh, GRAHⁿ-duh   grãd ʃãpaːɲ, grãdə

Grandes Marques
wine   GRAHⁿD MAHRK, GRAHⁿ-duh   grãd maːrk, grãdə

Grande-Terre
islands, Caribbean   gran-TER   græn'teᶜ

Grand Guignol
horror drama   grahⁿ gēn-YAWL, Ⓢ GRAHN gēn-YÔL   grã giːnjɔːl, Ⓢ ˌgran giːn'joːl

Grand Marais
village, MN   GRAN(D) muh-RĀ   ˌgræn(d) mə'reː

Grand Marnier
liqueur   GRAHⁿ mahrn-YĀ   grã maːrnjeː

Grand Pré
village, Nova Scotia   grahⁿ(n) PRĀ, Ⓢ GRAN PRĀ   grã(n) 'preː, Ⓢ 'græn 'preː

Grand Prix
auto race   grahⁿ PRĒ, gran(d) PRĒ   grã 'priː, græn(d) 'priː

Grand Teton
National Park, *Moose, WY*   gran(d) TĒ-TAHN   græn(d) 'tiːˌtɑn

Grand Traverse
county, MI   gran(d) TRAV-uhrs   græn(d) 'trævəᶜs

Grandy
Fred, *US actor, politician*   GRAN-dē   'grændi·

Grange, La
see La Grange

Granit
Ragnar, *Finnish-born Swedish*   grah-NĒT   grɑ'niːt
physiologist (Nobel 1967)

Granma
prov, Cuba   grahn-MAH   gran'ma

Key (col. 2):   a: fad   ā: fade   ah: father   ar: Mary   aw: law   e: fed   ē: feed   er: merry   i: hid   ī: hide   ō: coat   o͞o: boot
oi: boy   ow: now   u: put   uh: above   uhr: bird   ch: chop   ng: ring   sh: show   th: thick   <u>th</u>: this   zh: measure

Grant
  Ulysses S., *18th US president;* GRANT 'grænt
    pers. name
Granta
  river, Cambridgeshire, England GRANT-uh, ⓔ GRAHNT-uh 'græntə, ⓔ 'grɑːntə
Grantham
  town, England GRAN-thuhm, GRANT-uhm 'grænθəm, 'græntəm
Gratian
  Roman emperor GRĀ-sh(ē-)uhn 'greːʃ(iː)ən
Gratiot
  county, MI GRASH-uht 'græʃət
Grattan
  Henry, *Irish politician* GRAT-n 'grætn̩
Grau
  Shirley Ann, *US writer* GROW 'grɑu
Graubünden [Grisons]
  mtn. range, Switzerland grow-BUEN-duhn, grɑu'byndən,
    ⓢ grow-BIN-duhn, ⓢ grɑu'bindən,
    grow-BUN-duhn grɑu'bundən

Grau San Martín
  Ramón, *president, Cuba* GROW SAHN mahr-TĒN 'grɑu ˌsan mɑʳˈtiːn
Graustark
  novel, G. B. McCutcheon GROW-STAHRK 'grɑuˌstɑʳk
Gravenstein
  apple GRAV-uhn-STĒN, GRĀ-vuhn-STĪN, 'grævənˌstiːn, 'greːvənˌstɑin,
    -STĒN -ˌstiːn
Graves
  wine GRAHV 'grɑv
Graz
  city, Austria GRAHTS 'grɑts
Grazia
  pers. name, Italian GRAHTS-yah 'grɑtsjɑ
Graziano
  Rocky, *US boxer* GRAHT-sē-AHN-ō, GRAHS-ē-AHN-ō, ˌgrɑtsiːˈɑnoː, ˌgrɑsiːˈɑnoː,
    GRAHZ-ē-AHN-ō ˌgrɑziːˈɑnoː
Great Britain
  island, Europe grāt BRIT-n greːt 'britn̩
Great Pyrenees
  mts., France, Spain PIR-uh-NĒZ 'pirəˌniːz
Grebo
  lang., people, Liberia, Ivory Coast GRĀ-bō 'greːboː
Grecian
  pert. to Greece GRĒ-shuhn 'griːʃən
Greco, El
  Doménikos, *Spanish painter* el GREK-ō, el GRĀ-kō el 'grekoː, el 'greːkoː
Greco-Roman
  pert. to ancient Greece and Rome GREK-ō-RŌ-muhn ˌgrekoːˈroːmən
Greece
  republic, Europe GRĒS 'griːs
Greek
  lang., Greece, Cyprus, Turkey GRĒK 'griːk
Greeley
  Horace, *US politician; US pl.* GRĒ-lē 'griːliˑ
    name

Foreign Sounds: **ue**: *Fr.* **rue**, *Ger.* **füllen** **uh(r)**: *Fr.* **boeuf**, *Ger.* **Höhle** <u>kh</u>: *Ger.* **ich**, *Scot.* **loch** g̃: *Sp.* **amigo** v̧: *Sp.* **hablar**
hl: *Welsh* **Llanelli**. CAPITALS: primary stress. SMALL CAPS: secondary stress. ⓢ: U.S. pron. ⓔ: British pron.

Green
  college, Oxford Univ.   GRĒN   'griːn

Greenblatt
  Milton, *US psychiatrist*   GRĒN-BLAT   'griːn,blæt

Greenland
  island, North America   GRĒN-luhnd, GRĒN-LAND   'griːnlənd, 'griːn,lænd

Greenlander
  inhabitant of Greenland   GRĒN-luhn-duhr, -LAN-duhr   'griːnləndəʳ, -,lændəʳ

Greenlandic [Iniut]
  lang., Greenland, Canada, USA   grēn-LAN-dik, GRĒN-LAN-dik   griːn'lændik, 'griːn,lændik
  (AK)

Greenleaf
  pers. name   GRĒN-LĒF   'griːn,liːf

Greenlee
  county, AZ   GRĒN-lē   'griːniˑ

Greenock
  port, Scotland   GRĒ-nuhk, GRIN-uhk, GREN-uhk   'griːnək, 'grinək, 'grenək

Greenough
  pers. name   GRĒ-NŌ   'griː,noː

Greenpeace
  environmental organization   GRĒN-PĒS   'griːn,piːs

Greensboro
  city, NC   GRĒNZ-buhr-uh, GRĒNZ-buh-ruh   'griːnzbər-ə, 'griːnzbə-rə

Greenville
  US pl. name   GRĒN-vuhl, GRĒN-VIL   'griːnvəl, 'griːn,vil

Greenwich
  1. town, CT, RI   GREN-ich, GRĒN-WICH, GRIN-WICH   'grenitʃ, 'griːn,witʃ, 'grin,witʃ
  2. town, NY   GRĒN-WICH   'griːn,witʃ
  3. borough, London, England   GRIN-ij, GREN-ij, -ich   'grinidʒ, 'grenidʒ, -itʃ
  4. island, Shetland Islands   GREN-ich, GRIN-ich, -ij   'grenitʃ, 'grinitʃ, -idʒ

Greenwich Village
  area, New York City   GREN-ich VIL-ij, GREN-ij   'grenitʃ 'vilidʒ, 'grenidʒ

Greer
  Hershel, Stadium, *Nashville, TN*   GRIR   'griʳ

Greg
  pers. name   GREG, GRĀG   'greg, 'greːg

Grégoire
  pers. name, French   grā-GWAHR   greːgwɑːʳ

Gregor
  1. pers. name   GREG-uhr   'gregəʳ
  2. German   GRĀ-GAWR, grā-GAWR   'greː,gɔːʳ, greː'gɔːʳ

Gregorian
  pert. to any Pope Gregory   gri-GAWR-ē-uhn, greg-AWR-ē-uhn   gri'gɔːriːən, greg'ɔːriːən

Gregório
  pers. name, Portuguese   grā-GAWR-yōō   greː'gɔːrjuː

Gregorio
  1. pers. name, Italian   grā-GAWR-yō   greː'gɔːrjoː
  2. Spanish   grā-ĞŌR-yō   greː'ɣɔːrjoː

Gregorius
  pers. name, Latin   gri-GAWR-ē-uhs, greg-AWR-ē-uhs   gri'gɔːriːəs, greg'ɔːriːəs

Gregory
  pers. name   GREG(-uh)-rē   'greg(ə)riˑ

Grenache
  wine grape   gruh-NAHSH, gren-AHSH   grə'nɑʃ, gren'ɑʃ

Key (col. 2):   a: fad ā: fade ah: father ar: Mary aw: law e: fed ē: feed er: merry i: hid ī: hide ō: coat ōō: boot
oi: boy ow: now u: put uh: above uhr: bird ch: chop ng: ring sh: show th: thick t̲h̲: this zh: measure

Grenada
island, West Indies; county, city, MS — gruh-NĀD-uh — grə'neːdə

Grenadian
pert. to Grenada — gruh-NĀD-ē-uhn — grə'neːdiːən

Grenadine
pomegranate syrup — GREN-uh-DĒN, GREN-uh-DĒN — ˌgrenə'diːn, 'grenəˌdiːn

Grenadines
islands, West Indies — GREN-uh-DĒNZ — ˌgrenə'diːnz

Grendel
monster in Beowulf — GREND-l — 'grendḷ

Grenoble
city, France — gruh-NAWBL, Ⓢ gruh-NŌ-buhl — grənɔːbl, Ⓢ grə'noːbəl

Grenville
pers. name; county, Ontario; town, Grenada — GREN-VIL, GREN-vuhl — 'grenˌvil, 'grenvəl

Grenzquell
German beer — GRENTS-KVEL — 'grentsˌkvel

Gresham
pers. name; city, OR — GRESH-uhm — 'greʃəm

Greta
1. pers. name — GRET-uh, GRĒT-uh — 'gretə, 'griːtə
2. Swedish — GRÃ-tah — 'greːtɑː

Gretel
pers. name — GRET-l — 'gretḷ

Gretna
city, LA; district, Scotland — GRET-nuh — 'gretnə

Gretna Green
village, Scotland — GRET-nuh GRĒN — ˌgretnə 'griːn

Gretzky
Wayne, Canadian hockey player — GRET-skē — 'gretskiˑ

Grey
pers. name — GRÃ — 'greː

Grgich Hills
winery, CA — GUHR-gich HILZ — 'gəᵣgitʃ 'hilz

Grieg
Edvard, Norwegian composer — GRIG, Ⓢ GRĒG — 'grig, Ⓢ 'griːg

Grier
pers. name — GRIR — 'griᵣ

Griffin
mythical beast; pers. name — GRIF-uhn — 'grifən

Griffith
pers. name — GRIF-uhth — 'grifəθ

Griffiths
pers. name — GRIF-uh(th)s — 'grifə(θ)s

Griffon
mythical beast; breed of dog — GRIF-uhn — 'grifən

Grignard
Victor, French chemist (Nobel 1912) — grēn-YAHR — griːnjɑr

Grigori, -ry
pers. name, Russian — gri-GAWR-yi — gri'gɔːrjij

Grimaldi
royal family, Monaco; crater on Moon — gruh-MAWL-dē, gruh-MAHL-dē, gruh-MAL-dē — grə'mɔːldiˑ, grə'mɑldiˑ, grə'mældiˑ

Foreign Sounds: ue: *Fr.* **rue**, *Ger.* **füllen** uh(r): *Fr.* **boeuf**, *Ger.* **Höhle** kh: *Ger.* **ich**, *Scot.* **loch** g̃: *Sp.* **amigo** v: *Sp.* **hablar** hl: *Welsh* **Llanelli**. CAPITALS: primary stress. SMALL CAPS: secondary stress. Ⓢ: U.S. pron. Ⓛ: British pron.

Grimes
  pers. name; county, TX   GRĪMZ   'grɑimz
Grimm
  Jacob *and* Wilhelm, *German*   GRIM   'grim
    linguists, fairy tale collectors
Grimsby
  pers. name; town, Ontario;   GRIMZ-bē   'grimzbiˑ
    borough, England
Grindel [Éluard]
  Eugène, *French poet*   greⁿ-DEL   grẽdel
Grinnell
  George, *US naturalist;* College,   gruh-NEL   grə'nel
    IA; pl. name, US, Canada
Gris
  Juan, *Spanish artist*   GRẼS   'griːs
Grisons [Graubünden]
  mtn. range, Switzerland   grē-ZAWⁿ   griːzõ
Griswold
  pers. name   GRIZ-wuhld, -WŌLD, -WAWLD   'grizwəld, -ˌwoːld, -ˌwɔːld
Grodin
  Charles, *US actor, writer, director*   GRŌD-n   'groːdn̩
Groening
  Matt, *US cartoonist*   GRĀ-ning   'greːniŋ
Grofé
  Ferde, *US composer*   GRŌ-FĀ   'groːˌfeː
Grogan
  Steven, *football player*   GRŌ-guhn   'groːgən
Grolier
  US publisher   GRŌL-yuhr, GRŌ-lē-uhr   'groːljəʳ, 'groːliːəʳ
Grolier de Servières
  Jean, *French bibliophile*   grawl-yā duh ser-VYER   grɔːljeː də servjer
Gromyko
  Andrei, *president, USSR*   gruh-MĒ-kō   grə'miːkoː
Gronchi
  Giovanni, *president, Italy*   GRAHNG-kē   'grɑŋkiˑ
Groningen
  prov & town, Netherlands   GRŌ-ning-uhn   'groːniŋən
Gropius
  Walter, *German architect*   GRŌ-pē-uhs   'groːpiːəs
Grosbeak
  songbird   GRŌS-BĒK   'groːsˌbiːk
Grosseto
  prov, Italy   grō-SĀT-ō   groː'seːtoː
Grossmont
  College, *CA*   GRŌ-smahnt   'groːsmant
Grosvenor
  pers. name   GRŌV-nuhr, GRŌ-vuh-nuhr   'groːvnəʳ, 'groːvənəʳ
Gros Ventre
  N. American people   grō-VAHNT   groː'vant
Grosz
  George, *US artist*   GRŌS   'groːs
Grotius
  Hugo, *Dutch statesman*   GRŌ-sh(ē-)uhs   'groːʃ(iː)əs
Groton
  town, CT, MA; village, NY   GRAHT-n   'grɑtn̩

Key (col. 2):   a: fad   ā: fade   ah: father   ar: Mary   aw: law   e: fed   ē: feed   er: merry   i: hid   ī: hide   ō: coat   ōō: boot
oi: boy   ow: now   u: put   uh: above   uhr: bird   ch: chop   ng: ring   sh: show   th: thick   th: this   zh: measure

Groucho
   pers. name (G. Marx)   GROW-chō   'grautʃoː

Groundsel
   plant   GROWN(D)-suhl   'graun(d)səl

Grover
   pers. name   GRŌ-vuhr   'groːvəʳ

Grozny
   city, Russia   GRAWZ-nē, GRAHZ-nē   'groːzniˑ, 'grazniˑ

Grudziądz
   city, Poland   GROO-JAWⁿTS   'gruːˌdʒɔ̃ts

Grundig
   German radio co.   GRUN-dig, GRUHN-dig   'grundig, 'grəndig

Grundy
   pl. name, US   GRUHN-dē   'grəndiˑ

Grus
   constellation   GROOS, GRUHS   'gruːs, 'grəs

Gruyère
   district, Switzerland; cheese   groo-YER, grē-(Y)ER   gruː'jeʳ, griː'(j)eʳ

Gruzinian
   lang., Georgia   groo-ZIN-ē-uhn, groo-ZIN-yuhn   gruː'ziniːən, gruː'zinjən

Grzegorz
   pers. name, Polish   GZHEG-awsh   'gʒegɔːʃ

Gstaad
   city, Switzerland   guh-SHTAHT   gə'ʃtat

Guadalajara
   prov & town, Mexico; prov &   gwahth-ah-lah-KHAHR-ah,   gwaðala'xara,
      town, Spain   ⑤ GWAHD-l-uh-HAHR-uh   ⑤ ˌgwadl̩ə'harə

Guadalcanal
   island, Pacific   GWAHD-l-kuh-NAL,   ˌgwadl̩kə'næl, ˌgwadəkə'næl
       GWAHD-uh-kuh-NAL

Guadalquivir
   river, Spain   gwahth-ahl-kē-VIR,   gwaðalki:'βir,
       ⑤ GWAHD-l-ki-VIR   ⑤ ˌgwadl̩ki'viʳ

Guadalupe
   1. Mountains National Park, *TX;*   GWAHD-l-OOP, GWAHD-l-OO-pē   'gwadl̩ˌuːp, ˌgwadl̩'uːpiˑ
       county, NM, TX
   2. pers. name, Spanish   gwahth-ah-LOO-pā   gwaða'luːpeˑ

Guadalupe Hidalgo
   city, Mexico   GWAHTH-ah-LOO-pā ē-THAHL-gō,   ˌgwaða'luːpeˑ iˑ'ðalyoː,
       ⑤ GWAHD-l-OOP(-ē) hi-DAL-gō   ⑤ 'gwadl̩ˌuːp(iˑ) hi'dælgoː

Guadeloupe
   islands, West Indies   GWAHD-l-OOP, GWAHD-l-OOP   'gwadl̩ˌuːp, ˌgwadl̩'uːp

Guadeloupian
   pert. to Guadeloupe   GWAHD-l-OO-pē-uhn   ˌgwadl̩'uːpiːən

Guadix
   city, Spain   gwah-DĒKH, gwah-DĒKS   gwa'diːç, gwa'diːks

Guahibo
   lang., Colombia, Venezuela   gwah-(H)Ē-vō   gwa'(h)iːβoː

Guairá [Sete Quedas]
   waterfall, S. America   gwī-RAH   gwai'ra

Guam
   island, Pacific   GWAHM   'gwam

Guan
   S. & Cen. American bird   GWAHN   'gwan

Foreign Sounds: **ue**: *Fr.* **rue**, *Ger.* **füllen**   **uh**(r): *Fr.* **b**oeuf, *Ger.* **Höhle**   **kh**: *Ger.* i**ch**, *Scot.* lo**ch**   **ḡ**: *Sp.* ami**g**o   **v**: *Sp.* ha**b**lar
hl: *Welsh* **Ll**anelli.   CAPITALS: primary stress.   SMALL CAPS: secondary stress.   ⑤: U.S. pron.   ⓛ: British pron.

Guanajuato
  state, city, Mexico   gwahn-ah-<u>KH</u>WAHT-ō,   gwana'xwaṭoː,
           Ⓢ GWAHN-uh-(H)WAHT-ō   Ⓢ ˌgwanə'(h)waṭoː

Guangdong, Kwangtung
  prov, China   GWAHNG-DUNG   'gwaŋ'duŋ

Guangxi [Kwangsi Chuang]
  region, China   GWAHNG-SĒ, GWAHNG-SHĒ   'gwaŋ'siː, 'gwaŋ'ʃiː

Guangzhou, Kwangchow [Canton]
  city, China   GWAHNG-JŌ   'gwaŋ'dʒoː

Guantánamo
  prov & bay, Cuba   gwahn-TAHN-uh-mō   gwan'tanəmoː

Guaporé
  river, S. America   gwahp-uh-RĀ   gwapə'reː

Guaraní
  lang., people, S. America   GWAHR-uh-NĒ   ˌgwarə'niː

Guardi
  Francesco *and* Giovanni, *Italian*   GWAHR-dē   'gwaʳdiˑ
    painters

Guardia, La
  see La Guardia

Guarneri
  family of Italian violin makers   gwahrn-YER-ē   gwaʳn'jeriˑ

Guarnerius
  Latin form of Guarneri   gwahr-NIR-ē-uhs   gwaʳ'niriːəs

Guatemala
  republic, Cen. America   GWAHT-uh-MAHL-uh   ˌgwaṭə'malə

Guatemalan
  pert. to Guatemala   GWAHT-uh-MAHL-uhn   ˌgwaṭə'malən

Guató
  S. American people   gwah-TŌ   gwa'toː

Guayaná
  S. American people   GĪ-uh-NAH   ˌgaiə'nɑ

Guayaquil
  city, Ecuador   GWĪ-uh-KĒL   ˌgwaiə'kiːl

Guayas
  prov, Ecuador   GWĪ-uhs   'gwaiəs

Guaymí
  Cen. American people   gwī-MĒ   gwai'miː

Gucci
  fashion designers   GOO-chē   'guːtʃiˑ

Gudea
  Sumerian ruler of Lagash   goo-DĒ-uh   guː'diːə

Guderian
  Heinz, *German militarist*   goo-DER-ē-uhn   guː'deriːən

Gudmund
  pers. name, Swedish   GOOD-MUHND   'guːd,mənd

Gudmundur
  pers. name, Icelandic   GVUE<u>TH</u>-MUEN-duer   'gvyð,myndyr

Gudrun
  wife of Sigurd & Atli in Norse   GUD-RŌŌN   'gud,ruːn
    myth

Guelph
  town, Canada   GWELF   'gwelf

Guenoc
  winery, CA   gwuh-NAHK   gwə'nɑk

Key (col. 2):   a: fad   ā: fade   ah: father   ar: Mary   aw: law   e: fed   ē: feed   er: merry   i: hid   ī: hide   ō: coat   ōō: boot
oi: boy   ow: now   u: put   uh: above   uhr: bird   ch: chop   ng: ring   sh: show   th: thick   <u>th</u>: this   zh: measure

Guérard
  Michel, *French chef* — gä-RAHR — geːrɑːr
Guerlain
  French perfume — ger-LE^n — gerlɛ̃
Guernica
  town, Spain; painting, Picasso — ger-NĒ-kuh, ⑤ GWER-ni-kuh, GER-ni-kuh — geʳˈniːkə, ⑤ ˈgweʳnikə, ˈgeʳnikə
Guernsey
  island, English channel — GUHRN-zē — ˈgəʳnziː
Guerrero
  state, Mexico — ger-RER-ō — gerˈreroː
Guevara
  Che, *Cuban revolutionary* — gä-VAHR-uh, ⑤ gwuh-VAHR-uh — geːˈβarə, ⑤ gwəˈvaʳə
Guggenheim
  Solomon R., *museum, New York City* — GUG-uhn-HĪM, GOO-guhn-HĪM — ˈgugən,haim, ˈguːgən,haim
Guglielmo
  pers. name, Italian — gool-YEL-mō — guːlˈjelmoː
Gui
  pers. name, French — GĒ — giː
Guiana
  region, S. America — gē-AN-uh, gē-AHN-uh, gī-AN-uh — giːˈænə, giːˈɑnə, gaiˈænə
Guianese
  pert. to Guiana — GĪ-uh-NĒZ, GĒ-uh-, -NĒS — ˌgaiəˈniːz, ˌgiːə-, -ˈniːs
Guido
  1. pers. name — GĒD-ō, GWĒD-ō — ˈgiːdoː, ˈgwiːdoː
  2. Dutch — ĞĒ-DŌ — ˈɣiː,doː
  3. Italian — GWĒ-dō — ˈgwiːdoː
  4. German — goo-Ē-dō, GĒ-dō — guːˈiːdoː, ˈgiːdoː
Guidry
  Ron, *US baseball player* — GID-rē — ˈgidriː
Guildenstern
  character in Hamlet, *Shakespeare* — GIL-duhn-STUHRN — ˈgildən,stəʳn
Guildford
  town, England — GIL-fuhrd — ˈgilfəʳd
Guilford
  county, college, NC; town, CT, ME — GIL-fuhrd — ˈgilfəʳd
Guilherme
  pers. name, Portuguese — gēl-YER-muh, -mä — giːlˈjermə, -meː
Guilin, Kuei-lin, Kweilin
  city, China — GWĀ-LIN — ˈgweːˈlin
Guillain-Barré
  medical syndrome — gē-YA^n-buh-RĀ — giːˈjæbəˈreː
Guillaume
  1. C. E., *Swiss physicist (Nobel 1920)* — gē-YŌM — giːˈjoːm
  2. Robert, *US entertainer* — gē-(Y)ŌM — giːˈ(j)oːm
  3. pers. name, French — gē-YŌM — giːjoːm
Guillemin
  Roger C. L., *French-born US physiologist (Nobel 1977)* — gē-(yuh)-ME^n — giːˈ(jə)mɛ̃
Guillemot
  sea bird — GIL-i-MAHT — ˈgili,mɑt

Foreign Sounds: ue: *Fr.* **rue**, *Ger.* **füllen** uh(r): *Fr.* **boeuf**, *Ger.* **Höhle** kh: *Ger.* **ich**, *Scot.* **loch** ğ: *Sp.* **amigo** v: *Sp.* **hablar**
hl: *Welsh* **Llanelli**. CAPITALS: primary stress. SMALL CAPS: secondary stress. ⑤: U.S. pron. ⑥: British pron.

Guillermo
   1. pers. name, Spanish   gē(l)-YER-mō   giː(l)'jermoː
   2. in Argentina, Paraguay,   gē-ZHER-mō, gē(l)-YER-mō   giː'ʒermoː, giː(l)'jermoː
    Uruguay
Guinea
   region, republic, gulf, Africa   GIN-ē   'giniː
Guinea-Bissau
   country, Africa   GIN-ē-bis-OW   ,giniːbis'au
Guinean
   pert. to Guinea   GIN-ē-uhn   'giniːən
Guinevere [Gwenhwyfar]
   Arthur's queen in legend   GWIN-uh-VIR, GWEN-   'gwinə,virʳ, 'gwen-
Guinness
   Irish stout   GIN-uhs   'ginəs
Guipúzcoa
   prov, Spain   gē-P$\overline{OO}$TH-kuh-wuh,   giː'puːθkəwə, giː'puːskəwə
                        gē-P$\overline{OO}$S-kuh-wuh
Guisborough
   town, England   GIZ-buh-ruh, GIZ-buhr-uh, GIZ-bruh   'gizbə-rə, 'gizbər-ə, 'gizbrə
Guise
   commune, France   G$\overline{E}$Z   giːz
Guiseley
   town, England   G$\overline{I}$Z-lē   'gaizliː
Guisewite
   Cathy, *US cartoonist*   G$\overline{I}$Z-W$\overline{I}$T   'gaiz,wait
Guislain
   pers. name, French   gēs-LE^n giːslẽ
Guiyang, Kuei-yang, Kweiyang
   city, China   GW$\overline{A}$-YAHNG   'gweː'jaŋ
Guizhou, Kweichow
   prov, China   GW$\overline{A}$-J$\overline{O}$ 'gweː'dʒoː
Gujarat
   state, India   G$\overline{OO}$-juh-RAHT, GUJ-uh-RAHT   ,guːdʒə'rat, ,gudʒə'rat
Gujarati
   lang., people, India   G$\overline{OO}$-juh-RAHT-ē, GUJ-uh-RAHT-ē   ,guːdʒə'ratiː, ,gudʒə'ratiː
GULAG
   USSR prison system   G$\overline{OO}$-LAHG   'guː,lag
Gulielmus
   pers. name, Latin   GY$\overline{OO}$-lē-EL-muhs   ,gjuːliː'elməs
Gullah
   black Americans on coast of SC,   GUHL-uh   'gələ
    GA, FL; their dialect of English
Gulliver
   Lemuel, *hero of* Gulliver's Travels,   GUHL-uh-vuhr   'gələvəʳ
    J. Swift
Gullstrand
   Allvar, *Swedish ophthamologist*   GUHL-STRAHN(D)   'gəl,straːn(d)
    (Nobel 1911)
Gulpener
   Dutch beer   ḠUL-puh-nuhr, GUL-   'ɣulpənər, 'gul-
Gum
   department store, Moscow   G$\overline{OO}$M   'guːm
Gumbel
   Bryant, *US TV broadcaster*   GUHM-buhl   'gəmbəl

Key (col. 2):   a: fad   ā: fade   ah: father   ar: Mary   aw: law   e: fed   ē: feed   er: merry   i: hid   ī: hide   ō: coat $\overline{oo}$: boot
oi: boy   ow: now   u: put   uh: above   uhr: bird   ch: chop   ng: ring   sh: show   th: thick   th̲: this   zh: measure

Gund
   US mfrs.   GUHND, GUND   'gənd, 'gund

Gundagai
   town, shire, Australia   GUHN-duh-GĪ   'gəndə‚gai

Gundel
   restaurant, Budapest, Hungary   GŌŌN-duhl   'guːndəl

Gunderson
   pers. name   GUHN-duhr-suhn   'gəndəʳsən

Gundlach-Bundschu
   winery, CA   GUND-lah<u>kh</u> BUND-SHŌŌ   'gundlɑx 'bund‚ʃuː

Gunga Din
   Kipling character   GUHNG-guh DIN   ‚gəŋgə 'din

Gunnar
   1. pers. name, Icelandic   GUEN-nahr   'gynnɑr
   2. Norwegian   GUN-nahr   'gunnɑr
   3. Swedish   GUHN-nahr   'gənnɑːr

Gunnbjorn
   mtn., Greenland   GUN-BYUHRN, Ⓢ GUN-BYAWRN   'gun‚bjœːrn, Ⓢ 'gun‚bjɔːʳn

Gunnedah
   town, Australia   GUHN-uh-dah   'gənədɑː

Gunther
   1. pers. name   GUHN-thuhr   'gənθəʳ
   2. German   GUN-tuhr   'guntəʳ

Günther
   pers. name, German   GUEN-tuhr   'gyntəʳ

Gurage
   lang., people, Ethiopia   gōō-RAH-gā   guː'rɑgeː

Guralnik
   David, *US lexicographer*   guh-RAL-nik   gə'rælnik

Gurdjieff
   Armenian Sufi mystic in West guhr-JEF, guhr-JĒF   gəʳ'dʒef, gəʳ'dʒiːf

Gurkha
   Nepalese soldier in British or GUR-kuh, GUHR-kuh   'guʳkə, 'gəʳkə
   Indian army

Gurkhali [Nepali]
   lang., Nepal, Sikkim   gur-KAHL-ē, GUHR-KAHL-ē   guʳ'kɑliˑ, ‚gəʳ'kɑliˑ

Gurma
   lang., people, Togo, Burkina Faso GUR-muh   'guʳmə

Gursel
   Cemal, *president, Turkey*   guhr-SEL   gəʳ'sel

Gus
   pers. name   GUHS   'gəs

Gusev, Gussev
   city, Russia   GŌŌ-suhf   'guːsəf

Gustaf
   1. pers. name, Finnish   GUS-TAHF   'gus‚tɑːf
   2. German   GUS-TAHF   'gus‚taf
   3. Swedish   GUHS-TAHV   'gəs‚tɑv

Gustav
   1. pers. name, Danish   GUS-TAHV   'gus‚tɑv
   2. German   GUS-TAHF   'gus‚taf
   3. Swedish   GUHS-TAHV   'gəs‚tɑv

Foreign Sounds: ue: *Fr.* **rue**, *Ger.* **füllen** uh(r): *Fr.* **boeuf**, *Ger.* **Höhle** <u>kh</u>: *Ger.* **ich**, *Scot.* **loch** ḡ: *Sp.* amiḡo v̱: *Sp.* hablar
hl: *Welsh* **Llanelli**. CAPITALS: primary stress. SMALL CAPS: secondary stress. Ⓢ: U.S. pron. Ⓛ: British pron.

Gustave

1. pers. name	GUS-TAHV	'gus,tav
2. French	gue-TAHV	gyːtaːv
3. German	GUS-TAHV-uh	'gus,tavə

Gustavo

1. pers. name, Portuguese	g͞oosh-TAH-v͞oo, g͞oos-	guːʃ'taːvuː, guːs-
2. Spanish	g͞oo-STAHV-ō	guː'stavoː

Gustavus

pers. name, Latin	guhs-TĀ-vuhs, gus-	gəs'teːvəs, gus-

Gustavus Adolphus

Swedish king; college, MN	guh-STAHV-uhs uh-DAHL-fuhs, uh-DAWL-fuhs	gə'stavəs ə'dalfəs, ə'dɔːlfəs

Gustaw

pers. name, Polish	G͞OOS-tahf	'guːstaːf

Gusztav

pers. name, Hungarian	GUS-tahv	'gustav

Gutenberg

Johannes, *German inventor of printing*	G͞OOT-n-BERK, $ G͞OOT-n-BUHRG	'guːtn̩,beʳk, $ 'guːtn̩,bəʳg

Guthrie

Arlo, *folk singer;* Woody, *folk singer & activist*	GUHTH-rē	'gəθriˑ

Gutians

ancient conquerors of Babylonia	G͞OO-sh(ē-)uhnz	'guːʃ(iː)ənz

Gutierre

pers. name, Spanish	g͞oo-TYER-ā	guː'tjereː

Gutzon

pers. name (G. Borglum)	GUHT-suhn	'gətsən

Guy

1. pers. name	GĪ	'gai
2. French	GĒ	giː

Guyana

republic, S. America	gī-AHN-uh, gī-AN-uh	gai'anə, gai'ænə

Guyanese

pert. to Guyana	GĪ-uh-NĒZ, -NĒS	ˌgaiə'niːz, -'niːs

Guyenne

prov, France	gē-EN	giːen

Guy Fawkes Day

English celebration of capture of G. Fawkes, November 5	GĪ FAWKS DĀ	ˌgai 'fɔːks ˌdeː

Guyra

town, Australia	GĪ-ruh	'gairə

Guzmán Blanco

Antonio, *Venezuelan politician*	g͞oo-SMAHN BLAHNG-kō	guː'sman 'blaŋkoː

Gwalior

city, India	GWAHL-ē-AWR	'gwaliːˌɔːʳ

Gwen

pers. name	GWEN	'gwen

Gwendolen, -lin, -lyn

pers. name	GWEN-duh-luhn, GWEN-dl-uhn	'gwendələn, 'gwendl̩ən

Gwendoline

pers. name	GWEN-duh-luhn, GWEN-dl-uhn, GWEN-duh-LĪN	'gwendələn, 'gwendl̩ən, 'gwendə,lain

Gwenhwyfar [Guinevere]

Arthur's queen in Welsh legend	gwen-HUI-VAHR	gwen'hui,vaʳ

Key (col. 2):   a: fad ā: fade ah: father ar: Mary aw: law e: fed ē: feed er: merry i: hid ī: hide ō: coat o͞o: boot
oi: boy   ow: now   u: put   uh: above   uhr: bird   ch: chop   ng: ring   sh: show   th: thick   <u>th</u>: this   zh: measure

Gwenllïan		
pers. name, Welsh	gwen-HLĒ-ahn	gwen'l̥iːɑn
Gwent		
county, ancient kingdom, Wales	GWENT	'gwent
Gwerful Mechain		
Welsh poetess	GWER-vil MEKH-ĪN	'gweʳvil 'mex,ɑin
Gwilym		
pers. name, Welsh	GWIL-im	'gwilim
Gwinnett		
county, GA	gwin-ET	gwin'et
Gwladys		
pers. name, Welsh	GWLAHD-is, [$] GLAD-uhs	'gwlɑdis, [$] 'glædəs
Gwyn		
pers. name	GWIN	'gwin
Gwynedd		
county, ancient kingdom, Wales	GWIN-eth, GWIN-uhth	'gwineð, 'gwinəð
Gwynedd-Mercy		
College, *PA*	GWIN-uhd-MUHR-sē, GWIN-uhth	'gwinəd'məʳsiˑ, 'gwinəð
Gwynne		
pers. name	GWIN	'gwin
Gyatso		
Tenzin, *Tibetan leader, the Dalai Lama (Nobel 1989)*	GYAHT-sō	'gjɑtsoː
Gyges		
king of Lydia	JĪ-JĒZ, GĪ-JĒZ	'dʒai,dʒiːz, 'gai,dʒiːz
Gymnasium		
1. Greek school	jim-NĀ-zē-uhm, -NĀ-zhuhm	dʒim'neːziːəm, -'neːʒəm
2. German school	gim-NAHZ-ē-um	gim'nɑziːum
Gympie		
city, Australia	GIM-pē	'gimpiˑ
Gyo		
pers. name (G. Obata)	GYŌ	'gjoː
Gyõngyõs		
city, Hungarian	DYUH(R)N-DYUH(R)S, [$] JUHRN-JUHRS	'd̦œːn,d̦œːs, [$] 'dʒəʳn,dʒəʳs
Győr		
city, Hungarian	DYUHR, [$] JUHR	'd̦œːʳ, [$] 'dʒəʳ
György		
pers. name, Hungarian	DYUHRD, [$] JUHR-jē	'd̦œrd̦, [$] 'dʒəʳdʒiˑ
Gypsophila		
plant	jip-SAHF-uh-luh	dʒip'sɑfələ
Gypsy [Romany]		
people, lang., South Asia, Near East, Europe, USA	JIP-sē	'dʒipsiˑ
Gyrfalcon		
hawk	JUHR-FAL-kuhn, -FAWL-kuhn, -FAW-kuhn	'dʒəʳ,fælkən, -,fɔːlkən, -,fɔːkən

H

Ha
  lang., Africa .... HAH .... 'hɑ
Haag, Den [Hague, The]
  city, Netherlands .... duhn HAHG̃ .... dən 'hɑːɣ
Häagen-Dazs
  ice cream brand .... HAHG-uhn-DAHZ, -DAHS ... 'hɑgən,dɑz, -,dɑs
Haakon
  county, SD .... HAK-uhn .... 'hækən
Haarlem, Harlem
  city, Netherlands .... HAHR-luhm .... 'hɑʳləm
Haavelmo
  Trygve, *Norwegian economist* .. HAHV-uhl-MŌ .... 'hɑvəl,moː
  (Nobel 1989)
Habacuc
  Old Testament book .... HAB-uh-KUHK, -KUK; huh-BAK-uhk ... 'hæbə,kək, -,kuk; hə'bækək
Habakkuk
  1. Old Testament book, pers. .. HAB-uh-KUHK, -KUK; huh-BAK-uhk ... 'hæbə,kək, -,kuk; hə'bækək
  name
  2. German .... HAH-bah-KŌOK, -KUK ...... 'hɑbɑ,kuːk, -,kuk
Habdank
  pers. name, Polish .... HAHB-DAHNGK .... 'hɑːb,dɑːŋk
Haber
  Fritz, *German chemist (Nobel* .. HAHB-uhr .... 'hɑbəʳ
  1918)
Habersham
  county, GA .... HAB-uhr-SHAM, HAB-uhr-shuhm ... 'hæbəʳ,ʃæm, 'hæbəʳʃəm
Habib
  Philip Charles, *US foreign service* .. hah-BĒB .... hɑ'biːb
  officer; pers. name, Arabic
Habsburg, Hapsburg
  German royal house .... HAHPS-BURK, ⑤ HAPS-BUHRG ... 'hɑps,buʳk, ⑤ 'hæps,bəʳg
Hachiro
  pers. name, Japanese .... hah-chē-rō .... hɑtʃiːroː
Hackensack
  city, NJ .... HAK-uhn-SAK .... 'hækən,sæk
Hacker-Pschorr
  German beer .... HAHK-uhrp-SHAWR .... 'hɑkəʳp,ʃɔːʳ
Hackett
  Buddy, *US comedian, actor* .. HAK-uht .... 'hækət
Hackman
  Gene, *US actor* .... HAK-muhn .... 'hækmən
Hackney
  borough, England; carriage .. HAK-nē .... 'hækniˑ

Key (col. 2): a: fad ā: fade ah: father ar: Mary aw: law e: fed ē: feed er: merry i: hid ī: hide ō: coat o͞o: boot
oi: boy ow: now u: put uh: above uhr: bird ch: chop ng: ring sh: show th: thick <u>th</u>: this zh: measure

Hadassah
Jewish women's benevolent organization — khuh-DAHS-uh, huh-DAHS-uh, hah-DAHS-uh — xəˈdɑsə, həˈdɑsə, haˈdɑsə

Haddam
town, CT — HAD-uhm — ˈhædəm

Hades
Greek god of the Underworld; abode of dead, Hell — HĀD-ĒZ — ˈheːd‚iːz

Hadid
pers. name — hah-DĒD — haˈdiːd

Hadj [Hajj]
pilgrimage to Mecca — HAHJ — ˈhadʒ

Hadji
one who has made a pilgrimage to Mecca — HAHJ-ē — ˈhadʒiˑ

Hadrian
Roman emperor — HĀ-drē-uhn — ˈheːdriːən

Hadrianus
pers. name, Dutch — HAH-drē-AHN-ues — ˌhɑdriːˈanys

Hadrosaurus
dinosaur — HA-druh-SAWR-uhs — ˌhædrəˈsɔːrəs

Haeckel
Ernest, German scientist — HEK-uhl — ˈhekəl

Haeckelism
doctrines of Haeckel — HEK-uh-LIZ-uhm — ˈhekəˌlizəm

Haemon
son of Creon — HĒ-muhn — ˈhiːmən

Haerhpin [Harbin]
city, China — HAH-UHR-BIN, HAH-ER-BIN — haˈəʳbin, haˈeʳbin

Hafez
pers. name, Arabic — khah-FEZ, hah-FEZ — xaˈfez, haˈfez

Haflinger
horse breed — HAF-ling-uhr — ˈhæfliŋəʳ

hafnium
element — HAF-nē-uhm — ˈhæfniːəm

Haganah
Jewish underground militia — KHAHG-uh-NAH, HAHG-uh-NAH — ˌxagəˈna, ˌhagəˈna

Hagar
pers. name — HĀ-guhr, HĀ-GAHR — ˈheːgəʳ, ˈheːˌgaʳ

Hagerstown
city, MD — HĀ-guhrz-TOWN — ˈheːgəʳzˌtaun

Hagerup
pers. name, Norwegian — HAH-guh-rup — ˈhagərup

Haggadah, the [Aggada]
part of Jewish Talmud — HAHG-uh-DAH, huh-GAHD-uh, huh-GAWD-uh — ˌhagəˈda, həˈgadə, həˈgɔːdə

Haggai
Old Testament book — HAG-ē-Ī, HAG-Ī — ˈhægiːˌai, ˈhægˌai

Haggard
Sir Henry Rider, English novelist; Merle, US singer, songwriter — HAG-uhrd — ˈhægəʳd

Haggerty
Dan, *actor* — HAG-uhrt-ē — ˈhægəʳţiˑ

Foreign Sounds: ue: *Fr.* **rue**, *Ger.* füllen uh(r): *Fr.* **b**oeuf, *Ger.* Höhle kh: *Ger.* i**ch**, *Scot.* lo**ch** g̃: *Sp.* ami**g**o v: *Sp.* ha**b**lar hl: *Welsh* **Ll**anelli. CAPITALS: primary stress. SMALL CAPS: secondary stress. ⓢ: U.S. pron. ⓑ: British pron.

Hagiographa		
a Jewish division of the Old Testament	HAG-ē-AHG-ruh-fuh	ˌhægiːˈɑgrəfə
Hagler		
Marvelous Marvin, *US boxer*	HAG-luhr	ˈhæglər
Hagman		
Larry, *US actor*	HAG-muhn	ˈhægmən
Hague, The		
city, Netherlands	thuh HĀG	ðə ˈheːg
Hahn		
Otto, *German chemist (Nobel 1944)*	HAHN	ˈhɑn
Haida		
N. American people	HĪD-uh	ˈhɑidə
Haifa		
district, Israel	KHĪ-fuh, HĪ-fuh	ˈxɑifə, ˈhɑifə
Haig		
pers. name	HĀG	ˈheːg
Haigh		
pers. name	HĀG, HĀ	ˈheːg, ˈheː
Haight-Ashbury		
San Francisco hippie district	HĀT-ASH-BER-ē	ˈheːt̬ˈæʃˌberiˑ
Haile		
pers. name	HĪ-lē	ˈhɑiliˑ
Hailey		
Arthur, *British/Canadian author*	HĀ-lē	ˈheːliˑ
Haim		
pers. name, Hebrew	khī-(Y)IM, KHĪ-(y)im	xɑiˈ(j)im, ˈxɑi(j)im
Hainan		
island, China	HĪ-NAHN	ˈhɑiˈnɑn
Hainaut		
prov, Belgium	(h)ā-NŌ	(h)eːˈnoː
Haines		
division, AK; pers. name	HĀNZ	ˈheːnz
Haiphong		
seaport, Vietnam	HĪ-FAWNG, HĪ-FAHNG	ˈhɑiˈfɔːŋ, ˈhɑiˈfɑŋ
Haiti		
republic, West Indies	HĀT-ē	ˈheːt̬iˑ
Haitian		
lang., native, Haiti	HĀ-shuhn, HĀT-ē-uhn	ˈheːʃən, ˈheːt̬iːən
Hajj [Hadj]		
pilgrimage to Mecca	HAHJ	ˈhɑdʒ
Hakeem		
pers. name (H. Olajuwon)	hah-KĒM	hɑˈkiːm
Hakka		
lang., China	HAHK-AH, HAK-uh	ˈhɑkˈɑ, ˈhækə
Hakluyt		
Richard, *English geographer*	HAK-LO͞OT, HAK-l-WIT, HAK-lit	ˈhækˌluːt, ˈhækl̩ˌwit, ˈhæklit
Hakodate		
island, Japan	hahk-ō-daht-ā	hɑkoːdɑteˑ
Hal		
pers. name	HAL	ˈhæl
Halab, Haleb		
city, Syria	huh-LEB	həˈleb

Key (col. 2): a: fad ā: fade ah: father ar: Mary aw: **law** e: fed ē: feed er: merry i: hid ī: hide ō: coat o͞o: boot oi: boy ow: now u: put uh: above uhr: bird ch: chop ng: ring sh: show th: thick th: this zh: measure

Halafian
    prehistoric Near Eastern culture   huh-LĀ-fē-uhn   hə'leːfiːən

Halakah, Halachah
    The, *part of Jewish Talmud*   HAHL-uh-<u>KH</u>AH, hah-LAW<u>KH</u>-uh,   ˌhalə'xa, ha'lɔːxə, hə'laxə
        huh-LAH<u>KH</u>-uh

Halas
    George, *sports personality*   HAL-uhs   'hæləs

Halberstam
    David, *US journalist, author*   HAL-buhr-STAM   'hælbəʳˌstæm

Halb-und-Halb
    orange liqueur   HAHLP-unt-HAHLP   'haːlpunt'haːlp

Haldan
    pers. name   HAWL-duhn, HAL-duhn, HAHL-duhn   'hɔːldən, 'hældən, 'haldən

Haldane
    J. B. S., *scientist; pers. name*   HAWL-DĀN, HAWL-duhn   'hɔːlˌdeːn, 'hɔːldən

Haldeman
    Harry R., *former US government*   HAWL-duh-muhn   'hɔːldəmən
        official; Joe William, *US novelist*

Hale
    pers. name   HĀL   'heːl

Haleakala
    National Park, *volcano, HI*   HAHL-ē-AHK-uh-LAH   ˌhaliːˌakə'la

Halevi
    pers. name   hah-LĀ-vē   ha'leːviˑ

Haley
    Alex, *US author; pers. name*   HĀ-lē   'heːliˑ

Halfdan
    1. pers. name, Danish   HAHLV-DAHN   'haːlvˌdaːn
    2. Norwegian   HAHLV-DAHN   'halvˌdan

Halicarnassus
    ancient city, Asia Minor   HAL-i-KAHR-NAS-uhs   ˌhæliˌkaʳ'næsəs

Halifax
    city, Canada; borough, England;   HAL-uh-FAKS   'hæləˌfæks
    US pl. name

Halirrhothius
    son of Poseidon and Euryte   HAL-uh-RŌ-thē-uhs   ˌhælə'roːθiːəs

Halldór
    pers. name, Icelandic   HAHD-l-DAWR   'hadlˌdɔːʳ

Halle
    Morris, *US linguist; county, city,*   HAHL-uh   'halə
    Germany

Halley
    Edmund, *English astronomer*   HAL-ē, HĀ-lē, HAW-lē   'hæliˑ, 'heːliˑ, 'hɔːliˑ

Halley's
    comet   HAL-ēz, HĀ-lēz, HAW-lēz   'hæliˑz, 'heːliˑz, 'hɔːliˑz

Hallgrimur
    pers. name, Icelandic   HAHD-l-GRĒ-muer   'hadlˌgriːmyr

Halliwell
    Park, *ballpark, Pocatello, ID*   HAL-uh-WEL, HAHL-uh-WEL, -wuhl   'hæləˌwel, 'haləˌwel, -wəl

Halloween
    October 31   HAL-uh-WĒN, HAHL-   ˌhælə'wiːn, ˌhal-

Hallstatt
    town, Austria; archaeological   HAWL-STAT, HAHL-SHTAHT   'hɔːlˌstæt, 'halˌʃtat
    period

Foreign Sounds: ue: *Fr.* **rue**, *Ger.* **füllen** uh(r): *Fr.* **boeuf**, *Ger.* **Höhle** kh: *Ger.* **ich**, *Scot.* lo**ch** g̃: *Sp.* a**mi**go v: *Sp.* ha**bl**ar
hl: *Welsh* **Ll**anelli. CAPITALS: primary stress. SMALL CAPS: secondary stress. ⑧: U.S. pron. ⓒ: British pron.

Halmahera
  island, sea, Pacific   HAL-muh-HER-uh, HAHL-   ˌhælmə'herə, ˌhɑl-

Hals
  Frans, *Dutch painter*   HAHLS   'hɑls

Halstead, -sted
  pers. name   HAWL-stuhd, -STED   'hɔːlstəd, -ˌsted

Hamadān
  city, Iran   HAHM-uh-DAHN, HAM-uh-DAN,   ˌhɑmə'dɑn, ˌhæmə'dæn,
        HAHM-uh-DAHN   'hɑməˌdɑn

Hamadryad
  tree nymph   HAM-uh-DRĪ-uhd, -DRĪ-AD   ˌhæmə'drɑiəd, -'drɑiˌæd

Hamamatsu
  town, Japan   hahm-ah-maht-soo̅   hɑmɑmɑtsuː

Haman
  Biblical name   HĀ-muhn   'heːmən

Hamar
  1. city, Norway   HAHM-AHR   'hɑmˌɑʳ
  2. pers. name   HĀ-muhr   'heːməʳ

Hambletonian
  horse   HAM-buhl-TŌ-nē-uhn   ˌhæmbəl'toːniːən

Hamburg
  1. city, Germany   HAHM-BURK, Ⓢ HAM-BUHRG   'hɑmˌbuʳk, Ⓢ 'hæmˌbəʳg
  2. US pl. name   HAM-BUHRG   'hæmˌbəʳg

Hamel
  Veronica, *US actress*   HAM-uhl   'hæməl

Hamelin
  town, Germany   HAM-(uh-)luhn   'hæm(ə)lən

Hameln [Hamelin]
  town, Germany   HAHM-uhln   'hɑməln

Hamilcar
  Carthaginian general   huh-MIL-KAHR, HAM-uhl-KAHR   hə'milˌkɑʳ, 'hæməlˌkɑʳ

Hamill
  Dorothy, *US figure skater;* Mark,   HAM-uhl   'hæməl
     US actor

Hamilton
  Alexander, *US politician; pl.*   HAM-uhl-tuhn, HAM-uhlt-n   'hæməltən, 'hæməltn̩
     name; pers. name

Hamish
  pers. name   HĀ-mish   'heːmiʃ

Hamite
  biblical tribe   HAM-ĪT   'hæmˌɑit

Hamito-Semitic
  Afroasiatic lang. group   HAM-uht-ō-suh-MIT-ik   ˌhæmətoːsə'miţik

Hamline
  University, *MN*   HAM-luhn   'hæmlən

Hamlisch
  Marvin, *US composer*   HAM-lish   'hæmliʃ

Hammacher Schlemmer
  NY retailers   HAM-uh-kuhr SHLEM-uhr   ˌhæməkəʳ 'ʃleməʳ

Hammarskjöld
  Dag, *Swedish statesman, U.N.*   HAHM-uhr-SHUHLD, HAM-, -SHULD,   'hɑməʳˌʃɔld, 'hæm-, -ˌʃuld,
     official (Nobel 1961)   -SHĒLD   -ˌʃiːld

Hammer
  Armand, *US oil co. executive*   HAM-uhr   'hæməʳ

Key (col. 2):   a: fad   ā: fade   ah: father   ar: **Mary**   aw: **law**   e: fed   ē: feed   er: **merry**   i: hid   ī: hide   ō: coat   o̅o̅: boot
oi: **boy**   ow: **now**   u: put   uh: above   uhr: **bird**   ch: **chop**   ng: **ring**   sh: **show**   th: **thick**   <u>th</u>: **this**   zh: **measure**

Hammerfest
  port, Norway HAHM-uhr-FEST, HAM-uhr-FEST 'hɑməʳˌfest, 'hæməʳˌfest
Hammersmith and Fulham
  borough, England HAM-uhr-SMITH uhn(d) FUL-uhm 'hæməʳˌsmiθ ən(d) 'fuləm
Hammerstein
  Oscar II, *US musical lyricist* HAM-uhr-STĪN, -STÊN 'hæməʳˌstɑin, -ˌstiːn
Hammett
  Dashiell, *US writer* HAM-uht 'hæmət
Hammond
  Jay Sterner, *US politician* HAM-uhnd 'hæmənd
Hammurabi
  Babylonian king, lawgiver HAM-uh-RAHB-ē, HAHM- ˌhæmə'rɑbiˑ, ˌhɑm-
Hampden
  county, MA; town, ME HAM-duhn 'hæmdən
Hampshire
  county, MA, WV, England HAM(P)-shuhr, -SHIR 'hæm(p)ʃəʳ, -ˌʃiʳ
Hampstead
  London borough HAM(P)-stid, HAM(P)-STED 'hæm(p)stid, 'hæm(p)ˌsted
Hampton
  US pl. name; pers. name HAM(P)-tuhn 'hæm(p)tən
Hampton Roads
  channel, VA HAM(P)-tuhn RŌDZ ˌhæm(p)tən 'roːdz
Hamstrom
  1st Sunday of Feb., Switzerland HAHM-STRAWM 'hɑmˌstrɔːm
Hamsun
  Knut, *(pseudonym of* Knut HAHM-suhn 'hɑmsən
  Pedersen*), Norwegian author*
  (Nobel 1920)
Hamtramck
  city, MI ham-TRAM-ik hæm'træmik
Han
  river, people, China HAHN, HAN 'hɑn, 'hæn
Hana Matsuri
  Flower Festival (April 8), Japan hah-nah maht-sur-ē hɑnɑ mɑtsuriˑ
Handel
  Georg Frideric, *British composer* HAN-dl 'hændl̩
Handelian
  pert. to Handel han-DĒ-lē-uhn, han-DEL-ē-uhn hæn'diːliːən, hæn'deliːən
Haneda
  airport, Tokyo hahn-uhd-uh, hah-nād-uh hɑnədə, hɑneːdə
Hanford
  pers. name HAN-fuhrd 'hænfəʳd
Hangchow, Hangzhou
  city, China HAHNG-JŌ, Ⓢ HANG-CHOW 'hɑŋ'dʒoː, Ⓢ 'hæŋ'tʃɑu
Hank
  pers. name HANGK 'hæŋk
Hankou, Hankow
  port, China HAHNG-KŌ, HAHN-KŌ, 'hɑŋ'koː, 'hɑn'koː,
    Ⓢ HANG-KOW   Ⓢ 'hæŋ'kɑu
Han Lu
  Chinese festival HAHN LŌŌ 'hɑn 'luː
Hanna, Hannah
  pers. name HAN-uh 'hænə
Hanna-Barbera Productions, Inc.
  US entertainment co. HAN-uh-bahr-BER-uh 'hænəbɑʳˌberə

Foreign Sounds: ue: *Fr.* **rue**, *Ger.* **füllen** uh(r): *Fr.* **boeuf**, *Ger.* **Höhle** kh: *Ger.* **ich**, *Scot.* **loch** g̃: *Sp.* **amigo** v: *Sp.* **hablar**
hl: *Welsh* **Llanelli**. CAPITALS: primary stress. SMALL CAPS: secondary stress. Ⓢ: U.S. pron. Ⓛ: British pron.

Hannes

   pers. name, Swedish   HAHN-is   ˈhɑːnis

Hannibal

   1. Carthaginian general; pers.   HAN-uh-buhl   ˈhænəbəl
    name

   2. Dutch   HAHN-i-bahl   ˈhɑnibɑl

Hanno

   Carthaginian admiral   HAN-ō   ˈhænoː

Hannover

   prov, city, Germany   hah-NŌ-fuhr, hah-NŌ-vuhr,   haˈnoːfəʳ, haˈnoːvəʳ,
                            Ⓢ HAN-ō-vuhr, HAN-uh-vuhr   Ⓢ ˈhæn,oːvəʳ, ˈhænəvəʳ

Hanns

   pers. name, German   HAHNS   ˈhɑns

Hanoi

   city, Vietnam   ha-NOI, huh-NOI   hæˈnɔi, həˈnɔi

Hanover

   British royal house; English form HAN-Ō-vuhr, HAN-uh-vuhr   ˈhæn,oːvəʳ, ˈhænəvəʳ
    of Hannover

Hanoverian

   pert. to Hanover *or* Hannover   HAN-uh-VIR-ē-uhn,   ,hænəˈviriːən, ,hænəˈveriːən
                         HAN-uh-VER-ē-uhn

Hans

   1. pers. name   HAHNZ, HAHNS   ˈhɑnz, ˈhɑns

   2. Danish, Swedish   HAHNS   ˈhɑːns

   3. Dutch, German, Norwegian HAHNS   ˈhɑns

Hansa

   merchant guild; Norwegian beer HAHN-suh   ˈhɑnsə

Hansard

   parliamentary proceedings   HAN-SAHRD, HAN-suhrd   ˈhæn,sɑʳd, ˈhænsəʳd

Hanseatic League

   league of German towns   HAN-sē-AT-ik   ,hænsiːˈæṭik

Hansel

   pers. name   HAN(T)-suhl, HAN-zuhl   ˈhæn(t)səl, ˈhænzəl

Hänsel and Gretel

   fairy tale   HAN(T)-suhl uhn(d) GRET-l,   ˈhæn(t)səl ən(d) ˈgretl̩,
                         HAN-zuhl   ˈhænzəl

Hansun

   Knute, *writer*   HAN-suhn, HAHN-suhn   ˈhænsən, ˈhɑnsən

Hants [Hampshire]

   county, England   HAN(T)S   ˈhæn(t)s

Hanukkah

   Jewish holiday   HAHN-uh-kuh, <u>KH</u>AHN-   ˈhɑnəkə, ˈxɑn-

Hanunóo

   lang., people, Philippine Islands HAHN-uh-NŌ   ,hɑnəˈnoː

Haole

   a non-Hawaiian   HOW-lē, HOW-lā   ˈhauliˑ, ˈhauleː

Hapi

   Egyptian god of the Nile   HAHP-ē   ˈhɑpiˑ

Hapsburg

   see Habsburg

Harabi

   people, Africa   HAHR-ah-BĒ   ,hɑrɑˈbiː

Key (col. 2): a: fad ā: fade ah: father ar: Mary aw: law e: fed ē: feed er: merry i: hid ī: hide ō: coat ōō: boot
oi: boy ow: now u: put uh: above uhr: bird ch: chop ng: ring sh: show th: thick <u>th</u>: this zh: measure

Harald
1. pers. name, Danish, Norwegian	HAHR-AHL	'hɑr,ɑl
2. German	HAH-RAHLT	'hɑ,rɑlt
3. Swedish	HAH-RAHLD	'hɑ,rɑːld

Harare
city, Zimbabwe	huh-RAH-RĀ	hə'rɑ,reː

Harbin [Haerhpin]
city, China	hahr-BIN, HAHR-buhn	hɑr'bin, 'hɑrbən

Harboe
Danish beer	HAHR-buh(r)	'hɑrbœ

Harcourt Brace Jovanovich
US publisher	HAHR-kuhrt BRĀS jō-VAHN-uh-VICH, HAHR-KAWRT	'hɑrkərt 'breːs dʒoː'vɑnə,vitʃ, 'hɑr,kɔːrt

Hard
pers. name	HAHRD	'hɑrd

Harden
Sir Arthur, English chemist (Nobel 1929)	HAHRD-n	'hɑrdn̩

Harding
Warren G., 29th US president	HAHRD-ing	'hɑrdiŋ

Hardin-Simmons
University, TX	HAHRD-n-SIM-uhnz	'hɑrdn̩'simənz

Hardouin
pers. name, French	ahr-DWEⁿ	ɑːrdwẽ

Hare
N. American people	HAR, HER	'hær, 'her

Harebell
flower	HAR-BEL, HER-BEL	'hær,bel, 'her,bel

Hare Krishna
religious sect	HAHR-ē KRISH-nuh, HAR-ē, HER-ē	,hɑriˑ 'kriʃnə, ,hæriˑ, ,heriˑ

Harewood
1. village, England	HER-WUD, HAHR-WUD	'her,wud, 'hɑr,wud
2. Earl of, English title	HAHR-WUD	'hɑr,wud

Haricot
vegetable	HAR-i-KŌ, AR-i-KŌ	'hæri,koː, 'æri,koː

Hariett
pers. name	HAR-ē-uht	'hæriːət

Hari-Kuyo
Japanese festival	hahr-ē-kōō-yō	hɑriˑkuːjoː

Haringey
borough, England	HAR-ing-gā	'hæriŋgeː

Harkin
Thomas R., US politician	HAHR-kuhn	'hɑrkən

Harlan
pers. name	HAHR-luhn	'hɑrlən

Harleian
pert. to Harley	HAHR-lē-uhn	'hɑrliːən

Harlem
river, NY; district, New York City	HAHR-luhm	'hɑrləm

Harlequin
type of duck	HAHR-li-k(w)uhn	'hɑrlik(w)ən

Harley
Sir Robert, English statesman; street, London; pers. name	HAHR-lē	'hɑrliˑ

Foreign Sounds: **ue**: *Fr.* **rue**, *Ger.* **füllen**   **uh(r)**: *Fr.* **boeuf**, *Ger.* **Höhle**   <u>kh</u>: *Ger.* i**ch**, *Scot.* lo**ch**   g̃: *Sp.* ami**g**o   v̱: *Sp.* ha**b**lar
hl: *Welsh* **Ll**anelli.   CAPITALS: primary stress.   SMALL CAPS: secondary stress.   Ⓢ: U.S. pron.   Ⓑ: British pron.

Harley-Davidson
  motorcycle co.   HAHR-lē-DĀ-vuhd-suhn   ˌhɑʳliˈdeːvədsən

Harlow, Harlowe
  pers. name   HAHR-lō   ˈhɑʳloː

Harmhab
  Egyptian king   HAHRM-HAB   ˈhɑʳmˌhæb

Harmodio
  pers. name, Spanish   ahr-MŌTH-yō   ɑrˈmoːðjoː

Harmondsworth
  town, England   HAHR-muhnz-WUHRTH   ˈhɑʳmənz,wəʳθ

Harmonia
  wife of Cadmus   hahr-MŌ-nē-uh   hɑʳˈmoːniːə

Harmost
  Spartan governor   HAHRM-ōst   ˈhɑʳmoːst

Harold
  pers. name   HAR-uhld   ˈhærəld

Harpalyce
  brigand daughter of King   hahr-PAL-uh-sē   hɑʳˈpæləsiˈ
    Harpalycus

Harpalycus
  king of Thrace   hahr-PAL-uh-kuhs   hɑʳˈpæləkəs

Harpies
  winged divinities who carried off   HAHR-pēz   ˈhɑʳpiˈz
    or befouled things

Harpinna
  mother of Oenomaus by Ares   hahr-PIN-uh   hɑʳˈpinə

Harpocrates
  Egyptian god, Horus depicted as a   hahr-PAHK-ruht-ēz   hɑʳˈpɑkrətiːz
    child

Harrap
  French publisher   HAR-uhp, HER-uhp   ˈhærəp, ˈherəp

Harrier
  marsh hawk   HAR-ē-uhr   ˈhæriːəʳ

Harriet, -ett, -ette
  pers. name   HAR-ē-uht   ˈhæriːət

Harriman
  W. Averell, US statesman   HAR-uh-muhn, HER-   ˈhærəmən, ˈher-

Harrington
  pers. name   HAR-ing-tuhn, HER-   ˈhæriŋtən, ˈher-

Harrison
  Benjamin, 23rd US president;   HAR-uh-suhn   ˈhærəsən
    William Henry, *9th US president;*
    pers. name

Harrogate
  town, England   HAR-uh-guht, HAR-uh-GĀT, HER-   ˈhærəgət, ˈhærəˌgeːt, ˈher-

Harrovian
  pert. to or a student at Harrow   huh-RŌ-vē-uhn   həˈroːviːən

Harrow
  borough & school, England   HAR-ō   ˈhæroː

Harry
  pers. name   HAR-ē   ˈhæriˈ

Hartford
  city, CT   HAHRT-fuhrd   ˈhɑʳtfəʳd

Hartley
  Mariette, *US actress*   HAHRT-lē   ˈhɑʳtliˈ

Key (col. 2):   a: fad   ā: fade   ah: father   ar: Mary   aw: law   e: fed   ē: feed   er: merry   i: hid   ī: hide   ō: coat   ōō: boot
oi: boy   ow: now   u: put   uh: above   uhr: bird   ch: chop   ng: ring   sh: show   th: thick   th: this   zh: measure

Hartline
  Haldan Keffer, *US biophysicist*   HAHRT-LĪN   ˈhɑʳt,lɑin
  (Nobel 1967)
Hartmann
  pers. name, German   HAHRT-MAHN   ˈhɑʳt,mɑn
Hartmut
  pers. name (H. Michel)   HAHRT-MUT   ˈhɑʳt,mut
Hartsfield
  Henry Warren, Jr., *US astronaut*   HAHRTS-FĒLD   ˈhɑʳts,fiːld
Harvard
  university, town, MA   HAHR-vuhrd   ˈhɑʳvəʳd
Harvey
  pers. name   HAHR-vē   ˈhɑʳviˑ
Harwich
  city, England   HAR-ij, HAR-ich, ⓢ HAHR-wich   ˈhæridʒ, ˈhæritʃ,
                                                                           ⓢ ˈhɑʳwitʃ
Harwich Port
  town, MA   HAHR-wich PŌRT, PAWRT   ˈhɑʳwitʃ ˌpoːʳt, ˌpɔːʳt
Haryana
  state, India   HAHR-ē-AHN-uh   ˌhɑriːˈɑnə
Harz
  mtn. group, Germany   HAHRTS   ˈhɑʳts
Hasaniya Arabic
  lang., Middle East   hah-SAH-nē-(y)uh   həˈsɑniː(j)ə
Hasbro
  toy co.   HAZ-brō   ˈhæzbroː
Hasdrubal
  Carthaginian general   HAZ-DRŌŌ-buhl, haz-DRŌŌ-buhl   ˈhæz,druːbəl, hæzˈdruːbəl
Hašek
  Jaroslav, *Czech writer*   HAH-shek   ˈhɑːʃek
Hasenpfeffer
  rabbit stew   HAHZ-uhn-FEF-uhr, HAHS-   ˈhɑzən,fefəʳ, ˈhɑs-
Hashemi
  pers. name (H. Rafsanjani)   HAHSH-uh-mē   ˈhɑʃəmiˑ
Hashemite
  member of an Arab dynasty   HASH-uh-MĪT   ˈhæʃə,mɑit
Hasid, Chasid, Hassid
  member of a Jewish sect   KHAHS-uhd, HAHS-uhd, KHAW-suhd   ˈxɑsəd, ˈhɑsəd, ˈxɔːsəd
Hasidic
  pert. to Hasidism   khah-SID-ik, hah-SID-ik, ha-SID-ik xɑˈsidik, hɑˈsidik, hæˈsidik
Hasidim
  plural of Hasid   khah-SĒD-uhm, hah-SĒD-uhm   xɑˈsiːdəm, hɑˈsiːdəm
Hasidism
  beliefs of the Hasidim   KHAHS-uhd-IZ-uhm, HAHS-, HAS-   ˈxɑsəd,izəm, ˈhɑs-, ˈhæs-
Haslemere
  town, England   HĀ-zuhl-MIR   ˈheːzəl,miʳ
Hassam
  Childe, *US painter*   HAS-uhm   ˈhæsəm
Hassan II
  King of Morocco   hah-SAHN   həˈsɑn
Hassel
  Odd, *Norwegian physical chemist*   HAHS-uhl   ˈhɑsəl
  (Nobel 1969)
Hasselblad
  camera co.   HAHS-uhl-BLAHT, HAS-uhl-BLAD   ˈhɑsəl,blɑt, ˈhæsəl,blæd

---

Foreign Sounds: **ue**: *Fr.* **rue**, *Ger.* f**ü**llen **uh(r)**: *Fr.* b**oeu**f, *Ger.* H**öh**le **kh**: *Ger.* i**ch**, *Scot.* lo**ch** **ḡ**: *Sp.* ami**g**o **v**: *Sp.* ha**b**lar
hl: *Welsh* **Ll**anelli. CAPITALS: primary stress. SMALL CAPS: secondary stress. ⓢ: U.S. pron. ⓔ: British pron.

Hassid
  see Hasid

Hastings
  pl. name   HĀ-stingz   'heːstiŋz

Hathaway
  Anne, *Shakespeare's wife*   HATH-uh-WĀ   'hæθə,weː

Hathor
  Egyptian sky goddess   HAH-TAWR, HAHTH-AWR   'hɑ,tɔːʳ, 'hɑθ,ɔːʳ

Hatikvah
  Israeli national anthem   hah-TIK-vah, -vuh   hɑ'tikvɑ, -və

Hatoyama
  Ichirō, *Japanese politician*   hah-tō-yah-mah   hɑtoːjɑmɑ

Hatshepsut
  Egyptian pharoah-queen   hat-SHEP-SOOT, -suht   hæt'ʃep,suːt, -sət

Hatteras
  cape, NC   HAT-uh-ruhs   'hæʈərəs

Hattiesburg
  city, MS   HAT-ēz-BUHRG   'hæʈiːz,bəʳg

Hatvan
  commune, Hungary   HAWT-VAWN   'hɔːt,vɔːn

Hauer
  Rutger, *entertainer*   HOW(-uh)r   'hɑu(ə)ʳ

Hauge
  pers. name, Norwegian   HOW-guh   'hɑugə

Haugesund
  port, Norway   HOW-guh-SUN   'hɑugə,sun

Haughey
  Charles, *Irish politician*   HAWKH-ē, HAW-hē   'hɔːxiˑ, 'hɔːhiˑ

Hauptman
  Herbert A., *US mathematical*   HOWP(T)-muhn   'hɑup(t)mən
    physicist (Nobel 1985)

Hauptmann
  Gerhart, *German author (Nobel*   HOWP(T)-MAHN   'hɑup(t),mɑn
    1912)

Hausa
  lang., people, Africa   HOW-suh, HOW-zuh   'hausə, 'hauzə

Haut Bailly
  wine   Ō bah-YĒ   oː bɑːjiː

Haut Batailley
  wine   Ō bah-tah-YE   oː bɑːtɑːje

Haut Brion
  wine   Ō brē-AWⁿ   oː briːɔ̃

Haute-Garonne
  dept, France   ōt-gah-RAWN   oːtgɑːrɔːn

Haute-Marne
  dept, France   ōt-MAHRN   oːtmɑːrn

Haute-Normandie
  region, France   ōt-nawr-mahⁿ-DĒ   oːtnɔːrmɑ̃diː

Haute-Savoie
  dept, France   ōt-sahv-WAH   oːtsɑːvwɑː

Hautes-Pyrénées
  dept, France   ōt-pē-rā-NĀ   oːtpiːreːneː

Haut-Rhin
  dept, France   ō-REⁿ   oːrẽ

Key (col. 2):   a: fad   ā: fade   ah: father   ar: **M**a**ry**   aw: **law**   e: fed   ē: feed   er: **merry**   i: hid   ī: hide   ō: coat   o͞o: boot
oi: **boy**   ow: **now**   u: **put**   uh: **above**   uhr: **bird**   ch: **chop**   ng: **ring**   sh: **show**   th: **thick**   <u>th</u>: **this**   zh: mea**s**ure

Hauts-de-Seine
    dept, France   ōd(-uh)-SEN   oːd(ə)sen

Havana
    city, Cuba; cigar   huh-VAN-uh   hə'vænə

Havarti
    place, Denmark; cheese   huh-VAHRT-ē   hə'vaˑ^rṭiˑ

Havasupai
    N. American people   HAHV-uh-S͞OO-PĪ   ˌhɑvə'suːˌpɑi

Havel
    Vaclav, *Czech writer & politician*   HAHV-uhl   'hɑvəl

Havelock
    pers. name   HAV-LAHK, HAV-luhk   'hævˌlɑk, 'hævlək

Haverford
    town, DE; College, *PA*   HAV-uhr-fuhrd, HAV-uh-fuhrd   'hævə^rfə^rd, 'hævəfərd

Haverhill
    city, MA; town, England   HĀ-v(uh-)ruhl   'heːv(ə)rəl

Havering
    borough, England   HĀV(-uh)-ring   'heːv(ə)riŋ

Haversham
    pers. name   HAV-uhr-shuhm, HAHR-shuhm   'hævə^rʃəm, 'hɑ^rʃəm

Haviland
    French china   HAV-uh-luhnd   ˌhævələnd

Havlicek
    John, *sports personality*   HAV-luh-CHEK   'hævləˌtʃek

Havre
    city, MT   HAV-uhr   'hævə^r

Havre, Le
    see Le Havre

Havre de Grace
    city, MD   HAV-uhr duh GRĀS, GRAS   ˌhævə^r də 'greːs, 'græs

Hawaii
    state, US   huh-WAH-(y)ē, huh-WĪ-(y)ē,   hə'wɑ-(j)iˑ, hə'wɑi-(j)iˑ,
         huh-WAW-(y)ē   hə'wɔː(j)iˑ

Hawaiian
    pert. to Hawaii   huh-WAH-yuhn, huh-WĪ-(y)uhn,   hə'wajən, hə'wai(j)ən,
         huh-WAW-yuhn   hə'wɔːjən

Hawarden
    1. city, IA; Viscount, *English peer*   HĀ-WAWRD-n   'heːˌwɔː^rdṇ
    2. parish, castle, Wales; Barony of   HAHRD-n   'hɑ^rdṇ
    Gladstone

Haweitat
    people, Africa   huh-WĀ-TAHT   hə'weːˌtɑt

Hawes
    pers. name   HAWZ   'hɔːz

Hawke
    Robert J.L., *Prime minister of*   HAWK   'hɔːk
    Australia

Hawn
    Goldie, *US actress*   HAWN   'hɔːn

Haworth
    Sir Walter N., *English chemist*   HAW(-uh)rth, HAW-wuhrth,   'hɔː(ə)^rθ, 'hɔːwə^rθ,
    (Nobel 1937); borough, NJ;   HOW(-uh)rth, HAH-wuhrth   'hau(ə)^rθ, 'hawə^rθ
    village, England (Brontës'
    home)

Hawthorne

Nathaniel, *US writer*   HAW-THAWRN   'hɔː,θɔːʳn

Haya de la Torre

Victor, *Peruvian politician*   AH-yah th̲ā lah TAWR-rā   'aja ðeː la 'tɔːrreː

Hayakawa

Sessue, *US politician, linguist*   HĪ-(y)uh-KOW-uh   ˌhai(j)ə'kauə

Hayashi

Teru, *Japanese diplomat*   hah-yah-shē   hajaʃiː

Hayato

pers. name, Japanese   hah-yah-tō   hajatoː

Hayden

pers. name   HĀD-n   'heːdn̩

Haydn

Franz Joseph, *Austrian composer*   HĪD-n   'haidn̩

Hayek

Friedrich A. von, *Austrian-born*   HĪ-(y)uhk   'hai(j)ək
British political economist
(Nobel 1974)

Hayim

pers. name, Hebrew   kh̲ī-(Y)IM, KH̲Ī-(y)im   xai'(j)im, 'xai(j)im

Hayley

pers. name   HĀ-lē   'heːliˑ

Haym

pers. name, Polish   HĬM   'haim

Haynes

pers. name   HĀNZ   'heːnz

Hayyim

pers. name, Hebrew   kh̲ī-(Y)IM, KH̲Ī-(y)im   xai'(j)im, 'xai(j)im

Hazlitt

William, *English essayist*   HAZ-luht   'hæzlət

Hearn

Lafcadio, *US writer*   HUHRN   'həʳn

Hearns

Thomas, *US boxer*   HUHRNZ   'həʳnz

Hearst

William R., *US publisher; pers.*   HUHRST   'həʳst
name

Heath

pers. name   HĒTH   'hiːθ

Heathcliff

character in Wuthering Heights, *E.*   HĒTH-KLIF   'hiːθˌklif
Brontë; *cartoon cat*

Heathcote

pers. name   HĒTH-kuht, -KŌT   'hiːθkət, -ˌkoːt

Heather

pers. name   HETH̲-uhr   'heðəʳ

Heathrow

airport, London, England   HĒ-THRŌ, Ⓔ HĒTH-RŌ   'hiːˌθroː, Ⓔ ˌhiːθ'roː

Heaton

Park, *stadium, Augusta, GA*   HĒT-n   'hiːtn̩

Hebe

Greek goddess of youth   HĒ-bē   'hiːbiˑ

Hebei [Hopeh]

prov, China   HUH-BĀ   'hə'beː

Key (col. 2): a: fad ā: fade ah: father ar: Mary aw: law e: fed ē: feed er: merry i: hid ī: hide ō: coat o͞o: boot
oi: boy ow: now u: put uh: above uhr: bird ch: chop ng: ring sh: show th: thick th̲: this zh: measure

Hébert
  Jacques-René, *French politician*   ā-BER   eːber
Hebraic
  pert. to Hebrew   hi-BRĀ-ik   hiˈbreːik
Hebraist
  scholar of Hebrew   HĒ-BRĀ-uhst   ˈhiːˌbreːəst
Hebrew
  Semitic lang., people, Israel, USA,   HĒ-broo   ˈhiːbruː
  Europe
Hebrews
  New Testament book   HĒ-brooz   ˈhiːbruːz
Hebrides
  islands, Scotland   HEB-ruh-DĒZ   ˈhebrəˌdiːz
Hebron
  city, Jordan   HĒ-bruhn   ˈhiːbrən
Hecale
  hostess to Theseus   HEK-uh-lē   ˈhekəliˑ
Hecataeus
  Greek traveler, historian   HEK-uh-TĒ-uhs   ˌhekəˈtiːəs
Hecate
  ancient Greek goddess of night   HEK-uht-ē, HEK-uht   ˈhekəṭiˑ, ˈhekət
  and the Underworld
Hecatoncheires
  fifty-headed, hundred-armed   HEK-uh-TAHN-KĪ-rēz   ˌhekəˌtɑnˈkairiːz
  giants
Hecht
  Anthony, *US poet;* Ben, *US writer*   HEKT   ˈhekt
Heckerism
  Catholic sect   HEK-uh-RIZ-uhm   ˈhekəˌrizəm
Heckler
  Margaret Mary, *US ambassador*   HEK-luhr   ˈheklərʳ
Hector
  1. Trojan hero; pers. name   HEK-tuhr   ˈhektərʳ
  2. French   ek-TAWR   ektɔːr
Héctor
  pers. name, Spanish   EK-tawr   ˈektɔːr
Hecuba
  wife of Priam   HEK-yuh-buh   ˈhekjəbə
Hedgecock
  Roger Allan, *US politician*   HEJ-KAHK   ˈhedʒˌkɑk
Hedmark
  county, Norway   HED-MAHRK, HĀD-MAHRK   ˈhedˌmɑʳk, ˈheːdˌmɑʳk
Hedvig
  pers. name, Swedish   HED-vig   ˈhedvig
Hedwig
  pers. name, German   HĀT-vikh   ˈheːtviç
Heffernan
  Nathan Stewart, *US jurist*   HEF-uhr-nuhn   ˈhefəʳnən
Heflin
  Howell Thomas, *US politician*   HEF-luhn   ˈheflən
Hefner
  Hugh, *US publisher*   HEF-nuhr   ˈhefnəʳ
Hegel
  Georg Wilhelm Friedrich, *German*   HĀ-guhl   ˈheːgəl
  philosopher

Foreign Sounds: ue: *Fr.* **rue**, *Ger.* **füllen**   uh(r): *Fr.* b**oeuf**, *Ger.* **Höhle**   <u>kh</u>: *Ger.* i**ch**, *Scot.* lo**ch**   ğ: *Sp.* ami**go**   v̲: *Sp.* ha**b**lar
hl: *Welsh* **Ll**anelli.   CAPITALS: primary stress.   SMALL CAPS: secondary stress.   Ⓢ: U.S. pron.   Ⓒ: British pron.

Hegelian
follower of Hegel — hā-GĀ-lē-uhn, huh-, -GĒ-lē-uhn — heː'geːliːən, hə-, -'giːliːən

Hegelianism
philosophy of Hegel — hā-GĀ-lē-uh-NIZ-uhm, huh-, -GĒ-lē-uh-NIZ-uhm — heː'geːliːə,nizəm, hə-, -'giːliːə,nizəm

Hegira
flight of Muhammad — hi-JĪ-ruh, HEJ-uh-ruh, hi-JĒ-ruh — hi'dʒairə, 'hedʒərə, hi'dʒiːrə

Hehe
lang., people, Africa — HĀ-hā — 'heːheː

Heidegger
Martin, *German philosopher* — HĪD-i-guhr, HĪ-DEG-uhr — 'haidigəʳ, 'hai,degəʳ

Heidelberg
1. Germany — HĪD-uhl-BERK, ⑤ HĪD-l-BUHRG, -BERG — 'haidəl,beʳk, ⑤ 'haidl̩,bəʳg, -,beʳg

2. town, PA, S. Africa; college, OH — HĪD-l-BUHRG — 'haidl̩,bəʳg

Heidenstam
Verner von, *Swedish author (Nobel 1916)* — HĀD-n-STAHM — 'heːdn̩,staːm

Heidi
pers. name — HĪD-ē — 'haidiˑ

Heifetz
Jascha, *US violinist* — HĪ-fuhts — 'haifəts

Heijo [P'yŏngyang]
city, N. Korea — hā-jō — heːdʒoː

Heike
pers. name, Dutch — HĀ-kuh — 'heːkə

Heikki
pers. name, Finnish — HĀK-ki — 'heːkki

Heilongjiang, Heilungkiang
prov, China — HĀ-LUNG-jē-AHNG — 'heː'luŋdʒiː'aŋ

Heimdall
Scandinavian watchman of heaven — HĪM-DAWL, HĪM-DAHL — 'haim,dɔːl, 'haim,dal

Heimlich maneuver
anti-choking procedure — HĪM-lik — 'haimlik

Heine
Heinrich, *German writer; pers. name* — HĪ-nuh, ⑤ HĪ-nē — 'hainə, ⑤ 'hainiː

Heineken
Dutch beer — HĪ-nuh-kuhn — 'hainəkən

Heinemann
Julius, Stadium, *New Orleans;* William, *British publisher* — HĪ-nuh-muhn — 'hainəmən

Heinlein
Robert, *US author* — HĪN-LĪN — 'hain,lain

Heinrich
1. pers. name, Danish — HĪN-rēkh — 'hainriːç
2. German — HĪN-rikh — 'hainriç

Heinz
1. tdmk for food products; pers. name — HĪNZ, HĪN(T)S — 'hainz, 'hain(t)s
2. German — HĪNTS — 'haints

Heisenberg
Werner, *German physicist (Nobel 1932)* — HĪ-zuhn-BERG, ⑤ -BUHRG — 'haizən,beʳg, ⑤ -,bəʳg

---

Key (col. 2):   a: fad ā: fade ah: father ar: Mary aw: law e: fed ē: feed er: merry i: hid ī: hide ō: coat ōō: boot
oi: boy   ow: now   u: put   uh: above   uhr: bird   ch: chop   ng: ring   sh: show   th: thick   th̲: this   zh: measure

Heisman
    John William, *US football coach;*   HĪS-muhn   'haismən
        college football trophy

Heitor
    pers. name, Portuguese   Ā-TAWR   'eː,tɔː^{r}

Hejaz
    region, Saudi Arabia   he-JAZ, hij-AZ   he'dʒæz, hidʒ'æz

Hekla
    Mount, *volcano, Iceland*   HEK-luh   'heklə

Hektemors
    Athenian farmers   hek-TĒ-MAWRZ   hek'tiː,mɔː^{r}z

Helen
    daughter of Zeus & Leda, wife of   HEL-uhn   'helən
        Menelaus, lover of Paris; pers.
        name

Helena
    1. city, MT   HEL-uh-nuh   'helənə
    2. pers. name   HEL-uh-nuh, huh-LĒ-nuh, hel-Ā-nuh   'helənə, hə'liːnə, hel'eːnə
    3. Dutch   hā-LĀ-nah   heː'leːnɑː
    4. German   HĀ-lā-NAH   'heːleː,nɑ

Helene
    1. pers. name   huh-LĒN, huh-LĀN   hə'liːn, hə'leːn
    2. German   hā-LĀ-nuh   heː'leːnə

Hélène
    pers. name, French   ā-LEN   eːlen

Helenus
    1. son of Priam & Hecuba, twin of   HEL-uh-nuhs   'helənəs
        Cassandra
    2. pers. name, Swedish   he-LĀ-nuhs   he'leːnəs

Helga
    pers. name, Swedish   HEL-guh   'helgə

Helge
    pers. name, Danish   HEL-guh   'helgə

Helgoland [Heligoland]
    island, North Sea   HEL-gō-LAHNT, Ⓢ HEL-gō-LAND   'helgoː,lɑnt, Ⓢ 'helgoː,lænd

Heliaea
    Athenian law courts   HEL-ē-Ē-uh   ,heliː'iːə

Helianthus
    flower   HĒ-lē-AN-thuhs   ,hiːliː'ænθəs

Helice
    guardian of Zeus   HEL-uh-sē   'heləsiː

Helicon
    Mount, *abode of Muses*   HEL-uh-KAHN, HEL-uh-kuhn   'helə,kan, 'heləkən

Heligoland [Helgoland]
    island, North Sea   HEL-uh-gō-LAND   'heləgoː,lænd

Heliogabalus
    Roman emperor   HĒ-lē-ō-GAB-uh-luhs   ,hiːliːoː'gæbələs

Heliopolis
    ancient Egyptian city   HĒ-lē-AHP-uh-luhs   ,hiːliː'apələs

Helios
    Greek sun god   HĒ-lē-uhs, HĒ-lē-ŌS   'hiːliːəs, 'hiːliː,oːs

helium
    element   HĒ-lē-uhm   'hiːliːəm

Hellas
    ancient name of Greece   HEL-uhs   'heləs

Foreign Sounds: **ue**: *Fr.* r**ue**, *Ger.* f**ü**llen   **uh(r)**: *Fr.* b**oeu**f, *Ger.* H**öh**le   <u>kh</u>: *Ger.* i<u>ch</u>, *Scot.* lo<u>ch</u>   ğ: *Sp.* ami**g**o   <u>v</u>: *Sp.* ha**b**lar
hl: *Welsh* **Ll**anelli.   CAPITALS: primary stress.   SMALL CAPS: secondary stress.   Ⓢ: U.S. pron.   Ⓑ: British pron.

Helle
   mythical Greek heroine drowned   HEL-ē   'heli·
    in the Hellespont

Hellen
   eponymous hero of the Greeks   HEL-uhn, HEL-ĒN   'helən, 'hel,iːn

Hellene
   a Greek   HEL-ĒN   'hel,iːn

Hellenic
   pert. to ancient Greece   huh-LEN-ik, huh-LĒ-nik, hel-EN-ik,   hə'lenik, hə'liːnik, hel'enik,
     hel-Ē-nik   hel'iːnik

Hellenism
   ancient Greek culture   HEL-uh-NIZ-uhm   'helə,nizəm

Hellenistic
   pert. to Greek civilization   HEL-uh-NIS-tik   ,helə'nistik

Hellenotamiae
   Athenian officials   HEL-uh-nō-TĀ-mē-ī   ,helənoː'teːmiː,ɑi

Heller
   Joseph, US writer   HEL-uhr   'heləʳ

Hellespont [Dardanelles]
   strait, Turkey   HEL-uh-SPAHNT   'helə,spɑnt

Helmholtz
   Hermann von, scientist   HELM-HŌLTS   'helm,hoːlts

Helmond
   Katherine, US actress   HEL-muhnd   'helmənd

Helms
   Jesse, US politician   HELMZ   'helmz

Helmsley
   US hoteliers   HELMZ-lē, HEMZ-lē   'helmzli·, 'hemzli·

Helmut, -muth
   pers. name, German   HEL-MOOT   'hel,muːt

Heloise
   US columnist; pers. name   HEL-uh-WĒZ   'helə,wiːz

Helots
   Spartan serfs   HEL-uhts   'heləts

Helsingfors [Helsinki]
   city, Finland   HEL-sing-FAWRZ   'helsiŋ,fɔːʳz

Helsingør [Elsinore]
   seaport, Denmark   HEL-seng-UHR, ⑤ HEL-sing-UHR   ,helseŋ'œːr, ⑤ ,helsiŋ'əʳ

Helsinki
   city, Finland   HEL-SING-kē, hel-SING-kē   'hel,siŋki·, hel'siŋki·

Helvetia
   Latin name for Switzerland   hel-VĒ-sh(ē-)uh   hel'viːʃ(iː)ə

Helvetic
   pert. to Helvetia   hel-VET-ik   hel'veṭik

Helvetica
   typeface   HEL-VET-i-kuh   ,hel'veṭikə

Helvetii
   ancient Celtic inhabitants of   hel-VĒ-shē-ī   hel'viːʃiː,ɑi
    Switzerland

Helvidius Priscus
   Roman philosopher   hel-VID-ē-uhs PRIS-kuhs   hel'vidiːəs 'priskəs

Hémeenlinna
   city, Finland   HAM-ĀN-LIN-nuh   'hæm,eːn,linnə

Hemel Hempstead
   town, England   HEM-uhl HEM(P)-stuhd   ,heməl 'hem(p)stəd

Key (col. 2):   a: fad   ā: fade   ah: father   ar: Mary   aw: law   e: fed   ē: feed   er: merry   i: hid   ī: hide   ō: coat   o͞o: boot
oi: boy   ow: now   u: put   uh: above   uhr: bird   ch: chop   ng: ring   sh: show   th: thick   th: this   zh: measure

Hemera
  ancient Greek personification of   HEM-uh-ruh   'hemərə
    the day

Hemicynes
  legendary half-dogs   HEM-ē-SĪ-nēz   ˌhemi'sɑiniːz

Hemingway
  Ernest, *US author (Nobel 1954);*   HEM-ing-WĀ   'hemiŋˌweː
    Margaux *and* Mariel, *US*
    actresses

Hempstead
  county, AR; town, NY; pers. name   HEM(P)-STED, HEM(P)-stuhd   'hem(p)ˌsted, 'hem(p)stəd

Hemsley
  Sherman, *US actor*   HEMZ-lē   'hemzliˑ

Henan [Honan]
  prov, town, China   HUH-NAHN   'hə'nɑn

Hench
  Philip S., *US physician (Nobel*   HENCH   'hentʃ
    1950)

Henderson
  Arthur, *British labor leader,*   HEN-duhr-suhn   'hendəʳsən
    politician (Nobel 1934)

Hendric
  pers. name   HEN-drik   'hendrik

Hendrick
  pers. name, Dutch   HEN-druhk   'hendrək

Hendricksz
  pers. name, Dutch   HEN-druhks   'hendrəks

Hendricus
  pers. name, Dutch   hen-DRĒ-kues   hen'driːkys

Hendrik
  pers. name, Dutch   HEN-druhk   'hendrək

Hendrix
  Jimi, *rock musician*   HEN-driks   'hendriks

Heneage
  pers. name   HEN-ij   'henidʒ

Hengist
  pers. name   HENG-guhst, -GIST   'heŋgəst, -ˌgist

Hengwrt
  Chaucer manuscript   HEN-gurt, HENG-gurt   'heŋguʳt, 'heŋguʳt

Henleigh, -ley
  pers. name   HEN-lē   'henliˑ

Henley-on-Thames
  town, England   HEN-lē ahn TEMZ   'henliˑ ɑn 'temz

Hennepin
  1. county, MN   HEN-uh-puhn   'henəpən
  2. Louis, *Belgian explorer*   en-uh-PEⁿ, Ⓢ HEN-uh-puhn   enəpẽ, Ⓢ 'henəpən

Henner
  Marilu, *actress*   HEN-uhr   'henəʳ

Hennessy
  tdmk for a cognac; pers. name   HEN-uh-sē   'henəsiˑ

Henning
  Doug, *Canadian magician*   HEN-ing   'heniŋ

Henninger
  German beer   HEN-ing-uhr   'heniŋəʳ

Foreign Sounds: ue: *Fr.* **rue**, *Ger.* **füllen**   uh(r): *Fr.* **boeuf**, *Ger.* **Höhle**   <u>kh</u>: *Ger.* **ich**, *Scot.* **loch**   ḡ: *Sp.* **amigo**   <u>v</u>: *Sp.* **hablar** hl: *Welsh* **Llanelli**.   CAPITALS: primary stress.   SMALL CAPS: secondary stress.   Ⓢ: U.S. pron.   Ⓛ: British pron.

Henri
1. pers. name, Flemish	HAHⁿ-rē	'hãriː
2. French	ahⁿ-RĒ	ãriː

Henrich
pers. name, German   HEN-ri<u>kh</u>   'henriç

Henrico
county, VA   hen-RĪ-kō   hen'raikoː

Henricus
1. pers. name, Dutch	hen-RĒ-kues	hen'riːkys
2. Latin	hen-RĪ-kuhs, hen-RĒ-kuhs	hen'raikəs, hen'riːkəs

Henrietta
pers. name   HEN-rē-ET-uh   ˌhenriː'eʈə

Henriette
1. pers. name, French	ahⁿr-YET	ãrjet
2. German	HEN-rē-ET-uh	ˌhenriː'eʈə

Henriëtte
pers. name, Dutch   HEN-rē-ET-uh   ˌhenriː'eʈə

Henrik
1. pers. name, Danish	HEN-rēk	'henriːk
2. Norwegian	HEN-rik	'henrik

Henrique
1. pers. name, Portuguese	ān-RĒ-kuh, -kā	ẽːn'riːkə, -keː
2. Spanish	ān-RĒ-kā	eːn'riːkeː

Henriques
pers. name, Portuguese   ān-RĒ-kish, -kis   ẽːn'riːkiʃ, -kis

Henry
1. pers. name, English, German	HEN-rē	'henriˑ
2. Flemish	HAHⁿ-rē	'hãriː
3. French	ahⁿ-RĒ	ãriː

Henryk
pers. name, Polish   HEN-rik   'henrik

Henslowe
cape, Solomon Islands   HENZ-LŌ   'henzˌloː

Henson
Jim, US puppeteer   HEN(T)-suhn   'hen(t)sən

Hen Wlad fy Nhadau
Welsh national anthem   HEN WLAHD vuhn HAHD-ī   'hen ˌwlad vən 'hadai

Hepatica
flower   hi-PAT-i-kuh   hi'pæʈikə

Hepatic Tanager
songbird   hi-PAT-ik TAN-uh-juhr   hi'pæʈik 'tænədʒə^r

Hepburn
Audrey, Belgian-born actress; Katharine, US actress; pers. name   HEP-BUHRN, ⓔ *also* HEB-uhrn   'hepˌbə^rn, ⓔ *also* 'hebə^rn

Hephaestus
Greek god of fire   hi-FES-tuhs, hi-FĒ-stuhs   hi'festəs, hi'fiːstəs

Hepplewhite
furniture style   HEP-uhl-(H)WĪT   'hepəlˌ(h)wait

Heptateuch
first seven books of Bible   HEP-tuh-T(Y)OOK   'heptəˌt(j)uːk

Hepzibah
pers. name   HEP-suh-BAH, HEP-suh-buh   'hepsəˌba, 'hepsəbə

Hera
Greek queen of the gods   HIR-uh, HER-uh, HĒ-ruh   'hirə, 'herə, 'hiːrə

Key (col. 2):   a: **fad**   ā: **fade**   ah: **father**   ar: **Mary**   aw: **law**   e: **fed**   ē: **feed**   er: **merry**   i: **hid**   ī: **hide**   ō: **coat**   oo: **boot**
oi: **boy**   ow: **now**   u: **put**   uh: **above**   uhr: **bird**   ch: **chop**   ng: **ring**   sh: **show**   th: **thick**   <u>th</u>: **this**   zh: **measure**

Heraclean
   pert. to Heracles   HER-uh-KLĒ-uhn   ˌherə'kliːən

Heracles, -kles [Hercules]
   mythical Greek hero   HER-uh-KLĒZ   'herəˌkliːz

Heraclids
   descendants of Heracles   HER-uh-KLIDZ   'herəˌklidz

Heraclitus
   Greek philosopher   HER-uh-KLĪT-uhs   ˌherə'klɑiţəs

Heraclius
   pers. name, Latin   huh-RAK-lē-uhs   hə'rækliːəs

Héraclius
   pers. name, French   ā-rah-klē-UES   eːrɑːkliːyːs

Heraklion
   dept & town, Greece   hi-RAK-lē-uhn   hi'rækliːən

Herat
   prov, city, Afghanistan   he-RAHT, huh-RAHT   he'rɑt, hə'rɑt

Hérault
   river, dept, France   ā-RŌ   eːroː

Herb
   pers. name   HUHRB   'həʳb

Herbert
   1. pers. name   HUHR-buhrt, HUHR-buht   'həʳbəʳt, 'həʳbət
   2. German   HER-BERT   'heʳˌbeʳt
   3. Swedish   HER-buhrt   'herbərt

Herbie
   pers. name   HUHR-bē   'həʳbiˑ

Herculaneum
   ancient Roman town buried by   HUHR-kyuh-LĀ-nē-uhm   ˌhəʳkjə'leːniːəm
     Vesuvius

Hercule
   pers. name, French   er-KUEL   erkyːl

Herculean
   pert. to Hercules   HUHR-kyuh-LĒ-uhn,   ˌhəʳkjə'liːən, ˌhəʳ'kjuːliːən
      HUHR-KYŌŌ-lē-uhn

Hercules
   1. Latin form of Heracles;   HUHR-kyuh-LĒZ   'həʳkjəˌliːz
     constellation; pers. name
   2. Dutch   HER-kue-luhs   'herkyːləs

Herder
   Gerhard, German ambassador   HERD-uhr   'heʳdəʳ

Hereford
   1. town, England   HER-uh-fuhrd   'herəfəʳd
   2. breed of cattle   HUHR-fuhrd, HER-uh-fuhrd   'həʳfəʳd, 'herəfəʳd
   3. town, MD   HER-fuhrd   'herfəʳd

Herefordshire
   former county, England   HER-uh-fuhrd-shuhr, -SHIR;   'herəfəʳdʃəʳ, -ˌʃiʳ;
      Ⓢ HUHR-fuhrd-   Ⓢ 'həʳfəʳd-

Herennius
   pers. name, Latin   huh-REN-ē-uhs   hə'reniːəs

Herero
   lang., people, Africa   huh-RER-ō, HER-uh-RŌ   hə'reroː, 'herəˌroː

Herforder
   German beer   HER-FAWR-duhr   'herˌfɔːʳdəʳ

Herkimer
   county, NY   HUHR-kuh-muhr   'həʳkəməʳ

Foreign Sounds: **ue:** *Fr.* **rue,** *Ger.* **füllen**   <u>uh</u>(r): *Fr.* **boeuf,** *Ger.* **Höhle**   <u>kh</u>: *Ger.* **ich,** *Scot.* **loch**   ḡ: *Sp.* **amigo**   <u>v</u>: *Sp.* **hablar**
<u>hl</u>: *Welsh* **Llanelli.**   CAPITALS: primary stress.   SMALL CAPS: secondary stress.   Ⓢ: U.S. pron.   Ⓣ: British pron.

Herman
1. *pers. name*	HUHR-muhn	'hə‵mən
2. *Danish, Finnish*	HER-MAHN	'her,mɑːn
3. *Dutch, Norwegian*	HER-MAHN	'her,mɑn
4. *German*	HER-MAHN	'he‵,mɑn

Hermann
1. *pers. name*	HUHR-muhn	'hə‵mən
2. *Danish*	HER-MAHN	'her,mɑːn
3. *Dutch, Icelandic*	HER-MAHN	'her,mɑn
4. *French*	er-MAHN	ermɑːn
5. *German*	HER-MAHN	'he‵,mɑn

Hermaphroditus
androgynous Greek deity	huhr-MAF-ruh-DĪT-uhs	hə‵,mæfrə'daiʈəs

Hermes
1. *Greek messenger god; asteroid; pers. name*	HUHR-MĒZ	'hə‵,miːz
2. *Portuguese*	ER-mish, ER-mis	'ermiʃ, 'ermis

Hermès
French fashion retailers	er-MES, HUHR-MĒZ	er'mes, 'hə‵,miːz

Hermes Trismegistus
Thoth or Hermes as author of magical works	HUHR-mēz TRIS-muh-JIS-tuhs	'hə‵miːz ,trismə'dʒistəs

Hermeticism
Gnostic writings & teachings	HUHR-MET-uh-SIZ-uhm	,hə‵'meʈə,sizəm

Hermione
1. *daughter of Menelaus & Helen; pers. name*	huhr-MĪ-uh-nē	hə‵'maiəni‵
2. *French*	erm-YAWN	ermjɔːn

Hermitage
museum, Leningrad	er-mē-TAHZH	ermiːtɑːʒ

Hermogenes
pers. name	huhr-MAHJ-uh-NĒZ	hə‵'mɑdʒə,niːz

Hermon
mtn. between Lebanon & Syria	HUHR-muhn	'hə‵mən

Hermosa
district, Philippines	er-MŌ-suh	e‵'moːsə

Hernán
pers. name, Spanish	er-NAHN	er'nan

Hernández
pers. name, Spanish	er-NAHN-dăs, -dăth	er'nandeːs, -deːθ

Hernando
1. *county, FL*	huhr-NAN-dō	hə‵'nændoː
2. *pers. name, Spanish*	er-NAHN-dō	er'nandoː

Hero
beloved of Leander in Greek mythology	HĒ-rō, HIR-ō	'hiːroː, 'hiroː

Herod
Biblical ruler	HER-uhd	'herəd

Herodias
Biblical name	huh-RŌD-ē-uhs	hə'roːdiːəs

Herodotus
Greek historian	huh-RAHD-uht-uhs	hə'radəʈəs

Herophile
the second sibyl	hē-RAHF-uh-lē, hir-AHF-uh-lē	hiː'rafəli‵, hir'afəli‵

Key (col. 2):   a: fad ā: fade ah: father ar: Mary aw: law e: fed ē: feed er: merry i: hid ī: hide ō: coat ō͞o: boot
oi: boy   ow: now   u: put   uh: above   uhr: bird   ch: chop   ng: ring   sh: show   th: thick   th: this   zh: measure

Herr		
Mr. *in German*	HER	'he^r
Herrenbräu		
German beer	HER-uhn-BROI	'herən,brɔi
Herrenhäuser		
German beer	HER-uhn-HOI-zuhr	'herən,hɔizə^r
Herrenvolk		
master race	HER-uhn-FAWLK	'herən,fɔːlk
Herriot		
1. James, *British writer*	HER-ē-uht	'heriːət
2. Édouard, *French politician*	er-YŌ	erjoː
Herrmann		
pers. name, German	HER-MAHN	'he^r,mɑn
Herschbach		
Dudley R., *US chemist (Nobel 1986)*	HUHRSH-BAK	'hə^rʃ,bæk
Herschel		
Sir William, *British astronomer; pers. name*	HUHR-shuhl	'hə^rʃəl
Herschel-Rigollet		
comet	HUHR-shuhl-RIG-uh-LĀ	'hə^rʃəl,rigə'leː
Hersey		
John, *US author*	HUHR-sē	'hə^rsiˑ
Hershel		
pers. name	HUHR-shuhl	'hə^rʃəl
Hershey		
Alfred D., *US biologist (Nobel 1969); city, PA; US candy co.*	HUHR-shē	'hə^rʃiˑ
Hershler		
Edgar J., *US politician*	HUHRSH-luhr	'hə^rʃlə^r
Herstmonceux, Hurstmonceux		
village, observatory site, England	HUHRST-muhn-S(Y)OO̅	,hə^rstmən's(j)uː
Hertford		
1. county, town, NC	HUHRT-fuhrd	'hə^rtfə^rd
2. county, England; college, Oxford Univ.	HAHR-fuhrd, HAHRT-fuhrd	'hɑ^rfə^rd, 'hɑ^rtfə^rd
3. Marquess of, English peer	HAHR-fuhrd	'hɑ^rfə^rd
Hertfordshire		
county, England	HAHR-fuhrd-shuhr, HAHRT-fuhrd-shuhr, -SHIR	'hɑ^rfə^rdʃə^r, 'hɑ^rtfə^rdʃə^r, -,ʃi^r
Herts		
Hertfordshire	HAHRTS	'hɑ^rts
Hertz		
1. Gustav, *German physicist (Nobel 1925)*	HERTS, Ⓢ HUHRTS	'he^rts, Ⓢ 'hə^rts
2. US car rental co.	HUHRTS	'hə^rts
Hertzog		
James, *S. African prime minister*	HUHRT-SAWG, HUHRT-SAHG	'hə^rt,sɔːg, 'hə^rt,sɑg
Hervé		
pers. name, French	er-VĀ	erveː
Hervey		
pers. name	HUHR-vē, Ⓛ HAHR-vē	'hə^rviˑ, Ⓛ 'hɑ^rviˑ
Herz		
pers. name	HUHRTS	'hə^rts

Foreign Sounds: ue: *Fr.* **rue**, *Ger.* f**ü**llen uh(r): *Fr.* **boeuf**, *Ger.* H**öh**le kh: *Ger.* i**ch**, *Scot.* lo**ch** ḡ: *Sp.* ami**g**o v: *Sp.* ha**b**lar hl: *Welsh* **Ll**anelli. CAPITALS: primary stress. SMALL CAPS: secondary stress. Ⓢ: U.S. pron. Ⓛ: British pron.

Herzberg
Gerhard, *German-born Canadian physical chemist (Nobel 1971)*	HUHRTS-BUHRG	ˈhəʳts͵bəʳg

Herzegovina
region, Bosnia and Herzegovina	HERT-suh-gō-VĒ-nuh, HERT-suh-GŌ-vuh-nuh, HUHRT-	͵heʳtsəgoːˈviːnə, ͵heʳtsəˈgoːvənə, ͵həʳt-

Herzl
Theodor, *Hungarian Zionist leader in Vienna*	HERT-suhl	ˈheʳtsəl

Hesba
pers. name	HEZ-buh	ˈhezbə

Heseltine
Michael, *English politician*	HES-uhl-TĪN, HEZ-uhl-TĪN	ˈhesəl͵tain, ˈhezəl͵tain

Heshvan
Jewish month	KHESH-vuhn, HESH-vuhn, HESH-VAHN	ˈxeʃvən, ˈheʃvən, ˈheʃ͵van

Hesiod
Greek poet	HĒ-sē-uhd, HES-ē-uhd	ˈhiːsiːəd, ˈhesiːəd

Hesione
wife of Telamon	he-SĪ-uh-nē	heˈsaiəniˑ

Hesperia
mythical West	he-SPIR-ē-uh	heˈspiriːə

Hesperian
pert. to Hesperia	he-SPIR-ē-uhn	heˈspiriːən

Hesperides
nymphs who guarded a tree of golden apples	he-SPER-uh-DĒZ	heˈsperə͵diːz

Hesperidin
pigment	he-SPER-uhd-n	heˈsperədn̩

Hesperus
spirit of the evening star; schooner in Longfellow poem	HES-puh-ruhs	ˈhespərəs

Hess
Rudolf, *German Nazi politician;* V. F., *Austrian-born US physicist (Nobel 1936);* Walter Rudolf, *Swiss physiologist (Nobel 1949)*	HES	ˈhes

Hesse
1. Hermann, *German author (Nobel 1946)*	HES-uh	ˈhesə
2. *prov., Germany*	HES, HES-uh	ˈhes, ˈhesə

Hesseman
Howard, *US actor*	HES-muhn	ˈhesmən

Hessen [Hesse]
prov., Germany	HES-n	ˈhesn̩

Hessian
pert. to the German prov. Hesse	HESH-uhn	ˈheʃən

Hesston
city, KS	HES-tuhn	ˈhestən

Hester
pers. name	HES-tuhr	ˈhestəʳ

Hestia
Greek goddess of the hearth	HES-tē-uh, HES-chuh, HESH-chuh	ˈhestiːə, ˈhestʃə, ˈheʃtʃə

Heston
Charlton, *US actor*	HES-tuhn	ˈhestən

Key (col. 2):   a: fad   ā: fade   ah: father   ar: Mary   aw: law   e: fed   ē: feed   er: merry   i: hid   ī: hide   ō: coat   ōō: boot
oi: boy   ow: now   u: put   uh: above   uhr: bird   ch: chop   ng: ring   sh: show   th: thick   th̲: this   zh: measure

Heteroousian

   pert. to or member of an Arian   HET-uh-rō-$\overline{OO}$-sē-uhn,   ,hetərɔːˈuːsiːən,
   sect.   HET-uh-rō-$\overline{OO}$-zh(ē-)uhn   ,hetərɔːˈuːʒ(iː)ən

Het Kapittel Watou Prior

   Belgian beer   HET KAHP-i-tuhl VAH-$\overline{TOO}$ PRĒ-awr   ,het ˈkapitəl ˈvɑ,tuː ˈpriːɔːr

Hettinger

   county, ND   HET-uhn-juhr, HET-n-juhr   ˈhetəndʒəʳ, ˈhetn̩dʒəʳ

Hevesy

   Georg von, *Hungarian chemist*   HEV-ESH-ē; HEV-uh-shē   ˈhev,eʃiˈ; ˈhevəʃiˈ
   (Nobel 1943)

Hewish

   Antony, *English radio astronomer*   H$\overline{YOO}$-ish   ˈhjuːiʃ
   (Nobel 1974)

Hewitt

   pers. name   H$\overline{YOO}$-uht   ˈhjuːət

Hewlett-Packard

   US computer co.   (H)Y$\overline{OO}$-luht-PAK-uhrd   ˈ(h)juːlətˈpækəʳd

Heyerdahl

   Thor, *Norwegian ethnologist*   HÃ-uhr-DAHL   ˈheːəʳ,dɑl

Heymans

   Corneille, *Belgian physiologist*   ā-MAHⁿS, Ⓢ ā-MAHNS, ā-MANS   eːmãs, Ⓢ eːˈmans, eːˈmæns
   (Nobel 1938)

Heyrovsky

   Jaroslav, *Czech physical chemist*   hā-RAWF-skē   heːˈrɔːfskiˈ
   (Nobel 1959)

Heyse

   Paul, *German author (Nobel 1910)*   HĪ-zuh   ˈhɑizə

Heyward

   DuBose, *US lyricist*   HÃ-wuhrd   ˈheːwəʳd

Hezbollah

   Palestinian military organization   HEZ-buh-LAH   ,hezbəˈlɑ

Hezekiah

   pers. name   HEZ-uh-KĪ-uh   ,hezəˈkɑiə

Hialeah

   town, FL   HĪ-uh-LĒ-uh   ,hɑiəˈliːə

Hiawatha

   legendary Onondaga chief   HĪ-uh-WAW-thuh, HĪ-uh-WAHTH-uh,   ,hɑiəˈwɔːθə, ,hɑiəˈwɑθə,
        HĒ-uh-   ,hiːə-

Hibernia

   ancient Latin name of Ireland   hī-BUHR-nē-uh   haiˈbəʳniːə

Hibernian

   pert. to Hibernia   hī-BUHR-nē-uhn   haiˈbəʳniːən

Hickok

   James ("Wild Bill"), *US*   HIK-AHK   ˈhik,ak
   frontiersman

Hicks

   Sir John R., *English economist*   HIKS   ˈhiks
   (Nobel 1972)

Hidalgo

   1. *county, NM, TX*   hid-AL-gō   hidˈælgoː
   2. *state, Mexico*   ē-THAHL-gō   iːˈðɑlɣoː

Hidatsa

   N. American people   hi-DAHT-suh, hi-DAT-suh   hiˈdɑtsə, hiˈdætsə

Hideki

   pers. name, Japanese   hē-dek-ē   hiːdekiː

Foreign Sounds: **ue**: *Fr.* **rue**, *Ger.* **füllen**   **uh(r)**: *Fr.* **boeuf**, *Ger.* **Höhle**   kh: *Ger.* **ich**, *Scot.* **loch**   ḡ: *Sp.* amigo   v̱: *Sp.* **hablar**   hl: *Welsh* **Llanelli**.   CAPITALS: primary stress.   SMALL CAPS: secondary stress.   Ⓢ: U.S. pron.   Ⓑ: British pron.

Hideyo, Hideo
  pers. name, Japanese   hē-de-yō   hiːdejoː

Hiera
  wife of Telephus   HĪ-uh-ruh   'haiərə

Hierax
  hero turned into a falcon   HĪ-uh-RAKS   'haiə,ræks

Hiero
  tyrants of Syracuse   HĪ-uh-rō   ,haiəroː

Hieronymus
  1. pers. name   HĪ-uh-RAHN-uh-muhs,   ,haiə'ranəməs, hə'ranəməs
           huh-RAHN-uh-muhs
  2. Dutch   HĒ-uh-RŌ-nē-mues   ,hiːə'roːniːmys
  3. German   HĒ-ā-RŌ-nue-mus   ,hiːeːr'roːnyːmus

Higginbotham
  Jay C., jazz musician   HIG-uhn-BAHTH-uhm   'higən,baθəm

Higgins
  Jack, British author   HIG-uhnz   'higənz

Highland
  US pl. name; region, Scotland   HĪ-luhnd   'hailənd

Hiiumaa
  island, Baltic Sea   HĒ-uh-MAH   'hiːə,ma

Hilaire
  pers. name   hil-AR, hil-ER; Ⓔ *also* HIL-ER   hil'ærʳ, hil'eʳ; Ⓔ *also* 'hil,eʳ

Hilarius
  pope   huh-LAR-ē-uhs   hə'læriːəs

Hilarus
  pope   HIL-uh-ruhs   'hilərəs

Hilary
  pers. name   HIL-uh-rē   'hiləriˑ

Hilbert
  David, German mathematician   HIL-buhrt   'hilbəʳt

Hilburn
  Robert, US music critic   HIL-BUHRN   'hil,bəʳn

Hilda
  pers. name   HIL-duh   'hildə

Hildebrand
  1. pers. name   HIL-duh-BRAND   'hildə,brænd
  2. Dutch, German   HIL-duh-BRAHNT   'hildə,brant

Hildegard
  pers. name, Finnish   HIL-de-GAHRD   'hilde,gard

Hildegarde
  pers. name   HIL-duh-GAHRD   'hildə,gaʳd

Hildesheim
  prov, Germany   HIL-duhs-HĪM   'hildəs,haim

Hiligaynon
  lang., people, Philippines   HIL-uh-GĪ-nuhn   ,hilə'gainən

Hill
  A. V., English physiologist (Nobel   HIL   'hil
    1922)

Hillary
  pers. name   HIL-uh-rē   'hiləriˑ

Hillel
  Jewish scholar   HIL-uhl, HIL-EL   'hiləl, 'hil,el

Key (col. 2):   a: fad   ā: fade   ah: father   ar: Mary   aw: law   e: fed   ē: feed   er: merry   i: hid   ī: hide   ō: coat   o͞o: boot
oi: boy   ow: now   u: put   uh: above   uhr: bird   ch: chop   ng: ring   sh: show   th: thick   th̲: this   zh: measure

Hiller
Arthur, *Canadian film director;* HIL-uhr 'hilə^r
Wendy, *British actress*
Hillerman
John, *US actor* HIL-uhr-muhn 'hilə^rmən
Hillingdon
borough, England HIL-ing-duhn 'hiliŋdən
Hilo
city, HI HĒ-lō 'hiːloː
Hilton
Conrad, *US hotelier; pers. name* HILT-n 'hiltṇ
Hilversum
city, Netherlands HIL-vuhr-suhm 'hilvə^rsəm
Himachal Pradesh
state, India huh-MAHCH-uhl pruh-DESH hə'matʃəl prə'deʃ
Himalayan
pert. to the Himalayas; *cat* HIM-uh-LĀ-uhn, ˌhimə'leːən, hə'mal(ə)jən
huh-MAHL-(uh-)yuhn
Himalayas
The, *mts., Asia* HIM-uh-LĀ-uhz, ˌhimə'leːəz, hə'mal(ə)jəz
huh-MAHL-(uh-)yuhz
Himalia
satellite of Jupiter huh-MĀ-lē-uh, huh-MĀL-yuh hə'meːliːə, hə'meːljə
Himerus
personification of sexual desire in HIM-uh-ruhs 'himərəs
Greek mythology
Himno Istmeño
national anthem, Panama ĒM-nō ēst-MĀN-yō 'iːmnoː iːst'meːnjoː
Hinano
Tahitian beer hē-NAHN-ō hiː'nanoː
Hinayana [Theravada]
branch of Buddhism HĒ-nuh-YAHN-uh ˌhiːnə'janə
Hinayanism
branch of Buddhism HĒ-nuh-YAHN-ɪz-uhm ˌhiːnə'jan,izəm
Hinckley
John, Jr., *US convict, attempted* HING-klē 'hiŋkli·
assassin
Hindemith
Paul, *German composer* HIN-duh-mit 'hindəmit
Hindenburg
Paul von, *president, Germany;* HIN-duhn-BURK, 'hindən,bu^rk,
German airship ⑤ HIN-duhn-BUHRG, -BURG ⑤ 'hindən,bə^rg, -ˌbu^rg
Hindes
pers. name HĪN(D)Z 'hain(d)z
Hindi
lang., India, Africa, Fiji, Surinam, HIN-dē 'hindi·
Guyanas
Hindu
Indian culture HIN-doo 'hinduː
Hindu Kush
mts., Asia HIN-doo KUSH, KUHSH ˌhinduː 'kuʃ, 'kəʃ
Hindustani
lang., N. India HIN-doo-STAN-ē, HIN-doo-STAHN-ē ˌhinduː'stæni·, ˌhinduː'stani·

Foreign Sounds: ue: *Fr.* **rue,** *Ger.* **füllen** uh(r): *Fr.* **boeuf,** *Ger.* **Höhle** kh: *Ger.* **ich,** *Scot.* **loch** g̃: *Sp.* **amigo** y: *Sp.* **hablar**
hl: *Welsh* **Llanelli.** CAPITALS: primary stress. SMALL CAPS: secondary stress. ⑤: U.S. pron. ⓣ: British pron.

Hinshelwood
Sir Cyril N., *English chemist*   HIN-chuhl-WUD   'hintʃəl,wud
(Nobel 1956)
Hippalus
Greek explorer   HIP-uh-luhs   'hipələs
Hipparchus
crater on Moon   hi-PAHR-kuhs   hi'pɑʳkəs
Hippe
daughter of Chiron   HIP-ē   'hipiˑ
Hippias
tyrant of Athens; Lesser *and*   HIP-ē-uhs   'hipiːəs
Greater, *dialogues of Plato*
Hipple
Eric, *US football player*   HIP-uhl   'hipəl
Hippocrates
Greek physician   hip-AHK-ruh-TĒZ   hip'ɑkrə,tiːz
Hippocratic
pert. to Hippocrates; *medical oath*   HIP-uh-KRAT-ik   ,hipə'krætik
Hippocrene
fountain of inspiration created by   HIP-uh-KRĒN, HIP-uh-KRĒ-nē   'hipə,kriːn, ,hipə'kriːniˑ
Pegasus on Mt. Helicon
Hippodamia
wife of Pelops   HIP-uh-duh-MĪ-uh   ,hipədə'maiə
Hippodamus
Greek architect   hip-AHD-uh-muhs   hip'adəməs
Hippodrome
New York City theater   HIP-uh-DRŌM   'hipə,droːm
Hippogriff
fabulous creature   HIP-uh-GRIF   'hipə,grif
Hippolyta
queen of Amazons   hip-AHL-uht-uh   hip'alətə
Hippolyte
pers. name, French   ē(p)-paw-LĒT   iː(p)pɔliːt
Hippolytus
son of Theseus   hip-AHL-uht-uhs   hip'alətəs
Hippomedon
one of Seven against Thebes   hi-PAHM-uhd-uhn,   hi'pamədən, hi'pamə,dan
                                          hi-PAHM-uh-DAHN
Hippomenes
suitor of Atalanta   hi-PAHM-uh-NĒZ   hi'pamə,niːz
Hippotes
father of Aletes   HIP-uht-ĒZ   'hipət,iːz
Hiram
township, OH; biblical ruler; pers.   HĪ-ruhm   'hairəm
name
Hirohito
emperor, Japan   HIR-uh-HĒT-ō   ,hirə'hiːtoː
Hiroshi
pers. name, Japanese   hē-rō-shē   hiːroːʃiː
Hiroshige
Ando, *Japanese painter*   hē-rō-shē-ge   hiːroːʃiːge
Hiroshima
city, Japan   hē-rō-shē-mah, Ⓢ HIR-uh-SHĒ-muh,   hiːroːʃiːma, Ⓢ ,hirə'ʃiːmə,
                                          huh-RŌ-shuh-muh   hə'roːʃəmə

Key (col. 2):   a: fad   ā: fade   ah: father   ar: Mary   aw: law   e: fed   ē: feed   er: merry   i: hid   ī: hide   ō: coat   o͞o: boot
oi: boy   ow: now   u: put   uh: above   uhr: bird   ch: chop   ng: ring   sh: show   th: thick   th: this   zh: measure

Hirsch
　　Judd, *US actor* 　　　　　　HUHRSH 　　　　　　　　　　　　　'hə�98ʃ
Hirschfeld
　　Al, *US cartoonist* 　　　　　HUHRSH-FELD 　　　　　　　　　'həʳʃ,feld
Hispania
　　Roman name for Spain 　　his-PAN-yuh, his-PAN-ē-uh 　　his'pænjə, his'pæniːə
Hispanic
　　pert. to Spain *and/or* Latin 　his-PAN-ik, *in running speech also* 　his'pænik, *in running*
　　　　America 　　　　　　　is-PAN-ik 　　　　　　　　*speech also* is'pænik
Hispaniola
　　island, West Indies 　　　HIS-puhn-YŌ-luh 　　　　　　,hispən'joːlə
Histiaeus
　　tyrant of Miletus 　　　　HIS-tuh-Ē-uhs 　　　　　　　,histə'iːəs
Hitachi
　　Japanese corp. 　　　　　hi-tahch-ē 　　　　　　　　　hitɑtʃiː
Hitchings
　　George H., *US chemist (Nobel* 　HICH-ingz 　　　　　　　　'hitʃiŋz
　　　1988)
Hitler
　　Adolf, *Nazi dictator* 　　　HIT-luhr 　　　　　　　　　'hitləʳ
Hitlerian
　　pert. to Hitler 　　　　　hit-LIR-ē-uhn, hit-LER-ē-uhn 　hit'liriːən, hit'leriːən
Hitlerism
　　adherence to practices of Nazi 　HIT-luh-RIZ-uhm 　　　　　'hitlə,rizəm
　　　party
Hitlerite
　　adherent of Hitlerism 　　HIT-luh-RĪT 　　　　　　　　'hitlə,rait
Hittite
　　ancient people of Asia Minor 　HI-TĪT 　　　　　　　　　'hi,tait
Hiwassee
　　river, US; college, dam, TN 　hī-WAHS-ē 　　　　　　　　hai'wɑsiˑ
Hjalmar
　　1. pers. name, Danish 　　YAHL-MAHR 　　　　　　　　'jɑːl,mɑr
　　2. Finnish, Swedish 　　　YAHL-MAHR 　　　　　　　　'jɑːl,mɑːr
　　3. Icelandic, Norwegian 　　YAHL-MAHR 　　　　　　　　'jɑl,mɑr
Hler
　　Scandinavian god 　　　　HLER 　　　　　　　　　　　'hleʳ, 'l̥eʳ
Hmong [Miao]
　　lang., people, China,Vietnam, 　(H)MAWNG, (H)MAHNG 　　'(h)mɔːŋ, '(h)mɑŋ
　　　Laos, Thailand
Ho
　　Don, *US entertainer* 　　　HŌ 　　　　　　　　　　　'hoː
Hoagy
　　pers. name (H. Carmichael) 　HŌ-gē 　　　　　　　　　　'hoːgiˑ
Hoatzin
　　South American bird 　　　wah(t)-SĒN 　　　　　　　　wɑ(t)'siːn
Hobart
　　1. pers. name 　　　　　HŌ-buhrt, HŌ-BAHRT, Ⓛ *also* 　'hoːbəʳt, 'hoː,bɑʳt, Ⓛ *also*
　　　　　　　　　　　　HUHB-uhrt 　　　　　　　　　'həbəʳt
　　2. pl. name, IN 　　　　HŌ-buhrt 　　　　　　　　　'hoːbəʳt
　　3. city, Tasmania 　　　　HŌ-BAHRT 　　　　　　　　'hoː,bɑʳt
Hobbes
　　Thomas, *British philosopher;* 　HAHBZ 　　　　　　　　　'hɑbz
　　　comic strip tiger

Foreign Sounds: **ue**: *Fr.* **rue**, *Ger.* **füllen**　**uh**(r): *Fr.* **boeuf**, *Ger.* **Höhle**　k̲h̲: *Ger.* i**ch**, *Scot.* lo**ch**　ḡ: *Sp.* ami**g**o　v̲: *Sp.* ha**b**lar
hl: *Welsh* **Ll**anelli.　CAPITALS: primary stress.　SMALL CAPS: secondary stress.　⑤: U.S. pron.　Ⓛ: British pron.

Hobbism
   philosophy of T. Hobbes   HAHB-IZ-uhm   'hab,izəm

Hoboken
   city, NJ; number designating F. J.   HŌ-bō-kuhn   'hoːboːkən
    Haydn compositions

Hobson-Jobson
   altered foreign borrowing   HAHB-suhn-JAHB-suhn   ,habsən'dʒabsən

Hobson's choice
   no real alternative   HAHB-suhnz CHOIS   ,habsənz 'tʃɔis

Hochheim
   commune, Germany   HŌ<u>KH</u>-HĪM, ⑤ HAHK-HĪM, HŌK-,   'hoːx,haim, ⑤ 'hak,haim,
                       HAWK-   'hoːk-, 'hɔːk-

Hochi
   Honolulu newspaper   HŌ-chē   'hoːtʃiˑ

Ho Chi Minh
   president, N. Vietnam   HŌ chē MIN, HŌ shē MIN   ,hoː tʃiˑ 'min, ,hoː ʃiˑ 'min

Ho Chi Minh City [Saigon]
   city, Vietnam   HŌ chē MIN SIT-ē, shē   ,hoː tʃiˑ ,min 'siṭiˑ, ʃiˑ

Hodding
   pers. name   HAHD-ing   'hadiŋ

Hodgkin
   Sir Alan Lloyd, English   HAHJ-kin   'hadʒkin
    physiologist (Nobel 1963);
    Dorothy Mary Crowfoot, *English*
    chemist (Nobel 1964)

Hodgkin's disease
   lymphatic cancer   HAHJ-kinz di-ZĒZ   'hadʒkinz di,ziːz

Hoechst Celanese
   US chemical co.   HŌKST SEL-uh-NĒZ, SEL-uh-NĒS   'hoːkst ,selə'niːz, ,selə'niːs

Hoegaarden
   Belgian beer   HOO̅-GAHRD-n   'huː,gaːrdn̩

Hoek van Holland
   prov, Netherlands   HOO̅K vahn HŌ-LAHNT   'huːk van 'hoː,lant

Hofbräu
   German beer   HAWF-BROI   'hɔːf,brɔi

Hoffman
   Dustin, *US actor*   HAHF-muhn, HAWF-muhn   'hafmən, 'hɔːfmən

Hoffmann
   Roald, *Polish-born US chemist*   HAHF-muhn, HAWF-muhn   'hafmən, 'hɔːfmən
    (Nobel 1981)

Hofmark Wurzig
   German beer   HAWF-MAHRK VURT-sikh   'hɔːf,maʳk 'vurtsiç

Hofstadter
   Robert, *US physicist (Nobel 1961)*   HŌF-STAT-uhr, HAHF-, HAWF-   'hoːf,stæṭəʳ, 'haf-, 'hɔːf-

Hofstra
   University, *NY*   HAHF-struh, HAWF-struh   'hafstrə, 'hɔːfstrə

Hogan
   Ben, *US golfer, business executive*   HŌ-guhn   'hoːgən

Hogarth
   William, *English artist*   HŌ-GAHRTH   'hoː,gaʳθ

Hogmanay
   Dec. 31, Scotland   HAHG-muh-NĀ   'hagmə,neː

Hoh
   N. American people   HŌ   'hoː

Key (col. 2):   a: **fad** ā: **fade** ah: **father** ar: **Mary** aw: **law** e: **fed** ē: **feed** er: **merry** i: **hid** ī: **hide** ō: **coat** oo̅: **boot**
oi: **boy** ow: **now** u: **put** uh: **above** uhr: **bird** ch: **chop** ng: **ring** sh: **show** th: **thick** <u>th</u>: **this** zh: **measure**

Hohenzollern
  German royal family   HŌ-uhnt-SAWL-uhrn   ˈhoːənt͵sɔːləʳn

Hohe Tauern
  Alpine mtn. range   HŌ-uh TOW-uhrn   ͵hoːə ˈtauəʳn

Hohokam
  Park, stadium, Mesa, AZ   hō-HŌ-kuhm   hoːˈhoːkəm

Hojatolislam
  pers. name, Arabic   HŌ-yuh-TOO̅-lis-LAHM   ͵hoːjəˈtuːlis͵lɑm

Hokkaidō
  island, Japan   haw(k)-kī-dō, Ⓢ hah-KĪD-ō   hɔː(k)kaidoː, Ⓢ haˈkaidoː

Hokkien
  lang., China   HAWK-kē-EN   ˈhɔːkkiːˈen

Hokusai Katsushika
  Japanese artist   hō-kus-ī kaht-sush-ē-kah   hoːkusai katsuʃiːka

Hola
  Hindu festival   HŌ-lah   ˈhoːlɑ

Holbein
  Hans, Jr. & Sr., German painters   HŌL-BĪN, HAWL-BĪN   ˈhoːl͵bain, ˈhɔːl͵bain

Holbrook
  Hal, US actor   HŌL-BRUK   ˈhoːl͵bruk

Holder
  Geoffrey, West Indian dancer,   HŌL-duhr   ˈhoːldəʳ
    actor

Holi
  Hindu festival   HŌ-lē   ˈhoːliˑ

Holiness
  title of the pope   HŌ-lē-nuhs   ˈhoːliˑnəs

Holinshed
  Raphael, English chronicler   HAHL-uhn-SHED, HAHL-uhnz-HED   ˈhalən͵ʃed, ˈhalənz͵hed

Holland
  The Netherlands; town, MI   HAHL-uhnd   ˈhalənd

Hollandaise
  egg-based sauce   HAHL-uhn-DĀZ   ˈhalən͵deːz

Hollands
  Dutch gin   HAHL-uhndz   ˈhaləndz

Hollerith
  Herman, US inventor   HŌL-uh-rith   ˈhoːləriθ

Holley
  Robert W., US biochemist (Nobel   HAHL-ē   ˈhaliˑ
    1968)

Holliman
  Earl, US actor   HAHL-uh-muhn   ˈhaləmən

Hollings
  Earnest Frederick, US politician   HAHL-ingz   ˈhaliŋz

Hollins College
  town, college, VA   HAHL-uhnz   ˈhalənz

Hollis
  pers. name   HAHL-uhs   ˈhaləs

Hollister
  pers. name   HAHL-uhs-tuhr   ˈhaləstəʳ

Holloway
  Stanley, English entertainer   HAHL-uh-WĀ   ˈhalə͵weː

Holly
  pers. name   HAHL-ē   ˈhaliˑ

Foreign Sounds: **ue**: *Fr.* **rue**, *Ger.* **füllen**   **uh(r)**: *Fr.* **boeuf**, *Ger.* **Höhle**   **kh**: *Ger.* **ich**, *Scot.* **loch**   **ḡ**: *Sp.* **amigo**   **v̱**: *Sp.* **hablar**
hl: *Welsh* **Llanelli**.   CAPITALS: primary stress.   SMALL CAPS: secondary stress.   Ⓢ: U.S. pron.   Ⓣ: British pron.

Hollywood
> *city, CA; town, FL* — HAHL-ē-WUD — 'hali‧,wud

Holm
> Celeste, *US actress* — HŌM — 'hoːm

Holmes
> *pers. name* — HŌMZ — 'hoːmz

Holmes, Sherlock
> *fictional detective by A. Conan Doyle* — SHUHR-luhk HŌMZ, SHUHR-LAHK, HŌLMZ — 'ʃəᵣlək 'hoːmz, 'ʃəᵣ,lak, 'hoːlmz

holmium
> *element* — HŌ(L)-mē-uhm — 'hoː(l)miːəm

Holocene
> *geologic epoch* — HŌ-luh-SĒN, HAHL-uh- — 'hoːlə,siːn, 'halə-

Holofernes
> *1. Biblical general beheaded by Judith* — HAHL-uh-FUHR-NĒZ, HŌ-luh-FUHR-NĒZ — ,halə'fəᵣ,niːz, ,hoːlə'fəᵣ,niːz
> *2. schoolmaster in* Love's Labour's Lost, *Shakespeare* — HAHL-uh-FAHR-NĒZ, HŌ-luh-FAHR-NĒZ, -FUHR-NĒZ — ,halə'faᵣ,niːz, ,hoːlə'faᵣ,niːz, -'fəᵣ,niːz

Holstein
> *1. region, Germany* — HŌL-SHTĪN, ⑤ HŌL-STĪN, HŌL-STĒN — 'hoːl,ʃtain, ⑤ 'hoːl,stain, 'hoːl,stiːn
> *2. cattle* — HŌL-STĒN, HŌL-STĪN — 'hoːl,stiːn, 'hoːl,stain

Holyhead
> *town, Wales* — HAHL-ē-HED — 'hali‧,hed

Holyoke
> *city, MA* — HŌ-lē-ŌK, *locally* HŌ(L)-YŌK — 'hoːliː,oːk, *locally* 'hoː(l),joːk

Holy Rood
> *cross of Jesus* — HŌ-lē R̄OOD — ,hoːli‧ 'ruːd

Holyrood
> *royal palace, Scotland* — HAHL-ē-R̄OOD — 'hali‧,ruːd

Holy See
> *papal court* — HŌ-lē SĒ — ,hoːli‧ 'siː

Holywell
> *town, Wales* — HAHL-ē-WEL, HAHL-ē-wuhl — 'haliː,wel, 'hali‧wəl

Homburg
> *city, Germany* — HAWM-BURK, ⑤ HAHM-BUHRG — 'hɔːm,buᵣk, ⑤ 'ham,bəᵣg

Home
> Earls of, *English family* — HYŌ͞OM — 'hjuːm

Homer
> *Greek epic poet; pers. name* — HŌ-muhr — 'hoːməᵣ

Homeric
> *pert. to* Homer — hō-MER-ik — hoː'merik

Homerton
> *society, Cambridge Univ.* — HAHM-uhrt-n — 'haməᵣtn̩

Homoousian
> *adherent of or pert. to the doctrine of the Nicene creed* — HŌ-mō-O͞O-sē-uhn, HŌ-mō-O͞O-zh(ē-)uhn — ,hoːmoː'uːsiːən, ,hoːmoː'uːʒ(iː)ən

Homo sapiens
> *human being* — HŌ-mō SAP-ē-uhnz, SĀ-pē-uhnz — ,hoːmoː 'sæpiːənz, 'seːpiːənz

Honan [Henan, Luoyang]
> *prov., town, China* — HUH-NAHN, ⑤ HŌ-NAHN — 'hə'nan, ⑤ 'hoː'nan

Honda
> *Japanese car co.* — HAHN-duh — 'handə

Honduran
> *pert. to* Honduras — hahn-D(Y)UR-uhn — han'd(j)urən

Key (col. 2):   a: fad   ā: fade   ah: father   ar: Mary   aw: law   e: fed   ē: feed   'er: merry   i: hid   ī: hide   ō: coat   o͞o: boot
oi: boy   ow: now   u: put   uh: above   uhr: bird   ch: chop   ng: ring   sh: show   th: thick   t͟h: this   zh: measure

Honduras
   republic, Cen. America   hahn-D(Y)UR-uhs   hɑn'd(j)urəs

Honecker
   Erich, *East German politician*   HŌ-nuh-kuhr   'hoːnəkəʳ

Honegger
   Arthur, *Swiss composer*   aw-nā-GER   ɔːneːger

Honeywell
   US corp.   HUHN-ē-WEL   'həniˑˌwel

Hong Kong
   British colony, SE Asia   HAHNG-KAHNG, HAHNG-KAHNG,   'haŋˌkaŋ, 'haŋ'kaŋ,
                       HAWNG-KAWNG, HAWNG-KAWNG   'hɔːŋˌkɔːŋ, 'hɔːŋ'kɔːŋ

Honiara
   town, Solomon Islands   HŌ-nē-AHR-uh   ˌhoːniˑ'ɑrə

Honolulu
   county, city, HI   HAHN-l-OO-loo, HŌN-l-OO-loo   ˌhɑnl'uːluː, ˌhoːnl'uːluː

Honor
   pers. name   AHN-uhr   'ɑnəʳ

Honorat
   pers. name, French   aw-naw-RAH   ɔːnɔːrɑː

Honoré
   1. pers. name   AHN-uh-RĀ, AHN-uh-RĀ   ˌɑnə'reː, 'ɑnəˌreː
   2. French   aw-naw-RĀ   ɔːnɔːreː

Honorius
   pope; pers. name, Latin   hō-NŌR-ē-uhs, huh-, -NAWR-ē-uhs   hoː'noːriːəs, hə-, -'nɔːriːəs

Honshū
   island, Japan   hawn-shoo, Ⓢ HAHN-shoo   hɔːnʃuː, Ⓢ 'hɑnʃuː

Hooch, Hoogh
   Pieter de, *Dutch painter*   HŌKH   'hoːx

Hooghly
   river, India   HOO-glē   'huːgliˑ

Hookham
   pers. name   HUK-uhm   'hukəm

Hoonah
   city, AK   HOO-nuh   'huːnə

Hoopa
   N. American people   HOO-puh, HUP-uh   'huːpə, 'hupə

Hoosier
   someone from Indiana   HOO-zhuhr   'huːʒəʳ

Hoover
   Herbert, *31st US president*   HOO-vuhr   'huːvəʳ

Hooverville
   Depression shantytown   HOO-vuhr-VIL   'huːvəʳˌvil

Hope
   town, AR; pers. name   HŌP   'hoːp

Hopeh [Hebei]
   prov, China   HUH-BĀ, Ⓢ HŌ-BĀ, HŌ-PĀ   'hə'beː, Ⓢ 'hoː'beː, 'hoː'peː

Hopfenperle
   Swiss beer   HAWP-fuhn-PER-luh   'hɔːpfən,peʳlə

Hopi
   N. American people   HŌ-pē   'hoːpiˑ

Hopkins
   Sir Frederick G., *English*   HAHP-kuhnz, -kinz   'hɑpkənz, -kinz
   biochemist (Nobel 1929); Gerard
   Manley, *English poet;* Johns, *US*
   financier

Foreign Sounds: ue: *Fr.* **rue**, *Ger.* **füllen**   uh(r): *Fr.* **boeuf**, *Ger.* **Höhle**   kh: *Ger.* **ich**, *Scot.* **loch**   g̃: *Sp.* **amigo**   v̱: *Sp.* **hablar**
hl: *Welsh* **Llanelli**.   CAPITALS: primary stress.   SMALL CAPS: secondary stress.   Ⓢ: U.S. pron.   Ⓛ: British pron.

Hopkinsianism
Christian sect   hahp-KIN-zē-uh-NIZ-uhm   hap'kinziːəˌnizəm

Hoplite
Greek heavy-armed soldier   HAHP-LĪT   'hapˌlait

Hopper
Dennis, *US actor, writer, film director*   HAHP-uhr   'hapəʳ

Hor
Egyptian god, aspect of Horus   HAWR   'hɔːʳ

Hora, Horah
Israeli and Romanian dance   HŌR-uh, HAWR-uh   'hoːrə, 'hɔːrə

Horace
1. Roman poet; pers. name   HAWR-uhs, HAHR-uhs   'hɔːrəs, 'harəs
2. French   aw-RAHS   ɔːrɑːs

Horae
Greek goddesses of the seasons   HŌR-Ē, HAWR-Ē, HŌR-Ī, HAWR-Ī   'hoːrˌiː, 'hɔːrˌiː, 'hoːrˌai, 'hɔːrˌai

Horatian
pert. to Horace   huh-RĀ-shuhn   hə'reːʃən

Horatii
legendary Roman heros   huh-RĀ-shē-Ē   hə'reːʃiːˌiː

Horatio
pers. name   huh-RĀ-sh(ē-)ō   hə'reːʃ(iː)oː

Horatius
pers. name   huh-RĀ-sh(ē-)uhs   hə'reːʃ(iː)əs

Horeb [Sinai]
mtn., Sinai peninsula   HŌR-EB, HAWR-EB   'hoːrˌeb, 'hɔːrˌeb

Horlicks
tdmk for a malted milk powder   HAWR-liks   'hɔːʳliks

Hormel
US food products co.   hawr-MEL   hɔːʳ'mel

Hormisdas
pope   hawr-MIZ-duhs   hɔːʳ'mizdəs

Hormuz
strait, Persian Gulf   HAWR-muhz, hawr-MŌŌZ   'hɔːʳməz, hɔːʳ'muːz

Hornblende
mineral   HAWRN-BLEND   'hɔːʳnˌblend

Hornsby
Bruce, *singer, songwriter*   HAWRNZ-bē   'hɔːʳnzbiˑ

Hornung
Paul, *sports personality*   HAWR-nuhng   'hɔːʳnəŋ

Horologium
constellation   HAWR-uh-LŌ-jē-uhm   ˌhɔːrə'loːdʒiːəm

Horovitz
Israel Arthur, *US playwright*   HAWR-uh-VITS, HAHR-uh-VITS   'hɔːrəˌvits, 'harəˌvits

Horowitz
Vladimir, *Russian pianist*   HAWR-uh-WITS, HAHR-uh-WITS   'hɔːrəˌwits, 'harəˌwits

Horry
county, SC   ō-RĒ, HAWR-ē   oː'riː, 'hɔːriˑ

Horsa
Jutish chief; British WWII glider   HAWR-suh   'hɔːʳsə

Horsley
pers. name   HAWRZ-lē, HAWRS-lē   'hɔːʳzliˑ, 'hɔːʳsliˑ

Horst
pers. name, German   HAWRST   'hɔːʳst

Key (col. 2):   a: fad   ā: fade   ah: father   ar: Mary   aw: law   e: fed   ē: feed   er: merry   i: hid   ī: hide   ō: coat   ō͞o: boot
oi: boy   ow: now   u: put   uh: above   uhr: bird   ch: chop   ng: ring   sh: show   th: thick   th̲: this   zh: measure

Horsted Keynes
  village, England HAWR-stuhd KĀNZ ˌhɔːʳstəd 'keːnz
Horst Wessel
  Nazi official song HAWRST VES-uhl 'hɔːʳst 'vesəl
Hortense
  1. pers. name HAWR-TENS, HAWR-TENS ˌhɔːʳtens, 'hɔːʳˌtens
  2. French awr-TAHⁿS ɔːrtãs
Hortensian Law
  Roman plebiscite law hawr-TEN-sē-uhn, -TEN-shuhn hɔːʳ'tensiːən, -'tenʃən
Hortensius
  Roman name hawr-TEN(T)-sē-uhs, hɔːʳ'ten(t)siːəs, hɔːʳ'tentʃəs
            hawr-TEN-chuhs
Horus
  Egyptian sun god HŌR-uhs, HAWR-uhs 'hoːrəs, 'hɔːrəs
Hosea
  biblical prophet, Old Testament hō-ZĀ-uh, hō-ZĒ-uh hoː'zeːə, hoː'ziːə
    book
Hosni
  pers. name, Arabic HAWS-nē 'hɔːsniˑ
Hostius
  husband of Hersilia HAHS-tē-uhs, HAHS-ch(ē-)uhs 'hɑstiːəs, 'hɑstʃ(iː)əs
Hostos
  Community College, *NY* Ō-stōs 'oːstoːs
Hoth
  Scandinavian god HAWTH 'hɔːθ
Hotpoint
  tdmk for home appliances HAHT-POINT 'hɑtˌpɔint
Hottentot
  S. African people HAHT-n-TAHT 'hɑtn̩ˌtɑt
Houdini
  Harry, *US magician* hoo-DĒ-nē huː'diːniˑ
Hough
  Emerson, *US novelist* HUHF 'həf
Houghton
  1. county, MI; college, NY HŌT-n 'hoːtn̩
  2. pers. name HŌT-n, HOWT-n, HAWT-n 'hoːtn̩, 'hautn̩, 'hɔːtn̩
Houghton Mifflin
  US publishing house HŌT-n MIF-luhn ˌhoːtn̩ 'miflən
Houma
  city, LA HŌ-muh, HOO-muh 'hoːmə, 'huːmə
Hounsfield
  Godfrey Newbold, *English* HOWNZ-FĒLD 'haunzˌfiːld
    electrical engineer (Nobel 1979)
Hounslow
  borough, England HOWNZ-lō 'haunzloː
Housatonic
  river, MA, CT HOO-suh-TAHN-ik, HOO-zuh- ˌhuːsə'tɑnik, ˌhuːzə-
Housman
  A.E., *British poet, scholar* HOW-smuhn 'hausmən
Houssay
  B. A., *Argentine physiologist* oo-SĪ uː'sai
    (Nobel 1947)

Foreign Sounds: ue: *Fr.* **rue**, *Ger.* füllen uh(r): *Fr.* **boeuf**, *Ger.* Höhle kh: *Ger.* i**ch**, *Scot.* lo**ch** g̃: *Sp.* ami**g**o v̲: *Sp.* ha**b**lar
hl: *Welsh* **Ll**anelli. CAPITALS: primary stress. SMALL CAPS: secondary stress. Ⓢ: U.S. pron. Ⓑ: British pron.

Houston
1. *pers. name*   (H)Y$\overline{OO}$-stuhn, H$\overline{OO}$-stuhn   '(h)juːstən, 'huːstən
2. Sam, *president of TX; pl. name,*   (H)Y$\overline{OO}$-stuhn   '(h)juːstən
     US
3. *street, New York City; county,*   HOWS-tuhn   'haustən
     GA

Houyhnhnms
     race of intelligent horses in   H$\overline{OO}$-uh-nuhmz, HWIN-uhmz,   'huːənəmz, 'hwinəmz,
     Gulliver's Travels, *J. Swift*   h$\overline{oo}$-IN-uhmz   huː'inəmz

Hovey
     pers. name   HUHV-ē   'həviˑ

Howard
     pers. name   HOW-uhrd   'hauəʳd

Howe
     Gordon, *Canadian hockey player*   HOW   'hau

Howell
     pers. name   HOW(-uh)l   'hau(ə)l

Howie
     pers. name   HOW-ē   'hauiˑ

Howland
     Island, *Pacific Ocean*   HOW-luhnd   'haulənd

Hoyle
     card game rules; Fred, *English*   HOIL   'hɔil
     astronomer

Hoyt
     Dewey Lamarr, *baseball player;*   HOIT   'hɔit
     pers. name

Hrvatska [Croatia]
     republic, E. Europe   huhr-VAHT-skah   həʳ'vatskɑ

Hsi
     see Xi

Hsia-men
     see Xiamen

Hsi Chiang
     see Xi Jiang

Hsin-hsiang
     see Xinxiang

Hsining
     see Xining

Hsüan Chiao
     Taoism   shue-AHN JOW   ʃyˈan 'dʒau

Huachuca
     Fort, *AZ*   wah-CH$\overline{OO}$-kuh   wɑ'tʃuːkə

Hua Guofeng, Hua Kuo-feng
     Chinese premier   HWAH GW$\overline{O}$-FUHNG   'hwɑ 'gwoː'fəŋ

Hualapai
     N. American people   WAHL-uh-PĪ   'wɑlə,pai

Huang He [Huang Ho]
     river, China   HWAHNG HUH   'hwɑŋ 'hə

Huang Ho, Hwang Ho
     river, China   HWAHNG HUH, HWAHNG H$\overline{O}$ 'hwɑŋ 'hə, 'hwɑŋ 'hoː

Huang-ti
     "Yellow Emperor" of China   HWAHNG-D$\overline{E}$ 'hwɑŋ'diː

Huascarán
     mtn., Peru   WAHS-kuh-RAHN   ,wɑskə'ran

Key (col. 2):   a: **fad**   ā: **fade**   ah: **father**   ar: **Mary**   aw: **law**   e: **fed**   ē: **feed**   er: **merry**   i: **hid**   ī: **hide**   ō: **coat** $\overline{oo}$: **boot**
oi: **boy**   ow: **now**   u: **put**   uh: **above**   uhr: **bird**   ch: **chop**   ng: **ring**   sh: **show**   th: **thick**   <u>th</u>: **this**   zh: **measure**

Huastec
  lang., Mexico   WAHS-TEK   'wɑs,tek

Huave
  lang., people, Mexico   WAHV-ē   'wɑviˑ

Hubble
  Edwin, *US astronomer; space*   HUHB-uhl   'həbəl
  telescope

Hubbs
  pers. name   HUHBZ   'həbz

Hubei, Hupeh
  prov, China   HOO-BĀ   'huː'beː

Hubel
  David H., *Canadian-born US*   (H)YOO-buhl   '(h)juːbəl
  neurophysiologist (Nobel 1981)

Huber
  Robert, *German chemist (Nobel*   HOO-buhr   'huːbəʳ
  1988)

Hubert
  1. *pers. name*   HYOO-buhrt   'hjuːbəʳt
  2. *Dutch*   HUE-buhrt   'hyːbərt
  3. *French*   ue-BER   yːber
  4. *German*   HOO-BERT   'huː,beʳt

Huck
  nickname for Huckleberry Finn   HUHK   'hək

Huckleberry Finn
  character, novel by Mark Twain   HUHK-uhl-BER-ē FIN   'həkəl,beriˑ 'fin

Huddie
  pers. name   HUHD-ē   'hədiˑ

Huddleston
  Walter Darlington, *US politician*   HUHD-l-stuhn   'hədl̩stən

Hudibras
  poem, S. Butler   HYOOD-uh-BRAHS   'hjuːdə,brɑs

Hudnut
  William Herbert III, *US politician*   HUHD-NUHT   'həd,nət

Hudson
  Henry, *English navigator; river,*   HUHD-suhn   'hədsən
  NY; bay, strait, Canada

Hué
  town, Vietnam   h(y)oo-Ā, (H)WĀ   h(j)uː'eː, '(h)weː

Huelva
  prov, Spain   WEL-ṿah, Ⓢ WEL-vuh   'welβɑ, Ⓢ 'welvə

Huerfano
  river, county, CO   AWR-fuh-NŌ, WUHR-fuh-NŌ,   'ɔːʳfə,noː, 'wəʳfə,noː,
                         WER-fuh-NŌ   'weʳfə,noː

Huerta
  Victoriano, *Mexican politician*   WER-tah   'weʳtɑ

Huesca
  prov, Spain   WES-kah   'weskɑ

Huey
  pers. name   HYOO-ē   'hjuːiˑ

Huggins
  Charles Brenton, *Canadian-born*   HUHG-uhnz   'həgənz
  US surgeon (Nobel 1966)

Hugh
  pers. name   HYOO   'hjuː

Foreign Sounds: ue: *Fr.* **rue**, *Ger.* **füllen** uh(r): *Fr.* **boeuf**, *Ger.* **Höhle** <u>kh</u>: *Ger.* **ich**, *Scot.* **loch** ḡ: *Sp.* **amigo** ṿ: *Sp.* **hablar**
hl: *Welsh* **Llanelli**. CAPITALS: primary stress. SMALL CAPS: secondary stress. Ⓢ: U.S. pron. Ⓒ: British pron.

Hugh Capet
 king of France   UEG kah-PE, ⑤ HYO͞O KĀ-puht,   yːg kɑːpe, ⑤ 'hjuː 'keːpət,
              KAP-uht, ka-PĀ   'kæpət, kæ'peː

Hughes
 Langston, US writer; pers. name   HYO͞OZ, YO͞OZ   'hjuːz, 'juːz

Hughes Hall
 society, Cambridge Univ.   HYO͞OZ HAWL   ˌhjuːz 'hɔːl

Hugo
 1. science fiction award; pers.   HYO͞O-gō   'hjuːgoː
  name
 2. Dutch   HUE-gō   'hyːgoː
 3. Finnish   HUG-ō   'hugoː
 4. German, Swedish   HO͞O-gō   'huːgoː
 5. Polish   HO͞O-gaw   'huːgɔː

Huguenot
 French Protestant sect   HYO͞O-guh-NAHT   'hjuːgə,nɑt

Huguenotism
 beliefs of the Huguenots   HYO͞O-guh-NAHT-IZ-uhm   'hjuːgə,nɑt,izəm

Hugues
 pers. name, French   UEG   yːg

Hui
 pers. name, Chinese   HO͞O-ē, HWĒ   'huːiˑ, 'hwiː

Huidzong, Hui-tsung
 Chinese emperor   HWĀD-ZUNG   'hweːd'zuŋ

Huie
 William Bradford, author   HYO͞O-ē   'hjuːiˑ

Huig
 pers. name, Dutch   HOIG̃   'hɔiɣ

Huila
 volcano, dept, Columbia   WĒ-lah   'wiːlɑ

Hui-tsung
 see Huidzong

Huizenga
 H. Wayne, US entrepreneur   (H)WĒ-zing-uh, HOI-zing-uh   '(h)wiːziŋə, 'hɔiziŋə

Huizinga
 Johan, Dutch scholar   HOI-zing-uh, ⑤ (H)WĒ-zing-uh   'hɔiziŋə, ⑤ '(h)wiːziŋə

Hull
 Cordell, US statesman (Nobel   HUHL   'həl
  1945); city, England

Hulme
 Thomas, English critic   HYO͞OM, YO͞OM   'hjuːm, 'juːm

Humbard
 Rex, US TV evangelist   HUHM-BAHRD   'həm,bɑʳd

Humber
 estuary, England; river, Canada   HUHM-buhr   'həmbəʳ

Humberside
 county, England   HUHM-buhr-SĪD   'həmbəʳ,said

Humberto
 pers. name, Portuguese   o͞om-BER-to͞o   ũːm'bertuː, uːm-

Humboldt
 1. Alexander von, German   HUM-BAWLT, ⑤ HUHM-BŌLT   'hum,bɔːlt, ⑤ 'həm,boːlt
  naturalist
 2. State University, CA; US pl.   HUHM-BŌLT   'həm,boːlt
  name

Key (col. 2): a: fad ā: fade ah: father ar: Mary aw: law e: fed ē: feed er: merry i: hid ī: hide ō: coat o͞o: boot
oi: boy ow: now u: put uh: above uhr: bird ch: chop ng: ring sh: show th: thick th̲: this zh: measure

Humboldtianum, Mare
 see Mare Humboldtianum

Humboldt penguin
 bird   HUHM-BŌLT PEN-gwuhn,   'həm,boːlt 'peŋgwən,
         PENG-gwuhn   'peŋgwən

Hume
 David, *Scottish philosopher; pers.*   HYO͞OM   'hjuːm
    name

Humorum, Mare
 see Mare Humorum

Humperdinck
 1. Engelbert, *German composer*   HUM-puhr-DINGK,   'humpəʳ,diŋk,
         HUHM-puhr-DINGK   'həmpəʳ,diŋk
 2. Engelbert, *US entertainer*   HUHM-puhr-DINGK   'həmpəʳ,diŋk

Humphrey
 Hubert, *US politician; pers. name*   HUHM(P)-frē   'həm(p)friˑ

Humpty Dumpty
 Mother Goose character   HUHM(P)-tē DUHM(P)-tē   ˌhəm(p)tiˑ 'dəm(p)tiˑ

Hunan
 prov., China   HO͞O-NAHN   'huːˈnɑn

Hungarian [Magyar]
 lang., people, Hungary   huhng-GAR-ē-uhn,   həŋ'gæriːən, həŋ'geriːən
         huhng-GER-ē-uhn

Hungary
 republic, Europe   HUHNG-g(uh-)rē   'həŋg(ə)riˑ

Hungnam
 port, N. Korea   hung-nahm   huŋnɑm

Hunsa
 lang., Africa   HUHN-suh   'hənsə

Huntingdonshire
 former county, England   HUHNT-ing-duhn-shuhr, -SHIR   'həntiŋdənʃəʳ, -ˌʃiʳ

Huntington
 Henry Edwards, *US railway*   HUHNT-ing-tuhn   'həntiŋtən
    executive & art collector;
    museum, library, CA

Huot
 pers. name, French   ue-Ō   yːoː

Hupa
 N. American people   HO͞O-puh   'huːpə

Hupeh
 see Hubei

Hural
 upper house of Mongolian   (H)YUR-uhl, (h)yur-AHL   '(h)jurəl, (h)jur'ɑl
    Parliament

Hurley
 Kathy, *actress, playwright*   HUHR-lē   'həʳliˑ

Hürlimann Stern
 Swiss beer   HUR-li-MAHN SHTERN   'hyʳliˌmɑn 'ʃteʳn

Huron
 pl. name, lake, people, N. America   (H)YUR-uhn, (H)YUR-AHN   '(h)jurən, '(h)jurˌɑn

Hurrians
 ancient Middle Eastern people   HUR-ē-uhnz   'huriːənz

Hurstmonceux
 see Herstmonceux

Foreign Sounds: **ue**: *Fr.* **rue**, *Ger.* f**ü**llen   **uh(r)**: *Fr.* b**oeu**f, *Ger.* H**ö**hle   <u>**kh**</u>: *Ger.* i**ch**, *Scot.* lo**ch**   ḡ: *Sp.* ami**g**o   <u>v</u>: *Sp.* ha**b**lar
hl: *Welsh* **Ll**anelli.   CAPITALS: primary stress.   SMALL CAPS: secondary stress.   ⑤: U.S. pron.   Ⓔ: British pron.

Hus, Huss		
Jan, *Czech religious reformer*	HO͞OS, Ⓢ HUS, HUHS	'huːs, Ⓢ 'hus, 'həs
Husák		
Gustav, *Czech politician*	H(Y)O͞O-sahk	'h(j)uːsɑk
Husch		
Vineyards, *winery, CA*	HUHSH	'həʃ
Hussein		
1. Ibrahim, *Kenyan marathoner; Jordanian king;* Saddam, *president, Iraq*	ho͞o-SĀN, hu-SĀN	huː'seːn, hu'seːn
2. pers. name, Turkish	hue-SĀN	hyː'seːn
Husserl		
Edmund, *German philosopher*	HUHS-uhrl	'həsə^{r}l
Hussite		
adherent of Hussitism	HUHS-ĪT, HUS-ĪT	'həs,ɑit, 'hus,ɑit
Hussitism		
movement begun by Hus	HUHS-uht-IZ-uhm, HUS-	'həsəṭ,izəm, 'hus-
Hussong's		
Mexican beer	HUS-AWNGZ, HO͞O-SAWNGZ	'hus,ɔːŋz, 'huː,sɔːŋz
Huston		
John, Walter, & Anjelica, *US entertainers*	(H)YO͞OS-tuhn	'(h)juːstən
Huston-Tillotson		
College, *TX*	(H)YO͞O-stuhn-TIL-uht-suhn	'(h)juːstən'tilətsən
Huszt [Khust]		
town, Ukraine	HUST	'hust
Hutterites		
Anabaptist sect	HUHT-uhr-ĪTS	'həṭə^{r},ɑits
Huw		
pers. name, Welsh	HYO͞O	'hjuː
Huxley		
Aldous, *English writer;* Andrew Fielding, *English physiologist (Nobel 1963);* Thomas Henry, *English biologist*	HUHKS-lē	'həksliˑ
Hu Yaobang		
Chinese Communist leader	HO͞O YOW-BAHNG	'huː 'jɑu'bɑŋ
Huygens		
Christian, *Dutch mathematician*	HĪ-guhnz, HOI-guhnz	'hɑigənz, 'hɔigənz
Hwang Hai		
sea, China	HWAHNG HĪ	'hwɑŋ 'hɑi
Hwang Ho		
see Huang Ho		
Hyacinthe		
pers. name, French	yah-SE^{n}T	jɑːsɛ̃t
Hyacinthids		
girls sacrificed for Athens	HĪ-uh-SIN-thidz	,hɑiə'sinθidz
Hyacinthus		
beloved of Apollo	HĪ-uh-SIN-thuhs	,hɑiə'sinθəs
Hyades		
nymphs who nursed Dionysus; star cluster in Taurus	HĪ-uh-DĒZ	'hɑiə,diːz
Hyannis		
town, MA; village, NE	hī-AN-uhs	hɑi'ænəs

Key (col. 2): a: **fad** ā: **fade** ah: **father** ar: **Mary** aw: **law** e: **fed** ē: **feed** er: **merry** i: **hid** ī: **hide** ō: **coat** o͞o: **boot** oi: **boy** ow: **now** u: **put** uh: **above** uhr: **bird** ch: **chop** ng: **ring** sh: **show** th: **thick** th: **this** zh: **measure**

Hyas
    brother of the Pleiades and   HĪ-uhs   'haiəs
    Hyades

Hyatt
    US hotel chain   HĪ-uht   'haiət

Hybris
    personification of insolence, hubris   HĪ-bruhs, HĒ-bruhs   'haibrəs, 'hiːbrəs

Hydaburg
    city, AK   HĪD-uh-BUHRG   'haidə‚bərg

Hyde
    pers. name   HĪD   'haid

Hyderabad
    city, India   HĪD(-uh)-ruh-BAD, -BAHD   'haid(ə)rə‚bæd, -‚bad

Hydra
    island, Greece; constellation;   HĪ-druh   'haidrə
    nine-headed monster killed by
    Heracles

hydrogen
    element   HĪ-druh-juhn   'haidrədʒən

Hydrus
    constellation   HĪ-druhs   'haidrəs

Hygeia, Hygiea
    Greek goddess of health   hī-JĒ-(y)uh   hai'dʒiː(j)ə

Hyginus
    pope   huh-JĪ-nuhs   hə'dʒainəs

Hyksos
    ancient nomadic people in Egypt   HIK-SŌS, -SAHS   'hik‚soːs, -‚sas

Hylaeus
    Arcadian centaur   HĪ-lē-uhs   'hailiːəs

Hylas
    legendary youth, accompanied   HĪ-luhs, HĒ-luhs   'hailəs, 'hiːləs
    Heracles on the Argo

Hyllus
    son of Heracles   HIL-uhs   'hiləs

Hyman
    Phyllis, *soul singer; pers. name*   HĪ-muhn   'haimən

Hymen
    Greek god of marriage; pers.   HĪ-muhn   'haimən
    name

Hymenaeus
    Greek personification of marriage;   HĪ-muh-NĒ-uhs, HĪ-muh-NĀ-uhs   ‚haimə'niːəs, ‚haimə'neːəs
    Greek marriage song

Hymettus
    mtn., Greece   hī-MET-uhs   hai'meţəs

Hymie
    pers. name   HĪ-mē   'haimiˑ

Hymnus
    Phrygian shepherd in Greek   HIM-nuhs   'himnəs
    mythology

Hypatia
    Greek philosopher   hī-PĀ-shuh   hai'peːʃə

Hyperboreans
    mythical northern race   HĪ-puhr-BŌR-ē-uhns, -BAWR-ē-uhns   ‚haipərˈboːriːənz, -'bɔːriːənz

---

Foreign Sounds: **ue:** *Fr.* **rue,** *Ger.* **füllen**   **uh(r):** *Fr.* **boeuf,** *Ger.* **Höhle**   **kh:** *Ger.* **ich,** *Scot.* **loch**   **ḡ:** *Sp.* **amigo**   **v:** *Sp.* **hablar**
hl: *Welsh* **Llanelli.**   CAPITALS: primary stress.   SMALL CAPS: secondary stress.   Ⓢ: U.S. pron.   Ⓛ: British pron.

Hyperion
   poem, Keats; titan in Greek   hī-PIR-ē-uhn   haiˈpiriːən
     mythology; satellite of Saturn
Hypermestra
   daughter of King Danaus   HĪ-puhr-MES-truh   ˌhaipəʳˈmestrə
Hypermnestra [Hypermestra]
   daughter of King Danaus   HĪ-puhrm-NES-truh   ˌhaipəʳmˈnestrə
Hypnus
   Greek god of sleep   HIP-nuhs   ˈhipnəs
Hypolite
   pers. name, French   ē-paw-LĒT   iːpɔːliːt
Hypsilophodon
   dinosaur   HIP-suh-LAHF-uh-DAHN   ˌhipsəˈlafəˌdan
Hypsipyle
   mistress of Jason   hip-SIP-uh-lē   hipˈsipəliˑ
Hypsistarianism
   Asian religious sect   HIP-suh-STAR-ē-uh-NIZ-uhm,   ˌhipsəˈstæriːəˌnizəm,
                     -STER-ē-uh-NIZ-uhm   -ˈsteriːəˌnizəm
Hyracoidea
   hyraxes   HĪ-ruh-KOID-ē-uh   ˌhairəˈkɔidiːə
Hyrax
   mammal   HĪ-RAKS   ˈhaiˌræks
Hyrcania
   ancient Persian province   HUHR-KĀ-nē-uh   ˌhəʳˈkeːniːə
Hyrieus
   father of Orion   HĪ-rē-uhs, hī-RĒ-uhs   ˈhairiːəs, haiˈriːəs
Hyundai
   Korean car co.   HUHN-DĀ   ˈhənˌdeː

I

Iacchus
   god of the Eleusian mysteries   ī-AK-uhs   aiˈækəs
Iacocca
   Lee A., *US businessman*   Ī-uh-KŌ-kuh   ˌaiəˈkoːkə
Iacopo
   pers. name, Italian   YAHK-ō-pō   ˈjakoːpoː
Iago
   1. character in Othello,   ē-AHG-ō   iːˈagoː
     Shakespeare
   2. pers. name, Welsh   YAHG-ō   ˈjagoː
Ialemus
   personification of the funeral dirge   ī-AL-uh-muhs   aiˈæləməs
Ialmenus
   Argonaut, suitor of Helen   ī-al-MĒ-nuhs, ī-al-MEN-uhs   ˌaiælˈmiːnəs, ˌaiælˈmenəs

Key (col. 2):   a: fad   ā: fade   ah: father   ar: Mary   aw: law   e: fed   ē: feed   er: merry   i: hid   ī: hide   ō: coat   o͞o: boot
oi: boy   ow: now   u: put   uh: above   uhr: bird   ch: chop   ng: ring   sh: show   th: thick   <u>th</u>: this   zh: measure

Iambe
  daughter of Pan and Echo ī-AM-bē ɑiˈæmbiˈ
Iamus
  mythical founder of Olympic ī-Ā-muhs, ī-AM-uhs ɑiˈeːməs, ɑiˈæməs
    games
Ian
  pers. name Ē-uhn ˈiːən
Iapetus
  Titan, father of Atlas and ī-AP-uht-uhs, ē-AP-uht-uhs ɑiˈæpətəs, iːˈæpətəs
    Prometheus; satellite of Saturn
Iapyx
  Cretan hero ī-Ā-piks ɑiˈeːpiks
Iarbas
  African king who loved Queen ī-AHR-buhs ɑiˈɑʳbəs
    Dido
Iasion
  son of Zeus and Electra ī-Ā-sē-uhn ɑiˈeːsiːən
Iasus
  king of Argos ī-Ā-suhs ɑiˈeːsəs
Ibadan
  city, Africa ē-BAHD-n iːˈbɑdn̩
Ibadhi [Islam]
  religion uh-BAHD-ē əˈbɑdiˈ
Ibanag
  lang., people, Philippine Islands Ē-buh-NAHG, Ē-buh-NAHG ˈiːbəˌnɑg, ˌiːbəˈnɑg
Iberia
  parish, LA; peninsula, Spain, ī-BIR-ē-uh ɑiˈbiriːə
    Portugal; airline, Spain
Iberian
  Peninsula, *Europe* ī-BIR-ē-uhn ɑiˈbiriːən
Ibis
  shore bird Ī-buhs ˈɑibəs
Ibiza, Iviza
  island, Mediterranean ē-V̲Ē-thah, ē-V̲Ē-sah, i-VĒ-thuh, iːˈβiːθa, iːˈβiːsa, iˈviːθə,
    Ⓢ ē-V̲Ē-zuh Ⓢ iːˈviːzə
Ibiza hound
  breed of dog i-VĒ-thuh iˈviːθə
Iblis
  Devil IB-luhs ˈibləs
Ibn Saud
  king, Saudi Arabia IB-uhn sah-O͞OD ˌibən sɑˈuːd
Ibo [Igbo]
  lang., people, Nigeria Ē-bō ˈiːboː
Ibrahim
  pers. name, Turkish IB-rah-HIM ˌibrɑˈhim
Ibsen
  Henrik, *Norwegian author* IP-suhn, Ⓢ IB-suhn ˈipsən, Ⓢ ˈibsən
Icadius
  son of Apollo and Lycia i-KĀD-ē-uhs, ī-KĀD-ē-uhs iˈkeːdiːəs, ɑiˈkeːdiːəs
Icahn
  Carl, *US businessman* Ī-KAHN ˈɑiˌkɑn
Icaria
  ancient name of Ikaria ī-KER-ē-uh, ī-KAR-ē-uh, ik-ER-ē-uh, ɑiˈkeriːə, ɑiˈkæriːə, ikˈeriːə,
    ik-AR-ē-uh ikˈæriːə

Foreign Sounds: ue: *Fr.* **rue**, *Ger.* **füllen** uh(r): *Fr.* **boeuf**, *Ger.* **Höhle** <u>kh</u>: *Ger.* i**ch**, *Scot.* lo**ch** ḡ: *Sp.* ami**g**o v̲: *Sp.* ha**b**lar
hl: *Welsh* **Ll**anelli. CAPITALS: primary stress. SMALL CAPS: secondary stress. Ⓢ: U.S. pron. Ⓛ: British pron.

Icarius
  father of Penelope   i-KAR-ē-uhs, ī-KAR-ē-uhs   iˈkæriːəs, aiˈkæriːəs
Icarus
  son of Daedalus   IK-uh-ruhs   ˈikərəs
Iceland
  island country, Atlantic   Ī-sluhnd   ˈaislənd
Icelander
  inhabitant of Iceland   Ī-sluhn-duhr, Ī-SLAN-duhr   ˈaisləndəʳ, ˈai‚slændəʳ
Icelandic
  lang., Iceland   ī-SLAN-dik   aiˈslændik
Iceni
  ancient Celtic tribe   ī-SĒ-nē   aiˈsiːniˑ
Ichabod
  pers. name   IK-uh-BAHD   ˈikə‚bad
I Ching
  ancient Chinese book   Ē JING, Ⓢ ē CHING   ˈiː ˈdʒiŋ, Ⓢ iː ˈtʃiŋ
Ichiro
  pers. name, Japanese   ē-chē-rō   iːtʃiːroː
Ichitaro
  pers. name, Japanese   ē-chē-tahr-ō   iːtʃiːtaroː
Ichthyocentaurs
  fish centaurs   IK-thē-ō-SEN-TAWRZ   ‚ikθiːoːˈsen‚tɔːʳz
Ida
  mtn., Turkey; county, IA;   ĪD-uh   ˈaidə
    guardian of Zeus; pers. name
Idaho
  state, US   ĪD-uh-HŌ   ˈaidə‚hoː
Idahoan
  pert. to Idaho   ĪD-uh-HŌ-uhn   ˈaidə‚hoːən
'Id al-Adha
  Islamic festival   ID ahl-AH<u>TH</u>-ah   ˈidalˈaða
'Id al-Fitr
  Islamic festival   ID ahl-FIT-uhr   ˈidalˈfitər
Idas
  Argonaut, killer of Castor   ĪD-uhs, ĒD-uhs   ˈaidəs, ˈiːdəs
Idd
  Moslem festival   ĒD   ˈiːd
Idhra [Hydra]
  island, Greece   Ē-<u>th</u>rah   ˈiːðra
Idi
  pers. name (I. Amin)   ID-ē, ĒD-ē   ˈidiˑ, ˈiːdiˑ
Iditarod
  dog sled race, AK   ī-DIT-uh-RAHD   aiˈdiţə‚rad
Idleyld Park
  city, OR   ĪD-l-WĪLDˑ PAHRK   ˈaidl‚waild ˈpaʳk
Idmon
  Argonaut; soothsayer   ID-muhn, ID-MAHN   ˈidmən, ˈid‚man
Ido
  revised form of Esperanto   Ē-dō   ˈiːdoː
Idomeneo
  opera, Mozart   Ē-dō-muh-NĀ-ō   ‚iːdoːməˈneːoː
Idomeneus
  king of Crete, suitor of Helen   ī-DAHM-uh-N(Y)O͞OS,   aiˈdamə‚n(j)uːs,
       ī-DAHM-uh-NĒ-uhs   ‚ai‚daməˈniːəs

Key (col. 2):   a: fad   ā: fade   ah: father   ar: Mary   aw: law   e: fed   ē: feed   er: merry   i: hid   ī: hide   ō: coat   o͞o: boot
oi: boy   ow: now   u: put   uh: above   uhr: bird   ch: chop   ng: ring   sh: show   th: thick   <u>th</u>: this   zh: measure

Iðunn
   Scandinavian goddess of youth   ITH-un   'iðun

Idwal
   pers. name, Welsh   ID-wahl, ⑤ ID-wuhl   'idwɑːl, ⑤ 'idwəl

Ieper [Ypres]
   town, Belgium   YĀ-puhr   'jeːpəʳ

Ieuan
   pers. name, Welsh   YĀ-yahn   'jeːjɑːn

Ifni
   Spanish prov., Morocco   ĒF-nē, IF-nē   'iːfniˑ, 'ifniˑ

Ifor
   1. pers. name   Ē-vuhr, Ī-vuhr   'iːvəʳ, 'ɑivəʳ
   2. pers. name, Welsh   Ē-vawr   'iːvɔr

Ifugao
   lang., people, Philippine Islands   Ē-foo-GOW, Ē-foo-GOW   'iːfuː,gɑu, ,iːfuː'gɑu

Igala
   lang., people, Nigeria, Benin   ē-GAHL-uh   iː'gɑlə

Igbirra
   lang., people, Nigeria   IG-buhr-uh   'igbərə

Igbo [Ibo]
   lang., people, Nigeria   IG-bō   'igboː

Igdrasil
   see Yggdrasil

Iggy
   pers. name   IG-ē   'igiˑ

Iglesias
   Julio, *entertainer*   ē-GLĀ-zē-uhs   iː'gleːziːəs

Ignace
   pers. name, French   ēn-YAHS   iːnjɑːs

Ignacio
   1. pers. name, Portuguese   ēg-NAHS-yoo   iːg'nɑːsjuː
   2. Spanish   ēḡ-NAHS-yō, -NAHTH-yō   iːɣ'nasjoː, -'naθjoː

Ignat
   pers. name, Russian   ēg-NAHT   iːg'nɑːt

Ignatian
   pert. to Ignatius   ig-NĀ-shuhn   ig'neːʃən

Ignatius
   pers. name   ig-NĀ-sh(ē-)uhs   ig'neːʃ(iː)əs

Ignatius Loyola
   Christian saint, Jesuit founder   ig-NĀ-sh(ē-)uhs loi-Ō-luh   ig'neːʃ(iː)əs lɔi'oːlə

Ignaz
   pers. name, German   IG-NAHTS, ig-NAHTS   'ig,nats, ig'nats

Ignazio
   pers. name, Italian   ēn-YAHT-syō   iːn'jatsjoː

Igor
   1. pers. name   Ē-GAWR   'iː,gɔːʳ
   2. Russian   Ē-guhr   'iːgər

Igorot
   people of Malay stock, Philippines   IG-uh-RŌT   ,igə'roːt

Igraine
   mother of King Arthur   i-GRĀN   i'greːn

Iguana
   lizard   ig-WAHN-uh   ig'wɑnə

Iguanodon
   dinosaur   ig-WAHN-uh-DAHN   ig'wɑnə,dɑn

Foreign Sounds: ue: *Fr.* **rue**, *Ger.* **füllen** uh(r): *Fr.* **boeuf**, *Ger.* **Höhle** <u>kh</u>: *Ger.* **ich**, *Scot.* **loch** ḡ: *Sp.* **amigo** <u>v</u>: *Sp.* **hablar**
hl: *Welsh* **Llanelli**. CAPITALS: primary stress. SMALL CAPS: secondary stress. ⑤: U.S. pron. ⑭: British pron.

Iguassú
  river, Brazil   Ē-gwah-SŌŌ   ˌiːgwaˈsuː

Ijaw
  lang., people, Nigeria   Ē-jaw   ˈiːdʒɔː

Ijo [Ijaw]
  lang., people, Nigeria   Ē-jō, Ē-jaw   ˈiːdʒɔː, ˈiːdʒɔː

Ijssel
  tributary, Netherlands   Ī-suhl   ˈaisəl

Ijsselmeer
  inlet, Netherlands   Ī-suhl-MER   ˈaisəlˌmeʳ

Ikangaa
  Juma, *Tanzanian marathoner*   i-KAHNG-guh   iˈkaŋgə

Ikaria
  island, Greece   Ē-kuh-RḖ-uh   ˌiːkəˈriːə

Ike
  pers. name   ĪK   ˈaik

Ikeda
  Hayato, *Japanese statesman*   ē-kā-dah, ē-ked-ah   iːkeːda, iːkeda

Ila
  lang., people, Africa   Ē-luh   ˈiːlə

Ile-de-France
  prov, France   ēl-duh-FRAHⁿS   iːldəfrãs

Iliad
  Greek epic poem   IL-ē-uhd, IL-ē-AD   ˈiliːəd, ˈiliːˌæd

Ilia [Rhea Silvia]
  mother of Romulus and Remus   Ē-lē-uh, IL-ē-uh   ˈiːliːə, ˈiliːə

Ilía [Elis]
  dept, Greece   ē-LḖ-uh   iːˈliːə

Ilie
  pers. name, Romanian   Ē-lē-uh   ˈiːliːə

Iliescu
  Ion, *Romanian politician*   il-YES-kōō   ilˈjeskuː

Ilimbos
  mts., Greece   ē-LIM-bōs   iːˈlimbɔːs

Ilione
  daughter of Priam, wife of   IL-ē-Ō-nē   ˌiliːˈoːniˈ
    Polymestor

Ilioneus
  Trojan killed by Diomedes   IL-ē-Ō-nē-uhs, IL-ē-ŌN-YŌŌS   ˌiliːˈoːniːəs, ˌiliːˈoːnˌjuːs

Ilium [Troy]
  ancient city, Asia Minor   IL-ē-uhm   ˈiliːəm

Illampu
  peak, Bolivia   ē-YAHM-pōō   iːˈjampuː

Illimani
  mtn., Bolivia   Ē-yuh-MAHN-uh   ˌiːjəˈmanə

Illinois
  state, US ; N. American people;   IL-uh-NOI, IL-uh-NOIZ   ˌiləˈnɔi, ˌiləˈnɔiz
    pers. name

Illinoisan
  pert. to Illinois   IL-uh-NOI-uhn, IL-uh-NOIZ-n   ˌiləˈnɔiən, ˌiləˈnɔizn̩

Illuminati
  enlightened ones   il-ŌŌ-muh-NAHT-ē   ilˌuːməˈnɑtiˈ

Illyria
  ancient country along Adriatic   il-IR-ē-uh   ilˈiriːə

Key (col. 2):   a: fad   ā: fade   ah: father   ar: Mary   aw: law   e: fed   ē: feed   er: merry   i: hid   ī: hide   ō: coat   ōō: boot
oi: boy   ow: now   u: put   uh: above   uhr: bird   ch: chop   ng: ring   sh: show   th: thick   th: this   zh: measure

Illyrian
   lang., people, pert. to Illyria   il-IR-ē-uhn   il'iriːən

Illyricum
   ancient Roman province, Balkan   il-IR-i-kuhm   il'irikəm
     Peninsula

Illyrius
   son of Cadmus   il-IR-ē-uhs   il'iriːəs

Ilmari
   pers. name, Finnish   IL-mah-rē   'ilmɑriˑ

Ilmen
   lake, Russia   IL-muhn   'ilmən

Il Moro di Venezia
   Italian racing yacht   il MŌR-ō dē vuh-NET-sē-uh   il 'moːroː diˑ və'netsiːə

Ilocano
   lang., people, Philippine Islands   Ē-lō-KAHN-ō   ˌiːloː'kɑnoː

Iloko [Ilocano]
   lang., Philippine Islands   ē-LŌ-kō   iː'loːkoː

Il Penseroso
   poem, J. Milton   IL PEN-suh-RŌ-sō   ˌil ˌpensə'roːsoː

Ilse
   pers. name, German   IL-zuh   'ilzə

Ilson
   Robert, *US-born British*   IL-suhn   'ilsən
     lexicographer

Il Trovatore
   Italian opera, Verdi   ĒL trō-vuh-TŌR-ā, TRŌ-vuh-TAWR-ā   ˌiˑl troːvə'toːreː, ˌtroːvə'tɔːreː

Ilus
   founder of Troy   IL-uhs, Ē-luhs   'iləs, 'iːləs

Ilya
   pers. name, Russian   il-YAH   il'jɑː

Ilyich
   pers. name, Russian   il-YĒCH   il'jiːtʃ

Ilyushin
   Russian aircraft   il-YOO-shin   il'juːʃin

Imamu
   pers. name   i-MAHM-oo   i'mɑmuː

Iman
   Somali-born fashion model   Ē-mahn   'iːmɑn

Imbolc
   Celtic pagan festival   IM-BAWL(-uh)g   'im,bɔːl(ə)g

Imbrium, Mare
   see Mare Imbrium

Imelda
   pers. name   i-MEL-duh   i'meldə

Imhotep
   Egyptian physician & sage   im-HŌ-TEP   im'hoː,tep

Immanuel
   1. pers. name   i-MAN-yuh(-wuh)l   i'mænjə(wə)l
   2. Dutch   ē-MAHN-uh-wuhl   iː'mɑːnəwəl
   3. German   i-MAHN-oo-EL   i'mɑnuː,el

Imogen
   pers. name   IM-uh-juhn   'imədʒən

Imogene
   pers. name   IM-uh-JĒN   'imə,dʒiːn

Foreign Sounds: ue: *Fr.* r**ue**, *Ger.* f**ü**llen uh(r): *Fr.* b**oeu**f, *Ger.* H**ö**hle <u>kh</u>: *Ger.* i**ch**, *Scot.* lo**ch** ḡ: *Sp.* ami**g**o <u>v</u>: *Sp.* ha**b**lar
hl: *Welsh* **Ll**anelli. CAPITALS: primary stress. SMALL CAPS: secondary stress. Ⓢ: U.S. pron. Ⓛ: British pron.

Imperator
  Roman title: commmander,   IM-puh-RAHT-uhr, -RAH-TAWR   ˌɪmpəˈrɑtəʳ, -ˈrɑˌtɔːʳ
  emperor
Imperium
  Roman term for official authority im-PIR-ē-uhm   ɪmˈpiriːəm
Imphal
  city, India   IMP-HUHL, IM-PUHL   ˈɪmpˌhəl, ˈɪmˌpəl
Imre
  pers. name, Hungarian   IM-re   ˈɪmre
Ina
  pers. name   Ī-nuh, Ē-nuh   ˈaɪnə, ˈiːnə
Inachus
  Greek river god, father of Io   IN-uh-kuhs   ˈɪnəkəs
Inagua
  island, British Virgin Islands   in-AHG-wuh   ɪnˈɑgwə
Inaja-Cosmit
  N. American people   IN-uh-ZHAH-KAHZ-muht   ˈɪnəˌʒɑˈkɑzmət
Inca
  S. American people   ING-kuh   ˈɪŋkə
Inchon
  city, S. Korea   IN-CHAHN   ˈɪnˌtʃɑn
Increase
  pers. name   IN-KRĒS, in-KRĒS   ˈɪnˌkriːs, ɪnˈkriːs
Incubi
  plural of Incubus   ING-kyuh-BĪ, ING-kyuh-BĒ, IN-   ˈɪŋkjəˌbaɪ, ˈɪŋkjəˌbiː, ˈɪn-
Incubus
  evil spirit of sleep   ING-kyuh-buhs, IN-kyuh-buhs   ˈɪŋkjəbəs, ˈɪnkjəbəs
India
  subcontinent, republic, Asia   IN-dē-uh   ˈɪndiːə
Indian
  pert. to India; *Native American;* IN-dē-uhn   ˈɪndiːən
  ocean
Indiana
  state, US   IN-dē-AN-uh   ˌɪndiːˈænə
Indianan
  pert. to Indiana   IN-dē-AN-uhn   ˌɪndiːˈænən
Indianapolis
  city, IN   IN-dē-uh-NAP-(uh-)luhs   ˌɪndiːəˈnæp(ə)ləs
Indic
  pert. to India   IN-dik   ˈɪndɪk
Indies
  islands (East and West)   IN-dēz   ˈɪndiːz
Indigetes
  obscure Roman divinities   in-DIJ-uht-ĒZ   ɪnˈdɪdʒətˌiːz
Indira
  pers. name (I. Gandhi)   in-DIR-uh   ɪnˈdɪrə
indium
  element   IN-dē-uhm   ˈɪndiːəm
Indo-Aryan
  Indic culture   IN-dō-AR-ē-uhn, -ER-ē-uhn,   ˌɪndoːˈæriːən, -ˈeriːən,
                                       -AHR-yuhn   -ˈɑrjən
Indochina
  peninsula, Asia   IN-dō-CHĪ-nuh   ˌɪndoːˈtʃaɪnə

Key (col. 2):   a: fad ā: fade ah: father ar: Mary aw: law e: fed ē: feed er: merry i: hid ī: hide ō: coat ōō: boot
oi: boy   ow: now   u: put   uh: above   uhr: bird   ch: chop   ng: ring   sh: show   th: thick   th: this   zh: measure

Indo-European
  prehistoric people of Eurasia; their   IN-dō-YUR-uh-PĒ-uhn   ˌindoːˌjurə'piːən
  lang.

Indo-Iranian
  Indo-European lang. group   IN-dō-ir-Ā-nē-uhn   ˌindoːir'eːniːən

Indonesia
  republic, Asia   IN-duh-NĒ-zhuh, -shuh   ˌində'niːʒə, -ʃə

Indonesian
  lang., Indonesia   IN-duh-NĒ-zhuhn, -NĒ-shuhn   ˌində'niːʒən, -'niːʃən

Indore
  city, India   IN-DŌR, IN-DAWR   'inˌdoːr, 'inˌdoːr

Indra
  supreme Vedic god   IN-druh   'indrə

Indre
  dept, river, France   EⁿDR, ⑤ Aⁿ-druh   ẽdr, ⑤ 'æ(n)drə

Indus
  eponymous hero of India; river,   IN-duhs   'indəs
  Asia

Indy, d'
  Vincent, *French composer*   deⁿ-DĒ, ⑤ dan-DĒ, DAN-dē   dẽdiː, ⑤ dæn'diː, 'dændiˑ

Inés
  pers. name, Spanish   ē-NĀS   iː'neːs

Inez
  1. Don Juan's mother; pers. name   Ē-NEZ, Ī-NEZ, Ê-NEZ   'iːˌnez, 'aiˌnez, ˌiː'nez
  2. Spanish   ē-NĀS, ē-NĀTH   iː'neːs, iː'neːθ

Inga
  pers. name   ING-uh   'iŋə

Inge
  1. William, US playwright   INJ   'indʒ
  2. William, English prelate, author   ING   'iŋ

Ingeborg
  1. pers. name, Danish   ĒNG-uh-BAWRǴ   'iːŋəˌbɔːrɣ
  2. German   ING-uh-BAWRKH   'iŋəˌbɔʳx

Ingels
  Marty, *US agent, TV and film*   ING-guhlz   'iŋəlz
  production executive

Ingenii, Mare
  see Mare Ingenii

Ingersoll
  Robert, *American orator*   ING-uhr-SAWL, ING-uhr-suhl   'iŋəʳˌsɔːl, 'iŋəʳsəl

Ingmar
  pers. name, Swedish   ING-MAHR   'iŋˌmaʳ

Ingram
  James, *US singer, songwriter*   ING-gruhm   'iŋgrəm

Ingres
  Jean Auguste, *French painter*   EⁿGR   ẽgr

Ingrid
  pers. name   ING-gruhd   'iŋgrəd

Ingush
  lang., people, Kazakhstan   IN-GUSH, in-GUSH   'inˌguʃ, in'guʃ

Inigo
  pers. name   IN-uh-gō   'inəgoː

Íñigo
  pers. name, Spanish   ĒN-yē-ḡō   'iːnjiːɣoː

Foreign Sounds: ue: *Fr.* **rue**, *Ger.* **füllen**   uh(r): *Fr.* **boeuf**, *Ger.* **Höhle**   <u>kh</u>: *Ger.* i**ch**, *Scot.* lo**ch**   ǵ: *Sp.* ami**g**o   ɣ: *Sp.* ha**b**lar
hl: *Welsh* **Ll**anelli.   CAPITALS: primary stress.   SMALL CAPS: secondary stress.   ⑤: U.S. pron.   ⑭: British pron.

Iniki
  pers. name, Hawaiian   i-NĒ-kē   i'niːkiˑ

Inkatha
  South African politicial movement   in-KAHT-uh   in'kɑʈə

Innes
  Scottish family name   IN-uhs   'inəs

Inno
  national hymn, Vatican City   IN-nō   'innoː

Inno di Mameli
  national anthem, Italy   IN-nō dē mah-MÃ-lē   'innoː diː mɑ'meːliː

Innsbruck
  city, Austria   IN(T)S-BRUK, INZ-BRUK   'in(t)s,bruk, 'inz,bruk

Ino
  guardian of Dionysus; Leucothea   Ī-nō   'ɑinoː

İnönü
  Ismet, president, Turkey   IN-uh(r)-NUE, ⑤ IN-uh-N(Y)OO   ,inœˑ'nyː, ⑤ ,inə'n(j)uː

Inouye
  Daniel K., *US politician*   IN-uh-WĀ, i-NŌ-wā   'inə,weː, i'noːweː

Insectivora
  insect-eaters   IN-SEK-TIV-uh-ruh   ,in,sek'tivərə

Intel
  US microprocessor co.   IN-TEL   'in,tel

Intelsat
  satellite consortium   IN-TEL-SAT   'in,tel,sæt

Interlaken
  town, Switzerland   INT-uhr-LAH-kuhn   'intəʳ,lakən

Internationale
  revolutionary anthem   INT-uhr-NASH-uh-NAHL   ,intəʳ,næʃə'nɑˑl

Interpol
  international police organization   INT-uhr-PŌL, INT-uhr-PAHL   'intəʳ,poːl, 'intəʳ,pɑl

Inuit
  people, lang., N. America   IN-(y)uh-wuht   'in(j)əwət

Inuktitut [Inuit]
  lang., Greenland, Canada, USA   i-NOOK-tuh-TUT   i'nuːktə,tut

Inulin
  carbohydrate   IN-yuh-luhn   'injələn

Inupiac [Inuit]
  lang., Greenland, Canada, USA   i-NOO-pē-AK   i'nuːpiːˌæk

Inverell
  town, Australia   IN-vuh-REL, IN-vuh-REL   ,invə'rel, 'invə,rel

Inver Hills
  Community College, *MN*   IN-vuhr HILZ   'invəʳ 'hilz

Inverness
  1. city, Scotland   IN-vuhr-NES   ,invəʳ'nes
  2. town, CA, FL, IL   IN-vuhr-NES, IN-vuhr-nuhs   'invəʳ,nes, 'invəʳnəs

INXS
  rock group   IN-ek-SES, IN-ik-SES   ,inek'ses, ,inik'ses

Inyo
  county, CA   IN-yō   'injoː

Io
  beloved of Zeus turned into a cow;   Ī-ō, Ē-ō   'ɑioː, 'iːoː
    satellite of Jupiter

Ioan
  1. pers. name, Romanian   YWAHN   'jwɑn
  2. Welsh   YŌ-ahn   'joːɑːn

Key (col. 2):   a: fad   ā: fade   ah: father   ar: Mary   aw: law   e: fed   ē: feed   er: merry   i: hid   ī: hide   ō: coat   ōō: boot
oi: boy   ow: now   u: put   uh: above   uhr: bird   ch: chop   ng: ring   sh: show   th: thick   <u>th</u>: this   zh: measure

Ioannes, Ioannis
    pers. name, Mod. Greek   yaw-AHN-yēs   jɔ'anjiːs

Iobates
    father of Sthenboea   Ī-uh-BĂT-ēz   ˌaiə'beːʧiːz

Iobes
    son of Heracles and Certhe   ī-Ō-bēz   ai'oːbiːz

iodine
    element   Ī-uh-DĪN, Ī-uhd-n, Ī-uh-DĒN   'aiəˌdain, 'aiədn̩, 'aiəˌdiːn

Iolani
    palace, HI   Ē-uh-LAHN-ē   ˌiːə'lani·

Iolanthe
    operetta, Gilbert & Sullivan   Ī-uh-LAN-thē   ˌaiə'lænθi·

Iole
    captive of Hercules   Ī-uh-lē, ē-Ō-lē   'aiəli·, iː'oːli·

Iolo
    pers. name, Welsh   YŌ-lō   'joːloː

Ion
    dialogue of Plato; eponymous   Ī-uhn, Ī-AHN   'aiən, 'aiˌan
      ancestor of Ionians

Iona
    island, Scotland; college, NY   ī-Ō-nuh   ai'oːnə

Ionesco
    Eugène, French playwright   yaw-nes-KŌ, Ⓢ Ē-uh-NES-kō   jɔːneskoː, Ⓢ ˌiːə'neskoː

Ionia
    ancient region, Asia Minor;   ī-Ō-nē-uh   ai'oːniːə
      county, MI

Ionian
    sea, Mediterranean; architectural   ī-Ō-nē-uhn   ai'oːniːən
      order; musical mode; pert. to
      Ionia; *Islands, Greece*

Ionic
    ancient Greek dialect; pert. to   ī-AHN-ik   ai'anik
      Ionian order

Iora
    Asian songbird   ī-Ō-ruh, ē-Ō-ruh   ai'oːrə, iː'oːrə

Ios
    island, Greece   Ī-AHS, Ē-AWS   'aiˌas, 'iːˌɔːs

Iosco
    county, MI   ī-AHS-kō   ai'askoː

Iosif
    pers. name, Russian   YAWS-yif, i-AWS-yif   'jɔːsjif, i'ɔːsjif

Iowa
    state, US ; river, IA; N. American   Ī-uh-wuh   'aiəwə
      people

Iowan
    pert. to Iowa   Ī-uh-wuhn   'aiəwən

Iphianassa [Iphigenia]
    daughter of Agamemnon   IF-ē-uh-NAS-uh   ˌifiːə'næsə

Iphicles
    twin brother of Heracles   IF-i-KLĒZ, Ē-fi-KLĒZ   'ifiˌkliːz, 'iːfiˌkliːz

Iphiclus
    Argonaut; conqueror of   IF-i-kluhs, Ē-fi-kluhs   'ifikləs, 'iːfikləs
      Phoenicians at Rhodes

Foreign Sounds: ue: *Fr.* **rue**, *Ger.* **füllen** uh(r): *Fr.* **boeuf**, *Ger.* **Höhle** kh: *Ger.* i**ch**, *Scot.* lo**ch** g̃: *Sp.* ami**g**o v: *Sp.* ha**b**lar
hl: *Welsh* **Ll**anelli. CAPITALS: primary stress. SMALL CAPS: secondary stress. Ⓢ: U.S. pron. Ⓛ: British pron.

Iphigenia, -neia
  daughter of Agamemnon and   IF-uh-juh-NĪ-uh, IF-uh-juh-NĒ-uh   ˌifədʒəˈnaiə, ˌifədʒəˈniːə
    Clytemnestra

Iphitus
  son of Eurytus   Ē-fuht-uhs   ˈiːfətəs

Ipiros [Epirus]
  region, Greece   Ē-pi-RAWS   ˈiːpiˌrɔːs

Ippolito
  pers. name, Italian   ēp-PAW-lē-tō   iːpˈpɔːliːtoː

Ippolitov-Ivanov
  Mikhail, Russian composer   IP-uhl-YĒ-tuhf-yi-VAH-nuhf   ˌipəlˈjiːtəfjiˈvaːnəf

Ipsus
  ancient Phrygian village   IP-suhs   ˈipsəs

Ipswich
  US pl. name; borough, England;   IP-swich   ˈipswitʃ
    city, Australia

Ipuwer
  ancient Egyptian prophet   ē-PYOO-uhr   iːˈpjuːəʳ

Iqaluit
  town, Northwest Territories,   i-KAHL-uh-wit   iˈkalə wit
    Canada

Iqbal
  Muhammad, Pakistani poet   ik-BAHL, Ⓢ IK-BAHL, IK-BAL   ikˈbal, Ⓢ ˈikˌbal, ˈikˌbæl

IRA
  1. Irish Republican Army   Ī-AHR-Ā   ˌaiˌarˈeː
  2. individual retirement account   Ī-AHR-Ā, Ī-ruh   ˌaiˌaʳˈeː, ˈairə

Ira
  pers. name   Ī-ruh   ˈairə

Iráklion
  dept & town, Greece   i-RAHK-lē-AWN   iˈrakliːˌɔːn

Iran
  country, SW Asia   i-RAHN, i-RAN, ī-RAN   iˈran, iˈræn, aiˈræn

Iranian
  pert. to Iran   i-RAHN-ē-uhn, i-RĀN-, i-RAN-,   iˈraniːən, iˈreːn-, iˈræn-,
    ī-RAN-   aiˈræn-

Iraq
  country, Middle East   i-RAHK, i-RAK, ī-   iˈrak, iˈræk, ai-

Iraqi
  pert. to Iraq   i-RAHK-ē, i-RAK-ē, ī-   iˈrakiˑ, iˈrækiˑ, ai-

Iráya
  lang., people, Philippine Islands   i-RĪ-uh, i-RAH-yuh   iˈraiə, iˈrajə

Irazú
  volcano, Costa Rica   IR-uh-ZOO, IR-uh-SOO   ˌirəˈzuː, ˌirəˈsuː

Iredell
  county, NC   ĪR-DEL   ˈairˌdel

Ireland [Eire]
  republic, Europe   ĪR-luhnd   ˈaiʳlənd

Irenaeus
  pers. name   Ī-ruh-NĒ-uhs   ˌairəˈniːəs

Irene
  1. pers. name   ī-RĒN, Ⓔ ī-RĒ-nē   aiˈriːn, Ⓔ aiˈriːniˑ
  2. German   ē-RĀ-nā   iːˈreːneː
  3. Latin   ī-RĒ-nē   aiˈriːniˑ

Irène
  pers. name, French   ē-REN   iːren

Key (col. 2):   a: fad ā: fade ah: father ar: **Mary** aw: **law** e: fed ē: feed er: **merry** i: hid ī: hide ō: coat o͞o: boot
oi: **boy** ow: **now** u: put uh: **above** uhr: **bird** ch: **chop** ng: **ring** sh: **show** th: **thick** <u>th</u>: **this** zh: measure

Irénée
    pers. name, French   ē-rā-NĀ   iːreːneː

Irgun
    militant Zionist underground   ir-GUN   iʳgun
      group

Irian Jaya
    prov, Indonesia   IR-ē-AHN JĪ-uh   ˈiriːˌɑn ˈdʒɑiə

iridium
    element   ir-ID-ē-uhm   irˈidiːəm

Iridum, Sinus
    see Sinus Iridum

Irion
    county, TX   IR-ē-uhn   ˈiriːən

Iris
    Greek goddess of the rainbow;   Ī-ruhs   ˈɑirəs
      pers. name

Irish
    lang., people, Ireland   Ī-rish   ˈɑiriʃ

Irish Free State [Ireland]
    republic, Europe   ĪR-ish FRĒ STĀT   ˌɑiriʃ ˈfriː ˌsteːt

Irish Gaelic
    lang., Ireland   ĪR-ish GĀ-lik   ˈɑiriʃ ˈgeːlik

Irkutsk
    city, Russia   ir-KO͞OTSK   iʳkuːtsk

Irma
    pers. name   UHR-muh   ˈəʳmə

Irminger
    current off west coast of Ireland   UHR-ming-uhr   ˈəʳmiŋəʳ

iron
    element   Ī(-uh)rn   ˈɑi(ə)ʳn

Irondequoit
    Bay, *inlet, Lake Ontario; town,*   ir-AHN-duh-KWOIT   irˈɑndəˌkwɔit
      NY

Iroquoian
    pert. to the Iroquois   IR-uh-KWOI-uhn   ˌirəˈkwɔiən

Iroquois
    Native American confederacy   IR-uh-KWOI, IR-uh-KWAH   ˈirəˌkwɔi, ˈirəˌkwɑ

Irra
    Babylonian god of disease   IR-uh   ˈirə

Irrawaddy
    river, Burma   IR-uh-WAHD-ē   ˌirəˈwɑdiˑ

Irredentist
    advocate of historical or ethnic   IR-uh-DENT-uhst   ˌirəˈdentəst
      political unity

Irtish
    river, Kazakhstan, Russia   ir-TISH, uhr-TISH   iʳˈtiʃ, əʳˈtiʃ

Irvine
    1. city, CA   UHR-VĪN   ˈəʳˌvɑin
    2. city, KY; city, Scotland   UHR-vuhn   ˈəʳvən

Irving
    pers. name   UHR-ving   ˈəʳviŋ

Irwin
    Hale S., *US golfer*   UHR-wuhn   ˈəʳwən

Foreign Sounds: **ue**: *Fr.* r**ue**, *Ger.* f**ü**llen   **uh(r)**: *Fr.* b**oeu**f, *Ger.* H**ö**hle   <u>kh</u>: *Ger.* i**ch**, *Scot.* lo**ch**   ğ: *Sp.* ami**g**o   <u>v</u>: *Sp.* ha**b**lar
hl: *Welsh* L**l**anelli.   CAPITALS: primary stress.   SMALL CAPS: secondary stress.   ⑨: U.S. pron.   ⑫: British pron.

Isaac
1. pers. name	Ī-zik, Ī-zuhk	'aizik, 'aizək
2. French	ē-ZAHK	iːzɑːk
3. German	Ē-zah-AHK, Ē-ZAHK	'iːzaˌak, 'iːˌzak
4. Polish	Ē-sahk	'iːsaːk
5. Russian	i-SAHK	i'saːk
6. Spanish	ē-sah-AHK	iːsa'ak

Isaacs
1. Isaac Alfred, *Australian jurist;* Katherine M., *US onomastician;* Rufus, *British politician*	Ī-zuhks, Ī-ziks	'aizəks, 'aiziks
2. Jorge, *Colombian author*	ē-SAHKS, ē-SAH-ahks	iː'saks, iː'sɑ-aks

Isaak
1. Chris, *rock singer*	Ī-zik	'aizik
2. German	Ē-zah-AHK, Ē-ZAHK	'iːzaˌak, 'iːˌzak

Isaäk, Isaak
pers. name, Dutch	Ē-sahk	'iːsak

Isabel
1. pers. name	IZ-uh-BEL	'izəˌbel
2. Spanish	ē-sah-BEL	iːsa'bel

Isabella
1. pers. name	ɪZ-uh-BEL-uh	ˌizə'belə
2. Dutch	Ē-sah-BEL-ah	ˌiːsaː'belaː
3. Italian	Ē-zah-BEL-lah	ˌiːza'bellɑ

Isabelle
1. pers. name	IZ-uh-BEL	'izəˌbel
2. French	ē-zah-BEL	iːzaːbel
3. German	Ē-zah-BEL-uh	ˌiːza'belə

Isador, Isadore
pers. name	IZ-uh-DŌR, -DAWR	'izəˌdoːʳ, -ˌdɔːʳ

Isadora
pers. name	ɪZ-uh-DŌR-uh, -DAWR-uh	ˌizə'doːrə, -'dɔːrə

Isagoras
Athenian politician	ī-SAG-uh-ruhs	ai'sægərəs

Isaiah
biblical prophet; Old Testament book; pers. name	ī-ZĀ-uh, Ⓔ ī-ZĪ-uh	ai'zeːə, Ⓔ ai'zaiə

Isaias
1. Old Testament book	ī-ZĀ-uhs, Ⓔ ī-ZĪ-uhs	ai'zeːəs, Ⓔ ai'zaiəs
2. pers. name, Spanish	ē-sah-Ē-ahs	iːsa'iːas

Isak
pers. name, Dutch	Ē-SAHK	'iːˌsaːk

Isanti
county, MN	i-SANT-ē	i'sænti·

Isar
Bavarian river	Ē-ZAHR	'iːˌzaʳ

Iscariot
see Judas Iscariot

Ischia
Italian island, west of Naples	IS-kē-uh	'iskiːə

Isenbeck
German beer	Ē-zuhn-BEK	'iːzənˌbek

Iser
Czech river	Ē-zuhr	'iːzəʳ

Key (col. 2):   a: fad   ā: fade   ah: father   ar: Mary   aw: law   e: fed   ē: feed   er: merry   i: hid   ī: hide   ō: coat   ōō: boot
oi: boy   ow: now   u: put   uh: above   uhr: bird   ch: chop   ng: ring   sh: show   th: thick   th: this   zh: measure

Isère
   river, dept, France   ē-ZER   iːzer
Iseult [Isolde]
   beloved of Tristram   is-O͞OLT, iz-O͞OLT   is'uːlt, iz'uːlt
Isfahan [Esfahān]
   prov & town, Iran   IS-fuh-HAHN   ˌisfə'hɑn
Ishbosheth
   Biblical name   ish-BŌ-shuhth   iʃ'boːʃəθ
Ishikawa
   prefecture, Japan   ish-i-kah-wah   iʃikɑwɑ
Ishmael
   Biblical son of Abraham & Hagar;   ISH-MĀ-uhl, ISH-mē-uhl   'iʃˌmeːəl, 'iʃmiːəl
    pers. name
Ishmaelite
   descendant of Ishmael   ISH-MĀ-uh-LĪT, ISH-mē-uh-LĪT   'iʃˌmeːəˌlait, 'iʃmiːəˌlait
Ishpeming
   city, MI   ISH-puh-ming   'iʃpəmiŋ
Ishtar
   Assyrian and Babylonian fertility   ISH-TAHR   'iʃˌtɑʳ
    goddess
Ishtar Terra
   highland on planet Venus   ISH-TAHR TER-uh   'iʃˌtɑʳ 'terə
Isidor, Isidore
   pers. name   IZ-uh-DŌR, -DAWR   'izəˌdoːʳ, -ˌdɔːʳ
Isin
   ancient Sumerian city   IS-n   'isn̩
Isis
   Egyptian queen of the gods   Ī-suhs   'ɑisəs
İskenderun
   gulf, Mediterranean Sea   IS-KEN-duh-RO͞ON   ˌis,kendə'ruːn
Islam
   religion   is-LAHM, iz-LAHM, -LAM; IS-LAHM,   is'lɑm, iz'lɑm, -'læm;
     IZ-LAHM, -LAM   'is,lɑm, 'iz,lɑm, -,læm
Islamabad
   city, Pakistan   is-LAHM-uh-BAHD, iz-LAM-uh-BAD   is'lɑməˌbɑd, iz'læməˌbæd
Islamic
   pert. to Islam   is-LAHM-ik, iz-LAHM-ik, is-LAM-ik,   is'lɑmik, iz'lɑmik,
     iz-LAM-ik   is'læmik, iz'læmik
Islamorada
   resort, FL   Ī-luh-mawr-AHD-uh,   ˌailəmɔːr'ɑdə, ˌisləmə'rɑdə
     IS-luh-muh-RAHD-uh
Island Carib
   lang., Honduras, Belize,   Ī-luhnd KAR-uhb   'ailənd 'kærəb
    Guatemala
Islay
   island, Scotland   Ī-luh, Ī-lā   'ailə, 'aileː
Isle au Haut
   island, ME   Ī-luh-HŌ(T), Ē-luh-HŌ   ˌailə'hoː(t), ˌiːlə'hoː
Isle la Motte
   island, Lake Champlain   ĪL luh MAHT   ˌail lə 'mɑt
Isle of Wight
   see Wight, Isle of
Isleta Pueblo
   Indian reservation, US   ēz-LĀT-uh po͞o-EB-lō, PWEB-lō,   iːz'leːtə puː'ebloː, 'pwebloː,
     pyo͞o-EB-lō   pju'ebloː

Foreign Sounds: **ue**: *Fr.* **rue**, *Ger.* f**ü**llen   **uh(r)**: *Fr.* b**oeuf**, *Ger.* H**öh**le   <u>kh</u>: *Ger.* i**ch**, *Scot.* lo**ch**   ğ: *Sp.* ami**g**o   <u>v</u>: *Sp.* ha**b**lar
hl: *Welsh* **Ll**anelli.   CAPITALS: primary stress.   SMALL CAPS: secondary stress.   ⑤: U.S. pron.   Ⓔ: British pron.

Islington
 borough, England   IZ-ling-tuhn   'izliŋtən
Islip
 town, NY; village, England Ī-sluhp   'aisləp
Ismael
 1. pers. name, German IS-mah-EL   'ismɑ,el
 2. Spanish   ēz-mah-ĀL   iːzmɑ'eːl
Ismaël
 pers. name, French   ēs-mah-EL   iːsmɑːel
Ismail
 1. pers. name, Albanian ēs-mah-ĒL   iːsmɑ'iːl
 2. Russian   yis-MAH-(y)il   jis'mɑ(j)il
Isma'īl
 pers. name, Arabic   is-mah-ĒL   ismɑ'iːl
Ismene
 daughter of Oedipus and Jocasta is-MĒ-nē   is'miːniˑ
İsmet
 pers. name   is-MET   is'met
Isobel
 pers. name   IZ-uh-BEL   'izə,bel
Isocrates
 Athenian orator   ī-SAHK-ruh-TĒZ   ai'sɑkrə,tiːz
Isolda
 pers. name   i-SŌL-duh, i-ZŌL-duh, Ⓔ i'soːldə, i'zoːldə, Ⓔ i'zɑldə
         i-ZAHL-duh
Isolde
 1. beloved of Tristram [Iseult]; i-SŌL-duh, ē-ZŌL-duh, i-SŌLD i'soːldə, iː'zoːldə, i'soːld
  pers. name
 2. German   i-ZAWL-duh   i'zɔːldə
I Solisti
 chamber orchestras, Zagreb, Ē sō-LIS-tē   ,iː soː'listiˑ
  Venice
Israel
 1. republic, ancient kingdom, IZ-rē-uhl, IZ-rā-uhl, IZ-ruhl, IS- 'izriːəl, 'izreːəl, 'izrəl, 'is-
  eastern Mediterranean; pers.
  name
 2. Dutch   IS-rah-EL   'isrɑː,el
 3. French   ēs-rah-EL   iːsrɑːel
 4. Swedish   ĒS-rah-uhl   'iːsrɑːəl
Israel ben Eliezer [Ba'al Shem-Tov]
 founder of Hasidism   IZ-rē-uhl BEN EL-ē-Ā-zuhr 'izriːəl ,ben ,eliː'eːzəʳ
Israeli
 from or pert. to Israel iz-RĀ-lē, IZ-ruh-Ā-lē   iz'reːliˑ, ,izrə'eːliˑ
Israelite
 inhabitant of or pert. to Israel IZ-r(ē-)uh-LĪT   'izr(iː)ə,lɑit
Issa
. *pers. name, Japanese* ē-sah   iːsɑ
Issaquena
 county, MS   IS-uh-KWĒ-nuh   ,isə'kwiːnə
Issus
 ancient town, Asia Minor IS-uhs   'isəs
Istanbul
 province, city, Turkey IS-tuhm-BO͞OL, -TAHM-, -TAM-, ,istəm'buːl, -,tɑm-, -,tæm-,
        -TAHN-, -TAN-, -BUL   -,tɑn-, -,tæn-, -'bul

Key (col. 2): a: fad ā: fade ah: father ar: Mary aw: law e: fed ē: feed er: merry i: hid ī: hide ō: coat o͞o: boot
oi: boy ow: now u: put uh: above uhr: bird ch: chop ng: ring sh: show th: thick th: this zh: measure

Isthmian
pert. to isthmus of Corinth or Panama | IS-mē-uhn | 'ismiːən

Istra [Istria]
peninsula, Croatia | Ē-struh | 'iːstrə

Istria
peninsula, Croatia | Ē-strē-uh, IS-trē-uh | 'iːstriːə, 'istriːə

Istrus
personification of the Danube River | IS-truhs | 'istrəs

István
pers. name, Hungarian | ISHT-vahn | 'iʃtvaːn

Isuzu
Japanese car co. | i-SOO-zoo | i'suːzuː

Italia [Italy]
republic, Europe | ē-TAHL-yah, ē-TAHL-yuh | iː'talja, iː'taljə

Italian
lang., Europe | i-TAL-yuhn | i'tæljən

Italianate
Italian in style | uh-TAL-yuh-NĀT, i-TAL- | ə'tæljə͵neːt, i'tæl-

Italian spinone
dog breed | i-TAL-yuhn spuh-NŌ-nā | i͵tæljən spə'noːneː

Italo-
combining form meaning Italian | IT-l-ō, uh-TAL-ō, i-TAL-ō | 'itl̩oː, ə'tæloː, i'tæloː

Italo
pers. name, Italian | Ē-tahl-ō | 'iːtaloː

Italus
hero of Italy | uh-TAL-uhs, i-TAL-uhs | ə'tæləs, i'tæləs

Italy
republic, Europe | IT-l-ē | 'itl̩iˑ

Itasca
lake, county, college, MN | ī-TAS-kuh | ai'tæskə

Itawamba
county, MS | IT-uh-WAHM-buh | ͵itə'wɑmbə

Ithaca
city, NY; island, Greece | ITH-i-kuh | 'iθikə

Ithacus
eponymous hero of Ithaca | ITH-i-kuhs | 'iθikəs

Ithome
mtn., Greece | i-THŌ-mē | i'θoːmiˑ

Ittmann
Majorie McCullough, *Girl Scout official* | IT-muhn | 'itmən

Iturbi
Jose, *Spanish musician* | ē-TOOR-ve̱ | iː'tuːrβiː

Ituri
pers. name, Spanish | ē-TOO-rē | iː'tuːriː

Itys
son of Procne and Tereus | ĪT-uhs | 'aiţəs

Iulus [Ascanius]
son of Aeneas | YOO-luhs | 'juːləs

Ius auxilii
Roman tribune's right of help | YOOS owk-SIL-ē-Ē | 'juːs ɑuk'siliː͵iː

Iuventas [Juventas]
Roman goddess of youth | yoo-VENT-uhs | juː'ventəs

Foreign Sounds: ue: *Fr.* **rue**, *Ger.* **füllen** uh(r): *Fr.* **boeuf**, *Ger.* **Höhle** kh: *Ger.* **ich**, *Scot.* **loch** g̱: *Sp.* **amigo** v̱: *Sp.* **hablar** hl: *Welsh* **Llanelli**. CAPITALS: primary stress. SMALL CAPS: secondary stress. Ⓢ: U.S. pron. Ⓑ: British pron.

Ivan
  1. pers. name   ē-VAHN, Ī-vuhn   iː'vɑn, 'aivən
  2. Bulgarian   ē-VAHN   iː'vɑːn
  3. Russian   i-VAHN   i'vɑːn
  4. Serbo-Croatian, Swedish   Ē-vahn   'iːvɑːn
Ivana
  pers. name   i-VAHN-uh   i'vɑnə
Ivanhoe
  novel, Sir Walter Scott   Ī-vuhn-HŌ   'aivən,hoː
Ivanovitch
  patronym, Russian   i-VAHN(-uhv)-YICH   i'vɑːn(əv),jitʃ
Ivanovo
  city, Russia   i-VAHN-uh-vuh   i'vɑːnəvə
Ivar
  1. pers. name, Norwegian   Ē-vahr   'iːvɑr
  2. Swedish   Ē-vahr   'iːvɑːr
Iveco
  truck co.   uh-VĀ-kō, i-VĀ-kō   ə've:koː, i've:koː
Ives
  pers. name   ĪVZ   'aivz
Iviza
  see Ibiza
Ivo
  pers. name, Serbo-Croatian   Ē-vaw   'iːvɔː
Ivor
  pers. name   Ē-vuhr, Ī-vuhr   'iːvəʳ, 'aivəʳ
Ivorian
  inhabitant of the Ivory Coast   i-VŌR-ē-uhn, i-VAWR-ē-uhn   i'voːriːən, i'vɔːriːən
Ivory Coast
  republic, Africa   Ī-v(uh-)rē   'aiv(ə)riˑ
Ivy
  pers. name   Ī-vē   'aiviˑ
Iwan
  1. pers. name, French   ē-VAHⁿ   iːvɑ̃
  2. German   ē-VAHN, Ē-VAHN   iː'vɑn, 'iː,vɑn
  3. Welsh   YOO-ahn   'juːɑːn
Iwo Jima
  island, Pacific   Ē-wuh JĒ-muh, Ē-wō   ,iːwə 'dʒiːmə, ,iːwoː
Ixia
  flower   IK-sē-uh   'iksiːə
Ixil
  lang., people, Guatemala   ē-SHĒL   iː'ʃiːl
Ixion
  king of Thessaly, tortured on   ik-SĪ-uhn   ik'saiən
  * wheel in Hades*
Ixtaccihuatl, Iztaccíhuatl
  volcano, Puebla-México   ĒS-tahk-SĒ-WAHT-l   ,iːstak'siː,watļ
Ixtacihuatl [Ixtaccihuatl]
  volcano, Mexico   Ē-stah-SĒ-WAHT-l   ,iːsta'siː,watļ
Iyar
  Jewish month   Ē-YAHR   'iː,jɑr
Izaak
  1. pers. name   Ī-zik, Ī-zuhk   'aizik, 'aizək
  2. Dutch   Ē-ZAHK   'iː,zak

Key (col. 2):   a: fad   ā: fade   ah: father   ar: Mary   aw: law   e: fed   ē: feed   er: merry   i: hid   ī: hide   ō: coat   ōō: boot
oi: boy   ow: now   u: put   uh: above   uhr: bird   ch: chop   ng: ring   sh: show   th: thick   th̲: this   zh: measure

Izard		
county, AR	IZ-uhrd	'izəʳd
İzmir [Smyrna]		
prov, Turkey	iz-MIR	iz'miʳ
Izod Lacoste		
tdmk for sportswear	Ī-ZAHD luh-KAHST, luh-KAWST	ˌaɪˌzɑd lə'kɑst, lə'kɔːst
Iztaccíhuatl		
see Ixtaccihuatl		
Izvestia		
official Soviet newspaper	iz-VES-tē-uh, iz-VES-chē-uh	iz'vestiːə, iz'vestʃiːə

J

Jabberwocky		
nonsense verse by Lewis Carroll	JAB-uhr-WAHK-ē	'dʒæbəʳˌwɑkiˑ
Jabez		
pers. name	JĀ-buhz	'dʒeːbəz
Jabiru		
stork	ZHAB-uh-ROO	ˌʒæbə'ruː
Jacaltec		
lang., people, Guatemala	HAHK-uhl-TĀK	ˌhɑkəl'teːk
Jacamar		
S. & Cen. American bird	ZHAK-uh-MAHR	'ʒækəˌmɑʳ
Jaçana, Jacana		
wading bird	ZHAS-n-Aⁿ, juh-KAHN-uh	ˌʒæsn̩'æ̃, dʒə'kɑnə
Jacaranda		
plant	JAK-uh-RAN-duh	ˌdʒækə'rændə
Jacint		
pers. name, Catalan	zhah-SĒNT	ʒɑː'siːnt
Jacinta		
1. pers. name	juh-SINT-uh	dʒə'sintə
2. Spanish	<u>kh</u>ah-SĒN-tah, <u>kh</u>ah-THĒN-tah	xɑ'siːntɑ, xɑ'θiːntɑ
Jacintha		
pers. name	juh-SIN-thuh	dʒə'sinθə
Jacinto		
pers. name, Spanish	<u>kh</u>ah-SĒN-tō, <u>kh</u>ah-THĒN-tō	xɑ'siːntoː, xɑ'θiːntoː
Jack		
pers. name	JAK	'dʒæk
Jackie		
pers. name	JAK-ē	'dʒækiˑ
Jackson		
pers. name	JAK-suhn	'dʒæksən

Foreign Sounds: ue: *Fr.* **rue**, *Ger.* **füllen**   uh(r): *Fr.* **boeuf**, *Ger.* **Höhle**   <u>kh</u>: *Ger.* **ich**, *Scot.* **loch**   g̵: *Sp.* ami**g**o   v̵: *Sp.* ha**b**lar
hl: *Welsh* **Ll**anelli.   CAPITALS: primary stress.   SMALL CAPS: secondary stress.   ⑤: U.S. pron.   ⑥: British pron.

Jacob
  1. pers. name   JĀ-kuhb   'dʒeːkəb
  2. Afrikaans, German, Norwegian,   YAH-KAWP   'jɑˌkɔːp
    Swedish
  3. Danish, Dutch   YAH-KAWP   'jɑːˌkɔːp
  4. François, French biochemist   zhah-KAWB   ʒɑːkɔːb
    (Nobel 1965); pers. name,
    French

Jacobean
  pert. to King James I of England   JAK-uh-BĒ-uhn   ˌdʒækə'biːən

Jacobi
  Derek, *British actor*   juh-KŌ-bē; JAK-uh-bē   dʒə'koːbiˑ; 'dʒækəbiˑ

Jacobian
  mathematical determinant   juh-KŌ-bē-uhn, yah-KŌ-bē-uhn   dʒə'koːbiːən, jɑ'koːbiːən

Jacobin
  Dominican friar; political   JAK-uh-buhn   'dʒækəbən
    extremist

Jacobins Gueuze
  Belgian beer   YAH-kawb-uhns GUH(R)-zuh   'jakɔːbəns 'gœːzə

Jacobins Kriek
  Belgian beer   YAH-kawb-uhns KRĒK   'jakɔːbəns 'kriːk

Jacobite
  English Tory party   JAK-uh-BĪT   'dʒækəˌbait

Jacobo
  pers. name, Spanish   khah-KŌ-v̱ō   xɑ'koːβoː

Jacobus
  1. pers. name   juh-KŌ-buhs   dʒə'koːbəs
  2. Dutch   yah-KŌ-bues   jɑ'koːbys
  3. German   yah-KŌ-bus   jɑ'koːbus

Jacoby
  pers. name   juh-KŌ-bē   dʒə'koːbiˑ

Jacopo
  pers. name, Italian   YAHK-ō-pō   'jakoːpoː

Jacquard
  Joseph Marie Charles, *French*   zhah-KAHR, ⑤ JAK-AHRD,   ʒɑːkɑːr, ⑤ 'dʒækˌɑʳd,
    inventor   juh-KAHRD   dʒə'kɑʳd

Jacqueline
  1. pers. name   JAK-(w)uh-luhn, -LĒN   'dʒæk(w)ələn, -ˌliːn
  2. French   zhah-KLĒN   ʒɑːkliːn

Jacquelyn
  pers. name   JAK-wuh-luhn, JAK-uh-luhn   'dʒækwələn, 'dʒækələn

Jacquerie
  French peasant revolt   ZHAHK-uh-RĒ, ZHAK-uh-RĒ   ˌʒakə'riː, ˌʒækə'riː

Jacques
  1. pers. name, Dutch, German   ZHAHK   'ʒak
  2. French   ZHAHK   ʒak

Jacquet
  Illinois, *jazz musician*   juh-KET   dʒə'ket

Jacquinot
  bay, Pacific Ocean   ZHAK-uh-NŌ   ˌʒækə'noː

Jacuzzi
  tdmk for a whirlpool bath or a   juh-KOO-zē   dʒə'kuːziˑ
    pool

Jaeger
  sea bird   YĀ-guhr   'jeːgəʳ

Key (col. 2):   a: fad   ā: fade   ah: father   ar: Mary   aw: law   e: fed   ē: feed   er: merry   i: hid   ī: hide   ō: coat   o͞o: boot
oi: boy   ow: now   u: put   uh: above   uhr: bird   ch: chop   ng: ring   sh: show   th: thick   th̲: this   zh: measure

Jael
  Biblical name   JĀ(-uh)l   'dʒeː(ə)l

Jaffa [Joppa]
  city, Israel   JAHF-uh, JAF-uh, YAHF-uh, YAF-uh   'dʒɑfə, 'dʒæfə, 'jɑfə, 'jæfə

Jägermeister
  German liqueur   YĀ-guhr-MĪ-stuhr, YEG-uhr-   'jeːgəʳˌmaistəʳ, 'jegəʳ-

Jägerwahl Das Bockbier
  US beer   YĀ-guhr-WAHL dahs BAHK-BIR,   'jeːgəʳˌwal das 'bakˌbiʳ,
                      YĀ-guhr-VAHL   'jeːgəʳˌval

Jagger
  Mick, *British singer, songwriter*   JAG-uhr   'dʒægəʳ

Jaguar
  British car co.   JAG(-yuh)-WAHR, JAG-wuhr, ⓔ   'dʒæg(jə)ˌwaʳ, 'dʒægwəʳ, ⓔ
                      JAG-yuh-wuhr   'dʒægjəwəʳ

Jahveh
  see Yahweh

Jaime
  pers. name, Spanish   <u>KH</u>Ī-mā   'xɑimeː

Jain
  adherent of Jainism   JĪN   'dʒɑin

Jainism
  religion   JĪ-NIZ-uhm   'dʒɑiˌnizəm

Jaipur
  city, India   JĪ-PUR   'dʒɑiˌpuʳ

Jakarta
  see Djakarta

Jakób
  pers. name, Polish   YAH-kōōp   'jɑːkuːp

Jakob
  1. pers. name, Danish, Dutch   YAH-KAWP   'jɑːˌkɔːp
  2. German, Swedish   YAH-KAWP   'jɑˌkɔːp

Jalālābād
  city, Afghanistan   juh-LAHL-uh-BAHD   dʒəˈlɑləˌbad

Jalap
  plant   JAL-uhp, JAHL-uhp   'dʒæləp, 'dʒaləp

Jalapa
  dept, Guatemala; city, Mexico   <u>kh</u>uh-LAHP-uh   xəˈlɑpə

Jalisco
  state, Mexico   <u>kh</u>ah-LĒ-skō   xɑˈliːskoː

Jamaica
  island, Caribbean; area, New York   juh-MĀ-kuh   dʒəˈmeːkə
    City

Jamaican
  pert. to Jamaica   juh-MĀ-kuhn   dʒəˈmeːkən

Jamal
  pers. name   juh-MAHL   dʒəˈmal

Jamberoo
  town, Australia   JAM-buh-ROO, JAM-buh-ROO   ˌdʒæmbəˈruː, 'dʒæmbəˌruː

James
  1. New Testament book; pers.   JĀMZ   'dʒeːmz
    name, English, German
  2. French   JEMS   dʒems

Jamesian
  pert. to Henry James   JĀM-zē-uhn   'dʒeːmziːən

Foreign Sounds: **ue**: *Fr.* **rue**, *Ger.* **füllen**   **uh(r)**: *Fr.* **boeuf**, *Ger.* **Höhle**   <u>**kh**</u>: *Ger.* **ich**, *Scot.* **loch**   g̱: *Sp.* ami**g**o   v̱: *Sp.* ha**b**lar
hl: *Welsh* **Llanelli**.   CAPITALS: primary stress.   SMALL CAPS: secondary stress.   Ⓢ: U.S. pron.   Ⓔ: British pron.

Jameson		
tdmk for an Irish whisky	JĀ-muh-suhn	'dʒeːməsən
Jamestown		
US pl. name	JĀMZ-TOWN	'dʒeːmz,taun
Jamie		
pers. name	JĀ-mē	'dʒeːmiˑ
Jammu-Kashmir		
state, India	JUHM-o͞o-KASH-MIR, -kash-MIR	'dʒəmuː'kæʃ,miʳ, -kæʃ'miʳ
Jan		
1. pers. name	JAN	'dʒæn
2. Czech, Polish	YAHN	'jaːn
3. Dutch, German, Latvian	YAHN	'jɑn
Janáček		
Leoš, *Czech composer*	YAHN-uh-CHEK	'jɑnə,tʃek
Jane		
pers. name	JĀN	'dʒeːn
Janet		
1. pers. name	JAN-uht, juh-NET	'dʒænət, dʒə'net
2. French	zhah-NE	ʒaːne
Janice, Janis		
pers. name	JAN-uhs	'dʒænəs
Janissary, Janizary		
soldier in Turkish army	JAN-uh-SER-ē, JAN-uh-ZER-ē	'dʒænə,seriˑ, 'dʒænə,zeriˑ
János		
pers. name, Hungarian	YAH-nawsh	'jaːnɔːʃ
Jansen		
1. Cornelis Otto, *Dutch theologian*	YAHN-suhn, [$] JAN(T)-suhn	'jɑnsən, [$] 'dʒæn(t)sən
2. tdmk for sportswear	JAN(T)-suhn	'dʒæn(t)sən
Jansenism		
doctrine of moral determinism	JAN-suh-NIZ-uhm	'dʒænsə,nizəm
Jantzen		
US sportswear co.	JAN(T)-suhn	'dʒæn(t)sən
Januarius		
1. pers. name	JAN-yuh-WER-ē-uhs	,dʒænjə'weriːəs
2. German	YAHN-o͞o-AHR-yus, -AHR-ē-us	jɑnuː'ɑrjus, -'ɑriːus
January		
month	JAN-yuh-WER-ē	'dʒænjə,weriˑ
Janus		
Roman gateway god; satellite of Saturn; pers. name	JĀ-nuhs	'dʒeːnəs
Jap		
abbreviation for Japan or Japanese	JAP	'dʒæp
Japan		
nation, Asia	juh-PAN	dʒə'pæn
Japanese		
lang., people, Asia	JAP-uh-NĒZ, -NĒS	,dʒæpə'niːz, -'niːs
Japheth		
Biblical name	JĀ-fuhth	'dʒeːfəθ
Japhetic		
pert. to Japheth	jā-FET-ik	dʒeː'feṭik
Japonica		
plant	juh-PAHN-i-kuh	dʒə'pɑnikə
Japurá		
river, S. America	ZHAHP-uh-RAH	,ʒɑpə'rɑ

Key (col. 2): a: **f**a**d** ā: **f**a**de** ah: **f**a**ther** ar: **M**a**ry** aw: **l**aw e: **f**e**d** ē: **f**ee**d** er: **m**e**rry** i: **h**i**d** ī: **h**i**de** ō: **c**oa**t** o͞o: **b**oo**t** oi: **b**oy ow: **n**ow u: **p**u**t** uh: **a**bove uhr: **b**ir**d** ch: **ch**op ng: **r**i**ng** sh: **sh**ow th: **th**ick t͟h: **th**is zh: **m**ea**s**ure

Jaques
1. *character in* As You Like It,   ⓔ JĀ-kwiz, ⓢ JĀ-kwuhz, JĀ-ᴋᴡᴇ̄ᴢ   ⓔ 'dʒeːkwiz, ⓢ 'dʒeːkwəz,
    Shakespeare   'dʒeː,kwiːz
2. *pers. name*   JĀKS, JAKS   'dʒeːks, 'dʒæks

Jardins des Plantes
botanical garden, Paris   zhahr-DEⁿ dā PLAHⁿT   ʒɑːrdẽ deˑ plɑ̃t

Jared
pers. name   JAR-uhd   'dʒærəd

Jarl
1. *pers. name, Finnish*   YAHRL   'jɑːrl
2. *Norwegian*   YAHRL   'jɑrl

Jarmila
pers. name, Czech   YAHR-mil-uh   'jɑːrmilə

Jarmo
prehistoric village site, Iraq   JAHR-mō   'dʒɑrmoː

Jaromir
pers. name, Czech   YAH-raw-ᴍɪʀ   'jɑːrɔ,mir

Jaron
pers. name   JAR-uhn, JER-uhn   'dʒærən, 'dʒerən

Jaroslav
pers. name, Czech   YAH-raw-ꜱʟᴀʜꜰ   'jɑrɔ,slɑːf

Jaroslaw
pers. name, German   YAHR-aw-ꜱʟᴀʜꜰ   'jɑrɔ,slɑf

Jarosław
pers. name, Polish   yah-RAW-slahf   jɑːˈrɔːsłɑːf

Jarreau
Al, *entertainer*   juh-RŌ   dʒəˈroː

Jarrell
Randall, *US writer*   juh-REL, ja-REL   dʒəˈrel, dʒæˈrel

Jarrett
Keith, *US pianist*   JAR-uht, JER-uht   'dʒærət, 'dʒerət

Jarriel
Tom, *US TV journalist*   JAR-uhl, JER-uhl   'dʒærəl, 'dʒerəl

Jarrott
Charles, *British film and TV*   JAR-uht, JER-uht   'dʒærət, 'dʒerət
    director

Jarrow
town, England   JAR-ō   'dʒæroː

Jaruzelski
Wojciech, *Polish political leader*   YAHR-uh-ZEL-skē   jɑrəˈzelskiˑ

Järvi
Neeme, *Estonian conductor*   YER-vē   'jerviˑ

Jarvik-7
artificial heart   JAHR-vik SEV-uhn   'dʒɑrvik 'sevən

Jarvis
pers. name   JAHR-vuhs   'dʒɑrvəs

Jascha
pers. name   YAHSH-uh   'jɑʃə

Jasmine
pers. name   JAZ-muhn, JAZ-ᴍɪ̄ɴ   'dʒæzmən, 'dʒæz,main

Jason
leader of Argonauts, husband of   JĀS-n   'dʒeːsn̩
    Medea; pers. name

Jaspar, Jasper
pers. name   JAS-puhr   'dʒæspəʳ

Foreign Sounds: ue: *Fr.* **rue**, *Ger.* **füllen** uh(r): *Fr.* **boeuf**, *Ger.* **Höhle** <u>kh</u>: *Ger.* **ich**, *Scot.* **loch** g̃: *Sp.* **amigo** v̲: *Sp.* **hablar**
hl: *Welsh* **Llanelli**. CAPITALS: primary stress. ꜱᴍᴀʟʟ ᴄᴀᴘꜱ: secondary stress. ⓢ: U.S. pron. ⓔ: British pron.

Jataka
  tales of Bhudda's births   JAHT-uh-kuh   'dʒɑʈəkə
Java
  Sea, *Asia*   JAHV-uh, JAV-uh   'dʒɑvə, 'dʒævə
Java, Jawa, Djawa
  island, Indonesia   JAHV-uh, JAV-uh   'dʒɑvə, 'dʒævə
Javanese
  lang., SE Asia   JAV-uh-NĒZ, JAHV-uh-NĒZ, -NĒS ˌdʒævə'niːz, ˌdʒɑvə'niːz, -'niːs
Javel
  town, France   zhah-VEL   ʒɑːvel
Javier
  pers. name, Spanish   k͟hahv-YER   xɑv'jer
Javits
  Jacob, *US politician*   JAV-uhts   'dʒævəts
Jawa
  see Java
Jawa Barat
  prov, Java   JAHV-uh buh-RAHT   ˌdʒɑvə bə'rɑt
Jawaharlal
  pers. name, north India   juh-WAH-huhr-LAHL   dʒə'wɑhərˌlɑl
Jawa Tengah
  prov, Java   JAHV-uh TENG-gah   ˌdʒɑvə 'teŋgɑ
Jawa Timur
  prov, Java   JAHV-uh TĒ-MUR   ˌdʒɑvə 'tiːˌmuʳ
Jaworski
  Leon, *US lawyer;* Ronald Vincent,   juh-WAWR-skē   dʒə'wɔːʳskiˑ
  US football player
Jay
  pers. name   JĀ   'dʒeː
Jayapura
  city, Indonesia   JAH-(y)uh-PUR-uh   ˌdʒɑ(j)ə'purə
Jaycee
  member of a junior chamber civic   JĀ-SĒ   ˌdʒeː'siː
  group
Jayne
  pers. name   JĀN   'dʒeːn
Jean
  1. pers. name   JĒN   'dʒiːn
  2. Finnish   ZHAHN   'ʒɑːn
  3. Flemish, German   ZHAHⁿ   'ʒɑ̃
  4. French   ZHAHⁿ   ʒɑ̃
Jean de Meun
  French poet   zhahⁿ duh MUH(R)ⁿ   ʒɑ̃ də mœ̃
Jeane
  pers. name   JĒN   'dʒiːn
Jeanette
  pers. name   juh-NET   dʒə'net
Jeanie, Jeannie
  pers. name   JĒ-nē   'dʒiːniˑ
Jean Lassale
  watchmakers   ZHAHⁿ luh-SAHL, luh-SAL   ˌʒɑ̃ lə'sɑːl, lə'sæl
Jeanne
  1. pers. name   JĒN   'dʒiːn
  2. French   ZHAHN, ZHAHN   ʒɑn, ʒɑːn

Key (col. 2):   a: fad ā: fade ah: father ar: Mary aw: law e: fed ē: feed er: merry i: hid ī: hide ō: coat ōō: boot
oi: boy ow: now u: put uh: above uhr: bird ch: chop ng: ring sh: show th: thick t͟h: this zh: measure

Jeanne d' Arc
  French saint — zhahn DAHRK — ʒɑːn dɑːrk

Jeanneret [Corbusier, Le]
  Charles Édouard, *Swiss architect* — zhahn(-uh)-RE — ʒɑːn(ə)re

Jeannette
  pers. name — juh-NET — dʒəˈnet

Jeannot
  pers. name, French — zhah-NŌ — ʒɑːnoː

Jeb
  pers. name — JEB — ˈdʒeb

Jebel Toubkal
  see Toubkal, Jebel

Jebu
  West African people — JĒ-b(y)o͞o, JEB-(y)o͞o — ˈdʒiːb(j)uː, ˈdʒeb(j)uː

Jebusa
  pers. name — juh-BYo͞o-suh, JEB-yu-suh — dʒəˈbjuːsə, ˈdʒebjusə

Jed
  pers. name — JED — ˈdʒed

Jedda [Jiddah, Gedda]
  city, Saudi Arabia — JED-uh — ˈdʒedə

Jedediah
  pers. name — JED-uh-DĪ-uh — ˌdʒedəˈdaiə

Jedi
  knights in Star Wars films — JED-ī — ˈdʒed,ai

Jedidiah
  pers. name — JED-uh-DĪ-uh — ˌdʒedəˈdaiə

Jeep
  tdmk for a vehicle — JĒP — ˈdʒiːp

Jeeves
  character in novels of P. G. — JĒVZ — ˈdʒiːvz
  Wodehouse

Jeff
  pers. name — JEF — ˈdʒef

Jefferson
  Thomas, *3rd US president; US pl.* — JEF-uhr-suhn — ˈdʒefəʳsən
  name; pers. name

Jeffery
  pers. name — JEF-(uh-)rē — ˈdʒef(ə)riˑ

Jehan
  pers. name, French — zhuh-AHN, -ZHAHN — ʒəɑn, ʒɑn

Jehoiakim
  Biblical name — juh-HOI-uh-kuhm, -KIM — dʒəˈhɔiəkəm, -ˌkim

Jehol
  region, city, China — juh-HŌL, RŌ-HŌ *[sic]* — dʒəˈhoːl, ˈroːˈhoː *[sic]*

Jehoshaphat
  pers. name — juh-HAHSH-uh-FAT, — dʒəˈhaʃə,fæt, dʒəˈhasə,fæt
  juh-HAHS-uh-FAT

Jehovah
  Old Testament name for God — juh-HŌ-vuh — dʒəˈhoːvə

Jehovism
  worship of Jehovah — juh-HŌ-VIZ-uhm — dʒəˈhoːˌvizəm

Jehu
  biblical ruler — JĒ-h(y)o͞o, JĒ-yo͞o, JĀ- — ˈdʒiːh(j)uː, ˈdʒiːjuː, ˈdʒeː-

Jehuda
  pers. name — juh-Ho͞oD-uh — dʒəˈhuːdə

Foreign Sounds: ue: *Fr.* **rue**, *Ger.* füllen   uh(r): *Fr.* **boeuf**, *Ger.* Höhle   kh: *Ger.* i**ch**, *Scot.* lo**ch**   g̱: *Sp.* ami**g**o   v̱: *Sp.* ha**b**lar
hl: *Welsh* **Ll**anelli.   CAPITALS: primary stress.   SMALL CAPS: secondary stress.   Ⓢ: U.S. pron.   Ⓛ: British pron.

Jehudi
  pers. name   juh-HOOD-ē   dʒəˈhuːdiˑ

Jekyll
  1. Henry, *character in* Dr. Jekyll   JEK-uhl, JĒ-kuhl   ˈdʒekəl, ˈdʒiːkəl
     and Mr. Hyde, *R. L. Stevenson*
  2. *island, GA*   JEK-uhl   ˈdʒekəl

Jemdet Nasr
  Sumerian site   JEM-duht NAS-uhr   ˈdʒemdət ˈnæsəʳ

Jemez
  N. American people   HĀ-muhs   ˈheːməs

Jemima
  pers. name   juh-MĪ-muh   dʒəˈmɑimə

Jena
  city, Germany   YĀ-nuh   ˈjeːnə

Jenever
  Dutch gin   JEN-uh-vuhr   ˈdʒenəvəʳ

Jenner
  Edward, *British physician*   JEN-uhr   ˈdʒenəʳ

Jennie, Jenny
  pers. name   JEN-ē   ˈdʒeniˑ

Jennifer, Jenifer
  pers. name   JEN-uh-fuhr   ˈdʒenəfəʳ

Jennings
  Peter, *US TV journalist; pers.*   JEN-ingz   ˈdʒeniŋz
     name

Jenő
  pers. name, Hungarian   YEN-uh(r)   ˈjenœː

Jenolan
  caves, Australia   juh-NŌ-luhn   dʒəˈnoːlən

Jens
  1. Salome, *US entertainer*   JENZ   ˈdʒenz
  2. *pers. name, Danish, German,*   YENS   ˈjens
     Norwegian

Jensen
  1. J. Hans Daniel, *German*   YEN-zuhn   ˈjenzən
     physicist (Nobel 1963)
  2. Johannes Vilhelm, *Danish*   YEN(T)-suhn, Ⓢ JEN(T)-suhn   ˈjen(t)sən, Ⓢ ˈdʒen(t)sən
     author (Nobel 1944)

Jeptha
  pers. name   JEP-thuh   ˈdʒepθə

Jerauld
  county, SD   juh-RAWLD   dʒəˈrɔːld

Jeremiah
  Old Testament book; pers. name   JER-uh-MĪ-uh   ˌdʒerəˈmɑiə

Jeremias
  Old Testament book   JER-uh-MĪ-uhs   ˌdʒerəˈmɑiəs

Jérémie
  pers. name, French   zhā-rā-MĒ   ʒeːreːmiː

Jeremy
  pers. name   JER-uh-mē   ˈdʒerəmiˑ

Jerez de la Frontera
  city, Spain   k͟huh-RĀS t͟hā lah frawn-TER-uh,   xəˈreːs ðeː lɑ frɔːnˈterə,
                                            Ⓢ huh-RĀS duh   Ⓢ həˈreːs də lə,frənˈterə
                                          luh-FRUHN-TER-uh

Jericho
   town, Jordan | JER-i-kō | 'dʒerikoː
Jerilderie
   town, Australia | juh-RIL-duh-rē | dʒə'rildəriˑ
Jermaine
   pers. name | juhr-MĀN | dʒəʳˈmeːn
Jermyn
   Henry, *English courtier* | JUHR-muhn | 'dʒəʳmən
Jerne
   Niels K., *Danish immunologist* | YER-nuh | 'jeʳnə
   (Nobel 1984)
Jeroboam
   Hebrew king; pers. name; bottle | JER-uh-BŌ-uhm | ˌdʒerə'boːəm
Jéroboam
   pers. name, French | zhā-raw-baw-AHM | ʒeːrɔːbɔːɑːm
Jerome
   pers. name | juh-RŌM, Ⓔ *also* JER-uhm | dʒə'roːm, Ⓔ *also* 'dʒerəm
Jérôme
   pers. name, French | zhā-RŌM | ʒeːroːm
Jerônimo
   pers. name, Portuguese | zhuh-RAW-nē-m$\overline{oo}$, zhā- | ʒə'rɔːniːmuː, ʒeː-
Jerónimo
   pers. name, Spanish | k͟hā-RŌ-nē-mō | xeː'roːniːmoː
Jerry
   pers. name | JER-ē | 'dʒeriˑ
Jersey
   county, IL; island, English | JUHR-zē | 'dʒəʳziˑ
   Channel
Jerusalem
   holy city, Israel | juh-R$\overline{OO}$-s(uh-)luhm, | dʒə'ruːs(ə)ləm,
      | juh-R$\overline{OO}$Z-(uh-)luhm | dʒə'ruːz(ə)ləm
Jerusha
   pers. name | juh-R$\overline{OO}$-shuh | dʒə'ruːʃə
Jervis
   pers. name | JUHR-vuhs, Ⓔ *also* JAHR-vis | 'dʒəʳvəs, Ⓔ *also* 'dʒɑʳvis
Jerzy
   pers. name, Polish | YEZH-i | 'jeʒi
Jespersen
   Otto, *Danish philologist* | YES-puhr-suhn | 'jespəʳsən
Jess
   pers. name | JES | 'dʒes
Jessamine
   county, KY | JES-uh-muhn | 'dʒesəmən
Jesse
   pers. name | JES-ē | 'dʒesiˑ
Jessica
   pers. name | JES-i-kuh | 'dʒesikə
Jessie
   pers. name | JES-ē | 'dʒesiˑ
Jesu
   literary term for Jesus | JĒ-z$\overline{oo}$, JĀ-z$\overline{oo}$, YĀ-z$\overline{oo}$, -s$\overline{oo}$ | 'dʒiːzuː, 'dʒeːzuː, 'jeːzuː, -suː
Jesuitic
   pert. to the Jesuits | JEZH-uh-WIT-ik, JEZ-(y)uh-WIT-ik | ˌdʒeʒə'wiţik, ˌdʒez(j)ə'wiţik
Jesuitism
   tenets of the Jesuits | JEZH-(uh-)wuht-IZ-uhm, JEZ- | 'dʒeʒ(ə)wəţˌizəm, 'dʒez-

---

Foreign Sounds: **ue**: *Fr.* **rue**, *Ger.* **füllen** **uh(r)**: *Fr.* **boeuf**, *Ger.* **Höhle** **k͟h**: *Ger.* **ich**, *Scot.* **loch** **g**: *Sp.* **amigo** **v**: *Sp.* **hablar**
hl: *Welsh* **Llanelli**. CAPITALS: primary stress. SMALL CAPS: secondary stress. Ⓢ: U.S. pron. Ⓔ: British pron.

Jesuits
  religious order | JEZH-uh-wuhts, JEZ- | 'dʒeʒəwəts, 'dʒez-
Jesus
  pers. name | JĒ-zuhs, JĒ-zuhz | 'dʒiːzəs, 'dʒiːzəz
Jesús
  pers. name, Spanish | khā-SŌŌS, ⑤ hā-SŌŌS, HĀ-SŌŌS | xeːˈsuːs, ⑤ heːˈsuːs, 'heːˌsuːs
Jesus Christ
  Christian religious leader | JĒ-zuhs KRĪST, JĒ-zuhz | 'dʒiːzəs 'kraist, 'dʒiːzəz
Jethro
  pers. name | JETH-rō | 'dʒeθroː
Jettora
  pers. name | JET-uh-ruh, juh-TAWR-uh | 'dʒeṭərə, dʒəˈtɔːrə
Jever
  German beer | YĀ-vuhr | 'jeːvəʳ
Jewett
  Sarah Orne, *US author* | JŌŌ-uht | 'dʒuːət
Jewish
  pert. to Judaism | JŌŌ-ish | 'dʒuːiʃ
Jewry
  Jewish people collectively | JUR-ē, JŌŌ-rē | 'dʒuriˑ, 'dʒuːriˑ
Jezebel
  Biblical name | JEZ-uh-BUHL | 'dʒezəˌbəl
Jezreel
  town, Samaria | JEZ-rē-EL, JEZ-RĒL | 'dʒezriːˌel, 'dʒezˌriːl
Jhansi
  town, India | JAHN(T)-sē | 'dʒɑn(t)siˑ
Jhelum
  river, Asia | JĀ-luhm | 'dʒeːləm
Jiangsu, Kiang-Su
  prov, China | jē-AHNG-SŌŌ | dʒiːˈaŋˈsuː
Jiangxi, Kiang-Si
  prov, China | jē-AHNG-SHĒ | dʒiːˈaŋˈʃiː
Jibuti
  see Djibouti
Jicarilla
  N. American people | HĒ-kuh-RĒ-(y)uh | ˌhiːkəˈriː(j)ə
Jiddah [Jedda]
  city, Saudi Arabia | JID-uh | 'dʒidə
Jihad
  Islamic Holy War | ji-HAHD, ji-HAD | dʒiˈhad, dʒiˈhæd
Jilin [Kirin]
  prov & town, China | JĒ-LIN | 'dʒiːˈlin
Jill
  pers. name | JIL | 'dʒil
Jim
  pers. name | JIM | 'dʒim
Jiménez
  Juan Ramón, *Spanish poet (Nobel 1956)* | khē-MĀ-nāth, -nās; ⑤ hē-MĀ-nuhs | çiːˈmeːneːθ, -neːs; ⑤ hiːˈmeːnəs
Jim Hogg
  county, TX | JIM HAWG, HAHG | 'dʒim 'hɔːg, 'hag
Jimmy, Jimmie, Jimmi, Jimi
  pers. name | JIM-ē | 'dʒimiˑ
Jinan, Chi-nan, Tsinan
  prov, China | JĒ-NAHN | 'dʒiːˈnan

Key (col. 2): a: fad ā: fade ah: father ar: Mary aw: law e: fed ē: feed er: merry i: hid ī: hide ō: coat ōō: boot
oi: boy ow: now u: put uh: above uhr: bird ch: chop ng: ring sh: show th: thick <u>th</u>: this zh: measure

Jinghpo [Kachin]
   lang., China, Burma, India   JING-BŌ, JING-PŌ   'dʒiŋ'boː, 'dʒiŋ'poː

Jingmen
   city, China   JING-MUHN   'dʒiŋ'mən

Jinnah
   Mohammed Ali, *governor-general,*   JIN-uh   'dʒinə
     Pakistan

Jinnie, Jinny
   pers. name   JIN-ē   'dʒiniˑ

Jipijapa
   1. city, Ecuador   khē-pē-<u>KHAH</u>-pah,   xiːpiː'xɑpɑ, ⑤ ˌhiːpi''hɑpə
           ⑤ HĒ-pē-HAHP-uh
   2. plant   HĒ-pē-HAHP-uh   ˌhiːpi''hɑpə

Jirajara
   S. American people   HIR-uh-HAHR-uh   ˌhirə'hɑrə

Jiři
   pers. name, Czech   YIR-zhē   'jirʒiː

Jiro
   pers. name, Japanese   jē-rō   dʒiːroː

Ji Si
   Chinese year (Snake)   JUHR SĒ   'dʒəʳ 'siː

Jívaro
   S. American people   HĒ-vuh-RŌ   'hiːvəˌroː

Jo
   1. pers. name   JŌ   'dʒoː
   2. Dutch   YŌ   'joː

Joab
   Biblical name   JŌ-AB   'dʒoːˌæb

Joachim
   1. pers. name   YŌ-uh-kim, JŌ-uh-KIM   'joːəkim, 'dʒoːəˌkim
   2. Danish   YŌ-ah-kēm   'joːɑːkiːm
   3. Dutch   YŌ-ah-<u>kh</u>uhm   'joːɑːxəm
   4. French   zhō-ah-KĒM   ʒoːɑːkiːm
   5. German   YŌ-ah<u>kh</u>-im   'joːɑxim
   6. Norwegian   YŌ-ah-kim   'joːɑkim
   7. Polish   yaw-AH-<u>kh</u>ēm   jɔ'ɑːçiːm

Joad
   Cyril, *British philosopher; family*   JŌD   'dʒoːd
     name, Steinbeck characters

Joan
   1. pers. name   JŌN, jō-AN   'dʒoːn, dʒoː'æn
   2. Spanish   <u>kh</u>ō-AHN   xoː'ɑn

Joanna
   pers. name   jō-AN-uh   dʒoː'ænə

Joanne
   pers. name   jō-AN   dʒoː'æn

Joannes
   1. pers. name   jō-AN-ēz, jō-AN-uhs   dʒoː'æniːz, dʒoː'ænəs
   2. Dutch   yō-AHN-uhs   joː'ɑnəs
   3. Mod. Greek   yaw-AHN-yēs   jɔː'ɑnjiːs

João
   pers. name, Portuguese   ZHWOWⁿ   'ʒwɑ̃ũ

Joaquim
   pers. name, Portuguese   zhwuh-KIⁿ   ʒwə'kĩː

Foreign Sounds: ue: *Fr.* r**ue**, *Ger.* f**ü**llen uh(r): *Fr.* b**oeu**f, *Ger.* H**öh**le <u>kh</u>: *Ger.* i**ch**, *Scot.* lo**ch** ḡ: *Sp.* ami**g**o v̲: *Sp.* ha**b**lar
hl: *Welsh* **Ll**anelli. CAPITALS: primary stress. SMALL CAPS: secondary stress. ⑤: U.S. pron. ⑥: British pron.

Joaquin
　pers. name .... wah-KĒN .... wɑˈkiːn
Joaquin
　pers. name, Spanish .... k̲hwah-KĒN .... xwɑˈkiːn
Joaquina
　pers. name, Spanish .... k̲hwah-KĒ-nah .... xwɑˈkiːnɑ
Job
　1. Old Testament book; pers. ... JŌB .... ˈdʒoːb
　name
　2. Dutch .... YAWP .... ˈjɔːp
Jobs
　Steven P., *US computer executive* ... JAHBZ .... ˈdʒɑbz
Jocasta
　wife and mother of Oedipus ... jō-KAS-tuh .... dʒoːˈkæstə
Jocelyn
　pers. name .... JAHS-(uh-)luhn .... ˈdʒɑs(ə)lən
Jock
　pers. name .... JAHK .... ˈdʒɑk
Jodhpur
　city, India .... JAHD-puhr, JAHD-PUR .... ˈdʒɑdpəʳ, ˈdʒɑd‚puʳ
Jodi, Jodie, Jody
　pers. name .... JŌD-ē .... ˈdʒoːdiˑ
Jodrell Bank
　site of radio telescope, England ... JAHD-ruhl BANGK .... ‚dʒɑdrəl ˈbæŋk
Joe
　pers. name .... JŌ .... ˈdʒoː
Joel
　1. Old Testament book; pers. ... JŌ(-uh)l .... ˈdʒoː(ə)l
　name
　2. Finnish .... YAW-el .... ˈjɔːel
Joël
　pers. name, French .... yaw-EL .... jɔːel
Jo Enlai
　see Chou En-Lai
Joey
　pers. name .... JŌ-ē .... ˈdʒoːiˑ
Joffe
　Charles, *US film producer* ...... JAHF-ē, JAW-fē .... ˈdʒɑfiˑ, ˈdʒɔːfiˑ
Joffrey
　Robert, *US choreographer* ...... JAHF-rē, JAW-frē .... ˈdʒɑfriˑ, ˈdʒɔːfriˑ
Jog Falls [Gersoppa]
　waterfall, India .... JŌG .... ˈdʒoːg
Jogjakarta
　autonomous district, Java ...... JAHG-yuh-KAHRT-uh, ... ‚dʒɑgjəˈkaʳʈə,
　　　　　　　　　　　　　　　　　　JAWK-juh-KAHRT-uh .... ‚dʒɔːkdʒəˈkaʳʈə
Jogues
　Isaac, *French missionary* .... ZHAWG, ZHŌG .... ʒɔːg, ʒoːg
Johan
　1. pers. name, Danish .... yu-HAHN .... juˈhɑːn
　2. Dutch, Norwegian .... yō-HAHN .... joːˈhɑn
　3. Estonian .... YŌ-HAHN .... ˈjoː‚hɑn
　4. Finnish, Swedish .... YOO-HAHN .... ˈjuː‚hɑn

---

Key (col. 2):   a: fad   ā: fade   ah: father   ar: Mary   aw: law   e: fed   ē: feed   er: merry   i: hid   ī: hide   ō: coat   o͞o: boot
oi: boy   ow: now   u: put   uh: above   uhr: bird   ch: chop   ng: ring   sh: show   th: thick   t̲h: this   zh: measure

Johann

1. pers. name	YŌ-HAHN	'joː,han
2. Danish	yu-HAHN	ju'haːn
3. Dutch, German	yō-HAHN	joː'han
4. Finnish, Swedish	YOO-HAHN	'juː,han

Jóhann

pers. name, Icelandic	YŌ-HAHN	'joː,han

Johanna

1. pers. name	jō-(H)AN-uh	dʒoː'(h)ænə
2. Dutch	yō-HAHN-ah	joː'hanaː
3. German	yō-HAHN-ah	joː'hana
4. Swedish	yō-HAHN-nah	joː'haːnnaː

Johannes

1. pers. name	jō-HAN-uhs	dʒoː'hænəs
2. Danish	yu-HAHN-uhs	ju'haːnəs
3. Dutch, German	yō-HAHN-uhs	joː'hanəs
4. Finnish	yu-HAHN-nes	ju'haːnnes
5. French	zhaw-ah-NES	ʒɔaːnes
6. Swedish	yō-HAHN-nuhs	joː'haːnnəs

Johannesburg

city, South Africa	jō-HAN-uhs-BUHRG,	dʒoː'hænəs,bəʳg,
	jō-HAHN-uhs-BUHRG	dʒoː'hanəs,bəʳg

Johannine

pert. to the apostle John	jō-HAN-uhn, jō-HAN-ĪN	dʒoː'hænən, dʒoː'hæn,ain

Johannisberg

city, Germany	yō-HAHN-uhs-BERG	joː'hanəs,beʳg

John

1. New Testament book; pers.	JAHN	'dʒan
name		
2. French	YAWN, ZHAWN	joːn, ʒɔːn

John Bull

personification for England	JAHN BUL	,dʒan 'bul

John Doe

anonymous man	JAHN DŌ	,dʒan 'doː

Johnny, Johnnie

pers. name	JAHN-ē	'dʒaniˑ

John o' Groats

northern point of Scotland	JAHN uh GRŌTS	,dʒan ə 'groːts

Johns

pers. name	JAHNZ	'dʒanz

Johnson

1. pers. name	JAHN-suhn	'dʒansən
2. Eyvind, Swedish author (Nobel 1974)	YOON-sawn	'juːnsɔːn

Johnsonian

pert. to Samuel Johnson	jahn-SŌ-nē-uhn, jahn-SŌN-yuhn	dʒan'soːniːən, dʒan'soːnjən

Johor, Johore

state, Asia	juh-HŌR, juh-HAWR	dʒə'hoːʳ, dʒə'hɔːʳ

Johor Baharu

city, Asia	juh-HŌR buh-HAHR-oo, juh-HAWR	dʒə'hoːʳ bə'haruː, dʒə'hɔːʳ

Joi

pers. name	JOI	'dʒɔi

Jojo

pers. name	JŌ-JŌ	'dʒoː,dʒoː

Jojoba		
shrub	hō-HŌ-buh, huh-HŌ-buh	hoːˈhoːbə, həˈhoːbə
Jókai		
Maurus, *Hungarian novelist*	YŌ-KOI	ˈjoːˌkɔi
Joliet		
1. Louis, *French explorer*	zhawl-YĀ	ʒɔːlˈjeː
2. city, IL	JŌ-lē-ET, *by outsiders also* JAHL-ē-ET	ˌdʒoːliːˈet, *by outsiders also* ˌdʒɑliːˈet
Joliette		
county, Quebec, Canada	ZHŌ-lē-ET	ˌʒoːliːˈet
Joliot-Curie		
Frédéric & Irène, *French physicists (Nobel 1935)*	zhōl-YŌ-kue-RĒ, Ⓢ -kyu-RĒ, -KYUR-ē	ʒoːljoːkyːriː, Ⓢ -kjuˈriː, -ˈkjuriˑ
Jolla, La		
see La Jolla		
Jolo		
island, Philippines	KHŌ-lō, HŌ-lō	ˈxoːloː, ˈhoːloː
Jolson		
Al, *US entertainer*	JŌL-suhn	ˈdʒoːlsən
Jomo		
pers. name (J. Kenyatta)	JŌ-mō	ˈdʒoːmoː
Jon		
1. pers. name	JAHN	ˈdʒɑn
2. Norwegian	YŌN, YAWN	ˈjoːn, ˈjɔːn
3. Romanian	YAWN	ˈjɔːn
Jonah		
Old Testament book; pers. name	JŌ-nuh	ˈdʒoːnə
Jonas		
1. Old Testament book; pers. name	JŌ-nuhs	ˈdʒoːnəs
2. Dutch, German, Norwegian	YŌ-nahs	ˈjoːnɑs
3. Lithuanian	YAW-nahs	ˈjɔːnɑs
4. Swedish	YŌŌ-nahs	ˈjuːnɑːs
Jónas		
pers. name, Icelandic	YŌ-NAHS	ˈjoːˌnɑs
Jonathan		
1. pers. name	JAHN-uh-thuhn	ˈdʒɑnəθən
2. German	YŌ-nah-TAHN	ˈjoːnɑˌtɑn
Jones		
family name	JŌNZ	ˈdʒoːnz
Jonestown		
former settlement, Guyana	JŌN-STOWN	ˈdʒoːnˌstɑun
Jong		
Erica, *US writer*	JAWNG, ZHAWNG	ˈdʒɔːŋ, ˈʒɔːŋ
Joni		
pers. name	JŌ-nē	ˈdʒoːniˑ
Jöns		
pers. name, Swedish	YUH(R)NS	ˈjœns
Jonson		
Ben, *English author*	JAHN-suhn	ˈdʒɑnsən
Joos		
pers. name, Dutch	YŌS	ˈjoːs
Joost		
pers. name	YŌST	ˈjoːst

Key (col. 2): a: **fad** ā: **fade** ah: f**a**ther ar: M**ar**y aw: **law** e: **fed** ē: **feed** er: m**err**y i: **hid** ī: **hide** ō: **coat** ōō: **boot** oi: **boy** ow: **now** u: **put** uh: **a**bove uhr: **bird** ch: **ch**op ng: ri**ng** sh: **sh**ow th: **th**ick th: **th**is zh: mea**s**ure

Joplin
Scott, *US composer;* Janis, *US*   JAHP-luhn   'dʒɑplən
    rock singer; town, MO

Joppa
ancient name of Jaffa   JAHP-uh   'dʒɑpə

Jordache
clothing co.   JAWR-DASH   'dʒɔːˈrˌdæʃ

Jordaens
Jacob, *Flemish painter*   YAWR-dahns   'jɔːˈrdɑːns

Jordan
country, river, Middle East; pers.   JAWRD-n   'dʒɔːˈrdn̩
    name

Jordanian
pert. to Jordan   jawr-DĀ-nē-uhn   dʒɔːˈrˈdeːniːən

Jörg
pers. name, German   YUHR<u>KH</u>   'jœˈrx

Jorge
1. pers. name, Portuguese   ZHAWR-zhuh, ZHAWR-zhā   'ʒɔːrʒə, 'ʒɔːrʒeː
2. Spanish   <u>KH</u>AWR-ḡā, ⑤ HAWR-HĀ   'xɔːrɣeː, ⑤ 'hɔːˈrˌheː

Jörgen, Jørgen
1. pers. name, Danish   YUHR-ḡuhn   'jœrɣən
2. Norwegian   YUHR-guhn   'jœrgən

Jorge Newbery Aeroparque
airport, Buenos Aires, Argentina   HAWR-hā N(Y)O̅O̅-buh-rē   'hɔːˈrheː 'n(j)uːbəriˈ
    Ā-rō-PAHRK   'eːroːˌpɑˈrk

José
1. pers. name   hō-ZĀ   hoːˈzeː
2. Portuguese   zho̅o̅-ZE   ʒuːˈze
3. Spanish   <u>kh</u>ō-SĀ, hō-SĀ   xoːˈseː, hoːˈseː

Jose Cuervo
brand of tequila   hō-ZĀ KWER-vō   hoːˌzeː 'kweˈrvoː

Josef
1. pers. name   JŌ-zuhf, JŌ-suhf   'dʒoːzəf, 'dʒoːsəf
2. Czech   YAW-SEF   'jɔːˌsef
3. Dutch   YŌ-SEF   'joːˌsef
4. German   YŌ-ZEF   'joːˌzef
5. Swedish   YO̅O̅-SEF   'juːˌsef

Joseph
1. pers. name   JŌ-zuhf, JŌ-suhf   'dʒoːzəf, 'dʒoːsəf
2. Dutch   YŌ-SEF   'joːˌsef
3. French   zhō-ZEF   ʒoːzef
4. German   YŌ-ZEF   'joːˌzef
5. Swedish   YO̅O̅-SEF   'juːˌsef

Josepha
pers. name   jō-SĒ-fuh   dʒoːˈsiːfə

Josephine
pers. name   JŌ-zuh-FĒN, JŌ-zuh-FĒN,   'dʒoːzəˌfiːn, ˌdʒoːzəˈfiːn,
    JŌ-suh-FĒN, JŌ-suh-FĒN   'dʒoːsəˌfiːn, ˌdʒoːsəˈfiːn

Josephinism
Austrian sect   JŌ-zuh-fuh-NIZ-uhm,   'dʒoːzəfəˌnizəm,
    JŌ-suh-fuh-NIZ-uhm, -FĒ-NIZ-uhm   'dʒoːsəfəˌnizəm,
        -ˌfiːˌnizəm

Josephson
Brian D., *Welsh physicist (Nobel*   JŌ-zuhf-suhn, JŌ-suhf-suhn   'dʒoːzəfsən, 'dʒoːsəfsən
    1973)

Foreign Sounds: ue: *Fr.* **rue**, *Ger.* **füllen**   uh(r): *Fr.* **boeuf**, *Ger.* **Höhle**   <u>kh</u>: *Ger.* **ich**, *Scot.* **loch**   ḡ: *Sp.* **amigo**   v: *Sp.* **hablar**
hl: *Welsh* **Llanelli.**   CAPITALS: primary stress.   SMALL CAPS: secondary stress.   ⑤: U.S. pron.   ⑪: British pron.

Josephus

   Flavius, *Jewish general/historian*   jō-SĒ-fuhs   dʒɔː'siːfəs

Josh

   pers. name   JAHSH   'dʒɑʃ

Joshua

   Old Testament book; pers. name   JAHSH-(uh-)wuh   'dʒɑʃ(ə)wə

Josiah

   pers. name   jō-SĪ-uh, jō-ZĪ-uh   dʒɔː'saiə, dʒɔː'zaiə

Josip

   pers. name, Serbo-Croatian   YAW-sēp   'jɔːsiːp

Jostens

   US education products co.   JAHS-tuhnz   'dʒɑstənz

Josue

   Old Testament book   JAHSH-uh-wē   'dʒɑʃəwiˑ

Jotunheimen

   mtn. range, Norway   YŌT-n-HĀ-muhn   'jɔːtn̩,heːmən

Joual

   French Canadian dialect   ZHWAHL, zhōō-AHL   'ʒwaːl, ʒuˈal

Jou Enlai

   see Chou En-Lai

Jouhaux

   Léon, *French labor leader,*   zhōō-Ō   ʒuːoː
   politician (Nobel 1951)

Joule

   1. James Prescott, *English*   JŌŌL, JOWL, JŌL   'dʒuːl, 'dʒaul, 'dʒɔːl
   physicist

   2. unit of energy   JŌŌL, JOWL   'dʒuːl, 'dʒaul

Jourdan

   Louis, *entertainer*   zhur-DEⁿ   ʒurdẽ

Jove

   supreme Roman god (Jupiter)   JŌV   'dʒɔːv

Jovian

   pert. to Jupiter   JŌ-vē-uhn   'dʒɔːviːən

Jowett

   Benjamin, *English scholar*   JŌ-uht   'dʒɔːət

Joyce

   pers. name   JOIS   'dʒɔis

Józef

   pers. name, Polish   YŌŌ-zef   'juːzef

Juab

   county, UT   JŌŌ-AB   'dʒuː,æb

Juan

   1. pers. name   (H)WAHN   '(h)wɑn
   2. French   ZHWAHⁿ   ʒɥã
   3. Spanish   KHWAHN   'xwɑn

Juan Fernández

   islands, Pacific   (H)WAHN fuhr-NAN-duhs   ,(h)wɑn fəʳ'næ007ndəs

Juang

   lang., people, India (Orissa)   JŌŌ-AHNG   'dʒuː,ɑŋ

Juanita

   1. pers. name   wuh-NĒT-uh, wah-NĒT-uh   wə'niːṭə, wɑ'niːṭə
   2. Spanish   khwah-NĒ-tah   xwɑ'niːtɑ

Juan-les-Pins

   resort, France   zhwahⁿ-lā-PEⁿ   ʒɥwãleːpẽ

Key (col. 2): a: fad ā: fade ah: father ar: Mary aw: law e: fed ē: feed er: merry i: hid ī: hide ō: coat ōō: boot
oi: boy ow: now u: put uh: above uhr: bird ch: chop ng: ring sh: show th: thick th: this zh: measure

Juarez
  Benito, *Mexican political leader*   KHWAHR-uhs   'xwɑrəs
Juárez, Ciudad
  town, Mexico   syo͞o-THAHTH KHWAHR-es   sju:'ðɑð 'xwares
Juba
  river, Africa; town, Sudan   JO͞O-buh   'dʒu:bə
Jubal
  pers. name   JO͞O-buhl   'dʒu:bəl
Jubilate
  hymn; prayer   yo͞o-buh-LAH-TĀ, JO͞O-buh-LĂT-ē   ju:bə'lɑ,te:, ˌdʒu:bə'leɪʈi·
Judaea
  see Judea
Judaeo-German [Yiddish]
  European Jewish language   jo͞o-DĀ-ō-JUHR-muhn   dʒu:'de:o:'dʒəʳmən
Judah
  pers. name   JO͞OD-uh   'dʒu:də
Judaic
  pert. to Judaism   jo͞o-DĀ-ik   dʒu:'de:ik
Judaica
  things pert. to Judaism   jo͞o-DĀ-i-kuh   dʒu:'de:ikə
Judaism
  Jewish religion   JO͞OD-uh-ɪz-uhm, JO͞OD-ē-ɪz-uhm   'dʒu:də,izəm, 'dʒu:di:,izəm
Judas
  pers. name, French   zhue-DAH   ʒy:dɑ
Judas Iscariot
  apostle who betrayed Christ   JO͞OD-uhs is-KAR-ē-uht   'dʒu:dəs is'kæri:ət
Judd
  pers. name   JUHD   'dʒəd
Jude
  New Testament book; pers. name   JO͞OD   'dʒu:d
Judea, Judaea
  ancient region, Palestine   ju-DĒ-uh, JU-DĀ-uh   dʒu'di:ə, ˌdʒu'de:ə
Judeo-
  combining form, Judaic or   jo͞o-DĀ-ō, jo͞o-DĒ-ō   dʒu'de:o:, dʒu'di:o:
  Judaism
Judezmo [Ladino]
  lang., Sephardic Jews   jo͞o-DES-mō, ju-DEZ-mō,   dʒu'desmo:, dʒu'dezmo:,
                                          ho͞o-DES-mō   hu:'desmo:
Judges
  Old Testament book   JUHJ-uhz   'dʒədʒəz
Judi
  pers. name   JO͞OD-ē   'dʒu:di·
Judith
  1. Old Testament book; pers.   JO͞OD-uhth   'dʒu:dəθ
  name
  2. Dutch   YUE-duht   'jy:dət
  3. French   zhue-DĒT   ʒy:di:t
  4. German   YO͞O-dit   'ju:dit
Judy
  pers. name   JO͞OD-ē   'dʒu:di·
Juggernaut
  idol of Krishna   JUHG-uhr-NAWT, -NAHT   'dʒəgəʳ,nɔ:t, -,nɑt
Jugoslav
  see Yugoslav

Jugoslavia
  see Yugoslavia

Jugurtha
  king of Numidia   ju-GUHR-thuh   dʒuˈgəʳθə

Juilliard
  School, The, *music school, NY*   JOOL-YAHRD, JOO-lē-AHRD   ˈdʒuːlˌjaʳd, ˈdʒuːliːˌaʳd

Jui [Puyi]
  lang., China   JOO-Ē   ˈdʒuːˈiː

Jukes
  family, focus of a sociological   JOOKS   ˈdʒuːks
     study

Jule
  pers. name   JOOL   ˈdʒuːl

Jules
  1. pers. name   JOOLZ   ˈdʒuːlz
  2. French   ZHUEL   ʒyːl

Julia
  1. Raul, *US actor; pers. name*   JOOL-yuh, JOO-lē-uh   ˈdʒuːljə, ˈdʒuːliːə
  2. Dutch   YUE-lē-ah   ˈjyːliːɑ
  3. Finnish   YOO-li-ah   ˈjuːliɑ
  4. French   zhuel-YAH   ʒyːljɑ

Julia Domna
  Roman empress   JOOL-yuh DAHM-nuh   ˌdʒuːljə ˈdɑmnə

Julia Luperca
  legendary Roman heroine   JOOL-yuh LOO-puhr-kuh   ˌdʒuːljə ˈluːpəʳkə

Julia Maesa
  sister of Julia Domna   JOOL-yuh MĪ-suh   ˌdʒuːljə ˈmaisə

Julia Mamaea
  mother of Roman emperor   JOOL-yuh mahm-Ē-uh, mahm-Ī-uh   ˌdʒuːljə mɑmˈiːə, mɑmˈaiə
     Alexander Severus

Julian
  1. pers. name   JOOL-yuhn   ˈdʒuːljən
  2. German   YOO-lē-AHN, yool-YAHN   juːliːˈan, juːlˈjan
  3. Polish   yool-YAHN   juːlˈjaːn

Julián
  pers. name, Spanish   khool-YAHN   xuːlˈjan

Juliana
  pers. name   JOO-lē-AN-uh   ˌdʒuːliːˈænə

Julian Alps
  Alpine mtn. range   JOOL-yuhn ALPS   ˈdʒuːljən ˈælps

Julian the Apostate
  Roman emperor   JOOL-yuhn thē uh-PAHS-TĀT   ˈdʒuːljən ðiˈ əˈpɑsˌteːt

Julie
  1. pers. name   JOO-lē   ˈdʒuːliˈ
  2. French   zhue-LĒ   ʒyːliː
  3. German   YOO-lē-uh, YOOL-yuh   ˈjuːliːə, ˈjuːljə

Julien
  1. pers. name   JOOL-yuhn   ˈdʒuːljən
  2. French   zhuel-YEⁿ   ʒyːljẽ

Juliet
  pers. name   JOOL-yuht, JOO-lē-ET, JOO-lē-ET   ˈdʒuːljət, ˌdʒuːliːˈet, ˈdʒuːliːˌet

Juliette
  1. pers. name   JOO-lē-ET   ˌdʒuːliːˈet
  2. French   zhuel-YET   ʒyːljet

Key (col. 2):   a: **fad**   ā: **fade**   ah: **father**   ar: **Mary**   aw: **law**   e: **fed**   ē: **feed**   er: **merry**   i: **hid**   ī: **hide**   ō: **coat**   ōō: **boot**
oi: **boy**   ow: **now**   u: **put**   uh: **above**   uhr: **bird**   ch: **chop**   ng: **ring**   sh: **show**   th: **thick**   th: **this**   zh: **measure**

Julilla
  Roman female name   juh-LIL-uh   dʒə'lilə
Julio
  pers. name, Spanish   KHO͞OL-yō   'xuːljoː
Júlio
  pers. name, Portuguese   ZHO͞OL-yo͞o   'ʒuːljuː
Julius
  1. pers. name   YO͞OL-yuhs, JO͞O-lē-uhs   'juːljəs, 'dʒuːliːəs
  2. Czech   YU-li-us   'julius
  3. Danish, German   YO͞O-lē-us   'juːliːus
  4. Dutch   YUE-lē-ues   'jyːliːys
Julius Echter Hefe-Weissbier
  German beer   YO͞O-lē-us EKH-tuhr HĀ-fuh-VĪS-BIR   'juːliːus 'eçtəʳ 'heːfə,vais,biʳ
July
  month   juh-LĪ   dʒə'lai
Jumada
  Islamic month   ju-MAHD-uh   dʒu'madə
Jumna [Yamuna]
  river, India   JUHM-nuh   'dʒəmnə
Junco
  songbird   JUHNG-kō   'dʒəŋkoː
June
  month; pers. name   JO͞ON   'dʒuːn
Juneau
  county, WI; division, AK   JO͞O-nō   'dʒuːnoː
Junee
  town, Australia   ju-NĒ, JO͞O-nē   dʒu'niː, 'dʒuːniˑ
Juneteenth
  June 19th celebrated in the US   jo͞on-TĒNTH   dʒuːn'tiːnθ
    South as a day of freedom from
    slavery
Jung
  Carl, Swiss psychiatrist   YUNG   'juŋ
Jungfrau
  mtn. peak, Switzerland   YUNG-FROW   'juŋ,frau
Jungian
  pert. to Jung   YUNG-ē-uhn   'juŋiːən
Juniata
  county, PA   JO͞O-nē-AT-uh   ,dʒuːniː'æṭə
Junipero
  pers. name, Spanish   kho͞o-NĒ-pā-rō, ⑤ ho͞o-NIP-uh-ruh   xuː'niːpeːroː, ⑤ huː'nipərə
Junius
  pers. name   JO͞ON-yuhs, JO͞O-nē-uhs   'dʒuːnjəs, 'dʒuːniːəs
Junker
  Prussian aristocrats   YUNG-kuhr   'juŋkəʳ
Juno
  Roman queen of the gods   JO͞O-nō   'dʒuːnoː
Junoesque
  stately, regal   JO͞O-nō-ESK   ,dʒuːnoː'esk
Jupiter
  supreme Roman god; planet; pers.   JO͞O-puht-uhr   'dʒuːpəṭəʳ
    name
Jura
  1. mtn. range, dept, France   zhue-RAH, ⑤ JUR-uh   ʒyːraː, ⑤ 'dʒurə
  2. island, Hebrides   JUR-uh   'dʒurə

Foreign Sounds: **ue:** *Fr.* **r**ue, *Ger.* f**ü**llen   **uh(r):** *Fr.* b**oeu**f, *Ger.* H**ö**hle   **kh:** *Ger.* i**ch**, *Scot.* lo**ch**   **g̃:** *Sp.* ami**g**o   **v̱:** *Sp.* ha**b**lar
hl: *Welsh* L**l**anelli.   CAPITALS: primary stress.   SMALL CAPS: secondary stress.   ⑤: U.S. pron.   ⑪: British pron.

Jurassic
  geologic period   juh-RAS-ik, jur-AS-   dʒəˈræsik, dʒurˈæs-
Jürgen
  1. pers. name, Danish   YUER-g̊uhn   ˈjyrɣən
  2. German   YUR-guhn   ˈjyᵍgən
Jurgensen
  Christian Adolph III, *US sports*   JUHR-guhn-suhn   ˈdʒəᵍgənsən
    commentator
Juris Doctor
  doctor of law, J.D.   JUR-uhs DAHK-TAWR, YUR-uhs,   ˈdʒurəs ˈdɑk‚tɔːʳ, ˈjurəs,
                                   DAHK-tuhr   ˈdɑktəʳ
Juruá
  river, S. America   ZHUR-uh-WAH, zhur-WAH   ‚ʒurəˈwɑ, ʒuʳˈwɑ
Justice
  pers. name   JUHS-tuhs   ˈdʒəstəs
Justin
  1. pers. name   JUHS-tuhn   ˈdʒəstən
  2. French   zhue-STEⁿ   ʒyːstɛ̃
  3. German   yus-TĒN   jusˈtiːn
Justine
  1. pers. name   JUH-STĒN   ‚dʒəˈstiːn
  2. French   zhue-STĒN   ʒyːstiːn
Justinian
  name, Eastern Roman emperors;   JUHS-TIN-ē-uhn   ‚dʒəsˈtiniːən
    pers. name
Justus
  1. pers. name   JUHS-tuhs   ˈdʒəstəs
  2. Dutch   YUES-tues   ˈjystyːs
  3. German   YUS-tus   ˈjustus
Jute
  member of a continental   JOOT   ˈdʒuːt
    Germanic tribe
Jutish
  having characteristics of a Jute   JOOT-ish   ˈdʒuːṭiʃ
Jutland
  Danish peninsula   JUHT-luhnd   ˈdʒətlənd
Juturna
  Roman nymph of the springs   ju-TUHR-nuh, yu-TUHR-nuh   dʒuˈtəʳnə, juˈtəʳnə
Juvenal
  Roman satirist   JOO-vuhn-l   ˈdʒuːvənḷ
Juventas [Iuventas]
  Roman goddess of youth   joo-VENT-uhs, yoo-VENT-uhs   dʒuːˈventəs, juːˈventəs
Juventius
  pers. name   joo-VEN-sh(ē-)uhs   dʒuːˈvenʃ(iː)əs
Juventus
  Italian soccer team   yoo-VEN-tuhs   juːˈventəs
Jylland [Jutland]
  Danish peninsula   YOO-LAHN   ˈjuː‚lɑːn

Key (col. 2):   a: fad   ā: fade   ah: father   ar: Mary   aw: law   e: fed   ē: feed   er: merry   i: hid   ī: hide   ō: coat   ōō: boot
oi: boy   ow: now   u: put   uh: above   uhr: bird   ch: chop   ng: ring   sh: show   th: thick   th̲: this   zh: measure

K

Kaaawa
    village, HI   KAH-AH-AH-wuh, KAH-uh-AH-wuh,   ˌkɑˌɑ'awə, ˌkɑə'awə,
                                 kuh-AH-AH-wuh   kəˌɑ'awə

Kaaba
    Islamic sacred building   KAHB-uh   'kɑbə

Kabardian
    lang., Caucasus Mts.   kuh-BAHR-dē-uhn   kə'bɑʳdiːən

Kabuki
    Japanese drama   kah-bo͞o-kē, Ⓢ kuh-BO͞O-kē,   kɑbuːkiˑ, Ⓢ kə'buːkiˑ,
                                KAHB-u-kē   'kɑbukiˑ

Kabul
    river, city, prov, Afghanistan   kah-BO͞OL, KAHB-uhl   kɑ'buːl, 'kɑbəl

Kabyle
    lang., people, Algeria   kuh-BĪL, kuh-BĒL   kə'bail, kə'biːl

Kachina
    Pueblo ancestral spirit   kuh-CHĒ-nuh   kə'tʃiːnə

Kachin [Jinghpo]
    lang., China, Burma, India   KAH-CHIN   'kɑ'tʃin

Kádár
    Janos, Hungarian political leader   KAH-DAHR   'kɑːˌdɑːʳ

Kaddish
    Jewish prayer for the dead   KAHD-ish   'kɑdiʃ

Kadesh
    ancient city, Syria   KĀ-DESH   'keːˌdeʃ

Kadett
    tdmk for a German automobile   kuh-DET   kə'det

Kaduna
    town, state, Nigeria   kuh-DO͞O-nuh   kə'duːnə

Kael
    Pauline, US film critic   KĀL   'keːl

Kaesŏng
    town, N. Korea   KĀ-SAWNG   'keːˌsɔːŋ

Kafa
    lang., people, Ethiopia, Kenya   KAHF-uh, KAF-uh   'kɑfə, 'kæfə

Kaffir, Kafir
    Bantu people   KAF-uhr   'kæfəʳ

Kaffiyeh
    Arab headdress   kah-FĒ-(y)uh, kuh-   kɑ'fiː(j)ə, kə-

Kaffraria
    region, S. Africa   kuh-FRAR-ē-uh, kuh-FRER-ē-uh   kə'fræriːə, kə'freriːə

Kafka
    Franz, Austrian writer   KAHF-kuh   'kɑfkə

Foreign Sounds: ue: *Fr.* **rue**, *Ger.* **füllen** uh(r): *Fr.* **boeuf**, *Ger.* **Höhle** kh: *Ger.* **ich**, *Scot.* **loch** ḡ: *Sp.* **amigo** v̱: *Sp.* **hablar**
hl: *Welsh* **Llanelli.** CAPITALS: primary stress. SMALL CAPS: secondary stress. Ⓢ: U.S. pron. Ⓛ: British pron.

Kafkaesque
  pert. to Kafka   KAHF-kuh-ESK, KAF-   ˌkɑfkə'esk, ˌkæf-

Kagawa
  prefecture, Japan   kah-gah-wah   kɑgɑwɑ

Kagoshima
  city, Japan   kah-gō-shē-mah   kagoːʃiːma

Kahanamoku
  Duke, *US surfer*   kuh-HAHN-uh-MŌ-koo   kəˌhanə'moːkuː

Kahane
  Meir, *activist rabbi*   kah-HAHN-ā, kuh-   kɑ'haneː, kə-

Kahlil
  pers. name   kuh-LĒL   kə'liːl

Kahlúa
  liqueur   kuh-LOO-uh   kə'luːə

Kahn
  Michael, *US stage director*   KAHN   'kɑn

Kahului
  city, airport, HI   KAH-hoo-LOO-ē   ˌkahuː'luːiː

Kai
  pers. name, Swedish   KĪ   'kai

Kaibab
  National Forest, *Indian*   KĪ-BAB   'kai,bæb
    reservation, AZ

Kaieteur
  waterfall, Guyana   KĪ-uh-TUR, KĪ-CHUR   'kaiəˌtuʳ, 'kaiˌtʃuʳ

Kaifeng, K'ai-feng
  city, China   KĪ-FUHNG   'kai'fəŋ

Kaifu
  Toshiki, *prime minister, Japan*   kī-foo   kaifuː

Kailua
  town, HI   kī-LOO-uh   kai'luːə

Kaiser
  title for a German or Austrian   KĪ-zuhr   'kaizəʳ
    emperor

Kaiserbräu Bamberg
  German beer   KĪ-zuhr-BROI BAHM-BERK   'kaizəʳˌbrɔi 'bɑmˌberk

Kaiserdom
  German beer   KĪ-zuhr-DAWM   'kaizəʳˌdɔːm

Kaiserdom Rauchbier
  German beer   KĪ-zuhr-DAWM ROWKH-BIR   'kaizəʳˌdɔːm 'rɑuxˌbiʳ

Kaiserslautern
  city, Germany   KĪ-zuhrz-LOWT-uhrn   ˌkaizəʳz'lauʈəʳn

Kai Tak
  airport, Hong Kong   KĪ TAHK, Ⓢ KĪ TAK   'kai 'tɑk, Ⓢ 'kai ˌtæk

Kake
  village, AK   KAK-ē, KAHK-ē   'kækiˑ, 'kakiˑ

Kakuei
  Tanaka, *prime minister, Japan*   kah-koo-ā   kakuːeː

Kalahari
  desert region, Africa   KAL-uh-HAHR-ē, KAHL-uh-HAHR-ē   ˌkælə'hariˑ, ˌkalə'hariˑ

Kalakaua
  avenue, Honolulu, HI   KAH-luh-KOW-uh   ˌkalə'kauə

Kalakh
  ancient Assyrian city   KAHL-AHKH   'kalˌax

Key (col. 2):   a: fad   ā: fade   ah: father   ar: Mary   aw: law   e: fed   ē: feed   er: merry   i: hid   ī: hide   ō: coat   ōō: boot
oi: boy   ow: now   u: put   uh: above   uhr: bird   ch: chop   ng: ring   sh: show   th: thick   th: this   zh: measure

Kalamazoo
  river, city, county, MI   KAL-uh-muh-ZOO   ˌkæləmə'zuː

Kalambo
  waterfall, Africa   kuh-LAHM-bō   kə'lɑmboː

Kalanchoe
  plant   KAL-uhn-KŌ-ē, kuh-LANG-kuh-wē   ˌkælən'koːiˑ, kə'læŋkəwiˑ

Kalashnikov
  Russian-designed automatic rifle   kuh-LAHSH-ni-KAWF, -KAWV, -KAHV   kə'laʃni,kɔːf, -,kɔːv, -,kɑv

Kalat
  former Indian state, town, Pakistan   kuh-LAHT   kə'lɑt

Kalaupapa
  leper colony, HI   kuh-LAH-u-PAHP-uh   kəˌlau'pɑpə

Kalawao
  county, HI   KAHL-uh-WOW   ˌkɑlə'wɑu

Kalb
  Marvin Leonard, radio and TV news correspondent   KALB   'kælb

Kalback
  Swedish beer   KAHL-BAHK   'kɑːl,bɑk

Kalevala
  national epic of Finland   KAHL-i-VAHL-uh   ˌkɑli'vɑlə

Kalgan
  city, China   KAHL-GAHN, $ KAL-GAN   'kɑl'gɑn, $ 'kæl'gæn

Kalgoorlie
  city, Australia   kal-GUR-lē   kæl'guʳliˑ

Kalinga
  lang., people, Philippine Islands   kuh-LING-guh   kə'liŋgə

Kalinin
  city, Russia   kuhl-YĒN-yēn, $ kuh-LĒ-nuhn   kəl'jiːnjiːn, $ kə'liːnən

Kalispel
  N. American people   KAL-uh-SPEL, KAL-uh-SPEL   'kælə,spel, ,kælə'spel

Kalispell
  town, MT   KAL-uh-SPEL, KAL-uh-SPEL   'kælə,spel, ,kælə'spel

Kalisz
  prov, Poland   KAH-lēsh   'kɑːliːʃ

Kalkaska
  county, MI   kal-KAS-kuh   kæl'kæskə

Kálmán
  pers. name, Hungarian   KAHL-mahn   'kɑːlmɑːn

Kalmuk [Kalmyk]
  lang., people, Russia   KAL-MUHK, kal-MUHK   'kæl,mək, kæl'mək

Kalmyk
  lang., people, Russia   KAL-mik   'kælmik

Kalpa Sutra
  Jain scripture   KUHL-puh SOO-truh   'kəlpə 'suːtrə

Kalpa Vruksha
  Hindu festival   KUHL-puhv RUHK-shuh   'kəlpəv 'rəkʃə

Kam
  lang., China   KAHM, KAM   'kɑm, 'kæm

Kamakura
  town, Japan   kahm-ah-kur-ah   kɑmɑkurɑ

Kama Sutra
  Indian erotic text   KAHM-uh SOO-truh   ˌkɑmə 'suːtrə

Foreign Sounds: ue: *Fr.* **rue**, *Ger.* **füllen**   uh(r): *Fr.* **boeuf**, *Ger.* **Höhle**   <u>kh</u>: *Ger.* **ich**, *Scot.* **loch**   g̃: *Sp.* **amigo**   <u>v</u>: *Sp.* **hablar**   hl: *Welsh* **Llanelli**.   CAPITALS: primary stress.   SMALL CAPS: secondary stress. $: U.S. pron.   £: British pron.

Kamba [Kikamba]
  lang., people, Africa   KAHM-buh   'kɑmbə
Kamchatka
  peninsula, Russia   kahm-CHAHT-kuh, kam-CHAT-kuh   kam'tʃatkə, kæm'tʃætkə
Kamehameha
  King of Hawaii   kuh-MĀ-uh-MĀ-hah   kə‚meːə'meːhɑ
Kamerlingh Onnes
  Heike, *Dutch physicist (Nobel 1913)*   KAHM-uhr-ling AWN-uhs   'kɑməʳliŋ 'ɔːnəs
Kamia
  N. American people   KAHM-ē-uh   'kɑmiːə
Kamil
  pers. name, Polish   KAHM-yēl   'kɑːmjiːl
Kamose
  Egyptian king   KAH-MŌS   'kɑ‚moːs
Kampala
  capital, Uganda   kahm-PAHL-uh   kam'pɑlə
Kampleman
  Max M., *US ambassador*   KAM-puhl-muhn   'kæmpəlmən
Kampuchea [Cambodia]
  republic, SE Asia   KAHM-puh-CHĒ-uh, KAM-   ‚kɑmpə'tʃiːə, ‚kæm-
Kampuchean
  pert. to Kampuchea   KAHM-puh-CHĒ-uhn, KAM-   ‚kɑmpə'tʃiːən, ‚kæm-
Kanabec
  county, MN   kuh-NĀ-bek, kuh-NAW-bek   kə'neːbek, kə'nɔːbek
Kanaka
  Hawaiian *"native" & derisive for "mainlander"*   *sg.* kuh-NAHK-uh, *pl.* KAHN-uh-kuh   *sg.* kə'nɑkə, *pl.* 'kɑnəkə
Kananga
  city, central Africa   kuh-NAHNG-guh   kə'naŋə
Kanara
  state, India   KAHN-uh-ruh   'kɑnərə
Kanarese [Kannada]
  lang., people, India   KAN-uh-RĒZ, -RĒS   ‚kænə'riːz, -'riːs
Kanawha
  river, county, WV; Park, *ballpark, Charleston, SC*   kuh-NAW-(w)uh, kuh-NOI   kə'nɔː(w)ə, kə'nɔi
Kanazawa
  port, Japan   kahn-ah-zah-wah   kɑnɑzɑwɑ
Kanchenjunga, Kangchenjunga [Kinchinjunga]
  mtn., Himalaya   KAN-chuhn-JUHNG-guh, -JUNG-guh   ‚kæntʃən'dʒəŋgə, -'dʒuŋgə
Kanda
  district, Japan   kahn-dah   kɑndɑ
Kāndāhār
  prov & town, Pakistan   KAHN-duh-HAHR, KAN-duh-HAHR   'kɑndə‚hɑʳ, 'kændə‚hɑʳ
Kandahār
  prov, Afghanistan   KAHN-duh-HAHR   'kɑndə‚hɑʳ
Kander
  John, *US composer*   KAN-duhr   'kændəʳ
Kandinsky
  Wassily, *Russian painter*   kuhn-DYĒN-skyi, Ⓢ kan-DIN(T)-skē   kən'djiːnskjij, Ⓢ kæn'din(t)skiˑ
Kandiyohi
  county, MN   KAN-duh-yō-HĪ   ‚kændəjoː'hai

Key (col. 2):   a: fad   ā: fade   ah: father   ar: **Mary**   aw: **law**   e: fed   ē: feed   er: **merry**   i: hid   ī: hide   ō: coat   ōō: boot
oi: **boy**   ow: **now**   u: put   uh: **above**   uhr: **bird**   ch: **chop**   ng: **ring**   sh: **show**   th: **thick**   t̲h̲: **this**   zh: measure

Kandy
   city, Sri Lanka   KAN-dē   'kændiˑ

Kaneohe
   city, HI   KAHN-ē-Ō-ē, KAHN-ē-Ō-hā   ˌkaniˑˈoːiː, ˌkaniˑˈoːheː

Kanesh [Kültepe]
   ancient Assyrian city, Turkey   KAHN-uhsh, KAHN-ESH   'kanəʃ, 'kanˌeʃ

Kangchenjunga
   see Kanchenjunga

KaNgwane
   state, South Africa   kahng-(G)WAH-nā   kaŋˈ(g)waneː

Kang Wu
   Chinese year (Horse)   KAHNG WŌO   'kaŋ 'wuː

Kanin
   peninsula, Barents Sea   KAN-uhn   'kænən

Kanjobal, Kanhobal
   lang., people, Guatemala   kahn-ō-V̲AHL   kanoːˈβal

Kankakee
   river, US; city, county, IL   KANG-kuh-KĒ   ˌkæŋkəˈkiː

Kankanay
   lang., people, Philippine Islands   KAHNG-kuh-NĪ, KAHNG-kuh-NĪ   ˌkaŋkəˈnai, 'kaŋkəˌnai

Kannada [Kanarese]
   lang., people, India   KAHN-uhd-uh, KAN-uhd-uh   'kanədə, 'kænədə

Kannapolis
   town, NC   kuh-NAP-(uh-)luhs   kəˈnæp(ə)ləs

Kannon
   Japanese festival   kahn-(n)awn   kan(n)ɔːn

Kano
   state, city, Nigeria; school of   KAHN-ō   'kanoː
     painters

Kanpur
   city, India   KAHN-PUR   'kanˌpuʳ

Kansa
   N. American people   KAN-zuh, KAN-suh   'kænzə, 'kænsə

Kansan
   pert. to Kansas   KAN-zuhn   'kænzən

Kansas
   state, river, US   KAN-zuhs   'kænzəs

Kansu
   see Gansu

Kant
   Immanuel, *German philosopher*   KAHNT, KANT   'kant, 'kænt

Kantian
   pert. to Kant   KAHNT-ē-uhn, KANT-ē-uhn   'kantiːən, 'kæntiːən

Kantianism
   adherence to Kantian philosophy   KANT-ē-uh-NIZ-uhm,   'kæntiːəˌnizəm,
                       KAHNT-ē-uh-NIZ-uhm,   'kantiːəˌnizəm,
                       KAN-chuh-NIZ-uhm,   'kæntʃəˌnizəm,
                       KAHN-chuh-NIZ-uhm   'kantʃəˌnizəm

Kantner
   Paul, *US rock singer, songwriter*   KANT-nuhr   'kæntnəʳ

Kanto
   region, Japan   kahn-tō   kantoː

Kanuri
   lang., people, Nigeria, Niger   kuh-NUR-ē   kəˈnuriˑ

Foreign Sounds: ue: *Fr.* **rue**, *Ger.* f**ü**llen   uh(r): *Fr.* b**oeu**f, *Ger.* H**öh**le   k̲h̲: *Ger.* i**ch**, *Scot.* lo**ch**   g̲: *Sp.* ami**g**o   v̲: *Sp.* ha**b**lar
hl: *Welsh* **Ll**anelli.   CAPITALS: primary stress.   SMALL CAPS: secondary stress.   ⓈＳ: U.S. pron.   Ⓛ: British pron.

Kao-hsiung
  city, Taiwan   GOW-shē-UNG, GOW-SHUNG   'gauʃiː'uŋ, 'gau'ʃuŋ

Kaolan [Lanzhou]
  city, China   KOW-LAHN   'kau'lɑn

Kaoru
  pers. name, Japanese   kah-ō-r$\overline{oo}$ kaoːruː

Kapadokya [Cappadocia]
  region, Turkey   KAHP-ah-DAWK-yah   ˌkapa'dɔːkja

Kapellmeister
  German for choirmaster   kuh-PEL-MĪ-stuhr, kah-   kə'pel,maistəʳ, ka-

Kaplan
  Gabriel, *actor, comedian*   KAP-luhn   'kæplən

Kaposi's sarcoma
  skin disease   KAHP-ō-SHĒZ sahr-KŌ-muh,   ˌkapoːˌʃiːz saʳ'koːmə,
                              KAHP-uh-SĒZ, kuh-PŌ-sēz,   ˌkapəˌsiːz, kəˌpoːsiːz,
                              kuh-PŌ-shēz   kəˌpoːʃiːz

Kapunda
  town, Australia   kuh-PUHN-duh   kə'pəndə

Kapuskasing
  town, Ontario   KAP-uh-SKÃ-sing   ˌkæpə'skeːsiŋ

Kapuziner
  "Capuchin," German beer   KAH-P$\overline{OO}$T-SĒ-nuhr   ˌka,puːt'siːnəʳ

Kara
  Sea, *Arctic*   KAHR-uh   'karə

Karachai
  former autonomous oblast, USSR   KAR-uh-CHĪ   ˌkærə'tʃai

Karachay [Balkar]
  lang., people, Caucasus Mts.   KAR-uh-CHĪ, KAR-uh-CHĪ   ˌkærə'tʃai, 'kærəˌtʃai

Karachi
  city, Pakistan   kuh-RAHCH-ē   kə'ratʃiː

Karadeniz Boğazı [Bosporus]
  strait, Turkey   KAHR-uh-duh-NĒZ bō-ĞAHZ-ē   ˌkarədə'niːz boː'ɣaziː

Karajan
  Herbert von, *Austrian conductor*   KAHR-uh-YAHN   'karəjan

Karakalpak
  lang., republic, Uzbekistan   KAR-uhk-uhl-PAK, KAR-uhk-ahl-PAK   ˌkærəkəl'pæk, ˌkærəkal'pæk

Karakoram Range
  mtn. range, Asia   KAR-uh-KŌR-uhm, -KAWR-uhm   ˌkærə'koːrəm, -'koːrəm

Karakul
  sheep breed   KAR-uh-kuhl   'kærəkəl

Kara Kum, Qara Qum
  desert, Turkmenistan   KAR-uh K$\overline{OO}$M, KAHR-uh K$\overline{OO}$M   ˌkærə 'kuːm, ˌkarə 'kuːm

Karamanlis
  Constantine, *president of Greece*   KAHR-uh-MAHN-LĒS,   ˌkarə,man'liːs,
                              KAHR-uh-MAHN-LĒS   ˌkarə'man,liːs

Karamazov
  see Brothers Karamazov, The

Karamchand
  pers. name, Gujarati   KUH-ruhm-CHUHND   'kərəm,tʃənd

Karame
  Rashid, *Lebanese statesman*   KAHR-uh-MÃ   'karə,meː

Karamojong
  lang., people, Uganda, Kenya   KAR-uh-MŌ-JAHNG   ˌkærə'moːˌdʒaŋ

Karankawa
  N. American people   kuh-RANG-kuh-WAW   kə'ræŋkə,wɔː

Key (col. 2):   a: fad   ã: fade   ah: father   ar: Mary   aw: law   e: fed   ē: feed   er: merry   i: hid   ī: hide   ō: coat $\overline{oo}$: boot
oi: boy   ow: now   u: put   uh: above   uhr: bird   ch: chop   ng: ring   sh: show   th: thick   <u>th</u>: this   zh: measure

Karawanken [Caravanche]
Alpine mtn. range   KAHR-uh-VAHNG-kuhn   ˌkɑrə'vaŋkən

Kareem
pers. name   kuh-RĒM   kə'riːm

Karel
  1. pers. name, Czech   KAH-REL   'kɑːˌrel
  2. Dutch   KAHR-uhl   'kɑːrəl

Karelian
lang., people, Russia   kuh-RĒ-lē-uhn, kuh-RĒL-yuhn   kə'riːliːən, kə'riːljən

Karen
  1. pers. name   KAR-uhn, KAHR-uhn   'kærən, 'kɑrən
  2. Danish, Norwegian   KAHR-uhn   'kɑrən
  3. lang., people, Burma, Thailand   kuh-REN   kə'ren

Karénina, Anna
  see Anna Karénina

Kareshkova
Valentina, *cosmonaut, USSR*   kuh-RESH-kuh-vuh   kə'reʃkəvə

Kari
lang., Chad, Cameroon, Central   KAR-ē, KAHR-ē   'kæriˑ, 'kɑriˑ
  African Rep.

Karin
pers. name   KAHR-uhn, KAR-uhn, KER-uhn,   'kɑrən, 'kærən, 'kerən,
      kuh-RIN   kə'rin

Karl
  1. pers. name, English, German   KAHRL   'kɑʳl
  2. Danish, Dutch, Norwegian,   KAHRL   'karl
    Swedish
  3. Finnish, Russian   KAHRL   'kɑːrl
  4. French   KAHRL   kɑːrl

Karle
Jerome, *US physicist (Nobel 1985)*   KAHRL   'kɑʳl

Karlfeldt
E. A., *Swedish poet (Nobel 1931)*   KAHRL-FELT   'kɑʳlˌfelt

Karlheinz
pers. name, German   KAHRL-HĪNTS   'kɑʳlˌhaints

Karl Marx Stadt [Chemnitz]
city, Germany   kahrl MAHRK SHTAHT   kɑʳl 'mɑʳk ʃtɑt

Karlovac
city, Croatia   KAHR-luh-VAHTS   'kɑːʳləˌvɑːts

Karlovacko
Yugoslavian beer   KAHR-lō-VAHT-skō   ˌkarloː'vatskoː

Karlsbad
city, Czech republic   KAHRLZ-BAHT   'kɑʳlzˌbat

Karlsruhe
city, Germany   KAHRLZ-ROO-uh   'kɑʳlzˌruːə

Karmal
Babrak, *president, Afghanistan*   KAHR-muhl   'kɑʳməl

Karnak
village, temple, Egypt   KAHR-NAK   'kɑʳˌnæk

Karnataka
state, India   kahr-NAHT-uh-kuh   kɑʳˈnɑtəkə

Karnische Alpen [Carnic Alps]
Alpine mtn. range   KAHR-nish-uh AHL-puhn   'kɑʳniʃə 'ɑlpən

Kärnten
state, Austria   KERNT-n   'keʳntn̩

Foreign Sounds: **ue:** *Fr.* r**ue**, *Ger.* f**ü**llen   **uh(r):** *Fr.* b**oeu**f, *Ger.* H**öh**le   <u>kh</u>: *Ger.* i**ch**, *Scot.* lo**ch**   ğ: *Sp.* ami**g**o   <u>v</u>: *Sp.* ha**b**lar
hl: *Welsh* **Ll**anelli.   CAPITALS: primary stress.   SMALL CAPS: secondary stress.   (Ⓢ): U.S. pron.   (Ⓔ): British pron.

Karok
   N. American people   kuh-RAHK   kəˈrɑk

Karol
   pers. name   KAR-uhl, KER-uhl   ˈkærəl, ˈkerəl

Károly
   pers. name, Hungarian   KAH-rōl(-yuh)   ˈkɑːroːlj

Karolyi
   Bela, *Hungarian gymnastics coach*   KAHR-uhl-yē, ⑤ kuh-RŌ-lē   ˈkɑrəljiˈ, ⑤ kəˈroːliˈ

Karpov
   Anatoly, *Russian chess master*   KAHR-PAWF   ˈkɑːʳˌpɔːf

Karras
   Alex, *US actor*   KAR-uhs, KER-uhs   ˈkærəs, ˈkerəs

Karrer
   Paul, *Swiss chemist (Nobel 1937)*   KAHR-uhr   ˈkɑrəʳ

Karsavina
   Tamara, *Russian dancer*   KUHR-SAHV-yuh-nuh   ˌkəʳˈsɑːvjənə

Karuah
   river, Australia   kuh-ROO-uh   kəˈruːə

Kasai
   river, Africa   kuh-SĪ   kəˈsai

Kasavubu
   Joseph, *Zairian political leader*   KAH-sah-VOO-BOO   ˌkɑsɑˈvuːˌbuː

Kasbah, Casbah
   Arab quarter of city, esp. Algiers   KAZ-BAH, KAHZ-BAH   ˈkæzˌbɑ, ˈkɑzˌbɑ

Kasel
   German wine   KAH-suhl   ˈkɑːsəl

Kashmir, Cashmere
   region, India   KASH-MIR, KAZH-MIR, kash-MIR, kazh-MIR   ˈkæʃˌmiʳ, ˈkæʒˌmiʳ, kæʃˈmiʳ, kæʒˈmiʳ

Kashmiri
   lang., people, India & Pakistan   kazh-MIR-ē, kash-   kæʒˈmiriˈ, kæʃ-

Kashubian [Cassubian]
   lang., Europe   kash-OO-bē-uhn   kæʃˈuːbiːən

Kasim
   pers. name, Persian   KAHS-im   ˈkɑːsim

Kasimir
   pers. name, German   KAHZ-ē-MIR   ˈkɑziːˌmiʳ

Kasiwihara
   Ken, *TV journalist*   KAHS-uh-wuh-HAR-uh, -HAHR-uh   ˌkɑsəwəˈhærə, -ˈhɑrə

Kaska
   N. American people   KAS-kuh   ˈkæskə

Kaskaskia
   river, college, IL   kas-KAS-kē-uh   kæsˈkæskiːə

Kaspar
   1. *pers. name, Danish*   KAHS-PAHR   ˈkɑːsˌpɑr
   2. *Dutch*   KAHS-PAHR   ˈkɑsˌpɑr
   3. *German*   KAHS-PAHR   ˈkɑsˌpɑʳ
   4. *Hungarian*   KAHSH-PAHR   ˈkɑʃˌpɑr

Kassebaum
   Nancy, *US politician*   KAS-uh-BAWM, -BOWM   ˈkæsəˌbɔːm, -ˌbaum

Kasserine
   village, Tunisia   KAHS-uh-RĒN   ˈkɑsəˌriːn

Kassites
   ancient people of Iran   KAS-ĪTS   ˈkæsˌaits

Key (col. 2):   a: fad   ā: fade   ah: father   ar: Mary   aw: law   e: fed   ē: feed   er: merry   i: hid   ī: hide   ō: coat   ōō: boot
oi: boy   ow: now   u: put   uh: above   uhr: bird   ch: chop   ng: ring   sh: show   th: thick   <u>th</u>: this   zh: measure

Kasten
Robert W., Jr., *US politician*   KAS-tuhn   'kæstən

Kastler
Alfred, *French physicist (Nobel*   kahst-LER   kɑːstler
1966)

Kastrioti [Scanderbeg]
George, *Albanian revolutionary*   KAHS-trē-ŌT-ē   ˌkɑstriˈoːʈiˈ
leader

Kastrup
airport, Copenhagen   KAHS-trup   'kɑstrup

Katahdin, Ktaadn
mtn., ME   kuh-TAHD-n   kə'tɑdn̩

Katanga
former name of Shaba, *Zaire*   kuh-TAHNG-guh, kuh-TANG-guh   kə'tɑŋgə, kə'tæŋgə

Katangese
pert. to Katanga   kuh-tahng-GĒZ, -GĒS   kətɑŋ'giːz, -'giːs

Katarina
pers. name, Russian   KAH-tah-RĒ-nah   ˌkɑːtɑ'riːnɑː

Kate
pers. name   KĀT   'keːt

Katerina
pers. name   KAT-uh-RĒ-nuh   ˌkæʈəˌriːnə

Katharevousa, Katharevusa
Modern Greek literary lang.   KAHTH-uh-REV-ōō-suh, KATH-   ˌkɑθə'revuːsə, ˌkæθ-

Katharina
1. character in Taming of the   KAT-uh-RĒ-nuh, KATH-   ˌkæʈə'riːnə, ˌkæθ-
Shrew, *Shakespeare; pers. name*
2. pers. name, German,   KAHT-ah-RĒ-nah   ˌkatɑ'riːnɑ
Hungarian

Katharine
1. pers. name   KATH-(uh-)ruhn   'kæθ(ə)rən
2. German   KAHT-ah-RĒ-nuh   ˌkatɑ'riːnə

Käthe
pers. name, German   KET-uh   'ketə

Katherine
1. river, town, Australia   KATH-uh-RĪN   'kæθəˌrɑin
2. pers. name   KATH-(uh-)ruhn   'kæθ(ə)rən

Kathie
pers. name   KATH-ē   'kæθiˈ

Kathleen
pers. name   kath-LĒN   kæθ'liːn

Kathryn
pers. name   KATH-ruhn   'kæθrən

Kathy
pers. name   KATH-ē   'kæθiˈ

Katie
pers. name   KĀT-ē   'keːtiˈ

Katmai
National Park and Preserve, *King*   KAT-MĪ   'kætˌmɑi
Salmon, AK

Katmandu
city, Nepal   KAT-man-DŌŌ, KAHT-mahn-DŌŌ, -muhn-DŌŌ   ˌkætmæn'duː, ˌkatman'duː, -mən'duː

Katoikiai
Seleucid rural colonies   kah-TOI-kē-Ī   ka'tɔikiːˌai

Foreign Sounds: ue: *Fr.* **rue,** *Ger.* f**ü**llen   uh(r): *Fr.* b**oeu**f, *Ger.* H**ö**hle   k<u>h</u>: *Ger.* i**ch**, *Scot.* lo**ch**   ḡ: *Sp.* ami**g**o   <u>v</u>: *Sp.* ha**b**lar
hl: *Welsh* **Ll**anelli.   CAPITALS: primary stress.   SMALL CAPS: secondary stress.   ⑤: U.S. pron.   ⑫: British pron.

Katoomba
  waterfall, Australia   kuh-TOOM-buh   kə'tuːmbə

Katowice
  city, Poland   KAHT-uh-VĒT-suh   ˌkaːtə'viːtsə

Katrina
  pers. name   kuh-TRĒ-nuh, ka-TRĒ-nuh   kə'triːnə, kæ'triːnə

Katrine
  loch, Scotland   KA-truhn   'kætrən

Katsunori
  pers. name, Japanese   kaht-su-nō-rē   katsunoːriː

Katsunosuke
  pers. name, Japanese   kaht-su-nō-su-ke   katsunoːsuke

Katsushika
  pers name, Japanese   kaht-soo-shē-kah   katsuːʃiːka

Kattegat, Cattegat
  Sound & Belts, North Sea   KAT-i-GAT, KAHT-i-GAHT   'kæti̯ˌgæt, 'kati̯ˌgat

Katy
  city, TX; pers. name   KĀT-ē   'keːti·

Katz
  Bernard, German-born British   KATS   'kæts
    biophysicist (Nobel 1970)

Katzenjammer Kids
  comic strip   KAT-suhn-JAM-uhr   'kætsənˌdʒæməʳ

Kauai
  county, HI   KOW-ī   'kauˌai

Kaufman
  George S., US dramatist   KAWF-muhn   'kɔːfmən

Kaufmann's
  US department store chain   KAWF-muhnz, KAHF-muhnz, KOWF-   'kɔːfmənz, 'kafmənz, 'kauf-

Kaukauna
  city, WI; cheese spread   kaw-KAW-nuh   kɔː'kɔːnə

Kaunas [Kovno]
  city, Lithuania   KOW-nuhs, -NAHS   'kaunəs, -ˌnas

Kaunda
  Kenneth, president, Zambia   kah-OON-duh   ka'uːndə

Kavanaugh
  Field, ballpark, Little Rock, AR   KAV-uh-NAW   'kævəˌnɔː

Kavkaz [Caucasus]
  mtn. range, between Europe and   KUHF-KAHZ   ˌkəf'kaz
    Asia

Kaw
  N. American people; usual Kansan   KAW   'kɔː
    name of Kansas River

Kawabata
  Yasunari, Japanese author (Nobel   kah-wah-bah-tah,   kawabata, Ⓢ ˌkawə'batə,
    1968)   Ⓢ KAH-wuh-BAHT-uh,   kə'wabətə
         kuh-WAHB-uht-uh

Kawasaki
  1. city, Japan   kah-wah-sahk-ē   kawasaki·
  2. tdmk for a motorcycle   KAH-wuh-SAHK-ē, KOW-uh-SAHK-ē   ˌkawə'saki·, ˌkauə'saki·

Kazak, Kazakh
  lang., people, Kazakhstan, China,   kuh-ZAHK, kuh-ZAK   kə'zak, kə'zæk
    Mongolian PR, Afghanistan

Kazakh
  republic, Asia   kuh-ZAHK, kuh-ZAK   kə'zak, kə'zæk

Key (col. 2):   a: fad   ā: fade   ah: father   ar: Mary   aw: law   e: fed   ē: feed   er: merry   i: hid   ī: hide   ō: coat   oo: boot
oi: boy   ow: now   u: put   uh: above   uhr: bird   ch: chop   ng: ring   sh: show   th: thick   th: this   zh: measure

Kazakhstan [Kazakh]
  republic, Asia   kuh-ZUH<u>KH</u>-STAHN,   kə,zɑx'stɑn, kəzak'stɑn,
                                 kuh-zahk-STAHN, kuh-zak-STAN   kəzæk'stæn

Kazakistan [Kazakh]
  republic, Asia   kuh-zahk-uh-STAHN,   kəzakə'stɑn, kəzækə'stæn
                                 kuh-zak-uh-STAN

Kazan
  1. Elia, US actor; river, Canada   kuh-ZAN   kə'zæn
  2. city, Russia   kuh-ZAHN(-yuh)   kə'zɑːn(jə)

Kazantzakis
  Nikos, Greek writer   KAHZ-ahn(t)-ZAHK-ēs,   ,kazɑn(t)'zakiːs,
                                  KAHZ-ahn(t)-SAHK-ēs   ,kazɑn(t)'sakiːs

Kazbek
  peak, Caucasus Mts.   kuhz-BYEK   kəz'bjek

Kazimierz
  pers. name, Polish   kah-ZĒM-yesh   kɑː'ziːmjeʃ

Kazimir
  pers. name, Russian   kuhz-yim-YIR   kəzjim'jir

Kea
  parrot   KĒ-uh   'kiːə

Kéa [Keos]
  island, Greece   KĀ-uh, KĒ-uh   'keːə, 'kiːə

Keach
  Stacy, Jr., US entertainer   KĒCH   'kiːtʃ

Kean
  Edmund, English actor; Thomas   KĒN   'kiːn
    H., *US politician*

Keanu
  pers. name (K. Reeves)   kē-AN-o͞o   kiː'ænuː

Kearney
  1. county, city, state college, NE   KAHR-nē   'kɑʳniˑ
  2. street, San Francisco, CA   KUHR-nē   'kəʳniˑ

Kearny
  county, KS; town, NJ   KAHR-nē   'kɑʳniˑ

Keating
  Thomas Arthur, US football player KĒT-ing   'kiːt̬iŋ

Keaton
  Diane, US actress; Michael, *US*   KĒT-n   'kiːtn̩
    actor

Keats
  John, English poet   KĒTS   'kiːts

Keatsian
  pert. to Keats   KĒT-sē-uhn   'kiːtsiːən

Keb [Geb]
  Egyptian earth god   KEB   'keb

Keble
  college, Oxford Univ.   KĒ-buhl   'kiːbəl

Kedah
  state, Malaysia   KED-uh   'kedə

Kedar
  Biblical name   KĒD-uhr   'kiːdəʳ

Kedron [Kidron]
  valley, Jordan   KED-ruhn, KĒ-druhn   'kedrən, 'kiːdrən

Keebler
  US baking co.   KĒ-bluhr   'kiːbləʳ

Foreign Sounds: ue: *Fr.* **rue**, *Ger.* **fü**llen uh(r): *Fr.* **b**oeuf, *Ger.* **Hö**hle <u>kh</u>: *Ger.* i**ch**, *Scot.* lo**ch** ğ: *Sp.* ami**g**o <u>v</u>: *Sp.* ha**b**lar
hl: *Welsh* **Ll**anelli. CAPITALS: primary stress. SMALL CAPS: secondary stress. Ⓢ: U.S. pron. Ⓛ: British pron.

Keeshond
   dog breed   KĀS-HAWNT   'keːs,hɔːnt

Keewatin
   district, Canada   kē-WĂT-n   kiːˈweːtn̩

Kefallinía [Cephalonia]
   region, Greece   KEF-uh-lē-NĒ-uh   ˌkefəliːˈniːə

Keffer
   pers. name   KEF-uhr   'kefəʳ

Keflavik
   port, Iceland   KYEB-luh-VĒK, ⑤ KEF-luh-VĒK   'kjeblə,viːk, ⑤ 'keflə,viˈk

Keijo
   Japanese for Seoul, *S. Korea*   kā-jō   keːdʒoː

Keillor
   Garrison, *US broadcaster*   KĒ-luhr   'kiːləʳ

Keir
   pers. name   KIR   'kiʳ

Keisha
   pers. name   KĒ-shuh   'kiːʃə

Keishiro
   pers. name, Japanese   kā-shē-rō   keːʃiːroː

Keisuke
   pers. name, Japanese   kā-suk-e   keːsuke

Keith
   pers. name   KĒTH   'kiːθ

Kekchi, Quekchi
   lang., people, Guatemala   KEK-chē   'kektʃiˈ

Kekkonen
   Urho, *president, Finland*   KEK-uh-NEN, KEK-uh-nuhn   'kekə,nen, 'kekənən

Kekulé von Stradonitz
   Friedrich August, *German chemist*   KĀ-k͞oo-LĀ fawn SHTRAHD-ō-nits   'keːkuː,leː fɔːn 'ʃtradoːnits

Kelley, Kellie
   pers. name   KEL-ē   'keliˈ

Kellogg
   Frank B., *US jurist, statesman*   KEL-AHG, KEL-AWG   'kel,ɑg, 'kel,ɔːg
   (Nobel 1929); US cereal co.

Kells
   city, Ireland   KELZ   'kelz

Kelly
   pers. name   KEL-ē   'keliˈ

Kelson
   pers. name   KEL-suhn   'kelsən

Kelvin
   temperature scale; pers. name   KEL-vuhn   'kelvən

Kelvinator
   tdmk for home appliances   KEL-vuh-NĀT-uhr   'kelvə,neːt̬əʳ

Kemal Atatürk
   Turkish political leader   ke-MAHL AH-tah-TUERK,   ke'mal ˌɑtaˈtyːrk, ⑤ kə'mæl
                     ⑤ kuh-MAL AT-uh-TUHRK   'ætə,təʳk

Kemi
   river, port, Finland   KEM-ē   'kemiˈ

Kemp
   Jack F., *US politician*   KEMP   'kemp

Kempis
   Thomas à, *German ecclesiastic,*   KEM-puhs   'kempəs
   author

Key (col. 2):   a: fad   ā: fade   ah: father   ar: Mary   aw: law   e: fed   ē: feed   er: merry   i: hid   ī: hide   ō: coat   o͞o: boot
oi: boy   ow: now   u: put   uh: above   uhr: bird   ch: chop   ng: ring   sh: show   th: thick   <u>th</u>: this   zh: measure

Ken
   pers. name   KEN   'ken

Kenai Fjords
   National Park, *Kenai, AK*   KĒ-NĪ FYAWRDZ   ,kiː,nɑi 'fjɔːʳdz

Kenai Peninsula
   division, AK   KĒ-NĪ   'kiː,nɑi

Kendall
   Edward C., *US chemist (Nobel*   KEN-dl   'kendl̩
     1950); Henry W., *US physicist*
     (Nobel 1990)

Kendra
   pers. name   KEN-druh   'kendrə

Kendrew
   Sir John Cowdrey, *English*   KEN-drōō   'kendruː
     biochemist (Nobel 1962)

Kendrick
   pers. name   KEN-drik   'kendrik

Kenelm
   pers. name   KEN-ELM   'ken,elm

Kenesaw
   pers. name   KEN-uh-SAW   'kenə,sɔː

Kenichi
   pers. name, Japanese   ken-ē-chē   keniˑtʃiˑ

Kenilworth
   town, England   KEN-l-WUHRTH   'kenl̩,wəʳθ

Kenji
   pers. name, Japanese   ken-jē   kendʒiː

Kennebec
   river, county, ME   KEN-uh-BEK, KEN-uh-BEK   ,kenə'bek, 'kenə,bek

Kennebunk
   town, ME   KEN-uh-BUHNGK, KEN-ē-;   'kenə,bəŋk, 'keniˑ-;
                     KEN-uh-BUHNGK, KEN-ē-   ,kenə'bəŋk, ,keni-

Kennebunkport
   town, ME   KEN-uh-BUHNGK-PŌRT, KEN-ē-,   ,kenə'bəŋk,pɔːʳt, ,keni-,
                     -PAWRT   -,pɔːʳt

Kennedy
   Edward Moore, *US senator;* John   KEN-uhd-ē   'kenədiˑ
     F., *35th US president;* Robert
     F., *US attorney general*

Kennesaw
   city, mtn., college, GA   KEN-uh-saw   'kenəsɔː

Kenneth
   pers. name   KEN-uhth   'kenəθ

Kenny
   pers. name   KEN-ē   'keniˑ

Kenosha
   city, county, WI   kuh-NŌ-shuh   kə'noːʃə

Kensington
   pers. name   KEN-zing-tuhn   'kenziŋtən

Kensington and Chelsea
   borough, England   KEN-zing-tuhn uhn CHEL-sē   'kenziŋtən ən 'tʃelsiˑ

Kent
   county, England; pers. name   KENT   'kent

Kentaro
   pers. name, Japanese   ken-tah-rō   kentɑroː

Kentucky
  state, US   kuhn-TUHK-ē, ken-TUHK-ē   kən'təkiˑ, ken'təkiˑ

Kenya
  mtn., republic, Africa   KEN-yuh, *(esp. before independence)* KĔN-yuh   'kenjə, *(esp. before independence)* 'kiːnjə

Kenyan
  adj.   KEN-yuhn, KĔN-yuhn   'kenjən, 'kiːnjən

Kenyapithecus Wickeri
  early hominid   KEN-yuh-PITH-i-kuhs WIK-uhr-ē, KĔN-yuh-   ˌkenjə'piθikəs 'wikəriˑ, ˌkiːnjə-

Kenyatta
  Jomo, president, Kenya   ken-YAHT-uh   ken'jɑtə

Kenyon
  John, US phonetician   KEN-yuhn   'kenjən

Keogh
  savings plan   KĒ-ō   'kiːoˑ

Keohane
  Nannerl O., US college president   kō-HĂN, kō-HAN   koˑ'heːn, koˑ'hæn

Keokuk
  county, IA   KĒ-uh-KUHK   'kiːə,kək

Keos [Kéa]
  island, Greece   KĒ-AHS, KĒ-AWS   'kiː,ɑs, 'kiː,ɔːs

Kepler
  Johannes, German astronomer   KEP-luhr   'keplər

Ker
  William Paton, British scholar   KER, KUHR, KAHR   'keʳ, 'kəʳ, 'kɑʳ

Kerala
  state, India   KER-uh-luh   'kerələ

Kerang
  lake district, Australia   kuh-RANG   kə'ræŋ

Kerch
  peninsula, port, Crimea   KERCH   'keʳtʃ

Keres
  1. people, lang., N. America   KĂ-rās   'keːreːs
  2. the Greek fates or destinies   KER-ēz   'keriːz

Keresan
  N. American people   KER-uh-suhn   'kerəsən

Kerguelen
  archipelago, Indian Ocean   KUHR-guh-luhn, KUHR-guh-LEN   'kəʳgələn, ˌkəʳgə'len

Kérkira [Corfu]
  island, Greece   KER-ki-ruh   'kerkirə

Kermān [Kirman]
  prov, city, Iran   kuhr-MAHN, ker-MAHN   kəʳ'mɑn, keʳ'mɑn

Kermit
  television and movie frog; pers. name   KUHR-muht, KUHR-MIT   'kəʳmət, 'kəʳ,mit

Kermode
  Frank, US literary critic   KAHR-muhd-ē   'kɑʳmədiˑ

Kern
  Jerome, US composer   KUHRN   'kəʳn

Kerouac
  Jack, US novelist   KER-uh-WAK   'kerə,wæk

Kerr
  1. Deborah, US entertainer   KAHR, KER, KUHR   'kɑʳ, 'keʳ, 'kəʳ
  2. pers. name   KUHR, Ⓔ KUHR, KAHR, KER   'kəʳ, Ⓔ 'kəʳ, 'kɑʳ, 'keʳ

Key (col. 2):   a: fad ā: fade ah: father ar: Mary aw: law e: fed ē: feed er: merry i: hid ī: hide ō: coat o͞o: boot
oi: boy   ow: now   u: put   uh: above   uhr: bird   ch: chop   ng: ring   sh: show   th: thick   th: this   zh: measure

Kerrigan
Thomas Anthony, *US poet, editor,*   KER-uh-guhn   'kerəgən
  translator

Kerry
pers. name   KAR-ē, KER-ē   'kæriˑ, 'keriˑ

Kershner
Irvin, *film director*   KUHRSH-nuhr   'kəʳʃnəʳ

Kesey
Ken, *US writer*   KĒ-zē   'kiːziˑ

Keszthely
commune, Hungary   KEST-HĀ   'kest,heː

Ket
lang., people, river, Russia   KET   'ket

Ketcham
Henry King, *US cartoonist*   KECH-uhm   'ketʃəm

Ketchikan
town, AK   KECH-i-KAN   'ketʃi,kæn

Kettering
city, OH   KET-uh-ring   'ketəriŋ

Keturah
Biblical name   kuh-TUR-uh   kə'turə

Keuka
lake, NY   KYOO-kuh, kā-YOO-kuh   'kjuːkə, keˑ'juːkə

Kevin
pers. name   KEV-uhn   'kevən

Kew
parish, gardens, London, England;   KYOO   'kjuː
  city, Australia

Kewaunee
county, WI   ki-WAHN-ē   ki'waniˑ

Keweenaw
county, MI   KĒ-wuh-NAW   'kiːwə,nɔː

Keya Paha
river, county, NE   KĒ-(y)uh PAH-hah   'kiː(j)ə 'pahɑ

Keynes
1. John, *English economist*   KĀNZ   'keːnz
2. *see* Horsted Keynes, Milton
  Keynes

Keynesian
pert. to J. Keynes   KĀN-zē-uhn   'keːnziːən

Khabarovsk
city, Russia   <u>kh</u>uh-BAHR-uhfsk   xə'baːrəfsk

Khabarovsk Krai
territory, Russia   <u>kh</u>uh-BAHR-uhfsk KRĪ   xə'baːrəfsk 'krai

Khachaturian
Aram, *Armenian composer*   <u>KH</u>UHCH-i-tur-YAHN,   ,xətʃitur'jaːn,
      Ⓢ KAHCH-uh-TUR-ē-uhn, KACH-   Ⓢ ,katʃə'turiːən, ,kætʃ-

Khadafy
see Qadhafi

Khakas, Khakass
lang., people, region, Russia   <u>kh</u>uh-KAHS, Ⓢ kuh-KAS, kuh-KAHS   xə'kɑs, Ⓢ kə'kæs, kə'kɑs

Khaled, King
airport, Riyadh, Saudi Arabia   king <u>kh</u>ah-LED, hah-LED   kiŋ xɑ'led, hɑ'led

---

Foreign Sounds: **ue**: *Fr.* **r**u**e**, *Ger.* f**ü**llen   **uh(r)**: *Fr.* b**oeu**f, *Ger.* H**ö**hle   <u>kh</u>: *Ger.* i**ch**, *Scot.* lo**ch**   ḡ: *Sp.* ami**g**o   v̲: *Sp.* ha**b**lar
hl: *Welsh* **Ll**anelli.   CAPITALS: primary stress.   SMALL CAPS: secondary stress.   Ⓢ: U.S. pron.   Ⓔ: British pron.

Khalkha Mongol
   lang., Mongolia   KAL-kuh-MAHNG-guhl, MAHN-GŌL,   'kælkə'maŋgəl, 'man,goːl,
                            MAHNG-GŌL   'maŋ,goːl

Khalkidhiki [Chalcidice]
   peninsula, Greece   KHAHL-kē-thē-KĒ, KAHL-kuh-thē-KĒ   ˌxɑlkiːðiː'kiː, ˌkɑlkəðiː'kiː

Khalkis [Chalcis]
   city, Greece   khahl-KĒS, kahl-KĒS   xɑl'kiːs, kɑl'kiːs

Khamenei
   Hojatolislam Ali, Iranian Islamic   khah-MĀ-nē, hah-MĒ-nē   xa'meːniˑ, ha'miːniˑ
     leader

Khan
   Asian title, Cen. Asian people   KAHN, KHAHN   'kɑn, 'xɑn

Khanaqin
   town, Iraq   KHAHN-uh-KĒN   ˌxɑnə'kiːn

Khandeshi
   lang., India   kahn-DĀ-shē   kɑn'deːʃiˑ

Khaniá [Canea]
   town, Greece   khahn-YAH, kahn-YAH   xɑn'ja, kɑn'ja

Khanty [Ostyak]
   lang., Khanti-Mansi region,   KAHNT-ē   'kɑːntiˑ
    Russia

!Khara
   African people   KAHR-uh   'karə, 'ǀʰarə

Kharg [Khark]
   island, Iran   KHAHRG, KAHRG   'xɑʳg, 'kɑʳg

Kharia
   lang., people, India   KAHR-ē-uh   'kariːə

Khark [Kharg]
   island, Iran   KHAHRK   'xɑʳk

Kharkov
   city, Ukraine   KHAHR-kuhf, KAHR-KAWF,   'xarkəf, 'kaʳˌkɔːf, 'kaʳˌkɔːv,
                       KAHR-KAWV, KAHR-kuhf   'kaʳkəf

Khartoum
   capital, Sudan   kahr-TOOM   kar'tuːm

Khasi
   lang., India   KAHS-ē   'kasiˑ

Khattians
   pre-Hittite people of Anatolia   KHAHT-ē-uhnz, KAT-ē-uhnz   'xatiːənz, 'kætiːənz

Khattusha
   Hittite capital city   khah-TOO-shuh   xa'tuˑʃə

Khayyám
   see Omar Khayyám

Khe Sanh
   US marine outpost, Vietnam   kā sahn   keː san

Khíos
   island, Greece   KHĒ-AWS, KĒ-AWS   'xiːˌɔːs, 'kiːˌɔːs

Khmer [Cambodian]
   lang., people, Indochina   kuh-MER   kə'meʳ

Khmer Rouge
   communist group, Cambodia   kuh-MER ROOZH, ROOJ   kə'meʳ 'ruːʒ, 'ruːdʒ

Khmu'
   lang., people, Laos, Thailand   kuh-MOO   kə'muː

Khnum
   Egyptian creator god   KHNUM, khuh-NUM   'xnum, xə'num

Key (col. 2):   a: fad   ā: fade   ah: father   ar: Mary   aw: law   e: fed   ē: feed   er: merry   i: hid   ī: hide   ō: coat   oo: boot
oi: boy   ow: now   u: put   uh: above   uhr: bird   ch: chop   ng: ring   sh: show   th: thick   th: this   zh: measure

Khnum-Re
  Egyptian god, aspect of Khnum   KHNUM-RĀ, khuh-NUM-RĀ   'xnum're:, xə'num're:

Khoisan
  African lang. family   koi-SAHN, koi-SAN   kɔi'sɑn, kɔi'sæn

Khomeini
  Ruholla Mussaui, *Iranian*   khō-MĀ-nē, kō-, hō-; KHŌ-mā-NĒ   xoː'meːniˑ, koː-, hoː-;
    ayatollah   ,xoːmeː'niː

Khorana
  H. Gobind, *Indian-born US*   kō-RAHN-uh   koː'rɑnə
    molecular chemist (Nobel 1968)

Khordad'sal
  Zoroastrian festival   KAWR-duhd-SAHL   'kɔːʳdəd,sɑl

Khristian
  pers. name, Russian   khrēs-ti-AHN   xriːsti̩'ɑːn

Khrushchev
  Nikita, *premier, USSR*   khrōōsh-CHAWF,   xruːʃ'tʃɔːf, ⑤ kruːʃ'(tʃ)ɔːf,
                  ⑤ krōōsh-(CH)AWF,   'kruːʃ̩(tʃ)ev
                  KRŌŌSH-(CH)EV

Khufu [Cheops]
  Egyptian pharoah   KŌŌ-FŌŌ   'kuː,fuː

Khuri
  pers. name, Arabic   KHŌŌ-rē   'xuːriː

Khust, Chust [Huszt]
  town, Ukraine   KHŌŌST   'xuːst

Khuzistan
  prov, Iran   KHŌŌ-zuh-STAHN   ,xuːzə'stɑn

Khyber
  mtn. pass   KĪ-buhr   'kaibəʳ

Ki
  1. pers. name, Indonesian   KĒ   'kiː
  2. Japanese   kē   kiː

Kiang-si
  see Jiangxi

Kiang-su
  see Jiangsu

Kickapoo
  N. American people   KIK-uh-PŌŌ   'kikə,puː

Kiddush
  Jewish blessing over wine   KID-uhsh, KID-ish, kid-ŌŌSH   'kidəʃ, 'kidiʃ, kid'uːʃ

Kidnis
  Igor, *harpsichordist*   KID-nuhs   'kidnəs

Kidron [Kedron]
  valley, Jordan   KID-ruhn, KĪ-druhn   'kidrən, 'kaidrən

Kiefer
  pers. name   KĒ-fuhr   'kiːfəʳ

Kiel
  city, canal, Germany   KĒL   'kiːl

Kierkegaard
  Sören, *Danish philosopher*   KIR-kuh-GAHR(D), KIR-kuh-GAWR   'kiʳkə,gɑʳ(d), 'kiʳkə,gɔːʳ

Kiernan
  Edward J., *labor union official*   KIR-nuhn   'kiʳnən

Kieta
  district, Papua New Guinea   kē-ĀT-uh   kiː'eːṭə

Kiev, Kiyev, Kiyiv
  city, Ukraine   KĒ-(Y)EF, KĒ-(Y)EV, KĒ-(y)uhf   'kiː̩(j)ef, 'kiː̩(j)ev, 'kiː(j)əf

---

Foreign Sounds: **ue**: *Fr.* **rue**, *Ger.* **füllen** **uh(r)**: *Fr.* **boeuf**, *Ger.* **Höhle** **kh**: *Ger.* **ich**, *Scot.* **loch** **g̃**: *Sp.* **amigo** **v̲**: *Sp.* **hablar**
hl: *Welsh* **Llanelli**. CAPITALS: primary stress. SMALL CAPS: secondary stress. ⑤: U.S. pron. ⑥: British pron.

Kigali
  capital, Rwanda   ki-GAHL-ē   ki'gɑliˑ
Kiichi
  pers. name, Japanese   kē-ē-chē   kiːiːtʃiː
Kiichiro
  pers. name, Japanese   kē-ē-chē-rō   kiːiːtʃiːroː
Kijuro
  pers. name, Japanese   kē-ju-rō   kiːdʒuroː
Kikamba [Kamba]
  lang., Africa   ki-KAHM-buh   ki'kɑmbə
Kikládhes [Cyclades]
  Aegean islands   ki-KLAHTH-is   ki'klɑðis
Kikongo
  lang., Cen. Africa   kē-KAHNG-gō   kiˑ''kɑŋgoː
Kikujiro
  pers. name, Japanese   kē-kuj-ē-rō   kiːkudʒiːroː
Kikuyu
  lang., people, Africa   kē-K̄O̅O̅-yoo   kiˑ''kuːju
Kilauea
  Mount, volcano, HI   KĒ-LOW-Ā-uh, KIL-uh-WĀ-uh   ˌkiːˌlɑu'eːə, ˌkilə'weːə
Kildare
  county, Dublin   kil-DAR, kil-DER   kil'dæʳ, kil'deʳ
Kilgore
  College, TX   KIL-GŌR, KIL-GAWR   'kilˌgoːʳ, 'kilˌgɔːʳ
Kilimanjaro
  Mount, Tanzania   KIL-uh-muhn-JAHR-ō, -JAR-ō   ˌkiləmən'dʒɑroː, -'dʒæroː
Kilkenny
  prov & town, Irish Republic   kil-KEN-ē   kil'keniˑ
Killanin
  Michael Morris, Lord, Irish author kuh-LAN-uhn   kə'lænən
Killarney
  town, Irish Republic   kil-AHR-nē   kil'ɑʳniˑ
Killebrew
  Gwendolyn, US opera singer;   KIL-uh-BR̄O̅O̅   'kiləˌbruː
  Harmon, US baseball player
Killian
  pers. name, Dutch   KĒ-lē-AHN   'kiːliːˌɑːn
Killiecrankie
  mtn. pass, Scotland   KIL-ē-KRANG-kē   ˌkiliˑ''kræŋkiˑ
Kilmarnock
  burgh, Scotland   kil-MAHR-nuhk   kil'mɑʳnək
Kim
  pers. name   KIM   'kim
Kimbanguist
  religion   kim-BAHNG-gwist   kim'baŋgwist
Kimberly
  pers. name   KIM-buhr-lē   'kimbəʳliˑ
Kim Il-sung
  president, N. Korea   kim il-sung, kim il-suhng   kim ilsuŋ, kim ilsəŋ
Kimmochi
  pers. name, Japanese   kēm-mō-chē   kiːmmoːtʃiː
Kimpo
  airport, Seoul   kim-pō   kimpoː
Kinabalu
  mts., natl. park, Malaysia   KIN-uh-buh-L̄O̅O̅   ˌkinəbə'luː

Key (col. 2): a: fad ā: fade ah: father ar: **M**a**ry** aw: **l**a**w** e: fed ē: feed er: **merry** i: hid ī: hide ō: coat ō̅o̅: boot
oi: **b**o**y** ow: **n**o**w** u: put uh: **a**bove uhr: b**ir**d ch: **ch**op ng: ri**ng** sh: **sh**ow th: **th**ick th̲: **th**is zh: mea**s**ure

Kinchinjunga [Kanchenjunga]
  mtn., Himalaya   KIN-chuhn-JUHNG-guh, -JUNG-guh   ˌkintʃən'dʒəŋgə, -'dʒuŋgə

Kindl
  German beer   KIND-l   'kindl̩

Kindrick
  Legion Field, *ballpark, Helena,*   KIN-drik   'kindrik
  MT

King
  Martin Luther, Jr., *US civil rights*   KING   'kiŋ
  leader (Nobel 1964); pers. name

King Eider
  duck   king ĪD-uhr   kiŋ 'aidəʳ

King's College
  Cambridge Univ.   KINGZ   'kiŋz

Kingsley
  Ben, *British actor*   KINGZ-lē   'kiŋzliˑ

Kingston
  pl. name   KING-stuhn   'kiŋstən

Kingston-upon-Thames
  borough, England   KING-stuhn uh-PAHN TEMZ   'kiŋstən əˌpɑn 'temz

Kingstown
  city, Ireland; city, St. Vincent &   KING-STOWN   'kiŋˌstɑun
  the Grenadines

Kingwana
  lang., Zaire   king-WAHN-uh   kiŋ'wɑnə

Kingyarwanda [Rwanda]
  lang., Africa   KING-yuhr-WAHN-duh   ˌkiŋjəʳ'wɑndə

Kinkajou
  mammal   KING-kuh-JOO   'kiŋkəˌdʒuː

Kinki
  island, Japan   kin-kē, king-kē   kinkiˑ, kiŋkiˑ

Kinnan
  pers. name   KIN-uhn   'kinən

Kinnock
  Neil, *British politician*   KIN-uhk   'kinək

Kinro-Kansha-No-Hi
  Labor Thanksgiving Day (Nov.   kin-rō-kahn-shah-nō-hē   kinroːkanʃanoːhiː
  23), Japan

Kinsey
  Alfred, *US sexologist, zoologist*   KIN-zē   'kinziˑ

Kinshasa
  city, Zaire   kin-SHAHS-uh   kin'ʃɑsə

Kinski
  Klaus & Nastassia, *entertainers*   KIN-skē   'kinskiˑ

Kioga
  see Kyoga

Kiowa
  1. county, CO   KĪ-uh-WAH   'kaiəˌwa
  2. N. American people   KĪ-uh-WAW, -WAH, -WĀ   'kaiəˌwɔː, -ˌwa, -ˌweː

Kipling
  Rudyard, *English author (Nobel*   KIP-ling   'kipliŋ
  1907)

Kiplingesque
  pert. to Kipling   KIP-ling-ESK   ˌkipliŋ'esk

Foreign Sounds: ue: *Fr.* **rue**, *Ger.* **füllen**   uh(r): *Fr.* **boeuf**, *Ger.* **Höhle**   <u>kh</u>: *Ger.* **ich**, *Scot.* **loch**   ḡ: *Sp.* **amigo**   <u>v</u>: *Sp.* **hablar**
hl: *Welsh* **Llanelli.**   CAPITALS: primary stress.   SMALL CAPS: secondary stress.   Ⓢ: U.S. pron.   Ⓑ: British pron.

Kir
   alcoholic drink   KĒR, $ KIR   'kiːr, $ 'kiʳ
Kirby
   pers. name   KUHR-bē   'kəʳbiˑ
Kirghiz, Kirgiz
   lang., people, republic, mtn. range,   kir-GĒZ   kiʳ'giːz
     Asia
Kirghizia, Kirgizia
   republic, Europe   kir-GĒ-zh(ē-)uh, kir-GĒ-zē-uh   kiʳ'giːʒ(iː)ə, kiʳ'giːziːə
Kiri
   pers. name (K. Te Kanawa)   KIR-ē   'kiriˑ
Kiribatian
   pert. to Kiribati   KIR-uh-BAS-ē-uhn *[sic]*   ˌkirə'bæsiːən *[sic]*
Kiribati [Gilbert]
   islands, lang., people, Pacific   KIR-uh-BAS *[sic]*   'kirəˌbæs *[sic]*
Kiril
   pers. name, Bulgarian   kē-RĒL   kiː'riːl
Kirill
   pers. name, Russian   kyir-YĒL   kjir'jiːl
Kirin
   Japanese beer   kir-in   kirin
Kirin [Jilin]
   prov & town, China   KĒ-RIN   'kiː'rin
Kiritimati Atoll [Christmas]
   islands, Pacific   kuh-RIS-muhs, $ KRIS-muhs *[sic]*   kə'rismǝs, $ 'krismǝs *[sic]*
Kirk
   James Tiberius, *Star Trek captain;*   KUHRK   'kəʳk
    pers. name
Kirkcaldy
   city, Scotland   kuh-KAHD-ē, kuh-KAWD-ē, kuhr-;   kə'kɑdiˑ, kə'kɔːdiˑ, kər-;
                    $ kuhr-KAWL-dē $ kəʳ'kɔːldiˑ
Kirkcudbright
   town, Scotland   kuhr-KŌŌ-brē *[sic]*   kəʳ'kuːbriˑ *[sic]*
Kirke
   pers. name   KUHRK   'kəʳk
Kirkland
   Gelsey, *US ballet dancer*   KUHRK-luhnd   'kəʳklǝnd
Kirkpatrick
   Jeane, *US political scientist*   KUHRK-PA-trik, KUHR-PA-trik   ˌkəʳk'pætrik, ˌkəʳ'pætrik
Kirkuk
   town, Iraq   kir-KŌŌK   kiʳ'kuːk
Kirman [Kermān]
   prov, city, Iran   kuhr-MAHN, kir-MAHN   kəʳ'mɑn, kiʳ'mɑn
Kirov
   city, Russia   KĒ-RAWF   'kiːˌrɔːf
Kirschwasser
   cherry brandy   KIRSH-VAHS-uhr   'kiʳʃˌvasəʳ
Kirsten
   1. pers. name   KIRS-tuhn   'kiʳstǝn
   2. Norwegian   <u>KH</u>YISH-tuhn, <u>KH</u>YIRS-tuhn,   'xjiʃtǝn, 'xjirstǝn, $ 'kiʃtǝn
                    $ KISH-tuhn
Kirstie, Kirsty
   pers. name   KIR-stē, KUHR-stē   'kiʳstiˑ, 'kəʳstiˑ
Kirundi
   lang., Burundi   kē-RŌŌN-dē, kē-RUN-dē   kiˑ'ruːndiˑ, kiˑ'rundiˑ

Key (col. 2):   a: fad   ā: fade   ah: father   ar: Mary   aw: law   e: fed   ē: feed   er: merry   i: hid   ī: hide   ō: coat   ōō: boot
oi: boy   ow: now   u: put   uh: above   uhr: bird   ch: chop   ng: ring   sh: show   th: thick   <u>th</u>: this   zh: measure

Kish
   ancient Sumerian & Akkadian   KISH   'kiʃ
    city

Kishi
   Nobusuke, *Japanese statesman*   kē-shē   kiːʃiˈ

Kishinev
   city, Moldavia   KISH-uh-NEF   'kiʃəˌnef

Kishwaukee
   College, *IL*   kish-WAW-kē   kiʃ'wɔːkiˈ

Kiska
   island, AK   KIS-kuh   'kiskə

Kislev
   Jewish month   KIS-luhf, kē-SLEV   'kisləf, kiː'slev

Kislimu
   Babylonian month   KIS-lim-o͞o   'kislimuː

Kismet
   fate, destiny   KIZ-MET, KIZ-muht   'kizˌmet, 'kizmət

Kissimmee
   town, river, FL   kis-IM-ē   kis'imiˈ

Kissinger
   Henry A., *German-born US civil*   KIS-n-juhr   'kisn̩dʒəʳ
    servant (Nobel 1973)

Kistna [Krishna]
   river, India   KIS(T)-nuh   'kis(t)nə

Kiswahili
   lang., Africa   KIS-WAH-HĒ-lē   ˌkisˌwɑ'hiːliˈ

Kit
   pers. name   KIT   'kit

Kitagawa Utamaro
   Japanese artist   kē-tah-gah-wah ut-ah-mahr-ō   kiːtɑgɑwɑ uṭɑmɑroː

Kitchener
   Horatio H., *British militarist*   KICH-(uh-)nuhr   'kitʃ(ə)nəʳ

Kitsap
   county, WA   KIT-suhp   'kitsəp

Kittikachorn
   Thanom, *premier, Thailand*   KĒT-ē-kuh-CHAWRN   ˌkiːṭiˈkə'tʃɔːʳn

Kittitas
   county, WA   KIT-i-tuhs   'kiṭitəs

Kittiwake
   sea bird (gull)   KIT-ē-WĀK   'kiṭiˈˌweːk

Kitto
   pers. name   KIT-ō   'kiṭoː

Kittsian
   person from St. Kitts   KIT-sē-uhn   'kitsiːən

Kitty
   pers. name   KIT-ē   'kiṭiˈ

Kitzbühel
   city, Austria   KITS-BUE-uhl, Ⓢ KITS-B(Y)o͞o(-uh)l   'kitsˌbyːəl, Ⓢ 'kitsˌb(j)uː(ə)l

Kivu
   lake, province, Zaire   KĒ-vo͞o   'kiːvuː

Kiwanian
   member of Kiwanis club   kuh-WAHN-ē-uhn   kə'wɑniːən

Kiwanis
   business organization   kuh-WAHN-uhs   kə'wɑnəs

Foreign Sounds: ue: *Fr.* **rue**, *Ger.* **füllen**   uh(r): *Fr.* **boeuf**, *Ger.* **Höhle**   <u>kh</u>: *Ger.* i**ch**, *Scot.* lo**ch**   g̃: *Sp.* ami**g**o   <u>v</u>: *Sp.* ha**b**lar
hl: *Welsh* **Ll**anelli.   CAPITALS: primary stress.   SMALL CAPS: secondary stress.   Ⓢ: U.S. pron.   Ⓛ: British pron.

Kiwi
   New Zealand bird; fruit   KĒ-wē   'kiːwiˑ
Kiyev, Kiyiv
   see Kiev
Kiyoshi
   pers. name, Japanese   kē-yō-shē   kiːjoˑʃiː
Kizzy
   pers. name   KIZ-ē   'kiziˑ
Klaberjass
   game   KLAHB-uhr-YAHS   'klabəʳˌjas
Klagenfurt
   city, Austria   KLAHG-uhn-FURT   'klagən,fuʳt
Klallam
   see Clallam
Klamath
   county, OR; N. American people   KLAM-uhth   'klæməθ
Klaus
   pers. name, German   KLOWS   'klɑus
Klawock
   village, AK   KLAW-wuhk, KLOW-uhk   'klɔːwək, 'klɑuək
Kléber
   Jean, *French general*   klā-BER   kleːber
Kleberg
   county, TX   KLĀ-BUHRG   'kleːˌbəʳg
Klee
   Paul, *Swiss painter*   KLĀ   'kleː
Kleenex
   tdmk for a facial tissue   KLĒ-NEKS   'kliːˌneks
Klein
   Lawrence R., *US economist*   KLĪN   'klaɪn
   (Nobel 1980); bottle,
   single-sided surface
Kleine Munsterlander
   dog breed   KLĪ-nuh MUN-stuhr-LAHN-duhr   ˌklaɪnə 'munstəʳˌlandəʳ
Klemens
   1. pers. name, German   KLĀ-MENS   'kleːˌmens
   2. Polish   KLEM-ens   'klemens
Klement
   pers. name, Czech   KLEM-ent   'klement
Klemperer
   Otto, *German conductor;* Werner,   KLEM-puh-ruhr   'klempərəʳ
   US actor
Kliban
   Bernard, *US cartoonist*   KLĒ-BAN   'kliːˌbæn
Klickitat
   county, WA   KLIK-i-TAT   'kliki,tæt
Klikitat
   N. American people   KLIK-uh-TAT   'klikə,tæt
Kliment
   1. pers. name, Bulgarian   KLĒ-mänt   'kliːmeːnt
   2. Russian   KLĒM-yint   'kḷiːmjint
Klimenti, -ty
   pers. name, Russian   klēm-YEN-ti   kḷiːm'jenṭij
Klimt
   Gustav, *Austrian painter*   KLIM(P)T   'klim(p)t

Key (col. 2): a: fad ā: fade ah: father ar: Mary aw: law e: fed ē: feed er: merry i: hid ī: hide ō: coat ōō: boot
oi: boy ow: now u: put uh: above uhr: bird ch: chop ng: ring sh: show th: thick <u>th</u>: this zh: measure

Klingon
   alien race, Star Trek   KLING-AHN   'kliŋ‚ɑn

Klitzing
   Klaus von, *German physicist*   KLITS-ing   'klitsiŋ
   (Nobel 1985)

Klondike
   region, river, Canada   KLAHN-DĪK   'klɑn‚dɑik

Kloster
   German beer   KLAWS-tuhr   'klɔːstəʳ

Klosters
   resort, Switzerland   KLŌ-stuhrz   'klɔːstəʳz

Klotz
   Florence, *US costume designer* KLAHTS   'klɑts

Klug
   Aaron, *Lithuanian-born British* KLŌOG   'kluːg
   biophysicist (Nobel 1982)

Kluger
   Richard, *US author, editor, critic* KLŌO-guhr   'kluːgəʳ

Klugman
   Jack, *US actor*   KLUHG-muhn   'kləgmən

Knauer
   Virginia Harrington, *US*   NOW(-uh)r   'nɑu(ə)ʳ
   government official

Knesset
   Israeli parliament   KNES-uht, kuh-NES-uht, KNES-et   'knesət, kə'nesət, 'kneset

Knickerbocker
   a New Yorker   NIK-uhr-BAHK-uhr   'nikəʳ‚bɑkəʳ

Knieval
   Evel, *US daredevil*   kuh-NĒ-vuhl, KNĒ-vuhl   kə'niːvəl, 'kniːvəl

Knipperlé
   wine grape variety   kuh-NIP-uhr-lē, -LĀ   kə'nipəʳliˑ, -‚leː

Knokke-Heist
   resort, Belgium   KNAWK-uh-HĪST   'knɔːkə'hɑist

Knollys
   Sir Francis, *Elizabethan courtier* NŌLZ   'noːlz

Knopf, Alfred A.
   US publishing co.   AL-fruhd Ā (kuh)-NAHPF,   ‚ælfrəd ‚eː (kə)'nɑpf, kə'nəpf
                          kuh-NUHPF

Knossos
   city, Crete   NAHS-uhs   'nɑsəs

Knott
   family name   NAHT   'nɑt

Knowles
   John, *author*   NŌLZ   'noːlz

Knud
   1. pers. name, Danish   KNŌOTH   'knuːð
   2. Norwegian   KNŌOT   'knuːt

Knut
   pers. name, Norwegian, Swedish KNŌOT   'knuːt

Knute
   pers. name   NŌOT   'nuːt

Koala
   marsupial   kō-AHL-uh, kuh-WAHL-uh   koː'ɑlə, kə'wɑlə

Koasati
   N. American people   KŌ-uh-SAHT-ē   ‚koːə'sɑtiˑ

Foreign Sounds: ue: *Fr.* **rue**, *Ger.* f**ü**llen uh(r): *Fr.* b**oeu**f, *Ger.* H**öh**le kh: *Ger.* i**ch**, *Scot.* lo**ch** g̃: *Sp.* ami**g**o v: *Sp.* ha**b**lar
hl: *Welsh* **Ll**anelli. CAPITALS: primary stress. SMALL CAPS: secondary stress. $: U.S. pron. £: British pron.

Kobarid
　village, Slovenia　　　　　　　KŌ-buh-RĒD　　　　　　　'koːbəˌriːd
Kobbé
　Gustave, *opera guide author*　　kaw-BĀ　　　　　　　　　kɔː'beː
Kobe
　city, Japan　　　　　　　　　kō-bā, Ⓢ KŌ-bē, KŌ-bā　　koːbeː, Ⓢ 'koːbiˑ, 'koːbeː
København [Copenhagen]
　Denmark　　　　　　　　　　KUH(R)-buhn-HOWN　　　　ˌkœːbən'haun
Koblenz, Coblenz
　prov, Germany　　　　　　　KŌ-BLEN(T)S　　　　　　　'koːˌblen(t)s
Kobuk
　division, AK　　　　　　　　kō-BUK　　　　　　　　　　koː'buk
Kobuk Valley
　National Park, *AK*　　　　　　kō-BUK　　　　　　　　　　koː'buk
Koch
　1. Edward I., *US politician*　　KAHCH　　　　　　　　　　'katʃ
　2. Robert, *German physician,*　KAW<u>KH</u>　　　　　　　　'kɔːx
　　bacteriologist (Nobel 1905)
　3. Bill, *US yachtsman*　　　　KŌK　　　　　　　　　　　'koːk
　4. pers. name, US　　　　　　KAHCH, KAHK, KUK, KŌK　'katʃ, 'kak, 'kuk, 'koːk
Köchel
　number, designation of Mozart　KUH(R)<u>KH</u>-uhl, Ⓢ KUHR-shuhl,　'kœçəl, Ⓢ 'kəʳʃəl, 'kəʳkəl
　　compositions　　　　　　　KUHR-kuhl
Kocher
　Emil T., *Swiss surgeon (Nobel*　KŌ<u>KH</u>-uhr　　　　　　　'koːxəʳ
　　1909)
Kodachrome
　tdmk for a positive color　　　KŌD-uh-KRŌM　　　　　　'koːdəˌkroːm
　　transparency
Kodagu [Coorg]
　lang., people, India　　　　　KŌD-uh-GOO　　　　　　　'koːdəˌguː
Kodak
　tdmk for photographic supplies　KŌD-AK　　　　　　　　　'koːdˌæk
Kodály
　Zoltán, *Hungarian composer*　　KAW-DĪ(-ē), KŌ-DĪ(-ē)　　'kɔːˌdai(-iː), 'koːˌdai(-iː)
Kodiak
　island, division, AL　　　　　KŌD-ē-AK　　　　　　　　'koːdiːˌæk
Kodok [Fashoda]
　village, Sudan　　　　　　　KŌD-AHK　　　　　　　　　'koːdˌɑk
Koestler
　Arthur, *British writer*　　　　KES(T)-luhr　　　　　　　'kes(t)ləʳ
Koff
　Finnish beer　　　　　　　　KAWF　　　　　　　　　　'kɔːf
Kohinoor
　diamond　　　　　　　　　　KŌ-uh-NUR, KŌ-uh-NUR　　'koːəˌnuʳ, ˌkoːə'nuʳ
Kohl
　Helmut, *German Chancellor*　　KŌL　　　　　　　　　　　'koːl
Kohler
　Georges J. F., *German*　　　　KŌ-luhr　　　　　　　　　'koːləʳ
　　immunologist (Nobel 1984)
Koine
　Hellenistic Greek lang.; a　　koi-NĀ, KOI-nē　　　　　　kɔi'neː, 'kɔiniˑ
　　standardized dialect
Kojak
　US television character　　　　KŌ-JAK　　　　　　　　　'koːˌdʒæk

Key (col. 2):　a: fad　ā: fade　ah: father　ar: Mary　aw: law　e: fed　ē: feed　er: merry　i: hid　ī: hide　ō: coat　ōō: boot
oi: boy　ow: now　u: put　uh: above　uhr: bird　ch: chop　ng: ring　sh: show　th: thick　th̲: this　zh: measure

Kojonup
   town, Australia   KŌ-juh-NUHP   'koːdʒə,nəp
Kokama, Cocama
   lang., Peru, Colombia, Brazil   kō-KAHM-uh   koː'kɑmə
Kokanee
   Canadian beer   KŌ-kuh-nē, KŌ-kuh-nā   'koːkəniˑ, 'koːkəneˑ
Koko
   Lord High Executioner in The   KŌ-kō   'koːkoː
      Mikado*; US gorilla trained in*
      sign lang.
Kokomo
   city, IN   KŌ-kuh-MŌ   'koːkə,moː
Kokoschka
   Oskar, *Austrian painter*   kuh-KAWSH-kuh   kə'kɔːʃkə
Kolami
   lang., India   kuh-LAHM-ē   kə'lɑmiˑ
Kolkhoz
   collective farm in USSR   KUHL-<u>KH</u>AWZ, Ⓢ kahl-KAWZ,   ,kəl'xɔːz, Ⓢ kɑl'kɔːz,
       kahl-KAWS   kɑl'kɔːs
Kolkhoznik
   member of a kolkhoz   KUHL-<u>KH</u>AWZ-nik, Ⓢ kahl-KAWZ-nik   ,kəl'xɔːznik, Ⓢ kɑl'kɔːznik
Kolkhozy
   pl. of Kolkhoz   KUHL-<u>KH</u>AW-zē, Ⓢ kahl-KAW-zē   ,kəl'xɔːziˑ, Ⓢ kɑl'kɔːziˑ
Kollwitz
   Käthe, *German artist*   KAWL-VITS   'kɔːl,vits
Köln [Cologne]
   city, Germany   KUH(R)LN   'kœln
Kol Nidre
   Jewish prayer for Yom Kippur   kōl NID-rā, NID-ruh, nē-DRĀ, kawl   koːl 'nidreː, 'nidrə, niː'dreː,
       kɔːl
Kolyma
   river, Russia   kuh-LĒ-muh   kə'liːmə
Komárno
   town, Slovakia   KAW-mahr-NAW   'kɔːmɑʳ,nɔː
Komatsu
   Japanese manufacturing co.   kō-maht-so͞o   koːmɑtsuː
Kombu
   seaweed   KAHM-bo͞o   'kɑmbuː
Komi [Zyryan]
   lang., people, Russia   KŌ-mē   'koːmiˑ
Kommunizma, Pik
   mtn. peak, Tadzhikistan   PĒK KAHM-yuh-NĒZ-muh   'piːk ,kɑmjə'niːzmə
Komodo dragon
   Indonesian lizard   kuh-MŌD-ō DRAG-uhn   kə,moːdoː 'drægən
Komondor
   dog breed   KAHM-uhn-DAWR, KŌ-muhn-DAWR   'kɑmən,dɔːʳ, 'koːmən,dɔːʳ
Komsomol
   communist youth organization,   KUHM-suh-MAWL,   ,kəmsə'mɔːl,
      USSR   Ⓢ KAHM-suh-MAWL, -MŌL   Ⓢ 'kɑmsə,mɔːl, -,moːl
Konakri
   see Conakry
Konde [Makonde]
   lang., people, Africa   KŌN-dā   'koːndeː
Kondrati
   pers. name, Russian   KUHN-DRAH-ti   ,kən'drɑːt̮ij

Foreign Sounds: ue: *Fr.* **rue**, *Ger.* füllen   uh(r): *Fr.* **boeuf**, *Ger.* Höhle   <u>kh</u>: *Ger.* i**ch**, *Scot.* lo**ch**   ḡ: *Sp.* amigo   v: *Sp.* hablar
hl: *Welsh* **Llanelli**.   CAPITALS: primary stress.   SMALL CAPS: secondary stress.   Ⓢ: U.S. pron.   Ⓔ: British pron.

Kong Kristian
   national anthem, Denmark   KAWNG KRĒST-yahn   ˈkɔːŋ ˈkriːstjan
Kongo
   lang., people, Africa   KAHNG-gō   ˈkɑŋgoː
Konica
   tdmk for a camera   KAHN-i-kuh   ˈkɑnikə
König-Pilsener
   German beer   KUH(R)-ni<u>kh</u> PIL-suh-nuhr   ˈkœːniç ˈpilsənəʳ
Konigsberg
   Allen, *orig. name of* Woody Allen,   KŌ-nigz-BUHRG   ˈkoːnigz,bəʳg
     US filmmaker
Königsberg
   city, Germany; city, region, Russia   KUH(R)-niks-BERK   ˈkœːniks,beʳk
Koninck, De
   see De Koninck
Kónitsa
   commune, Greece   KAWN-yit-SAH   ˈkɔːnjit,sɑ
Konkani
   lang., India   KAHNG-kuh-nē, KAWNG-kuh-nē   ˈkɑŋkəniˑ, ˈkɔːŋkəniˑ
Konkow
   N. American people   KAHNG-kō   ˈkɑŋkoː
Kono
   lang., people, Liberia, Mali, Sierra   KŌ-nō   ˈkoːnoː
     Leone
Konrád
   pers. name, Icelandic   KAWN-ROWD   ˈkɔːn,rɑud
Konrad
   1. pers. name, Danish   KAWN-RAHD   ˈkɔːn,rɑd
   2. German   KAWN-RAHT   ˈkɔːn,rɑt
   3. Polish   KAWN-RAHT   ˈkɔːn,rɑːt
   4. Romanian   KAWN-RAHD   ˈkɔːn,rɑd
Konstantin
   1. pers. name, Czech   KAWN-stahn-CHIN   ˈkɔːnstɑn,tʃin
   2. Danish   KAWN-stahn-TĒN   ˌkɔːnstɑːnˈtiːn
   3. Estonian   KAWN-stahn-TIN   ˈkɔːnstɑn,tin
   4. German   KAWN-stahn-TĒN, KAWN-stahn-TĒN   ˌkɔːnstɑnˈtiːn, ˈkɔːnstɑn,tiːn
   5. Russian   kuhn-STUHN-TĒN   kən,stənˈt̞iːn
Konstanty
   pers. name, Polish   kawn-STAHN-ti   kɔːnˈstɑːnti
Konstanz, Constance
   prov, Germany   KAWN-STAHN(T)S   ˈkɔːn,stɑn(t)s
Kon Tiki
   raft, Thor Heyerdahl   kahn TĒ-kē   kɑn ˈtiːkiˑ
Koochiching
   county, MN   K͞OO-chuh-CHING   ˈkuːtʃə,tʃiŋ
Kookaburra
   Australian bird   KUK-uh-BUHR-uh, KUK-uh-BUH-ruh   ˈkukə,bər-ə, ˈkukə,bə-rə
Kookynie
   town, Australia   ku-KĪ-nē   kuˈkɑiniˑ
Koopmans
   Tjalling C., *Dutch-born US*   K͞OOP-muhnz   ˈkuːpmənz
     economist (Nobel 1975)
Kooringa
   Australia   ku-RING-guh   kuˈriŋgə

Key (col. 2):   a: fad ā: fade ah: father ar: Mary aw: law e: fed ē: feed er: merry i: hid ī: hide ō: coat o͞o: boot
oi: boy ow: now u: put uh: above uhr: bird ch: chop ng: ring sh: show th: thick <u>th</u>: this zh: measure

Kootenai
   1. county, ID   K $\overline{OO}$ T-n-ā, K $\overline{OO}$ T-n-ē   'kuːtn̩ˌeː, 'kuːtn̩i·
   2. see Kutenai
Kootenay, -ai
   river, N. America; lake, Canada   K $\overline{OO}$ T-n-ā, K $\overline{OO}$ T-n-ē   'kuːtn̩eː, 'kuːtn̩i·
Kopechne
   Mary Jo   kuh-PEK-nē   kə'pekni·
Kopernik [Copernicus]
   Mikołaj, Polish astronomer   kaw-PER-nēk   kɔː'peʳniːk
Kopit
   Arthur, playwright   KAHP-uht   'kɑpət
Koppel
   Ted, US newscaster   KAHP-uhl   'kɑpəl
Koppell
   Bernie, actor   KAHP-uhl   'kɑpəl
Koppernigk [Copernicus]
   Niklas, Polish astronomer   KAHP-uhr-nik   'kɑpəʳnik
Koran
   holy book of Islam   kuh-RAN, kuh-RAHN, KŌR-AN,   kə'ræn, kə'rɑn, 'koːrˌæn,
                      KAWR-AN   'kɔːrˌæn
Koranic
   pert. to the Koran   kuh-RAN-ik, kawr-AN-ik   kə'rænik, kɔːr'ænik
Korbel
   champagne winery, CA   kawr-BEL   kɔːʳ'bel
Korbut
   Olga, sports personality   KAWR-buht   'kɔːʳbət
Kordestān
   prov, Iran   KAWRD-uh-STAHN, -STAN   ˌkɔːʳdə'stɑn, -'stæn
Korea
   country, Asia   kuh-RẼ-uh, kō-, kaw-   kə'riːə, koː-, kɔː-
Korean
   lang., people, Asia   kuh-RẼ-uhn, kō-, kaw-   kə'riːən, koː-, kɔː-
Kórinthos [Corinth]
   city, Greece   KŌ-rin-THAWS   'koːrinˌθɔːs
Korman
   Harvey, US actor, comedian   KAWR-muhn   'kɔːʳmən
Kornberg
   Arthur, US biochemist (Nobel   KAWRN-BUHRG   'kɔːʳnˌbəʳg
   1959)
Kornelis
   pers. name, Dutch   kawr-NẼ-luhs   kɔːr'neːləs
Korney
   pers. name, Russian   kawrn-YÃ   kɔːʳn'jeː
Kornilov
   Lavrenti, Russian militarist   kawr-N(Y)Ẽ-luhf   kɔːʳ'n(j)iːləf
Korumburra
   town, Australia   KAHR-uhm-BUHR-uh   ˌkɑrəm'bərə
Koryak
   lang., people, region, Russia   KAWR-yak   'kɔːʳjæk
Korzeniowski
   Józef, orig. name of Joseph   KAW-zhen-YAWF-skē   ˌkɔːʒen'jɔːfski·
   Conrad, *British novelist*
Korzybski
   Alfred, US semanticist   kaw-ZHIP-skē, $ kawr-ZIP-skē   kɔː'ʒipski·, $ kɔːʳ'zipski·

Foreign Sounds: **ue**: *Fr.* **rue**, *Ger.* **füllen** **uh(r)**: *Fr.* **boeuf**, *Ger.* **Höhle** **kh**: *Ger.* **ich**, *Scot.* **loch** **g̃**: *Sp.* **amigo** **v**: *Sp.* **hablar**
hl: *Welsh* **Llanelli**. CAPITALS: primary stress. SMALL CAPS: secondary stress. $: U.S. pron. ⓛ: British pron.

Kós, Cos		
Greek island	KAHS, KAWS	'kɑs, 'kɔːs
Kosar		
Bernie, *football player*	KŌ-ZAHR	'koː,zɑʳ
Kosciusko		
1. county, IN; city, MS	KAHS-ē-UHS-kō, KAHZ-ē-UHS-kō	,kɑsiː'əskoː, ,kɑziː'əskoː
2. Mount, *Australia*	KAHZ-ē-UHS-kō	,kɑziː'əskoː
3. bridge, NY	KAHS-kē-UHS-kō	,kɑskiː'əskoː
Kosciuszko		
Tadeusz, *Polish militarist*	kawsh-CHUSH-kō, Ⓢ KAHS-ē-UHS-kō, KAHZ-ē-UHS-kō	kɔːʃ'tʃuʃkoː, Ⓢ ,kɑsiː'əskoː, ,kɑziː'əskoː
Košice		
city, Slovakia	KAW-shuht-SĀ	'kɔːʃət,seː
Kosovo		
province, Serbia	KAW-suh-VŌ	'kɔːsə,voː
Kossel		
Albrecht, *German physiological chemist (Nobel 1910)*	KAWS-uhl	'kɔːsəl
Kossuth		
1. county, IA	kuh-SO͞OTH	kə'suːθ
2. Lajos, *Hungarian political leader*	KAW-SHUT, Ⓢ KAHS-O͞OTH, kah-SO͞OTH	'kɔː,ʃut, Ⓢ 'kɑs,uːθ, kɑ'suːθ
Kostelanetz		
Richard, *US writer, artist*	KAHS-tuh-LAHN-uhts	,kɑstə'lɑnəts
Kosygin		
Alexei, *premier, USSR*	kuh-SIG-yin, Ⓢ kuh-SĒ-guhn	kə'sigjin, Ⓢ kə'siːgən
Kota		
lang., people, South India; lang., people, Africa	KŌT-uh	'koːtə
Kota Kinabalu		
city, Malaysia	KŌT-uh KIN-uh-buh-LO͞O	,koːṭə ,kinəbə'luː
Kotex		
tdmk for feminine hygiene products	KŌ-TEKS	'koː,teks
Kotka		
port, Finland	KAWT-kuh	'kɔːtkə
Kotoko		
lang., people, Chad	kuh-TŌ-kō	kə'toːkoː
Kotzebue		
city, AK	KAHT-suh-BYO͞O	'kɑtsə,bjuː
Koussevitzky		
Serge, *US/Russian conductor*	KO͞O-suh-VIT-skē	,kuːsə'vitskiˑ
Kovno [Kaunas]		
city, Lithuania	KAWV-nō	'kɔːvnoː
Kowloon		
peninsula, Hong Kong	KOW-LO͞ON	'kɑu'luːn
Koyukon		
N. American people	kō-YO͞O-KAHN	koː'juː,kɑn
Kozinski		
Jerzy, *Polish writer*	kuh-ZIN(T)-skē	kə'zin(t)skiˑ
Kpa		
lang., Africa	kuh-PAH	kə'pɑ
Kpelle		
lang., people, Liberia, Guinea	kuh-PEL-uh	kə'pelə

Kra
  Isthmus of, *Thailand*   KRAH   'krɑ
Krafft-Ebing
  Richard, *German neurologist*   KRAHFT-Ā-bing, KRAFT-Ā-bing,   'krɑft'eːbiŋ, 'kræft'eːbiŋ,
                                        KRAFT-EB-ing   'kræft'ebiŋ
Kragerø
  port, *Norway*   KRAHG-uh-RUH(R)   'krɑgə,rœː
Kragujevac
  city, *former capital, Serbia*   KRAH-gōō-yuh-VAHTS   'krɑːguʼjə,vɑːts
Krahn
  lang., *Liberia, Ivory Coast*   KRAHN   'krɑn
Krajina
  region, *Croatia*   krah-YĒ-nuh   krɑːʼjiːnə
Krakatau, -tao [Krakatoa]
  island, *volcano, Indonesia*   KRAK-uh-TOW   ˌkrækəʼtɑu
Krakatoa
  island, *volcano, Indonesia*   KRAK-uh-TŌ-uh   ˌkrækəʼtoːə
Kraków, Cracow
  city, *Poland*   KRAH-KŌŌF, Ⓢ KRAHK-OW,   'krɑːˌkuːf, Ⓢ 'krɑk,ɑu,
                                        KRAK-OW   'kræk,ɑu
Krakus
  Polish beer   KRAH-kus   'krɑːkus
Kramer
  Stanley E., *US film maker*   KRĀ-muhr   'kreːməʳ
Krantz
  Judith, *US novelist*   KRAN(T)S   'kræn(t)s
Kraprayoon
  Suchinda, *Thai politician*   KRAHP-RĪ-(Y)ŌŌN   ˌkrɑp,raiʼ(j)uːn
Krasnodar
  city, *Russia*   KRAHS-nuh-DAHR   'krɑsnə,dɑʳ
Krasnoyarsk
  city, *Russia*   KRAHS-nuh-YAHRSK   ˌkrɑsnəʼjɑʳsk
Kravchuk
  Leonid Makarovich, *Ukrainian*   KRAHV-chuk   'krɑvtʃuk
    political leader
Krebs
  Sir Hans A., *German-born British*   KREBZ   'krebz
    biochemist (Nobel 1953)
Krefeld
  city, *Germany*   KRĀ-FELT   'kreːˌfelt
Kreisky
  Bruno, *Austrian chancellor*   KRĪ-skē   'krɑiskiˑ
Kreisler
  Fritz, *US violinist*   KRĪ-sluhr   'krɑisləʳ
Kreps
  Juanita Morris, *US secretary of*   KREPS   'kreps
    commerce
Kreskin
  US mentalist   KRES-kuhn   'kreskən
Kreutzer
  Sonata, *Beethoven violin sonata*   KROIT-suhr   'krɔitsəʳ
Kreymborg
  Alfred, *US writer*   KRĀM-BAWRG   'kreːm,bɔːʳg
Krieg
  Dave, *football player*   KRĒG   'kriːg

Foreign Sounds: **ue**: *Fr.* **rue**, *Ger.* **füllen** **uh(r)**: *Fr.* **boeuf**, *Ger.* **Höhle** **kh**: *Ger.* **ich**, *Scot.* **loch** **g̃**: *Sp.* **amigo** **v**: *Sp.* **hablar**
hl: *Welsh* **Llanelli**. CAPITALS: primary stress. SMALL CAPS: secondary stress. Ⓢ: U.S. pron. Ⓛ: British pron.

Kriegspiel
  game   KRĒG-SHPĒL, KRĒG-SPĒL   'kriːgˌʃpiːl, 'kriːgˌspiːl
Kriemhild
  wife of Siegfried   KRĒM-HILD   'kriːmˌhild
Krimmler Wasserfälle
  waterfall, Austria   KRIM-luhr VAHS-uhr-FEL-uh   'krimləʳ 'vasəʳˌfelə
Krio
  lang., Sierra Leone   KRĒ-ō   'kriːoː
Kris
  pers. name   KRIS   'kris
Krishna
  Hindu incarnation of Vishnu;   KRISH-nuh   'kriʃnə
     river, India; pers. name
Krishnaism
  religion   KRISH-nuh-IZ-uhm   'kriʃnəˌizəm
Krista
  pers. name   KRIS-tuh   'kristə
Kristen
  pers. name   KRIS-tuhn   'kristən
Kristi, Kristie
  pers. name   KRIS-tē   'kristiˑ
Kristian
  1. pers. name, Danish   KRĒS-TYAHN   'kriːsˌtjan
  2. Dutch   KRIS-tē-AHN   'kristiːˌan
  3. Finnish   KRIS-ti-AHN   'kristiˌaːn
Kristiansand
  port, Norway   KRIS-chuhn-SAN(D),   'kristʃənˌsæn(d),
                              KRISH-chuhn-SAN(D)   'kriʃtʃənˌsæn(d)
Kristiansen
  Ingrid, *Norwegian marathoner* KRIST-yahn-suhn,   'kristjansən, Ⓢ 'kristʃənsən
                              Ⓢ KRIS-chuhn-suhn
Kristiansund
  port, Norway   KRIS-chuhn-SUN(D),   'kristʃənˌsun(d),
                              KRISH-chuhn-SUN(D)   'kriʃtʃənˌsun(d)
Kristin
  pers. name   KRIS-tuhn   'kristən
Kristofer
  pers. name, Norwegian, Swedish kris-TAW-fuhr   kris'toːfər
Kristoffer
  1. pers. name, Danish   krēs-TAWF-uhr   kriːs'toːfər
  2. Norwegian, Swedish   kris-TAWF-fuhr   kris'toːffər
Kristofferson
  Kris, *US entertainer*   kri-STAW-fuhr-suhn,   kri'stoːfəʳsən, kri'stafəʳsən
                              kri-STAHF-uhr-suhn
Kristy
  pers. name   KRIS-tē   'kristiˑ
Kríti [Crete]
  island, Greece   KRĒ-tē   'kriːtiˑ
Krk
  island, Croatia   KUHRK   'kəʳk
Krka
  river, Croatia   KUHR-kuh   'kəʳkə
Krnov
  town, Czech republic   KUHR-NAWF   'kəʳˌnoːf

Key (col. 2): a: **fad** ā: **fade** ah: **father** ar: **Mary** aw: **law** e: **fed** ē: **feed** er: **merry** i: **hid** ī: **hide** ō: **coat** o͞o: **boot**
oi: **boy** ow: **now** u: **put** uh: **above** uhr: **bird** ch: **chop** ng: **ring** sh: **show** th: **thick** th̲: **this** zh: **measure**

Kroc
Ray A., *US businessman*   KRAHK   'krɑk

Kroeber
Alfred L., *US anthropologist*   KRŌ-buhr   'kroːbəʳ

Krogh
S. A. S., *Danish physiologist*   KRAWḠ   'krɔːɣ
(Nobel 1920)

Krona
monetary unit, Sweden, Iceland,   KROO-nah, ⑤ KRŌ-nuh   'kruːnɑː, ⑤ 'kroːnə
Faeroe Islands

Krone
Danish monetary unit   KRŌ-nuh   'kroːnə

Kronen
German beer   KRŌ-nuhn   'kroːnən

Kronenbourg
French beer   kraw-neⁿ-BOOR   krɔːnẽbuːr

Kronos
Titan   KRŌ-nuhs, KRŌ-nōs   'kroːnəs, 'kroːnoːs

Kronstadt
city, Romania   krahn-SHTAHT, ⑤ KRŌN-STAT   krɑn'ʃtɑt, ⑤ 'kroːn,stæt

Kroonstad
town, Orange Free State   KRŌN-STAT   'kroːn,stæt

Kropf Edel
German beer   KRAWPF ĀD-l   'krɔːpf 'eːdl̩

Kropotkin
Pyotr, *Russian political leader*   kruh-PAHT-k(y)in   krə'pɑtk(j)in

Krueger
Freddy, *horror movie character*   KROO-guhr   'kruːgəʳ

Kruger
1. Jerome, *US government official*   KROO-guhr   'kruːgəʳ
2. Paul, *S. African statesman*   KRUE-uhr, ⑤ KROO-guhr   'kryːəʳ, ⑤ 'kruːgəʳ

Krugerrand
gold coin, South Africa   KROO-guh-RAND   'kruːgə,rænd

Kru-Krawi
lang., Liberia, Ivory Coast   KROO-KROW-ē   'kruː'krɑuiˑ

Kru [Kru-Krawi]
lang., Liberia, Ivory Coast   KROO   'kruː

Krupa
Gene, *US jazz drummer*   KROO-puh   'kruːpə

Krupp
German manufacturing co.   KRUP, KRUHP   'krup, 'krəp

Krups
appliances   KRUHPS   'krəps

Krupske
Danya, *US director, choreographer*   KRUHP-skē   'krəpskiˑ

Kruševac
town, Serbia   KROO-shuh-VAHTS   'kruːʃə,vɑːts

Krym [Crimea]
peninsula, Ukraine   KRIM   'krim

Krypton
fictional planet in Superman   KRIP-TAHN   'krip,tɑn
comics; element

Krzyzewski
Mike, *US college basketball coach*   shuh-SHEV-skē   ʃə'ʃevskiˑ

Foreign Sounds: ue: *Fr.* **rue**, *Ger.* **füllen**   uh(r): *Fr.* **boeuf**, *Ger.* **Höhle**   <u>kh</u>: *Ger.* **ich**, *Scot.* **loch**   ḡ: *Sp.* **amigo**   ɣ: *Sp.* **hablar**   hl: *Welsh* **Llanelli**.   CAPITALS: primary stress.   SMALL CAPS: secondary stress.   ⑤: U.S. pron.   ⑥: British pron.

Ktaadn
  see Katahdin

Kuala Lumpur
  city, Malaysia   KWAHL-uh LUM-PUR, ku-AHL-uh,   ˌkwɑlə 'lum,puʳ, ku'ɑlə,
                          LUHM-PUR, lum-PUR   'ləm,puʳ, lum'puʳ

Kua [Makua]
  lang., people, Africa   KWAH   'kwɑ

Kubango
  river, Africa   koo-BAHNG-gō   kuːˈbɑŋgoː

Kubek
  Tony, *US baseball player*   K(Y)OO-BEK   'k(j)uː,bek

Kublai Khan
  Mongol leader   koo-bluh KAHN, koo-BLĪ KAHN   ˌkuːblə 'kan, ˌkuː,blai 'kan

Kubler-Ross
  Elisabeth, *US physician & author*   KOO-bluhr-RAWS   'kuːbləʳrɔːs

Kubrick
  Stanley, *US film director*   K(Y)OO-brik   'k(j)uːbrik

Kučera
  Henry, *US linguist*   KOO-chuh-ruh   'kuːtʃərə

Kudzu
  vine   KUD-zoo   'kudzuː

Kuebler's
  Park, *St. Louis, MO*   K(Y)OOB-luhrz   'k(j)uːbləʳz

Kuei-lin
  see Guilin

Kuei-yang
  see Guiyang

Kufic
  Arabic script   K(Y)OO-fik   'k(j)uːfik

Kuhn
  Bowie, *US attorney, baseball*   K(Y)OON   'k(j)uːn
    commissioner

Kui
  lang., people, India   KOO-ē   'kuːiˑ

Kuibyshev
  city, Russia   KWĒ-buh-SHEF, KOO-ē-buh-SHEF   'kwiːbə,ʃef, 'kuːiːbə,ʃef

Ku Klux Klan
  white-supremacist organization   K(Y)OO KLUHKS KLAN, KLOO   ˌk(j)uː ˌkləks 'klæn, ˌkluː

Kulmbacher Mönchshof
  German beer   KULM-BAHKH-uhr   'kulm,bɑxəʳ 'mœːnçs,hɔːf
                       MUH(R)NKHS-HAWF

Kültepe [Kanesh]
  ancient Assyrian city, Turkey   KUL-tuh-PĀ   ˌkultə'peː

Kumbh Mela
  Indian festival   KUM-muh-LAH   'kummə,lɑ

Kümmel
  liqueur   KIM-uhl, KUEM-uhl   'kiməl, 'kyməl

Kumyk
  lang., people, Caucasus Mts.   koo-MIK   kuːˈmik

Kun
  Béla, *Hungarian political leader*   KOON   'kuːn

Kunama
  lang., Ethiopia   koo-NAHM-uh   kuːˈnɑmə

Kundera
  Milan, *Czech-born French novelist*   kun-DER-uh   kun'derə

Key (col. 2):   a: fad   ā: fade   ah: father   ar: Mary   aw: law   e: fed   ē: feed   er: merry   i: hid   ī: hide   ō: coat   oo: boot
oi: boy   ow: now   u: put   uh: above   uhr: bird   ch: chop   ng: ring   sh: show   th: thick   th: this   zh: measure

!Kung
  African people   khuⁿ, Ⓢ KUNG   ǀxũ, Ⓢ 'kuŋ

K'ung Fu-tzu [Confucius]
  Chinese philosopher   KUNG FŌŌD-ZŌŌ   'kuŋ 'fuːd'zuː

Kunimatsu
  pers. name, Japanese   kun-ē-maht-su   kuniːmɑtsu

Kunin
  Madeleine May, US politician.   KYŌŌ-nuhn   'kjuːnən

Kunming, K'ung-ming
  city, China   KUN-MING   'kun'miŋ

Kuno
  pers. name, German   KŌŌ-nō   'kuːnoː

Kuomintang
  political party, Taiwan   GWŌ-MIN-TAHNG   'gwoː'min'tɑŋ

Küppers Kölsch
  German beer   KUEP-uhrs KUH(R)LSH   'kypəʳs 'kœlʃ

Kura
  river, Turkey, Georgia, Azerbaijan   kuh-RAH, KUR-uh   kə'rɑ, 'kurə

Kuralt
  Charles, US TV personality   kuh-RAWLT, kuh-RAHLT   kə'rɔːlt, kə'rɑlt

Kurath
  Hans, US linguist   KUR-AHT, KYUR-AHT   'kur‚ɑt, 'kjur‚ɑt

Kurd
  1. people, Middle East, Europe   KUHRD, KURD   'kəʳd, 'kuʳd
  2. pers. name, German   KURT   'kuʳt

Kurdish
  lang., Middle East, Europe   KUHRD-ish, KURD-ish   'kəʳdiʃ, 'kuʳdiʃ

Kurdistan
  region, Middle East; rug   KUHRD-uh-STAHN, KURD-uh-STAHN, -ŚTAN   ‚kəʳdə'stɑn, ‚kuʳdə'stɑn, -'stæn

Kure
  city, Japan   kōō-rā   kuːreː

Kuril
  Islands, Pacific   KYUR-ĒL, kyu-RĒL   'kjur‚iːl, kju'riːl

Kuri [Lezghian]
  lang., people, Caucasus Mts.   KUR-ē   'kuriˑ

Kuril'skiye Ostrova [Kuril]
  Pacific   ku-RĒL-skuh-yuh AWS-truh-vuh   ku'riːlskəjə 'ɔːstrəvə

Kurku
  lang., people, India   KUR-kōō   'kuʳkuː

Kurosawa
  Japanese film director   KUR-uh-SAH-wuh   ‚kurə'sɑwə

Kurri Kurri
  town, Australia   KUHR-ē KUHR-ē   'kəriˑ ‚kəriˑ

Kursk
  city, Russia   KURSK   'kuʳsk

Kurt
  1. pers. name   KUHRT   'kəʳt
  2. German   KURT   'kuʳt
  3. Swedish   KUHRT   'kərt

Kurukh
  lang., people, India   KUR-uhk   'kurək

Kurukhi
  lang., India   KUR-uh-kē   'kurəkiˑ

Foreign Sounds: ue: *Fr.* **rue**, *Ger.* **füllen** uh(r): *Fr.* **boeuf**, *Ger.* **Höhle** <u>kh</u>: *Ger.* **ich**, *Scot.* **loch** ḡ: *Sp.* **amigo** <u>v</u>: *Sp.* **hablar**
hl: *Welsh* **Llanelli**. CAPITALS: primary stress. SMALL CAPS: secondary stress. Ⓢ: U.S. pron. Ⓛ: British pron.

Kurumba
   lang., people, Burkina Faso   kuh-R$\overline{OO}$M-buh   kə'ruːmbə

Kurzweil
   tdmk for optical scanning devices   KUHRT-swīl, KUHRZ-wīl   'kəʳt‚swail, 'kəʳz‚wail

Kusch
   Polykarp, *German-born US*   KUSH   'kuʃ
     physicist (Nobel 1955)

Kush, Cush
   ancient country on Nile   KUHSH, KUSH   'kəʃ, 'kuʃ

Kuskokwim
   river, AK   KUHS-kuh-KWIM   'kəskə‚kwim

Kusu
   lang., Africa   K$\overline{OO}$-s$\overline{oo}$ 'kuːsuː

Kutchin
   N. American people   k$\overline{oo}$-CHIN   kuː'tʃin

Kutenai, Kootenai
   N. American people   K$\overline{OO}$T-n-ā, K$\overline{OO}$T-n-ē   'kuːtn̩eː, 'kuːtn̩iˑ

Kutuzov
   Mikhail, *Russian militarist*   k$\overline{oo}$-T$\overline{OO}$-zuhf, -ZAWF, -ZAWV   kuː'tuːzəf, -‚zɔːf, -‚zɔːv

Kutztown
   borough, PA   KUTS-TOWN   'kuts‚taun

Kuvasz
   dog breed   K$\overline{OO}$-VAHS   'kuː‚vas

Kuwait
   country, Persian Gulf   kuh-WĀT   kə'weːt

Kuwaiti
   pert. to Kuwait   kuh-WĀT-ē   kə'weːtiˑ

Kuybyshev
   city, Russia   K$\overline{OO}$-i-buh-SHEF   'kuːibə‚ʃef

Kuzmich
   pers. name, Russian   K$\overline{OO}$Z-myēch   'kuːʐmjiːtʃ

Kuznets
   Simon, *Russian-born US*   KUHZ-NETS   'kəz‚nets
     economist (Nobel 1971)

Kuznetsk
   former name of Novokuznetsk   kuz-NETSK   kuz'netsk

Kwaa
   lang., Liberia   KWAH   'kwa

Kwajalein
   atoll, Marshall Islands   KWAHJ-uh-luhn, KWAHJ-uh-LĀN   'kwadʒələn, 'kwadʒə‚leːn

Kwak
   Belgian beer   KWAHK   'kwaːk

Kwakiutl
   N. American people   KWAHK-ē-$\overline{OO}$T-l, kwahk-Y$\overline{OO}$T-l   ‚kwakiː'uːtl̩, kwak'juːtl̩

Kwame
   pers. name (K. Nkrumah)   KWAHM-ā   'kwameː

KwaNdebele
   state, South Africa   KWAHN-duh-BÃ-lā   ‚kwandə'beːleː

Kwangchow
   see Guangzhou

Kwango
   river, Africa   KWAHNG-gō   'kwaŋgoː

Kwangsi Chuang [Guangxi]
   region, China   GWAHNG-SĒ chuh-WAHNG   'gwaŋ'siː tʃə'waŋ

Key (col. 2): a: fad ā: fade ah: father ar: Mary aw: law e: fed ē: feed er: merry i: hid ī: hide ō: coat $\overline{oo}$: boot
oi: boy ow: now u: put uh: above uhr: bird ch: chop ng: ring sh: show th: thick <u>th</u>: this zh: measure

Kwangtung
  see Guangdong

Kwangwa
  African people   KWAHNG-gwuh   'kwaŋgwə

Kwan-Ichi
  pers. name, Japanese   kwahn-ē-chē   kwaniːtʃiː

Kwantung
  territory, China   GWAHN-DUNG   'gwan'duŋ

Kwanza
  see Cuanza

Kwanzaa, -za
  African-American festival   KWAHN-zuh   'kwanzə

Kwapa [Quapaw]
  N. American people   KWAW-PAW   'kwɔːˌpɔː

KwaZulu
  state, South Africa   kwah-Z̄OO-l̄oo   kwa'zuːluː

Kweichow
  see Guizhou

Kweilin
  see Guilin

Kweiyang
  see Guiyang

Kweni
  lang., Ivory Coast   KWĀ-nē   'kweːniː

Ky
  see Nguyen Cao Ky

Kyd
  Thomas, *English dramatist*   KID   'kid

Kyeretwi
  pers. name, Twi   KYER-e-TWĒ   'kjereˌtwiː

Kyle
  pers. name   KĪL   'kail

Kynuna
  town, Australia   kī-N̄OO-nuh   kai'nuːnə

Kyocera
  Japanese electronics co.   kē-ō-SER-uh   kiːoː'serə

Kyoga, Kioga
  lake, Uganda   kē-Ō-guh   kiː'oːgə

Kyŏngju
  town, S. Korea   kē-AWNG-J̄OO   kiː'ɔŋ'dʒuː

Kyoto, Kyōto
  city, Japan   kē-ō-tō, Ⓢ kē-ŌT-ō   kiːoːtoː, Ⓢ kiː'oʈoː

Kyowa Saitama
  Japanese bank   kē-ō-(w)ah sī-tahm-ah   kiːoː(w)a saitama

Kyrie eleison
  liturgical prayer, section of the   KIR-ē-Ā uh-LĀ(-uh)-SAHN,   'kiriːˌeː ə'leː(ə)ˌsan,
    Mass   uh-LĀ(-uh)-suhn   ə'leː(ə)sən

Kyrillos
  pers. name, Mod. Greek   KYĒ-rē-LAWS   'kjiːriːˌlɔːs

Kyūshū
  island, Japan   kē-̄oo-sh̄oo   kiːuːʃuː

Kyzylkum, Peski
  desert, Uzbekistan, Kazakhstan   PESH-kyē kuh-ZIL-K̄OOM   'peʃkjiː kəˌzil'kuːm

Kyzyl Kum, Qizil Qum
  desert, Uzbekistan, Kazakhstan   kuh-ZIL K̄OOM   kə'zil 'kuːm

---

Foreign Sounds: ue: *Fr.* **rue**, *Ger.* **füllen**   uh(r): *Fr.* **boeuf**, *Ger.* **Höhle**   kh: *Ger.* **ich**, *Scot.* **loch**   g̃: *Sp.* **amigo**   v: *Sp.* **hablar**   hl: *Welsh* **Llanelli**.   CAPITALS: primary stress.   SMALL CAPS: secondary stress.   Ⓢ: U.S. pron.   Ⓛ: British pron.

L

Laban
  Biblical name   LĀ-buhn   'leːbən

Labatt
  Canadian brewing co.   luh-BAT   lə'bæt

La Bayamesa
  national anthem, Cuba   lah BAH-yah-mā-sah   la 'bajameːsa

Labdacus
  father of Laius   LAB-duh-kuhs   'læbdəkəs

Labelle
  Patti, *US singer*   luh-BEL   lə'bel

La Belle Strasbourgeoise
  French beer   lah BEL strahs-bōōr-ZHWAHZ   laː bel straːsbuːrӡwaːz

Labette
  Community College, *KS*   luh-BET   lə'bet

L'Abidjanaise
  national anthem, Ivory Coast   lah-bēd-zhah-NEZ   laːbiːdӡaːnez

La Bohème
  see Bohème, La

Laboure
  Junior College, *MA*   luh-BUR   lə'buᴿ

Labov
  William, *US linguist*   luh-BŌV, luh-BUHV   lə'boːv, lə'bəv

Labovian
  pert. to Labov   luh-BŌ-vē-uhn, luh-BUHV-ē-uhn   lə'boːviːən, lə'bəviːən

La Brabançonne
  national anthem, Belgium   lah brah-bah^n-SAWN   laː braːbãsɔːn

Labrador
  prov, Canada; dog breed   LAB-ruh-DAWR   'læbrə,dɔːᴿ

La Brea
  Tar Pits, *CA*   luh BRĀ-uh   lə 'breːə

Labuan
  island, Malaysia   luh-BŌO-uhn   lə'buːən

Laburnum
  tree   luh-BUHR-nuhm   lə'bəᴿnəm

Laccadive [Lakshadweep]
  Islands, *Arabian Sea*   LAK-uh-DĪV   'lækə,daiv

Lac Courte Oreilles
  Indian reservation, US   lahk KURT aw-RĀ(Y)   lak 'kuᴿt ɔː'reː(j)

Lac Du Flambeau
  Indian reservation, US   LAHK dōō flam-BŌ   'lak duˈ flæm'boː

Lacedaemonia
  ancient region, Greece   LAS-uhd-uh-MŌ-nē-uh   ˌlæsədə'moːniːə

Key (col. 2):   a: fad   ā: fade   ah: father   ar: Mary   aw: law   e: fed   ē: feed   er: merry   i: hid   ī: hide   ō: coat   ōō: boot
oi: boy   ow: now   u: put   uh: above   uhr: bird   ch: chop   ng: ring   sh: show   th: thick   <u>th</u>: this   zh: measure

Lacedaemon [Sparta]
  ancient city, country, Greece   LAS-uh-DĒ-muhn   ˌlæsə'diːmən
Lacerta
  constellation   luh-SUHRT-uh   lə'səʳtə
Lacey
  pers. name   LĀ-sē   'leːsiˑ
Laches
  dialogue of Plato   LĀ-KĒZ   'leːˌkiːz
Lachesis
  mythological Fate   LAK-uh-suhs   'lækəsəs
Lachlan
  pers. name   LAK-luhn, LAHK-luhn   'læklən, 'lɑklən
Lachryma Christi
  see Lacrima Christi
Lackawanna
  county, PA; city, NY   LAK-uh-WAHN-uh   ˌlækə'wɑnə
Laclede
  county, MO; Park, *former*   luh-KLĒD, luh-KLED   lə'kliːd, lə'kled
     ballpark, St. Louis, MO
La Concepción
  town, Panama   lah kawn-seps-YAWN   lɑ kɔːnseps'jɔːn
Laconia
  city, NH; region, Greece   luh-KŌ-nē-uh, luh-KŌN-yuh   lə'koːniːə, lə'koːnjə
La Coruña
  prov & city, Spain   lah kuh-ROON-yuh   lɑ kə'ruːnjə
Lac Qui Parle
  lake, county, MN   LAK ē PAHRL   ˌlæk iː 'pɑʳl
Lacrima Christi, Lachryma Christi
  Italian wine   LAHK-ruh-muh KRIS-tē, LAK-   'lɑkrəmə 'kristiˑ, 'læk-
La Crosse
  city, county, WI   luh KRAWS   lə 'krɔːs
Lactantius
  early Christian writer   lak-TAN-sh(ē-)uhs   læk'tænʃ(iː)əs
Lacy
  Beatrice Cates, *psychophysiologist* LĀ-sē   'leːsiˑ
Ladakh, Ladak
  district, Jammu and Kashmir   luh-DAHK   lə'dɑk
Lade
  island off Miletus   LAHD-ā   'lɑdeː
La Dessalinienne
  national anthem, Haiti   lah dā-sah-lēn-YEN   lɑː deːsɑːliːnjen
Lādhiqīyah, Al
  city, Syria   AHL LAH-tuh-KĒ-(y)uh, AL   ˌɑːl ˌlɑtə'kiː(j)ə, ˌæl
Ladin
  lang., Italy   luh-DĒN   lə'diːn
Ladino
  lang., Sephardic Jews   lah-THĒ-nō, Ⓢ luh-DĒ-nō   lɑ'ðiːnoː, Ⓢ lə'diːnoː
Ladislas
  1. pers. name   LAD-uhs-luhs, LAD-uhs-LAHS   'lædəsləs, 'lædəsˌlɑs
  2. French   lah-dē-SLAHS   lɑːdiːslɑːs
Ladislaus
  pers. name, German   LAHD-is-LOWS   'lɑdisˌlaus
Ladislav
  pers. name, Czech   LAHJ-is-LAHF   'lɑːdʒisˌlɑːf

Foreign Sounds: ue: *Fr.* **rue**, *Ger.* **füllen** uh(r): *Fr.* **boeuf**, *Ger.* **Höhle** <u>kh</u>: *Ger.* i<u>ch</u>, *Scot.* lo<u>ch</u> g̃: *Sp.* ami**g**o v̧: *Sp.* ha**b**lar
hl: *Welsh* **Ll**anelli.   CAPITALS: primary stress.   SMALL CAPS: secondary stress.   Ⓢ: U.S. pron.   Ⓛ: British pron.

Ladoga
   lake, Russia   LAHD-uh-guh, LAD-uh-guh   'lɑdəgə, 'lædəgə

Ladon
   dragon guarding the apples of the   LĀD-n, LĀ-DAHN   'leːdn̩, 'leːˌdɑn
      Hesperides; Greek river god

Ladozhskoye Ozero [Ladoga]
   lake, Russia   LAHD-uhsh-(s)kuh-yuh UHZ-YER-ō   'lɑːdəʃ(s)kəjə ˌəz'jeroː

Lady Margaret Hall
   college, Oxford Univ.   LĀD-ē MAHR-g(uh-)ruht HAWL   ˌleːdiˑ 'mɑrg(ə)rət 'hɔːl

Lae
   port, New Guinea   LAH-Ā   'lɑˌeː

Laertes
   father of Odysseus; Ophelia's   lā-UHRT-ēz   leˑ'əʳʈiːz
      brother in Hamlet, *Shakespeare*

Laestrygonians
   giant cannibals met by Odysseus   LES-truh-GŌ-nē-uhnz   ˌlestrə'goːniːənz

Laetare Sunday
   4th Sunday of Lent   lā-TAHR-ē SUHN-dē, lā-TAR-ē, leˑ'taʳiˑ 'səndiˑ, leˑ'tæriˑ,
                       SUHN-dā   'səndeː

Laetitia
   pers. name   li-TISH-(ē-)uh   li'tiʃ(iː)ə

Laetrile
   controversial drug   LĀ-uh-TRIL, LĀ-uh-truhl, Ⓔ   'leːə,tril, 'leːətrəl, Ⓔ
                       LĀ-uh-TRĬL   'leːə,trail

La Farge
   Mme., character in Tale of Two   luh FAHRJ, luh FAHRZH, lah   lə 'fɑrdʒ, lə 'fɑrʒ, lɑ 'fɑrʒ
      Cities, *Dickens*   FAHRZH

La Fayette
   city, GA   luh-FET   lə'fet

Lafayette
   1. Marquis de, French general   lah-fah-YET, Ⓢ LAHF-ē-ET, LAF-ē-ET lɑːfɑːjet, Ⓢ ˌlɑfiː'et, ˌlæfiː'et
   2. US pl. name   LAHF-ē-ET, LAF-ē-ET, LAHF-ī-ET, ˌlɑfiː'et, ˌlæfiː'et, ˌlɑfˌai'et,
                       LAF-ī-ET, *esp. in southeastern US* ˌlæfˌai'et, *esp. in*
                       LĀ-fē-ET, luh-FĀ(-uh)t   *southeastern US* ˌleːfiː'et,
                                             lə'feː(ə)t

Lafcadio
   pers. name   lahf-KAHD-ē-ō   laf'kɑdiːoː

La Fête de la Madeleine
   Provençal festival   lah FET duh lah mahd-LEN   lɑː fet də lɑː mɑːdlen

Lafferty
   Perry Francis, *TV executive*   LAF-uhrt-ē   'læfəʳʈiˑ

Lafite
   wine   lah-FĒT   lɑːfiːt

Lafite-Rothschild
   wine   lah-FĒT-rawt-SHĒLD   lɑːfiːtrɔːtʃiːld

Lafleur
   Guy, *sports personality*   luh-FLUHR   lə'fləʳ

LaFollette
   Robert M., *US politician*   luh-FAHL-uht   lə'fɑlət

La Fontaine
   Henri, *Belgian politician (Nobel* lah fawⁿ-TEN; Ⓢ luh fahn-TĀN, luh lɑː fɔ̃ten; Ⓢ lə fan'teːn, lə
      1913)   FAHN-TĀN   'fan,teːn

Lafourche
   bayou, parish, LA   luh-FOOSH   lə'fuːʃ

Key (col. 2): a: fad ā: fade ah: father ar: Mary aw: law e: fed ē: feed er: merry i: hid ī: hide ō: coat ōō: boot
oi: boy ow: now u: put uh: above uhr: bird ch: chop ng: ring sh: show th: thick th̲: this zh: measure

Lagash
  Sumerian city — LĀ-GASH — 'leːˌgæʃ

Lag b'Omer
  Jewish holiday — LAHG BŌ-muhr, buh-Ō-muhr, buh-Ō-mer — 'lɑg 'boːməʳ, bə'oːməʳ, bə'oːmeʳ

Lagerfeld
  Karl Otto, *European fashion designer* — LAHG-uhr-FELT — 'lɑgəʳˌfelt

Lagerkvist
  Pär F., *Swedish author (Nobel 1951)* — LAHG-uhrk-FIST — 'lɑgəʳkˌfist

Lagerlöf
  Selma, *Swedish author (Nobel 1909)* — LAH-guhr-LUH(R)V — 'lɑːgəʳˌlœːv

La Gioconda
  see Gioconda, La

Lagomorpha
  hares & rabbits — LAG-uh-MAWR-fuh — ˌlægə'mɔːʳfə

Lagos
  city, state, Nigeria — LĀ-GAHS, LAHG-ŌS, LAHG-uhs — 'leːˌgɑs, 'lɑgˌoːs, 'lɑgəs

La Grange
  pl. name, US — luh GRĀNJ — lə 'greːndʒ

LaGrave
  Field, *former ballpark, Fort Worth, TX* — luh-GRĀV — lə'greːv

Lágrima
  Spanish wine — LAHG-rē-muh — 'lɑgriːmə

Lagthing, Lagting [Storting]
  parliamentary body, Norway, Faeroe Islands — LAHG-ting — 'lɑgtiŋ

La Guardia
  Fiorello, *New York City mayor; airport, New York City* — luh GWAHR-dē-uh — lə 'gwɑʳdiːə

Laguna
  1. pueblo, village, NM; N. American people; Indian Reservation, US — luh-GOO-nuh — lə'guːnə
  2. city, Brazil; prov, Philippines — lah-GOO-nah, Ⓢ luh-GOO-nuh — lɑ'guːnɑ, Ⓢ lə'guːnə

Laguna Beach
  city, CA — luh-GOO-nuh BĒCH — lə,guːnə 'biːtʃ

Laguna Hills
  city, CA — luh-GOO-nuh HILZ — lə,guːnə 'hilz

Lahnda
  lang., India, Pakistan — LAHN-duh — 'lɑndə

Lahore
  prov, Pakistan — luh-HŌR, luh-HAWR — lə'hoːʳ, lə'hɔːʳ

Lahr
  Bert, *US comedian;* John, *US author* — LAHR — 'lɑʳ

Laidlaw
  William, *Scottish poet; US publisher* — LĀD-LAW — 'leːdˌlɔː

Laighton
  pers. name — LĀT-n — 'leːtn̩

Foreign Sounds: ue: *Fr.* **rue**, *Ger.* **füllen** uh(r): *Fr.* **boeuf**, *Ger.* **Höhle** kh: *Ger.* i**ch**, *Scot.* lo**ch** g: *Sp.* ami**go** v: *Sp.* ha**b**lar hl: *Welsh* **Ll**anelli. CAPITALS: primary stress. SMALL CAPS: secondary stress. Ⓢ: U.S. pron. Ⓔ: British pron.

Lailat al Miraj
Islamic festival   lī-LAHT ahl mir-AHZH, al   lai'lɑt ɑːl mir'ɑʒ, æl

Laine
Cleo, *British singer*   LĀN   'leːn

Laird
pers. name   LARD, LERD   'læ˞d, 'le˞d

Laius
father of Oedipus   LĀ-(y)uhs, LĪ-uhs   'leː(j)əs, 'laiəs

La Jolla
resort area, CA   luh HOI-uh   lə 'hɔiɐ

Lajos
pers. name, Hungarian   LAH-yawsh, LOI-ŌSH   'lajɔːʃ, 'lɔi,oːʃ

La Junta
city, CO   luh HUHNT-uh, luh HUN-tuh   lə 'həntə, lə 'huntə

Lak, Lakh, Lakk
lang., people, Caucasus Mts.   LAHK, LAK   'lɑk, 'læk

Lakeisha
pers. name   luh-KĒ-shuh   lə'kiːʃə

Lakisha
pers. name   luh-KĒ-shuh, luh-KISH-uh   lə'kiːʃə, lə'kiʃə

Lakmé
opera, Delibes   lahk-MĀ   lɑːkmeː

Lakonia [Laconia]
region, Greece   LAHK-uh-NĒ-uh   ˌlɑkə'niːə

Lakshadweep [Laccadive]
islands, Arabian Sea   luhk-SHAHD-WĒP   lək'ʃad,wiːp

Lakshmi
pers. name, Sanskrit   LUHK-shmē   'ləkʃmiˑ

Lal
pers. name, Hindi   LAHL   'lɑl

Lalage
character, Horatian ode   LAL-uh-gē, LAL-uh-jē   'læləgiˑ, 'lælədʒiˑ

LaLanne
Jack, *US fitness expert*   luh-LĀN   lə'leːn

La Leche
League for the promotion of   lah LĀ-chā, lah LĀ-shā   lɑ 'leːtʃeː, lɑ 'leːʃeː
breast-feeding

Lalia
lang., Africa   LĀ-lē-uh   'leːliːə

Lalique
crystal   lah-LĒK   lɑ'liːk

Lallans
Lowland Scots dialect   LAL-uhnz   'lælənz

L'Allegro
poem, J. Milton   luh-LEG-rō, lah-   lə'legroː, lɑ-

Lalo
Edouard Victor, *French composer*   lah-LŌ   lɑːloː

Lamachus
Athenian general   LAM-uh-kuhs   'læməkəs

Lamade
Stadium, *Williamsport, PA*   luh-MĀD   lə'meːd

La Madeleine
city, France   lah mahd(-uh)-LEN,   lɑː mɑːd(ə)len,
     ⑤ luh-MAD-l-ĀN   ⑤ lə,mædl'eːn

Key (col. 2):   a: fad   ā: fade   ah: father   ar: Mary   aw: law   e: fed   ē: feed   er: merry   i: hid   ī: hide   ō: coat   o͞o: boot
oi: boy   ow: now   u: put   uh: above   uhr: bird   ch: chop   ng: ring   sh: show   th: thick   <u>th</u>: this   zh: measure

Lamaism
   Tibetan Buddhism   LAHM-uh-IZ-uhm   'lɑmə,izəm
Lamaistic Buddhism
   religion   LAHM-uh-IS-tik B̅O̅O̅D-IZ-uhm,   ,lɑmə,istik 'buːd,izəm,
                                   BUD-IZ-uhm   'bud,izəm
La Mancha
   region, Spain   luh MAHN-chuh   lə 'mɑntʃə
La Manche [English Channel]
   strait between England & France   lah MAHⁿSH   lɑː mãʃ
Lamanism
   Buddhist sect   LÃ-muh-NIZ-uhm   'leːmə,nizəm
Lamar
   Community College, CO;   luh-MAHR   lə'mɑʳ
     University, TX; county, AL; pers.
     name
Lamarck
   Jean Baptiste de, French   lah-MAHRK, Ⓢ luh-MAHRK   lɑːmɑːrk, Ⓢ lə'mɑʳk
     naturalist
Lamarckian
   pert. to Lamarckism   luh-MAHR-kē-uhn   lə'mɑʳkiːən
Lamarckism
   theory of environmentally caused   luh-MAHR-KIZ-uhm   lə'mɑʳ,kizəm
     evolutionary change
Lamarr
   pers. name   luh-MAHR   lə'mɑʳ
La Marseillaise
   national anthem, France   lah mahr-se-YEZ   lɑː mɑːrsejez
Lamartine
   Alphonse de, French writer   lah-mahr-TĒN, Ⓢ LAM-uhr-TĒN   lɑːmɑːrtiːn, Ⓢ ,læməʳ'tiːn
Lamas
   Fernando, entertainer   LAHM-uhs   'lɑməs
Lamaze
   birthing method   luh-MAHZ   lə'mɑz
Lamb
   Charles, English essayist; Willis E.,   LAM   'læm
     Jr., US physicist (Nobel 1955)
Lamba
   lang., people, Africa   LAM-buh, LAHM-buh   'læmbə, 'lɑmbə
Lambeosaurus
   dinosaur   LAM-bē-uh-SAWR-uhs   ,læmbiːə'sɔːrəs
Lambert
   1. airport, St. Louis, MO; pers.   LAM-buhrt   'læmbəʳt
     name
   2. Dutch   LAHM-buhrt   'lɑmbərt
   3. French   lahⁿ-BER   lãber
Lambeth
   borough, England   LAM-buhth   'læmbəθ
Lamborghini
   Italian car   LAM-buhr-GĒ-nē   ,læmbəʳ'giːniˑ
Lambretta
   tdmk for an Italian motorbike   lam-BRET-uh   læm'breʈə
Lambrusco
   Italian wine   lam-BRO̅O̅S-kō, lahm-   læm'bruːskoː, lɑm-
Lambuth
   College, TN   LAM-buhth   'læmbəθ

Foreign Sounds: ue: *Fr.* **rue**, *Ger.* **füllen**   uh(r): *Fr.* **boeuf**, *Ger.* **Höhle**   <u>kh</u>: *Ger.* i**ch**, *Scot.* lo**ch**   ğ: *Sp.* ami**g**o   <u>v</u>: *Sp.* ha**b**lar
hl: *Welsh* **Ll**anelli.   CAPITALS: primary stress.   SMALL CAPS: secondary stress.   Ⓢ: U.S. pron.   Ⓔ: British pron.

Lamech
  biblical patriarch   LAM-uhk   'læmək
Lamedon
  king of Sicyon   LAM-uh-DAHN   'læmə,dɑn
Lamentations
  Old Testament book   LAM-uhn-TĀ-shuhnz   ,læmən'teːʃənz
La Mesa
  city, CA   luh MĀ-suh   lə 'meːsə
Lamesa
  city, TX   luh-MĒ-suh   lə'miːsə
Lamia
  mythical Greek woman who   LĀ-mē-uh   'leːmiːə
    devoured children; poem, Keats
Lamian War
  Greece, 4th cent. B.C.   luh-MĒ-uhn   lə'miːən
Lamm
  Richard Douglas, US politician   LAM   'læm
Lammas
  English Christian festival, August   LAM-uhs   'læməs
    1st
Lammermuir Hills
  hills, Scotland   LAM-uhr-MYUR HILZ   ,læməʳ,mjuʳ 'hilz
Lamoille
  county, VT   luh-MOIL   lə'mɔil
Lamont
  Corliss, US philosophy educator,   luh-MAHNT   lə'mɑnt
    author
La Moure
  county, ND   luh MUR   lə 'muʳ
Lampasas
  county, TX   lam-PAS-uhs   læm'pæsəs
Lampedusa
  Giuseppe di, Italian writer   LAHM-pā-DŌO-sah,   ,lampeː'duːsa,
                                            ⑤ LAM-puh-DŌO-suh, -zuh   ⑤ ,læmpə'duːsə, -zə
Lampung
  province, Indonesia   LAHM-PUNG   'lɑm,puŋ
Lamut [Even]
  lang., people, East Siberia   luh-MŌOT   lə'muːt
LAN
  local area network   LAN   'læn
Lanai
  island, HI   luh-NĪ   lə'nɑi
Lanark
  county, Scotland; county, Ontario,   LAN-uhrk   'lænəʳk
    Canada
Lancashire
  county, England   LANG-kuh-shuhr, -SHIR   'læŋkəʃəʳ, -,ʃiʳ
Lancaster
  1. US pl. name; town, England;   LANG-kuh-stuhr, LAN-KAS-tuhr,   'læŋkəstəʳ, 'læn,kæstəʳ,
    English noble family   LANG-KAS-tuhr   'læŋ,kæstəʳ
  2. Burt, US actor   LAN-KAS-tuhr, LANG-KAS-tuhr   'læn,kæstəʳ, 'læŋ,kæstəʳ
Lancastrian
  pert. to the house of Lancaster   lang-KAS-trē-uhn, lan-KAS-trē-uhn   læŋ'kæstriːən, læn'kæstriːən
Lance
  pers. name   LANS   'læns

Key (col. 2):   a: fad   ā: fade   ah: father   ar: Mary   aw: law   e: fed   ē: feed   er: merry   i: hid   ī: hide   ō: coat   ōō: boot
oi: boy   ow: now   u: put   uh: above   uhr: bird   ch: chop   ng: ring   sh: show   th: thick   th: this   zh: measure

Lancelot
  Arthurian hero; pers. name — LAN(T)-suh-LAHT, LAHN(T)-, -s(uh-)luht — ˈlæn(t)sə‚lɑt, ˈlɑn(t)-, -s(ə)lət

Lanchow
  see Lanzhou

Lancia
  Italian car — LAN(T)-sē-uh — ˈlæn(t)siːə

Lancome
  tdmk for cosmetics — lahng-KŌM — lɑŋˈkoːm

Landers
  Ann, *US advice columnist* — LAN-duhrz — ˈlændəʳz

Landesberg
  Steve, *US actor* — LAN-duhs-BUHRG — ˈlændəs‚bəʳg

Landis
  John, *US film writer, director* — LAN-duhs — ˈlændəs

Ländler
  dance — LENT-luhr — ˈlentləʳ

Landnámabók
  Icelandic "Book of Settlements" — LAHND-NAHM-uh-BŌK — ˈlɑnd‚nɑmə‚boːk

Lando
  pope — LAHN-dō — ˈlɑndoː

Landon
  Michael, *US actor, TV director* — LAN-duhn — ˈlændən

Land-Rover
  tdmk for a vehicle — LAND-RŌ-vuhr — ˈlænd‚roːvəʳ

Landry
  Tom, *US football coach* — LAN-drē — ˈlændriˑ

Landsbergis
  Vytautas, *president, Lithuania* — LAHNZ-BER-guhs — ˈlɑnz‚beʳgəs

Land's End
  cape, England; US clothing co. — LAN(D)Z END — ˈlæn(d)z ˈend

Landsteiner
  Karl, *Austrian-born US pathologist (Nobel 1930)* — LAHNT-SHTĪ-nuhr, Ⓢ LAN(D)-STĪ-nuhr — ˈlɑnt‚ʃtainəʳ, Ⓢ ˈlæn(d)‚stainəʳ

Lane
  pers. name — LĀN — ˈleːn

Lange
  1. C. L., *Norwegian pacifist (Nobel 1921); pers. name, Norwegian* — LAHNG-uh — ˈlɑŋə
  2. Jessica, *US actress* — LANG — ˈlæŋ

Langella
  Frank, *US actor* — lan-JEL-uh — lænˈdʒelə

Langerhans islets
  pancreatic cell clusters — LAHNG-uhr-HAHNZ Ī-luhts, LAHNG-uhr-HAHN(T)S — ˈlɑŋəʳ‚hanz ˈailəts, ˈlɑŋəʳ‚han(t)s

Langfield
  Joanna, *radio talk show host* — LANG-FĒLD — ˈlæŋ‚fiːld

Langlade
  county, WI — LANG-LĀD — ˈlæŋ‚leːd

Langland
  William, *English poet* — LANG-luhnd — ˈlæŋlənd

Langley
  Samuel, *US astronomer* — LANG-lē — ˈlæŋliˑ

Foreign Sounds: ue: *Fr.* **rue**, *Ger.* **füllen** uh(r): *Fr.* **boeuf**, *Ger.* **Höhle** k͟h: *Ger.* i**ch**, *Scot.* lo**ch** g̅: *Sp.* ami**g**o ꝟ: *Sp.* ha**b**lar hl: *Welsh* **Ll**anelli. ꟅAPITALS: primary stress. SMALL CAPS: secondary stress. Ⓢ: U.S. pron. Ⓒ: British pron.

Langlois
1. pers. name	LANG-LOIS	'læŋ₁lɔis
2. French	lah^{n}g-LWAH	lãglwaː

Langmuir
Irving, *US chemist (Nobel 1932)*	LANG-MYUR	'læŋ₁mjuˈr

Lango
lang., people, Uganda	LAHNG-gō	'lɑŋgoː

Langobardic
pert. to Lombardy; *ancient Germanic lang.*	LANG-gō-BAHRD-ik	₁læŋgoː'baˈrdik

Langston
pers. name	LANG-stuhn	'læŋstən

Languedoc [Provençal]
lang., prov, France	lah^{n}g-DAWK, ⑤ lahng-DAWK	lãgdɔːk, ⑤ laŋ'dɔːk

Languedoc-Roussillon
region, France	lah^{n}g-DAWK-r$\overline{oo}$-sē-YAW^n	lãgdɔːkruːsiːjõ

Lanier
Sidney, *US poet; county, GA; pers. name*	luh-NIR	lə'niˈr

Lanneau
pers. name	LAN-ō	'lænoː

Lanphier
Park, *ballpark, Springfield, IL*	LAN-FIR	'læn₁fiˈr

Lansbury
Angela, *British actress*	LANZ-b(uh-)rē, ⑤ LANZ-BER-ē	'lænzb(ə)riˈ, ⑤ 'lænz₁beriˈ

Lansdowne
street, Boston	LANZ-DOWN	'lænz₁dɑun

L'Anse
Indian reservation, US	LANS	'læns

Lansing
Robert Howell, *US actor, director; city, MI*	LAN(T)-sing	'læn(t)siŋ

lanthanum
element	LAN(T)-thuh-nuhm	'læn(t)θənəm

Lantz
Walter, *US cartoonist*	LAN(T)S	'læn(t)s

Lanza
Mario, *US entertainer*	LAHN-zuh	'lɑnzə

Lanzhou, Lanchow [Kaolan]
city, China	LAHN-JŌ	'lɑn'dʒoː

Laoag
river, port, Philippines	luh-WAHG	lə'wɑg

Laocoön
Trojan priest	lā-AHK-uh-WAHN	leː'akə₁wɑn

Laodamas
king of Thebes	lā-AHD-uh-muhs	leː'adəməs

Laodamia
mother of Sarpedon by Zeus; wife of Protesilaus	LĀ-uhd-uh-MĪ-uh, -MĒ-(y)uh	₁leːədə'maiə, -'miː(j)ə

Laodice
daughter of Priam and Hecuba; daughter of Agamemnon and Clytemnestra	lā-AHD-uh-sē	leː'adəsiˈ

Laodicea
ancient name of Latakia	lā-AHD-uh-SĒ-uh	leː₁adə'siːə

Key (col. 2): a: fad ā: fade ah: father ar: Mary aw: law e: fed ē: feed er: merry i: hid ī: hide ō: coat $\overline{oo}$: boot
oi: boy ow: now u: put uh: above uhr: bird ch: chop ng: ring sh: show th: thick <u>th</u>: this zh: measure

Laodocus
   son of Apollo and Phthia   lā-AHD-uh-kuhs   leːˈɑdəkəs
Lao [Laotian]
   lang., people, Laos, Thailand   LOW, LAH-ō   ˈlau, ˈlɑ-oː
Laomedon
   father of Priam   lā-AHM-uh-DAHN   leːˈamə,dɑn
Laon, La
   town, France   lah LAH^n   lɑː lɑ̃
Laos
   republic, Asia   LOWS, LĀ-AHS, LAH-ōs   ˈlaus, ˈleː,as, ˈlɑ-oːs
Laotian [Lao]
   lang., people, Laos, Thailand   LOW-shuhn, lā-Ō-shuhn,   ˈlauʃən, leːˈoːʃən, lɑˈoːʃən
       lah-Ō-shuhn
Lao-tzu
   Chinese philosopher   LOWD-ZU, LOWD-Z͞OO   ˈlaudˈzu, ˈlaudˈzuː
La Paz
   1. county, AZ   luh PAZ   lə ˈpæz
   2. S. American pl. name   luh PAHZ, luh PAHS, luh PAZ   lə ˈpaz, lə ˈpas, lə ˈpæz
Lapeer
   county, MI   luh-PIR   ləˈpiʳ
Laphroaig
   Scotch whiskey   luh-FROIG, la-FROIG   ləˈfrɔig, læˈfrɔig
Lapiths
   mythological people of Thessaly   LĀ-puhths, LAP-uhths   ˈleːpəθs, ˈlæpəθs
Lapland, Lappland
   prov, Finland   LAP-LAND, LAP-luhnd   ˈlæp,lænd, ˈlæplənd
La Plata
   county, CO   luh PLAT-uh, luh PLAHT-uh   lə ˈplæṭə, lə ˈplaṭə
La Porte
   county, IN   luh PŌRT, luh PAWRT   lə ˈpoːʳt, lə ˈpɔːʳt
La Posta
   Indian reservation, US   luh PŌ-stuh   lə ˈpoːstə
Lapp
   lang., people, N. Europe   LAP   ˈlæp
Lappi
   prov, Finland   LAHP-pē   ˈlaːppiˑ
Lappic [Lapp]
   lang., N. Europe   LAP-ik   ˈlæpik
Lappish [Lapp]
   lang., N. Europe   LAP-ish   ˈlæpiʃ
Lappland
   see Lapland
Lapsang Souchong
   tea   LAP-SANG S͞OO-CHAWNG   ˈlæp,sæŋ ˈsuː,tʃɔːŋ
Laptev
   Sea, Arctic   LAP-TEF, LAP-TEV   ˈlæp,tef, ˈlæp,tev
Laputa
   flying island in Gulliver's Travels,   luh-PY͞OOT-uh   ləˈpjuːṭə
       J. Swift
Laputan
   inhabitant of Laputa   luh-PY͞OOT-uhn   ləˈpjuːtən
La Quinta
   US motor inn chain   luh KĒN-tuh   lə ˈkiːntə
Lar
   singular of Lares   LAHR   ˈlaʳ

Foreign Sounds: ue: *Fr.* **rue**, *Ger.* **füllen**   uh(r): *Fr.* **boeuf**, *Ger.* **Höhle**   k͟h: *Ger.* i**ch**, *Scot.* lo**ch**   ḡ: *Sp.* ami**g**o   v̲: *Sp.* ha**b**lar
hl: *Welsh* **Ll**anelli.   CAPITALS: primary stress.   SMALL CAPS: secondary stress.   Ⓢ: U.S. pron.   Ⓔ: British pron.

Lara
  1. mother of the Lares by Mercury   LAR-uh   'lærə
  2. pers. name   LAHR-uh, LAR-uh   'lɑrə, 'lærə

Laramie
  river, US; city, county, WY   LAR-uh-mē, LER-uh-mē   'lærəmiˑ, 'lerəmiˑ

Lardner
  Ring Wilmer, Jr., US author   LAHRD-nuhr   'lɑʳdnəʳ

Laredo
  city, TX   luh-RĀD-ō   lə'reːdoː

La Renaissance
  national anthem, Central African   lah ruh-nes-AHⁿS; lahr-nes-AHⁿS   lɑː rənesɑ̃s; lɑːrnesɑ̃s
    Republic

Lares
  Roman household spirits   LĀ-RĒZ, LAR-ēz, LER-ēz   'leːˌriːz, 'læriːz, 'leriːz

Larisa
  pers. name   luh-RIS-uh   lə'risə

Larissa
  mother or daughter of Pelasgus;   luh-RIS-uh   lə'risə
    pers. name

Larnaca
  dist, Cyprus   LAHR-nuh-kuh   'lɑʳnəkə

La Roche
  College, PA   luh-RŌSH   lə'roːʃ

La Rochefoucauld
  François de, French moralist   lah rawsh-fōō-KŌ   lɑː rɔːʃfuːkoː

La Rochelle
  city, France   lah raw-SHEL   lɑː rɔːʃel

Larousse
  Pierre Athanase, French   lah-RŌŌS, Ⓢ luh-RŌŌS   lɑːruːs, Ⓢ lə'ruːs
    grammarian, lexicographer;
    dictionary imprint

Larousse Gastronomique
  cookery book   lah-RŌŌS gahs-traw-naw-MÊK,   lɑːruːs gɑːstrɔːnɔːmiːk,
        Ⓢ luh-RŌŌS GAS-truh-NAHM-ÊK   Ⓢ lə'ruːs ˌgæstrəˌnam'iːk

Larry
  pers. name   LAR-ē   'læriˑ

Lars
  1. pers. name   LAHRZ   'lɑʳz
  2. Latin   LAHRZ, LAHRS   'lɑʳz, 'lɑʳs
  3. Swedish   LAHZH, Ⓢ LAHRZH, LAHRSH   'lɑʒ, Ⓢ 'lɑʳʒ, 'lɑʳʃ

Larsa
  ancient Babylonian city   LAR-suh, LAHR-suh   'læʳsə, 'lɑʳsə

Larson
  Glen, TV producer, writer   LAHR-suhn   'lɑʳsən

Lars Porsena
  king of Clusium   lahrs PAWR-suh-nuh   lɑʳs 'pɔːʳsənə

Larvik
  port, Norway   LAHR-vik, LAHR-VĒK   'lɑʳvik, 'lɑʳˌviːk

La Salle
  University, PA   luh SAL   lə 'sæl

La Salle, Sieur de
  René Robert, French explorer   SYUH(R) duh lah SAHL, Ⓢ SYUHR   sjœʳ də lɑː sɑːl, Ⓢ 'sjəʳ də lə
        duh luh SAL   'sæl

Las Animas
  county, CO   las AN-uh-muhs, lahs   læs 'ænəməs, lɑs

Key (col. 2): a: fad ā: fade ah: father ar: Mary aw: law e: fed ē: feed er: merry i: hid ī: hide ō: coat ōō: boot
oi: boy ow: now u: put uh: above uhr: bird ch: chop ng: ring sh: show th: thick t̲h̲: this zh: measure

La Scala
   opera house, Milan   lah SKAHL-uh, luh   lɑ ˈskɑlə, lə
Lascăr
   pers. name, Romanian   LAHS-kuhr   ˈlɑskər
Lascaux
   cave with prehistoric paintings,   lah-SKŌ, Ⓢ las-KŌ   lɑːskoː, Ⓢ læsˈkoː
   France
Lascelles
   pers. name   LAS-uhlz   ˈlæsəlz
Las Cruces
   city, NM   lahs KROO-suhs   lɑs ˈkruːsəs
Lasell
   Junior College, *MA*   luh-SEL   ləˈsel
Lashio
   town, Burma   LAHSH-ō, LAHSH-ē-ō   ˈlaʃoː, ˈlaʃiːˌoː
Lasorda
   Tom Charles, *US baseball team*   luh-SAWRD-uh   ləˈsɔːrdə
   manager
Las Palmas
   province, Spain   lahs PAHL-mahs, Ⓢ lahs PAHL-muhs   lɑs ˈpɑlmɑs, Ⓢ lɑs ˈpɑlməs
Las Palmas de Gran Canaria
   city, Spain   lahs PAHL-mahs t͟hā grahn   lɑs ˈpɑlmɑs ðeː grɑn
        kah-NAHR-yah   kɑˈnɑrjɑ
La Spezia
   prov, Italy   lah SPET-sē-uh   lɑ ˈspetsiːə
Lassa fever
   African viral disease   LAS-uh FĒ-vuhr, LAH-suh   ˌlæsə ˈfiːvəʳ, ˌlɑːsə
Lassen
   volcano, county, college, CA   LAS-uhn   ˈlæsən
Lasser
   Louise, *US actress*   LAS-uhr   ˈlæsəʳ
Lassie
   young girl; fictional dog   LAS-ē   ˈlæsiˑ
Lasswell
   Fred, *US cartoonist*   LAS-WEL   ˈlæsˌwel
La Sueur
   county, MN   luh SUR   lə ˈsuʳ
Las Vegas
   city, NV   lahs VĀ-guhs   lɑs ˈveːgəs
László
   pers. name, Hungarian   LAHS-lō   ˈlaːsloː
Latah
   county, ID   LĀ-TAH, luh-TAH   ˈleːˌta, ləˈta
Latakia
   port, governorate, Syria   LAT-uh-KĒ-uh   ˌlætəˈkiːə
Latasha
   pers. name   luh-TAHSH-uh, luh-TASH-uh   ləˈtaʃə, ləˈtæʃə
La Tène
   archaeological site, Switzerland   lah TEN, lah TÄN   lɑ ˈten, lɑ ˈteːn
Lateran, St. John
   church in Rome   sänt JAHN LAT-uh-ruhn, suhnt   seːnt ˈdʒɑn ˈlætərən, sənt
Latham
   pers. name   LĀ-thuhm, LĀ-t͟huhm   ˈleːθəm, ˈleːðəm
Lathrop
   pers. name   LĀ-thruhp   ˈleːθrəp

Foreign Sounds: ue: *Fr.* **rue**, *Ger.* f**ü**llen   uh(r): *Fr.* b**oeu**f, *Ger.* H**öh**le   k͟h: *Ger.* i**ch**, *Scot.* lo**ch**   ḡ: *Sp.* ami**g**o   v̱: *Sp.* ha**b**lar
hl: *Welsh* **Ll**anelli.   CAPITALS: primary stress.   SMALL CAPS: secondary stress.   Ⓢ: U.S. pron.   Ⓛ: British pron.

Latifundia
   Roman plantations   LAT-uh-FUHN-dē-uh   ˌlæt̮ə'fəndiːə

Latimer
   Hugh, English Protestant bishop;   LAT-uh-muhr   'læt̮əməʳ
   pers. name

Latin
   lang. of Romans   LAT-n   'lætn̩

Latinate
   pert. to Latin   LAT-n-ĀT   'lætn̩ˌeːt

Latino
   person of Hispanic descent   la-TĒ-nō, luh-TĒ-nō   læ'tiːnoː, lə'tiːnoː

Latinus
   eponymous king of the Latins   luh-TĪ-nuhs   lə'tɑinəs

Latinus Silvius
   son of Aeneas Silvius   luh-TĪ-nuhs SIL-vē-uhs   lə,tɑinəs 'silviːəs

Latisha
   pers. name   luh-TISH-uh, luh-TĒ-shuh   lə'tiʃə, lə'tiːʃə

Latium [Lazio]
   ancient country, autonomous   LĀ-sh(ē-)uhm   'leːʃ(iː)əm
     region, Italy

Latonya
   pers. name   luh-TAHN-yuh   lə'tɑnjə

Latour
   pers. name, French   lah-TŌŌR   lɑːtuːr

Latoya
   pers. name   luh-TOI-uh   lə'tɔiə

Latrobe
   city, Pennsylvania   luh-TRŌB   lə'troːb

Latvia
   Baltić republic   LAT-vē-uh   'lætviːə

Latvian
   lang., Latvia   LAT-vē-uhn   'lætviːən

Latviskaya
   Russian form of Latvia   LUHT-VĒ-skuh-yuh   ˌlət'viːskəjə

L'Aube Nouvelle
   national anthem, Benin   LŌB noo-VEL   loːb nuːvel

Lauder
   Estee, *see* Estée Lauder

Lauderdale
   county, AL, MS, TN   LAWD-uhr-DĀL   'lɔːdəʳˌdeːl

Laudianism
   doctrines of Laud   LAWD-ē-uh-NIZ-uhm   'lɔːdiːəˌnizəm

Laue
   Max von, *German physicist (Nobel* LOW-uh   'lɑuə
    1914)

Laughton
   Charles, *British actor*   LAWT-n   'lɔːtn̩

Launcelot
   pers. name   LAWN-suh-LAHT, LAHN-, LAN-, 'lɔːnsəˌlɑt, 'lɑn-, 'læn-,
                               -s(uh-)luht   -s(ə)lət

Lauper
   Cyndi, *rock musician*   LOW-puhr   'lɑupəʳ

Key (col. 2): a: fad ā: fade ah: father ar: Mary aw: law e: fed ē: feed er: merry i: hid ī: hide ō: coat ōō: boot
oi: boy ow: now u: put uh: above uhr: bird ch: chop ng: ring sh: show th: thick <u>th</u>: this zh: measure

Laura
1. pers. name	LAWR-uh, LAHR-uh	'lɔːrə, 'lɑrə
2. Italian	LOW-rah	'laurɑ
3. Swedish	LOW-rah	'laurɑː

Laurasia
Mesozoic supercontinent	lawr-Ā-zhuh, lawr-Ā-shuh	lɔːr'eːʒə, lɔːr'eːʃə

Laurasian
pert. to Laurasia	lawr-Ā-zhuhn, lawr-Ā-shuhn	lɔːr'eːʒən, lɔːr'eːʃən

Laure
pers. name, French	LAWR	lɔːr

Laurel
pers. name	LAWR-uhl, LAHR-uhl	'lɔːrəl, 'lɑrəl

Lauren
1. pers. name	LAWR-uhn, LAHR-uhn	'lɔːrən, 'lɑrən
2. Ralph, *fashion designer*	LAWR-uhn, LAHR-uhn, luh-REN, law-REN	'lɔːrən, 'lɑrən, lə'ren, lɔː'ren

Laurence
pers. name	LAWR-uhn(t)s, LAHR-uhn(t)s	'lɔːrən(t)s, 'lɑrən(t)s

Laurencin
Marie, *French artist*	law-rahⁿ-SEⁿ	lɔːrɑ̃sɛ̃

Laurens
1. county, GA, SC; city, SC	LAWR-uhnz, LAHR-uhnz	'lɔːrənz, 'lɑrənz
2. pers. name	LAWR-uhnz, LAHR-uhnz, -uhn(t)s	'lɔːrənz, 'lɑrənz, -ən(t)s

Laurent
pers. name, French	law-RAHⁿ	lɔːrɑ̃

Laurentian
hills, Canada; pert. to Laurence, Laurentius, *or* Lawrence	law-REN-chuhn, luh-	lɔː'rentʃən, lə-

Laurentius
1. pers. name, Latin	law-REN-sh(ē-)uhs	lɔː'renʃ(iː)əs
2. Swedish	low-RENT-sē-uhs	lau'rentsiːəs

Lauretta
pers. name	luh-RET-uh, lawr-ET-uh	lə'reţə, lɔːr'eţə

Laureum
site of Athenian silver mines	LAWR-ē-uhm, LAHR-ē-uhm	'lɔːriːəm, 'lɑriːəm

Lauri
pers. name, Finnish	LOW-rē	'lauriː

Laurie
pers. name	LAWR-ē, LAHR-ē	'lɔːriˑ, 'lɑriˑ

Laurits, Lauritz
1. pers. name, Danish	LOW-rēts	'lauriːts
2. Norwegian	LOW-rits	'laurits

Lauro
pers. name, Italian	LOW-rō	'lauroː

Lausanne
resort, Switzerland	lō-ZAHN, lō-ZAN	loː'zan, loː'zæn

Lavaca
county, TX	luh-VAK-uh	lə'vækə

Laval
1. Pierre, *French politician; town, France*	lah-VAHL	lɑːvɑːl
2. town, Canada	lah-VAHL, luh-VAL	lɑːvɑːl, lə'væl
3. pers. name	luh-VAL	lə'væl

Laver
seaweed	LAHV-uhr, LĀ-vuhr	'lavəʳ, 'leːvəʳ

Laveran

  C. L. A., *French physician (Nobel*   lah-vuh-RAH^n, lahv-RAH^n lɑːvərã, lɑːvrã
  1907)

Lavern, Laverne

  pers. name   luh-VUHRN   ləˈvəʳn

La Verne

  University of, *CA; pers. name*   luh-VUHRN   ləˈvəʳn

Lavin

  Linda, *US actress*   LAV-uhn   ˈlævən

Lavinia

  1. wife of Aeneas; pers. name   luh-VIN-ē-uh   ləˈviniːə
  2. Italian   lah-VĒN-yah   laˈviːnja

Lavoisier

  Antoine, *French scientist*   lahv-wahz-YĀ, ⑤ luhv-WAHZ-ē-Ā   lɑːvwɑːzjeː, ⑤ ləvˈwɑziː,eː

Lavrenti

  pers. name, Russian   LUHV-REN-ti   ,ləvˈrentjij

Lawrence

  D. H., *English writer;* E. O., *US*   LAWR-uhn(t)s, LAHR-uhn(t)s   ˈlɔːrən(t)s, ˈlɑrən(t)s
  physicist (Nobel 1939);
  T(homas) E(dward), *British*
  adventurer & writer; pers. name

lawrencium

  element   law-REN(T)-sē-uhm   lɔːˈren(t)siːəm

Lawrentian

  pert. to D. H. Lawrence   law-REN-chuhn, luh-   lɔːˈrentʃən, lə-

Laxalt

  Paul, *US politician*   LAK-SAWLT   ˈlæk,sɔːlt

Laxness

  Halldór K., *Icelandic author (Nobel* LAHK-snuhs, LAHK-snes   ˈlaksnəs, ˈlaksnes
  1955)

Layamon

  English poet   LĪ-uh-muhn, LĀ-uh-muhn   ˈlaiəmən, ˈleːəmən

Layton

  Joe, *US director, choreographer* LĀT-n   ˈleːtn̩

Lazar

  pers. name, Russian   LAH-zuhr   ˈlɑːzər

Lázár

  pers. name, Hungarian   LAH-zahr   ˈlɑːzɑːr

Lazare

  pers. name, French   lah-ZAHR   lɑːzɑːr

Lázaro

  pers. name, Spanish   LAHS-ahr-ō, LAHTH-ahr-ō   ˈlasaroː, ˈlaθaroː

Lazarus

  Biblical name; Mell, *US*   LAZ-uh-ruhs   ˈlæzərəs
  cartoonist; pers. name

LA-Z-Boy

  US chair co.   LĀ-zē-BOI   ˈleːziˈ,bɔi

Lazio [Latium]

  autonomous region, Italy   LAHT-sē-ō   ˈlatsiːoː

Lazuli Bunting

  songbird   LAZ-uh-lē BUHNT-ing, LAZ-uh-LĪ   ˈlæzəliˈ ˈbəntiŋ, ˈlæzə,lai

Lazzaro

  pers. name, Italian   LAHD-dzahr-ō   ˈladdzaroː

L-dopa

  anti-Parkinson's disease drug   el-DŌ-puh   elˈdoːpə

Key (col. 2): a: fad ā: fade ah: father ar: Mary aw: law e: fed ē: feed er: merry i: hid ī: hide ō: coat ōō: boot
oi: boy ow: now u: put uh: above uhr: bird ch: chop ng: ring sh: show th: thick <u>th</u>: this zh: measure

Leach
    Robin, *TV host*   LĒCH   'liːtʃ

Leachman
    Cloris, *US actress*   LĒCH-muhn   'liːtʃmən

Lead
    city, SD   LĒD   'liːd

lead
    element   LED   'led

Leah
    Biblical name; pers. name   LĒ-uh   'liːə

Leahy
    Patrick Joseph, *US politician*   LĀ-hē, LĀ-ē   'leːhiː, 'leːiː

Leakey
    Louis, Mary, & Richard, *British anthropologists*   LĒ-kē   'liːkiˑ

Leamington
    town, Canada   LĒ-ming-tuhn   'liːmiŋtən

Leamington Spa
    resort, England   LEM-ing-tuhn SPAH   'lemiŋtən 'spɑ

Leander
    1. beloved of Hero in Greek myth; pers. name   lē-AN-duhr   liː'ændəʳ
    2. German   lā-AHN-duhr   leː'ɑndəʳ

Leandro
    pers. name, Italian, Spanish   lā-AHN-drō   leː'ɑndroː

Leanne
    pers. name   lē-AN   liː'æn

Lear
    Edward, *English poet;* Norman, *US film, TV writer, producer; Shakespearean character*   LIR   'liʳ

Learned
    pers. name   LUHR-nuhd   'ləʳnəd

Leary
    Timothy, *US psychologist, author*   LIR-ē   'liriˑ

Leavenworth
    city, county, KS; US penitentiary   LEV-uhn-WUHRTH   'levən,wəʳθ

Leavitt
    pers. name   LEV-it   'levit

Lebanese
    pert. to Lebanon   leb-uh-NĒZ, -NĒS   lebə'niːz, -'niːs

Lebanon
    republic, Middle East   LEB-uh-nuhn, -NAHN   'lebənən, -,nɑn

Lebensraum
    additional territory wanted by a nation   LĀ-buhnz-ROWM, LĀ-buhn(t)s-ROWM   'leːbənz,rɑum, 'leːbən(t)s,rɑum

Leberecht
    pers. name, German   LĀ-buh-REKHT   'leːbə,reçt

Le Bourget
    city, France   luh bur-ZHE   lə burʒe

Lebrecht
    1. pers. name, Danish   LIB-REKHT   'lib,reçt
    2. German   LĀ-PREKHT, LĀ-BREKHT   'leː,preçt, 'leː,breçt

Lebrija
    commune, Spain   lā-BRĒ-khah   leː'briːxɑ

Foreign Sounds: ue: *Fr.* **rue**, *Ger.* **füllen** uh(r): *Fr.* **boeuf**, *Ger.* **Höhle** kh: *Ger.* **ich**, *Scot.* **loch** g̃: *Sp.* **amigo** v: *Sp.* **hablar**
hl: *Welsh* **Llanelli**. CAPITALS: primary stress. SMALL CAPS: secondary stress. Ⓢ: U.S. pron. Ⓛ: British pron.

Le Carré
  John, *pseudonym of* D. J. M.   ℗ luh KAR-Ā, ⑤ luh kahr-Ā   ℗ lə 'kær,eː, ⑤ lə kar'eː
  Cornwall, *British writer*
Lech
  pers. name, Polish   LE<u>KH</u>, ⑤ LEK   'lex, ⑤ 'lek
Lechtal Alps
  mtn. range, Austria   LE<u>KH</u>-tuhl, LE<u>KH</u>-TAHL   'lextəl, 'lex,tɑl
Lecithin
  food ingredient   LES-uh-thuhn   'lesəθən
Le Claire
  pers. name   luh KLAR, luh KLER   lə 'klæʳ, lə 'kleʳ
Le Clerc, Leclerc
  pers. name, French   luh-KLER   ləkler
Le Corbusier
  see Corbusier, Le
Leçzyca
  commune, Poland   leⁿ-CHIT-suh, ⑤ len-CHIT-suh   lẽ'tʃitsə, ⑤ len'tʃitsə
Leda
  beloved of Zeus in Greek myth;   LĒD-uh   'liːdə
  satellite of Jupiter
Lederberg
  Joshua, *US biologist, geneticist*   LĀD-uhr-BUHRG   'leːdəʳ,bəʳg
  (Nobel 1958)
Lederle
  US pharmaceutical co.   LED-uhr-lē   'ledəʳliˑ
Lederman
  Leon M., *US physicist (Nobel*   LED-uhr-muhn   'ledəʳmən
  1988)
Le Duc Tho
  Vietnamese statesman (Nobel   LĀ DUHK TŌ   ,leː ,dək 'toː
  1973)
Lee
  pers. name   LĒ   'liː
Leeds
  town, England   LĒDZ   'liːdz
Lee Kuan Yew
  prime minister, Singapore   LĒ KWAHN YOO   'liː 'kwɑn 'juː
Leelanau
  county, MI   LĒ-luh-NAW   'liːlə,nɔː
Lee Tsung-Dao
  Chinese physicist (Nobel 1957)   LĒ DZUNG-DOW   'liː 'dzuŋ'dau
Leeuw
  Dutch beer   LĀ-oo   'leːuː
Leeuwarden
  city, Netherlands   LĀ-VAHRD-n   'leː,vɑʳdn̩
Leeuwenhoek
  Antonie von, *Dutch scientist*   LĀ-oo-vuhn-HOOK, ⑤ LĀ-vuhn-HUK   'leːuːvən,huːk, ⑤ 'leːvən,huk
Leevi
  pers. name, Finnish   LĀ-vi   'leːvi
Leeward
  Islands, *Pacific, Caribbean*   LĒ-wuhrd, LOO-uhrd   'liːwəʳd, 'luːəʳd
Le Fanu
  Sheridan, *Irish writer, editor*   LEF-uhn-yoo, luh-FAHN-yoo   'lefənjuː, lə'fɑˑnjuː

Key (col. 2):   a: fad   ā: fade   ah: father   ar: Mary   aw: law   e: fed   ē: feed   er: merry   i: hid   ī: hide   ō: coat   oo: boot
oi: boy   ow: now   u: put   uh: above   uhr: bird   ch: chop   ng: ring   sh: show   th: thick   <u>th</u>: this   zh: measure

Le Fèvre		
1. pers. name	luh FĀV(-ruh), luh FEV	lə 'feːv(rə), lə 'fev
2. French	luh FEVR	lə fevr
Leffe Blonde		
Belgian beer	LEF-uh BLAW^{n}D	'lefə 'blɔ̃d
Le Gallienne		
Eva, *English actress;* Richard, *English writer*	luh GAL-yuhn, luh GAL-YEN	lə 'gæljən, lə 'gæl,jen
Léger		
Alexis St.-Léger, *French poet, diplomat (Nobel 1960)*	lā-ZHĀ	leːʒeː
Legh		
pers. name	LĒ	'liː
Leghorn [Livorno]		
prov, Italy	LEG-HAWRN	'leg,hɔː^{r}n
Légier		
pers. name, French	lāzh-YĀ	leːʒjeː
Lego		
tdmk for toy building blocks	LEG-ō, LĀ-gō	'legoː, 'leːgoː
Legree		
Simon, *character in* Uncle Tom's Cabin, *H. B. Stowe*	luh-GRĒ	lə'griː
Le Guin		
Ursula, *US writer*	luh GWIN	lə 'gwin
Legum Baccalaureus		
bachelor of laws, LL.B.	LĀ-guhm BAK-uh-LŌR-ē-uhs, -LAWR-ē-uhs	'leːgəm ,bækə'loːriːəs, -'lɔːriːəs
Lehár		
Franz, *Hungarian composer*	LĀ-HAHR	'leː,hɑ^{r}
Le Havre		
seaport, France	luh HAHV(-ruh)	lə hɑv(rə)
Lehigh		
river, county, university, PA	LĒ-HĪ	'liː,hɑi
Lehman		
Christopher M., *US government official*	LĀ-muhn	'leːmən
Lehn		
Jean-Marie, *French chemist (Nobel 1987)*	LE^{n}	lẽ(n)
Lehrer		
Jim, *US newscaster;* Tom, *US mathematician & entertainer*	LER-uhr, LER	'lerə^{r}, 'le^{r}
Leibman		
Ron, *US actor*	LĒB-muhn	'liːbmən
Leibnitz, Leibniz		
Gottfried, *German philosopher*	LĪP-nits, [$] LĪB-nuhts	'lɑipnits, [$] 'lɑibnəts
Leibnizianism		
philosophy of Leibnitz	līp-NIT-sē-uh-NIZ-uhm	lɑip'nitsiːə,nizəm
Leica		
brand of 35mm camera	LĪ-kuh	'lɑikə
Leicester		
town, MA; city, England	LES-tuhr	'lestə^{r}
Leicestershire		
county, England	LES-tuhr-shuhr, -SHIR	'lestə^{r}ʃə^{r}, -,ʃi^{r}

Leiden, Leyden
  city, Netherlands   LĀ-yuh, LĀD-n, Ⓢ LĪD-n   'leːjə, 'leːdn̩, Ⓢ 'laidn̩

Leif
  pers. name   LĒF, LĀF   'liːf, 'leːf

Leigh
  pers. name   LĒ   'liː

Leighton
  pers. name   LĀT-n   'leːtn̩

Leighton Buzzard
  town, England   LĀT-n buh-ZAHRD, BUHZ-uhrd   ˌleːtn̩ bə'zaʳd, 'bəzəʳd

Leila
  pers. name   LĒ-luh, LĀ-luh   'liːlə, 'leːlə

Leinsdorf
  Erich, *US conductor*   LĪNZ-DAWRF, LĪN(T)S-DAWRF   'lainz,dɔːʳf, 'lain(t)s,dɔːʳf

Leinster
  1. prov., Ireland   LEN-stuhr   'lenstəʳ
  2. Duke of, British title   LIN-stuhr   'linstəʳ

Leipsic
  town, DE   LĪP-sik   'laipsik

Leipzig
  city, Germany   LĪPT-si<u>kh</u>, Ⓢ LĪP-sig, LĪP-sik   'laiptsiç, Ⓢ 'laipsig, 'laipsik

Leith
  port, Scotland   LĒTH   'liːθ

Leland
  pers. name   LĒ-luhnd   'liːlənd

Lele
  lang., Africa   LĀ-lā   'leːleˑ

Leloir
  Luis Federico, *French-born Argentine biochemist (Nobel 1970)*   lā-LWAHR   leˑ'lwar

Lely
  Sir Peter, *Dutch painter*   LĀ-lē, Ⓢ LĒ-lē   'leːliˑ, Ⓢ 'liːliˑ

Léman, Lac [Geneva]
  lake, Switzerland   lahk lā-MAHⁿ   laːk leːmã

Le Mans
  city, auto race, France   luh MAHⁿ, Ⓢ luh MAHN   lə mã, Ⓢ lə 'man

Lemass
  Sean, *prime minister, Ireland*   luh-MAHS   lə'maˑs

Lemhi
  county, ID   LEM-HĪ   'lem,hai

Lemmon
  Jack, *US actor*   LEM-uhn   'lemən

Lemnitzer
  Lyman, *US militarist*   LEM-nuht-suhr   'lemnətsəʳ

Lemnos [Límnos]
  island, Greece   LEM-NAHS, LEM-nuhs   'lem,nas, 'lemnəs

Le Moyne
  College, *NY*   luh MOIN   lə 'mɔin

Lemuel
  pers. name   LEM-yuh(-wuh)l   'lemjə(wə)l

Lemures
  Roman spirits of the dead   LEM-uh-RĀS, LEM-yuh-RĒZ   'leməˌreːs, 'lemjəˌriːz

---

Key (col. 2):   a: fad   ā: fade   ah: father   ar: Mary   aw: law   e: fed   ē: feed   er: merry   i: hid   ī: hide   ō: coat   ōō: boot
oi: boy   ow: now   u: put   uh: above   uhr: bird   ch: chop   ng: ring   sh: show   th: thick   <u>th</u>: this   zh: measure

Lena
   1. pers. name   LĒ-nuh   'liːnə
   2. river, Russia   LÃ-nuh, LĒ-nuh   'leːnə, 'liːnə
Lenape
   see Lenni-Lenape
Lenard
   Philipp, *German physicist (Nobel*   LÃ-NAHRT   'leːˌnɑ^rt
   1905)
Lenawee
   county, MI   LEN-uh-WĒ   'lenəˌwiː
Lenca
   Cen. American people   LENG-kuh   'leŋkə
Lendl
   Ivan, *Czechoslovakian tennis*   LEN-dl   'lendl̩
   player
Lendu
   lang., people, Uganda, Zaire   LEN-doo   'lenduː
L'Enfant
   Pierre, *designer of Washington,*   lahⁿ-FAHⁿ   lãfã
   DC
L'Engle
   Madeleine, *US writer*   LENG-guhl   'leŋgəl
Lenglen
   Suzanne, *French tennis player*   lahⁿ-GLEN, Ⓢ LENG-(g)luhn,   lãglen, Ⓢ 'leŋ(g)lən,
           LANG-(g)luhn   'læŋ(g)lən
Leni
   pers. name   LEN-ē   'leniˑ
Lenin
   premier, USSR; orig. Vladimir   LÃN-yin, Ⓢ LEN-uhn   'leːnjin, Ⓢ 'lenən
   Ilyich Ulyanov
Leningrad [St. Petersburg]
   city, Russia   LUHN-yin-GRAHT, Ⓢ LEN-uhn-GRAD   ˌlənjin'grɑt, Ⓢ 'lenənˌgræd
Leninism
   form of Communism taught by   LEN-uh-NIZ-uhm   'lenəˌnizəm
   Lenin
Lennie
   pers. name   LEN-ē   'leniˑ
Lenni-Lenape
   N. American people   LEN-ē luh-NAHP-ē, LEN-ē LEN-uh-pē   ˌleniˑ lə'nɑpiˑ, ˌleniˑ 'lenəpiˑ
Lennon
   John, *& his son* Julian, *British*   LEN-uhn   'lenən
   musicians
Lennox
   city, CA, SD; family name   LEN-uhks, LEN-iks   'lenəks, 'leniks
Lenny
   pers. name   LEN-ē   'leniˑ
Leno
   Jay, *US entertainer*   LEN-ō   'lenoː
Lenoir
   county, NC; pers. name   luh-NŌR, luh-NAWR   lə'noːʳ, lə'nɔːʳ
Lenoir-Rhyne
   College, NC   luh-NŌR-RĪN, luh-NAWR-   ləˌnoːʳrain, ləˌnɔːʳ-
Lenore
   pers. name   luh-NŌR, luh-NAWR   lə'noːʳ, lə'nɔːʳ

Foreign Sounds: ue: *Fr.* **rue**, *Ger.* **füllen** uh(r): *Fr.* **boeuf**, *Ger.* **Höhle** <u>kh</u>: *Ger.* i**ch**, *Scot.* lo**ch** ḡ: *Sp.* ami**go** <u>v</u>: *Sp.* ha**b**lar
hl: *Welsh* **Ll**anelli. CAPITALS: primary stress. SMALL CAPS: secondary stress. Ⓢ: U.S. pron. Ⓔ: British pron.

Lenox
  town, MA; tdmk for china   LEN-uhks, LEN-iks   'lenəks, 'leniks
Lentulus
  Roman cognomen   LEN-chuh-luhs, LENT-yuh-luhs   'lentʃələs, 'lentjələs
Lenya
  Lotte, *entertainer*   LEN-yuh   'lenjə
Leo
  1. constellation; pers. name   LĒ-ō   'liːoː
  2. Dutch, German   LĀ-ō   'leːoː
  3. Finnish   LE-aw   'leoː
  4. Italian   LE-ō   'leoː ·
Léo
  pers. name, French   lā-Ō   leːoː
Leofric
  pers. name   lā-AHF-rik, lā-Ō-frik   leː'afrik, leː'oːfrik
Leo Minor
  constellation   LĒ-ō MĪ-nuhr   'liːoː 'mainəʳ
Leominster
  1. city, MA   LEM-uhn-stuhr   'lemənstəʳ
  2. borough, England   LEM(P)-stuhr, LEM-uhn-stuhr   'lem(p)stəʳ, 'lemənstəʳ
Leon
  1. pers. name   LĒ-AHN, LĒ-uhn   'liː,an, 'liːən
  2. Italian   lā-ŌN   leː'oːn
León
  1. town, Mexico; pers. name,   lā-AWN   leː'ɔːn
    Spanish
  2. pers. name, French   lā-AWⁿ   leːõ
Leona
  pers. name   lē-Ō-nuh   liː'oːnə
Leonard
  1. pers. name   LEN-uhrd   'lenəʳd
  2. Dutch   LĀ-ō-NAHRT   'leːoː,nart
  3. German   LĀ-ō-NAHRT   'leːoː,naʳt
  4. Polish   le-AW-nahrt   le'ɔːnaːrt
  5. Swedish   LĀ-aw-NAHRD   'leːɔː,naːrd
Léonard
  pers. name, French   lā-aw-NAHR   leːɔːnaːr
Leonardo
  1. pers. name, Italian   LĀ-ō-NAHR-dō, Ⓢ LĒ-uh-NAHRD-ō,   ,leːoː'nardoː, Ⓢ ,liːə'naʳdoː,
         LĀ-uh-   ,leːə-
  2. Spanish   lā-ō-NAHR-<u>th</u>ō   leːoː'narðoː
Leonardo da Vinci
  Italian scientist, artist   LĀ-uh-NAHRD-ō duh VĒN-chē,   ,leːə'naʳdoː də 'viːntʃiˑ,
         LĒ-uh-NAHRD-ō, VIN-chē   ,liːə'naʳdoː, 'vintʃiˑ
Leonberger
  dog breed   LĀ-ahn-BER-guhr   'leːan,beʳgəʳ
Leoncavallo
  Ruggero, *Italian composer*   LĀ-ŌN-kuh-VAHL-ō   ,leː,oːnkə'valoː
Leone
  pers. name, Italian   lā-Ō-nā   leː'oːneː
Leonhard
  1. pers. name, German   LĀ-awn-HAHRT   'leːɔːn,haʳt
  2. Swedish   LĀ-aw-NAHRD   'leːɔː,naːrd
Leonid
  pers. name, Russian   li-UHN-YĒT, Ⓢ LĀ-uh-nid, LĒ-uh-nid   ļi,ən'jiːt, Ⓢ 'leːənid, 'liːənid

---

Key (col. 2):   a: fad   ā: fade   ah: father   ar: Mary   aw: law   e: fed   ē: feed   er: merry   i: hid   ī: hide   ō: coat   o͞o: boot
oi: boy   ow: now   u: put   uh: above   uhr: bird   ch: chop   ng: ring   sh: show   th: thick   <u>th</u>: this   zh: measure

Leonidas
  1. king of Sparta; pers. name   lē-AHN-uhd-uhs   liː'anədəs
  2. Spanish   lā-ō-NĒ-<u>th</u>ahs   leːɔː'niːðɑs
Léonide
  pers. name, French   lā-aw-NĒD   leːɔːniːd
Leonides
  meteor shower   lē-AHN-uh-DĒZ   liː'anə,diːz
Leonids
  meteor shower   LĒ-uh-nuhdz   'liːənədz
Léonie
  1. pers. name   LĒ-uh-nē   'liːəniˑ
  2. French   lā-aw-NĒ   leːɔːniː
Leonor
  pers. name   LĒ-uh-NŌR, -NAWR   'liːə,noːʳ, -,nɔːʳ
Leonora
  pers. name   LĒ-uh-NŌR-uh, -NAWR-uh   ,liːə'noːrə, -'nɔːrə
Leonteus
  chief of the Lapiths   lē-AHNT-ē-uhs   liː'ɑntiːəs
Leontief
  Wassily, *Russian-born US*   lē-AWNT-yuhf   liː'ɔːntjəf
  economist (Nobel 1973)
Leontyne
  pers. name   lē-AHN-TĒN, LĒ-uhn-TIN,   liː'ɑn,tiːn, 'liːən,tin,
           LĀ-uhn-TĒN   'leːən,tiːn
Leopardi
  Giacomo, *Italian poet*   LĀ-uh-PAHRD-ē   ,leːə'paʳdiˑ
Leopold
  1. pers. name   LĒ-uh-PŌLD   'liːə,poːld
  2. Dutch, German   LĀ-ō-PAWLT   'leːoː,poːlt
  3. Finnish   LE-aw-PAWLT   'leɔː,poːlt
  4. Polish   le-AW-pawlt   le'ɔːpoːlt
  5. Belgian beer   LĀ-ō-PAWLT   'leːoː,poːlt
Léopold
  pers. name, French   lā-aw-PAWL(D)   leːɔːpoːl(d)
Leopoldo
  1. pers. name, Italian   LĀ-ō-PAWL-dō   ,leːoː'poːldoː
  2. Spanish   lā-ō-PAWL-dō   leːoː'poːldoː
Léopoldville
  former name for Kinshasa   LĒ-uh-PŌLD-VIL, LĀ-uh-PŌLD-VIL   'liːə,poːld,vil, 'leːə,poːld,vil
Leos
  son of Orpheus   LĒ-AHS   'liː,ɑs
Leoš
  pers. name, Czech   LE-AWSH   'le,ɔːʃ
Lepanto
  port, gulf, Greece   luh-PAHN-tō, luh-PAN-tō   lə'pantoː, lə'pæntoː
Le Pen
  Jacques, *French politician*   luh PEⁿ   lə pɛ̃
Lepidus
  Roman family name (cognomen)   LEP-uhd-uhs   'lepədəs
Lepontine Alps
  Alpine mtn. range   li-PAHN-TĪN, LEP-uhn-TĪN   li'pan,tain, 'lepən,tain
Leppard
  Raymond, *English conductor*   LEP-AHRD   'lep,ɑʳd
Leptis Magna
  Roman seaport, Africa   LEP-tuhs MAG-nuh   'leptəs 'mægnə

Foreign Sounds: **ue**: *Fr.* **rue**, *Ger.* **füllen**   **uh(r)**: *Fr.* **boeuf**, *Ger.* **Höhle**   **kh**: *Ger.* **ich**, *Scot.* **loch**   **ḡ**: *Sp.* **amigo**   **v̶**: *Sp.* **hablar**
hl: *Welsh* **Llanelli**.   CAPITALS: primary stress.   SMALL CAPS: secondary stress.   Ⓢ: U.S. pron.   Ⓑ: British pron.

Lepus		
constellation	LĒ-puhs, LEP-uhs	'liːpəs, 'lepəs
Le Puy		
city, France	luh PWĒ, Ⓢ luh PWĒ	lə pɥiː, Ⓢ lə 'pwiː
Lermontov		
Mikhail, *writer*	LYER-muhn-tuhf	'ljermәntәf
Lerner		
Louis Abraham, *US ambassador, newspaper publisher;* Alan Jay, *US lyricist*	LUHR-nuhr	'lə^{r}nə^r
Leroy, Le Roy		
pers. name	li-ROI, LĒ-ROI	li'rɔi, 'liːˌrɔi
Les		
pers. name	LES	'les
Lesage		
Alain-René, *French writer*	lā-SAHZH	leːsɑːʒ
Lesbos		
island, dept, Greece	LEZ-BAHS, LEZ-buhs	'lezˌbɑs, 'lezbəs
Leschetizky, Leszetycki		
Theodor, *Polish pianist*	LESH-ā-TIT-skē	ˌleʃeˑ'titskiˑ
Les Invalides		
soldiers' home, tomb of Napoleon, Paris, France	lez e^n-vah-LĒD	lez ẽvɑːliːd
Lesley, Leslie		
pers. name	LES-lē, LEZ-lē	'lesliˑ, 'lezliˑ
Lesotho [Basutoland]		
country, S. Africa	luh-SŌŌ-tōō, luh-SŌ-tō	lə'suːtuː, lə'soːtoː
Lespedeza		
plant	LES-puh-DĒ-zuh	ˌlespə'diːzə
Lesseps		
Ferdinand de, *French political leader*	lā-SEPS, les-EPS Ⓢ LES-uhps	leːseps, leseps Ⓢ 'lesəps
Lessing		
Gotthold, *German writer*	LES-ing	'lesiŋ
Lester		
pers. name	LES-tuhr	'lestə^r
Les Trois Glorieuses		
national anthem, Congo	lā TRWAH glawr-YUH(R)Z	leː trwɑː glɔːrjœːz
Lésvos [Lesbos]		
island, dept, Greece	LEZ-VAWS	'lezˌvɔːs
Leszetycki		
see Leschetizky		
Leta		
pers. name	LĒT-uh	'liːtə
Lethbridge		
city, Canada	LETH-brij	'leθbridʒ
Lethe		
river of forgetfulness in Hades	LĒ-thē	'liːθiˑ
Letitia		
pers. name	li-TISH-(ē-)uh	li'tiʃ(iː)ə
Letizia		
pers. name, Italian	lā-TĒT-syah	leː'tiːtsjɑ
Leto		
mother of Apollo and Artemis	LĒT-ō	'liːt̬oː

Key (col. 2): a: **f**a**d** ā: **f**a**de** ah: **f**a**ther** ar: **M**a**ry** aw: **l**a**w** e: **f**e**d** ē: **f**e**ed** er: **m**e**rry** i: **h**i**d** ī: **h**i**de** ō: **c**o**at** ōō: **b**oo**t** oi: **b**oy ow: **n**ow u: **p**u**t** uh: **a**bove uhr: **b**ir**d** ch: **ch**op ng: **r**i**ng** sh: **sh**ow th: **th**ick th: **th**is zh: mea**s**ure

LeTourneau
    University, *TX*   luh-TUR-NŌ, luh-TUR-NŌ   lə'tuᵣˌnoː, lə,tuᵣ'noː

Letterman
    David, *US TV personality*   LET-uhr-muhn   'leṱəᵣmən

Lettie
    pers. name   LET-ē   'leṱiˑ

Lettish
    pert. to the Letts   LET-ish   'leṱiʃ

Letzebuergesch [Luxemburgish]
    lang., Luxemburg   LET-suh-BUR-guhsh   'letsəˌbyᵣgəʃ

Leucadius
    son of Icarius and Polycaste   lo͞o-KĀD-ē-uhs   luː'keːdiːəs

Leucaria
    wife of King Italus   lo͞o-KAR-ē-uh   luː'kæriːə

Leuce
    nymph loved by Hades   LO͞O-sē   'luːsiˑ

Leucippe
    mother of Priam   lo͞o-SIP-ē   luː'sipiˑ

Leucippidae
    daughters of Leucippus   lo͞o-SIP-uhd-ē   luː'sipədiˑ

Leucippus
    king of Messina   lo͞o-SIP-uhs   luː'sipəs

Leucothea
    Greek sea-goddess   LO͞O-kuh-THĒ-uh   ˌluːkə'θiːə

Leuctra
    ancient village, Greece   LO͞OK-truh   'luːktrə

Leucus
    foster-child and betrayer of   LO͞O-kuhs   'luːkəs
      Idomeneus

Leuven [Louvain]
    city, Belgium   LUH(R)-vuhn   'lœːvən

Lev
    pers. name, Russian   lef   l̰ef

Levant, The
    eastern Mediterranean shores   thuh luh-VANT   ðə lə'vænt

Levantine
    pert. to the Levant   LEV-uhn-TĪN, luh-VAN-TĪN, -TĒN   'levənˌtɑin, lə'vænˌtɑin, -ˌtiːn

Levar
    pers. name   luh-VAHR   lə'vɑᵣ

Leven, Loch
    see Loch Leven

Leventhal
    Harold, *talent manager, producer*   LEV-uhn-THAWL, LEV-uhn-THAHL   'levənˌθɔːl, 'levənˌθɑl

Leveson-Gower
    Granville George & *his uncle*   LO͞O-suhn-GAWR   'luːsən'gɔːᵣ
      George Granville, *English*
      politicians

Levesque
    Rene, *Canadian political leader*   luh-VEK   ləvek

Levi
  1. Jacob's son; Hebrew tribe; pers.   LĒ-VĪ   'liː,vai
     name
  2. Carlo, Italian writer, artist,   LÃ-vē   'leːviˑ
     physician
  3. family name   LEV-ē, LĒ-vē   'leviˑ, 'liːviˑ
Levice
  town, Slovakia   LEV-uht-SÄ   'levət,seː
Levi-Montalcini
  Rita, *Italian-born US*   LEV-ē-MAHNT-l-SĒ-nē   ,leviˑ,mantlʲ'siːniˑ
     neurobiologist (Nobel 1986)
Levin
  1. pers. name   LEV-uhn   'levən
  2. German   LÃ-vuhn   'leːvən
Levine
  James, *US opera director*   luh-VĪN   lə'vain
Levi's
  tdmk for clothing   LĒ-VĪZ   'liː,vaiz
Lévis-Lauzon
  College, *Canada*   lā-VĒ-lō-ZAWⁿ   leː,viːloˑ'zõ
Levi Strauss
  US clothing co.   LĒ-VĪ STROWS   ,liː,vai 'straus
Levite
  descendant of Levi   LĒ-VĪT   'liː,vait
Leviticus
  Old Testament book   luh-VIT-i-kuhs   lə'viṭikəs
Levittown
  town, NY   LEV-uht-TOWN   'levət,taun
Levitz
  US furniture corp.   LEV-uhts   'levəts
Levulin
  carbohydrate   LEV-yuh-luhn   'levjələn
Levy
  1. Louis, US chess master   LEV-ē   'leviˑ
  2. pers. name   LEV-ē, LĒ-vē   'leviˑ, 'liːviˑ
Lévy-Bruhl
  Lucien, *French philosopher*   lā-vē-BRUEL   leːviːbryːl
Lew
  pers. name   LOO̅   'luː
Lewellyn
  pers. name   luh-WEL-uhn   lə'welən
Lewes
  town, DE   LOO̅-uhs   'luːəs
Lewin
  Kurt, *US psychologist*   LOO̅-uhn   'luːən
Lewis
  pers. name   LOO̅-uhs   'luːəs
Lewisham
  borough, England   LOO̅-uh-shuhm   'luːəʃəm
Lex
  pers. name   LEKS   'leks
Lexan
  tdmk for synthetic resin   LEK-SAN   'lek,sæn
Lex Canuleia
  Roman marriage law   LEKS KAN-yuh-LÃ-uh   'leks ,kænjə'leːə

Key (col. 2):   a: fad ā: fade ah: father ar: Mary aw: law e: fed ē: feed er: merry i: hid ī: hide ō: coat oo̅: boot
oi: boy   ow: now   u: put   uh: above   uhr: bird   ch: chop   ng: ring   sh: show   th: thick   th̲: this   zh: measure

Lex Frumentaria
   Roman grain law   LEKS FR͞OO-muhn-TAR-ē-uh,   'leks ˌfruːmənˈtæriːə, -ˈteriːə
                                 -TER-ē-uh

Lexington
   city, KY; town, MA   LEK-sing-tuhn, LEK-suhn-tuhn   'leksiŋtən, 'leksəntən

Lex Provinciae
   Roman provincial charter   LEKS pruh-VIN-sē-ī   'leks prə'vinsiːˌai

Leyden
   1. town, MA   LĪD-n   'laidn̩
   2. see Leiden

Leyden jar
   electrical condenser   LĪD-n JAHR   'laidn̩ 'dʒɑr

Leyland
   town, England   LĀ-luhnd   'leːlənd

Leyte
   gulf, island, Philippines LĂT-ē, LĂT-ā   'leːti˙, 'leːteː

Lezghian [Kuri]
   lang., people, Caucasus Mts. LEZ-gē-uhn   'lezgiːən

Lezgi
   lang., people, Daghestan, Georgia, LEZ-gē   'lezgi˙
     Azerbaijan

Lhasa
   city, Tibet   LAHS-uh, LAS-uh   'lasə, 'læsə

Lhasa apso
   dog breed   LAHS-uh AHP-sō, LAS-uh AP-sō ˌlasə 'apsoː, ˌlæsə 'æpsoː

Lhotse
   Mount, Himalayas   (H)LŌT-SĀ   '(h)loːt'seː

Lhuyd
   Edward, Welsh antiquarian HLU-ēd   'l̥ui˙d

Li
   lang., people, China   LĒ   'liː

Liam
   pers. name   LĒ-uhm   'liːəm

Liao
   river, China   lē-OW   liː'au

Liaoning
   prov, China   lē-OW-NING   liː'au'niŋ

Libbie
   pers. name   LIB-ē   'libi˙

Libby
   W. F., US chemist (Nobel 1960); LIB-ē   'libi˙
     pers. name

Liber
   Roman wine god   LĒ-buhr, LĒ-BER   'liːbər, 'liːˌber

Liberace
   US entertainer   LIB-uh-RAHCH-ē   ˌlibə'ratʃi˙

Liberia
   republic, Africa   lī-BIR-ē-uh   lai'biriːə

Liberian
   pert. to Liberia   lī-BIR-ē-uhn   lai'biriːən

Liberius
   pope   lī-BIR-ē-uhs   lai'biriːəs

Libitina
   Roman goddess of rites for the LIB-uh-TĪ-nuh, LIB-uh-TĒ-nuh ˌlibə'tainə, ˌlibə'tiːnə
     dead

Foreign Sounds: ue: *Fr.* **rue**, *Ger.* **füllen**   uh(r): *Fr.* **boeuf**, *Ger.* **Höhle**   <u>kh</u>: *Ger.* **ich**, *Scot.* **loch**   ḡ: *Sp.* **amigo** <u>v</u>: *Sp.* **hablar**
hl: *Welsh* **Llanelli.**   CAPITALS: primary stress.   SMALL CAPS: secondary stress.   ⓢ: U.S. pron.   ⓛ: British pron.

Libra
   constellation, sign of the zodiac   LĒ-bruh   'liːbrə

Libreville
   city, Gabon   LĒ-bruh-VIL   'liːbrə,vil

Librium
   tdmk for a drug   LIB-rē-uhm   'libriːəm

Libya
   republic, Africa   LIB-ē-uh   'libiːə

Libyan
   pert. to Libya   LIB-ē-uhn   'libiːən

Licania
   plant   li-KĀ-nē-uh, lī-KĀ-nē-uh   li'keːniːə, lai'keːniːə

Lichfield
   town, England   LICH-FĒLD   'litʃ,fiːld

Li Chun
   Chinese spring observance   LĒ CHŌŌN   'liː 'tʃuːn

Licinian-Sextian
   Roman Laws, 367 B.C.   lī-SIN-ē-uhn-SEK-stē-uhn   lai'siniːən'sekstiːən

Licinius
   Roman emperor; pers. name,   li-SIN-ē-uhs   li'siniːəs
     Latin

Licorice
   spice; candy   LIK-(uh-)rish, LIK-(uh-)ruhs   'lik(ə)riʃ, 'lik(ə)rəs

Liddell
   Henry, *English classical scholar;*   LID-l   'lidḷ
     his daughter Alice, *the*
     inspiration for Alice in
     Wonderland

Lidice
   1. village, Czechoslovakia   LĒ-duht-SĀ, LID-yuht-SĀ   'liːdət,seː, 'lidjət,seː
   2. village, IL   LID-uh(t)-sē, LID-uh(t)-SĀ   'lidə(t)si', 'lidə(t),seː

Lidiya
   pers. name, Russian   LĒ-dē-yah   'ḷiːḍiːjaː

Lido
   Adriatic resort   LĒD-ō   'liːdoː

Liebfraumilch
   wine   LĒP-FROW-MILKH, ⑤ -MILK   'liːp,frau,milx, ⑤ -,milk

Liebmann
   pers. name, German   LĒP-MAHN   'liːp,man

Liechtenstein
   principality, Europe   LIKH-tuhn-SHTĪN; ⑤ LIK-tuhn-STĪN,   'liçtən,ʃtain;
       -SHTĪN   ⑤ 'liktən,stain, -,ʃtain

Liechtensteiner
   pert. to Liechtenstein   LIKH-tuhn-SHTĪ-nuhr;   'liçtən,ʃtainəʳ;
       ⑤ LIK-tuhn-STĪ-nuhr, -SHTĪ-nuhr   ⑤ 'liktən,stainəʳ,
         -,ʃtainəʳ

Liederkranz
   cheese   LĒD-uhr-KRAN(T)S,   'liːdəʳ,kræn(t)s,
       LĒD-uhr-KRAHN(T)S   'liːdəʳ,kran(t)s

Liège
   prov, Belgium   LYEZH, ⑤ lē-ĀZH, lē-EZH   ljeʒ, ⑤ liː'eːʒ, liː'eʒ

Ligonier
   city, IN; borough, PA   LIG-uh-NIR   ,ligə'niʳ

Liguria
   autonomous region, Italy   luh-GYUR-ē-uh   lə'gjuriːə

Key (col. 2):   a: fad   ā: fade   ah: father   ar: Mary   aw: law   e: fed   ē: feed   er: merry   i: hid   ī: hide   ō: coat   ōō: boot
oi: boy   ow: now   u: put   uh: above   uhr: bird   ch: chop   ng: ring   sh: show   th: thick   <u>th</u>: this   zh: measure

Ligurian		
Alps, *Alpine mtn. range;* Sea, *branch of Mediterranean*	li-GYUR-ē-uhn	li'gjuriːən
Likud		
political party, Israel	li-KOŌD	li'kuːd
Lili		
1. pers. name, French	lē-LĒ	liːliː
2. German	LIL-ē	'liliː
Lilian		
pers. name	LIL-ē-uhn, LIL-yuhn	'liliːən, 'liljən
Lilith		
mythological female demon; Adam's first wife	LIL-uhth	'liləθ
Liliuokalani		
queen, Hawaii	li-LĒ-uh-WŌ-kuh-LAHN-ē	li,liːə,woːkə'laniˑ
Lille		
city, France	LĒL	liːl
Lillehammer		
city, Norway	LIL-uh-HAHM-uhr	'lilə,hɑməʳ
Lilli		
pers. name, German	LIL-ē	'liliː
Lillian		
pers. name	LIL-ē-uhn, LIL-yuhn	'liliːən, 'liljən
Lillibullero		
English tune	LIL-ē-buh-LER-ō	,liliˑbə'leroː
Lillie		
pers. name	LIL-ē	'liliˑ
Lilliput		
island in Gulliver's Travels, *J. Swift*	LIL-i-puht	'lilipət
Lilliputians		
tiny inhabitants of Lilliput	LIL-uh-PYOŌ-shuhnz	,lilə'pjuːʃənz
Lilly		
pers. name	LIL-ē	'liliˑ
Lilly, Eli		
US pharmaceutical firm	Ē-LĪ LIL-ē	,iː,lai 'liliˑ
Lilongwe		
city, Malawi	li-LAWNG-wā	li'loŋweː
Lily		
1. pers. name, English, German	LIL-ē	'liliˑ
2. French	lē-LĒ	liːliː
Lima		
1. city, OH	LĪ-muh	'laimə
2. city, Peru	LĒ-muh	'liːmə
Limba		
lang., people, Guinea, Sierra Leone	LIM-buh	'limbə
Limbaugh		
Rush, *US conservative radio personality*	LIM-baw, LIM-bō	'limbɔː, 'limboː
Limburger		
cheese	LIM-BUHR-guhr	'lim,bəʳgəʳ
Limerick		
city, Irish Republic	LIM-(uh-)rik	'lim(ə)rik

Foreign Sounds: ue: *Fr.* **rue**, *Ger.* füllen uh(r): *Fr.* **boeuf**, *Ger.* Höhle k̲h̲: *Ger.* i**ch**, *Scot.* lo**ch** ḡ: *Sp.* ami**g**o y: *Sp.* ha**b**lar
hl: *Welsh* **Ll**anelli. CAPITALS: primary stress. SMALL CAPS: secondary stress. ⑤: U.S. pron. ⑫: British pron.

Limes
  Roman fortified frontier   LĪ-MĒZ   'laɪ,miːz
Limites
  plural of Limes   LIM-uh-TĒZ   'lɪmə,tiːz
Límnos [Lemnos]
  island, Greece   LĒM-NAWS   'liːm,nɔːs
Limoges
  town, France   lē-MŌZH   liːmoːʒ
Limousin
  prov, France   lē-moo-ZEⁿ   liːmuːzɛ̃
Limpopo
  river, Africa   lim-PŌ-pō   lɪm'poːpoː
Linacre
  college, Oxford Univ.   LIN-uh-kuhr   'lɪnəkəʳ
Linate
  airport, Milan   lē-NAH-tā   liː'naːteː
Lincoln
  Abraham, *16th US president; city,*   LING-kuhn   'lɪŋkən
  NE
Lincolnshire
  county, England   LING-kuhn-shuhr, -SHIR   'lɪŋkənʃəʳ, -,ʃiʳ
Linda
  pers. name   LIN-duh   'lɪndə
Lindbergh
  Charles, *US aviator; his wife*   LIN(D)-BUHRG   'lɪn(d),bəʳg
  Anne, *US writer*
Lindemans Faro
  Belgian beer   LIN-duh-MAHNS FAHR-ō   'lɪndə,mɑns 'faroː
Linden
  Hal, *US actor*   LIN-duhn   'lɪndən
Lindesay
  pers. name   LIN(D)-zē   'lɪn(d)ziˑ
Lindisfarne
  island, England   LIN-duhs-FAHRN   'lɪndəs,faʳn
Lindsay
  pers. name   LIN(D)-zē   'lɪn(d)ziˑ
Lindsey
  Benjamin, *US jurist; pers. name*   LIN(D)-zē   'lɪn(d)ziˑ
Lindy
  jitterbug dance   LIN-dē   'lɪndiˑ
Lingala
  lang., Cen. Africa   ling-GAHL-uh   lɪŋ'gɑlə
Lingayen
  gulf, city, Philippines   LING-gah-YEN   ,lɪŋɡa'jen
Linguaphone
  tdmk for a language-teaching   LING-gwuh-FŌN   'lɪŋgwə,foːn
  system
Linkletter
  Art, *Canadian radio, TV*   LING-KLET-uhr   'lɪŋ,kletəʳ
  broadcaster
Linlithgow
  former name of West Lothian   lin-LITH-gō   lɪn'lɪθgoː
Linnaean
  pert. to Linnaeus   luh-NĒ-uhn, luh-NĀ-uhn   lə'niːən, lə'neɪən

---

Key (col. 2): a: fad ā: fade ah: father ar: Mary aw: law e: fed ē: feed er: merry i: hid ī: hide ō: coat o͞o: boot
oi: boy ow: now u: put uh: above uhr: bird ch: chop ng: ring sh: show th: thick <u>th</u>: this zh: measure

Linnaeus
  Carolus, *Latin name of* Carl von   luh-NĒ-uhs, luh-NĀ-uhs   lə'niːəs, lə'neːəs
    Linné, *Swedish botanist; pers.*
    name
Linné [Linnaeus]
  Carl von, *Swedish botanist*   lin-Ā   lin'eː
Linnell
  pers. name   luh-NEL   lə'nel
Linnet
  songbird   LIN-uht   'linət
Linotype
  typesetting machine   LĪ-nuh-TĪP   'lainə,taip
Lin Piao
  Chinese politician   LIN bē-OW   'lin biː'au
Linus
  pope; son of Psamathe & Apollo in   LĪ-nuhs   'lainəs
    Greek myth; comic strip
    character; pers. name
Lin Yutang
  Chinese author   LIN YŌO-TAHNG   'lin ˌjuː'taŋ
Linz
  town, Austria   LIN(T)S   'lin(t)s
Linzer torte
  sweet filled pastry   LIN(T)-suhr TAWRT, LIN(D)-zuhr   'lin(t)səʳ ˌtɔːʳt, 'lin(d)zəʳ
Lionel
  1. pers. name   LĪ-uhn-l, LĪ-uh-NEL   'laiənḷ, 'laiə,nel
  2. tdmk for toy trains   LĪ-uh-NEL, LĪ-uhn-l   ˌlaiə'nel, 'laiənḷ
Lipan
  N. American people   lē-PAHN   liˈʼpɑn
Lipari
  island group, Tyrrhenian Sea   LIP-uh-rē   'lipəriˑ
Liparus
  son of Auson   LIP-uh-ruhs   'lipərəs
Lipe
  S. American people   LĒ-pā   'liːpeː
Li Peng
  premier, China   LĒ PUHNG   'liː 'pəŋ
Lipmann
  F. A., German-born US biochemist   LIP-muhn   'lipmən
    (Nobel 1953)
Li Po [Li Tai Po]
  Chinese poet   LĒ BŌ   'liː 'boː
Lippard
  pers. name   LIP-AHRD   'lip,ɑʳd
Lippe
  river, state, Germany   LIP-uh   'lipə
Lippi
  Fra Filippo *& his son* Filippo *or*   LIP-ē   'lipiˑ
    Filippino, *Florentine painters*
Lippizaner
  horse breed   LIP-uh-ZAHN-uhr   'lipə,zɑnəʳ
Lippman
  Gabriel, *French physicist (Nobel*   lēp-MAHN   liːpmɑːn
    1908)

Foreign Sounds: ue: *Fr.* **rue**, *Ger.* **füllen**   uh(r): *Fr.* **boeuf**, *Ger.* **Höhle**   <u>kh</u>: *Ger.* i**ch**, *Scot.* lo**ch**   ğ: *Sp.* ami**g**o   <u>v</u>: *Sp.* ha**b**lar
hl: *Welsh* **Ll**anelli.   CAPITALS: primary stress.   SMALL CAPS: secondary stress.   Ⓢ: U.S. pron.   Ⓛ: British pron.

Lippmann
   Walter, *US journalist*   LIP-muhn   'lipmən

Lippo
   pers. name, Italian   LĒP-pō   'liːppoː

Lipscomb
   Mance, *US blues guitarist;* William   LIP-skuhm   'lipskəm
     Nunn, *US inorganic chemist*
     (Nobel 1976)

Lipton
   Sir Thomas, *Scottish merchant;*   LIP-tuhn   'liptən
     US tea & food co.

Lisa
   1. pers. name   LĒ-suh, LĪ-zuh   'liːsə, 'laizə
   2. German, Italian   LĒ-zah   'liːza

Lisbeth
   pers. name, German   LĒS-bet   'liːsbet

Lisboa [Lisbon]
   city, Portugal   lēzh-VŌ-uh   liːʒ'voːə

Lisbon
   city, Portugal   LIZ-buhn   'lizbən

Lise
   pers. name, German   LĒ-zuh   'liːzə

Lisle
   1. city, France   LĒL, LIL   liːl, lil
   2. village, IL; pers. name   LĪL   'lail

Lister
   Joseph, *English surgeon*   LIS-tuhr   'listəʳ

Listerine
   tdmk for a mouthwash   LIS-tuh-RĒN, LIS-tuh-RĒN   ,listə'riːn, 'listə,riːn

Lisu
   lang., people, China   LĒ-SOO, LĒ-SOO   'liː'suː, 'liː,suː

Liszt
   Franz, *Hungarian composer*   LIST   'list

Li Tai Po [Li Po]
   Chinese poet   LĒ TĪ BŌ   'liː 'tai 'boː

Litchfield
   town, county, CT   LICH-FĒLD   'litʃ,fiːld

Lithgow
   John, *US actor*   LITH-GŌ   'liθ,goː

Lithium
   anti-depressant drug; element LITH-ē-uhm   'liθiːəm

Lithuania
   republic, Europe   LITH-(y)uh-WĀ-nē-uh, -nyuh ,liθ(j)ə'weːniːə, -njə

Lithuanian
   lang., Lithuania   LITH-(y)uh-WĀ-nē-uhn, -nyuhn ,liθ(j)ə'weːniːən, -njən

Litsea
   plant   LIT-sē-uh   'litsiːə

Litterarum Baccalaureus
   bachelor of letters   LIT-uh-RAR-uhm BAK-uh-LŌR-ē-uhs, ,litə'rærəm ,bækə'loːriːəs,
                       -LAWR-ē-uhs   -'loːriːəs

Litterarum Doctor
   doctor of letters, Litt.D.   LIT-uh-RAR-uhm DAHK-TAWR   ,litə'rærəm 'dak,tɔːʳ

Key (col. 2):   a: fad ā: fade ah: father ar: Mary aw: law e: fed ē: feed er: merry i: hid ī: hide ō: coat oo: boot
oi: boy ow: now u: put uh: above uhr: bird ch: chop ng: ring sh: show th: thick th: this zh: measure

Litterarum Humaniorum Doctor		
doctor of humanities, L.H.D.	LIT-uh-RAR-uhm h(y)u-MAN-ē-AWR-uhm, yu-MAN-	ˌliṭə'rærəm h(j)uˌmæniː'ɔːrəm, juˌmæn-
Litton		
US manufacturing co.	LIT-n	'litn̩
Litva [Lithuania]		
republic, Europe	LIT-vuh	'litvə
Litvinov		
Maxim, *Russian political leader*	lyit-VYĒ-nuhf, [$] lit-VĒ-nuhf	ljit'vjiːnəf, [$] lit'viːnəf
Liu Shao-chi		
Chinese politician	lē-OO SHOW-JĒ	liː'uː 'ʃau'dʒiː
Liv		
pers. name, Swedish	LĒV, LIV	'liːv, 'liv
Liverpool		
seaport, England	LIV-uhr-POOL	'livəʳˌpuːl
Liverpudlian		
pert. to Liverpool	LIV-uhr-PUHD-lē-uhn, *locally* LIV-uhr-PUD-lē-uhn	ˌlivəʳ'pədliːən, *locally* ˌlivəʳ'pudliːən
Livia		
wife of Roman emperor Augustus; pers. name	LIV-ē-uh	'liviːə
Livius		
pers. name, Latin	LIV-ē-uhs	'liviːəs
Livonia		
city, MI	luh-VŌ-nē-uh, luh-VŌN-yuh	lə'voːniːə, lə'voːnjə
Livorno [Leghorn]		
prov, Italy	lē-VAWR-nō	liː'vɔːʳnoː
Livy		
Roman historian	LIV-ē	'liviˑ
Li Xiannian		
Chinese politician	LĒ shē-AHN-YAHN	'liː ʃiː'an'jan
Liz		
pers. name	LIZ	'liz
Liza		
pers. name	LĪ-zuh	'laizə
Lizzie		
pers. name	LIZ-ē	'liziˑ
Ljubljana		
city, Slovenia	LYOOB-lyah-nah, [$] lē-OO-blē-AHN-uh, lē-OO-blē-uh-NAH	'ljuːbljana, [$] liːˌuːbliː'anə, liː'uːbliːəˌna
Ljubomir		
pers. name, Serbo-Croatian	LYOO-baw-MĒR	'ljuːbɔːˌmiːr
Ljudevit		
pers. name, Serbo-Croatian	LYOO-de-VĒT	'ljuːdeˌviːt
Lladró		
Spanish porcelain	(L)YAHTH-rō	'(l)jaðroː
Llanberis		
village, mtn. pass, Wales	hlahn-BER-is	l̥an'beris
Llanelli		
town, Wales	hlah-NEHL-ē	l̥a'nel̥iˑ
Llanera		
commune, Spain	(l)yah-NĀ-ruh	(l)ja'neːrə

Foreign Sounds: ue: *Fr.* **rue**, *Ger.* **füllen** uh(r): *Fr.* **boeuf**, *Ger.* **Höhle** kh: *Ger.* **ich**, *Scot.* **loch** g: *Sp.* ami**g**o v: *Sp.* ha**b**lar hl: *Welsh* **Llanelli**. CAPITALS: primary stress. SMALL CAPS: secondary stress. [$]: U.S. pron. [£]: British pron.

Llanfairpwllgwyngyll
  village, Wales (short form)   HLAHN-vīr-PUHL-GWIN-gihl   ˌl̦anvair'pul̦ˌgwingil̦

Llanfairpwll-
  gwyngyllgogery-
  chwyrndrobwllll-
  andysiliogogogoch
  village, Wales (full form)   HLAHN-vīr-PUHL-   ˌl̦anvair'pul̦ˌ
                  GWIN-gihl-GŌ-ger-uh-   ˌgwingil̦ˌgoːgerə-
                  K̲H̲WUHRN-DRŌ-buhl-HLAHN   'xwərn'droːbul̦ˌl̦-
                  -duh-SIL-yō-GŌ-gō-GŌK̲H̲   andə'siljoːˌgoːgoː'goːx

Llangollen
  town, Wales   hlahn-GAWHL-en   l̦an'gɔːl̦en

Llano
  river, county, TX   LAN-ō   'lænoː

Llareggub
  fictional Welsh town in Under Milk   hlah-REG-ib   l̦a'regib
    Wood, *D. Thomas*

Llewelyn
  pers. name, Welsh   hle-WEL-in, hlyo͞o-EL-in   l̦e'welin, l̦juː'elin

Llewelyn, Llewellyn
  pers. name   luh-WEL-uhn   lə'welən

Lleyn
  peninsula, Wales   HLĒN   'l̦iːn

Lloyd
  pers. name   LOID   'lɔid

Llull
  Ramón, *Catalan poet*   LYO͞OL   'ljuːl̦

Llullaillaco
  volcano, Chile   yo͞o-yī-YAHK-ō   juːjai'jakoː

Llywelyn
  1. pers. name   luh-WEL-uhn   lə'welən
  2. Welsh   hlyo͞o-EL-in   l̦juː'elin

Löb
  pers. name, German   LUH(R)P   'lœːp

Lobelia
  plant   lō-BĒL-yuh, lō-BĒ-lē-uh   loː'biːljə, loː'biːliːə

Lobito
  port, Angola   lō-BĒT-ō   loː'biːțoː

Locarno
  commune, Switzerland   lō-KAHR-nō   loː'kaʳnoː

Lochinvar
  romantic suitor in Marmion, *Sir*   LAHK̲H̲-uhn-VAHR, LAHK-uhn-VAHR   ˌlaxən'vaʳ, ˌlakən'vaʳ
    Walter Scott

Loch Leven
  lake, Scotland   LAHK̲H̲ LĒ-vuhn, LAHK   ˌlax 'liːvən, ˌlak

Loch Lomond
  lake, Scotland   lahk̲h̲ LŌ-muhnd, lahk   lax 'loːmənd, lak

Loch Morar
  lake, Scotland   LAHK̲H̲ MAWR-uhr, LAHK   ˌlax 'mɔːrəʳ, ˌlak

Loch Ness
  lake, Scotland   LAHK̲H̲ NES, LAHK   ˌlax 'nes, ˌlak

Loch Rannoch
  lake, Scotland   LAHK̲H̲ RAN-uhk̲h̲, RAN-uhk, LAHK   ˌlax 'rænəx, 'rænək, ˌlak

---

Key (col. 2): a: fad ā: fade ah: father ar: Mary aw: law e: fed ē: feed er: merry i: hid ī: hide ō: coat o͞o: boot
oi: boy ow: now u: put uh: above uhr: bird ch: chop ng: ring sh: show th: thick t̲h̲: this zh: measure

Locke
  John, *English philosopher;*   LAHK   ˈlɑk
  Sondra, *US actress*
Lockerbie
  town, Scotland   LAHK-uhr-bē   ˈlɑkəʳbiˑ
Lockhart
  pers. name   LAHK-HAHRT, LAHK-uhrt   ˈlɑk͜hɑʳt, ˈlɑkəʳt
Lockheed
  US aircraft manufacturer   LAHK-ĒD, LAHK-HĒD   ˈlɑk͜iːd, ˈlɑk͜hiːd
Locris
  district, Greece   LŌ-kruhs   ˈloːkrəs
Locrus
  builder of Thebes   LŌ-kruhs   ˈloːkrəs
Lodewijk, -wyck
  pers. name, Dutch   LŌ-duh-VĪK   ˈloːdə͜vɑik
Lodge
  Henry Cabot, *US politician*   LAHJ   ˈlɑdʒ
Lodi
  1. city, CA, NJ   LŌ-DĪ   ˈloːˌdɑi
  2. commune, Italy   LAWD-ē   ˈlɔːdiˑ
Lodovico
  pers. name, Italian   LŌ-dō-VĒ-kō   ˌloːdoːˈviːkoː
Łódź
  city, Poland   LŌOJ, Ⓢ LAHDZ   ˈłuːdʒ, Ⓢ ˈlɑdz
Loeb
  1. classical text series; pers. name   LŌB   ˈloːb
  2. German   LUH(R)P   ˈlœːp
Loesser
  Frank, *US composer*   LES-uhr   ˈlesəʳ
Loew
  US theater chain   LŌ, LŌ-ē   ˈloː, ˈloːiˑ
Loewi
  Otto, *German-born US*   LŌ-ē   ˈloːiˑ
  pharmacologist (Nobel 1936)
Lofoten
  island group, Norway   LŌ-FŌT-n   ˈloːˌfoːtn̩
Lofsöngur
  national anthem, Iceland   LAWF-SUH(R)NG-guhr   ˈlɔːfˌsœŋgər
Lofton
  James David, *US football player*   LAWF-tuhn   ˈlɔːftən
Logan
  pers. name; US pl. name   LŌ-guhn   ˈloːgən
Loggia
  Robert, *US actor*   LŌ-j(ē-)uh   ˈloːdʒ(iː)ə
Loggins
  Kenny, *US singer, songwriter*   LAW-guhnz, LAHG-uhnz   ˈlɔːgənz, ˈlagənz
Logo
  lang., Sudan, Zaire   LŌ-gō   ˈloːgoː
Logroño
  town, Spain   lō-GRŌN-yō   loːˈgroːnjoː
Lohengrin
  knight in German legend; opera,   LŌ-uhn-GRIN   ˈloːənˌgrin
  R. Wagner
Lohrer
  German beer   LŌR-uhr, LAWR-uhr   ˈloːrəʳ, ˈlɔːrəʳ

Loire
   river, region, dept, France   LWAHR, ⑤ luh-WAHR   lwɑːr, ⑤ lə'waʳ

Loire-Atlantique
   dept, France   LWAHR-aht-lahⁿ-TĒK   lwarɑːtlãtiːk

Loire-et-Cher
   dept, France   LWAHR-ā-SHER   lwareːʃer

Loiret
   dept, France   lwah-RE   lwaːre

Lois
   pers. name   LŌ-uhs   'loːəs

Loki
   Scandinavian adversary of the gods   LŌ-kē   'loːkiˑ

Lok Sabha
   lower house of Indian parliament   LAHK SAHB-uh, LAWK   'lak 'sabə, 'lɔːk

Lola
   pers. name   LŌ-luh   'loːlə

Lolita
   novel, V. Nabokov   lō-LĒT-uh   loː'liːtə

Lollard
   English or Scottish follower of J. Wyclif   LAHL-uhrd, ⑤ LAHL-AHRD   'laləʳd, ⑤ 'lal,aʳd

Lollardism
   teachings of J. Wyclif   LAHL-uhr-DIZ-uhm   'laləʳ,dizəm

Lollobrigida
   Gina, *entertainer*   LŌ-luh-BRIJ-uhd-uh   ,loːlə'bridʒədə

Loma
   lang., people, Liberia, Guinea   LŌ-muh   'loːmə

Loma Linda
   city, CA   LŌ-muh LIN-duh   ,loːmə 'lində

Lomax
   John Avery *& his son,* Alan, *US folklorists*   LŌ-MAKS   'loː,mæks

Lombard
   Carol, *US actress;* Longobard; *person from Lombardy*   LAHM-BAHRD, LAHM-buhrd   'lam,baʳd, 'lambəʳd

Lombardi
   Vince, *US coach*   luhm-BAHRD-ē, lahm-   ləm'baʳdiˑ, lam-

Lombardia [Lombardy]
   prov, Italy   LAHM-buhr-DĒ-uh   ,lambəʳdiːə

Lombardy
   prov, Italy   LAHM-BAHRD-ē, LAHM-buhrd-ē   'lam,baʳdiˑ, 'lambəʳdiˑ

Lombok
   island, Indonesia   LAHM-BAHK   'lam,bak

Lombrosian
   pert. to C. Lombroso   lahm-BRŌ-zē-uhn, lahm-BRŌ-sē-uhn   lam'broːziːən, lam'broːsiːən

Lombroso
   Cesare, *Italian criminologist*   lahm-BRŌ-sō   lam'broːsoː

Lomé
   city, Togo   lō-MĀ   loː'meː

Lomond, Loch
   see Loch Lomond

Lompoc
   city, CA   LAHM-PAHK   'lam,pak

Key (col. 2):   a: fad   ā: fade   ah: father   ar: Mary   aw: law   e: fed   ē: feed   er: merry   i: hid   ī: hide   ō: coat   o͞o: boot
oi: boy   ow: now   u: put   uh: above   uhr: bird   ch: chop   ng: ring   sh: show   th: thick   t͟h: this   zh: measure

Londinium
    ancient name of London   LUHN-DIN-ē-uhm, lahn-DIN-ē-uhm   ˌlən'diniːəm, lɑn'diniːəm

London
    city, England   LUHN-duhn   'ləndən

Londonderry
    city, Ireland   LUHN-duhn-DER-ē,   ˌləndən'deriˑ, 'ləndənˌderiˑ
        LUHN-duhn-DER-ē

Londoner
    inhabitant of London   LUHN-duh-nuhr   'ləndənəʳ

Long Beach
    city, NJ, CA   LAWNG BĒCH   'lɔːŋ ˌbiːtʃ

Longfellow
    Henry Wadsworth, *US poet*   LAWNG-FEL-ō, -FEL-uh   'lɔːŋˌfeloː, -ˌfelə

Longinus
    Dionysius, *Greek philosopher*   lahn-JĪ-nuhs, lawn-JĪ-nuhs   lɑn'dʒainəs, lɔːn'dʒainəs

Long Island
    island, NY   lawng Ī-luhnd, *locally also* lawng   lɔːŋ 'ailənd, *locally also* lɔːŋ
        GĪ-luhnd   'gailənd

Longisquamata
    dinosaur   LAHN-juh-SKWAHM-uht-uh   ˌlandʒə'skwɑmətə

Longman
    English family of book publishers   LAWNG-muhn   'lɔːŋmən

Longobard
    one of an ancient German tribe in   LAWNG-guh-BAHRD,   'lɔːŋgəˌbɑʳd, 'laŋgəˌbɑʳd
        Italy   LAHNG-guh-BAHRD

Longobardi
    plural of Longobard   LAWNG-guh-BAHRD-Ī,   ˌlɔːŋgə'bɑʳdˌai,
        LAHNG-guh-BAHRD-Ī, -BAHRD-ē   ˌlaŋgə'bɑʳdˌai, -'bɑʳdiˑ

Long Sault
    scenic parkway, Ontario   LAWNG S͞OO   'lɔːŋ 'suː

Longueuil
    town, Canada   lawng-GĀL   lɔːŋ'geːl

Longueville
    pers. name   LAWNG-VIL   'lɔːŋˌvil

Longus
    Greek author   LAHNG-guhs, LAWNG-guhs   'laŋgəs, 'lɔːŋgəs

Lon Morris
    College, *TX*   LAHN MAWR-uhs, MAHR-uhs   'lan 'mɔːrəs, 'marəs

Lonnie
    pers. name   LAHN-ē   'laniˑ

Lonoke
    county, AR   LŌ-NŌK   'loːˌnoːk

Loomis
    pers. name   L͞OO-mis   'luːmis

Lope
    pers. name, Spanish   LŌ-pā   'loːpeː

Lopes
    pers. name, Portuguese   LŌ-pēsh, LŌ-pēs   'loːpiːʃ, 'loːpiːs

López
    pers. name, Spanish   LŌ-pās, LŌ-pāth   'loːpeːs, 'loːpeːθ

Lopez-Cobos
    Jesus, *Spanish conductor*   lō-pāth-KŌ-vos, lō-PĀS-   loːpeːθ'koːβos, loːˈpeːs-

López Mateos
    Adolfo, *president, Mexico*   LŌ-pās mah-TĀ-ōs   'loːpeːs mɑ'teːoːs

---

Foreign Sounds: ue: *Fr.* **rue**, *Ger.* füllen uh(r): *Fr.* **boeuf**, *Ger.* Höhle <u>kh</u>: *Ger.* ich, *Scot.* loch ḡ: *Sp.* ami**g**o <u>v</u>: *Sp.* hablar
hl: *Welsh* Llanelli. CAPITALS: primary stress. SMALL CAPS: secondary stress. ⑤: U.S. pron. ⑥: British pron.

Lora
  pers. name   LŌR-uh, LAWR-uh   'lɔːrə, 'lɔːrə'

Lorain
  town, county, OH   luh-RĀN, law-RĀN   lə'reɪn, lɔː'reɪn

Loral
  US defense electronics co. lōr-AL, lawr-AL   loːr'æl, lɔːr'æl

Loran
  tdmk for a long range   LŌR-AN, LAWR-AN   'loːr,æn, 'lɔːr,æn
    navigational system

Lorber
  Jeff, *recording artist*   LAWR-buhr   'lɔːʳbəʳ

Lorca
  1. *city, Spain*   LAWR-kuh   'lɔːʳkə
  2. *see* García Lorca

Lord's Prayer
  prayer, "Our Father"   LAWRDZ PRAR, PRER   ,lɔːʳdz 'præʳ, 'preʳ

L'Oreal
  tdmk for cosmetics   LŌR-ē-AL, LAWR-ē-AL   ,loːriː'æl, ,lɔːriː'æl

Loredana
  pers. name, Italian   LAWR-e-DAHN-ah   ,lɔːre'dɑnɑ

Lorelei
  nymph of the Rhine; pers. name LŌR-uh-LĪ, LAWR-uh-LĪ 'loːrə,laɪ, 'lɔːrə,laɪ

Loren
  1. *pers. name*   LŌR-uhn, LAWR-uhn, LAHR-uhn 'loːrən, 'lɔːrən, 'lɑrən
  2. Sophia, *Italian actress* luh-REN, law-REN   lə'ren, lɔː'ren

Lorentz
  1. H. A., *Dutch physicist (Nobel* LŌR-en(T)S, LAWR-en(T)S 'loːr,en(t)s, 'lɔːr,en(t)s
    1902)
  2. *pers. name, Danish*   LAWR-uhns   'lɔːrəns
  3. *Norwegian*   LŌR-uhns   'loːrəns

Lorenz
  Konrad, *Austrian zoologist,* LŌ-rens, Ⓢ LŌR-en(T)S, 'loːrens, Ⓢ 'loːr,en(t)s,
    ethologist (Nobel 1973); pers.   LAWR-en(T)S   'lɔːr,en(t)s
    name

Lorenzo
  1. *pers. name*   luh-REN-zō   lə'renzoː
  2. *Italian*   lō-RENT-sō   loː'rentsoː
  3. *Spanish*   lō-RĀN-sō, -thō   loː'reːnsoː, -θoː
  4. *Swedish*   law-RENT-sō   lɔː'rentsoː

Loreto
  pers. name, Italian   lō-RĀ-tō   loː'reːtoː

Loretta
  pers. name   luh-RET-uh   lə'reɾə

Lori, Lorie
  pers. name   LAWR-ē   'lɔːriˑ

Lorica
  port, Colombia   luh-RĒ-kuh   lə'riːkə

Lorikeet
  parrot   LAWR-i-KĒT, LAHR-i-KĒT 'lɔːri,kiːt, 'lɑri,kiːt

Lorimer
  pers. name   LAWR-uh-muhr, LŌR-   'lɔːrəməʳ, 'loːr-

Lorin
  pers. name   LŌR-uhn, LAWR-uhn   'loːrən, 'lɔːrən

Loring
  pers. name   LŌ-ring, LAWR-ing   'loːriŋ, 'lɔːriŋ

Key (col. 2): a: fad ā: fade ah: father ar: Mary aw: law e: fed ē: feed er: merry i: hid ī: hide ō: coat ōō: boot
oi: boy   ow: now   u: put   uh: above   uhr: bird   ch: chop   ng: ring   sh: show   th: thick   th: this   zh: measure

Lorna		
pers. name	LAWR-nuh	'lɔːʳnə
Lorrain, Lorraine		
pers. name	luh-RĀN, law-RĀN	lə'reːn, lɔː'reːn
Lorraine		
prov, France	law-REN, [$] luh-RĀN	lɔːren, [$] lə'reːn
Lorre		
Peter, *US actor*	LAWR-ē, LAHR-ē	'lɔːriˑ, 'lɑriˑ
Lory		
parrot	LŌR-ē, LAWR-ē	'loːriˑ, 'lɔːriˑ
Los Alamos		
county, town, NM	laws AL-uh-MŌS	lɔːs 'ælə,moːs
Los Andes [Andes]		
mtn. range, S. America	laws AHN-dās	lɔːs 'ɑndeːs
Los Angeles		
1. city, CA	laws AN-juh-luhs, AN-juh-LĒZ, ANG-g(uh-)luhs	lɔːs 'ændʒələs, 'ændʒə,liːz, 'æŋg(ə)ləs
2. city, Chile	laws AHNG-hel-ās	lɔːs 'ɑŋheleːs
Los Coyotes		
Indian reservation, US	LAWS kī-ŌT-ēz, laws KĪ-ŌT-ēz	,lɔːs kɑi'oːtiˑz, lɔːs 'kɑi,oːtiˑz
Los Gatos		
city, CA	laws GAT-uhs	lɔːs 'gæt̬əs
Los Lobos		
rock band	laws LŌ-bōs, lahs	lɔːs 'loːboːs, lɑs
Lotario		
pers. name, Italian	lō-TAHR-yō	loː'tɑrjoː
Lothar		
pers. name, German	lō-TAHR, LŌ-TAHR	loː'tɑʳ, 'loː,tɑʳ
Lothario		
seducer; character in The Fair Penitent, *N. Rowe*	lō-THAR-ē-Ō, lō-THER-ē-Ō, lō-THAHR-ē-Ō	loː'θæriː,oː, loː'θeriː,oː, loː'θɑriː,oː
Lothian		
region, Scotland	LŌ-t͟hē-uhn	'loːðiːən
Loti		
Pierre, *French novelist*	lō-TĒ	loːtiː
Lotis		
nymph loved by Priapus	LŌT-uhs	'loːt̬əs
Lotophagi		
lotus-eaters, hosts of Odysseus	LŌT-uh-FĀ-JĪ	,loːt̬ə'feː,dʒɑi
Lotta		
1. pers. name	LAHT-uh	'lɑt̬ə
2. Finnish	LAWT-tah	'lɔːttɑ
Lotte		
pers. name, German	LAWT-uh	'lɔːt̬ə
Lottie		
pers. name	LAHT-ē	'lɑt̬iˑ
Lotuko		
lang., people, Sudan	luh-TO͞O-kō	lə'tuːkoː
Lou		
pers. name	LO͞O	'luː
Loudon		
county, TN; pers. name	LOWD-n	'lɑudn̩
Loudoun		
county, VA	LOWD-n	'lɑudn̩

Louella
pers. name   luh-WEL-uh   lə'welə

Louganis
Greg, *US Olympic diver*   lōō-GĀ-nuhs, lōō-GAHN-uhs   lu:'ge:nəs, lu:'ganəs

Loughborough
town, England   LUHF-b(uh-)ruh, LUHF-BUH-ruh,   'ləfb(ə)rə, 'ləf,bə-rə,
                                        LUHF-BUHR-uh   'ləf,bər-ə

Lough Derg
lake, Ireland   lawkh DYERG̃, $ lahkh DUHRG,   lɔːx 'djerɣ, $ lɑx 'dəʳg, lɑk
                                        lahk

Loughlin
family name   LAHK-luhn, LAHKH-luhn   'lɑklən, 'lɑxlən

Louiche
pers. name, French   LWĒSH   lwiːʃ

Louie
pers. name   LŌŌ-ē   'luːiˑ

Louis
1. pers. name   LŌŌ-uhs, LŌŌ-ē   'luːəs, 'luːiˑ
2. Dutch   lōō-Ē   luː'iː
3. French   LWĒ   lwiː
4. German, Swedish   LŌŌ-ē   'luːiː
5. Norwegian   LŌŌ-ē, LŌŌ-is   'luːiː, 'luːis

Louisa
1. city, KY; county, VA; pers.   luh-WĒ-zuh   lə'wiːzə
name
2. county, IA   luh-WĪ-zuh   lə'waizə
3. pers. name, Dutch   lōō-Ē-zuh   luː'iːzə

Louise
1. lake, Canada; pers. name   luh-WĒZ, lu-ĒZ   lə'wiːz, lu'iːz
2. Danish   lu-Ē-suh   lu'iːsə
3. Dutch   lōō-Ē-suh   luː'iːsə
4. French   LWĒZ   lwiːz
5. German   lōō-Ē-zuh   luː'iːzə

Louisiana
state, US   lōō-Ē-zē-AN-uh, LŌŌ-uh-zē-AN-uh, luˑiːziˑ'ænə, ,luːəziˑ'ænə,
                                        LŌŌ-zē-AN-uh   ,luːziˑ'ænə

Louis Quatorze
pert. to French king Louis XIV   lwē kah-TAWRZ, $ LŌŌ-ē   lwiˑ kɑːtɔːrz, $,luːiˑ
                                        kuh-TAWRZ, luh-WĒ   kə'tɔːʳz, lə,wiː

Louis Quinze
pert. to French king Louis XV   lwē KEⁿZ, $ LŌŌ-ē KAⁿZ, luh-WĒ,   lwiˑ kẽz, $,luːiˑ 'kæ̃(n)z,
                                        KANZ   lə,wiː, 'kænz

Louis Seize
pert. to French king Louis XVI   lwē SEZ, $ LŌŌ-ē SEZ, luh-WĒ   lwiˑ 'sez, $,luːiˑ 'sez, lə,wiː

Louis Treize
pert. to French king Louis XIII   lwē TREZ, $ LŌŌ-ē TREZ, luh-WĒ   lwiˑ 'trez, $,luːiˑ 'trez, lə,wiˑ

Louisville
city, KY   LŌŌ-i-VIL, LŌŌ-i-vuhl, lōō-uh-vuhl 'luːiˌvil, 'luˑivəl, luˑəvəl

Lourdes
1. town, France   LURD, $ LURD(Z)   lurd, $ 'luʳd(z)
2. College, OH   LURD(Z)   'luʳd(z)

Lourenço
pers. name, Portuguese   lō-REⁿ-sōō   loˑrẽːsuː

Key (col. 2):   a: fad ā: fade ah: father ar: Mary aw: law e: fed ē: feed er: merry i: hid ī: hide ō: coat ōō: boot
oi: boy   ow: now   u: put   uh: above   uhr: bird   ch: chop   ng: ring   sh: show   th: thick   th: this   zh: measure

Louth
  1. *county, Ireland* — LOW<u>TH</u>, LOWTH — ˈlauð, ˈlauθ
  2. *town, England* — LOWTH — ˈlauθ
Louvain [Leuven]
  city, Belgium — lo͞o-VEⁿ — luːvẽ
Louvre
  museum, art gallery, Paris, — LO͞OVR, Ⓢ LO͞OV(-ruh) — luːvr, Ⓢ ˈluːv(rə)
    France
Loveland
  city, CO — LUHV-luhnd — ˈləvlənd
Lovell
  pers. name — LUHV-uhl — ˈləvəl
Lowchen
  dog breed — LŌ-CHUHN, -CHEN — ˈloːtʃən, -ˈtʃen
Lowe
  Arthur, *English actor;* E. Nobles, — LŌ — ˈloː
    US lawyer; Rob, *US actor*
Lowell
  Amy, *US poet;* James Russell, *US* — LŌ-uhl — ˈloːəl
    writer; Robert, *US poet; city,*
    MA; pers. name
Lowenbrau, Löwenbräu
  US beer — LŌ-uhn-BROW — ˈloːən,brɑu
Löwenbräu
  Swiss, German beers — LUH(R)-vuhn-BROI, Ⓢ LŌ-uhn-BROW — ˈlœːvən,brɔi, Ⓢ ˈloːən,brɑu
Lower Brule
  Indian reservation, US — BRO͞OL, BRO͞O-lē — ˈbruːl, ˈbruːliˑ
Lower Elwah
  Indian reservation, US — EL-WAH — ˈel,wɑ
Lowestoft
  town, England — LŌ-STAWFT, LŌ-stuhf(t), LŌ-i- — ˈloː,stɔːft, ˈloːstəf(t), ˈloːi-
Lowndes
  county, AL, GA, MS — LOWN(D)Z — ˈlaun(d)z
Lowrie, Lowry
  pers. name — LOWR-ē — ˈlauriˑ
Lowthian
  pers. name — LŌ-thē-uhn, LŌTH-yuhn — ˈloːθiːən, ˈloːθjən
Lowy
  Jay Stanton, *US music publisher* — LŌ-ē — ˈloːiˑ
Loxahatchee
  National Wildlife Refuge, FL — LAHK-suh-HACH-ē — ˌlaksəˈhætʃiˑ
Loy
  Myrna, *US actress* — LOI — ˈlɔi
Lo-yang
  see Luoyang
Loy Krathong
  Thai festival — LOI KRAH-tawng — ˈlɔi ˈkrɑtɔːŋ
Loyola
  University, *LA, IL;* College, *MD* — loi-Ō-luh — lɔiˈoːlə
Lozi
  lang., people, Africa — LŌ-zē — ˈloːziˑ
Lua
  Roman goddess of plague or — LO͞O-uh — ˈluːə
    defilement

Foreign Sounds: **ue**: *Fr.* **rue**, *Ger.* **füllen** **uh(r)**: *Fr.* **boeuf**, *Ger.* **Höhle** **kh**: *Ger.* **ich**, *Scot.* **loch** **g̃**: *Sp.* **amigo** **v**: *Sp.* **hablar** **hl**: *Welsh* **Llanelli**. CAPITALS: primary stress. SMALL CAPS: secondary stress. Ⓢ: U.S. pron. Ⓑ: British pron.

Luanda
  city, Angola   lōō-AHN-duh, lōō-AN-duh   luːˈɑndə, luːˈændə
Luang
  pers. name, Thai   lōō-AHNG   luːˈaŋ
Luang Prabang
  prov & town, Laos   lōō-AHNG pruh-BAHNG   luːˌaŋ prəˈbaŋ
Luba
  lang., people, Africa   LŌŌ-buh   ˈluːbə
Luba-Lulua
  lang., people, Africa   LŌŌ-buh-LŌŌ-lōō-uh   ˌluːbəˈluːluːə
Lubang
  group of islands, Philippines   lōō-BAHNG   luːˈbaŋ
Lubavitcher
  Jewish Hassidic movement   lōō-BAHV-uh-chuhr   luːˈbavətʃəʳ
Lubbock
  city, TX   LUHB-uhk   ˈləbək
Lübeck
  seaport, Germany   LUE-BEK   ˈlyːˌbek
Lubitsch
  Ernst, US film director   LŌŌ-bich   ˈluːbitʃ
Lübke
  Heinrich, president, W. Germany   LUEP-kuh   ˈlypkə
Lublin
  city, Poland   LŌŌ-bluhn, LŌŌ-BLĒN   ˈluːblən, ˈluːˌbliːn
Lubor
  pers. name, Czech   LŌŌ-bawr   ˈluːbɔːr
Lubrizol
  US chemical co.   LŌŌ-bruh-ZAWL, -ZAHL   ˈluːbrəˌzɔːl, -ˌzal
Lubu
  lang., East Sumatra   LŌŌ-bōō   ˈluːbuː
Luc
  pers. name, French   LUEK   lyːk
Luca
  ancient Roman colony, Italy   LŌŌ-kuh   ˈluːkə
Lucan
  Roman poet   LŌŌ-kuhn   ˈluːkən
Lucania
  Mount, *Canada*   lōō-KĀ-nē-uh, lōō-KĀN-yuh   luːˈkeːniːə, luːˈkeːnjə
Lucas
  1. pers. name   LŌŌ-kuhs   ˈluːkəs
  2. Dutch   LUE-KAHS   ˈlyːˌkas
  3. French   lue-KAH   lyːkɑ
  4. German   LŌŌ-KAHS   ˈluːˌkas
  5. Spanish   LŌŌ-kahs   ˈluːkɑs
Lucayo
  Bahamian people   lōō-KĪ-ō, lōō-KĀ-ō   luːˈkaiɔː, luːˈkeːɔː
Lucazi
  lang., Africa   lōō-KAHZ-ē   luːˈkɑziˑ
Lucca
  prov, Italy   LŌŌ-kuh   ˈluːkə
Lucci
  Susan, US actress   LŌŌ-chē   ˈluːtʃiˑ

Key (col. 2):   a: fad ā: fade ah: father ar: Mary aw: law e: fed ē: feed er: merry i: hid ī: hide ō: coat ōō: boot
oi: boy   ow: now   u: put   uh: above   uhr: bird   ch: chop   ng: ring   sh: show   th: thick   th̲: this   zh: measure

Luce

   1. Henry *and* Clare B., *US*   LOOS   'luːs
     publishers; county, MI; pers.
     name

   2. river, France; pers. name,   LUES   lyːs
     French

Lučenec

   town, Slovakia   LUCH-uh-NETS   'lutʃə,nets

Lucerne [Luzern]

   lake, canton, city, Switzerland   loo-SUHRN   luːˈsəᴿn

Lucia

   1. pers. name   LOO-sh(ē-)uh   'luːʃ(iː)ə

   2. Italian   loo-CHĒ-ah   luːˈtʃiːɑ

Lucian

   1. Greek satirist; pers. name   LOO-shuhn   'luːʃən

   2. German   LOOT-sē-AHN, loots-YAHN   ,luːtsiˈɑn, luːtsˈjɑn

   3. Polish   LOOTS-yahn   'luːtsjɑːn

   4. Romanian   loo-CHAHN   luːˈtʃɑn

Luciano

   1. pers. name, Italian   loo-CHAHN-ō   luːˈtʃɑnoː

   2. Portuguese   loos-YAH-noo   luːsˈjɑːnuː

   3. Spanish   loos-YAHN-ō, looth-   luːsˈjanoː, luːθ-

Lucie

   1. pers. name   LOO-sē   'luːsiˈ

   2. French   lue-SĒ   lyːsiː

Lucien

   1. pers. name   LOO-shuhn   'luːʃən

   2. French   lues-YE[n]   lyːsˈjẽ

Lucifer

   Satan; planet Venus when a   LOO-suh-fuhr   'luːsəfəᴿ
     morning star

Lucilius

   Roman name   lu-SIL-ē-uhs   luˈsiliːəs

Lucille

   pers. name   loo-SĒL   luːˈsiːl

Lucina

   Roman goddess of birth; midwife   loo-SĪ-nuh   luːˈsɑinə

Lucinda

   pers. name   loo-SIN-duh   luːˈsində

Lucinde

   pers. name, French   lue-SE[n]D   lyːsẽd

Lucite

   tdmk for a clear plastic   LOO-sīt   'luː,sɑit

Lucius

   Roman praenomen; pers. name   LOO-sh(ē-)uhs   'luːʃ(iː)əs

Łuck

   see Lutsk

Lucknow

   city, India   LUHK-NOW   'lək,nɑu

Lucrece, The Rape of

   poem, Shakespeare   loo-KRĒS, LOO-krēs   luːˈkriːs, 'luː,kriːs

Lucrecia

   pers. name, Spanish   loo-KRĀS-yah, loo-KRĀTH-   luːˈkreːsjɑ, luːˈkreːθ-

Lucretia

   Roman matron, pers. name   loo-KRĒ-sh(ē-)uh   luːˈkriːʃ(iː)ə

Lucretius
  Roman philosopher   lo͞o-KRĒ-sh(ē-)uhs   luːˈkriːʃ(iː)əs
Lucrezia
  pers. name, Italian   lo͞o-KRET-syah   luːˈkretsjɑ
Lucullan
  pert. to Lucullus   lo͞o-KUHL-uhn   luːˈkələn
Lucullus
  Lucius Licinius, *Roman epicure &*   lo͞o-KUHL-uhs   luːˈkələs
  general
Lucy
  pers. name   LO͞O-sē   ˈluːsiˑ
Lucy Cavendish
  College, *Cambridge Univ.*   LO͞O-sē KAV-uhn-dish   ˈluːsiˑ ˈkævəndiʃ
Luddite
  one opposed to technological   LUHD-īT   ˈlədˌait
  change
Ludlow
  town, England; town, MA   LUHD-lō   ˈlədloː
Ludmilla
  pers. name, German   lo͞ot-MIL-ah   luːtˈmilɑ
Ludovic
  1. pers. name   LO͞OD-uh-VIK   ˈluːdəˌvik
  2. French   lue-daw-VĒK   lyːdɔːviːk
Ludovico
  pers. name, Italian   LO͞O-dō-VĒ-kō   ˌluːdoːˈviːkoː
Ludvig
  1. pers. name, Danish   LO͞OTH-vē   ˈluːðviː
  2. Swedish   LUHD-vig   ˈlədvig
Ludwig
  1. pers. name   LUHD-wig, LO͞OD-wig   ˈlədwig, ˈluːdwig
  2. Danish   LO͞OTH-vē   ˈluːðviː
  3. German   LO͞OT-vikh   ˈluːtviç
  4. Swedish   LUHD-vig   ˈlədvig
Ludwik
  pers. name, Polish   LO͞OD-vēk   ˈluːdviːk
Lufthansa
  German airline   LUFT-HAHN-suh, -zuh   ˈluftˌhɑnsə, -zə
Luftwaffe
  German airforce, WWII   LUFT-VAHF-uh, Ⓢ LUFT-WAHF-uh   ˈluftˌvɑfə, Ⓢ ˈluftˌwɑfə
Lug, Lugh
  Celtic hero-god   LO͞OG, LUḠ   ˈluːg, ˈluɣ
Lugal
  title, Sumerian kings   LO͞O-guhl   ˈluːgəl
Lugalzaggisi
  Mesopotamian king, 24th c. BC   LO͞O-guhl-ZAG-uh-sē   ˌluːgəlˈzægəsiˑ
Luganda
  Bantu lang., Africa   lo͞o-GAHN-duh, lo͞o-GAN-duh   luːˈgɑndə, luːˈgændə
Lugandan
  lang., Africa   lo͞o-GAHN-duhn, lo͞o-GAN-duhn   luːˈgɑndən, luːˈgændən
Lugano
  town, Switzerland; lake, Italy,   lo͞o-GAHN-ō   luːˈgɑnoː
  Switzerland
Lugar
  Richard G., *US politician*   LO͞O-guhr   ˈluːgəʳ

Key (col. 2):   a: fad   ā: fade   ah: father   ar: Mary   aw: law   e: fed   ē: feed   er: merry   i: hid   ī: hide   ō: coat   o͞o: boot
oi: boy   ow: now   u: put   uh: above   uhr: bird   ch: chop   ng: ring   sh: show   th: thick   th̲: this   zh: measure

Lugbara
  lang., people, Uganda, Zaire   lug-BAHR-uh   lugˈbɑrə

Lugdunum [Lyons]
  Roman city   lug-DOO-nuhm, LUHG-   lugˈduːnəm, ˌləg-

Luger
  German pistol   LOO-guhr   ˈluːgə^r

Lugh
  see Lug

Lughnasa, Dancing at
  Broadway play   lug-NAHS-uh, LOO-nuhs-uh   lugˈnɑsə, ˈluːnəsə

Luigi
  pers. name   loo-É-jē   luːˈiːdʒiˑ

Luis
  1. pers. name, Portuguese   loo-ÉSH, loo-ÉS   luːˈiːʃ, luːˈiːs
  2. Spanish   loo-ÉS   luːˈiːs

Luís
  pers. name, Portuguese   loo-ÉSH, loo-ÉS   luːˈiːʃ, luːˈiːs

Luisa
  pers. name, Italian   loo-É-zah   luːˈiːzɑ

Luise
  1. pers. name, Danish   lu-É-suh   luːˈiːsə
  2. German   loo-É-zuh   luːˈiːzə

Luiseño
  N. American people   LOO-ē-SĀN-yō   ˌluːiˈseːnjoː

Luis Muñoz Marin
  Airport, San Juan, Puerto Rico   loo-ÉS moon-YŌS mah-RÉN   luːˈiːs muːnˈjoːs mɑˈriːn

Luitpold
  pers. name, German   LOO-it-PAWLT   ˈluːitˌpɔːlt

Lukács
  George, *Hungarian literary critic,*   LOO-KAHCH   ˈluːˌkɑtʃ
    philosopher

Luke
  Christian apostle; New Testament   LOOK   ˈluːk
    book; pers. name

Luken
  Charles, *US politician*   LOO-kuhn   ˈluːkən

Lukl
  pers. name, Czech   LOO-kuhl   ˈluːkəl

Łuków
  commune, Poland   LOO-KOOF   ˈɫuːˌkuːf

Lulu
  pers. name   LOO-LOO   ˈluːˌluː

Lumet
  Sidney, *entertainer*   loo-MET, luh-MET   luˈmet, ləˈmet

Lumm
  Herman Tsui Fai, *US jurist*   LUHM   ˈləm

Lummi
  N. American people   LUHM-ē   ˈləmiˑ

Lumumba
  Patrice, *politician, Zaire*   luh-MUHM-buh, luh-MUM-buh   ləˈməmbə, ləˈmumbə

Luna
  Roman moon goddess   LOO-nuh   ˈluːnə

Lund
  city, Sweden   LUHND   ˈlənd

Foreign Sounds: ue: *Fr.* **r**ue, *Ger.* f**ü**llen uh(r): *Fr.* b**œu**f, *Ger.* H**ö**hle <u>kh</u>: *Ger.* i**ch**, *Scot.* lo**ch** ğ: *Sp.* ami**g**o <u>v</u>: *Sp.* ha**b**lar
hl: *Welsh* **Ll**anelli. CAPITALS: primary stress. SMALL CAPS: secondary stress. Ⓢ: U.S. pron. Ⓛ: British pron.

Lunda
  lang., people, Africa   LO͞ON-duh, LUN-duh   'luːndə, 'lundə

Lunden
  Joan, *TV host*   LUHN-duhn   'ləndən

Lundu
  lang., Africa   LO͞ON-do͞o, LUN-do͞o   'luːnduː, 'lunduː

Lüneburg
  prov & town, Germany   LUE-nuh-BURK, Ⓢ LO͞O-nuh-BURG   'lyːnə,buʳk, Ⓢ 'luːnə,buʳg

Lunenburg
  county, VA; town, MA; county, town, Canada   LO͞O-nuhn-BUHRG   'luːnən,bəʳg

Lungkiang
  former name of Qiqihar   LUNG-jē-AHNG   'luŋdʒiːˈɑŋ

Luo
  lang., people, Kenya, Tanzania   luh-WŌ   ləˈwoː

Luoyang, Lo-yang [Honan]
  town, China   LO͞O-YAHNG, Ⓢ LŌ-YAHNG   'luːˈjɑŋ, Ⓢ 'loːˈjɑŋ

Lupercal
  cave near Rome   LO͞O-puhr-KAL   'luːpəʳ,kæl

Lupercalia
  ancient Roman fertility festival   LO͞O-puhr-KĀL-yuh, -KĀ-lē-uh   ,luːpəʳˈkeːljə, -ˈkeːliːə

Luperci
  Roman priests of Faunus Lupercus   lo͞o-PUHR-SĪ, lo͞o-PUHR-KĪ   luːˈpəʳ,sai, luːˈpəʳ,kai

Lupercio
  pers. name, Spanish   lu-PER-syō, -thyō   luˈpersjoː, -θjoː

Lupine
  plant   LO͞O-puhn, LO͞O-PĪN   'luːpən, 'luː,pain

Lupus
  constellation   LO͞O-puhs   'luːpəs

Lurcher
  dog breed   LUHR-chuhr   'ləʳtʃəʳ

Lurex
  tdmk for a metallic yarn   LUR-EKS, Ⓔ LYUR-EKS   'lur,eks, Ⓔ 'ljur,eks

Luria
  A. R., *Russian neuropsychologist;* Salvador E., *Italian-born US biologist (Nobel 1969)*   LUR-ē-uh   'luriːə

Lurleen
  pers. name   luhr-LĒN   ləʳˈliːn

Lusaka
  city, Zambia   lo͞o-SAHK-uh   luːˈsɑkə

Lusatia
  region, Germany, Poland   lo͞o-SĀ-sh(ē-)uh   luːˈseːʃ(iː)ə

Lusatian [Sorbian]
  lang., Germany   lo͞o-SĀ-shuhn   luːˈseːʃən

Lushai
  lang., people, Burma   LO͞O-SHĪ, lo͞o-SHĪ   'luː,ʃai, luːˈʃai

Lusitania
  Roman province, Europe; Cunard liner sunk 1915   LO͞O-suh-TĀ-nē-uh, -TĀN-yuh   ,luːsəˈteːniːə, -ˈteːnjə

Lutatius
  pers. name   lo͞o-TĀ-sh(ē-)uhs   luːˈteːʃ(iː)əs

Lute
  musical instrument   LO͞OT   'luːt

Key (col. 2):   a: fad   ā: fade   ah: father   ar: Mary   aw: law   e: fed   ē: feed   er: merry   i: hid   ī: hide   ō: coat   o͞o: boot
oi: boy   ow: now   u: put   uh: above   uhr: bird   ch: chop   ng: ring   sh: show   th: thick   th̲: this   zh: measure

Lutece
French restaurant, New York City lue-TES, l(y)o͞o-TES lyːtes, l(j)uːˈtes

Lutetia
ancient name of Paris, France lo͞o-TĒ-sh(ē-)uh luːˈtiːʃ(iː)ə

lutetium
element lo͞o-TĒ-sh(ē-)uhm luːˈtiːʃ(iː)əm

Luther
Martin, *German religious* LO͞O-thuhr ˈluːθəʳ
  reformer; pers. name

Lutheran
pert. to Luther; *member of* LO͞O-th(uh-)ruhn ˈluːθ(ə)rən
  Lutheran Church

Lutheranism
doctrines of Luther & his followers LO͞O-th(uh-)ruh-NIZ-uhm ˈluːθ(ə)rə,nizəm

Luthuli
Albert J., *South African activist* lo͞o-TO͞O-lē, lo͞o-THO͞O-lē luːˈtuːliˑ, luːˈθuːliˑ
  (Nobel 1960)

Lutomer
Yugoslavian wine L(Y)O͞OT-uh-muhr ˈl(j)uːtəməʳ

Lutsk, Łuck
city, Ukraine LO͞OTSK ˈluːtsk

Lutyens
Sir Edwin L., *English architect* LUHT-yuhnz, LUHCH-uhnz ˈlətjənz, ˈlətʃənz

Luwi
ancient Anatolian people LO͞O-wē ˈluːwiˑ

Luwian
ancient Anatolian lang. LO͞O-ē-uhn ˈluːiːən

Luxembourg, -burg
grand duchy, city, Europe LUHK-suhm-BUHRG, ˈləksəm,bəʳg, ˈluksəm,buʳg
  LUK-suhm-BURG

Luxembourger, -burger
pert. to Luxembourg LUHK-suhm-BUHR-guhr, ˈləksəm,bəʳgəʳ,
  LUK-suhm-BUR-guhr ˈluksəm,buʳgəʳ

Luxemburgish
lang., Luxembourg LUHK-suhm-BUHR-gish, ˈləksəm,bəʳgiʃ,
  LUK-suhm-BUR-gish ˈluksəm,buʳgiʃ

Luxor
town, Egypt LUHK-SAWR, LUK-SAWR ˈlək,sɔːʳ, ˈluk,sɔːʳ

Luzerne
county, town, PA lu-ZUHRN luˈzəʳn

Luzern [Lucerne]
lake, canton, city, Switzerland lo͞ot-SERN luːtˈseʳn

Luzon
island, Philippines lo͞o-ZAHN luːˈzɑn

Lvov [Lwów]
city, Ukraine LVAWF, ⑤ luh-VAWF, luh-VAWV ˈlvɔːf, ⑤ ləˈvɔːf, ləˈvɔːv

Lwena
lang., people, Africa luh-WĀ-nuh ləˈweːnə

Lwo, Lwoo
lang., Uganda luh-WŌ ləˈwoː

Lwoff
André, *French biochemist (Nobel* LVAWF, ⑤ LWAWF, luh-WAWF lvɔːf, ⑤ ˈlwɔːf, ləˈwɔːf
  1965)

Lwów
Polish name for Lvov LVO͞OF, ⑤ luh-VO͞OF, luh-VO͞OV ˈlvuːf, ⑤ ləˈvuːf, ləˈvuːv

---

Foreign Sounds: **ue**: *Fr.* **rue**, *Ger.* **füllen** **uh(r)**: *Fr.* **boeuf**, *Ger.* **Höhle** **kh**: *Ger.* **ich**, *Scot.* **loch** **g̱**: *Sp.* **amigo** **v̱**: *Sp.* **hablar**
hl: *Welsh* **Llanelli**. CAPITALS: primary stress. SMALL CAPS: secondary stress. ⑤: U.S. pron. ⑥: British pron.

Lycaon
 son of Pelasgus   lī-KĀ-uhn   laiˈkeːən
Lycaonia
 ancient country, Asia Minor LIK-ā-Ō-nē-uh, LĪ-kā-Ō-nē-uh ˌlikeːˈoːniːə, ˌlaikeːˈoːniːə
Lycastus
 son of Ares and Phylonome lī-KAS-tuhs   laiˈkæstəs
Lyceum
 educational institution, esp. that lī-SĒ-uhm   laiˈsiːəm
  of Aristotle
Lycia
 ancient district, Asia Minor LISH-(ē-)uh   ˈliʃ(iː)ə
Lycian
 pert. to Lycia   LISH-(ē-)uhn   ˈliʃ(iː)ən
Lycidas
 elegy, J. Milton   LIS-uhd-uhs, ⓔ LIS-i-DAS ˈlisədəs, ⓔ ˈlisiˌdæs
Lycomedes
 Dolopian king; host of Achilles LĪ-kuh-MĒD-ēz   ˌlaikəˈmiːdiːz
Lycoming
 county, PA   lī-KŌ-ming   laiˈkoːmiŋ
Lycra
 tdmk for an elastic cloth LĪ-kruh   ˈlaikrə
Lycurgus
 Spartan lawgiver; Athenian orator; lī-KUHR-guhs   laiˈkəˤgəs
  king of Thrace
Lycus
 founder of the cult of Lycian LĪ-kuhs   ˈlaikəs
  Apollo
Lydgate
 John, *English monk, poet,* LID-GĀT, LIG-ĀT   ˈlidˌgeːt, ˈligˌeːt
  translator
Lydia
 1. ancient country, Asia Minor; LID-ē-uh   ˈlidiːə
  pers. name
 2. German   LUED-yah, LUE-dē-ah ˈlyːdjɑ, ˈlyːdiːɑ
Lydian
 musical mode   LID-ē-uhn   ˈlidiːən
Lyell
 pers. name   LĪL   ˈlail
Lyle
 pers. name   LĪL   ˈlail
Lyly
 John, *English author*   LIL-ē   ˈliliˑ
Lyman
 pers. name   LĪ-muhn   ˈlaimən
Lymphae
 Latin divinities of springs LIM(P)-fē   ˈlim(p)fiˑ
Lympne
 village, England   LIM   ˈlim
Lynceus
 husband of Hypermestra LING-kē-uhs   ˈliŋkiːəs
Lynch
 William Dennis, Jr., *US broadcast* LINCH   ˈlintʃ
  journalist
Lynde
 pers. name   LIND   ˈlind

Key (col. 2): a: fad ā: fade ah: father ar: Mary aw: law e: fed ē: feed er: merry i: hid ī: hide ō: coat o͞o: boot
oi: boy ow: now u: put uh: above uhr: bird ch: chop ng: ring sh: show th: thick th̲: this zh: measure

Lyndhurst		
town, NJ; city, OH	LIND-HUHRST	'lind,hə^{r}st
Lyndon		
pers. name	LIN-duhn	'lindən
Lynen		
Feodor, *German biochemist (Nobel 1964)*	LUE-nuhn	'lyːnən
Lynette		
pers. name	luh-NET	lə'net
Lynley		
Carol Ann, *US actress*	LIN-lē	'linliˑ
Lynn, Lynne		
pers. name	LIN	'lin
Lynsey		
pers. name	LIN-zē	'linziˑ
Lynx		
constellation	LINGKS	'liŋks
Lynyrd Skynyrd		
rock group	LIN-uhrd SKIN-uhrd	'linə^{r}d 'skinə^{r}d
Lyon		
pl. name, US; pers. name	LĪ-uhn	'laiən
Lyonel		
pers. name	LĪ-uhn-l, LĪ-uh-NEL	'laiənl̩, 'laiə,nel
Lyon [Lyons]		
city, France	LYAW^{n}	ljɔ̃
Lyonnais		
prov, France	lyaw-NE, [$] LĒ-uh-NĀ	ljɔːne, [$] ,liːə'neː
Lyonnaise		
brown onion sauce	LĪ-uh-NĀZ, LĒ-uh-NĀZ, -NEZ	,laiə'neːz, ,liːə'neːz, -'nez
Lyonnesse		
mythical region in Arthurian legend	LĪ-uh-NES	,laiə'nes
Lyons		
1. city, France	LYAW^{n}, [$] lē-AW^{n}, LĪ-uhnz	ljɔ̃, [$] liː'ɔ̃, 'laiənz
2. pl. name, US; family name	LĪ-uhnz	'laiənz
Lyra		
constellation	LĪ-ruh	'lairə
Lyrebird		
Australian bird	LĪR-BUHRD	'lai^{r},bə^{r}d
Lys		
French-Belgian river	LĒS	'liːs
Lysander		
Spartan military commander; pers. name	lī-SAN-duhr	lai'sændə^{r}
Lysenko		
Trofim, *Russian biologist*	lī-SENG-kuh	lai'seŋkə
Lysias		
Athenian orator	LIS-ē-uhs, LIS-ē-AS	'lisiːəs, 'lisiː,æs
Lysidice		
daughter of Pelops	lī-SID-uh-sē	lai'sidəsiˑ
Lysippus		
Greek sculptor	lī-SIP-uhs	lai'sipəs
Lysis		
dialogue of Plato	LĪ-suhs	'laisəs

Foreign Sounds: ue: *Fr.* **rue**, *Ger.* **füllen** uh(r): *Fr.* **boeuf**, *Ger.* **Höhle** kh: *Ger.* **ich**, *Scot.* **loch** g̃: *Sp.* ami**g**o v̠: *Sp.* ha**b**lar hl: *Welsh* **Llanelli**. CAPITALS: primary stress. SMALL CAPS: secondary stress. [$]: U.S. pron. [£]: British pron.

Lysistrata
   comedy, Aristophanes   LIS-uh-STRAHT-uh, lī-SIS-truht-uh   ,lisə'strɑṭə, lai'sistrəṭə
Lysithea
   satellite of Jupiter   lī-SITH-ē-uh   lai'siθiːə
Lysol
   tdmk for a disinfectant   LĪ-SAWL, LĪ-SAHL   'lai,sɔːl, 'lai,sal
Lystra
   town, Asia Minor   LIS-truh   'listrə
Lytham St. Anne's
   town, England   LĪ-thuhm suhnt ANZ, sănt   'laiðəm sənt 'ænz, seːnt
Lytton
   pers. name   LIT-n   'litṇ

M

Maarten
   pers. name, Dutch   MAHR-tuhn   'mɑːrtən
Maas
   Dutch name for river Meuse   MAHS   'mɑs
Maasai
   see Masai
Maastricht
   city, Netherlands; European   MAH-STRIKHT   'mɑː,strixt
     Community treaty site
Maazel
   Lorin, *US conductor*   mah-ZEL   mɑ'zel
Mab
   fairy queen of English and Irish MAB   'mæb
     folklore
Mabel
   pers. name   MĀ-buhl   'meːbəl
Mabinogi
   medieval Welsh story cycle MAB-uh-NAWG-ē   ,mæbə'nɔːgiˑ
Mabinogion
   collection of Welsh tales   MAB-uh-NAWG-ē-uhn   ,mæbə'nɔːgiːən
Mac-
   see also Mc-
Macalester
   College, *MN*   muh-KAL-uhs-tuhr   mə'kæləstəʳ
Macanese
   pert. to Macao   MAK-uh-NĒZ, -NĒS   ,mækə'niːz, -'niːs
Macao, Macau
   colony, Portugal   muh-KOW   mə'kau
Macapagal
   Diosdado, *president, Philippines* MAHK-uh-puh-GAHL   ,makəpə'gal

---

Key (col. 2):   a: fad ā: fade ah: father ar: Mary aw: law e: fed ē: feed er: merry i: hid ī: hide ō: coat oo: boot
oi: boy ow: now u: put uh: above uhr: bird ch: chop ng: ring sh: show th: thick th: this zh: measure

MacArthur
  Douglas, *US general;* James, *US*   muh-KAHR-thuhr   mə'kɑ^rθə^r
  actor

Macassarese
  lang., Asia   muh-KAS-uh-RĒZ, -RĒS   mə,kæsə'riːz, -'riːs

Macassar oil
  hairdressing preparation   muh-KAS-uhr OIL   mə'kæsə^r ‚oil

Macau
  see Macao

Macaulay, -ley
  pers. name   muh-KAW-lē   mə'kɔːliˑ

Macaw
  parrot   muh-KAW   mə'kɔː

Macbeth
  play, Shakespeare; pers. name   muhk-BETH   mək'beθ

MacBride
  Seán, *Irish civil rights activist*   muhk-BRĪD   mək'braid
  (Nobel 1974); pers. name

Maccabaean, -bean
  pert. to Maccabaeus *or*   MAK-uh-BĒ-uhn   ‚mækə'biːən
  Maccabees

Maccabaeus
  Judas, *Judean patriot*   MAK-uh-BĒ-uhs   ‚mækə'biːəs

Maccabees
  Apocryphal book   MAK-uh-BĒZ   'mækə‚biːz

Macchio
  Ralph, *US actor*   MAHK-ē-ō   'makiːoː

Macclesfield
  town, district, England   MAK-uhlz-FĒLD   'mækəlz‚fiːld

Macdonald
  pers. name   muhk-DAHN-uhld   mək'danəld

MacDougal
  pers. name   muhk-DŌO-guhl   mək'duːgəl

Macédoine
  fruit dessert   MAS-uh-DWAHN   ‚mæsə'dwan

Macedon
  ancient country, NW of Aegean   MAS-uhd-uhn, MAS-uh-DAHN   'mæsədən, 'mæsə‚dan
  Sea

Macedonia [Macedon]
  country, Europe; region, Greece;   MAS-uh-DŌ-nē-uh, -DŌN-yuh   ‚mæsə'doːniːə, -'doːnjə
  ancient country, NW of Aegean
  Sea

Macedonian
  pert. to Macedon; *Balkan lang*   MAS-uh-DŌ-nē-uhn,   ‚mæsə'doːniːən,
                                             MAS-uh-DŌN-yuhn   ‚mæsə'doːnjən

Macedonianism
  Christian heresy   MAS-uh-DŌ-nē-uh-NIZ-uhm   ‚mæsə'doːniːə‚nizəm

Macedonio
  pers. name, Italian   MAH-chä-DAWN-yō   ‚matʃeː'doːnjoː

Macfarlane
  pers. name   muhk-FAHR-luhn   mək'fɑ^rlən

Macgillycuddy's Reeks
  mtn. range, Ireland   MAG-li-KUHD-ēz RĒKS, Ⓢ *also*   ‚mægli‚kədiˑz 'riːks, Ⓢ *also*
                                    muh-GIL-uh-KUHD-ēz RĒKS   mə‚gilə‚kədiˑz 'riːks

---

Foreign Sounds: ue: *Fr.* **rue**, *Ger.* **füllen**   uh(r): *Fr.* **boeuf**, *Ger.* **Höhle**   <u>kh</u>: *Ger.* **ich**, *Scot.* **loch**   g: *Sp.* **amigo**   <u>v</u>: *Sp.* **hablar**
hl: *Welsh* **Llanelli.** CAPITALS: primary stress. SMALL CAPS: secondary stress. Ⓢ: U.S. pron. Ⓑ: British pron.

MacGraw
  Ali, *US actress*   muh-GRAW   mə'grɔː

Macgregor
  pers. name   muh-GREG-uhr   mə'gregəʳ

Mach
  Ernst, *Austrian physicist;*   MAH<u>KH</u>, MAHK   'mɑx, 'mɑk
    supersonic scale

Machabees
  Old Testament book   MAK-uh-bēz   'mækəbiːz

Machaon
  son of Asclepius   muh-KĀ-uhn, muh-KĀ-AHN   mə'keːən, mə'keːˌɑn

Machel
  Samora Moisés, *president,*   mah-SHEL   mɑ'ʃel
    Mozambique

Machias
  town, ME   muh-CHĪ-uhs   mə'tʃaiəs

Machiavelli
  Niccolò, *Italian political writer* MAK-ē-uh-VEL-ē, MAHK-   ˌmækiːə'veliˑ, ˌmɑk-

Machiavellian
  pert. to Machiavelli   MAK-ē-uh-VEL-ē-uhn, MAHK-,   ˌmækiːə'veliːən, ˌmɑk-,
                                       -VEL-yuhn   -'veljən

Machiguenga
  lang., people, Peru   MAHCH-uh-GENG-guh   ˌmatʃə'gengə

Machu Picchu
  ruined Inca city, Peru   MAHCH-o͞o PĒK-cho͞o, PĒ-cho͞o   ˌmatʃuː 'piːktʃuː, 'piːtʃuː

Machynlleth
  town, Wales   muh-<u>KH</u>UHN-hluhth   mə'xənl̥əθ

Maciej
  pers. name, Polish   MAH-chā   'maːtʃeː

Maciejowice
  commune, Poland   MAHT-suh-yaw-VĒT-suh,   ˌmaːtsəjɔː'viːtsə,
                                       MAHCH-uh-yaw-VĒT-suh   ˌmaːtʃəjɔː'viːtsə

MacInnes
  Helen, *British writer*   muh-KIN-uhs   mə'kinəs

Macintosh
  family name; tdmk for computers MAK-uhn-TAHSH   'mækənˌtaʃ

Mack
  pers. name; US truck co.   MAK   'mæk

Mackay
  pers. name   muh-KĪ, muh-KĀ, MAHK-ē   mə'kai, mə'keː, 'mɑkiˑ

Mackenzie
  pers. name   muh-KEN-zē   mə'kenziˑ

Mackie
  Bob, *US costume and fashion*   MAK-ē   'mækiˑ
    designer

Mackinac
  1. *island, straits, MI*   MAK-uh-NAK, MAK-uh-NAW   'mækəˌnæk, 'mækəˌnɔː
  2. *county, MI*   MAK-uh-NAW   'mækəˌnɔː

Mackinaw
  river, IL   MAK-uh-NAW   'mækəˌnɔː

Mackintosh
  pers. name   MAK-uhn-TAHSH   'mækənˌtaʃ

Macklin
  pers. name   MAK-luhn   'mæklən

Key (col. 2):   a: fad ā: fade ah: father ar: Mary aw: law e: fed ē: feed er: merry i: hid ī: hide ō: coat o͞o: boot
oi: boy   ow: now   u: put   uh: above   uhr: bird   ch: chop   ng: ring   sh: show   th: thick   <u>th</u>: this   zh: measure

Maclaine
   Shirley, *US actress, author*   muh-KLĀN   məˈkleːn

MacLean
   pers. name   muh-KLĀN   məˈkleːn

MacLeish
   Archibald, *US poet*   muh-KLĒSH   məˈkliːʃ

MacLeod
   J. J. R., *Scottish physiologist*   muh-KLOWD   məˈklɑud
     (*Nobel 1923*); *pers. name*

Macmillan
   publishing house; pers. name   muhk-MIL-uhn   məkˈmilən

MacMurray
   Fred, *US actor*   muhk-MUHR-ē, muhk-MUH-rē   məkˈmər-iˑ, məkˈmə-riˑ

MacNamara
   Donal Eoin Joseph, *US*   MAK-nuh-MAR-uh   ˈmæknə,mærə
    criminologist

Macnamara
   Robert, *US statesman*   MAK-nuh-MAR-uh, -MER-uh   ˈmæknə,mærə, -,merə

Macnee
   Patrick, *British actor*   muhk-NĒ   məkˈniː

Macneil
   Robert, *Canadian broadcast*   muhk-NĒL   məkˈniːl
    journalist

Macomb
   pl. name, US   muh-KŌM   məˈkoːm

Macon
   pl. name; pers. name   MĀ-kuhn   ˈmeːkən

Mâcon
   city, France   mah-KAWⁿ   makɔ̃

Mâconnais
   French wine   mah-kaw-NE   makɔːne

Macoupin
   county, IL   muh-KOO-puhn   məˈkuːpən

Macquarie
   Lachlan, *Scottish soldier, colonial*   muh-KWAHR-ē, Ⓢ *also*   məˈkwariˑ, Ⓢ *also*
    governor   muh-KWAWR-ē   məˈkwɔːriˑ

MacRae
   Gordon, *singer, actor*   muh-KRĀ   məˈkreː

Macready
   pers. name   muh-KRĒD-ē   məˈkriːdiˑ

Macrinus
   Roman emperor   muh-KRĪ-nuhs   məˈkrɑinəs

Macris
   guardian of Dionysus   MAK-ruhs   ˈmækrəs

Macrobius
   Ambrosius, *Latin grammarian*   muh-KRŌ-bē-uhs   məˈkroːbiːəs

Macú
   S. American people   mah-KOO, muh-KOO   maˈkuː, məˈkuː

Macy's
   US department store   MĀ-sēz   ˈmeːsiˑz

Madagascan
   pert. to Madagascar   MAD-uh-GAS-kuhn   ,mædəˈgæskən

Madagascar
   island, country, Indian Ocean   MAD-uh-GAS-kuhr   ,mædəˈgæskəʳ

Foreign Sounds: ue: *Fr.* **rue**, *Ger.* f**ü**llen   uh(r): *Fr.* b**oeu**f, *Ger.* H**öh**le   kh: *Ger.* i**ch**, *Scot.* lo**ch**   ḡ: *Sp.* ami**g**o   v: *Sp.* ha**b**lar
hl: *Welsh* **Ll**anelli.   CAPITALS: primary stress.   SMALL CAPS: secondary stress.   Ⓢ: U.S. pron.   Ⓔ: British pron.

Madame

French term of address for a
married woman
  mah-DAHM, ⑤ MAD-uhm,
  muh-DAHM, muh-DAM
  mɑːdɑːm, ⑤ 'mædəm,
  mə'dɑm, mə'dæm

Madang

dist, New Guinea   MAHD-AHNG   'mɑd,aŋ

Madden

John, *US TV sports commentator*   MAD-n   'mædn̩

Maddock

pers. name   MAD-uhk   'mædək

Madeira

*islands, Atlantic; river, Brazil;
wine*   muh-DIR-uh, muh-DER-uh   mə'dirə, mə'derə

Madeleine

1. *pers. name*   MAD-l-uhn   'mædlən
2. *French*   mahd-LEN   mɑːdlen

Madeleine, La

see La Madeleine

Madeleine, La Fête de la

see La Fête de la Madeleine

Madeline

pers. name   MAD-l-uhn   'mædlən

Mademoiselle

French term of address for an
unmarried woman
  mahd-mwah-ZEL, mahn-mwah-ZEL,
  ⑤ MAD-uh-m(w)uh-ZEL,
  MAD-m(w)uh-ZEL
  mɑːdmwɑːzel,
  mɑːnmwɑːzel,
  ⑤ ,mædəm(w)ə'zel,
  ,mædm(w)ə'zel

Madera

1. *county, CA*   muh-DER-uh   mə'derə
2. *town, Mexico; volcano,
Nicaragua*   mah-<u>TH</u>Ā-rah   ma'ðeːra

Madge

pers. name   MAJ   'mædʒ

Madhya Bharat

state, India   MUHD-yuh BUH-ruht, BUHR-uht   ,mədjə 'bə-rət, 'bər-ət

Madhya Pradesh

state, India   MUHD-yuh pruh-DESH   ,mədjə prə'deʃ

Madi

lang., people, Uganda, Sudan   MAHD-ē   'mɑdiˑ

Madīnah, Al [Medina]

city, Saudi Arabia   AHL mah-DĒ-nuh, AL ma-DĒ-nuh   ,ɑːl ma'diːnə, ,æl mæ'diːnə

Madison

James, *4th US president; US pl.
name*   MAD-uh-suhn   'mædəsən

Madlock

William, Jr., *US baseball player*   MAD-LAHK   'mæd,lak

Madoc

pers. name, Welsh   MAH-dawg   'mɑːdɔːg

Madonna

*the Virgin Mary; US singer,
actress*   muh-DAHN-uh   mə'danə

Madras

1. *city, India*   muh-DRAS, muh-DRAHS   mə'dræs, mə'drɑs
2. *fabric*   MA-druhs, muh-DRAS, muh-DRAHS   'mædrəs, mə'dræs, mə'drɑs

---

Key (col. 2):   a: **fad**   ā: **fade**   ah: **father**   ar: **Mary**   aw: **law**   e: **fed**   ē: **feed**   er: **merry**   i: **hid**   ī: **hide**   ō: **coat**   o͞o: **boot**
oi: **boy**   ow: **now**   u: **put**   uh: **above**   uhr: **bird**   ch: **chop**   ng: **ring**   sh: **show**   th: **thick**   <u>th</u>: **this**   zh: **measure**

Madrid
   1. city, province, Spain   mah-<u>THRĒTH</u>, ⑤ muh-DRID   mɑ'ðriːð, ⑤ mə'drid
   2. city, IA   MAD-ruhd   'mædrəd

Madrid Hurtado
   see de la Madrid Hurtado

Madrigal
   song   MAD-ri-guhl   'mædrigəl

Madrilène
   consommé   MAD-ruh-LEN, MAD-ruh-LĀN   ,mædrə'len, ,mædrə'leːn

Madura
   1. city, India   MAHJ-uh-ruh, MAJ-uh-ruh   'mɑdʒərə, 'mædʒərə
   2. island, Indonesia   muh-DUR-uh   mə'durə

Madurese
   lang., people, Madura, Indonesia   MAD-uh-RĒZ, MAJ-uh-RĒZ, -RĒS   ,mædə'riːz, ,mædʒə'riːz,
                                                             -'riːs

Mae
   pers. name   MĀ   'meː

Maecenas
   Roman statesman, literary patron   mī-SĒ-nuhs   mɑi'siːnəs

Maecilius
   pers. name   mē-SIL-ē-uhs   miː'siliːəs

Máel
   pers. name, Irish Gaelic   MOIL   'mɔil

Maelstrom
   current, whirlpool, Norwegian Sea MĀL-struhm, MĀL-STRAHM   'meːlstrəm, 'meːl,strɑm

Maenads
   female followers of Dionysus   MĒ-NADZ   'miː,nædz

Maenalus
   son of Lycaon or Arcas   MĒN-l-uhs   'miːnḷəs

Maeon
   ancestor of Homer   MĒ-AHN   'miː,ɑn

Maera
   dog of Icarius; constellation   MĒ-ruh, MIR-uh   'miːrə, 'mirə

Maeterlinck
   Maurice, Belgian author (Nobel MĀT-uhr-LINGK, MET-, MAT-   'meːtəʳ,liŋk, 'met-, 'mæt-
   1911)

Mae West
   inflatable lifejacket   MĀ WEST   ,meː 'west

Mafeking
   town, S. Africa   MAF-uh-king   'mæfəkiŋ

Maffeo
   pers. name, Italian   mahf-FE-ō   mɑfˈfeoː

Mafia
   criminal organization   MAHF-ē-uh, MAF-ē-uh   'mɑfiːə, 'mæfiːə

Magahi
   lang., India   MAG-uh-hē   'mægəhiˑ

Magallanes [Punta Arenas]
   city, Chile   mah-ḡah-YAH-nās   mɑɣɑ'jɑneːs

Magda
   pers. name, Romanian   MAHG-dah   'mɑgdɑ

Magdala
   ancient town, Palestine   MAG-duh-luh   'mægdələ

Magdalen
   college, Oxford Univ.   MAWD-luhn   'mɔːdlən

Foreign Sounds: ue: *Fr.* **rue**, *Ger.* **füllen** uh(r): *Fr.* **boeuf**, *Ger.* **Höhle** <u>kh</u>: *Ger.* i**ch**, *Scot.* lo**ch** ḡ: *Sp.* ami**g**o v̠: *Sp.* ha**b**lar
hl: *Welsh* **Ll**anelli. CAPITALS: primary stress. SMALL CAPS: secondary stress. ⑤: U.S. pron. Ⓛ: British pron.

Magdalena
  1. river, dept., Colombia; island,   MAG-duh-LĀ-nuh   ˌmægdə'leːnə
    Pacific
  2. pers. name, German   MAHG-dah-LĀ-nah   ˌmɑgda'leːna

Magdalene
  college, Cambridge Univ.   MAWD-luhn   'mɔːdlən

Magdalenian
  Paleolithic culture   MAG-duh-LĒ-nē-uhn   ˌmægdə'liːniːən

Magdeburg
  city, Germany   MAHG-duh-BURK,   'mɑgdə,buʳk,
     Ⓢ MAG-duh-BUHRG   Ⓢ 'mægdə,bəʳg

Magellan
  Ferdinand, *Portuguese navigator*   muh-JEL-uhn   mə'dʒelən

Magellanic cloud
  galaxy   MAJ-uh-LAN-ik KLOWD, Ⓔ   'mædʒə,lænik 'klaud, Ⓔ
     MAG-uh-LAN-ik   ˌmægə,lænik

Magellanic penguin
  bird   MAJ-uh-LAN-ik PEN-gwuhn,   'mædʒə,lænik 'pengwən,
     PENG-gwuhn, Ⓔ MAG-uh-LAN-ik   'pengwən, Ⓔ ˌmægə,lænik

Magen David, Mogen David
  hexagram symbol of Judaism   MAW-guhn DAW-vuhd, MAHG-uhn   ˌmɔːgən 'dɔːvəd, ˌmɑgən
     DAHV-uhd, mah-GEN dah-VĒD   'dɑvəd, mɑ'gen dɑ'viːd

Maggie
  pers. name   MAG-ē   'mægiˑ

Maggiore
  lake, Italy, Switzerland   mahd-JŌR-ā, Ⓢ muh-JŌR-ē,   mɑd'dʒɔːreː, Ⓢ mə'dʒɔːriˑ,
     muh-JAWR-ē   mə'dʒɔːriˑ

Magh Mela
  Hindu pilgrimage   MAHG MĀ-luh   'mɑg 'meːlə

Maghreb, Maghrib
  northwestern Africa   MUHG-ruhb   'məgrəb

Magi
  Biblical visitors of Christ child;   MĀ-JĪ, MAJ-Ī   'meːˌdʒai, 'mædʒˌai
    plural of Magus

Magill
  pers. name   muh-GIL   mə'gil

Magindanao
  Moro people of Mindanao,   muh-GĒN-duh-NOW,   mə,giːndə'nau,
    Philippines   muh-GĒN-duh-NAH-ō   mə,giːndə'naoː

Maginot
  André, *French war minister*   mah-zhē-NŌ   mɑːʒiːnoː

Maginot Line
  French defensive line, WWII   MAZH-uh-NŌ LĪN, MAJ-uh-NŌ   'mæʒə,noː 'lain, 'mædʒə,noː

Maglie
  Sal, Stadium, *Niagara Falls, NY*   MAG-lē   'mægliˑ

Magna Carta
  English charter of liberties   MAG-nuh KAHRT-uh   ˌmægnə 'kɑʳtə

Magna cum laude
  with great praise   MAHG-nuh KUM LOWD-uh, MAG-nuh   ˌmɑgnə ˌkum 'laudə,
     KUHM LAWD-ē   ˌmægnə ˌkəm 'lɔːdiˑ

Magna Graecia
  Greek settlements in southern   MAG-nuh GRĒ-shuh   ˌmægnə 'griːʃə
    Italy

Magnani
  Anna, *Italian actress*   mahn-YAHN-ē   mɑn'jɑniˑ

Key (col. 2):   a: fad   ā: fade   ah: father   ar: Mary   aw: law   e: fed   ē: feed   er: merry   i: hid   ī: hide   ō: coat   o͞o: boot
oi: boy   ow: now   u: put   uh: above   uhr: bird   ch: chop   ng: ring   sh: show   th: thick   <u>th</u>: this   zh: measure

Magnavox

   tdmk of a radio/TV mfg co   MAG-nuh-VAHKS   'mægnə,vɑks

Magnesia

   ancient city, Asia Minor   mag-NĒ-zhuh, mag-NĒ-shuh   mæg'niːʒə, mæg'niːʃə

magnesium

   element   mag-NĒ-zē-uhm, mag-NĒ-zhuhm   mæg'niːziːəm, mæg'niːʒəm

Magnificat

   canticle; hymn of praise   mag-NIF-i-KAT, mag-NIF-i-KAHT,   mæg'nifi,kæt, mæg'nifi,kɑt,
         mahn-YIF-i-KAHT   mɑn'jifi,kɑt

Magnifico

   chianti bottle   mahg-NIF-ē-kō, mag-   mɑg'nifiːkoː, mæg-

Magnus

   1. pers. name   MAG-nuhs   'mægnəs

   2. Danish   MAHĜ-nus   'mɑɣnus

   3. German   MAHG-nus   'mɑgnus

   4. Norwegian   MANG-nus   'mæŋnus

   5. Swedish   MAHNG-nus   'mɑːŋnus

Magoffin

   county, KY   muh-GAHF-uhn   mə'gafən

Magog

   Biblical people descended from   MĀ-GAHG   'meː,gɑg
     Japheth

Magritte

   René, *Belgian painter*   muh-GRĒT   mə'griːt

Magsaysay

   Ramón, *president, Philippines*   mahg-SĪ-sī, mahg-sī-SĪ   mag'sai,sai, mag,sai'sai

Mag Tured

   site of mythological Irish battle   moi T(Y)UR-uh   mɔi 't(j)urə

Magus

   Zoroastrian priest   MĀ-guhs   'meːgəs

Magyar [Hungarian]

   people, lang., Hungary   MAG-YAHR, MAHG-YAHR,   'mægjɑ^r, 'magjɑ^r,
         MAHD-YAHR, MAHJ-AHR   'mad,jɑ^r, 'madʒ,ɑ^r

Magyarorszag [Hungary]

   republic, Europe   MAHD-yahr-AWR-SAHG,   'madjɑr,ɔː^r,sag,
         MAHJ-AHR-AWR-SAHG   'madʒ,ɑr,ɔː^r,sag

Mahabharata

   epic poem of India   muh-HAH-BAHR-uh-tuh   mə,hɑ'barətə

Mahalia

   pers. name   muh-HĀL-yuh   mə'heːljə

Maharashtra

   state, India   MAH-huh-RAHSH-truh   ,mɑhə'raʃtrə

Maharbanji

   pers. name, Parsi   MUH-huhr-BAHN-jē   ,məhər'bandʒiˑ

Maharishi

   Hindu teacher   MAH-huh-RĒ-shē, muh-HAHR-ē-SHĒ   ,mɑhə'riːʃiː, mə'hariˑ,ʃiː

Mahashivarati

   Hindu festival   muh-HAH-SHIV-uh-RAH-tē   mə,hɑ,ʃivə'ratiˑ

Mahaska

   county, IA   muh-HAS-kuh   mə'hæskə

Mahatma

   Brahman sage   muh-HAHT-muh, muh-HAT-muh   mə'hatmə, mə'hætmə

Mahavira

   Jain teacher   mah-hah-VĒ-ruh   mɑhɑ'viːrə

Foreign Sounds: ue: *Fr.* **rue**, *Ger.* **füllen**   uh(r): *Fr.* **boeuf**, *Ger.* **Höhle**   <u>kh</u>: *Ger.* i**ch**, *Scot.* lo**ch**   ĝ: *Sp.* a**m**igo   <u>v</u>: *Sp.* ha**b**lar
hl: *Welsh* **Ll**anelli.   CAPITALS: primary stress.   SMALL CAPS: secondary stress.   Ⓢ: U.S. pron.   Ⓛ: British pron.

Mahavira Jayanti
  Jain festival   muh-hah-VĒ-ruh JĪ-(Y)AHN-tē   məha'vi:rə 'dʒai,(j)anti·

Mahayana
  branch of Buddhism   MAH-huh-YAHN-uh   ,mahə'janə

Mahayanism
  tenets of Mahayana Buddhism   MAH-huh-YAHN-IZ-uhm   ,mahə'jan,izəm

Mahdi
  Muslim messiah   MAHD-ē   'madi·

Mahendra Bir Bikram Shah Deva
  king, Nepal   muh-HEN-druh BIR bi-KRUHM   mə'hendrə 'biʳ bi'krəm 'ʃa
                                          SHAH dē-VAH   di:'va

Maher
  1. Frank A., *US psychologist;* Field,   MĀ(-uh)r, MER, MAHR, MAH-huhr   'meː(ə)ʳ, 'meʳ, 'maʳ,
  ballpark, Roanoke, VA   'mahəʳ
  2. John, *US drug rehabilitation*   MAH-huhr   'mahəʳ
  worker

Mahfouz
  Naguib, *Egyptian author (Nobel*   MAH-FŌŌZ   'ma,fuːz
  1988)

Mahican
  N. American people   muh-HĒ-kuhn   mə'hiːkən

Mahler
  Donald, *US ballet master;* Gustav,   MAHL-uhr   'maləʳ
  Austrian composer

Mahmud
  pers. name, Turkish   mah-MŌŌD   ma'muːd

Mahnomen
  county, MN   maw-NŌ-muhn   mɔː'noːmən

Mahomet
  pers. name   muh-HŌ-muht   mə'hoːmət

Mahon
  Derek, *Irish poet*   MAHN, ⑤ MAN   'maːn, ⑤ 'mæn

Mahoney
  J. Daniel, *US judge; pers. name*   muh-HŌ-nē   mə'hoːni·

Mahoning
  county, OH   muh-HŌ-ning   mə'hoːniŋ

Mahore
  island, Indian Ocean   muh-HŌR, muh-HAWR   mə'hoːʳ, mə'hɔːʳ

Mahorian
  lang., Comoros Islands   muh-HŌR-ē-uhn, muh-HAWR-ē-uhn   mə'hoːriːən, mə'hɔːriːən

Mahratti, Mahrati
  see Marathi

Maia
  mother of Hermes   MĪ-uh   'maiə

Maiasaurus
  dinosaur   MĪ-uh-SAWR-uhs   ,maiə'sɔːrəs

Maida
  pers. name   MĀD-uh, MĪD-uh   'meːdə, 'maidə

Maidanek
  Nazi concentration camp, Poland   MĪD-uh-NEK   'maidə,nek

Maidstone
  town, England   MĀD-stuhn, MĀD-STŌN   'meːdstən, 'meːd,stoːn

Maidu
  N. American people   MĪD-ōō   'maiduː

Key (col. 2): a: fad ā: fade ah: father ar: Mary aw: law e: fed ē: feed er: merry i: hid ī: hide ō: coat ōō: boot
oi: boy ow: now u: put uh: above uhr: bird ch: chop ng: ring sh: show th: thick th̲: this zh: measure

Maigret

   Inspector, *fictional detective of G.*   me-GRE, Ⓢ mā-GRĀ, Ⓔ MĀ-GRĀ   megre, Ⓢ meːˈgreː, Ⓔ
   Simenon   'meːˌgreː

Mailer

   Norman, US author   MĀ-luhr   'meːləʳ

Mailgram

   tdmk for electronic mail   MĀL-GRAM   'meːlˌgræm

Maillol

   Aristide, French sculptor   mah-YAWL   maːjɔːl

Maimonides

   Jewish philosopher   mī-MAHN-uh-DĒZ   maiˈmanəˌdiːz

Main

   river, Germany   MĪN   'main

Mainbocher

   US fashion designer   meⁿ-bō-SHĀ, MEN-bō-SHĀ   mẽboːʃeː, ˌmenboːˈʃeː

Maine

   1. state, US   MĀN   'meːn

   2. river, France   MEN   men

Mainwaring

   British family name   MAN-uh-ring, MĀN-WER-ing,   'mænəriŋ, 'meːnˌweriŋ,
      MĀN-wuh-ring   'meːnwəriŋ

Mainz

   city, Germany   MĪN(T)S   'main(t)s

Mair

   1. pers. name   MAR, MER   'mæʳ, 'meʳ

   2. Welsh   MĪR   'mair

Mairead

   pers. name, Irish   MOI-ruh   'mɔirə

Màiri

   pers. name, Scots Gaelic   MAHR-uh   'maʳə

Maisel

   German beer   MĪ-zuhl   'maizəl

Maiselbräu

   German beer   MĪ-zuhl-BROI   'maizəlˌbrɔi

Maithili

   lang., India, Nepal   MĪT-uh-lē, MĪT-l-ē   'maitəliˑ, 'maitl̩iˑ

Maitland

   Frederic W., English jurist   MĀT-luhnd   'meːtlənd

Maius Imperium

   Roman term for higher authority   MĪ-uhs im-PIR-ē-uhm, -PER-ē-uhm   'maiəs imˈpiriːəm, -ˈperiːəm

Majlis

   parliamentary chamber, Iran, Iraq   maj-LIS, MAHJ-lis   mædʒ'lis, 'maːdʒlis

Majolica

   earthenware   muh-JAHL-i-kuh   məˈdʒalikə

Majorca

   pers. name   muh-YAWR-kuh, muh-JAWR-kuh,   məˈjɔːʳkə, məˈdʒɔːʳkə,
      mī-AWR-kuh   maiˈɔːʳkə

Majorca [Mallorca]

   island, Spain   mah-YAWR-kah, Ⓢ muh-JAWR-kuh,   maˈjɔːrka, Ⓢ məˈdʒɔːʳkə,
      mī-AWR-kuh   maiˈɔːʳkə

Majulah Singapura

   national anthem, Singapore   MAHJ-ul-ah SING-(g)ah-PUR-ah   'madʒula ˌsiŋ(g)aˈpura

Makah

   N. American people   MAH-kah   'maka

Foreign Sounds: ue: *Fr.* **rue**, *Ger.* **füllen** uh(r): *Fr.* **boeuf**, *Ger.* **Höhle** kh: *Ger.* **ich**, *Scot.* **loch** g̃: *Sp.* **amigo** v̱: *Sp.* **hablar**
hl: *Welsh* **Llanelli**. CAPITALS: primary stress. SMALL CAPS: secondary stress. Ⓢ: U.S. pron. Ⓔ: British pron.

Makalu
   Mount, *Himalayas*   MUHK-uh-LO͞O   'məkə,luː

Makara Sankranti
   Indian festival   MAHK-uh-ruh sahn-KRAHN-tē,   'makərə san'krantiˑ,
                               sahng-KRAHN-tē   saŋ'kranti·

Makarios III
   Cypriot political leader   mah-KAHR-yaws   mə'karjɔːs

Makarova
   Natalia, *USSR-born ballerina*   muh-KAHR-uh-vuh   mə'karəvə

Makarovich
   patronym, Ukrainian   muh-KAHR(-uhv)-yich   mə'kar(əv)jitʃ

Makedhonia [Macedonia]
   region, Greece   MAHK-uh-<u>th</u>uh-NĒ-uh   ,makəðə'niːə

Makepeace
   pers. name, (William M. Thackeray)   MĀK-PĒS   'meːk,piːs

Makhachkala
   city, Russia   muh-<u>KHAHCH</u>-kuh-LAH   mə,xaːtʃkə'la

Makkah [Mecca]
   city, Saudi Arabia   MAK-uh   'mækə

Makonde [Konde]
   lang., people, Africa   muh-KŌN-dā   mə'koːndeː

Makoto
   pers. name, Japanese   mah-kō-tō   makoːtoː

Maksim
   pers. name, Russian   MUHK-SYĒM   ,mək'sjiːm

Maksimilian
   pers. name, Russian   MUHK-syēm-yēl-YAHN   ,məksjiːmjiːl'jaːn

Makua [Kua]
   lang., people, Africa   muh-KWAH   mə'kwa

Malabar
   district, India   MAL-uh-BAHR   'mælə,baʳ

Malabo
   town, Equatorial Guinea   muh-LAHB-ō   mə'laboː

Malacca
   Strait of, *Asia*   muh-LAHK-uh, muh-LAK-uh   mə'lakə, mə'lækə

Malachi
   Old Testament book; pers. name   MAL-uh-KĪ   'mælə,kai

Malachias
   Old Testament book   MAL-uh-KĪ-uhs   ,mælə'kaiəs

Málaga
   prov, city, Spain; wine   MAHL-uh-g̃uh, Ⓢ MAL-uh-guh   'maləɣə, Ⓢ 'mæləɡə

Malagasy
   lang., people, Madagasar   MAL-uh-GAS-ē, MAHL-uh-GAHS-ē   ,mælə'gæsiˑ, ,malə'gasiˑ

Malagueña
   dance   MAL-uh-GĀN-yuh, MAHL-   ,mælə'geːnjə, ,mal-

Malamud
   Bernard, *US novelist*   MAL-uh-MUHD, MAL-uh-muhd   'mælə,məd, 'mæləməd

Malamute
   dog breed   MAL-uh-MYO͞OT   'mælə,mjuːt

Malaprop
   Mrs., *character in* The Rivals,   MAL-uh-PRAHP   'mælə,prap
     Sheridan

Malathion
   insecticide   MAL-uh-THĪ-uhn, -THĪ-AHN   ,mælə'θaiən, -'θai,an

---

Key (col. 2):   a: **fad** ā: **fade** ah: **father** ar: **Mary** aw: **law** e: **fed** ē: **feed** er: **merry** i: **hid** ī: **hide** ō: **coat** o͞o: **boot**
oi: **boy**   ow: **now**   u: **put**   uh: **above**   uhr: **bird**   ch: **chop**   ng: **ring**   sh: **show**   th: **thick**   <u>th</u>: **this**   zh: **measure**

Malawi [Nyasa]
  country, lake, Africa   muh-LAH-wē, muh-LOW-ē   mə'lɑwiˑ, mə'lɑuiˑ

Malawian
  pert. to Malawi   muh-LAH-wē-uhn, muh-LOW-ē-uhn   mə'lɑwiːən, mə'lɑuiːən

Malay
  Archipelago, island group, Pacific   muh-LĀ, MĀ-lā   mə'leˑ, 'meːleˑ
  & Indian Oceans; lang., people,
  Malaysia

Malaya
  part of Malaysia   muh-LĀ-uh   mə'leːə

Malayalam
  lang., India   MAHL-uh-YAHL-uhm,   ˌmalə'jaləm, ˌmaliː'aləm
                MAHL-ē-AHL-uhm

Malayan
  lang., Malaysia   muh-LĀ-uhn   mə'leːən

Malaysia
  federation, Asia   muh-LĀ-zh(ē-)uh, -sh(ē-)uh   mə'leːʒ(iː)ə, -ʃ(iː)ə

Malaysian
  pert. to Malaysia   muh-LĀ-zh(ē-)uhn, -sh(ē-)uhn   mə'leːʒ(iː)ən, -ʃ(iː)ən

Malcolm
  pers. name   MAL-kuhm   'mælkəm

Malden
  Karl, *US actor; city, MA, MO*   MAWL-duhn   'mɔːldən

Maldives
  islands, Indian Ocean   MAWL-DĒVZ, mawl-DĪVZ   'mɔːlˌdiːvz, mɔːlˌdaivz

Maldivian
  lang., Maldives   mawl-DIV-ē-uhn, mawl-DĒ-vē-uhn   mɔːl'diviːən, mɔːl'diːviːən

Maldon
  borough, battlesite, England   MAWL-duhn   'mɔːldən

Male
  1. *lang., people, Ethiopia*   MAHL-ā, MAHL-ē   'maleˑ, 'maliˑ
  2. *atoll, city, Maldives*   MAHL-ē   'maliˑ

Malecite
  N. American people   MAL-uh-SĒT, MAL-uh-SĒT   'mæləˌsiːt, ˌmælə'siːt

Malenkov
  Georgi, *premier, USSR*   MUHL-yin-KAWF, ⑤ MAL-uhn-KAWF,   ˌməljin'kɔːf, ⑤ ˌmælən'kɔːf,
                MAHL-   ˌmal-

Malesherbes
  pers. name   MAL-ZUHRB   ˌmæl'zəʳb

Maletsunyane
  river, falls, Lesotho   MAHL-uht-sun-YAHN-ē   ˌmalətsun'janiˑ

Malfi, The Duchess of
  play by Webster   MAL-fē   'mælfiˑ

Malheur
  river, county, OR   mal-HUR   mæl'huʳ

Mali
  republic, Africa   MAHL-ē, MAL-ē   'maliˑ, 'mæliˑ

Malian
  pert. to Mali   MAHL-ē-uhn, MAL-ē-uhn   'maliːən, 'mæliːən

Malibu
  beach, California   MAL-uh-BOO   'mæləˌbuː

Malik
  pers. name, Arabic   MAH-lēk   'maliːk

Malines [Mechelen]
  city, Belgium   mah-LĒN   maliːn

Foreign Sounds: ue: *Fr.* **rue**, *Ger.* füllen   uh(r): *Fr.* **boeuf**, *Ger.* **Höhle**   <u>kh</u>: *Ger.* i<u>ch</u>, *Scot.* lo<u>ch</u>   ḡ: *Sp.* ami**g**o   <u>v</u>: *Sp.* ha**b**lar
hl: *Welsh* **Ll**anelli.   CAPITALS: primary stress.   SMALL CAPS: secondary stress.   ⑤: U.S. pron.   Ⓔ: British pron.

Malinka [Malinke]
  lang., people, West Africa   muh-LING-kuh   mə'liŋkə

Malinke [Malinka, Mandingo]
  lang., people, West Africa   muh-LING-kā, muh-LING-kuh   mə'liŋkeː, mə'liŋkə

Malinowski
  Bronislaw, *Polish anthropologist*   MAL-uh-NAWF-skē, MAHL-,   ˌmælə'nɔːfskiˑ, ˌmɑl-,
         -NAWV-skē   -'nɔːvskiˑ

Maliseet
  N. American people   MAL-uh-SĒT, MAL-uh-SĒT   'mæləˌsiːt, ˌmælə'siːt

Malkovich
  John, *US actor*   MAL-kuh-VICH, MAWL-kuh-VICH   'mælkəˌvitʃ, 'mɔːlkəˌvitʃ

Mall
  London district   MAL   'mæl

Mallacoota
  township, Australia   MAL-uh-KOOT-uh   ˌmælə'kuːtə

Mallarmé
  Stéphane, *French writer*   mah-lahr-MĀ   mɑːlɑːrmeː

Mallorca [Majorca]
  island, Spain   mah(l)-YAWR-kuh,   mɑ(l)'jɔːʳkə, mə(l)'jɔːʳkə,
         muh(l)-YAWR-kuh, mī-YAWR-kuh   maiˈjɔːʳkə

Mallory
  pers. name   MAL-(uh-)rē   'mæl(ə)riˑ

Malmédy
  commune, Belgium   mahl-mā-DĒ   mɑːlmeːdiː

Malmesbury
  borough, England   MAHMZ-b(uh-)rē,   'mɑːmzb(ə-)riˑ,
         MAH(L)MZ-b(uh-)rē   'mɑ(l)mzb(ə-)riˑ

Malmö
  city, Sweden   MAHL-muh(r)   'mɑlmœː

Malmsey
  wine   MAH(L)M-zē, MAHM-zē   'mɑ(l)mziˑ, 'mɑːmziˑ

Malone
  Moses, *US basketball player*   muh-LŌN   mə'loːn

Malope
  plant   MAL-uh-pē   'mæləpiˑ

Malory
  Sir Thomas, *English author*   MAL-uh-rē, MAL-rē   'mæləriˑ, 'mælriˑ

Malpas
  Robert, *English business executive*   MAL-puhs   'mælpəs

Malpighi
  Marcello, *Italian anatomist*   mahl-PĒ-gē, mal-   mɑl'piːgiˑ, mæl-

Malpighian
  pert. to Malpighi   mal-PIG-ē-uhn, mal-PĒ-gē-uhn   mæl'pigiːən, mæl'piːgiːən

Malraux
  André, *French writer*   mahl-RŌ, Ⓢ mal-RŌ   mɑːlroː, Ⓢ mæl'roː

Malta
  island state, Mediterranean   MAWL-tuh   'mɔːltə

Maltaise
  orange sauce   mawl-TEZ   mɔːl'tez

Maltan
  pert. to Malta   MAWL-tuhn   'mɔːltən

Maltese
  lang., Malta   mawl-TĒZ, mawl-TĒS   mɔːl'tiːz, mɔːl'tiːs

Key (col. 2):   a: fad   ā: fade   ah: father   ar: Mary   aw: law   e: fed   ē: feed   er: merry   i: hid   ī: hide   ō: coat   o͞o: boot
oi: boy   ow: now   u: put   uh: above   uhr: bird   ch: chop   ng: ring   sh: show   th: thick   <u>th</u>: this   zh: measure

Malthus
    Thomas Robert, *English*   MAL-thuhs, MAWL-thuhs   'mælθəs, 'mɔːlθəs
    economist

Malthusian
    pert. to Malthus   mal-TH(Y)O̅O̅-zhuhn,   mæl'θ(j)uːʒən,
                      mawl-TH(Y)O̅O̅-zhuhn   mɔːl'θ(j)uːʒən

Malto
    lang., people, India   MAL-tō   'mæltoː

Maluku [Moluccas]
    islands, Indonesia   muh-LO̅O̅-ko̅o̅   mə'luːkuː

Malvern
    1. US pl. name   MAL-vuhrn   'mælvəʳn
    2. urban area, England   MAW(L)-vuhrn   'mɔː(l)vəʳn
    3. city, Australia   MAWL-vuhrn   'mɔːlvəʳn

Malvern Hills
    urban area, England   MAW(L)-vuhrn HILZ   ,mɔː(l)vəʳn 'hilz

Malvi
    lang., India   MAL-vē   'mælviˑ

Malvina
    pers. name   mal-VĒ-nuh   mæl'viːnə

Malvinas, Islas [Falkland]
    islands, Atlantic   ĒZ-lahs mahl-VĒ-nahs   'iːzlɑs mɑl'βiːnɑs

Malvolio
    character in Twelfth Night,   mal-VŌ-lē-ō   mæl'voːliː,oː
    Shakespeare

Mam
    lang., people, Guatemala, Mexico   MAHM   'mɑm

Mama
    informal for mother   MAHM-uh, ⓔ muh-MAH   'mɑmə, ⓔ mə'mɑː

Mamaroneck
    city, NY   muh-MAR-uh-NEK, muh-MAR-uh-nik   mə'mærə,nek, mə'mærənik

Mamba
    snake   MAHM-buh, MAM-buh   'mɑmbə, 'mæmbə

Mambo
    dance   MAHM-bō   'mɑmboː

Mamelukes
    military class that controlled   MAM-uh-LO̅O̅KS   'mæmə,luːks
    Turkey

Mamenchisaurus
    dinosaur   MAM-EN-kī-SAWR-uhs   ,mæm,enkɑi'sɔːrəs

Mamercus
    Roman praenomen   MAHM-uhr-kuhs   'mɑməʳkəs

Mamie
    pers. name   MĀ-mē   'meːmiˑ

Mamilius
    pers. name, Latin   muh-MIL-ē-uhs   mə'miliːəs

Mamma Leone's
    restaurant, New York City   MAHM-uh lē-Ō-nēz   ,mɑmə liː'oːniˑz

Mammon
    greed or riches personified   MAM-uhn   'mæmən

Mamurius
    shield-maker for Numa   mam-(Y)UR-ē-uhs   mæm'(j)uriːəs

Managua
    city, dept, Nicaragua   mah-NAHG̅-wah, ⓢ muh-NAHG̅-wuh mɑ'nɑɣwɑ, ⓢ mə'nɑgwə

Foreign Sounds: ue: *Fr.* **rue**, *Ger.* **füllen**   uh(r): *Fr.* **boeuf**, *Ger.* **Höhle**   kh: *Ger.* i**ch**, *Scot.* lo**ch**   g̅: *Sp.* ami**g**o   v: *Sp.* ha**b**lar
hl: *Welsh* **Ll**anelli.   CAPITALS: primary stress.   SMALL CAPS: secondary stress.   ⓢ: U.S. pron.   ⓔ: British pron.

Manama
  town, Bahrain   muh-NAM-uh   mə'næmə

Manaslu
  mtn., Himalayas   muh-NAHS-lo͞o   mə'nɑslu:

Manassas
  county, VA   muh-NAS-uhs   mə'næsəs

Manasseh
  Prayer of, *Apocryphal book; pers.*   muh-NAS-uh   mə'næsə
    name

Manasses
  Prayer of, *Apocryphal book*   muh-NAS-uhs, muh-NAS-ēz   mə'næsəs, mə'næsi:z

Manatee
  county, FL   MAN-uh-TĒ, MAN-uh-TĒ   ˌmænə'ti:, 'mænəˌti:

Mance
  pers. name (M. Lipscomb)   MAN(T)S   'mæn(t)s

Mancha, La
  see La Mancha

Manche
  dept, France   MAHⁿSH   mɑ̃ʃ

Manchester
  US pl. name; borough, England   MAN-CHES-tuhr, MAN-chuh-stuhr   'mænˌtʃestəʳ, 'mæntʃəstəʳ

Manchu
  dynasty, China; ancient lang.,   man-CHO͞O   mæn'tʃu:
    China

Manchukuo
  former state, Asia   MAHN-CHO͞O-KWŌ   'mɑn'tʃu:'kwo:

Manchuria
  region, China   man-CHUR-ē-uh   mæn'tʃuri:ə

Mancini
  Henry, *composer*   man-SĒ-nē   mæn'si:ni'

Manco Capac, Manqo Qhapaq
  traditional founder of Inca   MAHNG-kō KAH-PAHK   'maŋko: 'kɑˌpɑk
    dynasty, Peru

Mancunian
  pert. to Manchester, *England*   man-KYO͞O-nē-uhn,   mæn'kju:ni:ən,
                mang-KYO͞O-nē-uhn   mæŋ'kju:ni:ən

Mancuso
  Nick, *actor, director*   man-KO͞O-sō, man-KO͞O-zō   mæn'ku:so:, mæn'ku:zo:

Mandala
  Hindu symbol   MUHN-duh-luh   'mʌndələ

Mandalay
  city, division, Burma   MAN-duh-LĀ   ˌmændə'le:

Mandan
  N. American people   MAN-DAN, MAN-duhn   'mænˌdæn, 'mændən

Mandarin
  lang., China   MAN-duh-ruhn   'mændərən

Mandé
  pers. name   mahⁿ-DĀ   mɑ̃de:

Mandela
  Nelson, *S. African political leader*   man-DEL-uh   mæn'delə

Mandell
  pers. name   MAN-dl, man-DEL   'mændl̩, mæn'del

Mandelstam
  Osip, *Russian writer*   MUHN-dyil-SHTAHM   ˌmənd jil'ʃtɑ:m

---

Key (col. 2): a: fad ā: fade ah: father ar: Mary aw: law e: fed ē: feed er: merry i: hid ī: hide ō: coat o͞o: boot
oi: boy ow: now u: put uh: above uhr: bird ch: chop ng: ring sh: show th: thick <u>th</u>: this zh: measure

Mandingo [Malinke]
 lang., people, Africa   man-DING-gō   mæn'diŋgoː
Mandinka
 lang., W. Africa   man-DING-kuh   mæn'diŋkə
Mandrell
 Barbara, *US country singer*   man-DREL   mæn'drel
Mandy
 pers. name   MAN-dē   'mændiˑ
Manes
 1. *husband of Callirhoe in Roman*   MĀ-nēz   'meːniːz
  mythology
 2. *Roman souls of the dead*   MAHN-ĀS, MĀ-NĒZ   'mɑn‚eːs, 'meː‚niːz
Manet
 Edouard, *French painter*   mah-NE, ⑤ ma-NĀ, mah-NĀ   mɑːne, ⑤ mæ'neː, mɑ'neː
Manfred
 1. *pers. name*   MAN-fruhd   'mænfrəd
 2. *German*   MAHN-FRĀT   'mɑn‚freːt
Manfredo
 pers. name, Italian   mahn-FRĀ-dō   mɑn'freːdoː
manganese
 element   MANG-guh-NĒZ, MANG-guh-NĒS   'mæŋgə‚niːz, 'mæŋgə‚niːs
Mangano
 Silvana, *Italian entertainer*   mahn-GAHN-ō   mɑn'gɑnoː
Mangbetu
 lang., people, Uganda, Zaire   mahng-BE-too   mɑŋ'betuː
Mangione
 Chuck, *US musician*   MAN-jē-Ō-nē, man-JŌ-nē   ‚mændʒiˈoːniˑ, mæn'dʒoːniˑ
Mangosuthu
 pers. name, S. Africa   MAHNG-gō-SOO-too   ‚mɑŋgoːˈsuːtuː
Manhattan
 island, NY   man-HAT-n, muhn-HAT-n   mæn'hætn̩, mən'hætn̩
Mania
 personification of madness   MĀ-nē-uh, MĀN-yuh   'meːniːə, 'meːnjə
Manichaean
 adherent of Manichaeanism   MAN-uh-KĒ-uhn   ‚mænə'kiːən
Manichaeanism [Manichaeism]
 religious or philosophical dualism   MAN-i-KĒ-uh-NIZ-uhm   ‚mæni'kiːə‚nizəm
Manichaeism [Manichaeanism]
 religious or philosophical dualism   MAN-i-kē-IZ-uhm   'mæniki:‚izəm
Manila
 city, Philippines   muh-NIL-uh   mə'nilə
Manilow
 Barry, *US entertainer*   MAN-l-ō   'mænl̩‚oː
Manipur
 river, Burma; state, India   MUHN-uh-PUR, MAHN-uh-PUR,   ‚mənə'puʳ, ‚mɑnə'puʳ,
         MAN-uh-PUR   ‚mænə'puʳ
Manipuri [Meithei]
 lang., people, India   MUHN-uh-PUR-ē, MAHN-uh-PUR-ē,   ‚mənə'puriˑ, ‚mɑnə'puriˑ,
        MAN-uh-PUR-ē   ‚mænə'puriˑ
Manischewitz
 kosher food & wine co.   MAN-uh-SHEV-uhts   ‚mænə'ʃevəts
Manistee
 river, county, MI   MAN-uh-STĒ   ‚mænə'stiː
Manitoba
 lake, province, Canada   MAN-uh-TŌ-buh   ‚mænə'toːbə

Foreign Sounds: **ue**: *Fr.* **rue**, *Ger.* **füllen**   **uh(r)**: *Fr.* **boeuf**, *Ger.* **Höhle**   <u>kh</u>: *Ger.* **ich**, *Scot.* **loch**   **g**: *Sp.* **amigo**   **v**: *Sp.* **hablar**
hl: *Welsh* **Llanelli**.   CAPITALS: primary stress.   SMALL CAPS: secondary stress.   ⑤: U.S. pron.   ⑭: British pron.

Manitoulin
  Islands, *Lake Huron*   MAN-uh-TŌŌ-luhn   ,mænə'tuːlən

Manitowoc
  city, county, WI   MAN-uht-uh-WAHK   'mænətə,wɑk

Manius
  pers. name, Latin   MÃ-nē-uhs   'meːniːəs

Mankato
  city, MN   man-KĀT-ō   mæn'keːtoː

Manley
  pers. name   MAN-lē   'mænliˑ

Manlius
  pers. name   MAN-lē-uhs   'mænliːəs

Mann
  1. Horace, *US education reformer* MAN   'mæn
  2. Thomas, *German author (Nobel MAHN   'mɑn
    1929)*

Manne
  pers. name, Swedish   MAHN-ne   'mɑːnne

Mannerheim
  Baron Carl Gustav, *Finnish*   MAHN-uhr-HĀM, -HĪM   'mɑnəʳ,heːm, -,hɑim
    politician

Mannes
  College of Music, *NY*   MANZ   'mænz

Mannheim
  1. Karl, *Hungarian historian*   MAHN-HĪM   'mɑn,hɑim
  2. port, Germany   MAHN-HĪM, Ⓢ MAN-HĪM 'mɑn,hɑim, Ⓢ 'mæn,hɑim

Mano
  lang., people, Liberia, Guinea MAHN-ō   'mɑnoː

Manoah
  Biblical name   muh-NŌ-uh   mə'noːə

Manoel
  pers. name, Portuguese   muhn-WEL, mahn-WEL   mən'wel, mɑːn'wel

Manolete
  cognomen of Manuel Rodriguez   mahn-ō-LÃ-tā   mɑnoː'leːteː
    Sánchez, *Spanish bullfighter*

Manon
  pers. name, French   mah-NAWⁿ   mɑːnõ

Manon Lescaut
  opera, Puccini   mah-NAWⁿ les-KŌ   mɑːnõ leskoː

Manqo Qhapaq
  see Manco Capac

Mans, Le
  see Le Mans

Mansi [Vogul]
  lang., people, Russia   MAHN-sē   'mɑnsiˑ

Manson
  Charles, *US mass murderer*   MAN-suhn   'mænsən

Mansur
  pers. name, Persian   mahn-SŌŌR   mɑːn'suːr

Mantegna
  Andrea, *Italian painter*   mahn-TEN-yah   mɑn'tenjɑ

Mantinea
  ancient village, Greece   MANT-n-Ē-uh   ,mæntn̩'iːə

Mantle
  Mickey, *US baseball player*   MANT-l   'mæntl̩

Key (col. 2): a: fad ā: fade ah: father ar: Mary aw: law e: fed ē: feed er: merry i: hid ī: hide ō: coat ōō: boot
oi: boy ow: now u: put uh: above uhr: bird ch: chop ng: ring sh: show th: thick th̲: this zh: measure

Manto
  prophetic daughter of Tiresias   MAN-tō   'mæntoː
Mantoux
  TB test   mah^n-TOO, mahn-TOO   mãtuː, man'tuː
Mantova [Mantua]
  prov, Italy   MAHNT-uh-vuh   'mantəvə
Mantovani
  Annunzio, *US entertainer*   MAHNT-uh-VAHN-ē   ˌmantə'vaniˑ
Mantua
  1. prov, Italy   MAN-chuh-wuh, MANT-uh-wuh   'mæntʃəwə, 'mæntəwə
  2. city, Cuba   MAHN-twuh   'mantwə
Manuel
  1. pers. name   MAN-yuh(-wuh)l, MAN-yuh-WEL   'mænjə(wə)l, 'mænjəˌwel
  2. Portuguese   muhn-WEL, mahn-WEL   mən'wel, maːn'wel
  3. Spanish   mahn-WEL   man'wel
Manx
  Celtic lang. of Isle of Man   MANGKS   'mæŋks
Man [Yao]
  lang., people, SE Asia   MAHN   'man
Manzanillo
  port, Cuba   MAHN-zuh-NĒ-(y)ō   ˌmanzə'niː(j)oː
Manzanita
  N. American people; shrub   MAN-zuh-NĒT-uh   ˌmænzə'niːt̬ə
Maoism
  political philosophy of Mao Zedong   MOW-IZ-uhm   'mauˌizəm
Maoist
  follower of Maoism   MOW-uhst   'mauəst
Maoke Range
  mts., Indonesia   MOW-kā   'maukeː
Maori
  New Zealand people   MOWR-ē   'mauriˑ
Maotai
  town, China   MOW-TĪ   'mau'tai
Mao Tse Tung
  see Mao Zedong
Mao Zedong, Mao Tse Tung
  Chinese leader   MOWD-ZUH-DUNG   'maud'zə'duŋ
Mapplethorpe
  Robert, *US photographer*   MĀ-puhl-THAWRP   'meːpəlˌθɔːʳp
Mapuche [Araucanian]
  lang., S. America   muh-POO-chā   mə'puːtʃeː
Maputo
  river, prov, Mozambique   muh-POOT-ō   mə'puːtoː
Maquis
  French resistance group, WWII   mah-KĒ, ⓢ muh-KĒ, mah-KĒ   maːkiː, ⓢ mə'kiː, maˈkiː
Mara
  1. evil Hindu god   MAHR-uh   'marə
  2. pers. name   MAR-uh, MAHR-uh   'mærə, 'marə
Marabou
  bird   MAR-uh-BOO   'mærəˌbuː
Maracaibo
  lake, city, Venezuela   MAR-uh-KĪ-bō   ˌmærə'kaiboː
Marajó
  island, Amazon River   MAR-uh-ZHŌ   ˌmærə'ʒoː

Foreign Sounds: ue: *Fr.* **rue**, *Ger.* **füllen**   uh(r): *Fr.* **boeuf**, *Ger.* **Höhle**   kh: *Ger.* i**ch**, *Scot.* lo**ch**   ḡ: *Sp.* ami**g**o   v̄: *Sp.* ha**b**lar hl: *Welsh* **Ll**anelli.   CAPITALS: primary stress.   SMALL CAPS: secondary stress.   ⓢ: U.S. pron.   ⓛ: British pron.

Maraschino
preserved cherry   MAR-uh-SKĒ-nō, -SHĒ-nō   ˌmærə'skiːnoː, -'ʃiːnoː

Mărăseşti
commune, Romania   MUHR-uh-SHEST(-ē)   ˌmərə'ʃest(iˑ)

Marat
Jean Paul, French political leader   mah-RAH   maːraː

Maratha
people, India   muh-RAHT-uh   mə'raṭə

Marathi, Mahratti, Mahrati
Indic lang.   muh-RAHT-ē   mə'raṭiˑ

Marathon
plain & ancient town, Greece   MAR-uh-THAHN, MAR-uh-thuhn   'mærəˌθan, 'mærəθən

Marattia
plant   muh-RAT-ē-uh   mə'rætiːə

Marawi
municipality, Philippines   muh-RAH-wē   mə'rawiˑ

Marbella
port, Spain   mahr-BĀ(L)-yah   mar'beː(l)ja

Marburg
city, Germany   MAHR-BURK, $ MAHR-BURG, MAHR-BUHRG   'maʳˌbuʳk, $ 'maʳˌburg, 'maʳˌbəʳg

Marc
1. pers. name   MAHRK   'maʳk
2. French   MAHRK   maːrk

Marceau
Marcel, French mime   mahr-SŌ   maːrsoː

Marcel
1. pers. name   mahr-SEL   maʳ'sel
2. French   mahr-SEL   maːrsel

Marcellinus
pope   MAHR-suh-LĪ-nuhs   ˌmaʳsə'lainəs

Marcello
pers. name, Italian   mahr-CHEL-lō   mar'tʃelloː

Marcellus
1. pope; pers. name   mahr-SEL-uhs   maʳseləs
2. Dutch   mahr-SEL-ues   mar'selys

March
month   MAHRCH   'maʳtʃ

Marchand
Nancy, US actress   mahr-SHAND, mahr-SHAHND   maʳ'ʃænd, maʳ'ʃand

Marcha Real
national anthem, Spain   MAHR-chah rā-AHL   'martʃa reː'al

Marcia
pers. name   MAHR-shuh   'maʳʃə

Marcial
pers. name, Spanish   mahr-SYAHL, mahr-THYAHL   mar'sjal, mar'θjal

Marciano
Rocco "Rocky," US boxer   MAHR-sē-AN-ō, MAHR-shē-AN-ō, -AHN-ō   ˌmaʳsiː'ænoː, ˌmaʳʃiː'ænoː, -'anoː

Marcia Pontificale
national anthem, Vatican City   MAHR-chah PAWN-tē-fē-KAH-lā   'martʃa ˌpoːntiːfiː'kaːleː

Marcionism
Gnostic sect   MAHR-suh-NIZ-uhm   'maʳsəˌnizəm

Marcius
pers. name, Latin   MAHR-sh(ē-)uhs   'maʳʃ(iː)əs

Key (col. 2):   a: fad   ā: fade   ah: father   ar: Mary   aw: law   e: fed   ē: feed   er: merry   i: hid   ī: hide   ō: coat   o͞o: boot
oi: boy   ow: now   u: put   uh: above   uhr: bird   ch: chop   ng: ring   sh: show   th: thick   <u>th</u>: this   zh: measure

Marco
   1. pers. name   MAHR-kō   'maʳkoː
   2. French   mahr-KŌ   mɑːrkoː
   3. Italian, Spanish   MAHR-kō   'markoː

Marconi
   Guglielmo, *Italian physicist,*   mahr-KŌ-nē   maʳkoːniˑ
     inventor (Nobel 1909)

Marcos
   1. Philippine political family; pers.   MAHR-kōs   'maʳkoːs
     name, Spanish
   2. Portuguese   MAHR-kō͞osh   'mɑːrkuːʃ

Marcus
   1. pers. name   MAHR-kuhs   'maʳkəs
   2. Dutch   MAHR-kues   'markys
   3. German   MAHR-kus   'maʳkus
   4. Norwegian   MAHR-kus   'markus
   5. Swedish   MAHR-kuhs   'maːrkəs

Marcus Aurelius
   Roman emperor & philosopher   MAHR-kuhs aw-RĒL-yuhs,   'maʳkəs ɔː'riːljəs, ɔː'riːliːəs
                             aw-RĒ-lē-uhs

Marcuse
   Herbert, *US political philosopher*   mahr-KŌ͞O-zuh   maʳ'kuːzə

Marcy
   pers. name   MAHR-sē   'maʳsiˑ

Mardi Gras
   New Orleans festival   MAHRD-ē GRAH, GRAW   'maʳdiˑ ˌgrɑ, ˌgrɔː

Mardonius
   Persian general   mahr-DŌ-nē-uhs   maʳ'doːniːəs

Marduk
   supreme Babylonian god   MAHR-DŌ͞OK   'maʳˌduːk

Mare Australe
   'sea' on Moon   MAHR-ā aw-STRĀ-lē, ahs-TRĀ-   ˌmareː ɔː'streːliˑ, ɑs'treː-

Mare Crisium
   'sea' on Moon   MAHR-ā KRIS-ē-uhm, KRĒ-sē-uhm,   'mareː 'krisiːəm, 'kriːsiːəm,
                     KRISH-(ē-)uhm   'kriʃ(iː)əm

Maredudd, -dydd
   pers. name, Welsh   me-RED-i<u>th</u>   me'redið

Mare Fecunditatis
   'sea' on Moon   MAHR-ā fuh-KUHN-duh-TAHT-uhs   'mareː fəˌkəndə'taʈəs

Mare Frigoris
   'sea' on Moon   MAHR-ā fri-GŌR-uhs, -GAWR-uhs   'mareː fri'goːrəs, -'goːrəs

Mare Humboldtianum
   'sea' on Moon   MAHR-ā HUHM-BŌL-tē-Ā-nuhm   'mareː ˌhəmˌboːltiː'eːnəm

Mare Humorum
   'sea' on Moon   MAHR-ā (H)YŌ͞O-MŌR-uhm,   'mareː ˌ(h)juː'moːrəm,
                     -MAWR-uhm   -'moːrəm

Mare Imbrium
   'sea' on Moon   MAHR-ā IM-brē-uhm   'mareː 'imbriːəm

Mare Ingenii
   'sea' on Moon   MAHR-ā in-JEN-ē-Ē, -ē-Ī   'mareː in'dʒeniːˌiː, -iːˌai

Mare Marginis
   'sea' on Moon   MAHR-ā mahr-JĪ-nuhs   'mareː maʳ'dʒainəs

Maremma
   Italian sheepdog   muh-REM-uh   mə'remə

Mare Moscoviense
  'sea' on Moon   MAHR-ā MAHS-kōv-YEN-sē   ˈmareː ˌmaskoːvˈjensiˑ

Mare Nectaris
  'sea' on moon   MAHR-ā NEK-tuh-ruhs   ˈmareː ˈnektərəs

Marengo
  1. county, AL; chicken dish   muh-RENG-gō   məˈrengoː
  2. village, Italy   mah-RENG-gō   maˈrengoː

Mare Nubium
  'sea' on Moon   MAHR-ā N(Y)O͞O-bē-uhm   ˈmareː ˈn(j)uːbiːəm

Mare Orientale
  'sea' on Moon   MAHR-ā AWR-ē-uhn-TĀ-lē   ˈmareː ˌɔːriːənˈteːliˑ

Mare Serenitatis
  'sea' on Moon   MAHR-ā suh-REN-uh-TAHT-uhs ˈmareː səˌrenəˈtatəs

Mare Smythii
  'sea' on Moon   MAHR-ā SMITH-ē-Ē   ˈmareː ˈsmiθiːˌiː

Mare Tranquillitatis
  'sea' on Moon   MAHR-ā TRAN-kwil-uh-TAHT-uhs ˈmareː ˌtrænkwiləˈtatəs

Mare Undarum
  'sea' on Moon   MAHR-ā UHN-DAHR-uhm   ˈmareː ˌənˈdarəm

Mare Vaporum
  'sea' on Moon   MAHR-ā vā-PŌR-uhm, -PAWR-uhm ˈmareː veːˈpoːrəm, -ˈpoːrəm

Marfeh
  Mideast Christian festival   MAHR-fe   ˈmaʳfe

Margaret
  pers. name   MAHR-g(uh-)ruht   ˈmaʳg(ə)rət

Margareta
  pers. name, Swedish   MAHR-gah-RĀ-tah   ˌmaːrgaːˈreːtaː

Margarete
  pers. name, German   MAHR-guh-RĀ-tuh   ˌmaʳgəˈreːtə

Margaretha
  pers. name, Dutch   MAHR-gah-RĀ-tah   ˌmargaˈreːta

Margaretta
  pers. name   MAHR-guh-RET-uh   ˌmaʳgəˈreṭə

Margarita
  cocktail; pers. name   MAHR-guh-RĒT-uh   ˌmaʳgəˈriːṭə

Margaux
  French wine; pers. name   mahr-GŌ   maːrgoː

Marge
  pers. name   MAHRJ   ˈmaʳdʒ

Margery
  pers. name   MAHR-juh-rē, MAHRJ-rē   ˈmaʳdʒəriˑ, ˈmaʳdʒriˑ

Margherita
  pers. name, Italian   MAHR-gā-RĒ-tah   ˌmargeːˈriːta

Margi
  lang., sub-Saharan Africa MAHR-gē   ˈmaʳgiˑ

Margie
  pers. name   MAHR-jē, MAHR-gē   ˈmaʳdʒiˑ, ˈmaʳgiˑ

Marginis, Mare
  see Mare Marginis

Margo
  pers. name   MAHR-gō   ˈmaʳgoː

Margot
  1. pers. name   MAHR-gō, MAHR-guht   ˈmaʳgoː, ˈmaʳgət
  2. French   mahr-GŌ   margoː

Key (col. 2): a: fad ā: fade ah: father ar: Mary aw: law e: fed ē: feed er: merry i: hid ī: hide ō: coat o͞o: boot
oi: boy ow: now u: put uh: above uhr: bird ch: chop ng: ring sh: show th: thick t͟h: this zh: measure

Marguerite
  1. pers. name   MAHR-guh-RĒT   ˌmɑˡgəˈriːt
  2. French   mahr-guh-RĒT   mɑːrgəriːt

Mari
  lang., people, Russia [Cheremis];   MAHR-ē   ˈmɑriˑ
    ancient Mesopotamian city

Maria
  1. pers. name   muh-RĒ-uh, muh-RĪ-uh   məˈriːə, məˈraiə
  2. Dutch, Finnish   mah-RĒ-ah   mɑːˈriːɑː
  3. German, Italian   mah-RĒ-ah   mɑˈriːɑ
  4. Polish   MAHR-yah   ˈmɑːrjɑː
  5. Portuguese   muh-RĒ-uh, mah-RĒ-ah   məˈriːə, mɑːˈriːɑː
  6. Russian   MUHR-YĒ-(y)uh   ˌmərˈjiː(j)ə
  7. Swedish   mah-RĒ-ah   mɑːˈriːɑː

María
  pers. name, Spanish   mah-RĒ-ah   mɑˈriːɑ

Mariah
  pers. name   muh-RĪ-uh   məˈraiə

Marian
  pers. name   MER-ē-uhn, MAR-ē-uhn   ˈmeriːən, ˈmæriːən

Mariana
  Trench, *Pacific; pers. name*   MAR-ē-AN-uh, MER-ē-AN-uh,   ˌmæriːˈænə, ˌmeriːˈænə,
     MAHR-ē-AHN-uh   ˌmɑriːˈɑnə

Marianas
  islands, Pacific   MAR-ē-AN-uhz, MER-ē-AN-uhz,   ˌmæriːˈænəz, ˌmeriːˈænəz,
     MAHR-ē-AHN-uhz   ˌmɑriːˈɑnəz

Marianism
  Christian veneration of Mary   MER-ē-uh-NIZ-uhm, MAR-ē-, MĀ-rē-   ˈmeriːəˌnizəm, ˈmæriː-,
          ˈmeːriː-

Marianna
  pers. name, Portuguese   muh-rē-AH-nuh, mah-rē-AH-nah   məriːˈɑːnə, mɑːriːˈɑːnɑː

Marianne
  1. pers. name   MER-ē-AN, MAR-   ˌmeriːˈæn, ˌmær-
  2. German   MAHR-ē-AHN-uh, mahr-YAHN-uh   ˌmɑriːˈɑnə, mɑˡjɑnə

Mariano
  pers. name, Italian, Spanish   mahr-YAHN-ō   mɑrˈjɑnoː

Maricopa
  county, mtn. range, AZ; N.   MAR-uh-KŌ-puh   ˌmærəˈkoːpə
    American people

Marie
  1. pers. name   muh-RĒ, Ⓔ *also* MAHR-ē, MAR-ē   məˈriː, Ⓔ *also* ˈmɑriˑ, ˈmæriˑ
  2. Danish, German   mah-RĒ(-uh)   mɑˈriː(ə)
  3. Dutch, Swedish   mah-RĒ   mɑːˈriː
  4. French   mah-RĒ   mɑːriː
  5. Norwegian   mah-RĒ-uh   mɑˈriːə

Marie Antoinette
  queen of France, wife of Louis   mah-RĒ ahⁿ-twah-NET, Ⓢ muh-RĒ   mɑːriː ɑ̃twɑːnet, Ⓢ məˌriː
    XVI   AN-twuh-NET, AN-tuh-NET   æntwəˈnet, ˌæntəˈnet

Mariel
  pers. name (M. Hemingway)   MAR-ē-uhl, MER-ē-uhl   ˈmæriːəl, ˈmeriːəl

Maries
  county, MO   MAR-ēz   ˈmæriˑz

Marietta
  1. pers. name   MER-ē-ET-uh, MAR-   ˌmeriːˈetə, ˌmær-
  2. Italian   MAHR-ē-ĀT-tah   ˌmɑriːˈeːtta

Mariette
   pers. name   MAR-ē-ET, MER-ē-ET, MAR-ē-ET,   ˌmæriː'et, ˌmeriː'et,
                                  MER-ē-ET   'mæriːˌet, 'meriːˌet

Marilu
   pers. name (M. Henner)   MAR-ē-LOO, MER-ē-LOO   ˌmæriː'luː, ˌmeriː'luː

Marilyn
   pers. name   MAR-uh-luhn, MER-uh-luhn   'mærələn, 'merələn

Marimba
   musical instrument   muh-RIM-buh   mə'rimbə

Marin
   1. county, CA   muh-RIN   mə'rin
   2. pers. name, Serbo-Croatian   MAHR-in   'maːrin

Marín
   commune, Spain   muh-RẼN   mə'riːn

Marinelli
   Field, *ballpark, Rockford, IL*   MAR-uh-NEL-ē   ˌmærə'neliː

Marinette
   county, WI   MAR-uh-NET, MER-   ˌmærə'net, ˌmer-

Marino
   pers. name, Italian   mah-RẼ-nō   ma'riːnoː

Marinus
   pope   muh-RĪ-nuhs   mə'rɑinəs

Mario
   1. pers. name   MER-ē-ō, MAR-   'meriːoː, 'mær-
   2. French   mahr-YŌ   maːrjoː
   3. Italian, Spanish   MAHR-yō   'marjoː

Mário
   pers. name, Portuguese   MAHR-yoo   'maːrjuː

Mariolatry
   veneration of the Virgin Mary   MER-ē-AHL-uh-trē, MAR-ē-, MÃ-rē-   ˌmeriː'alətriː, ˌmæriː-,
                                                                       ˌmeːriː-

Mariology
   doctrine relating to the Virgin   MER-ē-AHL-uh-jē, MAR-ē-, MÃ-rē-   ˌmeriː'alədʒiː, ˌmæriː-,
     Mary   ˌmeːriː-

Marion
   pl. name, US; pers. name   MER-ē-uhn, MAR-   'meriːən, 'mær-

Mariposa
   county, CA   MAR-uh-PŌ-suh, -PŌ-zuh   ˌmærə'poːsə, -'poːzə

Marist
   Roman Catholic religious order   MAR-uhst, MER-uhst   'mærəst, 'merəst

Maritain
   Jacques, *French diplomat*   mah-rē-TE[n]   maːriːtẽ

Maritime Alps
   Alpine mtn. range   MAR-uh-TĪM   'mærəˌtaim

Marius
   1. Gaius, Roman general; pers.   MER-ē-uhs, MAR-   'meriːəs, 'mær-
    name
   2. Dutch   MAH-rē-ues   'maːriːys
   3. French   mahr-YUES   maːrjyːs
   4. German   MAHR-yus, MAH-rē-us   'maʳjus, 'mariːus
   5. Norwegian   MAH-rē-us   'mariːus

Mariveles
   municipality, Philippines   MAHR-uh-VÃ-luhs   ˌmaʳə'veːləs

Mariya
   pers. name, Russian   MUHR-YẼ-(y)uh   ˌmər'jiː(j)ə

Key (col. 2):   a: fad   ā: fade   ah: father   ar: Mary   aw: law   e: fed   ē: feed   er: merry   i: hid   ī: hide   ō: coat   oo: boot
oi: boy   ow: now   u: put   uh: above   uhr: bird   ch: chop   ng: ring   sh: show   th: thick   <u>th</u>: this   zh: measure

Marjoribanks
  British family name   MAHRCH-BANGKS   'mɑ^rtʃ,bæŋks

Marjorie, Marjory
  pers. name   MAHR-juh-rē, MAHRJ-rē   'mɑ^rdʒəri', 'mɑ^rdʒri'

Mark
  1. New Testament book; pers.   MAHRK   'mɑ^rk
  name
  2. Dutch   MAHRK   'mɑrk
  3. Russian   MAHRK   'mɑːrk

Markos
  pers. name, Mod. Greek   MAHR-kaws   'mɑrkɔːs

Markova
  1. Alicia, English ballet dancer   mahr-KŌ-vuh   mɑ^rkoːvə
  2. Olga, Russian marathoner   MAHR-kuh-vuh   'mɑː^rkəvə

Markov process
  statistical procedure   MAHR-KAWF PRAHS-ES, PRŌ-SES   'mɑ^r,kɔːf ,prɑs,es, ,proː,ses

Markowitz
  Harry M., US economist (Nobel   MAHRK-uh-WITS   'mɑ^rkə,wits
  1990)

Marlboro, Marlborough
  pers. name; pl. name   MAHRL-BUHR-uh, MAHRL-BUH-ruh,   'mɑ^rl,bər-ə, 'mɑ^rl,bə-rə,
                                         MAHRL-bruh   'mɑ^rlbrə

Marlene
  1. pers. name   mahr-LĒN   mɑ^rliːn
  2. German   mahr-LĀ-nuh   mɑ^rleːnə

Marlin
  pers. name   MAHR-luhn   'mɑ^rlən

Marlon
  pers. name   MAHR-luhn   'mɑ^rlən

Marlow, Marlowe
  pers. name   MAHR-LŌ   'mɑ^r,loː

Marmaduke
  pers. name   MAHR-muh-D(Y)O͞OK   'mɑ^rmə,d(j)uːk

Marmara
  Sea of, Turkey   MAHR-muh-ruh   'mɑ^rmərə

Marmara Denizi
  sea, Turkey   MAHR-muh-RAH DEN-i-ZĒ   'mɑrmə,ra ,deni'ziː

Marmax
  suitor of Hippodamia   MAHR-MAKS   'mɑ^r,mæks

Marmoset
  monkey   MAHR-muh-SET, MAHR-muh-ZET   'mɑ^rmə,set, 'mɑ^rmə,zet

Marmot
  rodent   MAHR-muht   'mɑ^rmət

Marne
  river, France   MAHRN   mɑːrn

Marnie
  pers. name   MAHR-nē   'mɑ^rni'

Maronism
  Uniat sect   MAR-uh-NIZ-uhm, MER-   'mærə,nizəm, 'mer-

Maronite
  religion   MAR-uh-NĪT   'mærə,nait

Marpessa
  beloved of Idas and Apollo   mahr-PES-uh   mɑ^rpesə

Marques
  pers. name, Portuguese   MAHR-kēsh, -kēs   'mɑːrkiːʃ, -kiːs

---

Foreign Sounds: ue: *Fr.* **rue**, *Ger.* füllen uh(r): *Fr.* **boeuf**, *Ger.* Höhle   kh: *Ger.* **ich**, *Scot.* loch ğ: *Sp.* amigo v̲: *Sp.* hablar
hl: *Welsh* Llanelli.   CAPITALS: primary stress.   SMALL CAPS: secondary stress.   Ⓢ: U.S. pron.   Ⓛ: British pron.

Marquesan
  lang., Oceania   mahr-KĀ-zuhn, mahr-KĀ-suhn   mɑrˈkeːzən, mɑrˈkeːsən

Marquesas
  islands, Pacific   mahr-KĀ-zuhz, -zuhs, -suhz, -suhs   mɑrˈkeːzəz, -zəs, -səz, -səs

Marquette
  1. county, MI, WI; univ., WI; city,   mahr-KET   mɑrˈket
    MI
  2. Jacques, French explorer   mahr-KET   mɑːrket

Márquez
  pers. name, Spanish; see also   MAHR-kās, MAHR-kāth   ˈmɑrkeːs, ˈmɑrkeːθ
    García Márquez

Marquis
  1. title   MAHR-kwuhs, mahr-KĒ   ˈmɑrkwəs, mɑrˈkiː
  2. French title   mahr-KĒ   mɑːrkiː

Marquises, Îles [Marquesas]
  islands, Pacific   ēl mahr-KĒZ   iːl mɑːrkiːz

Marquita
  pers. name   mahr-KĒT-uh   mɑrˈkiːtə

Marrakech, -kesh
  city, Morocco   MAR-uh-KESH, MAR-uh-KESH,   ˈmærə‚keʃ, ‚mærəˈkeʃ,
                       muh-RAHK-ish   məˈrɑkiʃ

Marriott
  US food service and hotel co.   MAR-ē-uht, MAR-ē-AHT, MER-   ˈmæriːət, ˈmæriːˌɑt, ˈmer-

Marron
  chestnut   ma-RŌ^n mæˈrõː

Mars
  Roman god of war; planet   MAHRZ   ˈmɑrz

Marsala
  seaport, Sicily; wine   mahr-SAHL-uh   mɑrˈsɑlə

Marsalis
  Wynton and Branford, *US*   mahr-SAL-uhs   mɑrˈsæləs
    musicians

Marseillaise, La
  see La Marseillaise

Marseille [Massilia]
  city, France   mahr-SE   mɑːrsej

Marseilles
  1. English form of Marseille   mahr-SĀ, mahr-SĀLZ   mɑrˈseː, mɑrˈseːlz
  2. city, IL   mahr-SĀLZ   mɑrˈseːlz

Marshall
  George C., US army officer,   MAHR-shuhl   ˈmɑrʃəl
    statesman (Nobel 1953); John,
    US chief justice; Thurgood, *US*
    jurist; Pacific islands; pers.
    name

Marshallese
  lang., Marshall Islands   MAHR-shuh-LĒZ, -LĒS   ‚mɑrʃəˈliːz, -ˈliːs

Marsupialia
  pouched animals   mahr-SOO-pē-Ā-lē-uh   mɑr‚suːpiːˈeːliːə

Marsyas
  mythical inventor of the double   MAHR-sē-uhs   ˈmɑrsiːəs
    flute

Martaban
  town, Burma   MAHRT-uh-BAHN, MAHRT-uh-BAN   ‚mɑrṭəˈban, ‚mɑrṭəˈbæn

---

Key (col. 2):   a: fad   ā: fade   ah: father   ar: Mary   aw: law   e: fed   ē: feed   er: merry   i: hid   ī: hide   ō: coat   oo: boot
oi: boy   ow: now   u: put   uh: above   uhr: bird   ch: chop   ng: ring   sh: show   th: thick   <u>th</u>: this   zh: measure

Martell
  cognac brand   mahr-TEL   mɑ^r'tel
Martha
  pers. name   MAHR-thuh   'mɑ^{r}θə
Marti
  pers. name   MAHRT-ē   'mɑ^{r}ṭiˑ
Martial
  Roman poet   MAHR-shuhl   'mɑ^{r}ʃəl
Martian
  pert. to Mars*; alien*   MAHR-shuhn   'mɑ^{r}ʃən
Martim
  pers. name, Portuguese   muhr-TI^n, mahr-TI^n mər'tĩː, mɑːr'tĩː
Martin
  1. A. J. P., English biochemist   MAHRT-n   'mɑ^{r}tn̩
    (Nobel 1952); pers. name
  2. Danish, Norwegian   MAHR-tēn   'mɑrtiːn
  3. Dutch   MAHR-tuhn, mahr-TĪN   'mɑrtən, mɑr'tɑin
  4. Finnish, Swedish   MAHR-tin   'mɑːrtin
  5. French   mahr-TE^n mɑːrtẽ
  6. German   MAHR-tēn   'mɑ^{r}tiːn
Martín
  pers. name, Spanish   mahr-TĒN   mɑr'tiːn
Martina
  pers. name   mahr-TĒ-nuh   mɑ^r'tiːnə
Martin du Gard
  Roger, *French author (Nobel*   mahr-TE^n due GAHR   mɑːrtẽ dyː gɑːr
    1937)
Martine
  pers. name, French   mahr-TĒN   mɑːrtiːn
Martinez
  city, CA   mahr-TĒ-nuhs, -nuhz   mɑ^r'tiːnəs, -nəz
Martínez
  pers. name, Spanish   mahr-TĒ-nās, -nāth   mɑr'tiːneːs, -neːθ
Martini
  Louis M., *winery, CA; alcoholic*   mahr-TĒ-nē   mɑ^r'tiːniˑ
    drink
Martiniquais
  pert. to Martinique   MAHR-TĒ-ni-KE   ˌmɑ^{r}ˌtiːni'ke
Martiniquaise
  fem. of Martiniquais   MAHR-TĒ-ni-KEZ   ˌmɑ^{r}ˌtiːni'kez
Martinique
  island, West Indies   MAHRT-n-ĒK   ˌmɑ^{r}tn̩'iːk
Martinmas
  November 11 festival for St.   MAHRT-n-muhs   'mɑ^{r}tn̩məs
    Martin
Martins
  pers. name, Portuguese   muhr-TI^{n}S, mahr-TI^{n}S   mər'tĩːs, mɑːr'tĩːs
Martinson
  Harry, *Swedish author (Nobel*   MAHR-tēn-sawn   'mɑ^{r}tiːnsɔːn
    1974)
Martinus
  1. pers. name   mahr-TĪ-nuhs   mɑ^r'tɑinəs
  2. Dutch   mahr-TĒ-nues   mɑr'tiːnys
Marty
  pers. name   MAHRT-ē   'mɑ^{r}ṭiˑ

Foreign Sounds: ue: *Fr.* **rue**, *Ger.* f**ü**llen   uh(r): *Fr.* b**oeu**f, *Ger.* H**öh**le   <u>kh</u>: *Ger.* i**ch**, *Scot.* lo**ch**   g̃: *Sp.* ami**g**o   v̲: *Sp.* ha**b**lar
hl: *Welsh* **Ll**anelli.   CAPITALS: primary stress.   SMALL CAPS: secondary stress.   Ⓢ: U.S. pron.   Ⓑ: British pron.

Marvel
  tdmk for comic books   MAHR-vuhl   'maʳvəl
Marvell
  Andrew, *English poet*   MAHR-vuhl   'maʳvəl
Marvin
  pers. name   MAHR-vuhn   'maʳvən
Marwari [Rajasthani]
  lang., India, Pakistan   mahr-WAHR-ē   maʳ'wari·
Marx
  Karl, *German political and*   MAHRKS   'maʳks
    economic theorist; Groucho,
    Harpo, Chico, Zeppo, *US*
    comedians
Marxism
  philosophy of Karl Marx   MAHRK-SIZ-uhm   'maʳk,sizəm
Marxist
  pert. to Marx   MAHRK-suhst, MAHRK-sist   'maʳksəst, 'maʳksist
Mary
  pers. name   MER-ē, MAR-ē, MĀ-rē   'meri·, 'mæri·, 'meːri·
Maryland
  state, US   MER-uh-luhnd   'merələnd
Marylebone
  1. district, London   MAR-uh-luh-buhn, MAR-uh-luh-BŌN,   'mærələbən, 'mærələ,boːn,
          MAR-uh-buhn, MAHR-luh-buhn   'mærəbən, 'maʳləbən
  2. St., parish church, London   MAR-uh-luh-buhn   'mærələbən
Marylhurst
  College for Lifelong Learning   MAR-uhl-HUHRST, MER-uhl-   'mærəl,həʳst, 'merəl-
Marymount Palos Verdes
  College, *CA*   MAR-ē-MOWNT PAL-uhs VUHRD-ēz,   'mæri·,maunt ˌpæləs
          MER-ē-, MĀ-rē-   'vəʳdiːz, 'meri·-, 'meːri·-
Masa
  lang., Chad, Cameroon   MAHS-uh   'masə
Masada
  mountaintop fortress in Israel   muh-SAHD-uh   mə'sadə
Masai, Maasai
  lang., people, Tanzania, Kenya   muh-SĪ   mə'sai
Masaryk
  Tomáš, *president, Czechoslovakia*   MAH-sah-rik   'maːsaːrik
Masa's
  restaurant, San Francisco, CA   MAHS-uhz, MAS-uhz   'masəz, 'mæsəz
Masayoshi
  pers. name, Japanese   mah-sah-yō-shē   masajoːʃiː
Masbate
  island, prov, Philippines   mahs-BAHT-ē   mas'baʈi·
Mascagni
  Pietro, *Italian composer*   mahs-KAHN-yē   mas'kanji·
Mas Canosa
  Jorge, *Cuban activist*   mahs kah-NŌ-sah   mas ka'noːsa
Mascara
  dept, Algeria   MAS-kuh-ruh   'mæskərə
Mascerene
  islands, Indian Ocean   MAS-kuh-RĒN   ˌmæskə'riːn
Masefield
  John, *English poet*   MĀS-FĒLD, MĀZ-FĒLD   'meːs,fiːld, 'meːz,fiːld

---

Key (col. 2):   a: fad   ā: fade   ah: father   ar: Mary   aw: law   e: fed   ē: feed   er: merry   i: hid   ī: hide   ō: coat   oo̅: boot
oi: boy   ow: now   u: put   uh: above   uhr: bird   ch: chop   ng: ring   sh: show   th: thick   th̲: this   zh: measure

Maserati
  Italian car marque   MAHZ-uh-RAHT-ē, MAZ-uh-RAT-ē   ˌmɑzə'rɑţiˑ, ˌmæzə'ræţiˑ

Maseru
  town, Lesotho   MAHZ-uh-R$\overline{OO}$ 'mɑzəˌruː

Mashantucket Pequot
  N. American people   MASH-uhn-TUHK-uht PĒ-KWAHT   ˌmæʃən'təkət 'piːˌkwɑt

Masharbrum, Masherbrum
  peak, Himalayas   MUHSH-uhr-BRUM   'məʃəʳˌbrum

Mashhad
  city, Iran   muh-SHAD   mə'ʃæd

Masinissa
  king of Numidia   MAS-uh-NIS-uh   ˌmæsə'nisə

Maso
  pers. name, Italian   MAHZ-ō   'mɑzoː

Mason
  pers. name   MĀS-n   'meːsṇ

Mason-Dixon line
  boundary between PA and MD   MĀS-n-DIK-suhn LĪN   ˌmeːsṇ'diksən ˌlain

Masonic
  pert. to the Freemasons   muh-SAHN-ik   mə'sɑnik

Masonite
  tdmk for a hardboard   MĀS-n-ĪT   'meːsṇˌait

Masora, Masorah
  critical notes on Hebrew Old   muh-SŌR-uh, muh-SAWR-uh   mə'soːrə, mə'sɔːrə
  Testament

Masorete, Massorete
  one versed in the Masora   MAS-uh-RĒT   'mæsəˌriːt

Masotho
  plural of Basotho   mah-SŌT-ō, mah-S$\overline{OO}$T-$\overline{oo}$ mə'soːţoː, mə'suːţuː

Masqat
  city, Oman   MUHS-KAHT   'məsˌkɑt

Mass
  Christian liturgy   MAS   'mæs

Massac
  county, IL   MAS-AK, MAS-uhk   'mæsˌæk, 'mæsək

Massachuset [Massachusetts]
  N. American people   MAS-uh-CH$\overline{OO}$-suht, -zuht, *esp. in SE*   ˌmæsə'tʃuːsət, -zət, *esp. in*
      US -TY$\overline{OO}$-   *SE US* -'tjuː-

Massachusetts
  state, US; N. American people   MAS-uh-CH$\overline{OO}$-suhts,   ˌmæsə'tʃuːsəts,
      MAS-uh-CH$\overline{OO}$-zuhts, *esp. in SE*   ˌmæsə'tʃuːzəts, *esp. in SE*
      US MAS-uh-TY$\overline{OO}$-suhts   *US* ˌmæsə'tjuːsəts

Massapequa
  town, NY   MAS-uh-PĒ-kwuh   ˌmæsə'piːkwə

Massasoit
  Community College, *lake, MA; N.*   MAS-uh-SOI-it, MAS-uh-SOIT,   ˌmæsə'sɔi-it, 'mæsəˌsɔit,
    American people   MAS-uh-SOIT   ˌmæsə'sɔit

Massenet
  Jules, *French composer*   mah-SNE, Ⓢ MAS-n-Ā, mas-NĀ   mɑːsne, Ⓢ ˌmæsṇ'eː,
          mæs'neː

Massif Central
  ancient rocks, France   mah-SĒF sahⁿ-TRAHL   mɑːsiːf sãtrɑːl

Massilia
  ancient name of Marseilles   muh-SIL-ē-uh   mə'siliːə

Foreign Sounds: ue: *Fr.* **rue**, *Ger.* f**ü**llen   uh(r): *Fr.* b**oeuf**, *Ger.* H**öh**le   kh: *Ger.* i**ch**, *Scot.* lo**ch**   ḡ: *Sp.* ami**g**o   ṿ: *Sp.* ha**b**lar
hl: *Welsh* **Ll**anelli.   CAPITALS: primary stress.   SMALL CAPS: secondary stress.   Ⓢ: U.S. pron.   Ⓛ: British pron.

Massillon
   town, OH   MAS-uh-luhn, MAS-uh-LAHN   'mæsələn, 'mæsə,lɑn

Massine
   Léonide, *Russian ballet dancer/*   MUHS-YĒN   ˌməs'jiːn
     choreographer

Masson, Paul
   winery, CA   PAWL muh-SAHN, ma-SAHN   ˌpɔːl mə'sɑn, mæ'sɑn

Massorete
   see Masorete

Mastaba
   Egyptian tomb   MAS-tuh-buh   'mæstəbə

MasterCard
   tdmk for a bank credit card   MAS-tuhr-KAHRD, MAH-stuh-KAHD   'mæstəʳˌkaʳd, 'mɑːstəˌkɑːd

Mastrantonio
   Mary Elizabeth, *US actress*   MAHS-trahn-TŌ-nē-ō, -TŌN-yō   ˌmɑstran'toːniːˌoː, -'toːnjoː

Mastroianni
   Marcello, *Italian actor*   MAHS-troi-AHN-ē   ˌmɑstrɔi'aniˑ

Masur
   Kurt, *German conductor*   MAHZ-UR, mah-ZUR   'mɑzˌuʳ, mɑ'zuʳ

Matabele
   Bantu people, lang.   MAT-uh-BĀ-lä, MAT-uh-BĒ-lē   ˌmætə'beːleː, ˌmætə'biːliˑ

Mataco
   S. American people   muh-TAHK-ō   mə'takoː

Matagalpa
   dept, Nicaragua   maht-ah-ḠAHL-pah,   mata'ɣalpa, ⑤ ˌmætə'gælpə
                 ⑤ MAT-uh-GAL-puh

Matagorda
   county, TX   MAT-uh-GAWRD-uh   ˌmætə'gɔːʳdə

Mata Hari
   cognomen of Margaretha Zelle   MAHT-uh HAHR-ē, MAT-uh HAR-ē   ˌmɑtə 'hariˑ, ˌmætə 'hæriˑ
     MacLeod, Dutch dancer & spy

Matamoros
   town, Mexico   MAT-uh-MŌR-uhs,   ˌmætə'moːrəs, ˌmætə'mɔːrəs
               MAT-uh-MAWR-uhs

Matane
   county, Quebec   muh-TAN   mə'tæn

Matanuska-Susitna
   division, AK   MAT-uh-NOO-skuh-su-SIT-nuh   ˌmætə'nuːskəsu'sitnə

Matanzas
   prov, Cuba   muh-TAN-zuhs   mə'tænzəs

Matapan
   cape, Greece   MAT-uh-PAN   'mætəˌpæn

Matawan
   borough, NJ   MAT-uh-WAHN   'mætəˌwɑn

Maté
   plant   MAH-TĀ   'mɑˌteː

Matecumbe, Upper
   key, FL   MAT-uh-KUHM-bē   ˌmætə'kəmbiˑ

Mateo
   pers. name, Spanish   mah-TĀ-ō   mɑ'teːoː

Mater Dei
   College, NY   MAHT-uhr DĀ-ē   'mɑtəʳ 'deːiː

Mathäus
   pers. name, German   mah-TE-us   mɑ'teus

Key (col. 2):   a: fad   ä: fade   ah: father   ar: **Mary**   aw: **law**   e: fed   ē: feed   er: **merry**   i: hid   ī: hide   ō: coat   ōō: boot
oi: **boy**   ow: **now**   u: put   uh: **above**   uhr: **bird**   ch: **chop**   ng: **ring**   sh: **show**   th: **thick**   <u>th</u>: **this**   zh: measure

Mather
  Richard, Increase, Cotton, *US*   MA<u>TH</u>-uhr   'mæðəˈ
    clergymen; pers. name
Matheson
  Scott M., *US lawyer, politician*   MATH-uh-suhn   'mæθəsən
Mathew
  pers. name   MATH-yo͞o   'mæθjuː
Mathias
  1. pers. name   muh-THĪ-uhs   mə'θaiəs
  2. German, Norwegian   mah-TĒ-ahs   ma'tiːas
  3. Portuguese   muh-TĒ-uhsh, mah-TĒ-ahs   mə'tiːəʃ, maːˈtiːaːs
  4. French   mah-TYAHS   maːtjaːs
Mathieu
  pers. name, French   mah-TYUH(R)   maːtjœː
Mathilde
  1. pers. name, French   mah-TĒLD   maːtiːld
  2. German   mah-TIL-duh   ma'tildə
  3. Russian   muh-TIL-duh   mə'țildə
Mathis
  Johnny, *US singer*   MATH-uhs   'mæθəs
Matilda
  1. pers. name   muh-TIL-duh   mə'tildə
  2. Italian   mah-TĒL-dah   ma'tiːlda
Matilde
  pers. name, French   mah-TĒLD   maːtiːld
Matisse
  Henri, *French artist*   mah-TĒS   maːtiːs
Mato Grosso
  plateau, state, Brazil   MAT-uh GRŌ-sō   ˌmæțə 'groːsoː
Matosinhos, -zinhos
  parish, Portugal   MAHT-uh-ZĒN-yo͞osh   ˌmaːțə'ziːnjuːʃ
Matreyevna
  patronym, Russian   MUH-TRĀ-yev-nuh   ˌmə'treːjevnə
Matrūh
  city, Egypt   muh-TRO͞O, MA-tro͞o   mə'truː, 'mætruː
Ma-tsu
  island, China   MAHT-SO͞O   'mat'suː
Matsuo [Basho]
  Munefusa, *Japanese poet*   maht-so͞o-ō   matsuːoː
Matsuoka
  Yōsuke, *Japanese statesman*   maht-su-ō-kah   matsuoːka
Matsushima
  Satoshi, *US astronomer, educator*   mat-SO͞O-shim-uh,   mæt'suːʃimə, ˌmætsuːˈʃiːmə
                             MAT-so͞o-SHĒ-muh
Matsushita
  Japanese corp.   maht-su-shi-tah,   matsuʃita, Ⓢ ˌmætsuːˈʃiːțə
               Ⓢ MAT-so͞o-SHĒT-uh
Matswana
  plural of Tswana or Batswana   maht-SWAHN-uh   mat'swɑnə
Matt
  pers. name   MAT   'mæt
Mattapony
  N. American people   MAT-uh-PŌ-nē, MAT-uh-PŌ-nē   'mæțəˌpoːniˈ, ˌmæțə'poːniˈ
Mattatuck
  Community College, *CT*   MAT-uh-TUHK   'mæțəˌtək

Foreign Sounds: ue: *Fr.* **rue**, *Ger.* **füllen**   uh(r): *Fr.* **boeuf**, *Ger.* **Höhle**   <u>kh</u>: *Ger.* **ich**, *Scot.* **loch**   g̃: *Sp.* **amigo**   <u>v</u>: *Sp.* **hablar**
hl: *Welsh* **Llanelli**.   CAPITALS: primary stress.   SMALL CAPS: secondary stress.   Ⓢ: U.S. pron.   Ⓔ: British pron.

Mattel
  US toy co.   muh-TEL   mə'tel
Matteo
  pers. name, Italian   maht-TE-ō   mɑt'teoː
Matterhorn
  mtn., Switzerland, Italy   MAT-uhr-HAWRN, MAHT-   'mætəʳˌhɔːʳn, 'mɑt̮-
Matterhorn Peak
  mtn., CO   MAT-uhr-HAWRN PĒK   ˌmætəʳˌhɔːʳn 'piːk
Matthau
  Walter, US actor   MATH-ow   'mæθˌɑu
Matthäus
  pers. name, Dutch, German   mah-TE-us   mɑ'teus
Matthew
  New Testament book; pers. name   MATH-yoo̅   'mæθjuː
Matthias
  1. pers. name   muh-THĪ-uhs   mə'θɑiəs
  2. Finnish   mah-TĒ-ahs   mɑ'tiːɑːs
  3. German, Norwegian   mah-TĒ-ahs   mɑ'tiːɑs
Matthías
  pers. name, Icelandic   MAHT-TĒ-ahs   'mɑtˌtiːɑs
Mattie
  pers. name   MAT-ē   'mæt̮iˑ
Mattingly
  Mack F., US politician; Don,   MAT-ing-lē   'mæt̮iŋliˑ
    baseball player
Maud, Maude
  pers. name   MAWD   'mɔːd
Maugham
  Somerset, English author   MAWM   'mɔːm
Maui
  island, county, HI   MOW-ē   'mauiˑ
Mau Mau
  Kikuyu rebels in Kenya   MOW MOW   'mau ˌmau
Maumee
  city, OH; river, IN, OH   maw-MĒ, MAW-mē   mɔ'miː, 'mɔːmiˑ
Mauna Kea
  extinct volcano, HI   MOW-nuh KĀ-uh, MAW-nuh   ˌmaunə 'keːə, ˌmɔːnə
Mauna Loa
  volcano, HI   MOW-nuh LŌ-uh, MAW-nuh   ˌmaunə 'loːə, ˌmɔːnə
Maundy Thursday
  Christian holy day   MAWN-dē THUHRZ-dē, THUHRZ-dā   'mɔːndiˑ 'θəʳzdiˑ, 'θəʳzdeː
Maupassant
  Guy de, French writer   mō-pah-SAHⁿ   moːpɑːsã
Maur
  pers. name   MAWR   'mɔːʳ
Maureen
  pers. name   maw-RĒN, muh-RĒN   mɔ'riːn, mə'riːn
Mauretania
  ancient country, Africa   MAWR-uh-TĀ-nē-uh, MAHR-,   ˌmɔːrə'teːniːə, ˌmɑr-, -'teːnjə
                                      -TĀN-yuh
Mauriac
  François, French author (Nobel   mawr-YAHK   mɔːrjɑːk
    1952)

Key (col. 2):   a: fad   ā: fade   ah: father   ar: **M**ar**y**   aw: **l**aw   e: fed   ē: feed   er: merry   i: hid   ī: hide   ō: coat   oo̅: boot
oi: **b**oy   ow: **n**ow   u: put   uh: a**b**ove   uhr: **b**ird   ch: **ch**op   ng: ri**ng**   sh: **sh**ow   th: **th**ick   t̲h: **th**is   zh: mea**s**ure

Maurice
1. pers. name	MAWR-uhs, MAHR-uhs, maw-RĒS	'mɔːrəs, 'marəs, mɔː'riːs
2. French	maw-RĒS	mɔriːs

Mauritania
republic, Africa	MAWR-uh-TĀ-nē-uh, MAHR-, -nyuh	ˌmɔːrə'teːniːə, ˌmar-, -njə

Mauritanian
pert. to Mauritania	MAWR-uh-TĀ-nē-uhn, MAHR-, -nyuhn	ˌmɔːrə'teːniːən, ˌmar-, -njən

Mauritian
pert. to Mauritius	maw-RISH-(ē-)uhn	mɔː'riʃ(iː)ən

Mauritius
island, Indian Ocean	maw-RISH-(ē-)uhs	mɔː'riʃ(iː)əs

Maurits
pers. name, Dutch	MOW-rits	'maurits

Mauritz
pers. name, Dutch, Norwegian,	MOW-rits	'maurits
Swedish		

Maurizio
pers. name, Italian	mow-RĒT-syō	mau'riːtsjoː

Mauser
German gun	MOW-zuhr	'mauzəʳ

Mausoleum
tomb of Mausolus at	MAW-suh-LĒ-uhm, MAW-zuh-	ˌmɔːsə'liːəm, ˌmɔːzə-
Halicarnassus		

Mausolus
Persian satrap of Caria	maw-SŌ-luhs	mɔː'soːləs

Mawlid al-Nabi
Islamic festival	MOW-lid ahl-NAHB-ē, al-	'maulid al'nabiː, æl-

Max
1. pers. name	MAKS	'mæks
2. Dutch, German	MAHKS	'maks
3. French	MAHKS	maːks

Maxim
pers. name, Russian	MUHK-SYĒM	ˌmək'sjiːm

Maxime
1. pers. name	mak-SĒM	mæk'siːm
2. French	mahk-SĒM	maːksiːm

Maximianus
Roman emperor	MAK-SIM-ē-Ā-nuhs	ˌmækˌsimiː'eːnəs

Maximilian
1. pers. name	MAK-suh-MIL-yuhn	ˌmæksə'miljən
2. German	MAHK-sē-MĒL-yahn, -MĒ-lē-ahn	ˌmaksiː'miːljan, -'miːliːan
3. Norwegian	MAHK-sē-MĒ-lē-AHN	ˌmaksiːˌmiːliː'an
4. Polish	MAHK-si-MĒL-yahn	ˌmaːksi'miːljaːn

Maximilien
pers. name	mahk-sē-mēl-YEⁿ	maːksiːmiːljɛ̃

Maximinus
name, Roman emperors	MAK-suh-MĒ-nuhs	ˌmæksə'miːnəs

Maximus
pers. name, Latin	MAK-suh-muhs	'mæksəməs

Maxine
pers. name	mak-SĒN	mæk'siːn

Maxwell
pers. name	MAK-SWEL, MAK-swuhl	'mækˌswel, 'mækswəl

May
month; pers. name	MĀ	'meː

Foreign Sounds: ue: *Fr.* **rue**, *Ger.* **füllen**   uh(r): *Fr.* **boeuf**, *Ger.* **Höhle**   <u>kh</u>: *Ger.* i**ch**, *Scot.* lo**ch**   g̱: *Sp.* ami**g**o   v̱: *Sp.* ha**b**lar
hl: *Welsh* **Ll**anelli.   CAPITALS: primary stress.   SMALL CAPS: secondary stress.   Ⓢ: U.S. pron.   Ⓔ: British pron.

Mayacamas		
winery, CA	MĪ-(y)uh-KAHM-uhs	ˌmai(j)ə'kaməs
Mayaguana		
island, British Virgin Islands	MĀ-uh-GWAHN-uh	ˌmeːə'gwanə
Mayagüez		
city, Puerto Rico	mī-uh-ḠWĂS	maiə'ɣweːs
Mayakovsky		
Vladimir, *writer*	MAH-yuh-KAWF-skē, MĪ-uh-	ˌmajə'kɔːfskiˑ, ˌmaiə-
Mayall		
John, *English blues musician*	MĀ-AWL	'meːˌɔːl
Mayan		
pert. to the Maya	MĪ-(y)uhn	'mai(j)ən
Maya [Yucatec]		
lang., people, Guatemala, Mexico,	MĪ-(y)uh	'mai(j)ə
British Honduras; pers. name		
Mayberry		
pers. name	MĀ-BER-ē	'meːˌberiˑ
Mayenne		
dept & river, France	mah-YEN	maːjen
Mayer		
1. Maria Goeppert, *German-born*	MĪ(-uh)r	'mai(ə)ʳ
US physicist (Nobel 1963)		
2. pers. name	MĪ-uhr, MĀ-uhr	'maiəʳ, 'meːəʳ
3. German	MĪ-uhr	'maiəʳ
Mayet [Ma'at]		
Egyptian goddess of truth and	MAH-yuht, MĪ-uht	'majət, 'maiət
justice		
Mayfair		
district, London, England	MĀ-FAR, MĀ-FER	'meːˌfæʳ, 'meːˌfeʳ
Mayflower		
Pilgrim ship	MĀ-FLOW(-uh)r	'meːˌflau(ə)ʳ
Maynard		
pers. name	MĀ-nuhrd, MĀ-NAHRD	'meːnəʳd, 'meːˌnaʳd
Mayo		
1. Charles H., William J., *US*	MĀ-ō	'meːoː
surgeons; clinic, MN		
2. county, Irish Republic	MĀ-ō, *in Ireland also* mā-Ō	'meːoː, *in Ireland also*
		meː'oː
3. mtn., Chile; river, Mexico	MĪ-ō	'maioː
Mayon		
volcano, Philippines	mah-YŌN	ma'joːn
Mayonnaise		
condiment	MĀ-uh-NĀZ, MĀ-uh-NĀZ	'meːəˌneːz, ˌmeːə'neːz
Mayotte		
island, Indian Ocean	mah-YAWT	ma'jɔːt
Mazahua		
lang., people, Mexico	muh-ZAH-wuh	mə'zawə
Mazarin		
Jules, *French political leader*	mah-zah-RE[n]	maːzaːrɛ̃
Mazatec		
lang., people, Mexico	MAHZ-uh-TEK, MAHZ-uh-TEK	'mazəˌtek, ˌmazə'tek
Mazateco [Mazatec]		
lang., people, Mexico	MAHZ-uh-TĀ-kō	ˌmazə'teːkoː
Mazatlán		
seaport, Mexico	MAHZ-uh-TLAHN	ˌmazə'tlan

Key (col. 2):   a: f**a**d   ā: f**a**de   ah: f**a**ther   ar: M**a**ry   aw: l**a**w   e: f**e**d   ē: f**ee**d   er: m**e**rry   i: h**i**d   ī: h**i**de   ō: c**oa**t   ōō: b**oo**t
oi: b**oy**   ow: n**ow**   u: p**u**t   uh: **a**bove   uhr: b**i**rd   ch: **ch**op   ng: ri**ng**   sh: **sh**ow   th: **th**ick   th: **th**is   zh: mea**s**ure

Mazda
  Japanese car co.   MAHZ-duh   'mɑzdə

Mazda, Ahura
  see Ahura Mazda

Mazdaism
  religion   MAZ-duh-ɪz-uhm, MAHZ-   'mæzdə,izəm, 'mɑz-

Mazowiecki
  Tadeusz, *Polish politician*   MAHZ-uhv-YET-skē   ˌmɑzəv'jetskiˑ

Mazurka
  dance   muh-ZUHR-kuh, muh-ZUR-kuh   mə'zəʳkə, mə'zuʳkə

Mazzini
  Giuseppe, *Italian philosopher*   maht-SĒ-nē, mahd-ZĒ-nē   mɑt'siːniˑ, mɑd'ziːniˑ

Ma'at
  Egyptian goddess of truth and justice   MAH-AHT   'mɑˌɑt

Mba
  lang., Congo   m-BAH, uhm-BAH, em-BAH   m̩'bɑ, əm'bɑ, em'bɑ

Mbaama
  lang., Africa   m-BAHM-uh, uhm-BAHM-uh, em-BAHM-uh   m̩'bɑmə, əm'bɑmə, em'bɑmə

Mbabane
  town, Swaziland   m-buh-BAHN, EM-buh-BAHN   m̩bə'ban, ˌembə'ban

Mbai
  lang., Chad, Central African Republic   m-BĪ, uhm-BĪ, em-BĪ   m̩'bai, əm'bai, em'bai

Mbati
  lang., Africa   m-BAHT-ē, uhm-BAHT-ē, em-BAHT-ē   m̩'batiˑ, əm'bɑṭiˑ, em'bɑṭiˑ

Mbaya
  S. American people   m-buh-YAH, EM-buh-YAH   m̩bə'ja, ˌembə'ja

Mbete
  lang., Africa   m-BĀT-ā, uhm-BĀT-ā, em-BĀT-ā   m̩'beˑṭeː, əm'beˑṭeː, em'beˑṭeː

Mbimu
  lang., Africa   m-BĒ-mo͞o, uhm-BĒ-mo͞o, em-BĒ-mo͞o   m̩'biːmuː, əm'biːmuː, em'biːmuː

Mbo
  lang., Africa   m-BŌ, uhm-BŌ, em-BŌ   m̩'boː, əm'boː, em'boː

Mbole
  lang., Africa   m-BŌ-lā, uhm-BŌ-lā, em-BŌ-lā   m̩'boːleː, əm'boːleː, em'boːleː

Mboya
  Tom, *Kenyan political leader*   m-BOI-uh, uhm-BOI-uh, em-BOI-uh   m̩'bɔiə, əm'bɔiə, em'bɔiə

Mbunda
  lang., Africa   m-BO͞ON-duh, uhm-BO͞ON-duh, em-BO͞ON-duh   m̩'buˑndə, əm'buˑndə, em'buˑndə

Mbundu [Ovimbundu]
  lang., people, Africa   m-BO͞ON-do͞o, uhm-BO͞ON-do͞o, em-BO͞ON-do͞o   m̩'buˑnduː, əm'buˑnduː, em'buˑnduː

Mbwera
  lang., Africa   m-BWER-uh, uhm-BWER-uh, em-BWER-uh   m̩'bwerə, əm'bwerə, em'bwerə

Mc-
  see also Mac-

Foreign Sounds: ue: *Fr.* **rue**, *Ger.* **füllen**   uh(r): *Fr.* **boeuf**, *Ger.* **Höhle**   <u>kh</u>: *Ger.* **ich**, *Scot.* **loch**   ḡ: *Sp.* **amigo**   <u>v</u>: *Sp.* **hablar**
hl: *Welsh* **Llanelli**.   CAPITALS: primary stress.   SMALL CAPS: secondary stress.   Ⓢ: U.S. pron.   Ⓛ: British pron.

McAdoo
   Bob, *basketball player*   MAK-uh-DŌŌ   'mækə,duː
McCaffrey
   Anne, *US author*   muh-KAF-rē   mə'kæfriˈ
McCallum
   David, *British actor*   muh-KAL-uhm   mə'kæləm
McCarthy
   Eugene, *US writer, politician;*   muh-KAHR-thē, muh-KAHRT-ē   mə'kɑʳθiˈ, mə'kɑʳʈiˈ
     Joseph, *US politician*
McCarthyism
   political intolerance   muh-KAHR-thē-ɪz-uhm,   mə'kɑʳθiː,izəm,
                      muh-KAHRT-ē-ɪz-uhm   mə'kɑʳʈiː,izəm
McCartney
   Paul, *British musician, songwriter*   muh-KAHRT-nē   mə'kɑʳtniˈ
McClanahan
   Rue, *US actress*   muh-KLAN-uh-HAN   mə'klænə,hæn
McClintock
   Barbara, *US geneticist, biologist*   muh-KLIN-tuhk   mə'klintək
     (Nobel 1983); Jessica, *US*
     fashion designer
McClure
   James A., *US politician;* Doug,   muh-KLUR   mə'kluʳ
     US actor
McConnell
   Addison Mitchell, Jr., *US politician*   muh-KAHN-l   mə'kɑnl̩
McCormack
   Cyrus, *US industrialist;* Richard   muh-KAWR-mik   mə'kɔːʳmik
     Thomas Fox, *US government*
     official
McCovey
   Willie, *US baseball player*   muh-KUHV-ē   mə'kəviˈ
McCown's longspur
   bird   muh-KOWNZ LAWNG-SPUHR   mə'kɑunz 'lɔːŋ,spəʳ
McCoy
   pers. name   muh-KOI   mə'kɔi
McCrae, McCrea
   family name   muh-KRĀ   mə'kreː
McCulloch, McCullough
   pers. name   muh-KUHL-uhk, muh-KUHL-uh<u>kh</u>   mə'kələk, mə'kələx
McDermott
   pers. name   muhk-DUHR-muht   mək'dəʳmət
McDiarmid
   Hugh, *Scottish poet*   muhk-DUHR-muhd,   mək'dəʳməd, mək'dəʳmət
                      muhk-DUHR-muht
McDonagh
   Donagh, *Irish dramatist;* Thomas,   muhk-DAHN-uh   mək'dɑnə
     Irish poet
McDonald
   pers. name   muhk-DAHN-uhld   mək'dɑnəld
McDonough
   family name   muhk-DUHN-uh, muhk-DAHN-uh   mək'dənə, mək'dɑnə
McDowell
   Roddy, *British actor*   muhk-DOW(-uh)l   mək'dɑu(ə)l
McElroy
   family name   MAK-uhl-ROI, muh-KEL-ROI   'mækəl,rɔi, mə'kel,rɔi

---

Key (col. 2):   a: fad   ā: fade   ah: father   ar: Mary   aw: law   e: fed   ē: feed   er: merry   i: hid   ī: hide   ō: coat   ōō: boot
oi: boy   ow: now   u: put   uh: above   uhr: bird   ch: chop   ng: ring   sh: show   th: thick   <u>th</u>: this   zh: measure

McEnroe
   John, *US tennis player*   MAK-uhn-RŌ   'mækən‚roː

McEntire
   Reba, *US country western singer*   MAK-uhn-TĪR   'mækən‚taiʳ

McEvoy
   family name   MAK-uh-VOI   'mækə‚vɔi

McEwan, McEwen
   family name   muh-KYOO-uhn   mə'kjuːən

McGavin
   Darren, *US actor*   muh-GAV-uhn   mə'gævən

McGee
   Willie, *US baseball player*   muh-GĒ   mə'giː

McGhee
   Walter Brownie, *blues singer,*   muh-GĒ   mə'giː
     guitarist

McGovern
   George, *US politician*   muh-GUHV-uhrn   mə'gəvəʳn

McGregor
   pers. name   muh-GREG-uhr   mə'gregəʳ

McGuffey
   William Holmes, *US educator*   muh-GUHF-ē   mə'gəfiˑ

McGuigan
   family name   muh-GWĒ-guhn, muh-GWIG-uhn   mə'gwiːgən, mə'gwigən

McGuire
   Dorothy, *US actress*   muh-GWĪR   mə'gwaiʳ

McIntosh
   1. *pers. name; apple; US pl. name*   MAK-uhn-TAHSH   'mækən‚taʃ
   2. *county, GA*   MAK-uhn-tuhsh, MAK-uhn-TAHSH   'mækəntəʃ, 'mækən‚taʃ

McKay
   Jim, *US TV sports commentator*   muh-KĀ   mə'keː

McKean
   Michael, *US actor*   muh-KĒN   mə'kiːn

McKechnie
   Field, *ballpark, Bradenton, FL*   muh-KEK-nē   mə'kekniˑ

McKendree
   College, *IL*   muh-KEN-drē   mə'kendriˑ

McKinley [Denali]
   Mount, *AK*   muh-KIN-lē   mə'kinliˑ

McKinley
   William, *25th US president; pers.*   muh-KIN-lē   mə'kinliˑ
     name

McKinsey, McKinzey
   pers. name   muh-KIN-zē   mə'kinziˑ

McKuen
   Rod, *US poet, composer, author*   muh-KYOO-uhn   mə'kjuːən

McLaglen
   pers. name   muh-KLAHK-luhn, muh-GLAHK-luhn   mə'klaklən, mə'glaklən

McLaughlin
   John, *English musician*   muh-KLAHK-luhn,   mə'klaklən, mə'glaklən
              muh-GLAHK-luhn,   mə'klaxlən, mə'glaxlən
              muh-KLAH<u>KH</u>-luhn,
              muh-GLAH<u>KH</u>-luhn

McLeod
   county, MN; pers. name   muh-KLOWD   mə'klaud

Foreign Sounds: ue: *Fr.* **rue**, *Ger.* f**ü**llen uh(r): *Fr.* b**oeu**f, *Ger.* H**ö**hle <u>kh</u>: *Ger.* i**ch**, *Scot.* lo**ch** ğ: *Sp.* ami**g**o v̲: *Sp.* ha**b**lar
hl: *Welsh* **Ll**anelli. CAPITALS: primary stress. SMALL CAPS: secondary stress. Ⓢ: U.S. pron. Ⓔ: British pron.

McIver, McIvor
  family name   muh-KĪ-vuhr   məˈkɑivəʳ
McMahon
  1. Ed, US TV personality   muhk-MAN   məkˈmæn
  2. pers. name   muhk-MĀ-uhn, muhk-MAN,   məkˈmeːən, məkˈmæn,
       muhk-MAH(-uh)n   məkˈmɑ(ə)n
McManus
  William J., US political   muhk-MAN-uhs   məkˈmænəs
    organization executive
McMillan
  Edwin M., US physical chemist   muhk-MIL-uhn   məkˈmilən
    (Nobel 1951)
McNamara
  Robert, US government official   MAK-nuh-MAR-uh, MAK-nuh-MER-uh   ˈmæknə,mærə,
       ˈmæknə,merə
McNearney
  Stadium, Schenectady, NY   muhk-NIR-nē   məkˈnirniˑ
McNeil
  Freeman, football player   muhk-NĒL   məkˈniːl
McNichol
  Kristy, US actress   muhk-NIK-uhl   məkˈnikəl
McPherson
  Aimée Semple, US evangelist;   muhk-FUHR-suhn   məkˈfəʳsən
    James, Scottish poet
McRae
  Milton Alexander, US newspaper   muh-KRĀ   məˈkreː
    publisher
McRaney
  Gerald, US actor   muh-KRĀ-nē   məˈkreːniˑ
McVay, McVeagh, McVeigh, McVey
  family name   muhk-VĀ   məkˈveː
McVie
  Christine Perfect, British   muhk-VĒ   məkˈviː
    musician, singer; John,
    musician
McWethy
  John, US journalist   muh-KWETH-ē   məˈkweθiˑ
Mdina
  town, Malta   muh-DĒ-nuh   məˈdiːnə
Mélnik
  town, Czech republic   MYEL-NYĒK, MEL-nik   ˈmjel,njiːk, ˈmelnik
Mead
  Margaret, US anthropologist   MĒD   ˈmiːd
Meade
  George Gordon, US general;   MĒD   ˈmiːd
    James E., English economist
    (Nobel 1977)
Meagher
  county, MT   MAHR   ˈmɑʳ
Meara
  Anne, US actress   MIR-uh   ˈmirə
Mearns's gilded flicker
  bird   MUHRN-zuhz GILD-uhd FLIK-uhr   ˌməʳnzəz ˌgildəd ˈflikəʳ
Mearns's quail
  bird   MUHRN-zuhz KWĀL   ˌməʳnzəz ˈkweːl

Key (col. 2):   a: fad   ā: fade   ah: father   ar: Mary   aw: law   e: fed   ē: feed   er: merry   i: hid   ī: hide   ō: coat   ōō: boot
oi: boy   ow: now   u: put   uh: above   uhr: bird   ch: chop   ng: ring   sh: show   th: thick   <u>th</u>: this   zh: measure

Mears
 Rick, *US race car driver*   MIRZ   'miʳz

Mecca
 city, Saudi Arabia, center of Islam   MEK-uh   'mekə

Mechain
 1. Pierre, *French astronomer*   me-SHEⁿ   meʃẽ
 2. see Gwerful Mechain

Mechelen [Malines]
 city, Belgium   MEKH-uh-luh(n)   'mexələ(n)

Mechlin
 English form of Mechelen   MEK-luhn   'meklən

Mecklenburg
 1. county, NC, VA   MEK-luhn-BUHRG   'meklən,bəʳg
 2. former German state   MEK-luhn-BURK, -BURG   'meklən,buʳk, -,buʳg

Mecosta
 county, MI   mi-KAHS-tuh, mi-KAWS-tuh   mi'kɑstə, mi'kɔːstə

Medaglia d'Oro
 tdmk of a coffee co   muh-DAL-yuh DŌR-ō, DAWR-ō   mə'dæljə 'doːroː, 'dɔːroː

Medaille
 College, NY   muh-DĀL   mə'deːl

Medawar
 P. B., *British zoologist, immunologist (Nobel 1960)*   MED-uh-wuhr   'medəwəʳ

Medb
 Irish goddess of war   METHV, Ⓢ MEV, māv   'meðv, Ⓢ 'mev, meːv

Mede
 ancient Persian   MĒD   'miːd

Medea
 wife of Jason; tragedy, Euripides   muh-DĒ-uh   mə'diːə

Médecine Sans Frontière
 international medical aid group   med-SIN sahⁿ frawⁿ-TYER   medsin sã frõtjer

Medellín
 city, Colombia   mā-thuh-YĒN, Ⓢ MED-uh-YĒN, MED-l-(Y)ĒN   meːðə'jiːn, Ⓢ ,medə'jiːn, ,medl̩'(j)iːn

Medger
 pers. name (M. Evers)   MED-guhr   'medgəʳ

Media
 ancient country, Asia   MĒD-ē-uh   'miːdiːə

Medici
 Florentine family   MĀ-dē-chē, Ⓢ MED-uh-chē, muh-DĒ-chē   'meːdiːtʃiː, Ⓢ 'medətʃi, mə'diːtʃi

Medicinae Doctor
 Doctor of Medicine, M.D.   MED-uh-SĒ-NĪ DAHK-TAWR   ,medə'siː,nɑi 'dɑk,tɔːʳ

Medii, Sinus
 see Sinus Medii

Medina
 1. city, county, OH; character in Faerie Queen, *Spenser*   muh-DĪ-nuh   mə'dɑinə
 2. river, county, TX; city, Saudi Arabia   muh-DĒ-nuh   mə'diːnə

MEDIQ
 US healthcare services co.   MED-ik   'medik

Mediterranean
 Sea   MED-uh-tuh-RĀ-nē-uhn, -RĀN-yuhn   ,medətə'reːniːən, -'reːnjən

---

Foreign Sounds: ue: *Fr.* **rue**, *Ger.* f**ü**llen   uh(r): *Fr.* b**oeu**f, *Ger.* H**öh**le   kh: *Ger.* i**ch**, *Scot.* lo**ch**   g̅: *Sp.* ami**g**o   v: *Sp.* ha**b**lar
hl: *Welsh* **Ll**anelli.   CAPITALS: primary stress.   SMALL CAPS: secondary stress.   Ⓢ: U.S. pron.   Ⓔ: British pron.

Médoc
   district, France; wine variety　　mā-DAWK　　　　　meːdɔːk

Medusa
   Gorgon　　muh-D(Y)$\overline{\text{OO}}$-suh　　　　mə'd(j)uːsə

Meerendal
   S. African wine　　MER-uhn-DAHL, -DAL　　'meʳən,dɑl, -,dæl

Meese
   Edwin, III, *US government official*　　MĒS　　'miːs

Meg
   pers. name　　MEG　　'meg

Megacles
   Athenian politician　　MEG-uh-KLĒZ　　'megə,kliːz

Megaera
   one of the Greek Furies　　muh-GIR-uh　　mə'girə

Megalosaurus
   dinosaur　　MEG-uh-lō-SAWR-uhs　　,megəlɔːˈsɔːrəs

Megan
   1. pers. name　　MEG-uhn, MĀ-guhn, MĒ-guhn　　'megən, 'meːgən, 'miːgən
   2. Welsh　　MEG-ahn　　'megɑːn

Megara
   daughter of Creon; ancient city,　　MEG-uh-ruh　　'megərə
   state, Africa

Mégara, Megara
   city, Greece　　MEG-uh-ruh　　'megərə

Megasthenes
   Greek explorer　　muh-GAS-thuh-NĒZ　　mə'gæsθə,niːz

Meghan
   pers. name　　MEG-uhn　　'megən

Megiddo
   archaeological site, Israel　　mi-GID-ō　　mi'gidoː

Meharry
   Medical College, *TN*　　muh-HAR-ē, muh-HER-ē　　mə'hæriˑ, mə'heriˑ

Mehemed, Mehemet
   pers. name, Turkish　　me-MET　　me'met

Mehitabel
   literary cat　　muh-HIT-uh-BEL　　mə'hitə,bel

Mehmed
   1. pers. name, Serbo-Croatian　　MEM-ed　　'memed
   2. Turkish　　me-MET　　me'met

Mehmet
   pers. name, Albanian, Turkish　　me-MET　　me'met

Mehta
   Zubin, *US conductor*　　MĀT-uh　　'meːʈə

Meier
   pers. name　　MĪ-uhr　　'maiəʳ

Meiji
   district, Japan　　mā-jē　　meːdʒiː

Meiklejohn
   Alexander, *US educator*　　MIK-uhl-JAHN, MĪ-kuhl-JAHN　　'mikəl,dʒɑn, 'maikəl,dʒɑn

Meineke
   US muffler co.　　MĪ-nuh-kē　　'mainəkiˑ

Meinen
   Field, *ballpark, Peoria, IL*　　MĪ-nuhn　　'mainən

Mein Kampf
   autobiography, Adolf Hitler　　mīn KAHM(P)F　　main 'kɑm(p)f

Key (col. 2):　a: fad　ā: fade　ah: father　ar: Mary　aw: law　e: fed　ē: feed　er: merry　i: hid　ī: hide　ō: coat　ōō: boot
oi: boy　ow: now　u: put　uh: above　uhr: bird　ch: chop　ng: ring　sh: show　th: thick　th: this　zh: measure

Meir
　Golda, *Israeli prime minister;*　　me-IR　　　　　　　　　me'iʳ
　　pers. name, Hebrew
Meissen
　town, Germany; porcelain　　　　MĪS-n　　　　　　　　　'maisn̩
Meister Bräu
　US beer　　　　　　　　　　　MĪ-stuhr BROW, MĪ-stuhr BROI　　'maistəʳ ˌbrɑu, 'maistəʳ
　　　　　　　　　　　　　　　　　　　　　　　　　　　　　　ˌbrɔi

Meistersinger
　member of a German poetry &　　MĪ-stuhr-SING-uhr, -ZING-uhr　　'maistəʳˌsiŋəʳ, -ˌziŋəʳ
　　music guild
Meithei [Manipuri]
　lang., people, India　　　　　MĀ-THĀ　　　　　　　　　'meːˌθeː
Meitner
　Lise, *Austrian nuclear physicist*　MĪT-nuhr　　　　　　　　'maitnəʳ
Mekele
　city, Ethiopia　　　　　　　MĀ-kuh-LĀ　　　　　　　　'meːkəˌleː
Meklong
　river, Thailand　　　　　　MĀ-KLAWNG　　　　　　　'meː'klɔːŋ
Meknès
　city, Morocco　　　　　　　mek-NES　　　　　　　　　mek'nes
Mekong
　river, Asia　　　　　　　　MĀ-KAWNG, MĀ-KAHNG　　'meː'kɔːŋ, 'meː'kɑŋ
Mel
　pers. name　　　　　　　　MEL　　　　　　　　　　　'mel
Melampus
　Greek prophet　　　　　　　muh-LAM-puhs　　　　　　mə'læmpəs
Melanchthon
　Philipp, *German scholar*　　　mā-LAHNKH-tawn　　　　　meː'lɑnxtɔːn
Melanchthon, Melancthon
　pers. name　　　　　　　　muh-LANG(K)-thuhn, -tuhn　mə'læŋ(k)θən, -tən
Melanesia
　Pacific islands　　　　　　MEL-uh-NĒ-zhuh, MEL-uh-NĒ-shuh　ˌmelə'niːʒə, ˌmelə'niːʃə
Melanesian
　pert. to Melanesia　　　　　MEL-uh-NĒ-zhuhn,　　　　ˌmelə'niːʒən, ˌmelə'niːʃən
　　　　　　　　　　　　　　MEL-uh-NĒ-shuhn

Melanie
　pers. name　　　　　　　　MEL-uh-nē　　　　　　　　'meləniˑ
Melanippe
　sister of Queen Hippolyta;　　MEL-uh-NIP-ē　　　　　　ˌmelə'nipiˑ
　　daughter of Hippe and Aeolus
Melanippus
　killer of Tydeus, killed by　　MEL-uh-NIP-uhs　　　　　ˌmelə'nipəs
　　Amphiaraus
Melantho
　mother of Delphus by Poseidon　muh-LAN(T)-thō　　　　　mə'læn(t)θoː
Melanthus
　killer of Xanthus　　　　　muh-LAN(T)-thuhs　　　　mə'læn(t)θəs
Melba
　pers. name　　　　　　　　MEL-buh　　　　　　　　　'melbə
Melbourne
　1. city, Australia; town, FL　　MEL-buhrn, *by outsiders or*　'melbəʳn, *by outsiders or*
　　　　　　　　　　　　　　non-Australians also MEL-BAWRN　*non-Australians also*
　　　　　　　　　　　　　　　　　　　　　　　　　　　　　'melˌbɔːʳn
　2. town, England　　　　　MEL-bawrn　　　　　　　　'melbɔːʳn

Foreign Sounds: ue: *Fr.* **rue**, *Ger.* f**ü**llen　uh(r): *Fr.* b**oeu**f, *Ger.* H**öh**le　**kh**: *Ger.* i**ch**, *Scot.* lo**ch**　ḡ: *Sp.* ami**g**o　v̲: *Sp.* ha**b**lar
hl: *Welsh* **Ll**anelli.　CAPITALS: primary stress.　SMALL CAPS: secondary stress.　Ⓢ: U.S. pron.　Ⓛ: British pron.

Melcher
  John, *US politician* — MEL-chuhr — 'meltʃəʳ

Melchiades
  pope — mel-KĪ-uh-DĒZ — mel'kaiə,diːz

Melchior
  1. Lauritz, US tenor; pers. name — MEL-kē-awr — 'melkiːɔːʳ
  2. French — mel-KYAWR — melkjɔːr
  3. German — MELKH-yawr — 'melçjɔːʳ

Melchizedek, Melchisedec
  Biblical priest-king of Jerusalem — mel-KIZ-uh-DEK, mel-KĒ-zuh-DEK — mel'kizə,dek, mel'kiːzə,dek

Meleager
  killer of the Calydonian boar — MEL-ē-Ā-guhr — ˌmeliːˈeːgəʳ

Meleagrids
  sisters of Meleager — MEL-ē-Ā-gridz — ˌmeliːˈeːgridz

Meles
  Athenian loved by Timagoras — MĒ-lēz — 'miːliːz

Meliads
  nymphs of the ash tree — MĒ-lē-ADZ, MĒ-lē-uhdz — 'miːliːˌædz, 'miːliːədz

Melian
  Dialogue *on power, Thucydides* — MĒ-lē-uhn, MĒL-yuhn — 'miːliːən, 'miːljən

Meliboea
  daughter of Niobe; beloved of Alexis — MEL-uh-BĒ-uh — ˌmeləˈbiːə

Meliboeus
  guardian of Oedipus — MEL-uh-BĒ-uhs — ˌmeləˈbiːəs

Melicertes
  son of Ino, deified as Palaemon — MEL-uh-SUHRT-ēz — ˌmeləˈsəʳtiːz

Melilla
  port, Morocco — mā-LĒ-(y)uh — meːˈliː(j)ə

Melina
  pers. name — muh-LĒ-nuh — məˈliːnə

Melissa
  pers. name — muh-LIS-uh — məˈlisə

Melisseus
  king of Crete — muh-LIS-ē-uhs, muh-LIS-(Y)O͞OS — məˈlisiːəs, məˈlis,(j)uːs

Mell
  pers. name — MEL — 'mel

Mellencamp
  John Cougar, *rock musician* — MEL-uhn-KAMP — 'melən,kæmp

Mellette
  county, SD — muh-LET — məˈlet

Mellon
  Andrew, *US financier* — MEL-uhn — 'melən

Melnick
  Daniel, *US film producer* — MEL-nik — 'melnik

Melos [Mílos, Milo]
  island, Aegean — MĒ-LAHS — 'miːˌlɑs

Melpomene
  1. muse of tragedy — mel-PAHM-uh-nē — mel'pɑməniˑ
  2. street, New Orleans — MEL-puh-MĒN, mel-PAHM-uh-nē — 'melpə,miːn, mel'pɑməniˑ

Melrose
  city, Massachusetts; village, Scotland — MEL-RŌZ — 'mel,roːz

Melton Mowbray
  town, England — MELT-n MŌ-brā, MŌ-brē — 'meltn̩ 'moːbreː, 'moːbriˑ

Key (col. 2): a: fad ā: fade ah: father ar: Mary aw: law e: fed ē: feed er: merry i: hid ī: hide ō: coat o͞o: boot
oi: boy ow: now u: put uh: above uhr: bird ch: chop ng: ring sh: show th: thick t͟h: this zh: measure

Melus		
friend of Adonis	MĒ-luhs	'miːləs
Melvil		
pers. name	MEL-VIL, MEL-vuhl	'mel‚vil, 'melvəl
Melville		
Herman, *US writer*	MEL-VIL, MEL-vuhl	'mel‚vil, 'melvəl
Melvin		
pers. name	MEL-vuhn	'melvən
Memel		
river, city, Lithuania	MĀ-muhl	'meːməl
Memmius		
Roman name	MEM-ē-uhs	'memiːəs
Memnon		
Ethiopian ally of the Trojans	MEM-NAHN	'mem‚nɑn
Memphian		
resident of Memphis, *TN*	MEM(P)-fē-uhn	'mem(p)fiːən
Memphis		
city, TN; ancient capital of Egypt	MEM(P)-fuhs	'mem(p)fəs
Memphremagog		
lake, VT, Quebec	MEM-fri-MĀ-GAHG	‚memfri'meː‚gɑg
Menachem		
pers. name, Hebrew	muh-NAH<u>KH</u>-uhm	mə'nɑxəm
Menahem		
pers. name, German	MĀ-nah-HEM, mā-NAH-hem	'meːnɑ‚hem, meː'nɑhem
Menai		
strait, bridge between Anglesey and Welsh mainland	MEN-ī	'men‚ɑi
Menam, Me Nam		
English name of Chao Phraya	mā-NAHM	meː'nɑm
Menander		
Greek dramatist	muh-NAN-duhr	mə'nændə^r
Menard		
county, IL, TX	muh-NAHRD	mə'nɑ^rd
Menchú		
Rigoberta, *Guatemalan activist (Nobel, 1992)*	men-CHŌO	men'tʃuː
Mencius [Meng-tzu]		
Chinese philosopher	MEN-ch(ē-)uhs	'mentʃ(iː)əs
Mencken		
H.L., *US writer*	MENG-kuhn	'meŋkən
Mende		
1. lang., people, Africa	MEN-dē	'mendiˑ
2. town, France	MAHⁿD	mɑ̃d
Mendel		
Gregor, *Austrian botanist*	MEN-dl	'mendl̩
mendelevium		
element	MEN-duh-LĒ-vē-uhm, MEN-duh-LĀ-vē-uhm	‚mendə'liːviːəm, ‚mendə'leːviːəm
Mendeleyev, -leev		
Dmitri Ivanovitch, *Russian chemist*	MEN-duh-LĀ-uhf	‚mendə'leːəf
Mendelian		
pert. to G. Mendel	men-DĒ-lē-uhn, men-DĒL-yuhn	men'diːliːən, men'diːljən
Mendelssohn-Bartholdy		
Felix, *German composer*	MEN-dl-suhn-bahr-TAWL-dē	'mendl̩sənbɑ^r'tɔːldiˑ

Foreign Sounds: ue: *Fr.* **rue,** *Ger.* füllen   uh(r): *Fr.* **boeuf,** *Ger.* Höhle   <u>kh</u>: *Ger.* i**ch,** *Scot.* lo**ch**   ğ: *Sp.* amigo   v̱: *Sp.* hablar   hl: *Welsh* **Ll**anelli.   CAPITALS: primary stress.   SMALL CAPS: secondary stress.   Ⓢ: U.S. pron.   Ⓑ: British pron.

Menderes
  Turkish political leader; river, Asia   MEN-duh-RES   ˌmendə'res
  Minor
Mendes
  Sergio, *Brazilian entertainer*   MEN-DEZ, men-DĀS   'menˌdez, men'deːs
Méndez, Mendez
  1. pers. name   MEN-DEZ, men-DEZ   'menˌdez, men'dez
  2. Spanish   MĀN-dās, MĀN-dāth   'meːndeːs, 'meːndeːθ
Mendip Hills
  hill range, England   MEN-DIP HILZ   'menˌdip 'hilz
Mendocino
  county, CA   MEN-duh-SĒ-nō   ˌmendə'siːnoː
Mendoza
  river, prov, town, Argentina   men-DŌ-zuh, men-DŌ-sah   men'doːzə, men'doːsɑ
Menelaus
  king of Sparta & husband of   MEN-l-Ā-uhs   ˌmenḷ'eːəs
  Helen
Menelik
  emperor, Ethiopia   MĀ-nuh-lik, MEN-l-ik   'meːnəlik, 'menḷik
Menem
  Carlos Saul, *president, Brazil*   MEN-eⁿ   'menẽː
Menes
  1st king of Egypt, 3100 BC   MĒ-nēz   'miːniːz
Menestheus
  legendary Athenian leader   muh-NES-thē-uhs,   mə'nesθiːəs, mə'nesˌθ(j)uːs
                                                 muh-NES-TH(Y)O͞OS
Menexenus
  dialogue of Plato   muh-NEK-suh-nuhs, me-NEK-   mə'neksənəs, me'nek-
Mengele
  Joseph, *Nazi officer*   MENG-guh-luh   'meŋgələ
Meng-tzu [Mencius]
  Chinese philosopher   MUHNG-DZU, MUHNG-DZO͞O   'məŋ'dzu, 'məŋ'dzuː
Ménière's
  disease of the ear   MEN-ē-uhrz, MEN-yuhrz,   'meniːəʳz, 'menjəʳz,
                                                 muhn-YERZ   mən'jeʳz
Menifee
  county, KY   MEN-uh-fē   'menəfiˑ
Menindie
  Australia   muh-NIN-dē   mə'nindiˑ
Menjou
  Adolphe, *actor*   mahⁿ-ZHO͞O, MAHN-zho͞o   mãʒuː, 'manʒuː
Menkaure
  king of Egypt   men-KOW-rā   men'kɑureː
Menlo
  College, *CA*   MEN-lō   'menloː
Menlo Park
  city, CA   MEN-lō PAHRK   ˌmenloː 'pɑʳk
Menninger
  Karl Augustus, *US psychiatrist;*   MEN-ing-uhr   'meniŋəʳ
  clinic
Menno
  pers. name, Dutch   MEN-ō   'menoː
Mennonite
  Christian sect   MEN-uh-NĪT   'menəˌnɑit

Key (col. 2):   a: fad ā: fade ah: father ar: Mary aw: law e: fed ē: feed er: merry i: hid ī: hide ō: coat o͞o: boot
oi: boy   ow: now   u: put   uh: above   uhr: bird   ch: chop   ng: ring   sh: show   th: thick   th̲: this   zh: measure

Meno
dialogue of Plato — MĒ-nō — 'miːnoː

Menoetes
herdsman of the flocks of Hades — MEN-uh-WĒT-ēz — ˌmenə'wiːţiːz

Menoetius
Argonaut — MEN-uh-WĒ-sh(ē-)uhs — ˌmenə'wiːʃ(iː)əs

Menominee
county, MI, WI — muh-NAHM-uh-nē — mə'nɑməniˑ

Menominee, -ni
S. American people — muh-NAHM-uh-nē — mə'nɑməniˑ

Menomonee Falls
town, WI — muh-NAHM-uh-nē FAWLZ — mə'nɑməniˑ 'fɔːlz

Menorah
Jewish candelabrum — muh-NŌR-uh, muh-NAWR-uh — mə'noːrə, mə'nɔːrə

Menorca [Minorca]
island, Balearic Islands — mā-NAWR-kuh — meː'nɔːʳkə

Menotti
Gian Carlo, *Italian composer; pers. name, Italian* — mā-NAWT-tē — meː'nɔːttiː

Mensa
constellation; high IQ organization — MEN-suh — 'mensə

Menshevik
member of party opposing Bolsheviks — MEN-chuh-VIK — 'mentʃəˌvik

Mensheviki
plural of Menshevik — MEN-chuh-VĒ-kē, -VIK-ē — ˌmentʃə'viːkiˑ, -'vikiˑ

Menthe
nymph loved by Hades — MEN-thē — 'menθiˑ

Menthu-Hotep
name, kings of Egypt — MEN-tōō-HŌ-TEP — 'mentuː'hoːˌtep

Mentor
friend of Odysseus; pers. name — MEN-TAWR, MENT-uhr — 'menˌtɔːʳ, 'mentəʳ

Menuhin
Yehudi, *US violinist* — MEN-yuh-wuhn — 'menjəwən

Menzies
1. British family name — MEN-zēz, MEN-ziz; *in Scotland* MING-is, -iz — 'menˌziːz, 'menziz; *in Scotland* 'miŋis, -iz
2. Sir Robert G., *Australian prime minister* — MEN-zēz — 'menziˑz

Meo
see Miao

Mephisto
a devil — muh-FIS-tō — mə'fistoː

Mephistophelean
pert. to Mephisto or Mephistopheles — MEF-uh-STAHF-uh-LĒ-uhn, muh-FIS-tuh-FĒ-lē-uhn — ˌmefəˌstɑfə'liːən, məˌfistə'fiːliːən

Mephistopheles
a devil — MEF-uh-STAHF-uh-LĒZ — ˌmefə'stɑfəˌliːz

Mercator
Gerardus, *Flemish cartographer; map projection* — muhr-KĀT-uhr — məʳ'keːţəʳ

Merced
river, city, county, CA — muhr-SED — məʳ'sed

Mercedes-Benz
  German car marque   muhr-SĀD-ēz-BENZ, -BEN(T)S   məʳˌseːdiːzʼbenz, -ʼben(t)s
Mercer
  University, *GA*   MUHR-suhr   ˈməʳsəʳ
Mercia
  Anglo-Saxon kingdom   MUHR-shuh   ˈməʳʃə
Mercian
  pert. to Mercia   MUHR-shuhn   ˈməʳʃən
Mercier
  pers. name, French   mers-YĀ   mersjeː
Merck, Sharp, & Dohme
  division of Merck & Co., US   MUHRK SHAHRP uhn DŌM   ˈməʳk ˈʃɑʳp ən ˈdoːm
    pharmaceuticals co.
Mercouri
  Melina, *Greek actress*   muhr-K(Y)UR-ē   məʳˈk(j)uriˑ
Mercurius
  pers. name, Dutch   mer-KUE-rē-ues   merˈkyːriːys
Mercurochrome
  tdmk for an antiseptic   muhr-KYUR-uh-KRŌM   məʳˈkjurəˌkroːm
Mercury
  Roman messenger god; planet;   MUHR-kyuh-rē   ˈməʳkjəriˑ
    element
Mercutio
  character in Romeo and Juliet,   muhr-KYOO-shē-Ō, muhr-KYOO-shō   məʳˈkjuːʃiːˌoː, məʳˈkjuːʃoː
    Shakespeare
Mercy
  pers. name   MUHR-sē   ˈməʳsiˑ
Mercyhurst
  College, *PA*   MUHR-sē-HUHRST   ˈməʳsiˑˌhəʳst
Meredith
  Burgess, *US actor; pers. name*   MER-uhd-uhth, *in Wales*   ˈmerədəθ, *in Wales*
                                     muh-RED-ith   məˈrediθ
Meredydd
  pers. name, Welsh   me-RED-ith   meˈredi̱ð
Merengue
  dance   muh-RENG-gā   məˈreŋgeː
Merfyn
  pers. name   MUHR-vuhn   ˈməʳvən
Mergenthaler
  Ottmar, *US inventor*   MUHR-guhn-THAHL-uhr,   ˈməʳgənˌθɑləʳ,
                                     MER-guhn-TAHL-uhr   ˈmergənˌtɑləʳ
Mérida
  city, Mexico; commune, Spain;   MĀ-rē-thah, Ⓢ MER-uhd-uh   ˈmeːriːˌða, Ⓢ ˈmerədə
    state, Venezuela
Meriden
  city, CT   MER-uhd-n, MER-uhd-uhn   ˈmerədn̩, ˈmerədən
Mérimée
  Prosper, *French writer*   mā-rē-MĀ, Ⓢ MER-uh-MĀ   meːriːmeː, Ⓢ ˈmerəˌmeː
Merino
  sheep breed   muh-RĒ-nō   məˈriːnoː
Meriones
  companion of Idomeneus   MER-ē-Ō-nēz   ˌmeriˈoːniːz
Merionethshire
  former county, Wales   MER-ē-AHN-uhth-shuhr, -SHIR   ˌmeriˈanəθʃəʳ, -ˌʃiʳ

Key (col. 2): a: fad ā: fade ah: father ar: Mary aw: law e: fed ē: feed er: merry i: hid ī: hide ō: coat o͞o: boot
oi: boy   ow: now   u: put   uh: above   uhr: bird   ch: chop   ng: ring   sh: show   th: thick   th̲: this   zh: measure

Meriwether
  pers. name   MER-i-WE<u>TH</u>-uhr   ˈmeri͵weðəʳ

Merle
  pers. name   MUHRL, MUHR-uhl   ˈməʳl, ˈmərəl

Merlin
  wizard in Arthurian legend; pers.   MUHR-luhn   ˈməʳlən
    name

Merlot
  wine   mer-LŌ   merloː

Merneptah
  king of Egypt   MUHR-NEP-TAH   ˈməʳ͵nep͵ta

Meroë
  capital city, ancient Ethiopia   MER-uh-WĒ   ˈmerə͵wiˑ

Merope
  wife of Sisyphus; one of the   MER-uh-pē   ˈmerəpiˑ
    Pleiades

Merovingian
  Frankish dynasty   MER-uh-VIN-jē-uhn   ͵merəˈvindʒiːən

Merrifield
  R. Bruce, *US organic chemist*   MER-uh-FĒLD   ˈmerə͵fiːld
    (Nobel 1984)

Merrimack
  town, county, NH; river, NH, MA   MER-uh-MAK   ˈmerə͵mæk

Merriwether
  Lee, *US actress*   MER-i-WE<u>TH</u>-uhr   ˈmeri͵weðəʳ

Mersey
  river, England   MUHR-zē   ˈməʳziˑ

Merseyside
  county, England   MUHR-zē-SĪD   ˈməʳziˑ͵said

Merthyr Tydvil
  county borough, Wales   MUHR-thuhr TID-VIL   ͵məʳθəʳ ˈtid͵vil

Merton
  borough, England; college, Oxford   MUHRT-n   ˈməʳtn̩
    Univ.; pers. name

Mervin, -vyn
  pers. name   MUHR-vuhn   ˈməʳvən

Merwanji
  pers. name, Parsi   mär-VAHN-jē   meːrˈvandʒiː

Meryl
  pers. name   MER-uhl, MERL   ˈmerəl, ˈmerl

Mesa
  county, CO; town, AZ   MĀ-suh   ˈmeːsə

Mesa, La
  see La Mesa

Mesabi
  iron range, college, MN   muh-SAHB-ē   məˈsabiˑ

Mesa Grande
  Indian reservation, US   MĀ-suh GRAHN-dē   ͵meːsə ˈgrandiˑ

Mesa Verde
  National Park, CO   MĀ-suh VUHRD, VUHR-dē   ͵meːsə ˈvəʳd, ˈvəʳdiˑ

Mescalero
  N. American people   MES-kuh-LER-ō   ͵meskəˈleroː

Mesdames
  French, plural of Madame   mä-DAHM, ⓢ mä-DAHM, mä-DAM   meːdaːm, ⓢ meːˈdam,
                                                                                          meːˈdæm

---

Mesdemoiselles
  French, plural of Mademoiselle   mād-mwah-ZEL,   meːdmwaːzel,
       Ⓢ MĀD-uh-m(w)uh-ZEL,   Ⓢ ,meːdəm(w)ə'zel,
       MĀD-m(w)uh-ZEL   ,meːdm(w)ə'zel

Meshach
  Biblical name   MĒ-SHAK   'miː,ʃæk

Mesmer
  Franz, *German physician*   MEZ-muhr, MES-muhr   'mezmə^r, 'mesmə^r

Mesoamerica
  region of Mexico & Cen. America   MEZ-ō-uh-MER-i-kuh, MĒ-zō-   ,mezoːə'merikə, ,miːzoː-

Mesogeia
  Attic plain   MES-ō-GĀ-uh, MEZ-   ,mesoː'geːə, ,mez-

Mesolithic
  geologic era   MEZ-uh-LITH-ik, MĒZ-, MES-, MĒS-   ,mezə'liθik, ,miːz-, ,mes-, ,miːs-

Meson
  subatomic particle   MEZ-AHN, MES-AHN; MĀ-ZAHN,   'mez,an, 'mes,an; 'meː,zan,
       MĒ-ZAHN, -SAHN   'miː,zan, -,san

Mesopotamia
  region of early civilization, Near   MES-(uh-)puh-TĀ-mē-uh, -TĀM-yuh   ,mes(ə)pə'teːmiːə, -'teːmjə
  East

Mesozoic
  geologic era   MEZ-uh-ZŌ-ik, MĒZ-, MES-, MĒS-   ,mezə'zoːik, ,miːz-, ,mes-, ,miːs-

Mesquite
  town, TX   muh-SKĒT, me-SKĒT   mə'skiːt, me'skiːt

Messalim
  king of Lagash   MES-uh-luhm, MES-uh-LIM   'mesələm, 'mesə,lim

Messalina
  Valeria, *third wife of Claudius I*   MES-uh-LĪ-nuh, MES-uh-LĒ-nuh   ,mesə'lainə, ,mesə'liːnə

Messana [Messina]
  seaport, Sicily   muh-SAHN-uh   mə'sanə

Messenia
  region of ancient Greece   muh-SĒ-nē-uh, muh-SEN-yuh   mə'siːniːə, mə'siːnjə

Messerschmitt
  German WWII fighter plane   MES-uhr-SHMIT   'mesə^r,ʃmit

Messiah
  Jewish deliverer; Jesus Christ   muh-SĪ-uh   mə'saiə

Messianic
  pert. to a messiah   MES-ē-AN-ik   ,mesiː'ænik

Messidor
  month, French Revolutionary   mā-sē-DAWR   meːsiːdɔːr
  calendar

Messieurs
  French, plural of Monsieur   mā-SYUH(R), Ⓢ muhsh-YUHRZ,   meːsjœː, Ⓢ məʃ'jə^rz,
       muhs-YUHRZ, muh-SIRZ,   məs'jə^rz, mə'si^rz,
       mās-YUHRZ   meːs'jə^rz

Messina
  seaport, Sicily   muh-SĒ-nuh   mə'siːnə

Messius
  pers. name, Latin   MES-ē-uhs   'mesiːəs

Messrs.
  gentlemen, plural of Mr.   MES-uhrz   'mesə^rz

Mestra
  daughter of Erysichthon   MES-truh   'mestrə

Key (col. 2):   a: fad   ā: fade   ah: father   ar: Mary   aw: law   e: fed   ē: feed   er: merry   i: hid   ī: hide   ō: coat   ōō: boot
oi: boy   ow: now   u: put   uh: above   uhr: bird   ch: chop   ng: ring   sh: show   th: thick   th: this   zh: measure

Meštrović

Ivan, *Croatian-born American sculptor* — MESH-traw-VĒT, $ MESH-truh-VICH, MES- — 'meʃtrɔːˌviːʈ , $ 'meʃtrəˌvitʃ, 'mes-

Meta

1. *river, Colombia* — MĂT-uh — 'meːʈə
2. *pers. name* — MĒT-uh — 'miːʈə

Metabus

father of Camilla — MET-uh-buhs — 'meʈəbəs

Metallica

rock group — muh-TAL-i-kuh — mə'tælikə

Metanira

employer of Demeter — MET-uh-NĪ-ruh — ˌmeʈə'nairə

Metaxa

tdmk for a Greek brandy — me-TAK-suh, muh-TAK-suh, muh-TAHK-suh — me'tæksə, mə'tæksə, mə'taksə

Metaxas

Ioannis, *Greek dictator* — MET-ahk-SAHS, $ me-TAHK-SAHS — ˌmeʈak'sas, $ me,tak'sas

Metchnikoff

Elie, *Russian-born French zoologist, bacteriologist (Nobel 1908)* — MECH-ni-KAWF — 'metʃniˌkɔːf

Metellus

prominent Roman family — muh-TEL-uhs — mə'teləs

Meteor

French beer — mā-tā-AWR — meːteːɔːr

Methodism

doctrines of the Methodists — METH-uhd-IZ-uhm — 'meθədˌizəm

Methodist

religion — METH-uhd-uhst — 'meθədəst

Methodius

saint, apostle of the Slavs — me-THŌD-ē-uhs — me'θoːdiːəs

Methuen

1. *town, MA* — muh-TH(Y)OO̅-uhn — mə'θ(j)uːən
2. *pers. name* — METH-yuh-wuhn — 'meθjəwən

Methuselah

elderly ancestor of Noah; large wine bottle — muh-TH(Y)OO̅Z(-uh)-luh — mə'θ(j)uːz(ə)lə

Metics

aliens in Athens — MET-iks — 'meʈiks

Metis

Greek goddess of wisdom — MĒT-uhs — 'miːʈəs

Metlakatla

village, AK — MET-luh-KAT-luh — ˌmetlə'kætlə

Metoac

N. American people — muh-TŌ-AK — mə'toːˌæk

Metonic

cycle, 19-year cycle of the moon — muh-TAHN-ik, me-TAHN-ik — mə'tanik, me'tanik

Metternich

Clemens Wenzel, *Austrian statesman* — MET-uhr-ni<u>kh</u>, MET-uhr-nik — 'metəʳnix, 'metəʳnik

Metuchen

city, NJ — muh-TUHCH-uhn — mə'tətʃən

Metz

town, France — MES, $ METS — mes, $ 'mets

Foreign Sounds: ue: *Fr.* **rue**, *Ger.* **füllen** uh(r): *Fr.* **bœuf**, *Ger.* **Höhle** <u>kh</u>: *Ger.* **ich**, *Scot.* **loch** g̃: *Sp.* **amigo** v̶: *Sp.* **hablar** hl: *Welsh* **Llanelli**. CAPITALS: primary stress. SMALL CAPS: secondary stress. $: U.S. pron. £: British pron.

Metzenbaum
Howard, *US politician* | MET-suhn-BAWM, -BOWM | 'metsən,bɔːm, -,baum
Meun, de
see Jean de Meun
Meunier
Constantin, *Belgian sculptor* | muh(r)n-YĀ | mœːnjeː
Meursault
French wine | muhr-SŌ | mœrsoː
Meurthe
river, France | MUHRT | mœrt
Meurthe-et-Moselle
dept, France | MUHR-tā-mō-ZEL | mœrteːmoːzel
Meuse
river, Europe; dept., France | MUH(R)Z, ⑤ MYŌOZ | mœːz, ⑤ 'mjuːz
Mewari [Rajasthani]
lang., India, Pakistan | muh-WAHR-ē | mə'wariˑ
Me-Wuk
N. American people | MĒ-WUHK | 'miːˌwək
Mexicali
city, Mexico | MEK-si-KAL-ē | ˌmeksi'kæliˑ
Mexican
pert. to Mexico | MEK-si-kuhn | 'meksikən
Mexico, México
republic, N. America | MĀ-hē-kō, ⑤ MEK-si-KŌ | 'meˑhiːkoː, ⑤ 'meksiˌkoː
Mextitlaneca
N. American people | MEK-STĒT-luh-NĀ-kuh | ˌmekˌstiːtlə'neːkə
Meyer
pers. name | MĪ-uhr | 'maiəʳ
Meyerbeer
Giacomo, *German composer* | MĪR-BĀR, ⑤ MĪR-BIR | 'maiʳˌbeːʳ, ⑤ 'maiʳˌbiʳ
Meyerhof
Otto, *German physiologist (Nobel 1922)* | MĪ-uhr-HŌF | 'maiəʳˌhoːf
Meyerhoff
concert hall, Baltimore | MĪ-ER-hawf | 'maiˌeʳhɔːf
Mezada
mountaintop, Israel | muh-ZAHD-uh | mə'zadə
Mezentius
Etruscan king defeated by Aeneas | muh-ZEN-sh(ē-)uhs, muh-ZEN-ch(ē-)uhs | mə'zenʃ(iː)əs, mə'zentʃ(iː)əs
Mezzogiorno
region, Italy | MET-sō-JAWR-nō | ˌmetsoː'dʒɔːʳnoː
MIA
soldier listed as missing in action | EM-Ī-Ā | ˌemˌai'eː
Mia
pers. name | MĒ-uh | 'miːə
Miami
river, OH; city, FL; N. American people | mī-AM-ē, mī-AM-uh | mai'æmi, mai'æmə
Miao, Meo [Hmong]
lang., people, China, Vietnam, Laos, Thailand | mē-OW | miː'au
Micah
Old Testament book; pers. name | MĪ-kuh | 'maikə

Key (col. 2): a: fad ā: fade ah: father ar: M**a**ry aw: law e: fed ē: feed er: m**e**rry i: hid ī: hide ō: coat ōō: boot
oi: boy ow: now u: put uh: above uhr: bird ch: chop ng: ring sh: show th: thick th̲: this zh: measure

Micawber

Wilkins, *character in* David   mi-KAWB-uhr, mi-KAHB-uhr   miˈkɔːbəʳ, miˈkɑbəʳ
Copperfield, *Dickens*

Miccosukee

N. American people   MIK-uh-S͞OO-kē   ˌmikəˈsuːkiˑ

Michael

1. *pers. name*   MĪ-kuhl   ˈmaikəl
2. *Danish*   mi-KAHL, MĒK-kuhl   miˈkɑːl, ˈmiːkkəl
3. *Dutch*   MĒ-<u>kh</u>ah-EL   ˈmiːxɑːˌel
4. *Finnish*   MĒ-kah-EL   ˈmiːkɑːˌel
5. *German*   MI<u>KH</u>-ah-EL   ˈmiçaˌel
6. *Norwegian*   mē-KAHL   miːˈkal
7. *Serbo-Croatian*   MĒ-<u>kh</u>ah-el   ˈmiːxɑːel

Michaela

pers. name   muh-KĀ-luh   məˈkeːlə

Michaelmas

feast of St. Michael the Archangel,   MIK-uhl-muhs   ˈmikəlməs
Sept. 29th

Micheas

Old Testament book   MĪ-kē-uhs, mī-KĒ-uhs   ˈmaikiːəs, maiˈkiːəs

Michel

1. Hartmut, *German biochemist*   MI<u>KH</u>-uhl   ˈmiçəl
(Nobel 1988)
2. *pers. name*   MĪ-kuhl   ˈmaikəl
3. *French*   mē-SHEL   miːʃel
4. *German*   MI<u>KH</u>-uhl   ˈmiçəl

Michel Angelo, Michelangelo

1. *Italian artist; pers. name*   MĪ-kuh-LAN-juh-LŌ, MIK-uh-,   ˌmaikəˈlændʒəˌloː, ˌmikə-,
    MĒ-kuh-   ˌmiːkə-
2. *Italian*   MĒ-kā-LAHN-jā-LŌ   ˌmiːkeːˈlandʒeːˌloː

Michele

1. *pers. name*   mi-SHEL   miˈʃel
2. *Italian*   mē-KEL-ā   miːˈkeleː

Michelin

French tire manufacturer; travel   MISH-(uh-)luhn, MICH-uh-luhn   ˈmiʃ(ə)lən, ˈmitʃələn
guide

Michelle

1. *pers. name*   mi-SHEL   miˈʃel
2. *French*   mē-SHEL   miːʃel

Michelob

US beer   MIK-uh-LŌB   ˈmikəˌloːb

Michelson

Albert A., *German-born US*   MĪ-kuhl-suhn   ˈmaikəlsən
physicist (Nobel 1907)

Michener

James, *US novelist*   MICH-nuhr   ˈmitʃnəʳ

Michigan

lake, state, US   MISH-i-guhn   ˈmiʃigən

Michigander

inhabitant of Michigan   MISH-i-GAN-duhr   ˌmiʃiˈgændəʳ

Michiganite

inhabitant of Michigan   MISH-i-guh-NĪT   ˈmiʃigəˌnait

Michio

pers. name, Japanese   mē-chē-ō   miːtʃiːoː

Foreign Sounds: ue: *Fr.* **rue**, *Ger.* f**ü**llen   uh(r): *Fr.* b**oeu**f, *Ger.* H**ö**hle   <u>kh</u>: *Ger.* i**ch**, *Scot.* lo**ch**   ḡ: *Sp.* ami**g**o   <u>v</u>: *Sp.* ha**b**lar
hl: *Welsh* **Ll**anelli.   CAPITALS: primary stress.   SMALL CAPS: secondary stress.   ⑤: U.S. pron.   ⑥: British pron.

Michoacán
   state, Mexico   mē-chuh-wah-KAHN   miːtʃəwaˈkɑn

Mick
   pers. name   MIK   ˈmik

Mickey
   pers. name   MIK-ē   ˈmikiˑ

Mickey Finn
   drugged drink   MIK-ē FIN   ˌmikiˑ ˈfin

Micmac
   N. American people   MIK-MAK   ˈmikˌmæk

MicroGeneSys
   US biotechnology co.   MĪ-krō-JEN-uh-suhs   ˌmɑikroːˈdʒenəsəs

Micronesia
   islands of the western Pacific   MĪ-kruh-NĒ-zhuh, -NĒ-shuh   ˌmɑikrəˈniːʒə, -ˈniːʃə

Micronesian
   pert. to Micronesia   MĪ-kruh-NĒ-zhuhn, -NĒ-shuhn   ˌmɑikrəˈniːʒən, -ˈniːʃən

Microscopium
   constellation   MĪ-kruh-SKŌ-pē-uhm   ˌmɑikrəˈskoːpiːəm

Midas
   king of Phrygia with golden touch   MĪD-uhs   ˈmɑidəs

Middlebury
   town, CT, VT; College, *VT*   MID-l-BER-ē   ˈmidl̩ˌberiˑ

Middlemarch
   novel, George Eliot   MID-l-MAHRCH   ˈmidl̩ˌmɑʳtʃ

Middlesex
   former county, England; county,   MID-l-SEKS   ˈmidl̩ˌseks
    CT, MA, NJ, VA

Middletown
   town, NJ, CT, NY   MID-l-TOWN   ˈmidl̩ˌtɑun

Mid Glamorgan
   county, Wales   MID gluh-MAWR-guhn   ˌmid gləˈmɔːʳgən

Midi
   south of France   mē-DĒ   miːdiː

Midianite
   ancient Arabian people   MID-ē-uh-NĪT   ˈmidiːəˌnɑit

Midi-Pyrénées
   region, France   mē-dē-pē-rā-NĀ   miːdiːpiːreːneː

Midler
   Bette, *US entertainer*   MID-luhr   ˈmidləʳ

Midlothian
   1. town, IL   mid-LŌ-thē-uhn   midˈloːθiːən
   2. county, Scotland   mid-LŌ-<u>th</u>ē-uhn   midˈloːðiːən

Midori
   US violinist; melon liqueur   muh-DŌR-ē, muh-DAWR-ē   məˈdoːriˑ, məˈdɔːriˑ

Midsummer Day
   June 24   MID-SUHM-uhr DĀ   ˌmidˌsəməʳ ˈdeː

Midwest
   region, central US   mid-WEST   midˈwest

Midwestern
   pert. to the Midwest   mid-WES-tuhrn   midˈwestəʳn

Midwesterner
   inhabitant of the Midwest   mid-WES-tuhr-nuhr   midˈwestəʳnəʳ

Mieczysław
   pers. name, Polish   mye-CHIS-lahf   mjeˈtʃislɑːf

Key (col. 2):   a: fad   ā: fade   ah: father   ar: Mary   aw: law   e: fed   ē: feed   er: merry   i: hid   ī: hide   ō: coat   o͞o: boot
oi: boy   ow: now   u: put   uh: above   uhr: bird   ch: chop   ng: ring   sh: show   th: thick   <u>th</u>: this   zh: measure

Miesian
  pert. to Mies van der Rohe   MĒ-sē-uhn, MĒ-shuhn   'miːsiːən, 'miːʃən

Mies van der Rohe
  Ludwig, *US architect*   MĒS VAHN duh RŌ-uh, MĒZ   ˌmiːs ˌvɑn də 'roːə, ˌmiːz

Mifune
  Toshiro, *Japanese entertainer*   mē-fun-e   miːfune

MiG
  Russian fighter aircraft   MIG   'mig

Mignonette
  flower   MIN-yuh-NET   ˌminjə'net

Miguel
  1. pers. name, Portuguese   mē-GEL   miː'gel
  2. Spanish   mē-ĜEL   miː'ɣel

Mihai
  pers. name, Romanian   mē-HĪ   miː'hai

Mihail
  pers. name, Romanian   MĒ-hah-EL   ˌmiːhɑ'el

Mihály
  pers. name, Hungarian   MI-hahl   'mihɑːḷ

Mikado
  operetta, Gilbert & Sullivan   mi-KAHD-ō   mi'kadoː

Mike
  pers. name   MĪK   'maik

Mikhail
  1. pers. name, Bulgarian   MĒ-<u>kh</u>ah-ĒL, Ⓢ mi-KĪL   ˌmiːxɑ'iːl, Ⓢ mi'kail
  2. Russian   MI<u>KH</u>-UH-ĒL, Ⓢ mi-KĪL   ˌmiç,ə'iːl, Ⓢ mi'kail

Mikhailovich
  patronym, Russian   myi-<u>KH</u>ĪL(-uhv)-YICH,   mji'xail(əv)ˌjitʃ,
       Ⓢ mi-KĪ-luh-VICH   Ⓢ mi'kailə,vitʃ

Mikołaj
  pers. name, Polish   mē-KAWL-ī   miː'kɔːɫ,ai

Míkonos, Mykonos
  island, Greece   MĒ-kuh-NAWS   'miːkə,nɔːs

Mikoyan
  Anastas, *Soviet political leader*   MYĒ-kō-YAHN   ˌmjiːkoː'jɑːn

Milan
  1. city, Italy   muh-LAN, muh-LAHN   mə'læn, mə'lɑn
  2. US pl. name   MĪ-luhn   'mailən

Milanese
  pert. to Milan   MIL-uh-NĒZ, -NES   ˌmilə'niːz, -'niːs

Milano [Milan]
  city, Italy   mē-LAHN-ō   miː'lanoː

Mildred
  pers. name   MIL-druhd   'mildrəd

Mildura
  city, Australia   mil-DYUR-uh   mil'djurə

Miles
  pers. name   MĪLZ   'mailz

Milesian
  pert. to Miletus   mī-LĒ-zhuhn, mī-LĒ-shuhn   mai'liːʒən, mai'liːʃən

Miletus
  ancient city, Asia Minor   mī-LĒT-uhs, muh-LĒT-uhs   mai'liːṭəs, mə'liːṭəs

Milhaud
  Darius, *French composer*   mē-YŌ   miːjoː

Foreign Sounds: ue: *Fr.* **rue**, *Ger.* f**ü**llen   uh(r): *Fr.* b**oeu**f, *Ger.* H**öh**le   <u>kh</u>: *Ger.* i**ch**, *Scot.* lo**ch**   ĝ: *Sp.* ami**g**o   v̬: *Sp.* ha**b**lar
hl: *Welsh* **Ll**anelli.   CAPITALS: primary stress.   SMALL CAPS: secondary stress.   Ⓢ: U.S. pron.   Ⓛ: British pron.

Milhous
　　pers. name　　　　　　　　　MIL-HOWS　　　　　　　　'mil,haus

Millard
　　pers. name　　　　　　　　　MIL-uhrd　　　　　　　　'milərd

Millay
　　Edna St. Vincent, *US poet*　　mil-Ā　　　　　　　　　mil'eː

Mille Lacs
　　lake, county, Indian reservation,　mil (L)AK(S)　　　　　mil '(l)æk(s)
　　　MN; lake, Canada

Millet
　　Jean François, *French painter*　mē-YE, mē-LE　　　　　miːje, miːle

Millicent
　　pers. name　　　　　　　　　MIL-uh-suhnt　　　　　　'miləsənt

Millie
　　former First Dog; pers. name　MIL-ē　　　　　　　　　'miliˑ

Milligan
　　College, *TN*　　　　　　　　MIL-uh-guhn　　　　　　'miləgən

Millikan
　　Robert A., *US physicist (Nobel*　MIL-i-kuhn　　　　　　'milikən
　　　1923)

Millikin
　　University, *IL*　　　　　　　MIL-i-kuhn　　　　　　　'milikən

Millington
　　pers. name　　　　　　　　　MIL-ing-tuhn　　　　　　'miliŋtən

Milli Vanilli
　　lip-synching rock group　　　MIL-ē vuh-NIL-ē　　　　,miliˑ və'niliˑ

Millsaps
　　College, *MS*　　　　　　　　MIL-SAPS　　　　　　　'mil,sæps

Milly
　　pers. name　　　　　　　　　MIL-ē　　　　　　　　　'miliˑ

Milne
　　A. A., *British author; pers. name*　MILN, MIL　　　　　　'miln, 'mil

Milner
　　pers. name　　　　　　　　　MIL-nuhr　　　　　　　　'milnər

Milo
　　pers. name　　　　　　　　　MĪ-lō　　　　　　　　　'mailoː

Milo [Melos]
　　island, Aegean　　　　　　　MĒ-lō　　　　　　　　　'miːloː

Milos
　　pers. name, Czech　　　　　　MIL-aws　　　　　　　　'milɔːs

Milos [Melos]
　　island, Aegean　　　　　　　MĒ-LAHS, MĒ-LAWS　　'miː,las, 'miː,lɔːs

Miłosz
　　Czesław, *Lithuanian-born US*　MĒ-lawsh　　　　　　　'miːlɔːʃ
　　　poet, author (Nobel 1980)

Milovan
　　pers. name, Serbo-Croatian　　MĒ-law-VAHN　　　　　'miːlɔː,vaːn

Milpitas
　　city, CA　　　　　　　　　　mil-PĒT-uhs　　　　　　mil'piːʈəs

Milquetoast
　　Caspar, *comic strip character by*　MILK-TŌST　　　　　'milk,toːst
　　　H. T. Webster; timid person

Milsap
　　Ronnie, *US country musician*　MIL-SAP　　　　　　　'mil,sæp

Key (col. 2):　a: fad　ā: fade　ah: father　ar: Mary　aw: law　e: fed　ē: feed　er: merry　i: hid　ī: hide　ō: coat　o͞o: boot
oi: boy　ow: now　u: put　uh: above　uhr: bird　ch: chop　ng: ring　sh: show　th: thick　th̲: this　zh: measure

Milstein
    Cesar, *Argentine-born British*   MIL-STĪN   'mil,stain
      molecular biologist (Nobel
      1984)

Milt
    pers. name   MILT   'milt

Miltiades
    Athenian politician, general; pope   mil-TĪ-uh-DĒZ   mil'taiə,diːz

Milton
    John, *English poet; pers. name*   MILT-n   'miltṇ

Milton Keynes
    town, England   MILT-n KĒNZ   ,miltṇ 'kiːnz

Milvian Bridge
    ancient battle site north of Rome   MIL-vē-uhn BRIJ   'milviːən 'bridʒ

Milwaukee
    city, WI   mil-WAW-kē   mil'wɔːkiˑ

Mimas
    satellite of Saturn   MĪ-muhs   'maiməs

Mimi
    1. *lang., Sudan; pers. name*   MĒ-mē   'miːmiˑ
    2. *French*   mē-MĒ   miːmiː

Mimieux
    Yvette, *US entertainer*   mēm-YUH(R)   miːmjœː

Min
    Egyptian fertility god; lang.,   MIN   'min
      China

Mina
    lang., Togo   MĒ-nuh   'miːnə

Minamata
    disease, mercury poisoning   MIN-uh-MAHT-uh   ,minə'maṭə

Minan
    lang., China   MĒ-nuhn   'miːnən

Minangkabau
    lang., people, West Sumatra   MĒ-NAHNG-kuh-BOW   ,miːˌnaŋkə'bau

Minas Gerais
    state, Brazil   MĒ-nuhs zhuh-RĪS   ,miːnəs ʒə'rais

Minchia [Pai]
    lang., people, China   MIN-jē-AH   'mindʒiː'a

Mindanao
    island, Philippines   MIN-duh-NAH-ō, MIN-duh-NOW   ,mində'naoː, ,mində'nau

Mindoro
    island, Philippines   min-DŌR-ō, min-DAWR-ō   min'doːroː, min'dɔːroː

Mindy
    pers. name   MIN-dē   'mindiˑ

Mineola
    village, NY; city, TX   MIN-ē-Ō-luh   ,miniː'oːlə

Minerva
    Roman goddess of wisdom; pers.   muh-NUHR-vuh   mə'nərvə
      name

Minestrone
    soup   MIN-uh-STRŌ-nē   ,minə'stroːniˑ

Ming
    Chinese dynasty   MING   'miŋ

Minge
    pers. name   MINJ   'mindʒ

Foreign Sounds: ue: *Fr.* **rue**, *Ger.* füllen   uh(r): *Fr.* **boeuf**, *Ger.* Höhle   <u>kh</u>: *Ger.* i<u>ch</u>, *Scot.* lo<u>ch</u>   g̲: *Sp.* ami**g**o   v̲: *Sp.* ha**b**lar
hl: *Welsh* **Ll**anelli.   CAPITALS: primary stress.   SMALL CAPS: secondary stress.   Ⓢ: U.S. pron.   Ⓑ: British pron.

Mingus
Charles, *US jazz musician*   MING-guhs   'miŋgəs

Minho
river, Europe; prov., Portugal   MĒN-yōō   'miːnjuː

Minidoka
county, ID   MIN-uh-DŌ-kuh   ˌminə'doːkə

Minié
Claude-Étienne, *French militarist*   mēn-YĀ, Ⓢ MIN-ē-Ā   miːnjeː, Ⓢ 'miniːˌeː

Minié ball
muzzle-loading bullet   MIN-ē BAWL, MIN-ē-Ā BAWL   'mini· ˌbɔːl, 'miniːˌeː 'bɔːl

**Ministerium für Staatssicherheit
[Stasi]**
East German security   MIN-is-TER-yum fuer   ˌminis'teʳjum fyːʳ
   organization   SHTAHT-ZIKH-uhr-HĪT   'ʃtatˌziçəʳˌhait

Miniver
pers. name   MIN-uh-vuhr   'minəvəʳ

Minivet
bird   MIN-uh-VET   'minəˌvet

Minmi
Australia   MIN-MĪ   'minˌmai

Minneapolis
city, MN   MIN-ē-AP-(uh-)luhs   ˌminiː'æp(ə)ləs

Minnehaha
county, SD   MIN-ē-HAH-HAH   ˌminiː'haˌha

Minnelli
Liza, *US entertainer;* Vincent, *(her*   muh-NEL-ē   mə'neli·
   father) US director

Minnesota
state, US   MIN-uh-SŌT-uh   ˌminə'soːt̞ə

Minnesotan
pert. to Minnesota; *inhabitant of*   MIN-uh-SŌT-n   ˌminə'soːtn̩
   Minnesota

Minnetonka
lake, MN   MIN-uh-TAHNG-kuh   ˌminə'taŋkə

Minnie, -ny
pers. name   MIN-ē   'mini·

Minoan
ancient Cretan culture, lang.   muh-NŌ-uhn   mə'noːən

Minolta
Japanese camera co.   muh-NŌL-tuh, muh-NAHL-tuh   mə'noːltə, mə'naltə

Minorca
island, Balearic Islands   muh-NAWR-kuh   mə'nɔːʳkə

Minoru
pers. name, Japanese   mē-nō-rōō   miːnoːruː

Minos
legendary Cretan king   MĪ-nuhs   'mainəs

Minot
1. *city, ND*   MĪ-NAHT   'maiˌnat
2. G. R., *US physician (Nobel*   MĪ-nuht   'mainət
   1934); pers. name

Minotaur
half-man, half-bull of Greek myth   MIN-uh-TAWR, MĪ-nuh-TAWR   'minəˌtɔːʳ, 'mainəˌtɔːʳ

Minsk
city, Belorussia   MIN(T)SK   'min(t)sk

Key (col. 2):   a: fad   ā: fade   ah: father   ar: Mary   aw: law   e: fed   ē: feed   er: merry   i: hid   ī: hide   ō: coat   ōō: boot
oi: boy   ow: now   u: put   uh: above   uhr: bird   ch: chop   ng: ring   sh: show   th: thick   th̲: this   zh: measure

Minucius		
Roman name	muh-N(Y)O͞O-shē-uhs	məˈn(j)uːʃiːəs
Minuet		
dance	MIN-yuh-WET	ˌminjəˈwet
Minuit		
Peter, *Dutch colonist*	MIN-yuh-wuht	ˈminjəwət
Minuteman		
Revolutionary War militia; US ballistic missile	MIN-uht-MAN	ˈminətˌmæn
Minyads		
Minyas' daughters who offended Dionysus	MIN-YADZ, MIN-ē-ADZ	ˈminˌjædz, ˈminiːˌædz
Minyas		
king of Orchomenus	MIN-yuhs	ˈminjəs
Miocene		
geologic epoch	MĪ-uh-SĒN	ˈmaiəˌsiːn
MIPS		
million instructions per second	MIPS	ˈmips
Miquelon		
see Saint-Pierre & Miquelon		
Mirabeau		
pers. name	MIR-uh-BŌ	ˈmirəˌboː
Mira Costa		
College, *CA*	MIR-uh KAHS-tuh	ˈmirə ˈkastə
Miraflores		
village, lake, Panama	MIR-uh-FLŌR-uhs, MIR-uh-FLAWR-uhs	ˌmirəˈfloːrəs, ˌmirəˈflɔːrəs
Miramichi		
river, Canada	MIR-uh-muh-SHĒ	ˌmirəməˈʃiː
Miranda		
satellite of Uranus; US Supreme Court ruling; pers. name	muh-RAN-duh	məˈrændə
Mirani		
Australia	mir-AN-ē	mirˈæniˑ
Miriam		
pers. name	MIR-ē-uhm	ˈmiriːəm
Miró		
Joan, *Spanish artist*	mē-RŌ	miːˈroː
Mirro		
tdmk for cookware	MIR-ō	ˈmiroː
MIRV		
multiple independently targetable reentry vehicle	MUHRV	ˈmərv
Misbourne		
river, England	MIS-buhrn, MIZ-buhrn	ˈmisbərn, ˈmizbərn
Mischa		
pers. name, Russian	MĒ-shuh	ˈmiːʃə
Misenum		
headland on Bay of Naples	mī-SĒ-nuhm	maiˈsiːnəm
Misenus		
trumpeter drowned by Triton in the Aeneid	mī-SĒ-nuhs	maiˈsiːnəs
Misérables, Les		
novel, V. Hugo	lā mē-zā-RAHBL, [$] LĀ MIZ-uh-RAHB(-luh)	leː miːzeːrɑːbl, [$] ˌleː ˌmizəˈrɑb(lə)

Foreign Sounds: ue: *Fr.* **rue**, *Ger.* **fü**llen uh(r): *Fr.* b**oeu**f, *Ger.* H**ö**hle kh: *Ger.* i**ch**, *Scot.* lo**ch** g̃: *Sp.* ami**g**o v̰: *Sp.* ha**b**lar hl: *Welsh* **Ll**ane**ll**i. CAPITALS: primary stress. SMALL CAPS: secondary stress. [$]: U.S. pron. [£]: British pron.

Miserere
   prayer, Latin "have mercy"   MIZ-uh-RIR-ē, MIZ-uh-RER-ē,   ˌmizə'ririˈ, ˌmizə'reriˈ,
                       MIZ-uh-RÄ-rä   ˌmizə'reːreː

Mishna, -nah
   Jewish oral law   MISH-nuh   'miʃnə

Miskito [Mosquito]
   Cen. American people   muh-SKÊT-ō   mə'skiːtoː

Miss
   form of address for an unmarried   MIS, mis, muhs   'mis, mis, məs
    woman

Missa Brevis
   Latin "short mass"   MIS-uh BREV-uhs   ˌmisə 'brevəs

Missa Solemnis
   Latin "solemn mass"   MIS-uh suh-LEM-nuhs   ˌmisə sə'lemnəs

Missaukee
   county, MI   mi-SAW-kē   mi'sɔːkiˈ

Missenden
   former name of the Misbourne   MIS-n-duhn   'misn̩dən
    River, *England*

Mission Haut Brion, La
   wine   lah mēs-YAWⁿ ō brē-AWⁿ   lɑː miːsjɔ̃ oː briːɔ̃

Mississauga
   town, Canada   MIS-uh-SAW-guh   ˌmisə'sɔːgə

Mississippi
   river, state, US   MIS-(uh-)-SIP-ē   ˌmis(ə)'sipiˈ

Mississippian
   geologic period; pert. to Mississippi   MIS-(uh-)-SIP-ē-uhn   ˌmis(ə)'sipiːən

Missoula
   city, county, MT   muh-ZOO-luh   mə'zuːlə

Missouri
   state, US; N. American people   muh-ZUR-ē, muh-ZUR-uh   mə'zuriˈ, mə'zurə

Missourian
   pert. to Missouri; *inhabitant of*   muh-ZUR-ē-uhn   mə'zuriːən
    Missouri

Missy
   pers. name   MIS-ē   'misiˈ

Mister
   form of address for a man   MIS-tuhr, MIS-tuhr   'mistəʳ, ˌmistəʳ

Misti, El
   volcano, Peru   el MĒ-stē, el MIS-tē   el 'miːstiː, el 'mistiˈ

Mistral
   1. Frédéric, *Provençal poet (Nobel*   mē-STRAHL   miːstrɑːl
    1904)
   2. Gabriela, *Chilean poet,*   mē-STRAHL   miː'stral
    diplomat (Nobel 1945)
   3. wind   MIS-truhl   'mistrəl

Mita
   tdmk for a photocopying machine   MĒT-uh   'miːʈə

Mitanni
   ancient Mesopotamian people   muh-TAN-ē   mə'tæniˈ

Mitch
   pers. name   MICH   'mitʃ

Mitchell
   Peter, *English biochemist (Nobel*   MICH-uhl   'mitʃəl
    1978); pers. name

Key (col. 2):   a: fad   ā: fade   ah: father   ar: Mary   aw: law   e: fed   ē: feed   er: merry   i: hid   ī: hide   ō: coat   o͞o: boot
oi: boy   ow: now   u: put   uh: above   uhr: bird   ch: chop   ng: ring   sh: show   th: thick   <u>th</u>: this   zh: measure

Mitchum
Robert, *US actor*   MICH-uhm   'mitʃəm

Mithraism
ancient cult of Mithras   MITH-ruh-IZ-uhm, MITH-RĀ-IZ-uhm   'miθrə,izəm, 'miθ,reɪ,izəm

Mithras
supreme Persian god   MITH-ruhs   'miθrəs

Mithridates
king of Parthia   MITH-ruh-DĀT-ēz   ˌmiθrə'deːṭiːz

Mitla
ancient city, Mexico   MĒT-lah   'miːtlɑ

Mitsubishi
Japanese corp.   MIT-su-BĒ-shē   ˌmitsu'biːʃiˑ

Mitsui
Japanese trading co   MIT-so͞o-ē   'mitsuːiˑ

Mittagong
town, Australia   MIT-uh-GAHNG, -GAWNG   'miṭəˌgɑŋ, -ˌgɔːŋ

Mittelfranken
prov, Germany   MIT-l-FRAHNG-kuhn   'miṭlˌfrɑŋkən

Mittelheim
German wine   MIT-l-HĪM   'miṭlˌhɑim

Mittelmosel
German wine   MIT-l-MŌ-zuhl   'miṭlˌmoːzəl

Mittelrhein
German wine   MIT-l-RĪN   'miṭlˌrɑin

Mitterrand
François, *president, France*   mē-ter-AH[n]   miːterɑ̃

Mitty
Walter, *Thurber character*   MIT-ē   'miṭiˑ

Mitylene
see Mytilene

Mitzi
pers. name   MIT-sē   'mitsiˑ

Mixe
lang., people, Mexico   MĒ-HĀ   'miːˌheː

Mixolydian
musical mode   MIK-suh-LID-ē-uhn   ˌmiksə'lidiːən

Mixtec [Mixteco]
N. American people   MĒ-STEK   'miːˌstek

Mixteco [Mixtec]
N. American people   mē-STĀ-kō, mē-STEK-ō   miː'steːkoː, miː'stekoː

Miyazawa
Kiichi, *Japanese prime minister*   mē-ah-zah-wah, Ⓢ MĒ-uh-ZAH-wuh   miːɑzɑwɑ, Ⓢ ˌmiːə'zɑwə

Mizpah
towns, Palestine   MIZ-PAH, MIZ-puh   'mizˌpɑ, 'mizpə

Mladá Boleslav
town, Czech republic   MLAHD-uh BAW-luh-SLAHF, Ⓢ uhm-LAHD-uh   ˌmlɑdə 'bɔːlə,slɑf, Ⓢ əmˌlɑdə

Mmabatho
town, S. Africa   mah-BAH-tō   mɑ'bɑtoː

Mnemon
servant of Achilles   NĒ-MAHN, NĒ-muhn   'niːˌmɑn, 'niːmən

Mnemosyne
Greek goddess of memory, mother of the Muses   ni-MAHS-n-ē, ni-MAHZ-n-ē   ni'masni̩ˑ, ni'mazni̩ˑ

Foreign Sounds: ue: *Fr.* **r**ue, *Ger.* f**ü**llen   uh(r): *Fr.* b**oeu**f, *Ger.* H**öh**le   kh: *Ger.* i**ch**, *Scot.* lo**ch**   g̃: *Sp.* ami**g**o   v̱: *Sp.* ha**b**lar
hl: *Welsh* **Ll**anelli.   CAPITALS: primary stress.   SMALL CAPS: secondary stress.   Ⓢ: U.S. pron.   Ⓛ: British pron.

Mnestheus
   companion of Aeneas   NES-thē-uhs, NES-th(y)o͞os   'nesθiːəs, 'nesθ(j)uːs

Mo
   pers. name   MŌ   'moː

Moab
   ancient kingdom, Middle East;   MŌ-AB   'moːˌæb
   city, UT

Moabite
   native or inhabitant of Moab   MŌ-uh-BĪT   'moːə,bait

Moammar
   pers. name, Arabic   MŌ-uh-MAHR   'moːə,maʳ

Moana
   Municipal Stadium, *Reno, NV*   mō-AN-uh   moː'ænə

Moapa
   Indian reservation, NV   mō-AP-uh   moː'æpə

Moberly
   city, MO   MŌ-buhr-lē   'moːbəʳliˑ

Mobil
   US oil co.   MŌB-uhl   'moːbəl

Mobile
   river, city, county, AL   mō-BĒL, MŌ-BĒL   moː'biːl, 'moːˌbiːl

Möbius
   band or strip, one-sided surface   MUH(R)-bē-uhs, MŌ-bē-uhs   'mœːbiːəs, 'moːbiːəs

Mobutu Sese Seko
   president, Zaire   muh-BO͞O-to͞o SĀ-sä SĀ-kō   mə'buːtuː 'seːseː 'seːkoː

Moby Dick
   novel, H. Melville   MŌ-bē DIK   ˌmoːbiˑ 'dik

Mocha
   1. seaport, Yemen; chocolate/   MŌ-kuh   'moːkə
     coffee drink
   2. island, Pacific   MŌ-chuh   'moːtʃə

Moctezuma [Montezuma]
   Aztec emperor   MAHK-tuh-ZO͞O-muh   ˌmɑktə'zuːmə

Modelo Especial
   Mexican beer   mō-<u>TH</u>Ā-lō es-pes-YAHL   moː'ðeːloː espes'jal

Modem
   computer peripheral   MŌD-uhm, MŌ-DEM   'moːdəm, 'moːˌdem

Modena
   prov & town, Italy   MAW-den-AH, ⑤ MAWD-n-uh,   'mɔːdenˌɑ, ⑤ 'mɔːdnə,
                     MAWD-n-AH   'moːdn̩ˌɑ

Moderatus
   pers. name, Latin   MAHD-uh-RĀT-uhs   ˌmɑdə'reːʈəs

Modest
   pers. name, Russian   MUHD-YEST   ˌməd'jest

Modeste
   pers. name, French   maw-DEST   mɔːdest

Modesto
   1. city, CA   muh-DES-tō   mə'destoː
   2. pers. name, Spanish   mō-<u>TH</u>Ā-stō   moː'ðeːstoː

Modigliani
   Amedeo, *Italian artist;* Franco,   MŌ-dēl-YAHN-ē, MAWD-l-YAHN-ē   ˌmoːdiːl'janiˑ, ˌmɔːdl̩'janiˑ
   Italian-born US economist
   (Nobel 1985)

Modius Fabidius
   son of the Sabine god Quirinus   MŌD-ē-uhs fuh-BID-ē-uhs   ˌmoːdiːəs fə'bidiːəs

---

Key (col. 2):   a: fad   ā: fade   ah: father   ar: Mary   aw: law   e: fed   ē: feed   er: merry   i: hid   ī: hide   ō: coat   o͞o: boot
oi: boy   ow: now   u: put   uh: above   uhr: bird   ch: chop   ng: ring   sh: show   th: thick   <u>th</u>: this   zh: measure

Modjeska
  Helena, *US actress*   muh-JES-kuh   mə'dʒeskə

Modoc
  county, CA; N. American people   MŌD-AHK   'moːd,ɑk

Modred [Mordred]
  Arthurian villain   MŌ-druhd   'moːdrəd

Modrow
  Hans, *German politican*   MŌ-DRŌ   'moː,droː

Moesia
  ancient country of southern   MĒ-shuh, MĒ-sē-uh   'miːʃə, 'miːsiːə
    Europe

Moët & Chandon
  champagne   maw-ET ā shahⁿ-DAWⁿ, MWET   mɔːet eː ʃɑ̃dɔ̃, mwet

Moffat
  Donald, *British actor; pers. name*   MAHF-uht   'mɑfət

Mogadishu
  city, Somalia   MAHG-uh-DISH-ōō, MAWG-, -DĒSH-ōō   ,mɑgə'diʃuː, ,mɔːg-, -'diːʃuː

Mogador
  former name of Essaouira   MAHG-uh-DŌR, MAHG-uh-DAWR   ,mɑgə'doːʳ, ,mɑgə'dɔːʳ

Mogen David
  1. kosher food co.   MAW-guhn DAW-vuhd, MŌ-guhn   ,mɔːgən 'dɔːvəd, ,moːgən
     DAHV-uhd, DĀ-vuhd   'dɑvəd, 'deːvəd

  2. see Magen David

Mogollon
  mtn. range, AZ   MUHG-ē-ŌN, MŌ-guh-YŌN   ,məgiː'oːn, ,moːgə'joːn

Mogul, Moghul
  Indian Muslim of Mongol origin   MŌ-guhl, mō-GUHL   'moːgəl, moː'gəl

Mohács
  city, Hungary   MŌ-HAHCH   'moː,hɑtʃ

Mohammed
  1. pers. name   mō-HAM-uhd, mō-HAHM-uhd   moː'hæməd, moː'hɑməd
  2. Afghan   mō-HUHM-muhd   moː'həmməd
  3. Arabic   mu-HAM-muhd   mu'hæmməd
  4. Persian   maw-HAHM-mahd   mɔː'hɑmmɑːd

Mohammedan
  see Muhammedan

Mohammedanism
  see Muhammedanism

Mohammed Zahir
  king, Afghanistan   mō-HUHM-muhd zah-IR,   moː'həmməd zɑ'iʳ,
     Ⓢ mō-HAM-uhd, mō-HAHM-uhd   Ⓢ moː'hæməd,
          moː'hɑməd

Mohan
  pers. name   mō-HAHN   moː'hɑn

Mohandas
  pers. name, Gujarati   MŌ-huhn-DAHS   'moːhən,dɑs

Mohave
  county, AZ   muh-HAHV-ē, mō-   mə'hɑviˑ, moː-

Mohave, Mojave
  desert, CA; N. American people   muh-HAHV-ē, mō-   mə'hɑviˑ, moː-

Mohawk
  N. American people   MŌ-HAWK   'moː,hɔːk

Mohegan
  N. American people   mō-HĒ-guhn   moː'hiːgən

Foreign Sounds: **ue:** *Fr.* **rue**, *Ger.* **füllen**   **uh(r):** *Fr.* **boeuf**, *Ger.* **Höhle**   <u>kh</u>: *Ger.* **ich**, *Scot.* **loch**   **ğ:** *Sp.* **amigo**   **v:** *Sp.* **hablar**
hl: *Welsh* **Llanelli.**   CAPITALS: primary stress.   SMALL CAPS: secondary stress.   Ⓢ: U.S. pron.   Ⓛ: British pron.

Mohenjo-daro		
prehistoric city, Pakistan	mō-HEN-jō-DAHR-ō	moːˌhendʒoːˈdɑroː
Mohican		
N. American people; river, OH	mō-HĒ-kuhn	moːˈhiːkən
Moholy-Nagy		
László, *Hungarian artist*	MAW-HOI-NAHD, Ⓢ MAW-HOI-NAHZH, -NAHJ	ˈmɔːˌhɔiˈnɑd̦, Ⓢ ˈmɔːˌhɔiˈnɑʒ, -ˈnɑdʒ
Mohorovičić		
Andrija, *Croatian physicist*	maw-HAWR-uh-VĒ-CHĒCH, Ⓢ MŌ-huh-RŌ-vuh-CHICH	mɔːˌhɔːrəˈviːˌtʃiːtʃ, Ⓢ ˌmoːhəˈroːvəˌtʃitʃ
Mohs' scale		
scale of hardness	MŌZ SKĀL, MŌS, MŌ-zuhz	ˈmoːz ˌskeːl, ˈmoːs, ˈmoːzəz
Moi		
Daniel arap, *Kenyan leader*	MOI	ˈmɔi
Moira		
pers. name	MOI-ruh	ˈmɔirə
Moirae, Moirai		
the Fates	MOI-RĪ	ˈmɔiˌrɑi
Moïse		
pers. name, French	maw-ĒZ	mɔːiːz
Moisés		
pers. name	MOI-shās	ˈmɔiʃeːs
Moissan		
Henri, *French chemist (Nobel 1906)*	mwah-SAH^n	mwɑːsɑ̃
Mojave		
see Mohave		
Moji		
city, Japan	mō-jē	moːdʒiˑ
Mojo		
S. American people	MŌ-HŌ	ˈmoːˌhoː
Moktar		
pers. name, Arabic	MAHK-TAHR	ˈmɑkˌtɑ^r
Moldau		
river, E. Europe; region, Romania	MAWL-DOW, MŌL-DOW	ˈmɔːlˌdɑu, ˈmoːlˌdɑu
Moldavia		
republic, Europe; province, Romania	mahl-DĀ-vē-uh, -vyuh	mɑlˈdeːviːə, -vjə
Moldavian		
pert. to Moldavia	mahl-DĀ-vē-uhn, -vyuhn	mɑlˈdeːviːən, -vjən
Moldova [Moldavia]		
Eastern European republic	muhl-DŌ-vuh	məlˈdoːvə
Mole-Dagbani		
lang., Ghana	MŌ-lā-DAHG-BAHN-ē	ˌmoːleːˌdɑgˈbɑniˑ
Molière		
Jean Baptiste, *French playwright*	mawl-YER, Ⓢ mōl-YER, MŌL-YER	mɔːljer, Ⓢ moːlˈje^r, ˈmoːlˌje^r
Molina		
city, Chile	muh-LĒ-nuh	məˈliːnə
Moline		
town, IL	mō-LĒN	moːˈliːn
Molinism		
Christian sect	MŌ-luh-NIZ-uhm, MAHL-	ˈmoːləˌnizəm, ˈmɑl-
Molionidae		
twin brothers, Eurytus and Cteatus	MŌ-lē-AHN-uh-DĒ	ˌmoːliːˈɑnəˌdiː

Key (col. 2): a: **fad** ā: **fade** ah: **father** ar: **Mary** aw: **law** e: **fed** ē: **feed** er: **merry** i: **hid** ī: **hide** ō: **coat** o͞o: **boot** oi: **boy** ow: **now** u: **put** uh: **above** uhr: **bird** ch: **chop** ng: **ring** sh: **show** th: **thick** <u>th</u>: **this** zh: **measure**

Mollie, Molly
  pers. name   MAHL-ē   'mɑliˑ

Möllnir
  Thor's hammer in Scandinavian   MUH(R)D-l-NIR, MUH(R)L-nir   'mœd!ˌniʳ, 'mœlniʳ
  myth

Mollweide
  projection, map projection   MAWL-VĪD-uh, MÔL-WĪD-uh   'mɔːlˌvaidə, 'moːlˌwaidə

Molly
  see Mollie

Mollymauk
  sea bird (albatross)   MAHL-ē-MAWK   'mɑliˑˌmɔːk

Molnár
  Ferenc, *Hungarian writer*   MÔL-NAHR, MAWL-NAHR   'moːlˌnɑʳ, 'mɔːlˌnɑʳ

Moloch
  Canaanite god   MAHL-uhk, MŌ-LAHK   'mɑlək, 'moːˌlak

Molokai
  island, HI   MAHL-uh-KĪ, MŌ-luh-KĪ   ˌmɑlə'kai, ˌmoːlə'kai

Molong
  town, Australia   MŌ-LAHNG, MŌ-LAWNG   'moːˌlaŋ, 'moːˌlɔːŋ

Molossus
  son of Andromache and   mō-LAHS-uhs   moː'lasəs
  Neoptolemus

Molotov cocktail
  crude bomb   MAHL-uh-TAWF KAHK-TĂL,   ˌmaləˌtɔːf 'kak,teːl,
                        MAW-luh-TAWF, MŌ-luh-TAWF,   ˌmɔːləˌtɔːf, ˌmoːləˌtɔːf,
                        -TAWV   -ˌtɔːv

Moltke
  Helmuth von, *Prussian militarist*   MÔLT-kuh   'moːltkə

Molucca
  Sea, *Asia*   muh-LUHK-uh   mə'ləkə

Moluccas [Maluku]
  islands, Indonesia   muh-LUHK-uhz   mə'ləkəz

molybdenum
  element   muh-LIB-duh-nuhm   mə'libdənəm

Molyneux
  pers. name   MAHL-uhn-YŌŌ(KS), MUHL-   'malənˌjuː(ks), 'məl-

Mom
  informal for mother   MAHM, MUHM   'mɑm, 'məm

Momaday
  Navarre Scott, *US writer*   MAHM-uh-DĀ   'mɑməˌdeː

Mombasa
  island, city, Kenya   mahm-BAHS-uh   mɑm'bɑsə

Momma
  informal for mother   MAHM-uh, MUHM-uh   'mɑmə, 'məmə

Mommsen
  Theodor, *German historian (Nobel*   MÔM-zuhn   'moːmzən
  1902)

Mommy
  informal for mother   MAHM-ē, MUHM-ē   'mɑmiˑ, 'məmiˑ

Momus
  personification of sarcasm or   MŌ-muhs   'moːməs
  mockery

Mon [Talaing]
  lang., people, Burma, Thailand   MŌN   'moːn

Foreign Sounds: ue: *Fr.* **rue**, *Ger.* f**ü**llen uh(r): *Fr.* b**oeu**f, *Ger.* H**öh**le <u>kh</u>: *Ger.* i**ch**, *Scot.* lo**ch** ğ: *Sp.* ami**g**o <u>v</u>: *Sp.* ha**b**lar
hl: *Welsh* **Ll**anelli. CAPITALS: primary stress. SMALL CAPS: secondary stress. Ⓢ: U.S. pron. Ⓑ: British pron.

Mona
   pers. name   MŌ-nuh   'moːnə

Monacan
   pert. to Monaco   MAHN-uh-ᴋᴜʜɴ, muh-NAHK-uhn   'manə,kən, mə'nakən

Monaco
   principality, Europe   MAHN-uh-ᴋŌ, muh-NAHK-ō   'manə,koː, mə'nakoː

Monaco-Ville
   city, Monaco   MAHN-uh-ᴋŌ-VĒL, muh-NAHK-ō-   ,manə,koː'viːl, mə,nakoː-

Monadnock
   peak, NH   muh-NAD-ɴᴀʜᴋ   mə'næd,nak

Monaghan
   county, Ireland   MAHN-uh-huhn, Ⓢ MAHN-uh-ʜᴀɴ   'manəhən, Ⓢ 'manə,hæn

Mona Lisa [La Gioconda]
   da Vinci painting   MŌ-nuh LĒ-suh   ,moːnə 'liːsə

Monarch
   butterfly species   MAHN-uhrk, MAHN-ᴀʜʀᴋ   'manəʳk, 'man,aʳk

Monarchianism
   early Christian anti-Trinitarian muh-NAHR-kē-uh-ɴɪᴢ-uhm   mə'naʳkiːə,nizəm
     teachings

Mönchengladbach
   city, Germany   ᴍᴜʜ(ʀ)ɴ-<u>khuhn</u>-GLAHT-ʙᴀʜ<u>ᴋʜ</u> ,mœnçən'glat,bax

Mönchshof
   German beer   ᴍᴜʜ(ʀ)ɴ<u>ᴋʜꜱ</u>-ʜᴀᴡꜰ   'mœːnçs,hɔːf

Monck
   George, *English soldier*   MUHNGK   'məŋk

Moncrief
   Sidney, *US basketball player* mahn-KRĒF, MAHN-ᴋʀĒꜰ   man'kriːf, 'man,kriːf

Moncton
   town, Canada   MUHNG(K)-tuhn   'məŋ(k)tən

Mondale
   Walter, *US politician*   MAHN-ᴅĀʟ   'man,deːl

Mondavi
   Robert, *California vintner*   mahn-DAHV-ē   man'daviˑ

Monday
   day of the week   MUHN-dē, MUHN-dā   'məndiˑ, 'məndeː

Mondrian
   Piet, *Dutch artist*   MAWN-drē-ᴀʜɴ   'moːndriːˌan

Monegasque
   people of Monaco   MAHN-uh-GASK, MŌ-nuh-GAHSK ,manə'gæsk, ,moːnə'gaˑsk

Monel
   tdmk for a metal alloy   mō-NEL   moː'nel

Monet
   Claude, *French painter*   maw-NE, Ⓢ muh-NĀ   moːne, Ⓢ mə'neː

Moneta
   1. E. T., *Italian journalist, pacifist* mō-NĀT-uh   moː'neːtə
     (Nobel 1907)
   2. title of Juno   mō-NĒT-uh, mō-NĀT-uh, muh- moː'niːtə, moː'neːtə, mə-

Mongol
   people, Asia   MAHNG-guhl, MAHN-ɢŌʟ,   'maŋgəl, 'man,goːl,
                        MAHNG-ɢŌʟ   'maŋ,goːl

Mongolia
   region, Asia   mahn-GŌL-yuh, mahng-, -GŌ-lē-uh man'goːljə, maŋ-, -'goːliːə

Mongolian
   pert. to Mongols *or* Mongolia mahn-GŌL-yuhn, mahng-,   man'goːljən, maŋ-, -'goːliːən
                        -GŌ-lē-uhn

Key (col. 2): a: fad ā: fade ah: father ar: Mary aw: law e: fed ē: feed er: merry i: hid ī: hide ō: coat ōō: boot
oi: boy ow: now u: put uh: above uhr: bird ch: chop ng: ring sh: show th: thick <u>th</u>: this zh: measure

Mongoloid
 resembling the Mongols MAHNG-guh-LOID   'maŋgə,lɔid

Monguor
 lang., people, China MAHN-GWAWR, MAHNG-GWAWR 'man,gwɔːʳ, 'maŋ,gwɔːʳ

Monica
 pers. name MAHN-i-kuh   'manikə

Monique
 pers. name muh-NĒK, mō-NĒK   mə'niːk, moː'niːk

Moniteau
 county, MO MAHN-uh-TŌ   'manə,toː

Moniz
 see Egas Moniz

Mon-Khmer
 Austroasiatic lang. family MŌN-kuh-MER   ,moːnkə'meʳ

Mon-Lei
 Chinese beer MAHN-LĀ, MŌN-LĀ   'man'leː, 'moːn'leː

Monmouth
 pl. name, US & Britain MAHN-muhth, MUHN-muhth 'manməθ, 'mənməθ

Monmouthshire
 former county, England or Wales MAHN-muhth-shuhr, 'manməθʃəʳ, 'mənməθʃəʳ,
    MUHN-muhth-shuhr, -SHIR   -,ʃiʳ

Monnet
 Jean, *French economist* maw-NE, Ⓢ muh-NĀ moːne, Ⓢ mə'neː

Mono
 county, CA; river, Togo; island, MŌ-nō   'moːnoː
  Pacific; N. American people

Monoceros
 constellation muh-NAHS-uh-ruhs   mə'nasərəs

Monoclonius
 dinosaur MAHN-uh-KLŌ-nē-uhs   ,manə'kloːniːəs

Monod
 Jacques, *French biochemist* maw-NŌ   moːnoː
  (Nobel 1965)

Monona
 county, IA; lake, WI muh-NŌ-nuh   mə'noːnə

Monongahela
 river, WV, PA muh-NAHN-guh-HĒ-luh, mə,naŋgə'hiːlə, mə,naŋgə-,
    muh-NAHNG-guh-, -HĀ-luh   -'heːlə

Monongalia
 county, WV MAHN-uhn-GĀ-lē-uh, ,manən'geːliːə,
    MAHN-uhng-GĀ-lē-uh, -GĀL-yuh, ,manən'geːliːə, -'geːljə,
    locally also   *locally also*
    MAHN-guh-HĀL-ē(-uh)   ,mangə'heːliː(ə)

Monophysite
 adherent of Monophysitism muh-NAHF-uh-SĪT   mə'nafə,sait

Monophysitism
 doctrine of Christ's total divinity muh-NAHF-uh-SIT-IZ-uhm mə'nafə,sit,izəm

Monosodium glutamate
 food additive MAHN-uh-SŌD-ē-uhm ,manə'soːdiːəm 'gluːtə,meːt
    GLOOT-uh-MĀT

Monotremata
 egg-laying mammals MAHN-uh-TREM-uht-uh, ,manə'tremətə,
    MAHN-uh-TRĒ-muht-uh   ,manə'triːmətə

Monotype
 tdmk for a typesetting machine MAHN-uh-TĪP   'manə,taip

Foreign Sounds: ue: *Fr.* **rue**, *Ger.* f**ü**llen uh(r): *Fr.* b**oeu**f, *Ger.* H**ö**hle <u>kh</u>: *Ger.* i**ch**, *Scot.* lo**ch** g̶: *Sp.* ami**g**o <u>v</u>: *Sp.* ha**b**lar
hl: *Welsh* **Ll**anelli. CAPITALS: primary stress. SMALL CAPS: secondary stress. Ⓢ: U.S. pron. Ⓛ: British pron.

Monroe
   James, *5th US president;* Marilyn,   muhn-RŌ, MUHN-RŌ   mən'roː, 'mən,roː
     US actress; US pl. name; pers.
     name
Monrovia
   city, Liberia   muhn-RŌ-vē-uh   mən'roːviːə
Monsanto
   US chemical co.   mahn-SAN-tō   man'sæntoː
Monsarrat
   Nicholas, *English novelist*   MAHN-suh-RAHT, MAHN-suh-RAT, Ⓔ   ,mansə'rat, ,mansə'ræt, Ⓔ
                                MAHN-suh-RAT   'mansə,ræt
Monseigneur
   French title of honor   mawⁿ-sen-YUHR Ⓢ mawⁿ-SĀN-yuhr   mɔ̃seɲœr, Ⓢ mɔ̃'seːnjəʳ
Monsieur
   French form of address for a man   muhs-YUH(R), Ⓢ muhsh-YUHR,   məsjœː, Ⓢ məʃ'jəʳ, məs'jəʳ,
                             muhs-YUHR, muh-SIR   mə'siʳ
Monsignor
   title for certain prelates   mahn-SĒN-yuhr, muhn-SĒN-yuhr   man'siːnjəʳ, mən'siːnjəʳ
Monson
   town, MA   MUHN(T)-suhn   'mən(t)sən
Montagnais
   N. American people   MAHN-tuhn-YĀ   ,mantən'jeː
Montagu, -gue
   pers. name   MAHNT-uh-GYOO   'mantə,gjuː
Montaigne
   Michel, *French essayist*   mawⁿ-TEN-yuh   mɔ̃teɲ
Montalban
   Ricardo, *US actor*   mōn-tahl-VAHN, Ⓢ MAHNT-l-BAHN   moːntal'ßan, Ⓢ ,mantl'ban
Montalbana
   Italian chianti   MAWN-tahl-BAHN-uh   ,mɔːntal'banə
Montale
   Eugenio, *Italian poet (Nobel 1975)*   mōn-TAHL-ā   moːn'taleː
Montana
   state, US; Joe, *US football player*   mahn-TAN-uh   man'tænə
Montanism
   Christian heresy   MAHN-tuh-NIZ-uhm   'mantə,nizəm
Montauk Point
   eastern point of Long Island, NY   MAHN-TAWK POINT   ,man,tɔːk 'pɔint
Mont Blanc
   mtn., France; mfrs.   mawⁿ BLAHⁿ   mɔ̃ blã
Montcalm
   county, MI   mahnt-KAHM   mant'kam
Mont Cervin
   see Cervin, Mont
Monte Carlo
   tourist resort, Monaco   MAHNT-ē KAHR-lō   ,manti· 'kaʳloː
Monte Cassino
   abbey, Italy   MAHNT-ē kuh-SĒ-nō   ,manti: kə'siːnoː
Monte Cervino
   see Cervino, Monte
Monte Cristo
   1. island, Italy   MAWN-tā KRĒ-stō, Ⓢ MAHN-tē   ,mɔːnteː 'kriːstoː, Ⓢ ,manti·
                         KRIS-tō   'kristoː
   2. sandwich   MAHN-tē KRIS-tō   ,manti· 'kristoː

Key (col. 2):   a: fad ā: fade ah: father ar: Mary aw: law e: fed ê: feed er: merry i: hid ī: hide ō: coat ōō: boot
oi: boy ow: now u: put uh: above uhr: bird ch: chop ng: ring sh: show th: thick th: this zh: measure

Montefiascone

commune, Italy   MAWN-tä-fyah-SKŌ-nä,   ˌmɔːnteːfjaˈskoːneː,
        Ⓢ MAHNT-ē-fyah-SKŌ-nē   Ⓢ ˌmantiːfjaˈskoːniˑ

Montego Bay

city, Jamaica   mahn-TĒ-gō BĀ   manˈtiːgoː ˈbeː

Monteith

pers. name   mahn-TĒTH   manˈtiːθ

Montenegrin

pert. to Montenegro   MAHNT-uh-NĒ-gruhn, -NEG-ruhn,   ˌmantəˈniːgrən, -ˈnegrən,
        -NĀ-gruhn   -ˈneːgrən

Montenegro [Crna Gora]

republic, E. Europe (former   MAHNT-uh-NĒ-grō, -NEG-rō, -NĀ-grō   ˌmantəˈniːgroː, -ˈnegroː,
kingdom)   -ˈneːgroː

Montepulciano

commune, Italy   MAWNT-ä-pul-CHAHN-ō   ˌmɔːnteːpulˈtʃanoː

Monterey

city, county, CA   MAHNT-uh-RĀ   ˌmantəˈreː

Monterrey

city, Mexico   MAHNT-uh-RĀ   ˌmantəˈreː

Montesquieu

Baron de, Charles-Louis de   mawⁿ-tes-KYUH(R),   mõteskjœː, Ⓢ ˌmantəsˈkjuː
Secondat, *French philosopher*   Ⓢ MAHNT-uhs-KYŌŌ

Montessori

Maria, *Italian educator; teaching*   MAHNT-uh-SŌR-ē,   ˌmantəˈsoːriˑ, ˌmantəˈsoːriˑ
method   MAHNT-uh-SAWR-ē

Montevallo

town, AL   MAHNT-uh-VAL-ō   ˌmantəˈvæloː

Monteverdi

Claudio, *Italian composer*   MAHNT-uh-VERD-ē,   ˌmantəˈveʳdiˑ, ˌmantəˈvəʳdiˑ
        MAHNT-uh-VUHRD-ē

Montevideo

dept, city, Uruguay   MAHNT-uh-vuh-DĀ-ō, -VID-ē-ō   ˌmantəvəˈdeːoː, -ˈvidiːoː

Montezuma [Moctezuma]

Aztec emperor   MAHNT-uh-ZŌŌ-muh   ˌmantəˈzuːmə

Montfort

1. pers. name   MAHNT-fuhrt   ˈmantfəʳt
2. Simon de, French leader   mawⁿ-FAWR, Ⓢ MAHNT-fuhrt   mõfoːr, Ⓢ ˈmantfəʳt

Montgomerie, Montgomery

pers. name   muhn(t)-GUHM-(uh-)rē, mahn(t)-,   mən(t)ˈgəm(ə)riˑ, man(t)-,
        -GAHM-(uh-)rē   -ˈgam(ə)riˑ

Montgomery

US pl. name; borough, Wales   muhn(t)-GUHM-(uh-)rē, mahn(t)-,   mən(t)ˈgəm(ə)riˑ, man(t)-,
        -GAHM-(uh-)rē   -ˈgam(ə)riˑ

Montgomeryshire

former county, Wales   muhnt-GUHM-(uh-)rē-shuhr, -SHIR   məntˈgəm(ə)riˑʃəʳ, -ˌʃiʳ

Month

Egyptian war god   MAHNT, MAWNT   ˈmant, ˈmɔːnt

Monticello

Jefferson's home; US pl. name   MAHNT-uh-SEL-ō, -CHEL-ō   ˌmantəˈseloː, -ˈtʃeloː

Montmartre

section, Paris, France   mawⁿ-MAHRTR   mõmartr

Montmorency

1. county, MI; river, Canada   MAHNT-muh-REN(T)-sē   ˌmantməˈren(t)siˑ
2. commune, France   mawⁿ-maw-rahⁿ-SĒ   mõmɔːrãsiː

Foreign Sounds: **ue:** *Fr.* **rue,** *Ger.* **füllen** **uh(r):** *Fr.* **boeuf,** *Ger.* **Höhle** **kh:** *Ger.* **ich,** *Scot.* **loch** **g̃:** *Sp.* **amigo** **v:** *Sp.* **hablar**
hl: *Welsh* **Llanelli.** CAPITALS: primary stress. SMALL CAPS: secondary stress. Ⓢ: U.S. pron. Ⓛ: British pron.

Montour
  county, PA   mahn-TUR   mɑn'tuʳ
Montoya
  Carlos, *Spanish guitarist*   mahn-TOI-(y)uh   mɑn'tɔi(j)ə
Montpelier
  city, VT   mahnt-PĒL-yuhr   mɑnt'piːljəʳ
Montpellier
  city, France   mawⁿ-pel-YĀ   mɔ̃peljeː
Montrachet
  wine   mawⁿ-rah-SHE   mɔ̃rɑːʃe
Montreal
  city, Canada   mawⁿ-re-AHL, Ⓢ MAHN-trē-AWL, MUHN-   mɔ̃reɑːl, Ⓢ ˌmɑntriːˈɔːl, ˌmən-

Montreux
  town, Switzerland   mawⁿ-TRUH(R), Ⓢ mahn-TRŌ, MAHN-trō   mɔ̃trœː, Ⓢ mɑn'troː, 'mɑntroː
Mont-Saint-Michel
  islet near French coast; abbey and fortress   mawⁿ-seⁿ-mē-SHEL, Ⓢ MŌN-san-mē-SHEL   mɔ̃sẽmiːʃel, Ⓢ ˌmoːnsænmiˈʃel
Montserrat
  1. island, West Indies   MAHNT-suh-RAT, *locally* MAHNT-suh-RAT   ˌmɑntsə'ræt, *locally* 'mɑntsə,ræt
  2. mtn., Spain   mōnt-sā-RAHT, Ⓢ MAHNT-suh-RAT   moːntseːˈrɑt, Ⓢ ˌmɑntsə'ræt
Mont Tremblant
  park, Quebec   mawⁿ trahⁿ-BLAHⁿ   mɔ̃ trɑ̃blɑ̃
Montu [Month]
  Egyptian war god   MAHN-tōō, MAWN-tōō   'mɑntuː, 'mɔːntuː
Montu-Re [Month]
  Egyptian war god   MAHN-tōō-RĀ, MAWN-tōō-RĀ   'mɑntuːˈreː, 'mɔːntuːˈreː
Monty
  pers. name   MAHNT-ē   'mɑntiˑ
Monty Python
  British comedy troupe   MAHNT-ē PĪ-THAHN   ˌmɑntiˑ 'pai,θɑn
Monza
  city, Italy   MŌNT-sah, MAHN-zuh   'moːntsɑ, 'mɑnzə
Mooers
  Field, *ballpark, Richmond, VA*   MURZ, MŌRZ, MAWRZ   'muʳz, 'moːʳz, 'mɔːʳz
Moog
  tdmk for a music synthesizer   MŌG, MŌŌG   'moːg, 'muːg
Moon
  Sun Myung, *see* Sun Myung Moon
Moonbi
  mtn. range, Australia   MŌŌN-bē   'muːnbiˑ
Moonie
  follower of S. M. Moon *(derogatory)*   MŌŌ-nē   'muːniˑ
Moor
  Arab & Berber conquerors of Spain   MUR   'muʳ
Moore
  Henry, *British sculptor;* Marianne, *US poet;* Stanford, *US biochemist (Nobel 1972); pers. name*   MŌR, MAWR, MUR   'moːʳ, 'mɔːʳ, 'muʳ

Key (col. 2):   a: fad   ā: fade   ah: father   ar: Mary   aw: law   e: fed   ē: feed   er: merry   i: hid   ī: hide   ō: coat   ōō: boot
oi: boy   ow: now   u: put   uh: above   uhr: bird   ch: chop   ng: ring   sh: show   th: thick   <u>th</u>: this   zh: measure

Moorish
 pert. to the Moors   MUR-ish   'murɪʃ

Moosup
 town, CT   MOO-suhp   'muːsəp

Mopsus
 Argonaut; grandson of Tiresias   MAHP-suhs   'mɑpsəs

Mór
 pers. name, Hungarian   MAWR   'mɔːʳ

Moran
 family name   MAWR-uhn, MAHR-uhn, muh-RAN   'mɔːrən, 'mɑrən, mə'ræn

Morar, Loch
 see Loch Morar

Morava
 river, prov, Czech republic   MAWR-uh-vuh   'mɔːrəvə

Moravia
 prov, Czech republic   muh-RĀ-vē-uh   mə'reːviːə

Moravian
 College, *PA*   muh-RĀ-vē-uhn   mə'reːviːən

Moray
 eel   muh-RĀ, MAWR-ā   mə'reː, 'mɔːreː

Morbihan
 dept, France   mawr-bē-AHⁿ   mɔːrbiː㤭

Mordecai
 pers. name   MAWRD-i-кī   'mɔːʳdi,kɑi

Mordred [Modred]
 Arthurian villain   MAWR-druhd   'mɔːʳdrəd

Mordva
 lang., Russia   MAWRD-vuh   'mɔːʳdvə

Mordvin
 European people   MAWRD-vin   'mɔːʳdvin

Mordvinian
 European people   mawrd-VIN-ē-uhn, mawrd-VIN-yuhn   mɔːʳd'viniːən, mɔːʳd'vinjən

More
 Sir Thomas, *English humanist,*   MŌR, MAWR   'moːʳ, 'mɔːʳ
 statesman, saint

Moré [Mossi]
 lang., Ghana, Burkina Faso   muh-RĀ   mə'reː

Morea [Peloponnese]
 peninsula, Greece   muh-RĒ-uh   mə'riːə

Moreau
 1. *pers. name*   mawr-Ō, MŌR-ō, MAWR-ō   mɔːr'oː, 'moːroː, 'mɔːroː
 2. *French*   maw-RŌ   mɔːroː

Morecambe
 town, England   MAWR-kuhm   'mɔːʳkəm

Moree
 town, Australia   mawr-Ē   mɔːr'iː

Moreing
 Field, *ballpark, Sacramento, CA*   MŌR-ing, MAWR-ing   'moːriŋ, 'mɔːriŋ

Morelia
 city, Mexico   muh-RÂL-yuh   mə'reːljə

Morelos
 state, Mexico   muh-RĀ-luhs   mə'reːləs

Moreno
 Rita, *Puerto Rican actress*   maw-RĀ-nō, muh-RĒ-nō   mɔːˈreːnoː, mə'riːnoː

Foreign Sounds: ue: *Fr.* **rue**, *Ger.* **füllen** uh(r): *Fr.* **boeuf**, *Ger.* **Höhle** <u>kh</u>: *Ger.* i<u>ch</u>, *Scot.* lo<u>ch</u> ḡ: *Sp.* ami**g**o v̲: *Sp.* ha**b**lar
hl: *Welsh* **Ll**anelli. CAPITALS: primary stress. SMALL CAPS: secondary stress. Ⓢ: U.S. pron. Ⓔ: British pron.

Moretti
  Italian beer — mōr-ET-ē, mawr-ET-ē — mɔːr'eţiˑ, mɔːr'eţiˑ
Morgan
  John Pierpont *(father & son), US financiers;* Thomas H., *US geneticist (Nobel 1933); pers. name* — MAWR-guhn — 'mɔːʳgən
Morgenthau
  Henry, Jr., *US Secretary of the Treasury* — MAWR-guhn-THAW — 'mɔːʳgən,θɔː
Moriarty
  Michael, *US actor;* Professor, *opponent of Sherlock Holmes* — MAWR-ē-AHRT-ē — ,mɔːriˑ'aʳţiˑ
Moriches
  village, NY — muh-RICH-uhz — mə'ritʃəz
Morisot
  Berthe, *French painter* — maw-rē-SŌ — mɔːriːsoː
Moritz
  pers. name, German — MŌ-rits — 'mɔːrits
Morley
  pers. name — MAWR-lē — 'mɔːʳliˑ
Mormon
  member of the Church of Jesus Christ of Latter-day Saints — MAWR-muhn — 'mɔːʳmən
Mormonism
  religion — MAWR-muh-NIZ-uhm — 'mɔːʳmə,nizəm
Mornay
  white sauce with cheese — mawr-NĀ — mɔːʳneː
Moro
  Philippine Muslim — MŌR-ō, MAWR-ō — 'mɔːroː, 'mɔːroː
Moroccan
  pert. to Morocco — muh-RAHK-uhn — mə'rakən
Morocco
  kingdom, Africa — muh-RAHK-ō — mə'rakoː
Morón
  city, Argentina, Spain; town, Cuba — muh-RŌN — mə'roːn
Moroni
  town, Comoro Islands — maw-RŌ-nē — mɔ'roːniˑ
Morpheus
  Greek god of dreams — MAWR-fē-uhs, MAWR-F(Y)O͞OS — 'mɔːʳfiːəs, 'mɔːʳ,f(j)uːs
Morris
  1. *dance; pers. name* — MAWR-uhs, MAHR-uhs — 'mɔːrəs, 'marəs
  2. *Danish* — MAWR-ēs — 'mɔːriːs
Morrison
  Van, *Irish singer, composer* — MAWR-uh-suhn, MAHR-uh-suhn — 'mɔːrəsən, 'marəsən
Morse
  Samuel, *US inventor* — MAWRS — 'mɔːʳs
Mort
  pers. name — MAWRT — 'mɔːʳt
Morta
  Roman goddess of fate — MAWRT-uh — 'mɔːʳţə
Mortimer
  pers. name — MAWRT-uh-muhr — 'mɔːʳţəməʳ
Mortis, Lacus
  'lake' on Moon — LAHK-uhs MAWRT-uhs — 'lakəs 'mɔːʳţəs

Key (col. 2): a: **fad** ā: **fade** ah: **father** ar: **Mary** aw: **law** e: **fed** ē: **feed** er: **merry** i: **hid** ī: **hide** ō: **coat** o͞o: **boot** oi: **boy** ow: **now** u: **put** uh: **above** uhr: **bird** ch: **chop** ng: **ring** sh: **show** th: **thick** th̲: **this** zh: **measure**

Morton
   pers. name   MAWRT-n   'mɔːˈtn̩

Mort Subite Kriek
   Belgian beer   MAWRT SOO-bi-TĀ KRĔK   'mɔːrt 'suːbi,teː 'kriːk

Moru
   lang., people, Sudan   MŌ-roo, MAWR-oo   'mɔːruː, 'mɔːruː

Moruya
   town, Australia   muh-ROO-yuh   məˈruːjə

Mosaddeq
   see Mossadegh

Mosby
   pers. name   MŌZ-bē   'mɔːzbiˑ

Moscatel
   sweet wine   maw-skah-TEL   mɔːskɑːtel

Moscato
   Italian wine   maw-SKAHT-ō   mɔːˈskɑtoː

Moscoviense, Mare
   see Mare Moscoviense

Moscow
   city, Russia   MAHS-KOW, MAHS-kō   'mɑs,kau, 'mɑskoː

Mosel
   river, France, Germany; dept.,   MŌ-zuhl   'mɔːzəl
     France; wine

Moseley
   Mark, *US football player*   MŌZ-lē   'mɔːzliˑ

Moselle [Mosel]
   river, France, Germany   mō-ZEL   mɔːˈzel

Moses
   1. Hebrew prophet; pers. name   MŌ-zuhz, MŌ-zuhs   'mɔːzəz, 'mɔːzəs
   2. German   MŌ-zes   'mɔːzes

Moshe
   pers. name, Yiddish, Hebrew   MŌ-shuh, mō-SHE   'mɔːʃə, mɔːˈʃe

Moshoeshoe
   king, Lesotho   mō-SHOO-shoo   mɔːˈʃuːʃuː

Moskva
   Russian for Moscow   MUHSK-VAH, Ⓢ mahsk-VAH   ˌməskˈvɑː, Ⓢ mɑskˈvɑ

Moslem [Muslim]
   pert. to Islam; adherent of Islam   MAHZ-luhm, MAHS-luhm   'mɑzləm, 'mɑsləm

Mosquito [Miskito]
   Cen. American people   muh-SKĒT-ō   məˈskiːʈoː

Mosquito Coast
   region, Honduras, Nicaragua   muh-SKĒT-ō KŌST   mə,skiːʈoː 'koːst

Moss
   pers. name   MAWS, MAHS   'mɔːs, 'mɑs

Mossadegh, Mosaddeq
   Mohammed, *premier, Iran*   MAWS-uh-DEK   'mɔːsə,dek

Mössbauer
   R. L., *German-born US physicist*   MUH(R)S-BOW(-uh)r,   'mœs,bau(ə)ˈr,
     (Nobel 1961); effect, *gamma*   Ⓢ MAWS-BOW(-uh)r   Ⓢ 'mɔːs,bau(ə)ˈr
     radiation

Mossi [Moré]
   lang., people, Ghana, Burkina   MAHS-ē   'mɑsiˑ
     Faso

Mossmorran
   region, Scotland   maws-MAWR-uhn   mɔːsˈmɔːrən

Foreign Sounds: **ue**: *Fr.* **rue**, *Ger.* f**ü**llen   **uh(r)**: *Fr.* b**oeu**f, *Ger.* H**öh**le   <u>kh</u>: *Ger.* i**ch**, *Scot.* lo**ch**   **g̃**: *Sp.* ami**g**o   <u>v</u>: *Sp.* ha**b**lar
hl: *Welsh* **Ll**anelli.   CAPITALS: primary stress.   SMALL CAPS: secondary stress.   Ⓢ: U.S. pron.   Ⓛ: British pron.

Mostel
  Zero, *US entertainer*   muh-STEL, mahs-TEL   məˈstel, masˈtel

Mosul
  city, Iraq   mō-SŌŌL, MŌ-suhl   moːˈsuːl, ˈmoːsəl

Mota
  Rosa, *Portuguese marathoner*   MAW-tah   ˈmɔːtaː

Motilal
  pers. name, Kashmiri   MŌ-ti-LAHL   ˈmoːtiˌlal

Motilón
  S. American people   MŌT-uh-LŌN, MŌT-l-ŌN   ˌmoːtəˈloːn, ˌmoːtḷˈoːn

Motilónes
  plural of Motilón   MŌT-uh-LŌ-NĀS, MŌT-l-Ō-NĀS   ˌmoːtəˈloːˌneːs, ˌmoːtḷˈoːˌneːs

Motley Crue
  rock band   MAHT-lē KRŌŌ   ˌmatliˑ ˈkruː

Motown
  nickname for Detroit; musical style   MŌ-TOWN   ˈmoːˌtaun

Mott
  J. R., *US religious leader (Nobel 1946);* Sir Nevill F., *English physicist (Nobel 1977)*   MAHT   ˈmat

Mottelson
  Benjamin Roy, *US-born Danish physicist (Nobel 1975)*   MŌT-l-suhn, -sawn   ˈmoːtḷsən, -sɔːn

Motu
  Papuan people, lang.   MŌ-tōō   ˈmoːtuː

Mouache Ute
  N. American people   mōō-AHCH-ā YŌŌT   muːˈatʃeː ˈjuːt

Moulin à Vent
  French wine   mōō-LEⁿ ah VAHⁿ   muːlẽ aː vã

Moulinex
  tdmk for housewares   MŌŌL-uh-NEKS   ˈmuːləˌneks

Moulis
  French wine region   mōō-LĒ   muːliː

Moulmein
  port, Burma   mōōl-MĀN, mōl-MĀN, -MIN   muːlˈmeːn, moːlˈmeːn, -ˈmin

Moulton
  pers. name   MŌLT-n, MŌL-tuhn   ˈmoːltṇ, ˈmoːltən

Moultrie
  county, IL; city, GA   MŌL-trē   ˈmoːltriˑ

Mount Aloysius
  Junior College   MOWNT AL-uh-WISH-uhs   ˌmaunt ˌæləˈwiʃəs

Mount Athos
  mtn., theocratic republic, Greece   mownt ATH-AHS, Ā-THAHS   maunt ˈæθˌas, ˈeːˌθas

Mountbatten
  Louis, *British militarist*   mownt-BAT-n   mauntˈbætṇ

Mount Desert
  island, ME   MOWNT duh-ZUHRT, DEZ-uhrt   ˌmaunt dəˈzəʳt, ˈdezəʳt

Mount Holyoke
  College, *MA*   mownt HŌ-lē-ŌK, *locally* HŌ(L)-YŌK   maunt ˈhoːliːˌoːk, *locally* ˈhoˑ(l)ˌjoːk

Mountrail
  county, ND   MOWNT-RĀL   ˈmauntˌreːl

Key (col. 2):   a: fad   ā: fade   ah: father   ar: Mary   aw: law   e: fed   ē: feed   er: merry   i: hid   ī: hide   ō: coat   ōō: boot   oi: boy   ow: now   u: put   uh: above   uhr: bird   ch: chop   ng: ring   sh: show   th: thick   th̲: this   zh: measure

Mount Senario
  College, *WI*   MOWNT suh-NAR-ē-ō, suh-NER-ē-ō   ,maunt sə'næriːoː, sə'neriːoː

Mount Wachusett
  Community College, *MA*   MOWNT wah-CHOO-suht   ,maunt wɑ'tʃuːsət

Moure, La
  see La Moure

Mousehole
  town, Cornwall, England   MOWZ-l   'mauzl̩

Moussorgsky
  see Mussorgsky

Mousterian
  Paleolithic culture   moo-STIR-ē-uhn   muː'stiriːən

Mouton Baron Philippe
  wine   moo-TAWⁿ bah-RAWⁿ fē-LĒP   muːtɔ̃ barɔ̃ fiːliːp

Mouton Cadet
  wine   moo-TAWⁿ kah-DE   muːtɔ̃ kaːde

Mouton Rothschild
  wine   moo-TAWⁿ rawt-SHĒLD   muːtɔ̃ rɔːtʃiːld

Movado
  fashion designers   muh-VAHD-ō, mō-VAHD-ō   mə'vadoː, moː'vadoː

Movimento Popular de Libertaçao
  de Angola
  (MPLA), political party, Angola   MŌ-vē-MĀ(N)-too PUH-poo-LAHR   ,moːviː'mẽː(n)tuː ,pəpuː'laːr
        thā LĒ-ber-tah-SOWⁿ thā   ðeː ,liːberta'saũ ðeː
        ahng-GŌ-lah   aŋ'goːlaː

Mowbray
  pers. name   MŌ-BRĀ, MŌ-brē   'moː,breː, 'moːbriˑ

Mowgli
  character in Jungle Books, *R.*   MOW-glē, MŌ-glē   'maugliˑ, 'moːgliˑ
  Kipling

Moynihan
  Daniel P., US politician   MOI-nuh-HAN   'mɔinə,hæn

Moyra
  pers. name   MOI-ruh   'mɔirə

Mozambican
  pert. to Mozambique   MŌ-zuhm-BĒ-kuhn, MŌ-ZAM-BĒ-kuhn   ,moːzəm'biːkən,
               ,moː,zæm'biːkən

Mozambique
  channel, country, Africa   MŌ-zuhm-BĒK, MŌ-ZAM-BĒK   ,moːzəm'biːk, ,moː,zæm'biːk

Mozart
  Wolfgang Amadeus, Austrian   MŌT-SAHRT   'moːt,sɑʳt
  composer

Mozzarella
  cheese   MAHT-suh-REL-uh   ,matsə'relə

Mpumalanga
  city, S. Africa   em-poom-uh-LANG-guh   empuːmə'læŋgə

Mr.
  form of address to a man   MIS-tuhr, MIS-tuhr, *in rapid speech*   'mistəʳ, ,mistəʳ, *in rapid*
        esp. before a title mis(t)   *speech esp. before a title*
               mis(t)

Mrs.
  form of address to a married   MIS-iz, MIS-is, *in rapid speech* MIZ,   'misiz, 'misis, *in rapid*
  woman   MIS; *esp. southern US* MIZ-iz,   *speech* ,miz, ,mis; *esp.*
        MIZ-is   *southern US* 'miziz,
               'mizis

Foreign Sounds: ue: *Fr.* **rue**, *Ger.* **füllen** uh(r): *Fr.* **boeuf**, *Ger.* **Höhle** kh: *Ger.* **ich**, *Scot.* **loch** g̃: *Sp.* **amigo** v: *Sp.* **hablar** hl: *Welsh* **Llanelli**. CAPITALS: primary stress. SMALL CAPS: secondary stress. Ⓢ: U.S. pron. Ⓛ: British pron.

Ms.
   magazine; form of address to a   MIZ, ᴍɪᴢ   'miz, ˌmiz
   woman

MS-DOS
   tdmk for a microcomputer   EM-ES-DAHS, -DAWS   ˌem͵es'dɑs, -'dɔːs
   operating system

Mstislav
   pers. name, Russian   sti-SLAHV; Ⓢ MIS-tuh-SLAHV   sti'slɑːv; Ⓢ 'mistə͵slav

Muammar
   pers. name, Arabic   M͞OO-uh-MAHR   'muːə͵mɑʳ

Mubarak
   Hosni, *president, Egypt*   mu-BAHR-uhk   mu'bɑrək

Mucius
   pers. name, Latin   M(Y)͞OO-sh(ē-)uhs   'm(j)uːʃ(iː)əs

Mucius Scaevola
   Roman who fought Etruscans   MY͞OO-shuhs SEV-uh-luh   ˌmjuːʃəs 'sevələ

Muckleshoot
   N. American people   MUHK-uhl-SH͞OOT   'məkəl͵ʃuːt

Mudgee
   town, Australia   MUHJ-ē   'mədʒiˑ

Muenchen
   airport, Munich   MUEN-k͟huhn   'mynçən

Muenster
   cheese   MUHN-stuhr, M(Y)͞OON-stuhr,   'mənstəʳ, 'm(j)uːnstəʳ,
          MUN-stuhr   'munstəʳ

Muffy
   pers. name   MUHF-ē   'məfiˑ

Mufti
   Muslim religious leader   MUHF-tē, MUF-tē   'məftiˑ, 'muftiˑ

Mugabe
   Robert, *prime minister,*   mu-GAHB-ē   mu'gabiˑ
   Zimbabwe

Muhammad
   1. founder of Islam; pers. name,   mu-K͟HAM-muhd   mu'xæmməd
   Arabic
   2. Persian   mō-K͟HAHM-mahd   moː'xɑːmmɑːd
   3. Elijah, *US cleric*   m͞oo-HAHM-uhd   mu"hɑməd

Muhammedan, Mohammedan
   pert. to Muhammad *or* Islam;   mō-HAM-uhd-uhn,   moː'hæmədən,
   adherent of Islam   mō-HAHM-uhd-uhn, m͞oo-   moː'hɑmədən, mu'-

Muhammedanism,
Mohammedanism
   religion   mō-HAM-uhd-uh-ɴɪᴢ-uhm,   moː'hæmədə͵nizəm,
          mō-HAHM-uhd-uh-ɴɪᴢ-uhm, m͞oo-   moː'hɑmədə͵nizəm, mu'-

Muharram
   Islamic month   m͞oo-HAHR-uhm   muː'hɑrəm

Muhlenberg
   county, KY; college, PA   MY͞OO-luhn-BUHRG   'mjuːlən͵bəʳg

Mühlhausen
   town, Germany   MUEL-HOW-zuhn   'myːl͵hauzən

Muir
   John, *US naturalist; glacier, AK;*   MYUR, MY͞OO-uhr   'mjuʳ, 'mjuːəʳ
   pers. name

Mujeres, Isla
   island, Caribbean   ĒZ-lah m͞oo-K͟HER-ās   'iːzlɑ muː'xereːs

---

Key (col. 2):   a: fad   ā: fade   ah: father   ar: Mary   aw: law   e: fed   ē: feed   er: merry   i: hid   ī: hide   ō: coat   o͞o: boot
oi: boy   ow: now   u: put   uh: above   uhr: bird   ch: chop   ng: ring   sh: show   th: thick   t͟h: this   zh: measure

Mukačevo, Mukachevo
  town, Ukraine　　MUK-uh-CHEV-ō　　'mukə,tʃevoː
Mukden
  prov, China　　MUK-duhn, MUHK-duhn, muk-DEN　　'mukdən, 'məkdən,
　　　　　　　　　　　　muk'den

Mukhā, Al
  seaport, Yemen　　ahl mu-KHAH, al　　ɑːl mu'xɑ, æl
Muldaur
  Diana, US actress; Maria, *US*　　MUHL-DOWR, MUHL-DAWR　　'məl,dɑuʳ, 'məl,dɔːʳ
  singer
Muldoon
  Robert, *prime minister, New*　　MUHL-DOON　　,məl'duːn
  Zealand
Mulgrew
  Kate, *US actress*　　MUHL-GROO　　,məl'gruː
Mulhacén
  Mount, *Spain*　　MOO-lah-SĀN, -SEN　　,muːlɑ'seːn, -'sen
Mülhausen [Mulhouse]
  port, France　　MUEL-HOW-zuhn　　'myl,hɑuzən
Mulhouse
  port, France　　mue-LOOZ　　myːluːz
Müller
  K. Alex, *Swiss physicist (Nobel*　　MUEL-uhr; Ⓢ MYOO-luhr, MIL-uhr,　　'myləʳ; Ⓢ 'mjuːləʳ, 'miləʳ,
  1987); Max, *German philologist;*　　MUHL-uhr　　'mələʳ
  Paul H., *Swiss chemist (Nobel*
  1948)
Muller
  H. J., *US geneticist (Nobel 1946)*　　MUHL-uhr　　'mələʳ
Mullewa
  township, Australia　　MUHL-uh-WAW　　'mələ,wɔː
Mulligan
  Richard, *US actor*　　MUHL-uh-guhn　　'mələgən
Mulligatawny
  soup　　MUHL-i-guh-TAW-nē, -TAHN-ē　　,məligə'tɔːniˑ, -'tɑniˑ
Mulliken
  Robert S., *US chemist, physicist*　　MUHL-i-kuhn　　'məlikən
  (Nobel 1966)
Mullumbimby
  town, Australia　　MUHL-uhm-BIM-bē　　,mələm'bimbiˑ
Mulroney
  Brian, *prime minister, Canada*　　MUHL-RŌ-nē, MUHL-ROO-nē　　,məl'roːniˑ, ,məl'ruːniˑ
Multnomah
  county, OR; Stadium, *Portland,*　　MUHLT-NŌ-muh　　,məlt'noːmə
  OR
Munch
  Edvard, *Norwegian painter*　　MUNGK　　'muŋk
Munchausen
  anglicization of Münchhausen　　MUHN-CHOWZ-n, MUN-CHOWZ-n,　　'mən,tʃɑuzn̩, 'mun,tʃɑuzn̩,
　　　　　　　　　　　　-CHAWZ-n　　　　　-,tʃɔːzn̩
München [Munich]
  city, Germany　　MUEN-khuhn, Ⓢ MUN-chuhn,　　'mynçən, Ⓢ 'muntʃən,
　　　　　　　　　　　　MIN-chuhn　　　　　'mintʃən
Münchhausen
  Karl F. Hieronymus, *Baron von,*　　MUENKH-HOWZ-n　　'mynç,hɑuzn̩
  German soldier

Foreign Sounds:　ue: *Fr.* **rue,** *Ger.* f**ü**llen　uh(r): *Fr.* b**oeu**f, *Ger.* H**ö**hle　kh: *Ger.* i**ch,** *Scot.* lo**ch**　ğ: *Sp.* ami**g**o　v̩: *Sp.* ha**b**lar
hl: *Welsh* L**l**anelli.　CAPITALS: primary stress.　SMALL CAPS: secondary stress.　Ⓢ: U.S. pron.　Ⓛ: British pron.

Muncie	*city, IN*	MUHN(T)-sē	'mən(t)siˑ
Mundari	*lang., India*	MUHN-DAHR-ē	ˌmən'dɑriˑ
Mundelein	College, *IL*	MUHN-duh-LĪN	'məndəˌlɑin
Mundulla	*Australia*	MUHN-DUHL-uh	ˌmən'dələ
Mundurucú	*S. American people*	MO͞ON-do͞o-ro͞o-KO͞O	ˌmuːnduːruː'kuː
Munefusa	*pers. name, Japanese*	mo͞o-ne-fo͞o-sah	muːnefuːsɑ
Mungo	*pers. name*	MUHNG-gō	'məŋgoː
Mungunyah	*Australia*	MUHN-GUHN-yuh	ˌmən'gənjə
Munich	*city, Germany*	MYO͞O-nik, MYO͞O-nikh	'mjuːnik, 'mjuːnix
Munich-Riem	*airport, Munich*	MYO͞O-nik-RĒM, MYO͞O-nikh-	ˌmjuːnik'riːm, ˌmjuːnix-
Munichus	*king of Molossians*	MYO͞O-ni-kuhs	'mjuːnikəs
Munitus	*son of Laodice and Acamas*	MYO͞O-nuht-uhs	'mjuːnət̬əs
Muñoz Marín	Luis, *governor, Puerto Rico*	mo͞on-YŌS mah-RĒN	muːn'joːs mɑ'riːn
Munro, Munroe	*pers. name*	muhn-RŌ, MUHN-RŌ	mən'roː, 'mənˌroː
Munroe [Saki]	Hector Hugh, *Scottish writer*	muhn-RŌ	mən'roː
Munsee	*N. American people*	MUHN-sē	'mənsiˑ
Munsell	*pers. name*	MUHN-suhl	'mənsəl
Munson	Thurman, *US baseball player; pers. name*	MUHN-suhn	'mənsən
Munster	*prov, Ireland; town, IN; cartoon family*	MUHN(T)-stuhr	'mən(t)stəʳ
Münster	*city, Germany*	MUEN-stuhr, [S] MIN(T)-stuhr, MUN(T)-stuhr, MUHN(T)-stuhr	'mynstəʳ, [S] 'min(t)stəʳ, 'mun(t)stəʳ, 'mən(t)stəʳ
Münsterhof	*French beer*	MUEN-stuhr-HAWF	'mynstəʳˌhɔːf
Munthe	*pers. name*	MUN-tuh	'muntə
Mu'ò'ng, Muong	*lang., people, North Vietnam*	MWAHNG, muh-WAHNG	'mwɑŋ, mə'wɑŋ
Muon	*subatomic particle*	MYO͞O-AHN	'mjuːˌɑn
Muppets	*puppet characters*	MUHP-uhts	'məpəts
Mura	*S. American people*	MO͞O-ruh	'muːrə

Key (col. 2): a: fad ā: fade ah: father ar: Mary aw: law e: fed ē: feed er: merry i: hid ī: hide ō: coat o͞o: boot oi: boy ow: now u: put uh: above uhr: bird ch: chop ng: ring sh: show th: thick th: this zh: measure

Murasaki		
Shikibu, *Japanese poet*	mur-ah-sahk-ē	murasakiˑ
Murat		
1. Joachim, *French militarist*	mue-RAH, [$] myu-RAH, m(y)uh-RAT	myːraː, [$] mju'ra, m(j)ə'ræt
2. pers. name	m(y)uh-RAT	m(j)ə'ræt
3. river, Turkey	mu-RAHT	mu'rat
Murcia		
prov & town, Spain	MURTH-yah, [$] MUHR-sh(ē-)uh	'murθja, [$] 'məʳʃ(iː)ə
Murdoch		
Iris, *British writer;* Rupert, *Australian entrepreneur*	MUHR-duhk, MUHR-DAHK	'məʳdək, 'məʳˌdak
Murfreesboro		
city, TN	MUHR-f(r)ēz-BUHR-uh, -BUH-ruh	'məʳf(r)iːzˌbər-ə, -ˌbə-rə
Muriel		
pers. name	MYUR-ē-uhl	'mjuriːəl
Murillo		
Bartolomé Esteban, *Spanish painter*	mo͞o-RĒ(L)-yō, [$] m(y)u-RIL-ō, m(y)u-RĒ-ō	muː'riː(l)joː, [$] m(j)u'riloː, m(j)u'riːoː
Murmansk		
city, Russia	mur-MAHN(T)SK, mur-MAN(T)SK	muʳ'maːn(t)sk, muʳ'mæn(t)sk
Murmi [Bhutia]		
lang., India (Sikkim), Nepal	MUR-mē, MUHR-mē	'muʳmiˑ, 'məʳmiˑ
Murnane		
Field, *ballpark, Utica, NY*	muhr-NĀN, MUHR-NĀN	məʳ'neːn, 'məʳˌneːn
Murphy		
W. P., *US physician (Nobel 1934); pers. name*	MUHR-fē	'məʳfiˑ
Murray		
Sir James A. H., *British lexicographer;* Joseph E., *US surgeon (Nobel 1990); pers. name*	MUHR-ē, MUH-rē	'mər-iˑ, 'mə-riˑ
Murre		
sea bird	MUHR	'məʳ
Murree		
Pakistani beer	m(y)u-RĀ, M(Y)UR-Ā	m(j)u'reː, 'm(j)urˌeː
Murrelet		
sea bird	MUHR-luht	'məʳlət
Murrough		
pers. name	MUHR-ō, MUH-RŌ	'məroː, 'məˌroː
Murrumbidgee		
river, Australia	MUHR-uhm-BIJ-ē	ˌmərəm'bidʒiˑ
Murrumburrah		
town, Australia	MUHR-uhm-BUHR-uh	ˌmərəm'bərə
Murrurundi		
town, Australia	MUHR-uh-RUHN-DĪ	ˌmərə'rənˌdai
Mururoa		
atoll, Pacific	MO͞O-ro͞o-RŌ-uh	ˌmuˑruˑ'roːə
Murwillumbah		
town, Australia	muhr-WIL-uhm-buh	məʳ'wiləmbə
Musaeus		
legendary Greek musician and seer	myo͞o-ZĒ-uhs	mjuː'ziːəs

Foreign Sounds: ue: *Fr.* **rue**, *Ger.* **füllen** uh(r): *Fr.* **boeuf**, *Ger.* **Höhle** kh: *Ger.* **ich**, *Scot.* **loch** g̃: *Sp.* **amigo** v̲: *Sp.* **hablar** hl: *Welsh* **Llanelli**. CAPITALS: primary stress. SMALL CAPS: secondary stress. [$]: U.S. pron. [£]: British pron.

Musburger
   Brent, *US sportscaster*   MUHS-BUHR-guhr   'məs,bəˢgəˢ
Musca
   constellation   MUHS-kuh   'məskə
Muscadelle
   wine grape   mue-skah-DEL   myːskɑːdel
Muscadet
   wine grape   mue-skah-DE, Ⓢ MUHS-kuh-DĀ   myːskɑːde, Ⓢ ˌməskə'deː
Muscadine
   wine grape   MUHS-kuh-DĒN, -DĪN   'məskə,diːn, -,dain
Muscat
   1. city, Oman   MUHS-KAHT, MUHS-kuht   'məs,kɑt, 'məskət
   2. wine   mue-SKAH, Ⓢ MUHS-KAT, -KAHT, -kuht   myːskɑː, Ⓢ 'məs,kæt, -,kɑt, -kət
Muscat de Beaumes de Venise
   wine   mue-SKAH duh BŌM duh vuh-NĒZ   myːskɑː də boːm də vəniːz
Muscatel
   wine   MUHS-kuh-TEL   ˌməskə'tel
Muscatine
   city, county, IA   MUHS-kuh-TĒN   ˌməskə'tiːn
Muscovite
   person from Moscow   MUHS-kuh-VĪT   'məskə,vait
Muscovy
   former principality centered on Moscow; duck   MUHS-kuh-vē   'məskəviˑ
Muse
   one of nine Greek inspirational nymphs   MYŌŌZ   'mjuːz
Musgu
   lang., people, Chad, Cameroon   MUHS-GŌŌ   'məs,guː
Musica Antiqua Köln
   early music ensemble, Germany   MŌŌ-zēk-uh an-TĒ-kwuh KUH(R)LN   'muːziˑkə æn'tiːkwə 'kœln
Muskegon
   city, county, MI   muh-SKĒ-guhn   mə'skiːgən
Muskie
   Edmund, *US politician*   MUHS-kē   'məskiˑ
Muskingum
   river, county, OH   muh-SKING-guhm, muh-SKING-uhm   mə'skiŋgəm, mə'skiŋəm
Muskogean
   N. American lang. family   muh-SKŌ-gē-uhn   mə'skoːgiːən
Muskogee
   city, county, OK; N. American people   muh-SKŌ-gē   mə'skoːgiˑ
Muskoka
   Lake, *Canada*   muh-SKŌ-kuh   mə'skoːkə
Muslim [Moslem]
   pert. to Islam; *adherent of Islam*   MUHZ-luhm, MUS-luhm, MUZ-luhm   'məzləm, 'musləm, 'muzləm
Mussaui
   pers. name, Persian   muh-SOW-ē   mə'sauiˑ
Musset
   Alfred de, *French writer*   mue-SE, Ⓢ myōō-SĀ   myːse, Ⓢ mjuː'seː
Mussolini
   Benito, *Italian leader*   MŌŌ-suh-LĒ-nē, MUS-uh-LĒ-nē   ˌmuːsə'liːniˑ, ˌmusə'liːniˑ

Key (col. 2):   a: fad   ā: fade   ah: father   ar: Mary   aw: law   e: fed   ē: feed   er: merry   i: hid   ī: hide   ō: coat   ōō: boot
oi: boy   ow: now   u: put   uh: above   uhr: bird   ch: chop   ng: ring   sh: show   th: thick   th̲: this   zh: measure

Mussorgsky, Moussorgsky
  Modest, *Russian composer*   mu-SAWRG-skē, mu-ZAWRG-skē   muˈsɔːᵣgskiˑ, muˈzɔːᵣgskiˑ

Mustafa, Mustapha
  1. pers. name, Arabic   MUS-tah-fah   ˈmustɑfɑ
  2. Turkish   mus-tah-FAH   mustɑˈfɑ

Mut
  Egyptian sky goddess   MUT   ˈmut

Muti
  Riccardo, *US conductor*   MOOT-ē   ˈmuːt̬iˑ

Mutsuhito
  emperor, Japan   mut-su-hē-tō   mutsuhiːtoː

Muybridge
  Eadweard, *US motion-picture*   MĪ-BRIJ   ˈmɑi‚bridʒ
  pioneer

Muzak
  tdmk for recorded background   MYOO-ZAK   ˈmjuː‚zæk
  music

Mwami
  pers. name, Kirundi   MWAHM-ē   ˈmwɑmiˑ

Mwanbutsa
  Mwami, *king, Burundi*   mwahn-BOOT-suh   mwɑnˈbuːtsə

Mwanga
  lang., Africa   MWAHNG-guh   ˈmwɑŋgə

Mwera
  lang., Africa   MWER-uh   ˈmwerə

Mweru
  lake, Zaire, Zambia   MWER-oo   ˈmweruː

Myanmar [Burma]
  republic, Asia   myahn-MAH, mē-ahn-MAHR   mjɑnˈmɑ, miːɑnˈmɑᵣ

Myaungmya
  town, district, Burma   MYOWNG-MYAH   ˈmjauŋˈmjɑ

Mycale
  ancient promontory, Asia Minor   MIK-uh-lē   ˈmikəliˑ

Mycenae
  ancient city, Greece   mī-SĒ-nē   mɑiˈsiːniˑ

Mycenaean
  Bronze age culture   MĪ-suh-NĒ-uhn   ‚mɑisəˈniːən

Myceneus
  founder of Mycenae   mī-SĒ-nē-uhs   mɑiˈsiːniːəs

Mygdon
  Phrygian king, ally of Priam   MIG-duhn, MIG-DAHN   ˈmigdən, ˈmig‚dɑn

Mykonos
  see Míkonos

Mýkonos
  Greek island   MĒ-kuh-NAWS, ⑤ MIK-uh-NAHS,   ˈmiːkə‚nɔːs, ⑤ ˈmikə‚nɑs,
   MIK-uh-nuhs   ˈmikənəs

My Lai
  village, Vietnam   MĒ LĪ   ˈmiː ˈlɑi

Myles
  pers. name   MĪLZ   ˈmɑilz

Mynheer
  Dutch form of address for a man   muh-NER   məˈneᵣ

Myra
  pers. name   MĪ-ruh   ˈmɑirə

Foreign Sounds: ue: *Fr.* **rue**, *Ger.* f**ü**llen   uh(r): *Fr.* b**oeu**f, *Ger.* H**öh**le   <u>kh</u>: *Ger.* i**ch**, *Scot.* lo**ch**   g̃: *Sp.* ami**g**o   <u>v</u>: *Sp.* ha**b**lar
hl: *Welsh* **Ll**anelli.   CAPITALS: primary stress.   SMALL CAPS: secondary stress.   ⑤: U.S. pron.   ⑬: British pron.

Myrdal
  Alva, *Swedish peace activist (Nobel*   MUER-DAHL, Ⓢ MUHR-DAHL,   'myr‚dɑl, Ⓢ 'məʳ‚dɑl,
  1982); Gunnar *(her husband),*   MIR-DAHL   'miʳ‚dɑl
  Swedish economist (Nobel 1974)
Myrina
  Amazon queen who fought the   muh-RĪ-nuh   mə'rɑinə
  Gorgons
Myristica
  nutmeg   muh-RIS-ti-kuh, mī-RIS-ti-kuh   mə'ristikə, mai'ristikə
Myrmex
  girl changed into ant by Athena   MUHR-MEKS   'məʳ‚meks
Myrmidon
  subjects of Peleus & Achilles   MUHR-muh-DAHN,   'məʳmə‚dɑn, 'məʳmədən
                                            MUHR-muhd-uhn
Myrna
  pers. name   MUHR-nuh   'məʳnə
Myron
  Greek sculptor; pers. name   MĪ-ruhn   'mairən
Myrsus
  son of Aretus   MUHR-suhs   'məʳsəs
Myrtilus
  son of Hermes; charioteer   MUHRT-l-uhs   'məʳtləs
  constellation
Myrtle
  pers. name   MUHRT-l   'məʳtl̩
Myrto
  sister of Patroclus   MUHRT-ō   'məʳʈoː
Mysore
  city, India   mī-SŌR, mī-SAWR   mai'soːʳ, mai'soːʳ
Mystic
  town, CT; river, CT, MA   MIS-tik   'mistik
Mytilene, Mitylene [Lesbos]
  island, city, Greece   MIT-l-Ē-nē   ‚mitl̩'iːniˑ

N

NAACP
National Assoc. for the   EN DUHB-uhl Ā SĒ PĒ   ˌen ˌdəbəl ˌeː ˌsiː ˈpiː
   Advancement of Colored People
Nabataean
ancient Arab people   NAB-uh-TĒ-uhn   ˌnæbəˈtiːən
Nabisco
US food products co.   nuh-BIS-kō   nəˈbiskoː
Nablus
district, Israel   NAHB-luhs, NAB-luhs   ˈnɑbləs, ˈnæbləs
Nabokov
Vladimir, *Russian American writer*   nuh-BAW-kuhf, NAB-uh-KAWF   nəˈbɔːkəf, ˈnæbəˌkɔːf
Nabonidus
king of Babylonia   NAB-uh-NĪD-uhs   ˌnæbəˈnɑidəs
Nabopolassar
king of Babylonia   NAB-uh-puh-LAS-uhr   ˌnæbəpəˈlæsəʳ
Nabors
Jim, *US actor, singer*   NĀ-buhrz   ˈneːbəʳz
Naboth
Biblical name   NĀ-BAHTH   ˈneːˌbɑθ
Nachman
pers. name, Hebrew   NAHKH-mahn   ˈnɑːxmɑn
Nacogdoches
city, county, TX   NAK-uh-DŌ-chuhz   ˌnækəˈdoːtʃəz
Na-Dene, Na-Déné
N. American lang. family   NAH-DEN-ē, NAH-DEN-Ā   ˌnɑˈdeniˑ, ˌnɑˈdenˌeː
Nader
Ralph, *US consumer advocate*   NĀD-uhr   ˈneːdəʳ
Nadia
1. pers. name   NAHD-yuh, NAHD-ē-uh   ˈnɑdjə, ˈnɑdiːə
2. French   nahd-YAH   nɑːdjɑː
Nadine
pers. name   nā-DĒN   neːˈdiːn
Naera
pers. name, Maori   nah-Ā-rah   nɑˈeːrɑ
Naevius
Gnaeus, *Roman writer; pers.*   NĒ-vē-uhs   ˈniːviːəs
   name, Latin
NAFTA
North American Free Trade   NAF-tuh   ˈnæftə
   Agreement
Naftali
1. pers. name, French   nahf-tah-LĒ   nɑːftɑːliː
2. Hebrew   nahf-TAH-lē   nɑːfˈtɑːliː

Foreign Sounds: ue: *Fr.* **rue**, *Ger.* füllen   uh(r): *Fr.* **boeuf**, *Ger.* Höhle   kh: *Ger.* i**ch**, *Scot.* lo**ch**   ğ: *Sp.* ami**g**o   v̱: *Sp.* ha**b**lar
hl: *Welsh* **Ll**anelli.   CAPITALS: primary stress.   SMALL CAPS: secondary stress.   Ⓢ: U.S. pron.   Ⓛ: British pron.

Nafūd		
desert, Arabian Peninsula	nuh-FO͞OD	nə'fuːd
Naga		
lang., India, Burma; municipality, Philippines	NAHG-uh	'nɑgə
Nagambie		
town, Australia	nuh-GAM-bē	nə'gæmbiˑ
Nagasaki		
city, Japan	nahg-uh-sahk-ē, Ⓢ NAHG-uh-SAHK-ē, NAG-uh-SAK-ē	nɑgəsɑkiˑ, Ⓢ ˌnɑgə'sɑkiˑ, ˌnægə'sækiˑ
Nagasaki Takoage		
Japanese kite contest	nahg-uh-sahk-ē tahk-ō-ahg-ā	nɑgəsɑkiˑ tɑkoːɑgeː
Nagel		
pers. name, Norwegian	NAHG-uhl	'nɑgəl
Nagorno-Karabakh		
region, Azerbaijan	nuh-GAWR-nō-KAR-uh-BAHKH	nə'gɔː^{r}noːˌkærə'bɑx
Nagoya		
city, Japan	nuh-GOI-uh, NAHG-uh-yah	nə'gɔiə, 'nɑgəjɑ
Nagpur		
city, India	NAHG-PUR	'nɑgˌpu^{r}
Naguib		
pers. name, Arabic	NAH-GĒB, nah-GĒB	'nɑˌgiːb, nɑ'giːb
Nagy		
Imre, *Hungarian political leader*	NAHD, Ⓢ NAHZH, NAHJ	'nɑd̦, Ⓢ 'nɑʒ, 'nɑdʒ
Nahant		
town, bay, MA	nuh-HANT	nə'hænt
Nahor		
biblical patriarch	nuh-HAWR	nə'hɔː^{r}
Nahua		
ancient Central American people	NAH-wuh	'nɑwə
Nahuatl		
people, lang., Cen. America	NAH-WAHT-l	'nɑˌwɑtl̩
Nahuatlan		
lang. family, N. America	nah-WAHT-luhn	nɑ'wɑtlən
Nahum		
1. Old Testament book; pers. name	NĀ-(h)uhm, NĀ-HUHM	'neː(h)əm, 'neːˌhəm
2. German	NAH-HUM	'nɑˌhum
3. Hebrew	NAHKH-um	'nɑxum
Naiad		
water nymph	NĀ-uhd, NĪ-uhd, NĀ-AD, NĪ-AD	'neːəd, 'nɑiəd, 'neːˌæd, 'nɑiˌæd
Naiades		
plural of Naiad	NĀ-uh-DĒZ, NĪ-uh-DĒZ	'neːəˌdiːz, 'nɑiəˌdiːz
Naipaul		
V.J., *Trinidadian novelist*	nī-PAWL	nɑi'pɔːl
Nairobi		
city, Kenya	nī-RŌ-bē	nɑi'roːbiˑ
Naismith		
James, *Canadian-born US originator of basketball*	NĀ-smith	'neːsmiθ
Najd [Nejd]		
prov, Saudi Arabia	NAJD	'nædʒd
Najibullah		
Mohammad, *Afghan president*	NAHJ-ē-bu-LAH	ˌnɑdʒiˑbu'lɑ

Key (col. 2): a: **fad** ā: **fade** ah: **father** ar: **Mary** aw: **law** e: **fed** ē: **feed** er: **merry** i: **hid** ī: **hide** ō: **coat** o͞o: **boot** oi: **boy** ow: **now** u: **put** uh: **above** uhr: **bird** ch: **chop** ng: **ring** sh: **show** th: **thick** th: **this** zh: **measure**

Nakasone
    Yasuhiro, *prime minister, Japan*   nahk-ah-sō-nā   nɑkɑsoːneː

Nakhichevan
    town, Azerbaijan   NAHK-i-chuh-VAHN   ˌnɑkitʃə'vɑn

Nam, 'Nam
    informal reference to Vietnam   NAHM, NAM   'nɑm, 'næm

Nama
    lang., people, Namibia   NAHM-uh   'nɑmə

Namaqualand
    region, Southern Africa   nuh-MAHK-wuh-LAND   nə'mɑkwəˌlænd

Namath
    Joe, *US football player*   NĀ-muhth   'neːməθ

Nambe Pueblo
    Indian reservation, US   NAHM-bā poo-EB-lō, PWEB-lō,   'nambeː puː'ebloː, 'pwebloː,
                                     pyoo-EB-lō   pjuː'ebloː

Nambicuara
    S. American people   NAM-bē-KWAHR-uh, NAHM-   ˌnæmbiː'kwarə, ˌnɑm-

Nambucca
    river, Australia   nam-BUHK-uh   næm'bəkə

Namib
    desert, Africa   NAHM-ib   'nɑmib

Namibia
    territory, Africa   nuh-MIB-ē-uh   nə'mibiːə

Namoi
    river, Australia   NAM-OI   'næmˌɔi

Nampula
    prov, Mozambique   nam-POO-luh   næm'puːlə

Namur
    commune, prov, Belgium   nah-MUR   nɑ'muʳ

Nan
    pers. name   NAN   'næn

Nanaian
    pert. to Nanays   na-NĪ-uhn   næ'naiən

Nanango
    town, Australia   nuh-NANG-gō   nə'næŋgoː

Nanchang, Nan-ch'ang
    city, China   NAHN-CHAHNG   'nɑn'tʃɑŋ

Nancy
    1. pers. name   NAN-sē   'nænsiˑ
    2. city, France   nahⁿ-SẼ, ⓢ NAN-sē   nɑ̃siː, ⓢ 'nænsiˑ

Nanda Devan
    Indian festival   NAHN-duh DĀ-vuhn   'nɑndə 'deːvən

Nandi
    lang., people, Kenya, Uganda,   NAHN-DĒ   'nɑnˌdiː
      Tanzania

Nanette
    pers. name   nan-ET, nuh-NET   næn'et, nə'net

Nanga Parbat
    mtn., Himalayas   NUHNG-guh PUHR-buht   ˌnəŋgə 'pəʳbət

Nanjing [Nanking]
    city, China   NAHN-JING   'nɑn'dʒiŋ

Nanking
    city, China   NAHN-KING, ⓢ NAN-KING   'nɑn'kiŋ, ⓢ 'næn'kiŋ

Nannacus
    king of Phrygia   NAN-uh-kuhs   'nænəkəs

Foreign Sounds: ue: *Fr.* **r**u**e**, *Ger.* f**ü**llen   uh(r): *Fr.* b**oeu**f, *Ger.* H**öh**le   <u>kh</u>: *Ger.* i**ch**, *Scot.* lo**ch**   ḡ: *Sp.* ami**g**o   v̱: *Sp.* ha**b**lar
hl: *Welsh* **Ll**anelli.   CAPITALS: primary stress.   SMALL CAPS: secondary stress.   ⓢ: U.S. pron.   Ⓛ: British pron.

Nannerl		
pers. name, German	NAHN-uhrl	'nɑnə^{r}l
Nansemond		
stream, former county, VA	NAN(T)-sē-MUHN(D)	ˌnæn(t)siˈ'mən(d)
Nansen		
1. Fridtjof, *Norwegian explorer, zoologist, statesman (Nobel 1922)*	NAHN-suhn	'nɑnsən
2. Sound, *strait, Canada*	NAN-suhn	'nænsən
Nantes		
city, France	NAH^{n}T	nɑ̃t
Nanticoke		
river, MD; city, PA; N. American people	NANT-i-KŌK	'nænti,koːk
Nantucket		
island, county, MA	nan-TUHK-uht	næn'təkət
Nanuet		
town, NY	NAN-yuh-WET	ˌnænjə'wet
Naomi		
pers. name	nā-Ō-mē	neˑ'oːmiˑ
Naotake		
pers. name, Japanese	nā-ō-tah-ke	neːoːtɑke
NAPA		
auto parts chain	NAP-uh	'næpə
Napa		
city, county, valley, CA	NAP-uh	'næpə
Naphtali		
1. pers. name	NAF-tuh-LĪ	'næftə,lɑi
2. Russian	NUHF-TAHL-yi	ˌnəf'tɑljij
Napier		
pers. name	NĀ-pē-uhr, NĀ-PIR, nuh-PIR	'neːpiːə^{r}, 'neː,pi^{r}, nə'pi^{r}
Naples		
city, FL; city, prov, Italy	NĀ-puhlz	'neːpəlz
Napoleon		
1. custard-filled pastry; pers. name	nuh-PŌ-lē-uhn, nuh-PŌL-yuhn	nə'poːliːən, nə'poːljən
2. German	nah-PŌ-lā-awn, nah-PŌ-lā-aw^{n}	nɑ'poːleːɔːn, nɑ'poːleːɔ̃
Napoléon		
French emperor	nah-paw-lā-AW, [$] nuh-PŌ-lē-uhn	nɑːpɔːleːɔ, [$] nə'poːliːən
Napoleonic		
pert. to Napoléon	nuh-PŌ-lē-AHN-ik	nə,poːliː'ɑnik
Napoli [Naples]		
city, prov, Italy	NAHP-uh-lē	'nɑpəliˑ
Nara		
1. city, Japan	nahr-ah	nɑrɑ
2. lang., Ethiopia	NAHR-uh	'nɑrə
Naram-Sin		
king of Akkad	nah-RAHM-SIN	nɑ'rɑm'sin
Narasimha		
pers. name, Hindi	nuh-RAHS-im-HAH	nə'rɑsim,hɑ
Narayan		
pers. name	NAH-rī-(Y)AHN	ˌnɑrɑi'(j)ɑn
Narbada [Narmada]		
river, India	nuhr-BUHD-uh	nə^{r}'bədə
Narbo		
ancient name of Narbonne	NAHR-bō	'nɑ^{r}boː

Key (col. 2): a: **fad** ā: **fade** ah: **father** ar: **Mary** aw: **law** e: **fed** ē: **feed** er: **merry** i: **hid** ī: **hide** ō: **coat** o͞o: **boot** oi: **boy** ow: **now** u: **put** uh: **above** uhr: **bird** ch: **chop** ng: **ring** sh: **show** th: **thick** th: **this** zh: **measure**

Narbonensis		
region of Gaul	NAHR-buh-NEN-suhs	ˌnaʳbəˈnensəs
Narbonne		
commune, France	nahr-BAWN	naːrbɔːn
Narciso		
pers. name, Spanish	nahr-SĒ-sō, nahr-THĒ-sō	narˈsiːsoː, narˈθiːsoː
Narcissus		
handsome youth in Greek myth	nahr-SIS-uhs	naʳˈsisəs
Narita		
airport, Tokyo	nahr-ē-tah	nariːta
Narmada [Narbada]		
river, India	nuhr-MUHD-uh	nəʳˈmədə
Narmer		
king of Egypt	NAHR-mer	ˈnaʳmeʳ
Naropa		
Institute, *college, CO*	nuh-RŌ-puh	nəˈroːpə
Narrabri		
town, Australia	NAR-uh-BRĪ	ˈnærəˌbrai
Narraganset		
N. American people	NAR-uh-GAN-suht, NER-	ˌnærəˈgænsət, ˌner-
Narrandera		
town, Australia	nuh-RAN-druh	nəˈrændrə
Narva		
river, city, Estonia	NAHR-vuh	ˈnaʳvə
Narvik		
city, Norway	NAHR-vik, NAHR-VĒK	ˈnaʳvik, ˈnaʳˌviːk
NASA		
US space agency	NAS-uh	ˈnæsə
Nasca		
see Nazca		
Nashua		
city, NH	NASH-uh-wuh, NASH-uh-WĀ	ˈnæʃəwə, ˈnæʃəˌweː
Nasica		
Roman cognomen	NAHS-i-kuh	ˈnasikə
Naskapi		
N. American people	NAS-kuh-pē	ˈnæskəpiˑ
Nassau		
1. county, FL, NY; city, Bahamas; pers. name	NAS-aw	ˈnæsɔː
2. region, Germany	NAHS-OW	ˈnasˌau
Nasser		
Gamal Abdel, *president, Egypt*	NAHS-uhr	ˈnasəʳ
Nastase		
Ilie, *Romanian tennis player*	nahs-TAHZ-ē	nasˈtaziˑ
Nastassja		
pers. name (N. Kinski)	nuh-STAHS-yuh	nəˈstasjə
Nat		
pers. name	NAT	ˈnæt
Natal		
port, Brazil; prov, S. Africa	nah-TAHL, nuh-TAL	naːˈtaːl, nəˈtæl
Natalia, Natalya		
pers. name	nuh-TAHL-yuh	nəˈtaljə
Natalie		
pers. name	NAT-l-ē	ˈnætl̩iˑ

Foreign Sounds: ue: *Fr.* **rue**, *Ger.* **fü**llen uh(r): *Fr.* b**oeu**f, *Ger.* H**ö**hle kh: *Ger.* i**ch**, *Scot.* lo**ch** g: *Sp.* ami**g**o v: *Sp.* ha**b**lar hl: *Welsh* **Ll**ane**ll**i. CAPITALS: primary stress. SMALL CAPS: secondary stress. [$]: U.S. pron. [£]: British pron.

Natasha
   pers. name   nuh-TASH-uh, nuh-TAHSH-uh   nə'tæʃə, nə'tɑʃə

Natchez
   city, MS; N. American people   NACH-uhz   'nætʃəz

Natchitoches
   city, parish, LA   NAK-uh-TAHSH, NAK-(uh-)tuhsh   'nækə,tɑʃ, 'næk(ə)təʃ

Nathan
   1. pers. name   NĀ-thuhn   'neːθən
   2. German   NAH-tahn   'nɑtɑn
   3. Swedish   NAH-tahn   'nɑtɑːn

Nathanael
   1. pers. name   nuh-THAN-ā-uhl, nuh-THAN-ē-uhl nə'θæneːəl, nə'θæniːəl
   2. German   nah-TAHN-ah-EL   na'tɑnɑ,el

Nathaniel
   pers. name   nuh-THAN-yuhl   nə'θænjəl

Nathans
   Daniel, US microbiologist (Nobel NĀ-thuhnz   'neːθənz
   1978)

Natick
   town, MA; village, RI   NĀT-ik   'neːţik

Nationalrat
   Austrian parliament   NAHTS-yō-NAHL-RAHT   ,nɑtsjoː'nɑl,rɑt

NATO
   North Atlantic Treaty   NĀT-ō, NĀ-TŌ   'neːţoː, 'neː,toː
   Organization

Natrona
   county, WY   nuh-TRŌ-nuh   nə'troːnə

Natta
   Giulio, Italian chemist (Nobel   NAHT-tah   'nɑttɑ
   1963)

Natty
   pers. name   NAT-ē   'næti·

Natufian
   Mesolithic culture in Palestine nuh-TŌŌ-fē-uhn   nə'tuːfiːən

Natzler
   Otto, US ceramic artist   NAT-sluhr   'nætsləʳ

Naucratis, Naukratis
   ancient Greek city, Egypt   NAW-kruht-uhs   'nɔːkrətəs

Naugahyde
   tdmk for a vinyl upholstery fabric NAW-guh-HĪD, NAHG-uh-HĪD   'nɔːgə,haid, 'nɑgə,haid

Naugatuck
   town, CT   NAW-guh-TUHK   'nɔːgə,tək

Naupactus
   ancient seaport, Greece   naw-PAK-tuhs   nɔː'pæktəs

Nauplia
   town, Greece   NAW-plē-uh   'nɔːpliːə

Nauplion
   see Návplion

Nauplius
   father of Palamedes   NAW-plē-uhs   'nɔːpliːəs

Nauru
   island   nah-ŌŌ-rōō   nɑ'uːruː

Nauruan
   lang., Nauru   NAH-ŌŌ-RŌŌ-uhn, NOW-RŌŌ-uhn ,nɑ,uː'ruːən, ,nɑu'ruːən

---

Key (col. 2): a: fad ā: fade ah: father ar: **Mary** aw: **law** e: fed ē: feed er: **merry** i: hid ī: hide ō: coat ōō: boot
oi: **boy** ow: **now** u: put uh: **above** uhr: bird ch: **chop** ng: **ring** sh: **show** th: **thick** <u>th</u>: **this** zh: measure

Nauset
    N. American people   NAW-suht   ˈnɔːsət

Nausicaa
    daughter of Alcinous   NAW-si-kuh   ˈnɔːsikə

Nautes
    companion of Aeneas in Italy   NAW-TĒZ   ˈnɔːˌtiːz

Nautilus
    submarine   NAWT-l-uhs, NAHT-l-uhs   ˈnɔːtləs, ˈnatləs

Navajo, Navaho
    county, AZ; N. American people   NAV-uh-HŌ, NAHV-uh-HŌ   ˈnævəˌhoː, ˈnavəˌhoː

Navarra [Navarre]
    region, Spain   nah-VAHR-rah   naˈvɑrɑ

Navarre
    ancient kingdom, region, Spain   nuh-VAHR, *French* nah-VAHR   nəˈvaʳ, *French* naːvaːr

Navarro
    county, TX   nuh-VAHR-ō   nəˈvaroː

Návplion, Nauplion
    town, Greece   NAHF-plē-AWN   ˈnɑfpliːˌɔːn

Navratilova
    Martina, *sports personality*   NAV-ruh-tuh-LŌ-vuh, NAHV-   ˌnævrətəˈloːvə, ˌnav-

Naxi
    lang., China   NAH-SĒ, NAH-SHĒ   ˈnɑˈsiː, ˈnɑˈʃiː

Náxos
    island, Greece   NAHK-SAWS, ⓢ NAK-suhs, NAK-SAHS   ˈnɑkˌsɔːs, ⓢ ˈnæksəs, ˈnækˌsɑs

Nayarit
    state, Mexico   NĪ-uh-RĒT   ˌnaiəˈriːt

Nazarbayev
    Nursultan, *Kazakhstanian political leader*   NAHZ-uhr-BĪ-(y)uhf   ˌnazəʳˈbai(j)əf

Nazaré
    town, Portugal   NAHZ-uh-RÃ   ˌnazəˈreː

Nazarene
    native or inhabitant of Nazareth   NAZ-uh-RĒN   ˌnæzəˈriːn

Nazareth
    town, Israel; borough, PA   NAZ-(uh-)ruhth   ˈnæz(ə)rəθ

Nazca, Nasca
    Peruvian Indian culture   NAS-kuh   ˈnæskə

Nazi
    member of German fascist party   NAHT-sē, NAT-sē   ˈnatsiˈ, ˈnætsiˈ

Naziism
    principles or methods of the Nazis   NAHT-sē-IZ-uhm, NAT-sē-IZ-uhm   ˈnatsiːˌizəm, ˈnætsiːˌizəm

Nazism
    principles or methods of the Nazis   NAHT-SIZ-uhm, NAT-SIZ-uhm   ˈnatˌsizəm, ˈnætˌsizəm

Ndali
    lang., Africa   n-DAHL-ē, uhn-DAHL-ē, en-   n̩ˈdaliˈ, ənˈdaliˈ, en-

Ndamba
    lang., Africa   n-DAHM-buh, uhn-DAHM-buh, en-   n̩ˈdambə, ənˈdambə, en-

Ndandi
    lang., Africa   n-DAHN-dē, uhn-DAHN-dē, en-   n̩ˈdandiˈ, ənˈdandiˈ, en-

Ndebele
    people, Africa   n-duh-BĒ-lē, EN-duh-BĒ-lē   n̩dəˈbiːliˈ, ˌendəˈbiːliˈ

N'Djamena
    city, Chad   n-juh-MÃ-nuh, EN-juh-, -MĒ-nuh, -MEN-uh   n̩dʒəˈmeːnə, ˌendʒə-, -ˈmiːnə, -ˈmenə

Foreign Sounds: ue: *Fr.* **rue**, *Ger.* f**ü**llen   uh(r): *Fr.* b**oeu**f, *Ger.* H**öh**le   <u>kh</u>: *Ger.* i**ch**, *Scot.* lo**ch**   ḡ: *Sp.* ami**g**o   <u>v</u>: *Sp.* ha**b**lar
hl: *Welsh* **Ll**anelli.   CAPITALS: primary stress.   SMALL CAPS: secondary stress.   ⓢ: U.S. pron.   Ⓛ: British pron.

Ndo
   lang., Uganda, Zaire   n-DŌ, en-   ṇ'doː, en-

Ndonde
   lang., Africa   n-DŌN-dā, uhn-DŌN-dā, en-,   ṇ'doːndeː, ən'doːndeː, en-,
        -DAHN-dā   -'dɑndeː

Neagh Windermere, Lough
   N. Ireland   LAHK NĀ WIN-duhr-MIR, LAHKH   'lɑk 'neː 'windəʳ,miʳ, 'lɑx

Neahwa
   Park, *former name for* Damaschke   NĒ-uh-WAW, NĒ-uh-WAH, NĒ-uh-wuh   'niːə,wɔː, 'niːə,wɑ, 'niːəwə
   Field, *Oneonta, NY*

Neal, Neale
   pers. name   NĒL   'niːl

Neanderthal
   Paleolithic human subspecies   nē-AN-duhr-THAWL, -TAWL;   niː'ændəʳ,θɔːl, -,tɔːl;
        nā-AHN-duhr-TAHL   neː'ɑndəʳ,tɑl

Neapolis
   ancient name of Naples   nē-AP-uh-luhs   niː'æpələs

Neapolitan
   pert. to Naples   NĒ-uh-PAHL-uht-n   ,niːə'pɑlətṇ

Nearchus
   Macedonian soldier, explorer   nē-AHR-kuhs   niː'ɑʳkəs

Nebbiolo
   Italian wine grape   neb-BYŌ-lō   nebbjoːloː

Nebo
   Mount, *Jordan*   NĒ-bō   'niːboː

Nebraska
   state, US   nuh-BRAS-kuh   nə'bræskə

Nebuchadnezzar
   king of Babylon   NEB-(y)uh-kuhd-NEZ-uhr   ,neb(j)əkəd'nezəʳ

Nebuchadrezzar
   alternate form of Nebuchadnezzar   NEB-(y)uh-kuh-DREZ-uhr   ,neb(j)əkə'drezəʳ

Nebularum, Palus
   see Palus Nebularum

NEC
   Japanese electronics co.   NEK, EN-Ē-SĒ   'nek, ,en,iː'siː

Necchi
   sewing machine co.   NEK-ē   'nekiˑ

Necho
   Egyptian pharaoh   NĒ-kō   'niːkoː

Necronomicon
   ancient occult text, H.P. Lovecraft   NEK-ruh-NAHM-i-KAHN   ,nekrə'nɑmi,kɑn

Nectaris, Mare
   see Mare Nectaris

Ned
   pers. name   NED   'ned

Neðri Deild
   Icelandic legis. body   NETH-rē DĀLD   'neðriˑ 'deːld

Needham
   Hal, *US film writer; town, MA*   NĒD-uhm   'niːdəm

Néel
   Louis Eugène, *French physicist*   nā-EL   neːel
        (*Nobel 1970*)

Neeme
   pers. name, Estonian   nyi-ĀM-yuh, Ⓢ NĒ-muh   nji'eːmjə, Ⓢ 'niːmə

Key (col. 2):   a: fad   ā: fade   ah: father   ar: Mary   aw: law   e: fed   ē: feed   er: merry   i: hid   ī: hide   ō: coat   ō͞o: boot
oi: boy   ow: now   u: put   uh: above   uhr: bird   ch: chop   ng: ring   sh: show   th: thick   th̲: this   zh: measure

Nefertiti
  Egyptian queen   NEF-uhr-TĒT-ē   ˌnefəˈtiːˌtiˈ

Neftali
  pers. name, Spanish   nef-tah-LĒ   neftɑˈliː

Negev
  desert, Israel   NEG-EV   ˈnegˌev

Negra Modelo
  Mexican beer   NĀ-grah mō-DĀ-lō   ˈneːgrɑ moːˈdeːloː

Negress
  (formerly) woman of black African NĒ-gruhs   ˈniːgrəs
    race

Negrillo
  Pygmy   ni-GRĒ-(y)ō, ni-GRIL-ō   niˈgriː(j)oː, niˈgriloː

Negri Sembilan
  state, Malaysia   nuh-GRĒ sem-BĒ-luhn   nəˌgriː semˈbiːlən

Negrito
  small-statured people, Asia   nuh-GRĒT-ō   nəˈgriːtoː

Negro
  1. member of black African race NĒ-grō   ˈniːgroː
  2. Rio, river, S. America   NĀ-ḡrō, Ⓢ NEG-rō   ˈneːɣroː, Ⓢ ˈnegroː

Negroid
  pert. to Negro people   NĒ-GROID   ˈniːˌgrɔid

Negros
  island, Philippines   NĀ-grōs, NEG-rōs   ˈneːgroːs, ˈnegroːs

Negus
  title of sovereign in Ethiopia NĒ-guhs   ˈniːgəs

Nehemiah
  pers. name   NĒ-(h)uh-MĪ-uh   ˌniː(h)əˈmaiə

Neher
  Edwin, *German physicist (Nobel* NĀ-uhr, NER   ˈneːəˈ, ˈneˈ
    1991)

Nehru
  Jawaharlal, *Indian leader*   NER-o͞o, NĀ-ro͞o   ˈneruː, ˈneːruː

Neil
  pers. name   NĒL   ˈniːl

Neilson
  William Allen, *US educator*   NĒL-suhn   ˈniːlsən

Neiman
  Leroy, *US artist*   NĒ-muhn   ˈniːmən

Neiman-Marcus
  department store, US   NĒ-muhn-MAHR-kuhs   ˌniːmənˈmɑˈkəs

Nei-Meng-Gu, Nei-Meng-Ku, Nei Mongol
  Inner Mongolia, China   NĀ MUHNG-GO͞O   ˈneː ˈməŋˈguː

Neineva
  governorate, Iraq   NĀ-nuh-vuh   ˈneːnəvə

Neith
  Egyptian war goddess   NĀT, NĀTH   ˈneːt, ˈneːθ

Nejd [Najd]
  prov, Saudi Arabia   NEJD   ˈnedʒd

Nekhbet
  Egyptian guardian goddess   NE<u>KH</u>-buht   ˈnexbət

Nekhebet [Nekhbet]
  Egyptian guardian goddess   NE<u>KH</u>-uh-buht   ˈnexəbət

Foreign Sounds: ue: *Fr.* **rue**, *Ger.* **füllen**   uh(r): *Fr.* **boeuf**, *Ger.* **Höhle**   <u>kh</u>: *Ger.* **ich**, *Scot.* **loch**   ḡ: *Sp.* **amigo**   <u>v</u>: *Sp.* **hablar**   hl: *Welsh* **Llanelli**.   CAPITALS: primary stress.   SMALL CAPS: secondary stress.   Ⓢ: U.S. pron.   Ⓔ: British pron.

Nektar
  Yugoslavian beer   NEK-TAHR   'nek,tɑr

Neleus
  son of Tyro and Poseidon   NĒ-lē-uhs, NĒ-L(Y)O͞OS   'niːliːəs, 'niː,l(j)uːs

Nell
  pers. name   NEL   'nel

Nellie, Nelly
  pers. name   NEL-ē   'neliˑ

Nelligan
  Kate, *Canadian actress*   NEL-uh-guhn   'neləgən

Nelson
  pers. name   NEL-suhn   'nelsən

Nemaha
  river, US; county, KS, NE   NEM-uh-HAW, NĒ-muh-HAW   'nemə,hɔː, 'niːmə,hɔː

Neman
  river, Belorussia, Lithuania,   NEM-uhn   'nemən
    Russia

Nembutal
  tdmk for pentobarbital   NEM-byuh-TAWL   ˌnembjə'tɔːl

Nemea
  valley, ancient Greece   NĒ-mē-uh   'niːmiːə

Nemean
  pert. to **Nemea**   ni-MĒ-uhn, NEM-ē-uhn, NĒ-mē-uhn   ni'miːən, 'nemiːən,
                                                   'niːmiːən

Nemerov
  Howard, *US poet laureate*   NEM-uh-RAWV   'nemə,rɔːv

Nemesis
  Greek goddess of divine vengeance   NEM-uh-suhs   'neməsəs

Nemetz
  Nathaniel Theodore, *Canadian*   NEM-uhts   'neməts
    jurist

Nemi
  lake, Italy   NĀ-mē, NEM-ē   'neːmiˑ, 'nemiˑ

Nemo
  Captain, *character in 20,000*   NĒ-mō   'niːmoː
    Leagues Under the Sea, *Jules*
    Verne

Nene
  1. English river   NĒN, NEN   'niːn, 'nen
  2. Hawaiian goose   NĀ-nā   'neːneː

Nenets [Yurak]
  lang., region, Russia   nyuhn-YETS   njən'jets

Neocene
  geologic era   NĒ-uh-SĒN, NĒ-uh-SĒN   ˌniːə'siːn, 'niːə,siːn

neodymium
  element   NĒ-ō-DIM-ē-uhm   ˌniːoːˈdimiːəm

Neogaea
  biogeographical division, the   NĒ-uh-JĒ-uh   ˌniːə'dʒiːə
    Neotropical region

Neogene
  geologic period   NĒ-uh-JĒN   'niːə,dʒiːn

Neolithic
  prehistoric age   NĒ-uh-LITH-ik   ˌniːə'liθik

Neo-Melanesian [Tok Pisin]
  lang., Papua New Guinea   NĒ-ō-MEL-uh-NĒ-zhuhn, -NĒ-shuhn   ˌniːoːˌmelə'niːʒən, -'niːʃən

---

Key (col. 2):   a: **fad**   ā: **fade**   ah: **father**   ar: **Mary**   aw: **law**   e: **fed**   ē: **feed**   er: **merry**   i: **hid**   ī: **hide**   ō: **coat**   o͞o: **boot**
oi: **boy**   ow: **now**   u: **put**   uh: **above**   uhr: **bird**   ch: **chop**   ng: **ring**   sh: **show**   th: **thick**   <u>th</u>: **this**   zh: **measure**

neon		
element	NĒ-AHN	'niː,ɑn
Neoplatonism		
modified Platonism	NĒ-ō-PLĀT-n-ɪZ-uhm	,niːoː'pleːtn̩,izəm
Neoptolemus		
son of Achilles and Deidamia	NĒ-uhp-TAHL-uh-muhs	,niːəp'tɑləməs
Neosho		
river, county, KA	nē-Ō-shō, nē-Ō-shuh	niː'oːʃoː, niː'oːʃə
Nepal		
kingdom, Asia	nuh-PAWL, -PAHL, -PAL	nə'pɔːl, -'pɑl, -'pæl
Nepalese		
people, lang. Nepal	NEP-uh-LĒZ, -LĒS	,nepə'liːz, -'liːs
Nepali [Gurkhali]		
lang., Nepal, Sikkim	nuh-PAW-lē, nuh-PAHL-ē	nə'pɔːliˑ, nə'pɑliˑ
Nepean		
river, Australia	nuh-PĒ-uhn	nə'piːən
Nephele		
Greek mythical figure	NEF-uh-lē	'nefəliˑ
Nephelococcygia		
Cloud-cuckoo-land (Aristophanes)	NEF-uh-LŌ-kuh-SIJ-ē-uh, NEF-uh-LŌ-kuh-KIJ-ē-uh	,nefə,loːkə'sidʒiːə, ,nefə,loːkə'kidʒiːə
Nephthys		
Egyptian goddess of the dead	NEP-tuhs, NEF-thuhs	'neptəs, 'nefθəs
Nepomuk		
pers. name, Czech, German	NĀ-pō-MUK	'neːpoː,muk
Neptun		
Danish beer	nep-TUH(R)N	nep'tœn
Neptune		
Roman god of the sea; planet	NEP-T(Y)O͞ON	'nep,t(j)uːn
Neptunian		
pert. to Neptune	nep-T(Y)O͞O-nē-uhn	nep't(j)uːniːən
neptunium		
element	nep-T(Y)O͞O-nē-uhm	nep't(j)uːniːəm
Nereid		
sea nymph; satellite of Neptune	NIR-ē-uhd	'niriːəd
Nereids		
sea deities, daughters of Nereus	NIR-ē-uhdz	'niriːədz
Nereus		
sea-god in Greek mythology	NIR-ē-uhs	'niriːəs
Nerio		
personification of valor	NIR-ē-Ō	'niriː,oː
Nerites		
son of Nereus	nir-ĪT-ēz	nir'aițiːz
Nernst		
Walther, *German physicist, chemist (Nobel 1920)*	NERNST	'neʳnst
Nero		
Roman emperor	NĒ-rō, NIR-ō	'niːroː, 'niroː
Neruda		
Pablo, *Chilean poet, diplomat (Nobel 1971)*	nā-RO͞O-thah, Ⓢ nā-RO͞OD-uh	neː'ruːðɑ, Ⓢ neː'ruːdə
Nerva		
Roman emperor	NUHR-vuh	'nəʳvə
Nescafe, Nescafé		
tdmk for coffee	NES-kuh-FĀ, NES-kuh-FĀ	'neskə,feː, ,neskə'feː

Foreign Sounds: ue: *Fr.* **rue**, *Ger.* füllen uh(r): *Fr.* **b**o**euf**, *Ger.* Höhle kh: *Ger.* i**ch**, *Scot.* lo**ch** ḡ: *Sp.* ami**g**o v: *Sp.* ha**b**lar
hl: *Welsh* **Ll**anelli. CAPITALS: primary stress. SMALL CAPS: secondary stress. Ⓢ: U.S. pron. Ⓛ: British pron.

Neshoba
  county, MS   nuh-SHŌ-buh   nə'ʃoːbə

Ness, Loch
  see Loch Ness

Nesselrode
  1. Count Karl Robert, Russian   nyis-il-RAW-duh, Ⓢ NES-uhl-RŌD   njisil̹'rɔːdə, Ⓢ 'nesəl,roːd
    diplomat
  2. fruit-nut mixture   NES-uhl-RŌD   'nesəl,roːd

Nessus
  centaur   NES-uhs   'nesəs

Nesta
  pers. name   NES-tuh   'nestə

Nestlé
  Swiss food products co.   NES-lē, Ⓔ NES-uhl, NES-LĀ   'nesliˑ, Ⓔ 'nesəl, 'nes,leː

Néstor
  pers. name, Spanish   NĀ-stawr   'neːstɔːr

Nestor
  1. long-winded king of Pylos in   NES-tuhr, NES-TAWR   'nestəʳ, 'nes,tɔːʳ
    Greek mythology; pers. name
  2. Finnish   NES-TAWR   'nes,tɔːr
  3. French   nes-TAWR   nestɔːr

Nestorian
  pert. to Nestor   nes-TŌR-ē-uhn, nes-TAWR-ē-uhn   nes'toːriːən, nes'tɔːriːən

Netherlander
  inhabitant of the Netherlands   NE<u>TH</u>-uhr-LAN-duhr, -luhn-duhr   'neðəʳ,lændəʳ, -ləndəʳ

Netherlandic [Dutch]
  lang., Netherlands, Belgium,   NE<u>TH</u>-uhr-LAN-dik,   'neðəʳ,lændik,
    Suriname, Antilles   NE<u>TH</u>-uhr-LAN-dik   ,neðəʳ'lændik

Netherlands
  kingdom, Europe   NE<u>TH</u>-uhr-luhn(d)z   'neðəʳlən(d)z

Netherlands Antillean
  pert. to Netherlands Antilles   NE<u>TH</u>-uhr-luhn(d)z an-TIL-ē-uhn   'neðəʳlən(d)z æn'tiliːən

Netherlands Antilles
  islands, West Indies   NE<u>TH</u>-uhr-luhn(d)z an-TIL-ēz   'neðəʳlən(d)z æn'tiliːz

Nettleton
  Lois, *US actress*   NET-l-tuhn   'netl̹tən

Neuburger
  Austrian wine grape   NOI-BURG-uhr, -BUHRG-uhr   'nɔi,buʳgəʳ, -,bəʳgəʳ

Neuchâtel
  town, canton, Switzerland   nuh(r)-shah-TEL   nœːʃatel

Neuenburg [Neuchâtel]
  town, Switzerland   NOI-uhn-BURK   'nɔiən,buʳk

Neufchâtel
  town, France; cheese   nuh(r)-shah-TEL,   nœːʃatel, Ⓢ ,n(j)uːʃə'tel
         Ⓢ N(Y)O͞O-shuh-TEL

Neufeldt
  Victoria, *US lexicographer*   N(Y)O͞O-FELD, N(Y)O͞O-FELT   'n(j)uː,feld, 'n(j)uː,felt

Neuilly-sur-Seine
  suburb, Paris   nuh(r)-YĒ-suer-SEN   nœjiːsyːrsen

Neumann
  1. John N., *Czech-born US*   N(Y)O͞O-muhn   'n(j)uːmən
    clergyman, saint
  2. family name, German   NOI-MAHN   'nɔi,mɑn

Neusiedlersee
  lake, Austria, Hungary   NOI-ZĒD-luhr-ZĀ   'nɔi,ziːdləʳ,zeː

Key (col. 2):   a: **fad**   ā: **fade**   ah: **father**   ar: **Mary**   aw: **law**   e: **fed**   ē: **feed**   er: **merry**   i: **hid**   ī: **hide**   ō: **coat**   o͞o: **boot**
oi: **boy**   ow: **now**   u: **put**   uh: **above**   uhr: **bird**   ch: **chop**   ng: **ring**   sh: **show**   th: **thick**   <u>th</u>: **this**   zh: **measure**

Neuth [Nut]
  Egyptian sky goddess N(Y)OOT, N(Y)OOTH 'n(j)uːt, 'n(j)uːθ
Neutrino
  subatomic particle n(y)oo-TRĒ-nō n(j)uː'triːnoː
Neva
  river, Russia NĒ-vuh, NĂ-vuh 'niːvə, 'neːvə
Nevada
  state, US nuh-VAD-uh, nuh-VAHD-uh nə'vædə, nə'vɑdə
Nevil, Neville
  pers. name NEV-uhl, NEV-il 'nevəl, 'nevil
Nevis
  one of the Leeward Islands, West Indies NĒ-vuhs, NEV-uhs 'niːvəs, 'nevəs
Nevisian
  pert. to Nevis NEV-uh-SĒ-uhn ˌnevə'siːən
Newari
  lang., Central Nepal nuh-WAHR-ē nə'wɑriˑ
Newark
  1. city, CA, NJ, OH; village, NY; borough, England N(Y)OO-uhrk, N(Y)U(-uh)rk 'n(j)uːəʳk, 'n(j)u(ə)ʳk
  2. city, DE N(Y)OO-AHRK 'n(j)uːˌɑʳk
Newaygo
  county, MI ni-WĀ-gō ni'weːgoː
Newbold
  pers. name N(Y)OO-BŌLD 'n(j)uːˌboːld
New Brunswick
  city, NJ; province, Canada n(y)oo BRUHNZ-wik n(j)uˑ 'brənzwik
Newburgh
  city, NY N(Y)OO-BUHRG 'n(j)uːˌbəʳg
New Caledonia
  island, French territory, Pacific N(Y)OO KAL-uh-DŌ-nē-uh ˌn(j)uː ˌkælə'doːniːə
New Caledonian
  pert. to New Caledonia N(Y)OO KAL-uh-DŌ-nē-uhn ˌn(j)uː ˌkælə'doːniːən
Newcastle
  pl. name, US, England N(Y)OO-KAS-uhl, n(y)oo-KAS-uhl 'n(j)uːˌkæsəl, n(j)uː'kæsəl
New College
  college, Oxford Univ. N(Y)OO KAHL-ij 'n(j)uː ˌkɑlidʒ
New Delhi
  city, India n(y)oo DEL-ē n(j)uˑ 'deliˑ
New England
  region, Northeast US n(y)oo ING-gluhnd, ING-luhnd n(j)uˑ 'ingglənd, 'inlənd
New Englander
  inhabitant of New England n(y)oo ING-gluhn-duhr, ING-luhn-duhr n(j)uˑ 'inggləndəʳ, 'inləndəʳ
Newfie
  slang, inhabitant of Newfoundland N(Y)OO-fē 'n(j)uːfiˑ
Newfoundland
  island, province, Canada; dog breed N(Y)OO-fuhn(d)-luhnd, N(Y)OO-fuhn(d)-LAND, n(y)oo-FOWN(D)-luhnd; *in Canada usually* N(Y)OO-fuhn(d)-LAND 'n(j)uːfən(d)lənd, 'n(j)uːfən(d)ˌlænd, n(j)uː'faun(d)lənd; *in Canada usually* ˌn(j)uːfən(d)'lænd

---

Foreign Sounds: ue: *Fr.* **rue**, *Ger.* füllen uh(r): *Fr.* **boeuf**, *Ger.* **Höhle** <u>kh</u>: *Ger.* i<u>ch</u>, *Scot.* lo<u>ch</u> ḡ: *Sp.* ami**g**o v̱: *Sp.* ha**b**lar
hl: *Welsh* **Llanelli**. CAPITALS: primary stress. SMALL CAPS: secondary stress. ⑤: U.S. pron. ⓔ: British pron.

Newfoundlander

inhabitant of Newfoundland   N(Y)OO-fuhn(d)-luhn-duhr,   'n(j)u:fən(d)ləndəʳ,
    N(Y)OO-fuhn(d)-LAN-duhr,   'n(j)u:fən(d),lændəʳ,
    n(y)oo-FOWN(D)-luhn-duhr; *in*   n(j)u:'faun(d)ləndəʳ; *in*
    Canada usually   *Canada usually*
    N(Y)OO-fuhn(d)-LAN-duhr   ,n(j)u:fən(d)'lændəʳ

Newgrange

prehistoric burial site, Ireland   n(y)oo-GRĀNJ   n(j)u'greɪndʒ

New Guinea

island, Pacific   n(y)oo GIN-ē   n(j)u' 'gini·

New Hall

college, Cambridge Univ.   n(y)oo HAWL   n(j)u: 'hɔːl

Newham

borough, England   N(Y)OO-uhm   'n(j)u:əm

New Hampshire

state, US   n(y)oo HAM(P)-shuhr,   n(j)u' 'hæm(p)ʃəʳ,
    HAM(P)-SHIR   'hæm(p),ʃiʳ

New Hanover

county, NC   N(Y)OO han-Ō-vuhr; n(y)oo   ,n(j)u: hæn'oːvəʳ; n(j)u:
    HAN-Ō-vuhr, HAN-uh-vuhr   'hæn,oːvəʳ, 'hænəvəʳ

Newhart

Bob, US actor   N(Y)OO-HAHRT   'n(j)u:,haʳt

New Haven

city, county, CT   n(y)oo HĀ-vuhn, N(Y)OO HĀ-vuhn   n(j)u' 'heɪvən, 'n(j)u: ,heɪvən

Newhaven

port, England   n(y)oo-HĀ-vuhn, N(Y)OO-HĀ-vuhn   n(j)u'heɪvən, 'n(j)u:,heɪvən

Ne Win

Burmese leader   NĀ WIN   'neɪ 'win

New Jersey

state, US   n(y)oo JUHR-zē   n(j)u' 'dʒəʳzi·

Newley

Anthony, British actor, singer   N(Y)OO-lē   'n(j)u:li·

Newlin

Michael H., US ambassador   N(Y)OO-luhn   'n(j)u:lən

New Madrid

county, city, MO; earthquake   n(y)oo MAD-ruhd   n(j)u' 'mædrəd
fault, US

New Mexico

state, US   n(y)oo MEK-si-KŌ   n(j)u' 'meksi,koː

Newnes

Sir George, English publisher   N(Y)OONZ   'n(j)u:nz

Newnham

college, Cambridge Univ.   N(Y)OO-nuhm   'n(j)u:nəm

New Orleans

city, LA   n(y)oo AWR-lē-uhnz, AWRL-(y)uhnz;   n(j)u' ɔːʳli·ənz, 'ɔːʳl(j)ənz;
    mostly by outsiders N(Y)OO   *mostly by outsiders*
    awr-LĒNZ   ,n(j)u: ɔːʳ'liːnz

New Paltz

town, NY   N(Y)OO PAWLTS   'n(j)u: ,pɔːlts

Newport

city, RI   N(Y)OO-PŌRT, N(Y)OO-PAWRT   'n(j)u:,poːʳt, 'n(j)u:,pɔːʳt

Newport News

city, VA   N(Y)OO-PŌRT N(Y)OOZ,   ,n(j)u:,poːʳt 'n(j)u:z,
    N(Y)OO-PAWRT, N(Y)OO-puhrt   ,n(j)u:,pɔːʳt, ,n(j)u:pəʳt

Key (col. 2): a: fad ā: fade ah: father ar: Mary aw: law e: fed ē: feed er: merry i: hid ī: hide ō: coat oo: boot
oi: boy ow: now u: put uh: above uhr: bird ch: chop ng: ring sh: show th: thick th: this zh: measure

New Rochelle
    town, NY   N(Y)U ruh-SHEL, N(Y)OO rō-SHEL   ,n(j)u rə'ʃel, ,n(j)uː roː'ʃel
New South Wales
    state, Australia   N(Y)OO SOWTH WĂLZ   ,n(j)uː ,sauθ 'weːlz
Newt
    pers. name   N(Y)OOT   'n(j)uːt
Newton
    Sir Isaac, English philosopher,   N(Y)OOT-n   'n(j)uːtn̩
       mathematician; city, MA
Newtonian
    pert. to Newton *or his theories*   n(y)oo-TŌ-nē-uhn   n(j)uː'toːniːən
New York
    state, city, US   n(y)oo YAWRK   n(j)uː 'jɔːʳk
New Zealand
    island nation, Pacific   n(y)oo ZĒ-luhnd   n(j)uː 'ziːlənd
New Zealander
    inhabitant of New Zealand   n(y)oo ZĒ-luhn-duhr   n(j)uː 'ziːləndəʳ
Ney
    Michel, *French militarist*   NE, Ⓢ NĀ   ne, Ⓢ 'neː
Nez Perce
    county, ID; mtn., WY   NEZ PUHRS   'nez 'pəʳs
Nezperce
    village, ID   NEZ-PUHRS   'nez'pəʳs
Nez Percé
    1. N. American people   NEZ PUHRS, PERS   'nez 'pəʳs, 'peʳs
    2. French   nā per-SĀ   neː perseː
Ngadju, Ngaju
    lang., people, South Borneo   NGAHJ-oo, Ⓢ uhng-GAHJ-oo   'ŋadʒuː, Ⓢ əŋ'gadʒuː
Ngaio
    pers. name   NĪ-ō   'naioː
Ngo Dinh Diem
    president, South Vietnam   NŌ DIN dē-EM, NGŌ   'noː 'din diː'em, ŋoː
Ngoni
    lang., people, Africa   NGŌ-nē, Ⓢ uhng-GŌ-nē, eng-   'ŋoːniː, Ⓢ əŋ'goːni', eŋ-
Ngorongoro
    crater, Tanzania   NGŌR-ōng-GŌR-ō,   ,ŋoːroːŋ'goːroː,
          Ⓢ eng-GŌR-ōng-GŌR-ō,   Ⓢ eŋ,goːroːŋ'goːroː,
          eng-GAWR-ōng-GAWR-ō   eŋ,gɔːroːŋ'goːroː
Nguni
    lang., people, Africa   NGOO-nē, Ⓢ uhng-GOO-nē, eng-   'ŋuːni', Ⓢ əŋ'guːni', eŋ-
Nguyen Cao Ky
    military official, South Vietnam   NOO-yen KOW KĒ, NGOO-yen   'nuːjen 'kau 'kiː, 'ŋuːjen
Nguyen Van Thieu
    president, South Vietnam   NOO-yen VAN TOO, NGOO-yen   'nuːjen 'væn 'tuː, 'ŋuːjen
Niagara
    river, N. America; county, NY   nī-AG(-uh)-ruh   nai'æg(ə)rə
Niagara Falls
    falls, N. America; town, Canada   nī-AG(-uh)-ruh FAWLZ   nai,æg(ə)rə 'fɔːlz
Niall
    king of Ireland; pers. name, Irish   NĒL   'niːl
       Gaelic
Niamey
    city, Niger   nē-AHM-ā   niː'ameː
Niantic
    stream, inlet, town division, CT   nī-ANT-ik   nai'æntik

Foreign Sounds: ue: *Fr.* **rue**, *Ger.* **füllen** uh(r): *Fr.* **boeuf**, *Ger.* **Höhle** <u>kh</u>: *Ger.* **ich**, *Scot.* **loch** ḡ: *Sp.* **amigo** <u>v</u>: *Sp.* **hablar**
hl: *Welsh* **Llanelli**. CAPITALS: primary stress. SMALL CAPS: secondary stress. Ⓢ: U.S. pron. Ⓛ: British pron.

Nias
   island, lang., Indian Ocean   NĒ-AHS   'niːˌɑs

Nibelung
   dwarf in German legend; follower   NĒ-buh-LUNG   'niːbəˌluŋ
     of Siegfried

Nibelungenlied
   medieval German legend   NĒ-buh-LUNG-uhn-LĒD   ˌniːbə'luŋən,liːd

Nicaea
   ancient city, empire, Asia Minor;   nī-SĒ-uh   nɑi'siːə
     naiad pursued by Dionysus

Nicaragua
   republic, Cen. America   nē-kah-RAHG-wah,   niːkɑ'rɑɣwɑ,
                      Ⓢ NIK-uh-RAHG-wuh, Ⓔ   Ⓢ ˌnikə'rɑgwə, Ⓔ
                      NIK-uh-RAG-yuh-wuh   ˌnikə'rægjəwə

Nicaraguan
   pert. to Nicaragua   NIK-uh-RAHG-wuhn   ˌnikə'rɑgwən

Niccolò
   pers. name, Italian   NĒK-kō-LAW   ˌniːkkoː'lɔː

Nice
   resort, France   NĒS   niːs

Nicene
   pert. to Nicaea or to church   NĪ-SĒN, nī-SĒN   'nɑiˌsiːn, nɑi'siːn
     council held there

Nicene Creed
   statement of Christian belief   NĪ-SĒN KRĒD   ˌnɑiˌsiːn 'kriːd

Nichol
   William, *British physicist*   NIK-uhl   'nikəl

Nicholas
   pers. name   NIK-(uh-)luhs   'nik(ə)ləs

Nicholson
   Ben, *English artist;* Jack, *US actor* NIK-uhl-suhn   'nikəlsən

Nicias
   Athenian general   NIS-ē-uhs, NISH-ē-uhs   'nisiːəs, 'niʃiːəs

Nick
   pers. name   NIK   'nik

nickel
   element   NIK-uhl   'nikəl

Nicki
   pers. name   NIK-ē   'nikiˑ

Nicklaus
   Jack, *US golfer*   NIK-luhs   'nikləs

Nickleby
   Nicholas, *character by Dickens* NIK-uhl-bē   'nikəlbiˑ

Nickles
   Don, *US politician*   NIK-uhlz   'nikəlz

Nicky
   pers. name   NIK-ē   'nikiˑ

Nicobar
   Islands, *Bay of Bengal*   NIK-uh-BAHR   'nikə,bɑʳ

Nicobarese
   lang., people, Nicobar Islands NIK-uh-bahr-ĒZ, -ĒS   ˌnikəbɑr'iːz, -'iːs

Nicodemus
   1. pers. name   NIK-uh-DĒ-muhs   ˌnikə'diːməs
   2. Swedish   NIK-ō-DĀ-muhs   ˌnikoː'deːməs

Key (col. 2):   a: fad   ā: fade   ah: father   ar: **M**ary   aw: **l**aw   e: fed   ē: feed   er: merry   i: hid   ī: hide   ō: coat   ōō: boot
oi: **b**oy   ow: now   u: put   uh: above   uhr: bird   ch: chop   ng: ring   sh: show   th: thick   <u>th</u>: this   zh: measure

Niçoise
  salad   nē-SWAHZ   niːˈswɑz
Nicol
  pers. name   NIK-uhl   ˈnikəl
Nicola
  1. pers. name   NIK-uh-luh   ˈnikələ
  2. Italian   nē-KAW-lah   niːˈkɔːla
  3. see Nikola
Nicolaas
  see Nikolaas
Nicolae
  pers. name, Romanian   NĒ-kō-LĪ   ˌniːkoːˈlai
Nicolai
  1. pers. name, Danish   NĒ-kuh-LĪ   ˌniːkəˈlai
  2. Dutch   NĒ-kō-LAH-ē   ˌniːkoːˈlaːiː
  3. German   NĒ-kō-LAH-ē, NĒ-kō-LĪ   ˌniːkoːˈla-iː, ˈniːkoːˌlai
Nicolas
  1. pers. name   NIK-(uh-)luhs   ˈnik(ə)ləs
  2. Dutch   NĒ-kuh-lahs   ˈniːkəlɑːs
  3. French   nē-kaw-LAH   niːkɔːla
Nicolás
  pers. name, Spanish   nē-kō-LAHS   niːkoːˈlas
Nicolaus
  pers. name, Latin   NIK-uh-LĀ-uhs   ˌnikəˈleːəs
Nicole
  1. pers. name   ni-KŌL   niˈkoːl
  2. French   nē-KAWL   niːkɔːl
Nicolet
  Canada   NĒ-kuh-LĀ   ˌniːkəˈleː
Nicolette
  pers. name   NIK-uh-LET   ˌnikəˈlet
Nicolle
  C. J. H., French bacteriologist   nē-KAWL   niːkɔːl
  (Nobel 1928)
Nicollet
  county, MN; Park, *former*   NIK-uh-LET   ˈnikəˌlet
  ballpark, Minneapolis, MN
Nicolò
  pers. name, Italian   NĒ-kō-LAW   ˌniːkoːˈlɔː
Nicomachean Ethics
  Aristotelian treatise   NĪ-KAHM-uh-KĒ-uhn ETH-iks   ˌnɑiˌkaməˈkiːən ˈeθiks
Nicomedia
  ancient city, Asia Minor   NIK-uh-MĒD-ē-uh   ˌnikəˈmiːdiːə
Nicopolis
  ancient city, Greece; town,   ni-KAHP-uh-luhs, nī-   niˈkapələs, nɑi-
  Bulgaria
Nicosia
  city, district, Cyprus   NIK-uh-SĒ-uh   ˌnikəˈsiːə
Nicostratus
  son of Helen and Menelaus   nī-KAHS-truht-uhs   nɑiˈkastrətəs
Niebuhr
  1. Barthold Georg, *German*   NĒ-BO͞OR   ˈniːˌbuˑʳ
    historian
  2. Rheinhold, *US theologian*   NĒ-BUR, NĒ-buhr   ˈniːˌbuʳ, ˈniːbəʳ

Foreign Sounds: ue: *Fr.* **rue,** *Ger.* f**ü**llen   uh(r): *Fr.* b**oeu**f, *Ger.* H**ö**hle   <u>kh</u>: *Ger.* i**ch,** *Scot.* lo**ch**   g̃: *Sp.* ami**g**o   <u>v</u>: *Sp.* ha**b**lar
hl: *Welsh* **Ll**anelli.   CAPITALS: primary stress.   SMALL CAPS: secondary stress.   ⑤: U.S. pron.   ⑭: British pron.

Niedere Tauern
  mtn. range, Austria — NĒD-uhr-uh TOW-uhrn — ˌniːdərə ˈtauəʳn
Niederösterreich
  state, Austria — NĒD-uh-RUH(R)-stuhr-RĪ<u>KH</u> — ˌniːdəˈrœːstəʳˌraiç
Niedersachsen
  prov, Germany — NĒD-uhr-SAHK-suhn — ˈniːdəʳˌsaksən
Niels
  1. pers. name, Danish — NILS — ˈnils
  2. Norwegian — NĒLS — ˈniːls
Nielsen
  1. Carl August, *Danish composer* — NIL-suhn, Ⓢ NĒL-suhn — ˈnilsən, Ⓢ ˈniːlsən
  2. A.C., *TV ratings firm;* Erik H., — NĒL-suhn — ˈniːlsən
    Canadian politician
Niemeyer
  German publishing co. — NĒ-MĪ(-uh)r — ˈniːˌmai(ə)ʳ
Nietzsche
  Friedrich Wilhelm, *German* — NĒ-chuh, NĒ-chē — ˈniːtʃə, ˈniːtʃiˑ
    philosopher
Nietzscheism
  philosophy of Nietzsche — NĒ-chē-IZ-uhm — ˈniːtʃiːˌizəm
Nigel
  pers. name — NĪ-juhl — ˈnaidʒəl
Niger
  1. river, Africa; Roman general — NĪ-juhr — ˈnaidʒəʳ
  2. republic, Africa — nē-ZHER, NĪ-juhr — niːˈʒeʳ, ˈnaidʒəʳ
Nigeria
  republic, Africa — nī-JIR-ē-uh — naiˈdʒiriːə
Nigerian
  pert. to Nigeria — nī-JIR-ē-uhn — naiˈdʒiriːən
Nigerois
  inhabitant of Niger — nē-zher-WAH — niːʒerwaː
Nightingale
  Florence, *English nurse* — NĪT-n-GĀL, NĪT-ing-GĀL — ˈnaitn̩ˌgeːl, ˈnaiti̩ŋˌgeːl
Nihon
  Japanese name for Japan — nē-hawn — niːhɔːn
Niihau
  island, HI — NĒ-HOW, NĒ-ē-HOW — ˈniːˌhau, ˈniːiːˌhau
Nijinksky
  Vaslav, *Russian ballet dancer* — nuh-ZHIN-skē, nuh-JIN-skē — nəˈʒinskiˑ, nəˈdʒinskiˑ
Nijmegen
  city, Netherlands — NĪ-MĀ-ğuh(n) — ˈnaiˌmeːɣə(n)
Nike
  Greek goddess of victory; — NĪ-kē — ˈnaikiˑ
    sportswear mfrs.
Nikita
  pers. name, Russian — nyik-YĒ-tuh, Ⓢ ni-KĒT-uh — njikˈjiːtə, Ⓢ niˈkiːt̬ə
Nikkei Dow
  Japanese stock index — NĒ-KĀ DOW — ˌniːˌkeː ˈdau
Nikki
  pers. name — NIK-ē — ˈnikiˑ
Niklas
  pers. name, German — NĒ-klahs — ˈniːklas
Nikodemus
  pers. name, German — NĒ-kō-DĀ-mus — ˌniːkoːˈdeːmus

Key (col. 2): a: fad ā: fade ah: father ar: Mary aw: law e: fed ē: feed er: merry i: hid ī: hide ō: coat o͞o: boot
oi: boy ow: now u: put uh: above uhr: bird ch: chop ng: ring sh: show th: thick <u>th</u>: this zh: measure

Nikola, Nicola
   pers. name, Serbo-Croatian   NĒ-kaw-LAH   'niːkɔːˌlɑː

Nikolaas, Nicolaas
   pers. name, Dutch   NĒ-kuh-LAHS   'niːkəˌlɑːs

Nikolai
   1. pers. name, Danish   NĒ-kuh-LĪ   ˌniːkə'lai
   2. Russian   nyik-uh-LĪ   njikə'lai

Nikolaos
   pers. name, Greek   nyē-KAW-lah-aws   nji'ˈkɔːlɑːs

Nikon
   Japanese camera co.   NĒ-KAHN, NĪ-KAHN, NIK-AHN   'niːˌkɑn, 'naiˌkɑn, 'nikˌɑn

Nikos
   pers. name, Greek   NĒ-KAWS   'niːˌkɔːs

Niksicko Pivo
   Yugoslavian beer   NIK-SHIT-skō PĒ-vō   'nikˌʃitskɔː 'piːvɔː

Nile
   river, Africa   NĪL   'nail

Nilo-Hamitic
   lang., Africa   NĪ-lō-ha-MIT-ik   ˌnailɔːhæ'mitik

Nilo-Saharan
   African lang. family   NĪ-lō-suh-HAR-uhn, -suh-HER-uhn,   ˌnailɔːsə'hærən, -sə'herən,
                                 -suh-HAHR-uhn   -sə'harən

Nilotic
   lang., pert. to the Nile   nī-LAHT-ik   nai'laṭik

Nils
   1. pers. name, Danish, Swedish   NILS   'nils
   2. Norwegian   NĒLS   'niːls

Nilsson
   1. Birgit, *Swedish soprano*   NĒL-sawn   'niːlsɔːn
   2. Harry, *US singer, songwriter*   NIL-suhn, NĒL-suhn   'nilsən, 'niːlsən

Nilus
   god of the Nile River   NĪ-luhs, NĒ-luhs   'nailəs, 'niːləs

NIMBY
   not in my back yard   NIM-bē   'nimbiˑ

Nimeiry, al-
   Gaffar Mohammed, *president,*   AHL ni-MER-ē, AL   ˌɑːl ni'meriˑ, ˌæl
     Sudan

Nîmes
   town, France   NĒM   niːm

Nimitz
   Chester W., *US admiral*   NIM-its   'nimits

Nimmitabel
   town, Australia   NIM-uht-uh-BEL   'nimətəˌbel

Nimoy
   Leonard, *US actor, director*   NĒ-MOI   'niːˌmɔi

Nimrod
   great-grandson of Noah; great   NIM-RAHD   'nimˌrɑd
     hunter

Nimrud
   modern name, site of ancient   nim-ROOD   nim'ruːd
     Kalakh

Nin
   Anaïs, *US author*   NĒN, NIN   'niːn, 'nin

Foreign Sounds: ue: *Fr.* **rue**, *Ger.* **fü**llen   uh(r): *Fr.* b**oeu**f, *Ger.* H**öh**le   <u>kh</u>: *Ger.* i<u>ch</u>, *Scot.* lo<u>ch</u>   ḡ: *Sp.* ami**g**o   <u>v</u>: *Sp.* ha**b**lar
hl: *Welsh* **Ll**anelli.   CAPITALS: primary stress.   SMALL CAPS: secondary stress.   Ⓢ: U.S. pron.   Ⓛ: British pron.

Nina
  1. pers. name   NĒ-nuh, NĪ-nuh   'niːnə, 'nainə
  2. Russian   NYĒ-nuh   'njiːnə
Nineveh
  capital of Assyria   NIN-uh-vuh   'ninəvə
Ningxia Huizu
  admin. division, China   NING-shē-AH HWĀ-ZOO   'niŋʃiːˈa 'hweːˈzuː
Ninian
  pers. name   NIN-ē-uhn   'niniːən
Nino
  pers. name   NĒ-nō   'niːnoː
Niño
  Pedro Alonzo, Spanish explorer   NĒN-yō   'niːnjoː
Nintendo
  Japanese computer game co.   nin-TEN-dō   nin'tendoː
Ninus
  founder of Nineveh and   NĪ-nuhs   'nainəs
    Babylonian Empire
Niobe
  mother of Argos and Pelasgus   NĪ-uh-bē, NĪ-Ō-bē   'naiəbiˈ, 'nai,oːbiˈ
niobium
  element   nī-Ō-bē-uhm   nai'oːbiːəm
Niobrara
  county, WY   NĪ-uh-BRAR-uh, NĪ-uh-BRER-uh   ,naiə'brærə, ,naiə'brerə
Niort
  town, France   NYAWR   njoːr
Nipissing
  Canada   NIP-uh-SING   'nipə,siŋ
Nipmuc
  N. American people   NIP-MUHK   'nip,mək
Nippon [Japan]
  nation, Asia   nip-ahn   nipɑn
Nippondenso
  Japanese electronics co.   NIP-ahn-DEN(T)-sō   ,nipɑn'den(t)soː
Nipponese
  Japanese   NIP-uh-NĒZ, -NĒS   ,nipə'niːz, -'niːs
Nippur
  ancient Sumerian/Babylonian city   nip-UR   nip'uʳ
Nirenberg
  Marshall W., US biochemist (Nobel   NIR-uhn-BUHRG   'nirən,bəʳg
    1968)
Nisan
  Jewish month   NIS-n, nē-SAHN   'nisn̩, niːˈsɑn
Nisanu
  Babylonian month   nē-SAHN-oo   niːˈsɑnuː
Nisei
  Japanese-American or -Canadian   nē-SĀ, NĒ-SĀ   niːˈseː, 'niː,seː
Nishapur
  town, Iran   NĒ-shuh-PUR   ,niːʃə'puʳ
Nisqually
  N. American people   ni-SKWAHL-ē, niz-KWAHL-ē   ni'skwɑliˈ, niz'kwɑliˈ
Nissan
  Japanese car co.   NĒ-SAHN, NIS-AHN   'niː,sɑn, 'nis,ɑn
Nissen
  prefabricated hut   NIS-n   'nisn̩

Key (col. 2):   a: fad ā: fade ah: father ar: Mary aw: law e: fed ē: feed er: merry i: hid ī: hide ō: coat oo: boot
oi: boy   ow: now   u: put   uh: above   uhr: bird   ch: chop   ng: ring   sh: show   th: thick   th: this   zh: measure

Nisus		
father of Scylla	NĪ-suhs	'nɑisəs
Nita		
pers. name	NĒT-uh	'niːʈə
nitrogen		
element	NĪ-truh-juhn	'nɑitrədʒən
Niue		
island, Pacific Ocean	nē-O͞O-(w)ā	niː'uː(w)eː
Niuean		
lang., people, Niue	n(y)o͞o-(W)Ā-uhn	n(j)uː'(w)eːən
Nivea		
tdmk for a cosmetic cream	NIV-ē-uh	'niviːə
Niven		
David, *English actor*	NIV-uhn	'nivən
Nivkh [Gilyak]		
lang., people, Russia	NIV<u>KH</u>	'nivx
Nivôse		
month, French Revolutionary	nē-VŌZ	niːvoːz
calendar		
Nixon		
Richard Milhous, *37th US*	NIK-suhn	'niksən
president		
Njörð		
Scandinavian sea god	NYUHR<u>TH</u>	'njœrð
Nkore [Nyankole]		
lang., people, Africa	(uh)ng-KŌR-ā, eng-	(ə)ŋ'koːreː, eŋ-
Nkrumah		
Kwame, *president, Ghana*	ng-KRO͞O-muh, en-KRO͞O-muh	ŋ'kruːmə, en'kruːmə
Noah		
pers. name	NŌ-uh	'noːə
Noailles		
pers. name, French	naw-AHY, Ⓢ nō-Ī	nɔːaj, Ⓢ noː'ai
Noam		
pers. name	NŌ(-uh)m	'noː(ə)m
Nobel		
Alfred, *Swedish engineer*	nō-BEL	noː'bel
Nobelist		
winner of a Nobel Prize	nō-BEL-uhst	noː'beləst
nobelium		
element	nō-BĒ-lē-uhm	noː'biːliːəm
Nobel Prize		
annual prize established by A.	nō-BEL PRĪZ, NŌ-BEL	noːˌbel 'prɑiz, 'noːˌbel
Nobel		
Nobles		
pers. name (E. N. Lowe)	NŌ-buhlz	'noːbəlz
Noblia		
watchmakers	NŌ-blē-uh	'noːbliːə
Noboru		
pers. name, Japanese	nō-bō-ro͞o	noːboːruː
Nobusuke		
pers. name, Japanese	nō-bu-suk-e	noːbusuke
Noche Buena		
Mexican beer	NŌ-chā BWĀ-nah	'noːtʃeː 'bweːnɑ
Nodaway		
county, MO	NAHD-uh-WĀ	'nɑdəˌweː

Foreign Sounds: ue: *Fr.* **rue**, *Ger.* füllen   uh(r): *Fr.* **b**oeuf, *Ger.* H**ö**hle   <u>kh</u>: *Ger.* i**ch**, *Scot.* lo**ch**   ğ: *Sp.* ami**g**o   <u>v</u>: *Sp.* ha**b**lar
hl: *Welsh* **Ll**anelli.   CAPITALS: primary stress.   SMALL CAPS: secondary stress.   Ⓢ: U.S. pron.   Ⓑ: British pron.

Noël
  pers. name, French   naw-EL   nɔːel
Noel, Noël
  1. pers. name   NŌ-uhl   'noːəl
  2. Christmas; Christmas carol   nō-EL   noː'el
Noel-Baker
  Philip J., *English statesman (Nobel*   NŌ-uhl-BĀ-kuhr   ˌnoːəl'beːkəʳ
    1959)
Nogai
  lang., people, Caucasus Mts.   NŌ-GĪ   'noːˌgai
Nogales
  city, AZ; town, Mexico   nō-GAL-uhs, nō-GAHL-uhs, *Spanish*   noː'gæləs, noː'galəs, *Spanish*
                                      nō-ĠAHL-ās   noː'ɣaleːs
Noguchi
  Hideyo, *US bacteriologist*   nō-GOO-chē   noː'guːtʃiˑ
Noilly Prat
  wine   n(uh-)wah-YĒ PRAHT   n(ə)waːjiː praːt
Noir de Pressac
  wine   nwahr duh pres-AHK   nwaːr də presaːk
Nola
  pers. name   NŌ-luh   'noːlə
Nolan
  pers. name   NŌ-luhn   'noːlən
Nolte
  Nick, *US actor*   NŌL-tē   'noːltiˑ
Nomalacki
  N. American people   NŌ-muh-LAK-ē   ˌnoːmə'lækiˑ
Nomalaki-Wailaki
  N. American people   NŌ-muh-LAK-ē-WĪ-LAK-ē   ˌnoːmə'lækiˑˌwai'lækiˑ
Nomaoi Matsuri
  Japanese festival   nō-mah-oi maht-sur-ē   noːmaɔi matsuriˑ
Nomarch
  ancient Egyptian magistrate   NAHM-AHRK   'nɑmˌaʳk
Nome
  division, city, AK; ancient   NŌM   'noːm
    Egyptian administrative unit
Nonius
  Roman name   NŌ-nē-uhs   'noːniːəs
Nooksack
  N. American people   NUK-SAK   'nukˌsæk
Noord Brabant
  prov, Netherlands   NŌRT bruh-BAHNT   ˌnoːʳt brə'bant
Noord Holland
  prov, Netherlands   nōrt HŌ-lahnt   noːʳt 'hoːlant
Nootka
  N. American people   NUT-kuh, NOOT-kuh   'nutkə, 'nuːtkə
Noquet
  N. American people   NŌ-kwā   'noːkweː
Nora
  pers. name   NŌR-uh, NAWR-uh   'noːrə, 'nɔːrə
NORAD
  air defense system   NŌR-AD, NAWR-AD   'noːrˌæd, 'nɔːrˌæd

Key (col. 2):   a: fad   ā: fade   ah: father   ar: Mary   aw: law   e: fed   ē: feed   er: merry   i: hid   ī: hide   ō: coat   ōō: boot
oi: boy   ow: now   u: put   uh: above   uhr: bird   ch: chop   ng: ring   sh: show   th: thick   th̲: this   zh: measure

Norbert		
1. pers. name	NAWR-buhrt	'nɔː^{r}bə^{r}t
2. Czech	NAWR-bert	'nɔːrbert
3. French	nawr-BER	nɔːrber
4. German	NAWR-bert	'nɔː^{r}be^{r}t
Nord		
dept, France	NAWR	nɔːr
Nordahl		
pers. name, Norwegian	NAWR-dahl	'nɔːrdɑl
Nordeste		
region, Brazil	nawr-DES-tā	nɔː^{r}'desteː
Nordik Wölf		
Swedish beer	NAWR-dik VUH(R)LF	'nɔːrdik 'vœlf
Nordiques		
Quebec hockey team	nawr-DĒKS	nɔː^{r}'diːks
Nord-Pas-de-Calais		
region, France	nawr-PAH-duh-kah-LE	nɔːrpɑdəkɑle
Nordrhein-Westfalen		
prov, Germany	nōrt-RĪN-vest-FAHL-uhn	noː^{r}t,rɑinvest'fɑlən
Nordstrom		
US department store	NAWRD-struhm	'nɔː^{r}dstrəm
Noreen		
pers. name	nōr-ĒN, nawr-ĒN	noːr'iːn, nɔːr'iːn
Norell		
tdmk, perfume	nawr-EL	nɔːr'el
Norfolk		
city, NE, VA; county, MA; county, England	NAWR-fuhk, [$] *also* NAWR-FAWK	'nɔː^{r}fək, [$] *also* 'nɔː^{r},fɔːk
Norgay		
Tenzing, *Sherpa mountaineer*	NAWR-gā	'nɔː^{r}geː
Norge [Norway]		
kingdom, Europe	NAWR-guh	'nɔː^{r}gə
Noric		
Alps, *Alpine mtn. range*	NŌR-ik, NAWR-ik	'noːrik, 'nɔːrik
Noriega		
Manuel, *Panamanian leader*	nawr-YĀ-guh, NAWR-ē-Ā-guh	nɔː^{r}'jeːgə, ,nɔːriː'eːgə
Noriker		
German horse breed	NŌR-i-kuhr, NAWR-	'noːrikə^{r}, 'nɔːr-
Norische Alpen [Noric Alps]		
Alpine mtn. range	NŌ-rish-uh AHL-puhn	'noːriʃə 'ɑlpən
Noritake		
brand of china	NŌR-uh-TAHK-ē, NAWR-uh-TAHK-ē	,noːrə'tɑkiˑ, ,nɔːrə'tɑkiˑ
Norm		
pers. name	NAWRM	'nɔː^{r}m
Norma		
constellation; pers. name	NAWR-muh	'nɔː^{r}mə
Norman		
inhabitant of Normandy; pers. name	NAWR-muhn	'nɔː^{r}mən
Normande, potée		
three-meat dish	paw-TĀ nawr-MAH^{n}D	pɔːteː nɔːrmɑ̃d
Normandie [Normandy]		
prov, France	nawr-mah^{n}-DĒ	nɔːrmɑ̃diː
Normandy		
prov, France	NAWR-muhn-dē	'nɔː^{r}məndiˑ

Foreign Sounds: ue: *Fr.* **rue**, *Ger.* **füllen** uh(r): *Fr.* **boeuf**, *Ger.* **Höhle** kh: *Ger.* **ich**, *Scot.* **loch** g̃: *Sp.* **amigo** v̲: *Sp.* **hablar** hl: *Welsh* **Llanelli**. CAPITALS: primary stress. SMALL CAPS: secondary stress. [$]: U.S. pron. [£]: British pron.

Norodom Sihanouk
   Cambodian chief of state   NŌR-uh-DUM SĒ-uh-NUK   ˌnoːrəˈdum ˈsiːəˌnuk

Norrish
   Ronald George Wreyford, English   NAWR-ish   ˈnɔːriʃ
   chemist (Nobel 1967)

Norse
   lang., N. Europe; pert. to ancient   NAWRS   ˈnɔːʳs
   Scandinavia; Norwegian

Northampton
   US pl. name; town, England   nawr-THAM(P)-tuhn,   nɔːʳˈθæm(p)tən,
                         nawrth-HAM(P)-tuhn   nɔːʳθˈhæm(p)tən

Northamptonshire
   county, England   nawr-THAM(P)-tuhn-shuhr,   nɔːʳˈθæm(p)tənʃəʳ,
                         nawrth-HAM-tuhn-shuhr, -SHIR   nɔːʳθˈhæmtənʃəʳ, -ˌʃiʳ

Northanger Abbey
   novel, J. Austen   nawr-THANG-uhr AB-ē,   nɔːʳˌθæŋəʳ ˈæbi·, ˌnɔːʳθæŋəʳ
                         NAWR-thang-uhr

North Carolina
   state, US   NAWRTH KAR-uh-LĪ-nuh,   ˌnɔːʳθ ˌkærəˈlainə, kəʳˈlainə,
                         kuhr-LĪ-nuh, kar-LĪ-nuh   kæʳˈlainə

North Dakota
   state, US   NAWRTH duh-KŌT-uh   ˌnɔːʳθ dəˈkoːtə

Northern Sotho
   lang., Africa   NAWR-<u>th</u>uhrn SŌ-thō, SŌT-ō   ˈnɔːʳðəʳn ˈsoːθoː, ˈsoːtoː

Northrop
   J. H., US biochemist (Nobel   NAWR-thruhp   ˈnɔːʳθrəp
   1946); pers. name

North Slope
   division, AK   nawrth SLŌP   nɔːʳθ ˈsloːp

Northumberland
   1. county, England; county, PA   nawr-THUHM-buhr-luhnd   nɔːʳˈθəmbəʳlənd
   2. county, VA   nawr-THUHM-uhr-luhn(d),   nɔːʳˈθəməʳlən(d),
                         nawr-THUHM-buhr-luhnd   nɔːʳˈθəmbəʳlənd

Northumbria
   early English kingdom   nawr-THUHM-brē-uh   nɔːʳˈθəmbriːə

North Yorkshire
   county, England   nawrth YAWRK-shuhr, -SHIR   nɔːʳθ ˈjɔːʳkʃəʳ, -ˌʃiʳ

Norton
   pers. name   NAWRT-n   ˈnɔːʳtn̩

Norval
   pers. name   NAWR-vuhl   ˈnɔːʳvəl

Norwalk
   river, city, CT; city, CA   NAWR-WAWK   ˈnɔːʳˌwɔːk

Norway
   kingdom, Europe   NAWR-WĀ   ˈnɔːʳˌweː

Norwegian
   lang., Norway   nawr-WĒ-juhn   nɔːʳˈwiːdʒən

Norwegian buhund
   dog breed   nawr-WĒ-juhn BOO-HUNT   nɔːʳˌwiːdʒən ˈbuːˌhunt

Norwich
   1. town, CT, NY   NAWR-wich, NAHR-wich   ˈnɔːʳwitʃ, ˈnɑʳwitʃ
   2. town, England   NAWR-ij, NAWR-ich   ˈnɔːridʒ, ˈnɔːritʃ

Nosferatu
   fictional vampire   NAWS-fuh-RAH-TOO, NAHS-   ˌnɔːsfəˈrɑˌtuː, ˌnɑs-

---

Key (col. 2):   a: fad ā: fade ah: father ar: Mary aw: law e: fed ē: feed er: merry i: hid ī: hide ō: coat o͞o: boot
oi: boy   ow: now   u: put   uh: above   uhr: bird   ch: chop   ng: ring   sh: show   th: thick   <u>th</u>: this   zh: measure

Nostradamus
   French astrologer   NAHS-truh-DĀ-muhs,   ˌnɑstrəˈdeːməs,
                                 NAWS-truh-DAHM-uhs   ˌnɔːstrəˈdaməs

Notre Dame
   University, IN; bay, Newfoundland   NŌT-uhr DĂM   ˌnoːtəʳ ˈdeːm, -ˈdɑːm

Notre-Dame
   cathedral, Paris, France   naw-truh-DAHM, ⑤ NŌ-truh-DĂM,   nɔːtrədɑːm, ⑤ ˌnoːtrəˈdeːm,
                                 NŌT-uhr-DĂM, -DAHM   ˌnoːtəʳˈdeːm, -ˈdɑːm

Nottingham
   town, England   NAHT-ing-uhm   ˈnɑtiŋəm

Nottinghamshire
   county, England   NAHT-ing-uhm-shuhr, -SHIR   ˈnɑtiŋəmʃəʳ, -ˌʃiʳ

Nottoway
   river, county, VA   NAHT-uh-WĀ   ˈnɑtə,weː

Notts [Nottinghamshire]
   county, England   NAHTS   ˈnɑts

Notus
   Greek god of the south wind   NŌT-uhs   ˈnoːtəs

Nouakchott
   city, Mauritania   nu-AHK-SHAHT   nuˈɑkˌʃat

Nouméa
   town, New Caledonia   noo-MĀ-uh   nuːˈmeːə

Novak
   Kim, US actress   NŌ-VAK   ˈnoːˌvæk

Nova Scotia
   prov, Canada   NŌ-vuh SKŌ-shuh   ˌnoːvə ˈskoːʃə

Novatian
   antipope   nō-VĀ-shuhn   noːˈveːʃən

Novationism
   early Christian schism   no-VĀ-shuh-NIZ-uhm   noːˈveːʃə,nizəm

Novaya Zemlya
   islands, Russia   NŌ-vuh-yuh ZEM-lē-AH   ˈnoːvəjə ˌzemliːˈɑː

Novello
   1. pers. name   nuh-VEL-ō, nō-   nəˈveloː, noː-
   2. Italian   nō-VEL-lō   noːˈvelloː

November
   month   nō-VEM-buhr, nuh-VEM-buhr   noːˈvembəʳ, nəˈvembəʳ

Nové Zámky [Érsekújvár]
   town, Slovakia   NŌ-vā ZAHM(P)-kē   ˌnoːveː ˈzam(p)kiˑ

Novgorod
   city, Russia   NAHV-guh-RAHD   ˈnavgə,rad

Novi
   village, MI   NŌ-VĪ   ˈnoːˌvɑi

Novi Sad
   city, Serbia   NŌ-vē SAHD   ˌnoːviˑ ˈsaːd

Novocaine
   tdmk for procaine   NŌ-vuh-KĀN   ˈnoːvə,keːn

Novorossisk
   port, Russia   NŌ-vuh-ruh-SĒSK   ˌnoːvərəˈsiːsk

Novosibirsk
   city, Russia   NŌ-vuh-suh-BIRSK, NUH-vuh-   ˌnoːvəsəˈbiʳsk, ˌnəvə-

Novotný
   Antonin, president, Czechoslovakia   NAW-vawt-nē   ˈnɔːvɔːtniˑ

Nowa Huta
   suburb of Kraków, Poland   NŌ-vuh HOO-tuh   ˈnoːvə ,huːtə

Foreign Sounds: ue: *Fr.* **rue**, *Ger.* f**ü**llen uh(r): *Fr.* b**oeu**f, *Ger.* H**ö**hle <u>kh</u>: *Ger.* i**ch**, *Scot.* lo**ch** ğ: *Sp.* ami**g**o v̲: *Sp.* ha**b**lar
hl: *Welsh* L**l**anelli. CAPITALS: primary stress. SMALL CAPS: secondary stress. ⑤: U.S. pron. Ⓛ: British pron.

Nowata

county, OK nō-WAHT-uh nɔːˈwɑtə

Nox

Roman goddess of the night NAHKS ˈnɑks

Noxubee

river, county, MS NAHK-shuh-bē ˈnɑkʃəbiː

Nu [Nun]

Egyptian god or goddess, source of N$\overline{OO}$ ˈnuː
all life

Nuadu

Irish god, former leader of the N$\overline{OO}$-uh-th$\overline{oo}$ ˈnuːəðuː
Tuatha de Danaan

Nuba

mts., Sudan N(Y)$\overline{OO}$-buh ˈn(j)uːbə

Nubia

region in Nile valley N(Y)$\overline{OO}$-bē-uh ˈn(j)uːbiːə

Nubian

lang., desert, Africa N(Y)$\overline{OO}$-bē-uhn ˈn(j)uːbiːən

Nubium, Mare

see Mare Nubium

Nuckolls

county, NE NUHK-uhlz ˈnəkəlz

Nueces

river, county, TX n(y)u-Ā-suhs n(j)uˈeːsəs

Nuer

lang., people, Sudan, Ethiopia N$\overline{OO}$-uhr, NUR ˈnuːəʳ, ˈnuʳ

Nuevo León

state, Mexico nu-Ā-vō lā-ÓN nuˌeːvoː leːˈoːn

Nuffield

college, Oxford Univ. NUHF-ĒLD ˈnəfˌiːld

Nugent

pers. name N(Y)$\overline{OO}$-juhnt ˈn(j)uːdʒənt

Nuit

Egyptian god N(Y)$\overline{OO}$T, N(Y)$\overline{OO}$-uht ˈn(j)uːt, ˈn(j)uːət

Nuits-Saint-Georges

wine nwē-seⁿ-ZHAWRZH, nɥiːsẽˈʒɔːrʒ,
  Ⓢ nuh-WĒ-SĀNT-JAWRJ, NWĒ- Ⓢ nəˌwiːˌseɪntˈdʒɔːʳdʒ,
    ˌnwiː-

Nukualofa

city, Tonga N$\overline{OO}$-kuh-wuh-LAW-fuh, -LŌ-fuh ˌnuːkəwəˈlɔːfə, -ˈloːfə

Nuku Hiva

island, Marquesas N$\overline{OO}$-kuh HĒ-vuh ˌnuːkə ˈhiːvə

Nullarbor Plain

plateau, Australia NUHL-uh-BAWR PLĀN, ˌnələˌbɔːʳ ˈpleːn, ˌnələrˌbɔːr
  NUHL-uhr-BAWR

Numantia

ancient city, Spain n(y)$\overline{oo}$-MAN-ch(ē-)uh n(j)uˈmæntʃ(iː)ə

Numa Pompilius

legendary 2nd king of Rome N(Y)$\overline{OO}$-muh pahm-PIL-ē-uhs ˈn(j)uːmə pɑmˈpiliːəs

Numbers

Old Testament book NUHM-buhrz ˈnəmbəʳz

Numeri

formations of the Roman army N(Y)$\overline{OO}$-muh-RĪ, N(Y)$\overline{OO}$-muh-rē ˈn(j)uːməˌrɑi, ˈn(j)uːməriˑ

Numidia

ancient country, Africa n(y)$\overline{oo}$-MID-ē-uh n(j)uˈmidiːə

Key (col. 2): a: fad ā: fade ah: father ar: Mary aw: law e: fed ē: feed er: merry i: hid ī: hide ō: coat $\overline{oo}$: boot
oi: boy ow: now u: put uh: above uhr: bird ch: chop ng: ring sh: show th: thick th: this zh: measure

Numitor

    grandfather of Romulus and   N(Y)O̅O̅-muht-uhr,   'n(j)uːmətəʳ, 'n(j)uːmə,tɔːʳ
    Remus   N(Y)O̅O̅-muh-TAWR

Nun [Nu]

    Egyptian god or goddess, source of   NUN, NUHN   'nun, 'nən
    all life

Nunc Dimittis

    canticle   NUHNGK duh-MIT-uhs, NUNGK   ,nəŋk də'mitəs, ,nuŋk

Nuñez

    pers. name   NO̅O̅N-yăth, NO̅O̅N-yăs   'nuːnjeːθ, 'nuːnjeːs

Nung

    lang., people, Vietnam, South   NUNG   'nuŋ
    China

Nunn

    Sam, *US politician; pers. name*   NUHN   'nən

Nupe

    lang., people, Nigeria   NO̅O̅-pā   'nuːpeː

Nuremberg

    city, Germany   N(Y)UR-uhm-BUHRG   'n(j)urəm,bəʳg

Nureyev

    Rudolf, *Russian ballet dancer*   nur-YĀ-yif, Ⓢ nur-Ā-(y)uhf,   nur'jeːjif, Ⓢ nur'eː(j)əf,
          nur-Ā-(y)ev, NUR-ē-EF   nur'eː(j)ev, 'nuriː,ef

Nurmi

    Paavo, *Finnish athlete*   NUR-mē   'nuʳmiˑ

Nürnberg [Nuremberg]

    city, Germany   NUERN-BERK   'nyːʳn,beʳk

Nursultan

    pers. name (N. Nazarbayev)   nur-SUL-tahn, nur-sul-TAHN   nuʳ'sultɑn, nuʳsul'tɑn

Nut

    Egyptian sky goddess   NUT, NO̅O̅T, NUHT   'nut, 'nuːt, 'nət

NutraSweet

    tdmk for aspartame, a sweetener   NO̅O̅-truh-SWĒT   'nuːtrə,swiːt

Nuwara-Eliya

    city, Sri Lanka   NO̅O̅-wuh-ruh-Ā-lē-(y)uh   ,nuːwərə'eːliː(j)ə

Nuyen

    France, *US entertainer*   noo-YEN   nu'jen

Nuzi

    archaeological site, Iraq   NO̅O̅-zē   'nuːziˑ

Nyack

    town, NY   NĪ-AK   'nɑi,æk

Nyamwesi

    lang., people, Africa   nyahm-WĀ-zē   njam'weːzi

Nyanga

    lang., Africa   NYAHN-guh   'njangə˙

Nyanja [Chewa]

    lang., people, Africa   NYAHN-juh   'njandʒə

Nyankole [Nkore]

    lang., people, Africa   nyahng-KŌ-lā   njaŋ'koːleː

Nyasa [Malawi]

    lake, Africa   nī-AS-uh, nē-AS-uh   nɑi'æsə, niː'æsə

Nyborg

    town, Denmark   NUE-BAWRǦ   'nyː,bɔːrɣ

Nycteus

    father of Antiope   NIK-tē-uhs   'niktiːəs

Foreign Sounds: ue: *Fr.* **rue,** *Ger.* füllen   uh(r): *Fr.* b**oeu**f, *Ger.* H**öh**le   kh: *Ger.* i**ch,** *Scot.* lo**ch**   ǧ: *Sp.* ami**g**o   v: *Sp.* ha**b**lar
hl: *Welsh* **Ll**anelli.   CAPITALS: primary stress.   SMALL CAPS: secondary stress.   Ⓢ: U.S. pron.   Ⓒ: British pron.

Nyctimus
  son of Lycaon   NIK-tuh-muhs   'niktəməs

Nyerere
  Julius, *president, Tanzania*   nyuh-RER-ā   njə'rereː

Nyeri
  town, Kenya   nē-ER-ē   niː'eriˑ

Nygaarsdvold
  Johan, *prime minister, Norway*   NĪ-gawrs-VAWL   'naigɔːʳsˌvɔːl

Nyíreghyháza
  city, Hungary   NĒ-REJ-HAHZ-aw   'niːˌredʒˌhazɔː

Nyköping
  city, Sweden   NUE-KUH(R)-ping   'nyːˌkœːpiŋ

Nymphs
  Greek deities   NIM(P)FS   'nim(p)fs

NYNEX
  US telecommunications co.   NĪ-NEKS   'naiˌneks

Nyngan
  town, Australia   NING-guhn   'niŋgən

Nyoro
  lang., people, Africa   NYÔR-ō   'njoːroː

Nysa
  nursemaid of Dionysus; pers. name   NĒ-suh, NĪ-suh   'niːsə, 'naisə

Nysus
  adoptive father of Dionysus   NĪ-suhs   'naisəs

Nyx
  Greek goddess of night   NIKS   'niks

O

Oahe
  dam, lake, SD   ō-AH-hē   oː'ahiˑ

Oahu
  island, HI   uh-WAH-hoo, ō-AH-hoo   ə'wahuː, oː'ahuː

Oakley
  Annie, *US markswoman;* Robert, *US ambassador*   Ō-klē   'oːkliˑ

Oates
  John, *US musician;* Joyce Carol, *US writer;* Titus, *British traitor*   ŌTS   'oːts

Oaxaca
  state, Mexico   wah-<u>KH</u>AH-kah, ⑤ wuh-HAHK-uh   wa'xaka, ⑤ wə'hakə

Ob
  1. river, Russia   AHB, AWB   'ab, 'ɔːb
  2. Korean beer   ŌB, AHB   'oːb, 'ab

Key (col. 2):   a: fad   ā: fade   ah: father   ar: Mary   aw: law   e: fed   ē: feed   er: merry   i: hid   ī: hide   ō: coat   oo: boot   oi: boy   ow: now   u: put   uh: above   uhr: bird   ch: chop   ng: ring   sh: show   th: thick   <u>th</u>: this   zh: measure

Obadiah
   Old Testament book; pers. name   Ō-buh-DĪ-uh   ,oːbə'daiə

Obata
   Gyo, *US architect*   ō-BAHT-uh   oː'baʈə

Obed
   pers. name   Ō-buhd   'oːbəd

Obeid, El
   town, Sudan   EL ō-BĀD   ,el oː'beːd

Oberammergau
   resort, Passion play, Germany   ō-buh-RAHM-uhr-GOW,   ,oːbə'ramə^r,gau,
         Ⓢ Ō-buh-RAM-uhr-GOW   Ⓢ ,oːbə'ræmə^r,gau

Oberbayern
   prov, Germany   Ō-buhr-BĪ-uhrn   'oːbə^r,baiə^{r}n

Oberdorfer
   German beer   Ō-buhr-DAWR-fuhr   'oːbə^r,dɔː^{r}fə^r

Oberfranken
   prov, Germany   Ō-buhr-FRAHNG-kuhn   'oːbə^r,fraŋkən

Oberland
   mtn. region, Switzerland   Ō-buhr-LAHNT, Ō-buhr-LAND   'oːbə^r,lant, 'oːbə^r,lænd

Oberlin
   city, college, OH   Ō-buhr-luhn   'oːbə^{r}lən

Oberon
   Merle, *US entertainer; fairy king;*   Ō-buh-RAHN, -ruhn   'oːbə,ran, -rən
     satellite of Uranus

Oberösterreich
   state, Austria   Ō-buh-RUH(R)-stuhr-RĪKH   ,oːbə'rœːstə^r,raiç

Oberpfalz
   prov, Germany   Ō-buhr-FAHLTS   'oːbə^r,falts

Obey
   David, *US politician*   Ō-bē   'oːbiˑ

Obie
   off-Broadway award   Ō-bē   'oːbiˑ

Obion
   river, county, TN   ō-BĪ-uhn   oː'baiən

Ob-Irtysh
   river, Russia   AWB UHR-TISH, ir-TISH   'ɔːb ,ər'tiʃ, ir'tiʃ

Oblate
   College, *Washington, DC*   AHB-LĀT   'ab,leːt

Oblomov
   novel by Ivan Goncharov   uh-BLAW-mawf, AHB-luh-MAWF   ə'blɔːmɔːf, 'ablə,mɔːf

Oboe
   musical instrument   Ō-bō   'oːboː

O-Bon
   Japanese festival   ō-bōn   oːboːn

Obote
   Milton, *president, Uganda*   aw-BAW-TĀ   ɔː'bɔː,teː

Obregón
   Alvaro, *president, Mexico*   ō-vrā-GŌN   oːβreː'ɣoːn

O'Brien
   pers. name   ō-BRĪ-uhn   oː'braiən

Ocala
   city, FL   ō-KAL-uh   oː'kælə

Ocarina
   musical instrument   AHK-uh-RĒ-nuh   ,akə'riːnə

O'Casey
  Sean, *Irish playwright*   ō-KĀ-sē   oːˈkeːsiˑ

Occam, Ockham
  William of, *English philosopher*   AHK-uhm   ˈakəm

Occam's razor
  principle of logic   AHK-uhmz RĀ-zuhr   ˌakəmz ˈreːzəʳ

Occident
  western hemisphere   AHK-suhd-uhnt, AHK-suh-DENT   ˈaksədənt, ˈaksəˌdent

Occidental
  pert. to the western hemisphere   AHK-si-DENT-l   ˌaksiˈdentl̩

Occitan [Provençal]
  lang., France   awk-sē-TAHⁿ   oːksiːtã

Oceana
  county, MI   Ō-shē-AN-uh   ˌoːʃiːˈænə

Oceania
  Pacific islands   Ō-shē-AN-ē-uh, O-shē-Ā-nē-uh   ˌoːʃiːˈæniːə, ˌoʃiːˈeːniːə

Oceanica [Oceania]
  Pacific islands   Ō-shē-AN-i-kuh, Ō-shē-Ā-ni-kuh   ˌoːʃiːˈænikə, ˌoːʃiːˈeːnikə

Oceanids
  mythological daughters of Oceanus and Tethys   ō-SĒ-uh-nidz, ō-SHĒ-uh-nidz   oːˈsiːənidz, oːˈʃiːənidz

Oceanus
  Titan who rules the earth-encircling river   ō-SĒ-uh-nuhs   oːˈsiːənəs

Ochiltree
  county, TX   AHK-uhl-TRĒ   ˈakəlˌtriː

Ochoa
  Severo, *Spanish-born US biochemist (Nobel 1959)*   ō-CHŌ-uh   oːˈtʃoːə

Ochs
  Phil, *US folksinger*   ŌKS   ˈoːks

Ockeghem
  Jean d', *Flemish composer*   AHK-uh-guhm   ˈakəgəm

Ockham
  see Occam

Ocmulgee
  1. National Monument, *river, GA*   ōk-MUHL-gē   oːkˈməlgiˑ
  2. see Okmulgee

Ocnus
  rope-maker in Hades   AHK-nuhs   ˈaknəs

Oconee
  county, GA, SC   ō-KŌ-nē   oːˈkoːniˑ

O'Conor
  pers. name   ō-KAHN-uhr   oːˈkanəʳ

Oconto
  county, WI   ō-KAHN-tō   oːˈkantoː

Ocracoke
  island, inlet, NC   Ō-kruh-KŌK, Ō-kuhr-KŌK   ˈoːkrəˌkoːk, ˈoːkəʳˌkoːk

Octans
  constellation   AHK-TANZ   ˈakˌtænz

Octavia
  Roman matron (Augustus' sister), pers. name   ahk-TĀ-vē-uh   akˈteːviːə

Key (col. 2):   a: fad   ā: fade   ah: father   ar: Mary   aw: law   e: fed   ē: feed   er: merry   i: hid   ī: hide   ō: coat   ōō: boot
oi: boy   ow: now   u: put   uh: above   uhr: bird   ch: chop   ng: ring   sh: show   th: thick   <u>th</u>: this   zh: measure

Octavian
  1. Roman emperor, pers. name   ahk-TĀ-vē-uhn   ɑk'teːviːən
  2. Romanian   AWK-tahv-YAHN   ˌɔːktɑv'jɑn
Octavio
  pers. name, German   awk-TAHV-yō, awk-TAHV-ē-ō   ɔːk'tɑvjoː, ɔːk'tɑviːoː
Octavius
  Roman politician, emperor, pers. name   ahk-TĀ-vē-uhs   ɑk'teːviːəs
October
  month   ahk-TŌ-buhr   ɑk'toːbəʳ
Ocyrrhoe
  daughter of Chiron   ō-SIR-uh-wē   oː'sirəwiˑ
Odd
  pers. name, Norwegian   AWD   'ɔːd
Oddone
  pers. name, Italian   ōd-DŌ-nā   oːd'doːneː
Odell, Odelle
  pers. name   ō-DEL   oː'del
Odelsting
  Norwegian parliament   ŌD-l-STING   'oːdl̩ˌstiŋ
Odense
  town, Denmark   U-uhn-zuh *(local pron.)*, ŌD-n-suh   'uənzə *(local pron.)*, 'oːdn̩sə
Odeon
  tdmk for cognac, perfume; recording label   ŌD-ē-uhn   'oːdiːən
Oder
  river, Baltic   ŌD-uhr   'oːdəʳ
Oder-Neisse Line
  boundary between Poland and Germany   ŌD-uhr-NĪ-suh LĪN   ˌoːdəʳ'naisə ˌlain
Odessa
  city, TX; city, Ukraine   ō-DES-uh   oː'desə
Odet
  pers. name, French   aw-DE   ɔːde
Odets
  Clifford, writer   ō-DETS   oː'dets
Odetta
  US folk singer; pers. name   ō-DET-uh   oː'deţə
Odette
  pers. name, French   aw-DET   ɔːdet
Odeum
  hall or theater   ŌD-ē-uhm   'oːdiːəm
Odilon
  pers. name, French   aw-dē-LAWⁿ   ɔːdiːlõ
Odin
  supreme Scandinavian god   ŌD-n, Ō-thuhn   'oːdn̩, 'oːðən
Oðinn [Odin]
  supreme Scandinavian god   Ō-thuhn   'oːðən
Odo
  pers. name   ŌD-ō   'oːdoː
Odoacer
  barbarian king of Italy   ō-duh-WĀ-suhr   ˌoːdə'weːsəʳ
Odysseus [Ulysses]
  mythical Greek hero   ō-DIS-ē-uhs, ō-DIS-yuhs, ō-DISH-uhs, ō-DISH-ōōs   oː'disiːəs, oː'disjəs, oː'diʃəs, oː'diʃuːs

---

Foreign Sounds: ue: *Fr.* **r**ue, *Ger.* f**ü**llen uh(r): *Fr.* b**oeu**f, *Ger.* H**öh**le <u>kh</u>: *Ger.* i**ch**, *Scot.* lo**ch** ḡ: *Sp.* ami**g**o v̱: *Sp.* ha**b**lar
hl: *Welsh* **Ll**anelli. CAPITALS: primary stress. SMALL CAPS: secondary stress. Ⓢ: U.S. pron. Ⓑ: British pron.

Odyssey		
epic poem, Homer	AHD-uh-sē	'ɑdəsiˑ
Oedipal		
pert. to Oedipus	ED-uh-puhl, Ē D-uh-puhl	'edəpəl, 'iːdəpəl
Oedipus		
legendary king of Thebes	ED-uh-puhs, ĒD-uh-puhs	'edəpəs, 'iːdəpəs
Oekist		
founder of a Greek colony	Ē-kuhst	'iːkəst
Oeneus		
king of Calydon	Ē-nē-uhs, ĒN-YOOS	'iːniːəs, 'iːnˌjuːs
Oenomaus		
father of Hippodamia	Ē-nuh-MĀ-uhs	ˌiːnə'meːəs
Oenone		
wife of Paris, abandoned for Helen	ē-NŌ-nē	iː'noːniˑ
Oenopion		
son of Ariadne	ē-NŌ-pē-uhn	iː'noːpiːən
Oeonus		
cousin and companion of Heracles	ē-Ō-nuhs	iː'oːnəs
O'Faoláin		
Seán, *Irish writer*	ō-FĀ-luhn, ō-FAL-uhn	oː'feːlən, oː'fælən
Offenbach		
1. city, Germany	AW-fuhn-BAHKH, Ⓢ AW-fuhn-BAHK	'ɔːfənˌbɑx, Ⓢ 'ɔːfənˌbɑk
2. Jacques, *French composer*	aw-fen-BAHK, AW-fuhn-BAHK, -BAHKH	ɔːfenbɑːk, 'ɔːfənˌbɑk, -ˌbɑx
O'Flaherty		
Liam, *Irish novelist*	ō-FLAH-huhrt-ē, Ⓢ ō-FLĀ-uhrt-ē, ō-FLART-ē	oː'flɑːhəʳt̬iˑ, Ⓢ oː'fleːəʳt̬iˑ, oː'flæʳt̬iˑ
Ogasawara-shotō		
islands, Pacific Ocean	ō-GAHS-uh-WAHR-uh-SHŌ-tō	oːˌgɑsə'wɑrə'ʃoːtoː
Ogbomosho		
city, Nigeria	AHG-buh-MŌ-shō	ˌɑgbə'moːʃoː
Ogden		
city, UT; pers. name	AHG-duhn	'ɑgdən
Ogemaw		
county, MI	Ō-guh-MAW	'oːgəˌmɔː
Ogilvy		
pers. name	Ō-guhl-vē	'oːgəlviˑ
Oglala		
N. American people	ahg-LAHL-uh, ō-GLAHL-uh	ɑg'lɑlə, oː'glɑlə
Oglala Lakota		
N. American people	ahg-LAHL-uh luh-KŌT-uh, ō-GLAHL-uh	ɑg'lɑlə lə'koːt̬ə, oː'glɑlə
Oglala Sioux		
N. American people	ahg-LAHL-uh SOO, ō-GLAHL-uh	ɑg'lɑlə 'suː, oː'glɑlə
Oglethorpe		
James, *English colonizer of GA; county, city, GA*	Ō-guhl-THAWRP	'oːgəlˌθɔːʳp
O'Hara		
pers. name	ō-HAR-uh, ō-HER-uh	oː'hærə, oː'herə
O'Hare		
pers. name	ō-HAR, ō-HER	oː'hæʳ, oː'heʳ
Ohio		
river, state, US; county, IN, KY, WV	ō-HĪ-ō, uh-HĪ-uh	oː'hɑioː, ə'hɑiə

Key (col. 2): a: **fad** ā: **fade** ah: f**a**ther ar: M**ar**y aw: l**aw** e: f**e**d ē: f**ee**d er: m**err**y i: h**i**d ī: h**i**de ō: c**oa**t o͞o: b**oo**t oi: **boy** ow: n**ow** u: p**u**t uh: **a**bove uhr: b**ir**d ch: **ch**op ng: ri**ng** sh: **sh**ow th: **th**ick th: **th**is zh: mea**s**ure

Ohira
  Masayoshi, *prime minister, Japan*   ō-hē-rah   oːhiːrɑ

Ohlin
  Bertil, *Swedish economist,*   Ō-lin   'oːlin
    politician (Nobel 1977)

Ohm
  Georg S., *German physicist;*   ŌM   'oːm
    electrical unit

Ohrid
  lake, Albania, Macedonia   Ō<u>KH</u>-RĒD, Ō-KRĒD   'oːx‚riːd, 'oː‚kriːd

Oireachtas
  Irish parliament   AWR-yuh<u>kh</u>-tuhs   'ɔːrjəxtəs

Oise
  river, dept, France   WAHZ   wɑːz

Ojai
  city, CA   Ō-HĪ   'oː‚hai

Ojibwa [Chippewa]
  N. American people   ō-JIB-wā, -wuh   oː'dʒibweː, -wə

Ojos del Salado
  mtn., Argentina   Ō-hōz <u>th</u>el sah-LAH-<u>th</u>ō, Ⓢ Ō-hōz   'oːhoːz ðel sɑ'lɑðoː,
               DEL suh-LAHD-ō   Ⓢ 'oːhoːz ‚del sə'lɑdoː

Okaloosa
  county, FL   ō-kuh-LOO-suh   ‚oːkə'luːsə

Okaloosa-Walton
  junior college, FL   ō-kuh-LOO-suh-WAWLT-n, -WAHLT-n   ‚oːkə'luːsə'wɔːltn̩, -'wɑltn̩

Okanagan
  lake, college, Canada; river,   ō-kuh-NAHG-uhn   ‚oːkə'nɑgən
    Canada & US

Okanogan
  county, WA; US spelling of   ō-kuh-NAHG-uhn   ‚oːkə'nɑgən
    Okanagan

Okavango
  river, Africa   ō-kuh-VANG-gō   ‚oːkə'væŋgoː

Okayama
  city, Japan   ō-kah-yahm-ah   oːkɑjɑmɑ

Okeechobee
  lake, county, FL   ō-kuh-CHŌ-bē   ‚oːkə'tʃoːbiˑ

O'Keefe
  Miles, *actor*   ō-KĒF   oː'kiːf

O'Keeffe
  Georgia, *US artist*   ō-KĒF   oː'kiːf

Okefenokee
  swamp land, wildlife refuge, GA   ō-kē-fuh-NŌ-kē   ‚oːkiˑfə'noːkiˑ

Okfuskee
  county, OK   ōk-FUHS-kē   oːk'fəskiˑ

Okhotsk
  sea, Russia   UH-<u>KH</u>AWTSK, ō-<u>KH</u>AHTSK,   ‚ə'xɔːtsk, oː'xɑtsk,
           Ⓢ ō-KAHTSK   Ⓢ oː'kɑtsk

Oki
  Japanese electronics co.   Ō-kē   'oːkiˑ

Okie
  native or inhabitant of Oklahoma   Ō-kē   'oːkiˑ

Okinawa
  island, Pacific   Ō-kuh-NAH-wuh   ‚oːkə'nɑwə

Foreign Sounds: ue: *Fr.* **rue**, *Ger.* f**ü**llen   uh(r): *Fr.* b**oeu**f, *Ger.* H**öh**le   <u>kh</u>: *Ger.* i**ch**, *Scot.* lo**ch**   g̱: *Sp.* ami**g**o   v̱: *Sp.* ha**b**lar
hl: *Welsh* **Ll**anelli.   CAPITALS: primary stress.   SMALL CAPS: secondary stress.   Ⓢ: U.S. pron.   Ⓛ: British pron.

Okinawan
   pert. to Okinawa   ō-kuh-NAH-wuhn   ˌoːkəˈnawən

Oklahoma
   state, US   ō-kluh-HŌ-muh   ˌoːkləˈhoːmə

Okmulgee
   1. city, county, OK   ōk-MUHL-gē   oːkˈməlgiˑ
   2. see Ocmulgee

Okocim
   Polish beer   aw-KAW-chēm   ɔːˈkɔːtʃiːm

Oktibbeha
   county, MS   ahk-TIB-uh-HAW   akˈtibəˌhɔː

Oktoberfest
   German festival   ahk-TŌ-buhr-FEST   akˈtoːbəʳˌfest

Olaf
   1. pers. name   Ō-luhf, Ō-luhv   ˈoːləf, ˈoːləv
   2. Danish   Ō-LAHF   ˈoːˌlaːf
   3. Norwegian   Ō-LAHF   ˈoːˌlaf
   4. Swedish   OO-lahf, OO-lahv   ˈuːlɑːf, ˈuːlɑːv

Olajuwon
   Hakeem, *Nigerian basketball*   ō-LĪ-juh-wahn   oːˈlaidʒəwan
   player

Olathe
   city, KS   ō-LĀ-thuh   oːˈleːθə

Olaus
   1. pers. name, Danish   ō-LOWS   oːˈlaus
   2. German   ō-LAH-us, Ō-LOWS   oːˈla-us, ˈoːˌlaus
   3. Latin   uh-LĀ-uhs, ō-LĀ-uhs   əˈleːəs, oːˈleːəs
   4. Swedish   oo-LAH-uhs   uːˈlaəs

Olav
   pers. name, Norwegian   Ō-LAHV, Ō-LAHF   ˈoːˌlav, ˈoːˌlaf

Oldham
   town, England   ŌL-duhm   ˈoːldəm

Oldsmobile
   US automobile co.   ŌL(D)Z-mō-BĒL, ŌL(D)Z-muh-BĒL   ˈoːl(d)zmoːˌbiːl, ˈoːl(d)zməˌbiːl

Oldsquaw
   duck   ŌL(D)-SKWAW   ˈoːl(d)ˌskwɔː

Olduvai
   Gorge, *Tanzania*   ŌL-duh-WĀ, ŌL-duh-VĀ   ˈoːldəˌweː, ˈoːldəˌveː

Ole
   pers. name, Danish, Norwegian   Ō-luh   ˈoːlə

Oleander
   plant   Ō-lē-AN-duhr, ō-lē-AN-duhr   ˈoːliːˌændəʳ, ˌoːliːˈændəʳ

Oleg
   pers. name, Russian   AW-leg   ˈɔːleg

Oléron, Ile d'
   island, France   ēl daw-lā-RAWⁿ   iːl dɔːleːrɔ̃

Olga
   1. pers. name   AWL-guh, AHL-guh, ŌL-guh   ˈɔːlgə, ˈalgə, ˈoːlgə
   2. Russian   AWL-guh   ˈɔːlg̯ə

Oligocene
   geologic epoch   AHL-i-gō-SĒN, Ō-li-gō-, uh-LIG-uh-   ˈaligoːˌsiːn, ˈoːligoː-, əˈligə-

Olimbia [Olympia]
   village, Greece   ō-LIM-bē-uh   oːˈlimbiːə

Key (col. 2):   a: fad   ā: fade   ah: father   ar: Mary   aw: law   e: fed   ē: feed   er: merry   i: hid   ī: hide   ō: coat   ōō: boot
oi: boy   ow: now   u: put   uh: above   uhr: bird   ch: chop   ng: ring   sh: show   th: thick   th̲: this   zh: measure

Olin
US defense products co. | Ō-luhn | 'oːlən

Oliphant
Pat, *US cartoonist* | AHL-uh-fuhnt | 'aləfənt

Olivaceous
flycatcher | AHL-uh-VĀ-shuhs | ˌalə'veːʃəs

Olive
pers. name | AHL-iv, AHL-uhv | 'aliv, 'aləv

Oliver
pers. name | AHL-uh-vuhr | 'aləvəʳ

Olivetti
Italian manufacturing co. | AHL-uh-VET-ē | ˌalə'veţiˑ

Olivia
pers. name | uh-LIV-ē-uh, ō- | ə'liviːə, oː-

Olivier
1. Sir Laurence, *British actor;* | ō-LIV-ē-Ā, uh-LIV-ē-Ā | oː'liviːˌeː, ə'liviːˌeː
  pers. name
2. Dutch | Ō-li-VIR | 'oːliˌvir
3. French | aw-lēv-YĀ | ɔːliːvjeː

Ollie
pers. name | AHL-ē | 'aliˑ

Olmec
N. American people | AHL-MEK, ŌL-MEK, AWL-MEK | 'alˌmek, 'oːlˌmek, 'ɔːlˌmek

Olmos
Edward James, *US actor* | ŌL-muhs | 'oːlməs

Olof
pers. name, Swedish | O̅O̅-lawv, O̅O̅-lawf, $ Ō-luhf, Ō-LAHF | 'uːlɔːv, 'uːlɔːf, $ 'oːləf, 'oːˌlaf

Oloroso
type of sherry | ō-luh-RŌ-sō | oːlə'roːsoː

Olsen
Merlin, *US sports analyst, football* | ŌL-suhn | 'oːlsən
  player

Olus
giant in Etruscan legend | Ō-luhs | 'oːləs

Olympe
pers. name, French | aw-LEⁿP | ɔːlẽp

Olympia
city, WA; village, ancient city, | uh-LIM-pē-uh, ō- | ə'limpiːə, oː-
  Greece; pers. name

Olympiad
four-year period between Olympic | ō-LIM-pē-uhd, ō-LIM-pē-AD | oː'limpiːəd, oː'limpiːˌæd
  games

Olympian
pert. to Mount Olympus | ō-LIM-pē-uhn | oː'limpiːən

Olympias
Macedonian queen | uh-LIM-pē-uhs, ō- | ə'limpiːəs, oː-

Olympic
pert. to Olympic Games *or to* | ō-LIM-pik | oː'limpik
  Olympia

Olympus
mtn., Greece, home of Greek gods | uh-LIM-puhs, ō- | ə'limpəs, oː-

Olympus Mons
mtn., Mars, highest in solar | uh-LIM-puhs MAHNZ, ō-LIM-puhs, | ə'limpəs 'manz, oː'limpəs,
  system | MŌNZ | 'moːnz

Foreign Sounds: ue: *Fr.* **rue**, *Ger.* f**ü**llen uh(r): *Fr.* b**oeu**f, *Ger.* H**ö**hle kh: *Ger.* i**ch**, *Scot.* lo**ch** ḡ: *Sp.* ami**g**o v: *Sp.* ha**b**lar
hl: *Welsh* **Ll**anelli. CAPITALS: primary stress. SMALL CAPS: secondary stress. $: U.S. pron. Ⓛ: British pron.

Olynthus
  Macedonian town   ō-LIN-thuhs   oː'linθəs

Om
  Hindu mantra   ŌM   'oːm

Omagua
  S. American people   ō-MAH(G)-wuh, ō-MAHĜ-wah   oː'ma(g)wə, oː'maɣwa

Omaha
  city, NE; beach, France; N.   Ō-muh-HAW, Ō-muh-HAH   'oːmə,hɔː, 'oːmə,ha
    American people

Oman
  sultanate, Asia; Gulf of, *arm of*   ō-MAHN, ō-MAN   oː'man, oː'mæn
    Arabian Sea

Omani
  pert. to Oman   ō-MAHN-ē, ō-MAN-ē   oː'maniˑ, oː'mæniˑ

Omar
  1. pers. name   Ō-MAHR   'oː,maʳ
  2. French   aw-MAHR   ɔːmaːr

Omar Khayyám
  Persian writer, astronomer   Ō-MAHR KĪ-(Y)AHM, KĪ-(Y)AM   ,oː,maʳ ,kai'(j)am, ,kai'(j)æm

Omdurman
  city, Sudan   AHM-duhr-MAN   ,amdəʳ'mæn

Omega
  last letter of the Greek alphabet   ō-MEG-uh, ō-MĒ-guh, ō-MĀ-guh   oː'megə, oː'miːgə, oː'meːgə

Omer
  49 days from Passover to   Ō-muhr, Ō-MER, ō-MER   'oːməʳ, 'oː,meʳ, oː'meʳ
    Shabuoth

Omisoka
  Grand Last Day (Dec. 31), Japan   ō-mis-ō-kah   oːmisoːka

Omizutori
  Japanese ritual   ō-mē-zoo͞-tōr-ē   oːmiːzuːtoːriˑ

O-Mizutori Matsuri
  Japanese festival   ō-mē-zoo͞-tōr-ē maht-sur-ē   oːmiːzuːtoːriˑ mɑtsuriˑ

Omnigraphics
  US publishing co.   AHM-ni-GRAF-iks   ,amni'græfiks

Omoo
  novel, H. Melville   Ō-MOO͞   'oː,muː

Omphale
  wife of Heracles   AHM-fuh-lē   'amfəliˑ

OMRON
  Japanese co.   ŌM-RAHN   'oːm,rɑn

Omsk
  city, Russia   AWM(P)SK, AHM(P)SK   'ɔːm(p)sk, 'am(p)sk

Ona
  S. American people   Ō-nuh   'oːnə

Onam
  Hindu festival   Ō-nuhm   'oːnəm

Onan
  Biblical character, son of Judah   Ō-NAN, Ō-nuhn   'oː,næn, 'oːnən

Onassis
  Jacqueline Bouvier Kennedy, *US*   ō-NAS-uhs   oː'næsəs
    editor; Greek/US shipping
    family

Oncoba
  plant   AHNG-kuh-buh, AHN-kuh-buh   'aŋkəbə, 'ankəbə

Key (col. 2):   a: fad   ā: fade   ah: father   ar: Mary   aw: law   e: fed   ē: feed   er: merry   i: hid   ī: hide   ō: coat   oo͞: boot
oi: boy   ow: now   u: put   uh: above   uhr: bird   ch: chop   ng: ring   sh: show   th: thick   <u>th</u>: this   zh: measure

Ondine
  play, Giraudoux   awⁿ-DĒN   ɔdiːn

Onega
  lake, Europe   ōn-YEG-uh   oːnˈjegə

Oneida
  US pl. name; N. American people   ō-NĪD-uh   oːˈnaidə

O'Neill
  Eugene, *US playwright (Nobel   ō-NĒL   oːˈniːl
  1936)*

Oneiros
  *dream demon sent by Zeus to   ō-NĪ-ruhs   oːˈnairəs
  Agamemnon*

Oneonta
  city, AL, NY   Ō-nē-AHNT-uh   ˌoːniːˈantə

Onezhskoye, Ozero [Onega]
  lake, Europe   UHZ-YER-ō UHN-YESH-kuh-yuh   ˌəzˈjeroː ˌənˈjeʃkəjə

Onions
  Charles T., *English lexicographer UHN-yuhnz   ˈənjənz
  and philologist*

Onnes
  see Kamerlingh Onnes

Onondaga
  *lake, county, NY; N. American   AHN-uh(n)-DAHG-uh, -DÃ-guh   ˌanə(n)ˈdagə, -ˈdeːgə
  people*

Onsager
  Lars, *US chemist (Nobel 1968)*   AWN-SAHG-uhr, AHN-   ˈɔːnˌsagəʳ, ˈan-

Ons Hémécht
  national anthem, Luxembourg   AWNS HÃ-māk͟ht   ˈɔːns ˈheːmeːxt

Onslow
  county, NC   AHNZ-lō   ˈanzloː

Ontario
  province, Canada; county, NY   ahn-TER-ē-ō, ahn-TAR-ē-ō   anˈteriːoː, anˈtæriːoː

Ontonagon
  county, MI   AHN-tuh-NAW-guhn,   ˌantəˈnɔːgən, ˌantəˈnagən
                                      AHN-tuh-NAHG-uhn

Oodnadatta
  township, Australia   ŌŌD-nuh-DAT-uh   ˌuˑdnəˈdætə

Oona, Oonagh
  pers. name   ŌŌ-nuh   ˈuːnə

Oort Cloud
  'cloud' of comets   AWRT KLOWD, ŌRT   ˈɔːʳt ˌklaud, ˈoːʳt

Oostende [Ostend]
  prov & town, Belgium   ō-STEN-duh   oːˈstendə

Opatija
  town, Croatia   ō-PAHT-ē-(y)uh   oːˈpaṭiː(j)ə

OPEC
  *Organization of Petroleum   Ō-PEK   ˈoːˌpek
  Exporting Countries*

Opel
  tdmk for a German car   Ō-puhl   ˈoːpəl

Opéra
  French for opera   aw-pā-RAH   ɔːpeːraː

Ophelia
  character in Hamlet, *Shakespeare* ō-FĒL-yuh   oːˈfiːljə

Foreign Sounds: ue: *Fr.* **r**ue, *Ger.* f**ü**llen   uh(r): *Fr.* b**oeu**f, *Ger.* H**öh**le   k͟h: *Ger.* i**ch**, *Scot.* lo**ch**   ğ: *Sp.* ami**g**o   v̱: *Sp.* ha**b**lar
hl: *Welsh* **Ll**anelli.   CAPITALS: primary stress.   SMALL CAPS: secondary stress.   Ⓢ: U.S. pron.   Ⓔ: British pron.

Ophir
　Biblical land rich in gold　　　　Ō-fuhr　　　　　　　　'oːfər

Ophism
　Gnostic serpent worship　　　　AHF-ɪz-uhm, Ō-FɪZ-uhm　　　'af‚izəm, 'oː‚fizəm

Ophiuchids
　meteor shower　　　　Ō-fē-(Y)OO-kidz, AHF-ē-　　　‚oːfiː'(j)uːkidz, ‚afiː-

Ophiuchus
　constellation　　　　Ō-fē-(Y)OO-kuhs, AHF-ē-　　　‚oːfiː'(j)uːkəs, ‚afiː-

Opimius
　Lucius, Roman politician　　　　ō-PIM-ē-uhs　　　　oː'pimiːəs

Oporto [Porto]
　port city, Portugal　　　　ō-PŌRT-ō, ō-PAWRT-ō　　　oː'poːʳʈoː, oː'pɔːʳʈoː

Oppenheimer
　J. Robert, US physicist　　　　AHP-uhn-HĪ-muhr　　　'apən‚haiməʳ

Oprah
　pers. name (O. Winfrey)　　　　Ō-pruh　　　　'oːprə

Ops
　Roman goddess of plenty　　　　AHPS　　　　'aps

Optacon
　tdmk for reading machines for the　AHP-tuh-KAHN, AHP-tuh-kuhn　'aptə‚kan, 'aptəkən
　　blind

Optimates
　Roman senatorial faction　　　　AHP-tuh-MĀT-ēz　　　‚aptə'meːʈiːz

Optimator
　German beer　　　　AWP-ti-MAH-tawr　　　‚ɔpti'matɔʳ

Oradea
　city, Romania　　　　aw-RAHD-yah　　　ɔː'radja

Oran
　seaport, Algeria　　　　ō-RAHN　　　oː'ran

Orange
　1. *city, France*　　　　aw-RAHⁿZH　　　ɔːrãʒ
　2. *pl. name, US*　　　　AHR-inj, AHR-uhnj, AHRNJ,　'arindʒ, 'arəndʒ, 'aʳndʒ,
　　　　　　　　　　　　AWR-inj, AWR-uhnj, AWRNJ　　'ɔːrindʒ, 'ɔːrəndʒ, 'ɔːʳndʒ

Orangutan
　type of ape　　　　uh-RANG-uh-TANG,　　　ə'ræŋə‚tæŋ, ə'ræŋə‚tæn
　　　　　　　　　uh-RANG-uh-TAN

Oranjeboom
　Dutch beer　　　　aw-RAHN-yuh-BŌM　　　ɔː'ranjə‚boːm

Oraoni [Kurukh]
　lang., people, India　　　　ō-RAH-ō-nē　　　oː'ra‚oːniˑ

Oraon [Kurukh]
　lang., people, India　　　　ō-RAH-ŌN　　　oː'ra‚oːn

Orazio
　pers. name, Italian　　　　ō-RAHT-syō　　　oː'ratsjoː

Orbison
　Roy, rock musician　　　　AWR-buh-suhn　　　'ɔːʳbəsən

Orca
　killer whale　　　　AWR-kuh　　　'ɔːʳkə

Orcadian
　inhabitant of the Orkney Islands　awr-KĀD-ē-uhn　　　ɔːʳ'keːdiːən

Orcus [Dis]
　Roman god of the Underworld　　AWR-kuhs　　　'ɔːʳkəs

Ordoñez
　Antonio, Spanish bullfighter;　　awr-THAWN-yāth　　　ɔːr'ðɔːnjeːθ
　　Bartolomé, Spanish sculptor

Key (col. 2): a: fad　ā: fade　ah: father　ar: Mary　aw: law　e: fed　ē: feed　er: merry　i: hid　ī: hide　ō: coat　OO: boot
oi: boy　ow: now　u: put　uh: above　uhr: bird　ch: chop　ng: ring　sh: show　th: thick　th: this　zh: measure

Ordovician
  geologic period   awrd-uh-VISH-uhn   ɔːʳdə'viʃən

Ordzhonikidze
  city, Russia   AWR-JAHN-uh-KID-zuh   ˌɔːʳˌdʒɑnə'kidzə

Oregon
  state, US   AWR-uh-guhn, AHR-uh-guhn; *by*   'ɔːrəgən, 'ɑrəgən; *by*
      outsiders often AWR-uh-GAHN,   *outsiders often* 'ɔːrəˌgɑn,
      AHR-   'ɑr-

Oregonian
  pert. to Oregon   AWR-i-GŌ-nē-uhn, AHR-i-GŌ-nē-uhn,   ˌɔːri'goːniːən, ˌɑri'goːniːən,
      -GŌN-yuhn   -'goːnjən

Orel
  Russian port   awr-YAWL, aw-REL   ɔːʳ'jɔːl, ɔː'rel

Orem
  town, UT   ŌR-uhm, AWR-uhm   'oːrəm, 'ɔːrəm

Oren
  pers. name   Ō-ruhn, AWR-uhn   'oːrən, 'ɔːrən

Orense
  prov, Spain   ō-REN(T)-sā   oː'ren(t)seː

Oreo
  tdmk for a sandwich cookie   ŌR-ē-ō, AWR-ē-ō   'oːriːˌoː, 'ɔːriːˌoː

Oreopithicus
  genus of fossil primate   AWR-ē-uh-PITH-i-kuhs   ˌɔːriːə'piθikəs

Orest
  pers. name, Russian   UHR-YĀST   ˌər'jeːst

Oreste
  pers. name, Italian   ō-RES-tā   oː'resteː

Oresteia
  tragic trilogy, Aeschylus   AWR-uh-STĪ-uh, AWR-uh-STĀ-uh,   ˌɔːrə'staiə, ˌɔːrə'steːə,
      AWR-uh-STĒ-uh   ˌɔːrə'stiːə

Orestes
  son of Agamemnon and   uh-RES-tēz, aw-RES-tēz   ə'restiːz, ɔː'restiːz
  Clytemnestra; tragedy,
  Euripides; pers. name

Orff
  Carl, German composer   AWRF   'ɔːʳf

Oriel
  college, Oxford Univ.   AWR-ē-uhl   'ɔːriːəl

Orient
  Eastern hemisphere   ŌR-ē-uhnt, AWR-ē-uhnt, -ENT   'oːriːənt, 'ɔːriːənt, -ˌent

Oriental
  pert. to the Orient   ŌR-ē-ENT-l, AWR-ē-ENT-l   ˌoːriː'entḷ, ˌɔːriː'entḷ

Orientale, Mare
  see Mare Orientale

Oriente
  prov, Cuba   ōr-ē-EN-tā, Ⓢ ŌR-ē-ENT-ē,   oːriː'enteː, Ⓢ ˌoːriː'entiˑ,
      AWR-ē-ENT-ē   ˌɔːriː'entiˑ

Origen
  Christian theologian   AWR-i-juhn, AHR-i-juhn   'ɔːridʒən, 'ɑridʒən

Origenism
  adherence to the teachings of   AWR-uh-juh-NIZ-uhm, AHR-,   'ɔːʳədʒəˌnizəm, 'ɑʳ-,
      Origen   -JEN-IZ-uhm   -ˌdʒenˌizəm

Orinoco
  river, Venezuela   ŌR-uh-NŌ-kō, AWR-   ˌoːrə'noːkoː, ˌɔːr-

Foreign Sounds: ue: *Fr.* **r**ue, *Ger.* f**ü**llen uh(r): *Fr.* b**oeu**f, *Ger.* H**öh**le <u>kh</u>: *Ger.* i**ch**, *Scot.* lo**ch** g̃: *Sp.* ami**g**o <u>v</u>: *Sp.* ha**b**lar
hl: *Welsh* **Ll**anelli. CAPITALS: primary stress. SMALL CAPS: secondary stress. Ⓢ: U.S. pron. Ⓛ: British pron.

Oriole
  songbird   ŌR-ē-ŌL, AWR-, -ē-uhl   'ɔːriː,oːl, 'ɔːr-, -iːəl

Orion
  giant Boeotian hunter;   uh-RĪ-uhn, aw-RĪ-uhn   ə'raiən, ɔː'raiən
    constellation

Orionids
  meteor shower   AWR-ē-AHN-idz, uh-RĪ-uh-nidz   ,ɔriː'anidz, ə'raiənidz

Oriskany
  village, NY   aw-RIS-kuh-nē   ɔː'riskəniˑ

Orissa
  state, India   aw-RIS-uh   ɔː'risə

Oriya
  lang., people, India   aw-RĒ-(y)uh   ɔː'riː(j)ə

Orizaba [Citlaltépetl]
  mtn., city, Mexico   AWR-ē-SAH<u>V</u>-ah, ⑤ ŌR-uh-ZAHB-uh,   ,ɔːriː'saβa, ⑤ ,oːrə'zabə, ,ɔːr-
                           AWR-

Orkney
  islands, Scotland   AWRK-nē   'ɔːʳkniˑ

Orlando
  1. city, FL; pers. name   awr-LAN-dō, awr-LAHN-dō   ɔːʳ'lændoː, ɔːʳ'landoː
  2. Italian   ōr-LAHN-dō   oːr'landoː

Orléannais
  prov, France   awr-lā-ah-NE   ɔːrleːaːne

Orleans
  1. parish, LA   AWR-lē-uhnz, AWRL-(y)uhnz   'ɔːʳliˑənz, 'ɔːʳl(j)ənz
  2. county, NY   AWR-lēnz   'ɔːʳliːnz
  3. county, VT; town, MA   awr-LĒNZ   ɔːʳ'liːnz

Orléans
  town, France   awr-lā-AHⁿ   ɔːrleːã

Orlich
  Francisco, *president, Costa Rica*   awr-LĒCH   ɔːʳ'liːtʃ

Orlon
  tdmk for a synthetic acrylic   AWR-LAHN   'ɔːʳ,lan

Orlov trotter
  horse breed   AWR-LAHF, AWR-LAWF, awr-LAWF   'ɔːʳ,laf, 'ɔːʳ,lɔːf, ɔːʳ'lɔːf

Orly
  city, airport, France   awr-LĒ   ɔːrliː

Ormandy
  Eugene, *US conductor*   AWR-muhn-dē   'ɔːʳməndiˑ

Ormazd
  Zoroastrian god   AWR-MAHZD   'ɔːʳ,mazd

Orne
  1. river, dept, France   AWRN   ɔːrn
  2. pers. name (S. O. Jewett)   AWRN   'ɔːʳn

Ornithischia
  dinosaur order   AWR-nuh-THIS-kē-uh   ,ɔːʳnə'θiskiːə

Ornitholestes
  dinosaur   AWR-nuh-thō-LES-TĒZ   ,ɔːʳnəθoː'les,tiːz

Ornithomimus
  dinosaur   AWR-nuh-thō-MĪ-muhs   ,ɔːʳnəθoː'maiməs

Ornithopoda
  dinosaur suborder   AWR-nuh-THAHP-uhd-uh   ,ɔːʳnə'θapədə

Ornithosuchus
  dinosaur   AWR-nuh-THŌ-si-kuhs   ,ɔːʳnə'θoːsikəs

Key (col. 2):   a: fad   ā: fade   ah: father   ar: **Mary**   aw: **law**   e: fed   ē: feed   er: **merry**   i: hid   ī: hide   ō: coat   o͞o: boot
oi: boy   ow: **now**   u: put   uhr: **bird**   uh: **above**   ch: **chop**   ng: **ring**   sh: **show**   th: **thick**   <u>th</u>: **this**   zh: measure

Orokaiva
  lang., people, New Guinea   AWR-uh-KĪ-vuh   ˌɔːrəˈkɑivə

Orominga
  lang., Ethiopia   AWR-uh-MING-guh   ˌɔːrəˈmiŋgə

Oromo [Galla]
  lang., Ethiopia, Kenya   ŌR-uh-MŌ, AWR-uh-MŌ   ˈɔːrəˌmoː, ˈɔːrəˌmoː

Orontes
  mtn., Iran; river, Syria; Hindu   awr-AHN-TĒZ, ō-RAHN-TĒZ   ɔːrˈɑnˌtiːz, oːˈrɑnˌtiːz
    hero wounded by Dionysus

Orphean
  pert. to Orpheus   AWR-fē-uhn   ˈɔːʳfiːən

Orpheus
  mythogical Greek musician; pers.   AWR-FYŌŌS, AWR-fē-uhs   ˈɔːʳˌfjuːs, ˈɔːʳfiːəs
    name

Orphic
  pert. to Orpheus, *his music, or*   AWR-fik   ˈɔːʳfik
    cult of Dionysus

Orphism
  mystic Greek religion   AWR-FIZ-uhm   ˈɔːʳˌfizəm

Orpington
  breed of fowl   AWR-ping-tuhn   ˈɔːʳpiŋtən

Orr
  1. Robert G. (Bobby), *Canadian*   AWR   ˈɔːʳ
    hockey player
  2. see Boyd Orr

Orren
  pers. name   AWR-uhn, AHR-uhn   ˈɔːrən, ˈɑrən

Orson
  pers. name   AWR-suhn   ˈɔːʳsən

Ortega
  Saavedra Daniel, *president,*   awr-TĀ-ğah, Ⓢ awr-TĀ-guh   ɔːrˈteːɣɑ, Ⓢ ɔːʳˈteːgə
    Nicaragua

Ortega y Gasset
  Jose, *Spanish philosopher*   awr-TĀ-ğah ē ğah-SET   ɔːrˈteːɣɑ iː ɣɑˈset

Orthagoras
  tyrant of Sicyon   awr-THAG-uh-ruhs   ɔːʳˈθægərəs

Orthopolis
  king of Sicyon   awr-THAHP-uh-luhs   ɔːʳˈθɑpələs

Orthros
  dog of Geryon   AWR-THRŌS   ˈɔːʳˌθroːs

Oruro
  dept, Bolivia   aw-RUR-ō   ɔːˈruroː

Orust
  island, Sweden   ŌŌ-RUHST   ˈuːˌrəst

Orval
  Belgian beer   AWR-vahl   ˈɔːrvɑl

Orvieto
  commune, Italy   AWR-vē-ĀT-ō   ˌɔːʳviˈeːtoː

Orville
  pers. name   AWR-vuhl   ˈɔːʳvəl

Orvon
  pers. name (O. G. Autry)   AWR-vuhn, AWR-VAHN   ˈɔːʳvən, ˈɔːʳˌvɑn

---

Foreign Sounds: ue: *Fr.* **rue**, *Ger.* f**ü**llen   uh(r): *Fr.* b**oe**uf, *Ger.* H**ö**hle   <u>kh</u>: *Ger.* i**ch**, *Scot.* lo**ch**   ğ: *Sp.* ami**g**o   <u>v</u>: *Sp.* ha**b**lar
hl: *Welsh* **Ll**anelli.   CAPITALS: primary stress.   SMALL CAPS: secondary stress.   Ⓢ: U.S. pron.   Ⓑ: British pron.

Osage
  river, MO; county, KS, MO, OK;   ō-SĀJ, Ō-SĀJ   oː'seːdʒ, 'oːˌseːdʒ
  Plains, *geographic feature, US;*
  N. American people
Osaka
  city, Japan   ō-sahk-ah, ⓢ ō-SAHK-uh   oːsaka, ⓢ oː'sakə
Osami
  pers. name, Japanese   ō-sah-mē   oːsamiː
Osawatomie
  city, KS   Ō-suh-WAHT-uh-mē   ˌoːsə'waʈəmiˑ
Osbourne
  Ozzy, *rock singer*   AHZ-BAWRN, AHZ-BUHRN   'azˌbɔː�*n, 'azˌbəᵣn
Oscan
  ancient people, Italy   AHS-kuhn   'askən
Oscar
  1. pers. name   AHS-kuhr   'askəᵣ
  2. French   aws-KAHR   ɔːskaːr
  3. German   AWS-KAHR   'ɔːsˌkaᵣ
  4. Norwegian   AWS-KAHR   'ɔːsˌkar
  5. Polish, Swedish   AWS-KAHR   'ɔːsˌkaːr
  6. Russian   AWS-kuhr   'ɔːskər
Óscar
  pers. name, Spanish   Ō-skahr   'oːskar
Oscar de la Renta
  see de la Renta
Oscar Mayer
  US food co.   AHS-kuhr MĪ(-uh)r   ˌaskəᵣ 'maɪ(ə)ᵣ
Osceola
  US pl. name; N. American people Ō-sē-Ō-luh, AHS-ē-Ō-luh   ˌoːsiː'oːlə, ˌasiː'oːlə
Oscoda
  county, MI   ahs-KŌD-uh   as'koːdə
Osco-Umbrian
  ancient Italic lang. family   AHS-kō-UHM-brē-uhn   ˌaskoː'əmbriːən
Osee
  Old Testament book   Ō-ZĒ, ō-ZĀ-uh   'oːˌziː, oː'zeːə
Osgood
  Charles, *US broadcast journalist;* AHZ-GUD   'azˌgud
  pers. name
Oshawa
  town, Canada   AHSH-uh-wuh, AHSH-uh-WAH,   'aʃwə, 'aʃəˌwa, 'aʃəˌwɔː
                                     AHSH-uh-WAW
Oshkosh
  city, WI; tdmk for clothing   AHSH-KAHSH   'aʃˌkaʃ
Osijek
  city, Croatia   Ō-sē-(Y)EK   'oːsiːˌ(j)ek
Osip
  pers. name, Russian   AWS-yip   'ɔːsjip
Osiris
  Egyptian god of the Underworld   ō-SĪ-ruhs   oː'saɪrəs
Oskar
  1. pers. name   AHS-kuhr   'askəᵣ
  2. Finnish, Swedish   AWS-KAHR   'ɔːsˌkaːr
  3. German   AWS-KAHR   'ɔːsˌkaᵣ
  4. Norwegian   AWS-KAHR   'ɔːsˌkar

Key (col. 2):   a: fad   ā: fade   ah: father   ar: Mary   aw: law   e: fed   ē: feed   er: merry   i: hid   ī: hide   ō: coat   o͞o: boot
oi: boy   ow: now   u: put   uh: above   uhr: bird   ch: chop   ng: ring   sh: show   th: thick   th̲: this   zh: measure

Oslo
city, Norway — AHZ-lō, AHS-lō — 'azlo:, 'aslo:

Osman
Turkish emir, founder of Ottoman dynasty — AHZ-muhn, AHS-muhn, -MAHN — 'azmən, 'asmən, -ˌmɑn

Osmanli
an Ottoman; lang. of the Ottoman Turks — ahz-MAN-lē, ahs- — ɑz'mænli·, ɑs-

osmium
element — AHZ-mē-uhm — 'ɑzmiːəm

Osmond
Donny, Marie, US singers — AHZ-muhnd — 'ɑzmənd

Osnabruck, Osnabrück
city, Germany — AWS-nuh-BRUEK, Ⓢ AHZ-nuh-BRUK — 'ɔːsnəˌbryk, Ⓢ 'ɑznəˌbruk

Ossa
mtn., Greece — AHS-uh — 'ɑsə

Ossetia
region, Caucasus Mts. — ah-SĒ-sh(ē-)uh — ɑ'siːʃ(iː)ə

Ossetic
lang., Caucasus Mts. — uh-SET-ik — ə'setik

Ossian
Irish legendary hero; pers. name — AHSH-uhn, AHS-ē-uhn, AWSH-uhn — 'ɑʃən, 'ɑsiːən, 'ɔːʃən

Ossietzky
Carl von, German pacifist, author (Nobel 1935) — aws-YET-skē — ɔːs'jetski·

Ossining
town, NY — AHS-uh-ning, AW-suh-ning — 'ɑsəniŋ, 'ɔːsəniŋ

Ossip
pers. name, Russian — AWS-yip — 'ɔːsjip

Ostend
prov & town, Belgium — ahs-TEND, AHS-TEND — ɑs'tend, 'ɑsˌtend

Österreich [Austria]
republic, Europe — UH(R)-stuh-RĪKH — 'œːstəˌraiç

Ostia
port, Italy — AHS-tē-uh, AW-stē-uh — 'ɑstiːə, 'ɔːstiːə

Ostian Way
road from Rome to Ostia — AHS-tē-uhn WĀ, AW-stē-uhn — ˌɑstiːən 'weː, ˌɔːstiːən

Ostrava
city, Czech republic — AW-struh-vuh — 'ɔːstrəvə

Ostrogoth
easterly division of Goths — AHS-truh-GAHTH — 'ɑstrəˌgɑθ

Ostrowiec
commune, site of WWII concentration camp, Poland — aw-STRAWV-YETS — ɔː'strɔːvˌjets

Ostwald
Friedrich Wilhelm, German chemist (Nobel 1909) — AWST-VAHLT, Ⓢ AHST-WAWLD — 'ɔːstˌvalt, Ⓢ 'astˌwɔːld

Ostyak [Khanty]
lang., Khanti-Mansi region, Russia — AHS-tē-AK — 'ɑstiːˌæk

Ostyak Samoyed [Selkup]
lang., Khanti-Mansi region, Russia — AHS-tē-AK SAM-uh-YED, SAM-OI-ED, suh-MOI-(y)uhd — 'ɑstiːˌæk 'sæməˌjed, 'sæmˌɔiˌed, sə'mɔi(j)əd

---

Foreign Sounds: ue: *Fr.* **rue**, *Ger.* **füllen** uh(r): *Fr.* **boeuf**, *Ger.* **Höhle** <u>kh</u>: *Ger.* i**ch**, *Scot.* lo**ch** g: *Sp.* ami**g**o <u>v</u>: *Sp.* ha**b**lar hl: *Welsh* **Ll**anelli. CAPITALS: primary stress. SMALL CAPS: secondary stress. Ⓢ: U.S. pron. Ⓛ: British pron.

Oswald
   1. pers. name   AHZ-wuhld, AHZ-WAWLD   'ɑzwəld, 'ɑz,wɔːld
   2. German   AWS-VAHLT   'ɔːs,valt
Oswaldo
   pers. name, Portuguese   awzh-WAHL-do͞o, awz-   ɔːʒ'waldoː, ɔːz-
Oswego
   pl. name, US   ahs-WĒ-gō   ɑs'wiːgoː
Oświęcim [Auschwitz]
   commune, site of WWII   awsh-VYE^{n}T-sēm   ɔːʃ'vjẽtsiːm
      concentration camp, Poland
Osyth
   Christian saint   Ō-zuhth, Ō-suhth   'oːzəθ, 'oːsəθ
Otero
   county, CO, NM   ō-TER-ō   oː'teroː
Othello
   play, Shakespeare   uh-THEL-ō, ō-THEL-ō   ə'θeloː, oː'θeloː
Othmar
   pers. name, German   AWT-MAHR   'ɔːt,maʳ
Otho
   Roman emperor; pers. name   Ō-thō   'oːθoː
Othon
   pers. name, French   aw-TAW^{n} ɔːtõ
Otis
   pers. name   ŌT-uhs   'oːtəs
Otmar
   pers. name, German   AWT-MAHR   'ɔːt,maʳ
Oto, Otoe
   N. American people   ŌT-ō   'oːt̪oː
Otoe
   county, NE   ŌT-ō   'oːt̪oː
Otoe Missouria
   N. American people   ŌT-ō muh-ZUR-ē-uh   'oːt̪oː mə'zuriːə
Otomí
   N. American people   ŌT-uh-MĒ   ,oːt̪ə'miː
Oton
   pers. name, French   aw-TAW^{n} ɔːtõ
Otranto
   town, Italy   ō-TRAN-tō, AW-truhn-TŌ   oː'træntoː, 'ɔːtrən,toː
Otsego
   county, MI, NY   aht-SĒ-gō   ɑt'siːgoː
Ottavio
   pers. name, Italian   ōt-TAHV-yō   oːt'tavjoː
Ottawa
   city, Canada; N. American people   AHT-uh-wuh, -WAH, -WAW   'ɑt̪əwə, -,wa, -,wɔː
Otterbein
   University, OH   AHT-uhr-BĪN   'ɑt̪əʳ,bain
Ottmar
   pers. name, German   AWT-MAHR   'ɔːt,maʳ
Otto
   1. pers. name   AHT-ō   'ɑtoː
   2. Danish, Dutch, German   AW-tō   'ɔːtoː
   3. Estonian, Norwegian   AWT-tō   'ɔːttoː
   4. Finnish   AWT-taw   'ɔːttɔː
   5. Swedish   AWT-tu   'ɔːttu

Key (col. 2):   a: fad   ā: fade   ah: father   ar: Mary   aw: law   e: fed   ē: feed   er: merry   i: hid   ī: hide   ō: coat   o͞o: boot
oi: boy   ow: now   u: put   uh: above   uhr: bird   ch: chop   ng: ring   sh: show   th: thick   <u>th</u>: this   zh: measure

Ottoman
  pert. to Turks *or* Turkey   AHT-uh-muhn   'aṭəmən

Ottorino
  pers. name, Italian   ŌT-tō-RĒ-nō   ˌoːttoːˈriːnoː

Ottumwa
  city, IA   ah-TUHM-wuh, uh-TUHM-wuh   aˈtəmwə, əˈtəmwə

Ouachita
  river, mts., lake, pl. name, US   WAHSH-uh-TAW   ˈwaʃəˌtɔː

Ouadai, Wadai
  prefecture, Chad   WAH-DĪ   ˌwaˈdai

Ouagadougou
  city, Burkina Faso   WAHG-uh-DOO-goo   ˌwagəˈduːguː

Oudenaarde
  prov, Belgiuim   OWD-n-AHRD-uh   ˌaudn̩ˈaʳdə

Ouessant, Ile d' [Ushant]
  island, France   ēl dwe-SAHⁿ   iːl dwesã

Ouida
  pen name of Louise de la Ramée;   WĒD-uh   ˈwiːdə
    pers. name

Ouija
  tdmk for a board game   WĒ-juh, WĒ-jē   ˈwiːdʒə, ˈwiːdʒi'

Oulu
  river, city, prov, Finland   OW-loo   ˈauluː

Our
  river, Belgium   UR   ˈuʳ

Ouray
  county, CO   oo-RĀ   uːˈreː

Ourthe
  river, Belgium   URT   ˈuʳt

Ouse
  river, England   OOZ   ˈuːz

Ouspenskaya
  Maria, *entertainer*   OO-SPEN-SKĪ-uh   ˌuːˌspenˈskaiə

Outagamie
  county, WI   OWT-uh-GAM-ē   ˌautəˈgæmi'

Outer Hebrides
  islands, Scotland   OWT-uhr HEB-ruh-DĒZ   ˌautəʳ ˈhebrəˌdiːz

Ouzel
  songbird   OO-zuhl   ˈuːzəl

Ovaltine
  tdmk for a malt flavoring   Ō-vuhl-TĒN   ˈoːvəlˌtiːn

Ovambo [Ambo]
  lang., people, Angola, Namibia   ō-VAHM-bō   oːˈvamboː

Ovamboland
  region, Africa   ō-VAHM-bō-LAND   oːˈvamboːˌlænd

Overijsell
  prov, Netherlands   Ō-vuh-RĪ-suhl   ˌoːvəˈraisəl

Ovett
  Steve, *English runner*   ō-VET   oːˈvet

Ovid
  1. Roman poet; pers. name   AHV-uhd   ˈavəd
  2. village, NY   Ō-vuhd   ˈoːvəd

Ovide
  pers. name, French   aw-VĒD   ɔːviːd

Foreign Sounds: ue: *Fr.* rue, *Ger.* füllen   uh(r): *Fr.* boeuf, *Ger.* Höhle   <u>kh</u>: *Ger.* i**ch**, *Scot.* lo**ch**   ğ: *Sp.* ami**g**o   v̱: *Sp.* ha**b**lar
hl: *Welsh* **Ll**anelli.   CAPITALS: primary stress.   SMALL CAPS: secondary stress.   Ⓢ: U.S. pron.   Ⓛ: British pron.

Ovidian
   pert. to Ovid   ō-VID-ē-uhn, ah-VID-ē-uhn   oː'vidiːən, a'vidiːən

Oviedo
   prov, Spain   Ō-vē-Ā-<u>th</u>ō   ,oːviˈeːðoː

Ovimbundu [Mbundu]
   lang., people, Africa   Ō-vuhm-B$\overline{OO}$N-d$\overline{oo}$,oːvəmˈbuˈnduː

Owain
   pers. name, Welsh   Ō-WĪN, Ⓢ Ō-īn, Ō-uhn, Ō-ān   'oː,wain, Ⓢ 'oːain, 'oːən, 'oːeːn

Owen
   pers. name   Ō-uhn   'oːən

Owsley
   county, KY   OWZ-lē   'auzliˑ

Owyhee
   county, ID   ō-WĪ-(h)ē   oː'wai(h)iː

Oxbridge
   Oxford or Cambridge University,   AHKS-brij, AHKS-BRIJ   'aksbridʒ, 'aks,bridʒ
     or both

Oxford
   town, university, England   AHKS-fuhrd   'aksfəʳd

Oxfordshire
   county, England   AHKS-fuhrd-shuhr, -SHIR   'aksfəʳdʃəʳ, -,ʃiʳ

Oxnard
   city, CA   AHK-SNAHRD   'ak,snaʳd

Oxon
   abbr. for Oxoniensis "of Oxford"   AHK-SAHN   'ak,san

Oxonian
   pert. to Oxford   ahk-SŌ-nē-uhn   ak'soːniːən

Oxydol
   tdmk for a detergent   AHK-suh-DAWL, -DAHL   'aksə,dɔːl, -,dal

oxygen
   element   AHK-suh-juhn   'aksədʒən

Oxynius
   son of Hector   ahk-SIN-ē-uhs   ak'siniːəs

Oxynthes
   king of Athens   ahk-SIN-THĒZ   ak'sin,θiːz

Oxyrhynchus
   archaeological site, Egypt   AHK-si-RING-kuhs   ,aksi'riŋkəs

Oyo
   state, Nigeria   Ō-yō   'oːjoː

Oyvind
   pers. name, Norwegian   OI-vind   'ɔivind

Oz
   Frank, *British puppeteer, actor;*   AHZ   'az
    fictional land, Baum; Australian
    slang for Australia

Ozark
   county, MO; city, AL, AR; mtns.,   Ō-ZAHRK   'oː,zaʳk
    US

Ozaukee
   county, WI   ō-ZAW-kē   oː'zɔːkiˑ

Ozawa
   Seiji, *Japanese conductor*   ō-ZAH-wuh   oː'zawə

Ozero Baykal
   see Baykal, Ozero

Key (col. 2):   a: fad ā: fade ah: father ar: Mary aw: law e: fed ē: feed er: merry i: hid ī: hide ō: coat $\overline{oo}$: boot
oi: boy ow: now u: put uh: above uhr: bird ch: chop ng: ring sh: show th: thick <u>th</u>: this zh: measure

Ozero Onezhskoye
  see Onezhskoye, Ozero
Ozette
  lake, Indian reservation, WA   ō-ZET   oːˈzet
Ozick
  Cynthia, *US writer*   Ō-zik   ˈoːzik
Ozymandias
  sonnet by Shelley   AHZ-i-MAN-dē-uhs   ˌɑziˈmændiːəs
Ozzie, Ozzy
  pers. name   AHZ-ē   ˈɑziˑ

P

Paavo
  pers. name, Finnish   PAH-VAW   ˈpɑˌvɔː
Pablo
  pers. name, Spanish   PAHV-lō   ˈpaβloː
Pabst
  US beer   PABST, PAPST   ˈpæbst, ˈpæpst
Pacaraima, Sierra
  mtn. range, S. America   sē-ER-uh PAK-uh-RĪ-muh   siːˌerə ˌpækəˈraimə
Pachelbel
  Johann, *German composer*   pah<u>kh</u>-EL-BEL, PAH<u>KH</u>-uhl-BEL,   pɑxˈelˌbel, ˈpɑxəlˌbel,
                                    PAHK-uhl-BEL   ˈpɑkəlˌbel
Pachistima
  plant   puh-KIS-tuh-muh   pəˈkistəmə
Pachuca
  city, Mexico   puh-CHOO-kuh   pəˈtʃuːkə
Pachycephalosaurus
  dinosaur   PAK-uh-SEF-uh-lō-SAWR-uhs   ˌpækəˌsefəloːˈsɔːrəs
Pachyderm
  thick-skinned, hoofed mammal   PAK-i-DUHRM   ˈpækiˌdəʳm
Pacifica
  city, CA   puh-SIF-i-kuh   pəˈsifikə
Pacifico
  Mexican beer   pah-SĒ-fē-kō   paˈsiːfiːkoː
Pacino
  Al, *US actor*   puh-CHĒ-nō   pəˈtʃiːnoː
Packard
  US car co.   PAK-uhrd   ˈpækəʳd
Pac-man
  tdmk for a video game   PAK-MAN   ˈpækˌmæn
Pactolus
  river in Asia Minor   pak-TŌ-luhs   pækˈtoːləs
Padang
  island, city, Sumatra   PAHD-AHNG   ˈpɑdˌɑŋ

Foreign Sounds: ue: *Fr.* **rue**, *Ger.* **füllen**   uh(r): *Fr.* **boeuf**, *Ger.* **Höhle**   <u>kh</u>: *Ger.* **ich**, *Scot.* **loch**   ǥ: *Sp.* **amigo**   v̱: *Sp.* **hablar**
hl: *Welsh* **Llanelli**.   CAPITALS: primary stress.   SMALL CAPS: secondary stress.   Ⓢ: U.S. pron.   Ⓛ: British pron.

Paddy
   pers. name   PAD-ē   'pædiˑ

Paderewski
   Ignace, *Polish composer &*   PAHD-uh-REF-skē, PAD-uh-REV-skē   ˌpadəˈrefskiˑ, ˌpædəˈrevskiˑ
   statesman

Padouca
   N. American people   puh-D(Y)O̅O̅-kuh   pəˈd(j)uːkə

Padova [Padua]
   city, prov, Italy   PAHD-uh-vuh   'padəvə

Padraic, Padhraic, Padraig
   1. pers. name   PAH-drig, PAHD-rik, PAH<u>TH</u>-rig   'padrig, 'padrik, 'paðrig
   2. Irish Gaelic   PAWR-ig, PAW<u>TH</u>-rig, PAH-rig   'pɔːrig, 'pɔːðrig, 'parig

Padre
   Island, *TX*   PAHD-rē, PAD-rē   'padriˑ, 'pædriˑ

Padua
   city, Italy   PAJ-uh-wuh   'pædʒəwə

Paducah
   city, KY   puh-D(Y)O̅O̅-kuh   pəˈd(j)uːkə

Paean
   Greek god of healing; epithet of   PĒ-uhn   'piːən
   Apollo

Paeon
   grandson of Nestor   PĒ-uhn, PĒ-AHN   'piːən, 'piːˌan

Paestum
   ancient city, Italy   PES-tuhm, PĒ-stuhm   'pestəm, 'piːstəm

Paez
   lang., people, Colombia, Panama   pah-EZ   paˈez

Pagan
   temple city, Burma; island, Pacific   puh-GAHN   pəˈgan

Paganini
   Niccolo, *Italian composer*   PAHG-uh-NĒ-nē, PAG-uh-NĒ-nē   ˌpagəˈniːniˑ, ˌpægəˈniːniˑ

Paget
   pers. name   PAJ-uht   'pædʒət

Paglia
   Camille, *US writer*   PAHL-yuh, PAHG-lē-uh, PAG-lē-uh   'paljə, 'pagliːə, 'pægliːə

Pagliacci
   opera, Leoncavallo   pahl-YAHCH-ē   palˈjatʃiˑ

Pago Pago, Pango Pango
   town, American Samoa   PAHNG-(g)ō PAHNG-(g)ō, PAHG-ō   ˌpaŋ(g)oː 'paŋ(g)oː, ˌpagoː
                                   PAHG-ō   'pagoː

Pahang
   river, state, Malaysia   puh-HAHNG   pəˈhaŋ

Pahlavi
   Iranian lang.   PAHL-uh-vē, PAL-uh-vē   'paləviˑ, 'pæləviˑ

Pai [Bai, Minchia]
   lang., China   BĪ, PĪ   'bai, 'pai

Paige
   pers. name   PĀJ   'peːdʒ

Päijänne
   lake, Finland   PĀ-YAHN-ne   'peːˌjanne

Paisley
   Ian, *N. Irish politician; city,*   PĀZ-lē   'peːzliˑ
   Scotland; pattern

Pais Vasco
   region, Spain   pīs <u>V</u>AHS-kō   pais 'βaskoː

Key (col. 2):   a: fad ā: fade ah: father ar: Mary aw: law e: fed ē: feed er: merry i: hid ī: hide ō: coat o̅o̅: boot
oi: boy   ow: now   u: put   uh: above   uhr: bird   ch: chop   ng: ring   sh: show   th: thick   <u>th</u>: this   zh: measure

Paiute
    N. American people   PĪ-(Y)O͞OT   'pɑi,(j)uːt

Paiwan
    lang., Taiwan   pī-WAHN   pɑi'wɑn

Pajjusana
    Jain penitential period   pah-JO͞O-sahn-uh   pɑ'dʒuːsɑnə

Pajonism
    Christian sect   PAJ-uh-NIZ-uhm   'pædʒə,nizəm

Pakenham
    1. Sir Edward M., British soldier   PAK-(uh-)nuhm   'pæk(ə)nəm
    2. town, England   PĀ-kuh-nuhm, PĀK-nuhm   'peːkənəm, 'peːknəm

Pakhto [Pashto]
    lang., Afghanistan, Pakistan   PUHKH-tō   'pəxtoː

Pakistan
    republic, Asia   PAK-i-STAN, PAHK-i-STAHN,   ,pæki'stæn, ,pɑki'stɑn,
                 PAK-i-STAN   'pæki,stæn

Pakistani
    pert. to Pakistan   PAK-i-STAN-ē, PAHK-i-STAHN-ē   ,pæki'stæniˑ, ,pɑki'stɑniˑ

Pál
    pers. name, Hungarian   PAHL   'pɑːl

Pala
    Indian reservation, CA   PAL-uh   'pælə

Palade
    George Emil, Romanian-born US   puh-LAHD-ē   pə'lɑdiˑ
      cell biologist (Nobel 1974)

Palaemon
    son of Heracles; Argonaut   pal-Ē-muhn   pæl'iːmən

Palaestra
    Greek or Roman wrestling school   puh-LES-truh   pə'lestrə

Palais-Royal
    French 'royal palace'   pah-LE-raw-YAHL   pɑːleroːjɑːl

Palamedes
    legendary inventor in Greek   PAL-uh-MĒD-ēz   ,pælə'miːdiːz
      mythology

Palamon
    lover in The Knight's Tale,   PAL-uh-MAHN, PAL-uh-muhn   'pælə,mɑn, 'pæləmən
      Chaucer

Palatinate
    district, Germany   puh-LAT-n-ĀT   pə'lætn̩,eːt

Palatine
    hill, Rome, Italy; village, IL   PAL-uh-TĪN   'pælə,tain

Palatka
    city, FL   puh-LAT-kuh   pə'lætkə

Palau [Belau]
    islands, Pacific   puh-LOW   pə'lɑu

Palaung
    lang., people, Burma   puh-LOWNG   pə'lauŋ

Palaung-Wa
    division of Mon-Khmer lang.   puh-LOWNG-WAH   pə'lauŋ'wɑ
      group

Palawan
    island, Philippines   puh-LAH-wuhn   pə'lawən

Palazzo Venezia
    museum, Rome, Italy   puh-LAHT-sō vuh-NET-sē-uh   pə'latsoː və'netsiːə

Foreign Sounds: ue: *Fr.* **rue**, *Ger.* **füllen**   uh(r): *Fr.* **boeuf**, *Ger.* **Höhle**   kh: *Ger.* **ich**, *Scot.* **loch**   g̃: *Sp.* **amigo**   v: *Sp.* **hablar**
hl: *Welsh* **Llanelli**.   CAPITALS: primary stress.   SMALL CAPS: secondary stress.   Ⓢ: U.S. pron.   Ⓑ: British pron.

Palembang
  prov, Indonesia   PAHL-uhm-BAHNG   ‚paləm'baŋ

Palencia
  prov, Spain   puh-LEN-ch(ē-)uh   pə'lentʃ(iː)ə

Palenque
  city, Mexico   puh-LEN-kā   pə'lenkeː

Paleocene
  geologic epoch   PĀ-lē-uh-SĒN, Ⓔ PAL-ē-uh-   'peːliːə‚siːn, Ⓔ 'pæliːə-

Paleogene
  geologic period   PĀ-lē-uh-JĒN, Ⓔ PAL-ē-uh-   'peːliːə‚dʒiːn, Ⓔ 'pæliːə-

Paleolithic
  prehistoric age   PĀ-lē-uh-LITH-ik, Ⓔ PAL-ē-uh-   ‚peːliːə'liθik, Ⓔ ‚pæliːə-

Paleozoic
  geologic era   PĀ-lē-uh-ZŌ-ik, Ⓔ PAL-ē-uh-   ‚peːliːə'zoːik, Ⓔ ‚pæliːə-

Palermo
  prov, Sicilia   puh-LER-mō, puh-LUHR-mō   pə'leʳmoː, pə'ləʳmoː

Pales
  Roman guardian spirit of flocks   PĀ-LĒZ   'peː‚liːz

Palestine
  1. ancient country, site of Holy   PAL-uh-STĪN, -STĒN   'pælə‚stain, -‚stiːn
    Land
  2. city, TX   PAL-uh-STĒN   'pælə‚stiːn

Palestinian
  pert. to Palestine   PAL-uh-STIN-ē-uhn,   ‚pælə'stiniːən, ‚pælə'stinjən
          PAL-uh-STIN-yuhn

Palestrina
  Giovanni Pierluigi da, *Italian*   PAH-lā-STRĒ-nah,   ‚pɑleː'striːnɑ, Ⓢ ‚pælə'striːnə
    composer; commune, Italy   Ⓢ PAL-uh-STRĒ-nuh

Paley
  William S., *US broadcasting*   PĀ-lē   'peːliˑ
    executive

Pali
  lang., India   PAHL-ē   'paliˑ

Palin
  Michael, *British writer, comedian*   PĀ-luhn   'peːlən

Palinurus
  pilot of Aeneas   PAL-uhn-YUR-uhs   ‚pælən'jurəs

Palisades
  line of cliffs, NY, NJ   PAL-uh-SĀDZ   ‚pælə'seːdz

Palladian
  pert. to Palladio *or* Athena   puh-LĀD-ē-uhn, puh-LAHD-ē-uhn   pə'leːdiːən, pə'ladiːən

Palladio
  Andrea, *Italian architect*   pah-LAHD-yō   pɑ'ladjoː

Palladium
  statue of Pallas Athena which   puh-LĀD-ē-uhm   pə'leːdiːəm
    protected Troy; element

Pallantidae
  fifty sons of Pallas   puh-LANT-uh-DĒ   pə'læntə‚diː

Pallas
  1. epithet of Athena   PAL-uhs   'pæləs
  2. grandfather of Evander   PAL-uhs, PAL-AS, PAL-AHS   'pæləs, 'pæl‚æs, 'pæl‚as

Pallas Athena
  Greek goddess, protective aspect of   PAL-uhs uh-THĒ-nuh   'pæləs ə'θiːnə
    Athena; asteroid

Key (col. 2):   a: fad ā: fade ah: father ar: Mary aw: law e: fed ē: feed er: merry i: hid ī: hide ō: coat o͞o: boot
oi: boy   ow: now   u: put   uh: above   uhr: bird   ch: chop   ng: ring   sh: show   th: thick   <u>th</u>: this   zh: measure

Pallene		
daughter of Sithon	puh-LĒ-nē	pə'liːniˑ
Pall Mall		
1. street, London, England	PAL MAL, *formerly* PEL MEL, [$] PAWL MAWL	ˌpæl 'mæl, *formerly* ˌpel 'mel, [$] 'pɔːl 'mɔːl
2. brand of cigarettes	PAWL MAWL, PEL MEL	'pɔːl 'mɔːl, ˌpel 'mel
Palma de Mallorca		
city, Spain	PAHL-muh <u>th</u>ā mah(l)-YAWR-kuh	'palmə ðeː ma(l)'jɔː^{r}kə
Palme		
Olof, *prime minister, Sweden*	PAHL-muh	'paːlmə
Palmer		
Arnold, *US golfer; pers. name*	PAHM-uhr, PAHL-muhr	'paˑmə^{r}, 'paˑlmə^{r}
Palmolive		
tdmk for a soap	pah(l)-MAHL-uhv	pa(l)'maləv
Palmyra		
ancient city, Syria; pl. name, US	pal-MĪ-ruh	pæl'mairə
Palo Alto		
city, CA	PAL-ō AL-tō	ˌpæloː 'æltoː
Palomar		
Mount, *mtn., observatory, CA*	PAL-uh-MAHR	'pæləˌma^{r}
Palomino		
horse breed	PAL-uh-MĒ-nō	ˌpælə'miːnoː
Palos		
port, Spain	PAHL-ōs	'paloːs
Palus Nebularum		
feature on Moon	PĀ-luhs NEB-yuh-LAHR-uhm	'peːləs ˌnebjə'larəm
Palus Putredinis		
feature on Moon	PĀ-luhs pyo͞o-TRED-n-uhs	'peːləs pjuː'tredn̩əs
Palus Somnii		
feature on Moon	PĀ-luhs SAHM-nē-Ē	'peːləs 'samniːˌiː
Pam		
pers. name	PAM	'pæm
Pama-Nyungan		
Australian aboriginal lang. family	PAHM-uh-NYUNG-guhn	ˌpamə'njuŋgən
Pamela		
pers. name	PAM-uh-luh	'pæmələ
Pamfilo		
pers. name, Italian	PAHM-fē-lō	'pamfiːloː
Pamirs		
mtn. range, Asia	puh-MIRZ	pə'mi^{r}z
Pamlico		
river, county, sound, NC	PAM-li-KŌ	'pæmliˌkoː
Pampa, La		
prov, Argentina	lah PAHM-puh	la 'pampə
Pamphile		
pers. name, French	pah^{n}-FĒL, *in Canada* pah^{n}-FIL	pãfiːl, *in Canada* pãfil
Pamphylia		
ancient country, Asia Minor	pam-FIL-ē-uh	pæm'filiːə
Pamplona		
prov, Spain	pam-PLŌ-nuh	pæm'ploːnə
Pamunkey		
N. American people	puh-MUHNG-kē	pə'məŋkiˑ
Pan		
Greek god of shepherds & flocks	PAN	'pæn

Foreign Sounds: ue: *Fr.* **rue**, *Ger.* **füllen** uh(r): *Fr.* **boeuf**, *Ger.* **Höhle** <u>kh</u>: *Ger.* **ich**, *Scot.* **loch** g̃: *Sp.* **amigo** <u>v</u>: *Sp.* **hablar** hl: *Welsh* **Llanelli**. CAPITALS: primary stress. SMALL CAPS: secondary stress. [$]: U.S. pron. [£]: British pron.

Panacea
  Greek goddess of herbal healing   PAN-uh-SĒ-uh   ˌpænə'siːə

Panadol
  tdmk for an analgesic   PAN-uh-DAWL, PAN-uh-DAHL   'pænəˌdɔːl, 'pænəˌdɑl

Pan Am
  former US airline   pan AM   pæn 'æm

Panama
  republic, C. America   PAN-uh-MAH, -MAW; PAN-uh-MAH, -MAW   'pænəˌmɑ, -ˌmɔː; ˌpænə'mɑ, -'mɔː

Panamanian
  pert. to Panama   PAN-uh-MĀ-nē-uhn   ˌpænə'meːniːən

Panasonic
  electronics co.   PAN-uh-SAHN-ik, PAN-uh-SAHN-ik   ˌpænə'sɑnik, 'pænəˌsɑnik

Panathenaea
  ancient Athenian festival   PAN-ATH-uh-NĒ-uh   ˌpænˌæθə'niːə

Panathenaic
  festival, ancient Athens   PAN-ATH-uh-NĀ-ik   ˌpænˌæθə'neːik

Panay
  Philippine island   puh-NĪ   pə'nai

Panchayat
  council of elders or elected officials, India   PUHN-CHĪ-(y)uht   ˌpən'tʃai(j)ət

Pancho
  pers. name, Spanish   PAHN-chō   'pantʃoː

Pancratis
  sister of the Aloadae   pan-KRĀT-uhs, pang-KRĀT-uhs   pæn'kreːʈəs, pæŋ'kreːʈəs

Pandareus
  father of girls killed by harpies   pan-DAR-ē-uhs   pæn'dæriːəs

Pandarus
  Lycian who broke the truce at Troy   PAN-duh-ruhs   'pændərəs

Pandect
  Roman law; digest   PAN-DEKT   'pænˌdekt

Pandemonium
  capital of Hell in Paradise Lost, *Milton*   PAN-duh-MŌ-nē-uhm   ˌpændə'moːniːəm

Pandion
  father of Philomela and Procne   pan-DĪ-uhn   pæn'daiən

Pandit
  Vijaya Lakshmi, *Indian stateswoman*   PAHN-dit   'pandit

Pandora
  Greek mythical figure   pan-DŌR-uh, pan-DAWR-uh   pæn'doːrə, pæn'dɔːrə

Pandrosus
  daughter of Cecrops and Aglaurus   pan-DRŌ-suhs   pæn'droːsəs

Pánfilo
  pers. name, Spanish   PAHM-fē-lō   'pamfiːloː

Pangaea
  Paleozoic supercontinent   pan-JĒ-uh   pæn'dʒiːə

Pangaion Oros
  region, Greece   pahng-GĀ-uhn AWR-uhs   paŋˌgeːən 'ɔːrəs

Pangasinan
  lang., people, Philippine Islands   PAHN-GAHS-ē-NAHN   ˌpanˌgasiː'nan

Pangloss
  character, Voltaire   PAN-GLAHS, PAN-GLAWS   'pænˌglas, 'pænˌglɔːs

---

Key (col. 2):   a: fad   ā: fade   ah: father   ar: Mary   aw: law   e: fed   ē: feed   er: merry   i: hid   ī: hide   ō: coat   o͞o: boot
oi: boy   ow: now   u: put   uh: above   uhr: bird   ch: chop   ng: ring   sh: show   th: thick   t͟h: this   zh: measure

Panglossian
   pert. to Pangloss   pan-GLAHS-ē-uhn,   pæn'glɑsiːən, pæn'glɔːsiːən
                        pan-GLAW-sē-uhn

Pango Pango
   see Pago Pago

Panguingue
   game   pahng-GING-gē, pahng-GĒNG-gē   paŋ'giŋgi', paŋ'giːŋgi'

Panhellenism
   spirit of unity among ancient   PAN-HEL-uh-NIZ-uhm   ˌpæn'helə,nizəm
   Greeks

Panic
   Milan, *Yugoslav prime minister*   PAHN-ēts   'pɑniːts

Panides
   poetry judge who chose Hesiod   PAN-e-DĒZ   'pæne,diːz
   over Homer

Panini, Pānini
   Sanskrit grammarian   PAHN-uh-nē, PAHN-yuh-nē   'pɑnəni', 'pɑnjəni'

Panjab
   see Punjab

Panjabi
   see Punjabi

Pankhurst
   Emmeline *and* Christabel, *English*   PANGK-HUHRST   'pæŋk,həʳst
   suffragists

Pankush
   Hittite assembly   pan-KUSH, pang-KUSH   pæn'kuʃ, pæŋ'kuʃ

Panmunjom
   community between N. & S.   pahn-mun-juhm   pɑnmundʒəm
   Korea

Pannonia
   ancient country and Roman   puh-NŌ-nē-uh   pə'noːniːə
   province, Europe

Pano
   S. American people   PAHN-ō   'pɑnoː

Panola
   county, MS   puh-NŌ-luh   pə'noːlə

Panopeus
   twin brother of Crisus   pa-NŌ-pē-uhs   pæ'noːpiːəs

Pansatanism
   Gnostic doctrine   pan-SĀT-n-IZ-uhm   pæn'seːtn̩,izəm

Pantages
   Theater, *Los Angeles, CA*   pan-TĀ-juhz   pæn'teːdʒəz

Pantagruel
   giant in Pantagruel, *Rabelais*   pahⁿ-tah-grue-EL,   pɑ̃taːgryːel,
               Ⓢ PANT-uh-GRŌO(-uh)l,   Ⓢ ˌpæntə'gruː(ə)l,
               pan-TAG-ruh-WEL, -ruh-wuhl   pæn'tægrə,wel, -rəwəl

Pantagruelian
   pert. to Pantagruel   PANT-uh-grōo-EL-ē-uhn,   ˌpæntəgru'eliːən,
               PAN-TAG-ruh-WEL-ē-uhn   ˌpæn,tægrə'weliːən

Pantelleria
   island, Italy   PAN-TEL-uh-RĒ-uh   ˌpæn,telə'riːə

Pantheon
   ancient Roman building   PAN-thē-AHN   'pænθiː,ɑn

Panthéon
  national monument, Paris, France   pah^n-tā-AW^n, ⑤ PAN(T)-thē-AHN,   pãteːɔ̃, ⑤ 'pæn(t)θiː,ɑn,
                                       PAN(T)-thē-uhn   'pæn(t)θiːən

Panurge
  character in Pantagruel, *Rabelais*   pah-NUERZH, ⑤ PAN-UHRJ,   paːnyːrʒ, ⑤ 'pæn,əʳdʒ,
                                          pa-NURZH   pæ'nuʳʒ

Panza
  see Sancho Panza

Panzer
  German tank, WW II   PAN-zuhr, PAHN(T)-suhr   'pænzəʳ, 'pɑn(t)səʳ

Pao-an [Santa]
  lang., China   POW-AHN   'pɑu'ɑn

Paolo
  pers. name, Italian   PAH-ō-lō   'pɑ-oːloː

Papa
  father   PAHP-uh, Ⓔ puh-PAH   'pɑpə, Ⓔ pə'pɑː

Papago
  N. American people   PAP-uh-GŌ, PAHP-uh-GŌ   'pæpə,goː, 'pɑpə,goː

Papandreou
  Andreas, *prime minister, Greece*   PAHP-ahn-DRĀ-ōō   ,pɑpɑn'dreːuː

Papeete
  port, Tahiti   PAHP-ē-ĀT-ē, puh-PĒT-ē   ,pɑpiː'eːţi, pə'piːţi

Papen
  Franz von, *German political*   PAHP-uhn   'pɑpən
     leader

Paphlagonia
  ancient region, Asia Minor   PAF-luh-GŌ-nē-uh   ,pæflə'goːniːə

Paphos
  district, Cyprus   PĀ-FAHS   'peːˌfɑs

Papiamento [Papiamentu]
  lang., Dutch Antilles   PAHP-yuh-MEN-tō   ,pɑpjə'mentoː

Papiamentu [Papiamento]
  lang., Dutch Antilles   PAHP-yuh-MEN-tōō   ,pɑpjə'mentuː

Papillion
  city, NE   puh-PIL-yuhn   pə'piljən

Papillon
  dog breed   PAHP-ē-(Y)AW^n, PAP-   ,pɑpiː'(j)ɔ̃, ,pæp-

Papirius
  Lucius, *Roman consul, dictator*   puh-PIR-ē-uhs   pə'piriːəs

Papua New Guinea
  nation, island group, Pacific   PAHP-uh-wuh N(Y)ōō GIN-ē,   'pɑpəwə ,n(j)uˈ 'giniˈ,
                                     PAP-yuh-wuh   'pæpjəwə

Papua New Guinean
  pert. to Papua New Guinea   PAHP-uh-wuh N(Y)ōō GIN-ē-uhn,   'pɑpəwə ,n(j)uˈ 'giniːən,
                                PAP-yuh-wuh   'pæpjəwə

Pär
  pers. name, Swedish   PER   'peʳ

Paracelsus
  Swiss physician, alchemist   PAR-uh-SEL-suhs   ,pærə'selsəs

Paraclete
  Holy Spirit   PAR-uh-KLĒT   'pærəˌkliːt

Paradise
  garden of Eden   PAR-uh-DĪS, PAR-uh-DĪZ   'pærəˌdais, 'pærəˌdaiz

Paraguay
  republic, S. America   PAR-uh-GWĪ, -GWĀ   'pærəˌgwai, -ˌgweː

Key (col. 2): a: fad ā: fade ah: father ar: Mary aw: law e: fed ē: feed er: merry i: hid ī: hide ō: coat ōō: boot
oi: boy ow: now u: put uh: above uhr: bird ch: chop ng: ring sh: show th: thick th̲: this zh: measure

Paraguayan
  pert. to Paraguay   PAR-uh-GWĪ-uhn, -GWĀ-uhn   'pærə,gwaiən, -,gweːən

Paralipomenon
  Old Testament book   PAR-uh-luh-PAHM-uh-NAHN,   ,pærələ'pamə,nan,
                   PAR-uh-LĪ-PAHM-uh-NAHN   ,pærə,lai'pamə,nan

Paramaribo
  city, Suriname   PAR-uh-MAR-uh-BŌ   ,pærə'mærə,boː

Paramus
  city, NJ   puh-RAM-uhs   pə'ræməs

Paraná
  river; state, Brazil; city, Argentina   PAR-uh-NAH   ,pærə'na

Paranaíba
  river, Brazil   PAHR-uh-nah-Ē-buh,   ,paːrəna'iːbə, ⑤ ,pærənə'iːbə
          ⑤ PAR-uh-nuh-Ē-buh

Paraquat
  toxic herbicide   PAR-uh-KWAHT   'pærə,kwat

Parasaurolophus
  dinosaur   PAR-uh-saw-RAHL-uh-fuhs   ,pærəsɔː'raləfəs

Parcae
  Roman goddesses of destiny   PAHR-KĪ, PAHR-sē   'paʳ,kai, 'paʳsiˑ

Parcheesi
  tdmk for a board game   pahr-CHĒ-zē   paʳ'tʃiːziˑ

Pardalote
  Australian bird   PAHRD-l-ŌT   'paʳdḷ,oːt

Pardo
  Don, *US broadcasting announcer*   PAHRD-ō   'paʳdoː

Pareto
  Vilfredo, *Italian economist*   puh-RĀT-ō   pə'reːtoː

Parian
  pert. to Páros; *marble*   PAR-ē-uhn   'pæriːən

Paricutín
  volcano, former village, Mexico   puh-RĒ-ko͞o-TĒN   pə,riːku'tiːn

Parinarium
  plant   PAR-uh-NAR-ē-uhm   ,pærə'næriːəm

Paris
  1. *city, France*   pah-RĒ, ⑤ PAR-uhs   paːriː, ⑤ 'pærəs
  2. *Trojan who abducted Helen; US*   PAR-uhs   'pærəs
    pl. name

Parisian
  pert. to Paris   puh-RĒ-zhuhn, puh-RIZH-uhn,   pə'riːʒən, pə'riʒən,
              puh-RIZ-ē-uhn   pə'riziːən

Park Chung Hee
  president, S. Korea   pahrk chuhng hē   paʳk tʃəŋ hiː

Parke-Bernet
  auction gallery   PAHRK-BUHR-nuht   ,paʳk'bəʳnət

Parker
  Dorothy, *US writer; pers. name*   PAHR-kuhr   'paʳkəʳ

Parkinson
  C. N., *English historian;* James,   PAHR-kuhn-suhn   'paʳkənsən
    English physician

Parma
  prov, Italy; city, OH   PAHR-muh   'paʳmə

Parmenides
  Greek philosopher; dialogue of   pahr-MEN-uh-DĒZ   paʳ'menə,diːz
    Plato

Foreign Sounds: **ue**: *Fr.* **rue**, *Ger.* **füllen**   **uh(r)**: *Fr.* **boeuf**, *Ger.* **Höhle**   k͟h: *Ger.* **ich**, *Scot.* **loch**   ḡ: *Sp.* **amigo**   v̲: *Sp.* **hablar**
hl: *Welsh* **Llanelli.** CAPITALS: primary stress. SMALL CAPS: secondary stress. ⑤: U.S. pron. Ⓔ: British pron.

Parmenio
  Macedonian general   pahr-MḖ-nē-Ō, pahr-MĒN-yō   paʳmiːniːˌoː, paʳmiːnjoː
Parmentier
  food prepared or served with   PAHR-muhn-TYḀ̄   ˌpaʳmənˈtjeː
    potatoes
Parmesan
  pert. to Parma; *cheese*   PAHR-muh-ZAHN, PAHR-muh-ZHAHN,   ˈpaʳməˌzan, ˈpaʳməˌʒan,
                                          PAHR-muh-zuhn, PAHR-muh-ZAN   ˈpaʳməzən, ˈpaʳməˌzæn
Parmigiana
  made with Parmesan cheese   PAHR-mi-JAHN-uh, PAHR-mi-ZHAHN,   ˌpaʳmiˈdʒɑnə, ˈpaʳmiˌʒan,
                                          PAHR-mi-ZHAHN   ˌpaʳmiˈʒan
Parmigiano Reggiano
  Italian cheese   PAHR-mi-ZHAHN-ō rej-AHN-ō   ˌpaʳmiˈʒanoː redʒˈanoː
Parnassian
  pert. to Parnassus, *to poetry, to a* pahr-NAS-ē-uhn   paʳnæsiːən
    school of French poets
Parnassus
  mtn., Greece   pahr-NAS-uhs   paʳnæsəs
Parnell
  pers. name   pahr-NEL, PAHR-nl   paʳnel, ˈpaʳnl̩
Parnu
  bay, river, port, Estonia   PAHR-nōo   ˈpaʳnuː
Páros
  Greek island noted for white   PAH-RAWS, Ⓢ PAR-AHS, PER-AHS   ˈpaˌrɔːs, Ⓢ ˈpærˌas, ˈperˌas
    marble
Parrhasius
  Greek painter, 5th cent., BC   puh-RḀ̄-zh(ē-)uhs,   pəˈreːʒ(iː)əs, pəˈreːʃ(iː)əs
                                          puh-RḀ̄-sh(ē-)uhs
Parsee
  Indian Zoroastrian descended   pahr-SḖ, PAHR-sē   paʳsiː, ˈpaʳsiˈ
    from Persians
Parsi
  follower of Zoroastrianism;   PAHR-sē   ˈpaʳsiˈ
    Iranian dialect
Parsifal
  opera, R. Wagner; Arthurian   PAHR-suh-VAHL, PAHR-suh-vuhl   ˈpaʳsəˌval, ˈpaʳsəvəl
    romance hero
Parsiism
  religion   PAHR-SḖ-IZ-uhm   ˈpaʳˌsiːˌizəm
Parthenon
  Athenian temple   PAHR-thuh-NAHN   ˈpaʳθəˌnɑn
Parthenopaeus
  one of the Seven against Thebes   PAHR-thuh-nō-PḖ-(y)uhs   ˌpaʳθənoːˈpiː(j)əs
Parthenope
  a siren in Greek mythology   pahr-THEN-uh-pē   paʳˈθenəpiˈ
Parthenos
  epithet of Athena   PAHR-thuh-NŌS   ˈpaʳθəˌnoːs
Parthia
  ancient country, Asia   PAHR-thē-uh   ˈpaʳθiːə
Parthians
  inhabitants of Parthia   PAHR-thē-uhnz   ˈpaʳθiːənz
Partido Revolucionario Institucional
  political party, Mexico   pahr-TḖ-t͟hō rā-v͟o-lōos-yō-NAHR-yō   parˈtiːðoː reːβoːluːsjoːˈnarjoː
                                          in-stē-t͟oos-yō-NAHL   instiˈtuːsjoːˈnal

---

Key (col. 2):   a: fad   ā: fade   ah: father   ar: Mary   aw: law   e: fed   ē: feed   er: merry   i: hid   ī: hide   ō: coat   ōō: boot
oi: boy   ow: now   u: put   uh: above   uhr: bird   ch: chop   ng: ring   sh: show   th: thick   t͟h: this   zh: measure

Parton
    Dolly, *US singer, actress*   PAHRT-n   'pɑ^rtn̩

Parzival [Parsifal]
    Arthurian romance hero   PAHRT-suh-FAHL   'pɑ^rtsə,fɑl

Pas, The
    town, Manitoba   thuh PAH, thuh PAW   ðə 'pɑ, ðə 'pɔː

Pasadena
    city, CA, MD   PAS-uh-DĒ-nuh   ,pæsə'diːnə

Pasargadae
    ruined city, Persia   puh-SAHR-guh-DĒ   pə'sɑ^rgə,diː

Pascagoula
    river, city, MS   PAS-kuh-GOO-luh   ,pæskə'guːlə

Pascal
    1. Blaise, French philosopher   pahs-KAHL, Ⓢ pas-KAL   pɑːskɑːl, Ⓢ pæs'kæl
    2. programming lang.   pas-KAL, pahs-KAHL   pæs'kæl, pɑːs'kɑːl

Paschal
    antipope   pas-KAL, pahs-KAHL   pæs'kæl, pɑs'kɑl

Pasco-Hernando
    Community College, FL   PAS-kō-(h)er-NAHN-dō,   'pæskoː(h)e^r'nɑndoː,
                -huhr-NAN-dō   -hə^r'nændoː

Pascua, Isla de
    Easter Island   ĒZ-lah thā PAHS-kwah   'iːzlɑ ðeː 'pɑskwɑ

Pascual
    pers. name, Spanish   pahs-KWAHL   pɑs'kwɑl

Pascua Yaqui
    N. American people   PAS-kwuh YAHK-ē   'pæskwə 'jɑki·

Pas-de-Calais
    dept, France   pah-duh-kah-LE   pɑːdəkɑːle

Pasha
    Turkish title   PAHSH-uh, PASH-uh, puh-SHAH   'pɑʃə, 'pæʃə, pə'ʃɑ

Pashto
    lang., Afghanistan, Pakistan   PUHSH-tō   'pəʃtoː

Pashtu [Pashto]
    lang., Afghanistan, Pakistan   PASH-too, PAHSH-too   'pæʃtuː, 'pɑʃtuː

Pasiphaë
    wife of Minos, mother of the   puh-SIF-uh-Ē   pə'sifə,iː
        Minotaur; satellite of Jupiter

Paso Doble
    dance   PAHS-ō DŌ-blā   ,pɑsoː 'doːbleː

Pasquale
    pers. name, Italian   pahs-KWAHL-ā   pɑs'kwɑleː

Pasqueflower
    flower   PASK-FLOW-uhr   'pæsk,flauə^r

Pasquotank
    county, NC   PAS-kwuh-TANGK   'pæskwə,tæŋk

Passaic
    river, city, county, NJ   puh-SĀ-ik   pə'seːik

Passamaquoddy
    lang., people, N America   PAS-uh-muh-KWAHD-ē   ,pæsəmə'kwɑdi·

Passat
    tdmk for a German automobile   pa-SAHT, puh-SAT   pæ'sɑt, pə'sæt

Passau
    city, Germany   PAHS-OW   'pɑs,au

Passerine
    bird genus (English name)   PAS-uh-RĪN   'pæsə,rain

Foreign Sounds: ue: *Fr.* **rue**, *Ger.* **füllen** uh(r): *Fr.* **boeuf**, *Ger.* **Höhle** <u>kh</u>: *Ger.* **ich**, *Scot.* **loch** g̃: *Sp.* **amigo** y: *Sp.* **hablar**
hl: *Welsh* **Llanelli**. CAPITALS: primary stress. SMALL CAPS: secondary stress. Ⓢ: U.S. pron. Ⓛ: British pron.

Passiontide
   Passion Sunday to Holy Saturday   PASH-uhn-TĪD   'pæʃən,tɑid

Passon
   Field, *former ballpark,*   PAS-uhn   'pæsən
   Philadelphia, PA

Passover
   Jewish holiday   PAS-ō-vuhr   'pæs,oːvəʳ

Passy
   Frédéric, *French economist,*   pah-SĒ   pɑːsiː
   author (Nobel 1901)

Pasternak
   Boris L., *Russian author (Nobel*   PAS-tuhr-NAK   'pæstəʳ,næk
   1958)

Pasteur
   Louis, *French scientist*   pahs-TUHR, Ⓢ pas-TUHR   pɑːstœːr, Ⓢ pæs'təʳ

Pasto
   city, Colombia   PAHS-tō   'pɑstoː

Pastorale
   type of musical work   PAS-tuh-RAHL, PAS-tuh-RAL,   ˌpæstə'rɑl, ˌpæstə'ræl,
                     PAS-tuh-RAHL-ē   ˌpæstə'rɑliˑ

Pat
   pers. name   PAT   'pæt

Patagonia
   prov, Argentina   PAT-uh-GŌ-nē-uh, PAT-uh-GŌN-yuh   ˌpæʈə'goːniːə, ˌpæʈə'goːnjə

Patagonian Desert
   S. America   PAT-uh-GŌ-nē-uhn, -GŌN-yuhn   ˌpæʈə'goːniːən, -'goːnjən

Patarinism
   Christian heresy   PAT-uh-ruh-NIZ-uhm,   'pæʈərə,nizəm, -ə,riː,nizəm
                     -uh-RĒ-NIZ-uhm

Patavium
   Latin form of Padua   puh-TĀ-vē-uhm   pə'teːviːəm

Patchogue
   village, NY   PACH-AWG   'pætʃˌɔːg

Pate
   Jerome Kendrick, *US golfer*   PĀT   'peːt

Pater
   1. Walter H., *English author*   PĀT-uhr   'peːʈəʳ
   2. British term for father   PĀT-uhr   'peːʈəʳ
   3. see Pater Noster

Pater Noster
   Lord's Prayer   PAHT-uhr NAHS-tuhr, PAT-uhr   ˌpɑʈəʳ 'nɑstəʳ, 'pæʈəʳ
                     NAHS-tuhr, PAH-TER NAHS-TER   ˌnɑstəʳ, 'pɑ,teʳ 'nɑs,teʳ

Paterson
   city, NJ   PAT-uhr-suhn   'pæʈəʳsən

Pathetiqué
   sonata, Beethoven   PAH-thā-TĒK   ˌpɑθeː'tiːk

Pathet Lao
   communist group, Laos   PAHT-uht LOW, LAH-ō·   'pɑʈət 'lau, 'laoː

Patiala
   city, India   PUHT-ē-AHL-uh   ˌpəʈiː'ɑlə

Patinkin
   Mandy, *US actor*   puh-TING-kin   pə'tiŋkin

Pátmos, Patmos
   island, Greece   PAHT-maws, Ⓢ PAT-muhs   'pɑtmɔːs, Ⓢ 'pætməs

---

Key (col. 2): a: fad ā: fade ah: father ar: Mary aw: law e: fed ē: feed er: merry i: hid ī: hide ō: coat ōō: boot
oi: boy ow: now u: put uh: above uhr: bird ch: chop ng: ring sh: show th: thick th̲: this zh: measure

Patna
city, India	PUHT-nuh	'pɒtnə

Paton
Alan, *S. African novelist; pers.* *name*	PĀT-n	'peːtn̩

Patos
lake, Argentina	PAH-tōs	'pɑtoːs

Patrae
ancient form of Patras	PĀ-trē	'peːtriˑ

Pátrai
town, Greece	PAH-trā	'pɑtreː

Patras
town, Greece	puh-TRAS, PA-truhs	pə'træs, 'pætrəs

Patrice
pers. name, French	pah-TRĒS	pɑːtriːs

Patricia
pers. name	puh-TRISH-uh, puh-TRĒ-shuh	pə'triʃə, pə'triːʃə

Patricians
Roman aristocratic class	puh-TRISH-uhnz	pə'triʃənz

Patricio
pers. name, Spanish	pah-TRĒS-yō, pah-TRĒTH-yō	pɑ'triːsjoː, pɑ'triːθjoː

Patrick
pers. name	PA-trik	'pætrik

Patrimonium
Roman emperor's private estate	PA-truh-MŌ-nē-uhm	ˌpætrə'moːniːəm

Patripassianism
Christian heresy	PA-truh-PAS-ē-uh-NIZ-uhm, PA-truh-PĀ-sē-uh-NIZ-uhm	ˌpætrə'pæsiːəˌnizəm, ˌpætrə'peːsiːəˌnizəm

Patrizier
German beer	pah-TRĒTS-yuhr	pɑ'triːtsjəʳ

Patroclus
friend of Achilles	puh-TRŌ-kluhs	pə'troːkləs

Patsy
pers. name	PAT-sē	'pætsiˑ

Pattala
ancient city, Indus river delta	puh-TAHL-uh	pə'tɑlə

Patterson
Floyd, *US boxer, athletic* *commissioner*	PAT-uhr-suhn	'pætəʳsən

Patti, Pattie, Patty
pers. name	PAT-ē	'pæt̬iˑ

Patton
Gen. George Smith, *US general*	PAT-n	'pætn̩

Pau
city, France	PŌ	poː

Pauillac
French wine	paw-YAHK, pō-YAHK	poːjɑːk, poːjɑːk

Paul
1. pers. name	PAWL	'pɔːl
2. Afrikaans	PŌ-ul	'poːul
3. Danish, Dutch, German, *Norwegian, Swedish*	POWL	'paul
4. French	PAWL	pɔːl

Foreign Sounds: ue: *Fr.* **rue**, *Ger.* f**ü**llen   uh(r): *Fr.* b**oeu**f, *Ger.* H**öh**le   <u>kh</u>: *Ger.* i**ch**, *Scot.* lo**ch**   g̃: *Sp.* ami**g**o   v̲: *Sp.* ha**b**lar
hl: *Welsh* **Ll**anelli.   CAPITALS: primary stress.   SMALL CAPS: secondary stress.   Ⓢ: U.S. pron.   Ⓔ: British pron.

Paula
1. pers. name	PAW-luh	'pɔːlə
2. German, Spanish	POW-lah	'paula
3. Portuguese	POW-luh, POW-lah	'paulə, 'paulɑː

Paulaner
German beer	POW-LAHN-uhr	'pau͵lanəʳ

Paule
pers. name, French	PAWL	pɔːl

Paulette
pers. name	paw-LET	pɔː'let

Pauley
Jane, *US TV journalist*	PAW-lē	'pɔːliˑ

Pauli
Wolfgang, *Austrian-born US physicist (Nobel 1945)*	POW-lē	'pauliˑ

Pauline
1. pers. name	paw-LĒN, ⓔ PAW-LĒN	pɔː'liːn, ⓔ 'pɔː͵liːn
2. Dutch, German	pow-LĒ-nuh	pau'liːnə
3. French	paw-LĒN	pɔːliːn
4. pert. to St. Paul; *pupil of St. Paul's School, London*	PAW-LĪN	'pɔː͵lain

Pauling
Linus C., *US chemist (Nobel 1954), pacifist (Nobel 1962)*	PAW-ling	'pɔːliŋ

Paulinism
doctrines of St. Paul	PAW-luh-NIZ-uhm	'pɔːlə͵nizəm

Paulinus
pers. name	paw-LĪ-nuhs	pɔː'lainəs

Paulo
pers. name, Portuguese	POW-lo͞o	'pauluː

Paulo Afonso
waterfalls, Brazil	POW-lo͞o uh-FŌN-so͞o	'pauluː ə'fɔːnsuː

Paulus
1. pers. name, Afrikaans	PŌ-ul-uh(r)s	'pɔːulœs
2. German	POW-lus	'paulus

Paulus, Paullus
pers. name, Latin	PAW-luhs	'pɔːləs

Paung-daw-U
Burmese festival	POWNG-DOW-O͞O	'pauŋ'dau'uː

Pausanias
Spartan general	paw-SĀ-nē-uhs	pɔː'seːniːəs

Pavane
dance	puh-VAHN, puh-VAN	pə'van, pə'væn

Pavarotti
Luciano, *Italian tenor*	PAHV-ah-RAWT-tē, ⓢ PAHV-uh-RAHT-ē, PAV-	͵pavaˈrɔːttiː, ⓢ ͵pavəˈraţiˑ, ͵pæv-

Pavel
1. pers. name, Czech	PAH-VEL, PAHV-uhl	'paː͵vel, 'paːvəl
2. Russian	PAHV-yil	'paˌvjil

Pavia
prov, Italy	puh-VĒ-uh	pə'viːə

Pavillon Blanc
wine	pah-vē-yawⁿ BLAHⁿ	paːviːjɔ̃ blɑ̃

Pavlos
pers. name, Mod. Greek	PAHV-laws	'pavlɔːs

Key (col. 2):   a: fad ā: fade ah: father ar: Mary aw: law e: fed ē: feed er: merry i: hid ī: hide ō: coat o͞o: boot
oi: boy ow: now u: put uh: above uhr: bird ch: chop ng: ring sh: show th: thick <u>th</u>: this zh: measure

Pavlov
Ivan Petrovich, *Russian* — PAHV-LAWF, PAV-LAWF, -LAWV — 'pɑv‚lɔːf, 'pæv‚lɔːf, -‚lɔːv
physiologist (Nobel 1904)

Pavlova
Anna Matreyevna, *Russian ballet* — PAHV-luh-vuh, Ⓢ PAV-luh-vuh, — 'pɑːvləvə, Ⓢ 'pævləvə,
dancer — pav-LŌ-vuh — pæv'loːvə

Pavlovian
pert. to Pavlov; learned response — pav-LAW-vē-uhn, pav-LŌ-vē-uhn — pæv'lɔːviːən, pæv'loːviːən

Pavlovich
patronym, Russian — puhv-LAWV-yich — pəv'lɔːvjitʃ

Pavo
constellation — PĀ-vō, PAHV-ō — 'peːvoː, 'pɑvoː

Pawnee
N. American people — paw-NĒ, pah-NĒ — pɔː'niː, pɑ'niː

Pawtucket
city, RI — puh-TUHK-uht, paw-TUHK-uht — pə'təkət, pɔː'təkət

Pax
Roman personification of peace — PAKS, PAHKS — 'pæks, 'pɑks

Pax Christi
Latin for 'Peace of Christ' — paks KRIS-tē, pahks — pæks 'kristi', pɑks

Pax Romana
Roman political peace — PAKS rō-MAHN-uh, PAHKS — 'pæks roː'mɑnə, 'pɑks

Paxton
Tom, *US songwriter* — PAK-stuhn — 'pækstən

Payaguá
S. American people — PĪ-(y)uh-GWAH — ‚pai(j)ə'gwɑ

Payette
river, county, ID — pā-ET — peː'et

Pays de la Loire
region, France — pād lahl WAHR — peːd lɑːl waːr

Payton
Walter, *US football player* — PĀT-n — 'peːtn̩

Paz
1. Octavio, *Mexican poet (Nobel* — PAHS, Ⓢ PAHZ — 'pɑs, Ⓢ 'pɑz
1990)
2. pers. name, Spanish — PAHS, PAHTH — 'pɑs, 'pɑθ

Paz, La
see La Paz

Paz Estenssoro
Victor, *president, Bolivia* — PAHS es-ten-SAWR-ō — ‚pɑs esten'sɔːroː

Peabody
town, MA — PĒ-BAHD-ē, *esp. locally* PĒ-buhd-ē — 'piː‚bɑdiˑ, *esp. locally* 'piːbədiˑ

Peale
Norman Vincent, *US clergyman* — PĒL — 'piːl

Peano
Giuseppe, *Italian mathematician* — pā-AHN-ō — peː'ɑnoː

Pear
British family name — PIR — 'piʳ

Pearce
pers. name — PIRS — 'piʳs

Pearl
pers. name — PUHRL, PUHR-uhl — 'pəʳl, 'pərəl

Foreign Sounds: ue: *Fr.* **rue**, *Ger.* **füllen** uh(r): *Fr.* **boeuf**, *Ger.* **Höhle** kh: *Ger.* **ich**, *Scot.* **loch** ǧ: *Sp.* **amigo** v: *Sp.* **hablar**
hl: *Welsh* **Llanelli**. CAPITALS: primary stress. SMALL CAPS: secondary stress. Ⓢ: U.S. pron. Ⓛ: British pron.

Pears
1. Sir Peter, *British tenor*	PIRZ	'pi^rz
2. brand of soap	PERZ	'pe^rz

Pearsall
| *city, Texas* | PIR-SAWL | 'pi^rˌsɔːl |

Pearse
| *pers. name* | PIRS | 'pi^rs |

Pearson
| Lester B., *Canadian politician (Nobel 1957); airport, Toronto* | PIRS-n | 'pi^rsn̩ |

Peary
| Robert E., *US admiral, explorer* | PIR-ē | 'piriˑ |

Pecksniff
| Seth, *character in* Martin Chuzzlewit, *Dickens* | PEK-SNIF | 'pekˌsnif |

Pecksniffian
| *pert. to* Pecksniff; *a hypocrite* | pek-SNIF-ē-uhn | pek'snifiːən |

Pecorino Romano
| *Italian cheese* | PEK-uh-RĒ-nō rō-MAHN-ō | ˌpekə'riːnoː roː'mɑnoː |

Pecos
| *river, NM, TX; city, county, TX;* National Monument, *NM* | PĀ-kuhs | 'peːkəs |

Pécs
| *city, Hungary* | PĀCH | 'peːtʃ |

Peder
| *pers. name, Danish* | PI-<u>th</u>uhr | 'piðər |

Pedersen
| Charles J., *US chemist (Nobel 1987)* | PED-uhr-suhn, PĒD-uhr-suhn | 'pedə^rsən, 'piːdə^rsən |

Pedro
1. pers. name, Portuguese	PĀ-<u>th</u>ro͞o, ⑤ PĀ-drō	'peːðruː, ⑤ 'peːdroː
2. Spanish	PĀ-<u>th</u>rō, ⑤ PĀ-drō	'peːðroː, ⑤ 'peːdroː

Pedroncelli
| J., *winery, CA* | PED-ruhn-CHEL-ē | ˌpedrən'tʃeliˑ |

Pedro Ximenez
| *wine grape* | PĀ<u>TH</u>-rō hē-MĀ-neth | 'peːðroː hiː'meːneθ |

Pegasus
| *mythical flying horse; constellation* | PEG-uh-suhs | 'pegəsəs |

Peggy
| *pers. name* | PEG-ē | 'pegiˑ |

Pehr
| *pers. name, Finnish, Swedish* | PER | 'per |

Pei
| I. M., *US architect;* Mario, *US linguist* | PĀ | 'peː |

Peiping [Beijing]
| *city, China* | PĀ-PING | 'peː'piŋ |

Peipus
| *lake, Estonia, Russia* | PĪ-puhs | 'paipəs |

Peiraeus
| *see* Piraeus |

Peisistratus, Pisistratus
| *Athenian tyrant* | pi-SIS-truht-uhs, puh- | pi'sistrətəs, pə- |

Pekin
    city, IL   PĒ-kuhn, PĒ-KIN   'piːkən, 'piːˌkin

Peking [Beijing]
    city, China   PĒ-KING, PĀ-KING   'piːˈkiŋ, 'peːˈkiŋ

Pekingese
    pert. to Peking; *dog breed*   PĒ-kuh-NĒZ, -NĒS; PĒ-king-ĒZ, -ĒS   ˌpiːkə'niːz, -'niːs; ˌpiːkiŋ'iːz,
                                                                  -'iːs

Pelagian
    pert. to or a follower of Pelagius   puh-LĀ-jē-uhn   pə'leːdʒiːən

Pelagianism
    denial of original sin   puh-LĀ-jē-uh-NIZ-uhm   pə'leːdʒiːəˌnizəm

Pelagio
    pers. name, Spanish   pā-LAH-ḡyō   peː'laɣjoː

Pelagius
    pope   puh-LĀ-j(ē-)uhs   pə'leːdʒ(iː)əs

Pelasgus
    founder of the Pelasgians   puh-LAS-guhs   pə'læsgəs

Pele
    Hawaiian volcano goddess   PĀ-lā   'peːleː

Pelé
    Brazilian soccer player   PĀ-lā   'peːleː

Pelée
    volcano, Martinique   puh-LĀ   pə'leː

Peleliu
    island, Pacific   PEL-uh-LĒ-o͞o   ˌpelə'liːuː

Peleus
    father of Achilles   PĒ-lē-uhs, PĒL-Yo͞oS   'piːliːəs, 'piːˌljuːs

Pelham
    US pl. name; pers. name   PEL-uhm   'peləm

Pelias
    uncle of Jason   PEL-ē-uhs   'peliːəs

Pelion
    mtn., Greece   PĒ-lē-uhn   'piːliːən

Pelopia
    mother of Aegisthus   puh-LŌ-pē-uh   pə'loːpiːə

Pelopidas
    Theban general   puh-LAHP-uhd-uhs   pə'lapədəs

Peloponnese
    peninsula, Greece   PEL-uh-puh-NĒZ, -NĒS   'peləpəˌniːz, -ˌniːs

Peloponnesian
    pert. to the Peloponnesus   PEL-uh-puh-NĒ-zhuhn, -shuhn   ˌpeləpə'niːʒən, -ʃən

Peloponnesus
    peninsula, Greece   PEL-uh-puh-NĒ-suhs   ˌpeləpə'niːsəs

Pelopónnisos [Peloponnesus]
    peninsula, Greece   pel-uh-PAWN-uh-saws   pelə'pɔːnəsɔːs

Pelops
    father of Atreus   PĒ-LAHPS, PEL-AHPS   'piːˌlaps, 'pelˌaps

Peltier
    effect, electrical temperature   pel-TYĀ, PEL-tē-ā   pel'tjeː, 'peltiːˌeː
      change

Pelvoux, Massif du
    mtn., France   mah-SĒF due pel-Vo͞o   maːsiːf dyː pelvuː

Pemba
    island, Indian Ocean; town,   PEM-buh   'pembə
      Mozambique

Foreign Sounds: ue: *Fr.* **rue**, *Ger.* **füllen**   uh(r): *Fr.* **boeuf**, *Ger.* **Höhle**   <u>kh</u>: *Ger.* i**ch**, *Scot.* lo**ch**   ḡ: *Sp.* ami**g**o   ʋ: *Sp.* ha**b**lar
hl: *Welsh* **Ll**anelli.   CAPITALS: primary stress.   SMALL CAPS: secondary stress.   Ⓢ: U.S. pron.   Ⓑ: British pron.

Pembina
  county, ND   PEM-buh-nuh, PEM-buh-NAW   'pembənə, 'pembə,nɔː
Pembroke
  1. town, Wales; college, Oxford   PEM-bruk, PEM-bruhk, PEM-BRŌK   'pembruk, 'pembrək,
    Univ., Cambridge Univ.   'pem,broːk
  2. pl. name, US   PEM-BRŌK, PEM-BRUK   'pem,broːk, 'pem,bruk
Pembrokeshire
  former county, Wales   PEM-bruk-shuhr, PEM-bruhk-, -SHIR   'pembrukʃəʳ, 'pembrək-,
                                                     -,ʃiʳ
Pemiscot
  county, MO   PEM-i-SKAHT, PEM-i-SKŌ   'pemi,skat, 'pemi,skoː
Penang
  state, Malaysia   puh-NANG   pə'næŋ
Penates
  Roman household gods   puh-NĀT-ēz, puh-NAHT-ēz   pə'neːɾiːz, pə'nɑɾiːz
Pendergrass
  Teddy, US musician, singer,   PEN-duhr-GRAS   'pendəʳ,græs
    songwriter
Pendleton
  1. Austin, US actor, director   PEN-dl-tuhn   'pendl̩tən
  2. county, WV   PEN-dl-tuhn, PEN-l-tuhn   'pendl̩tən, 'penl̩tən
Pend Oreille
  county, WA   PAHN duh-RĀ   ,pɑn də'reː
Pendragon
  title of Uther, King Arthur's father   pen-DRAG-uhn, PEN-DRAG-uhn   pen'drægən, 'pen,drægən
Penelope
  faithful wife of Odysseus; pers.   puh-NEL-uh-pē   pə'neləpiˑ
    name
Penetanguishene
  city, Ontario   PEN-uh-TANG-gwuh-SHĒN   ,penə'tæŋgwə,ʃiːn
Peneus
  ancient name of Salambria   puh-NĒ-uhs   pə'niːəs
Peng-hu
  islands, Taiwan   PUHNG-HOO   'pəŋ'huː
P'eng-hu Lieh-tao [Pescadores]
  islands, Taiwan   PENG-HOO lē-E-DOW   'peŋ'huː liː'e'dau
Penina
  pers. name   pen-Ē-nuh, puh-NĒ-nuh   pen'iːnə, pə'niːnə
Pennacook
  N. American people   PEN-uh-KUK   'penə,kuk
Pennine
  Alps, Alpine mtn. range   PEN-ĪN   'pen,ain
Pennines, The
  mts., England   PEN-ĪNZ   'pen,ainz
Pennsylvania
  state, US   PEN(T)-suhl-VĀ-nyuh, -VĀ-nē-uh   ,pen(t)səl'veːnjə, -'veːniːə
Pennsylvanian
  geologic period   PEN-suhl-VĀ-nyuhn, -nē-uhn   ,pensəl'veːnjən, -niːən
Penny, Penney, Pennie
  pers. name   PEN-ē   'peniˑ
Penobscot
  river, bay, ME; N. American   puh-NAHB-skuht, -SKAHT   pə'nɑbskət, -,skat
    people
Penrhyn
  pers. name   PEN-rin, pen-RIN   'penrin, pen'rin

Key (col. 2):   a: fad   ā: fade   ah: father   ar: **Mary**   aw: **law**   e: fed   ē: feed   er: **merry**   i: hid   ī: hide   ō: coat   ōō: boot
oi: boy   ow: now   u: put   uh: above   uhr: bird   ch: chop   ng: ring   sh: show   th: thick   <u>th</u>: this   zh: measure

Pensacola
  city, FL; N. American people   PEN(T)-suh-KŌ-luh   ˌpen(t)sə'koːlə
Pentagon
  US Defense Dept bldg.   PENT-uh-GAHN   'pentəˌgɑn
Pentateuch
  first five books of Bible   PENT-uh-T(Y)O͞OK   'pentəˌt(j)uːk
Pentax
  tdmk for a Japanese camera   PEN-TAKS   'penˌtæks
Pentecost
  Christian holy day   PENT-uh-KAWST, -KAHST   'pentəˌkɔːst, -ˌkɑst
Penthesilea
  Amazon who fought Achilles   PEN-thuh-suh-LĒ-uh   ˌpenθəsə'liːə
Pentheus
  king of Thebes   PEN-thē-uhs, PEN-TH(Y)O͞OS   'penθiːəs, 'penˌθ(j)uːs
Pentothal
  tdmk for an anesthetic   PENT-uh-THAWL   'pentəˌθɔːl
Pentstemon
  plant   pent-STĒ-muhn, PEN(T)-stuh-muhn   pent'stiːmən, 'pen(t)stəmən
Penutian
  N. American lang. group   puh-N(Y)O͞O-sh(ē-)uhn,   pə'n(j)uːʃ(iː)ən,
    puh-N(Y)O͞OT-ē-uhn   pə'n(j)uːʈiːən
Penzance
  town, England   pen-ZAN(T)S, puhn-ZAN(T)S   pen'zæn(t)s, pən'zæn(t)s
Penzias
  Arno A., German-born US   PEN(T)-sē-uhs   'pen(t)siːəs
    astrophysicist (Nobel 1978)
Peoria
  city, IL; N. American people   pē-ŌR-ē-uh, pē-AWR-ē-uh   piː'oːriːə, piː'ɔːriːə
Pepe
  1. pers. name   PEP-Ā, PEP-ē   'pepˌeː, 'pepi·
  2. Spanish   PĀ-pā   'peːpeː
Pepin
  1. Frankish king, father of   PEP-uhn   'pepən
    Charlemagne
  2. county, WI   PIP-uhn, PEP-uhn   'pipən, 'pepən
Peppard
  George, US actor   pep-AHRD, puh-PAHRD   pep'ɑʳd, pə'pɑʳd
Pepperdine
  University, CA   PEP-uhr-DĪN   'pepəʳˌdɑin
Pepperidge Farm
  US food co.   PEP-(uh-)rij FAHRM   ˌpep(ə)ridʒ 'fɑʳm
Pepsi-Cola
  tdmk for a soft drink   PEP-sē-KŌ-luh   ˌpepsi·'koːlə
Pepsodent
  tdmk for dental care products   PEP-suhd-uhnt, PEP-suh-DENT   'pepsədənt, 'pepsəˌdent
Pepys
  1. Samuel, English diarist   PĒPS   'piːps
  2. current British family name   PEP-is, PEPS   'pepis, 'peps
Pequot
  N. American people   PĒ-KWAHT   'piːˌkwɑt
Per
  pers. name, Swedish   PER   'per
Perahia
  Murray, US pianist   puh-RĪ-uh   pə'rɑiə

Foreign Sounds: ue: *Fr.* **rue**, *Ger.* füllen   uh(r): *Fr.* **boeuf**, *Ger.* Höhle   <u>kh</u>: *Ger.* i<u>ch</u>, *Scot.* lo<u>ch</u>   g̃: *Sp.* ami**g**o   v̲: *Sp.* ha**b**lar
hl: *Welsh* **Ll**anelli.   CAPITALS: primary stress.   SMALL CAPS: secondary stress.   ⓢ: U.S. pron.   ⓑ: British pron.

Perak
  river, state, Malaysia   PER-uh, PIR-uh *[sic]*   'perə, 'pirə *[sic]*

Perceval
  pers. name   PUHR-suh-vuhl   'pəʳsəvəl

Percheron
  draft horse   PUHR-chuh-RAHN, PUHR-shuh-RAHN   'pəʳtʃə,ran, 'pəʳʃə,ran

Percival
  pers. name   PUHR-suh-vuhl   'pəʳsəvəl

Percy
  pers. name   PUHR-sē   'pəʳsiˑ

Perdiccas
  Macedonian king, general   puhr-DIK-uhs   pəʳ'dikəs

Perdue
  US food products co.   PUHR-D(Y)OO   ˌpəʳ'd(j)uː

Peregrine
  pers. name   PER-uh-gruhn, -GRĒN, -GRIN   'perəgrən, -ˌgriːn, -ˌgrin

Pereira
  1. William, US architect   puh-RÃ-ruh, puh-RER-uh   pə're:rə, pə'rerə
  2. pers. name, Portuguese   puh-RÃ-ruh   pə're:rə

Perelman
  S. J., US author   PER-uhl-muhn *(his own pron.)*,   'perəlmən *(his own pron.)*,
         PUHR-uhl-muhn, PUHRL-muhn   'pər-əlmən, 'pəʳlmən

Peres
  Shimon, Israeli politician   PER-ez   'per,ez

Pérez
  pers. name, Spanish   PÃ-räs, PÃ-räth   'pe:re:s, 'pe:re:θ

Pérez de Cuellar
  Javier, UN Secretary General   PÃ-räs thã KWÃ-(y)ahr   'pe:re:s ðe: 'kwe:(j)aʳ

Perfect
  pers. name (C. P. McVie)   PUHR-fikt   'pəʳfikt

Pergamon
  town, Turkey   PUHR-guh-MAHN   'pəʳgə,man

Pergamum
  city, ancient Greek kingdom, Asia   PUHR-guh-muhm   'pəʳgəməm
  Minor

Pergamus
  son of Andromache and   PUHR-guh-muhs   'pəʳgəməs
  Neoptolemus

Pergolesi
  Giovanni Battista, Italian   PER-gō-LÃ-sē   ˌpeʳgoː'le:siˑ
  composer

Periander
  Greek statesman   PER-ē-AN-duhr   ˌperiˑ'ændəʳ

Periclean
  pert. to Pericles   PER-i-KLĒ-uhn   ˌperi'kliːən

Pericles
  Athenian statesman   PER-i-KLĒZ   'peri,kliːz

Périgord
  prov, France   pã-rē-GAWR   pe:riːgɔːr

Périgueux
  town, France; sauce with truffles   pã-rē-GUH(R)   pe:riːgœ:

Perikles
  pers. name, Mod. Greek   per-ē-KLĒS   periˑ'kliːs

Perilla
  plant   puh-RIL-uh   pə'rilə

Key (col. 2):   a: fad   ā: fade   ah: father   ar: Mary   aw: law   e: fed   ē: feed   er: merry   i: hid   ī: hide   ō: coat   o͞o: boot
oi: boy   ow: now   u: put   uh: above   uhr: bird   ch: chop   ng: ring   sh: show   th: thick   <u>th</u>: this   zh: measure

Perioeci
   free inhabitants of Laconia   PER-ē-Ē-SĪ   ,peri:'i:,sɑi

Peripatetic
   pert. to the Aristotelian school of   PER-uh-puh-TET-ik   ,perəpə'teţik
     philosophy

Peripateticism
   Aristotelianism   PER-uh-puh-TET-uh-SIZ-uhm ,perəpə'teţə,sizəm

Periphetes
   brigand slain by Theseus   PER-uh-FĒT-ēz   ,perə'fi:ţi:z

Perissodactyla
   hoofed animals   puh-RIS-uh-DAK-tuh-luh   pə,risə'dæktələ

Perkins
   Anthony, *US actor*   PUHR-kuhnz   'pə^rkənz

Perlis
   state, Malaysia   PER-luhs   'pe^rləs

Perlman
   Rhea, *US actress*   PUHRL-muhn   'pə^rlmən

Perm
   city, Russia   PYERM, Ⓢ PUHRM, PERM   'pjerm, Ⓢ 'pə^rm, 'pe^rm

Permian
   geologic period   PUHR-mē-uhn   'pə^rmi:ən

Pernambuco
   state, Brazil   PER-nuhm-B̄O̅O̅-kō,   ,pe^rnəm'bu:ko:,
                           PUHR-nuhm-B(Y)O̅O̅-kō   ,pə^rnəm'b(j)u:ko:

Pernod
   tdmk for a liqueur   per-NŌ   pe^r'no:

Perón
   Juan *and* Evita, *Argentine political* pā-RŌN, puh-RŌN   pe:'ro:n, pə'ro:n
     leaders

Peroni
   Italian beer   pā-RŌ-nē   pe:'ro:ni:

Perot
   H. Ross, *US business executive*   puh-RŌ, PIR-ō   pə'ro:, 'piro:

Perpignan
   town, France   per-pēn-YAHⁿ   perpi:njã

Perquimans
   county, NC   puhr-KWIM-uhn(t)s   pə^r'kwimən(t)s

Perrault
   Charles, *French poet, author of* pe-RŌ, Ⓢ puh-RŌ, per-Ō pero:, Ⓢ pə'ro:, per'o:
     fairy tales

Perrier
   tdmk for mineral water   PER-ē-Ā, per-YĀ   'peri:,e:, per'je:

Perrin
   1. pers. name   PER-uhn   'perən
   2. J. B., French physicist (Nobel pe-REⁿ   perẽ
     1926)

Perrine
   Valerie, *US actress*   puh-RĪN   pə'rɑin

Perry
   pers. name   PER-ē   'peri·

Perseids
   meteor shower   PUHR-sē-uhdz   'pə^rsi:ədz

Persephone
   Greek goddess of the Underworld puhr-SEF-uh-nē   pə^r'sefəni·

Foreign Sounds: ue: *Fr.* **rue**, *Ger.* **füllen** uh(r): *Fr.* b**oeu**f, *Ger.* H**öh**le <u>kh</u>: *Ger.* i**ch**, *Scot.* lo**ch** ğ: *Sp.* ami**g**o ṿ: *Sp.* ha**b**lar
hl: *Welsh* **Ll**anelli. CAPITALS: primary stress. SMALL CAPS: secondary stress. Ⓢ: U.S. pron. Ⓛ: British pron.

Persepolis
  ancient Persian city   puhr-SEP-uh-luhs   pəʳˈsepələs

Perses
  father of Hecate   PUHR-sēz   ˈpəʳsiːz

Perseus
  mythological Greek hero;   PUHR-sē-uhs, PUHR-S(Y)O̅O̅S   ˈpəʳsiːəs, ˈpəʳˌs(j)uːs
    constellation; pers. name

Pershing
  John, *US general*   PUHR-shing, PUHR-zhing   ˈpəʳʃiŋ, ˈpəʳʒiŋ

Persia
  former name for Iran   PUHR-zhuh, PUHR-shuh   ˈpəʳʒə, ˈpəʳʃə

Persian
  pert. to Persia; *lang., Middle East*   PUHR-zhuhn, PUHR-shuhn   ˈpəʳʒən, ˈpəʳʃən

Perth
  city, Australia; city, Scotland   PUHRTH   ˈpəʳθ

Perth Amboy
  city, NJ   PUHRTH AM-BOI   ˌpəʳθ ˈæmˌbɔi

Pertinax
  Roman emperor   PUHRT-n-AKS   ˈpəʳtn̩ˌæks

Peru
  1. republic, S. America   pā-ROO, ⑤ puh-ROO   peːˈruː, ⑤ pəˈruː
  2. city, IL; city, IN   PĒ-ROO, puh-ROO   ˈpiːˌruː, pəˈruː

Perugia
  prov, Italy   puh-ROO-j(ē-)uh   pəˈruːdʒ(iː)ə

Perugino
  Italian painter   PER-oo-JĒ-nō   ˌperuːˈdʒiːnoː

Perutz
  M. F., *Austrian-born British*   puh-ROOTS   pəˈruːts
    biochemist (Nobel 1962)

Peruvian
  pert. to Peru   puh-ROO-vē-uhn   pəˈruːviːən

Pesach, Pesah [Passover]
  Jewish holiday   PĀ-SAHKH, PES-AHKH   ˈpeːˌsax, ˈpesˌax

Pescadores
  islands, Taiwan   PES-kuh-DŌR-ēz, -DAWR-ēz   ˌpeskəˈdoːriːz, -ˈdɔːriːz

Peshawar
  prov, Pakistan   puh-SHAH-wuhr, puh-SHOW(-uh)r   pəˈʃawəʳ, pəˈʃau(ə)ʳ

Pest
  county, Hungary   PESHT, ⑤ PEST   ˈpeʃt, ⑤ ˈpest

Pestalozzi
  Johann H., *Swiss educational*   PES-tuh-LAHT-sē   ˌpestəˈlatsiˈ
    reformer

Pétain
  Henri Philippe, *French militarist*   pā-TEⁿ   peːtẽ

Petaluma
  city, CA   PET-l-OO-muh   ˌpetl̩ˈuːmə

Petar
  pers. name, Serbo-Croatian   PE-tahr   ˈpetɑːr

Pete
  pers. name   PĒT   ˈpiːt

Key (col. 2):   a: fad   ā: fade   ah: father   ar: Mary   aw: law   e: fed   ē: feed   er: merry   i: hid   ī: hide   ō: coat   o̅o̅: boot
oi: boy   ow: now   u: put   uh: above   uhr: bird   ch: chop   ng: ring   sh: show   th: thick   th: this   zh: measure

Peter

   1. New Testament book; pers.   PĒT-uhr   'piːtəʳ
     name

   2. Danish   PI-tuhr   'pitər

   3. Dutch, Norwegian, Swedish   PÅ-tuhr   'peɪtər

   4. German   PE-tuhr   'petəʳ

Péter

   pers. name, Hungarian   PÅ-ter   'peɪter

Peterhouse

   college, Cambridge Univ.   PĒT-uhr-HOWS   'piːtəʳˌhaus

Petersham

   town, England; heavy woolen cloth PĒT-uhr-shuhm, -SHAM   'piːtəʳʃəm, -ˌʃæm
     for coats

Petit

   pers. name   PET-uht   'peṭət

Petite Champagne

   wine   puh-TĒT shahⁿ-PAHN-yuh pətiːt ʃɑ̃pɑːɲ

Petite Sirah

   wine grape   puh-TĒT suh-RAH   pəˌtiːt sə'rɑ

Petits pois

   peas   puh-tē PWAH   pətiː 'pwa

Petit Village

   wine   puh-TĒ vē-LAHZH   pətiː viːlɑːʒ

Petőfi

   Sándor, *Hungarian poet*   PET-uh(r)-fē, Ⓢ PET-uh-fē   'petœːfiˑ, Ⓢ 'peṭəfiˑ

Petr

   1. pers. name, Czech   PET-uhr   'peṭər

   2. Russian   PYAW-tuhr   'pjɔːtər

Pëtr

   pers. name, Russian   PYAW-tuhr   'pjɔːtər

Petra

   1. ruined city, Jordan   PĒ-truh, PE-truh   'piːtrə, 'petrə

   2. pers. name   PE-truh   'petrə

Petrarch

   Italian poet, scholar   PĒ-TRAHRK, PE-TRAHRK   'piːˌtrɑʳk, 'peˌtrɑʳk

Petrarchan

   pert. to Petrarch; *type of sonnet* pē-TRAHR-kuhn, pe-TRAHR-kuhn piˑ'trɑʳkən, pe'trɑʳkən

Petri

   J. R., *German bacteriologist;*   PĒ-trē, PE-trē   'piːtriˑ, 'petriˑ
     bacteria culture dish

Petrofina

   Belgian petroleum firm   PE-trō-FĒ-nuh   ˌpetroː'fiːnə

Petrograd

   former name of St. Petersburg, pyi-TRUH-GRAHT, Ⓢ PE-truh-GRAD pji,trə'grɑːt, Ⓢ 'petrəˌgræd
     Russia

Petronius

   Roman writer; pers. name, Latin puh-TRŌ-nē-uhs   pə'troːniːəs

Petropavlovsk

   city, Kazakhstan   PYI-truh-PAHV-luhfsk,   ˌpjitrə'pavləfsk,
                       Ⓢ PE-truh-PAV-LAWFSK   Ⓢ ˌpetrə'pæv,lɔːfsk

Petrópolis

   town, Brazil   puh-TRAHP-uh-luhs   pə'trapələs

Petros

   town, Romania   PE-truh-SHAHN(-ē)   ˌpetrə'ʃan(iˑ)

Petrouchka
   ballet, Stravinsky   pe-TRŌŌCH-kuh, puh-TRŌŌSH-kuh   pe'truːtʃkə, pə'truːʃkə

Petrovna
   pers. name, Russian   pyi-TRAWV-nuh   pji'trɔːvnə

Petrozavodsk
   city, Russia   PE-truh-suh-VAHTSK   ˌpetrəsə'vɑːtsk

Petruccio
   1. pers. name   puh-TRŌŌ-chē-ō, puh-TRŌŌ-chō   pə'truːtʃiːˌoː, pə'truːtʃoː
   2. Italian   pā-TRŌŌT-chō   peː'truːttʃoː

Petruchio
   character in Taming of the Shrew,   puh-TRŌŌ-kē-ō, puh-TRŌŌ-chē-ō,   pə'truːkiːoː, pə'truːtʃiːˌoː,
     Shakespeare   puh-TRŌŌ-chō   pə'truːtʃoː

Petrus
   1. pers. name, Dutch   PĀ-trues   'peːtrys
   2. Latin   PĒ-truhs   'piːtrəs
   3. Swedish   PĀ-truhs   'peːtrəs

Pétrus
   pers. name, French   pā-TRUES   peːtrys

Petsamo
   territory, Russia   PET-suh-MŌ   'petsəˌmoː

Petula
   pers. name   puh-T(Y)ŌŌ-luh   pə't(j)uːlə

Peugeot
   French car co.   puh(r)-ZHŌ, Ⓢ p(y)ōō-ZHŌ   pœːʒoː, Ⓢ p(j)uː'ʒoː

Pewee
   bird   PĒ-WĒ   'piːˌwiː

Peyton
   pers. name   PĀT-n   'peːtn̩

Pfaff
   Johann, *German mathematician;*   PFAHF   'pfɑf
     sewing machine co.

Pfeiffer
   Michelle, *US actress;* College, *NC*   FĪ-fuhr   'faifəʳ

Pfizer
   US chemical co.   FĪ-zuhr   'faizəʳ

Phaeacians
   mythical sailors   fē-Ā-shuhnz   fiː'eːʃənz

Phaedo
   Greek philosopher; dialogue of   FĒD-ō   'fiːdoː
     Plato

Phaedra
   wife of Theseus   FĒ-druh, FE-druh, FĀ-druh   'fiːdrə, 'fedrə, 'feːdrə

Phaedrus
   Greek philosopher; dialogue of   FĒ-druhs, FE-druhs, FĀ-druhs   'fiːdrəs, 'fedrəs, 'feːdrəs
     Plato

Phaestus
   1. ancient city, Crete   FES-tuhs, FĒ-stuhs   'festəs, 'fiːstəs
   2. son of Heracles   FĒ-stuhs   'fiːstəs

Phaëthon
   son of Helios   FĀ-uht-n, FĀ-uh-tuhn, FĀ-uh-THAHN   'feːətn̩, 'feːətən, 'feːəˌθɑn

Phaidon
   Cultural Guides, *imprint for a*   FĪD-n   'faidn̩
     book series

Phainopepla
   songbird   fā-ī-nuh-PEP-luh, FĪN-uh-PEP-luh   feːˌainə'peplə, ˌfainə'peplə

Key (col. 2):   a: fad   ā: fade   ah: father   ar: Mary   aw: law   e: fed   ē: feed   er: merry   i: hid   ī: hide   ō: coat   ōō: boot
oi: boy   ow: now   u: put   uh: above   uhr: bird   ch: chop   ng: ring   sh: show   th: thick   th: this   zh: measure

Phalange, Phalangist
  see Falange, Falangist

Phalanx
  brother of Arachne   FĀ-LANGKS, ⓔ FAL-ANGKS   'feɪ,læŋks, ⓔ 'fæl,æŋks

Phalarope
  shore bird   FAL-uh-RŌP   'fælə,roːp

Pham Van Dong
  prime minister, Vietnam   FAHM VAHN DAHNG   ,fam ,van 'daŋ

Phanerozoic
  eon that includes Paleozoic,   FAN-uhr-uh-ZŌ-ik   ,fænərə'zoːik
  Mesozoic, Cenozoic eras

Phaon
  legendary ferryman of Lesbos   FĀ-uhn, FĀ-AHN   'feɪən, 'feɪ,an

Pharaoh
  Egyptian ruler   FER-ō, FAR-ō, FĀ-rō   'feroː, 'færoː, 'feɪroː

Pharaonic
  like a Pharoah   FER-ā-AHN-ik, FAR-ā-AHN-ik   ,fereɪ'anik, ,færeɪ'anik

Pharisaic
  pert. to Pharisees   FAR-uh-SĀ-ik   ,færə'seɪik

Pharisee
  Jewish sect   FAR-uh-sē   'færəsiː

Phariseeism
  tenets of the Pharisees   FAR-uh-SĒ-IZ-uhm, FER-   'færə,siː,izəm, 'fer-

Pharos
  ancient lighthouse, Alexandria;   FAR-AHS, FER-AHS   'fær,as, 'fer,as
  pilot for Helen & Menelaus

Pharpar
  river, Damascus   FAHR-puhr   'faʳpəʳ

Pharsalia
  epic poem, Lucan   fahr-SĀ-lē-uh, fahr-SĀL-yuh   faʳ'seːliːə, faʳ'seːljə

Pharsalus
  battlesite, Greece   fahr-SĀ-luhs   faʳ'seːləs

Pheidias [Phidias]
  Greek sculptor   FID-ē-uhs, FĪD-ē-uhs   'fidiːəs, 'faidiːəs

Pheidippides
  Greek runner from Sparta to   fī-DIP-uhd-ĒZ   fai'dipəd,iːz
  Athens before battle of
  Marathon

Pheidon
  king of Argos   FĪ-DAHN   'fai,dan

Phelim
  pers. name, Irish Gaelic   FYĀ-lyim, ⓢ FĀ-lim   'fjeːljim, ⓢ 'feːlim

Phenix City
  city, AL   FĒ-niks SIT-ē   ,fiːniks 'sitiˑ

Phenomenology
  study of awareness; classification   fi-NAHM-uh-NAHL-uh-jē   fi,namə'nalədʒiˑ
  of phenomena

Pheops
  name, Egyptian kings   FĒ-AHPS   'fiː,aps

Pheres
  son of Medea and Jason   FER-ĒZ   'fer,iːz

Phi Beta Kappa
  academic honor society   FĪ BĀT-uh KAP-uh   ,fai ,beːʈə 'kæpə

Phidias [Pheidias]
  Greek sculptor   FID-ē-uhs   'fidiːəs

Foreign Sounds: ue: *Fr.* **rue**, *Ger.* **füllen**   uh(r): *Fr.* **boeuf**, *Ger.* **Höhle**   <u>kh</u>: *Ger.* **ich**, *Scot.* **loch**   ḡ: *Sp.* **amigo**   v̲: *Sp.* **hablar**   hl: *Welsh* **Llanelli**.   CAPITALS: primary stress.   SMALL CAPS: secondary stress.   ⓢ: U.S. pron.   ⓔ: British pron.

Phil
  pers. name   FIL   'fil

Philadanco
  dance co., PA   FIL-uh-DANG-kō, FIL-uh-DAN-kō   ˌfilə'dæŋkoː, ˌfilə'dænkoː

Philadelphia
  city, PA   FIL-uh-DEL-fyuh, -fē-uh   ˌfilə'delfjə, -fiːə

Philammon
  legendary poet and seer   fuh-LAM-uhn   fə'læmən

Philander
  1. pers. name   fuh-LAN-duhr   fə'lændəʳ
  2. Dutch   fē-LAHN-duhr   fiː'landər
  3. German   fē-LAHN-duhr   fiː'landəʳ

Philéas
  pers. name, French   fē-lā-AHS   fiːleːas

Philebus
  dialogue of Plato   fuh-LĒ-buhs, fī-LĒ-buhs   fə'liːbəs, fai'liːbəs

Philemon
  New Testament book; pers. name   fuh-LĒ-muhn, fī-   fə'liːmən, fai-

Philharmonia
  orchestra   FIL-uhr-MŌ-nē-uh,   ˌfiləʳ'moːniːə,
                FIL-(H)AHR-MŌ-nē-uh   ˌfil,(h)aʳ'moːniːə

Philharmonia Virtuosi
  symphony, NY   FIL-uhr-MŌ-nē-uh vuhr-chuh-WŌ-sē,   ˌfiləʳ'moːniːə vəʳtʃə'woːsi',
                FIL-(H)AHR-MŌ-nē-uh   ˌfil,(h)aʳ'moːniːə

Philip
  1. pers. name   FIL-uhp   'filəp
  2. Dutch   FĒ-luhp   'fiːləp
  3. German   FĒ-lip, FIL-ip   'fiːlip, 'filip
  4. Swedish   FĒ-lip   'fiːlip

Philipp
  1. pers. name   FIL-uhp   'filəp
  2. German   FĒ-lip, FIL-ip   'fiːlip, 'filip
  3. Russian   fyil-YĒP   fjil'jiːp
  4. Swedish   FĒ-lip   'fiːlip

Philippa
  pers. name   FIL-uh-puh, FI-LI-puh   'filəpə, ˌfi'lipə

Philippe
  pers. name, French   fē-LĒP   fiːliːp

Philippi
  1. ancient town, Macedonia   FIL-uh-PĪ, fuh-LIP-Ī   'filəˌpai, fə'lipˌai
  2. Civil War battle site, WV   FIL-uh-pē   'filəpiː

Philippians
  New Testament book   fuh-LIP-ē-uhnz   fə'lipiːənz

Philippics
  speeches of Demosthenes   fuh-LIP-iks   fə'lipiks

Philippines
  island nation, Pacific   FIL-uh-PĒNZ, FIL-uh-PĒNZ   ˌfilə'piːnz, 'filəˌpiːnz

Philippism
  doctrines of Philip Melanchthon   FIL-uh-PIZ-uhm   'filəˌpizəm

Philippus
  pers. name   fi-LIP-uhs   fi'lipəs

Philistia
  ancient region, Palestine   fuh-LIS-tē-uh   fə'listiːə

Key (col. 2):   a: fad   ā: fade   ah: father   ar: Mary   aw: law   e: fed   ē: feed   er: merry   i: hid   ī: hide   ō: coat   o͞o: boot
oi: boy   ow: now   u: put   uh: above   uhr: bird   ch: chop   ng: ring   sh: show   th: thick   <u>th</u>: this   zh: measure

Philistine
   inhabitant of Philistia   FIL-uh-STĒN, -STĪN; fuh-LIS-tuhn,   'filə,stiːn, -,stain; fə'listən,
                              FIL-uh-stuhn   'filəstən

Phillip
   pers. name   FIL-uhp   'filəp

Phillips
   pers. name   FIL-uhps   'filəps

Philly
   nickname for Philadelphia   FIL-ē   'fili·

Philo
   pers. name   FĪ-lō   'failoː

Philoctetes
   keeper of the bow and arrow of   fi-LAHK-tuh-TĒZ, FIL-ahk-TĒT-ēz   fi'laktə,tiːz, ˌfilak'tiːt̪iːz
      Heracles

Philomel
   poetic Latin name for the   FIL-uh-MEL   'filə,mel
      nightingale

Philomela
   sister of Procne   FIL-uh-MĒ-luh   ˌfilə'miːlə

Philomena
   Christian saint   FIL-uh-MĒ-nuh   ˌfilə'miːnə

Philosophiae Baccalaureus
   bachelor of philosophy, Ph.B.   fil-AHS-uh-FĒ-ī BAK-uh-LŌR-ē-uhs,   fil,asə'fiː,ai ,bækə'loːriːəs,
                               -LAWR-ē-uhs   -'loːriːəs

Philosophiae Doctor
   doctor of philosophy, Ph.D.   fil-AHS-uh-FĒ-ī DAHK-TAWR   fil,asə'fiː,ai 'dak,tɔːʳ

Philostratus
   Greek sophist at Rome   fuh-LAHS-truht-uhs   fə'lastrətəs

Philyra
   mother of Chiron by Cronus   fil-Ī-ruh   fil'airə

Phineas
   pers. name   FIN-ē-uhs   'finiːəs

Phineus
   uncle of Andromeda; king of   FIN-ē-uhs   'finiːəs
      Thrace

pHisoDerm
   tdmk for a medicated soap   FĪ-suh-DUHRM, FĪ-zuh-DUHRM   'faisə,dəʳm, 'faizə,dəʳm

Phix
   the Sphinx   FIKS   'fiks

Phlegethon
   river of Hades   FLEG-uh-THAHN   'flegə,θan

Phlias
   Argonaut   FLĒ-uhs   'fliːəs

Phlox
   flower   FLAHKS   'flaks

Phnom Penh
   city, Cambodia   (puh-)NAHM PEN   (pə)'nam 'pen

Phobos
   "Fear," son of Ares; satellite of   FŌ-BŌS, FŌ-buhs   'foː,boːs, 'foːbəs
      Mars

Phocaea
   ancient city, Asia Minor   fō-SĒ-uh   foː'siːə

Phocas
   pers. name, Latin   FŌ-kuhs   'foːkəs

Foreign Sounds: ue: *Fr.* **rue**, *Ger.* **füllen**   uh(r): *Fr.* **boeuf**, *Ger.* **Höhle**   <u>kh</u>: *Ger.* **ich**, *Scot.* **loch**   ḡ: *Sp.* **amigo** <u>v</u>: *Sp.* **hablar**
hl: *Welsh* **Llanelli**.   CAPITALS: primary stress.   SMALL CAPS: secondary stress.   ⓢ: U.S. pron.   ⓔ: British pron.

Phocis [Fokis]
  ancient district, dept., Greece   FŌ-suhs   'foːsəs
Phocus
  father of Callirhoe   FŌ-kuhs   'foːkəs
Phoebe
  Titaness in Greek myth; songbird; FĒ-bē   'fiːbiˑ
  satellite of Saturn; pers. name
Phoebus
  epithet of Apollo; pers. name   FĒ-buhs   'fiːbəs
Phoenice
  ancient city, Epirus   fi-NĪ-sē   fi'nɑisiˑ
Phoenicia
  ancient country, Syria   fi-NISH-(ē-)uh, fi-NĒ-sh(ē-)uh   fi'niʃ(iː)ə, fi'niːʃ(iː)ə
Phoenician
  lang., native of Phoenicia   fi-NISH-(ē-)uhn, fi-NĒ-sh(ē-)uhn   fi'niʃ(iː)ən, fi'niːʃ(iː)ən
Phoenicids
  meteor shower   FĒ-nuh-sidz   'fiːnəsidz
Phoenix
  city, AZ; mythical bird;   FĒ-niks   'fiːniks
  companion of Achilles;
  eponymous founder of
  Phoenicia; constellation
Pholidota
  pangolins   FAHL-uh-DŌT-uh   ˌfɑlə'doːtə
Pholus
  centaur, host of Heracles   FŌ-luhs   'foːləs
Phorcys
  Greek sea god, husband of Ceto   FAWR-kuhs   'fɔːʳkəs
Phosphorus
  morning star personified in Greek FAHS-f(uh-)ruhs   'fɑsf(ə)rəs
  myth; element
Photinianism
  Christian heresy   fō-TIN-ē-uh-NIZ-uhm   foː'tiniːəˌnizəm
Phraortes
  king of Media   frā-AWRT-ēz   freː'ɔːʳtiːz
Phra [Re]
  Egyptian sun god   PRAH, FRAH   'prɑ, 'frɑ
Phratry
  Greek "fraternal" group   FRĀ-trē   'freːtriˑ
Phrixus
  brother of Helle   FRIK-suhs   'friksəs
Phrygia
  ancient country, Asia Minor   FRIJ-(ē-)uh   'fridʒ(iː)ə
Phrygian
  pert. to Phrygia; musical mode   FRIJ-ē-uhn   'fridʒiːən
Phrygius
  king of Miletus   FRIJ-ē-uhs   'fridʒiːəs
Phthah
  see Ptah
Phthiotis, Fthiótis
  dept, Greece   thī-ŌT-uhs   θai'oːtəs
Phuket
  island near Thailand   PŌŌ-KET   ˌpuː'ket
Phyfe
  Duncan, US cabinetmaker   FĪF   'faif

Key (col. 2): a: fad ā: fade ah: father ar: Mary aw: law e: fed ē: feed er: merry i: hid ī: hide ō: coat ōō: boot
oi: boy ow: now u: put uh: above uhr: bird ch: chop ng: ring sh: show th: thick th: this zh: measure

Phylas
   opponent of Heracles   FĪ-luhs   ˈfailəs
Phyle
   Greek tribe   FĪ-lē   ˈfailiˑ
Phyleus
   son of Augeas   FĪ-lē-uhs, FĪ-L͞O͞OS   ˈfailiːəs, ˈfaiˌluːs
Phyllis
   pers. name   FIL-uhs   ˈfiləs
Phylloxera vastatrix
   grapevine pest   fī-LAHK-suh-ruh VAS-tuh-TRIKS   faiˈlaksərə ˈvæstəˌtriks
Pia
   pers. name (P. Zadora)   PĒ-uh   ˈpiːə
Piacenza
   prov, Italy   pyah-CHEN(T)-suh, -sah   pjaˈtʃen(t)sə, -sa
Piaf
   Edith, French singer   PYAHF, Ⓢ PĒ-AHF   pjaːf, Ⓢ ˈpiːˌaf
Piaget
   Jean, Swiss psychologist   pyah-ZHĀ   pjaˈʒeː
Piagetian
   pert. to theories of Jean Piaget   PĒ-uh-ZHĀ-uhn   ˌpiːəˈʒeːən
Piazza Venezia
   central square, Rome, Italy   pē-AHT-suh vuh-NET-sē-uh   piːˈatsə vəˈnetsiːə
Piazzi
   1. pers. name   pē-AZ-ē   piːˈæziˑ
   2. Italian   PYAHT-tsē   ˈpjattsiː
Pibroch
   see Piobaireachd
Picard
   Jean, French astronomer   pē-KAHR   piːkaːr
Picardie
   prov, France   pē-kahr-DĒ   piːkaːrdiː
Picardy
   prov, France   PIK-uhr-dē   ˈpikəʳdiˑ
Picasso
   Pablo, Spanish artist   pi-KAHS-ō, puh-KAS-ō   piˈkasoː, pəˈkæsoː
Picayune Rancheria
   Indian reservation, US   PIK-ē-(Y)O͞ON RAN-chuh-RĒ-uh, PIK-uh-Y͞O͞ON   ˌpikiːˈ(j)uːn ˌræntʃəˈriːə, ˌpikəˈjuːn
Piccadilly Circus
   landmark, London, England   PIK-uh-DIL-ē SUHR-kuhs   ˌpikəˌdiliˑ ˈsəʳkəs
Piccard
   Auguste, Swiss physicist   pē-KAHR   piːkaːr
Piccolo
   musical instrument   PIK-uh-LŌ   ˈpikəˌloː
Picenum
   ancient Roman province   pī-SĒ-nuhm   paiˈsiːnəm
Pichincha
   volcano, province, Ecuador   pē-CHĒN-chah, Ⓢ puh-CHIN-chuh   piːˈtʃiːntʃa, Ⓢ pəˈtʃintʃə
Pickaway
   county, OH   PIK-uh-WĀ   ˈpikəˌweː
Pickett
   George E., Confederate general   PIK-uht   ˈpikət
Pickwick
   Samuel, Dickens character   PIK-wik   ˈpikwik

Foreign Sounds: ue: *Fr.* **rue**, *Ger.* **füllen**   uh(r): *Fr.* **boeuf**, *Ger.* **Höhle**   <u>kh</u>: *Ger.* i**ch**, *Scot.* lo**ch**   ḡ: *Sp.* ami**g**o   <u>v</u>: *Sp.* ha**b**lar
hl: *Welsh* **Ll**anelli.   CAPITALS: primary stress.   SMALL CAPS: secondary stress.   Ⓢ: U.S. pron.   Ⓛ: British pron.

Pickwickian
   pert. to Pickwick   pik-WIK-ē-uhn   pik'wikiːən

Pico
   volcano, Azores   PĒ-kō   'piːkoː

Pict
   ancient people, northern Britain   PIKT   'pikt

Pictish
   pert. to the Picts; *lang. of the Picts*   PIK-tish   'piktiʃ

Pictor
   constellation   PIK-tuhr   'piktəʳ

Piculet
   woodpecker   PIK-yuh-LUHT   'pikjə,lət

Picuris Pueblo
   Indian reservation, US   pi-KYUR-uhs pōō-EB-lō, PWEB-lō,   pi'kjuʳəs puː'ebloː, 'pwebloː,
                                pyōō-EB-lō   pju:'ebloː

Picus
   legendary 1st king of Italy   PĒ-kuhs, PĪ-kuhs   'piːkəs, 'paikəs

Piebald
   horse   PĪ-BAWLD   'pai,bɔːld

Piedmont
   plateau region, US; region, Italy   PĒD-MAHNT   'piːd,mant

Piedmontese
   pert. to the Piedmont, *Italy*   PĒD-muhn-TĒZ, PĒD-mahn-TĒZ, -TĒS   ,piːdmən'tiːz, ,piːdmɑn'tiːz,
                                                         -'tiːs

Pied Piper
   German legendary character   PĪD PĪ-puhr   ,paid 'paipəʳ

Piegan
   N. American people   pē-GAN   piː'gæn

Pie Jesu
   hymn   PĒ-Ā YĀ-zōō, YĀ-sōō   ,piː,eː 'jeːzuː, 'jeːsuː

Piels
   US beer   PĒLZ   'piːlz

Piemonte [Piedmont]
   region, Italy   pyā-MAWN-tā   pjeː'mɔnteː

Pier
   1. pers. name, Danish   PIR   'pir
   2. Italian   PYER   'pjer

Pierce
   Franklin, *14th US president*   PIRS   'piʳs

Piercy
   Marge, *US writer*   PIR-sē   'piʳsiˑ

Pierfrancesco
   pers. name, Italian   PYER-frahn-CHĀS-kō   ,pjerfrɑn'tʃeːskoː

Piería
   dept, Greece   pī-IR-ē-uh   pai'iriːə

Pierian
   pert. to the Muses   pī-IR-ē-uhn, pī-ER-ē-uhn   pai'iriːən, pai'eriːən

Pierides
   nine maidens changed to magpies   pē-ER-uhd-ĒZ   piː'erəd,iːz
     by Muses

Pierluigi
   pers. name, Italian   PYER-lōō-Ē-jē   ,pjerluː'iːdʒiː

Piero
   pers. name, Italian   PYĀ-rō   'pjeːroː

Key (col. 2):   a: fad ā: fade ah: father ar: **M**ary aw: **l**aw e: fed ē: feed er: **m**erry i: hid ī: hide ō: coat ōō: boot
oi: **b**oy ow: new u: put uh: above uhr: bird ch: **ch**op ng: ring sh: **sh**ow th: thick <u>th</u>: this zh: measure

Pierpont
  pers. name PIR-PAHNT 'pi^r‚pɑnt

Pierre
  1. city, SD PĒR 'piːʳ
  2. pers. name pē-ER, PIR piː'eʳ, 'piʳ
  3. Flemish PYER 'pjer
  4. French PYER pjer

Pierres Dorés
  wine region PYER daw-RĀ pjer dɔːreː

Pierrot
  French pantomine character pye-RŌ, Ⓢ PĒ-uh-RŌ pjeroː, Ⓢ 'piːə‚roː

Piers
  pers. name PIRZ 'piʳz

Piers Plowman
  Middle English poem, Langland PIRZ PLOW-muhn 'piʳz 'plɑumən

Piešťany
  town, Slovakia PYESH-tuh-nē 'pjeʃtəniˑ

Piet
  pers. name, Dutch PĒT 'piːt

Pietà
  Mary mourning the dead Christ, PĒ-Ā-TAH, PYĀ-TAH ‚piː‚eː'tɑ, ‚pjeː'tɑ
    esp. Michelangelo's sculpture

Pietas
  Roman sense of duty PĒ-uh-TAHS 'piːə‚tɑs

Pieter
  pers. name, Dutch PĒ-ter 'piːter

Pietermaritzburg
  town, S. Africa PĒT-uhr-MAR-uhts-BUHRG ‚piːṭəʳ'mærəts‚bəʳg

Pietro
  pers. name, Italian PYE-trō 'pjetroː

Pigalle
  square in Paris, France pē-GAHL piːgɑːl

Pigmy
  see Pygmy

Pignola
  pine nut pēn-YŌ-luh piːn'joːlə

Pila
  lang., Benin PĒ-luh 'piːlə

Pila-pila
  lang., Benin PĒ-luh-PĒ-luh ‚piːlə'piːlə

Pilarczyk
  Daniel, archbishop of Cincinnati puh-LAHR-chik pə'lɑʳtʃik

Pilate
  Pontius, Roman procurator of PĪ-luht 'pɑilət
    Judea

Pilatus
  mtn. peak, Swiss Alps pē-LAH-TUS, Ⓢ puh-LAHT-uhs piː'lɑː‚tus, Ⓢ pə'lɑṭəs

Pilcomayo
  river, S. America PIL-kuh-MĪ-ō ‚pilkə'mɑioː

Pilgrim
  English Puritan settler in MA PIL-gruhm 'pilgrəm

Pilipino [Tagalog]
  lang., Philippine Islands PIL-uh-PĒ-nō ‚pilə'piːnoː

Pillsbury
  US food products co. PILZ-BER-ē, PILZ-b(uh-)rē 'pilz‚beriˑ, 'pilzb(ə)riˑ

Foreign Sounds: ue: *Fr.* **rue,** *Ger.* **füllen** uh(r): *Fr.* **boeuf,** *Ger.* **Höhle** <u>kh</u>: *Ger.* i<u>ch</u>, *Scot.* lo<u>ch</u> ḡ: *Sp.* ami**g**o ṿ: *Sp.* ha**b**lar
hl: *Welsh* **Llanelli.** CAPITALS: primary stress. SMALL CAPS: secondary stress. Ⓢ: U.S. pron. Ⓛ: British pron.

Pilobolus
US dance troupe   pi-LAHB-uh-luhs   pi'labələs

Pilsen
1. city, Czech republic   PIL-zuhn   'pilzən
2. Peruvian beer   PIL-suhn, PIL-zuhn   'pilsən, 'pilzən

Pilsner Urquell
Czech beer   PILZ-nuhr URK-vel   'pilznər 'urkvel

Piłsudski
Jósef, Polish political leader   pēl-SŌŌT-skē   piːɫ'suːtskiː

Piltdown
site of fraudulent early human bone fragments, England   PILT-DOWN   'pilt,daun

Pilumnus
Roman protector of newborn babies   puh-LUHM-nuhs   pə'ləmnəs

Pima
county, AZ; N. American people   PĒ-muh   'piːmə

Pima-Papago
lang., people, US, Mexico   PĒ-muh-PAHP-uh-GŌ, -PAP-uh-GŌ   'piːmə'papə,goː, -'pæpə,goː

Pimento
allspice   puh-MENT-ō   pə'mentoː

Pimiento
vegetable   puh-MENT-ō, puhm-YENT-ō   pə'mentoː, pəm'jentoː

Pimlico
district, London; race course, MD   PIM-li-KŌ   'pimli,koː

Pimpernel
plant   PIM-puhr-NEL, PIM-puhr-nuhl   'pimpəʳ,nel, 'pimpəʳnəl

Piña Colada
alcoholic drink   PĒN-yuh kuh-LAHD-uh   'piːnjə kə'ladə

Pinal
county, AZ   puh-NAL   pə'næl

Pinchas
pers. name   PING-kuhs, PIN-khuhs   'piŋkəs, 'pinxəs

Pindar
Greek lyric poet   PIN-duhr, PIN-DAHR   'pindəʳ, 'pin,daʳ

Pindaric
pert. to the style of Pindar   pin-DAR-ik, pin-DAHR-ik   pin'dærik, pin'darik

Pindus
mtn. range, Greece; son of Macedon   PIN-duhs   'pindəs

Pinellas
county, FL   pī-NEL-uhs   pai'neləs

Pinero
Sir Arthur W., English playwright, actor   puh-NIR-ō, puh-NER-ō   pə'niroː, pə'neroː

Pine Siskin
songbird   PĪN SIS-kuhn   'pain 'siskən

Piniella
Louis Victor, US baseball player   pin-EL-uh   pin'elə

Pinkham
pers. name   PING-kuhm   'piŋkəm

Pinkiang
former name of Harbin   BIN-jē-AHNG, BING-jē-AHNG   'bindʒiː'aŋ, 'biŋdʒiː'aŋ

Pinkus
German beer   PING-kuhs   'piŋkəs

Key (col. 2):   a: fad   ā: fade   ah: father   ar: Mary   aw: law   e: fed   ē: feed   er: merry   i: hid   ī: hide   ō: coat   ōō: boot
oi: boy   ow: now   u: put   uh: above   uhr: bird   ch: chop   ng: ring   sh: show   th: thick   th̲: this   zh: measure

Pinnipedia
   seals & walruses   PIN-uh-PĒD-ē-uh   ˌpinə'piːdiːə

Pinocchio
   fairy tale wooden puppet   puh-NŌ-kē-ō   pə'noːkiːˌoː

Pinochet Ugarte
   Augusto, president, Chile   pē-nō-CHET o͞o-ĜAHR-tä   piːnoː'tʃet uːˈɣarteː

Pinochle
   game   PĒ-NUHK-uhl   'piːˌnəkəl

Piñon, Pinyon
   pine nut   PIN-YŌN, pin-YŌN, PIN-YAHN,   'pinˌjoːn, pin'joːn, 'pinˌjan,
                           PIN-yuhn   'pinjən

Piñon jay
   bird   PIN-YŌN JĀ, PIN-YAHN, PIN-yuhn   'pinˌjoːn 'dʒeː, 'pinˌjan,
                                              'pinjən

Pinot
   wine; pers. name, French   pē-NŌ   piːnoː

Pinot Noir
   wine variety   pē-nō NWAHR   piːnoː nwaːr

Pinta
   one of Columbus' ships   PĒN-tah, ⓢ PINT-uh, PIN-tuh   'piːnta, ⓢ 'pint-ə, 'pin-tə

Pinter
   Harold, British playwright   PINT-uhr   'pintəʳ

Pinteresque
   pert. to Pinter or his style   PINT-uh-RESK   ˌpintə'resk

Pinyin
   transliteration system for Chinese   PIN-YIN   'pin'jin

Pinza
   Ezio, Italian singer   PĒN-zuh   'piˈnzə

Pinzgauer
   Austrian horse breed   PIN(T)S-GOWR   'pin(t)sˌgauʳ

Piobaireachd, Pibroch
   style of Scottish bagpipe music   PĒ-BRAHKH, -BRAWKH   'piːˌbrax, -ˌbrɔːx

Piotr
   pers. name, Polish, Russian   PYAW-tuhr   'pjɔːtər

Piper
   pers. name   PĪ-puhr   'paipəʳ

Pippa
   pers. name   PIP-uh   'pipə

Piqua
   city, OH   PIK-wā, PIK-wuh   'pikweː, 'pikwə

Piquet
   game   pē-KĀ   pi'keː

Piracicaba
   town, Brazil   PIR-uh-si-KAHB-uh   ˌpirəsi'kabə

Piraeus, Peiraeus
   seaport, Greece   pī-RĒ-uhs, pi-RĀ-uhs   pai'riːəs, pi'reːəs

Piraiévs [Piraeus]
   port, Greece   PĒ-re-EFS   ˌpiːre'efs

Pirandello
   Luigi, Italian author (Nobel 1934)   PIR-uhn-DEL-ō   ˌpirən'deloː

Piranesi
   Giambattista, Italian architect,   PIR-uh-NĀ-zē   ˌpirə'neːziˈ
     artist

Foreign Sounds: ue: *Fr.* **rue**, *Ger.* **füllen** uh(r): *Fr.* **boeuf**, *Ger.* **Höhle** kh: *Ger.* **ich**, *Scot.* **loch** ĝ: *Sp.* amigo ɣ: *Sp.* hablar
hl: *Welsh* **Llanelli**. CAPITALS: primary stress. SMALL CAPS: secondary stress. ⓢ: U.S. pron. ⓣ: British pron.

Pire		
Dominique Georges, *Belgian priest (Nobel 1958)*	PIR	pir
Pirene		
mother of Leches and Cenchrias	pī-RĒ-nē	pɑi'riːniˑ
Pirithous		
friend of Theseus	pī-RITH-o͞os, PIR-uh-THO͞OS	pɑi'riθuːs, 'pirəˌθuːs
Piro		
lang., Peru; lang., US & Mexico	PIR-ō	'piroː
Pisa		
prov & town, Italy	PĒ-sah, [S] PĒ-zuh	'piːsɑ, [S] 'piːzə
Piscataquis		
county, ME	pis-KAT-uh-kwis	pis'kætəkwis
Piscean		
pert. to the constellation Pisces	PĪ-sē-uhn, PIS-ē-uhn, PIS-kē-uhn	'pɑisiːən, 'pisiːən, 'piskiːən
Pisces		
constellation, sign of the zodiac	PĪ-SĒZ	'pɑiˌsiːz
Piscis Austrinus		
constellation	PĪ-suhs aw-STRĪ-nuhs	'pɑisəs ɔː'strɑinəs
Pisco		
seaport, Peru	PĒ-skō	'piːskoː
Piscopo		
Joseph Charles, *US actor, comedian*	PIS-kuh-pō	'piskəpoː
Pisgah		
Mount, *NY; mtn. ridge, Jordan*	PIZ-guh	'pizgə
Pisidia		
ancient Roman province, Asia Minor	pī-SID-ē-uh	pɑi'sidiːə
Pisistratus		
see Peisistratus		
Piso		
L. Calpurnius, *Roman politician*	PĪ-sō	'pɑisoː
Pissarro		
Camille, *French painter*	pē-sah-RŌ, [S] puh-SAHR-ō	piːsɑːroː, [S] pə'sɑroː
Pitcairn		
Island, *Pacific*	PIT-KARN, PIT-KERN	'pitˌkæ^{r}n, 'pitˌke^{r}n
Pitchblende		
uraninite	PICH-BLEND	'pitʃˌblend
Pithecanthropus		
hominid genus	PITH-i-KAN-thruh-puhs, PITH-i-KAN-THRŌ-puhs	ˌpiθi'kænθrəpəs, ˌpiθiˌkæn'θroːpəs
Pitlochry		
town, Scotland	pit-LAH<u>KH</u>-rē	pit'lɑxriˑ
Pitney Bowes		
US manufacturing co.	PIT-nē BŌZ	ˌpitniˑ 'boːz
Pitons, The		
mts., Caribbean	pē-TAW^{n}	piː'tɔ̃
Pitot tube		
flow measuring device	PĒ-TŌ, pē-TŌ	'piːˌtoː, piː'toː
Pitri		
Hindu legendary figure	PI-trē	'pitriˑ
Pitta		
songbird	PIT-uh	'pitə

Key (col. 2): a: **fad** ā: **fade** ah: **father** ar: **Mary** aw: **law** e: **fed** ē: **feed** er: **merry** i: **hid** ī: **hide** ō: **coat** o͞o: **boot** oi: **boy** ow: **now** u: **put** uh: **above** uhr: **bird** ch: **chop** ng: **ring** sh: **show** th: **thick** <u>th</u>: **this** zh: **measure**

Pitti		
gallery, Florence, Italy	PIT-ē	'pitiˑ
Pitts		
Zasu, *entertainer; aerobatic airplane marque*	PITS	'pits
Pittsburgh		
city, PA; county, OK	PITS-BUHRG	'pits,bəʳg
Pius		
name of 12 popes	PĪ-uhs	'pɑiəs
Piute		
county, UT	pī-(Y)O͞OT	pɑi'(j)uːt
Pizarro		
Francisco, *Spanish conquistador*	puh-ZAHR-ō	pə'zɑʳoː
Piz Bernina		
see Bernina, Piz		
Placentia		
city, CA	pluh-SEN-ch(ē-)uh	plə'sentʃ(iː)ə
Placid, Lake		
lake, village, NY	lāk PLAS-uhd	leːk 'plæsəd
Placide		
pers. name, French	plah-SĒD	plɑːsiːd
Plácido		
pers. name, Spanish	PLAHS-ē-t͟hō, PLAHTH-ē-t͟hō, [$] PLAHS-uh-dō	'plɑsiːðoː, 'plɑθiːðoː, [$] 'plɑsədoː
Plaid Cymru		
Welsh nationalist political party, United Kingdom	PLĪD KUHM-rē	,plɑid 'kəmriˑ
Plaistow		
1. town, NH	PLAS-tō	'plæstoː
2. various towns, England	PLĀ-stō, PLAS-tō, PLAHS-tō	'pleːstoː, 'plæstoː, 'plɑːstoː
Planck		
Max Karl Ernst, *German physicist (Nobel 1918)*	PLAHNGK	'plɑŋk
Planck's		
mathematical constant	PLANGKS, PLAHNGKS	'plæŋks, 'plɑŋks
Plano		
town, TX	PLĀ-nō	'pleːnoː
Plantagenet		
English ruling dynasty	plan-TAJ-uh-nuht	plæn'tædʒənət
Plaquemines		
parish, LA	PLAK-(uh-)muhnz	'plæk(ə)mənz
Plassey		
village, India	PLAS-ē	'plæsiˑ
Plasticine		
tdmk for a synthetic modeling material	PLAS-tuh-SĒN	'plæstə,siːn
Plata, La		
1. prov, Argentina	lah PLAHT-ah	lɑ 'plɑtɑ
2. see La Plata		
Plata, Río de la		
estuary, S. America	RĒ-ō t͟hā lah PLAHT-ah	,riːoː ðeː lɑ 'plɑtɑ
Plataea		
ancient city, Greece	pluh-TĒ-uh	plə'tiːə
Plate [Plata, Río de la]		
river, South America	PLĀT	'pleːt

Foreign Sounds: ue: *Fr.* **rue**, *Ger.* **fü**llen uh(r): *Fr.* b**oeu**f, *Ger.* H**ö**hle k͟h: *Ger.* i**ch**, *Scot.* lo**ch** ḡ: *Sp.* ami**g**o v̲: *Sp.* ha**b**lar hl: *Welsh* **Ll**ane**ll**i. CAPITALS: primary stress. SMALL CAPS: secondary stress. [$]: U.S. pron. [£]: British pron.

Plateau
　　N. American people　　　　　pla-TŌ　　　　　　　　　plæ'toː

Plateosaurus
　　dinosaur　　　　　　　　　　PLAT-ē-uh-SAWR-uhs　　　,plætiːə'sɔːrəs

Plath
　　Sylvia, *US poet*　　　　　　　PLATH　　　　　　　　　　'plæθ

platinum
　　element　　　　　　　　　　PLAT-nuhm, PLAT-n-uhm　　'plætnəm, 'plætn̩əm

Plato
　　Greek philosopher　　　　　　PLĀT-ō　　　　　　　　　　'pleːtoː

Platonic
　　pert. to Plato　　　　　　　　pluh-TAHN-ik, plā-TAHN-ik　plə'tanik, pleː'tanik

Platonism
　　philosophy of Plato　　　　　PLĀT-n-IZ-uhm　　　　　　'pleːtn̩,izəm

Plattdeutsch
　　Low German dialects　　　　PLAHT-DOICH　　　　　　　'plat,dɔitʃ

Platte
　　rivers, US　　　　　　　　　PLAT　　　　　　　　　　　'plæt

Plautus
　　Roman playwright　　　　　　PLAWT-uhs　　　　　　　　'plɔːţəs

Pleasence
　　Donald, *British actor*　　　　PLEZ-uhn(t)s　　　　　　　'plezən(t)s

Plebeians
　　Roman lower class　　　　　pluh-BĒ-uhnz, plē-BĒ-uhnz　plə'biːənz, pliː'biːənz

Pleiades
　　daughters of Atlas; star cluster in　PLĒ-uh-DĒZ, PLĀ-, Ⓔ PLĪ-　'pliːə,diːz, 'pleː-, Ⓔ 'plai-
　　Taurus

Pleiku
　　city, Vietnam　　　　　　　plā-k̄oo　　　　　　　　　　pleːkuː

Pleisthenes
　　son of Pelops　　　　　　　PLĪS-thuh-NĒZ　　　　　　'plaisθə,niːz

Pleistocene
　　geologic epoch　　　　　　PLĪ-stuh-SĒN　　　　　　　'plaistə,siːn

Plekhanov
　　Georgi, *Russian political leader*　pluh-KAHN-uhf, -AWF, -AWV　plə'kanəf, -,ɔːf, -,ɔːv

Plexiglas
　　tdmk for a thermoplastic polymer　PLEK-sē-GLAS　　　　'pleksiˑ,glæs

Plimpton
　　George, *US author, editor*　　PLIM(P)-tuhn　　　　　　'plim(p)tən

Pliny
　　name of two Roman authors　PLIN-ē　　　　　　　　　　'pliniˑ

Pliocene
　　geologic epoch　　　　　　PLĪ-uh-SĒN　　　　　　　　'plaiə,siːn

Plisetskaya
　　Maya, *ballet dancer, USSR*　pli-SET-skuh-yuh　　　　　pli'setskəjə

Ploies
　　city, Romania　　　　　　　plaw-YESHT(-ē)　　　　　　plɔˑ'jeʃt(iˑ)

Plotinus
　　Roman philosopher　　　　　plō-TĪ-nuhs　　　　　　　plɔˑ'tainəs

Plotius
　　Roman name　　　　　　　PLŌT-ē-uhs　　　　　　　　'plɔːţiːəs

Plotz-Brau
　　German beer　　　　　　　PLAWTS-BROW　　　　　　'plɔːts,brau

Key (col. 2): a: fad ā: fade ah: father ar: Mary aw: law e: fed ē: feed er: merry i: hid ī: hide ō: coat o̅o̅: boot
oi: boy ow: now u: put uh: above uhr: bird ch: chop ng: ring sh: show th: thick <u>th</u>: this zh: measure

Plough
   star cluster in Great Bear   PLOW   'plɑu
   constellation; US
   pharmaceutical co.

Plovdiv
   prov, Bulgaria   PLAWV-DIF, PLAWV-DIV   'plɔːv,dif, 'plɔːv,div

Plumas
   county, CA   PLOO-muhs   'pluːməs

Plumbago
   flower   PLUHM-BĀ-gō   ,pləm'beːgoː

Plumbeous gnatcatcher
   gnatcatcher   PLUHM-bē-uhs   'pləmbiːəs

Plummer
   Christopher, *Canadian actor*   PLUHM-uhr   'pləmər

Plunkett
   James William, Jr., *US football*   PLUHNG-kuht   'pləŋkət
   player

Plutarch
   Greek biographer   PLOO-TAHRK   'pluː,tɑʳk

Pluto
   Roman god of the Underworld;   PLUT-ō   'pluʈoː
   planet

Pluton
   title of Hades, god of the   PLOO-TAHN   'pluː,tɑn
   Underworld

Plutonian
   pert. to Pluto *or the lower world*   ploo-TŌ-nē-uhn   pluː'toːniːən

plutonium
   element   ploo-TŌ-nē-uhm   pluː'toːniːəm

Plutus
   personification of wealth   PLOOT-uhs   'pluːʈəs

Pluviôse
   month, French Revolutionary   pluev-YŌZ   plyːvjoːz
   calendar

Plymouth
   port, England; US pl. name; US PLIM-uhth   'pliməθ
   car make

Pnyx
   hill, Athens, Greece   NIKS   'niks

Po
   river, Italy   PŌ   'poː

Poarch Band
   N. American people (Creek)   PŌRCH, PAWRCH   'poːʳtʃ, 'pɔːʳtʃ

Pobeda
   peak between Kirghiz and China puh-B(Y)ED-uh   pə'b(j)edə

Pocahontas
   American Indian princess; county, PŌ-kuh-HAHNT-uhs, -HUHNT-uhs ,poːkə'hɑntəs, -'həntəs
   IA, WV

Poconos
   mtns., PA   PŌ-kuh-NŌZ   'poːkə,noːz

Podgorica
   former name for Titograd   PAHD-guh-RĒT-suh   'pɑdgə,riːtsə

Podgorny
   Nikolai, *president, USSR*   pahd-GAWR-nē   pɑd'gɔːʳniˑ

Podocarpus
  plant   PAHD-uh-KAHR-puhs   ˌpadə'kɑ^rpəs

Podokesaurus
  dinosaur   puh-DŌ-kuh-SAWR-uhs   pəˌdoːkə'sɔːrəs

Podunk
  village, CT   PŌ-DUHNGK   'poːˌdəŋk

Poe
  Edgar A., *US author*   PŌ   'poː

Po Hai, Bohai [Chihli]
  gulf, Yellow Sea   BŌ HĪ   'boː 'hai

Pohl
  Frederick, *US writer*   PŌL   'poːl

Pohlman
  Harry C., Field, *ballpark, Beloit,*   PŌL-muhn   'poːlmən
  WI

Poinciana
  festival, Miami, FL   POIN-sē-AN-uh, P(W)AHN-   ˌpɔinsiː'ænə, ˌp(w)ɑn-

Poinciano
  pers. name, Spanish   poin-SYAHN-ō, -THYAHN-ō   pɔin'sjɑnoː, -'θjɑnoː

Poinsett
  county, AR   POIN-SET, POIN-sit   'pɔinˌset, 'pɔinsit

Poinsettia
  plant   poin-SET-ē-uh, poin-SET-uh   pɔin'setiːə, pɔin'setə

Pointe Coupée
  parish, LA   POINT ko͞o-PĒ   'pɔint kuː'piː

Point Pelee
  National Park, *Ontario*   point PĒ-lē   pɔint 'piːliː

Poire Williams
  brand of pear liqueur   PWAHR WIL-yuhmz   'pwɑ^r 'wiljəmz

Poirot
  Hercule, *Agatha Christie's*   pwah-RŌ   pwɑ'roː
  detective

Poisson
  S. D., *French mathematician,*   pwah-SAWⁿ Ⓢ pwah-SŌN,   pwɑːsɔ̃ Ⓢ pwa'soːn,
  physicist   pwah-SAHN   pwa'sɑn

Poitier
  Sidney, *US actor*   pwaht-YĀ, PWAHT-ē-ā   pwɑt'jeː, 'pwaṭiːˌeː

Poitiers
  city, France   pwah-TYĀ   pwaːtjeː

Poitou-Charentes
  region, France   pwah-to͞o-shah-RAHⁿT   pwaːtuːʃaːrã̃t

Pojoaque Pueblo
  Indian reservation, US   pō-(H)WAHK-ē po͞o-EB-lō, PWEB-lō,   poː'(h)waki· puː'ebloː,
                                         pyo͞o-EB-lō   'pwebloː, pju·'ebloː

Pokhara
  valley, Nepal   PŌ-kuh-ruh   'poːkərə

Pokomam [Pokoman]
  lang., Cen. America   PŌ-kō-MAHM   ˌpoːkoː'mam

Pokoman
  lang., Cen. America   PŌ-kō-MAHN   ˌpoːkoː'man

Pokomo
  lang., people, Africa   puh-KŌ-mō   pə'koːmoː

Pokonchi
  lang., people, Guatemala   puh-KAHN-chē   pə'kantʃi·

Key (col. 2): a: fad ā: fade ah: father ar: **Mary** aw: **law** e: fed ē: feed er: **merry** i: hid ī: hide ō: coat o͞o: boot
oi: boy ow: **now** u: put uh: **above** uhr: **bird** ch: **chop** ng: **ring** sh: **show** th: **thick** <u>th</u>: **this** zh: measure

Polabian
 ancient Slavic people of Germany; pō-LÃ-bē-uhn, puh-   poːˈleːbiːən, pə-
  extinct language

Poland
 republic, Europe   PŌ-luhnd   ˈpoːlənd

Polanski
 Roman, *US filmmaker*   puh-LAN-skē   pəˈlænskiˑ

Polanyi
 John C., *Canadian chemist (Nobel*   puh-LAN-yē   pəˈlænjiˑ
  1986)

Polari
 English argot of theater and circus   puh-LAHR-ē   pəˈlariˑ

Polaris
 1. star Alpha Ursae Minoris   puh-LAR-uhs, puh-LAHR-uhs   pəˈlærəs, pəˈlarəs
 2. submarine missile   puh-LAR-uhs   pəˈlærəs

Polaroid
 tdmk for an instant camera   PŌ-luh-ROID   ˈpoːlə,rɔid

Pole
 inhabitant of Poland   PŌL   ˈpoːl

Poleis
 plural of Polis   PŌ-LĪS   ˈpoːˌlais

Polemarch
 Athenian general   PAHL-uh-MAHRK   ˈpaləˌmaʳk

Polhymnia [Polyhymnia]
 muse of mime; street, New   puh-LIM-nē-uh   pəˈlimniːə
  Orleans

Policarpo
 pers. name, Spanish   pō-lē-KAHR-pō   poːliːˈkarpoː

Poli-Grip
 tdmk for a denture adhesive   PAHL-ē-GRIP   ˈpaliˑˌgrip

Polis
 Greek city-state   PŌ-luhs   ˈpoːləs

Polish
 lang., Poland   PŌ-lish   ˈpoːliʃ

Politburo
 Communist executive committee   PAHL-uht-BYUR-ō, PŌ-luht-BYUR-ō,   ˈpalətˌbjuroː, ˈpoːlətˌbjuroː,
            puh-LIT-BYUR-ō   pəˈlitˌbjuroː

Polk
 James K., *11th US president*   PŌK   ˈpoːk

Polka
 dance   PŌL-kuh, PŌ-kuh   ˈpoːlkə, ˈpoːkə

Pollack
 Sydney, *US film director*   PAHL-uhk   ˈpalək

Pollio
 pers. name, Latin   PAHL-ē-ō, PAHL-yō   ˈpaliːˌoː, ˈpaljoː

Pollock
 Jackson, *artist*   PAHL-uhk   ˈpalək

Pollux
 twin of Castor; star Beta   PAHL-uhks   ˈpaləks
  Geminorum

Polly
 pers. name   PAHL-ē   ˈpaliˑ

Pollyanna
 character, Eleanor Porter   PAHL-ē-AN-uh   ˌpaliːˈænə

Foreign Sounds: ue: *Fr.* **rue**, *Ger.* f**ü**llen uh(r): *Fr.* b**oeu**f, *Ger.* H**öh**le <u>kh</u>: *Ger.* i**ch**, *Scot.* lo**ch** g̃: *Sp.* ami**g**o v̲: *Sp.* ha**b**lar
hl: *Welsh* L**l**anelli. CAPITALS: primary stress. SMALL CAPS: secondary stress. Ⓢ: U.S. pron. Ⓑ: British pron.

Pollyannaish
  excessively optimistic, as   PAHL-ē-AN-uh-ISH   ˌpaliːænəˌiʃ
  Pollyanna
Polo
  Marco, *Italian explorer*   PŌ-lō   'poːloː
Polonaise
  dance; butter-crumb sauce   PAHL-uh-NĀZ, PŌ-luh-NĀZ   ˌpalə'neːz, ˌpoːlə'neːz
polonium
  element   puh-LŌ-nē-uhm   pə'loːniːəm
Polonius
  character in Hamlet, *Shakespeare*   puh-LŌ-nē-uhs, puh-LŌN-yuhs   pə'loːniːəs, pə'loːnjəs
Pol Pot
  Cambodian dictator   PAHL PAHT, PŌL PAHT   ˌpal 'pat, ˌpoːl 'pat
Poltava
  city, Ukraine   puhl-TAHV-uh   pəl'tavə
Polybius
  Greek historian   puh-LIB-ē-uhs   pə'libiːəs
Polybus
  king of Thebes in Egypt; foster   PAHL-uh-buhs   'paləbəs
  father of Oedipus
Polycarp
  1. Christian saint   PAHL-ē-KAHRP   'paliˌkaʳp
  2. pers. name, German   PŌ-lue-KAHRP   ˌpoːlyː'kaʳp
Polycarpe
  pers. name, French   paw-lē-KAHRP   poːliːkaːrp
Polycaste
  daughter of Nestor; mother of   PAHL-i-KAS-tē   ˌpali'kæstiˈ
  Penelope
Polyclitus, Polycleitus
  Greek sculptor   PAHL-i-KLĪT-uhs   ˌpali'klaiṭəs
Polycrates
  tyrant of Samos   puh-LIK-ruh-TĒZ   pə'likrəˌtiːz
Polycrite
  heroine of Naxos   PAHL-i-KRĪT-ē   ˌpali'kraiṭiˈ
Polydectes
  man who sent Perseus for head of   PAHL-uh-DEK-tēz   ˌpalə'dektiːz
  Medusa
Polydora
  daughter of Peleus   PAHL-uh-DŌR-uh, PAHL-uh-DAWR-uh   ˌpalə'doːrə, ˌpalə'dɔːrə
Polydore
  1. pers. name   PAHL-i-DAWR   'paliˌdɔːʳ
  2. French   paw-lē-DAWR   poːliːdɔːr
Polydorus
  Greek sculptor; son of Priam; son   PAHL-uh-DŌR-uhs,   ˌpalə'doːrəs, ˌpalə'dɔːrəs
  of Cadmus and Harmonia   PAHL-uh-DAWR-uhs
Polygnotus
  Greek painter   PAHL-ig-NŌT-uhs   ˌpalig'noːṭəs
Polyhymnia
  1. muse of mime   PAHL-ē-HIM-nē-uh   ˌpaliˈhimniːə
  2. street, New Orleans   puh-LIM-nē-uh   pə'limniːə
Polykarp
  pers. name   PAHL-ē-KAHRP   'paliˈkaʳp
Polymede
  mother of Jason   PAHL-uh-MĒD-ē   ˌpalə'miːdiˈ

Key (col. 2):   a: fad   ā: fade   ah: father   ar: Mary   aw: law   e: fed   ē: feed   er: merry   i: hid   ī: hide   ō: coat   ōō: boot
oi: boy   ow: now   u: put   uh: above   uhr: bird   ch: chop   ng: ring   sh: show   th: thick   th̲: this   zh: measure

Polymestor
  king of Thrace PAHL-uh-MES-tuhr ˌpalə'mestəʳ
Polymnus
  Dionysus's guide to the puh-LIM-nuhs pə'limnəs
  Underworld
Polynesia
  central Pacific islands PAHL-uh-NĒ-zhuh, -shuh ˌpalə'niːʒə, -ʃə
Polynesian
  pert. to Polynesia PAHL-uh-NĒ-zhuhn, -shuhn ˌpalə'niːʒən, -ʃən
Polynices
  son of Oedipus PAHL-uh-NĪ-sēz ˌpalə'naisiːz
Polyphemus
  Cyclops blinded by Odysseus; PAHL-i-FĒ-muhs ˌpali'fiːməs
  Argonaut
Polyphonte
  girl changed into night bird by PAHL-uh-FAHNT-ē ˌpalə'fantiˑ
  Ares
Polypody
  plant PAHL-ē-PŌD-ē 'paliˑˌpoːdiˑ
Polyxena
  daughter of Priam puh-LIK-suh-nuh pə'liksənə
Polyxenus
  son of Jason and Medea puh-LIK-suh-nuhs pə'liksənəs
Polyxo
  wife of Tlepolemus puh-LIK-sō pə'liksoː
Pomarine jaeger
  sea bird PAHM-uh-RĪN YĀ-guhr 'paməˌrain 'jeːgəʳ
Pomerania
  region, Europe PAHM-uh-RĀ-nē-uh, -RĀN-yuh ˌpamə'reːniːə, -'reːnjə
Pomeranian
  pert. to Pomerania; dog breed PAHM-uh-RĀ-nē-uhn ˌpamə'reːniːən
Pomerol
  French wine pawm-RAWL poːmrɔːl
Pomeroy
  pers. name PAHM-(uh-)ROI, PUHM-(uh-)ROI 'pam(ə)ˌrɔi, 'pəm(ə)ˌrɔi
Pommard
  red wine variety paw-MAHR poːmaːr
Pomo
  N. American people PŌ-mō 'poːmoː
Pomona
  Roman goddess of fruit; city, CA puh-MŌ-nuh pə'moːnə
Pomo-Patwin
  N. American people PŌ-mō-PAT-wuhn 'poːmoː'pætwən
Pompano Beach
  town, FL PAHM-puh-NŌ BĒCH, PUHM-puh-NŌ ˌpampə,noː 'biːtʃ,
    ˌpəmpə,noː
Pompei
  commune, Italy pahm-PĂ(-Ē) pam'peː(ˌiː)
Pompeian, Pompeiian
  pert. to Pompeii or its culture pahm-PĂ-uhn pam'peːən
Pompeii
  ancient city, Italy pahm-PĂ, pahm-PĂ-Ē pam'peː, pam'peːˌiː
Pompeius
  pers. name, Latin pahm-PĒ-uhs pam'piːəs

Foreign Sounds: ue: *Fr.* **rue**, *Ger.* **füllen** uh(r): *Fr.* **boeuf**, *Ger.* **Höhle** kh: *Ger.* **ich**, *Scot.* **loch** ğ: *Sp.* **amigo** v̱: *Sp.* **hablar**
hl: *Welsh* **Llanelli**. CAPITALS: primary stress. SMALL CAPS: secondary stress. ⑤: U.S. pron. ⑥: British pron.

Pompeo
  pers. name, Italian   pōm-PE-Ō   poːmˈpe-oː

Pompey
  Roman statesman   PAHM-pē   ˈpɑmpiˑ

Pompey, Sextus
  son of Pompey   SEK-stuhs PAHM-pē   ˈsekstəs ˈpɑmpiˑ

Pompidou
  Georges, president, France   pawⁿ-pē-DOO͞   pɔ̃piːduː

Pomponius
  pers. name, Latin   pahm-PŌ-nē-uhs   pɑmˈpoːniːəs

Ponapean
  lang., people, Micronesia   PŌ-nuh-PĀ-uhn, PAHN-uh-PĀ-uhn   ˌpoːnəˈpeːən, ˌpɑnəˈpeːən

Ponca
  city, NE; N. American people PAHNG-kuh   ˈpɑŋkə

Ponca City
  city, OK   PAHNG-kuh SIT-ē   ˌpɑŋkə ˈsiţiˑ

Ponce
  1. city, Puerto Rico   PAWN(T)-sā   ˈpɔːn(t)seː
  2. pers. name, French   PAWⁿS   pɔ̃s

Ponce de Leon
  Juan, Spanish explorer   PAHN(T)S duh LĒ-uhn, PAHN(T)-suh   ˌpɑn(t)s də ˈliːən, ˌpɑn(t)sə
                          dā lē-ŌN   deː liːˈoːn

Ponchielli
  Amilcare, Italian composer PAWNG-kē-EL-lē   ˌpɔːŋkiːˈelliˑ

Pondera
  county, MT   PAHN-duh-RĀ   ˌpɑndəˈreː

Pondicherry
  territory, India   PAHN-duh-CHER-ē,   ˌpɑndəˈtʃeriˑ, ˌpɑndəˈʃeriˑ
                         PAHN-duh-SHER-ē

Ponta Delgada
  port, Azores   PAHNT-uh del-GAHD-uh   ˌpɑntə delˈgɑdə

Pontchartrain
  lake, LA   PAHN-chuhr-TRĀN,   ˈpɑntʃəʳˌtreːn, ˌpɑntʃəʳˈtreːn
                         PAHN-chuhr-TRĂN

Pontefract
  town, England   PAHNT-uh-FRAKT, *locally also*   ˈpɑntəˌfrækt, *locally also*
                         PUHM-fruht   ˈpəmfrət

Pontiac
  city, MI, IL; N. American people; PAHNT-ē-AK   ˈpɑntiːˌæk
    US car make

Pontian
  pope   PAHN-sh(ē-)uhn   ˈpɑnʃ(iː)ən

Pontifex maximus
  Roman high priest   PAHNT-uh-FEKS MAK-suh-muhs   ˈpɑntəˌfeks ˈmæksəməs

Pontifices
  Roman priests   pahn-TIF-uh-SĒZ   pɑnˈtifə ˌsiːz

Pontine Marshes
  marshy area near Rome, now PAHN-TĪN MAHR-shuhz   ˌpɑnˌtain ˈmɑʳʃəz
    drained

Pontius
  pers. name, Latin   PAHN-chuhs, PUHN-chuhs   ˈpɑntʃəs, ˈpəntʃəs

Pontius Pilate
  biblical Roman procurator, Judea PAHN-chuhs PĪ-luht, PUHN-chuhs   ˌpɑntʃəs ˈpailət, ˌpəntʃəs

Pont Neuf
  bridge, Paris, France   pawⁿ NUH(R)F   pɔ̃ nœf

Key (col. 2): a: fad ā: fade ah: father ar: Mary aw: law e: fed ē: feed er: merry i: hid ī: hide ō: coat o͞o: boot
oi: boy ow: now u: put uh: above uhr: bird ch: chop ng: ring sh: show th: thick <u>th</u>: this zh: measure

Pontoise		
town, France	paw^{n}-TWAHZ	pɔ̃twaːz
Pontoppidan		
Henrik, *Danish author (Nobel 1917)*	pahn-TAHP-uh-DAHN	pɑn'tɑpəˌdɑːn
Pontotoc		
county, MS, OK	PAHNT-uh-TAHK	'pɑntəˌtɑk
Pontus		
ancient country, Asia Minor; personification of the sea	PAHN-tuhs, PAHNT-uhs	'pɑn-təs, 'pɑnt-əs
Pooh-Bah		
character in the Mikado, *Gilbert and Sullivan; a high official*	PO͞O-BAH	'puːˌbɑ
Poona, Pune		
city, India	PO͞O-nuh	'puːnə
Poospatuck		
N. American people	po͞o-SPAT-uhk	puː'spætək
Pop		
informal for father	PAHP	'pɑp
Popayán		
city, Columbia	PŌ-puh-YAHN	ˌpoːpə'jɑn
Popeye		
cartoon character	PAHP-Ī	'pɑpˌɑi
Popocatepetl		
volcano, Mexico	PŌ-puh-KAT-uh-PET-l	ˌpoːpəˌkæt̪ə'petl̩
Popoloca		
lang., people, Mexico	PŌ-puh-LŌ-kuh	ˌpoːpə'loːkə
Popoluca		
lang., people, Mexico	PŌ-puh-LUHK-uh, PŌ-puh-LO͞O-kuh	ˌpoːpə'ləkə, ˌpoːpə'luːkə
Popov		
vodka brand	PAHP-AWF, PAHP-AWV	'pɑpˌɔːf, 'pɑpˌɔːv
Poppa		
informal for father	PAHP-uh	'pɑpə
Poppaea		
Sabina, *2nd wife of Nero*	pahp-Ē-uh	pɑp'iːə
Populares		
Roman popular leaders	PAHP-yuh-LĀ-rēz	ˌpɑpjə'leːriːz
Poquoson		
county, VA	puh-KWAW-suhn	pə'kwɔːsən
Porcella		
Roman cognomen	pawr-SEL-uh	pɔː^{r}'selə
Porcius		
pers. name, Latin	PAWR-sh(ē-)uhs	'pɔː^{r}ʃ(iː)əs
Poretti		
Italian beer	pō-RET-tē	poː'rettiː
Porgy		
character in Porgy & Bess, *Gershwin*	PAWR-gē	'pɔː^{r}giˑ
Pori		
port, Finland	PAWR-ē	'pɔːriˑ
Porsche		
German car make	PAWR-shuh, PAWRSH	'pɔː^{r}ʃə, 'pɔː^{r}ʃ
Porsena, Lars		
see Lars Porsena		

Foreign Sounds: ue: *Fr.* **rue**, *Ger.* **füllen** uh(r): *Fr.* **boeuf**, *Ger.* **Höhle** kh: *Ger.* **ich**, *Scot.* **loch** g̃: *Sp.* **amigo** v̱: *Sp.* **hablar** hl: *Welsh* **Llanelli**. CAPITALS: primary stress. SMALL CAPS: secondary stress. [$]: U.S. pron. [£]: British pron.

Port-au-Prince
city, Haiti   pawr-tō-PREⁿS; Ⓢ PŌRT-ō-PRINS,   pɔːrtoːprẽs; Ⓢ ˌpoːʳtoːˈprins,
                          PAWRT-, -PRANS   ˌpɔːʳt-, -ˈpræns

Port-de-Paix
town, Haiti   PAWR-duh-PĀ   ˌpɔːʳdəˈpeː

Port du Salut
Trappist monastery, France;   pawr due sah-LUE, Ⓢ PAWR duh   pɔːr dyː saːlyː, Ⓢ ˌpoːʳ də
cheese   suhl-(Y)O͞O   səlˈ(j)uː

Porte, La
see La Porte

Porteño
Spanish for one who lives on the   pawr-TĂN-yō   pɔːʳˈteːnjoː
coast

Porter
pers. name   PŌRT-uhr, PAWRT-uhr   ˈpoːʳtəʳ, ˈpɔːʳtəʳ

Port Gentil
city, Gabon   pawr zhahⁿ-TĒ   pɔːr ʒãtiː

Port Harcourt
city, Nigeria   pōrt HAHR-kuhrt, pawrt   poːʳt ˈhaʳkəʳt, pɔːʳt

Porthos
character in The Three   pawr-TŌS, Ⓢ PAWR-THŌS   pɔːrtoːs, Ⓢ ˈpoːʳˌθoːs
Musketeers, *A. Dumas*

Portia
pers. name   PAWR-shuh   ˈpɔːʳʃə

Portland
US pl. name   PŌRT-luhnd, PAWRT-luhnd   ˈpoːʳtlənd, ˈpɔːʳtlənd

Portlaoighise
city, Ireland   pawrt-LĂ-uh-shuh, pawrt-LĒSH   pɔːʳtˈleːəʃə, pɔːʳtˈliːʃ

Port Louis
city, Mauritius   pōrt LO͞O-uhs, pawrt, LO͞O-ē, lu-Ē   poːʳt ˈluːəs, pɔːʳt, ˈluːiˈ, luˈiː

Port Moresby
city, New Guinea   pōrt MŌRZ-bē, pawrt MAWRZ-   poːʳt ˈmoːʳzbiˈ, pɔːʳt ˈmɔːʳz-

Port Natal
seaport, Brazil   PŌRT nah-TAHL, PAWRT   ˌpoːʳt naˈtɑl, ˌpɔːʳt

Porto [Oporto]
port city, Portugal   PŌR-to͞o   ˈpoːʳtuː

Pôrto Alegre
city, Brazil   PAWR-to͞o uh-LĂG-ruh, PŌR-to͞o   ˌpɔːʳtuː əˈleˈgrə, ˌpoːʳtuː

Port-of-Spain
city, Trinidad   PŌRT-uhv-SPĀN, PAWRT-   ˌpoːʳtəvˈspeːn, ˌpɔːʳt-

Porto-Novo
port city, Benin   PŌRT-ō-NŌ-vō, PAWRT-   ˌpoːʳtoːˈnoːvoː, ˌpɔːʳt-

Porto Rico
former name of Puerto Rico   PAWRT-uh RĒ-kō   ˌpɔːʳtə ˈriːkoː

Port Pirie
port, South Australia pōrt PIR-ē, pawrt   poːʳt ˈpiriˈ, pɔːʳt

Port Said
seaport, Egypt   PŌRT sah-ĒD, PAWRT, SĪD   ˌpoːʳt saˈiːd, ˌpɔːʳt, ˈsaid

Portsmouth
city, England; city, NH, OH, VA   PŌRT-smuhth, PAWRT-smuhth   ˈpoːʳtsməθ, ˈpɔːʳtsməθ

Portugal
republic, Europe   PŌR-chi-guhl, PAWR-   ˈpoːʳtʃigəl, ˈpɔːʳ-

Portuguese
lang., Portugal, Brazil, parts of   PŌR-chuh-GĒZ, PAWR-, -GĒS   ˌpoːʳtʃəˈgiːz, ˌpɔːʳ-, -ˈgiːs
Africa

Key (col. 2):   a: fad   ā: fade   ah: father   ar: Mary   aw: law   e: fed   ē: feed   er: merry   i: hid   ī: hide   ō: coat   o͞o: boot
oi: boy   ow: now   u: put   uh: above   uhr: bird   ch: chop   ng: ring   sh: show   th: thick   th: this   zh: measure

Portulaca		
plant	PAWR-chuh-LAK-uh	ˌpɔːʳtʃə'lækə
Portunus		
Roman god of doors or harbors	pawr-T(Y)O͞O-nuhs	pɔːʳ't(j)uːnəs
Porus		
Indian king	PŌR-uhs	'poːrəs
Posada		
Nine Days of, *3rd week of Dec., Mexico*	pō-SAHT͟H-ah	poː'sɑðɑ
Poseidon		
Greek god of the sea	puh-SĪD-n	pə'sɑidn̩
Posen		
1. city, Poland	PŌ-zuhn	'poːzən
2. village, IL	PŌ-zuhn, PŌS-n	'poːzən, 'poːsn̩
Positron		
nuclear particle	PAHZ-uh-TRAHN	'pɑzəˌtrɑn
Posner		
Vladimir, *Russian commentator*	PŌZ-nuhr	'poːznəʳ
Posta, La		
see La Posta		
Poston		
Tom, *US actor*	PŌ-stuhn	'poːstən
Postumius		
pers. name, Latin	pahs-T(Y)O͞O-mē-uhs	pɑs't(j)uːmiːəs
Postumus		
Roman cognomen	PAHS-chuh-muhs	'pɑstʃəməs
potassium		
element	puh-TAS-ē-uhm	pə'tæsiːəm
Potawatomi		
N. American people	PAHT-uh-WAHT-uh-mē	ˌpɑtə'wɑtəmiˑ
Potemkin		
Grigori, *Russian nobleman*	puh-TYAWM-kyin, [$] pō-TEM(P)-kuhn	pə'tjɔːmkjin, [$] poː'tem(p)kən
Pothos		
personification of love and desire	PŌ-THŌS, PŌ-THAHS	'poːˌθoːs, 'poːˌθɑs
Potidaea		
ancient city, Macedonia	PAHT-uh-DĒ-uh	ˌpɑtə'diːə
Potiphar		
Biblical name	PAHT-uh-fuhr, PAHT-uh-FAHR	'pɑt̪əfəʳ, 'pɑt̪əˌfɑʳ
Potomac		
river, US	puh-TŌ-muhk, puh-TŌ-mik	pə'toːmək, pə'toːmik
Potoo		
S. & Cen. American bird	pō-TO͞O	poː'tuː
Potosi		
city, MO; mtn., NV, CO	puh-TŌ-sē	pə'toːsiˑ
Potosí		
dept, city, Bolivia	PŌT-uh-SĒ	ˌpoːt̪ə'siː
Potsdam		
county, Germany	PAHTS-DAM	'pɑtsˌdæm
Pottawatomie		
county, KA, OK	PAHT-uh-WAHT-uh-mē	ˌpɑt̪ə'wɑt̪əmiˑ
Pottawattamie		
county, IA	PAHT-uh-WAHT-uh-mē	ˌpɑt̪ə'wɑt̪əmiˑ
Poughkeepsie		
city, NY	puh-KIP-sē, pō-KIP-sē	pə'kipsiˑ, poː'kipsiˑ

Foreign Sounds: ue: *Fr.* **rue**, *Ger.* **fü**llen uh(r): *Fr.* b**oeu**f, *Ger.* H**ö**hle k͟h: *Ger.* i**ch**, *Scot.* lo**ch** g̃: *Sp.* ami**g**o v̲: *Sp.* ha**b**lar hl: *Welsh* **Ll**anelli. CAPITALS: primary stress. SMALL CAPS: secondary stress. [$]: U.S. pron. [£]: British pron.

Pouilly Fuissé
   wine   p$\overline{oo}$-YĒ fwē-SÃ, Ⓢ p$\overline{oo}$-YĒ fwē-SÃ   puːjiː fɥiːseː, Ⓢ puːˈjiː fwiːˈseː

Pouilly Fumé
   wine   p$\overline{oo}$-YĒ fue-MÃ, Ⓢ p$\overline{oo}$-YĒ f$\overline{oo}$-MÃ   puːjiː fyːmeː, Ⓢ puːˈjiː fuːˈmeː

Poul
   pers. name, Danish   POWL, PŌL   ˈpaul, ˈpoːl

Poulenc
   Francis, *French composer*   p$\overline{oo}$-LE^{n}K, Ⓢ P$\overline{OO}$-LANGK   puːlẽk, Ⓢ ˈpuːˌlæŋk

Powel
   pers. name   POW(-uh)l, Ⓔ *also* PŌ-uhl   ˈpau(ə)l, Ⓔ *also* ˈpoːəl

Powell
   1. Adam Clayton, *US politician;*   POW(-uh)l   ˈpau(ə)l
      Colin, *US general;* Lewis
      Franklin, *US jurist*
   2. Anthony, *British writer;* C. F.,   PŌ-uhl, POW(-uh)l   ˈpoːəl, ˈpau(ə)l
      English physicist (Nobel 1950)

Poweshiek
   county, IA   POW-uh-SHĒK   ˈpauəˌʃiːk

Powhatan
   1. American Indian leader; N.   POW-uh-TAN, POW-uh-TAN,   ˈpauəˌtæn, ˌpauəˈtæn,
      American people   pow-HAT-n   pauˈhætn̩
   2. county, VA   POW-uh-TAN   ˌpauəˈtæn
   3. town, AR   pow-HAT-n, POW-uh-TAN   pauˈhætn̩, ˌpauəˈtæn

Powis
   pers. name   PŌ-uhs, POW-uhs   ˈpoːəs, ˈpauəs

Powys
   1. county, ancient kingdom, Wales   PŌ-is, PUH-wis   ˈpoːis, ˈpəwis
   2. family name   POW-uhs, PŌ-uhs   ˈpauəs, ˈpoːəs
   3. John Cowper, *English writer*   PŌ-uhs   ˈpoːəs

Požarevac
   town, Serbia   pō-ZHAHR-uh-VAHTS   poːˈʒɑːrəˌvɑːts

Požega
   town, Croatia   PAW-zhuh-guh   ˈpɔːʒəgə

Poznán
   city, Poland   PŌZ-NAHN-yuh, Ⓢ PŌZ-NAN(-yuh)   ˈpoːzˌnaːn̠, Ⓢ ˈpoːzˌnæn(jə)

Prabhashankar
   pers. name, Hindi   PRUH-buh-SHUHNG-kuhr   ˌprəbəˈʃəŋkər

Prado
   museum, Madrid, Spain   PRAH<u>TH</u>-ō, PRAHD-ō   ˈprɑðoː, ˈprɑdoː

Praetorius
   Michael, *German composer*   pri-TŌR-ē-uhs, pri-TAWR-ē-uhs   priˈtoːriːəs, priˈtɔːriːəs

Prague
   city, Czech republic   PRAHG   ˈprɑg

Praha
   Czech name for Prague   PRAH-hah   ˈprɑhɑ

Praia
   city, Cape Verde Islands   PRĪ-uh   ˈpraiə

Prairial
   month, French Revolutionary   prer-YAHL   prerjɑːl
      calendar

Prajadhipok
   king, Siam   PRĪ-ahd-ē-PAWK   ˌpraiadiːˈpɔːk

Key (col. 2): a: fad ā: fade ah: father ar: Mary aw: law e: fed ē: feed er: merry i: hid ī: hide ō: coat $\overline{oo}$: boot
oi: boy ow: now u: put uh: above uhr: bird ch: chop ng: ring sh: show th: thick <u>th</u>: this zh: measure

Prakrit		
Indic lang.	PRAHK-rit	'prɑkrit
praseodymium		
element	PRĀ-zē-ō-DIM-ē-uhm, PRĀ-sē-	ˌpreːziːoː'dimiːəm, ˌpreːsiː-
Prather		
pers. name	PRATH-uhr	'præðər
Pratincole		
wading bird	PRAT-n-KŌL, PRAT-ing-KŌL, PRĀT-	'prætn̩ˌkoːl, 'prætiŋˌkoːl, 'preːt-
Pratt		
pers. name	PRAT	'præt
Pratt & Whitney		
US machine tools co.	PRAT n (H)WIT-nē	ˌpræt n̩ '(h)witniˑ
Pravda		
official Communist newspaper, USSR	PRAHV-duh	'prɑvdə
Praxede		
pers. name, German	prahk-SĀ-duh	prɑk'seːdə
Práxedes		
pers. name, Spanish	PRAHK-sā-thās	'prɑkseːðeːs
Praxiteles		
Greek sculptor	prak-SIT-l-ĒZ	præk'sitl̩ˌiːz
Precambrian		
geologic period	prē-KAM-brē-uhn, PRĒ-KAM-brē-uhn, -KĀM-brē-uhn	priː'kæmbriːən, 'priː'kæmbriːən, -'keːmbriːən
pre-Columbian		
pert. to the Americas before arrival of Columbus	PRĒ-kuh-LUHM-bē-uhn	ˌpriːkə'ləmbiːən
Pregl		
Fritz, *Austrian chemist (Nobel 1923)*	PRĀ-guhl	'preːgəl
Prelog		
Vladimir, *Yugoslav-born Swiss organic chemist (Nobel 1975)*	PREL-ŌG	'prelˌoːg
Prelude, The		
poem, Wordsworth	PREL-yo͞od, PRĀ-L(Y)O͞OD	'preljuːd, 'preːˌl(j)uːd
Premières Côtes de Bordeaux		
wine	pruhm-YER KŌT duh bawr-DŌ	prəmjer koːt də bɔːrdoː
Pre-Raphaelite		
member of a group of English artists	prē-RAF-(ē-)uh-LĪT, prē-RĀ-fē-uh-LĪT	priː'ræf(iː)əˌlɑit, priː'reːfiːəˌlɑit
Presbyterian		
Protestant church	PREZ-buh-TIR-ē-uhn, PRES-	ˌprezbə'tiriːən, ˌpres-
Presbyterianism		
Christian religion	PREZ-buh-TIR-ē-uh-NIZ-uhm, PRES-	ˌprezbə'tiriːəˌnizəm, ˌpres-
Prescott		
pers. name; US pl. name	PRES-kuht	'preskət
Preserved		
pers. name	pri-ZUHR-vuhd	pri'zərvəd
Presidente		
Dominican beer	prā-zi-DEN-tā	preːzi'denteː
Presidente Hayes		
dept, Paraguay	PRES-uh-THEN-tā ĪS	ˌpresəˌðenteː 'ɑis

Foreign Sounds: ue: *Fr.* **rue**, *Ger.* **füllen** uh(r): *Fr.* **boeuf**, *Ger.* **Höhle** kh: *Ger.* **ich**, *Scot.* **loch** g: *Sp.* **amigo** v: *Sp.* **hablar** hl: *Welsh* **Llanelli**. CAPITALS: primary stress. SMALL CAPS: secondary stress. [$]: U.S. pron. [£]: British pron.

Presidio

   military post, San Francisco, CA;   pruh-SID-ē-ō   prə'sidiːoː
   county, TX

Presley

   Elvis, *US musician; pers. name*   PREZ-lē, PRES-lē   'prezliˑ, 'presliˑ

Presocratics

   Greek philosophers before Socrates   PRĒ-suh-KRAT-iks   ˌpriːsə'krætʲiks

Presque Isle

   1. peninsula, bay, Lake Erie; city,   presk ĪL   presk 'ɑil
   ME

   2. county, MI   presk ĒL   presk 'iːl

Pressler

   Larry, *US politician*   PRES-luhr   'preslərˢ

Preston

   pers. name; US pl. name   PRES-tuhn   'prestən

Prestonpans

   seaside resort, Scotland   PRES-tuhn-PANZ   ˌprestən'pænz

Prestwick

   airport, Scotland   PREST-wik   'prestwik

Pretoria

   city, S. Africa   pri-TŌR-ē-uh, pri-TAWR-ē-uh   pri'toːriːə, pri'tɔːriːə

Pretorius

   Andries, *S. African colonizer*   pri-TŌR-ē-uhs, pri-TAWR-ē-uhs   pri'toːriːəs, pri'tɔːriːəs

Previn

   André, *US musician*   PREV-uhn   'prevən

Prévost

   Eugène Marcel, *French novelist*   prā-VŌ   preːvoː

Priam

   king of Troy   PRĪ-uhm, PRĪ-AM   'prɑiəm, 'prɑiˌæm

Priapus

   Greek god of fertility   prī-Ā-puhs, PRĪ-uh-puhs,   prɑi'eːpəs, 'prɑiəpəs,
                            PRĒ-uh-puhs   'priːəpəs

Pribilof

   islands, Bering Sea   PRIB-uh-LAWF   'pribəˌlɔːf

Prichard

   pers. name   PRICH-uhrd   'pritʃərˢd

Prideaux

   pers. name   prē-DŌ, PRID-ō   priː'doː, 'pridoː

Priene

   Ionian city   prī-Ē-nē   prɑi'iːniˑ

Prigogine

   Ilya, *Russian-born Belgian chemist*   pri-GAW-zhuhn, pri-gaw-ZHĒN   pri'gɔːʒən, prigɔː'ʒiːn
   (Nobel 1977)

Primo

   pers. name, Spanish   PRĒ-mō   'priːmoː

Prince Edward

   1. county, VA   prin(t)s ED-(w)uhrd   prin(t)s 'ed(w)ərˢd

   2. county, Ontario, Canada   prin(t)s ED-wuhrd   prin(t)s 'edwərˢd

Prince Edward Island

   island province, Canada   prin(t)s ED-wuhrd Ī-luhnd   prin(t)s ˌedwərˢd 'ɑilənd

Prince Gustaf Adolf

   Sea, *arm of the Arctic Ocean,*   prin(t)s GŌŌS-tahf Ā-DAHLF SĒ,   prin(t)s ˌguˑstaf ˌeːˌdɑlf 'siː,
   Canada   AD-AHLF   ˌædˌɑlf

Key (col. 2):   a: **fad**   ā: **fade**   ah: **father**   ar: **Mary**   aw: **law**   e: **fed**   ē: **feed**   er: **merry**   i: **hid**   ī: **hide**   ō: **coat**   o͞o: **boot**
oi: **boy**   ow: **now**   u: **put**   uh: **above**   uhr: **bird**   ch: **chop**   ng: **ring**   sh: **show**   th: **thick**   <u>th</u>: **this**   zh: **measure**

Prince of Wales-Outer Ketchikan
    division, AK   PRIN(T)S uhv WĀLZ OWT-uhr KECH-i-KAN   ˌprin(t)s əv ˌweːlz ˌauţəʳ ˈketʃi̥ˌkæn

Princeps
    term for Roman emperor   PRIN-SEPS, PRING-KEPS   ˈprinˌseps, ˈpriŋˌkeps

Princeton
    river, city, university, NJ   PRIN(T)-stuhn   ˈprin(t)stən

Príncipe
    island, São Tomé & Príncipe   PRI(N)-suh-puh, Ⓢ PRIN(T)-suh-puh   ˈprĩ(n)səpə, Ⓢ ˈprin(t)səpə

Principes
    plural of Princeps   PRIN-suh-PĒZ, PRING-kuh-PĀS   ˈprinsəˌpiːz, ˈpriŋkəˌpeːs

Principia
    College, IL   prin-SIP-ē-uh   prinˈsipiːə

Principia Mathematica
    scientific work, Newton   prin-SIP-ē-uh MATH-uh-MAT-i-kuh   prinˈsipiːə ˌmæθəˈmæţikə

Prine
    John, US singer, songwriter   PRĪN   ˈprɑin

Prinknash
    district, Gloucestershire, England   PRIN-ij *[sic]*   ˈprinidʒ *[sic]*

Pripet
    river, Belorussia, Ukraine   PRIP-ET, PRIP-uht   ˈpripˌet, ˈpripət

Priscian
    Latin grammarian   PRISH-(ē-)uhn   ˈpriʃ(iː)ən

Priscilla
    pers. name   pruh-SIL-uh   prəˈsilə

Priscillian
    Spanish religious reformer   pruh-SIL-ē-uhn, pruh-SIL-yuhn   prəˈsiliːən, prəˈsiljən

Priscillianism
    teachings of Priscillian   pruh-SIL-yuh-NIZ-uhm, -SIL-ē-uh-NIZ-uhm   prəˈsiljəˌnizəm, -ˈsiliːəˌnizəm

Pritchard
    pers. name   PRICH-uhrd   ˈpritʃəʳd

Privet
    bush   PRIV-uht   ˈprivət

Proboscidea
    elephants   PRŌ-buh-SID-ē-uh, prō-BAHS-uh-DĒ-uh   ˌproːbəˈsidiːə, proːˌbasəˈdiːə

Probus
    Roman emperor   PRŌ-buhs   ˈproːbəs

Procellarum, Oceanus
    'ocean' on Moon   Ō-shē-AN-uhs PRŌ-suh-LAHR-uhm, -LAR-uhm   ˌoːʃiːˈænəs ˌproːsəˈlarəm, -ˈlærəm

Procne
    sister of Philomela   PRAHK-nē   ˈprɑkniˑ

Procofieff
    pers. name, Russian   PRUH-KAWF-yif   ˌprəˈkɔːfjif

Procopius
    Greek historian   pruh-KŌ-pē-uhs   prəˈkoːpiːəs

Procris
    daughter of Erechtheus   PRŌ-kruhs   ˈproːkrəs

Procrustean
    pert. to Procrustes *and his bed*   p(r)uh-KRUHS-tē-uhn, prō-KRUHS-tē-uhn   p(r)əˈkrəstiːən, proːˈkrəstiːən

---

Foreign Sounds: ue: *Fr.* **rue**, *Ger.* **füllen** uh(r): *Fr.* **boeuf**, *Ger.* **Höhle** <u>kh</u>: *Ger.* i**ch**, *Scot.* lo**ch** ḡ: *Sp.* ami**g**o v̲: *Sp.* ha**b**lar hl: *Welsh* **Ll**anelli. CAPITALS: primary stress. SMALL CAPS: secondary stress. Ⓢ: U.S. pron. Ⓛ: British pron.

Procrustes
   cruel son of Poseidon   p(r)uh-KRUHS-tēz, prō-KRUHS-tēz   p(r)ə'krəstiːz, proː'krəstiːz

Procter
   Bryan, *(pseudonym* Barry   PRAHK-tuhr   'praktəʳ
     Cornwall*), English poet*

Procter & Gamble
   US co.   PRAHK-tuhr uhn(d) GAM-buhl   'praktəʳ ən(d) 'gæmbəl

Procul Harum
   rock group   PRŌ-kuhl HAR-uhm, HER-uhm   'proːkəl 'hærəm, 'herəm

Procyon
   star   PRŌ-sē-AHN   'proːsiːˌɑn

Prof.
   abbreviation of Professor   PRAHF   'praf

Professor
   academic title   pruh-FES-uhr, *in rapid speech*   prə'fesəʳ, *in rapid speech*
                            puh-FES-uhr   pə'fesəʳ

Profumo
   John, *English politician*   pruh-FYŌŌ-mō   prə'fjuːmoː

Prokhorov
   Alexander Mikhailovich, *Russian*   PRAW-<u>kh</u>uh-RAWF   ˌprɔːxə'rɔːf
     physicist (Nobel 1964)

Prokofiev
   Sergei, *Russian composer*   pruh-KAWF-yuhf, pruh-KAWF-YEF,   prə'kɔːfjəf, prə'kɔːfˌjef,
                           pruh-KAWF-YEV   prə'kɔːfˌjev

Prokopyevsk
   city, Russia   pruh-KAWP-yuhfsk   prə'kɔːpjəfsk

PROLOG
   programming lang.   PRŌ-LAWG, PRŌ-LAHG   'proːˌlɔːg, 'proːˌlag

PROM
   programmable read-only memory   PRAHM   'pram
     (computer chip)

Promethean
   pert. to Prometheus   pruh-MĒ-thē-uhn   prə'miːθiːən

Prometheus
   Titan who championed   pruh-MĒ-thē-uhs,   prə'miːθiːəs, prə'miːˌθ(j)uːs
     humankind; pers. name   pruh-MĒ-TH(Y)ŌŌS

promethium
   element   pruh-MĒ-thē-uhm, prō-   prə'miːθiːəm, proː-

Propertius
   Roman poet   prō-PUHR-sh(ē-)uhs   proː'pəʳʃ(iː)əs

Propontis
   sea, Turkey   prō-PAHNT-uhs   proː'pantəs

Propylaea
   entrance to Acropolis   PRŌ-puh-LĒ-uh, PRAHP-uh-LĒ-uh   ˌproːpə'liːə, ˌprapə'liːə

Prosauropoda
   dinosaur infraorder   PRŌ-suh-RAHP-uhd-uh   ˌproːsə'rapədə

Proserpina
   Roman goddess of Underworld   pruh-SUHR-puh-nuh   prə'səʳpənə

Proserpine
   anglicization of Proserpina   PRAHS-uhr-PĪN   'prasəʳˌpain

Proskynesis
   Persian ceremony of prostration   PRAHS-KĪ-NĒ-suhs   ˌprasˌkai'niːsəs

---

Key (col. 2):   a: fad   ā: fade   ah: father   ar: Mary   aw: law   e: fed   ē: feed   er: merry   i: hid   ī: hide   ō: coat   ōō: boot
oi: boy   ow: now   u: put   uh: above   uhr: bird   ch: chop   ng: ring   sh: show   th: thick   <u>th</u>: this   zh: measure

Prosper
  1. pers. name — PRAHS-puhr — 'prɑspəʳ
  2. French — praws-PER — prɔːsper
  3. German — PRAWS-puhr — 'prɔːspəʳ
Prospero
  1. Shakespearean enchanter; pers. — PRAHS-puh-rō — 'prɑspərɔː
  name
  2. Italian — PRAWS-pā-rō — 'prɔːspeːrɔː
Próspero
  pers. name, Spanish — PRŌ-spā-rō — 'proːspeːrɔː
Prostigmin
  tdmk for neostigmine — prō-STIG-muhn — proː'stigmən
protactinium
  element — PRŌT-AK-TIN-ē-uhm — ˌproːtˌæk'tiniːəm
Protagoras
  Greek philosopher; dialogue of — prō-TAG-uh-ruhs — proː'tægərəs
  Plato
Protean
  pert. to Proteus — PRŌT-ē-uhn, prō-TĒ-uhn — 'proːtiːən, proː'tiːən
Proterozoic
  geologic era — PRAHT-uh-ruh-ZŌ-ik, PRŌT- — ˌprɑtərə'zoːik, ˌproːt-
Protesilaus
  first Greek killed by Trojans — PRŌT-uh-suh-LĀ-(y)uhs — ˌproːtəsə'leː(j)əs
Protestant
  type of Christian — PRAHT-uh-stuhnt — 'prɑtəstənt
Protestantism
  branch of Christianity — PRAHT-uh-stuhnt-IZ-uhm — 'prɑtəstəntˌizəm
Proteus
  Greek sea god; pers. name — PRŌT-ē-uhs, PRŌ-T(Y)O͞OS — 'proːtiːəs, 'proːˌt(j)uːs
Prothonotary warbler
  bird — prō-THAHN-uh-TER-ē WAWR-bluhr, — proː'θɑnəˌteriˑ 'wɔːʳbləʳ,
        PRŌ-thuh-NŌT-uh-rē — ˌproːθə'noːtəriˑ
Protoceratops
  dinosaur — PRŌT-ō-SER-uh-TAHPS — ˌproːtoː'serəˌtɑps
Proto-Indo-European
  prehistoric parent lang. of — PRŌT-ō-IN-dō-YUR-uh-PĒ-uhn — ˌproːtoːˌindoːˌjurə'piːən
  Indo-European
Proud'hon
  Pierre Paul, French painter — proo-DAWⁿ — pruːdɔ̃
Proust
  Marcel, French writer — PROOST — pruːst
Proustian
  pert. to Proust — PROO-stē-uhn — 'pruːstiːən
Provençal [Languedoc, Occitan]
  lang., France — praw-vahⁿ-SAHL — prɔːvãsal
Provence
  prov, France — praw-VAHⁿS — prɔːvãs
Proverbs
  Old Testament book — PRAHV-UHRBZ — 'prɑvˌəʳbz
Providence
  divine guidance; US pl. name — PRAHV-uhd-uhn(t)s, — 'prɑvədən(t)s, 'prɑvədn̩(t)s,
        PRAHV-uhd-n(t)s, — 'prɑvəˌden(t)s
        PRAHV-uh-DEN(T)S
Provincetown
  town, MA — PRAHV-uhn-STOWN — 'prɑvənˌstɑun

Foreign Sounds: ue: *Fr.* **rue**, *Ger.* **füllen** uh(r): *Fr.* **boeuf**, *Ger.* **Höhle** kh: *Ger.* **ich**, *Scot.* **loch** ğ: *Sp.* **amigo** v̱: *Sp.* **hablar**
hl: *Welsh* **Llanelli**. CAPITALS: primary stress. SMALL CAPS: secondary stress. ⑤: U.S. pron. ⑭: British pron.

Provincias Vascongadas		
region, Spain	prō-VIN-sē-ahs v̲ahs-kawn-GAHT̲H̲-ahs	proː'vinsiːɑs βɑskoːn'gɑðɑs
Provo		
city, UT	PRŌ-vō	'proːvoː
Provolone		
cheese	PRŌ-vuh-LŌ-nē, PRŌ-vuh-LŌN	ˌproːvə'loːniˑ, ˌproːvə'loːn
Proxima Centauri		
star in Centaurus	PRAHK-sim-uh sen-TAWR-ē	'prɑksimə sen'tɔːriˑ
Proxmire		
William, *US politician*	PRAHK-SMĪR	'prɑkˌsmɑi^{r}
Prozac		
tdmk for anti-depressant drug	PRŌ-ZAK	'proːˌzæk
Prudence		
pers. name	PRO̅O̅D-ns	'pruːdn̩s
Prudencio		
pers. name, Spanish	pro̅o̅-T̲H̲Ā̲N-syō, -thyō	pruː'ðeˑnsjoː, -θjoː
Prudential-Bache		
US financial co.	pru-DEN-chuhl-BĀSH	pru'dentʃəl'beːʃ
Prudhoe		
bay, AK	PRUHD-(h)ō, PRO̅O̅D-ō	'prəd(h)oː, 'pruːdoː
Prufrock		
J. Alfred, *character in poem of T. S. Eliot*	PRO̅O̅-FRAHK	'pruːˌfrɑk
Prussia		
former German state	PRUHSH-uh	'prəʃə
Prussian		
pert. to Prussia	PRUHSH-uhn	'prəʃən
Pruszków		
commune, Poland	PRO̅O̅SH-ko̅o̅f	'pruːʃkuːf
Prut, Pruth		
river, Romania	PRO̅O̅T	'pruːt
Prynne		
Hester, *Hawthorne character*	PRIN	'prin
Pryor		
David Hampton, *US politician;* Richard, *US comedian*	PRĪ(-uh)r	'prɑi(ə)^{r}
Prytany		
panel of Athenian Council of 500	PRIT-n-ē	'pritn̩iˑ
Przybysz		
Polish family name	PSHI-bish, [S] SHĒ-bish, PRIZ-bē, PRIZ-BIZ	'pʃibiʃ, [S] 'ʃiːbiʃ, 'prizbiˑ, 'prizˌbiz
Psalms		
Old Testament book	SAHMZ, SAHLMZ	'sɑˑmz, 'sɑlmz
Psalter		
book of Psalms	SAWL-tuhr	'sɔːltə^{r}
Psaltery		
the Psalter	SAWL-tuh-rē, SAWL-trē	'sɔːltəriˑ, 'sɔːltriˑ
Psammetichus		
name, kings of Egypt	suh-MET-i-kuhs	sə'meţikəs
Psittacosaurus		
dinosaur	SIT-uh-kō-SAWR-uhs	ˌsiţəkoː'sɔːrəs
Psyche		
wife of Eros in Roman myth	SĪ-kē	'sɑikiˑ

Key (col. 2): a: fad ā: fade ah: father ar: Mary aw: law e: fed ē: feed er: merry i: hid ī: hide ō: coat o̅o̅: boot oi: boy ow: now u: put uh: above uhr: bird ch: chop ng: ring sh: show th: thick t̲h̲: this zh: measure

Ptah, Phthah		
Egyptian creator god	(P)TAH, puh-TAH	'(p)tɑ, pə'tɑ
Pterodactyl		
prehistoric, bird-like reptile	TER-uh-DAK-tl	ˌterə'dæktl̩
Pterosauria		
reptilian order	TER-uh-SAWR-ē-uh	ˌterə'sɔːriːə
Ptolemaeus		
crater on Moon	TAHL-uh-MĀ-uhs	ˌtɑlə'meːəs
Ptolemaic		
pert. to Ptolemy	TAHL-uh-MĀ-ik	ˌtɑlə'meːik
Ptolemy		
name, kings of Egypt; Alexandrian astronomer	TAHL-uh-mē	'tɑləmiˑ
Ptuj		
town, Slovenia	PTOO-ē, puh-TOO-ē	'ptuːiˑ, pə'tuːiˑ
Publicani		
Roman tax collectors	PUHB-li-KĀ-nē, -KĀ-NĪ	ˌpəbli'keːniˑ, -'keːˌnɑi
Publilius		
pers. name, Latin	PUHB-LIL-ē-uhs	ˌpəb'liliːəs
Publius		
pers. name, Latin	PUHB-lē-uhs	'pəbliːəs
Pucci		
Emilio, *Italian fashion designer*	POO-chē	'puːtʃiˑ
Puccini		
Giacomo, *Italian composer*	poo-CHĒ-nē	puː'tʃiːniˑ
Puebla		
state, Mexico	PWEV-lah	'pweβlɑ
Pueblo		
city, county, CO; N. American people	poo-EB-lō, PWEB-lō, pyoo-EB-lō	puː'ebloː, 'pwebloː, pjuː'ebloː
Puelche		
S. American people	PWEL-chē	'pweltʃiˑ
Puerto De la Cruz		
resort, Canary Islands	PWER-tō thā lah KROOTH	ˌpwertoː ðeː lɑ 'kruːθ
Puerto Plata		
prov, Dominican Republic	PWER-tō PLAHT-ah	ˌpwertoː 'plɑtɑ
Puerto Presidente Stroessner		
town, Paraguay	PWER-tō PREZ-i-THEN-tā STRES-nuhr	ˌpwertoː ˌpreziˌðenteː 'stresnəʳ
Puerto Rican		
pert. to or inhabitant of Puerto Rico	PŌRT-uh RĒ-kuhn, PAWRT-uh, PWERT-ō	ˌpoːʳt̬ə 'riːkən, ˌpɔːʳt̬ə, ˌpweʳt̬oː
Puerto Rico		
island, West Indies	PŌRT-uh RĒ-kō, PAWRT-uh, PWERT-ō	ˌpoːʳt̬ə 'riːkoː, ˌpɔːʳt̬ə, ˌpweʳt̬oː
Puerto Vallarta		
resort, Mexico	PWERT-ō vah-YAHRT-uh	ˌpweʳt̬oː vɑ'jɑʳt̬ə
Puget		
sound, WA	PYOO-juht	'pjuːdʒət
Pugh		
Robert L., *US ambassador*	PYOO	'pjuː
Puglia		
prov, Italy	POOL-yah	'puːljɑ
Pukapuka		
coral atoll, Cook Islands, Pacific	POO-kuh-POO-kuh	ˌpuːkə'puːkə

Pukaskwa
  National Park, *Ontario*   poo-KAHS-kwuh   puː'kɑskwə
Pulaski
  1. Kazimierz, *Polish nobleman*   poo-LAHS-kē, ⑤ puh-LAS-kē,   puː'lɑskiˌ, ⑤ pə'læskiˌ,
        pyu-LAS-kē   pju'læskiˌ
  2. pl. name, US   puh-LAS-kē, pyu-LAS-kē   pə'læskiˌ, pju'læskiˌ
Pulcher
  Roman cognomen   PUHL-kuhr   'pəlkərˡ
Puli
  dog breed   PUL-ē, P(Y)OO-lē   'puliˌ, 'p(j)uːliˌ
Puligny-Montrachet
  French wine   pue-lēn-YĒ-mawⁿ-trah-SHE   pyːliːnjiːmõtrɑːʃe
Pulitzer
  Joseph, *US journalist; literary/*   PUL-uht-suhr *(family's usual pron.),*   'pulətsərˡ *(family's usual*
    music prize   PYOO-luht-suhr   *pron.),* 'pjuːlətsərˡ
Pullman
  George, *US inventor; tdmk for a*   PUL-muhn   'pulmən
    railroad sleeping car
Pulteney
  pers. name   PUHLT-nē   'pəltniˌ
Pułtusk
  commune, Poland   POOL-TOOSK   'puːɫˌtuːsk
Punchinello
  puppet show character   PUHN-chuh-NEL-ō   ˌpəntʃə'neloː
Pune
  see Poona
Pungwe
  river, waterfall, Mozambique   PUNG-gwuh   'puŋgwə
Punic
  Carthaginian (adj.)   PYOO-nik   'pjuːnik
Punjab, Panjab
  prov., India & Pakistan   PUHN-JAHB, PUHN-JAHB   ˌpən'dʒɑb, 'pənˌdʒɑb
Punjabi, Panjabi
  lang., native of Punjab   PUHN-JAHB-ē   ˌpən'dʒɑbiˌ
Punt
  ancient name for part of Africa   PUNT   'punt
Punta, Cerro de
  island, Puerto Rico   SER-ō thā POON-tuh   ˌseroː ðeː 'puːntə
Punta Arenas [Magallanes]
  city, Chile   POON-tuh uh-RĀ-nuhs   ˌpuːntə ə'reːnəs
Punt e Mes
  Italian vermouth   PUNT ē MES   ˌpunt iː 'mes
Puntigam
  Austrian beer   PUN-ti-GAHM, PUN-ti-GAHM   'puntiˌgɑm, ˌpunti'gɑm
Punxsutawney
  borough, PA   PUHNGK-suh-TAW-nē   ˌpəŋksə'tɔːniˌ
Puppis
  constellation   PUHP-uhs   'pəpəs
Puran
  pers. name   poo-RAHN   puː'rɑn
Purcell
  1. E. M., *US physicist (Nobel*   puhr-SEL   pərˡ'sel
    1952)
  2. Henry, *English composer*   PUHR-suhl, puhr-SEL   'pərsəl, pərˡ'sel

---

Key (col. 2):   a: fad   ā: fade   ah: father   ar: **M**a**ry**   aw: law   e: fed   ē: feed   er: me**rry**   i: hid   ī: hide   ō: coat   oo: boot
oi: boy   ow: now   u: put   uh: above   uhr: bird   ch: chop   ng: ring   sh: show   th: thick   <u>th</u>: <u>th</u>is   zh: measure

Purdue		
University, *IN*	puhr-D(Y)O͞O	pəʳ'd(j)uː
Purim		
Jewish holiday	PUR-uhm, PO͞O-ruhm, pu-RIM	'purəm, 'puːrəm, pu'rim
Purina		
tdmk for pet food	pyur-Ē-nuh	pjur'iːnə
Puritan		
English Protestant group	PYUR-uht-n	'pjurətn̩
Puritanism		
beliefs of the Puritans	PYUR-uht-n-IZ-uhm	'pjurətn̩ˌizəm
Purolator Courier		
US corp.	PYUR-uh-LĀT-uhr KUR-ē-uhr, KUHR-ē-uhr, KUH-rē-uhr	'pjurəˌleːṭəʳ 'kuriːəʳ, 'kər-iːəʳ, 'kə-riːəʳ
Purus		
river, S. America	puh-RO͞OS	pə'ruːs
Purvis		
John, *US lawyer*	PUHR-vuhs	'pəʳvəs
Pusan		
city, S. Korea	po͞o-sahn	puːsɑn
Pusey		
Edward B., *English theologian*	PYO͞O-zē	'pjuːziˑ
Puseyism		
the theology of Pusey	PYO͞O-zē-IZ-uhm, PYO͞O-sē-	'pjuːziːˌizəm, 'pjuːsiː-
Puseyite		
follower of Pusey (Oxford Movement)	PYO͞O-zē-ĪT	'pjuːziːˌɑit
Pushkin		
Alexander S., *Russian author*	PO͞OSH-kyin, [$] PUSH-kin	'puːʃkjin, [$] 'puʃkin
Pushmataha		
county, OK	PUSH-muh-TAH-hah, -HAW	ˌpuʃmə'tɑhɑ, -ˌhɔː
Pushto [Pashto]		
lang., Afghanistan, Pakistan	PUSH-tō, PO͞OSH-tō	'puʃtoː, 'puːʃtoː
Pushtu [Pashto]		
lang., Afghanistan, Pakistan	PUSH-to͞o, PO͞OSH-to͞o	'puʃtuː, 'puːʃtuː
Puteoli		
ancient town near Naples	PO͞O-tā-Ō-lē	ˌpuːteː'oːliˑ
Puti tai nobio		
flower	PO͞OT-i TĪ NŌ-bē-ō	ˌpuːṭi ˌtai 'noːbiːoː
Putnam		
US publishing co.	PUHT-nuhm	'pətnəm
Putredinis, Palus		
see Palus Putredinis		
Putumayo		
river, S. America	PO͞OT-uh-MĪ-ō	ˌpuːṭə'maioː
Puyallup		
N. American people	pyo͞o-AL-uhp	pjuː'æləp
Puyang		
city, China	PO͞O-YAHNG	'puː'jɑŋ
Puy-de-Dôme		
dept, France	pwēd(-uh)-DŌM	pɥiːd(ə)doːm
Puyi [Buyi, Chung-chia, Jui]		
lang., China	BO͞O-YĒ, PO͞O-YĒ	'buː'jiː, 'puː'jiː
Puzo		
Mario, *US writer*	PO͞O-zō	'puːzoː

Foreign Sounds: ue: *Fr.* **rue**, *Ger.* **füllen** uh(r): *Fr.* **boeuf**, *Ger.* **Höhle** kh: *Ger.* **ich**, *Scot.* **loch** g̃: *Sp.* ami**g**o v̱: *Sp.* ha**b**lar hl: *Welsh* **Llanelli**. CAPITALS: primary stress. SMALL CAPS: secondary stress. [$]: U.S. pron. [£]: British pron.

Pwani
  region, Tanzania   PWAHN-ē   'pwɑni·

Pycnanthus
  plant   pik-NAN-thuhs   pik'nænθəs

Pydna
  town, Greece   PID-nuh   'pidnə

Pygmalion
  legendary sculptor & king of   pig-MĀL-yuhn, pig-MĀ-lē-uhn   pig'meːljən, pig'meːliːən
  Cyprus; play, G. B. Shaw

Pygmy, Pigmy
  people, equatorial Africa or SE PIG-mē   'pigmi·
  Asia

Pylades
  friend of Orestes   PĪ-luh-DĒZ   'pailə,diːz

Pylas
  king of Megara   PĪ-luhs   'pailəs

Pyle
  Denver, actor   PĪL   'pail

Pylos, Pylus
  ancient Greek city   PĪ-luhs   'pailəs

Pynchon
  Thomas, US writer; Park,   PIN-chuhn   'pintʃən
  ballpark, Springfield, MA

Pyongyang
  city, N. Korea   PYUHNG-YAHNG, PYUHNG-YANG   ,pjəŋ'jaŋ, ,pjəŋ'jæŋ

P'yŏngyang [Heijo]
  city, N. Korea   pyuhng-yahng   pjəŋjaŋ

Pyotr
  pers. name, Russian   PYAW-tuhr   'pjɔːtər

Pyramus
  mythological lover of Thisbe   PIR-uh-muhs   'pirəməs

Pyrene
  victim of Heracles   pī-RĒ-nē   pai'riːni·

Pyrenean
  pert. to the Pyrenees   PIR-uh-NĒ-uhn   ,pirə'niːən

Pyrenees
  mts., France, Spain   PIR-uh-NĒZ   'pirə,niːz

Pyrénées-Atlantiques
  dept, France   pē-rā-nā-zaht-lahⁿ-TĒK   piːreːneːzɑːtlãtiːk

Pyrénées-Orientales
  dept, France   pē-rā-nā-zawr-yahⁿ-TAHL   piːreːneːzɔːrjãtɑːl

Pyrex
  tdmk for heat resistant glassware   PĪ-REKS   'pai,reks

Pyrrha
  wife of Deucalion; Horace's   PIR-uh   'pirə
  beloved

Pyrrhic
  pert. to Pyrrhus   PIR-ik   'pirik

Pyrrhic victory
  costly victory   PIR-ik VIK-t(uh-)rē   ,pirik 'vikt(ə)ri·

Pyrrho
  Greek philosopher   PIR-ō   'pirɔː

Pyrrhus
  king of Epirus   PIR-uhs   'pirəs

Key (col. 2): a: fad ā: fade ah: father ar: Mary aw: law e: fed ē: feed er: merry i: hid ī: hide ō: coat ōō: boot
oi: boy ow: now u: put uh: above uhr: bird ch: chop ng: ring sh: show th: thick tẖ: this zh: measure

Pythagoras
  Greek philosopher, mathematician   puh-THAG-uh-ruhs, pī-   pə'θægərəs, pai-
Pythagoreanism
  doctrines of Pythagoras &   puh-THAG-uh-RĒ-uh-NIZ-uhm   pə,θægə'riːə,nizəm
    Pythagoreans
Pythagoreans
  followers of Pythagoras   puh-THAG-uh-RĒ-uhnz   pə,θægə'riːənz
Pytheas
  Greek explorer   PITH-ē-uhs, PĪ-thē-uhs, ⓔ *also*   'piθiːəs, 'paiθiːəs, ⓔ *also*
    PITH-ē-AS   'piθiː,æs
Pythia
  priestess of Apollo at Delphi   PITH-ē-uh   'piθiːə
Pythian
  pert. to Delphi *or* Pythia   PITH-ē-uhn   'piθiːən
Pythias
  friend of Damon in Greek legend   PITH-ē-uhs, ⓔ *also* PITH-ē-AS   'piθiːəs, ⓔ *also* 'piθiː,æs
Python
  dragon and oracle in Greek myth   PĪ-THAHN, PĪ-thuhn   'pai,θan, 'paiθən
Pythonesque
  pert. to Monty Python   PĪ-THAHN-ESK, PĪ-thuh-NESK   ,pai,θan'esk, ,paiθə'nesk
Pyxis
  constellation   PĪK-suhs, PIK-suhs   'paiksəs, 'piksəs

Q

Qadhafi, Qaddafi
  Moammar, *Libyan leader*   kuh-DAHF-ē   kə'dafiˈ
Qâhira, Al [Cairo]
  city, Egypt   ahl KAH-hē-RAW, al   aːl 'kahiː,rɔː, æl
Qaidam Pendi
  basin, China   CHĪ-DAHM PUHN-DĒ   'tʃai'dam 'pən'diː
Qalyûbîya
  governorate, Egypt   KAHL-yu-BĒ-(y)uh   ,kalju'biː(j)ə
Qantas
  Australian airline   K(W)AHNT-uhs   'k(w)antəs
Qara Qum
  see Kara Kum
Qatar
  sheikdom on Persian Gulf   KAHT-uhr, GAHT-uhr, GUHT-uhr,   'katər, 'gatər, 'gətər, kə'taˈ
    kuh-TAHR
Qatari
  pert. to Qatar   KAHT-uh-rē, GAHT-uh-rē,   'katəriˈ, 'gatəriˈ, 'gətəriˈ,
    GUHT-uh-rē, kuh-TAHR-ē   kə'tariˈ
Qattara
  Depression, *geographical feature,*   kuh-TAHR-uh   kə'tarə
    Egypt

Foreign Sounds: ue: *Fr.* **rue**, *Ger.* **füllen** uh(r): *Fr.* **boeuf**, *Ger.* **Höhle** kh: *Ger.* **ich**, *Scot.* **loch** ḡ: *Sp.* **amigo** v̲: *Sp.* **hablar**
hl: *Welsh* **Llanelli**. CAPITALS: primary stress. SMALL CAPS: secondary stress. ⓢ: U.S. pron. ⓔ: British pron.

Qeshm
  island, Iran   KESH-uhm   'keʃəm

Qilian Shan
  mtn. range, China   CHIL-YAHN SHAHN   'tʃil'jan 'ʃan

Qingdao, Tsingtao
  city, China   CHING-DOW   'tʃiŋ'dau

Qinghai, Tsinghai, Chinghai
  prov, China   CHING-HĬ   'tʃiŋ'hai

Qiqihar, Ch'i-ch'i-ha-erh, Tsitsihar
  prov, China   CHI-CHI-HAH(-UH)R   'tʃi'tʃi'ha('ə)ʳ

Qizil Qum
  see Kyzyl Kum

Qom
  town, Iran   KŌM   'koːm

Quaalude
  tdmk for methaqualone   KWĀ-LO͞OD   'kweːˌluːd

Quadragesima
  1st Sunday in Lent   KWAHD-ruh-JES-uh-muh   ˌkwadrə'dʒesəmə

Quadrans Muralis
  former constellation   KWAHD-ruhnz myu-RĀ-luhs,   'kwadrənz mju'reːləs,
      myu-RAL-uhs   mju'ræləs

Quadrantids
  meteor shower   kwah-DRANT-uhdz   kwa'dræntədz

Quahog
  clam   KŌ-HAWG, KWAW-HAWG, KWŌ-HAWG,   'koːˌhɔːg, 'kwɔːˌhɔːg,
      -HAHG   'kwoːˌhɔːg, -ˌhag

Quaid
  Dennis, *US actor*   KWĀD   'kweːd

Quai d'Orsay
  French Ministry of Foreign Affairs   kā dawr-SE   keː dɔːrse

Quaker
  member of Religious Society of   KWĀ-kuhr   'kweːkəʳ
  Friends

Quakerism
  Quaker beliefs   KWĀ-kuh-RIZ-uhm   'kweːkəˌrizəm

Quant
  Mary, *British designer*   KWAHNT   'kwant

Quantrill
  William Clark, *Confederate soldier*   KWAHN-truhl   'kwantrəl

Quapaw [Kwapa]
· *N. American people*   KWAW-PAW   'kwɔːˌpɔː

Quara
  lang., Ethiopia   K(W)AHR-uh   'k(w)arə

Quarles
  pers. name   KWAWRLZ, KWAHRLZ   'kwɔːʳlz, 'kwaʳlz

Quarnero
  gulf in Adriatic Sea   kwuhr-NER-ō   kwəʳneroː

Quasar
  distant star-like object; electronics   KWĀ-ZAHR, KWĀ-SAHR   'kweːˌzaʳ, 'kweːˌsaʳ
  brand

Quasimodo
  1. Salvatore, Italian poet, critic   KWAH-zē-MAW-dō   ˌkwazi'mɔːdoː
  (Nobel 1959)
  2. the Sunday after Easter;   KWAHZ-ē-MŌD-ō   ˌkwazi'mɔːdoː
  fictional hunchback

Key (col. 2):   a: fad ā: fade ah: father ar: Mary aw: law e: fed ē: feed er: merry i: hid ī: hide ō: coat o͞o: boot
oi: boy ow: now u: put uh: above uhr: bird ch: chop ng: ring sh: show th: thick t͟h: this zh: measure

Quaternary
   geologic period   KWAHT-uh(r)-NER-ē,   'kwɑʈə(r),neriˑ, kwə'təʳnəriˑ
        kwuh-TUHR-nuhr-ē

Quathlamba [Drakensberg]
   mtn. range, S. Africa   kwaht-LAM-buh   kwɑt'læmbə

Quattro Stagioni
   classical vocal quartet   KWAH-trō stahg-YŌ-nē   'kwɑtroː stɑg'joːniˑ

Quay
   county, NM   KWĀ   'kweː

Quayle
   James Danforth, *US vice president*   KWĀL   'kweːl

Québec, Quebec
   prov, Canada   kā-BEK, ⓈⒸ kwi-BEK, ki-BEK   keːbek, Ⓢ kwi'bek, ki'bek

Quebecer
   inhabitant of Quebec   kwi-BEK-uhr, ki-BEK-uhr   kwi'bekəʳ, ki'bekəʳ

Québecois
   inhabitant of Québec   KĀ-buh-KWAH, KĀ-BE-KWAH   ,keːbə'kwɑ, ,keː,be'kwɑ

Quechan
   people, N. America   KECH-wuhn   'ketʃwən

Quechua
   people, lang., S. America   KECH-wuh   'ketʃwə

Queensberry
   Sir John S. Douglas, *Scottish*   KWĒNZ-b(uh-)rē, Ⓢ KWĒNZ-BER-ē   'kwiːnzb(ə)riˑ,
      Marquis; boxing rules   Ⓢ 'kwiːnz,beriˑ

Queensland
   state, Australia   KWĒNZ-luhnd, -LAND   'kwiːnzlənd, -,lænd

Quekchi
   see Kekchi

Quelpart
   former name of Cheju, S. Korea   KWEL-PAHRT   'kwel,pɑʳt

Queluz
   town, Portugal   ki-LŌŌZH   ki'luːʒ

Quemoy
   island, Formosa Strait   k(w)i-MOI, KWĒ-MOI   k(w)i'mɔi, 'kwiː,mɔi

Quentin
   1. pers. name   KWENT-n   'kwentṇ
   2. Dutch   KVIN-tuhn, KVEN-; kvin-TIN, kven-   'kvintən, 'kven-; kvin'tin,
                                           kven-
   3. French   kahⁿ-TEⁿ   kɑ̃tẽ

Querandí
   S. American people   KĀ-ruhn-DĒ   ,keːrən'diː

Querétaro
   state, Mexico   kuh-RĀT-uh-RŌ   kə're̞ʈə,roː

Quesnay
   Francois, *French economist*   kā-NE, Ⓢ kā-NĀ   keːne, Ⓢ keːneː

Questel
   Mae, *US actress*   KWES-tl   'kwestḷ

Quetta
   town, Pakistan   KWET-uh   'kwe̞ʈə

Quetzal
   Central American bird   ket-SAHL, ket-SAL   ket'sɑl, ket'sæl

Quetzalcoatl
   Aztec & Toltec creator god   ket-SAHL-KWAHT-l,   ket'sɑl,kwɑtḷ, ket'sɑlkə,wɑtḷ
        ket-SAHL-kuh-WAHT-l

Foreign Sounds: ue: *Fr.* **rue**, *Ger.* **füllen**   uh(r): *Fr.* **boeuf**, *Ger.* **Höhle**   kh: *Ger.* **ich**, *Scot.* **loch**   g̶: *Sp.* **amigo**   y: *Sp.* **hablar**
hl: *Welsh* **Llanelli**.   CAPITALS: primary stress.   SMALL CAPS: secondary stress.   Ⓢ: U.S. pron.   Ⓒ: British pron.

Quezon City
  city, Philippines   KĀ-SŌN SIT-ē   'keɪˌsoɪn 'siˌt͡iʼ
Quiche
  1. S. American people   KĒ-chā   'kiːt͡ʃeɪ
  2. custard pie   KĒSH   'kiːʃ
Quiche Lorraine
  quiche with cheese & bacon or   KĒSH luh-RĀN, luh-REN, law-REN   ˌkiːʃ ləˈreɪn, ləˈren, lɔːˈren
  ham
Quiche-Mayan
  lang., C. America   KĒ-chā-MĪ-uhn   'kiːt͡ʃeɪˈmaiən
Quidde
  Ludwig, *German historian,*   KFID-uh, ⑤ KWID-uh   'kfidə, ⑤ 'kwidə
  politician (Nobel 1927)
Quileute
  N. American people   KWIL-uh-YŌ͞OT   'kwiləˌjuːt
Quiller-Couch
  Sir Arthur T., *English author*   KWIL-uhr-KŌ͞OCH   ˌkwiləʳˈkuːt͡ʃ
Quimper
  city, France   keⁿ-PER   kẽper
Quinault
  N. American people   kwuh-NUHLT   kwəˈnəlt
Quinctius
  pers. name, Latin   KWING(K)-sh(ē-)uhs   'kwiŋ(k)ʃ(iː)əs
Quincy
  1. city, FL, IL; town, WA; village,   KWIN(T)-sē   'kwin(t)siʼ
  CA
  2. city, MA   KWIN-zē   'kwinziʼ
  3. pers. name   KWIN-zē, KWIN(T)-sē   'kwinziʼ, 'kwin(t)siʼ
Quinebaug
  river, MA, CT   KWIN-uh-BAWG   'kwinəˌbɔːg
Quinn
  Aidan, *actor;* Anthony, *US actor*   KWIN   'kwin
Quinnipiac
  river, CT   KWIN-uh-pē-AK   ˌkwinəpiːˈæk
Quinquagesima
  Sunday before Lent   KWING-kwuh-JES-uh-muh,   ˌkwiŋkwəˈd͡ʒesəmə,
            -JĀ-zuh-muh   -ˈd͡ʒeɪzəmə
Quinsigamond
  Community College, *lake, MA*   kwin-SIG-uh-muhnd   kwinˈsigəmənd
Quintana Roo
  state, Mexico   kēn-TAHN-ah RŌ   kiːnˌtɑnɑ 'roː
Quintilian
  Roman rhetorician   kwin-TIL-ē-uhn   kwinˈtiliːən
Quintilianus
  pers. name, Latin   kwin-TIL-ē-Ā-nuhs   kwinˌtiliːˈeɪnəs
Quintilius
  pers. name, Latin   kwin-TIL-ē-uhs, kwin-TIL-yuhs   kwinˈtiliːəs, kwinˈtiljəs
Quintius
  pers. name, Latin   KWIN-sh(ē-)uhs, KWINT-ē-uhs   'kwinʃ(iː)əs, 'kwintiːəs
Quintus
  pers. name, Latin   KWINT-uhs   'kwintəs
Quirinal
  hill, Rome, Italy   KWIR-uhn-l   'kwirənl̩
Quirindi
  town, Australia   kwuh-RIN-DĪ   kwəˈrinˌdɑi

Key (col. 2):   a: fad   ā: fade   ah: father   ar: Mary   aw: law   e: fed   ē: feed   er: merry   i: hid   ī: hide   ō: coat   o͞o: boot
oi: boy   ow: now   u: put   uh: above   uhr: bird   ch: chop   ng: ring   sh: show   th: thick   <u>th</u>: this   zh: measure

Quirino
  pers. name, Italian   kwē-RĒ-nō   kwiː'riːnoː
Quirinus
  1. Sabine/Roman god of war   kwuh-RĪ-nuhs, kwuh-RĒ-nuhs   kwə'rɑinəs, kwə'riːnəs
  2. pers. name, Dutch   kvē-RĒ-nues   kviː'riːnys
  3. German   kvē-RĒ-nus   kviː'riːnus
Quirites
  citizens of ancient Rome   kwuh-RĪT-ēz   kwə'rɑiţiːz
Quisenberry
  Dan, *US baseball player*   KWIZ-uhn-BER-ē   'kwizən,beriˑ
Quisling
  Vidkun, *Norwegian army officer &*   KFIS-ling, KWIZ-ling   'kfisliŋ, 'kwizliŋ
    Nazi politician
Quito
  city, Ecuador   KĒ-tō   'kiːtoː
Qum
  town, Iran   KUM   'kum
Qunaytirah, El
  governorate, Syria   EL ko͞o-NĀ-truh   ,el ku''neːtrə
Quonset
  naval base, RI; tdmk for a   KWAHN(T)-suht, KWAHN-zuht   'kwɑn(t)sət, 'kwɑnzət
    prefabricated shelter
Quo Vadis
  novel, Henry Sienkiewicz   kwō VAHD-uhs   kwoː 'vɑdəs
Qur'ân, al- [Koran]
  holy book of Islam   ahl kuh-RAN, al, kuh-RAHN, kur-AN,   ɑːl kə'ræn, æl, kə'rɑn,
                                             kur-AHN   kur'æn, kur'ɑn
QwaQwa
  state, South Africa   KWAH-KWAH   'kwɑ'kwɑ
QWERTY
  standard keyboard layout   KWUHRT-ē   'kwəˡţiˑ

R

Ra [Re]
  Egyptian sun god   RAH   'rɑ
Raban
  pers. name   RĀ-BAN   'reː,bæn
Rabat
  city, Morocco; town, Malta   ruh-BAHT   rə'bɑt
Rabaul
  town, New Guinea   ruh-BOWL   rə'bɑul
Rabb
  Ellis, *US actor, director, writer*   RAB   'ræb
Rabelais
  Françoise, *French writer*   rah-BLE, Ⓢ RAB-uh-LĀ, RAB-uh-LĀ   rɑːble, Ⓢ ,ræbə'leː, 'ræbə,leː

Foreign Sounds: ue: *Fr.* **rue**, *Ger.* **füllen**   uh(r): *Fr.* **boeuf**, *Ger.* **Höhle**   <u>kh</u>: *Ger.* **ich**, *Scot.* **loch**   g̃: *Sp.* **amigo**   v̱: *Sp.* **hablar** hl: *Welsh* **Llanelli**.   CAPITALS: primary stress.   SMALL CAPS: secondary stress.   Ⓢ: U.S. pron.   Ⓛ: British pron.

Rabelaisian

   pert. to Rabelais   RAB-uh-LĀ-zhuhn, RAB-uh-LĀ-zē-uhn   ,ræbə'leːʒən, ,ræbə'leːziːən

Rabi

   1. I. I., Austrian-born US physicist   RAHB-ē   'rɑbiˑ

   (Nobel 1944)

   2. Islamic month   RUHB-ē   'rəbiˑ

Rabi Al-Awal

   Islamic holiday   RUHB-ē ahl-AH-wahl   'rəbiː al'awal

Rabin

   Yitzhak, *prime minister, Israel*   rah-BĒN   ra'biːn

Rabindranath

   pers. name, Bengali   ruh-BIN-druh-NAHT   rə'bindrə,nɑt

Rabinowitz

   Sholem, *US author, aka* Shalom   ruh-BIN-uh-WITS   rə'binə,wits

   Aleichem

Rabun

   county, GA   RĀ-buhn   'reːbən

Racal

   British communications co.   RĀ-KAWL   'reː,kɔːl

Rachel

   1. pers. name   RĀ-chuhl   'reːtʃəl

   2. Dutch   RAH-<u>KHEL</u>   'rɑː,xel

   3. French   rah-SHEL   raːʃel

   4. Hebrew   rah-<u>KHEL</u>   ra'xel

Rachins

   Alan, *US actor*   RĀ-shuhnz   'reːʃənz

Rachmaninoff

   Sergei, *Russian composer*   RU<u>HKH</u>-MAHN-yi-nuhf,   ,rəx'mɑːnjinəf,

                             Ⓢ rahk-MAHN-uh-NAWF   Ⓢ rak'manə,nɔːf

Racine

   1. city, county, WI   ruh-SĒN, rā-SĒN   rə'siːn, reː'siːn

   2. Jean Baptiste, French   rah-SĒN, Ⓢ ra-SĒN, ruh-SĒN   raːsiːn, Ⓢ ræ'siːn, rə'siːn

   playwright

Racine, Hector

   Stadium, *Montreal, Canada*   ek-TAWR ra-SĒN, HEK-tuhr ruh-SĒN   ek'tɔːʳ ræ'siːn, 'hektəʳ

                                                              rə'siːn

Rackham

   Arthur, *English illustrator*   RAK-uhm   'rækəm

Racovianism

   Christian heresy   ruh-KŌ-vē-uh-NIZ-uhm   rə'koːviːə,nizəm

Rădăut

   town, Romania   RAHD-uh-O͞OTS, RAHD-uh-O͞OT-sē   ,rɑdə'uːts, ,rɑdə'uːtsiˑ

Radcliffe

   College, MA   RAD-klif   'rædklif

Radeberger

   German beer   RAHD-uh-BER-guhr   'rɑdə,beʳgəʳ

Radhakrishnan

   Sarvepalli, *president, India*   RAHD-uh-KRISH-nuhn   ,rɑdə'kriʃnən

radium

   element   RĀD-ē-uhm   'reːdiːəm

Radko

   pers. name, Bulgarian   RAHT-kō   'rɑːtkoː

Radner

   Gilda, *US comedienne*   RAD-nuhr   'rædnəʳ

Key (col. 2): a: fad ā: fade ah: father ar: **M**ary aw: law e: fed ē: feed er: merry i: hid ī: hide ō: coat o͞o: boot
oi: **b**oy ow: now u: put uh: above uhr: bird ch: chop ng: ring sh: show th: thick th: this zh: measure

Radnor
town, PA; former county, Wales — RAD-nuhr — 'rædnəʳ

Radnorshire
former county, Wales — RAD-nuhr-shuhr, -SHIR — 'rædnəʳʃəʳ, -ˌʃiʳ

Radó
pers. name, Hungarian — RAH-dō — 'rɑdoː

Radom
province, city, Poland — RAHD-AWM — 'rɑːdˌɔːm

Radomir
pers. name, Serbo-Croatian — RAH-daw-MĒR — 'rɑːdɔːˌmiːr

radon
element — RĀ-DAHN — 'reɪˌdɑn

Rae
Charlotte, US actress; pers. name — RĀ — 'reɪ

Rafael
pers. name, Spanish — rahf-ah-EL — rɑfɑ'el

Rafah
district, occupied West Bank, Israel — RAHF-uh — 'rɑfə

Raffaello
pers. name, Italian — RAHF-fah-EL-lō — ˌrɑffɑ'elloː

Raffi
US children's singer — RAF-ē, RAHF-ē — 'ræfiˑ, 'rɑfiˑ

Raffin
Deborah, actress — RAF-uhn — 'ræfən

Raffo
Italian beer — RAHF-fō — 'rɑffoː

Rafkin
Alan, US TV director — RAF-kuhn — 'ræfkən

Rafsanjani
Hashemi, president, Iran — RAHF-suhn-JAHN-ē — ˌrɑfsən'dʒɑniˑ

Ragbrai
Iowa bicycle ride — RAG-BRĀ — 'rægˌbreː

Ragnar
pers. name, Swedish — RAHNG-nahr — 'rɑːŋnɑːr

Ragnarök
fall of the gods in Scandinavian myth — RAHG-nuh-RUH(R)K, Ⓢ RAG-nuh-RAHK, -ruhk — 'rɑgnəˌrœk, Ⓢ 'rægnəˌrɑk, -rək

Ragu
US food brand — rag-OO — ræg'uː

Ragusa
prov, Italy — ruh-GOO-zuh — rə'guːzə

Rahway
town, NJ — RAW-WĀ, RAH-WĀ — 'rɔːˌweː, 'rɑˌweː

Raimond
pers. name, French — re-MAWⁿ — remɔ̃

Raimondo
pers. name, Italian — rī-MŌN-dō — rai'moːndoː

Raimund
pers. name, German — RĪ-munt — 'raimunt

Raimundo
1. pers. name, Portuguese — rī-MOO(N)-doo — rai'mũː(n)duː
2. Spanish — rī-MOON-dō — rai'muːndoː

Raine
pers. name — RĀN — 'reɪn

Foreign Sounds: **ue**: *Fr.* **rue**, *Ger.* **füllen**   **uh(r)**: *Fr.* **boeuf**, *Ger.* **Höhle**   <u>kh</u>: *Ger.* **ich**, *Scot.* **loch**   ğ: *Sp.* **amigo**   v̲: *Sp.* **hablar**
hl: *Welsh* **Llanelli**.   CAPITALS: primary stress.   SMALL CAPS: secondary stress.   Ⓢ: U.S. pron.   Ⓛ: British pron.

Rainer		
1. pers. name, Dutch	RĪ-nuhr	'rɑinər
2. German	RĪ-nuhr	'rɑinəʳ
Raines		
Tim, *US baseball player*	RĀNZ	'reːnz
Rainier		
1. mtn., WA	ruh-NIR, rā-NIR	rə'niʳ, reː'niʳ
2. prince of Monaco; pers. name	ren-YĀ, [$] rā-NIR	renjeː, [$] reː'niʳ
Rainwater		
James, *US physicist (Nobel 1975)*	RĀN-WAWT-uhr, RĀN-WAHT-uhr	'reːn,wɔːt̬əʳ, 'reːn,wɑt̬əʳ
Raisa		
pers. name, Russian	ruh-Ē-suh, [$] rī-Ē-suh, rā-Ē-suh	rə'iːsə, [$] rɑi'iːsə, reː'iːsə
Raïssa		
pers. name, French	rah-ē-SAH	rɑiːsɑː
Raitt		
Bonnie, *US singer*	RĀT	'reːt
Raj		
pers. name, Hindi	RAHJ, RAHZH	'rɑdʒ, 'rɑʒ
Rajab		
Islamic month	ruh-JAB	rə'dʒæb
Rajahmundry		
city, India	RAHJ-uh-MUHN-drē	,rɑdʒə'məndriˑ
Rajasthan		
state, India	RAHJ-uh-STAHN	'rɑdʒə,stɑn
Rajasthani [Marwari, Mewari]		
lang., India, Pakistan	RAHJ-uh-STAHN-ē	,rɑdʒə'stɑniˑ
Rajiv		
pers. name, India	RAHJ-iv, rahj-ĒV	'rɑdʒiv, rɑdʒ'iːv
Rajput		
people, India	RAHJ-PUT, RAHZH-PUT	'rɑdʒ,put, 'rɑʒ,put
Rajputana		
region, India	RAHJ-puh-TAHN-uh	,rɑdʒpə'tɑnə
Rajshahi		
region, Bangladesh	rahj-SHAH-hē	rɑdʒ'ʃɑhiˑ
Raksha Bandha		
Indian festival	RUHK-shuh BUHN-duh	'rəkʃə 'bəndə
Raleigh		
1. Sir Walter, *English courtier, poet, explorer; pers. name*	RAW-lē, RAHL-ē, RAL-ē	'rɔːliˑ, 'rɑliˑ, 'ræliˑ
2. pl. name, NC, WV	RAW-lē, RAHL-ē	'rɔːliˑ, 'rɑliˑ
3. British bicycle co.	RAW-lē, RAHL-ē, [£] RAL-ē	'rɔːliˑ, 'rɑliˑ, [£] 'ræliˑ
Ralph		
pers. name	RALF, [£] RALF, RĀF	'rælf, [£] 'rælf, 'reːf
Ralston		
city, NE	RAWL-stuhn	'rɔːlstən
Ralston Purina		
US food co.	RAWL-stuhn pyu-RĒ-nuh	,rɔːlstən pju'riːnə
RAM		
random-access memory	RAM	'ræm
Rama		
incarnation of Vishnu; pers. name, Sanskrit	RAHM-uh	'rɑmə
Ramachandra		
hero of the Ramayana	RAHM-uh-CHUHN-druh	,rɑmə'tʃəndrə

Ramada
   US hotel chain   ruh-MAHD-uh   rə'mɑdə

Ramadan
   Islamic month   RAHM-uh-DAHN, RAM-uh-DAN   'rɑmə,dɑn, 'ræmə,dæn

Ramah
   N. American people   RAHM-uh   'rɑmə

Ramaism
   worship of Rama   RAHM-uh-IZ-uhm   'rɑmə,izəm

Ramallah
   district, Israel   ruh-MAHL-uh   rə'mɑlə

Raman
   Sir Chandrasekhara V., Indian   RAHM-uhn   'rɑmən
      physicist (Nobel 1930)

Ramapo
   river, mts., NJ, NY   RAM-uh-PŌ   'ræmə,poː

Ramaswami
   pers. name, Sanskrit   RAHM-uh-SWAHM-ē   ,rɑmə'swɑmiː

Ramat Gan
   town, Israel   ruh-MAHT GAHN, RAHM-aht GAHN   rə'mɑt 'gɑn, 'rɑmɑt 'gɑn

Ramayana
   Indian epic   ruh-MAH-yuh-nuh,   rə'mɑjənə, ,rɑmə'jɑnə,
                     RAHM-uh-YAHN-uh,   rə'mɑiənə
                     ruh-MĪ-uh-nuh

Rambo
   Stallone film character   RAM-BŌ   'ræm,boː

Rambouillet
   1. town, France   rahⁿ-boo-YE   rɑ̃buːje
   2. sheep breed   RAM-buh-LĀ, RAM-boo-YĀ   ,ræmbə'leː, ,ræmbuː'jeː

Ramchandra
   pers. name, Sanskrit   ruhm-CHUHN-druh   rəm'tʃəndrə

Ramée [Ouida]
   Louise de la, English novelist   ruh-MĀ   rə'meː

Rameses [Ramses]
   Egyptian king   RAM-uh-SĒZ   'ræmə,siːz

Ramírez
   pers. name, Spanish   rah-MĒ-res, -reth   rɑ'miːres, -reθ

Ramism
   doctrines of Ramée   RĀ-MIZ-uhm   'reː,mizəm

Ramji
   pers. name, Marathi   RAHM-jē   'rɑmdʒiː

Ramla
   district, Israel   RAHM-luh   'rɑmlə

Ramón
   pers. name, Spanish   rah-MAWN, Ⓢ ruh-MŌN   rɑ'mɔːn, Ⓢ rə'moːn

Ramona
   pers. name   ruh-MŌ-nuh   rə'moːnə

Ramón y Cajal
   Santiago, Spanish physician,   rah-MAWN ē kah-KHAHL,   rɑ'mɔːn iː kɑ'xɑl,
     histologist (Nobel 1906)   Ⓢ ruh-MŌN ē kuh-HAHL   Ⓢ rə'moːn iː kə'hɑl

Rampal
   Jean-Pierre, French flautist   rahⁿ-PAHL   rɑ̃paːl

Ramsay
   Sir William, Scottish chemist   RAM-zē   'ræmziː
     (Nobel 1904); pers. name

Foreign Sounds: ue: *Fr.* **rue**, *Ger.* **füllen** uh(r): *Fr.* **boeuf**, *Ger.* **Höhle** <u>kh</u>: *Ger.* **ich**, *Scot.* **loch** ḡ: *Sp.* **amigo** <u>v</u>: *Sp.* **hablar**
hl: *Welsh* **Llanelli**. CAPITALS: primary stress. SMALL CAPS: secondary stress. Ⓢ: U.S. pron. Ⓔ: British pron.

Ramses [Rameses]
  Egyptian king   RAM-sēz   'ræmsiːz

Ramsey
  Norman F., Jr., *US physicist*   RAM-zē   'ræmziˑ
  (Nobel 1989)

Ramsgate
  town, England   RAMZ-GĀT, RAMZ-guht   'ræmz,geɪt, 'ræmzgət

Rancagua
  prov, Chile   rahn-KAHḠ-wuh, rahng-KAHḠ-wuh   ran'kɑɣwə, raŋ'kɑɣwə

Rancho Palos Verdes
  city, CA   RAN-chō PAL-uhs VUHRD-ēz   ˌræntʃoː 'pæləs 'vəʳdiːz

Randal, Randall
  pers. name   RAN-dl   'rændl̩

Randers
  seaport, Denmark   RAHN-uhrz   'ranəʳz

Randolph
  pers. name   RAN-DAHLF, RAN-DAWLF   'ræn,dalf, 'ræn,dɔːlf

Randolph-Macon
  College, VA   RAN-DAHLF-MĀ-kuhn, RAN-DAWLF-   ˌræn,dalf'meɪkən, ˌræn,dɔːlf-

Randstad
  conurbation, Netherlands   RAHN-STAHD   'ran,stad

Randy
  pers. name   RAN-dē   'rændiˑ

Rangel
  Charles B., *US politician*   RANG-guhl   'ræŋgəl

Rangoon
  river, city, Burma   ran-GOON, rang-   ræn'guːn, ræŋ-

Rangpur
  region, Bangladesh   RUHNG-PUR   'rəŋ,puʳ

Rank
  Otto, *Austrian psychoanalyst*   RAHNGK   'raŋk

Rannoch, Loch
  see Loch Rannoch

Ransom
  pers. name   RAN-suhm   'rænsəm

Ranulf, Ranulph
  pers. name   RĀ-nuhlf, RAN-uhlf   'reːnəlf, 'rænəlf

Rao
  P.V. Narasimha, *Indian prime*   ROW   'rɑu
  minister

Rao, Rau
  Santha Rama, *Indian writer*   ROW   'rɑu

Raoul
  1. pers. name, French   rah-OOL   rɑːuːl
  2. German, Spanish   rah-OOL   ra'uːl

Rapallo
  port, Italy   ruh-PAHL-ō   rə'paloː

Raphael
  1. Italian painter   RAF-ē-uhl, RĀ-fē-uhl, RAHF-ē-uhl,   'ræfiːəl, 'reːfiːəl, 'rɑfiːəl,
       RAHF-ī-EL   ˌrɑfai'el
  2. archangel; pers. name   RĀ-fē-uhl, RAF-ē-uhl, RAF-Ā-uhl,   'reːfiːəl, 'ræfiːəl, 'ræf,eːəl,
       RĀF-yuhl   'reːfjəl
  3. Dutch   RAH-FEL   'raː,fel
  4. French   rah-fah-EL   raːfaːel
  5. German   RAH-fah-EL   'rafa,el

Key (col. 2):   a: fad ā: fade ah: father ar: Mary aw: law e: fed ē: feed er: merry i: hid ī: hide ō: coat o͞o: boot
oi: boy ow: now u: put uh: above uhr: bird ch: chop ng: ring sh: show th: thick th̲: this zh: measure

Raphia
   ancient town, Gaza & Egypt   ruh-FĪ-uh   rə'faiə
Rapidan
   river, VA   RAP-uh-DAN   ˌræpə'dæn
Rapides
   parish, LA   rah-PĒD   rɑ'piːd
Rappahannock
   river, county, VA   RAP-uh-HAN-uhk   ˌræpə'hænək
Rapunzel
   fairy tale character   ruh-PUHN-zuhl   rə'pənzəl
Raquel
   1. pers. name   rah-KEL, ra-KEL   rɑ'kel, ræ'kel
   2. Spanish   rah-KEL   rɑ'kel
Raritan
   river, borough, NJ   RAR-uht-n   'rærətn̩
Rarotonga
   island, Cook Islands   RAR-uh-TAHNG-guh   ˌrærə'tɑŋgə
Ra's al Khaymah
   emirate, United Arab Emirates   RAHS ahl KHĪ-muh, al   ˌrɑs aːl 'xaimə, æl
Rashi
   French Hebrew scholar   rah-SHĒ   rɑːʃiː
Rashid
   pers. name   rah-SHĒD, ra-SHĒD   rɑ'ʃiːd, ræ'ʃiːd
Rask
   Rasmus, *Danish philologist*   RAHSG, ⑤ RASK, RAHSK   'rɑːsg, ⑤ 'ræsk, 'rɑsk
Rasmus
   pers. name, Danish, Norwegian   RAHS-mus   'rɑsmus
Rasmussen
   Knud, *Danish explorer*   RAHS-MUS-n, ⑤ RAS-muh-suhn   'rɑsˌmusn̩, ⑤ 'ræsməsən
Rasputin
   Grigori, *Russian mystic*   ruh-SPOOT-yin, ⑤ ra-SP(Y)OOT-n, ra-SPUT-n   rə'spuːtjin, ⑤ ræ'sp(j)uːtn̩, ræ'sputn̩
Ras Shamra
   site of Ugarit   RAHS SHAM-rah   ˌrɑs 'ʃæmrɑ
Rastafari
   pert. to Rastafarianism   RAS-tuh-FAR-ē, RAHS-, -FER-ē, -FAHR-ē   ˌræstə'færiˑ, ˌrɑs-, -'feriˑ, -'fariˑ
Rastafarian
   pert. to Rastafarianism   RAS-tuh-FAR-ē-uhn, RAHS-, -FER-ē-uhn, -FAHR-ē-uhn   ˌræstə'færiːən, ˌrɑs-, -'feriːən, -'fariːən
Rastafarianism
   religion   RAS-tuh-FAR-ē-uh-NIZ-uhm, RAHS-, -FER-ē-uh-NIZ-uhm, -FAHR-ē-uh-NIZ-uhm   ˌræstə'færiːəˌnizəm, ˌrɑs-, -'feriːəˌnizəm, -'fariːəˌnizəm
Rastus
   pers. name   RAS-tuhs   'ræstəs
Ratatouille
   vegetable dish   RA-TA-TOO-ē, RAH-TAH-TOO-ē, RAT-uh-TWĒ   ˌræˌtæ'tuːiˑ, ˌrɑˌtɑ'tuːiˑ, ˌrætə'twiː
Ratcliffe
   pers. name   RAT-KLIF   'rætˌklif
Rathbone
   pers. name   RATH-BŌN, RATH-buhn   'ræθˌboːn, 'ræθbən
Rathlin
   island, Ireland   RATH-luhn   'ræθlən

Foreign Sounds: ue: *Fr.* **rue**, *Ger.* **füllen**   uh(r): *Fr.* **boeuf**, *Ger.* **Höhle**   <u>kh</u>: *Ger.* **ich**, *Scot.* **loch**   ğ: *Sp.* **amigo**   <u>v</u>: *Sp.* **hablar** hl: *Welsh* **Llanelli**.   CAPITALS: primary stress.   SMALL CAPS: secondary stress.   ⑤: U.S. pron.   ⑫: British pron.

Rätische Alpen [Rhaetian Alps]
  Alpine mtn. range   RĀ-tish-uh AHL-puhn   ˌreːtiʃə ˈɑlpən
Rau
  see Rao
Rauber Skat
  game   ROI-buhr SKAHT, ROW-buhr SKAT   ˈrɔibəʳ ˈskat, ˈraubəʳ ˈskæt
Rauchenfels
  German beer   ROW-<u>kh</u>uhn-FELS   ˈrauxənˌfels
Raúl
  pers. name, Spanish   rah-O͞OL   rɑˈuːl
Rauschenberg
  Robert, *US artist*   ROW-shuhn-BUHRG   ˈrauʃənˌbəʳg
Ravalli
  county, MT   ruh-VAL-ē   rəˈvæliˑ
Ravel
  Maurice, *French composer*   rah-VEL, Ⓢ ruh-VEL   rɑːvel, Ⓢ rəˈvel
Ravenna
  prov, city, Italy   ruh-VEN-uh   rəˈvenə
Ravindranatha
  pers. name, Sanskrit   ruh-VIN-druh-NAH-tah   rəˈvindrəˌnɑtɑ
Rawalpindi
  prov, Pakistan   RAH-wuhl-PIN-dē, rowl-PIN-dē   ˌrawəlˈpindiˑ, raulˈpindiˑ
Rawlings
  Lester, *US actor;* Marjorie Kinnan, RAW-lingz   ˈrɔːliŋz
    *US author; US sporting goods
    co.*
Rawlins
  city, WY   RAW-luhnz, RAHL-uhnz   ˈrɔːlənz, ˈrɑlənz
Rawls
  Lou, *US singer*   RAWLZ   ˈrɔːlz
Ray
  1. Satyajit, *Indian film maker* RĪ, RĀ   ˈrai, ˈreː
  2. pers. name   RĀ   ˈreː
Ray-Ban
  tdmk for sunglasses   RĀ-BAN   ˈreːˌbæn
Rayburn
  Gene, *US TV performer*   RĀ-BUHRN   ˈreːˌbəʳn
Rayleigh
  J. W. S., *English physicist (Nobel* RĀ-lē   ˈreːliˑ
    1904)
Raymond
  1. pers. name   RĀ-muhnd   ˈreːmənd
  2. French   re-MAWⁿ   remɔ̃
Raymund
  pers. name, German   RĪ-munt   ˈraimunt
Raymundo
  pers. name, Portuguese   rī-MO͞O(N)-do͞o   raiˈmũː(n)duː
Rayovac
  US corp.   RĀ-ō-VAK, RĀ-uh-VAK   ˈreːoːˌvæk, ˈreːəˌvæk
Re
  Egyptian sun god   RĀ   ˈreː
Rea
  pers. name   RĀ   ˈreː

Key (col. 2): a: fad ā: fade ah: father ar: Mary aw: law e: fed ē: feed er: merry i: hid ī: hide ō: coat o͞o: boot
oi: boy ow: now u: put uh: above uhr: bird ch: chop ng: ring sh: show th: thick <u>th</u>: this zh: measure

Reading
railroad, US; city, PA; city,   RED-ing   'rediŋ
  England

Reagan
1. Ronald, *40th US president*   RĀ-guhn; *now rarely* RĒ-guhn   'reːgən; *now rarely* 'riːgən
2. *county, TX*   RĀ-guhn   'reːgən

Real Madrid
Spanish soccer team   rā-AHL mah-<u>THRĒTH</u>   reː'al ma'ðriːð

Reasoner
Harry, *US TV news reporter*   RĒZ-nuhr, RĒ-zuh-nuhr   'riːznəʳ, 'riːzənəʳ

Reate
ancient form of Rieti   rē-ĀT-ē   riː'eːṭiˑ

Reba
pers. name (R. McEntire)   RĒ-buh   'riːbə

Rebecca, Rebekah
pers. name   ri-BEK-uh   ri'bekə

Recife
city, Brazil   ruh-SĒ-fuh   rə'siːfə

Red
pers. name   RED   'red

Redbridge
borough, England   RED-BRIJ   'red₁bridʒ

Reddy
Helen, *Australian singer*   RED-ē   'rediˑ

Redemptorist
religious order   ruh-DEM(P)-t(uh-)ruhst   rə'dem(p)t(ə)rəst

Redenbacher
Orville, *US popcorn magnate*   RED-n-BAK-uhr, RED-n-BAHK-uhr   'redn̩₁bækəʳ, 'redn̩₁bɑkəʳ

Redfern
pers. name   RED-FUHRN   'red₁fəʳn

Redford
Robert, *US actor, director*   RED-fuhrd   'redfəʳd

Redgrave
British acting family   RED-GRĀV   'red₁greːv

Redjang
lang., people, Sumatra   rā-ZHAHNG, rā-ZHANG   reː'ʒɑŋ, reː'ʒæŋ

Redlands
city, CA   RED-luhn(d)z   'redlən(d)z

Redon
Odilon, *French artist*   ruh-DAWⁿ   rədɔ̃

Redondo Beach
city, CA   ri-DAHN-dō BĒCH   ri₁dɑndoː 'biːtʃ

Reebok
US footwear co.   RĒ-BAHK   'riː₁bɑk

Reese
Della, *US singer*   RĒS   'riːs

Reeve
Christopher, *US actor*   RĒV   'riːv

Reeves
Keanu, *US actor*   RĒVZ   'riːvz

Refugio
county, town, TX   ruh-F(Y)UR-ē-ō *[sic]*   rə'f(j)uriːoː *[sic]*

Reg
pers. name   REJ   'redʒ

Foreign Sounds: **ue**: *Fr.* **rue**, *Ger.* **füllen**   **uh(r)**: *Fr.* **boeuf**, *Ger.* **Höhle**   <u>kh</u>: *Ger.* **ich**, *Scot.* **loch**   ğ̵: *Sp.* **amigo**   v̱: *Sp.* **hablar**
hl: *Welsh* **Llanelli**.   CAPITALS: primary stress.   SMALL CAPS: secondary stress.   Ⓢ: U.S. pron.   Ⓑ: British pron.

Regan
  Donald, *US government official;*   RĒ-guhn   'riːgən
    character in King Lear,
    Shakespeare

Régence
  style of French furnishings   rä-ZHAHⁿS   reːʒãs

Regency
  pert. to styles of 1811-20; genre of   RĒ-juhn-sē   'riːdʒənsiˑ
    romance novel

Regensburg
  city, Germany   RĀ-guhnz-BURK, ⑤ RĀ-guhnz-BUHRG   'reːgənz,buᵊk,
                                             ⑤ 'reːgənz,bəᵊg

Regenstein
  Joseph, Library, *Chicago*   RĀ-guhn-STĪN, REG-uhn-STĪN   'reːgən,stain, 'regən,stain

Reggie
  pers. name   REJ-ē   'redʒiˑ

Reggio di Calabria
  prov & town, Italy   RED-j(ē-)ō DĒ kah-LAHB-rē-ah   'reddʒ(iː)oː ˌdiː kaˈlabriːa

Reggio nell'Emilia
  prov, Italy   RED-j(ē-)ō NEL le-MĒL-yah   'reddʒ(iː)oː ˌnel leˈmiːlja

Regia
  Roman home of Numa Pompilius   RĒ-jē-uh   'riːdʒiːə

Regina
  1. city, Canada   ri-JĪ-nuh   riˈdʒainə
  2. pers. name   ri-JĒ-nuh, Ⓔ ri-JĪ-nuh   riˈdʒiːnə, Ⓔ riˈdʒainə
  3. Italian   rä-JĒ-nah   reːˈdʒiːnɑ

Reginald
  pers. name   REJ-uhn-ld   'redʒənl̩d

Régine
  pers. name, French   rä-ZHĒN   reːʒiːn

Regis
  College, *CO, MA; pers. name*   RĒ-juhs   'riːdʒəs

Régis
  pers. name, French   rä-ZHĒS   reːʒiːs

Regius
  royal professorship   RĒ-j(ē-)uhs   'riːdʒ(iː)əs

Regulus
  Roman hero   REG-yuh-luhs   'regjələs

Rehnquist
  William Hubbs, *US Supreme Court*   REN-kwist, RENG-kwist   'renkwist, 'reŋkwist
    justice

Rehoboam
  king of Judah   RĒ-(h)uh-BŌ-uhm   ˌriː(h)əˈboːəm

Rehoboth
  US pl. name   ri-HŌ-buhth   riˈhoːbəθ

Rehovot
  district, Israel   ruh-KHAW-VAWT, ⑤ RĀ-hō-VŌT   rəˈxɔːvɔːt, ⑤ 'reːhoː,voːt

Reich
  German regime   RĪKH, ⑤ RĪK   'raiç, ⑤ 'raik

Reichenbach
  waterfall, Switzerland   RĪ-khuhn-BAHKH, ⑤ RĪ-kuhn-BAHK   'raiçən,bax, ⑤ 'raikən,bak

Reichstag
  German parliament   RĪKH-STAHK, ⑤ RĪK-STAHG   'raiç,stak, ⑤ 'raik,stag

---

Key (col. 2):   a: fad   ā: fade   ah: father   ar: Mary   aw: law   e: fed   ē: feed   er: merry   i: hid   ī: hide   ō: coat   ōō: boot
oi: boy   ow: now   u: put   uh: above   uhr: bird   ch: chop   ng: ring   sh: show   th: thick   <u>th</u>: this   zh: measure

Reichstein

Tadeus, *Polish-born Swiss chemist* RĪKH-SHTĪN, Ⓢ RĪK-STĪN 'raiç‚ʃtain, Ⓢ 'raik‚stain
  (Nobel 1950)

Reid

Kate, *British actress* RĒD 'riːd

Reigate

suburb of London, England RĪ-GĀT, RĪ-git 'rai‚geːt, 'raigit

Reijiro

pers. name, Japanese rā-jē-rō reːdʒiːroː

Reilly

pers. name RĪ-lē 'raili·

Reims, Rheims

town, France REⁿS, Ⓢ RĒMZ rẽs, Ⓢ 'riːmz

Reiner

Carl, *US comedian, writer, & his* RĪ-nuhr 'rainəʳ
  son Rob, *US actor, writer*

Reinhard

pers. name, German RĪN-HAHRT 'rain‚haʳt

Reinhardt

Django, *French jazz musician;* RĪN-HAHRT 'rain‚haʳt
  College, *GA*

Reinhart

pers. name, Dutch RĪN-HAHRT 'rain‚hart

Reinheitsgebot

German beer purity laws RĪN-HĪTS-guh-BŌT 'rain‚haitsgə‚boːt

Reinhold

1. pers. name RĪN-HŌLD 'rain‚hoːld
2. German RĪN-HAWLT 'rain‚hoːlt

Rek

lang., Sudan, Ethiopia RĂK 'reˑk

Religio Medici

meditative writings of Sir Thomas rē-LIJ-ē-ō MED-uh-chē ri·'lidʒiːoː 'medətʃi·
  Browne

REM

rapid eye movement REM, AHR-Ē-EM 'rem, ‚ar‚iː'em

Remarque

Erich, *German novelist* ruh-MAHRK rə'maʳk

Rembrandt

1. pers. name REM-BRANT 'rem‚brænt
2. Dutch REM-BRAHNT 'rem‚brant

Rembrandt van Rijn

Dutch painter REM-BRAHNT vahn RĪN, 'rem‚brant van 'rain,
  Ⓢ REM-BRANT van RĪN Ⓢ 'rem‚brænt væn 'rain

Remi

1. pers. name, French ruh-MĒ, rā-MĒ rəmiː, reːmiː
2. ancient Gaulish people RĒ-MĪ 'riː‚mai
3. lang., Africa RĀ-mē 'reːmi·

Remick

Lee, *US actress* REM-ik 'remik

Remigio

pers. name, Spanish rā-MĒĜ-yō reː'miːɣjoː

Remigius

pers. name, German rā-MĒG-yus, rā-MĒ-gē-us reː'miːgjus, reː'miːgiːus

---

Foreign Sounds: ue: *Fr.* **rue,** *Ger.* f**ü**llen uh(r): *Fr.* b**oeu**f, *Ger.* H**ö**hle kh: *Ger.* i**ch,** *Scot.* lo**ch** ĝ: *Sp.* ami**g**o v: *Sp.* ha**b**lar
hl: *Welsh* **Ll**anelli. CAPITALS: primary stress. SMALL CAPS: secondary stress. Ⓢ: U.S. pron. Ⓛ: British pron.

Remington

Frederic, *US painter; US rifle manufacturer* — REM-ing-tuhn — 'remiŋtən

Remus

1. *twin brother of Romulus; pers. name* — RĒ-muhs — 'riːməs

2. *German* — RĀ-mus — 'reːmus

Rémy

pers. name, French — rä-MĒ — reːmiː

Remy Martin

cognac — ruh-MĒ mahr-TEⁿ, ⑤ REM-ē MAHRT-n — rəmiː maːrtẽ, ⑤ 'remi·'mɑʳtn̩

Renaissance

period of intellectual & artistic activity — REN-uh-SAHN(T)S, -ZAHN(T)S, -SAHⁿS, -ZAHⁿS, Ⓔ ri-NĀS-n(t)s — 'renə,sɑn(t)s, -,zɑn(t)s, -,sãs, -,zãs, Ⓔ ri'neːsn̩(t)s

Renaissance, La

see La Renaissance

Renata

pers. name — ruh-NAHT-uh — rə'nɑtə

Renato

pers. name — ri-NAHT-ō, rä- — ri'nɑtoː, reː-

Renatus

pers. name, Latin — ri-NĀT-uhs — ri'neːtəs

Renaud

pers. name, French — ruh-NŌ — rənoː

Renault

1. *French automobile* — ruh-NŌ; ⑤ ruh-NŌ, ruh-NAWLT — rənoː; ⑤ rə'noː, rə'nɔːlt

2. *Louis, French jurist, pacifist (Nobel 1907)* — ruh-NŌ — rənoː

Rene

pers. name — ruh-NĀ, Ⓔ REN-Ā, RUHN-Ā, REN-ē — rə'neː, Ⓔ 'ren,eː, 'rən,eː, 'reni·

René

1. *pers. name, English, German* — ruh-NĀ, Ⓔ REN-Ā, RUHN-Ā, REN-ē — rə'neː, Ⓔ 'ren,eː, 'rən,eː, 'reni·

2. *French* — ruh-NĀ — rəneː

Renée

1. *pers. name* — ruh-NĀ — rə'neː

2. *French* — ruh-NĀ — rəneː

Reni

Guido, *Italian painter* — REN-ē — 'reni·

Rennes

city, France — REN — ren

Rennie

pers. name — REN-ē — 'reni·

Reno

1. *city, NV; county, KS; pers. name* — RĒ-nō — 'riːnoː

2. *river, Italy* — RĀ-nō, REN-ō — 'reːnoː, 'renoː

Renoir

Jean, *French film director, son of Pierre Auguste, French painter* — ruhn-WAHR, ⑤ REN-WAHR, ruhn-WAHR — rənwɑːr, ⑤ 'ren,wɑʳ, rən'wɑʳ

Rensselaer

1. *town,* Polytechnic Institute, *NY* — REN(T)-suh-LIR, REN(T)-s(uh-)luhr — ,ren(t)sə'liʳ, 'ren(t)s(ə)ləʳ

2. *pers. name* — REN(T)-suh-LIR — 'ren(t)sə,liʳ

Key (col. 2):   a: fad   ā: fade   ah: father   ar: Mary   aw: law   e: fed   ē: feed   er: merry   i: hid   ī: hide   ō: coat   o͞o: boot
oi: boy   ow: now   u: put   uh: above   uhr: bird   ch: chop   ng: ring   sh: show   th: thick   <u>th</u>: this   zh: measure

Repsol
    Spanish oil co.   REP-SŌL   'rep,soːl

Republican
    US political party   ri-PUHB-li-kuhn   ri'pəblikən

République
    French for republic   rā-pue-BLĒK   reːpyːbliːk

Requiem
    mass for the dead   REK-wē-uhm, RĀ-kwē-uhm   'rekwiːəm, 'reːkwiːəm

Res gestae
    autobiography of Augustus   RĀS JES-TĪ, GES-TĪ   'reːs 'dʒes,tai, 'ges,tai

Resighini Rancheria
    Indian reservation, US   RES-uh-GĒ-nē RAN-chuh-RĒ-uh   ,resə'giːni· ,ræntʃə'riːə

Respighi
    Ottorino, *Italian composer*   ruh-SPĒ-gē, res-PĒ-gē   rə'spiːgi·, res'piːgi·

Restigouche
    river, Canada   RES-ti-GŌŌSH   'resti,guːʃ

Reston
    James, *Scottish-born US journalist; city, VA*   RES-tuhn   'restən

Reticulum
    constellation   ri-TIK-yuh-luhm   ri'tikjələm

Retsina
    Greek resinated wine   ret-SĒ-nuh   ret'siːnə

Reuben
    sandwich; pers. name   RŌŌ-buhn   'ruːbən

Réunion
    island, Indian Ocean   rē-YŌŌN-yuhn   ri·'juːnjən

Reunionese
    lang., pert. to Réunion   rē-YŌŌN-yuh-NĒZ, -NĒS   ri·,juːnjə'niːz, -'niːs

Reuters
    British news agency   ROIT-uhrz   'rɔiʈərz

Reuther
    Walter, *US labor leader*   RŌŌ-thuhr   'ruːθər

Revelation
    New Testament book   REV-uh-LĀ-shuhn   ,revə'leːʃən

Revere
    Paul, *American patriot; town, MA*   ri-VIR   ri'viʳ

Reverend
    title for a member of the clergy   REV-(uh-)ruhnd, REV-uhrnd   'rev(ə)rənd, 'revəʳnd

Revlon
    US cosmetics co.   REV-LAHN   'rev,lɑn

Rex
    pers. name   REKS   'reks

Reye's
    syndrome, medical disorder   RĪZ, RĀZ   'rɑiz, 'reːz

Reykjavik
    city, Iceland   RĀK-yuh-VIK, -VĒK   'reːkjə,vik, -,viːk

Reymont
    Władysław Stanisław, *Polish author (Nobel 1924)*   RĀ-MAHNT   'reː,mɑnt

Reynaldo
    pers. name, Spanish   rā-NAHL-dō   reː'nɑldoː

Reynard
    fox in medieval stories   RĀ-nuhrd, REN-uhrd, RĀ-NAHR(D)   'reːnəʳd, 'renəʳd, 'reː,nɑʳ(d)

Foreign Sounds: ue: *Fr.* **rue**, *Ger.* f**ü**llen   uh(r): *Fr.* b**oeuf**, *Ger.* H**öh**le   <u>kh</u>: *Ger.* i**ch**, *Scot.* lo**ch**   ḡ: *Sp.* ami**g**o   <u>v</u>: *Sp.* ha**b**lar hl: *Welsh* **Ll**anelli.   CAPITALS: primary stress.   SMALL CAPS: secondary stress.   Ⓢ: U.S. pron.   Ⓑ: British pron.

Reynaud
    Paul, *French political leader*   re-NŌ   renoː

Reynella
    Australian wine   ren-EL-uh   ren'elə

Reynolds
    Burt, *US actor;* Debbie, *US actress*   REN-l(d)z   'renḷ(d)z

Reza Shah Pahlavi
    shah, Iran   ri-ZAH SHAH PAHL-uh-vē   ri'za 'ʃa 'paləviˑ

Rhadamanthine
    pert. to Rhadamanthys   RAD-uh-MAN(T)-thuhn,   ˌrædə'mæn(t)θən,
         RAD-uh-MAN-THĪN   ˌrædə'mæn,θain

Rhadamanthys, -thus
    judge of the Underworld in Greek   RAD-uh-MAN(T)-thuhs   ˌrædə'mæn(t)θəs
       mythology

Rhaetia
    ancient Roman province, Europe   RĒ-sh(ē-)uh   'riːʃ(iː)ə

Rhaetian
    lang., Switzerland, Italy, Austria;   RĒ-sh(ē-)uhn   'riːʃ(iː)ən
       Alps, *mtn. range*

Rhaetic
    pert. to Rhaetia   RĒT-ik   'riːtik

Rhaeto-Romanic
    Romance lang.   RĒT-ō-rō-MAN-ik   ˌriːtoːroː'mænik

Rhea
    1. Greek goddess, mother of Zeus;   RĒ-uh   'riːə
       satellite of Saturn; S. American
       flightless bird
    2. pers. name   RĒ, RĀ, RĒ-uh   'riː, 'reː, 'riːə

Rhea Silvia [Ilia]
    mother of Romulus and Remus   RĒ-uh SIL-vē-uh   ˌriːə 'silviːə

Rhee
    Syngman, *Korean political leader*   RĒ   'riː

Rheims
    see Reims

Rhein
    see Rhine

Rheingold, Das
    opera, R. Wagner   dahs RĪN-GŌLD   dɑs 'rain,goːld

Rheinhessen-Pfalz
    prov, Germany   RĪN-HES-uhn-(P)FAHLTS   ˌrain,hesən'(p)falts

Rheinisches Schiefergebirge
    plateau, Germany   RĪ-nuh-shuhs SHĒ-fuhr-guh-BIR-guh   'rainəʃəs 'ʃiːfərˌgə,birgə

Rheinland-Pfalz
    prov, Germany   RĪN-LAHNT-(P)FAHLTS   'rain,lant'(p)falts

Rheinpfalz
    prov, Germany   RĪN-(P)FAHLTS   'rain,(p)falts

Rhenish
    pert. to the Rhine   REN-ish   'reniʃ

Rhenish Slate
    plateau, Germany   REN-ish SLĀT   'reniʃ 'sleːt

rhenium
    element   RĒ-nē-uhm   'riːniːəm

Rhenus
    Latin name of the Rhine   RĒ-nuhs   'riːnəs

Key (col. 2):   a: fad   ā: fade   ah: father   ar: Mary   aw: law   e: fed   ē: feed   er: merry   i: hid   ī: hide   ō: coat   ōō: boot
oi: boy   ow: now   u: put   uh: above   uhr: bird   ch: chop   ng: ring   sh: show   th: thick   <u>th</u>: this   zh: measure

Rhesus		
mythical Thracian; monkey genus	RĒ-suhs	'ri:səs
Rhett		
pers. name	RET	'ret
Rhin [Rhine]		
river, Europe; dept, France	RE^{n}	rẽ
Rhine, Rhein, Rijn		
river, Europe	RĪN	'rɑin
Rhineland		
region, Germany	RĪN-luhnd, -LAND	'rɑinlənd, -ˌlænd
Rhineland-Palatinate		
prov, Germany	RĪN-luhnd-puh-LAT-n-uht	'rɑinləndpə'lætn̩ət
Rhoda		
pers. name	RŌD-uh	'ro:də
Rhodanus		
Latin name of the Rhone	RAHD-n-uhs	'rɑdn̩əs
Rhode Island		
state, US	rōd Ī-luhnd, ruh-DĪ-luhnd	ro:d 'ɑilənd, rə'dɑilənd
Rhodes		
Cecil John, *British financier; island, Aegean*	RŌDZ	'ro:dz
Rhodesia		
region, central Africa, now Zambia and Zimbabwe	rō-DĒ-zh(ē-)uh	ro:'di:ʒ(i:)ə
rhodium		
element	RŌD-ē-uhm	'ro:di:əm
Rhodolite		
garnet	RŌD-l-ĪT	'ro:dl̩ˌɑit
Rhodonite		
mineral	RŌD-n-ĪT	'ro:dn̩ˌɑit
Rhodope		
1. region, Greece; mtn. range, Europe	RAHD-uh-pē	'rɑdəpi·
2. legendary Ephesian heroine	rō-DŌ-pē, ruh-DŌ-pē	ro:'do:pi·, rə'do:pi·
Rhodus		
wife of Helios	RŌD-uhs	'ro:dəs
Rhön		
mtn. range, Germany	RUH(R)N	'rœ:n
Rhonda		
pers. name	RAHN-duh	'rɑndə
Rhondda		
valley, district, Wales	HRAHN-thuh, Ⓢ RAHN-thuh	'r̥ɑnðə, Ⓢ 'rɑnðə
Rhône		
river, Europe	RŌN	'ro:n
Rhône-Alpes		
region, France	RŌN-AHLP	ro:nɑ:lp
Rhumba		
see Rumba		
Rhymney, Rhymni		
river, Wales	HRUHM-nē, Ⓢ RUHM-nē	'r̥əmni·, Ⓢ 'rəmni·
Rhys		
1. pers. name	RĒS	'ri:s
2. Welsh	HRĒS, Ⓢ RĒS	'r̥i:s, Ⓢ 'ri:s

Foreign Sounds: ue: *Fr.* **rue**, *Ger.* **füllen** uh(r): *Fr.* **boeuf**, *Ger.* **Höhle** kh: *Ger.* **ich**, *Scot.* **loch** ḡ: *Sp.* ami**g**o v: *Sp.* ha**b**lar hl: *Welsh* **Llanelli**. CAPITALS: primary stress. SMALL CAPS: secondary stress. Ⓢ: U.S. pron. [£]: British pron.

Rialto

  1. city, CA   rē-AL-tō   riːˈæltoː

  2. street, Venice   rē-AHL-tō, ⑤ rē-AL-tō   riːˈaltoː, ⑤ riːˈæltoː

Ribbonism

  precepts of an Irish secret society   RIB-uh-NIZ-uhm   ˈribə͵nizəm
    opposing landlords

Ricardo

  1. David, British economist   ri-KAHR-dō   riˈkaʳdoː

  2. pers. name, Spanish   rē-KAHR-<u>th</u>ō   riːˈkarðoː

Riccardo

  1. pers. name   rik-AHRD-ō   rikˈaʳdoː

  2. Italian   rēk-KAHR-do   riːkˈkardo

Ricci

  Marco, *Italian painter;* Nina,   RĒT-chē, ⑤ RĒ-chē   ˈriːttʃiˑ, ⑤ ˈriːtʃiˑ
    Italian designer; Sebastiano,
    Italian painter

Rice

  University, *TX; pers. name*   RĪS   ˈrais

Rice-a-Roni

  tdmk for rice and stuffing mixes   RĪ-suh-RŌ-nē   ͵raisəˈroːniˑ

Rich

  pers. name   RICH   ˈritʃ

Richard

  1. pers. name   RICH-uhrd   ˈritʃəʳd

  2. Dutch   RĒ-SHAHRT   ˈriː͵ʃart

  3. French   rē-SHAHR   riːˈʃaːr

  4. German   RI<u>KH</u>-AHRT   ˈriç͵aʳt

Richards

  D. W., Jr., *US physician (Nobel*   RICH-uhrdz   ˈritʃəʳdz
    1956); T. W., *US chemist (Nobel*
    1914)

Richardson

  Sir Owen W., *English physicist*   RICH-uhrd-suhn   ˈritʃəʳdsən
    (Nobel 1928); Sir Ralph, *English*
    actor

Richelieu

  1. Duc de, French cardinal   rē-shuh-LYUH(R),   riːʃəljœː, ⑤ ˈriʃəl͵(j)uː
                          ⑤ RISH-uhl-(Y)O͞O

  2. river, Canada   RISH-uhl-(Y)O͞O   ˈriʃəl͵(j)uː

Richet

  C. R., *French physiologist (Nobel*   rē-SHĀ   riːˈʃeː
    1913)

Richie

  Lionel B., Jr., *US singer*   RICH-ē   ˈritʃiˑ

Richmond

  pl. name; pers. name   RICH-muhnd   ˈritʃmənd

Richmond-upon-Thames

  borough, England   RICH-muhn-duh-puhn-TEMZ   ˈritʃməndəpənˈtemz

Richter

  Burton, *US particle physicist*   RIK-tuhr   ˈriktəʳ
    (Nobel 1976); Francis, *US*
    seismologist; earthquake scale

Rick

  pers. name   RIK   ˈrik

Key (col. 2):   a: fad   ā: fade   ah: father   ar: **Mary**   aw: **law**   e: fed   ē: feed   er: **merry**   i: hid   ī: hide   ō: coat   o͞o: boot
oi: **boy**   ow: **now**   u: **put**   uh: **above**   uhr: **bird**   ch: **chop**   ng: **ring**   sh: **show**   th: **thick**   <u>th</u>: **this**   zh: measure

Rickenbacker
    Edward, *US military aviator*   RIK-uhn-BAK-uhr   'rikən,bækə^r
Rickles
    Don, *US comedian*   RIK-uhlz   'rikəlz
Rickover
    Hyman, *US admiral*   RIK-ō-vuhr   'rik,oːvə^r
Ricky, Rickey, Ricki, Rickie
    pers. name   RIK-ē   'rikiˑ
Rico
    pers. name   RĒ-kō   'riːkoː
Ricoh
    tdmk for watches   RĒ-kō   'riːkoː
Ricotta
    cheese   ri-KAHT-uh   ri'kɑʈə
Rideau
    lake, river, canal, Canada   ri-DŌ   ri'doː
Rider
    pers. name   RĪD-uhr   'raidə^r
Ridley
    pers. name   RID-lē   'ridliˑ
Riegle
    Donald W., Jr., *US politician*   RĒ-guhl   'riːgəl
Riemann
    Bernhard, *German mathematician*   RĒ-MAHN   'riː,mɑn
Riesling
    wine   RĒZ-ling, RĒ-sling   'riːzliŋ, 'riːsliŋ
Rieti
    city, Italy   rē-ĀT-ē, rē-ET-ē   riː'eːʈiˑ, riː'eʈiˑ
Riff
    lang., Algeria, Morocco   RIF   'rif
Riga
    city, Latvia; gulf, Baltic Sea   RĒ-guh   'riːgə
Rigakushi
    pers. name, Japanese   rē-gah-kōō-shē   riːgakuːʃiː
Rigby
    Cathy, *US gymnast*   RIG-bē   'rigbiˑ
Rigel
    star   RĪ-juhl, RĪ-guhl   'raidʒəl, 'raigəl
Rigoberta
    pers. name (R. Menchú)   rē-ḡō-VER-tah, Ⓢ RIG-uh-BERT-uh   riːɣoː'βerta, Ⓢ ,rigə'be^rʈə
Rigoletto
    opera, Verdi   RIG-uh-LET-ō   ,rigə'leʈoː
Rigsdag
    former Parliament, Denmark   RIGZ-DAHG   'rigz,dɑg
Rig-Veda
    Hindu book of hymns   rig-VĀD-uh   rig've:də
Riis
    Jacob, *US reformer*   RĒS   'riːs
Rijeka [Fiume]
    city, Croatia   rē-YEK-uh   riː'jekə
Rijks
    museum, Amsterdam, Netherlands   RĪKS   'raiks
Rijn
    see **Rhine**

Foreign Sounds: ue: *Fr.* **rue**, *Ger.* **füllen**   uh(r): *Fr.* **boeuf**, *Ger.* **Höhle**   k̲h: *Ger.* **ich**, *Scot.* **loch**   g̲: *Sp.* **amigo**   v̲: *Sp.* **hablar** hl: *Welsh* **Llanelli**.   CAPITALS: primary stress.   SMALL CAPS: secondary stress.   Ⓢ: U.S. pron.   Ⓛ: British pron.

Rikki		
pers. name	RIK-ē	'rikiˑ
Rikki-Tiki-Tavi		
fictional mongoose, Kipling	RIK-ē-TIK-ē-TAHV-ē, -TĀ-vē, -TAV-ē	ˌrikiˑˌtikiˑ'tɑviˑ, -'teːviˑ, -'tæviˑ
Riksdag		
parliament, Sweden	RĒKS-DAHG	'riːksˌdɑːg
Riley		
James Whitcomb, *US poet;* Pat, *US basketball coach*	RĪ-lē	'rɑiliˑ
Rilke		
Rainer Maria, *German poet*	RIL-kuh	'rilkə
Rima		
pers. name	RĒ-muh	'riːmə
Rimbaud		
Arthur, *French writer*	re^{n}-BŌ, Ⓢ ram-BŌ, RAM-bō	rɛ̃boː, Ⓢ ræm'boː, 'ræmboː
Rimini		
port, Italy	RIM-uh-nē, RĒ-muh-nē	'riməniˑ, 'riːməniˑ
Rimouski		
city, Canada	ruh-M$\overline{\text{OO}}$-skē	rə'muːskiˑ
Rimsky-Korsakov		
Nikolai, *Russian composer*	RĒM-ski-KAWR-suh-KUHF, Ⓢ RIM(P)-skē-KAWR-suh-KAWF, -KAWR-suh-KAWF	'riːmskʲij'kɔː^{r}səˌkəf, Ⓢ ˌrim(p)skiˑ'kɔː^{r}səˌkɔːf, -ˌkɔː^{r}sə'kɔːf
Rina		
pers. name	RĒ-nuh	'riːnə
Rinaldo		
1. pers. name	ri-NAHL-dō, ri-NAL-dō	ri'nɑldoː, ri'nældoː
2. Italian	rē-NAHL-dō	riː'nɑldoː
Rincon		
Indian reservation, US	RING-kahn, ring-KŌN	'riŋkɑn, riŋ'koːn
Ring		
pers. name	RING	'riŋ
Ringnes		
Norwegian beer	RING-nuhs	'riŋnəs
Rio Amazonas [Amazon]		
river, S. America	RĒ-$\overline{\text{oo}}$ AHM-uh-ZŌ-nuhs	'riːuː ˌɑmə'zoːnəs
Rio Arriba		
county, NM	RĒ-ō uh-RĒ-buh	ˌriːoː ə'riːbə
Rio Blanco		
county, CO	RĒ-ō BLANG-kō	ˌriːoː 'blæŋkoː
Rio Bravo		
Mexican name for Rio Grande	RĒ-ō BRAHV̲-ō	ˌriːoː 'brɑβoː
Rio de Janeiro		
state, city, Brazil	RĒ-ō DĀ zhuh-NER-ō, DĒ, juh-NER-ō	'riːoː ˌdeː ʒə'neroː, ˌdiː, dʒə'neroː
Rio de Oro		
bay, Sahara	RĒ-ō dē ŌR-ō, AWR-ō	ˌriːoː diː 'oːroː, 'ɔːroː
Rio Gallegos		
port, Argentina	RĒ-ō gah-ZHĀ-gōs, Ⓢ RĒ-ō gah-YĀ-guhs, gī-Ā-guhs	ˌriːoː gɑ'ʒeːɣoːs, Ⓢ ˌriːoː gɑ'jeːgəs, gɑi'eːgəs
Rio Grande		
1. county, CO	RĒ-ō GRAND(-ē), RĪ-ō GRAND	ˌriːoː 'grænd(iˑ), ˌrɑioː 'grænd
2. river, Africa; river, Brazil	RĒ-$\overline{\text{oo}}$ GRAHN-duh	ˌriːuː 'grɑndə

Key (col. 2): a: **fad** ā: **fade** ah: **father** ar: **Mary** aw: **law** e: **fed** ē: **feed** er: **merry** i: **hid** ī: **hide** ō: **coat** $\overline{\text{oo}}$: **boot** oi: **boy** ow: **now** u: **put** uh: **above** uhr: **bird** ch: **chop** ng: **ring** sh: **show** th: **thick** th̲: **this** zh: **measure**

Río Grande, Rio Grande
    river, US & Mexico   RĒ-ō GRAND(-ē), RĪ-ō GRAND   ˌriːoː 'grænd(iˑ), ˌrɑioː 'grænd

Rio Hondo
    College, CA   RĒ-ō (H)AHN-dō   ˌriːoː '(h)andoː

Rioja, La
    region, Spain; wine variety   lah rē-AW-hah   lɑ riː'ɔːhɑ

Rio Muni
    prov, Equatorial Guinea   RĒ-ō M‾O‾O-nē   ˌriːoː 'muːniˑ

Riordan
    family name   RIRD-n   'riʳdn̩

Ripon
    town, England   RIP-uhn   'ripən

RISC
    reduced instruction set [computer]   RISK   'risk
    chip

Risë
    pers. name   RĒ-suh   'riːsə

Risorgimento
    political movement, Italy   rē-ZAWR-ji-MEN-tō, rē-SAWR-   riːˌzɔːʳdʒi'mentoː, riːˌsɔːʳ-

Risotto
    cooked rice dish   ri-SAWT-ō, ri-ZAWT-ō, ri-ZAHT-ō   ri'sɔːtoː, ri'zɔːtoː, ri'zɑtoː

Rissole
    small pastry   RIS-ōL   'ris,oːl

Rita
    pers. name   RĒT-uh   'riːt̬ə

Ritchie
    pers. name   RICH-ē   'ritʃiˑ

Ritter
    John, US actor; German beer   RIT-uhr   'rit̬əʳ

Ritz
    César, Swiss founder of luxury   RITS   'rits
    hotels

Riva
    Belgian beer   RĒ-vuh   'riːvə

Rivas
    dept, town, Nicaragua   RĒ-vahs   'riːβɑs

Rivera
    Chita, US actress, singer; Geraldo,   ruh-VER-uh   rə'verə
    US TV interviewer

Rivier
    College, NH   ri-VIR   ri'viʳ

Riviera, The
    region, Mediterranean   RIV-ē-ER-uh   ˌriviː'erə

Rivière
    pers. name, French   rē-VYER   riːvjer

Rivoli's
    hummingbird   RIV-uh-lēz   'rivəliˑz

Riyadh
    city, Saudi Arabia   rē-(Y)AHD   riː'(j)ɑd

Rizal
    prov, Philippines   ri-ZAHL, ri-SAHL   ri'zɑl, ri'sɑl

Rizos
    pers. name, Mod. Greek   RI-zaws   'rizɔːs

Foreign Sounds: ue: *Fr.* **rue**, *Ger.* **füllen** uh(r): *Fr.* **boeuf**, *Ger.* **Höhle** <u>kh</u>: *Ger.* i**ch**, *Scot.* lo**ch** ḡ: *Sp.* ami**g**o v̱: *Sp.* ha**b**lar
hl: *Welsh* **Ll**anelli. CAPITALS: primary stress. SMALL CAPS: secondary stress. Ⓢ: U.S. pron. Ⓔ: British pron.

Rizzoli		
bookstore, publisher, New York City	ri-ZŌ-lē	riˈzoːliˑ
Roald		
pers. name, Norwegian	RŌ-ahl	ˈroːɑl
Roanoke		
river, city, county, VA; island, NC; N. American people	RŌ-(uh-)-NŌK	ˈroː(ə)ˌnoːk
Roanoke-Chowan		
Technical College, *NC*	RŌ-(uh-)-NŌK-chuh-WAHN	ˈroː(ə)ˌnoːktʃəˈwɑn
Rob		
pers. name	RAHB	ˈrɑb
Robards		
Jason, *US actor*	RŌ-BAHRDZ	ˈroːˌbɑʳdz
Robb		
Charles Spittal, *US politician*	RAHB	ˈrɑb
Robbie		
pers. name	RAHB-ē	ˈrɑbiˑ
Robbins		
F. C., *US physiologist, pediatrician (Nobel 1954)*	RAHB-uhnz	ˈrɑbənz
Robert		
1. pers. name	RAHB-uhrt	ˈrɑbəʳt
2. Danish	RŌ-BERT	ˈroːˌbert
3. Dutch	RAWB-uhrt	ˈrɔːbərt
4. Finnish	RAW-BERT	ˈrɔːˌbert
5. French	rō-BER	roːber
6. German	RŌ-BERT	ˈroːˌbeʳt
7. Russian	RUHB-YERT, RAWB-yirt	ˌrəbˈjert, ˈrɔːbjirt
8. Swedish	RAWB-buhrt	ˈrɔːbbərt
Roberta		
pers. name	ruh-BUHRT-uh	rəˈbəʳt̬ə
Roberto		
1. pers. name, Italian	rō-BER-tō	roːˈbertoː
2. Spanish	rō-V̲ER-tō	roːˈβertoː
Robertson		
Cliff, *US actor, writer*	RAHB-uhrt-suhn	ˈrɑbəʳtsən
Robeson		
Paul, *US singer, actor*	RŌB-suhn	ˈroːbsən
Robespierre		
Maximilien, *French revolutionary*	raw-bes-PYER, [$] RŌBZ-PIR, RŌBZ-PYER	rɔːbespjer, [$] ˈroːbzˌpiʳ, ˈroːbzˌpjeʳ
Robigo		
Roman divinity of wheat	rō-BĪ-gō, rō-BĒ-gō	roːˈbɑigoː, roːˈbiːgoː
Robin		
pers. name	RAHB-uhn	ˈrɑbən
Robinson		
college, Cambridge Univ.; pers. name	RAHB-uhn-suhn	ˈrɑbənsən
Robinson Crusoe		
character, novel, Defoe	RAHB-uhn-suhn KRŌŌ-sō, KRŌŌ-zō	ˌrɑbənsən ˈkruːsoː, ˈkruːzoː
Robur Carolinum		
former constellation	RŌ-buhr KAR-uh-LĪ-nuhm, RŌ-bur	ˈroːbəʳ ˌkærəˈlɑinəm, ˈroːbuʳ
Rocco		
pers. name	RAHK-ō	ˈrɑkoː

Key (col. 2): a: fad ā: fade ah: father ar: Mary aw: **law** e: fed ē: feed er: merry i: hid ī: hide ō: coat ōō: boot oi: boy ow: **now** u: put uh: **above** uhr: **bird** ch: **chop** ng: ri**ng** sh: **show** th: **thick** th̲: **this** zh: mea**sure**

Rocha
  city, dept, Uruguay   RAW-chuh   'rɔːtʃə
Rochambeau
  Conte de, *French general*   raw-shahⁿ-BŌ   rɔːʃãboː
Rochdale
  borough, England   RAHCH-DĀL   'ratʃˌdeːl
Roche
  pers. name   RAWSH, RŌSH, RŌCH   'rɔːʃ, 'roːʃ, 'rɔːtʃ
Roche, La
  see La Roche
Rochefoucauld, La
  see La Rochefoucauld
Rochelle, La
  see La Rochelle
Rochester
  pl. name, England, US   RAHCH-uh-stuhr, RAHCH-ES-tuhr 'ratʃəstəʳ, 'ratʃˌestəʳ
Rockefeller
  noted US family   RAHK-uh-FEL-uhr, RAHK-FEL-uhr 'rakəˌfeləʳ, 'rakˌfeləʳ
Rockies
  mtn. range, N. America   RAHK-ēz   'rakiˑz
Rockingham
  county, NC, NH, VA   RAHK-ing-HAM   'rakiŋˌhæm
Rockne
  Knute, *US football coach*   RAHK-nē   'rakniˑ
Rockwell
  Norman, *US painter; pers. name*   RAHK-WEL, RAHK-wuhl   'rakˌwel, 'rakwəl
Rocky
  Mountains, *mtn. range, N.*   RAHK-ē   'rakiˑ
    America; pers. name
Rococo
  ornate style of art and music   ruh-KŌ-kō, RŌ-kuh-KŌ   rə'koːkoː, ˌroːkə'koː
Rod, Rodd
  pers. name   RAHD   'rad
Roddy
  pers. name   RAHD-ē   'radiˑ
Rodenbach
  Belgian beer   RŌD-n-BAHKH   'roːdn̩ˌbax
Rodentia
  gnawing mammals   rō-DEN-ch(ē-)uh, rō-DENT-ē-uh roː'dentʃ(iː)ə, roː'dentiːə
Roderic, -ick
  pers. name   RAHD-uhr-ik, RAHD-rik   'radərik, 'radrik
Roderich
  pers. name, German   RŌ-duh-ri̲k̲h̲   'roːdəriç
Rodgers
  Richard, *US composer*   RAHJ-uhrz   'radʒəʳz
Ródhos [Rhodes]
  island, Greece   RAW-T̲H̲AWS   'rɔːˌðoːs
Rodin
  Auguste, *French sculptor*   raw-DEⁿ, Ⓢ RŌ-DA(N)   rɔːdẽ, Ⓢ 'roːˌdæ̃(n)
Rodney
  pers. name   RAHD-nē   'radniˑ
Rodolfo
  1. pers. name, Italian   rō-DAWL-fō   roː'dɔːlfoː
  2. Spanish   rō-T̲H̲AWL-fō   roː'ðɔːlfoː

Foreign Sounds: **ue:** *Fr.* **rue**, *Ger.* **füllen**   **uh(r):** *Fr.* **boeuf**, *Ger.* **Höhle**   **kh:** *Ger.* **ich**, *Scot.* **loch**   **g̃:** *Sp.* **amigo**   **v:** *Sp.* **hablar**
hl: *Welsh* **Llanelli**.   CAPITALS: primary stress.   SMALL CAPS: secondary stress.   Ⓢ: U.S. pron.   Ⓛ: British pron.

Rodolphe
  pers. name, French   raw-DAWLF   rɔːdɔːlf

Rodôpi [Rhodope]
  region, Greece   raw-THAW-pē   rɔː'ðɔːpiˑ

Rodrigo
  1. pers. name   rahd-RĒ-gō   rɑd'riːgoː
  2. Italian   rō-DRĒ-gō   roː'driːgoː
  3. Spanish   rō-THRĒ-ḡō   roː'ðriːɣoː

Rodrigues
  pers. name, Portuguese   rōō-DRĒ-gish, -gis   ruː'driːgiʃ, -gis

Rodríguez
  pers. name, Spanish   raw-THRĒ-gās, -gāth; ⑤ rahd-RĒ-gez   rɔː'ðriːgeːs, -geːθ; ⑤ rɑd'riːgez

Rodríguez Sánchez [Manolete]
  Manuel, *Spanish bullfighter*   rawth-RĒ-ḡāth SAHN-chāth   rɔːð'riːɣeːθ 'sɑntʃeːθ

Roebling
  John Augustus, *US engineer*   RŌ-bling   'roːbliŋ

Roentgen, Röntgen
  Wilhelm Conrad von, *German physicist (Nobel 1901)*   RUH(R)NT-guhn, ⑤ RENT-guhn, RUHNT-guhn, REN-chuhn   'rœntgən, ⑤ 'rentgən, 'rəntgən, 'rentʃən

Roethke
  Theodore, *US writer*   RET-kē, RETH-kē   'retkiˑ, 'reθkiˑ

Roger
  1. pers. name   RAHJ-uhr   'rɑdʒəʳ
  2. French   raw-ZHĀ   rɔːʒeː

Roget
  Peter Mark, *English thesaurus compiler*   rō-ZHĀ, RŌ-ZHĀ   roː'ʒeː, 'roːˌʒeː

Rogue
  Community College, *OR*   RŌG   'roːg

Rohrer
  Heinrich, *Swiss physicist (Nobel 1986)*   RAWR-uhr   'rɔːrəʳ

Roh Tae Woo
  S. Korean leader   nō tā wōō *[sic]*   noː teː wuː *[sic]*

Roissy [Charles de Gaulle]
  airport, Paris   rwah-SĒ   rwɑːsiː

Rokusai Nembutsu
  Japanese festival   rō-kōō-sī nem-bōōt-sōō   roːkuːsɑi nembuːtsuː

Roland
  1. pers. name   RŌ-luhnd   'roːlənd
  2. French   raw-LAHⁿ   rɔːlɑ̃
  3. German; beer   RŌ-LAHNT   'roːˌlɑnt

Rolando
  pers. name, Italian   rō-LAHN-dō   roː'lɑndoː

Rolette
  county, ND   rō-LET   roː'let

Rolex
  tdmk for watches   RŌ-LEKS   'roːˌleks

Rolf
  pers. name   RAHLF, RAWLF   'rɑlf, 'rɔːlf

Rolland
  Romain, *French musicologist, author (Nobel 1915)*   raw-LAHⁿ   rɔːlɑ̃

Key (col. 2):   a: fad   ā: fade   ah: father   ar: **Mary**   aw: **law**   e: fed   ē: feed   er: **merry**   i: hid   ī: hide   ō: coat   ōō: boot
oi: **boy**   ow: **now**   u: put   uh: above   uhr: **bird**   ch: **chop**   ng: **ring**   sh: **show**   th: **thick**   tẖ: **this**   zh: measure

Rollei		
tdmk for photographic equipment	RŌ-LĪ	'roːˌlai
Rollo		
pers. name	RAHL-ō	'rɑloː
Rolls-Royce		
tdmk for an English car	RŌLZ-ROIS	ˌroːlz'rɔis
Rolo		
tdmk for a candy	RŌ-lō	'roːloː
Rolodex		
tdmk for a rotary card file system	RŌ-luh-DEKS	'roːləˌdeks
Rölvaag		
Ole, *US novelist*	RŌL-VAHG	'roːlˌvɑg
ROM		
read-only memory	RAHM	'rɑm
Rom		
gypsy man or boy	RŌM, RAHM	'roːm, 'rɑm
Roma [Rome]		
city, Italy	RŌ-muh	'roːmə
Romaic		
modern Greek vernacular	rō-MĀ-ik	roː'meːik
Romain		
pers. name, French	raw-ME^{n}	rɔːmẽ
Romaine		
lettuce; pers. name	rō-MĀN	roː'meːn
Romains		
Jules, *pen name of* Louis Farigoule, *French writer*	raw-ME^{n}	rɔːmẽ
Roman		
1. pert. to Rome *or the* Roman Catholic Church*; pers. name*	RŌ-muhn	'roːmən
2. Polish	RAW-MAHN	'rɔːˌmɑːn
3. Russian	RUH-MAHN	ˌrə'mɑːn
Romanesque		
architectural style	RŌ-muh-NESK	ˌroːmə'nesk
Romania		
republic, Europe	rō-MĀ-nē-uh, -nyuh	roː'meːniːə, -njə
Romanian		
lang., Romania	rō-MĀ-nē-uhn, -nyuhn	roː'meːniːən, -njən
Romanic		
derived from Latin	rō-MAN-ik	roː'mænik
Romanism		
Roman Catholicism	RŌ-muh-NIZ-uhm	'roːməˌnizəm
Romano		
cheese	ruh-MAHN-ō, rō-MAHN-ō	rə'mɑnoː, roː'mɑnoː
Romanov, Romanoff		
Russian dynasty	ruh-MAHN-uhf, [$] rō-MAHN-AWF, RŌ-muh-NAWF	rə'mɑːnəf, [$] roː'mɑnˌɔːf, 'roːməˌnɔːf
Romans		
New Testament book	RŌ-muhnz	'roːmənz
Romansch, -sh, -tsch		
lang., Switzerland, Italy	rō-MAHNCH, rō-MANCH	roː'mɑntʃ, roː'mæntʃ
Romanus		
pope	rō-MĀ-nuhs	roː'meːnəs

Romany, Romani [Gypsy]
 people, lang., South Asia, Near RAHM-uh-nē, RŌ-muh-nē   'raməni', 'roːməni'
  East, Europe, USA
Rome
 city, Italy   RŌM   'roːm
Romeo
 Shakespearean character; pers. RŌ-mē-ō   'roːmiːoː
  name
Romero
 1. Cesar, entertainer   rō-MER-ō, ruh-   roː'meroː, rə-
 2. pers. name, Spanish   rō-MĀ-rō, ⑤ ruh-MER-ō roː'meːroː, ⑤ rə'meroː
Romish
 pert. to Rome as center of the RŌ-mish   'roːmiʃ
  Roman Catholic Church
Rommel
 Erwin, *German general*   RAHM-uhl   'raməl
Romolo
 pers. name, Italian   RŌ-mō-LŌ   'roːmoː,loː
Romulan
 alien race, Star Trek   RAHM-yuh-luhn   'ramjələn
Romulo
 Carlos, *Philippine diplomat* RAHM-yuh-LŌ   'ramjə,loː
Romulus
 eponymous founder of Rome; pers. RAHM-yuh-luhs   'ramjələs
  name
Romulus Augustulus
 last Western Roman emperor RAHM-yuh-luhs aw-GUHS-chuh-luhs 'ramjələs ɔː'gəstʃələs
Ron
 1. lang., Nigeria   RŌN, RAHN   'roːn, 'ran
 2. pers. name   RAHN   'ran
Rona
 pers. name   RŌ-nuh   'roːnə
Ronald
 1. pers. name   RAHN-ld   'ranļd
 2. Norwegian   RŌ-NAHL(D)   'roː,nal(d)
 3. Portuguese   roo-NAHLD   ruː'nald
Roncesvalles
 village, Spain   rawn(t)-suhs-VAH(L)-YĀS rɔːn(t)səs'va(l),jeːs
Roncevaux
 French for Roncesvalles   rawⁿs(-uh)-VŌ   rɔ̃s(ə)voː
Ronga
 lang., people, Africa   RAHNG-guh   'raŋgə
Ronnie, Ronny
 pers. name   RAHN-ē   'rani'
Ronsard
 Pierre de, *French writer*   rawⁿ-SAHR   rɔ̃sar
Ronstadt
 Linda, *US singer*   RAHN-STAT   'ran,stæt
Röntgen
 see Roentgen
Roodepoort-Maraisburg
 city, S. Africa   ROOD-uh-PURT-mah-RĀ-BURK 'ruːdə,puˈrtmaˈreː,buˈrk
Roone
 pers. name   ROON   'ruːn

Key (col. 2): a: fad ā: fade ah: father ar: Mary aw: law e: fed ē: feed er: merry i: hid ī: hide ō: coat o͞o: boot
oi: boy ow: now u: put uh: above uhr: bird ch: chop ng: ring sh: show th: thick th̲: this zh: measure

Rooney
  Mickey, *US actor; pers. name*   R$\overline{OO}$-nē   'ruːniˑ

Roosevelt
  Eleanor, *US humanitarian (wife of*   RŌ-zuh-vuhlt *(family's usual pron.),*   'roːzəvəlt *(family's usual*
    FDR); Franklin Delano, 32d US   RŌ-zuh-VELT, R$\overline{OO}$-   *pron.),* 'roːzəˌvelt, 'ruː-
    president; Theodore, 26th US
    president (Nobel 1906); pers.
    name

Root
  Elihu, *US jurist, statesman (Nobel*   R$\overline{OO}$T, RUT   'ruːt, 'rut
    1912)

Roquefort
  1. town, France   rawk-FAWR   rɔːkfɔːr
  2. tdmk for a cheese   RÔK-fuhrt   'roːkfəˑrt

Roris, Sinus
  see Sinus Roris

Rorschach test
  psychological inkblot test   RAWR-SHAHK   'rɔːrˌʃak

Rory
  pers. name   RÔR-ē, RAWR-ē   'roːriˑ, 'rɔːriˑ

Ros
  1. pers. name, short for Rosalind,   RAHZ   'raz
    Rosaline
  2. family name   RAWS, RAHS   'rɔːs, 'ras

Rosa
  1. pers. name   RÔ-zuh   'roːzə
  2. French   rō-ZAH   roːzaː
  3. German   RÔ-zah   'roːza
  4. Italian   RAW-zah   'rɔːza
  5. Spanish   RÔ-sah   'roːsa

Rosalie
  1. pers. name   RÔ-z(uh-)lē   'roːz(ə)liˑ
  2. French   raw-zah-LÉ   rɔːzaːliː

Rosalind
  pers. name   RAHZ-(uh-)lind, RÔZ-(uh-)lind,   'raz(ə)lind, 'roːz(ə)lind,
         -LĪND   -ˌlaind

Rosaline
  pers. name   RAHZ-(uh-)lin, RÔZ-(uh-)lin, -LĪN   'raz(ə)lin, 'roːz(ə)lin, -ˌlain

Rosalyn, Rosalynn
  pers. name   RÔZ-(uh-)luhn, RAHZ-   'roːz(ə)lən, 'raz-

Rosamond, -mund
  pers. name   RAHS-(uh-)muhnd, RÔZ-   'ras(ə)mənd, 'roːz-

Rosanna
  pers. name   rō-ZAN-uh   roː'zænə

Rosanne
  pers. name   rō-ZAN   roː'zæn

Rosario
  city, Argentina   rō-SAHR-ē-ō, rō-ZAHR-ē-ō   roː'sariːoː, roː'zariːoː

Roscoe
  pers. name   RAHS-kō   'raskoː

Roscommon
  county, MI; county, Ireland   rah-SKAHM-uhn   ra'skamən

Rose
  1. pers. name   RŌZ   'roːz
  2. French   RŌZ   roːz

Foreign Sounds: ue: *Fr.* **rue**, *Ger.* **füllen**   uh(r): *Fr.* **boeuf**, *Ger.* **Höhle**   kh: *Ger.* **ich**, *Scot.* **loch**   ḡ: *Sp.* **amigo**   v̱: *Sp.* **hablar**
hl: *Welsh* **Llanelli**.   CAPITALS: primary stress.   SMALL CAPS: secondary stress.   ⑤: U.S. pron.   ⑫: British pron.

Rosé
  wine   rō-ZĀ   roːˈzeː

Roseau
  county, MN   rō-ZŌ   roːˈzoː

Rosecrans
  pers. name   RŌZ-KRANS   ˈroːz,kræns

Rosemarie
  pers. name   RŌZ-muh-RĒ, RŌZ-muh-RĒ   ,roːzməˈriː, ˈroːzmə,riː

Rosemary
  pers. name   RŌZ-MER-ē, RŌZ-MAR-ē, RŌZ-MĀ-rē   ˈroːz,meriˈ, ˈroːz,mæriˈ, ˈroːz,meːriˈ

Rosemonde
  pers. name, French   rawz-MAW^{n}D   rɔːzmɔ̃d

Rosemontag
  German festival   RŌ-zuh-MŌN-TAHK   ˈroːzə,moːn,taːk

Rosencrantz
  character in Hamlet, *Shakespeare*   RŌ-zuhn-KRAN(T)S   ˈroːzən,kræn(t)s

Rosetta
  Stone, *ancient inscribed tablet*   rō-ZET-uh   roːˈzețə

Rosh Hashanah
  Jewish New Year   RAWSH hah-shuh-NAH, RŌSH (h)uh-SHAW-nuh, RAHSH, RUHSH, (h)uh-SHAHN-uh   ,rɔːʃ haʃəˈna, ,roːʃ (h)əˈʃɔːnə, ,raʃ, ,rəʃ, (h)əˈʃanə

Rosicrucian
  member of an esoteric spiritual movement   RŌ-zuh-KRO͞O-shuhn, RAHZ-uh-KRO͞O-shuhn   ,roːzəˈkruːʃən, ,razəˈkruːʃən

Rosicrucianism
  tenets of the Rosicrucians   RŌ-zuh-KRO͞O-shuh-NIZ-uhm, RAHZ-uh-   ,roːzəˈkruːʃə,nizəm, ,razə-

Rosie
  pers. name   RŌ-zē   ˈroːziˈ

Rosinante
  Don Quixote's horse   RAHZ-uh-NANT-ē, RŌ-zuh-NANT-ē   ,razəˈnæntiˈ, ,roːzəˈnæntiˈ

Rosita
  pers. name   rō-ZĒT-uh   roːˈziːțə

Roskilde
  prov & town, Denmark   RUHS-KIL-uh   ˈrəs,kilə

Roslyn
  pers. name   RAHZ-luhn   ˈrazlən

Rosminianism
  philosophy   rahz-MIN-ē-uh-NIZ-uhm, rahz-MĒ-nē-uh-NIZ-uhm   razˈminiːə,nizəm, razˈmiːniːə,nizəm

Ross
  pers. name   RAWS, RAHS   ˈrɔːs, ˈras

Rossano
  pers. name, Italian   rō-SAHN-ō   roːˈsanoː

Rossellini
  Roberto, *Italian film director*   RŌS-sāl-LĒ-nē   ,roːsseːlˈliːniˈ

Rosser
  John B., *US mathematician*   RAHS-uhr   ˈrasə^r

Rossetti
  Dante Gabriel, *English painter, poet;* Christina, *English poet*   rō-ZET-ē, rō-SET-ē   roːˈzețiˈ, roːˈsețiˈ

Rossignol
  ski manufacturer   RAHS-ēn-YŌL, RAHS-ig-NAHL   ,rasiːnˈjoːl, ˈrasig,nal

---

Key (col. 2):   a: fad   ā: fade   ah: father   ar: Mary   aw: law   e: fed   ē: feed   er: merry   i: hid   ī: hide   ō: coat   o͞o: boot   oi: boy   ow: now   u: put   uh: above   uhr: bird   ch: chop   ng: ring   sh: show   th: thick   <u>th</u>: this   zh: measure

Rossini
  Gioacchino, *Italian composer* — raw-SĒ-nē, ruh-SĒ-nē — rɔːˈsiːniˈ, rəˈsiːniˈ
Rossiyskaya
  SSR, *Russian republic, USSR* — raw-SĒ-skuh-yuh — rɔːˈsiːskəjə
Rostand
  Edmond, *French playwright* — raw-STAHⁿ, Ⓢ RAHS-TAND — rɔːstã, Ⓢ ˈrɑsˌtænd
Rostenkowski
  Dan, *US politician* — RAHS-tuhn-KOW-skē — ˌrɑstənˈkɑuskiˈ
Rostock
  county, Germany — RAHS-TAHK, RAW-STAWK — ˈrɑsˌtɑk, ˈrɔːˌstɔːk
Rostock-Warnemünde
  city, Germany — RAHS-TAHK-VAHR-nuh-MUEN-duh, RAW-STAWK- — ˌrɑsˌtɑk,vɑʳnəˈmyndə, ˌrɔːˌstɔːk-
Rostov
  principality, town, Russia — ruh-STAWF, ruh-STAWV — rəˈstɔːf, rəˈstɔːv
Rostropovich
  Mstislav, *Russian cellist/conductor* — ruhs-TRUH-PAWV-yēch, Ⓢ RAHS-truh-PŌ-vich — rəsˌtrəˈpɔːvjiˈtʃ, Ⓢ ˌrɑstrəˈpɔːvitʃ
Rotarian
  member of Rotary Club — rō-TAR-ē-uhn, rō-TER-ē-uhn — rɔːˈtæriːən, rɔːˈteriːən
Rotary
  business club — RŌT-uh-rē — ˈrɔːtəriˈ
Roth
  David Lee, *rock singer;* Philip, *US writer* — RAWTH, RAHTH — ˈrɔːθ, ˈrɑθ
Rothko
  Mark, *Russian-born US painter* — RAHTH-kō — ˈrɑθkɔː
Rothschild
  European family financial dynasty — RAWTHS-CHĪLD, RAWTH-CHĪLD, RAWS-, *German* RŌT-SHILT — ˈrɔːθs,tʃaild, ˈrɔːθ,tʃaild, ˈrɔːs-, *German* ˈroːt,ʃilt
Roto-Rooter
  US co. — RŌT-ō-RŌOT-uhr, RŌT-ō-RŌOT-uhr — ˌrɔːtɔːˈruːtəʳ, ˈrɔːtɔːˌruːtəʳ
Rototiller
  tdmk for a rotary cultivator — RŌT-uh-TIL-uhr — ˈrɔːtə,tiləʳ
Rotterdam
  city, Netherlands — RAHT-uhr-DAM — ˈrɑtəʳ,dæm
Rottweiler
  dog breed — RAHT-WĪ-luhr, RAWT-VĪ-luhr — ˈrɑt,wailəʳ, ˈrɔːt,vailəʳ
Rouault
  Georges, *French artist* — RWŌ, Ⓢ rōo-Ō — rwoː, Ⓢ ruːˈoː
Roubaix
  city, France — rōo-BE — ruːbe
Rouen
  city, France — RWAHⁿ, Ⓢ ru-AHⁿ, ru-AHN — rwã, Ⓢ ruˈã, ruˈɑn
Rouget de Lisle
  Claude Joseph, *French composer* — rōo-ZHE duh LĒL — ruːʒe də liːl
Rough Tor
  granite hill, Cornwall, England — ROW TAWR — ˈrɑu ˌtɔːʳ
Roundhead
  member of Parliamentary Party, English Civil War — ROWND-HED — ˈrɑund,hed
Rous
  Francis Peyton, *US pathologist (Nobel 1966)* — ROWS — ˈrɑus

---

Foreign Sounds: ue: *Fr.* **rue**, *Ger.* füllen uh(r): *Fr.* **boeuf**, *Ger.* Höhle <u>kh</u>: *Ger.* i<u>ch</u>, *Scot.* lo<u>ch</u> g̃: *Sp.* ami<u>g</u>o v̱: *Sp.* ha<u>b</u>lar
hl: *Welsh* L<u>l</u>anelli. CAPITALS: primary stress. SMALL CAPS: secondary stress. Ⓢ: U.S. pron. Ⓛ: British pron.

Rousseau
   Jean Jacques, *French philosopher*   rōō-SŌ   ruːsoː

Roussillon
   prov, France   rōō-sē-YAWⁿ   ruːsiːjõ

Routledge
   British publishing co.   RUHT-lij, ROWT-lij   'rətlidʒ, 'rautlidʒ

Routt
   county, CO   ROWT   'raut

Rovno
   town, Ukraine   RAWV-nuh   'rɔːvnə

Rowan
   1. tree   RŌ-uhn, ROW-uhn   'roːən, 'rauən
   2. pers. name   RŌ-uhn, RŌ-AN   'roːən, 'roː‚æn

Rowe
   Nicholas, *English poet, dramatist*   RŌ   'roː

Rowena
   pers. name   rō-Ē-nuh   roː'iːnə

Rowenta
   tdmk for cookware   rō-ENT-uh   roː'entə

Rowland
   pers. name   RŌ-luhnd   'roːlənd

Rowley
   pers. name   ROW-lē, RŌ-lē   'rauliˑ, 'roːliˑ

Roxana
   pers. name   rahk-SAN-uh   rɑk'sænə

Roxanna
   pers. name   rahk-SAN-uh   rɑk'sænə

Roxanne
   pers. name   rahk-SAN   rɑk'sæn

Roxburgh
   pers. name   RAHKS-buhr-uh, RAHKS-buh-ruh,   'rɑksbər-ə, 'rɑksbə-rə,
        RAHKS-bruh   'rɑksbrə

Roxy
   pers. name   RAHK-sē   'rɑksiˑ

Roy
   pers. name   ROI   'rɔi

Roz
   pers. name   RAHZ   'rɑz

Rozelle
   Pete, *US football commissioner*   rō-ZEL   roː'zel

Ruadh
   pers. name, Scots Gaelic   RŌŌ-uhth   'ruːəð

Ruaidhri
   pers. name, Irish Gaelic   RŌŌ-uh-rē   'ruːəriˑ

Ruanda
   former name of Rwanda   ruh-WAHN-duh, ru-AHN-duh   rə'wɑndə, ru'ɑndə

Ruanda-Urundi
   former territory, Africa   rōō-AHN-duh-u-RŌŌN-dē   ruː'ɑndəu'ruːndiˑ

Rubaiyat
   poem, Omar Khayyam   RŌŌ-bē-AHT, RŌŌ-BĪ-AHT, -AT   'ruːbiː‚at, 'ruː‚bai‚at, -‚æt

Rub al Khālī
   desert, Saudi Arabia   RUB ahl KHAHL-ē, al KAHL-ē   ‚rub aːl 'xaːliˑ, æl 'kaliˑ

Rubbia
   Carlo, *Italian-born US physicist*   RŌŌB-bē-uh   'ruːbbiːə
   (Nobel 1984)

Key (col. 2):   a: fad   ā: fade   ah: father   ar: Mary   aw: law   e: fed   ē: feed   er: merry   i: hid   ī: hide   ō: coat   ōō: boot
oi: boy   ow: now   u: put   uh: above   uhr: bird   ch: chop   ng: ring   sh: show   th: thick   th: this   zh: measure

Rube		
pers. name	RO͞OB	'ru:b
Rubén		
pers. name, Spanish	ro͞o-V̲Ā̲N	ru:'βe:n
Rubens		
Peter Paul, *Flemish painter*	RUE-buhns, [$] RO͞O-buhnz	'ry:bəns, [$] 'ru:bənz
Rubicon		
river, Italy	RO͞O-bi-KAHN	'ru:bi,kɑn
rubidium		
element	ro͞o-BID-ē-uhm	ru:'bidi:əm
Rubik		
Erno, *Hungarian mathematician*	RO͞O-bik	'ru:bik
Rubik's cube		
puzzle	RO͞O-biks	'ru:biks
Rubin		
pers. name	RO͞O-buhn	'ru:bən
Rubino		
Italian wine	ro͞o-BĒ-nō	ru:'bi:no:
Rubinstein		
1. Anton, *Russian pianist & composer*	RO͞OB-yin-SHTĪN, [$] RO͞O-buhn-STĪN	,ru:bjin'ʃtɑin, [$] 'ru:bən,stɑin
2. Artur, *US pianist*	RO͞O-buhn-STĪN	'ru:bən,stɑin
Ruby		
pers. name	RO͞O-bē	'ru:bi'
Rudbeckia		
flower	RUHD-BEK-ē-uh, ro͞od-BEK-ē-uh	,rəd'beki:ə, ru:d'beki:ə
Rüdesheim		
German wine	RUE-duhs-HĪM	'ry:dəs,hɑim
Rudi		
pers. name	RO͞OD-ē	'ru:di'
Rüdiger		
pers. name, German	RUE-di-guhr	'ry:digə^{r}
Rudman		
Warren Bruce, *US politician*	RUHD-muhn	'rədmən
Rudolf		
1. pers. name	RO͞O-DAHLF, RO͞O-DAWLF	'ru:,dɑlf, 'ru:,dɔ:lf
2. Czech, Finnish	RUD-AWLF	'rud,ɔ:lf
3. Dutch	RUE-dawlf	'ry:dɔ:lf
4. German, Swedish	RO͞O-DAWLF	'ru:,dɔ:lf
Rudolph		
1. pers. name	RO͞O-DAHLF, RO͞O-DAWLF	'ru:,dɑlf, 'ru:,dɔ:lf
2. Dutch	RUE-dawlf	'ry:dɔ:lf
3. German, Norwegian	RO͞O-DAWLF	'ru:,dɔ:lf
Rudolphe		
pers. name, French	rue-DAWLF	ry:dɔ:lf
Rudy		
pers. name	RO͞OD-ē	'ru:di'
Rudyard		
pers. name	RUHD-yuhrd	'rədjə^{r}d
Rue		
pers. name	RO͞O	'ru:
Rueil-Malmaison		
suburb, France	rwel-mahl-me-ZAW^{n}	rɥelmɑ:lmezɔ̃
Rue Morgue		
Murders in the, *story, E. A. Poe*	RO͞O MAWRG	'ru: 'mɔ:^{r}g

Foreign Sounds: ue: *Fr.* **rue**, *Ger.* **fü**llen uh(r): *Fr.* b**oeu**f, *Ger.* H**öh**le k̲h̲: *Ger.* i**ch**, *Scot.* lo**ch** g̃: *Sp.* ami**g**o v̲: *Sp.* ha**b**lar
hl: *Welsh* **Ll**anelli. CAPITALS: primary stress. SMALL CAPS: secondary stress. [$]: U.S. pron. [£]: British pron.

Rufino
　pers. name, Spanish　　　　　roo-FĒ-nō　　　　　　　　ruːˈfiːnoː

Rufinus
　Roman cognomen　　　　　　roo-FĪ-nuhs　　　　　　　ruːˈfɑinəs

Rufus
　pers. name　　　　　　　　ROO-fuhs　　　　　　　　ˈruːfəs

Rugby
　town, school, England; ball game　RUHG-bē　　　　　　　　ˈrəgbiˑ

Ruggero, Ruggiero
　pers. name, Italian　　　　　rood-JER-ō　　　　　　　ruːdˈdʒeroː

Ruhollah
　pers. name, Persian　　　　　ru-HŌ-luh　　　　　　　ruˈhoːlə

Ruhr
　river, industrial area, Germany　RUR　　　　　　　　　ˈruʳ

Rui
　pers. name, Portuguese, Spanish　ROO-i　　　　　　　　ˈruːi

Ruiz
　pers. name, Spanish　　　　　roo-ĒS, roo-ĒTH　　　　　ruːˈiːs, ruːˈiːθ

Rukeyser
　Louis, *television economist*　　ROO-KĪ-zuhr, RUK-Ī-zuhr　ˈruːˌkɑizəʳ, ˈrukˌaizəʳ

Rumanian [Romanian]
　lang., Romania　　　　　　roo-MĀ-nē-uhn　　　　　ruˈmeːniːən

Rumantsch [Romansch]
　lang., Switzerland, North Italy　roo-MANCH, roo-MAHNCH　ruˈmæntʃ, ruˈmɑntʃ

Rumba, Rhumba
　dance　　　　　　　　RUHM-buh, RUM-buh, ROOM-buh　ˈrəmbə, ˈrumbə, ˈruːmbə

Rumelia
　division of the Turkish Empire　roo-MĒL-yuh, roo-MĒ-lē-uh　ruːˈmiːljə, ruːˈmiːliːə

Rumpelstiltskin
　fairytale character　　　　RUHM-puhl-STIL(T)-skuhn　ˌrəmpəlˈstil(t)skən

Runcie
　Robert, *archbishop of Canterbury*　RUHN(T)-sē　　　　　ˈrən(t)siˑ

Rundgren
　Todd, *US musician, record*　RUHN(D)-gruhn, RUHNG-gruhn　ˈrən(d)grən, ˈrəŋgrən
　　producer

Rundi
　lang., people, Africa　　　ROON-dē　　　　　　　ˈruːndiˑ

Rundstedt
　Karl von, *German militarist*　RUN(T)-SHTET　　　　　ˈrun(t)ˌʃtet

Runnymede
　meadow, England　　　　RUHN-ē-MĒD　　　　　ˈrəniˑˌmiːd

Runyon
　Damon, *US author*　　　　RUHN-yuhn　　　　　　ˈrənjən

Rupert
　1. pers. name　　　　　ROO-puhrt　　　　　　ˈruːpəʳt
　2. German　　　　　　ROO-PERT　　　　　　ˈruːˌpeʳt
　3. Swedish　　　　　ROO-puhrt　　　　　　ˈruːpərt

Ruppert
　Stadium, *Kansas City, MO*　ROO-puhrt　　　　　　ˈruːpəʳt

Rurik, Ryurik
　Scandinavian founder of Russian　RYOOR-yik, Ⓢ RUR-ik　ˈrjuːrjik, Ⓢ ˈrurik
　　dynasty

Key (col. 2):　a: fad　ā: fade　ah: father　ar: Mary　aw: law　e: fed　ē: feed　er: merry　i: hid　ī: hide　ō: coat　oo: boot
oi: boy　ow: now　u: put　uh: above　uhr: bird　ch: chop　ng: ring　sh: show　th: thick　th̲: this　zh: measure

Ruritania

   fictional country in The Prisoner   RUR-uh-TĂ-nē-uh, -TĂN-yuh   ˌrurəˈteːniːə, -ˈteːnjə
   of Zenda, *A. Hope; state ruled*
   by reactionary court

Rushdi

   pers. name, Turkish   ruesh-TUE, Ⓢ RUHSH-dē   ryːʃˈtyː, Ⓢ ˈrəʃdiˑ

Rushdie

   Salman, *British author*   RUHSH-dē, RUSH-dē *(his own pron.)*   ˈrəʃdiˑ, ˈruʃdiˑ *(his own pron.)*

Rushmore

   Mount, *National Memorial, SD*   RUHSH-MŌR, RUHSH-MAWR   ˈrəʃˌmoːˑ, ˈrəʃˌmoːˑ

Rusk

   Dean, *US educator, government*   RUHSK   ˈrəsk
   official

Ruska

   Ernest, *German physicist (Nobel*   RUS-kuh   ˈruskə
   1986)

Ruskin

   John, *English author*   RUHS-kuhn   ˈrəskən

Russ

   Viking people   RUHS, RŌŌS, RUS   ˈrəs, ˈruːs, ˈrus

Russel

   pers. name   RUHS-uhl   ˈrəsəl

Russell

   Bertrand, *British intellectual*   RUHS-uhl   ˈrəsəl
   (Nobel 1950); pers. name

Russia

   republic, Europe, Asia   RUHSH-uh   ˈrəʃə

Russian

   pert. to Russia   RUHSH-uhn   ˈrəʃən

Russification

   process of making Russian   RUHS-uh-fi-KĂ-shuhn   ˌrəsəfiˈkeːʃən

Russo-

   combining form, Russia or   RUHS-uh, RUHS-uh, RUHSH-uh,   ˌrəsə, ˈrəsə, ˌrəʃə, ˈrəʃə, -oː
   Russian   RUHSH-uh, -ō

Russophile

   lover of Russia   RUHS-uh-FĪL, RUHSH-uh-FĪL   ˈrəsəˌfail, ˈrəʃəˌfail

Russophobe

   hater of Russia   RUHS-uh-FŌB, RUHSH-uh-FŌB   ˈrəsəˌfoːb, ˈrəʃəˌfoːb

Rustin

   Bayard, *US activist*   RUHS-tuhn   ˈrəstən

Rust-Oleum

   US corp.   RUHST-Ō-lē-uhm   ˌrəstˈoːliːəm

Rustom

   pers. name   RŌŌ-stuhm, RUHS-tuhm   ˈruːstəm, ˈrəstəm

Rutger

   pers. name   RUHT-guhr   ˈrətgəˑ

Rutgers

   University, *NJ*   RUHT-guhrz   ˈrətgəˑz

Ruth

   Old Testament book; pers. name   RŌŌTH   ˈruːθ

Ruthenia

   region, E. Europe   rōō-THĔN-yuh, rōō-THĔ-nē-uh   ruːˈθiːnjə, ruːˈθiːniːə

ruthenium

   element   rōō-THĔ-nē-uhm   ruːˈθiːniːəm

Foreign Sounds: ue: *Fr.* **rue**, *Ger.* **füllen**   uh(r): *Fr.* **boeuf**, *Ger.* **Höhle**   <u>kh</u>: *Ger.* **ich**, *Scot.* **loch**   ğ: *Sp.* **amigo**   ᴠ: *Sp.* **hablar**
hl: *Welsh* **Llanelli**.   CAPITALS: primary stress.   SMALL CAPS: secondary stress.   Ⓢ: U.S. pron.   Ⓔ: British pron.

Rutherford
  borough, NJ; pers. name   RUH<u>TH</u>-uhr-fuhrd, RUHTH-   'rəðəˈfəˈd, 'rəθ-
Ruthven
  village, Scotland   RIV-uhn, ROͦOͦTH-vuhn,   'rivən, 'ruːθvən, 'rəθvən
       RUHTH-vuhn
Rutilius
  Roman name   roͦo-TIL-ē-uhs   ruːˈtiliːəs
Rutland
  town, VT; former county, England   RUHT-luhnd   'rətlənd
Rutuli
  tribe of Turnus   roͦo-TOͦO-lē   ruˈtuːliˑ
Ruwenzori
  mts., Uganda, Zaire   ROͦO-(w)uhn-ZŌR-ē,   ˌruː(w)ən'zoːriˑ,
       ROͦO-(w)uhn-ZAWR-ē   ˌruː(w)ən'zoːriˑ
Ruy
  1. pers. name, Portuguese   ROͦO-ē   'ruːiˑ
  2. Spanish   roͦo-Ē   ruˈˈiˑ
Ružička
  Leopold, Yugoslav chemist (Nobel   ROͦO-ZHICH-kuh, ROͦO-ZICH-kuh,   'ruːˌʒitʃkə, 'ruːˌzitʃkə,
  1939)   ROͦO-ZHITS-kuh   'ruːˌʒitskə
Rwanda
  country, lang., Africa   ruh-WAHN-duh, ru-AHN-duh, ⓔ   rə'wɑndə, ru'ɑndə, ⓔ
       ru-AN-duh   ru'ændə
Rwandan
  pert. to Rwanda   ruh-WAHN-duhn, ru-AHN-duhn, ⓔ   rə'wɑndən, ru'ɑndən, ⓔ
       ru-AN-duhn   ru'ændən
Ry
  pers. name (R. Cooder)   RĪ   'rɑi
Ryan
  pers. name   RĪ-uhn   'rɑiən
Ryazan
  city, Russia   RĒ-uh-ZAHN(-yuh)   ˌriːə'zɑːn(jə)
Ryle
  Martin, *English radio astronomer*   RĪL   'rɑil
  (Nobel 1974)
Ryokei
  pers. name, Japanese   ryō-kā   rjoːkeː
Ryther
  pers. name   RĪ-<u>th</u>uhr   'rɑiðəˈ
Ryukyu
  islands, Pacific   rē-(Y)OͦO-k(y)oͦo   riː'(j)uːk(j)uː
Rzeszów
  city, Poland   ZHESH-OͦOF   'ʒeʃˌuːf

Key (col. 2):   a: fad   ā: fade   ah: father   ar: Mary   aw: law   e: fed   ē: feed   er: merry   i: hid   ī: hide   ō: coat   oͦo: boot
oi: boy   ow: now   u: put   uh: above   uhr: bird   ch: chop   ng: ring   sh: show   th: thick   <u>th</u>: this   zh: measure

S

Saab
    Swedish automobile   SAHB   'sɑb

Saad
    pers. name, Arabic   sah-AHD   sɑ'ɑd

Saale
    river, Germany   ZAHL-uh, SAHL-uh   'zɑlə, 'sɑlə

Saarbrücken
    city, Germany   zahr-BRUEK-uhn, sahr-   zaʳ'brykən, sɑʳ-

Saarinen
    Eero, *US architect*   SAHR-uh-nuhn   'sɑrənən

Saarland
    prov, Germany   ZAHR-LAHNT, Ⓢ ZAHR-LAND,   'zɑʳˌlɑnt, Ⓢ 'zɑʳˌlænd,
                                SAHR-LAND   'sɑʳˌlænd

Saar [Sarre]
    European river   SAHR, ZAHR   'sɑʳ, 'zɑʳ

Saatchi & Saatchi
    British advertising co.   SAH-chē uhn(d) SAH-chē   ˌsɑːtʃiˈ ən(d) 'sɑːtʃiˈ

Saavedra Lamas
    Carlos, *Argentine jurist (Nobel*   sah-VĀTH-rah LAHM-ahs,   sɑ'veːðrɑ 'lɑmɑs,
        1936)   Ⓢ suh-VĀ-druh LAHM-uhs   Ⓢ sə'veːdrə 'lɑməs

Saba
    island, Netherland Antilles SĀ-buh, SAHB-uh   'seːbə, 'sɑbə

Šabac
    town, Serbia   SHAH-BAHTS   'ʃɑːˌbɑːts

Sabaean
    pert. to Saba   suh-BĒ-uhn, SĀ-bē-uhn, SAHB-ē-uhn   sə'biːən, 'seːbiːən, 'sɑbiːən

Sabaoth
    1. Biblical name   SAB-ē-AHTH, SAB-ā-AHTH,   'sæbiːˌɑθ, 'sæbeːˌɑθ,
                             sa-BĀ-uhth   sæ'beːəθ
    2. Sabbath   SAH-bah-ōt   'sɑbɑoːt

Sabaragamuwa
    prov, Sri Lanka   SAHB-uh-ruh-GAHM-o͞o-vuh   ˌsɑbərə'gɑmuˈvə

Sabatier
    Paul, *French chemist (Nobel 1912)* sah-bah-TYĀ   sɑːbɑːtjeː

Sabatini
    Rafael, *English writer;* Gabriela,   SAB-uh-TĒ-nē, SAHB-uh-TĒ-nē   ˌsæbə'tiːniˈ, ˌsɑbə'tiːniˈ
        tennis player

Sabato
    1. pers. name   suh-BAT-ō, SAB-uht-ō   sə'bæṭoː, 'sæbəṭoː
    2. Italian   SAH-bah-tō   'sɑbɑtoː

Sabazius
    Phrygian god of agriculture   suh-BĀ-zē-uhs   sə'beːziːəs

---

Foreign Sounds: ue: *Fr.* **rue**, *Ger.* füllen uh(r): *Fr.* **boeuf**, *Ger.* Höhle <u>kh</u>: *Ger.* i<u>ch</u>, *Scot.* lo<u>ch</u> g̃: *Sp.* ami**g**o v: *Sp.* ha**b**lar
hl: *Welsh* L**l**anelli. CAPITALS: primary stress. SMALL CAPS: secondary stress. Ⓢ: U.S. pron. Ⓛ: British pron.

Sabbath
   day of worship & rest   SAB-uhth   'sæbəθ

Sabbatical
   pert. to the Sabbath   suh-BAT-i-kuhl   sə'bæţikəl

Sabellian
   group of early Italian peoples &   suh-BEL-ē-uhn   sə'beliːən
   langs.

Sabellianism
   early Christian theological   suh-BEL-ē-uh-NIZ-uhm   sə'beliːə,nizəm
   doctrine

Sabena
   Belgian airline   suh-BĒ-nuh, suh-BĀ-nuh   sə'biːnə, sə'beːnə

Sabianism
   star-worshipping religion   SĀ-bē-uh-NIZ-uhm   'seːbiːə,nizəm

Sabin
   polio vaccine   SĀ-buhn   'seːbən

Sabina
   pers. name, Latin   suh-BĒ-nuh   sə'biːnə

Sabine
   1. river, US; county, TX; parish,   suh-BĒN   sə'biːn
   LA
   2. ancient people of the Apennines   SĀ-BĪN, Ⓔ SAB-ĪN   'seː,bain, Ⓔ 'sæb,ain
   3. pers. name   SĀ-BĪN, SĀ-buhn, Ⓢ SAB-ĪN,   'seː,bain, 'seːbən,
                        SAB-uhn   Ⓢ 'sæb,ain, 'sæbən
   4. French   sah-BĒN   saːbiːn

Sabinian
   pope   suh-BIN-ē-uhn   sə'biniːən

Sabinus
   pers. name, Latin   suh-BĪ-nuhs, suh-BĒ-nuhs   sə'bainəs, sə'biːnəs

Sables Saint Émilion
   wine   SAHB-luh SEⁿ tā-mēl-YAWⁿ   saːblə sẽ teːmiːljõ

Sabra
   refugee camp, Lebanon; native   SAHB-ruh, SAHB-rah   'sabrə, 'sabra
   Israeli

Sabrina
   pers. name   suh-BRĒ-nuh, suh-BRĪ-nuh   sə'briːnə, sə'brainə

Sabus
   son of Sancus   SĀ-buhs   'seːbəs

Sac
   N. American people   SAK   'sæk

Sacagawea, -jawea
   Shoshone interpreter   SAK-uh-juh-WĒ-uh, -WĀ-uh;   ,sækədʒə'wiːə, -'weːə;
                        SAK-uh-JAH-wē-uh   ,sækə'dʒawiːə

Saccharin
   artificial sweetener   SAK-(uh-)ruhn   'sæk(ə)rən

Sacco
   Nicola, *Italian anarchist executed*   SAK-ō   'sækoː
   in US

Sacha
   pers. name, French   sah-SHAH   saːʃaː

Sacher torte, Sachertorte
   chocolate-apricot cake   ZAH<u>KH</u>-uhr-TAWR-tuh,   'zaxəʳ,tɔːʳtə, Ⓢ 'zakəʳ,tɔːʳt,
                      Ⓢ ZAHK-uhr-TAWRT,   'sakəʳ,tɔːʳt
                      SAHK-uhr-TAWRT

Key (col. 2):   a: fad   ā: fade   ah: father   ar: Mary   aw: law   e: fed   ē: feed   er: merry   i: hid   ī: hide   ō: coat   o͞o: boot
oi: boy   ow: now   u: put   uh: above   uhr: bird   ch: chop   ng: ring   sh: show   th: thick   <u>th</u>: this   zh: measure

Sacheverell		
pers. name	suh-SHEV(-uh)-ruhl	sə'ʃev(ə)rəl
Sachs		
Hans, *German Meistersinger;* Nelly, *German-born Swedish author (Nobel 1966)*	ZAHKS, SAKS	'zɑks, 'sæks
Sackville		
pers. name	SAK-vuhl, SAK-VIL	'sækvəl, 'sæk,vil
Saco		
river, NH, ME; city, ME	SAW-kō, SAHK-ō	'sɔːkoː, 'sɑkoː
Sacrae Theologiae Baccalaureus		
bachelor of sacred theology, S.T.B.	SA-KRĒ THĒ-uh-LŌ-jē-Ē BAK-uh-LŌR-ē-uhs, -LAWR-ē-uhs	'sæ,kriː ,θiːə'loːdʒiː,iː ,bækə'loːriːəs, -'lɔːriːəs
Sacramento		
city, CA	SAK-ruh-MENT-ō	,sækrə'mentoː
Sacré Cœur		
basilica, Paris, France	sah-krā KUHR	sɑːkreː kœr
Sadakichi		
pers. name, Japanese	sah-dah-kē-chē	sɑdɑkiːtʃiː
Sadao		
pers. name, Japanese	sah-dah-ō	sɑdɑ-oː
Sadat, al-		
Anwar, *Egyptian statesman (Nobel 1978)*	AHL-suh-DAHT, AL-suh-DAHT, AL-suh-DAT	,ɑːlsə'dɑːt, ,ælsə'dɑt, ,ælsə'dæt
Saddam		
pers. name, Arabic	sahd-AHM, [$] suh-DAHM, SAD-uhm, SAHD-uhm	sɑːd'ɑm, [$] sə'dɑm, 'sædəm, 'sɑdəm
Sadducee		
Jewish sect	SAJ-uh-SĒ, SAD-yuh-SĒ	'sædʒə,siː, 'sædjə,siː
Sadducean		
pert. to Sadducees	SAJ-uh-SĒ-uhn, SAD-yuh-SĒ-uhn	,sædʒə'siːən, ,sædjə'siːən
Sadduceeism		
tenets of the Sadducees	SAJ-uh-SĒ-IZ-uhm, SAD-yuh-SĒ-	'sædʒə,siː,izəm, 'sædjə,siː-
Sade		
Marquis de, *French novelist*	SAHD	sɑːd
Sadie		
pers. name	SĀD-ē	'seːdiˑ
Sadowa		
village, Czech republic	SAHD-uh-VAH	'sɑdə,vɑ
Safar		
Islamic month	suh-FAHR	sə'fɑ^{r}
Safer		
Morley, *Canadian-born TV journalist*	SĀ-fuhr	'seːfə^{r}
Safid Rud		
river, Iran	sa-FĒD ROOD	sæ'fiːd 'ruːd
Safire		
William, *US columnist*	SAF-ĪR	'sæf,ɑi^{r}
Sagadahoc		
county, ME	SAG-uhd-uh-HAHK	,sægədə'hɑk
Sagaing		
city, Burma	suh-GĪNG	sə'gɑiŋ
Sagan		
1. Carl, *US astronomer*	SĀ-guhn	'seːgən
2. Françoise, *French writer*	sah-GAH^{n}	sɑːgɑ̃

Foreign Sounds: ue: *Fr.* **rue**, *Ger.* **füllen** uh(r): *Fr.* **boeuf**, *Ger.* **Höhle** kh: *Ger.* **ich**, *Scot.* lo**ch** g: *Sp.* ami**g**o v: *Sp.* ha**b**lar hl: *Welsh* **Llanelli**. CAPITALS: primary stress. SMALL CAPS: secondary stress. [$]: U.S. pron. [£]: British pron.

Saginaw
　city, county, MI　　　　　SAG-uh-NAW　　　　　　　'sægə,nɔː

Sagitta
　constellation　　　　　　suh-JIT-uh, SAJ-uht-uh　　　sə'dʒiţə, 'sædʒəţə

Sagittarius
　constellation, sign of the zodiac　SAJ-uh-TER-ē-uhs　　　,sædʒə'teriːəs

Sagres
　Portuguese beer　　　　SAH-grish, SHAH-gris　　　'saːgriʃ, 'ʃaːgris

Saguache
　county, CO　　　　　　suh-WAHCH　　　　　　　sə'watʃ

Saguaro
　cactus　　　　　　　　suh-WAHR-uh, suh-(G)WAHR-ō　sə'warə, sə'(g)waroː

Saguenay
　river, Canada　　　　　SAG-uh-NĀ, SAG-uh-NÃ　　'sægə,neː, ,sægə'neː

Saguenay-Lac-St.-Jean
　College, Canada　　　　SAG-uh-NÃ-LAHK-seⁿ-ZHAHⁿ　,sægə'neː,laˑksẽ'ʒã

Saguntum
　Greek settlement, Spain　suh-GUHN-tuhm　　　　　sə'gəntəm

Sahachiro
　pers. name, Japanese　sah-hah-chē-rō　　　　　sahatʃiːroː

Sahara
　desert, Africa　　　　　suh-HAR-uh, suh-HER-uh,　sə'hærə, sə'herə, sə'harə
　　　　　　　　　　　　suh-HAHR-uh

Sahel
　desert, Africa　　　　　suh-HĀL, suh-HĒL, SAH-HEL　sə'heːl, sə'hiːl, 'sa,hel

Sahl
　Mort, *Canadian comedian*　SAHL, SAWL　　　　　　'sal, 'sɔːl

Saïda [Sidon]
　city, Lebanon　　　　　SĪD-uh　　　　　　　　'saidə

Saigon [Ho Chi Minh City]
　city, Vietnam　　　　　sī-GAHN, SĪ-GAHN　　　sai'gan, 'sai,gan

Sailer
　German beer　　　　　ZĪ-luhr　　　　　　　　'zailəʳ

Sainsbury
　British retailers　　　　SÃNZ-b(uh-)rē, Ⓢ SÃNZ-BER-ē　'seːnzb(ə)riˑ, Ⓢ 'seːnz,beriˑ

Saint, St.
　as an element in US & British　Ⓢ *usually* SĀNT; Ⓔ *usually* suhnt　Ⓢ *usually* ,seːnt; Ⓔ *usually*
　names　　　　　　　　　　　　　　　　　　　sənt

St. Albans
　town, England　　　　suhnt AWL-buhnz, Ⓢ sānt　sənt 'ɔːlbənz, Ⓢ seːnt

Saint Alphonsus
　College, *CT*　　　　　SĀNT al-FAHN-suhs　　　,seːnt æl'fansəs

Saint Ambrose
　College, *IA*　　　　　sānt AM-BRŌZ　　　　　seːnt 'æm,broːz

St. Andrews
　town, Scotland　　　　suhnt AN-drōōz, Ⓢ sānt　sənt 'ændruːz, Ⓢ seːnt

St. Anne's
　college, Oxford Univ.　suhnt ANZ, Ⓢ sānt　　　sənt 'ænz, Ⓢ seːnt

Saint Anthony's fire
　skin disease　　　　　SĀNT AN(T)-thuh-nēz FĪR, Ⓔ　,seːnt æn(t)θəniˑz 'faiʳ, Ⓔ
　　　　　　　　　　　AN-tuh-nēz　　　　　　　æntəniˑz

St. Antony's
　college, Oxford Univ.　suhnt AN-tuh-nēz, Ⓢ sānt ANT-n-ēz　sənt 'æntəniˑz, Ⓢ seːnt
　　　　　　　　　　　　　　　　　　　　　　　'æntni̩z

Key (col. 2):　a: fad　ā: fade　ah: father　ar: Mary　aw: law　e: fed　ē: feed　er: merry　i: hid　ī: hide　ō: coat　ōō: boot
oi: boy　ow: now　u: put　uh: above　uhr: bird　ch: chop　ng: ring　sh: show　th: thick　t̲h̲: this　zh: measure

St. Asaph
   city, cathedral, Wales   suhnt AS-uhf, sānt   sənt 'æsəf, seːnt

St. Augustine
   1. early Christian philosopher   SĀNT AW-guhs-TĒN, suhnt,   ,seːnt 'ɔːgəs,tiːn, sənt,
           aw-GUHS-tuhn, uh-GUHS-tuhn   ɔː'gəstən, ə'gəstən
   2. city, FL   SĀNT AW-guhs-TĒN, suhnt   ,seːnt 'ɔːgəs,tiːn, sənt

St. Austell
   town, England   suhnt AWS-tl, Ⓢ sānt   sənt 'ɔːstl̩, Ⓢ seːnt

Saint Bernard
   dog breed   SĀNT buhr-NAHRD   ,seːnt bəʳ'nɑʳd

Saint Bonaventure
   University, NY   sānt BAHN-uh-VEN-chuhr   seːnt 'bɑnə,ventʃəʳ

St. Catharine's
   college, Cambridge Univ.   suhnt KATH-(uh-)ruhnz, Ⓢ sānt   sənt 'kæθ(ə)rənz, Ⓢ seːnt

St. Catherine's
   college, Oxford Univ.   suhnt KATH-(uh-)ruhnz, Ⓢ sānt   sənt 'kæθ(ə)rənz, Ⓢ seːnt

Saint Christopher-Nevis
   independent state, West Indies   sānt KRIS-tuh-fuhr-NĒ-vuhs, suhnt,   seːnt 'kristəfəʳ'niːvəs, sənt,
           -NEV-uhs   -'nevəs

Saint Clair, St. Clair
   pers. name   sānt KLAR, KLER; Ⓛ suhnt KLER,   seːnt 'klæʳ, 'kleʳ; Ⓛ sənt
           SING-KLER, SIN-KLER   'kleʳ, 'siŋ,kleʳ, 'sin,kleʳ

St. Cloud
   1. city, MN   sānt KLOWD, suhnt   seːnt 'klɑud, sənt
   2. city, France   seⁿ KLOO, Ⓢ sang KLOO   sẽ kluː, Ⓢ sæŋ 'kluː

St. Croix
   island, West Indies; county, WI   sānt KROI, suhnt   seːnt 'krɔi, sənt

St. Cross
   college, Oxford Univ.   suhnt KRAWS, Ⓢ sānt   sənt 'krɔːs, Ⓢ seːnt

St. Denis
   city, France; city, Réunion Island   seⁿd-NĒ, seⁿ-duh-NĒ, Ⓢ SAN duh-NĒ   sẽdniː, sẽdəniː, Ⓢ ,sæn
               də'niː

St. Dogmaels
   village, Wales   suhnt DAWG-muhlz, sānt,   sənt 'dɔːgməlz, seːnt,
           DAHG-muhlz   'dɑgməlz

St. Donat's
   village, Wales   suhnt DAHN-uhts, sānt   sənt 'dɑnəts, seːnt

St. Edmund Hall
   college, Oxford Univ.   suhnt ED-muhnd HAWL, Ⓢ sānt   sənt 'edmənd 'hɔːl, Ⓢ seːnt

St. Edmund's House
   college, Cambridge Univ.   suhnt ED-muhn(d)z HOWS, Ⓢ sānt   sənt 'edmən(d)z ,hɑus,
               Ⓢ seːnt

Sainte Foy
   town, Canada   seⁿt FWAH   sẽt 'fwɑː

Saint Elias
   mtn. range, N. America   SĀNT-l-Ī-uhs   ,seːntl̩'ɑiəs

Saint Elmo's fire
   electrical discharge in storms   SĀNT EL-mōz FĪR   ,seːnt ,elmɔːz 'fɑiʳ

Saint Émilion
   wine   seⁿ tā-mēl-YAWⁿ   sẽ teːmiːljõ

Saintes, Îles des
   islands, Caribbean   ēl duh SEⁿT   iːl də sẽt

St.-Étienne
   town, France   seⁿ-tā-TYEN   sẽteːtjen

Foreign Sounds: ue: *Fr.* **rue**, *Ger.* **füllen** uh(r): *Fr.* **boeuf**, *Ger.* **Höhle** k̲h̲: *Ger.* i**ch**, *Scot.* lo**ch** ḡ: *Sp.* ami**g**o v̲: *Sp.* ha**b**lar
hl: *Welsh* **Ll**anelli. CAPITALS: primary stress. SMALL CAPS: secondary stress. Ⓢ: U.S. pron. Ⓛ: British pron.

Saint-Exupéry
    Antoine de, *French writer*   se^n-täg-zue-pā-RḔ   sẽteːgzyːpeːriː
St. Francois
    county, MO   sänt FRAN(T)-suhs   seːnt 'fræn(t)səs
St. Gall
    canton, Switzerland   sänt GAWL, suhnt, GAHL   seːnt 'gɔːl, sənt, 'gɑl
St. Gallen [St Gall]
    canton, Switzerland   zahng(k)t GAHL-uhn   zɑŋ(k)t 'gɑlən
Saint-Gaudens
    Augustus, *US sculptor*   sänt-GAWD-nz   seːnt'gɔːdṇz
Ste. Genevieve
    county, MO   sänt JEN-uh-VĒV, suhnt   seːnt 'dʒenə,viːv, sənt
Saint Georges
    town, Grenada   sänt JAWR-juhz, suhnt   seːnt 'dʒɔːʳdʒəz, sənt
St. Gotthard
    mtn. range, Switzerland   se^n guh-TAHR, ⑤ sänt GAHT-uhrd,   sẽ gətɑːr, ⑤ seːnt 'gatəʳd,
         suhnt   sənt
St. Helena
    island, Atlantic; parish, LA; city,   SĀNT-l-Ē-nuh, SĀNT-huh-LĒNUH   ,seːntḷ'iːnə, ,seːnthə'liːnə
    CA
St. Helens
    Mount, *volcano, WA*   SĀNT HEL-uhnz   ,seːnt 'helənz
St. Helier
    city, Channel Islands   suhnt HEL-yuhr, ⑤ sänt   sənt 'heljəʳ, ⑤ seːnt
St. Hilda's
    college, Oxford Univ.   suhnt HIL-duhz, ⑤ sänt   sənt 'hildəz, ⑤ seːnt
St. Hugh's
    college, Oxford Univ.   suhnt HYO͞OZ, ⑤ sänt   sənt 'hjuːz, ⑤ seːnt
Saint-Hyacinthe
    College, *MA*   sänt-HĪ-uh-SINTH, suhnt-   seːnt'haiə,sinθ, sənt-
St. Ives
    town, England   suhnt ĪVZ, ⑤ sänt   sənt 'ɑivz, ⑤ seːnt
Saint Jérôme
    Canada   SE^n zhā-RŌM   ,sẽ ʒeː'roːm
St. John
    pers. name   sänt-JAHN, ⓔ SIN-juhn   seːnt'dʒɑn, ⓔ 'sindʒən
Saint John's
    city, Canada; University, *NY*   sänt JAHNZ, suhnt   seːnt 'dʒɑnz, sənt
St. John's
    college, Oxford Univ., Cambridge   suhnt JAHNZ, ⑤ sänt   sənt 'dʒɑnz, ⑤ seːnt
    Univ.
St. Kitts-Nevis
    state, Caribbean   sänt KITS-NĒ-vuhs, suhnt, -NEV-uhs   seːnt 'kits'niːvəs, sənt,
                                                     -'nevəs
St. Laurent
    see Yves Saint Laurent
Saint-Laurent
    city, Canada   SE^n luh-RAH^n, SANT law-RENT   ,sẽ lə'rã, ,sænt lɔː'rent
St. Lawrence
    county, NY; river, US & Canada   sänt LAWR-uhn(t)s, LAHR-uhn(t)s,   seːnt 'lɔːrən(t)s, 'lɑrən(t)s,
         suhnt   sənt
St. Leger
    1. pers. name   sänt LEJ-uhr, ⓔ suhnt LEJ-uhr   seːnt 'ledʒəʳ, ⓔ sənt 'ledʒəʳ
    2. family name   sänt LEJ-uhr, ⓔ suhnt LEJ-uhr,   seːnt 'ledʒəʳ, ⓔ sənt 'ledʒəʳ,
         SEL-in-juhr   'selindʒəʳ

Key (col. 2):   a: **fad** ā: **fade** ah: **father** ar: **Mary** aw: **law** e: **fed** ē: **feed** er: **merry** i: **hid** ī: **hide** ō: **coat** o͞o: **boot**
oi: **boy** ow: **now** u: **put** uh: **above** uhr: **bird** ch: **chop** ng: **ring** sh: **show** th: **thick** <u>th</u>: **this** zh: **measure**

St. Léonard

   town, Canada   se^n lā-aw-NAHR; sänt LEN-uhrd,   sẽ leːɔːnɑːr; seːnt ˈlenəʳd,
                                suhnt   sɑnt

St.-Lô

   town, France   se^n-LŌ   sẽloː

St. Louis

   1. city, MO; river, MN   sänt LOO-uhs, suhnt   seːnt ˈluːəs, sənt

   2. city, France; city, Réunion; city,   se^n LWẼ   sẽ lwiː
    Senegal

St. Louis encephalitis

   a viral encephalitis   SĀNT LOO-uhs in-SEF-uh-LĪT-uhs   ˌseːnt ˌluːəs inˌsefəˈlɑiʦəs

Saint Lucia

   island, West Indies   sänt LOO-shuh, suhnt; SĀNT   seːnt ˈluːʃə, sənt; ˌseːnt
                                loo-SĒ-uh   luːˈsiːə

Saint Lucian

   pert. to St. Lucia   sänt LOO-shuhn, suhnt; SĀNT   seːnt ˈluːʃən, sənt; ˌseːnt
                                  loo-SĒ-uhn   luːˈsiːən

St. Lucie

   county, FL   sänt LOO-sē, suhnt   seːnt ˈluːsiˑ, sənt

St.-Malo

   seaport, France   se^n-mah-LŌ   sẽmɑːloː

St. Martin

   island, Caribbean; parish, LA   sänt MAHRT-n, suhnt   seːnt ˈmɑʳtn̩, sənt

Saint Meinrad

   College, *IN*   SĀNT MĪN-RAD   ˌseːnt ˈmain,ræd

St.-Mihiel

   commune, France   se^n-mē-EL, se^n-MYEL   sẽmiːel, sẽmjel

St.-Moritz

   commune, Switzerland   se^n-maw-RĒTS, Ⓢ SĀNT muh-RITS   sẽmɔːriːts, Ⓢ ˌseːnt məˈrits

St.-Nazaire

   town, France   se^n-nah-ZER   sẽnɑːzer

St. Neots

   town, England   suhnt NĒTS, Ⓢ sänt   sənt ˈniːts, Ⓢ seːnt

Saint Olaf

   College, *MN*   SĀNT Ō-luhf, Ō-luhv   ˌseːnt ˈoːləf, ˈoːləv

St. Olaves

   village, England   suhnt AHL-uhvz, Ⓢ sänt   sənt ˈɑləvz, Ⓢ seːnt

St.-Ouen

   commune, France   se^n-TWAH^n, se^n-TWE^n sẽtwɑ̃, sẽtwẽ

St. Pancras

   Christian saint; former borough,   suhnt PANG-kruhs, Ⓢ sänt   sənt ˈpæŋkrəs, Ⓢ seːnt
    London, England

St. Pauli Girl

   beer   sänt PAW-lē GUHRL   seːnt ˈpɔːliˑ ˈgəʳl

St. Peter's

   church, Vatican City; college,   sänt PĒT-uhrz, suhnt   seːnt ˈpiːʦəʳz, sənt
    Oxford Univ.

St. Petersburg

   city, FL; city, Russia [Leningrad]   sänt PĒT-uhrz-BUHRG, suhnt   seːnt ˈpiːʦəʳz,bəʳg, sənt

St.-Pierre

   town, Réunion   se^n-PYER, Ⓢ sänt-PIR, suhnt-PIR,   sẽpjer, Ⓢ seːntˈpiʳ, səntˈpiʳ,
                                 SĀNT-pē-ER   ˌseːntpiːˈeʳ

Foreign Sounds: ue: *Fr.* **rue**, *Ger.* **füllen**   uh(r): *Fr.* **boeuf**, *Ger.* **Höhle**   <u>kh</u>: *Ger.* **ich**, *Scot.* **loch**   ḡ: *Sp.* **amigo**   <u>v</u>: *Sp.* **hablar**
hl: *Welsh* **Llanelli**.   CAPITALS: primary stress.   SMALL CAPS: secondary stress.   Ⓢ: U.S. pron.   Ⓔ: British pron.

Saint-Pierre & Miquelon
　islands, N Atlantic　　　　　　　se^n-PYER ā mē-KLAW^n, ⑤ sānt-PIR　　　sẽpjer eː miːklõ, ⑤ seːnt'pir
　　　　　　　　　　　　　　　　　uhn(d) MIK-uh-LAHN, suhnt,　　　　　 ən(d) 'mikəˌlan, sənt,
　　　　　　　　　　　　　　　　　pē-ER　　　　　　　　　　　　　　　piːˈer
Saint-Saëns
　Camille, French composer　　　 se^n-SAH^{n}S　　　　　　　　　　　　sẽsãs
St. Sixtus
　Belgian beer　　　　　　　　　sānt SIK-stuhs　　　　　　　　　　　 seːnt 'sikstəs
St.-Tropez
　resort, France　　　　　　　　se^n-traw-PÃ　　　　　　　　　　　　 sẽtrɔːpeː
Saint Vincent and the Grenadines
　nation, West Indies　　　　　　sānt VIN(T)-suhnt uhn(d) <u>th</u>uh　　seːnt 'vin(t)sənt ən(d) ðə
　　　　　　　　　　　　　　　　　GREN-uh-DĒNZ, suhnt　　　　　　　ˌgrenə'diːnz, sənt
Saint Vincentian
　pert. to Saint Vincent　　　　　SĀNT vin-SENT-ē-uhn, suhnt,　　　 ˌseːnt vin'sentiːən, sənt,
　　　　　　　　　　　　　　　　　vin-SEN-shuhn　　　　　　　　　　 vin'senʃən
St. Weonards
　town, England　　　　　　　　suhnt WEN-uhrdz　　　　　　　　　 sənt 'wenəʳdz
Saipan
　island, Pacific　　　　　　　　sī-PAN, sī-PAHN, SĪ-PAN, SĪ-PAHN　sai'pæn, sai'pan, 'saiˌpæn,
　　　　　　　　　　　　　　　　　　　　　　　　　　　　　　　　'saiˌpan
Sakalava
　people, Madagascar　　　　　　SAHK-uh-LAHV-uh　　　　　　　　ˌsakə'lavə
Sakhalin
　island, Sea of Okhotsk　　　　SU<u>H</u>K<u>H</u>-UHL-YĒN, ⑤ SAK-uh-LĒN,　ˌsəxˌəl'jiːn, ⑤ 'sækəˌliːn,
　　　　　　　　　　　　　　　　　SAK-uh-luhn, SAK-uh-LĒN　　　　 'sækələn, ˌsækə'liːn
Sakharov
　Andrei D., *Russian physicist,*　 SAH<u>KH</u>-uh-RAWF, SAHK-, -RAWV　'saxəˌrɔːf, 'sak-, -ˌrɔːv
　　dissident (Nobel 1975)
Saki
　pen name of H.H. Munro　　　　SAHK-ē　　　　　　　　　　　　　'sakiˑ
Sakmann
　Bert, *German physician (Nobel*　ZAHK-muhn, ZAHK-mahn　　　　　'zakmən, 'zakman
　　1991)
Sakura
　Japanese bank　　　　　　　　sah-kur-ah, ⑤ suh-KUR-uh　　　　　sakura, ⑤ sə'kurə
Sala
　pers. name　　　　　　　　　 SAL-uh　　　　　　　　　　　　　'sælə
Salacia
　Roman sea goddess　　　　　　suh-LÃ-sh(ē-)uh　　　　　　　　　sə'leːʃ(iː)ə
Saladin
　Muslim hero & sultan　　　　　SAL-uhd-n, SAL-uh-DIN　　　　　 'sælədn̩, 'sæləˌdin
Salado
　river, Cuba; river, Mexico　　 suh-LAH<u>TH</u>-ō　　　　　　　　　 sə'laðoː
Salado, Río
　rivers, Argentina　　　　　　 RĒ-ō suh-LAH<u>TH</u>-ō　　　　　　　 ˌriːoː sə'laðoː
Salam
　Abdus, *Pakistani physicist (Nobel*　sah-LAHM　　　　　　　　　　 sa'lam
　　1979)
Salamanca
　1. city, university, Spain; prov &　SAHL-uh-MAHNG-kuh,　　　　 ˌsalə'maŋkə, ˌsælə'mæŋkə
　　town, Mexico　　　　　　　　SAL-uh-MANG-kuh
　2. city, NY　　　　　　　　　SAL-uh-MANG-kuh　　　　　　　 ˌsælə'mæŋkə
Salambria
　river, Greece　　　　　　　　SAHL-ahm-BRĒ-uh, suh-LAM-brē-uh　ˌsalam'briːə, sə'læmbriːə

Key (col. 2):　a: fad　ā: fade　ah: father　ar: Mary　aw: law　e: fed　ē: feed　er: merry　i: hid　ī: hide　ō: coat　o͞o: boot
oi: boy　ow: now　u: put　uh: above　uhr: bird　ch: chop　ng: ring　sh: show　th: thick　<u>th</u>: this　zh: measure

Salamis
 island, town, Aegean; ancient city, SAL-uh-muhs 'sæləməs
 Cyprus
Salang
 island, Taiwan sah-LAHNG sɑ'lɑŋ
Salazar
 Alberto, *US runner* SAL-uh-ZAHR 'sælə,zɑˤ
Salem
 US pl. name SĀ-luhm 'seːləm
Salerno
 prov & town, Italy suh-LER-nō, suh-LUHR-nō sə'leˤnoː, sə'ləˤnoː
Salesian
 religious order suh-LĒ-zhuhn, sā- sə'liːʒən, seː-
Salian Franks
 ancient Frankish people SĀ-lē-uhn FRANGKS ˌseːliːən 'fræŋks
Salic
 pert. to Salian Franks SĀ-lik, SAL-ik 'seːlik, 'sælik
Salida
 city, CO suh-LĪD-uh sə'lɑidə
Salieri
 Antonio, *Italian composer* sahl-YER-ē sɑl'jeriˑ
Salina
 1. city, KS suh-LĪ-nuh sə'lɑinə
 2. island, Tyrrhenian Sea suh-LĒ-nuh sə'liːnə
Salinan
 N. American people suh-LĒ-nuhn sə'liːnən
Salinas
 river, city, CA suh-LĒ-nuhs sə'liːnəs
Saline
 pl. name, US suh-LĒN sə'liːn
Salinger
 J.D., US writer SAL-uhn-juhr 'sæləndʒəˤ
Salisbury
 city, England; pl. name, US; pers. SAWLZ-BER-ē, SAWLZ-b(uh-)rē, 'sɔːlzˌberiˑ, 'sɔːlzb(ə)riˑ,
 name SALZ- 'sælz-
Salish
 people, lang., N. America SĀ-lish 'seːliʃ
Salishan
 N. American lang. family SĀ-lish-uhn 'seːliʃən
Salius
 companion of Aeneas SĀ-lē-uhs 'seːliːəs
Salk
 Jonas, *US physician, scientist* SAW(L)K 'sɔː(l)k
Salle, La
 see La Salle
Salle, Sieur de La
 see La Salle, Sieur de
Sallust
 Roman historian SAL-uhst 'sæləst
Sally
 pers. name SAL-ē 'sæliˑ
Salman
 pers. name SAL-muhn 'sælmən

Foreign Sounds: ue: *Fr.* **rue**, *Ger.* **füllen** uh(r): *Fr.* **boeuf**, *Ger.* **Höhle** <u>kh</u>: *Ger.* **ich**, *Scot.* **loch** ḡ: *Sp.* amiḡo v̲: *Sp.* hab̲lar
hl: *Welsh* **Llanelli**. CAPITALS: primary stress. SMALL CAPS: secondary stress. Ⓢ: U.S. pron. Ⓛ: British pron.

Salmon
   1. pers. name   SAL-muhn   'sælmən
   2. French   sahl-MAW^n saːlmɔ̃
Salmoneus
   father of Tyro   sal-MŌ-nē-uhs, sal-MŌ-n(y)o͞os   sæl'moːniːəs, sæl'moːn(j)uːs
Salomé
   opera, R. Strauss   ZAHL-ō-mä   'zaloːmeː
Salome
   niece of Herod Antipas; pers.   suh-LŌ-mē   sə'loːmiˑ
     name
Salomon
   1. pers. name, Dutch   SAH-lō-MAWN   'saːloːˌmɔːn
   2. French   sah-law-MAW^n saːlɔːmɔ̃
   3. German   ZAH-lō-MAWN   'zaloːˌmɔːn
   4. Swedish   SAH-lo͞o-MAWN   'saluːˌmɔːn
Salonica, -ika
   city, Greece   suh-LAHN-i-kuh, SAL-uh-NĒ-kuh   sə'lanikə, ˌsælə'niːkə
Salop [Shropshire]
   former county, England   SAL-uhp   'sæləp
Salopian
   pert. to Salop   suh-LŌ-pē-uhn   sə'loːpiːən
Salsify
   plant   SAL-suh-fē, SAL-suh-FĪ   'sælsəfiˑ, 'sælsəˌfai
SALT
   Strategic Arms Limitation Treaty   SAWLT   'sɔːlt
Salta
   prov & town, Argentina   SAHL-tuh   'saltə
Saltillo
   city, Mexico   sahl-TĒ-(y)ō   sal'tiː(j)oː
Salto
   prov & town, Uruguay   SAHL-tō   'saltoː
Salton Sea
   lake, CA   SAWLT-n SĒ   ˌsɔːltn̩ 'siː
Saltopus
   dinosaur   SAWL-tuh-puhs   'sɔːltəpəs
Saluda
   river, county, SC   suh-LO͞OD-uh   sə'luːdə
Saluki
   dog breed   suh-LO͞O-kē   sə'luːkiˑ
Salus
   Roman goddess, protector of   SĀ-luhs   'seːləs
     health
Salut, Îles du
   islands, S. America   ēl due sah-LUE   iːl dyː saːlyː
Salvador
   1. city, Brazil   SAL-vuh-DAWR, SAL-vuh-DAWR   'sælvəˌdɔːr, ˌsælvə'dɔːr
   2. pers. name, Spanish   sahl-vah-<u>TH</u>AWR, Ⓢ SAL-vuh-DAWR   salva'ðɔːr, Ⓢ 'sælvəˌdɔːr
Salvador, El
   see El Salvador
Salvadoran
   pert. to Salvador   SAL-vuh-DAWR-uhn   ˌsælvə'dɔːrən
Salvator
   pers. name, Italian   SAHL-vah-TŌR   ˌsalva'toːr
Salvatore
   pers. name, Italian   SAHL-vah-TŌ-rä   ˌsalva'toːreː

Key (col. 2):   a: fad ā: fade ah: father ar: Mary aw: law e: fed ē: feed er: merry i: hid ī: hide ō: coat o͞o: boot
oi: boy ow: now u: put uh: above uhr: bird ch: chop ng: ring sh: show th: thick <u>th</u>: this zh: measure

Salve Regina
  College, *MA*   SAL-vā ruh-JĪ-nuh   ˈsælveː rəˈdʒainə
Salween
  river, Asia   SAL-WĒN   ˈsælˌwiːn
Salyut
  Soviet space station   SUHL-YŌOT, sal-YŌOT   ˌsəlˈjuːt, sælˈjuːt
Salzburg
  state, city, Austria   ZAHLTS-BURK; ⑤ SAWLZ-BUHRG, SAHLZ-, -BURG   ˈzaltsˌbuʳk; ⑤ ˈsɔːlzˌbəʳg, ˈsalz-, -ˌbuʳg
Salzkammergut
  Alpine region, Austria   ZAHLT-SKAHM-uhr-GŌOT   ˈzaltˌskaməʳˌguːt
SAM
  surface-to-air missile   SAM, ES-ā-EM   ˈsæm, ˌeseːˈem
Sam
  pers. name   SAM   ˈsæm
Samantha
  pers. name   suh-MAN-thuh   səˈmænθə
Samar
  island, Philippines   SAHM-AHR   ˈsamˌaʳ
Samaranch
  Juan Antonio, *president, International Olympic Committee*   SAHM-uh-RAHNCH   ˌsaməˈrantʃ
Samaria
  ancient city, region, Palestine   suh-MAR-ē-uh, suh-MER-ē-uh   səˈmæriːə, səˈmeriːə
Samaritan
  lang., people, Samaria; generous helper   suh-MAR-uht-n, suh-MER-uht-n   səˈmærətn̩, səˈmerətn̩
Samaritanism
  religious doctrine of the Samaritans   suh-MAR-uht-n-IZ-uhm, suh-MER-   səˈmærətn̩ˌizəm, səˈmer-
samarium
  element   suh-MER-ē-uhm, suh-MAR-ē-uhm   səˈmeriːəm, səˈmæriːəm
Samarkand
  city, Uzbekistan   suh-MUHR-KAHNT, ⑤ SAM-uhr-KAND, SAM-uhr-KAND   səˌmərˈkant, ⑤ ˈsæməʳˌkænd, ˌsæməʳˈkænd
Samarra
  town, Iraq   suh-MAHR-uh   səˈmarə
Samba
  dance   SAHM-buh   ˈsambə
Sambuca Romana
  liqueur   sam-BŌO-kuh rō-MAHN-uh   sæmˈbuːkə roːˈmanə
Samhain
  Celtic pagan festival   SOW-uhn   ˈsauən
Samhita
  Hindu prayers & hymns   SUHM-hi-TAH   ˌsəmhiˈta
Samian
  pert. to Samos   SĀ-mē-uhn   ˈseːmiːən
Samichlaus
  "Santa Claus," Swiss beer   ZAHM-ikh-LOWS   ˈzamiçˌlaus
Sammy, Sammie
  pers. name   SAM-ē   ˈsæmiˑ
Samnite
  ancient people of Samnium   SAM-NĪT   ˈsæmˌnait

Foreign Sounds: ue: *Fr.* **rue**, *Ger.* **füllen** uh(r): *Fr.* **boeuf**, *Ger.* **Höhle** kh: *Ger.* **ich**, *Scot.* **loch** g̃: *Sp.* ami**g**o v̲: *Sp.* ha**b**lar
hl: *Welsh* **Llanelli**. CAPITALS: primary stress. SMALL CAPS: secondary stress. ⑤: U.S. pron. Ⓛ: British pron.

Samnium

    ancient country, central Italy   SAM-nē-uhm   'sæmniːəm

Samoa

    island, Pacific   suh-MŌ-uh   sə'moːə

Samoan

    lang., Samoa Islands, New   suh-MŌ-uhn   sə'moːən
      Zealand, USA

Samora

    pers. name, Kirundi   sah-MAWR-uh   sɑ'mɔːrə

Sámos, Samos

    island, Greece   SAH-MAWS, Ⓢ SĀ-MAHS   'sɑˌmɔːs, Ⓢ 'seɪˌmɑs

Samothrace

    island, Aegean Sea   SAM-uh-THRĀS, *in ancient context*   'sæməˌθreɪs, *in ancient*
      SAM-uh-THRĀ-sē   *context* ˌsæmə'θreɪsiˑ

Samothráki [Samothrace]

    island, Aegean Sea   SAHM-ō-THRAHK-ē   ˌsɑmoːˈθrɑkiˑ

Samoyed [Selkup]

    lang., Khanti-Mansi region,   SAM-uh-YED, SAM-OI-ED,   'sæməˌjed, 'sæmˌɔiˌed,
      Russia; dog breed   SAM-uh-YED, SAM-OI-ED,   ˌsæmə'jed, ˌsæmˌɔi'ed,
      suh-MOI-(y)uhd   sə'mɔi(j)əd

Sampang

    town, Indonesia   SAHM-PAHNG   'sɑmˌpaŋ

Samphire

    plant   SAM(P)-FĪR   'sæm(p)ˌfaiʳ

Sampras

    Pete, US tennis player   SAHM-pruhs, SAM-pruhs   'sɑmprəs, 'sæmprəs

Sampson

    pers. name   SAM(P)-suhn   'sæm(p)sən

Samson

    1. pers. name   SAM(P)-suhn   'sæm(p)sən

    2. German   ZAHM-ZAWN   'zamˌzɔːn

Samson Agonistes

    drama, J. Milton   SAM-suhn AG-uh-NIS-TĒZ   'sæmsən ˌægə'nisˌtiːz

Samsonite

    tdmk for luggage   SAM(P)-suh-NĪT   'sæm(p)səˌnait

Samsonov

    Aleksandr, Russian militarist   SUHM-SAW-nuhf   ˌsəm'sɔːnəf

Samsun

    prov & town, Turkey   sahm-SOO̅N   sɑm'suːn

Samsung

    tdmk of a Korean electronics firm   sahm-sawng, Ⓢ SAM-SUHNG,   sɑːmsɔːŋ, Ⓢ 'sæmˌsəŋ,
      SAM-suhng   'sæmsəŋ

Samuel

    1. Old Testament book; pers.   SAM-yuh(-wuh)l   'sæmjə(wə)l
      name

    2. Dutch   SAH-mue-EL   'saːmyːˌel

    3. French   sah-MWEL   saːmyɛl

    4. German   ZAHM-oo̅-EL   'zamuːˌel

    5. Polish   sah-MOO̅-el   saːˈmuːel

    6. Spanish   sahm-WEL   sɑm'wel

Samuelson

    Paul A., US economist (Nobel   SAM-yuh(-wuh)l-suhn   'sæmjə(wə)lsən
      1970)

Key (col. 2): a: fad ā: fade ah: father ar: Mary aw: law e: fed ē: feed er: merry i: hid ī: hide ō: coat oo̅: boot
oi: boy ow: now u: put uh: above uhr: bird ch: chop ng: ring sh: show th: thick th̲: this zh: measure

Samuelsson
 Bengt I., *Swedish medical chemist* SAHM-uh-wuhl-SAWN   'saməwəl,sɔːn
 (Nobel 1982)

San [Bushman]
 lang., people, Angola   SAHN   'san

San [Zan]
 lang., people, Caucasus Mts.,   SAHN   'san
 Georgia, Turkey

Sanaa
 city, Saudi Arabia   san-AH, SAN-AH   sæn'ɑ, 'sæn,ɑ

San Agustín
 cape, Philippines   SAN AHG-u-STĒN   ,sæn ,ɑgu'stiːn

San Andreas
 village, CA   SAN an-DRĀ-uhs   ,sæn æn'dreːəs

San Andreas Fault
 geological fault line, CA   SAN an-DRĀ-uhs FAWLT   ,sæn æn,dreːəs 'fɔːlt

San Andrés
 island, town, Caribbean   SAN uhn-DRES   ,sæn ən'dres

San Angelo
 city, TX   san AN-juh-lō   sæn 'ændʒəloː

San Antonio
 river, city, TX   SAN an-TŌ-nē-ō, uhn-TŌ-nē-ō   ,sæn æn'toːniːoː, ən'toːniːoː

San Augustine
 county, TX   san AW-guh-STĒN   sæn 'ɔːgə,stiːn

San Benito
 county, CA   SAN buh-NĒT-ō   ,sæn bə'niːt̮oː

San Bernardino
 city, county, CA   SAN BUHR-nuh(r)-DĒ-nō,   ,sæn ,bərnə(r)'diːnoː,
         BUHR-nuhr-DĒ-nō   ,bərⁿnərᵊ'diːnoː

Sanborn
 David, *singer, songwriter*   SAN-BAWRN   'sæn,bɔːʳn

San Bruno
 city, CA   san BRŌŌ-nō   sæn 'bruːnoː

San Buenaventura
 city, CA   SAN BWEN-uh-ven-T(Y)UR-uh   ,sæn ,bwenəven't(j)urə

San Carlos
 river, AZ; N. American people;   san KAHR-luhs, KAHR-LŌS   sæn 'kɑʳləs, 'kɑʳ,loːs
 city, CA, Philippines

Sánchez
 pers. name, Spanish   SAHN-chās, SAHN-chāth   'santʃeːs, 'santʃeːθ

Sancho Panza
 character in Don Quixote,   SAHN-chō PAHN-zuh   ,santʃoː 'panzə
 Cervantes

San Clemente
 city, CA   SAN kluh-MENT-ē   ,sæn klə'mentiˑ

San Cristóbal
 Latin American pl. name   sahn krē-STŌ-vahl, Ⓢ SAN   san kriː'stoːβal, Ⓢ ,sæn
         kris-TŌ-buhl   kris'toːbəl

Sancti Spiritus
 prov & town, Cuba   SAHNG(K)-tē SPIR-uh-TŌŌS   ,saŋ(k)tiː 'spirə,tuːs

Sanctus
 Christian liturgical hymn, part of   SANG(K)-tuhs, SAHNG(K)-tuhs,   'sæŋ(k)təs, 'saŋ(k)təs,
 the Mass   SAHNG(K)-TŌŌS   'saŋ(k),tuːs

Sancus
 Sabine god of oath-keeping   SANG-kuhs   'sæŋkəs

Foreign Sounds: ue: *Fr.* **rue**, *Ger.* **füllen**   uh(r): *Fr.* **boeuf**, *Ger.* **Höhle**   <u>kh</u>: *Ger.* i**ch**, *Scot.* lo**ch**   ḡ: *Sp.* ami**g**o   <u>v</u>: *Sp.* ha**b**lar
hl: *Welsh* **Ll**anelli.   CAPITALS: primary stress.   SMALL CAPS: secondary stress.   Ⓢ: U.S. pron.   Ⓛ: British pron.

Sand

  George, *pseudonym of A.*   sahⁿd, sahⁿ, ⓢ SAND   sãd, sã, ⓢ 'sænd
    Dudevant, *French writer*

Sandarac

  tree   SAN-duh-RAK   'sændə,ræk

Sandawe

  lang., people, Tanzania   sahn-DAH-wā   sɑn'dɑweˑ

Sandefjord

  port, Norway   SAHN-uh-FYUR   'sɑnə,fjuʳ

Sandeman

  Port wine   SAHN-duh-mahn, ⓢ SAN-duh-muhn   'sɑndəmɑn, ⓢ 'sændəmən

Sanders

  Richard, *US actor*   SAN-duhrs   'sændəʳs

Sandhurst

  Royal Military Academy, *England*   SAND-HUHRST   'sænd,həʳst

Sandia

  N. American people   san-DĒ-uh   sæn'diːə

San Diego

  city, county, CA   SAN dē-Ā-gō   ˌsæn diː'eːgoː

San Diego Miramar

  College, *CA*   SAN dē-Ā-gō MIR-uh-MAHR   ˌsæn diː'eːgoː 'mirə,mɑʳ

Sandinista

  political party, Nicaragua   sahn-dē-NĒ-stah,   sɑndiː'niːstɑ,
         ⓢ SAN-duh-NĒ-stuh   ⓢ ˌsændə'niːstə

Sandino

  Augusto César, *Nicaraguan*   sahn-DĒ-nō, san-DĒ-nō   sɑn'diːnoː, sæn'diːnoː
    revolutionary

Sandø

  pers. name, Danish   SAHN-nuh(r)   'sɑːnnœː

Sándor

  pers. name, Hungarian,   SHAHN-dawr   'ʃɑːndɔːʳ
    Serbo-Croatian

Sandoval

  county, NM   SAN-duh-VAHL, san-DŌ-vuhl   'sændə,vɑl, sæn'doːvəl

Sandra

  pers. name   SAN-druh, SAHN-druh   'sændrə, 'sɑˑndrə

Sandro

  pers. name, Italian   SAHN-drō   'sɑndroː

Sandusky

  river, city, county, OH   suhn-DUHS-kē, san-DUHS-kē   sən'dəskiˑ, sæn'dəskiˑ

Sandvic

  Swedish manufacturing co.   SAHND-vik, ⓢ SAN(D)-vik   'sɑːndvik, ⓢ 'sæn(d)vik

Sandy

  pers. name   SAN-dē   'sændiˑ

Sandys

  Edwin, *British prelate;* George,   SAN(D)Z   'sæn(d)z
    English colonist, poet

San Fernando

  pl. name   SAN fuhr-NAN-dō   ˌsæn fəʳ'næmdoː

Sanford

  Isabel, *US actress; pers. name*   SAN-fuhrd   'sænfəʳd

San Francisco

  city, county, CA   SAN fruhn-SIS-kō, fran-SIS-kō   ˌsæn frən'siskoː, fræn'siskoː

Key (col. 2):   a: fad   ā: fade   ah: father   ar: Mary   aw: law   e: fed   ē: feed   er: merry   i: hid   ī: hide   ō: coat   o͞o: boot
oi: boy   ow: now   u: put   uh: above   uhr: bird   ch: chop   ng: ring   sh: show   th: thick   t̲h̲: this   zh: measure

San Francisco, Rio
   river, NM, AZ   RĒ-ō SAN fruhn-SIS-kō, fran-SIS-kō   'riːoː ˌsæn frən'siskoː, fræn'siskoː

San Francisco de Macoris
   town, Dominican Republic   SAN fruhn-SIS-kō dā MAHK-uh-RIS, fran-SIS-kō   ˌsæn frən'siskoː deː ˌmɑkə'ris, fræn'siskoː

San Francisco Gotera
   city, El Salvador   SAN fruhn-SIS-kō gō-TĀ-ruh, fran-SIS-kō   ˌsæn frən'siskoː goː'teːrə, fræn'siskoː

San Gabriel
   river, city, CA   san GĀ-brē-uhl   sæn 'geːbriːəl

Sangamon
   State University, river, county, IL   SANG-guh-muhn   'sæŋgəmən

San Gennaro
   Italian name for St. Januarius   SAN je-NAR-ō, je-NER-ō   ˌsæn dʒe'næroː, dʒe'neroː

Sanger
   1. Frederick, English biochemist (Nobel 1958, 1980); Margaret, US women's rights leader   SANG-uhr   'sæŋəʳ
   2. pers. name   SANG-uhr, SANG-guhr   'sæŋəʳ, 'sæŋgəʳ

Sangir
   lang., people, Sangihe, Talaud, Philippine Islands   SAHNG-IR   'sɑŋˌiʳ

Sango
   lang., Africa   SAHNG-gō   'sɑŋgoː

Sangre
   alcoholic drink   SAHNG-grā   'sɑŋgreː

Sangre de Cristo
   mtn. range, CO, NM   SANG-grē duh KRIS-tō   ˌsæŋgriː də 'kristoː

Sangria
   alcoholic drink   sang-GRĒ-uh, sahng-   sæŋ'griːə, sɑŋ-

Sanhedrin
   ancient Jewish council   san-HED-ruhn, sahn-HED-ruhn, san-HĒ-druhn   sæn'hedrən, sɑn'hedrən, sæn'hiːdrən

Sanilac
   county, MI   SAN-l-AK   'sænlˌæk

San Ildefonso
   N. American people   SAN IL-duh-FAHN(T)-sō   ˌsæn ˌildə'fɑn(t)soː

San Jacinto
   US pl. name   SAN juh-SINT-ō, SAN huh-SINT-ō, -SINT-uh   ˌsæn dʒə'sintoː, ˌsæn hə'sintoː, -'sintə

San Joaquin
   river, valley, county, CA   SAN wah-KĒN, san waw-KĒN   ˌsæn wɑ'kiːn, sæn wɔː'kiːn

San Jorge
   Latin American pl. name   sahn KHAWR-ğā, Ⓢ san HAWR-hä   sɑn 'xɔːrɣeː, Ⓢ sæn 'hɔːʳheː

San José
   1. city, CA   SAN ō-ZĀ, SAN uh-ZĀ   ˌsæn oː'zeː, ˌsæn ə'zeː
   2. prov., city, Costa Rica; dept., Uruguay   sahn haw-SĀ, Ⓢ SAN ō-ZĀ, SAN uh-ZĀ   sɑn hɔː'seː, Ⓢ ˌsæn oː'zeː, ˌsæn ə'zeː

San Juan
   pl. name   san (H)WAHN   sæn '(h)wɑn

Sankhya
   system of Hindu philosophy   SAHNGK-yuh   'sɑŋkjə

San Leandro
   city, CA   SAN lē-AN-drō   ˌsæn liː'ændroː

Foreign Sounds: ue: *Fr.* **rue**, *Ger.* füllen   uh(r): *Fr.* **boeuf**, *Ger.* Höhle   <u>kh</u>: *Ger.* **ich**, *Scot.* loch   ğ: *Sp.* amigo   <u>v</u>: *Sp.* hablar   hl: *Welsh* **Llanelli**.   CAPITALS: primary stress.   SMALL CAPS: secondary stress.   Ⓢ: U.S. pron.   Ⓛ: British pron.

San Lucas, Cabo
  southernmost point of Baja   KAH-y̱ō sahn LOO-kahs   ˌkaβoː san ˈluːkas
    California, Mexico

San Luis
  1. prov & town, Argentina; city,   sahn lu-ĒS   san luˈiːs
    Cuba
  2. city, CO   san LOO-uhs   sæn ˈluːəs

San Luiseño
  Band, N. American people   SAN LOO-i-SĀN-yō   ˌsæn ˌluːiˈseːnjoː

San Luis Obispo
  city, county, CA   SAN LOO-uhs uh-BIS-pō   ˌsæn ˌluːəs əˈbispoː

San Luis Potosí
  state, Mexico   SAHN lu-ĒS PŌT-uh-SĒ   ˌsan luˌiːs ˌpoːʈəˈsiː

San Manuel
  Indian reservation, US   SAN muhn-WEL, mahn-WEL   ˌsæn mənˈwel, manˈwel

San Marcos
  1. city, CA, TX   san MAHR-kuhs   sæn ˈmaʳkəs
  2. Guatemala   sahn MAHR-kōs   san ˈmarkoːs

San Marinese, Sanmarinese
  pert. to San Marino   SAN-MAR-uh-NĒZ, -NĒS   ˌsænˌmærəˈniːz, -ˈniːs

San Marino
  repuplic, city, Europe   SAN muh-RĒ-nō   ˌsæn məˈriːnoː

San Martín
  town, Argentina   SAN mahr-TĒN   ˌsæn maʳˈtiːn

San Mateo
  city, county, CA   SAN muh-TĀ-ō   ˌsæn məˈteːoː

San Miguel
  1. river, CO; county, CO, NM   SAN muh-GIL   ˌsæn məˈgil
  2. city, El Salvador; island,   sahn mē-ĞEL, Ⓢ SAN muh-GEL   san miːˈɣel, Ⓢ ˌsæn məˈgel
    Philippines; Philippine beer

San Pasqual
  Indian reservation, US   SAN puh-SKWAWL, puh-SKWAHL   ˌsæn pəˈskwɔːl, pəˈskwal

San Patricio
  county, TX   SAN puh-TRISH-ē-ō   ˌsæn pəˈtriʃiːˌoː

Sanpete
  county, UT   SAN-PĒT   ˈsænˌpiːt

San Quentin
  prison, town, CA   san KWENT-n, sang   sæn ˈkwentn̩, sæŋ

San Rafael
  1. city, CA; river, UT   SAN ruh-FEL   ˌsæn rəˈfel
  2. town, Argentina; national park,   SAN RAH-fē-EL   ˌsæn ˌrafiːˈel
    Chile

San Remo
  1. port, Italy   sahn RĀ-mō, san RĒ-mō   san ˈreːmoː, sæn ˈriːmoː
  2. community, NY   san RĒ-mō   sæn ˈriːmoː

San Saba
  county, TX   san SAB-uh   sæn ˈsæbə

San Salvador
  island, Bahamas   sahn sahl-vah-THAWR, Ⓢ san   san salvaˈðɔːr, Ⓢ sæn
                            SAL-vuh-DAWR   ˈsælvəˌdɔːʳ

San Sebastián
  pl. name   SAN suh-bast-YAHN, SAN   ˌsæn səbæstˈjan, ˌsæn
                            suh-BAS-chuhn   səˈbæstʃən

Sanskrit
  ancient lang., India   SAN-SKRIT, SAN-skruht   ˈsænˌskrit, ˈsænskrət

---

Key (col. 2): a: fad ā: fade ah: father ar: Mary aw: law e: fed ē: feed er: merry i: hid ī: hide ō: coat o͞o: boot
oi: boy ow: now u: put uh: above uhr: bird ch: chop ng: ring sh: show th: thick t͟h: this zh: measure

Sanskritic
  pert. to Sanskrit   san-SKRIT-ik   sæn'skriʈik
Santa
  1. see Santa Claus
  2. pers. name, Italian, Spanish   SAHN-tah   'sɑntɑ
Santa [Pao-an]
  lang., China   SAHN-TAH   'sɑn'tɑ
Santa Ana
  1. city, CA; strong, hot wind in CA   SANT-uh AN-uh   ˌsæntə 'ænə
  2. prov & town, El Salvador   SAHNT-uh AHN-uh   ˌsɑntə 'ɑnə
Santa Barbara
  city, county, CA   SANT-uh BAHR-b(uh-)ruh   ˌsæntə 'bɑʳb(ə)rə
Santa Catalina
  islands, CA   SANT-uh KAT-l-Ē-nuh   ˌsæntə ˌkætl'iːnə
Santa Clara
  1. river, city, county, CA; N. American people   SANT-uh KLAR-uh, KLER-uh   ˌsæntə 'klærə, 'klerə
  2. city, Cuba   sahn-tah KLAHR-ah   sɑntɑ 'klɑrɑ
Santa Claus
  Christmas folk figure   SANT-uh KLAWZ, SANT-ē KLAWZ   'sæntə ˌklɔːz, 'sænti· ˌklɔːz
Santa Cruz
  1. river, AZ; county, AZ, CA; city, CA   SANT-uh KRŌOZ, SANT-uh KRŌOZ   'sæntə ˌkruːz, ˌsæntə 'kruːz
  2. pl. name, S. America, Philippines; islands, Pacific   sahn-tah KRŌOS   sɑntɑ 'kruːs
Santa Cruz de Mayo
  Philippine festival   SAHN-tah KRŌOS thā MĪ-ō   ˌsɑntɑ 'kruːs ðeː 'maioː
Santa Cruz de Tenerife
  prov, Canary Islands   SAHN-tah KRŌOS thā TEN-uh-RĒ-fā   ˌsɑntɑ 'kruːs ðeː ˌtenə'riːfeː
Santa Fe
  city, NM   SANT-uh FĀ, SANT-uh FĀ   ˌsæntə 'feː, 'sæntə ˌfeː
Santali
  lang., India   SUHN-TAHL-ē   ˌsən'tɑliˑ
Santa Maria
  pl. name   SANT-uh muh-RĒ-uh   ˌsæntə mə'riːə
Santa Monica
  city, CA   SANT-uh MAHN-i-kuh   ˌsæntə 'mɑnikə
Santana
  Carlos, *rock guitarist*   san-TAN-uh   sæn'tænə
Santander
  prov & town, Colombia   SAHN-tahn-DER   ˌsɑntɑn'der
Santarém
  prov & town, Brazil   SAHNT-uh-REM   ˌsɑntə'rem
Santa Rosa
  city, CA   SANT-uh RŌ-zuh   ˌsæntə 'roːzə
Santayana
  George, *Spanish philosopher*   SANT-uh-YAHN-uh, SANT-ē-AHN-uh, SAHNT-   ˌsæntə'jɑnə, ˌsæntiː'ɑnə, ˌsɑnt-
Santa Ynez
  Band, *N. American people*   SANT-uh ē-NEZ   ˌsæntə iː'nez
Santee
  N. American people   san-TĒ   sæn'tiː
Santeria
  Voodoo sect   SAHNT-uh-RĒ-uh   ˌsɑntə'riːə

Foreign Sounds: ue: *Fr.* **rue**, *Ger.* **füllen** uh(r): *Fr.* **boeuf**, *Ger.* **Höhle** <u>kh</u>: *Ger.* i<u>ch</u>, *Scot.* lo<u>ch</u> ġ: *Sp.* ami<u>g</u>o <u>v</u>: *Sp.* ha<u>b</u>lar hl: *Welsh* **Llanelli**. CAPITALS: primary stress. SMALL CAPS: secondary stress. ⑤: U.S. pron. ⑪: British pron.

Santha
  pers. name, Bengali   SHAHN-tuh   'ʃantə

Santiago
  1. city, Chile   sahn-TYAHG̃-ō, Ⓢ SAHNT-ē-AHG-ō,   san'tjaɣoː, Ⓢ ˌsantiː'aɡoː,
       SANT-ē-AHG-ō   ˌsæntiː'aɡoː

  2. pers. name, Spanish   sahn-TYAHG̃-ō   san'tjaɣoː

Santiago de Cuba
  prov & town, Cuba   sahn-TYAHG̃-ō thā KO͞O-buh,   san'tjaɣoː ðeː 'kuːbə,
       Ⓢ SANT-ē-AHG-ō duh KYO͞O-buh   Ⓢ ˌsæntiː'aɡoː də 'kjuːbə

Santiago Fiesta
  Puerto Rican festival   SANT-ē-AHG-ō fē-EST-uh   ˌsæntiː'aɡoː fiː'estə

Santo Domingo
  city, Dominican Republic   sahn-tō thaw-MING-gō, Ⓢ SANT-uh   santoː ðɔː'miŋɡoː, Ⓢ ˌsæntə
       duh-MING-gō   də'miŋɡoː

Santorin [Thera]
  island, Greece   SANT-uh-RĒN   ˌsæntə'riːn

Santorini [Thera]
  island, Greece   SANT-uh-RĒ-nē   ˌsæntə'riːniˑ

Santos
  1. city, Brazil   SAHN-tōs, Ⓢ SANT-uhs   'santoːs, Ⓢ 'sæntəs
  2. pers. name, Spanish   SAHN-tōs   'santoːs

San Vicente
  dept, El Salvador   sahn bē-THĀN-tā, bē-SĀN-tā, Ⓢ SAN   san biː'θeːnteː, biː'seːnteː,
       vuh-SENT-ē   Ⓢ ˌsæn və'sentiˑ

San Xavier
  Indian reservation, US   SAN hahv-YER, sahn khahv-YER   ˌsæn hav'jeʳ, san xav'jer

Sanyo
  Japanese electronics co.   sahn-yō, Ⓢ SAN-yō   sanjoː, Ⓢ 'sænjoː

São Francisco
  island, river, city, Brazil   SOW(M) fruhn-SIS-ko͞o   ˌsaũ(m) frən'siskuː

São Luis
  island, seaport, Brazil   SOW^n lu-ĒS   ˌsaũ lu'iːs

São Miguel
  island, Azores   SOW^n mi-GEL   ˌsaũ mi'gel

Saône
  river, France   SŌN   soːn

São Paulo
  state, city, Brazil   sow(m) POW-lo͞o, -lō   saũ(m) 'pauluː, -loː

Saorstat Eireann
  Gaelic name for Irish Free State   SĀR-STAWT ER-(y)uhn   ˌseːʳˌstɔːt 'er(j)ən

São Salvador
  port, Brazil   SOW^n sahl-vuh-DAWR, sow^n ˌsaũ saːlvə'dɔːʳ, saũ
       SAHL-vuh-DAWR   'saːlvəˌdɔːʳ

São Tiago
  islands, Cape Verde   sow^n(n) TYAHG-o͞o   saũ(n) 'tjaguː

São Tomé
  island, Africa   SOW^n(N) tuh-MĀ   ˌsaũ(n) tə'meː

Sao Tomean
  pert. to São Tomé   SOW^n(N) tuh-MĀ-uhn   ˌsaũ(n) tə'meːən

Sao Tome and Principe
  republic, Africa   SOW^n(N) tuh-MĀ uhn(d)   ˌsaũ(n) tə'meː ən(d)
       PRIN-suh-puh   'prinsəpə

São Tomé e Príncipe
  republic, Africa   SOW^n(N) tuh-ME ā PRI^n(N)-suh-puh   ˌsaũ(n) tə'me eː 'prĩ(n)səpə

Key (col. 2):   a: **fad**   ā: **fade**   ah: **father**   ar: **Mary**   aw: **law**   e: **fed**   ē: **feed**   er: **merry**   i: **hid**   ī: **hide**   ō: **coat**   o͞o: **boot**
oi: **boy**   ow: **now**   u: **put**   uh: **above**   uhr: **bird**   ch: **chop**   ng: **ring**   sh: **show**   th: **thick**   <u>th</u>: **this**   zh: **measure**

Sapir
Edward, *US anthropologist,*   suh-PIR   sə'piʳ
  linguist

Sapodilla
tree   SAP-uh-DIL-uh, SAP-uh-DĒ-(y)uh   ‚sæpə'dilə, ‚sæpə'diː(j)ə

Sapphic
pert. to Sappho   SAF-ik   'sæfik

Sapphira
Biblical name   suh-FĪ-ruh   sə'fɑirə

Sappho
Greek poet   SAF-ō   'sæfoː

Sapporo
city, Japan; tdmk for a Japanese   sahp-pōr-ō   sɑppoːroː
  beer

Saqqara
village, Egypt   suh-KAHR-uh   sə'kɑrə

Sara
1. African people   SAHR-uh   'sɑʳə
2. pers. name   SER-uh, SAR-uh, SĀ-ruh   'serə, 'særə, 'seːrə
3. French   sah-RAH   sɑːrɑː

Saracen
nomadic people, Syria, Arabia;   SAR-uh-suhn   'særəsən
  former name for Arabs

Saracenic
pert. to the Saracens   SAR-uh-SEN-ik   ‚særə'senik

Saracoğlu
Şükrü, *Turkish politician*   suh-RAHJ-ō-GLUE   sə'rɑdʒoː‚glyː

Saragossa
prov, city, Spain   SAR-uh-GAHS-uh   ‚særə'gɑsə

Sarah
1. pers. name   SER-uh, SAR-uh, SĀ-ruh   'serə, 'særə, 'seːrə
2. French   sah-RAH   sɑːrɑː

Sarajevo
city, Bosnia and Herzegovina   SAHR-uh-ye-VAW, ⑤ SAR-uh-YĀ-vō   'sɑrəje‚vɔː, ⑤ ‚særə'jeːvoː

Sarakole
African people   SAR-uh-KŌL, SAR-uh-KŌL   ‚særə'koːl, 'særə‚koːl

Saranac
river, lakes, NY   SAR-uh-NAK   'særə‚næk

Sarandon
Susan, *US actress;* Chris, *US actor*   suh-RAN-duhn   sə'rændən

Sarasota
city, FL   SAR-uh-SŌT-uh   ‚særə'soːţə

Saratoga
city, CA; race track, NY   SAR-uh-TŌ-guh   ‚særə'toːgə

Saratov
city, region, Russia   suh-RAHT-uhf   sə'rɑːţəf

Sarawak
state, Malaysia   suh-RAH-wah(k), suh-RAH-WAK   sə'rɑwɑ(k), sə'rɑ‚wæk

Sarbanes
Paul Spyros, *US politician*   SAHR-BĀNZ   'sɑʳ‚beːnz

Sardanapalian
pert. to Sardanapalus   SAHRD-n-uh-PĀ-lē-uhn,   ‚sɑʳdṇə'peːliːən, ‚sɑʳdənə-
                                SAHR-duh-nuh-

Foreign Sounds: ue: *Fr.* **rue,** *Ger.* **füllen** uh(r): *Fr.* **boeuf,** *Ger.* **Höhle** <u>kh</u>: *Ger.* i**ch,** *Scot.* lo**ch** g̱: *Sp.* ami**go** v̱: *Sp.* ha**b**lar
hl: *Welsh* **Ll**anelli. CAPITALS: primary stress. SMALL CAPS: secondary stress. ⑤: U.S. pron. ⓑ: British pron.

Sardanapalus
   legendary decadent Assyrian king   SAHRD-n-AP-uh-luhs,   ˌsɑʳdn̩ˈæpələs,
      SAHR-duh-NAP-uh-luhs   ˌsɑʳdəˈnæpələs

Sardegna [Sardinia]
   island, Mediterranean   sahr-DĀN-yuh   sɑʳdeːnjə

Sardes
   ancient city, Asia Minor   SAHRD-ēz   ˈsɑʳdiːz

Sardinia
   island, Mediterranean   sahr-DIN-ē-uh, sahr-DIN-yuh   sɑʳdiniːə, sɑʳdinjə

Sardinian
   pert. to Sardinia   sahr-DIN-ē-uhn, sahr-DIN-yuhn   sɑʳdiniːən, sɑʳdinjən

Sardis
   ancient city, Asia Minor   SAHRD-uhs   ˈsɑʳdəs

Sargasso Sea
   region of Atlantic Ocean   sahr-GAS-ō SĒ   sɑʳˌgæsoː ˈsiː

Sargeant, Sargent
   pers. name   SAHR-juhnt   ˈsɑʳdʒənt

Sargon
   ruler of Akkad; king of Assyria   SAHR-GAHN, SAHR-guhn   ˈsɑʳˌgɑn, ˈsɑʳgən

Sarmatia
   ancient region, eastern Europe   sahr-MĀ-shuh   sɑʳˈmeːʃə

Sarmatian
   pert. to Sarmatia   sahr-MĀ-shuhn   sɑʳˈmeːʃən

Sarnia
   port, Ontario, Canada   SAHR-nē-uh   ˈsɑʳniːə

Saronic
   pert. to saros, 18-year   suh-RAHN-ik   səˈrɑnik
     astronomical period

Saroyan
   William, US writer   suh-ROI-(y)uhn   səˈrɔi(j)ən

Sarpedon
   Lycian hero in Odyssey   sahr-PĒD-n   sɑʳˈpiːdn̩

Sarre
   French name of Saar   SAHR   sɑːr

Sarsi
   N. American people   SAHR-sē   ˈsɑʳsiˑ

Sarto, del
   Andrea, Florentine artist   del SAHR-tō   del ˈsɑʳtoː

Sartre
   Jean Paul, French philosopher   SAHRTR, Ⓢ SAHRT, SAHR-truh   sɑːrtr, Ⓢ ˈsɑʳt, ˈsɑʳtrə
     (Nobel 1964)

Sarvepalli
   pers. name, Hindi   SUHR-vuh-PUHL-lē   ˌsəʳvəˈpəlliˑ

SASE
   self-addressed stamped envelope   ES-Ā-ES-Ē, SĀ-zē   ˌesˌeːˌesˈiː, ˈseːziˑ

Sasha
   pers. name   SAHSH-uh, SASH-uh   ˈsɑʃə, ˈsæʃə

Saskatchewan
   river, province, Canada   suh-SKACH-uh-wuhn, sas-KACH-,   səˈskætʃəwən, sæsˈkætʃ-,
      -uh-WAHN   -əˌwɑn

Saskatoon
   town, Canada   SAS-kuh-TOON   ˌsæskəˈtuːn

Sasquatch [Big Foot]
   legendary manlike creature   SAS-KWACH, SAS-KWAHCH   ˈsæsˌkwætʃ, ˈsæsˌkwɑtʃ

Key (col. 2): a: fad ā: fade ah: father ar: Mary aw: law e: fed ē: feed er: merry i: hid ī: hide ō: coat ōō: boot
oi: boy ow: now u: put uh: above uhr: bird ch: chop ng: ring sh: show th: thick <u>th</u>: this zh: measure

Sassanid
  Persian dynasty suh-SAHN-uhd, suh-SAN-uhd, sə'sɑnəd, sə'sænəd, 'sæsənid
  SAS-uh-nid

Sassari
  prov & town, Sardinia SAHS-uh-rē 'sɑsəri·

Sassenach
  Irish/Scots disparaging term for SAH-suh-nuhkh, Ⓢ SAS-n-AK, 'sɑːsənəx, Ⓢ 'sæsn̩ˌæk,
  English SAS-n-AHKH 'sæsn̩ˌɑx

Sassoon
  Siegfried, English author; Vidal, suh-SOON, sa-SOON sə'suːn, sæ'suːn
  British hair styling executive

Satan
  adversary of God, devil SĀT-n 'seɪtn̩

Satanic
  pert. to Satan suh-TAN-ik, sā-TAN-ik sə'tænik, seɪ'tænik

Satanism
  worship of Satan SĀT-n-IZ-uhm 'seɪtn̩ˌizəm

Satanist
  worshipper of Satan SĀT-n-uhst 'seɪtn̩əst

Sathanas
  the Devil SAT-uh-nuhs, SĀT-n-uhs 'sæθənəs, 'seɪtn̩əs

Satie
  Erik, French composer sah-TĒ sɑ'tiː

Satis
  Egyptian goddess SAHT-uhs, SĀT-uhs 'sɑtəs, 'seɪtəs

Sato
  Eisaku, Japanese politician (Nobel sah-tō sɑtoː
  1974)

Satoshi
  pers. name, Japanese sah-tō-shē sɑtoːʃiː

Satsuma
  prov, Japan; porcelain; tree saht-soo-mah, Ⓢ sat-SOO-muh, satsuːma, Ⓢ sæt'suːmə,
  SAT-suh-muh 'sætsəmə

Sattui
  V., winery, CA suh-TOO-ē sə'tuːi·

Saturday
  day of the week SAT-uhr-dē, SAT-uhr-dā, *rapidly also* 'sætərdi·, 'sætərdeː, *rapidly*
  SAR-dē, SAD-dē *also* 'særdi·, 'sæddi·

Saturn
  Roman god, father of Jupiter; SAT-uhrn 'sætərn
  planet

Saturnalia
  Roman festival SAT-uhr-NĀL-yuh, -NĀ-lē-uh ˌsætərˈneːljə, -'neːliːə

Saturnian
  pert. to Saturn sa-TUHR-nē-uhn, suh- sæ'tərniːən, sə-

Saturninus
  Roman politician SAT-uhr-NĪ-nuhs ˌsætərˈnainəs

Satyagraha
  passive resistance, India suh-TYAHG-ruh-huh sə'tjɑgrəhə

Satyendra
  pers. name, Bengali sawt-YĀN-draw, Ⓢ suht-YEN-druh sɔːt'jeɪndrɔː, Ⓢ sət'jendrə

Satyendranath
  pers. name, Bengali sawt-YĀN-druh-nuht sɔːt'jeɪndrənət

Satyrs
  Greek sylvan deities SĀT-uhrz, SAT-uhrz 'seɪtərz, 'sætərz

Foreign Sounds: ue: *Fr.* **rue**, *Ger.* füllen uh(r): *Fr.* boeuf, *Ger.* Höhle kh: *Ger.* ich, *Scot.* loch ğ: *Sp.* amigo v̱: *Sp.* hablar
hl: *Welsh* Llanelli. CAPITALS: primary stress. SMALL CAPS: secondary stress. Ⓢ: U.S. pron. Ⓔ: British pron.

Saud
  royal family, Saudi Arabia   sah-$\overline{OO}$D   sɑˈuːd

Saudi
  pert. to Saudi Arabia   SOWD-ē, SAWD-ē, sah-$\overline{OO}$D-ē   ˈsaudiˌ, ˈsɔːdiˌ, sɑˈuːdiˌ

Saudi Arabia
  kingdom, Arabian Peninsula   SOWD-ē uh-RĀ-bē-uh, SAWD-ē, sah-$\overline{OO}$D-ē   ˌsaudiː əˈreːbiːə, ˌsɔːdiˌ, sɑˌuːdiː

Saudi Arabian
  pert. to Saudi Arabia   SOWD-ē uh-RĀ-bē-uhn, SAWD-ē, sah-$\overline{OO}$D-ē   ˌsaudiː əˈreːbiːən, ˌsɔːdiˌ, sɑˌuːdiː

Saugus
  town, MA   SAW-guhs, SAHG-uhs   ˈsɔːgəs, ˈsɑgəs

Sauk
  county, WI; N. American people   SAWK   ˈsɔːk

Sauk-Fox
  Indian reservation, US   SAWK-FAHKS   ˈsɔːkˈfɑks

Sauk-Suiattle
  Indian reservation, US   SAWK-S$\overline{OO}$-ē-AT-l   ˈsɔːkˌsuːiˈætl̩

Saul
  king of Israel; pers. name   SAWL   ˈsɔːl

Sault Ste. Marie
  city, MI; N. American people   S$\overline{OO}$ SĀNT muh-RĒ   ˌsuː ˌseːnt məˈriː

Saunders
  pers. name   SAWN-duhrz, SAHN-duhrz   ˈsɔːndə^{r}z, ˈsɑndə^{r}z

Saurashtra
  state, India   sow-RAHSH-truh   sauˈraʃtrə

Saurischia
  dinosaur order   saw-RIS-kē-uh   sɔːˈriskiːə

Saurolophus
  dinosaur   saw-RAHL-uh-fuhs   sɔːˈrɑləfəs

Sauropoda
  dinosaur infraorder   saw-RAHP-uhd-uh   sɔːˈrɑpədə

Sauropodomorpha
  dinosaur suborder   saw-RAHP-uhd-uh-MAWR-fuh   sɔːˌrɑpədəˈmɔː^{r}fə

Saussure
  Ferdinand de, *Swiss linguist*   sō-SUER, Ⓢ sō-SIR, sō-SUR   sɔːˈsyːr, Ⓢ sɔːˈsi^r, sɔːˈsu^r

Saussurean, Saussurian
  pert. to Saussure   sō-SIR-ē-uhn, sō-SUR-ē-uhn, sō-SHUR-ē-uhn   sɔːˈsiriːən, sɔːˈsuriːən, sɔːˈʃuriːən

Sauternes
  wine   sō-TERN, Ⓢ sō-TUHRN, saw-   sɔːˈtern, Ⓢ sɔːˈtə^{r}n, sɔː-

Sauvignon Blanc
  wine   sō-vēn-yaw^n BLAH^n sɔːviːnjõ blã

Sava, Save
  river, Serbia   SAHV-uh   ˈsavə

Savaii, Savai'i
  island, Samoa   suh-VĪ-ē   səˈvaiiː

Savalas
  Telly, *US entertainer*   suh-VAL-uhs, suh-VAHL-uhs   səˈvæləs, səˈvɑləs

Savannah
  city, GA   suh-VAN-uh   səˈvænə

Savarin
  flavored cake; brand of coffee   SAV-uh-ruhn   ˈsævərən

Savigny-sur-Orge
  commune, France   sah-vēn-YĒ-suer-AWRZH   sɑːviːnjiːsyːrɔːrʒ

Key (col. 2):   a: fad   ā: fade   ah: father   ar: Mary   aw: law   e: fed   ē: feed   er: merry   i: hid   ī: hide   ō: coat $\overline{oo}$: boot
oi: boy   ow: now   u: put   uh: above   uhr: bird   ch: chop   ng: ring   sh: show   th: thick   <u>th</u>: this   zh: measure

Savile, Saville
   pers. name — SAV-uhl, SAV-il — 'sævəl, 'sævil

Savile Row
   street, London, England — SAV-uhl RŌ, SAV-il RŌ — ˌsævəl 'roː, ˌsævil 'roː

Savin
   US copier co. — SAV-uhn, SĀ-vuhn — 'sævən, 'seːvən

Savinien
   pers. name, French — sah-vēn-YE[n] — saːviːnjẽ

Savoie [Savoy]
   region, France, Italy — sahv-WAH, Ⓢ sav-WAH, suh-VOI — saːvwaː, Ⓢ sæv'wɑ, sə'vɔi

Savona
   prov & town, Italy — suh-VŌ-nuh — sə'voːnə

Savonarola
   Girolamo, Italian religious leader — SAV-uh-nuh-RŌ-luh, suh-VAHN-uh-RŌ-luh — ˌsævənə'roːlə, sə,vɑnə'roːlə

Savoy
   theatre, street, London, England; anglicization of Savoie; Alps, *mtn. range* — suh-VOI — sə'vɔi

Savoyard
   inhabitant of or pert. to Savoy; *fan of Gilbert & Sullivan operas* — SAV-OI-AHRD, suh-VOI-AHRD, SAV-wah-YAHR(D) — ˌsæv,ɔi'ɑ[r]d, sə'vɔi,ɑ[r]d, ˌsævwa'jɑ[r](d)

Savoyarde
   cookery preparation — SAV-OI-AHRD, suh-VOI-AHRD, SAV-wah-YAHRD — ˌsæv,ɔi'ɑ[r]d, sə'vɔi,ɑ[r]d, ˌsævwa'jɑ[r]d

Sawatch
   mtn. range, CO — suh-WAHCH — sə'watʃ

Sawu Sea, Savu Sea
   region of Indian Ocean — SAHV-o͞o SĒ — ˌsavuː 'siː

Saw-whet
   owl — SAW-(H)WET — 'sɔːˌ(h)wet

Sawyer
   Diane, US TV journalist; pers. name — SAW-yuhr, SOI(-uh)r — 'sɔːjə[r], 'sɔi(ə)[r]

Saxe-Coburg-Gotha
   British royal family — SAKS-KŌ-BUHRG-GŌ-thuh — ˌsæks,koːˌbə[r]g'goːθə

Saxifrage
   plant — SAK-suh-frij, SAK-suh-FRĀJ — 'sæksəfridʒ, 'sæksəˌfreːdʒ

Saxo Grammaticus
   Danish historian, poet — SAK-sō gruh-MAT-i-kuhs — 'sæksoː grə'mætikəs

Saxon
   a Germanic people — SAK-suhn — 'sæksən

Saxony
   state, Germany — SAK-suh-nē — 'sæksəniˑ

Saxophone
   musical instrument — SAK-suh-FŌN — 'sæksəˌfoːn

Sayan
   mtn. range, Russia — suh-YAHN — sə'jan

Sayer
   Leo, musician, singer — SĀ(-uh)r — 'seː(ə)[r]

Sazerac
   tdmk for a cocktail — SAZ-uh-RAK — 'sæzəˌræk

Sbarro
   US restaurant chain — SPAHR-ō — 'sparoː

Foreign Sounds: ue: *Fr.* **rue**, *Ger.* **füllen** uh(r): *Fr.* **boeuf**, *Ger.* **Höhle** <u>kh</u>: *Ger.* i**ch**, *Scot.* lo**ch** g̃: *Sp.* ami**g**o <u>v</u>: *Sp.* ha**b**lar
hl: *Welsh* **Ll**anelli. CAPITALS: primary stress. SMALL CAPS: secondary stress. Ⓢ: U.S. pron. Ⓛ: British pron.

Scaasi
  Arnold, *US fashion designer*   SKAHS-ē, SKAHZ-ē   'skɑsiˑ, 'skɑziˑ

Scabious
  flower   SKĀ-bē-uhs, SKAB-ē-uhs   'skeːbiːəs, 'skæbiːəs

Scaevola
  Roman cognomen   SĒ-vuh-luh, SEV-uh-luh   'siːvələ, 'sevələ

Scafell
  mtn., England   SKAW-FEL   'skɔːˌfel

Scaggs
  Boz, *US musician*   SKAGZ   'skægz

Scala, La
  see La Scala

Scaldis
  Belgian beer   SKAHL-duhs   'skɑldəs

Scaliger
  J. C., *Italian scholar in France;*   SKAL-uh-juhr   'skælədʒəʳ
  his son, J. J., French scholar

Scamander
  river of Troy   skuh-MAN-duhr   skə'mændəʳ

Scammony
  plant   SKAM-uh-nē   'skæməniˑ

Scanderbeg [Kastrioti]
  Albanian revolutionary leader   SKAHN-duhr-BEG, SKAN-   'skɑndəʳˌbeg, 'skæn-

Scandia
  Danish beer   SKAHN-dē-uh, ⓢ SKAN-dē-uh   'skɑndiːə, ⓢ 'skændiːə

Scandian
  a Scandinavian   SKAN-dē-uhn   'skændiːən

Scandinavia
  region, North Europe   SKAN-duh-NĀ-vē-uh, -NĀV-yuh   ˌskændə'neːviːə, -'neːvjə

scandium
  element   SKAN-dē-uhm   'skændiːəm

Scapa Flow
  area of water, Orkney Islands   SKAP-uh FLŌ   ˌskæpə 'floː

Scaramouch, -che
  braggart character in Commedia   SKAR-uh-MŌŌSH, -MŌŌCH, -MOWCH   'skærə,muːʃ, -,muːtʃ,
  dell' Arte   -,mautʃ

Scaramuccia
  pers. name, Italian   SKAHR-ah-MŌŌT-chah   ˌskɑrɑ'muːttʃɑ

Scarborough
  town, England   SKAHR-BUHR-uh, -BUH-ruh, -bruh   'skɑʳˌbər-ə, -ˌbə-rə, -brə

Scarlatti
  Alessandro, *Italian composer*   skahr-LAHT-ē   skaʳ'lɑţiˑ

Scarlett
  pers. name   SKAHR-luht   'skɑʳlət

Scarritt
  College for Christian Education,   SKAR-uht, SKER-uht   'skærət, 'skerət
  TN

Scaup
  duck   SKAWP   'skɔːp

Scaurus
  Roman cognomen   SKŌR-uhs, SKAWR-uhs   'skoːrəs, 'skɔːrəs

Scawen
  pers. name   SKŌ-uhn   'skoːən

Scelidosaurus
  dinosaur   SEL-uhd-uh-SAWR-uhs   ˌselədə'sɔːrəs

Key (col. 2): a: **fad** ā: **fade** ah: **father** ar: **Mary** aw: **law** e: **fed** ē: **feed** er: **merry** i: **hid** ī: **hide** ō: **coat** ōō: **boot**
oi: **boy** ow: **now** u: **put** uh: **above** uhr: **bird** ch: **chop** ng: **ring** sh: **show** th: **thick** <u>th</u>: **this** zh: **measure**

Schacht
    Hjalmar, *German economist*   SHAH<u>KHT</u>   'ʃɑxt
Schaffhausen
    canton, Switzerland   shahf-HOWZ-n   ʃafʰhauzn̩
Schafkopf
    game   SHAHF-KAWPF   'ʃaf,kɔːpf
Schally
    Andrew V., *Polish-born US*   SHAL-ē   'ʃæli·
        biochemist (Nobel 1977)
Schaumburg
    village, IL   SHAWM-BUHRG   'ʃɔːm,bəʳg
Schawlow
    Arthur, *US physicist (Nobel 1981)*   SHAW-lō   'ʃɔːloː
Scheherazade, Sh-
    symphonic suite,   shuh-HER-uh-ZAHD-uh, -ZAHD   ʃə,herə'zɑdə, -'zɑd
        Rimsky-Korsakov
Scheidemann
    Philipp, *German political leader*   SHĪD-uh-MAHN   'ʃaidə,man
Schelde
    river, Europe   SKEL-duh   'skeldə
Scheldt [Schelde]
    river, Europe   SKELT   'skelt
Schell
    Maximilian, *Australian actor*   SHEL   'ʃel
Schelling
    Friedrich Wilhelm, *German*   SHEL-ing   'ʃeliŋ
        philosopher
Schellingism
    philosophy of F. W. Schelling   SHEL-ing-IZ-uhm   'ʃeliŋ,izəm
Schenectady
    city, county, NY   skuh-NEK-tuhd-ē   skə'nektədi·
Schenkel
    Chris, *US sportscaster*   SHENG-kuhl   'ʃeŋkəl
Schering-Plough
    US drug co.   SHIR-ing-PLOW   'ʃiriŋ,plau
Schermerhorn
    1. Kenneth, *US conductor*   SHUHR-muhr-HAWRN   'ʃəʳməʳ,hɔːʳn
    2. *street, New York City*   SKUHR-muhr-HAWRN, SKER-   'skəʳməʳ,hɔːʳn, 'skeʳ-
Scherzo
    musical passage   SKERT-sō   'skeʳtsoː
Schiaparelli
    Elsa, *fashion designer*   SKYAHP-uh-REL-ē, SKAP-, SHAP-   ,skjɑpə'reli·, ,skæp-, ,ʃæp-
Schiava
    Italian wine grape   skē-AHV-uh   skiː'ɑvə
Schick
    test for diphtheria; razor mfr.   SHIK   'ʃik
Schickel
    Richard, *US writer*   SHIK-uhl   'ʃikəl
Schickele
    1. Peter, *US composer, aka*   SHIK-uh-lē   'ʃikəli·
        "P.D.Q. Bach"
    2. René, *German writer*   SHIK-uh-luh   'ʃikələ
Schieffer
    Bob, *US journalist*   SHĒ-fuhr   'ʃiːfəʳ

Foreign Sounds: **ue**: *Fr.* **rue**, *Ger.* **füllen**   **uh(r)**: *Fr.* **boeuf**, *Ger.* **Höhle**   <u>kh</u>: *Ger.* **ich**, *Scot.* **loch**   ḡ: *Sp.* **amigo**   <u>v</u>: *Sp.* **hablar**
hl: *Welsh* **Llanelli**.   CAPITALS: primary stress.   SMALL CAPS: secondary stress.   Ⓢ: U.S. pron.   Ⓛ: British pron.

Schiele
Egon, *Austrian painter*	SHĒ-luh	'ʃiːlə

Schiff
pers. name	SHIF	'ʃif

Schild
US beer	SHILD, SHILT	'ʃild, 'ʃilt

Schildkraut
Joseph & Rudolf, *German actors*	SHILT-KROWT	'ʃilt,kraut

Schiller
Friedrich von, *German writer*	SHIL-uhr	'ʃiləʳ

Schiphol
airport, Amsterdam	SHIP-ŌL	'ʃip,oːl

Schipperke
dog breed	SKIP-uhr-kē, SHIP-, -uhrk, -uhr-kuh	'skipəʳkiˑ, 'ʃip-, -əʳk, -əʳkə

Schippers
Thomas, *US conductor*	SHIP-uhrz	'ʃipəʳz

Schlafly
Phyllis, *US author, activist*	SHLAF-lē	'ʃlæfliˑ

Schlage
lock	SHLĀG, SLĀG, SLĀJ, SHLĀJ	'ʃleːg, 'sleːg, 'sleːdʒ, 'ʃleːdʒ

Schlegel
A. W. von, *German author;* F. von, *German author*	SHLĀ-guhl	'ʃleːgəl

Schleicher
county, TX	SHLĪ-kuhr, SLĪ-kuhr	'ʃlaikəʳ, 'slaikəʳ

Schlesinger
1. Arthur Meier *(father & son), US historians*	SHLĀ-zing-uhr	'ʃleːziŋəʳ
2. James, *US cabinet officer*	SLES-ing-(g)uhr, SLES-in-juhr	'slesiŋ(g)əʳ, 'slesindʒəʳ

Schleswig-Holstein
prov, Germany	SHLES-vikh-HŌL-SHTĪN, ⑤ SLES-vig-HŌL-STĪN	'ʃlesviç'hoːl,ʃtain, ⑤ 'slesvig'hoːl,stain

Schley
county, GA	SLĪ	'slai

Schliemann
Heinrich, *German archaeologist*	SHLĒ-MAHN	'ʃliːˌman

Schmidt
Helmut, *German chancellor;* Michael, *US baseball player; pers. name*	SHMIT	'ʃmit

Schmierkase
cheese	SHMIR-KĀ-zuh, SHMIR-KĀS	'ʃmiʳ,keːzə, 'ʃmiʳ,keːs

Schmitt
Harrison Hagan, *US astronaut, politician*	SHMIT	'ʃmit

Schnapps
liquor	SHNAPS, SHNAHPS	'ʃnæps, 'ʃnaps

Schnauzer
dog breed	SHNOW-zuhr, SNOW-; SHNOWT-suhr	'ʃnauzəʳ, 'snau-; 'ʃnautsəʳ

Schnitzel
meat cutlet	SHNIT-suhl, SNIT-suhl	'ʃnitsəl, 'snitsəl

Schoene
Field, *airport, Germany*	SHUH(R)-nuh	'ʃœnə

Key (col. 2):   a: fad   ā: fade   ah: father   ar: Mary   aw: law   e: fed   ē: feed   er: merry   i: hid   ī: hide   ō: coat   o͞o: boot
oi: boy   ow: now   u: put   uh: above   uhr: bird   ch: chop   ng: ring   sh: show   th: thick   th̲: this   zh: measure

Schoenling
US beer — SHEN-ling — ˈʃɛnlɪŋ

Schoharie
county, NY — skō-HAR-ē — skɔːˈhæriˑ

Scholasticism
medieval philosophical system — skuh-LAS-tuh-SIZ-uhm — skəˈlæstəˌsɪzəm

Schopenhauer
Arthur, German philosopher — SHŌ-puhn-HOW-uhr — ˈʃoːpənˌhaʊəʳ

Schorling
Park, former ballpark, Chicago, IL — SHAWR-ling — ˈʃɔːʳlɪŋ

Schottische
dance — SHAHT-ish, shah-TĒSH — ˈʃɑtɪʃ, ʃɑˈtiːʃ

Schramberg
city, Germany — SHRAHM-BERK — ˈʃrɑmˌbeʳk

Schramsberg
winery, CA — SHRAMZ-BUHRG — ˈʃræmzˌbəʳg

Schreiffer
John Robert, US physicist (Nobel 1972) — SHRĒ-fuhr, SRĒ-fuhr — ˈʃriːfəʳ, ˈsriːfəʳ

Schreiner
College, TX — SHRĪ-nuhr — ˈʃraɪnəʳ

Schrödinger
Erwin, Austrian physicist (Nobel 1933) — SHRUH(R)D-ing-uhr, Ⓢ SHRĀD-ing-uhr, SHRŌD-ing-uhr, SRĀD-, SRŌD- — ˈʃrœːdɪŋəʳ, Ⓢ ˈʃreːdɪŋəʳ, ˈʃroːdɪŋəʳ, ˈsreːd-, ˈsroːd-

Schroeder
Patricia, US politician — SHRŌD-uhr — ˈʃroːdəʳ

Schubert
Franz, Austrian composer — SHOO-buhrt, SHOO-BERT — ˈʃuːbəʳt, ˈʃuːˌbeʳt

Schuller
Gunther, US composer — SHUL-uhr — ˈʃuləʳ

Schultz
Theodore W., US economist (Nobel 1979) — SHULTS — ˈʃults

Schulz
Charles, US cartoonist — SHULTS — ˈʃults

Schumacher
pers. name, Danish — SHOO-mahkh-uhr — ˈʃuːmɑːxər

Schumann
Robert, German composer — SHOO-MAHN, SHOO-muhn — ˈʃuːˌmɑn, ˈʃuːmən

Schumpeter
Joseph, US economist — SHUM-PĀT-uhr — ˈʃumˌpeːtəʳ

Schuschnigg
Kurt von, Austrian politician — SHUSH-nik — ˈʃuʃnɪk

Schutz
French beer — SHUTS — ʃuts

Schutzenburger
French beer — shut-suhn-boor-GER, SHUT-suhn-BUR-guhr — ʃutsənbuːrger, ˈʃutsənˌburgəʳ

Schutzenfeste
German festival — SHUT-suhn-FES-tuh — ˈʃutsənˌfestə

Schutzstaffel
elite Nazi military unit — SHUT-STAHF-uhl — ˈʃutˌstɑfəl

Schuyler
county, IL, MO, NY; pers. name — SKĪ-luhr — ˈskaɪləʳ

Foreign Sounds: ue: *Fr.* **rue**, *Ger.* **füllen** uh(r): *Fr.* **boeuf**, *Ger.* **Höhle** <u>kh</u>: *Ger.* **ich**, *Scot.* **loch** g̱: *Sp.* **amigo** v̱: *Sp.* **hablar**
hl: *Welsh* **Llanelli**. CAPITALS: primary stress. SMALL CAPS: secondary stress. Ⓢ: U.S. pron. Ⓔ: British pron.

Schuylkill
  river, county, PA   SK$\overline{OO}$L-KIL, SK$\overline{OO}$(L)-kuhl   'skuːl,kil, 'skuː(l)kəl

Schwaben [Swabia]
  prov, Germany   SHFAHB-uhn   'ʃfabən

Schwann
  1. *Theodor, German zoologist*   SHFAHN, Ⓢ SHWAHN   'ʃfɑn, Ⓢ 'ʃwɑn
  2. *music catalogue*   SHWAHN   'ʃwɑn

Schwartz
  Melvin, US physicist (Nobel 1988)   SHWAWRTS   'ʃwɔːʳts

Schwarzenegger
  Arnold, Austrian actor in US   SHWAWRT-suh-NEG-uhr, -NĀ-guhr   'ʃwɔːʳtsə,negəʳ, -,neːgəʳ

Schwarzkopf
  Norman, US general   SHWAWRTS-KAW(P)F,   'ʃwɔːʳts,kɔ(p)f,
       SHWAWRTS-KAH(P)F, SWAWRTS-   'ʃwɔːʳts,ka(p)f, 'swɔːʳts-

Schwarzwald
  Black Forest, Germany   SHFAHRTS-VAHLT   'ʃfaʳts,valt

Schweitzer
  Albert, Alsatian doctor (Nobel 1952)   SHFĪT-suhr, Ⓢ SHWĪT-suhr   'ʃfaitsəʳ, Ⓢ 'ʃwaitsəʳ

Schweizerhofbrau
  German beer   SHFĪT-suhr-HAWF-BROW   'ʃfaitsəʳ,hɔːf,brau

Schweiz [Switzerland]
  republic, Europe   SHFĪTS   'ʃfaits

Schwenkfeld
  Kaspar von, German religious leader   SHFENGK-FELT   'ʃfeŋk,felt

Schweppes
  soft drink co.   SHWEPS, SWEPS   'ʃweps, 'sweps

Schwerin
  county, Germany   shfā-RĒN   ʃfeːˈriːn

Schwinger
  Julian Seymour, US physicist (Nobel 1965)   SHWING-uhr   'ʃwiŋəʳ

Schwinn
  US bicycle co.   SHWIN   'ʃwin

Schwyz
  mtn., canton, Switzerland   SHFĒTS   'ʃfiːts

Scientology
  tdmk for a US group   SĪ-uhn-TAHL-uh-jē   ,saiənˈtalədʒiˑ

Scilly
  Isles of, islands, England   SIL-ē   'siliˑ

Scioto
  river, county, OH   sī-ŌT-uh   saiˈoːțə

Scipio Aemilianus Africanus
  Roman general   SIP-ē-ō i-MIL-ē-Ā-nuhs   'sipiː,oˑ i,miliːˈeːnəs
       AF-ri-KĀ-nuhs, SKIP-ē-ō   æfri'keːnəs, 'skipiː,oˑ

Scipio Africanus
  Roman general   SIP-ē-ō AF-ri-KĀ-nuhs, SKIP-ē-ō   'sipiː,oˑ æfri'keːnəs, 'skipiː,oˑ

Scipion
  pers. name, French   sēp-YAWⁿ   siːpjɔ̃

Sciron
  brigand killed by Theseus   SKĪ-ruhn, SKĪ-RAHN, SKIR-uhn,   'skairən, 'skai,ran, 'skirən,
       SKIR-AHN   'skir,an

Scituate
  town, MA   SICH-(uh-)wuht   'sitʃ(ə)wət

Key (col. 2):   a: fad   ā: fade   ah: father   ar: Mary   aw: law   e: fed   ē: feed   er: merry   i: hid   ī: hide   ō: coat $\overline{oo}$: boot
oi: boy   ow: now   u: put   uh: above   uhr: bird   ch: chop   ng: ring   sh: show   th: thick   <u>th</u>: this   zh: measure

Scleromochlus
  dinosaur   SKLER-uh-MAHK-luhs   ˌsklerə'mɑkləs
Scofield
  Paul, *English actor*   SKŌ-FĒLD   'skoːˌfiːld
Scone
  Stone of, *Scottish coronation*   SKO͞ON   'skuːn
    stone
Scopas
  Greek sculptor   SKŌ-puhs   'skoːpəs
Scorpio
  sign of the zodiac   SKAWR-pē-Ō   'skɔːʳpiːˌoː
Scorpius
  constellation   SKAWR-pē-uhs   'skɔːʳpiːəs
Scorsese
  Martin, *entertainer*   skawr-SĀ-zē   skɔːʳ'seːziˑ
Scot
  inhabitant of Scotland   SKAHT   'skɑt
Scotch
  pert. to Scotland *or* Scots;   SKAHCH   'skɑtʃ
    whiskey; tdmk for adhesive tape
Scotch-Irish
  mixed Scottish and Irish descent   skahch-Ī-rish   skɑtʃ'airiʃ
Scoter
  duck   SKŌT-uhr   'skoːʈəʳ
Scotia Sea
  region, South Atlantic ocean   SKŌ-shuh SĒ   ˌskoːʃə 'siː
Scotism
  doctrines of Duns Scotus   SKŌT-IZ-uhm   'skoːʈˌizəm
Scotland
  northern part of Great Britain   SKAHT-luhnd   'skɑtlənd
Scots
  form of English spoken in   SKAHTS   'skɑts
    Scotland
Scott
  pers. name   SKAHT   'skɑt
Scotticism
  Scots term   SKAHT-uh-SIZ-uhm   'skɑtəˌsizəm
Scottish
  pert. to Scotland   SKAHT-ish   'skɑtiʃ
Scottish Gaelic
  lang., Scotland   SKAHT-ish GĀ-lik   'skɑtiʃ 'geːlik
Scottsdale
  city, AZ   SKAHTS-DĀL   'skɑtsˌdeːl
Scotty
  pers. name   SKAHT-ē   'skɑtiˑ
Scotus
  pers. name, Latin   SKŌT-uhs   'skoːʈəs
Scowcroft
  Brent, *US politician*   SKŌ-KRAWFT   'skoːˌkrɔːft
Scrabble
  tdmk for a board game   SKRAB-uhl   'skræbəl
Scranton
  William, *US politician; city, PA*   SKRANT-n   'skræntn̩
Screven
  county, GA   SKRIV-uhn   'skrivən

Foreign Sounds: ue: *Fr.* **rue**, *Ger.* **füllen**   uh(r): *Fr.* **boeuf**, *Ger.* **Höhle**   <u>kh</u>: *Ger.* i**ch**, *Scot.* lo**ch**   ḡ: *Sp.* amiḡo   v̠: *Sp.* hab̠lar
hl: *Welsh* **Llanelli**.   CAPITALS: primary stress.   SMALL CAPS: secondary stress.   Ⓢ: U.S. pron.   Ⓛ: British pron.

Scriabin
   Aleksandr, *Russian composer*   SKRYAHB-yin, skrē-AHB-uhn   'skrjɑːbjin, skriː'ɑbən
Scrooge
   Ebenezer, *Dickens character*   SKRŌŌJ   'skruːdʒ
SCSI
   small computer system interface   SKUHZ-ē   'skəziˑ
Scud
   missile   SKUHD   'skəd
Scudamore
   pers. name   SKUHD-uh-MŌR, -MAWR   'skədə,moːʳ, -,mɔːʳ
Scully
   Vin, *US sportscaster*   SKUHL-ē   'skəliˑ
Sculptor
   constellation   SKUHLP-tuhr   'skəlptəʳ
Scuppernong
   river, lake, NC; grape; wine   SKUHP-uhr-NAWNG, -NAHNG,   'skəpəʳ,nɔːŋ, -,nɑŋ, -,nəŋ
                       -NUHNG
Scutari
   lake, Europe   SKŌŌT-uh-rē   'skuːțəriˑ
Scutum
   constellation   SK(Y)ŌŌT-uhm   'sk(j)uːțəm
Scylax
   Greek explorer   SĪ-LAKS   'sɑi,læks
Scylla
   sea monster   SIL-uh   'silə
Scythia
   ancient regions of Europe & Asia   SITH-ē-uh, SI<u>TH</u>-ē-uh   'siθiːə, 'siðiːə
Scythian
   inhabitant of Scythia   SITH-ē-uhn, SI<u>TH</u>-ē-uhn   'siθiːən, 'siðiːən
Seaborg
   Glenn T., *US nuclear chemist*   SĒ-BAWRG   'siː,bɔːʳg
    (Nobel 1951)
Seagal
   Steven, *US actor*   si-GAHL, si-GAL   si'gɑl, si'gæl
Seagram
   liquor co.   SĒ-gruhm   'siːgrəm
Sealyham
   terrier breed   SĒ-lē-HAM, Ⓔ SĒ-lē-uhm   'siːliˑ,hæm, Ⓔ 'siːliːəm
Seamus
   pers. name, Irish   SHĀ-muhs   'ʃeːməs
Sean, Seán
   pers. name, Irish Gaelic   SHAWN, SHAHN   'ʃɔːn, 'ʃɑn
Seaned Eireann
   Irish legislative body   SHAH-nuh<u>th</u> ER-(y)uhn   ˌʃɑːnəð 'er(j)ən
Searcy
   city, county, AR   SUHR-sē   'səʳsiˑ
Sears Roebuck
   US retail chain   SIRZ RŌ-BUHK, RŌ-buhk   ˌsiʳz 'roː,bək, 'roːbək
Sea-Tac
   airport, Seattle-Tacoma, WA   SĒ-TAK   'siː,tæk
SEATO
   South-East Asian Treaty   SĒT-ō   'siːțoː
    Organization
Seattle
   city, WA   sē-AT-l   siː'ætl̩

Key (col. 2): a: fad ā: fade ah: father ar: Mary aw: law e: fed ē: feed er: merry i: hid ī: hide ō: coat ōō: boot
oi: boy ow: now u: put uh: above uhr: bird ch: chop ng: ring sh: show th: thick <u>th</u>: this zh: measure

Seaver
  Tom, *US baseball player*   SĒ-vuhr   'siːvəʳ
Seb
  pers. name   SEB   'seb
Seb [Geb]
  Egyptian earth god   SEB   'seb
Sebastian
  1. pers. name   suh-BAS-chuhn, suh-BASH-chuhn   sə'bæstʃən, sə'bæʃtʃən
  2. Dutch, Norwegian   sä-BAHS-tē-ahn   seː'bastiːan
  3. German   zä-BAHS-tyahn, -tē-ahn   zeː'bastjan, -tiːan
  4. Polish   se-BAHS-tyahn   se'baːstjaːn
Sebastián
  pers. name, Spanish   sä-v̲ahs-TYAHN   seːβas'tjan
Sebastiani
  winery   suh-BAS-tē-AHN-ē   sə,bæstiː'aniˑ
Sebastiano
  pers. name, Italian   SÄ-bahs-TYAH-nō   ,seːbas'tjanoː
Sebastianus
  pers. name, Latin   suh-BAS-chē-Ā-nuhs, suh-BASH-   sə,bæstʃiː'enəs, sə,bæʃ-
Sebastião
  pers. name, Portuguese   suh-buhsh-TYOWⁿ, sä-bahs-TYOWⁿ   səbəʃ'tjaũ, seːbaːs'tjaũ
Sebastopol
  1. city, CA   suh-BAS-tuh-P\overline{OO}L, -PŌL   sə'bæstə,puːl, -,poːl
  2. see Sevastopol
Sebek, Sebeq
  Egyptian crocodile god   SEB-uhk, SÄ-buhk   'sebək, 'seːbək
Sebeok
  Thomas, *US linguist*   SĒ-bē-AHK   'siːbiː,ak
Sebring
  city, FL   SĒ-bring   'siːbriŋ
Sebuano, Cebuano [Bisaya]
  lang., people, Philippine Islands   sä-BWAHN-ō   seː'bwanoː
Secaucus
  town, NJ   si-KAW-kuhs   si'kɔːkəs
Secessio
  Roman plebeian walkout   suh-SESH-ō   sə'seʃoː
Seconal
  tdmk for secobarbital   SEK-uh-NAWL, SEK-uhn-l   'sekə,nɔːl, 'sekənl̩
Secondat
  pers. name, French   suh-gawⁿ-DAH   səgõdaː
Secunderabad
  town, India   si-KUHN-duhr-uh-BAHD, -BAD   si'kəndərə,bad, -,bæd
Secundus
  pers. name, Latin   si-KUHN-duhs, si-KUN-duhs   si'kəndəs, si'kundəs
Sedaka
  Neil, *rock musician*   suh-DAK-uh   sə'dækə
Sedalia
  city, MO   si-DĀL-yuh   si'deːljə
Sedan
  city, KS   si-DAN   si'dæn
Sedang
  lang., people, South Vietnam   sä-DAHNG, suh-DANG   seː'daŋ, sə'dæŋ
Seder
  Passover meal   SĀD-uhr   'seːdəʳ

Foreign Sounds: ue: *Fr.* **rue**, *Ger.* füllen   uh(r): *Fr.* **boeuf**, *Ger.* Höhle   k̲h̲: *Ger.* i**ch**, *Scot.* lo**ch**   ḡ: *Sp.* ami**g**o   v̲: *Sp.* ha**b**lar
hl: *Welsh* **Ll**anelli.   CAPITALS: primary stress.   SMALL CAPS: secondary stress.   Ⓢ: U.S. pron.   Ⓔ: British pron.

Sedgwick *pers. name*	SEJ-wik	'sedʒwik
Sedum *plant*	SĒD-uhm	'siːdəm
Seebohm *pers. name*	SĒ-BŌM	'siːˌboːm
Seeger *family of US musicologists, singers*	SĒ-guhr	'siːgə^{r}
Seferiades Giorgios Stylianou, *orig. name of* George Seferis	SEF-ER-YAHTH-ēs	ˌsefˌer'jɑðiːs
Seferis George *(pseudonym of* G. S. Seferiades*), Greek poet, diplomat (Nobel 1963)*	se-FER-ēs	se'feriːs
Sega *tdmk for video games*	SĀ-guh	'seːgə
Segal George, *US actor;* Erich, *US author*	SĒ-guhl	'siːgəl
Segesta *ancient city, Sicily*	si-JES-tuh	si'dʒestə
Sego *lily*	SĒ-gō	'siːgoː
Segovia *prov, Spain;* Andrés, *Spanish guitarist*	sā-ḠŌ-vyah, [S] si-GŌ-vē-uh	seː'ɣoːβjɑ, [S] si'goːviːə
Segrè Emilio, *Italian-born US physicist (Nobel 1959)*	suh-GRĀ, sā-GRĀ	sə'greː, seː'greː
Seguidilla *dance*	SEG-uh-DĒ-(y)uh, SEG-uh-DĒL-yuh	ˌsegə'diː(j)ə, ˌsegə'diːljə
Seidlitz *laxative powders*	SED-luhts	'sedləts
Seifert Jaroslav, *writer*	SĪ-fuhrt	'sɑifə^{r}t
Seihin *pers. name, Japanese*	sā-hin	seːhin
Seiichiro *pers. name, Japanese*	sā-ē-chē-rō	seiːtʃiːroː
Seiji *pers. name, Japanese*	sā-jē	seːdʒiː
Seiko *tdmk, Japanese watches*	SĀ-kō	'seːkoː
Seim, Sejm, Seym *river, Russia*	SĀM	'seːm
Seine *river, France*	SEN, [S] SĀN, SEN	sen, [S] 'seːn, 'sen
Seine-et-Marne *dept, France*	sen-ā-MAHRN	seneːmaːrn
Seine-Maritime *dept, France*	sen-mah-rē-TĒM	senmɑːriːtiːm
Seine-Saint-Denis *dept, France*	sen-se^{n}d-NĒ	sensẽdniː

Key (col. 2): a: **fad** ā: **fade** ah: **father** ar: **Mary** aw: **law** e: **fed** ē: **feed** er: **merry** i: **hid** ī: **hide** ō: **coat** o͞o: **boot** oi: **boy** ow: **now** u: **put** uh: **above** uhr: **bird** ch: **chop** ng: **ring** sh: **show** th: **thick** th: **this** zh: **measure**

Seisachtheia		
Solon's debt cancellation	SĪ-suhk-THĀ-(y)uh	ˌsaisək'θeː(j)ə
Seishiro		
pers. name, Japanese	sā-shē-rō	seːʃiːroː
Sejanus		
Roman conspirator	si-JĀ-nuhs	si'dʒeːnəs
Sejm		
see Seim		
Seker Bayrami		
Turkish festival	SĀ-kuhr bī-RAHM-ē	'seːkəʳ bai'rami·
Sekhet [Sekhmet]		
Egyptian goddess of war	SEKH-uht, SEK-uht	'sexət, 'sekət
Sekhmet		
Egyptian goddess of war	SEKH-muht, SEK-, -met	'sexmət, 'sek-, -met
Selah		
pers. name	SĒ-luh	'siːlə
Selangor		
state, Malaysia	suh-LANG-uhr	sə'læŋəʳ
Selassie		
Haile, *emperor, Ethiopia*	suh-LAS-ē, suh-LAHS-ē	sə'læsi·, sə'lasi·
Selena		
pers. name	suh-LĒ-nuh	sə'liːnə
Selene		
Greek goddess of the moon	suh-LĒ-nē	sə'liːni·
selenium		
element	suh-LĒ-nē-uhm	sə'liːniːəm
Seleucia		
ancient city, Asia Minor	suh-LOO-sh(ē-)uh	sə'luːʃ(iː)ə
Seleucid		
Greek dynasty in Syria	suh-LOO-suhd, suhl-YOO-suhd	sə'luːsəd, səl'juːsəd
Seleucus		
Seleucid king	suh-LOO-kuhs	sə'luːkəs
Selig		
1. pers. name	SĒ-lig	'siːlig
2. German	ZĀ-likh	'zeːliç
Selim		
1. pers. name	SĒ-luhm	'siːləm
2. Finnish	SĀ-lim	'seːlim
Selina		
pers. name	suh-LĒ-nuh, suh-LĪ-nuh	sə'liːnə, sə'lainə
Seljuk		
pert. to a Turkish dynasty	SEL-JOOK, sel-JOOK	'sel,dʒuːk, sel'dʒuːk
Selkirk		
mts., Canada; burgh, Scotland	SEL-KUHRK	'sel,kəʳk
Selkup		
lang., Khanti-Mansi region, Russia	SEL-KUHP	'sel,kəp
Selleck		
Tom, *US actor*	SEL-ik	'selik
Selma		
1. city, AL; pers. name	SEL-muh	'selmə
2. Swedish	SEL-mah	'selmaː
Selwyn		
pers. name	SEL-wuhn, SEL-win	'selwən, 'selwin

Selznick
  David O., *US film producer*   SELZ-nik   'selznɪk
Semarang
  port, Java   suh-MAHR-AHNG   sə'mɑr͵ɑŋ
Semele
  mother of Dionysus by Zeus   SEM-uh-lē   'seməli·
Semen, Semën
  pers. name, Russian   syim-YAWN   sjim'jɔːn
Semenov
  Nikolai N., *Russian physicist*   syim-YAWN-uhf   sjim'jɔːnəf
  (Nobel 1956)
Seminole
  N. American people   SEM-uh-NŌL   'semə͵noːl
Semi-Pelagianism
  doctrine that man needs God's   SEM-ē-puh-LĀ-jē-uh-NIZ-uhm, SEM-Ī-   ͵semi·pə'leːdʒiːə͵nizəm,
    special help   ͵sem͵ɑi-
Semiramis
  Assyrian queen   suh-MIR-uh-muhs   sə'mirəməs
Semite
  Semitic people; descendant of   SEM-ĪT, Ⓔ SĒ-MĪT   'sem͵ɑit, Ⓔ 'siː͵mɑit
    Shem
Semitic
  lang. family; pert. to Semites, *esp.*   suh-MIT-ik   sə'miṭik
    Jews
Semitics
  study of Semitic peoples & langs. suh-MIT-iks   sə'miṭiks
Semitism
  Semitic characteristics   SEM-uh-TIZ-uhm   'semə͵tizəm
Semitist
  Semitic scholar   SEM-uht-uhst   'seməṭəst
Semple
  pers. name (A. S. McPherson)   SEM-puhl   'sempəl
Sempronius
  pers. name, Latin   sem-PRŌ-nē-uhs   sem'proːniːəs
Semyon
  pers. name, Russian   syim-YAWN   sjim'jɔːn
Senatus consultum ultimum
  final decree of the Roman Senate suh-NĀT-uhs kuhn-SUHL-tuhm   sə'neːṭəs kən'səltəm
                                      UHL-tuh-muhm   'əltəməm
Sendai
  city, Japan   sen-dī   sendɑi
Sendak
  Maurice, *US author, illustrator*   SEN-dak   'sendæk
Seneca
  Roman writer; N. American   SEN-i-kuh   'senikə
    people
Senecan
  pert. to Seneca   SEN-i-kuhn   'senikən
Senegal
  republic, Africa   SEN-i-GAWL   ͵seni'gɔːl
Senegalese
  pert. to Senegal   SEN-i-guh-LĒZ, -LĒS   ͵senigə'liːz, -'liːs
Senegambia
  confederation, Africa   SEN-i-GAHM-bē-uh,   ͵seni'gɑmbiːə, ͵seni'gæmbiːə
                                      SEN-i-GAM-bē-uh

Key (col. 2):   a: fad   ā: fade   ah: father   ar: Mary   aw: law   e: fed   ē: feed   er: merry   i: hid   ī: hide   ō: coat   ōō: boot
oi: boy   ow: now   u: put   uh: above   uhr: bird   ch: chop   ng: ring   sh: show   th: thick   th̲: this   zh: measure

Senghor
Leopold, *president, Senegal*   sahⁿ-GAWR, sen-GAWR   sɑ̃'gɔːr, sen'gɔːr

Senlac
hill, England   SEN-LAK   'sen,læk

Sennacherib
Assyrian king   suh-NAK-uh-ruhb, -RIB   sə'nækərəb, -,rib

Señor
Spanish form of address for a man   sān-YAWR, sen-YAWR   seːn'jɔːr, sen'jɔːr

Señora
Spanish form of address for a married woman   sān-YŌR-ah, sān-YAWR-uh, sen-   seːn'joːrɑ, seːn'joːrə, sen-

Señores
plural of Señor   sān-YŌR-ās, sān-YAWR-ās, sen-   seːn'joːreːs, seːn'joːreːs, sen-

Señorita
Spanish form of address for an unmarried woman   sān-yaw-RĒ-tah, ⑤ SĀN-yuh-RĒT-uh, SEN-   seːnjɔː'riːtɑ, ⑤ ,seːnjə'riːt̪ə, ,sen-

Sensodyne
tdmk for toothpaste   SEN(T)-suh-DĪN   'sen(t)sə,dɑin

Sentinum
ancient town, Italy   sen-TĪ-nuhm   sen'tɑinəm

Seoul
city, S. Korea   sōl   soːl

Sephardi
Jew from Spain, Portugal, or N. Africa   suh-FAHRD-ē   sə'fɑʳdiˑ

Sephardic
pert. to the Sephardim   suh-FAHRD-ik   sə'fɑʳdik

Sephardim
plural of Sephardi   suh-FAHRD-im   sə'fɑʳdim

Sepik
river, New Guinea   SĀ-pik   'seːpik

Septante
French beer   sep-TAHⁿT   septɑ̃t

September
month   sep-TEM-buhr   sep'tembəʳ

Sept-Îles
city, Canada   se-TĒL   se'tiːl

Septimius
pers. name, Latin   sep-TIM-ē-uhs   sep'timiːəs

Septimius Severus
Roman emperor   sep-TIM-ē-uhs suh-VIR-uhs   sep'timiːəs sə'virəs

Septimus
pers. name, Latin   SEP-tuh-muhs   'septəməs

Septuagesima
3rd Sunday before Lent   SEP-tuh-wuh-JES-uh-muh, -JĀ-zuh-muh   ,septəwə'dʒesəmə, -'dʒeːzəmə

Septuagint
Greek version of the Old Testament   sep-T(Y)OO-uh-juhnt, SEP-tuh-wuh-JINT   sep't(j)uːədʒənt, 'septəwə,dʒint

Sepúlveda
Juan Gines de, *Spanish historian*   sā-POOL-vā-thah, ⑤ suh-PUL-vuhd-uh, suh-PUHL-vuhd-uh   seː'puːlβeːðɑ, ⑤ sə'pulvədə, sə'pəlvədə

Foreign Sounds: ue: *Fr.* **rue**, *Ger.* füllen   uh(r): *Fr.* **boeuf**, *Ger.* Höhle   k̲h̲: *Ger.* i**ch**, *Scot.* lo**ch**   g̲: *Sp.* ami**g**o   v̲: *Sp.* ha**b**lar
hl: *Welsh* **Ll**anelli.   CAPITALS: primary stress.   SMALL CAPS: secondary stress.   ⑤: U.S. pron.   ⑪: British pron.

Sepulveda
　Boulevard, *Los Angeles, CA*　　suh-PUHL-vuhd-uh,　　　　sə'pəlvədə, sə'pulvədə
　　　　　　　　　　　　　　　　　suh-PUL-vuhd-uh
Sequatchie
　river, county, TN　　　　　　si-KWAHCH-ē　　　　　　si'kwɑtʃiˑ
Sequim
　town, WA　　　　　　　　　SKWIM, suh-KWIM　　　　'skwim, sə'kwim
Sequoia
　Cherokee scholar; park, CA　si-KWOI-(y)uh　　　　　　si'kwɔi(j)ə
Sequoyah
　county, OK　　　　　　　　si-KWOI-(y)uh　　　　　　si'kwɔi(j)ə
Serafin
　Barry, *US TV news correspondent*　SER-uh-fin, SER-uh-fuhn　'serəfin, 'serəfən
Serafino
　pers. name, Italian　　　　　SĀ-rah-FĒ-nō　　　　　　ˌseːrɑ'fiːnoˑ
Seram
　see Ceram
Serang
　island, town, Indonesia　　　SĀ-RAHNG　　　　　　　'seːˌrɑŋ
Seraphim
　order of angels　　　　　　SER-uh-FIM　　　　　　　'serəˌfim
Séraphin
　pers. name, French　　　　　sā-rah-FEⁿ　　　　　　　seːrɑːfẽ
Seraphina
　seraphine, reed instrument　·　SER-uh-FĒ-nuh　　　　　ˌserə'fiːnə
Séraphine
　pers. name, French　　　　　sā-rah-FĒN　　　　　　　seːrɑːfiːn
Serapis
　Ptolemaic Egyptian god　　　suh-RĀ-puhs　　　　　　sə're:pəs
Serb
　a native of Serbia　　　　　SUHRB　　　　　　　　'səʳb
Serban
　pers. name, Romanian　　　　sher-BAHN　　　　　　　ʃeʳ'bɑn
Serbia
　republic, E. Europe　　　　　SUHR-bē-uh　　　　　　'səʳbiːə
Serbian
　pert. to Serbia　　　　　　SUHR-bē-uhn　　　　　　'səʳbiːən
Serbo-Croatian
　Slavonic lang., Europe　　　SUHR-bō-KRŌ-Ā-shuhn　　ˌsəʳboːˌkroː'e:ʃən
Serengeti
　natl. park, Tanzania　　　　SER-uhn-GET-ē　　　　　ˌserən'geţiˑ
Serenitatis, Mare
　see Mare Serenitatis
Serer
　lang., people, Senegal, Gambia　suh-RER　　　　　　　sə'reʳ
Serestus
　companion of Aeneas　　　　suh-RES-tuhs　　　　　　sə'restəs
Serge
　1. *pers. name*　　　　　　　SUHRJ, SERZH, SERJ　　'səʳdʒ, 'seʳʒ, 'seʳdʒ
　2. *French*　　　　　　　　　SERZH　　　　　　　　serʒ
Sergei, Sergey
　pers. name, Russian　　　　syir-GYĀ(-ē), Ⓢ ser-GĀ, SER-gā　sjir'gjeː(iː), Ⓢ seʳ'geː, 'seʳgeː
Sergestus
　companion of Aeneas　　　　suhr-JES-tuhs　　　　　　səʳ'dʒestəs

Key (col. 2):　a: fad　ā: fade　ah: father　ar: **M**ary　aw: law　e: fed　ē: feed　er: **merry**　i: hid　ī: hide　ō: coat　o͞o: boot
oi: boy　ow: now　u: put　uh: above　uhr: bird　ch: chop　ng: ring　sh: show　th: thick　th: this　zh: measure

Sergio
   pers. name   SER-khyō, Ⓢ SUHR-jē-ō   'serxjoː, Ⓢ 'sərdʒiːoː

Sergius
   pope   SUHR-jē-uhs   'sərdʒiːəs

Seriema
   South American bird   SER-ē-Ē-muh, SER-ē-Ā-muh   ˌseriˈiːmə, ˌseriˈeːmə

Seringapatam
   town, Karnataka, India   suh-RING-guh-puh-TAHM, -TAM   səˌriŋɡəpəˈtɑm, -ˈtæm

Seriphos
   island, Greece   si-RĪ-fuhs, SER-i-FAWS   siˈraifəs, 'seriˌfɔːs

Serkin
   Rudolf, *Austrian-born US pianist*   SUHR-kuhn   'sərkən

Serov
   city, Russia   SER-uhf   'serəf

Serpens
   constellation   SUHR-puhnz, SUHR-PENZ   'sərpənz, 'sərˌpenz

Serra
   Junípero, *Spanish missionary in California*   SER-rah, Ⓢ SER-uh   'serrɑ, Ⓢ 'serə

Sertorius
   Roman general   SUHR-TŌR-ē-uhs, SUHR-TAWR-ē-uhs   ˌsərˈtoːriːəs, ˌsərˈtoːriːəs

Servian Reform
   Roman reorganization, 6th cent., BC   SUHR-vē-uhn   'sərviːən

Servilia
   pers. name, Latin   suhr-VIL-ē-uh   sərˈviliːə

Servilius
   pers. name, Latin   suhr-VIL-ē-uhs, suhr-VIL-yuhs   sərˈviliːəs, sərˈviljəs

Servius
   pers. name, Latin   SUHR-vē-uhs   'sərviːəs

Servius Tullius
   sixth king of Rome   SUHR-vē-uhs TUHL-ē-uhs   'sərviːəs 'təliːəs

Sesame Street
   TV program   SES-uh-mē STRĒT   'sesəmiˑ ˌstriːt

Seshat
   Egyptian goddess of writing   SESH-uht   'seʃət

Sesostris
   king of Egypt   suh-SAHS-truhs   sə'sɑstrəs

Sesotho
   Bantu lang., Lesotho   suh-SŌŌT-ōō, suh-SŌŌ-tōō   sə'suːtuː, sə'suːtuː

Sessue
   pers. name   SES-(y)ōō   'ses(j)uː

Set [Seth]
   evil Egyptian god   SET   'set

Setekh [Seth]
   evil Egyptian god   SET-uhkh, SET-uhk   'seţəx, 'seţək

Sete Quedas [Guairá]
   waterfall, S. America   SĀT-uh KĀ-thuhsh   ˌseːţə ˈkeːðəʃ

Setesh [Seth]
   evil Egyptian god   SET-uhsh   'seţəʃ

Seth
   1. evil Egyptian god; pers. name   SETH   'seθ
   2. German   ZÄT   'zeːt

Seti
   king of Egypt   SET-ē   'seţiˑ

Foreign Sounds: ue: *Fr.* **rue**, *Ger.* **füllen**   uh(r): *Fr.* **boeuf**, *Ger.* **Höhle**   <u>kh</u>: *Ger.* i**ch**, *Scot.* lo**ch**   g̱: *Sp.* ami**g**o   ṿ: *Sp.* ha**b**lar   hl: *Welsh* **Ll**anelli.   CAPITALS: primary stress.   SMALL CAPS: secondary stress.   Ⓢ: U.S. pron.   Ⓛ: British pron.

Seton
Elizabeth, *US educator*   SĒT-n   'siːtn̩

Seto Naikai
Inland Sea, Japan   se-tō nī-kī   setoː naikai

Seton Hall
University, *NJ*   SĒT-n HAWL   ˌsiːtn̩ 'hɔːl

Setsubun
Bean-throwing Festival (Feb. 3),   set-sōō-bun   setsuːbun
Japan

Setswana [Tswana]
lang., Africa   set-SWAHN-uh   set'swanə

Se⁺úbal
prov & town, Portugal   suh-TŌŌ-buhl   sə'tuːbəl

Seurat
Georgeꞙ *French painter*   suh(r)-RAH   sœːraː

Seuss
Dr., *pseudonym of* Theodore   SŌŌS   'suːs
Geisel, *US writer*

Sevareid
Eric, *US journalist*   SEV-uh-RĪD   'sevəˌraid

Sevastopol, Sebastopol
port, Ukraine   SYEV-uh-STAW-puhl,   ˌsjevə'stɔːpəl,
                                          Ⓢ suh-VAS-tuh-PŌL, -PAWL   Ⓢ sə'væstəˌpoːl, -ˌpɔːl

Seve
pers. name, Spanish   SĀ-vā   'seːβeː

Sevechorus
grandfather of Gilgamesh   suh-VEK-uh-ruhs   sə'vekərəs

Severan Dynasty
Roman imperial dynasty   suh-VIR-uhn   sə'virən

Severinsen
Doc, *US musician*   SEV-(uh-)ruhn-suhn   'sev(ə)rənsən

Severinus
pope; pers. name, Latin   SEV-uh-RĪ-nuhs   ˌsevə'rainəs

Severn
river, Gt. Britain   SEV-uhrn   'sevᵊrn

Severnaya Zemlya
island group, Arctic Ocean   SEV-uhr-nuh-YAH ZEM-lē-AH   'sevᵊrnəja ˌzemliː'a

Severo
pers. name, Spanish   sā-VĀ-rō   seː'βeːroː

Severus Alexander
Roman emperor   se-VIR-uhs AL-ig-ZAN-duhr, EL-ig-   se'virəs ˌælig'zændəʳ, ˌelig-

Sevier
river, UT; county, AR, TN, UT   suh-VIR   sə'viʳ

Sevilla
city, prov, Spain   sā-VẼ(L)-yah   seː'βiː(l)ja

Seville [Sevilla]
city, prov, Spain   suh-VIL   sə'vil

Sèvres
commune, France   SEVR   sevr

Seward
1. William Henry, *US politician;*   SŌŌ-uhrd, SURD   'suːᵊʳd, 'suʳd
US pl. name
2. pers. name   SŌŌ-uhrd, SURD, Ⓔ *also* SĒ-wuhrd   'suːᵊʳd, 'suʳd, Ⓔ *also*
                                                                                       'siːwəʳd

---

Key (col. 2):   a: fad   ā: fade   ah: father   ar: Mary   aw: law   e: fed   ē: feed   er: merry   i: hid   ī: hide   ō: coat   ōō: boot
oi: boy   ow: now   u: put   uh: above   uhr: bird   ch: chop   ng: ring   sh: show   th: thick   th̲: this   zh: measure

Sexagesima
    2nd Sunday before Lent   SEK-suh-JES-uh-muh   ˌseksə'dʒesəmə

Sextans
    constellation   SEK-STANZ, -stuhnz   'sek,stænz, -stənz

Sextus
    pers. name, Latin   SEK-stuhs   'sekstəs

Seychelles
    islands, Indian Ocean   sā-SHEL(Z)   seɪ'ʃel(z)

Seychellois
    inhabitant(s) of Seychelles   sā-shel-WAH   seɪʃelwaɪ

Seym
    see Seim

Seymour
    family name; pers. name   SĒ-MŌR, SĒ-MAWR, Ⓔ SĒ-muhr,   'siːˌmoːʳ, 'siːˌmɔːʳ, Ⓔ 'siːməʳ,
        SĒ-MAWR, SĀ-muhr   'siːˌmɔːʳ, 'seɪməʳ

Sforza
    ruling family of Milan, Italy   SFAWRT-sah   'sfɔːʳtsɑ

Sgaw
    lang., people, Burma, Thailand   SKAW   'skɔː

's-Gravenhage [Hague, The]
    city, Netherlands   S(K)RAHV-uhn-HAH-ğuh   ˌs(k)rɑvən'hɑɣə

Shaanxi
    see Shanxi

Shaba [Katanga]
    prov, Zaire   SHAHB-uh   'ʃɑbə

Sha'ban
    Islamic month   shuh-BAHN   ʃə'bɑn

Shabatu
    Babylonian month   shuh-BAHT-ōō   ʃə'bɑṭuː

Shabbat
    Jewish Sabbath   shuh-BAHT, SHAHB-uhs   ʃə'bat, 'ʃabəs

Shabuoth, Shavuoth
    Jewish festival   SHAHV-ōō-AWT, shuh-VŌŌ-ŌT,   ˌʃɑvuː'ɔːt, ʃə'vuːˌɔːt,
        shuh-VŌŌ-ŌTH, shuh-VŌŌ-ŌS,   ʃə'vuːˌɔːθ, ʃə'vuːˌɔːs,
        shuh-VŌŌ-uhs   ʃə'vuːəs

Shackelford
    Ted, *US actor*   SHAK-uhl-fuhrd   'ʃækəlfəʳd

Shaddai
    Hebrew name for God inscribed in   SHAHD-ī   'ʃad,ai
    a mezuzah

Shadrach
    pers. name   SHAD-RAK   'ʃæd,ræk

SHAEF
    Supreme Headquarters, Allied   SHĀF   'ʃeɪf
    Expeditionary Force

Shaeffer
    Peter, *English playwright; US pen*   SHĀ-fuhr   'ʃeɪfəʳ
    co.

Shaemas
    pers. name, Irish Gaelic   SHĀ-muhs   'ʃeɪməs

Shafi'i
    school of Islam   SHAF-ē-Ē, SHAHF-ē-Ē   'ʃæfiːˌiː, 'ʃɑfiːˌiː

Shaftesbury
    Earl of, *British reformer*   SHAHF(T)S-b(uh-)rē,   'ʃɑːf(t)sb(ə)riˑ,
        Ⓢ SHAF(T)S-b(uh-)rē   Ⓢ 'ʃæf(t)sb(ə)riˑ

Foreign Sounds: **ue**: *Fr.* **rue**, *Ger.* **füllen**   **uh(r)**: *Fr.* **boeuf**, *Ger.* **Höhle**   <u>kh</u>: *Ger.* **ich**, *Scot.* **loch**   ğ: *Sp.* **amigo**   <u>v</u>: *Sp.* **hablar**
hl: *Welsh* **Llanelli**.   CAPITALS: primary stress.   SMALL CAPS: secondary stress.   Ⓢ: U.S. pron.   Ⓔ: British pron.

Shahada
  Islamic profession of faith   shuh-HAHD-uh   ʃəˈhadə

Shahjahanpur
  city, India   SHAH-juh-HAHN-PUR, SHAW-   ˌʃadʒəˈhanˌpuʳ, ˌʃɔː-

Shaitan
  evil jinni or spirit   shā-TAHN, shī-TAHN   ʃeːˈtan, ʃaiˈtan

Shakerism
  religion   SHĀ-kuh-RIZ-uhm   ˈʃeːkəˌrizəm

Shakespeare
  William, *English poet; pers. name*   SHĀK-SPIR   ˈʃeːkˌspiʳ

Shakespearean
  pert. to Shakespeare   shāk-SPIR-ē-uhn   ʃeːkˈspiriːən

Shakespeareana
  things pert. to Shakespeare   SHĀK-SPIR-ē-AN-uh, -AHN-uh   ˌʃeːkˌspiriːˈænə, -ˈɑːnə

Shakopee Mdewakanton Sioux
  N. American people   SHAK-uh-pē EM-duh-WAW-kuhn-TŌN   ˈʃækəpiˑ ˌemdəˈwɔːkənˌtoːn
       SO͞O, MED-uh-WAW-kuhn-TŌN   ˈsuː, ˌmedəˈwɔːkənˌtoːn

Shakta
  adherent of Shaktism   SHAHK-tuh   ˈʃaktə

Shakti
  Hindu embodiment of female   SHAHK-tē   ˈʃaktiˑ
    creative energy; cosmic energy

Shaktism
  Hindu worship of Shakti   SHAHK-TIZ-uhm   ˈʃakˌtizəm

Shalit
  Gene, *US TV commentator*   SHAL-uht   ˈʃælət

Shalmaneser
  king of Assyria   SHAL-muh-NĒ-zuhr   ˌʃælməˈniːzəʳ

Shalom
  pers. name, Hebrew   shah-LŌM, *for S. Aleichem often*   ʃaˈloːm, *for S. Aleichem*
       SHAW-luhm   *often* ˈʃɔːləm

Shamanism
  religion   SHAHM-uh-NIZ-uhm,   ˈʃaməˌnizəm, ˈʃeːməˌnizəm,
       SHĀ-muh-NIZ-uhm,   ˈʃæməˌnizəm
       SHAM-uh-NIZ-uhm

Shamir
  Yitzhak, *Israeli prime minister*   shah-MIR, shuh-MIR   ʃaˈmiʳ, ʃəˈmiʳ

Shan
  S. Asian people   SHAHN, SHAN   ˈʃan, ˈʃæn

Shandong
  prov, peninsula, China   SHAHN-DUNG   ˈʃanˈduŋ

Shang
  dynasty, China   SHAHNG, SHANG   ˈʃaŋ, ˈʃæŋ

Shanghai
  city, China   shang-HĪ, SHANG-HĪ   ʃæŋˈhai, ˈʃæŋˌhai

Shangri-La
  imaginary paradise   SHANG-gri-LAH   ˌʃæŋgriˈlɑ

Shannon
  river, Ireland; pers. name   SHAN-uhn   ˈʃænən

Shansi
  see Shanxi

Shanti
  pers. name   SHAHN-tē   ˈʃantiˑ

Shanxi, Shaanxi, Shansi
  prov, China   SHAHN-SHĒ, SHAHN-SĒ   ˈʃanˈʃiː, ˈʃanˈsiː

Key (col. 2):   a: fad ā: fade ah: father ar: Mary aw: law e: fed ē: feed er: merry i: hid ī: hide ō: coat o͞o: boot
oi: boy   ow: now   u: put   uh: above   uhr: bird   ch: chop   ng: ring   sh: show   th: thick   th̲: this   zh: measure

Shapur
   Persian king   shah-P$\overline{OO}$R, shuh-PUR   ʃɑːˈpuːʳ, ʃəˈpuʳ

Shaqra [Ash-Shaqra]
   town, Saudi Arabia   shuh-KRAH   ʃəˈkrɑ

Shaquille
   pers. name   shah-KĒL   ʃɑˈkiːl

Shara
   a Mongol people   SHAHR-uh   ˈʃɑrə

Shari
   see Chari

Sharif
   Omar, *Egyptian actor*   shuh-RĒF   ʃəˈriːf

Sharjah
   emirate, town, United Arab   SHAHR-zhuh, SHAHR-juh   ˈʃɑrʒə, ˈʃɑʳdʒə
     Emirates

Sharon
   1. district, Israel; US pl. name;   SHAR-uhn, SHER-uhn   ˈʃærən, ˈʃerən
     pers. name
   2. Ariel, Israeli politician   shah-RŌN   ʃɑˈroːn

Sharpe
   William F., *US economist (Nobel*   SHAHRP   ˈʃɑʳp
     1990)

Shar Pei
   dog breed   shahr PĀ   ʃɑʳ ˈpeː

Sharpeville
   prov, South Africa   SHAHRP-VIL   ˈʃɑʳpˌvil

Shasta
   N. American people; Mount,   SHAS-tuh   ˈʃæstə
     volcano, CA

Shatner
   William, *Canadian-born actor,*   SHAT-nuhr   ˈʃætnəʳ
     director

Shatt al'Arab
   river channel, Iraq   SHAHT ahl-AHR-ahb, SHAT al-AR-uhb   ˌʃɑːt ɑːlˈɑːrɑːb, ˌʃæt ælˈærəb

Shaun
   pers. name   SHAWN, SHAHN   ˈʃɔːn, ˈʃɑn

Shavian
   pert. to G. B. Shaw   SHĀ-vē-uhn   ˈʃeːviːən

Shavonne
   pers. name   shuh-VAHN   ʃəˈvɑn

Shavuoth
   see Shabuoth

Shaw
   G. B., *Irish author (Nobel 1925)*   SHAW   ˈʃɔː

Shawano
   county, WI   SHAW-nō   ˈʃɔːnoː

Shawinigan
   city, Canada   shuh-WIN-uh-guhn   ʃəˈwinəgən

Shawn
   pers. name   SHAWN   ˈʃɔːn

Shawnee
   N. American people; US pl. name;   shaw-NĒ, shah-NĒ   ʃɔːˈniː, ʃɑˈniː
     college, IL

Shawwal
   Islamic month   shuh-WAHL   ʃəˈwɑl

Foreign Sounds: ue: *Fr.* **rue**, *Ger.* **füllen**   uh(r): *Fr.* **boeuf**, *Ger.* **Höhle**   kh: *Ger.* **ich**, *Scot.* **loch**   ğ: *Sp.* a**m**igo   v: *Sp.* ha**b**lar
hl: *Welsh* **Llanelli**.   CAPITALS: primary stress.   SMALL CAPS: secondary stress.   Ⓢ: U.S. pron.   Ⓛ: British pron.

Shcharansky
  Anatoly, *mathematician, USSR* — sh(ch)uh-RAHN-skē — ʃ(tʃ)ə'rɑːnskiˑ

Shcherbakov
  city, Russia — SH(CH)ER-buh-KAWF — ˌʃ(tʃ)eʳbə'kɔːf

She
  Chinese people — SHUH, SHĀ, SHĒ — 'ʃə, 'ʃeː, 'ʃiː

Shea
  1. William A., *Stadium, New York City* — SHĀ — 'ʃeː
  2. tree; pers. name — SHĒ, SHĀ — 'ʃiː, 'ʃeː

Shearing
  George, *US pianist, composer* — SHIR-ing — 'ʃiriŋ

Shearson Lehman Brothers
  US financial co. — SHIR-suhn LĀ-muhn — ˌʃiʳsən 'leːmən

Sheba
  ancient country, Arabian Peninsula — SHĒ-buh — 'ʃiːbə

Shebat, Shevat
  Jewish month — shuh-BAHT, shuh-VAHT — ʃə'bɑt, ʃə'vɑt

Shebelle, -bele, -beli
  river, Africa — shuh-BEL-ē — ʃə'beliˑ

Sheboygan
  city, county, WI — shi-BOI-guhn — ʃi'bɔigən

Shechinah
  manifestation of God's presence on Earth in Judaism — shuh-<u>KH</u>Ē-nuh, shuh-KĒ-nuh, shuh-KĪ-nuh — ʃə'xiːnə, ʃə'kiːnə, ʃə'kainə

Sheehan
  David, *US entertainment critic; pers. name* — SHĒ-uhn — 'ʃiːən

Sheen
  Martin, *US actor* — SHĒN — 'ʃiːn

Sheena
  pers. name — SHĒ-nuh — 'ʃiːnə

Sheetrock
  tdmk for a plasterboard — SHĒT-RAHK — 'ʃiːt,rɑk

Sheffield
  William Jennings, *US politician; city, AL; city, England* — SHEF-ēld — 'ʃefiːld

Sheherazade
  see Scheherazade

Shehu
  Mehmet, *Albanian politician* — she-HOO — ʃe'huː

Sheila
  pers. name — SHĒ-luh — 'ʃiːlə

Shel
  pers. name — SHEL — 'ʃel

Sheldon
  pers. name — SHEL-duhn — 'ʃeldən

Sheldonian
  Theatre, *Oxford University, England* — shel-DŌ-nē-uhn — ʃel'dɔːniːən

Shelley
  Mary Wollstonecraft, *English writer;* Percy Bysshe, *English poet; pers. name* — SHEL-ē — 'ʃeliˑ

Key (col. 2):   a: fad   ā: fade   ah: father   ar: Mary   aw: law   e: fed   ē: feed   er: merry   i: hid   ī: hide   ō: coat   ōō: boot
oi: boy   ow: now   u: put   uh: above   uhr: bird   ch: chop   ng: ring   sh: show   th: thick   <u>th</u>: this   zh: measure

Shemini Atzereth
  Jewish holiday shuh-MĒ-nē aht-SER-uht, SHMĒ-nē, ʃəˈmiːniː atˈserət, ˈʃmiːniː,
  aht-SER-uhth, -uhs atˈserəθ, -əs
Shemtob, Shem Tov
  pers. name, Hebrew shem-TŌV, shem-TAWV ʃemˈtoːv, ʃemˈtɔːv
Shenandoah
  river, VA, WV; US pl. name SHEN-uhn-DŌ-uh, SHAN-uhn-DŌ-uh ˌʃenənˈdoːə, ˌʃænənˈdoːə
Shenyang
  prov, China SHUHN-YAHNG ˈʃənˈjaŋ
Sheol
  Hebrew abode of the dead shē-ŌL, SHĒ-ŌL ʃiːˈoːl, ˈʃiːˌoːl
Shepard, Shepherd
  pers. name SHEP-uhrd ˈʃepəʳd
Sheraton
  Thomas, *English furniture* SHER-uht-n ˈʃerətn̩
  designer; US hotel chain
Sheremetyevo
  airport, Moscow SHER-yuhm-yuh-TYĀ-vō ˌʃerjəmjəˈtjeːvoː
Sherente
  S. American people shuh-RĀN-tä ʃəˈreːnteː
Sheri, Sheree
  pers. name SHER-ē ˈʃeriˈ
Sheridan
  Philip Henry, *US general;* Richard SHER-uhd-n ˈʃerədn̩
  B., *Irish dramatist; pers. name*
Sherlock
  pers. name (S. Holmes) SHUHR-luhk, SHUHR-LAHK ˈʃəʳlək, ˈʃəʳˌlak
Sherman
  William T., *US general; pers. name* SHUHR-muhn ˈʃəʳmən
Sherpa
  people of Tibet SHER-puh, SHUHR-puh ˈʃeʳpə, ˈʃəʳpə
Sherr
  Lynn, *US journalist* SHUHR ˈʃəʳ
Sherri, Sherree
  pers. name SHER-ē ˈʃeriˈ
Sherrington
  Sir Charles, *English physiologist* SHER-ing-tuhn ˈʃeriŋtən
  (Nobel 1932)
Sherry
  pers. name; wine SHER-ē ˈʃeriˈ
's-Hertogenbosch
  city, Netherlands SER-tō-ğuh(n)-BAWS ˈseʳtoːɣə(n)ˌbɔːs
Sherwin
  pers. name SHUHR-wuhn ˈʃəʳwən
Sherwood
  pers. name SHUHR-WUD, SHER-WUD ˈʃəʳˌwud, ˈʃeʳˌwud
Sheryl
  pers. name SHER-uhl ˈʃerəl
Shetland
  islands, Scotland SHET-luhnd ˈʃetlənd
Shevardnadze
  Eduard, *foreign minister, USSR* SHEV-uhrd-NAHD-zuh ˌʃevəʳdˈnɑdzə
Shevat
  see Shebat

Foreign Sounds: ue: *Fr.* **rue**, *Ger.* **füllen** uh(r): *Fr.* **boeuf**, *Ger.* **Höhle** <u>kh</u>: *Ger.* i<u>ch</u>, *Scot.* lo<u>ch</u> ğ: *Sp.* ami**g**o v: *Sp.* ha**b**lar
hl: *Welsh* **Ll**anelli. CAPITALS: primary stress. SMALL CAPS: secondary stress. Ⓢ: U.S. pron. Ⓑ: British pron.

Shi'a
  branch of Islam   SHĒ-ah, SHĒ-uh   ˈʃiːɑ, ˈʃiːə

Shiawassee
  river, county, MI   SHĒ-uh-WAW-sē, SHĒ-uh-WAHS-ē   ˌʃiːəˈwɔːsiˑ, ˌʃiːəˈwasiˑ

Shibe
  Park, former ballpark,   SHĪB   ˈʃaib
    Philadelphia, PA

Shih Hwang-ti
  Chinese emperor   SHIR HWAHNG-DĒ   ˈʃiʳ ˈhwaŋˈdiː

Shih Tzu
  dog breed   SHĒD ZOO, SHIRD ZOO, SHI TSOO   ˈʃiːd ˈzuː, ˈʃiʳd ˈzuː, ˈʃit ˈsuː

Shiism
  tenets of Shi'a   SHĒ-IZ-uhm   ˈʃiːˌizəm

Shiite
  adherent of Shi'a   SHĒ-ĪT   ˈʃiːˌait

Shikibu
  pers. name, Japanese   shē-kē-bu   ʃiːkiːbu

Shikoku
  island, Japan   shi-kō-koo   ʃikoːkuː

Shillong
  city, India   shi-LAWNG   ʃiˈlɔːŋ

Shilluk
  lang., people, Sudan   shuh-LOOK   ʃəˈluːk

Shiloh
  ancient ruins; site of Civil War   SHĪ-lō   ˈʃailoː
    battle, TN

Shimer
  College, IL   SHĪ-muhr   ˈʃaiməʳ

Shimizu
  port, Japan   shim-ē-zoo   ʃimiːzuː

Shimon
  pers. name (S. Peres)   shi-MŌN   ʃiˈmoːn

Shimonoseki
  port, Japan   shim-ō-nō-sek-ē   ʃimoːnoːsekiˑ

Shinichiro
  pers. name, Japanese   shēn-ē-chē-rō   ʃiˈniːtʃiːroː

Shinnecock
  N. American people   SHIN-uh-KAHK   ˈʃinəˌkak

Shintaro
  pers. name, Japanese   shin-tahr-ō   ʃintaroː

Shinto
  Japanese religion   SHIN-tō   ˈʃintoː

Shintoism
  Japanese religion   SHIN-tō-IZ-uhm   ˈʃintoːˌizəm

Shīrāz
  city, Iran   shi-RAHZ   ʃiˈraz

Shirley
  pers. name   SHUHR-lē   ˈʃəʳliˑ

Shiva
  see Siva

Shizuoka
  city, Japan   shiz-oo-ō-kah   ʃizuːoːka

Shlomo
  pers. name   SHLŌ-mō   ˈʃloːmoː

Key (col. 2):   a: fad   ā: fade   ah: father   ar: Mary   aw: law   e: fed   ē: feed   er: merry   i: hid   ī: hide   ō: coat   o͞o: boot
oi: boy   ow: now   u: put   uh: above   uhr: bird   ch: chop   ng: ring   sh: show   th: thick   <u>th</u>: this   zh: measure

Shluh
   lang., people, Morocco,   SHL$\overline{OO}$, shuh-L$\overline{OO}$ 'ʃluː, ʃə'luː
   Mauritania

Shmuel
   pers. name   SHM$\overline{OO}$-uhl, SHM$\overline{OO}$-EL   'ʃmuːəl, 'ʃmuːˌel

Shockley
   W. B., English-born US physicist   SHAHK-lē   'ʃɑkliˑ
   (Nobel 1956)

Sholapur
   city, India   SH$\bar{O}$-luh-PUR   'ʃoːləˌpuʳ

Sholem
   pers. name, Yiddish   SH$\bar{O}$-luhm   'ʃoːləm

Sholokhov
   Mikhail A., Russian author (Nobel   SHAW-luh-<u>KHAWF</u>,   'ʃɔːlə,xɔːf, Ⓑ 'ʃɔːlə,kɔːf,
   1965)   Ⓢ SHAW-luh-KAWF, -KAWV   -ˌkɔːv

Sholom
   pers. name, Hebrew   SH$\bar{O}$-luhm   'ʃoːləm

Shona
   lang., southern Africa   SH$\bar{O}$-nuh   'ʃoːnə

Shor
   lake, Asia   SHAWR   'ʃɔːʳ

Shoreham
   port, England   SH$\bar{O}$R-uhm, SHAWR-uhm   'ʃoːrəm, 'ʃɔːrəm

Shoshana
   pers. name, Hebrew   shō-SHAHN-uh   ʃoː'ʃɑnə

Shoshone, -ni
   N. American people   shuh-SH$\bar{O}$-nē, shō-SH$\bar{O}$-nē   ʃə'ʃoːniˑ, ʃoː'ʃoːniˑ

Shoshonean
   lang., N. America   shō-SH$\bar{O}$-nē-uhn, SH$\bar{O}$-shuh-N$\bar{E}$-uhn   ʃoː'ʃoːniːən, ˌʃoːʃə'niːən

Shostakovich
   Dmitri, Russian composer; Maxim,   shuhs-tuh-KAWV-yich,   ʃəstə'kɔːvjitʃ,
   Russian conductor   Ⓢ SHAHS-tuh-K$\bar{O}$-vich,   Ⓢ ˌʃɑstə'koːvitʃ,
                  SHAW-stuh-KAW-vich   ˌʃɔːstə'kɔːvitʃ

Shoyu
   soy sauce   SH$\bar{O}$-y$\overline{oo}$ 'ʃoːjuː

Shreveport
   city, LA   SHR$\bar{E}$V-P$\bar{O}$RT, SHR$\bar{E}$V-PAWRT, *esp.*   'ʃriːvˌpoːʳt, 'ʃriːvˌpɔːʳt, *esp.*
                  southeastern US SR$\bar{E}$V-   *southeastern US* 'sriːv-

Shrewsbury
   1. US pl. name   SHR$\overline{OO}$Z-BER-ē, *esp. southeastern US*   'ʃruːzˌberiˑ, *esp.*
                  SR$\overline{OO}$Z-BER-ē   *southeastern US*
                                       'sruːzˌberiˑ

   2. borough, England   SHR$\bar{O}$Z-b(uh-)rē, SHR$\overline{OO}$Z-b(uh-)rē,   'ʃroːzb(ə)riˑ, 'ʃruːzb(ə)riˑ,
                  Ⓢ SHR$\overline{OO}$Z-BER-ē, *esp.*   Ⓢ 'ʃruːzˌberiˑ, *esp.*
                  southeastern US SR$\overline{OO}$Z-BER-ē   *southeastern US*
                                         'sruːzˌberiˑ

Shriver
   Maria, US newscaster; Pamela, *US*   SHR$\bar{I}$-vuhr, *esp. southeastern US*   'ʃraivəʳ, *esp. southeastern*
   tennis player   SR$\bar{I}$-vuhr   *US* 'sraivəʳ

Shropshire
   county, England   SHRAHP-shuhr, -SHIR, *esp.*   'ʃrɑpʃəʳ, -ˌʃiʳ, *esp.*
                  southeastern US SRAHP-   *southeastern US* 'srɑp-

Shrove Tuesday
   day before Ash Wednesday   SHR$\bar{O}$V, *esp. southeastern US* SR$\bar{O}$V   'ʃroːv, *esp. southeastern*
                                         US 'sroːv

Foreign Sounds: ue: *Fr.* **rue**, *Ger.* **füllen**   uh(r): *Fr.* **boeuf**, *Ger.* **Höhle**   <u>kh</u>: *Ger.* **ich**, *Scot.* **loch**   ḡ: *Sp.* **amigo**   <u>v</u>: *Sp.* **hablar**   hl: *Welsh* **Llanelli**.   CAPITALS: primary stress.   SMALL CAPS: secondary stress.   Ⓢ: U.S. pron.   Ⓑ: British pron.

Shrovetide
   the three days before Ash   SHRŌV-TĪD, *esp. southeastern US*   'ʃroːv,taid, *esp.*
     Wednesday   SRŌV-TĪD   *southeastern US*
                                                                'sroːv,taid

Shu
   Egyptian god of the air   SHŌŌ   'ʃuː

Shughni
   lang., Afghanistan   SHUG-nē   'ʃugniˑ

Shula
   Don, *US football coach*   SHŌŌ-luh   'ʃuːlə

Shulamit
   pers. name, Hebrew   shōō-LAHM-it, shōō-LAHM-is   ʃuː'lamit, ʃuː'lamis

Shulamite
   Biblical name   SHŌŌ-luh-MĪT   'ʃuːlə,mait

Shulgi
   Sumerian king   SHUL-gē   'ʃulgiˑ

Shultheiss
   German beer   SHULT-HĪS   'ʃult,hais

Shultz
   George Pratt, *US government*   SHULTS   'ʃults
    official

Shunroku
   pers. name, Japanese   shun-rŏ-kōō   ʃunroːkuː

Shuppiluliumash
   Hittite king   shuh-PIL-ōō-LĒ-ōō-MAHSH   ʃə,piluː'liːuˑ,maʃ

Shushkevich
   Stanislav, *Belorussian political*   SHUSH-kyuhv-YICH   'ʃuʃkjəv,jitʃ
    leader

Shuzo
   pers. name, Japanese   SHUZ-ō   'ʃuzoː

Shylock
   character in Merchant of Venice,   SHĪ-LAHK   'ʃai,lak
    Shakespeare

Si
   see Xi

Sialkot
   city, India   sē-AHL-KŌT   siː'al,koːt

Siam
   former name of Thailand   sī-AM   sai'æm

Siamese
   pert. to Siam   sī-uh-MĒZ, -MĒS   ,saiə'miːz, -'miːs

Sian
   1. pers. name   SHAHN   'ʃaˑn
   2. see Xian

Sibelius
   Jean, *composer*   suh-BĀL-yuhs, suh-BĀ-lē-uhs   sə'beːljəs, sə'beːliːəs

Siberia
   region, Russia   sī-BIR-ē-uh   sai'biriːə

Sibert
   pers. name   SĪ-buhrt   'saibəʳt

Sibyl
   ancient priestess; pers. name   SIB-uhl   'sibəl

Sibylla
   pers. name, German   zē-BUEL-ah   ziː'byla

Key (col. 2):   a: fad   ā: fade   ah: father   ar: Mary   aw: law   e: fed   ē: feed   er: merry   i: hid   ī: hide   ō: coat   ōō: boot
oi: boy   ow: now   u: put   uh: above   uhr: bird   ch: chop   ng: ring   sh: show   th: thick   th̲: this   zh: measure

Sibylle
  pers. name, French   sē-BĚL   siːbiːl

Sichuan [Szechuan]
  prov, China   SICH-WAHN   'sitʃ'wɑn

Sichuan Pendi
  basin, China   SICH-WAHN PUHN-DĚ   'sitʃ'wɑn 'pən'diː

Sicilia [Sicily]
  island, Mediterranean   *Ital.* sē-CHĚL-yah, *Lat.* si-KIL-yuh, si-SIL-yuh   *Ital.* siː'tʃiːlja, *Lat.* si'kiljə, si'siljə

Sicilian
  pert. to Sicily   si-SIL-yuhn   si'siljən

Sicily
  island, Mediterranean   SIS-(uh-)lē   'sis(ə)liˑ

Siculus
  Roman cognomen   SIK-yuh-luhs   'sikjələs

Sicyon
  ancient city, Greece   SIS-ē-AHN, SISH-ē-AHN, SIK-ē-AHN   'sisiːˌɑn, 'siʃiːˌɑn, 'sikiːˌɑn

Sid
  pers. name   SID   'sid

Siddhartha Gautama
  the Buddha   si-DAHRT-uh GOWT-uh-muh, GAWT-uh-muh   si'dɑʳtə 'ɡautəmə, 'ɡɔːʈəmə

Sīdī Barrāni
  village, Egypt   SĒD-ē buh-RAHN-ē   ˌsiːdiˑ bə'rɑniˑ

Sidney
  pers. name   SID-nē   'sidniˑ

Sidney Sussex
  college, Cambridge Univ.   SID-nē SUHS-uhks   'sidniˑ 'səsəks

Sidon
  city, Lebanon   SĪD-n   'saidn̩

Sidonian
  pert. to Sidon   sī-DŌ-nē-uhn   sai'doːniːən

Sidonie
  1. pers. name, French   sē-daw-NĚ   siːdɔːniˑ
  2. German   zē-DŌ-nē-uh   ziː'doːniːə

Sidra
  gulf, Libya   SID-ruh   'sidrə

Siefert
  Jaroslav, *Czech author (Nobel 1984)*   SĒ-FERT   'siːˌfeʳt

Siegbahn
  Kai Manne, *Swedish physicist (Nobel 1981);* Karl Manne Georg, *Swedish physicist (Nobel 1924)*   SĒG-BAHN   'siːɡˌbɑn

Siegen
  city, Germany   ZĒ-guhn   'ziːɡən

Siegfried
  1. dragon-slayer in German mythology; pers. name   SIG-FRĒD, SĒG-FRĒD   'siɡˌfriːd, 'siːɡˌfriːd
  2. German   ZĒ**KH**-FRĒT   'ziːçˌfriːt

Sieglinde
  mother of Siegfried in German mythology   ZĒ**KH**-LIN-duh   'ziːçˌlində

Foreign Sounds: ue: *Fr.* **rue**, *Ger.* **füllen**   uh(r): *Fr.* **boeuf**, *Ger.* **Höhle**   <u>kh</u>: *Ger.* **ich**, *Scot.* **loch**   ğ: *Sp.* **amigo**   v̱: *Sp.* **hablar** hl: *Welsh* **Llanelli**.   CAPITALS: primary stress.   SMALL CAPS: secondary stress.   Ⓢ: U.S. pron.   Ⓛ: British pron.

Siegmund
   pers. name, German   ZI<u>KH</u>-MUNT   'ziç,munt

Siemens
   Ernst Werner von, *German*   ZĒ-muhnz, Ⓢ SĒ-muhnz   'ziːmənz, Ⓢ 'siːmənz
     industrialist; German electronics
     co.

Siena
   commune, Italy; college, NY   sē-EN-uh   siː'enə

Sienkiewicz
   Henryk, *Polish author (Nobel*   shen-KYĀ-vich   ʃen'kjeːvitʃ
     1905)

Sierra
   county, CA, NM   sē-ER-uh   siː'erə

Sierra Leone
   republic, Africa   sē-ER-uh lē-ŌN, SIR-uh   siː,erə liː'oːn, ,sirə

Sierra Leonean
   pert. to Sierra Leone   sē-ER-uh lē-Ō-nē-uhn, SIR-uh   siː,erə liː'oːniːən, ,sirə

Sierra Madre
   mts., WY; city, CA   sē-ER-uh MAHD-rē, MAHD-rā   siː,erə 'mɑdriˑ, 'mɑdreː

Sierra Nevada
   1. *mts., CA*   sē-ER-uh nuh-VAD-uh, nuh-VAHD-uh   siː,erə nə'vædə, nə'vɑdə
   2. *mts., Spain*   sē-ER-ah nā-VAH<u>TH</u>-ah   siː,erɑ neː'vɑðɑ

Sierra Popoloca
   lang., Mexico   sē-ER-uh PŌ-puh-LŌ-kuh   siː,erə ,poːpə'loːkə

Sieur de La Salle
   see La Salle, Sieur de

Sigbjörn
   pers. name, Norwegian   SIG-byuhrn   'sigbjœːrn

Sigfrid
   pers. name, German   ZĒ<u>KH</u>-FRĒT   'ziːç,friːt

Sighişoara
   city, Romania   SĒ-guh-SHWAHR-uh   ,siːgə'ʃwɑrə

Sigismond
   pers. name, French   sē-zhēs-MAW^n   siːʒiːsmɔ̃

Sigismund
   pers. name, German   ZĒ-gis-munt   'ziːgismunt

Sigmund
   1. *pers. name*   SIG-muhnd   'sigmənd
   2. *German*   ZĒ<u>KH</u>-munt   'ziːçmunt

Signor
   Italian form of address for a man   sēn-YAWR, SĒN-YAWR   siːn'jɔːʳ, 'siːnjɔːʳ

Signora
   Italian form of address for a   sēn-YŌR-uh, sēn-YAWR-uh   siːn'joːrə, siːn'jɔːrə
     married woman

Signoret
   Simone, *entertainer*   SĒN-yuh-RĀ   ,siːnjə'reː

Signorina
   Italian form of address for an   SĒN-yaw-RĒ-nuh, SĒN-yuh-RĒ-nuh   ,siːnjɔː'riːnə, ,siːnjə'riːnə
     unmarried woman

Sigourney
   1. *town, IA*   SIG-uhr-nē   'sigəʳniˑ
   2. *pers. name*   si-GUHR-nē, si-GAWR-nē   si'gəʳniˑ, si'gɔːʳniˑ

Key (col. 2):   a: fad   ā: fade   ah: father   ar: Mary   aw: law   e: fed   ē: feed   er: merry   i: hid   ī: hide   ō: coat   ōō: boot
oi: boy   ow: now   u: put   uh: above   uhr: bird   ch: chop   ng: ring   sh: show   th: thick   <u>th</u>: this   zh: measure

Sigrid
   1. pers. name, German   ZĒ-grit, ZĒ-GRĒT   'ziːgrit, 'ziːˌgriːt
   2. Norwegian   SIG-rē   'sigriˑ
   3. Swedish   SĒ-grid   'siːgrid

Sigurð [Sigurd]
   legendary Scandinavian hero   SIG-ur<u>th</u>   'sigurð

Sigurd
   1. legendary Scandinavian hero   SIG-urd, SIG-uhrd   'siguʳd, 'sigəʳd
   2. pers. name, Norwegian   SIG-urd   'sigurd

Sihanouk
   see Norodom Sihanouk

Sikandarabad
   town, India   si-KUHN-duh-ruh-BAHD, -BAD   si'kəndərəˌbɑd, -ˌbæd

Sikh
   adherent of Sikhism   SĒK   'siːk

Sikhism
   religion   SĒ-KIZ-uhm   'siːˌkizəm

Sikhote-Alin
   mtn. range, Russia   SYĒ-<u>kh</u>ō-TĀ uh-LĒN   ˌsjiːxoːˌteː ə'liːn

Sikinos
   island, Greece   SIK-uh-NAWS, -NAHS   'sikəˌnɔːs, -ˌnɑs

Sikkim
   state, India   SIK-uhm   'sikəm

Sikorsky
   1. Igor, *Russian-born US*   syi-KAWR-skyi, $ suh-KAWR-skē   sji'kɔːʳskjij, $ sə'kɔːʳskiˑ
   aeronautical inventor
   2. US helicopter co.   suh-KAWR-skē   sə'kɔːʳskiˑ

Silas
   pers. name   SĪ-luhs   'sailəs

Silenus
   satyr who reared Dionysus   sī-LĒ-nuhs   sai'liːnəs

Siles
   Hernan, *president, Bolivia*   SĒ-lās   'siːleːs

Silesia
   region, central Europe   sī-LĒ-zh(ē-)uh, sī-LĒ-sh(ē-)uh, suh-   sai'liːʒ(iː)ə, sai'liːʃ(iː)ə, sə-

Silesian
   pert. to Silesia   sī-LĒ-zh(ē-)uhn, sī-LĒ-sh(ē-)uhn, suh-   sai'liːʒ(iː)ən, sai'liːʃ(iː)ən, sə-

Siletz
   Indian reservation, US   SĪ-luhts   'sailəts

silicon
   element   SIL-i-kuhn, SIL-uh-KAHN   'silikən, 'siləˌkɑn

Sillanpää
   Frans Eemil, *Finnish author*   SIL-ahn-PAH, $ SIL-uhn-PA   'silɑːnˌpɑ, $ 'silənˌpæ
   (Nobel 1939)

Sillus
   grandson of Nestor   SIL-uhs   'siləs

Siloam
   spring near Jerusalem   sī-LŌ-uhm   sai'loːəm

Siloam Springs
   city, AR   SĪ-lōm SPRINGZ, SĪ-luhm   ˌsailoːm 'spriŋz, ˌsailəm

Silurian
   geologic period   suh-LUR-ē-uhn, sī-   sə'luriːən, sai-

Silvan
   pers. name   SIL-vuhn   'silvən

Foreign Sounds: ue: *Fr.* **rue**, *Ger.* füllen   uh(r): *Fr.* **boeuf**, *Ger.* Höhle   <u>kh</u>: *Ger.* i**ch**, *Scot.* lo**ch**   ğ: *Sp.* ami**g**o   Ꜯ: *Sp.* ha**b**lar
hl: *Welsh* Llanelli.   CAPITALS: primary stress.   SMALL CAPS: secondary stress. $: U.S. pron.   ©: British pron.

Silvana
  pers. name, Italian   sēl-VAHN-uh   siːl'vɑnə

Silvanus
  Roman divinity of the woods; pers.   sil-VĂ-nuhs   sil'veːnəs
    name

silver
  element   SIL-vuhr   'silvəʳ

Silverius
  pope   sil-VIR-ē-uhs   sil'viriːəs

Silverstein
  Shel, *US humorist*   SIL-vuhr-STĪN, -STĒN   'silvəʳˌstain, -ˌstiːn

Silvester
  pers. name   sil-VES-tuhr   sil'vestəʳ

Silvestre
  1. pers. name, French   sēl-VESTR   siːlvestr
  2. Spanish   sēl-VĂ-strā   siːl'βeːstreː

Silvestro
  pers. name, Italian   sēl-VES-trō   siːl'vestroː

Silvia
  pers. name   SIL-vē-uh   'silviːə

Silvio
  1. pers. name   SIL-vē-ō   'silviːoː
  2. German   ZIL-vyō, ZIL-vē-ō   'zilvjoː, 'zilviːoː
  3. Italian   SĒL-vyō   'siːlvjoː

Silvius
  king of Alba   SIL-vē-uhs   'silviːəs

Simanu
  Babylonian month   suh-MAHN-o͞o   sə'mɑnuː

Simão
  pers. name, Portuguese   sē-MOWⁿ   siː'maũ

Simbirsk [Ulyanovsk]
  city, Russia   syim-BYIRSK   sjim'bjiʳsk

Simchas Torah
  Jewish festival   sim-<u>KHA</u>HT tawr-AH, SIM-<u>kh</u>uhs   sim'xat tɔːr'a, ˌsimxəs 'toːrə,
                   TŌR-uh, TAWR-uh   'tɔːrə

Simenon
  Georges, *French writer*   sē-me-NAWⁿ   siːmenɔ̃

Simeon
  1. pers. name   SIM-ē-uhn   'simiːən
  2. Russian   syim-yi-AWN   sjimji'ɔːn
  3. Spanish   sē-mā-ŌN   siːmeˈoːn

Siméon
  pers. name, French   sē-mā-AWⁿ   siːmeːɔ̃

Simferopol
  city, Ukraine   S(Y)IM(P)-fuh-RAW-puhl,   ˌs(j)im(p)fə'rɔːpəl,
                   SIM(P)-fuh-RŌ-puhl   ˌsim(p)fə'roːpəl

Simi Valley
  city, CA   si-MĒ VAL-ē   si,miː 'væliˑ

Simmel
  George, *German sociologist*   ZIM-uhl   'ziməl

Simmons
  College, *MA*   SIM-uhnz   'simənz

Key (col. 2):   a: fad   ā: fade   ah: father   ar: Mary   aw: law   e: fed   ē: feed   er: merry   i: hid   ī: hide   ō: coat   o͞o: boot
oi: boy   ow: now   u: put   uh: above   uhr: bird   ch: chop   ng: ring   sh: show   th: thick   <u>th</u>: this   zh: measure

Simon

1. Herbert A., *US economist*   SĪ-muhn   'saimən
   (Nobel 1978); pers. name
2. Claude, *French author (Nobel*   sē-MAWⁿ   si:mɔ̃
   1985); pers. name, French
3. *German*   ZĒ-mawn   'zi:mɔːn
4. *Russian*   SYĒ-muhn   'sji:mən
5. *Serbo-Croatian*   SĒ-mawn   'si:mɔːn

Simón

pers. name, Spanish   sē-MAWN   si:'mɔːn

Simon & Schuster

US publisher   SĪ-muhn uhn(d) SHOO-stuhr,   ,saimən ən(d) 'ʃuːstəʳ,
                        SHUS-tuhr   'ʃustəʳ

Simón Bolívar Maiquetia

airport, Caracas, Venezuela sē-MŌN bō-LĒ-vahr mī-KĀT-yah si:'mɔːn boː'liːβar mai'keːtja

Simone

1. *pers. name*   si-MŌN   si'mɔːn
2. *French*   sē-MAWN   si:mɔːn
3. *Italian*   sē-MŌ-nā   si:'moːneː

Simonides

Greek poet   SĪ-MAHN-uhd-ĒZ   sai'manəd,iːz

Simpatico

German beer   zim-PAHT-i-kō   zim'paṭikoː

Simplice

pers. name, French   seⁿ-PLĒS   sẽpliːs

Simplicius

pope   sim-PLISH-(ē-)uhs   sim'pliʃ(iː)əs

Simplon Pass

Alpine pass   SIM-PLAHN PAS   'sim,plan 'pæs

Simpson

Alan K., US politician   SIM(P)-suhn   'sim(p)sən

Sinai [Horeb]

peninsula, mtn., desert, Egypt SĪ-NĪ   'sai,nai

Sinaloa

state, Mexico   SĒ-nuh-LŌ-uh   ,si:nə'loːə

Sinanthropus

early hominid, "Peking man" sī-NAN-thruh-puhs,   sai'nænθrəpəs,
                       sī-nan-THRŌ-puhs   ,sainæn'θroːpəs

Sinarquist

member of a Mexican political SIN-AHR-kist   'sin,aʳkist
movement

Sinarquista

Spanish form of Sinarquist sin-ahr-KĒ-stah   sinar'kiːsta

Sinatra

Frank, US singer, actor   suh-NAH-truh   sə'natrə

Sinbad

hero, Arabian Nights   SIN-BAD   'sin,bæd

Sinclair

pers. name   SIN-KLAR, SIN-KLER, SING-; 'sin,klæʳ, 'sin,kleʳ, 'siŋ-;
                  sin-KLAR, sin-KLER, sing-   sin'klæʳ, sin'kleʳ, siŋ-

Sind, Sindh

prov, Pakistan   SIND   'sind

Si Ndebele

lang., Africa   SĒN-duh-BĒ-lē, SĒ EN-duh-BĒ-lē ,si:ndə'biːliˈ, ,si: ,endə'biːliˈ

Foreign Sounds: ue: *Fr.* **rue**, *Ger.* **füllen** uh(r): *Fr.* **boeuf**, *Ger.* **Höhle** <u>kh</u>: *Ger.* i**ch**, *Scot.* lo**ch** g̃: *Sp.* ami**g**o v̲: *Sp.* ha**b**lar
hl: *Welsh* L**l**anelli. CAPITALS: primary stress. SMALL CAPS: secondary stress. Ⓢ: U.S. pron. Ⓑ: British pron.

Sindhi		
people, lang., India	SIN-dē	'sindiˑ
Sineád		
pers. name, Irish	SHIN-Ā-uh, [S] shuh-NĀD, shuh-NĀ-uhd	'ʃin,eːə, [S] ʃə'neːd, ʃə'neːəd
Singapore		
republic, city, Asia	SING-(g)uh-PŌR, -PAWR	'siŋ(g)ə,poːʳ, -,pɔːʳ
Singaporean		
pert. to Singapore	SING-(g)uh-PŌR-ē-uhn, -PAWR-ē-uhn	,siŋ(g)ə'poːriːən, -'pɔːriːən
Singaraja, Singaradja		
town, Bali	SING-guh-RAHJ-uh	,siŋgə'rɑdʒə
Singer		
Isaac Bashevis, *Polish-born US author (Nobel 1978)*	SING-uhr	'siŋəʳ
Singh		
pers. name	SING	'siŋ
Singha		
Thai beer	SING-HAH, SING-(h)uh	'siŋ'hɑ, 'siŋ(h)ə
Singhalese		
see Sinhalese		
Singhji		
pers. name, Hindi	SING-jē	'siŋdʒiˑ
Singleton		
pers. name	SING-guhl-tuhn	'siŋgəltən
Sinhala		
Sri Lankan New Year	SIN-huh-luh	'sinhələ
Sinhalese, Singhalese		
Sri Lankan people, lang.	SING-guh-LĒZ, SIN-(h)uh-LĒZ, -LĒS	,siŋgə'liːz, ,sin(h)ə'liːz, -'liːs
Sinicism		
characteristic of the Chinese	SĪ-nuh-SIZ-uhm, SIN-uh-SIZ-uhm	'sɑinə,sizəm, 'sinə,sizəm
Sinitic		
pert. to the Chinese	sī-NIT-ik, suh-NIT-ik	sɑi'niţik, sə'niţik
Sinkiang		
see Xinjiang		
Sinkiang Uighur		
see Xingjiang Uygur		
Sinn Fein		
Irish political party	SHIN FĀN	,ʃin 'feːn
Sino-		
combining form meaning 'Chinese'	SĪ-nō, SĪ-nuh, SĪ-nō	'sɑinoː, 'sɑinə, ,sɑinoː
Sinology		
study of things Chinese	sī-NAHL-uh-jē, suh-NAHL-uh-jē	sɑi'nɑlədʒiˑ, sə'nɑlədʒiˑ
Sinon		
Greek spy at Troy	SĪ-NAHN, SĪ-nuhn	'sɑi,nɑn, 'sɑinən
Sinope		
ancient seaport, Turkey; satellite of Jupiter	suh-NŌ-pē	sə'noːpiˑ
Sino-Tibetan		
S. Asian lang. family	SĪ-nō-tuh-BET-n	,sɑinoːtə'betṇ
Sinte Gleska		
College, *SD*	SINT-uh GLES-kuh	,sintə 'gleskə
Sint-Niklaas		
prov, Belgium	sint-NĒ-kluhs	sint'niːkləs

Key (col. 2): a: fad ā: fade ah: father ar: Mary aw: law e: fed ē: feed er: merry i: hid ī: hide ō: coat o͞o: boot oi: boy ow: now u: put uh: above uhr: bird ch: chop ng: ring sh: show th: thick th: this zh: measure

Sinuhe
  Egyptian politician   SIN-(y)uh-HĀ   'sin(j)ə,heː

Sinus Iridum
  'bay' on Moon   SĪ-nuhs IR-uh-duhm   'sainəs 'irədəm

Sinus Medii
  'bay' on Moon   SĪ-nuhs MED-ē-Ē, MED-ē-Ī   'sainəs 'mediː,iː, 'mediː,ai

Sinus Roris
  'bay' on moon   SĪ-nuhs RŌR-uhs, RAWR-uhs   'sainəs 'roːrəs, 'rɔːrəs

Siobhan
  pers. name, Irish   shuh-VAHN   ʃə'van

Siôn
  pers. name, Welsh   SYAWN, Ⓢ SHAWN, SHAHN   'sjɔːn, Ⓢ 'ʃɔːn, 'ʃan

Siouan
  pert. to the Sioux   SOO-uhn   'suːən

Sioux
  N. American people   SOO   'suː

Siqueiros
  David, *Mexican painter*   sē-KĀ-rōs   siː'keːroːs

Siracusa
  prov, Italy   SIR-uh-KOO-zuh   ,sirə'kuːzə

Sirenia
  dugongs & manatees   sī-RĒ-nē-uh   sai'riːniːə

Sirens
  Greek legendary sea demons   SĪ-ruhnz   'sairənz

Siret
  river, Europe   sē-RET   siː'ret

Sirhan
  Sirhan, *US assassin; pers. name*   sir-HAHN, SIR-HAHN   siʳ'han, 'siʳ,han

Siricius
  pope   suh-RISH-(ē-)uhs   sə'riʃ(iː)əs

Sirimavo
  pers. name, Sinhalese   SIR-uh-MAHV-ō   ,sirə'mavoː

Sirionó
  S. American people   SIR-ē-uh-NŌ   ,siriːə'noː

Sirius
  star Alpha Canis Majoris   SIR-ē-uhs   'siriːəs

Síros
  island, Greece   SĒ-RAWS   'siː,rɔːs

Sirte
  gulf, Africa; town, Libya   SIR-TĀ   'siʳ,teː

Sisinnius
  pope   suh-SIN-ē-uhs   sə'siniːəs

Siskel
  Gene, *US film critic*   SIS-kuhl   'siskəl

Siskiyou
  county, CA; mts., US   SIS-ki-YOO   'siski,juː

Siskiyous
  College of the, *CA*   SIS-ki-YOOZ   'siski,juːz

Sisseton
  N. American people   SIS-uht-n   'sisətn̩

Sissy
  pers. name   SIS-ē   'sisiˑ

Sistine
  Chapel, *the Vatican*   SIS-TĒN   'sis,tiːn

Foreign Sounds: ue: *Fr.* **rue**, *Ger.* **f**ü**llen**   uh(r): *Fr.* b**oeuf**, *Ger.* H**öh**le   <u>kh</u>: *Ger.* i**ch**, *Scot.* lo**ch**   ḡ: *Sp.* ami**g**o   v̲: *Sp.* ha**b**lar
hl: *Welsh* **Ll**anelli.   CAPITALS: primary stress.   SMALL CAPS: secondary stress.   Ⓢ: U.S. pron.   Ⓛ: British pron.

Sisto
  pers. name, Italian   SĔS-tō   'siːstoː
siSwati [Swazi]
  lang., Africa   si-SWAHT-ē   si'swaʈiˑ
Sisyphean
  pert. to Sisyphus or his labors   suh-SIF-ē-uhn, SIS-uh-FĒ-uhn   sə'sifiːən, ˌsisə'fiːən
Sisyphus
  man condemned to roll rock uphill in Hades   SIS-uh-fuhs   'sisəfəs
Sitar
  musical instrument   si-TAHR, SI-TAHR   si'tɑ^r, 'si,tɑ^r
Sitka
  city, division, AK; N. American people   SIT-kuh   'sitkə
Sittang
  river, Burma   SI-TAHNG   'si,taŋ
Sitting Bull
  N. American Indian warrior   SIT-ing BUL   ˌsiʈiŋ 'bul
Sittwe [Akyab]
  town, Burma   SIT-wē   'sitwiˑ
Siva, Shiva
  Hindu god, member of the supreme triad   SHIV-uh, SHĒ-vuh   'ʃivə, 'ʃiːvə
Sivaism
  worship of Siva   SHIV-uh-IZ-uhm, SHĒ-vuh-IZ-uhm   'ʃivə,izəm, 'ʃiːvə,izəm
Sivan
  Jewish month   SIV-uhn, SĒ-VAHN   'sivən, 'siːˌvɑn
Sivas
  city, prov, Turkey   si-VAHS   si'vɑs
Siwa
  town, Egypt   SĒ-wuh   'siːwə
Sixtine
  pert. to Pope Sixtus or to Sistine Chapel   SIK-STĒN   'sik,stiːn
Sixtus
  pope   SIK-stuhs   'sikstəs
Sjælland [Zealand]
  island, Denmark   SHEL-AHN   'ʃel,ɑn
Skaði
  Scandinavian goddess   SKAHTH-ē   'skɑði·
Skagen
  town, Denmark   SKAHG-uhn   'skɑgən
Skagerrak
  arm of North Sea   SKAG-uh-RAK   'skægə,ræk
Skaggs
  Ricky, US country musician   SKAGS   'skægs
Skagit
  river, bay, county, WA; N. American people   SKAJ-uht   'skædʒət
Skagway-Yakutat-Angoon
  division, AK   SKAG-WĀ-YAK-uh-TAT-ang-GOON   'skæg,weːˈjækəˌtæʈæŋ'guːn
Skamania
  county, WA   skuh-MĀN-yuh   skə'meːnjə
Skaneateles
  town, NY   SKIN-ē-AT-luhs, SKAN-ē-AT-luhs   ˌskiniːˈætləs, ˌskæniːˈætləs

---

Key (col. 2):   a: fad   ā: fade   ah: father   ar: Mary   aw: law   e: fed   ē: feed   er: merry   i: hid   ī: hide   ō: coat   o͞o: boot
oi: boy   ow: now   u: put   uh: above   uhr: bird   ch: chop   ng: ring   sh: show   th: thick   th: this   zh: measure

Skara Brae
    excavated Neolithic village,   SKAR-uh BRĀ   ˌskærə ˈbreː
    Orkney Islands

Skeat
    Walter, *English philologist,*   SKĒT   ˈskiːt
    lexicographer

Skeena
    river, Canada   SKĒ-nuh   ˈskiːnə

Skene
    pers. name   SKĒN   ˈskiːn

Skiathos, Skiathos
    island, Greece   SKĒ-uh-THAWS, Ⓢ SKĪ-uh-THAHS   ˈskiːəˌθɔːs, Ⓢ ˈskɑiəˌθɑs

Skinner
    Burrhus Frederic, *US psychologist,*   SKIN-uhr   ˈskinəʳ
    educator

Skinnerian
    pert. to Skinner *or behaviorist*   ski-NIR-ē-uhn, ski-NER-ē-uhn   skiˈniriːən, skiˈneriːən
    theories

Skiros
    island, Greece   SKĒ-RAWS   ˈskiːˌrɔːs

Skoda, Škoda
    J., *Austrian physician;* Emil von,   SHKŌ-dah, Ⓢ SKŌD-uh, SHKŌD-uh   ˈʃkoːdɑː, Ⓢ ˈskoːdə, ˈʃkoːdə
    Czech engineer

Skokie
    town, IL   SKŌ-kē   ˈskoːkiˑ

Skokomish
    N. American people   skō-KŌ-mish   skoːˈkoːmiʃ

Skol
    tdmk for vodka, tobacco   SKŌL, SKAWL   ˈskoːl, ˈskɔːl

Skopje
    city, Macedonia   SKAWP-ye, SKAWP-yā   ˈskɔːpje, ˈskɔːpjeː

Skoplje [Skopje]
    city, Macedonia   SKAWP-lye, SKAWP-lē-Ā   ˈskɔːplje, ˈskɔːpliːˌeː

Skua
    sea bird   SKYOO-uh   ˈskjuːə

Skye
    island, Scotland   SKĪ   ˈskɑi

Skylab
    US space station   SKĪ-LAB   ˈskɑiˌlæb

Slatkin
    Leonard, *US conductor*   SLAT-kin   ˈslætkin

Slaughter
    pers. name   SLAWT-uhr   ˈslɔːʈəʳ

Slav
    European ethnic group   SLAHV   ˈslɑv

Slave
    river, Canada; N. American people   SLĀV   ˈsleːv

Slavic
    pert. to Slavs; *branch of*   SLAHV-ik   ˈslɑvik
    Indo-European langs.

Slavonia
    region, Croatia   sluh-VŌN-yuh, sluh-VŌ-nē-uh   sləˈvoːnjə, sləˈvoːniːə

Slavonic
    Slavic   sluh-VAHN-ik   sləˈvɑnik

Foreign Sounds: ue: *Fr.* **rue,** *Ger.* füllen   uh(r): *Fr.* b**oe**uf, *Ger.* H**öh**le   <u>kh</u>: *Ger.* i**ch,** *Scot.* lo**ch**   ğ: *Sp.* ami**g**o   v̱: *Sp.* ha**b**lar
hl: *Welsh* L**l**anelli.   CAPITALS: primary stress.   SMALL CAPS: secondary stress.   Ⓢ: U.S. pron.   Ⓔ: British pron.

Slavophile	*admirer of the Slavs*	SLAV-uh-FĪL, SLAHV-uh-FĪL	'slævə,fail, 'slɑvə,fail
Slavophobe	*hater of the Slavs*	SLAV-uh-FŌB, SLAHV-uh-FŌB	'slævə,foːb, 'slɑvə,foːb
Slayton	Donald Kent, *US astronaut*	SLĀT-n	'sleːtn̩
Slazenger	*tdmk for sport racquets*	SLĀ-zuhn-juhr	'sleːzəndʒəʳ
Sleigh	*pers. name*	SLĀ	'sleː
Slezak	Leo, *Czech tenor;* Walter, *US actor*	SLEZ-AHK, [$] SLĀ-ZAK	'slez,ɑːk, [$] 'sleː,zæk
Slidell	*pers. name*	SLĪD-l, slī-DEL	'slɑidl̩, slɑi'del
Sligh	*pers. name*	SLĪ	'slɑi
Sligo	*pers. name*	SLĪ-gō	'slɑigoː
Slivovitz	*Balkan plum brandy*	SLIV-uh-VITS, SLĒ-vuh-VITS, SHLIV-uh-VITS, -WITS	'slivə,vits, 'sliːvə,vits, 'ʃlivə,vits, -,wits
Slobodan	*pers. name, Serbo-Croatian*	slaw-BAW-dahn	slɔː'bɔːdɑːn
Slough	*town, England*	SLOW	'slɑu
Slough of Despond	*bog in* Pilgrim's Progress, *J. Bunyan; depression*	SLOW uhv di-SPAHND, [$] *also* SLOO	,slɑu əv di'spɑnd, [$] *also* ,sluː
Slovak	*lang., people, E. Europe*	SLŌ-VAHK, SLŌ-VAK	'sloː,vɑk, 'sloː,væk
Slovakia	*republic, E. Europe*	slō-VAHK-ē-uh, slō-VAK-ē-uh	sloː'vɑkiːə, sloː'vækiːə
Slovene	*lang., people, Slovenia*	SLŌ-VĒN	'sloː,viːn
Slovenia	*republic, E. Europe*	slō-VĒN-yuh, slō-VĒ-nē-uh	sloː'viːnjə, sloː'viːniːə
Slovenian [Slovene]	*lang., Slovenia*	slō-VĒ-nē-uhn, slō-VĒN-yuhn	sloː'viːniːən, sloː'viːnjən
Slovenija [Slovenia]	*republic, E. Europe*	slō-VEN-ē-(Y)AH	sloː'veniː,(j)ɑ
Slovensko [Slovakia]	*republic, E. Europe*	slō-VEN-skō	sloː'venskoː
Smedley	*pers. name*	SMED-lē	'smedliˑ
Smenkhare	*king of Egypt*	smeng-KAHR-uh	smeŋ'kɑrə
Smerdis	*Persian noble*	SMUHR-duhs	'sməʳdəs
Smetana	Bedřich, *Czech composer*	SMET-n-uh	'smetn̩ə
Smith	*pers. name*	SMITH	'smiθ
Smithson	James, *English chemist, mineralogist*	SMITH-suhn	'smiθsən

Key (col. 2): a: fad ā: fade ah: father ar: Mary aw: law e: fed ē: feed er: merry i: hid ī: hide ō: coat oo: boot oi: boy ow: now u: put uh: above uhr: bird ch: chop ng: ring sh: show th: thick th: this zh: measure

Smithsonian
    Institution, *US natl. museum*   smith-SŌ-nē-uhn   smiθ'soːniːən
Smolensk
    city, Russia   SMUHL-YEN(T)SK, Ⓢ smō-LEN(T)SK   ˌsməl'jen(t)sk, Ⓢ smoː'len(t)sk
Smollett
    Tobias G., *English author*   SMAHL-uht   'smɑlət
Smothers
    Dick *and* Tom, *US comedians*   SMUH<u>TH</u>-uhrz   'sməðəʳz
Smucker's
    US jam co.   SMUHK-uhrz   'sməkəʳz
Smuts
    Jan, *South African statesman*   SMUETS, Ⓢ SMUHTS   'smyːts, Ⓢ 'sməts
Smyrna
    mother of Adonis in Greek myth;   SMUHR-nuh   'sməʳnə
    ancient city, Asia Minor; prov,
    Turkey; pl. name, US
Smyth
    pers. name   SMITH, SMĪTH   'smiθ, 'smaiθ
Smythe
    pers. name   SMĪ<u>TH</u>, SMĪTH   'smaið, 'smaiθ
Smythii, Mare
    see Mare Smythii
Smyth-sewn
    bookbinding   SMITH-SŌN, SMĪTH-SŌN   'smiθˌsoːn, 'smaiθˌsoːn
SNCC
    Student Non-Violent Coordinating   SNIK   'snik
    Committee
Snead
    Sam, *US golfer*   SNĒD   'sniːd
Snell
    George D., *US immunologist*   SNEL   'snel
    (Nobel 1980)
SNET
    Southern New England Telephone   ES-EN-Ē-TĒ, SNET   ˌesˌenˌiː'tiː, 'snet
    Co.
SNOBOL
    programming lang.   SNŌ-BAWL   'snoːˌbɔl
Snohomish
    river, county, WA; N. American   snō-HŌ-mish   snoː'hoːmiʃ
    people
Snoopy
    cartoon beagle   SNO͞OP-ē   'snuːpiˑ
Snoqualmie
    river, WA   snō-KWAHL-mē   snoː'kwɑlmiˑ
Snowdonia
    region, natl. park, Wales   snō-DŎN-yuh, snō-DŌ-nē-uh   snoː'dɔnjə, snoː'doːniːə
Soame
    pers. name   SŌM   'soːm
Soave
    wine   SWAHV-ā, suh-WAHV-ā   'swɑveː, sə'wɑveː
Sobek-Re
    Egyptian god   SAWB-uhk-RĀ, SAHB-uhk-RĀ   'sɔbək're˞ː, 'sabək'reː
Sobhuza
    king of Swaziland   sō-BO͞O-zuh   soː'buːzə

Foreign Sounds: ue: *Fr.* **rue**, *Ger.* f**ü**llen   uh(r): *Fr.* b**oeu**f, *Ger.* H**öh**le   kh: *Ger.* i**ch**, *Scot.* lo**ch**   g̃: *Sp.* ami**g**o   v̱: *Sp.* ha**b**lar
hl: *Welsh* **Ll**anelli.   CAPITALS: primary stress.   SMALL CAPS: secondary stress.   Ⓢ: U.S. pron.   Ⓛ: British pron.

Sobk [Sebek]
  Egyptian crocodile god   SAHB-uhk, SAWB-uhk   'sabək, 'sɔːbək
Soboba
  Band, N. American people   sō-BŌ-buh   soː'boːbə
Sochi
  port, Russia   SŌ-chē   'soːtʃiˑ
Socinian
  follower of Socinus   suh-SIN-ē-uhn   sə'siniˑən
Socinianism
  religious beliefs of Socinus   suh-SIN-ē-uh-NIZ-uhm   sə'siniˑə,nizəm
Socinus
  Faustus, Protestant theologian   sō-SĪ-nuhs, suh-SĪ-nuhs   soː'sainəs, sə'sainəs
Socorro
  county, NM   suh-KAWR-ō   sə'kɔːroː
Socotra
  island, Indian Ocean   suh-KŌ-truh   sə'koːtrə
Socrates
  1. Greek philosopher; pers. name   SAHK-ruh-TĒZ   'sakrə,tiːz
  2. Mod. Greek   saw-KRAH-tēs   sɔː'kratiːs
Socratic
  pert. to Socrates   suh-KRAT-ik, sō-KRAT-ik   sə'kræṭik, soː'kræṭik
Socraticism
  a characteristic of Socrates   suh-KRAT-uh-SIZ-uhm   sə'kræṭə,sizəm
Socratism
  philosophy or method of Socrates   SAHK-ruh-TIZ-uhm   'sakrə,tizəm
Soddy
  Frederick, English chemist (Nobel 1921)   SAHD-ē   'sadiˑ
Söderblom
  Nathan, Swedish churchman (Nobel 1930)   SUH(R)D-uhr-BLOOM   'sœːdəʳ,bluːm
sodium
  element   SŌD-ē-uhm   'soːdiːəm
Sodom
  Biblical city   SAHD-uhm   'sadəm
Sodomite
  inhabitant of Sodom   SAHD-uh-MĪT   'sadə,mait
Soerabaja
  see Surabaja
Sofia
  1. pers. name   suh-FĒ-uh, suh-FĪ-uh, sō-FĒ-uh   sə'fiːə, sə'faiə, soː'fiːə
  2. Swedish   su-FĒ-ah   su'fiːaː
Sofonisba
  pers. name, Italian   sō-fō-NĒZ-bah   ˌsoːfoː'niːzba
Soga
  lang., people, Africa   SŌ-guh   'soːgə
Sogdian
  extinct Iranian lang.   SAHG-dē-uhn   'sagdiːən
Sogdiana
  region, Uzbekistan   SAHG-dē-AHN-uh, SAHG-dē-AN-uh, SAHG-dē-Ā-nuh   ˌsagdiː'anə, ˌsagdiː'ænə, ˌsagdiː'eːnə
Soho, SoHo
  district, NY & London, England   SŌ-HŌ   'soː,hoː
Soissons
  city, France   swah-SAWⁿ   swasɔ̃

Key (col. 2):   a: fad   ā: fade   ah: father   ar: Mary   aw: law   e: fed   ē: feed   er: merry   i: hid   ī: hide   ō: coat   o͞o: boot
oi: boy   ow: now   u: put   uh: above   uhr: bird   ch: chop   ng: ring   sh: show   th: thick   <u>th</u>: this   zh: measure

Sojourner
   pers. name   SŌ-JUHR-nuhr, sō-JUHR-nuhr   'soːˌdʒəʳnəʳ, soːˈdʒəʳnəʳ
Sojourner-Douglas
   College, MD   SŌ-JUHR-nuhr-DUHG-luhs,   'soːˌdʒəʳnəʳˈdəgləs,
        sō-JUHR-nuhr-   soːˈdʒəʳnəʳ-
Sokagoan Chippewa
   N. American people   SŌ-kuh-GŌ-uhn CHIP-uh-WAW, -WAH,   ˌsoːkəˈgoːən 'tʃipəˌwoː, -ˌwɑ,
        -WĂ, -wuh   -ˌweː, -wə
Sokar
   Egyptian god of the dead   SAWK-uhr, SAHK-uhr   'soːkəʳ, 'sɑkəʳ
Sol
   Roman sun god   SAWL, SAHL, SŌL   'soːl, 'sɑl, 'soːl
Solano
   county, CA   suh-LAHN-ō   sə'lɑnoː
Solāpur
   city, India   sō-LAH-PUR   soː'lɑˌpuʳ
Soledad
   1. *city, CA*   SAHL-uh-DAD, SŌ-luh-DAD   'sɑləˌdæd, 'soːləˌdæd
   2. *town, Colombia*   SAW-luh-THAH(TH)   ˌsoːlə'ða(ð)
   3. *city, Mexico*   SAW-luh-DAHD, SAW-luh-THAH(TH)   ˌsoːlə'dad, ˌsoːlə'ða(ð)
Solent, The
   channel between Isle of Wight &   thuh SŌ-luhnt   ðə 'soːlənt
   England
Sol Especial
   Mexican beer   SŌL es-pes-YAHL   'soːl espes'jɑl
Soli
   lang., Africa   SŌ-lē   'soːliˑ
Solidarnosc
   "Solidarity" political party,   SAWL-ē-DAHR-NAWSH   ˌsoːliˑ'dɑːrˌnoːʃ
   Poland
Solingen
   city, Germany   ZŌ-ling-uhn, SŌ-ling-uhn   'zoːliŋən, 'soːliŋən
Solo
   river, Indonesia; former name of   SŌ-lō   'soːloː
   Surakarta; Han, *hero of Star*
   Wars
Sologne
   basin, France   saw-LAWN-yuh   soːloːɲ
Solomon
   king of Israel; Islands, *Pacific;*   SAHL-uh-muhn   'sɑləmən
   pers. name
Solon
   Athenian statesman; pers. name   SŌ-luhn, SŌ-LAHN   'soːlən, 'soːˌlɑn
Solothurn
   canton, Switzerland   ZŌ-luh-TURN, SŌ-luh-TURN   'zoːləˌtuʳn, 'soːləˌtuʳn
Solow
   Robert M., US economist (Nobel   SŌ-lō   'soːloː
   1987)
Solti
   Sir Georg, Hungarian conductor   SHŌL-tē   'ʃoːltiˑ
Solvay
   1. *Ernest, Belgian chemist*   sawl-VE, Ⓢ SAHL-VĀ   soːlve, Ⓢ 'sɑlˌveː
   2. *village, NY*   SAHL-VĀ   'sɑlˌveː
Solway Firth
   arm of Irish Sea   SAHL-wā FUHRTH   ˌsɑlweː 'fəʳθ

Foreign Sounds: ue: *Fr.* **rue**, *Ger.* **füllen**   uh(r): *Fr.* **boeuf**, *Ger.* **Höhle**   kh: *Ger.* **ich**, *Scot.* **loch**   g̶: *Sp.* **amigo**   v̶: *Sp.* **hablar**
hl: *Welsh* **Llanelli**.   CAPITALS: primary stress.   SMALL CAPS: secondary stress.   Ⓢ: U.S. pron.   Ⓑ: British pron.

Solzhenitsyn		
Alexandr I., *Russian author (Nobel 1970)*	SAWL-zhuhn-YĒT-syin, [S] SŌL-zhuh-NĒT-suhn, SAWL-	ˌsɔːlʒən'jiːtsjin, [S] ˌsoːlʒə'niːtsən, ˌsɔːl-
Somali		
people, lang., Africa	suh-MAHL-ē, sō-	sə'maliˑ, soː-
Somalia		
republic, Africa	sō-MAHL-ē-uh, suh-, -MAHL-yuh	soː'maliːə, sə-, -'maljə
Somaliland		
region, Africa	sō-MAHL-ē-LAND, suh-	soː'maliˑˌlænd, sə-
Somers		
John, *1st Baron, English statesman;* Suzanne, *US actress*	SUHM-uhrz	'səməʳz
Somerset		
county, England; pers. name	SUHM-uhr-SET, SUHM-uhr-suht	'səməʳˌset, 'səməʳsət
Somerville		
town, MA, NJ, TN; college, Oxford Univ.	SUHM-uhr-VIL	'səməʳˌvil
Somme		
river, dept., France	SAWM, [S] SUHM, SAHM	sɔːm, [S] 'səm, 'sam
Sommer		
Elke, *German actress*	ZAWM-uhr, [S] SUHM-uhr	'zɔːməʳ, [S] 'səməʳ
Somnii, Palus		
see Palus Somnii		
Somniorum, Lacus		
feature on Moon	LAHK-uhs SAHM-nē-AWR-uhm	'lakəs ˌsamniː'ɔːrəm
Somnus		
Roman personification of sleep	SAHM-nuhs	'samnəs
Somoza		
Nicaraguan political family	suh-MŌ-suh, suh-MŌ-zuh	sə'moːsə, sə'moːzə
Sønderborg		
town, Denmark	SUH(R)N-uhr-BAWRḠ	'sœnəʳˌbɔːʳɣ
Sondheim		
Stephen, *US composer*	SAHND-HĪM	'sandˌhaim
Sondra		
pers. name	SAHN-druh	'sandrə
Songhai		
lang., people, Africa	sahng-GĪ	saŋ'gai
Songkran		
Buddhist New Year	SAWNG-KRAHN	'sɔːŋˌkran
Songo		
lang., Africa	SAHNG-gō, SAWNG-gō	'saŋgoː, 'sɔːŋgoː
Sonia, Sonja, Sonya		
1. pers. name	SŌN-yuh, SAHN-yuh	'soːnjə, 'sanjə
2. Russian	SAWN-yuh	'sɔːnjə
Sonnambula, La		
opera, Bellini	LAH saw-NAHM-byu-lah, LAH suh-NAM-byuh-luh	ˌla sɔː'nambjula, ˌla sə'næmbjələ
Sonny		
pers. name	SUHN-ē	'səniˑ
Sonoma		
county, CA	suh-NŌ-muh	sə'noːmə
Sonora		
city, CA, TX; river, state, Mexico	suh-NŌR-uh, suh-NAWR-uh	sə'noːrə, sə'nɔːrə
Sony		
Japanese corp.	SŌ-nē	'soːniˑ

Key (col. 2): a: **fad** ā: **fade** ah: **father** ar: **Mary** aw: **law** e: **fed** ē: **feed** er: **merry** i: **hid** ī: **hide** ō: **coat** o͞o: **boot** oi: **boy** ow: **now** u: **put** uh: **above** uhr: **bird** ch: **chop** ng: **ring** sh: **show** th: **thick** t͟h: **this** zh: **measure**

Sonya
  see Sonja
Soochow
  see Suzhou
Sophia
  1. pers. name suh-FĒ-uh, suh-FĪ-uh, sō-FĒ-uh, səˈfiːə, səˈfaiə, soːˈfiːə, ˈsoːfiːə
    SŌ-fē-uh
  2. Danish, Swedish su-FĒ-ah suˈfiːaː
  3. German zō-FĒ-ah zoːˈfiːa
  4. Russian SAWF-yuh ˈsoːfjə
Sophianism
  Orthodox Christian sect sō-FĒ-uh-NIZ-uhm, SŌ-fē-uh-, soːˈfiːə͵nizəm, ˈsoːfiːə-,
    SAHF-ē-uh- ˈsafiːə-
Sophie
  1. pers. name SŌ-fē ˈsoːfiˑ
  2. French saw-FĒ soːfiː
  3. German zō-FĒ(-uh) zoːˈfiː(ə)
  4. Swedish su-FĒ suˈfiː
Sophist
  dialogue of Plato SAHF-uhst ˈsafəst
Sophistic
  ancient Greek rhetorical sah-FIS-tik, suh- saˈfistik, sə-
    movement
Sophoclean
  pert. to Sophocles SAHF-uh-KLĒ-uhn ͵safəˈkliːən
Sophocles
  1. Greek playwright; pers. name SAHF-uh-KLĒZ ˈsafə͵kliːz
  2. Mod. Greek saw-faw-KLĒS soːfɔːˈkliːs
Sophonias
  Old Testament book SAHF-uh-NĪ-uhs, SŌ-fuh-NĪ-uhs ͵safəˈnaiəs, ͵soːfəˈnaiəs
Sophonisba
  pers. name SAHF-uh-NIZ-buh, SŌ-fuh- ͵safəˈnizbə, ͵soːfə-
Sophronia
  Roman wife of Maxentius suh-FRŌ-nē-uh səˈfroːniːə
Sophy
  pers. name SŌ-fē ˈsoːfiˑ
Sopron
  city, Hungary SHŌ-PRŌN ˈʃoː͵proːn
Sopwith
  British-designed aircraft SAHP-with ˈsapwiθ
Sora
  bird SŌR-uh, SAWR-uh ˈsoːrə, ˈsoːrə
Sorata
  mtn., village, Bolivia sō-RAHT-uh soːˈratə
Sorbian [Lusatian]
  lang., Germany SAWR-bē-uhn ˈsoːʳbiːən
Sorbonne
  university, Paris, France sawr-BAWN, Ⓢ sawr-BUHN, soːrbɔːn, Ⓢ soːʳbən, soːʳban
    sawr-BAHN
Søren, Sören
  pers. name, Danish SUH(R)-ruhn ˈsœːrən
Sorensen
  Theodore, *US public figure* SAWR-uhn-suhn, SAHR-uhn-suhn ˈsoːrənsən, ˈsarənsən

---

Foreign Sounds: ue: *Fr.* **rue**, *Ger.* **füllen** uh(r): *Fr.* **boeuf**, *Ger.* **Höhle** <u>kh</u>: *Ger.* **ich**, *Scot.* **loch** g̱: *Sp.* **amigo** v̱: *Sp.* **hablar**
hl: *Welsh* **Llanelli.** CAPITALS: primary stress. SMALL CAPS: secondary stress. Ⓢ: U.S. pron. Ⓛ: British pron.

Soroptimist
  member of an international   saw-RAHP-tuh-muhst,   sɔ'raptəməst, sɔ'raptə,mist
     women's organization   saw-RAHP-tuh-MIST

Sorrel
  plant   SAWR-uhl, SAHR-uhl   'sɔːrəl, 'sarəl

Sorrento
  port, Italy   suh-REN-tō   sə'rentoː

Sorvino
  Paul, *US actor*   sawr-VĒ-nō   sɔːʳ'viːnoː

Sosnowiec
  city, Poland   saw-SNŌV-YETS   sɔ'snoːv‚jets

Soter
  pope   SŌT-uhr   'soːʈəʳ

Sotheby
  auction house, London & New   SUHTH-uh-bē   'səðəbiˑ
     York City

Sotho
  Bantu lang. group, Africa   SŌ-thō, SŌT-ō   'soːθoː, 'soːʈoː

Souphanouvong
  president, Laos   su-FAHN-ōō-VAWNG   su'fanuˑ,vɔːŋ

Soûr [Tyre]
  fishing port, Lebanon   SUR   'suʳ

Souris
  river, Manitoba   SUR-uhs   'surəs

Sousa
  John Philip, *US composer*   SŌŌ-zuh   'suːzə

Sousaphone
  musical instrument   SŌŌ-zuh-FŌN   'suːzə,foːn

Souter
  David, *US Supreme Court Justice*   SŌŌT-uhr   'suːʈəʳ

South Africa
  republic, Africa   sowth AF-rik-uh   sauθ 'æfrikə

South African
  pert. to South Africa   sowth AF-rik-uhn   sauθ 'æfrikən

Southall
  1. *British family name*   SUHTH-AWL, SUHTH-uhl   'səð,ɔːl, 'səðəl
  2. *location, London, England*   SOW-THAWL   'sau,θɔːl

Southampton
  1. *city, former county, England*   sowth-HAM(P)-tuhn,   sauθ'hæm(p)tən,
                            sow-THAM(P)-tuhn,   sau'θæm(p)tən,
                            suh-THAM(P)-tuhn,   sə'θæm(p)tən,
                            suh-THAM(P)-tuhn   sə'ðæm(p)tən
  2. *pl. name, US*   sowth-HAM(P)-tuhn,   sauθ'hæm(p)tən,
                sow-THAM(P)-tuhn   sau'θæm(p)tən

South Carolina
  state, US   SOWTH KAR-uh-LĪ-nuh, kuhr-LĪ-nuh,   ‚sauθ ‚kærə'lainə, kəʳ'lainə,
              kar-LĪ-nuh   kæʳ'lainə

Southcote
  pers. name   SOWTH-kuht, SOWTH-KŌT   'sauθkət, 'sauθ,koːt

South Dakota
  state, US   SOWTH duh-KŌT-uh   ‚sauθ də'koːʈə

Southend-on-Sea
  town, England   SOW-THEN-dawn-SĒ   ‚sau‚θendɔːn'siː

Southern Sotho
  lang., Africa   SUHTH-uhrn SŌ-thō, SŌT-ō   'səðəʳn 'soːθoː, 'soːʈoː

Key (col. 2):   a: fad   ā: fade   ah: father   ar: Mary   aw: law   e: fed   ē: feed   er: merry   i: hid   ī: hide   ō: coat   ōō: boot
oi: boy   ow: now   u: put   uh: above   uhr: bird   ch: chop   ng: ring   sh: show   th: thick   <u>th</u>: this   zh: measure

Southey		
Robert, *English poet*	SOW-thē, SUHTH-ē	'sɑuðiˑ, 'səðiˑ
South Glamorgan		
county, Wales	SOWTH gluh-MAWR-guhn	ˌsɑuθ glə'mɔː^{r}gən
Southwark		
borough, England	SUHTH-uhrk, [$] SOWTH-WUHRK	'səðə^{r}k, [$] 'sɑuθˌwə^{r}k
Southwick		
1. town, MA	SOWTH-wik	'sɑuθwik
2. town, England	SOWTH-wik, SUHTH-ik	'sɑuθwik, 'səðik
South Yorkshire		
county, England	sowth YAWRK-shuhr, -SHIR	sɑuθ 'jɔː^{r}kʃə^r, -ˌʃi^r
Souvanna Phouma		
premier, Laos	so͞o-VAHN-uh PO͞O-muh	suˑ'vɑnə 'puːmə
Souverain Cellars		
winery, CA	SO͞O-vuh-RĀN SEL-uhrz	'suːvəˌreːn 'selə^{r}z
Soviet		
Russian Communist system	SŌ-vē-ET, SAHV-ē-, -uht	'soːviːˌet, 'sɑviː-, -ət
Sowerby		
pers. name	SŌ-uhr-bē	'soːə^{r}biˑ
Soweto		
prov, South Africa	suh-WET-ō, suh-WĀT-ō	sə'wet̪oː, sə'weːt̪oː
Soyinka		
Wole, *Nigerian author (Nobel 1986)*	swoi-(Y)ING-kuh	swɔi'(j)iŋkə
Soyuz		
Soviet spacecraft	SUH-YO͞OS, [$] soi-O͞OZ, SOI-O͞OZ	ˌsə'juːs, [$] sɔi'uːz, 'sɔiˌuːz
Spaatz		
Carl, *US militarist*	SPAHTS	'spɑts
Spacek		
Sissy, *US actress*	SPĀ-SEK	'speːˌsek
Spain		
kingdom, Europe	SPĀN	'speːn
Spalding		
Albert, *US violinist; US sporting goods co.*	SPAWL-ding	'spɔːldiŋ
Spam		
tdmk for a meat product	SPAM	'spæm
Spandau		
city, Germany	SHPAHN-DOW, [$] SPAN-DOW	'ʃpɑnˌdɑu, [$] 'spænˌdɑu
Spaniard		
inhabitant of Spain	SPAN-yuhrd	'spænjə^{r}d
Spanish		
lang., Spain, the Americas	SPAN-ish	'spæniʃ
Sparta		
ancient city, country, Greece [Lacedaemon]; *pl. name, US*	SPAHRT-uh	'spɑ^{r}t̪ə
Spartacus		
Roman rebel slave	SPAHRT-uh-kuhs	'spɑ^{r}t̪əkəs
Spartoi		
mythical men from dragon's teeth	SPAHR-TOI	'spɑ^{r}ˌtɔi
Spassky		
Tower, *Moscow*	SPAHS-kyuh, [$] SPAS-kē	'spɑskjəi, [$] 'spæskiˑ
Spaten		
German beer	SHPAHT-n	'ʃpɑtn̩

Spector
   Phil, *US record producer*   SPEK-tuhr   'spektəʳ
Speidel
   tdmk for watchbands   spī-DEL   spɑi'del
Speke
   John, *British explorer*   SPĒK   'spiːk
Spelman
   College, *GA*   SPEL-muhn   'spelmən
Spemann
   Hans, *German zoologist (Nobel*   SHPĀ-MAHN   'ʃpeːˌmɑn
   1935)
Spencer
   Herbert, *English philosopher;*   SPEN(T)-suhr   'spen(t)səʳ
   British noble family; pers. name
Spencerianism
   philosophy of Herbert Spencer   spen-SIR-ē-uh-NIZ-uhm   spen'siriːəˌnizəm
Spener
   Phillip Jacob, *German theologian*   SHPĀ-nuhr   'ʃpeːnəʳ
Spenerism
   teaching of P. J. Spener   SHPĀ-nuh-RIZ-uhm, SPĀ-   'ʃpeːnəˌrizəm, 'speː-
Spengler
   Oswald, *German philosopher*   SHPENG-gluhr, SPENG-gluhr   'ʃpeŋgləʳ, 'speŋgləʳ
Spenser
   Edmund, *English poet; pers. name*   SPEN(T)-suhr   'spen(t)səʳ
Spenserian
   pert. to Spenser   spen(t)-SIR-ē-uhn,   spen(t)'siriːən,
                                             spen(t)-SER-ē-uhn   spen(t)'seriːən
Sperry
   Roger W., *US neurobiologist*   SPER-ē   'speriˑ
   (Nobel 1981)
Spertus
   College of Judaica, *IL*   SPUHRT-uhs   'spəʳʈəs
Spes
   Roman goddess of hope   SPĀS, SPĀZ   'speːs, 'speːz
Spezia, La
   see La Spezia
Sphacteria
   island, Greece   sfak-TIR-ē-uh   sfæk'tiriːə
Sphaerus
   charioteer of Pelops   SFĒ-ruhs, SFIR-uhs   'sfiːrəs, 'sfirəs
Sphinx
   mythical riddler; Egyptian stone   SFINGKS   'sfiŋks
   colossus
Spica
   star   SPĪ-kuh   'spɑikə
Spiegel
   US mail order co.; pers. name   SPĒ-guhl   'spiːgəl
Spiegel, Der
   see Der Spiegel
Spielberg
   Steven, *US film maker*   SPĒL-BUHRG   'spiːlˌbəʳg
Spillane
   Mickey, *US writer*   spuh-LĀN   spə'leːn
Spinifex
   Australian songbird   SPĪ-nuh-FEKS, SPIN-uh-FEKS   'spɑinəˌfeks, 'spinəˌfeks

---

Key (col. 2):   a: **fad**   ā: **fade**   ah: **father**   ar: **Mary**   aw: **law**   e: **fed**   ē: **feed**   er: **merry**   i: **hid**   ī: **hide**   ō: **coat**   o͞o: **boot**
oi: **boy**   ow: **now**   u: **put**   uh: **above**   uhr: **bird**   ch: **chop**   ng: **ring**   sh: **show**   th: **thick**   th̲: **this**   zh: **measure**

Spinks
  Michael, *US boxer*   SPINGKS   'spiŋks
Spinoza
  Benedict (Baruch), *Dutch*   spi-NŌ-zuh   spi'noːzə
    philosopher
Spinozism
  philosophy of Spinoza   spuh-NŌ-zɪz-uhm   spə'noːˌzizəm
Spirea
  plant   spī-RĒ-uh   spɑi'riːə
Spiridon
  see Spyridon
Spiro
  pers. name   SPIR-ō, SPĪ-rō   'spiroː, 'spɑiroː
Spitsbergen
  archipelago, Arctic Ocean SPITS-BUHR-guhn   'spits,bəʳgən
Spittal
  pers. name   SPIT-l   'spitl̩
Spitteler
  C. F. G., *Swiss author (Nobel* SHPIT-l-uhr, SHPIT-luhr 'ʃpitl̩əʳ, 'ʃpitləʳ
    1919)
Split
  city, Croatia   SPLIT   'split
Spock
  Benjamin, *US physician;* Mr., SPAHK   'spɑk
    character, Star Trek
Spode
  tdmk for china   SPŌD   'spoːd
Spokane
  river, city, county, WA; N. spō-KAN   spoː'kæn
    American people
Spoleto
  town, Italy; music festival, SC spuh-LĀT-ō   spə'leːtoː
Sporades
  islands, Greece   SPAWR-uh-DĒZ, SPAHR-uh-DĒZ 'spoːrəˌdiːz, 'spɑrəˌdiːz
Sporádhes [Sporades]
  islands, Greece   spaw-RAH-thās   spɔː'rɑðeːs
Spotsylvania
  county, village, VA   SPAHT-suhl-VĀN-yuh   ˌspɑtsəl'veːnjə
Sprague
  pers. name   SPRĀG   'spreːg
Springboks
  South African rugby team SPRING-BAHKS   'spriŋˌbɑks
Springsteen
  Bruce, *US rock musician* SPRING-STĒN   'spriŋˌstiːn
Spruance
  Raymond, *US militarist* SPROO-uhn(t)s   'spruːən(t)s
Spruille
  pers. name   SPROO-uhl   'spruːəl
Spurius
  pers. name, Latin   SPUR-ē-uhs   'spuriːəs
Sputnik
  Soviet space satellite   SPUT-nik, SPUHT-nik, SPOOT-nik 'sputnik, 'spətnik, 'spuːtnik
Spuyten Duyvil
  creek, NY; district, New York City SPĪT-n DĪ-vuhl 'spɑitn̩ ˌdɑivəl

---

Foreign Sounds: ue: *Fr.* **rue**, *Ger.* **fü**llen uh(r): *Fr.* **b**oeuf, *Ger.* H**öh**le <u>kh</u>: *Ger.* i**ch**, *Scot.* lo**ch** g̶: *Sp.* ami**g**o v̠: *Sp.* ha**b**lar
hl: *Welsh* **Ll**anelli.   CAPITALS: primary stress.   SMALL CAPS: secondary stress.   ⑤: U.S. pron.   ⑫: British pron.

Spyridon, Spiridon
  pers. name, Mod. Greek   spē-RĒ-<u>th</u>awn   spiː'riːðɔːn

Spyro Gyra
  rock group   SPĪ-rō JĪ-ruh   ˌspairoː 'dʒairə

Spyros
  pers. name, Greek   SPĒ-raws, SPĒ-rōs   'spiːrɔːs, 'spiːroːs

Squab
  bird   SKWAHB   'skwab

Squacco
  heron   SKWAHK-ō, SKWAW-kō   'skwakoː, 'skwɔːkoː

Squaxin Island
  Indian reservation, US   SKWAHK-suhn   'skwaksən

Sranan Tongo
  lang., S. America   SRAHN-uhn TAWNG-gō, TAHNG-gō   ˌsranən 'tɔːŋgoː, 'taŋgoː

Srbija [Serbia]
  republic, E. Europe   SUHR-bē-AH   'sərbiːˌa

Sri
  Hindu prosperity goddess; pers.   SHRĒ, SRĒ   'ʃriː, 'sriː
    name

Sri-Jayawardenapura
  city, Sri Lanka   SRĒ-JĪ-uh-wuhr-duhn-uh-PUR-uh,   'sriːˌdʒaiəwəʳdənə'purə,
            SHRĒ-   'ʃriː-

Sri Lanka [Ceylon]
  island state, Indian Ocean   srē LAHNG-kuh, shrē   sriː 'laŋkə, ʃriː

Sri Lankan
  pert. to Sri Lanka   srē LAHNG-kuhn, shrē   sriː 'laŋkən, ʃriː

Srinagar
  city, India   sri-NUHG-uhr, shri-   sri'nəgəʳ, ʃri-

Srinivasa
  pers. name   SRĒ-nuh-VAHS-uh, SHRĒ-   ˌsriːnə'vasə, ˌʃriː-

St.
  see under Saint

Staatliche Weinbaudomäne
  German wine concern   SHTAHT-li<u>kh</u>-uh   'ʃtatliçə 'vainˌbaudoːˌmenə
            VĪN-BOW-dō-MEN-uh

Stabat Mater
  Latin hymn   STAHB-AHT MAHT-uhr   'stab,at 'matəʳ

Stabler
  Kenny, *US football player*   STĀ-bluhr   'steːbləʳ

Stacey, Stacy
  pers. name   STĀ-sē   'steːsiˑ

Stade Olympique
  stadium, Montreal, Canada   STAHD aw-leⁿ-PĒK   staːd ɔːlẽpiːk

Stafford
  Robert Theodore, *US politician;*   STAF-uhrd   'stæfəʳd
    borough, England; US pl. name

Staffordshire
  county, England   STAF-uhrd-shuhr, -SHIR   'stæfəʳdʃəʳ, -ˌʃiʳ

Stahl
  Lesley, *US journalist*   STAHL   'stal

Stakhanovism
  Soviet system to increase   stuh-KAHN-uh-VIZ-uhm   stə'kanəˌvizəm
    production

Key (col. 2):   a: fad   ā: fade   ah: father   ar: Mary   aw: law   e: fed   ē: feed   er: merry   i: hid   ī: hide   ō: coat   ōō: boot
oi: boy   ow: now   u: put   uh: above   uhr: bird   ch: chop   ng: ring   sh: show   th: thick   <u>th</u>: this   zh: measure

Stakhanovite
   Soviet worker who surpasses   stuh-KAHN-uh-VĪT   stə'kanə,vait
     quotas

Stalin
   Joseph, *leader, USSR*   STAHL-yin, Ⓢ STAHL-uhn,   'staːljin, Ⓢ 'stalən, 'stal,iːn,
                               STAHL-ĒN, STAL-uhn   'stælən

Stalingrad [Volgograd]
   city, Russia   STUHL-yin-GRAHT,   ,stəljin'grat, Ⓢ 'stalən,græd,
            Ⓢ STAHL-uhn-GRAD, -GRAHD   -,grad

Stalinism
   communist principles associated   STAHL-uh-NIZ-uhm, STAL-   'stalə,nizəm, 'stæl-
     with Stalin

Stalinist
   pert. to Stalin; *advocate of*   STAHL-uh-nuhst   'stalənəst
     Stalinism

Stallone
   Sylvester, *US actor*   stuh-LŌN   stə'loːn

Stamboul, Stambul
   part of Istanbul, Turkey   stahm-B͞OOL, stam-B͞OOL   stam'buːl, stæm'buːl

Stamford
   city, CT   STAM-fuhrd   'stæmfəʳd

Stan
   pers. name   STAN   'stæn

Stanburrough
   pers. name   STAN-BUHR-uh, STAN-bruh   'stæn,bərə, 'stænbrə

Standish
   pers. name   STAN-dish   'stændiʃ

Stanford
   University, *CA; pers. name*   STAN-fuhrd   'stænfəʳd

Stanford-Binet
   psychological test   STAN-fuhrd-buh-NĀ   ,stænfəʳdbə'neː

Stanislas
   1. pers. name   STAN-uh-SLAWS, -SLAHS   'stænə,slɔːs, -,slas
   2. French   stah-nē-SLAHS   staːniːslas

Stanislaus
   1. pers. name   STAN-uh-SLAWS, -SLOWS   'stænə,slɔːs, -,slaus
   2. German   SHTAHN-is-LOWS, STAHN-   'ʃtanis,laus, 'stan-

Stanislav
   pers. name, Czech   STAHN-yis-LAHF   'staːnjis,laːf

Stanislavski, -sky
   Konstantin, *Russian actor,*   STUHN-yi-SLAHF-ski,   ,stənji'slaːfsḳij,
     producer, director   Ⓢ STAN-uh-SLAHV-skē   Ⓢ ,stænə'slavski·

Stanisław
   pers. name, Polish   stah-NĒ-slahf   staːˈniːsɫaːf

Stanko
   pers. name, Serbo-Croatian   STAHNG-kaw   'staːŋkɔː

Stanley
   pers. name; tdmk for tools   STAN-lē   'stænli·

Stanovoi
   mtn. range, Russia   STAHN-uh-VOI, STAN-uh-VOI   'stanə,vɔi, 'stænə,vɔi

Stansfield
   pers. name (S. Turner)   STANZ-FĒLD   'stænz,fiːld

Stanton
   pers. name   STANT-n, Ⓔ STAN-tuhn   'stæntn̩, Ⓔ 'stæntən

Foreign Sounds: ue: *Fr.* **rue**, *Ger.* **füllen**   uh(r): *Fr.* **boeuf**, *Ger.* **Höhle**   <u>kh</u>: *Ger.* **ich**, *Scot.* **loch**   g̃: *Sp.* **amigo**   <u>v</u>: *Sp.* **hablar**
hl: *Welsh* **Llanelli**.   CAPITALS: primary stress.   SMALL CAPS: secondary stress.   Ⓢ: U.S. pron.   Ⓔ: British pron.

Stanwyck
   Barbara, *US actress*   STAN-wik   'stænwik

Staples
   pers. name   STĀ-puhlz   'steːpəlz

Stapleton
   Jean, *US actress*   STĀ-puhl-tuhn   'steːpəltən

Stark
   Johannes, *German physicist*   SHTAHRK   'ʃtaʳk
   (Nobel 1919)

Starkað
   legendary Scandinavian hero   STAHR-KAH<u>TH</u>, STAHR-kuh<u>th</u>   'staʳˌkað, 'staʳkəð

Stasi [Ministerium für Staatssicherheit]
   East German security   SHTAHZ-ē   'ʃtaziˑ
   organization

Stassen
   Harold E., *US politician*   STAS-uhn   'stæsən

Staten Island
   borough, New York City   STAT-n Ī-luhnd   ˌstætn̩ 'ailənd

Statius
   Roman poet   STĀ-sh(ē-)uhs   'steːʃ(iː)əs

Statler
   Brothers, *country music group;*   STAT-luhr   'stætləʳ
   hotel, New York City

Staubach
   Roger, *US football player*   STOW-BAHK   'stauˌbak

Staubbach
   waterfall, Switzerland   SHTOWP-BAH<u>KH</u>, Ⓢ STOWP-BAHK   'ʃtaupˌbax, Ⓢ 'staupˌbak

Stauder
   German beer   SHTOWD-uhr   'ʃtaudəʳ

Staudinger
   Hermann, *German organic*   SHTOWD-ing-uhr   'ʃtaudiŋəʳ
   chemist (Nobel 1953)

Staunton
   1. *city, IL*   STAWNT-n, STAHNT-n   'stɔːntn̩, 'stantn̩
   2. *city, VA*   STANT-n   'stæntn̩

Stavanger
   port, Norway   stuh-VAHNG-uhr   stə'vaŋəʳ

Stavropol [Tol'yatti]
   city, Russia   stahv-RAW-puhl, stahv-RŌ-puhl   staːv'rɔːpəl, stav'roːpəl

Stearns
   pers. name   STUHRNZ   'stəʳnz

Steele
   pers. name   STĒL   'stiːl

Steen
   1. Jan, *Dutch painter*   STĀN   'steːn
   2. Marguerite, *English novelist*   STĒN   'stiːn
   3. *pers. name, Danish*   STIN   'stin

Steenburgen
   Mary, *US actress*   STĒN-BUHR-guhn   'stiːnˌbəʳgən

Stefan
   1. *pers. name, Bulgarian, Polish*   STEF-ahn   'stefaːn
   2. *German*   SHTEF-ahn   'ʃtefan

Stefán
   pers. name, Icelandic   STE-FOWN   'steˌfaun

Key (col. 2):   a: fa**d**   ā: fa**d**e   ah: f**a**ther   ar: **Mary**   aw: l**aw**   e: f**e**d   ē: f**ee**d   er: m**erry**   i: h**i**d   ī: h**i**de   ō: c**oa**t   ōō: b**oo**t
oi: b**oy**   ow: n**ow**   u: p**u**t   uh: **a**bove   uhr: b**ir**d   ch: **ch**op   ng: ri**ng**   sh: **sh**ow   th: **th**ick   <u>th</u>: **th**is   zh: mea**s**ure

Ṡtefan
   pers. name, Romanian   shte-FAHN   ʃteˈfɑn

Stefanie
   see Stephanie

Stefano
   pers. name, Italian   STĀ-fahn-ō, STEF-ahn-ō   ˈsteːfɑnoː, ˈstefɑnoː

Steffi
   pers. name   SHTEF-ē   ˈʃtefiˑ

Steffl
   Austrian beer   SHTEF-uhl   ˈʃtefəl

Stegner
   pers. name   STEG-nuhr   ˈstegnəʳ

Stegosauria
   dinosaur suborder   STEG-uh-SAWR-ē-uh   ˌstegəˈsɔːriːə

Stegosaurus
   dinosaur   STEG-uh-SAWR-uhs   ˌstegəˈsɔːrəs

Steichen
   Edward, *US photographer*   STĪ-kuhn   ˈstɑikən

Steiermark
   state, Austria   SHTĪR-MAHRK   ˈʃtaiʳˌmɑʳk

Steiger
   Rod, *US actor*   STĪ-guhr   ˈstɑigəʳ

Stein
   1. Gertrude, *US writer;* William Howard, *US biochemist (Nobel 1972); pers. name*   STĪN   ˈstɑin
   2. Norwegian   STĀN   ˈsteːn

Steinbeck
   John, *US author (Nobel 1962)*   STĪN-BEK   ˈstɑinˌbek

Steinberg
   David, *Canadian comedian, actor*   STĪN-BUHRG   ˈstɑinˌbəʳg

Steinberger
   Jack, *German-born US physicist (Nobel 1988)*   STĪN-BUHR-guhr   ˈstɑinˌbəʳgəʳ

Steinbrenner
   George, *US businessman*   STĪN-BREN-uhr   ˈstɑinˌbrenəʳ

Steinem
   Gloria, *US feminist, writer, editor*   STĪ-nuhm   ˈstɑinəm

Steinhäuser
   German beer   SHTĪN-HOI-zuhr   ˈʃtɑinˌhɔizəʳ

Steinlager
   New Zealand beer   STĪN-LAH-guhr, SHTĪN-   ˈstɑinˌlɑˈgəʳ, ˈʃtɑin-

Steinway
   piano manufacturer   STĪN-WĀ   ˈstɑinˌweː

Stella Artois
   Belgian beer   STEL-uh ahr-TWAH   ˈstelə ɑʳˈtwɑ

Stellenbosch
   town, South Africa   STEL-uhn-BAWS, STEL-uhn-BUSH   ˈstelənˌbɔːs, ˈstelənˌbuʃ

Sten
   pers. name, Norwegian, Swedish   STĀN   ˈsteːn

Stendhal
   pseudonym of Marie Henri Beyle   steⁿ-DAHL, Ⓢ sten-DAHL, stan-DAHL   stẽdɑːl, Ⓢ stenˈdɑl, stænˈdɑl

---

Foreign Sounds: ue: *Fr.* **rue**, *Ger.* **füllen**   uh(r): *Fr.* **bœuf**, *Ger.* **Höhle**   kh: *Ger.* i**ch**, *Scot.* lo**ch**   g̃: *Sp.* ami**g**o   v̦: *Sp.* ha**b**lar
hl: *Welsh* **Ll**anelli.   CAPITALS: primary stress.   SMALL CAPS: secondary stress.   Ⓢ: U.S. pron.   Ⓛ: British pron.

Stengel-Huggins
   Field, *former ballpark, St.*   STENG-guhl-HUHG-uhnz   'steŋgəl'həgənz
    Petersburg, FL

Stennis
   John Cornelius, *US politician*   STEN-uhs   'stenəs

Stentor
   Thracian herald in Trojan War   STEN-TAWR, STENT-uhr   'sten,tɔːʳ, 'stentəʳ

Stepan
   1. pers. name, Russian   styi-PAHN   stji'paːn
   2. Serbo-Croatian   STEP-ahn   'stepaːn

Stephan
   1. pers. name, German   SHTEF-ahn   'ʃtefan
   2. Norwegian   STĀ-fahn   'steːfan

Stéphane
   pers. name, French   stā-FAHN   steːfaːn

Stéphanie
   pers. name, French   stā-fah-NĒ   steːfaːniː

Stephanie, Stefanie
   pers. name   STEF-uh-nē   'stefaniˑ

Stephanopoulos
   George, *US government official* STEF-uh-NAHP-uh-luhs   ,stefə'napələs

Stephanos
   pers. name, Mod. Greek   STEF-ah-naws   'stefanɔːs

Stephanus
   pers. name, Dutch   stā-FAHN-ues   steː'faːnys

Stephen
   1. pers. name   STĒ-vuhn   'stiːvən
   2. French   stā-FEN   steːfen
   3. German   SHTEF-uhn   'ʃtefən

Stéphen
   pers. name, French   stā-FEN   steːfen

Sterculia
   plant   stuhr-K(Y)OO-lē-uh   stəʳk(j)uːliːə

Sterling
   pers. name   STUHR-ling   'stəʳliŋ

Stern
   1. Isaac, *US violinist;* Otto,   STUHRN   'stəʳn
    German-born US physicist
    (Nobel 1943)
   2. German beer   SHTERN   'ʃteʳn

Sterne
   Laurence, *English writer*   STUHRN   'stəʳn

Sterner
   pers. name   STUHR-nuhr   'stəʳnəʳ

Sterope
   mother of Oenomaus; star in STER-uh-pē, STIR-uh-pē   'sterəpiˑ, 'stirəpiˑ
    Pleiades

Steropes
   a Cyclops   STER-uh-PĒZ, STIR-uh-PĒZ 'sterə,piːz, 'stirə,piːz

Stesemann
   Gustav, *political leader*   SHTĀ-zuh-MAHN   'ʃteːzə,man

Stetson
   tdmk for a hat; pers. name   STET-suhn   'stetsən

Stettin
   German form of Szczecin   shte-TĒN   ʃte'tiːn

Key (col. 2):   a: fad ā: fade ah: father ar: Mary aw: law e: fed ē: feed er: merry i: hid ī: hide ō: coat ōō: boot
oi: boy ow: now u: put uh: above uhr: bird ch: chop ng: ring sh: show th: thick th̲: this zh: measure

Stettinius
  Edward R., Jr., *US political leader*   stuh-TIN-ē-uhs, ste-   stə'tiniːəs, ste-
Steuben
  1. *county, IN, NY; pers. name*   st(y)o͞o-BEN, ST(Y)O͞O-buhn   st(j)uː'ben, 'st(j)uːbən
  2. *US glassmakers*   st(y)o͞o-BEN   st(j)uː'ben
  3. *Friedrich von, Baron, Prussian*   SHTOI-buhn   'ʃtɔibən
     soldier in US
Steubenville
  city, OH   ST(Y)O͞O-buhn-VIL   'st(j)uːbən,vil
Stevan
  pers. name, Serbo-Croatian   STEV-ahn   'stevɑːn
Steve
  pers. name   STĒV   'stiːv
Steven
  pers. name   STĒ-vuhn   'stiːvən
Stevie
  pers. name   STĒ-vē   'stiːviˑ
Stewart
  pers. name   ST(Y)O͞O-uhrt, ST(Y)U-uhrt,   'st(j)uːəʳt, 'st(j)uəʳt, 'st(j)uʳt
           ST(Y)URT
Sthenelas
  son of Evadne   STHEN-l-uhs   'sθenl̩əs
Sthenelus
  companion of Heracles; son of   STHEN-l-uhs   'sθenl̩əs
     Perseus and Andromeda
Stheno
  Gorgon   STHEN-ō   'sθenoː
Stich
  Michael, German tennis player   SHTĒKH, Ⓢ STĒK   'ʃtiːç, Ⓢ 'ʃtiːx, 'stiːk
Stieglitz
  Alfred, US photographer   STĒG-luhts   'stiːgləts
Stieng
  lang., people, South Vietnam   STĒNG   'stiːŋ
Stiers
  David Ogden, US actor   STĪRZ   'staiʳz
Stigler
  George J., US economist (Nobel   STIG-luhr   'stigləʳ
     1982)
Stigwood
  Robert, Australian film, record   STIG-WUD, STIG-wuhd   'stig,wud, 'stigwəd
     producer
Stijn
  pers. name, Dutch   STĪN   'stain
Stillaguamish
  Indian reservation, US   STIL-uh-GWAHM-ish   ,stilə'gwɑmiʃ
Stiller
  Jerry, US actor   STIL-uhr   'stiləʳ
Stillingia
  plant   stuh-LING-ē-uh, stuh-LIN-j(ē-)uh   stə'liŋiːə, stə'lindʒ(iː)ə
Stillwell, Stilwell
  pers. name   STIL-WEL, STIL-wuhl   'stil,wel, 'stilwəl
Stilton
  English cheese   STILT-n   'stiltn̩
Stith
  pers. name   STITH   'stiθ

Foreign Sounds: ue: *Fr.* **rue**, *Ger.* **füllen**   uh(r): *Fr.* **boeuf**, *Ger.* **Höhle**   kh: *Ger.* **ich**, *Scot.* **loch**   g̱: *Sp.* **amigo**   v: *Sp.* **hablar**
hl: *Welsh* **Llanelli**.   CAPITALS: primary stress.   SMALL CAPS: secondary stress.   Ⓢ: U.S. pron.   Ⓛ: British pron.

Stoa
  Greek colonnade   STŌ-uh   'stoːə

Stockard
  pers. name (S. Channing)   STAHK-uhrd   'stakəʳd

Stockholm
  city, Sweden   STAHK-HŌ(L)M   'stak,hoː(l)m

Stockton
  Dick, *US sports broadcaster; city,*   STAHK-tuhn   'staktən
    CA

Stoddard
  Brandon, *US TV and film co.*   STAHD-uhrd   'stadəʳd
    executive

Stoic
  adherent of Stoicism   STŌ-ik   'stoːik

Stoicism
  philosophy of Zeno of Citium   STŌ-uh-SIZ-uhm   'stoːə,sizəm

Stojan
  pers. name, Serbo-Croatian   STAW-yahn   'stɔːjɑːn

Stokowski
  Leopold, *US conductor*   stuh-KAWF-skē, stuh-KAWV-skē,   stə'kɔːfskiʳ, stə'kɔːvskiʳ,
                               stuh-KOW-skē   stə'kauskiʳ

STOL
  short takeoff and landing   STAHL, ES-tahl   'stal, 'estal

Stolichnaya
  vodka brand   stuh-LICH-nuh-yuh,   stə'litʃnəjə, ˌstəlitʃ'nai(j)ə
                               STUHL-ich-NĪ-(y)uh

Stone
  Sir Richard, *English economist*   STŌN   'stoːn
    (Nobel 1984)

Stonehenge
  megalithic monument, England   STŌN-HENJ   'stoːn,hendʒ

Stoppard
  Tom, *Czech-born British*   STAHP-AHRD, STAHP-uhrd   'stap,ɑʳd, 'stapəʳd
    playwright

Store Bededag
  Danish prayer day   STŌR-uh BĀD-uh-DAHK   'stoːrə 'beːdə,dak

Storting [Lagthing]
  parliament, Norway   STAWR-ting   'stɔːʳtiŋ

Stouffer
  US food products co.   STŌ-fuhr   'stoːfəʳ

Stoughton
  city, MA   STŌT-n   'stoːtn̩

Stour
  1. *river, Suffolk & Essex, England*   STUR   'stuʳ
  2. *river, Kent, England*   STUR, STOWR   'stuʳ, 'stauʳ
  3. *river, Warwickshire, England*   STOWR, STŌR   'stauʳ, 'stoːʳ
  4. *other rivers, England*   *usually* STOWR   *usually* 'stauʳ

Stowe
  urban area, PA; city, VT   STŌ   'stoː

Stow-on-the-Wold
  town, England   STŌ-AHN-<u>thuh</u>-WŌLD   ˌstoːˌanðə'woːld

Stoyan
  pers. name, Bulgarian   staw-YAHN   stɔː'jɑːn

Strabo
  Greek geographer   STRĀ-bō   'streːboː

Key (col. 2):   a: fad   ā: fade   ah: father   ar: Mary   aw: law   e: fed   ē: feed   er: merry   i: hid   ī: hide   ō: coat   o͞o: boot
oi: boy   ow: now   u: put   uh: above   uhr: bird   ch: chop   ng: ring   sh: show   th: thick   <u>th</u>: this   zh: measure

Strachan

   pers. name   STRAWN, STRAH<u>KH</u>-uhn   'strɔːn, 'strɑxən

Strachey

   Lytton, *English writer*   STRĀ-chē   'streːtʃiˑ

Stradivari

   Antonio, *Italian violin maker*   STRAHD-uh-VAHR-ē,   ,strɑdə'vɑˡiˑ, ,strædə'væriˑ,
                       STRAD-uh-VAR-ē, STRAD-uh-VER-ē   ,strædə'veri·

Stradivarius

   Antonius, *Latin form of* A.   STRAD-uh-VAR-ē-uhs,   ,strædə'væˡiːəs,
   Stradivari   STRAD-uh-VER-ē-uhs   ,strædə'veriːəs

Stram

   Hank Louis, *US football coach,*   STRAM   'stræm
   commentator

Strasberg

   Susan, *US actress*   STRAS-BUHRG, STRAHS-BUHRG   'stræs,bəˡg, 'strɑs,bəˡg

Strasbourg

   city, France   strahs-B̄OOR, Ⓢ STRAHS-BURG,   strɑːsbuːr, Ⓢ 'strɑs,buˡg,
                   STRAHZ-   'strɑz-

Strasbourgeoise, La Belle

   see La Belle Strasbourgeoise

Strasbrau

   German beer   SHTRAHS-BROW   'ʃtrɑs,brɑu

Strassburg

   German form of Strassbourg   SHTRAHS-BURK   'ʃtrɑs,buˡk

Strategia

   Athenian generalship   stra-TĒ-jē-uh   stræ'tiːdʒiːə

Stratford-on-Avon

   town, England   STRAT-fuhrd-AHN-Ā-vuhn,   ,strætfəˡd,ɑn'eːvən,
                   Ⓢ -Ā-VAHN   Ⓢ -'eː,vɑn

Stratford-upon-Avon

   town, England   STRAT-fuhrd-uh-PAHN-Ā-vuhn, ,strætfəˡdə,pɑn'eːvən,
                   Ⓢ -Ā-VAHN   Ⓢ -'eː,vɑn

Strathclyde

   medieval Celtic kingdom; region, strath-KLĪD   stræθ'klaid
   Scotland

Strauss

   1. *family of Austrian composers* SHTROWS   'ʃtrɑus
   2. Levi, *US clothing manufacturer;* STROWS   'strɑus
   Peter, *US actor*

Stravinsky

   Igor, *US composer*   struhv-YĒN-skyi,   strəv'jiːnskjij,
                   Ⓢ struh-VIN(T)-skē   Ⓢ strə'vin(t)skiˑ

Středočeský

   region, Czech republic   STRED-uh-CHES-kē   'stredə,tʃeskiˑ

Streep

   Meryl, *US actress*   STRĒP   'striːp

Strega

   tdmk for a liqueur   STRĀ-guh   'streːgə

Streisand

   Barbra, *US singer, actress*   STRĪ-zuhnd, STRĪ-ZAND   'straizənd, 'strai,zænd

Stresemann

   Gustav, *German statesman (Nobel* SHTRĀ-zuh-MAHN   'ʃtreːzə,man
   1926)

Foreign Sounds: ue: *Fr.* **rue**, *Ger.* **füllen** uh(r): *Fr.* **boeuf**, *Ger.* **Höhle** <u>kh</u>: *Ger.* i**ch**, *Scot.* lo**ch** g̃: *Sp.* ami**g**o <u>v</u>: *Sp.* ha**b**lar
hl: *Welsh* **Ll**anelli. CAPITALS: primary stress. SMALL CAPS: secondary stress. Ⓢ: U.S. pron. Ⓔ: British pron.

Strindberg
  August, *Swedish writer*   STRIN-BER, Ⓢ STRIN(D)-BUHRG, STRIN-BER-ē   'strin‚ber, Ⓢ 'strin(d)‚bəᴿg, 'strin‚beriʳ

Stroessner
  Alfredo, *president, Paraguay*   STRES-nuhr   'stresnəʳ

Stroganoff
  beef dish   STRŌ-guh-NAWF   'stroːgə‚nɔːf

Stroheim
  see Von Stroheim

Stroh's
  US beer   STRŌZ   'stroːz

Strom
  pers. name   STRAHM   'strɑm

Stromboli
  island, volcano, Italy   strahm-BŌ-lē   strɑm'boːliʲ

strontium
  element   STRAHN-ch(ē-)uhm, STRAHNT-ē-uhm   'strɑntʃ(iː)əm, 'strɑntiːəm

Strophanthus
  plant   struh-FAN-thuhs   strə'fænθəs

Strophius
  son of Crisus   STRŌ-fē-uhs   'stroːfiːəs

Struthers
  pers. name   STRUHTH-uhrz   'strəðəʳz

Struthiomimus
  dinosaur   STROO-thē-ō-MĪ-muhs   ‚struːθiːoː'maiməs

Stu
  pers. name   STOO   'stuː

Stuart
  pers. name   ST(Y)OO-uhrt, ST(Y)U-uhrt, ST(Y)URT   'st(j)uːəʳt, 'st(j)uəʳt, 'st(j)uʳt

Stubai Alps
  mtn. range, Austria   st(y)oo-BĪ, shtoo-BĪ   st(j)uː'bai, ʃtuː'bai

Stubaier Alpen
  mtn. range, Austria (German)   shtoo-BĪ-uhr AHL-puhn   ʃtuː'baiər 'alpən

Studebaker
  US car   STOOD-uh-BĀ-kuhr   'stuːdə‚beːkəʳ

Studs
  pers. name   STUHDZ   'stədz

Stuka
  German warplane   SHTOO-kuh, STOO-kuh   'ʃtuːkə, 'stuːkə

Stumpf
  Field, *former ballpark, Lancaster, PA*   STUHM(P)F   'stəm(p)f

Stundism
  evangelical Russian protestant movement   SHTUN-DIZ-uhm, STUN-, STUHN-   'ʃtun‚dizəm, 'stun-, 'stən-

Sturm und Drang
  style of German literature   SHTURM unt DRAHNG, STURM   ‚ʃtuʳm unt 'drɑŋ, ‚stuʳm

Sturtevant
  Alfred H., *US geneticist*   STUHRT-uh-vuhnt   'stəʳţəvənt

Stuttgart
  1. prov & town, Germany   SHTUT-GAHRT, Ⓢ STUHT-GAHRT, STOOT-GAHRT   'ʃtut‚gɑʳt, Ⓢ 'stət‚gɑʳt, 'stuːt‚gɑʳt
  2. city, AR   STUHT-GAHRT, STUHT-guhrt   'stət‚gɑʳt, 'stətgəʳt

---

Key (col. 2):   a: fad   ā: fade   ah: father   ar: Mary   aw: law   e: fed   ē: feed   er: merry   i: hid   ī: hide   ō: coat   oo: boot
oi: boy   ow: now   u: put   uh: above   uhr: bird   ch: chop   ng: ring   sh: show   th: thick   th: this   zh: measure

Stuyvesant

    1. Peter, *Dutch official in America*   STUH(R)-vuh-SAHNT,   'stœivə‚sɑnt, ⑤ 'stɑivəsənt
                      ⑤ STĪ-vuh-suhnt

    2. pers. name   STĪ-vuh-suhnt   'stɑivəsənt

Stygian

    pert. to the river Styx *or* Hades   STIJ-ē-uhn   'stidʒiːən

Stylian

    pers. name, Albanian   STĒL-yahn   'stiːljɑn

Stylianou

    pers. name, Greek   stil-YAHN-ōo   stil'jɑnuː

Styne

    Jule, *US composer, producer*   STĪN   'stɑin

Styr

    river, Ukraine   STIR   'stiʳ

Styracosaurus

    dinosaur   stuh-RAK-uh-SAWR-uhs,   stə‚rækə'sɔːrəs,
              STĪ-RAK-uh-SAWR-uhs   ‚stɑi‚rækə'sɔːrəs

Styrofoam

    tdmk for expanded plastic   STĪ-ruh-FŌM   'stɑirə‚foːm

Styx

    stream, Greece; Underworld river   STIKS   'stiks
      in Greek myth

Suakin

    port, Sudan   SWAHK-uhn   'swɑkən

Suarez

    Xavier Louis, *US politician*   SWAHR-ĀS, SWAHR-EZ   'swɑr‚eːs, 'swɑr‚ez

Subang

    airport, Kuala Lumpur, Malaysia   sōo-BAHNG   suː'bɑŋ

Subanun

    lang., people, Philippine Islands   sōo-BAH-NŌON   suː'bɑ‚nuːn

Subaru

    tdmk of a Japanese car co.   SŌO-buh-RŌO   'suːbə‚ruː

Subhas

    pers. name, Bengali   shub-HAHSH, sub-HAHSH   ʃub'hɑʃ, sub'hɑʃ

Subic

    bay, city, Philippines   SŌO-bik   'suːbik

Sublette

    county, WY   suh-BLET   sə'blet

Subotica, Subotitsa

    city, Serbia   SŌO-buh-TĒT-suh   'suːbə‚tiːtsə

Subrahmanyan

    pers. name (S. Chandrasekhar)   SUB-ruh-MAHN-yuhn   ‚subrə'mɑnjən

Subura

    district of ancient Rome   SUHB-(y)uh-ruh   'səb(j)ərə

Succoth

    see Sukkoth

Suceava

    river, county, town, Romania   sōo-CHAHV-uh   suː'tʃɑvə

Suchinda

    pers. name, Thai   su-CHIN-duh   su'tʃində

Suchos [Sebek]

    Egyptian crocodile god   SUKH-uhs, SŌO-khuhs   'suxəs, 'suːxəs

Su-chou, Suchow

    see Suzhou

Foreign Sounds: ue: *Fr.* **rue**, *Ger.* füllen uh(r): *Fr.* **boeuf**, *Ger.* Höhle <u>kh</u>: *Ger.* ich, *Scot.* loch g̃: *Sp.* amigo v̲: *Sp.* hablar
hl: *Welsh* Llanelli. CAPITALS: primary stress. SMALL CAPS: secondary stress. ⑤: U.S. pron. Ⓛ: British pron.

Sucre
   city, Bolivia   SOO-krā   'suːkreː

Sudan
   region, republic, Africa   soo-DAN, soo-DAHN   suː'dæn, suː'dɑn

Sudanese
   pert. to Sudan *or to the Republic*   SOOD-n-ĒZ, -ĒS   ‚suːdn̩'iːz, -'iːs
    of Sudan

Sudanic
   former lang. family   soo-DAN-ik, soo-DAHN-ik   suː'dænik, suː'dɑnik

Sudbury
   1. town, Canada, England   SUHD-b(uh-)rē   'sədb(ə)riˑ
   2. town, MA   SUHD-BER-ē, SUHD-b(uh-)rē   'səd‚beriˑ, 'sədb(ə)riˑ

Sudeste
   region, Brazil   soo-DES-tā   suː'desteː

Sudeten
   mountainous region, Europe   soo-DĀT-n   suː'deːtn̩

Sudetenland
   mountainous region, Europe   soo-DĀT-n-LAHNT,   suː'deːtn̩‚lɑnt,
       Ⓢ soo-DĀT-n-LAND   Ⓢ suː'deːtn̩‚lænd

Sudetes
   mtn. range, Czech republic   soo-DIT-ēz   suː'diṭiˑz

Sue
   pers. name   SOO   'suː

Suetonius
   Roman historian   swē-TŌ-nē-uhs, SOO-uh-TŌ-nē-uhs   swiː'toːniːəs, ‚suːə'toːniːəs

Sueur, La
   see La Sueur

Suez
   gulf, canal, isthmus, city, Middle   soo-EZ, SOO-EZ, Ⓔ SOO-iz   suː'ez, 'suː‚ez, Ⓔ 'suːiz
    East

Suffolk
   county, England; county, MA, NY   SUHF-uhk, Ⓢ *also* SUHF-AWK   'səfək, Ⓢ *also* 'səf‚ɔːk

Sufi
   member, Muslim sect   SOO-fē   'suːfiˑ

Sufiism
   religion   SOO-fē-IZ-uhm   'suːfiː‚izəm

Sufism
   religion   SOO-FIZ-uhm   'suː‚fizəm

Suharo
   pers. name, Japanese   soo-hahr-ō   suːhɑroː

Suharto
   president, Indonesia   su-HAHRT-ō   su'hɑʳṭoː

Suisse, La [Switzerland]
   republic, Europe   lah SWĒS   lɑː sᵫiːs

Sukarno
   Indonesian political leader   su-KAHR-nō   su'kɑʳnoː

Sukenori
   pers. name, Japanese   suk-en-ō-rē   sukenoːriˑ

Sukhothai
   city, Thailand   SUK-uh-TĪ   'sukə'tai

Sukiro
   pers. name, Japanese   suk-ē-rō   sukiːroː

Sukkoth, Succoth
   Jewish holiday   SUK-uhs, SUK-ōt, SUK-ōs, soo-KŌS,   'sukəs, 'sukoːt, 'sukoːs,
       soo-KAWT   su''koːs, su''kɔːt

Key (col. 2):   a: fad   ā: fade   ah: father   ar: Mary   aw: law   e: fed   ē: feed   er: merry   i: hid   ī: hide   ō: coat   oo: boot
oi: boy   ow: now   u: put   uh: above   uhr: bird   ch: chop   ng: ring   sh: show   th: thick   th: this   zh: measure

Şükrü
  pers. name, Turkish   shue-KRUE   ʃyː'kryː

Suku
  lang., people, Africa   suh-KOO   sə'kuː

Sukuma
  lang., people, Africa   suh-KOO-muh   sə'kuːmə

Sul
  region, Brazil   SOOL   'suːl

Sulawesi [Celebes]
  island, Indonesia   SOO-luh-WĀ-sē   ˌsuːlə'weːsiˈ

Sulawesi Selatan
  prov, Indonesia   SOO-luh-WĀ-sē sā-LAH-TAHN   ˌsuːlə'weːsiˈ seː'la,tɑn

Sulawesi Tengah
  prov, Indonesia   SOO-luh-WĀ-sē TENG-guh   ˌsuːlə'weːsiˈ 'teŋgə

Sulawesi Tenggara
  prov, Indonesia   SOO-luh-WĀ-sē TENG-guh-ruh   ˌsuːlə'weːsiˈ 'teŋgərə

Sulawesi Utara
  prov, Indonesia   SOO-luh-WĀ-sē OOT-uh-ruh   ˌsuːlə'weːsiˈ 'uːtərə

Suleiman
  pers. name, Turkish   sue-lā-MAHN   syːleː'man

sulfur
  element   SUHL-fuhr   'səlfəʳ

Sulla
  Roman politician   SUHL-uh, SUL-uh   'sələ, 'sulə

Sullivan
  family name   SUHL-uh-vuhn   'sələvən

Sully-Prudhomme
  R. F. A., French poet (Nobel 1901)   suel-LĒ-prue-DAWM   syːlliːpryːdɔːm

Sulpicia
  pers. name, Latin   suhl-PISH-(ē-)uh   səl'piʃ(iː)ə

Sulpicius
  pers. name, Latin   suhl-PISH-(ē-)uhs   səl'piʃ(iː)əs

Sul Ross
  State University, TX   SUHL RAWS, RAHS   'səl 'rɔːs, 'ras

Sultan
  sovereign of Turkey   SUHLT-n, SUHL-tuhn   'səltn̩, 'səltən

Sulu
  archipelago, sea, Philippines;   SOO-loo   'suːluː
  Hikaru, *character, Star Trek*

Sumac
  Yma, *entertainer*   SOO-MAK, SHOO-MAK   'suːˌmæk, 'ʃuːˌmæk

Sumatra
  island, Indonesia   su-MAH-truh   su'matrə

Sumba
  island, Indonesia   SOOM-buh   'suːmbə

Sumbawa
  island, Indonesia   soom-BAH-wuh   suːm'bawə

Sumer
  ancient kingdom, Asia   SOO-muhr   'suːməʳ

Sumerian
  native of Sumer; ancient lang.   soo-MER-ē-uhn, soo-MIR-ē-uhn   suː'meriːən, suː'miriːən

Sumitomo
  Japanese bank   soo-mē-tō-mō   suːmiːtoːmoː

Foreign Sounds: ue: *Fr.* **rue**, *Ger.* **füllen**   uh(r): *Fr.* **boeuf**, *Ger.* **Höhle**   <u>kh</u>: *Ger.* **ich**, *Scot.* lo<u>ch</u>   g̃: *Sp.* ami**g**o   v̱: *Sp.* ha**b**lar
hl: *Welsh* **Ll**anelli.   CAPITALS: primary stress.   SMALL CAPS: secondary stress.   Ⓢ: U.S. pron.   Ⓛ: British pron.

Summa cum laude
  with highest praise   SUM-uh KUM LOWD-uh, SUHM-uh   ,sumə ,kum 'laudə, ,səmə
                                KUHM LAWD-ē, SOO-muh, LOWD-ē   ,kəm 'lɔːdiˑ, ,suːmə, 'laudiˑ

Summerall
  Pat, *US sportscaster*   SUHM-uh-RAWL   'səmə,rɔːl

Sumner
  J. B., US biochemist (Nobel 1946)   SUHM-nuhr   'səmnəʳ

Sumter
  county, AL   SUHM(P)-tuhr   'səm(p)təʳ

Sunda
  Deep, *Indian Ocean*   SUHN-duh, SOON-duh   'səndə, 'suːndə

Sundanese
  lang., West Java   SUHN-duh-NĒZ, -NĒS   ,səndə'niːz, -'niːs

Sunday
  day of the week   SUHN-dē, SUHN-dā   'səndiˑ, 'səndeː

Sune
  pers. name, Swedish   SOO-nuh   'suːnə

Sung
  Chinese dynasty   SUNG, SUHNG   'suŋ, 'səŋ

Sunkist
  US food products co.   SUHN-KIST   'sən,kist

Sun Lik
  Hong Kong beer   SUN LIK, SUHN   'sun 'lik, 'sən

Sun Myung Moon
  Korean religious group leader SUHN MYUHNG MOON   'sən 'mjəŋ 'muːn

Sunna
  traditional Muslim law   SUN-uh, SUHN-uh   'sunə, 'sənə

Sunni
  adherents of a branch of Islam SUN-(n)ē   'sun(n)iˑ

Sunnism
  religious tenets of the Sunni SUN-IZ-uhm   'sun,izəm

Sunnite
  pert. to the Sunni   SUN-(N)ĪT   'sun,(n)ait

Sunny
  pers. name   SUHN-ē   'səniˑ

Sunnyvale
  city, CA   SUHN-ē-VĀL   'səniˑ,veːl

SUNOCO
  Sun Oil Co., US   suh-NŌ-kō   sə'noːkoː

Suntory
  Japanese beverage co.   sun-tō-rē, sun-tawr-ē   suntɔːriː, suntɔːriː

Sununu
  John H., US politician   suh-NOO-noo   sə'nuːnuː

SUNY
  State University of New York SOO-nē   'suːniˑ

Sun Yat-sen
  Chinese leader   SUN YAHT-SEN, SUHN YAT-SEN 'sun 'jat'sen, 'sən 'jæt'sen

Suomenlinna
  fortress, Helsinki, Finland   SWAW-muhn-LIN-nuh   'swɔːmən,linnə

Suomi
  College, *MI*   suh-WAW-mē, SWAW-mē   sə'wɔːmiˑ, 'swɔːmiˑ

Suomi [Finland]
  republic, Europe   SWAW-mē   'swɔːmiˑ

Superior
  lake, N. America; city, WI   su-PIR-ē-uhr   su'piriˑəʳ

Key (col. 2): a: fad ā: fade ah: father ar: Mary aw: law e: fed ē: feed er: merry i: hid ī: hide ō: coat ōō: boot
oi: boy ow: now u: put uh: above uhr: bird ch: chop ng: ring sh: show th: thick th: this zh: measure

Suquamish
   N. American people | suh-KWAHM-ish, SKWAHM-ish, | sə'kwɑmiʃ, 'skwɑmiʃ,
     | suh-KWAW-mish, SKWAW-mish | sə'kwɔːmiʃ, 'skwɔːmiʃ

Sura
   lang., Nigeria; section of the | SUR-uh | 'surə
     Koran

Surabaja, Soerabaja, Surabaya
   seaport, Java, Indonesia | SUR-uh-BĪ-uh | ˌsurə'baiə

Surakarta
   native principality, city, Java | SUR-uh-KAHRT-uh | ˌsurə'kɑrţə

Surat
   city, Gujarat, India | SUR-uht, suh-RAT | 'surət, sə'ræt

Surendranath
   1. pers. name, Bengali | su-RĀN-draw-NAWT, -druh-NAHT | su'reːndrɔːˌnɔːt, -drə,nɑt
   2. Hindi | suh-REN-druh-NAHT | sə'rendrə,nɑt

Suribachi
   volcano, Iwo Jima | SUR-uh-BAHCH-ē | ˌsurə'bɑtʃiˑ

Surinam [Suriname]
   republic, S. America | SUR-uh-NAM | 'surə,næm

Suriname
   river, republic, S. America | SUR-uh-NAHM-uh, SUR-uh-NAM | ˌsurə'nɑmə, ˌsurə'næm

Surinamer
   inhabitant of Suriname | SUR-uh-NAM-uhr, SUR-uh-NAHM-uhr | 'surə,næməʳ, ˌsurə'nɑməʳ

Surinamese
   pert. to Suriname | SUR-uh-nuh-MĒZ, -MĒS | ˌsurənə'miːz, -'miːs

Surrey
   county, England | SUHR-ē, SUH-rē | 'sər-iˑ, 'sə-riˑ

Surridge
   pers. name | SUHR-ij | 'səridʒ

Surry
   pl. name, US | SUHR-ē, SUH-rē | 'sər-iˑ, 'sə-riˑ

Sursum Corda
   exhortation to worship in the mass | SUR-suhm KAWRD-uh, KAWR-DAH | ˌsuʳsəm 'kɔːʳdə, 'kɔːʳ,dɑ

Surtees
   pers. name | SUHR-TĒZ | 'səʳ,tiːz

Susa
   ancient city, Iran | SOO-suh, SOO-zuh | 'suːsə, 'suːzə

Susan
   pers. name | SOO-zuhn | 'suːzən

Susanna, -nah
   Apocryphal book; pers. name | soo-ZAN-uh | suː'zænə

Susanne
   pers. name, German | zoo-ZAHN-uh | zuː'zɑnə

Susie, Susy
   pers. name | SOO-zē | 'suːziˑ

Suslov
   Mikhail, *government official, USSR* | SUS-LAWF | 'sus,lɔːf

Susquehanna
   river, US; N. American people; | SUHS-kwuh-HAN-uh | ˌsəskwə'hænə
     county, univ., PA

Susse Chalet
   US hotel chain | SOOS sha-LĀ | ˌsuːs ʃæ'leː

Sussex
   former county, England | SUHS-iks | 'səsiks

Foreign Sounds: ue: *Fr.* **rue**, *Ger.* **füllen** uh(r): *Fr.* **boeuf**, *Ger.* **Höhle** <u>kh</u>: *Ger.* i**ch**, *Scot.* lo**ch** ğ: *Sp.* ami**g**o <u>v</u>: *Sp.* ha**b**lar
hl: *Welsh* **Ll**anelli. CAPITALS: primary stress. SMALL CAPS: secondary stress. Ⓢ: U.S. pron. Ⓑ: British pron.

Susskind
    David, *TV, film, theater producer*   SUHS-KĪND   'səs,kaind
Susu
    lang., people, Africa   SŌŌ-SŌŌ   'suː,suː
Susumu
    pers. name, Japanese   sus-um-u   susumu
Sutherland
    pers. name   SU<u>TH</u>-uhr-luhnd   'səðəʳlənd
Sutlej
    river, India   SUHT-LEJ   'sət,ledʒ
Sutter
    Howard, *US baseball player*   SUHT-uhr   'sətəʳ
Suttner
    Baroness Bertha von, *Austrian*   ZUT-nuhr, SUT-nuhr   'zutnəʳ, 'sutnəʳ
    author, pacifist (Nobel 1905)
Sutton
    Don, *US baseball player; borough,*   SUHT-n   'sətn̦
    England
Suva
    town, Fiji   SŌŌ-vuh   'suːvə
Suvorov
    island, Pacific Ocean   su-VAWR-uhf   su'vɔːrəf
Suwannee [Swanee]
    river, GA, FL; county, FL   suh-WAHN-ē, SWAHN-ē   sə'waniˑ, 'swaniˑ
Suwŏn
    town, S. Korea   sōō-wuhn   suːwən
Suzan
    pers. name   SŌŌ-zuhn   'suːzən
Suzanna, Suzannah
    pers. name   sōō-ZAN-uh   suː'zænə
Suzanne
    1. pers. name   sōō-ZAN   suː'zæn
    2. French   sue-ZAHN   syːzaːn
Suzette
    pers. name   sōō-ZET   suː'zet
Suzhou, Su-chou, Suchow,
** Soochow**
    city, China   SŌŌ-JŌ, Ⓢ SŌŌ-CHOW   'suːdʒɔː, Ⓢ 'suː'tʃau
Suzie, Suzy
    pers. name   SŌŌ-zē   'suːziˑ
Suzuki
    1. Japanese motor vehicle co.;   suz-uk-ē, Ⓢ suh-ZŌŌ-kē   suzukiː, Ⓢ sə'zuːkiˑ
    pers. name, Japanese
    2. method of music instruction   suh-ZŌŌ-kē   sə'zuːkiˑ
Suzy
    see Suzie
Svalbard
    islands, Arctic   SFAHL-BAHR   'sfal,baʳ
Svan
    lang., people, Caucasus Mts.   SFAHN, SVAHN   'sfan, 'svan
Svedberg
    Theodor, *Swedish physical chemist*   SFED-BER, Ⓢ SFED-BUHRG, -BER-ē   'sfed,ber, Ⓢ 'sfed,bəʳg,
    (Nobel 1926)   -,beriˑ
Svein
    pers. name, Norwegian   SVĀN   'sveːn

Key (col. 2): a: fad ā: fade ah: father ar: Mary aw: law e: fed ē: feed er: merry i: hid ī: hide ō: coat ōō: boot
oi: boy ow: now u: put uh: above uhr: bird ch: chop ng: ring sh: show th: thick <u>th</u>: this zh: measure

Sveinbjörn
  pers. name, Icelandic SVĀN-BYUH(R)D-n 'sveːn,bjœdn̩

Sveinn
  pers. name, Icelandic SVĀD-n 'sveːdn̩

Sven
  pers. name, Danish, Norwegian, SVEN 'sven
  Swedish

Svengali
  evil dominator sfeng-GAHL-ē, sfen-GAHL-ē sfeŋ'gɑliˑ, sfen'gɑliˑ

Svenska [Sweden]
  kingdom, Europe SFEN-skah 'sfenskɑː

Svenson
  Bo, *US actor* SFEN-suhn 'sfensən

Sverdlovsk
  city, region, Russia sferd-LAWFSK sfeʳd'lɔːfsk

Sverige [Sweden]
  kingdom, Europe SFAR-yuh 'sfærjə

Svetlana
  pers. name, Russian sfet-LAHN-uh sfet'lɑːnə

Svizzera [Switzerland]
  republic, Europe ZVĒT-tsā-rah 'zviːttseːrɑ

Swabia
  medieval duchy, prov, Germany SWĀ-bē-uh 'sweːbiːə

Swabian Jura
  mtn. range, Germany SWĀ-bē-uhn JUR-uh ˌsweːbiːən 'dʒurə

Swadeshi
  political independence movement, swah-DĀ-shē, swah-DESH-ē swɑ'deːʃiˑ, swɑ'deʃiˑ
  India

Swaggart
  Jimmy, *US TV evangelist* SWAG-uhrt 'swægəʳt

Swahili
  lang., people, Africa swah-HĒ-lē swɑ'hiːliˑ

Swainson's
  hawk SWĀN-suhnz 'sweːnsənz

Swanee [Suwannee]
  river, GA, FL SWAHN-ē 'swɑniˑ

Swansea
  city, Wales; town, IL, MA SWAHN-zē, SWAHN(T)-sē 'swɑnziˑ, 'swɑn(t)siˑ

SWAPO
  South-West Africa People's SWAHP-ō 'swɑpoː
  Organization, political party,
  Namibia

Swaraj
  national or local home rule, India swuh-RAHJ swə'rɑdʒ

Swarthmore
  College, *town, PA* SWAWRTH-MŌR, SWAHTH-, -MAWR 'swɔːʳθˌmoːʳ, 'swɑθ-, -ˌmɔːʳ

SWAT
  Special Weapons and Tactics SWAHT 'swɑt
  police team

Swat
  river, region, Pakistan SWAHT 'swɑt

Swati [Swazi]
  lang., people, South Africa, SWAHT-ē 'swɑt̪iˑ
  Swaziland

Foreign Sounds: **ue**: *Fr.* **rue**, *Ger.* f**ü**llen **uh(r)**: *Fr.* b**oeu**f, *Ger.* H**öh**le <u>kh</u>: *Ger.* i**ch**, *Scot.* lo**ch** ğ: *Sp.* ami**g**o <u>v</u>: *Sp.* ha**b**lar
hl: *Welsh* L**l**anelli. CAPITALS: primary stress. SMALL CAPS: secondary stress. ⑤: U.S. pron. ⓔ: British pron.

Swayne
  Noah H., Field, *former ballpark,*   SWĀN   'sweːn
    Toledo, OH

Swayze
  Patrick, *US actor*   SWĀ-zē   'sweːziˑ

Swazi
  lang., people, South Africa,   SWAHZ-ē   'swɑziˑ
    Swaziland

Swaziland
  kingdom, Africa   SWAHZ-ē-LAND   'swɑziˑ,lænd

Swede
  inhabitant of Sweden   SWĒD   'swiːd

Sweden
  kingdom, Europe   SWĒD-n   'swiːdn̩

Swedenborg
  Emanuel, *Swedish mystic*   SVĀ-duhn-BAWR-yuh,   'sveːdən,bɔːrj,
                       Ⓢ SWĒD-n-BAWRG   Ⓢ 'swiːdn̩,bɔːʳg

Swedenborgian
  pert. to teachings of Swedenborg   SWĒD-n-BAWR-jē-uhn,   ,swiːdn̩'bɔːʳdʒiːən,
                       SWĒD-n-BAWR-gē-uhn   ,swiːdn̩'bɔːʳgiːən

Swedish
  lang., Scandinavia; pert. to   SWĒD-ish   'swiːdiʃ
    Sweden

Swinburne
  A.C., *English poet*   SWIN-BUHRN   'swin,bəʳn

Swinkels
  Dutch beer   SVING-kuhls   'sviŋkəls

Swinomish
  N. American people   swuh-NŌ-mish   swə'noːmiʃ

Swiss
  pert. to Switzerland   SWIS   'swis

Swissair
  Swiss airline co.   SWIS-AR, SWIS-ER, swis-AR, swis-ER   'swis,æʳ, 'swis,eʳ, swis'æʳ,
                                                      swis'eʳ

Swithin, Swithun
  English saint   SWITH-uhn   'swiðən

Switzerland
  republic, Europe   SWIT-suhr-luhnd   'switsəʳlənd

Sybaris
  ancient city, Italy   SIB-uh-ruhs   'sibərəs

Sybarite
  inhabitant of Sybaris; *sensualist*   SIB-uh-RĪT   'sibə,rɑit

Sybaritic
  pert. to Sybaris *or* Sybarites;   SIB-uh-RIT-ik   ,sibə'riṭik
    luxurious

Sybil
  pers. name   SIB-uhl   'sibəl

Sycuan
  Band, *N. American people*   si-KYOO-uhn   si'kjuːən

Sydney
  city, Australia; pers. name   SID-nē   'sidniˑ

Sylacauga
  city, AL   SIL-uh-KAW-guh   ,silə'kɔːgə

Sylphides, Les
  ballet, Chopin   lā sēl-FĒD   leː siːlfiːd

Key (col. 2):   a: fad   ā: fade   ah: father   ar: Mary   aw: law   e: fed   ē: feed   er: merry   i: hid   ī: hide   ō: coat   o͞o: boot
oi: boy   ow: now   u: put   uh: above   uhr: bird   ch: chop   ng: ring   sh: show   th: thick   <u>th</u>: this   zh: measure

Sylvanus
  pers. name sil-VĀ-nuhs sil'veːnəs
Sylvester
  pers. name sil-VES-tuhr sil'vestəʳ
Sylvestre
  pers. name, French sēl-VESTR siːlvestr
Sylvia
  pers. name SIL-vē-uh 'silviːə
Sylvio
  pers. name SIL-vē-ō 'silviːoː
Syme
  Sir Ronald, *New Zealand historian* SĪM 'saim
Symington
  W. Stuart, *US senator* SĪ-ming-tuhn 'saimiŋtən
Symmachus
  Roman politician; pope SIM-uh-kuhs 'siməkəs
Symms
  Steven Douglas, *US politician* SIMZ 'simz
Symonds
  John Addington, *English poet,* SIM-uhn(d)z 'simən(d)z
    essayist, critic
Symons
  Arthur, *British poet, critic* SIM-uhn(d)z 'simən(d)z
Symposium
  dialogue of Plato sim-PŌ-zē-uhm sim'poːziːəm
Syng
  pers. name SING 'siŋ
Synge
  John Millington, *Irish writer;* SING 'siŋ
    Richard Laurence Millington,
    English biochemist (Nobel
    1952); pers. name
Syngman
  pers. name, Korean SING-muhn, SIG-muhn 'siŋmən, 'sigmən
Syracusan
  pert. to Syracuse; *native or* SIR-uh-KYOO-zuhn, Ⓔ ˌsirə'kjuːzən, Ⓔ
    inhabitant of Syracuse SĪR-uh-KYOO-zuhn ˌsairə'kjuːzən
Syracuse
  1. city, Sicily SIR-uh-KYOOS, -KYOOZ, Ⓔ 'sirəˌkjuːs, -ˌkjuːz, Ⓔ
      SĪ-ruh-KYOOS 'sairəˌkjuːs
  2. city, county, NY SIR-uh-KYOOS, -KYOOZ, *locally often* 'sirəˌkjuːs, -ˌkjuːz, *locally*
      SER- *often* 'ser-
Syr Darya
  river, Kazakhstan, Kirghiz, sir DAHR-yuh siʳ 'daʳjə
    Uzbekistan
Syria
  1. country, Middle East SIR-ē-uh 'siriːə
  2. town, VA sī-RĒ-uh sai'riːə
Syriac
  literary & liturgical form of SIR-ē-AK 'siriːˌæk
    Aramaic
Syrian
  pert. to Syria SIR-ē-uhn 'siriːən
Syringa
  flower suh-RING-guh sə'riŋgə

Foreign Sounds: ue: *Fr.* **rue**, *Ger.* **füllen** uh(r): *Fr.* **boeuf**, *Ger.* **Höhle** kh: *Ger.* **ich**, *Scot.* **loch** ḡ: *Sp.* amigo v̱: *Sp.* hablar
hl: *Welsh* **Llanelli.** CAPITALS: primary stress. SMALL CAPS: secondary stress. Ⓢ: U.S. pron. Ⓔ: British pron.

Syrinx
  hamadryad loved by Pan   SIR-ingks   'siriŋks

Syro-Hittites
  ancient peoples, Cilicia & Syria   SĪ-rō-HI-TĪTS, SIR-ō-   ˌsairoːˈhiˌtaits, ˌsiroː-

Syros
  island, Greece   SĪ-RAHS   'saiˌrɑs

Syrtis
  area in northern hemisphere of   SUHRT-uhs   'səᵣțəs
  Mars

SYSOP
  system operator   SIS-AHP   'sisˌɑp

Syssition
  Spartan military unit   sī-SIT-ē-uhn   sai'sitiːən

Szczęsny
  pers. name, Polish   SHCHEⁿS-ni   'ʃtʃẽsni

Szczecin
  prov, seaport, Poland   SHCHET-SĒN   'ʃtʃetˌsiːn

Szechuan, Szechwan [Sichuan]
  prov, China; regional cookery style   SECH-WAHN   'setʃ'wɑn

Szeged
  city, Hungary   SEG-ED   'seg,ed

Szell
  George, *US conductor*   SEL, ZEL   'sel, 'zel

Szent-Györgyi
  Albert von, *Hungarian-born US*   sānt-JAWRJ(-ē)   seːnt'dʒɔːᵣdʒ(iˑ)
  biochemist (Nobel 1937)

Szilard
  Leo, *US physicist*   ZIL-AHRD, zuh-LAHRD, SIL-AHRD   'zilˌɑᵣd, zə'lɑᵣd, 'silˌɑᵣd

Szoka
  Edmund Cardinal, *archbishop,*   SHŌ-kuh   'ʃoːkə
  Detroit

Szold
  Henrietta, *US Zionist*   ZŌLD   'zoːld

Szolnok
  county, city, Hungary   SHŌL-NŌK   'ʃoːlˌnoːk

Szombathely
  city, Hungary   SŌM-BAWT-HĀ *[sic]*   'soːmˌbɔːtˌheː *[sic]*

Szymon
  pers. name, Polish   SHIM-awn   'ʃimɔːn

Key (col. 2):   a: fad ā: fade ah: father ar: **M**a**ry** aw: **law** e: fed ē: feed er: **merry** i: hid ī: hide ō: coat o͞o: boot
oi: boy ow: now u: put uh: above uhr: bird ch: chop ng: ring sh: show th: thick th: this zh: measure

T

Taal
1. *volcano, city, Philippines*   tah-AHL, TAHL   taˈɑl, ˈtɑl
2. *Afrikaans*   TAHL   ˈtɑl
Ta'anit Esther
  Jewish fast day   TAH-uh-NĒT es-TER, TAHN-it   ˌtɑəˈniːt esˈteʳ, ˈtɑnit ˈestəʳ,
                                       ES-tuhr, TAHN-is   ˈtɑnis

Tabasco
1. *river, state, Mexico*   tah-V̱AHS-kō, ⑤ tuh-BAS-kō   tɑˈβɑskoː, ⑤ təˈbæskoː
2. *tdmk for a hot pepper sauce*   tuh-BAS-kō   təˈbæskoː
Tabaski
  Islamic festival   tah-BAHS-kē   tɑˈbɑskiˑ
Tabitha, Tabatha
  pers. name   TAB-uh-thuh   ˈtæbəθə
Tabor
1. *biblical mtn.; college, KS*   TĀ-buhr   ˈteːbəʳ
2. *Czech republic*   TAHB-AWR   ˈtɑbˌɔːʳ
Tabrīz
  city, Iran   tuh-BRĒZ   təˈbriːz
Tabuleiros
  Portuguese festival   TAHB-yu-LĀ-r͞oos   ˌtɑbjuˈleːruːs
Tache
  N. American people   TASH, TACH-ē   ˈtæʃ, ˈtætʃiˑ
Tacitus
  Roman historian   TAS-uht-uhs   ˈtæsətəs
Tacna
  town, Chile; dept., Peru   TAHK-nah, ⑤ TAK-nuh   ˈtɑknɑ, ⑤ ˈtæknə
Tacoma
  city, WA   tuh-KŌ-muh   təˈkoːmə
Taconic
  mtn. range, northeast US   tuh-KAHN-ik   təˈkɑnik
Tacubaya
  district, Mexico City   tah-k͞oo-BAH-yah   tɑkuːˈbɑjɑ
Taddeo
  pers. name, Italian   tahd-DE-ō   tɑdˈdeoː
Tadeo
  pers. name, Spanish   tah-ṮHĀ-ō   tɑˈðeːoː
Tadeus
  pers. name, German   tah-DĀ-us   tɑˈdeːus
Tadeusz
  pers. name, Polish   tah-DE-͞oosh   tɑːˈdeuːʃ
Tadmur
  ancient city, Syria   TAD-MUR, TAD-muhr   ˈtædˌmuʳ, ˈtædməʳ

Foreign Sounds: ue: *Fr.* **rue**, *Ger.* füllen   uh(r): *Fr.* b**oeu**f, *Ger.* H**öh**le   k̲h̲: *Ger.* i**ch**, *Scot.* lo**ch**   g̱: *Sp.* ami**g**o   v̱: *Sp.* ha**b**lar
hl: *Welsh* **Ll**anelli.   CAPITALS: primary stress.   SMALL CAPS: secondary stress.   ⑤: U.S. pron.   ⑥: British pron.

Tadzhik
  lang., people, central Asia   tah-JIK, tah-JĒK, tuh-   tɑ'dʒik, tɑ'dʒiːk, tə-
Tadzhikistan, Tajikistan
  republic, central Asia   tah-JIK-i-STAHN, tah-JĒK-i-STAHN,   tɑ,dʒiki'stɑn, tɑ,dʒiːki'stɑn,
                                          -STAN   -'stæn

Taegu
  city, S. Korea   tag-o͞o   tæguː
Taejŏn
  city, S. Korea   taj-awn   tædʒɔːn
Taft
  William Howard, 27th US president   TAFT   'tæft
Tagakaolo
  lang., people, Philippine Islands   TAHG-uh-KOW-lō   ,tagə'kauloː
Tagalog [Pilipino]
  lang., people, Philippine Islands   tuh-GAHL-uhg, tuh-GAHL-AWG,   tə'galəg, tə'gal,ɔːg, tə'gal,ag
                                          tuh-GAHL-AHG

Taganrog
  seaport, Russia   TAG-uhn-RAHG   'tægən,rɑg
Tagbanuwa
  lang., people, Philippines   TAHG-bahn-uh-WAH   ,tagbanə'wa
Tage
  pers. name, Swedish   TAHG-uh   'tagə
Tages
  Etruscan prophet   TĀ-jēz   'teːdʒiːz
Tagliabue
  Paul, US football commissioner   TAG-lē-uh-Bo͞o   'tæɡliːə,buː
Tagore
  Sir Rabindranath, Indian author,   tuh-GŌR, tuh-GAWR   tə'gɔːr, tə'gɔːr
    philosopher (Nobel 1913)
Tagus [Tajo, Tejo]
  river, Spain, Portugal   TĀ-guhs   'teːgəs
Tahini
  sesame paste   tuh-KHĒ-nuh, Ⓢ tuh-HĒ-nē   tə'xiːnə, Ⓢ tə'hiːniˑ
Tahiti
  island, Pacific   tuh-HĒT-ē   tə'hiːt̬iˑ
Tahitian
  pert. to Tahiti   tuh-HĒ-shuhn   tə'hiːʃən
Tahoe
  lake, CA, NV   TAH-HŌ   'tɑ,hoː
Tai
  Asian lang. family; pers. name   TĪ   'tai
T'ai-chung
  city & town, Taiwan   TĪ-CHUNG   'tai'tʃuŋ
Ta'if, At
  town, Saudi Arabia   aht TAH-if   at 'tɑ-if
Taimyr, Taimir
  district, peninsula, Russia   TĪ-MIR   ,tai'mir
T'ai-nan [Tainan]
  city, Taiwan   TĪ-NAHN   'tai'nan
Tainan
  city, Taiwan   TĪ-NAHN, DĪ-NAHN   'tai'nan, 'dai'nan
Táin Bó Cuailnge
  ancient Irish epic   TOIN BŌ KO͞O-ling-uh *[sic]*   'tɔin 'boː 'kuːliŋə *[sic]*
Taine
  Hippolyte, French historian   TEN   ten

Key (col. 2):   a: fad ā: fade ah: father ar: Mary aw: law e: fed ē: feed er: merry i: hid ī: hide ō: coat o͞o: boot
oi: boy ow: now u: put uh: above uhr: bird ch: chop ng: ring sh: show th: thick th: this zh: measure

Taino
    West Indian people   TĪ-nō   'taino:

Taipei
    city, Taiwan   TĪ-PĀ, -BĀ   'tai'pe:, -'be:

Taiping
    river, China, Burma; city,   TĪ-PING, TĪ-BING   'tai'piŋ, 'tai'biŋ
    Malaysia

Tairona
    S. American people   TAH-Ē-RŌ-nuh   ,ta-i:'ro:nə

Taisho
    reign of Emperor Yoshihito of   tī-shō   taiʃo:
    Japan

Taittinger
    champagne brand   te-te^n-ZHĀ   tetẽʒe:

Taiwan
    island nation, SE Asia   TĪ-WAHN, tī-WAHN   'tai'wan, tai'wan

Taïyetos Oros
    mtn. range, Greece   TĪ-ye-TAWS AW-RAWS   'taije,tɔ:s 'ɔ:,rɔ:s

Taiyo
    Japanese fishing co.   tī-(y)ō   tai(j)o:

Taiyuan
    city, China   TĪ-yoo-AHN   'taiju:'an

Taizz
    city, Yemen   ta-IZ   tæ'iz

Tajik [Tadzhik]
    people, Tadzhikistan, Afghanistan,   tah-JIK, tah-JĒK   ta'dʒik, ta'dʒi:k
    Turkestan

Tajikistan
    see Tadzhikistan

Taj Mahal
    mausoleum, India; Indian beer;   TAHZH MUH-HAHL, TAHJ   ,taʒ mə'hal, ,tadʒ
    US musician

Tajo [Tagus]
    river, Spain, Portugal   TAH-hō, TAH-khō   'ta·ho:, 'taxo:

Takamatsu
    port, Japan   tahk-ah-maht-soo   takamatsu:

Takamori
    pers. name, Japanese   tah-kah-mō-rē   takamo:ri:

Takao
    city, Taiwan   tah-KAH-ō, tah-KOW   ta'kao:, ta'kau

Takashi
    pers. name, Japanese   tah-kah-shē   takaʃi:

Takeda
    Japanese chemical co.   tah-kā-dah, Ⓢ tuh-KĀD-uh   take:da, Ⓢ tə'ke:də

Takehito
    pers. name, Japanese   tah-ke-hē-tō   takehi:to:

Takeshita
    Noboru, *Japanese prime minister*   tah-ke-shē-tah   takeʃi:ta

Takkakaw
    waterfall, Canada   TAK-uh-KAW   'tækə,kɔ:

Takla Makan
    desert, China   TAHK-luh muh-KAHN   ,taklə mə'kan

Talaing [Mon]
    lang., people, Burma, Thailand   tah-LĪNG   ta'laiŋ

Foreign Sounds: ue: *Fr.* **r**ue, *Ger.* füllen   uh(r): *Fr.* b**oeu**f, *Ger.* Höhle   kh: *Ger.* i**ch**, *Scot.* lo**ch**   ğ: *Sp.* ami**g**o   v: *Sp.* ha**b**lar
hl: *Welsh* **Ll**anelli.   CAPITALS: primary stress.   SMALL CAPS: secondary stress.   Ⓢ: U.S. pron.   Ⓑ: British pron.

Talamanca, Cordillera de

  mtn. range, Central America   kawr-dē(l)-YER-ah dā   kɔːʳdiː(l)ˈjerɑ deː
                     tahl-ah-MAHNG-kah   talɑˈmɑŋka

Talassio

  ritual cry at ancient Roman   tuh-LAS-ē-ō, tuh-LAHS-ē-ō   təˈlæsiːoː, təˈlɑsiːoː
  marriages

Talber

  pers. name   TAWL-buhr, TAL-buhr   ˈtɔːlbəʳ, ˈtælbəʳ

Talbot

  pers. name   TAWL-buht, TAL-buht   ˈtɔːlbət, ˈtælbət

Talbots

  US apparel co.   TAWL-buhts, TAL-buhts   ˈtɔːlbəts, ˈtælbəts

Talcahuano

  port, Chile   TAHL-kuh-<u>KH</u>WAHN-ō   ˌtalkəˈxwanoː

Taliaferro

  1. county, GA   TAHL-uh-vuhr   ˈtaləvəʳ
  2. pers. name   TAHL-uh-vuhr, TAHL-yuh-FER-ō   ˈtaləvəʳ, ˌtaljəˈferoː

Taliesin

  Welsh bard; home of Frank Lloyd   tahl-YES-in, TAL-ē-ES-uhn   talˈjesin, ˌtæliːˈesən
  Wright

Talladega

  city, county, AL   TAL-uh-DĒ-guh, TAL-uh-DĀ-guh   ˌtæləˈdiːgə, ˌtæləˈdeːgə

Tallahassee

  city, FL   TAL-uh-HAS-ē   ˌtæləˈhæsiˑ

Tallahatchie

  river, county, MS   TAL-uh-HACH-ē   ˌtæləˈhætʃiˑ

Tallapoosa

  river, county, AL   TAL-uh-POO-suh   ˌtæləˈpuːsə

Tallinn

  city, Estonia   TAHL-yin, Ⓢ TAL-uhn, TAHL-uhn   ˈtaljin, Ⓢ ˈtælən, ˈtalən

Tallis

  Thomas, *English composer*   TAL-uhs   ˈtæləs

Tallulah

  pers. name   tuh-LOO-luh   təˈluːlə

Talmadge

  pers. name   TAL-mij   ˈtælmidʒ

Talmud

  Jewish rabbinical law   TAHL-MUD, TAL-muhd   ˈtal,mud, ˈtælməd

Talmudic

  pert. to Jewish law   tahl-MUD-ik, tal-M(Y)OOD-ik   talˈmudik, tælˈm(j)uːdik

Talos

  mythical guardian of Crete   TAL-uhs   ˈtæləs

Talysh

  lang., Iran, Azerbaijan   tuh-LISH   təˈliʃ

Tama

  lang., Sudan, Chad   TAHM-uh   ˈtamə

Tamar

  Biblical name   TĀ-muhr   ˈteːməʳ

Tamara

  1. pers. name   TAM-uh-ruh   ˈtæmərə
  2. Russian   tuh-MAH-ruh   təˈmaːrə

Tamari

  soy sauce   tuh-MAHR-ē   təˈmariˑ

Tamashek [Tuareg]

  lang., N Africa   TAM-uh-SHEK   ˈtæmə,ʃek

Key (col. 2):   a: fad ā: fade ah: father ar: **Mary** aw: **law** e: fed ē: **feed** er: **merry** i: hid ī: hide ō: coat o͞o: boot
oi: **boy** ow: **now** u: **put** uh: **above** uhr: **bird** ch: **chop** ng: **ring** sh: **show** th: **thick** <u>th</u>: **this** zh: measure

Tamatave
   port, Madagascar — TAHM-uh-TAHV, TAM-uh-TAHV — ˌtaməˈtɑv, ˌtæməˈtɑv
Tamaulipas
   1. state, Mexico — tahm-ow-LĒ-pahs — tɑmauˈliːpɑs
   2. thrush, songbird — tuh-MAW-luh-puhs — təˈmɔːləpəs
Tamazight
   lang., Morocco — TAHM-uh-ZIKHT — ˈtaməˌziçt
Tambora
   Mount, *volcano, Indonesia* — TAHM-buh-ruh — ˈtɑmbərə
Tamburlaine [Tamerlane, Timur]
   Tartar conqueror — TAM-(b)uhr-LĀN — ˈtæm(b)əʳˌleːn
Tamerlane [Tamburlaine]
   Tartar conqueror — TAM-uhr-LĀN — ˈtæməʳˌleːn
Tamil
   lang., people, Asia — TAHM-uhl, TAM-uhl, -il — ˈtaməl, ˈtæməl, -il
Tamil Nadu
   state, India — TAHM-uhl NAHD-o͞o, TAM-uhl, -il — ˌtaməl ˈnɑduː, ˌtæməl, -il
Tamkarum
   Babylonian trader — tam-KAHR-uhm — tæmˈkɑrəm
Tammany Hall
   corrupt Democratic political — TAM-uh-nē HAWL — ˌtæməniˑ ˈhɔːl
    organization
Tammuz
   Jewish month — TAHM-uz — ˈtɑmˌuz
Tammy
   pers. name — TAM-ē — ˈtæmiˑ
Tam o' Shanter
   1. poem, R. Burns — TAM uh SHANT-uhr — ˌtæm ə ˈʃæntəʳ
   2. Scottish cap — TAM uh SHANT-uhr — ˈtæm ə ˌʃæntəʳ
Tampa
   city, FL — TAM-puh — ˈtæmpə
Tampere
   city, Finland — TAHM-puh-RĀ, TAM-puh-RĀ — ˈtɑmpəˌreː, ˈtæmpəˌreː
Tampico
   city, IL; port, Mexico — tam-PĒ-kō — tæmˈpiːkoː
Tamworth
   city, Australia — TAM-WUHRTH — ˈtæmˌwəʳθ
Tana [Tsana]
   lake, Ethiopia; river, Kenya — TAHN-uh — ˈtɑnə
Tanager
   songbird — TAN-uh-juhr — ˈtænədʒəʳ
Tanagra
   town, ancient Greece — TAN-uh-gruh — ˈtænəgrə
Tanaina
   N. American people — tuh-NĪ-nuh — təˈnainə
Tanaka
   pers. name, Japanese — tahn-ahk-ah — tɑnɑkɑ
Tanakh, Tanach
   Hebrew scriptures — tah-NAHKH — tɑˈnɑx
Tanana
   1. Frank, US baseball player — tuh-NAN-uh — təˈnænə
   2. river, city, AK — TAN-uh-NAW — ˈtænəˌnɔː
Tananarive
   former name of Antananarivo — tuh-NAN-uh-RĒV — təˈnænəˌriːv

---

Foreign Sounds: **ue:** *Fr.* **rue,** *Ger.* **füllen** **uh(r):** *Fr.* **boeuf,** *Ger.* **Höhle** **kh:** *Ger.* **ich,** *Scot.* **loch** **ḡ:** *Sp.* **amigo** **v:** *Sp.* **hablar**
hl: *Welsh* **Llanelli.** CAPITALS: primary stress. SMALL CAPS: secondary stress. Ⓢ: U.S. pron. Ⓛ: British pron.

Tancred
　　Norman crusader; king of Sicily　　TANG-kruhd　　'tæŋkrəd

Tancrède
　　pers. name, French　　tahⁿ-KRED　　tɑ̃kred

Tandy
　　Jessica, *British actress*　　TAN-dē　　'tændi·

Tanesha
　　pers. name　　tuh-NĒ-shuh　　tə'niːʃə

Tang
　　Chinese dynasty　　TAHNG　　'taŋ

Tanganyika
　　lake, Africa　　TAN-guhn-YĒ-kuh,　　‚tæŋgən'jiːkə, ‚tæŋgən'jiːkə,
　　　　TANG-guhn-YĒ-kuh, -guh-NĒ-kuh　　-gə'niːkə

Tanger [Tangier]
　　seaport, Morocco　　*French* tahⁿ-ZHĀ, *German*　　*French* tɑ̃ʒeː, *German*
　　　　TAHN-juhr, TAHNG-uhr　　'tandʒəʳ, 'taŋəʳ

Tangier
　　seaport, Morocco　　tan-JIR　　tæn'dʒiʳ

Tangiers [Tangier]
　　seaport, Morocco　　tan-JIRZ　　tæn'dʒiʳz

Tangipahoa
　　parish, LA　　TAN-juh-puh-HŌ(-uh)　　‚tændʒəpə'hoː(ə)

Tangshan, T'angshan
　　city, China　　TAHNG-SHAHN　　'taŋ'ʃɑn

Tanguy
　　Yves, *French painter*　　tahⁿ-GĒ　　tɑ̃giː

Tania
　　pers. name　　TAHN-yuh　　'tɑnjə

Tanis
　　city, Egypt　　TĀ-nuhs　　'teːnəs

Tannhäuser
　　opera, R. Wagner　　TAHN-HOI-zuhr　　'tɑn‚hɔizəʳ

Tannu Tuva
　　region, Russia　　TAHN-ōō TŌŌ-vuh　　‚tɑnuː 'tuːvə

Tano-Tewa
　　N. American people　　TAHN-ō-TĒ-wuh, TAHN-ō-TĀ-wuh　　‚tɑnoː'tiːwə, ‚tɑnoː'teːwə

Tano-Tigua
　　N. American people　　TAHN-ō-TĒ-wuh　　‚tɑnoː'tiːwə

Tanqueray
　　tdmk for gin　　TANG-kuh-RĀ　　'tæŋkə‚reː

tantalum
　　element　　TANT-l-uhm　　'tæntl̩əm

Tantalus
　　son of Zeus condemned to eternal
　　　thirst　　TANT-l-uhs　　'tæntl̩əs

Tantra
　　Hindu doctrine　　TAHN-truh, TUHN-truh, TAN-truh　　'tɑntrə, 'təntrə, 'tæntrə

Tantrism
　　school of Mahayana Buddhism　　TUHN-TRIZ-uhm　　'tən‚trizəm

Tanzania
　　republic, Africa　　TAN-zuh-NĒ-uh, TAHN-　　‚tænzə'niːə, ‚tɑːn-

Tanzanian
　　pert. to Tanzania　　TAN-zuh-NĒ-uhn, TAHN-　　‚tænzə'niːən, ‚tɑːn-

Tao
　　a doctrine of Taoism　　DOW　　'dɑu

Key (col. 2):　a: fad　ā: fade　ah: father　ar: Mary　aw: law　e: fed　ē: feed　er: merry　i: hid　ī: hide　ō: coat　ōō: boot
oi: boy　ow: now　u: put　uh: above　uhr: bird　ch: chop　ng: ring　sh: show　th: thick　th̲: this　zh: measure

Taoiseach
  Irish prime minister — THĒ-shuh<u>kh</u>, TĒ-shuh<u>kh</u>, TĒ-shuhk — 'θiːʃəx, 'tiːʃəx, 'tiːʃək

Taoism
  religion — DOW-ɪz-uhm, TOW-ɪz-uhm — 'dɑu,izəm, 'tɑu,izəm

Taos
  town, county, NM; N. American people; Indian reservation, US — TOWS, TAH-ōs — 'tɑus, 'tɑoːs

Tao-te-ching
  basic text of Taoism — DOW-DĀ-JING — 'dɑu'deː'dʒiŋ

Tapaculo
  S.American songbird — TAP-uh-KOO-lō — ,tæpə'kuːloː

Tapajós, Tapajoz
  river, Brazil — TAHP-uh-ZHAWS, -ZHAWSH — ,tɑpə'ʒɔːs, -'ʒɔːʃ

Tappan
  1. village, NY — tap-AN — tæp'æn
  2. US appliance co. — tap-AN, TAP-uhn — tæp'æn, 'tæpən

Tappan Zee Bridge
  Hudson River, NY — TAP-an ZĒ BRIJ, TAP-uhn ZĒ — ,tæpæn ,ziː 'bridʒ, ,tæpən ,ziː

Tara
  1. ancient Irish capital; plantation in Gone with the Wind; *pers. name* — TAR-uh, TER-uh, TAHR-uh — 'tærə, 'terə, 'tɑrə
  2. lang., Central Sulawesi (Celebes) — TAHR-uh — 'tɑrə

Tarabulus
  see Trâblous

Tarahumara
  lang., people, Mexico — TAHR-uh-hoo-MAHR-uh — ,tɑrəhuː'mɑrə

Taranto
  prov & town, Italy — TAHR-uhn-TŌ, tuh-RANT-ō — 'tɑrən,toː, tə'ræntoː

Tarascan
  N. American people — tuh-RAS-kuhn, tuh-RAHS-kuhn — tə'ræskən, tə'rɑskən

Tarasco
  lang., Mexico — tuh-RAHS-kō, tuh-RAS-kō — tə'rɑskoː, tə'ræskoː

Tarawa
  atoll, Kiribati — tuh-RAH-wuh, TAR-uh-WAH — tə'rɑwə, 'tærə,wɑ

Taree
  town, Australia — tah-RĒ — tɑː'riː

Tarentum
  ancient seaport, Italy — tuh-RENT-uhm — tə'rentəm

Targum
  Aramaic translation of the Old Testament — TAHR-GUM, TAHR-GOOM — 'tɑʳ,gum, 'tɑʳ,guːm

Tarim He
  river, China — DAH-RĒM HUH, TAH-RĒM — 'dɑ'riːm 'hə, 'tɑ'riːm

Tarim Pendi
  basin, China — DAH-RĒM PUHN-DĒ, TAH-RĒM — 'dɑ'riːm 'pən'diː, 'tɑ'riːm

Tariq
  pers. name, Arabic — tah-RĒK — tɑ'riːk

Tarkanian
  Jerry, *US basketball coach* — tahr-KĀ-nē-uhn — tɑʳ'keːniːən

Tarkenton
  Fran, *US football player, sportscaster* — TAHR-kuhn-tuhn — 'tɑʳkəntən

---

Foreign Sounds: ue: *Fr.* **rue**, *Ger.* **füllen**   uh(r): *Fr.* **boeuf**, *Ger.* **Höhle**   <u>kh</u>: *Ger.* **ich**, *Scot.* **loch**   ğ: *Sp.* **amigo**   <u>v</u>: *Sp.* **hablar**   hl: *Welsh* **Llanelli.**   CAPITALS: primary stress.   SMALL CAPS: secondary stress.   ⓈⓈ: U.S. pron.   ⒷⒷ: British pron.

Tarkio
  pl. name, US   TAHR-kē-ō   'taʳkiːoː

Tarleton
  pers. name   TAHRL-tuhn, TAHRLT-n   'taʳltən, 'taʳltn̩

Tarpeia
  legendary Roman traitor   tahr-PĒ-uh   taʳ'piːə

Tarpeian Rock
  Roman execution site   tahr-PĒ-uhn RAHK   taʳ'piːən 'rɑk

Tarquin
  king of Rome   TAHR-kwin   'taʳkwin

Tarquinii
  ancient town, Italy   tahr-KWIN-ē-ī   taʳ'kwiniːˌai

Tarquinius
  name of two early Roman kings   tahr-KWIN-ē-uhs   taʳ'kwiniːəs

Tarragona
  prov & town, Spain   TAR-uh-GŌ-nuh   ˌtærə'goːnə

Tarrant
  county, TX   TAR-uhnt   'tærənt

Tarrytown
  town, NY   TAR-ē-TOWN, TER-ē-TOWN   'tæriːˌtaun, 'teriːˌtaun

Tarshish
  Biblical name   TAHR-shish   'taʳʃiʃ

Tarsus
  town, Turkey   TAHR-suhs   'tɑrsəs

Tartar
  Asian tribal people   TAHRT-uhr   'taʳʈəʳ

Tartarus
  portion of Hades in Roman myth   TAHRT-uh-ruhs   'taʳʈərəs

Tartary
  region overrun by Tatars, Europe   TAHRT-uh-rē   'taʳʈəriˑ
  and Asia

Tartessus
  ancient kingdom, Spain   tahr-TES-uhs   taʳ'tesəs

Tartikoff
  Brandon, US entertainment   TAHRT-i-KAWF, TAHRT-i-KAHF   'taʳʈiˌkɔːf, 'taʳʈiˌkaf
  executive

Tartu
  city, Estonia   TAHR-tōō   'taʳtuː

Tartuffe
  comedy, Molière   tahr-TUEF, Ⓢ tahr-TUF, tahr-TŌŌF   taːrtyːf, Ⓢ taʳ'tuf, taʳ'tuːf

Tarzan
  character, E. R. Burroughs   TAHR-zuhn, TAHR-ZAN   'taʳzən, 'taʳˌzæn

Tasha
  pers. name   TAHSH-uh, Ⓔ TASH-uh   'taʃə, Ⓔ 'tæʃə

Tashkent, Tashkend
  city, Uzbekistan   tash-KENT, tash-KEND, tahsh-   tæʃ'kent, tæʃ'kend, taʃ-

Tashritu
  Babylonian month   tahsh-RĒ-tōō   taʃ'riːtuː

Tasman
  Sea, between New Zealand &   TAZ-muhn   'tæzmən
  Australia

Tasmania
  island, state, Australia   taz-MĀ-nē-uh, taz-MĀN-yuh   tæz'meːniːə, tæz'meːnjə

Key (col. 2):   a: fad   ā: fade   ah: father   ar: Mary   aw: law   e: fed   ē: feed   er: merry   i: hid   ī: hide   ō: coat   ōō: boot
oi: boy   ow: now   u: put   uh: above   uhr: bird   ch: chop   ng: ring   sh: show   th: thick   <u>th</u>: this   zh: measure

Tasmanian devil
  marsupial — taz-MĀ-nē-uhn DEV-uhl, — tæz͵meːniːən 'devəl,
    taz-MĀN-yuhn — tæz'meːnjən

Tass
  news agency, USSR — TAHS, TAS — 'tɑs, 'tæs
Tat
  lang., people, Caucasus Mts. — TAHT — 'tɑt
Tatar
  lang., people, Eurasia — TAHT-uhr — 'tɑtəʳ
Tate
  pers. name — TĀT — 'teːt
Tatiana
  pers. name — tah-TYAHN-uh — ta'tjɑnə
Tatius
  second king of Rome — TĀ-sh(ē-)uhs — 'teːʃ(iː)əs
Tatler
  British periodical by Steele, — TAT-luhr — 'tætləʳ
    Addison, and Swift
Tatra
  mts., E. Europe — TAH-truh — 'tɑtrə
Tatry [Tatra]
  mts., E. Europe — TAH-trē — 'tɑtriˑ
Tattnall
  county, GA — TAT-nl — 'tætnl̩
Tatum
  E. L., US biochemist (Nobel — TĀT-uhm — 'teːʈəm
    1958); pers. name
Ta-t'ung
  see Datong
Taube
  Henry, *Canadian-born US* — TAWB, TOWB — 'tɔːb, 'tɑub
    inorganic chemist (Nobel 1983)
Taulipang
  S. American people — TOW-luh-PAHNG, TOW-luh-PAHNG — 'tɑulə͵paŋ, ͵taulə'paŋ
Taumotu
  archipelago, Pacific — tow-MŌ-tōō — tɑu'moːtuː
Taungthu
  lang., people, Burma, Thailand — TOWNG-TU — 'tauŋ͵tu
Taunus
  mtn. range, Germany — TOW-nuhs — 'taunəs
Taurids
  meteor shower — TAWR-idz — 'tɔːridz
Taurt [Taweret]
  Egyptian goddess of childbirth — TOWRT — 'tauʳt
Taurus
  constellation, sign of the zodiac; — TAWR-uhs — 'tɔːrəs
    mts., Turkey
Taussig
  Frank W., *US economist* — TOW-sig — 'tausig
Tawe
  river, Wales — TAH-wā, Ⓢ , Ⓔ TOW-ē — 'tɑːweː, Ⓢ , Ⓔ 'tauiˑ
Taweret [Taurt]
  Egyptian goddess of childbirth — TOW(-uh)r-uht — 'tau(ə)rət
Taxco
  city, Mexico — TAHS-kō — 'tɑskoː

Foreign Sounds: ue: *Fr.* **rue**, *Ger.* **füllen** uh(r): *Fr.* **boeuf**, *Ger.* **Höhle** <u>kh</u>: *Ger.* i**ch**, *Scot.* lo**ch** g̱: *Sp.* ami**g**o v̱: *Sp.* ha**b**lar hl: *Welsh* **Ll**anelli. CAPITALS: primary stress. SMALL CAPS: secondary stress. Ⓢ: U.S. pron. Ⓔ: British pron.

Taxila
  ancient town, Indus valley   TAK-suh-luh   'tæksələ

Taxiles
  king of Taxila   TAK-suh-lēz   'tæksəliːz

Tay
  river, Scotland   TĀ   'teː

Tayal [Atayal]
  Malayasian people, lang.   tuh-YAHL   tə'jɑl

Tayback
  Vic, *US actor*   TĀ-BAK   'teːˌbæk

Taygete
  mother of Lacedaemon by Zeus   tā-IJ-uht-ē   teː'idʒəţiˑ

Taygetus
  mtn. range, Greece   tā-IJ-uht-uhs   teː'idʒəţəs

Taylor
  pers. name   TĀ-luhr   'teːlərˡ

Tay-Sachs
  disease   TĀ-SAKS   'teː'sæks

Tayside
  region, Scotland   TĀ-SĪD   'teːˌsaid

Tazewell
  county, VA   TAZ-WEL, TAZ-wuhl   'tæzˌwel, 'tæzwəl

Tbilisi [Tiflis]
  city, Georgia   tuh-bil-Ē-sē, tuh-BIL-uh-sē   təbil'iːsiˑ, tə'biləsiˑ

Tchaikovsky, Tsch-
  Peter Ilyich, *Russian composer*   chī-KAWF-skē, chī-KAWV-skē   tʃai'kɔːfskiˑ, tʃai'kɔːvskiˑ

Tchibanga
  city, Gabon   CHĒ-BAHNG-GAH   ˌtʃiːˌbaŋ'ga

Tczew
  commune, Poland   CHEF   'tʃef

Tebaldi
  Renata, *Italian soprano*   tā-BAHL-dē, Ⓢ tuh-BAWL-dē   teː'baldiˑ, Ⓢ tə'bɔːldiˑ

Tebet, Tevet
  Jewish month   tā-VET, TĀ-VĀS, TĀ-VĀT   teː'vet, 'teːˌveːs, 'teːˌveːt

Tebetu
  Babylonian month   tā-BĀ-tōō   teː'beːtuː

Tecate
  Mexican beer   tā-KAHT-ā   teː'kɑţeː

technetium
  element   tek-NĒ-sh(ē-)uhm   tek'niːʃ(iː)əm

Technicolor
  tdmk for a color motion picture system   TEK-ni-KUHL-uhr   'tekniˌkələrˡ

Tecmessa
  girl abducted by Great Ajax   tek-MES-uh   tek'mesə

Tecumseh
  Shawnee leader; pers. name   tuh-KUHM-suh, -sē   tə'kəmsə, -siˑ

Ted
  pers. name   TED   'ted

Teda
  lang., people, Chad, Libya   TĀD-uh   'teːdə

Teddy, Teddie
  pers. name   TED-ē   'tediˑ

Te Deum
  Christian hymn of praise   tā DĀ-uhm, tē DĒ-uhm   teː 'deːəm, tiː 'diːəm

---

Key (col. 2):   a: fad   ā: fade   ah: father   ar: Mary   aw: law   e: fed   ē: feed   er: merry   i: hid   ī: hide   ō: coat   ōō: boot
oi: boy   ow: now   u: put   uh: above   uhr: bird   ch: chop   ng: ring   sh: show   th: thick   th: this   zh: measure

Teej
   Indian festival   TĒJ   'tiːdʒ
Teena
   pers. name   TĒ-nuh   'tiːnə
Tees
   river, England   TĒZ   'tiːz
TEFL
   Teaching English as a Foreign   TEF-uhl   'tefəl
     Language
Teflon
   tdmk for a synthetic resin   TEF-LAHN   'tef,lɑn
Tefnut, Tefnet
   Egyptian rain goddess   TEF-nuht   'tefnət
Tegal
   port, Java   tā-GAHL   teː'gɑl
Tegeates
   mythical son of Lycaon & founder   tuh-JĒ-uht-ēz   tə'dʒiːəʈiːz
     of Tegea
Tegel
   airport, Germany   TĀ-guhl   'teːgəl
Tegucigalpa
   dept, city, Honduras   tā-ḡo͞o-sē-ḠAHL-pah,   teːɣuːsiː'ɣɑlpɑ,
      Ⓢ tuh-GO͞O-suh-GAL-puh,   Ⓢ tə,guːsə'gælpə, -'gɑlpə
      -GAHL-puh
Tehachapi
   mtn. range, city, CA   tuh-HACH-uh-pē   tə'hætʃəpiˑ
Tehama
   county, CA   ti-HĀ-muh   ti'heːmə
Teheran, Tehran
   city, Iran   TĀ(-uh)-RAN, TĀ(-uh)-RAHN   ,teː(ə)'ræn, ,teː(ə)'rɑn
Tehuantepec
   town, Mexico   tā-<u>KH</u>WAHN-tā-pek,   teː'xwanteːpek,
      Ⓢ tuh-(H)WAHN-tuh-PEK   Ⓢ tə'(h)wantə,pek
Tehuelche
   S. American people   tuh-WEL-chē, te-WEL-chā   tə'weltʃiˑ, te'weltʃeː
Teicher
   see Ferrante & Teicher
Teide, Teyde
   mtn., Canary Islands   TĀD-ē   'teːdiˑ
Teign
   river, England   TIN, TĒN   'tin, 'tiːn
Teignmouth
   town, England   TIN-muhth, TĒN-muhth, TIM-uhth   'tinməθ, 'tiːnməθ, 'timəθ
Teilhard de Chardin
   Pierre, French philosopher   tā-YAHR duh shahr-DE[n]   teːjɑːr də ʃɑːrdẽ
Teixeira
   pers. name, Portuguese   tā-SHĀ-ruh, -rah   teː'ʃeːrə, -rɑː
Tejo [Tagus]
   river, Spain, Portugal   TĀ-zho͞o   'teːʒuː
Te Kanawa
   Kiri, *New Zealand soprano*   tā KAHN-uh-wuh, tuh   teː 'kɑnəwə, tə
Telamon
   father of Great Ajax and Teucer   TEL-uh-MAHN   'telə,man
Tel Aviv
   city, Israel   TEL uh-VĒV   ,tel ə'viːv

Foreign Sounds: **ue**: *Fr.* **rue**, *Ger.* **füllen**   **uh(r)**: *Fr.* **boeuf**, *Ger.* **Höhle**   <u>kh</u>: *Ger.* i<u>ch</u>, *Scot.* lo<u>ch</u>   ḡ: *Sp.* ami**g**o   <u>v</u>: *Sp.* ha**b**lar
hl: *Welsh* **Llanelli**.   CAPITALS: primary stress.   SMALL CAPS: secondary stress.   Ⓢ: U.S. pron.   Ⓑ: British pron.

Tel Aviv-Jaffa
  cities, Israel   TEL UH-VĒV-JAHF-uh, -YAHF-uh   ˌtel ə'viːv'dʒafə, -'jafə
Tel Aviv-Yafo
  cities, Israel   TEL uh-VĒV-YAH-fō   ˌtel ə'viːv'jafoː
Telecleia
  mother of Hecuba   TEL-uh-KLĒ-uh, TEL-uh-KLĪ-uh   ˌtelə'kliːə, ˌtelə'klaiə
Teledyne
  US co.   TEL-uh-DĪN   'telə,dain
Teléfonos de Mexico
  Mexican phone co.   tel-Ā-fō-nōs thā MĀ-hē-kō   tel'eːfoːnoːs ðeː 'meˑhiːkoː
Telegonus
  son of Odysseus and Circe   tuh-LEG-uh-nuhs   tə'legənəs
Telemachus
  son of Odysseus and Penelope   tuh-LEM-uh-kuhs   tə'leməkəs
Telemann
  Georg Philipp, German composer   TĀ-luh-MAHN   'teːlə,man
Telemark
  region, county, Norway   TEL-uh-MAHRK   'telə,maʳk
Telephassa
  mother of Cadmus, Europa, Cilix, TEL-uh-FAS-uh   ˌtelə'fæsə
  Phoenix
Telephus
  son of Heracles   TEL-uh-fuhs   'teləfəs
Telescopium
  constellation   TEL-uh-SKŌ-pē-uhm   ˌtelə'skoːpiːəm
Telesphorus
  pope   tuh-LES-fuh-ruhs   tə'lesfərəs
tellurium
  element   tuh-LUR-ē-uhm, te-LUR-ē-uhm   tə'luriːəm, te'luriːəm
Tellus
  Roman earth goddess   TEL-uhs   'teləs
Telly
  pers. name   TEL-ē   'teliˑ
TelPrompTer
  tdmk for a TV cueing device   TEL(-uh)-PRAHM(P)-tuhr   'tel(ə),pram(p)təʳ
Telstar
  tdmk for a communication   TEL-STAHR   'tel,staʳ
  satellite
Telugu
  lang., people, India, Malaysia   TEL-uh-GOO   'telə,guː
Tem
  lang., Ghana, Benin, Togo   TEM   'tem
Tem [Atum]
  Egyptian creator god   TEM   'tem
Temenus
  a Heraclid, conqueror of Argos   TEM-uh-nuhs   'temənəs
Temin
  Howard M., US virologist (Nobel   TEM-uhn   'temən
  1975)
Temne
  people, lang., Africa   TEM-nē   'temniˑ
Te-Moak
  N. American people   TĀ-MŌ-uhk   ˌteː'moːək

Key (col. 2):   a: fad   ā: fade   ah: father   ar: Mary   aw: law   e: fed   ē: feed   er: merry   i: hid   ī: hide   ō: coat   ōō: boot
oi: boy   ow: now   u: put   uh: above   uhr: bird   ch: chop   ng: ring   sh: show   th: thick   th̲: this   zh: measure

Tempe
  1. city, AZ   tem-PĒ   temˈpiː
  2. valley, Greece   TEM-pē   ˈtempiˑ

Templar
  member of a religious military   TEM-pluhr   ˈtempləʳ
    order

Temuco
  city, Chile   tā-MOO̅-kō   teːˈmuːkoː

Temujin [Genghis Khan]
  Mongol leader   TEM-yuh-juhn   ˈtemjədʒən

Tenafly
  borough, NJ   TEN-uh-FLĪ   ˈtenəˌflɑi

Tène, La
  see La Tène

Tenebrae
  morning services during Christian   TEN-uh-BRĀ, TEN-uh-BRĪ,   ˈtenəˌbreː, ˈtenəˌbrɑi,
    Holy Week   TEN-uh-BRĒ   ˈtenəˌbriː

Tenedos
  ancient name of Bozcaada   TEN-uh-DAHS   ˈtenəˌdɑs

Tenerife, Teneriffe
  largest Canary Island   TEN-uh-RĒ-fē, TEN-uh-RĒ-fā,   ˌtenəˈriːfiˑ, ˌtenəˈriːfeˑ,
                         TEN-uh-RIF, TEN-uh-RĒF   ˌtenəˈrif, ˌtenəˈriːf

Tenes
  son of Procleia   TĒ-nēz, TĒ-nēs   ˈtiːniːz, ˈtiːniːs

Teng Hsiao-p'ing, Teng Hsiao-ping
  see Deng Xiaoping

Teniers
  David *&* *his son* David, *Flemish*   tuh-NĒRS, Ⓢ TEN-yuhrz   təˈniːrs, Ⓢ ˈtenjəʳz
    painters

Tennant
  Victoria, *actress*   TEN-uhnt   ˈtenənt

Tenneco
  US corp.   TEN-uh-KŌ   ˈtenəˌkoː

Tennessean, Tennesseean
  pert. to Tennessee; *native of*   TEN-uh-SĒ-uhn, TEN-uh-SĒ-uhn   ˌtenəˈsiːən, ˈtenəˌsiːən
    Tennessee

Tennessee
  river, state, US; pers. name (T.   TEN-uh-SĒ, TEN-uh-SĒ   ˌtenəˈsiː, ˈtenəˌsiː
    Williams)

Tenney
  pers. name   TEN-ē   ˈteniˑ

Ten Nhat
  Vietnamese New Year   ten HAHT   ten ˈhɑt

Tenniel
  Sir John, *British illustrator*   TEN-ē-uhl   ˈteniːəl

Tennille
  Toni, *US entertainer*   tuh-NĒL   təˈniːl

Tennyson
  Alfred, Lord, *English poet; pers.*   TEN-uh-suhn   ˈtenəsən
    name

Tennysonian
  pert. to Tennyson   TEN-uh-SŌ-nē-uhn   ˌtenəˈsoːniːən

Tensas
  river, AL; parish, LA   TEN-SAW   ˈtenˌsɔː

Foreign Sounds: ue: *Fr.* **rue**, *Ger.* **füllen**   uh(r): *Fr.* **boeuf**, *Ger.* **Höhle**   <u>kh</u>: *Ger.* **ich**, *Scot.* **loch**   ḡ: *Sp.* **amigo**   v: *Sp.* **hablar**
hl: *Welsh* **Llanelli**.   CAPITALS: primary stress.   SMALL CAPS: secondary stress.   Ⓢ: U.S. pron.   Ⓛ: British pron.

Tenzin
   pers. name, Tibetan   TEN-zin, TEN-sin   'tenzin, 'tensin
Tenzing
   pers. name, Nepalese   TEN-zing, TEN-sing   'tenziŋ, 'tensiŋ
Teobaldo
   pers. name, Italian   TĀ-ō-BAHL-dō   ,teːoː'bɑldoː
Teodor
   1. pers. name, Polish   te-AW-dawr   te'ɔːdɔːr
   2. Swedish   TĀ-aw-DAWR   'teːɔː,dɔːr
Teodoro
   1. pers. name, Italian   TĀ-ō-DAWR-ō   ,teːoː'dɔːroː
   2. Spanish   tā-ō-<u>TH</u>ŌR-ō   teːoː'ðoːroː
Teofil
   pers. name, Polish   tā-AW-fēl   teː'ɔːfiːl
Teófilo
   pers. name, Portuguese   tā-AW-fē-l$\overline{oo}$ teː'ɔːfiːluː
Teofilo
   pers. name, Italian   tā-AW-fē-lō   teː'ɔːfiːloː
Teotihuacán
   town, Toltec ruins, Mexico TĀ-uh-TĒ-wah-KAHN   ,teːə,tiːwɑ'kɑn
terbium
   element   TUHR-bē-uhm   'təʳbiːəm
Terbrugghen
   Hendrik, *Dutch painter*   tuhr-BR$\overline{OO}$-guhn   təʳ'bruːgən
Terceira
   island, Azores   tuhr-SIR-uh, tuhr-SER-uh təʳ'sirə, təʳ'serə
Terence
   Roman playwright; pers. name TER-uhn(t)s   'terən(t)s
Terentius
   pers. name, Latin   tuh-REN-sh(ē-)uhs   tə'renʃ(iː)əs
Teresa
   1. Mother, *Albanian religious* tuh-RĒ-suh, tuh-RĀ-suh   təˈriːsə, təˈreːsə
     (Nobel 1979); pers. name
   2. Italian   tā-REZ-ah   teː'rezɑ
   3. Spanish   tā-RĀ-sah   teː'reːsɑ
Terese
   pers. name   tuh-RĒZ, tuh-RĀZ   təˈriːz, təˈreːz
Tereshkova
   Valentina, *cosmonaut, USSR* TUHR-(y)uhsh-KAW-vuh, TER- ,tər(j)əʃ'kɔːvə, ,ter-
Terkel
   Studs, *US writer*   TUHR-kuhl   'təʳkəl
Terminus
   Roman god of the boundaries of TUHR-muh-nuhs   'təʳmənəs
    fields
Ternate
   island, Indonesia   tuhr-NAHT-ē   təʳ'nɑtiˑ
Terpander
   Greek musician & poet   tuhr-PAN-duhr   təʳ'pændəʳ
Terpsichore
   1. muse of light verse & dance tuhrp-SIK-uh-rē   təʳp'sikəriˑ
   2. street, New Orleans   TUHRP-si-KŌR, -KAWR   'təʳpsi,koːʳ, -,kɔːʳ
Terpsichorean
   pert. to Terpsichore   TUHRP-sik-uh-RĒ-uhn,   ,təʳpsikə'riːən,
                        TUHRP-si-KŌR-ē-uhn,   ,təʳpsi'koːriːən,
                        TUHRP-si-KAWR-ē-uhn   ,təʳpsi'kɔːriːən

---

Key (col. 2):   a: fad ā: fade ah: father ar: Mary aw: law e: fed ē: feed er: merry i: hid ī: hide ō: coat $\overline{oo}$: boot
oi: boy ow: now u: put uh: above uhr: bird ch: chop ng: ring sh: show th: thick <u>th</u>: this zh: measure

Terra

   Latin for 'earth' or 'land'   TER-uh   'terə

Terramycin

   tdmk for oxytetracycline   TER-uh-MĪS-n   ˌterə'maisn̩

Terrance

   pers. name   TER-uhns   'terəns

Terrebonne

   parish, LA; county, town, Quebec,   TER-uh-BAHN   'terəˌbɑn
     Canada

Terre Haute

   city, IN   TER-uh HŌT, TER-ē, HUHT, HAWT   ˌterə 'hoːt, ˌteriˑ, 'hət, 'hɔːt

Terremare

   culture, *Italian Bronze Age*   TER-uh-MAHR-ā   ˌterə'mareː
     settlements

Terri, Terry

   pers. name   TER-ē   'teriˑ

Tertiary

   geologic period   TUHR-shē-ER-ē, TUHR-shuh-rē   'təʳʃiːˌeriˑ, 'təʳʃəriˑ

Tertius

   Roman name   TUHR-sh(ē-)uhs   'təʳʃ(iː)əs

Tertullian

   Latin Church Father   TUHR-TUHL-yuhn,   ˌtəʳ'təljən, ˌtəʳ'təliːən
      TUHR-TUHL-ē-uhn

Tertullianism

   teachings of Tertullian   TUHR-TUHL-ē-uh-NIZ-uhm,   ˌtəʳ'təliːəˌnizəm, təʳ'tuːliː-
      tuhr-TŌŌ-lē-

Teru

   pers. name, Japanese   ter-u   teru

TESL

   Teaching English as a Second   TES-uhl   'tesəl
     Language

Tesla

   Nikola, *US inventor*   TES-luh   'teslə

Teso

   lang., people, Uganda   TĀ-sō   'teːsoː

TESOL

   Teaching English to Speakers of   TĒ-SAWL, TĒ-SAHL, TES-AWL,   'tiːˌsoːl, 'tiːˌsɑl, 'tesˌɔːl, 'tesəl
     Other Languages   TES-uhl

Tess

   pers. name   TES   'tes

Tessa

   pers. name   TES-uh   'tesə

Tessie

   pers. name   TES-ē   'tesiˑ

Tessin [Ticino]

   canton, Switzerland   te-SEⁿ   tesẽ

Tesuque

   N. American people   tuh-SŌŌ-kē   tə'suːkiˑ

Tet

   Vietnamese New Year   TET   'tet

Tethys

   Greek sea divinity; satellite of   TĒ-thuhs   'tiːθəs
     Saturn

Foreign Sounds: **ue:** *Fr.* **rue**, *Ger.* **füllen**   **uh(r):** *Fr.* **boeuf**, *Ger.* **Höhle**   **kh:** *Ger.* **ich**, *Scot.* **loch**   **ḡ:** *Sp.* **amigo**   **v:** *Sp.* **hablar**
hl: *Welsh* **Llanelli.**   CAPITALS: primary stress.   SMALL CAPS: secondary stress.   Ⓢ: U.S. pron.   Ⓑ: British pron.

Teton
  river, MT; mtn. range, WY;   TĒ-TAHN, TĒT-n   'tiːˌtɑn, 'tiːtn̩
  county, ID, MT, WY; N.
  American people
Tetradenia
  plant   TE-truh-DĒ-nē-uh   ˌtetrə'diːniːə
Tetragrammaton
  the 4 letters YHWH, a Hebrew   TE-truh-GRAM-uh-TAHN   ˌtetrə'græməˌtɑn
    name of God
Tetrazzini
  1. baked dish in cream sauce   TE-truh-ZĒ-nē   ˌtetrə'ziːniˈ
  2. Luisa, Italian soprano   TĀ-traht-TSĒ-nē   ˌteːtrɑt'tsiːniˈ
Tetuán
  city, Morocco   tā-TWAHN, tuh-TWAHN   teː'twɑn, tə'twɑn
Teucer
  Trojan ancestor   T(Y)O͞O-suhr   't(j)uːsəʳ
Teucher
  Swiss chocolate mfrs.   TOI-shuhr   'tɔiʃəʳ
Teutarus
  teacher of archery to Heracles   T(Y)O͞OT-uh-ruhs   't(j)uːt̬ərəs
Teuton
  early European people; a German   T(Y)O͞OT-n   't(j)uːtn̩
Teutones
  Latin name of Teutons   t(y)o͞o-TŌ-nēz   t(j)uː'toːniːz
Teutonic
  pert. to Teutons; Germanic   t(y)o͞o-TAHN-ik   t(j)uː'tɑnik
Tevere [Tiber]
  river, Italy   TĀ-vă-rā   'teːveːreː
Tevet
  see Tebet
Tewa
  N. American people   TĀ-wuh, TĒ-wuh   'teːwə, 'tiːwə
Tewkesbury
  borough, England   T(Y)O͞OKS-b(uh-)rē,   't(j)uːksb(ə)riˈ,
                                         ⑤ T(Y)O͞OKS-BER-ē   ⑤ 't(j)uːksˌberiˈ
Tewksbury
  town, MA   TUKS-b(uh-)rē, *by outsiders often*   'tuksb(ə)riˈ, *by outsiders*
                                         T(Y)O͞OKS-BER-ē   *often* 't(j)uːksˌberiˈ
Tex
  abbreviation for Texan or Texas;   TEKS   'teks
    pers. name
Texaco
  US oil co.   TEK-si-KŌ   'teksiˌkoː
Texan
  pert. to Texas; inhabitant of Texas   TEK-suhn   'teksən
Texarkana
  twin cities, AK, TX   TEK-sahr-KAN-uh, TEK-suhr-KAN-uh   ˌteksɑʳ'kænə, ˌteksəʳ'kænə
Texas
  state, US   TEK-suhs, TEK-siz   'teksəs, 'teksiz
Tex-Mex
  Texas-Mexican culture   TEK-SMEKS   'tek'smeks
Tey
  Josephine *(pseudonym of*   TĀ   'teː
    Elizabeth Mackintosh*), British*
    mystery writer

Key (col. 2):   a: fad   ā: fade   ah: father   ar: Mary   aw: law   e: fed   ē: feed   er: merry   i: hid   ī: hide   ō: coat   o͞o: boot
oi: boy   ow: now   u: put   uh: above   uhr: bird   ch: chop   ng: ring   sh: show   th: thick   th̲: this   zh: measure

Teyde
  see Teide

Tezcatlipoca
  Aztec warrior god tez-KAT-luh-PŌ-kuh tez'kætlə,poːkə

Thackeray
  William Makepeace, *English* THAK-(uh-)rē, THAK-uh-RĀ 'θæk(ə)riˑ, 'θækə,reː
  novelist

Thad
  pers. name THAD 'θæd

Thaddeus, Thadeus
  pers. name THAD-ē-uhs 'θædiːəs

Thadingyut
  Buddhist penitential period tah-DING-GYŌŌT tɑ'diŋ,gjuːt

Thai
  lang., people, SE Asia TĪ 'tɑi

Thailand
  kingdom, Asia TĪ-LAND, TĪ-luhnd 'tɑi,lænd, 'tɑilənd

Thaipusam
  Hindu festival TĪ-PŌŌ-juhm, TĪ-PŌŌ-suhm 'tɑi,puːdʒəm, 'tɑi,puːsəm

Thaïs
  1. *Athenian courtesan* THĀ-uhs 'θeːəs
  2. *opera, Massenet* tah-ĒS tɑːiːs

Thales
  Greek philosopher THĀ-LĒZ 'θeː,liːz

Thalhimers
  US department store chain TAWL-HĪ-muhrz 'tɔːl,hɑiməʳz

Thalia
  1. *muse of comedy; one of the* thuh-LĪ-uh θə'lɑiə
  Graces
  2. *street, New Orleans* THĀ-lē-uh 'θeːliːə
  3. *pers. name* THĀ-lē-uh, THAL-yuh, THAHL-yuh 'θeːliːə, 'θæljə, 'θɑljə

thallium
  element THAL-ē-uhm 'θæliːəm

Thames
  1. *rivers, England, Canada* TEMZ 'temz
  2. *river, CT; street, Newport, RI* THĀMZ, TEMZ, TĀMZ 'θeːmz, 'temz, 'teːmz
  3. *pers. name* THĀMZ 'θeːmz

Thamyris
  mythical Thracian musician THAM-uh-ruhs 'θæmərəs

Thanatos
  Greek personification of death THAN-uh-TAHS, -TŌS 'θænə,tɑs, -,toːs

Thanet
  Isle of, *region, England* THAN-uht 'θænət

Thanksgiving
  November holiday, US; October thangks-GIV-ing θæŋks'giviŋ
  holiday, Canada

Thanom
  pers. name, Thai tah-NAWM tɑ'nɔːm

Thant
  U, *former UN Secretary General* THAHNT, THANT 'θɑnt, 'θænt

Thapsus
  ancient town, Tunisia THAP-suhs 'θæpsəs

Thar
  desert region, India, Pakistan TAHR, TUHR 'tɑʳ, 'təʳ

Foreign Sounds: **ue:** *Fr.* **rue**, *Ger.* **füllen** **uh(r):** *Fr.* **boeuf**, *Ger.* **Höhle** **kh:** *Ger.* **ich**, *Scot.* **loch** **g̠:** *Sp.* **amigo** **v:** *Sp.* **hablar**
hl: *Welsh* **Llanelli.** CAPITALS: primary stress. SMALL CAPS: secondary stress. Ⓢ: U.S. pron. Ⓛ: British pron.

Tharp
    Twyla, *US dancer, choreographer*   THAHRP   'θɑʳp

Thásos
    island, Greece   THAH-saws, ⑤ THĀ-SAHS   'θɑ,sɔːs, ⑤ 'θeː,sɑs

Thasus
    brother of Cadmus and Europa   THĀ-suhs   'θeːsəs

Thatcher
    Margaret, *British politician*   THACH-uhr   'θætʃəʳ

Thatcherism
    policies of M. Thatcher   THACH-uh-RIZ-uhm   'θætʃə,rizəm

Thaumas
    primordial sea divinity   THAW-muhs   'θɔːməs

Thayer
    pers. name   THER, THĀ-uhr   'θeʳ, 'θeːəʳ

Thea
    1. *pers. name*   THĒ-uh   'θiːə
    2. *German*   TĀ-ah   'teːɑ

Theaetetus
    dialogue of Plato   thē-ĒT-uht-uhs, THĒ-uh-TĒT-uhs   θiː'iːtətəs, ,θiːə'tiːtəs

Theatines
    religious order   THĒ-uh-tuhnz, THĒ-uh-TĒNZ   'θiːətənz, 'θiːə,tiːnz

Thebaid
    epic poem, Statius   thuh-BĪ-uhd   θə'baiəd

Theban
    pert. to Thebes   THĒ-buhn   'θiːbən

Thebe
    wife of Heracles; satellite of   THĒ-bē   'θiːbiˑ
    Jupiter

Thebes
    ancient city, Egypt; ancient city,   THĒBZ   'θiːbz
    Greece

Thecodontia
    reptilian order   THĒ-kuh-DAHN-chuh   ,θiːkə'dantʃə

Theda
    pers. name   THĀD-uh, THĒD-uh   'θeːdə, 'θiːdə

Theia
    mother of Helios, Eos, and Selene   THĒ-uh, THĪ-uh   'θiːə, 'θaiə

Theias
    father of Adonis   THĒ-uhs, THĪ-uhs   'θiːəs, 'θaiəs

Theiler
    Max, *South African-born US*   TĪ-luhr   'tailəʳ
    bacteriologist (Nobel 1951)

Themis
    Greek goddess, personification of   THĒ-muhs   'θiːməs
    justice

Themisto
    wife of Athamas   thuh-MIS-tō   θə'mistoː

Themistocles
    1. *Athenian statesman; pers. name*   thuh-MIS-tuh-KLĒZ   θə'mistə,kliːz
    2. *Mod. Greek*   the-mē-staw-KLĒS   θemiːstɔːˈkliːs

Theo
    1. *pers. name*   THĒ-ō   'θiːoː
    2. *Dutch*   TĀ-ō   'teːoː

Théobald
    pers. name, French   tā-aw-BAHLD   teːɔːbɑːld

Key (col. 2):   a: fad   ā: fade   ah: father   ar: Mary   aw: law   e: fed   ē: feed   er: merry   i: hid   ī: hide   ō: coat   ōō: boot
oi: boy   ow: now   u: put   uh: above   uhr: bird   ch: chop   ng: ring   sh: show   th: thick   <u>th</u>: this   zh: measure

Theobald
  pers. name   THĒ-uh-BAWLD, TIB-uhld   'θiːə,bɔːld, 'tibəld

Theocritus
  Greek poet   thē-AHK-ruht-uhs   θiːˈɑkrətəs

Theoderic
  antipope   thē-AHD-uh-rik   θiːˈɑdərik

Théodor
  pers. name, French   tā-aw-DAWR   teːɔːdɔːr

Theodor
  1. pers. name   THĒ-uh-DŌR, THĒ-uh-DAWR,   'θiːə,doːr, 'θiːə,dɔːr, 'θiːədər
         THĒ-uhd-uhr
  2. Danish, Dutch   TĀ-ō-DAWR   'teːoː,dɔːr
  3. German   TĀ-ō-DŌR   'teːoː,doːr
  4. Norwegian   TĀ-ō-DŌR   'teːoː,doːr
  5. Swedish   TĀ-aw-DAWR   'teːɔ,dɔːr

Theodora
  Byzantine empress; pers. name   THĒ-uh-DŌR-uh, THĒ-uh-DAWR-uh   ,θiːə'doːrə, ,θiːə'dɔːrə

Théodore
  pers. name, French   tā-aw-DAWR   teːɔːdɔːr

Theodore
  pers. name   THĒ-uh-DŌR, THĒ-uh-DAWR,   'θiːə,doːr, 'θiːə,dɔːr, 'θiːədər
         THĒ-uhd-uhr

Theodoric
  pers. name   thē-AHD-uh-rik   θiːˈɑdərik

Theodorus
  pers. name, Latin   THĒ-uh-DŌR-uhs, THĒ-uh-DAWR-uhs   ,θiːə'doːrəs, ,θiːə'dɔːrəs

Theodosia
  pers. name   THĒ-uh-DŌ-shuh   ,θiːə'doːʃə

Theodosius
  1. the Great, Roman emperor   THĒ-uh-DŌ-sh(ē-)uhs   ,θiːə'doːʃ(iː)əs
  2. pers. name, German   TĀ-ō-DŌZ-yus, -DŌ-zē-us   ,teːoː'doːzjus, -'doːziːus

Theodric
  pers. name   thē-AHD-rik   θiːˈɑdrik

Theognis
  Greek poet   thē-AHG-nuhs   θiːˈɑgnəs

Theoni
  pers. name, Greek   thā-AW-nē   θeːˈɔːniː

Theopaschitism
  Christian heresy   THĒ-uh-PAS-KĪT-IZ-uhm   ,θiːə'pæs,kaiṭ,izəm

Theophane
  mother of ram with golden fleece   thē-AHF-uh-nē   θiːˈɑfəniˑ

Théophile
  pers. name, French   tā-aw-FĒL   teːɔːfiːl

Theophilus
  1. crater on Moon   thē-AHF-uh-luhs, tā-AHF-   θiːˈɑfələs, teːˈaf-
  2. pers. name   thē-AHF-uh-luhs   θiːˈɑfələs
  3. Danish   tē-Ō-fē-lus   tiːˈoːfiːlus
  4. German   tā-Ō-fē-lus   teːˈoːfiːlus

Théophraste
  pers. name, French   tā-aw-FRAHST   teːɔːfrɑːst

Theophrastus
  1. Greek philosopher   THĒ-uh-FRAS-tuhs   ,θiːə'fræstəs
  2. pers. name, German   TĀ-ō-FRAHS-tus   ,teːoː'frɑstus

Foreign Sounds: **ue**: *Fr.* **rue**, *Ger.* **füllen**   **uh(r)**: *Fr.* **boeuf**, *Ger.* **Höhle**   <u>**kh**</u>: *Ger.* **ich**, *Scot.* **loch**   **g̱**: *Sp.* **amigo**   **v**: *Sp.* **hablar**
hl: *Welsh* **Llanelli**.   CAPITALS: primary stress.   SMALL CAPS: secondary stress.   Ⓢ: U.S. pron.   Ⓑ: British pron.

Theorell
  A. H. T., *Swedish biochemist*   TE-u-REL, Ⓢ TĀ-uh-REL   ˌteu'rel, Ⓢ ˌteːə'rel
  (Nobel 1955)

Theosophism
  belief in Theosophy   thē-AHS-uh-FIZ-uhm   θiː'asə,fizəm

Theosophy
  system of esoteric thought   thē-AHS-uh-fē   θiː'asəfiˑ

Thera, Thíra [Santoríni]
  island, Greece   THIR-uh   'θirə

Theramenes
  Athenian politician   thi-RAM-uh-NĒZ   θi'ræmə,niːz

Theras
  descendant of Oedipus   THIR-uhs   'θirəs

Theravada [Hinayana]
  branch of Buddhism   THER-uh-VAHD-uh   ˌθerə'vadə

Thérésa
  pers. name, French   tā-rā-ZAH   teːreːzaː

Theresa
  pers. name   tuh-RĒ-suh, tuh-RĒ-zuh   tə'riːsə, tə'riːzə

Thérèse
  pers. name, French   tā-REZ   teːrez

Therese
  pers. name, German   tā-RĀ-zuh   teː'reːzə

Thermidor
  month, French Revolutionary   ter-mē-DAWR   termiːdɔːr
  calendar

Thermopylae
  pass, battle site, Greece   THUHR-MAHP-uh-lē   ˌθəʳ'mapəliˑ

Theropoda
  dinosaur suborder   thi-RAHP-uhd-uh   θi'rapədə

Theroux
  Paul, *US writer*   thuh-R̅O̅O̅   θə'ruː

Thersander
  one of the Epigoni   thuhr-SAN-duhr   θəʳ'sændəʳ

Thersites
  ugliest and most abusive Greek at   thuhr-SĪT-ēz   θəʳ'saiṭiːz
  Troy

Theseus
  mythological king of Athens   THĒ-sē-uhs, THĒ-S(Y)O̅O̅S   'θiːsiːəs, 'θiː,s(j)uːs

Thesmothetai
  Athenian magistrates   THES-mō-THĒ-TĪ   ˌθesmoː'θiː,tai

Thespiae
  ancient town, Greece   THES-pē-Ē   'θespiː,iː

Thespian
  pert. to Thespiae, Thespis, *or to*   THES-pē-uhn   'θespiːən
  drama

Thespis
  Greek poet   THES-puhs   'θespəs

Thespius
  king of Boeotia   THES-pē-uhs   'θespiːəs

Thessalia [Thessaly]
  region, Greece   THĀ-suh-LĒ-uh   ˌθeːsə'liːə

Thessalian
  pert. to Thessaly   the-SĀ-lē-uhn   θe'seːliːən

Key (col. 2):   a: fad   ā: fade   ah: father   ar: Mary   aw: law   e: fed   ē: feed   er: merry   i: hid   ī: hide   ō: coat   o̅o̅: boot
oi: boy   ow: now   u: put   uh: above   uhr: bird   ch: chop   ng: ring   sh: show   th: thick   <u>th</u>: this   zh: measure

Thessalonians

   New Testament book — THES-uh-LŌN-yuhnz, -LŌ-nē-uhnz — ˌθesəˈloːnjənz, -ˈloːniːənz

Thessalonica

   official name of Salonika — THES-uh-luh-NĪ-kuh, THES-uh-LAHN-i-kuh — ˌθesələˈnɑikə, ˌθesəˈlɑnikə

Thessaloníki

   region, Greece — THES-ah-law-NĒ-kē — ˌθesɑlɔːˈniːkiˑ

Thessaly

   region, Greece — THES-uh-lē — ˈθesəliˑ

Thestor

   father of Calchas, Leucippe, and Theonoe — THES-tuhr, THES-TAWR — ˈθestəʳ, ˈθesˌtɔːʳ

Thetes

   Athenian lowest class — THĒT-ēz — ˈθiːʈiːz

Thetis

   Greek sea goddess, mother of Achilles — THĒT-uhs — ˈθiːʈəs

Thibodaux

   city, LA — TIB-uh-DŌ — ˈtibəˌdoː

Thiel

   College, PA — TĒL, THĒL — ˈtiːl, ˈθiːl

Thierry

   pers. name, French — tye-RĒ — tjeriː

Thiers

   Louis, *president, France; city, France* — tē-ER — tiːer

Thieu

   see Nguyen Van Thieu

Thimphu

   city, Butan — thim-P̄O̅O̅ — θimˈpuː

Thingvellir

   plain, Iceland (site of Althing, 930-1880) — THING(G)-VET-LIR — ˈθiŋ(g)ˌvetˌliʳ

Thingyan

   Burmese festival — THING-GYAHN — ˈθiŋˌgjɑn

Thiokol

   tdmk for synthetic rubber products — THĪ-uh-KAWL, -KŌL — ˈθɑiəˌkɔːl, -ˌkoːl

Thira

   see Thera

Thisbe

   mythological lover of Pyramus — THIZ-bē — ˈθizbiˑ

Thívai [Thebes]

   town, Greece — THĒ-vä — ˈθiːveː

Tho

   lang., people, Vietnam — TŌ — ˈtoː

Thoas

   son of Ariadne — THŌ-uhs — ˈθoːəs

Thohoyandou

   capital city, Venda — tuh-HOI-AHN-d̄o̅o̅ — təˈhɔiˌɑnduː

Thom

   pers. name — TAHM — ˈtɑm

Foreign Sounds: **ue:** *Fr.* **rue**, *Ger.* füllen **uh(r):** *Fr.* **b**oeuf, *Ger.* Höhle <u>kh</u>: *Ger.* i**ch**, *Scot.* lo**ch** ḡ: *Sp.* ami**g**o v̲: *Sp.* ha**b**lar **hl:** *Welsh* **Ll**anelli. CAPITALS: primary stress. SMALL CAPS: secondary stress. ⑤: U.S. pron. ⑪: British pron.

Thomas
1. pers. name	TAHM-uhs	'taməs
2. Danish	TAW-MAHS	'tɔːˌmɑːs
3. Dutch, German	TŌ-MAHS	'toːˌmas
4. French	taw-MAH	tɔmɑ
5. Norwegian	TAWM-AHS	'tɔːmˌɑs
6. Swedish	TOO̅-MAHS	'tuːˌmɑːs

Thomasena, Thomasina
pers. name	TAHM-uh-SĒ-nuh	ˌtaməˈsiːnə

Thomasin
pers. name	TAHM-uh-suhn	'taməsən

Thomism
philosophy of Thomas Aquinas	TŌ-MIZ-uhm	'toːˌmizəm

Thom McAn
US shoe co.	TAHM muh-KAN	ˌtam məˈkæn

Thompson
James Robert, *US politician*	TAHM(P)-suhn	'tam(p)sən

Thomson
Sir George P., *English physicist (Nobel 1937); his father* Sir Joseph, *English physicist (Nobel 1906)*	TAHM(P)-suhn	'tam(p)sən

Thor
1. Scandinavian god of thunder	THAWR	'θɔːʳ
2. pers. name, Icelandic	THAWR	'θɔːr

Thorazine
tdmk for a tranquilizer	THŌR-uh-ZĒN, THAWR-	'θoːrəˌziːn, 'θɔːr-

Thoreau
Henry David, *US writer*	thuh-RŌ, thaw-RŌ, THAWR-ō	θəˈroː, θɔːˈroː, 'θɔːroː

thorium
element	THŌR-ē-uhm, THAWR-ē-uhm	'θoːriːəm, 'θɔːriːəm

Thornburgh
Dick Lewis, *US politician*	THAWRN-BUHRG	'θɔːʳnˌbəʳg

Thornton
pers. name	THAWRNT-n	'θɔːʳntn̩

Thorshavn
capital, Faroe Islands	tawrs-HOWN	tɔːʳsˈhaun

Thorstein
pers. name	THAWR-STĪN	'θɔːʳˌstain

Thorvald
pers. name, Danish	TUR-VAHL	'tuʳˌvɑːl

Thorvaldur
pers. name, Icelandic	THAWR-vahl-duer	'θɔːʳvaldyːr

Thoth
Egyptian god of wisdom	TŌT, TŌTH, THŌTH	'toːt, 'toːθ, 'θoːθ

Thothmes
name, Egyptian pharoahs	TŌT-muhs, TAHT-muhs, tuh-HUHT-muhs	'toːtməs, 'tatməs, təˈhɑtməs

Thrace
region, Greece	THRĀS, *in ancient context* THRĀ-sē	'θreːs, *in ancient context* 'θreːsiˑ

Thracian
pert. to Thrace	THRĀ-shuhn	'θreːʃən

Key (col. 2): a: fad ā: fade ah: father ar: Mary aw: law e: fed ē: feed er: merry i: hid ī: hide ō: coat o̅o̅: boot oi: boy ow: now u: put uh: above uhr: bird ch: chop ng: ring sh: show th: thick <u>th</u>: this zh: measure

Thraco-Phrygian
  hypothetical branch of   THRĀ-kō-FRIJ-ē-uhn   ˌθreːkoːˈfridʒiːən
  Indo-European lang.
Thráki [Thrace]
  region, Greece   THRAHK-(y)ē   ˈθrɑk(j)iˑ
Thrale
  Hester L., *Welsh author*   THRĀL   ˈθreːl
Thrasyboulos
  Athenian general   thras-IB-uh-luhs   θræsˈibələs
Thrasymedes
  son of Nestor   thruh-SIM-uhd-ēz   θrəˈsimədiːz
Threefin Blenny
  Icelandic skeptic   THRĀ-fin BLED-nue   ˈθreːfin ˈbled_nyː
Thucydidean
  pert. to Thucydides   TH(Y)OO-SID-uh-DĒ-uhn   ˌθ(j)uːˌsidəˈdiːən
Thucydides
  Greek historian   th(y)oo-SID-uh-DĒZ   θ(j)uːˈsidəˌdiːz
Thule
  ancient northern world;   T(Y)OO-lē, TH(Y)OO-lē, TH(Y)OOL   ˈt(j)uːliˑ, ˈθ(j)uːliˑ, ˈθ(j)uːl
  settlement, Greenland; N.
  American Eskimo culture
thulium
  element   TH(Y)OO-lē-uhm   ˈθ(j)uːliːəm
Thun
  lake, commune, Switzerland   TOON   ˈtuːn
Thuner See
  lake, Switzerland   TOO-nuhr ZĀ   ˈtuːnəʳ ˌzeː
Thunor [Thor]
  Scandinavian god of thunder   THUN-AWR   ˈθunˌɔːʳ
Thurber
  James, *US humorist*   THUHR-buhr   ˈθəʳbəʳ
Thurgood
  pers. name   THUHR-GUD   ˈθəʳˌgud
Thurii
  Athenian colony, Italy   TH(Y)UR-ē-Ī   ˈθ(j)uriːˌai
Thüringer Wald
  Thuringian Forest   TUE-ring-uhr VAHLT   ˈtyːriŋəʳ ˌvalt
Thuringia
  former state, Germany   th(y)ur-IN-j(ē-)uh   θ(j)urˈindʒ(iː)ə
Thuringian
  Forest, *region, Germany*   th(y)u-RIN-j(ē-)uhn   θ(j)uˈrindʒ(iː)ən
Thurlow
  pers. name   THUHR-lō   ˈθəʳloː
Thurman
  pers. name   THUHR-muhn   ˈθəʳmən
Thurmond
  Strom, *US politician*   THUHR-muhnd   ˈθəʳmənd
Thursday
  day of the week   THUHRZ-dē, THUHRZ-dā   ˈθəʳzdiˑ, ˈθəʳzdeː
Thurston
  pers. name   THUHR-stuhn   ˈθəʳstən
Thutmose
  Egyptian ruler   thoot-MŌ-suh, tuh-HUT-muh-suh   θuːtˈmoːsə, təˈhutməsə
Thyatira
  ancient city, Asia Minor   THĪ-uh-TĪ-ruh   ˌθɑiəˈtairə

Foreign Sounds: **ue**: *Fr.* **rue**, *Ger.* **füllen**   **uh(r)**: *Fr.* **boeuf**, *Ger.* **Höhle**   **kh**: *Ger.* i**ch**, *Scot.* lo**ch**   **g̅**: *Sp.* ami**g**o   **v̲**: *Sp.* ha**b**lar
hl: *Welsh* **Ll**anelli.   CAPITALS: primary stress.   SMALL CAPS: secondary stress.   Ⓢ: U.S. pron.   Ⓛ: British pron.

Thyestean
  pert. to Thyestes   thī-ES-tē-uhn   θai'estiːən

Thyestes
  twin brother of Atreus   thī-ES-tēz   θai'estiːz

Thymoetes
  husband of Cilla   THĪ-muh-WĒT-ēz   ,θaimə'wiːʈiːz

Thyone
  mother of Dionysus   thī-Ō-nē   θai'oːniˑ

Thyssen
  Fritz, *German industrialist*   TUES-uhn, Ⓢ TĒ-suhn   'tysən, Ⓢ 'tiːsən

Tia
  pers. name   TĒ-uh   'tiːə

Tia Juana
  city, Mexico   TĒ-uh WAHN-uh   ,tiːə 'wanə

Tia Maria
  tdmk for a liqueur   TĒ-uh muh-RĒ-uh   ,tiːə mə'riːə

Tiananmen
  Square, *public square, Beijing* TYEN-uh(n)-MEN,   'tjenə(n),men,
                              tē-EN-uh(n)-muhn,   tiː'enə(n)mən,
                              tē-AHN-uh(n)-MEN   tiː'anə(n),men

Tianjin [Tientsin]
  city, China   tē-AHN-JIN, tē-EN-JIN   tiː'an'dʒin, tiː'en'dʒin

Tian Shan [Tien Shan]
  mts., Asia   tē-AHN SHAHN, tē-EN SHAHN tiː'an 'ʃan, tiː'en 'ʃan

Tiber
  river, Italy   TĪ-buhr   'taibəʳ

Tiberias [Galilee]
  sea, city, Israel   tī-BIR-ē-uhs   tai'biriːəs

Tiberinus
  eponymous hero of the Tiber River TĪ-buh-RĪ-nuhs   ,taibə'rainəs

Tiberius
  1. Roman emperor; pers. name tī-BIR-ē-uhs   tai'biriːəs
  2. Dutch   tē-BĀ-rē-ues   tiː'beːriːys

Tibet
  region, China   tuh-BET   tə'bet

Tibetan
  pert. to Tibet   tuh-BET-n   tə'betn̩

Tibullus
  Roman poet   tuh-BUHL-uhs   tə'bələs

Ticino [Tessin]
  canton, Switzerland   ti-CHĒ-nō   ti'tʃiːnoː

Ticonderoga
  fort, former village, NY   TĪ-KAHN-duh-RŌ-guh   ,tai,kandə'roːgə

Tiegs
  Cheryl, *US fashion model*   TĒGZ   'tiːgz

T'ien-Ching
  city, China   tē-EN-JING   tiː'en'dʒiŋ

Tien Shan
  mts., Asia   tē-EN SHAHN   tiː'en 'ʃan

Tientsin [Tianjin]
  city, China   tē-EN(T)-SIN, TIN(T)-SIN tiː'en(t)'sin, 'tin(t)'sin

Tierney
  pers. name   TIR-nē   'tiʳniˑ

Tierra del Fuego
  island territory, Argentina   tē-ER-uh del FWĀ-gō   tiː'erə del 'fweːgoː

Key (col. 2):   a: fad ā: fade ah: father ar: Mary aw: law e: fed ē: feed er: merry i: hid ī: hide ō: coat o͞o: boot
oi: boy ow: now u: put uh: above uhr: bird ch: chop ng: ring sh: show th: thick th̲: this zh: measure

Tiffany
   US jewelry co.; pers. name   TIF-uh-nē   'tifəniˑ

Tiflis [Tbilisi]
   city, Georgia   TIF-luhs, tuh-FLĒS   'tiflǝs, tǝ'fliːs

Tigellinus
   Roman politician, adviser of Nero   TIJ-uh-LĪ-nuhs   ,tidʒǝ'lainǝs

Tiglath-Pileser
   Assyrian king   TIG-LATH-pī-LĒ-zuhr   'tig,læθpai'liːzǝʳ

Tigray
   see Tigre

Tigre
   river, S. America; city, Argentina   TĒ-ḡrā   'tiːɣreː

Tigre, Tigray
   lang., region, Ethiopia   ti-GRĀ   ti'greː

Tigrinya
   Semitic lang.   tuh-GRĒN-yuh   tǝ'griːnjǝ

Tigris
   river, Asia Minor   TĪ-gruhs   'taigrǝs

Tigua
   N. American people   TĒ-wuh, TĒḠ-wuh   'tiːwǝ, 'tiːɣwǝ

Tijuana
   town, Baja California Norte,   tē-HWAHN-ah, Ⓢ TĒ-uh-WAHN-uh,   tiː'hwɑnɑ, Ⓢ ,tiːǝ'wɑnǝ,
     Mexico   ti-WAHN-uh   ti'wɑnǝ

Tijuca
   mtn., Brazil; Brazilian beer   ti-ZHO͞O-kuh   ti'ʒuːkǝ

Tilburg
   city, Netherlands   TIL-BUHRG   'til,bǝʳg

Tillamook
   county, OR; N. American people   TIL-uh-muhk, TIL-uh-MUK   'tilǝmǝk, 'tilǝ,muk

Till Eulenspiegel
   German lengendary character   TIL OI-luhn-SHPĒ-guhl   'til ɔilǝn,ʃpiːgǝl

Tillinghast
   pers. name   TIL-ing-HAST   'tiliŋ,hæst

Tillis
   Melvin, *US musician, songwriter*   TIL-uhs   'tilǝs

Tilsit
   cheese   TIL-suht, TIL-zuht   'tilsǝt, 'tilzǝt

Tim
   pers. name   TIM   'tim

Timaeus
   Greek astronomer; dialogue of   tī-MĒ-uhs   tai'miːǝs
    Plato

Timandra
   mother of Evander   tuh-MAN-druh   tǝ'mændrǝ

Timba-Sha
   Indian reservation, US   TIM-buh-SHAH   'timbǝ'ʃɑ

Timbira
   S. American people   tim-BĒ-ruh   tim'biːrǝ

Timbuktu
   ancient city, town, Mali   TIM-BUHK-TO͞O   ,tim,bǝk'tuː

Times-Picayune
   newspaper, New Orleans, LA   TĪMZ PIK-ē-YO͞ON   'taimz ,piki'juːn

Timex
   US watch co.   TĪ-MEKS   'tai,meks

Foreign Sounds: ue: *Fr.* r**ue**, *Ger.* f**ü**llen uh(r): *Fr.* b**oeu**f, *Ger.* H**öh**le <u>kh</u>: *Ger.* i<u>ch</u>, *Scot.* lo<u>ch</u> ḡ: *Sp.* ami**g**o <u>v</u>: *Sp.* ha**b**lar
hl: *Welsh* L**l**anelli. CAPITALS: primary stress. SMALL CAPS: secondary stress. Ⓢ: U.S. pron. Ⓔ: British pron.

Timişoara
city, Romania   TĒ-mish-WAHR-uh   ˌtiːmiʃ'warə

Timoleon
Greek statesman   tuh-MŌ-lē-uhn, tī-   tə'moːliːən, taɪ-

Timon
Shakespearean character   TĪ-muhn   'taɪmən

Timor
island, sea, Indonesia   TĒ-MAWR, tē-MAWR   'tiːˌmɔːʳ, tiː'mɔːʳ

Timor Timur
eastern half of Timor island,   TĒ-MAWR TĒ-MUR, tē-MAWR tē-MUR   ˌtiːˌmɔːʳ 'tiːˌmuʳ, tiːˌmɔːʳ
Indonesia   tiː'muʳ

Timoshenko
Semyon, Russian militarist   tyim-uh-SHENG-kō   tjimə'ʃeŋkoː

Timothée
pers. name, French   tē-maw-TÃ   tiːmɔːteː

Timothy
New Testament book; pers. name   TIM-uh-thē   'timəθiˑ

Timucua
N. American people   TIM-uh-KŌŌ-uh   ˌtimə'kuːə

Timur [Tamburlaine]
Tartar conqueror   TIM-UR, TĒ-MUR   'tim,uʳ, 'tiːˌmuʳ

tin
element   TIN   'tin

T'in, Tin
lang., people, Laos, Thailand   TIN   'tin

Tina
1. pers. name   TĒ-nuh   'tiːnə
2. German   TĒ-nah   'tiːna

Tinamou
South American bird   TIN-uh-MŌŌ   'tinəˌmuː

Tinbergen
Jan, Dutch economist (Nobel   TIN-BER-ğuh(n)   'tin,beʳɣə(n)
1969); his brother Nikolaas,
Dutch zoologist (Nobel 1973)

Tindale, Tyndale
William, English New Testament   TIN-dl, TIN-DĀL   'tindl̩, 'tinˌdeːl
translator

Ting
Samuel Chao Chung, US physicist   TING   'tiŋ
(Nobel 1976)

Tinggian
lang., people, Philippine Islands   TING-gē-AHN   ˌtiŋgiː'an

Tinian
island, Pacific   TIN-ē-AN, TIN-ē-uhn   ˌtiniː'æn, 'tiniːən

Tintern
ruined abbey, England   TIN-tuhrn   'tintəʳn

Tintoretto
Jacopo, Italian painter   TIN-tuh-RET-ō   ˌtintə'reṭoː

Tioga
river, county, NY, PA   tī-Ō-guh   taɪ'oːgə

Tiomkin
Dimitri, US composer   TYAWM-kyin, ⑤ tē-AHM(P)-kuhn   'tjɔːmkjin, ⑤ tiː'am(p)kən

Tiphys
pilot of the Argo   TĪ-fuhs, TĒ-fuhs   'taɪfəs, 'tiːfəs

Key (col. 2):   a: fad   ā: fade   ah: father   ar: Mary   aw: law   e: fed   ē: feed   er: merry   i: hid   ī: hide   ō: coat   ōō: boot
oi: boy   ow: now   u: put   uh: above   uhr: bird   ch: chop   ng: ring   sh: show   th: thick   <u>th</u>: this   zh: measure

Tippah
county, MS — TIP-uh — 'tɪpə

Tippecanoe
river, county, IN — TIP-uh-kuh-N$\overline{OO}$ — ˌtɪpəkə'nuː

Tipperary
prov & town, Irish Republic — TIP-uh-RER-ē — ˌtɪpə'reriˑ

Tippetarius
Queen of Oz — TIP-uh-TAR-ē-uhs, TIP-uh-TER-ē-uhs — ˌtɪpə'tæriːəs, ˌtɪpə'teriːəs

Tirana, Tiranë
city, Albania — ti-RAHN-uh — ti'rɑnə

Tiresias
soothsayer at Thebes — tī-RĒ-sē-uhs, tī-RĒ-zē-uhs — tai'riːsiːəs, tai'riːziːəs

Tirol, Tyrol
state, Austria — tuh-RŌL, TĪ-RŌL, tī-RŌL, TIR-uhl — tə'roːl, 'tai,roːl, tai'roːl, 'tirəl

Tiros
satellites — TĪ-RŌS — 'tai,roːs

Tirpitz
Alfred von, German militarist — TIR-puhts — 'tiʳpəts

Tiruray
lang., people, Philippine Islands — TIR-uh-RĪ, TIR-uh-RĪ — 'tirə,rai, ˌtirə'rai

Tiryns
ancient city, Greece — TIR-uhnz, TĪ-ruhnz — 'tirənz, 'tairənz

Tirzah
ancient Canaanite town — TUHR-zuh — 'təʳzə

Tisch
Preston, US government official — TISH — 'tiʃ

Tiselius
Arne, Swedish chemist (Nobel 1948) — tuh-SÃ-lē-uhs, tuh-ZÃ-lē-uhs — tə'seːliːəs, tə'zeːliːəs

Tish Ab B'ab
Jewish holiday — TISH uh BAHV, BAWV — 'tiʃ ə ˌbɑv, ˌbɔːv

Tishah Be'av
Jewish holiday — TISH-uh buh-AHV, buh-AWV — 'tiʃə bə'ɑv, bə'ɔːv

Tishomingo
county, MS — TISH-uh-MING-gō — ˌtiʃə'miŋgoː

Tishri
Jewish month — TISH-rē, TISH-rā — 'tiʃriˑ, 'tiʃreˑ

Tisiphone
one of the Greek Furies — tī-SIF-uh-nē, tuh-SIF-uh-nē — tai'sifəniˑ, tə'sifəniˑ

Tisza
river, Europe — TIS-AW — 'tis,ɔː

Titan
giant in Greek myth; satellite of Saturn — TĪT-n — 'taitn̩

Titania
fairy queen in A Midsummer Night's Dream, Shakespeare; satellite of Uranus — tuh-TÃN-yuh, tuh-TAHN-yuh, tī-TÃN-yuh — tə'teːnjə, tə'tɑnjə, tai'teːnjə

Titanic
British ocean liner — tī-TAN-ik — tai'tænik

Titanides
daughters of Uranus and Gaia — tī-TAN-uh-DĒZ — tai'tænə,diːz

titanium
element — tī-TÃ-nē-uhm, tuh-, -TAN-ē-uhm — tai'teːniːəm, tə-, -'tæniːəm

---

Foreign Sounds: ue: *Fr.* **rue**, *Ger.* **füllen**   uh(r): *Fr.* **boeuf**, *Ger.* **Höhle**   kh: *Ger.* i**ch**, *Scot.* lo**ch**   ḡ: *Sp.* ami**g**o   v̲: *Sp.* ha**b**lar   hl: *Welsh* **Ll**anelli.   CAPITALS: primary stress.   SMALL CAPS: secondary stress.   ⑤: U.S. pron.   ⓒ: British pron.

Titanosaurus
  dinosaur   TĪ-TAN-uh-SAWR-uhs,   ˌtaiˌtænəˈsɔːrəs, ˌtaitn̩əˈsɔːrəs
                                    TĪT-n-uh-SAWR-uhs

Tithonus
  brother of Priam   tī-THŌ-nuhs   taiˈθoːnəs

Titian
  Italian painter; pers. name   TISH-uhn   ˈtiʃən

Titicaca
  lake, Peru   TIT-i-KAHK-uh, TĒT-ē-KAHK-uh   ˌtiţiˈkakə, ˌtiːţiːˈkakə

Titius
  Roman name   TISH-uhs   ˈtiʃəs

Tito
  1. Josip Broz, Yugoslav leader TĒ-taw, ⑤ TĒT-ō   ˈtiːtɔː, ⑤ ˈtiːţoː
  2. pers. name, Italian   TĒ-tō   ˈtiːtoː

Titograd [Podgorica]
  city, Montenegro   TĒT-ō-GRAD, -GRAHD   ˈtiːţoːˌgræd, -ˌgrad

Titus
  *New Testament book; Roman   TĪT-uhs   ˈtaitəs
   emperor; pers. name*

Titus Andronicus
  play, Shakespeare   TĪT-uhs an-DRAHN-i-kuhs   ˈtaitəs ænˈdranikəs

Tityus
  son of Zeus who attacked Leto   TIT-ē-uhs   ˈtiţiːəs

Tiv
  lang., people, Nigeria   TIV   ˈtiv

Tivoli
  1. town, Roman resort, Italy   TĒ-vō-lē, ⑤ TIV-uh-lē   ˈtiːvoːliˑ, ⑤ ˈtivəliˑ
  2. entertainment park,   TIV-uh-lē   ˈtivəliˑ
   Copenhagen

Tiy
  Queen of Egypt   TĒ   ˈtiː

Tjalling
  pers. name, Dutch   TYAHL-ing   ˈtjaliŋ

Tlapanec
  lang., people, Mexico   TLAHP-uh-NEK, TLAHP-uh-NEK   ˈtlapəˌnek, ˌtlapəˈnek

Tlaxcala
  state, Mexico   tlah-SKAHL-uh   tlaˈskalə

Tlepolemus
  son of Heracles   tlep-AHL-uh-muhs   tlepˈaləməs

Tlingit
  N. American people   TLING-(g)uht, TLING-kuht   ˈtliŋ(g)ət, ˈtliŋkət

Toba
  lang., people, Sumatra [Batak]; TŌ-buh   ˈtoːbə
   lang., people, Argentina

Tobago
  see Trinidad and Tobago

Tobagonian
  pert. to Tobago; *native or   TŌ-buh-GŌ-nē-uhn   ˌtoːbəˈgoːniːən
   inhabitant of* Tobago

Tobiah
  Biblical name   tuh-BĪ-uh   təˈbaiə

Key (col. 2): a: fad ā: fade ah: father ar: **M**ary aw: law e: fed ē: feed er: me**rr**y i: hid ī: hide ō: coat o͞o: boot
oi: boy ow: now u: put uh: above uhr: bird ch: chop ng: ri**ng** sh: **sh**ow th: **th**ick th: **th**is zh: measure

Tobias

   1. Old Testament book, pers.   tuh-BĪ-uhs   tə'baiəs
     name

   2. Dutch, German   tō-BĒ-ahs   toː'biːɑs

   3. Swedish   tu-BĒ-ahs   tu'biːɑːs

Tobin

   James, *US economist (Nobel*   TŌ-buhn   'toːbən
     1981); pers. name

Tobit

   Apocryphal book   TŌ-buht   'toːbət

Toblerone

   tdmk for a candy bar   TŌ-bluh-RŌN, TAHB-luh-RŌN   ,toːblə'roːn, ,tɑblə'roːn

Tobruk

   prov, Libya   TŌ-BRUK, tō-BRUK   'toː,bruk, toː'bruk

Toby

   pers. name   TŌ-bē   'toːbiˑ

Tocai [Tokay]

   wine   TŌ-kī   'toːkai

Tocantins

   river, Brazil   TŌ-kuhn-TIⁿS   ,toːkən'tĩːs

Toccoa

   river, city, falls, GA   tuh-KŌ-uh   tə'koːə

Tocharian, Tokharian

   ancient Asian people, lang.   tō-KAR-ē-uhn, tō-KER-ē-uhn,   toː'kæriːən, toː'keriːən,
                      tō-KAHR-ē-uhn   toː'kɑriːən

Tocqueville, de

   Alexis, *French writer*   duh tawk-VĒL   də toːkviːl

Tod

   pers. name   TAHD   'tad

Toda

   1. lang., people, South India   TŌD-uh   'toːdə

   2. Japanese construction co.   tō-dah   toːdɑ

Todd

   Sir Alexander R., *Scottish chemist*   TAHD   'tad
     (Nobel 1957); pers. name

Todor

   pers. name (T. Zhivkov)   TAW-DAWR   'tɔː,dɔːʳ

Tody

   Caribbean bird   TŌD-ē   'toːdiˑ

TOEFL

   Test of English as a Foreign   TŌ-fuhl   'toːfəl
     Language

Togo

   republic, Africa   TŌ-gō   'toːgoː

Togolese

   pert. to Togo   TŌ-guh-LĒZ, -LĒS   ,toːgə'liːz, -'liːs

Tōhoku

   mtn. region, Japan   tō-hō-ko͞o   toːhoːkuː

Tohono O'odham

   N. American people   tō-HŌ-nō ō-ŌD-uhm   toː'hoːnoː oː'oːdəm

Tojolabal

   lang., people, Mexico   TŌ-<u>kh</u>ō-luh-BAHL   ,toːxoːlə'bɑl

Tokai

   Japanese bank   tō-kī   toːkɑi

Foreign Sounds: ue: *Fr.* **rue**, *Ger.* **fü**llen uh(r): *Fr.* b**oeu**f, *Ger.* H**öh**le <u>kh</u>: *Ger.* i**ch**, *Scot.* lo**ch** ḡ: *Sp.* ami**g**o v̲: *Sp.* ha**b**lar
hl: *Welsh* **Ll**anelli. CAPITALS: primary stress. SMALL CAPS: secondary stress. Ⓢ: U.S. pron. Ⓑ: British pron.

Tokaj [Tokay]
   town, Hungary   TAW-KĪ   'tɔːˌkɑi

Tokay
   1. town, Hungary   TAW-KĪ, Ⓢ TŌ-KĪ, TŌ-KĀ, tō-KĀ   'tɔːˌkɑi, Ⓢ 'toːˌkɑi, 'toːˌkeː, toːˈkeː

   2. wine   tō-KĀ, TŌ-KĀ, TŌ-KĪ   toːˈkeː, 'toːˌkeː, 'toːˌkɑi

Tokay d'Alsace
   wine   taw-KE dahl-SAHS   tɔːke dɑːlsɑːs

Tokelau
   islands, Pacific   TŌ-kuh-LOW   'toːkəˌlɑu

Tokelauan
   pert. to Tokelau   TŌ-kuh-LOW-uhn   ˌtoːkəˈlauən

Tokharian
   see Tocharian

Toklas
   Alice B., *US author*   TŌ-kluhs   'toːkləs

Tok Pisin [Neo-Melanesian]
   lang., Papua New Guinea   TAWK PĒ-suhn, TAHK   'tɔːk 'piːsən, 'tɑk

Tokyo
   city, Japan   TŌ-kē-ō, TŌ-kyō   'toːkiːˌoː, 'toːkjoː

Toland
   John, *US author*   TAHL-uhnd   'tɑlənd

Toledo
   1. US pl. name   tuh-LĒD-ō, tuh-LĒD-uh   təˈliːdoː, təˈliːdə
   2. prov & town, Spain; district,   tō-LĀ-tħō, Ⓢ tuh-LĒD-ō, tuh-LĒD-uh   toːˈleːðoː, Ⓢ təˈliːdoː, təˈliːdə
      Belize

Tolkien
   J.R.R., *English writer*   TAHL-KĒN, Ⓢ TŌL-KĒN   'tɑlˌkiːn, Ⓢ 'toːlˌkiːn

Tolland
   county, town, CT   TAHL-uhnd   'tɑlənd

Tolstoy, Tolstoi
   Lev (Leo), *Russian novelist*   TUHL-STOI, Ⓢ TAWL-STOI, TŌL-,   ˌtəlˈstɔi, Ⓢ 'tɔːlˌstɔi, 'toːl-,
                     TAHL-   'tɑl-

Toltec
   N. American people   TŌL-TEK, TAHL-TEK   'toːlˌtek, 'tɑlˌtek

Toluca
   city, volcano, Mexico   tuh-LOO-kuh   təˈluːkə

Tol'yatti [Stavropol]
   city, Russia   tawl-YAHT-ē   tɔːlˈjɑːʈiˑ

Tom
   pers. name   TAHM   'tɑm

Toma
   pers. name, Romanian   TAW-mah   'tɔːmɑ

Tomáš
   pers. name, Czech   TAW-MAHSH   'tɔːˌmɑʃ

Tomás
   pers. name, Spanish   tō-MAHS   toːˈmas

Tomasz
   pers. name, Polish   TAW-mahsh   'tɔmɑːʃ

Tomaz
   pers. name, Portuguese   tōō-MAHSH   tuːˈmɑːʃ

Tombigbee
   river, MS, AL   tahm-BIG-bē   tɑmˈbigbiˑ

Tombouctou [Timbuktu]
   town, Mali   tawⁿ-bōōk-TOO   tõbuːktuː

Key (col. 2):   a: fad   ā: fade   ah: father   ar: Mary   aw: law   e: fed   ē: feed   er: merry   i: hid   ī: hide   ō: coat   ōō: boot
oi: boy   ow: now   u: put   uh: above   uhr: bird   ch: chop   ng: ring   sh: show   th: thick   <u>th</u>: this   zh: measure

Tomini
Gulf of, *Molucca Sea* — tō-MĒ-nē — toːˈmiːniˑ

Tomlin
Lily, *US actress* — TAHM-luhn — ˈtɑmlən

Tommaso
pers. name, Italian — tōm-MAHZ-ō — toːmˈmɑzoː

Tommy, Tommie
pers. name — TAHM-ē — ˈtɑmiˑ

Tomomi
pers. name, Japanese — tō-mō-mē — toːmoːmiː

Tomonaga
Shinichiro, *Japanese physicist (Nobel 1965)* — tō-mō-nahg-ah — toːmoːnɑgɑ

Tomoyuki
pers. name, Japanese — tō-mō-yuk-ē — toːmoːjukiː

Tomoyushi
pers. name, Japanese — tō-mō-yush-ē — toːmoːjuʃiː

Tonawanda
town, NY — TAHN-uh-WAHN-duh — ˌtɑnəˈwɑndə

Tonegawa
Susumu, *Japanese biologist (Nobel 1987)* — tō-nā-gah-wah — toːneːgɑwɑ

Tonga
1. *island kingdom, Pacific* — TAHNG-(g)uh, TAWNG-(g)uh — ˈtɑŋ(g)ə, ˈtɔːŋ(g)ə
2. *lang., people, Africa* — TAHNG-guh, TAWNG-guh — ˈtɑŋgə, ˈtɔːŋgə

Tongan
lang., people, Tonga — TAHNG-(g)uhn — ˈtɑŋ(g)ən

Tongan-Samoan
lang., Polynesia — TAHNG-(g)uhn-suh-MŌ-uhn — ˈtɑŋ(g)ənsəˈmoːən

Toni
pers. name — TŌ-nē — ˈtoːniˑ

Tonia
pers. name — TŌN-yuh — ˈtoːnjə

Tonka
tdmk for toys — TAWNG-kuh, TAHNG-kuh — ˈtɔːŋkə, ˈtɑŋkə

Tonkawa
N. American people — TAHNG-kuh-wuh — ˈtɑŋkəwə

Tonkin
gulf, China Sea; region, Vietnam — TAHNG-kuhn, TAHN-KIN, TAHNG-KIN — ˈtɑŋkən, ˈtɑnˈkin, ˈtɑŋˈkin

Tonle Sap
lake, Cambodia — TAHN-lā SAHP, SAP — ˌtɑnleː ˈsɑp, ˈsæp

Tonowanda
N. American people — TAHN-uh-WAHN-duh — ˌtɑnəˈwɑndə

Tønsberg
port, Norway — TUH(R)NZ-BER-yuh, Ⓢ TUHRNZ-BAR — ˈtœːnzˌberj, Ⓢ ˈtəʳnzˌbæʳ

Tonto
river, Mexico; Lone Ranger's companion — TAHN-tō — ˈtɑntoː

Tony
1. *pers. name* — TŌ-nē — ˈtoːniˑ
2. *French* — taw-NĒ — tɔːniː

Tooele
county, UT — tu-EL-uh, tuh-WEL-uh — tuˈelə, təˈwelə

Foreign Sounds: ue: *Fr.* **rue**, *Ger.* **füllen** uh(r): *Fr.* **boeuf**, *Ger.* **Höhle** kh: *Ger.* i**ch**, *Scot.* lo**ch** ğ: *Sp.* ami**go** v: *Sp.* ha**b**lar
hl: *Welsh* **Ll**anelli. CAPITALS: primary stress. SMALL CAPS: secondary stress. Ⓢ: U.S. pron. Ⓛ: British pron.

Toowoomba
city, Australia tuh-WUM-buh tə'wumbə

Topa'zio
Portuguese beer tō-PAHZ-yō toː'paːzjoː

Topeka
city, KS tuh-PĒ-kuh tə'piːkə

Topham
pers. name TAHP-uhm 'tɑpəm

Tophet
Biblical place TŌ-fuht, TŌ-FET 'toːfət, 'toː,fet

Toppan
Japanese printing co. tō-pahn toːpɑn

Tor
pers. name, Swedish TO͞OR 'tuːʳ

Torah
Jewish scripture & law TŌR-uh, TAWR-uh, TOI-ruh, 'toːrə, 'tɔːrə, 'tɔirə, tɔː'rɑ
  taw-RAH

Torbay
borough, England TAWR-BĀ ,tɔːʳ'beː

Torcuato
pers. name, Spanish tawr-KWAH-tō tɔːr'kwɑtoː

Tordesillas
village, Spain tawr-thā-SĒ(L)-yahs, tɔːrðeː'siː(l)jɑs,
  ⑤ TAWRD-uh-SĒ-(y)uhs, ⑤ ,tɔːʳdə'siː(j)əs,
  TAWRD-uh-SĒL-yuhs ,tɔːʳdə'siːljəs

Torii
Shinto symbol TŌR-ē(-Ē), TAWR-ē(-Ē) 'toːriː(,iː), 'tɔːriː(,iː)

Torino [Turin]
prov & town, Italy tō-RĒ-nō toː'riːnoː

Torme
Mel, US entertainer tawr-MĀ tɔːʳ'meː

Torne
river, Sweden TAWR-nuh 'tɔːʳnə

Tornio
port, Finland TAWR-nē-ō 'tɔːʳniː,oː

Toro
lang., Africa TŌR-ō, TAWR-ō 'toːroː, 'tɔːroː

Toronto
1. city, Canada tuh-RAHNT-ō, -uh; TRAHN(T)-ō tə'rɑntoː, -ə; 'tran(t)oː
2. city, OH tuh-RAHNT-ō, -uh tə'rɑntoː, -ə

Torosaurus
dinosaur TAWR-uh-SAWR-uhs ,tɔːrə'sɔːrəs

Toros Dağları [Taurus]
mtn. range, Turkey taw-RAWS DAHǦ-lah-RĒ tɔː,rɔːs ,dɑɣlɑ'riː

Torquato
pers. name, Italian tawr-KWAH-tō tɔːʳ'kwɑtoː

Torquay
former borough, England, now tawr-KĒ tɔːʳ'kiː
  part of Torbay

Torquemada
Juan de, Spanish inquisitor tawr-kā-MAH-thah tɔːʳkeː'mɑðɑ

Torrance
city, CA; county, NM TAWR-uhn(t)s, TAHR-uhn(t)s 'tɔːrən(t)s, 'tɑrən(t)s

---

Key (col. 2): a: fad ā: fade ah: father ar: Mary aw: law e: fed ē: feed er: merry i: hid ī: hide ō: coat o͞o: boot
oi: boy ow: now u: put uh: above uhr: bird ch: chop ng: ring sh: show th: thick t̲h̲: this zh: measure

Torremolinos
 town, Spain   tawr-rā-mō-LĒ-nōs,   tɔːrreːmoːˈliːnoːs,
                                  ⑤ TAWR-uh-muh-LĒ-nōs   ⑤ ˌtɔːrəməˈliːnoːs

Torrens
 lake, Australia   TAWR-uhnz, TAHR-uhnz   ˈtɔːrənz, ˈtɑrənz

Torres-Martinez
 N. American people   TAWR-ās-mahr-TĒ-nez   ˌtɔːreːsmɑˑˈtiːnez

Torres Vedras
 town, Portugal   TAWR-uhs VĀ-druhs   ˌtɔːrəs ˈveːdrəs

Torrey
 pers. name   TAWR-ē   ˈtɔːriˑ

Torrijos Herrera
 Omar, *Panamanian general*   tawr-RĒ-khōs er-RĀ-rah   tɔːrˈriːxoːs erˈreːrɑ

Torsten
 pers. name, Swedish   TAWR-stuhn   ˈtɔːˑstən

Tortola
 island, British Virgin Islands tawr-TŌ-luh   tɔːˑˈtoːlə

Tortoni
 dessert   tawr-TŌ-nē   tɔːˑˈtoːniˑ

Tortuga
 island, Haiti   tawr-TŌO-guh   tɔːˑˈtuːgə

Tory
 political party, England & TŌR-ē, TAWR-ē   ˈtoːriˑ, ˈtɔːriˑ
  Canada; pers. name

Toscana [Tuscany]
 region, Italy   tō-SKAHN-uh, taw-SKAHN-uh   toːˈskɑnə, tɔːˈskɑnə

Toscanini
 Arturo, *Italian conductor* TAHS-kuh-NĒ-nē, TAWS-   ˌtɑskəˈniːniˑ, ˌtɔːs-

Toshiba
 Japanese electronics co.   tuh-SHĒ-buh   təˈʃiːbə

Toshiki
 pers. name, Japanese   tō-shē-kē   toːʃiːkiː

Toshiro
 pers. name, Japanese   tō-shē-rō   toːʃiːroː

Tosk
 lang., Albania   TAHSK   ˈtɑsk

Toto
 pop music group; dog in The   TŌT-ō   ˈtoːʈoː
  Wizard of Oz, *F. Baum*

Totonac
 N. American people   TŌT-n-AHK   ˌtoːtn̩ˈɑk

Totowa
 city, NJ   TŌT-uh-wuh   ˈtoːʈəwə

Tottenham
 former borough, England   TAHT-n-uhm, TAHT-nuhm   ˈtɑtn̩əm, ˈtɑtnəm

Toubkal, Jebel
 mtn., Morocco   JEB-uhl tōob-KAHL   ˌdʒebəl tuːbˈkɑl

Toucouleur, Tukulör
 people, lang., Africa   TŌO-kuh-LUHR   ˌtuːkəˈləˑ

Toulon
 city, France   tōo-LAWⁿ   tuːlɔ̃

Toulouse
 city, France   tu-LŌOZ   tuluːz

Toulouse-Lautrec
 Henri de, *French painter*   tōo-lōoz-lō-TREK   tuːluːzloːtrek

---

Foreign Sounds: ue: *Fr.* **rue**, *Ger.* **füllen**   uh(r): *Fr.* **boeuf**, *Ger.* **Höhle**   kh: *Ger.* **ich**, *Scot.* **loch**   ğ: *Sp.* **amigo**   v: *Sp.* **hablar**
hl: *Welsh* **Llanelli**.   CAPITALS: primary stress.   SMALL CAPS: secondary stress.   ⑤: U.S. pron.   ⓛ: British pron.

Toungoo
  district, town, Burma   TOWNG-(G)ŌŌ   'tauŋ,(g)uː

Touraine
  prov, France   tōo-REN   tuːren

Tour Blanche, La
  wine   lah tōor BLAHⁿSH   laː tuːr blɑ̃ʃ

Tour de France
  French bicycle race   tōor duh FRAHⁿS, Ⓢ TUR duh   tuːr də frɑ̃s, Ⓢ ,tuʳ də 'frɑ̃s,
                             FRAHⁿS, TUR duh FRAN(T)S   ,tuʳ də 'fræn(t)s

Tour Haut Brion, La
  wine   lah TŌOR ō brē-AWⁿ   laː tuːr oː briːɔ̃

Tour Martillac, La
  wine   lah TŌOR mahr-tē-YAHK   laː tuːr maːrtiːjaːk

Tournai
  district, Belgium   tur-NĀ   tuʳneː

Tourneau
  jewelers   tur-NŌ   tuʳnoː

Touro
  College, NY   TUR-ō   'turoː

Tours
  city, France   TŌOR   tuːr

Tours-sur-Marne
  town, France   TŌOR-suer-MAHRN   tuːrsyːrmaːrn

Toushi
  fermented black beans   TŌO-shē   'tuːʃiˑ

Toussaint
  pers. name, French   tōo-SEⁿ   tuːsẽ

Toussaint L'Ouverture
  François, *Haitian political leader*   tōo-seⁿ lōo-ver-TUER   tuːsẽ luːvertyːr

Tower Hamlets
  borough, England   TOW(-uh)r HAM-luhts   'tau(ə)ʳ 'hæmləts

Towhee
  songbird   TŌ-HĒ, TŌ-ē, tō-HĒ   'toː,hiː, 'toːiː, toː'hiː

Townes
  Charles Hard, *US physicist (Nobel 1964)*   TOWNZ   'taunz

Townsend
  Francis E., *US physician*   TOWN-zuhnd   'taunzənd

Townshend
  family of British politicians; Peter,   TOWN-ZEND, TOWN-zuhnd   'taun,zend, 'taunzənd
  British rock musician

Towong
  Australia   tuh-WAHNG, tuh-WAWNG   tə'waŋ, tə'wɔŋ

Towson
  town, MD   TOWS-n   'tausn̩

Toya, Toyah
  pers. name   TOI-uh   'tɔiə

Toynbee
  Arnold, *British historian*   TOIN-bē   'tɔinbiˑ

Toyota
  Japanese car co.   toi-ŌT-uh   tɔi'oːʈə

Toys "R" Us
  US toy co.   TOI-ZAHR-UHS, TOI-zuh-RUHS   ,tɔi,zɑr'əs, ,tɔizə'rəs

Trâblous, Tarabulus [Tripoli]
  city, Lebanon   tuh-RAHB-uh-luhs   tə'rabələs

Key (col. 2): a: fad ā: fade ah: father ar: **M**ary aw: **l**aw e: fed ē: feed er: **m**erry i: hid ī: hide ō: coat ōō: boot
oi: **b**oy   ow: **n**ow   u: put   uh: above   uhr: b**i**rd   ch: **ch**op   ng: ri**ng**   sh: **sh**ow   th: **th**ick   th: **th**is   zh: mea**s**ure

Tracey
   pers. name   TRĀ-sē   'treːsiˑ

Trachodon
   dinosaur   trak-uh-DAHN, TRĀ-kuh-DAHN   trækəˌdɑn, 'treːkəˌdɑn

Tractarian
   supporter of Tractarianism   trak-TAR-ē-uhn   træk'tæriːən

Tractarianism
   Oxford Movement toward   trak-TAR-ē-uh-NIZ-uhm   træk'tæriːəˌnizəm
   Anglo-Catholicism

Tracy
   US pl. name; pers. name   TRĀ-sē   'treːsiˑ

Trafalgar
   Square, *London, England*   truh-FAL-guhr   trə'fælgəʳ

Trafalgar, Cabo
   cape, Spain   KAH<u>V</u>-ō trah-fahl-G̃AHR   'kaβoː trafal'ɣar

Traherne
   Thomas, *English author*   truh-HUHRN   trə'həʳn

Traill's flycatcher
   bird   TRĀLZ   'treːlz

Train à Grand Vitesse
   high-speed French train   TREN ah GRAH^n vē-TES   trẽn aː grã viːtes

Trajan
   Roman emperor   TRĀ-juhn   'treːdʒən

Trakehner
   wine   truh-KĀ-nuhr   trə'keːnəʳ

Tralee
   seaport, Ireland   truh-LĒ   trə'liː

Traminer
   wine   TRAM-uh-nuhr, TRAHM-uh-nuhr,   'træmənəʳ, 'tramənəʳ,
        truh-MĒ-nuhr   trə'miːnəʳ

Tramore
   town, Ireland   truh-MAWR   trə'mɔːʳ

Tranquillitatis, Mare
   see Mare Tranquillitatis

Transcaucasia
   region, Caucasus Mts.   TRAN(T)S-kaw-KĀ-zh(ē-)uh, TRANZ-   ˌtræn(t)skɔː'keːʒ(iː)ə, ˌtrænz-

Transcendentalism
   philosophical movement   TRAN-SEN-DENT-l-iz-uhm,   ˌtræn,sen'dentḷizəm,
        TRAN-suhn-   ˌtrænsən-

Transjordan
   part of kingdom of Jordan   tranz-JAWRD-n, tran(t)s-   trænz'dʒɔːʳdṇ, træn(t)s-

Transkei
   independent territory, South   tran(t)-SKĪ, -SKĀ; tranz-KĪ, -KĀ   træn(t)'skai, -'skeː;
   Africa   trænz'kai, -'keː

Trans-Siberian
   across Siberia, Russia, esp. the   tran(z)-sī-BIR-ē-uhn   træn(z)sai'biriːən
   railroad

Transvaal
   prov, South Africa   tran(t)s-VAHL, tranz-VAHL   træn(t)s'val, trænz'val

Transylvania
   prov, Romania; county, NC   TRAN-suhl-VĀ-nē-uh,   ˌtrænsəl've ːniːə,
        TRAN-suhl-VĀN-yuh   ˌtrænsəl'veːnjə

Trapani
   prov, port, Sicily   TRAHP-uh-nē   'trɑpəniˑ

Foreign Sounds: **ue:** *Fr.* **rue,** *Ger.* **füllen**   **uh(r):** *Fr.* **boeuf,** *Ger.* **Höhle**   <u>kh</u>: *Ger.* **i<u>ch</u>,** *Scot.* **lo<u>ch</u>**   **g̃:** *Sp.* **ami<u>g</u>o**   <u>v</u>: *Sp.* **ha<u>b</u>lar**
hl: *Welsh* **Llanelli.**   CAPITALS: primary stress.   SMALL CAPS: secondary stress.   ⑤: U.S. pron.   ⑥: British pron.

Trapier
   pers. name   truh-PIR   trə'piʳ

Trappist
   religious order   TRAP-uhst   'træpəst

Trasimene
   lake, central Italy   TRAS-uh-MĒN   'træsə,miːn

Trasimeno [Trasimene]
   lake, central Italy   TRAHZ-i-MĀ-nō   ˌtrɑzi'meːnoː

Traubel
   Helen, *US soprano*   TROW-buhl   'trɑubəl

Traugott
   1. pers. name   TROW-guht   'trɑugət
   2. German   TROW-GAWT   'trɑuˌgɔːt

Traun
   river, Austria   TROWN   'trɑun

Traun See
   lake, Austria   TROWN ZĀ   'trɑun ˌzeː

Travancore
   former state, India   TRAV-uhn-KAWR, TRAV-uhn-KAWR   ˌtrævən'kɔːʳ, 'trævənˌkɔːʳ

Travelodge
   tdmk for a US hotel/motel chain   TRAV-uh-LAHJ   'trævəˌlɑdʒ

Traverse
   county, MN; lake, SD, MI   TRAV-uhrs   'trævəʳs

Traviata, La
   opera, Verdi   lah TRAHV-ē-AHT-uh   lɑ ˌtraviː'aţə

Travis
   pers. name   TRAV-uhs   'trævəs

Travolta
   John, *US actor*   truh-VŌL-tuh   trə'voːltə

Treat
   pers. name   TRĒT   'triːt

Trebbiano
   Italian wine   treb-YAHN-ō   treb'janoː

Trebizond
   Greek empire   TREB-uh-ZAHND   'trebəˌzɑnd

Treblinka
   Nazi concentration camp, Poland   truh-BLING-kuh   trə'blinkə

Trefethen
   winery, CA   truh-FETH-uhn   trə'feθən

Trego
   county, KA   TRĒ-gō   'triːgoː

Treitschke
   Heinrich von, *German historian*   TRĪCH-kuh   'traitʃkə

Trelawney
   pers. name   tri-LAW-nē   tri'lɔːniˑ

Trematoda
   class of flatworms   truh-MAT-uhd-uh   trə'mæţədə

Tremayne
   pers. name   truh-MĀN   trə'meːn

Tremiti Islands
   prov. & islands, Italy   TRĀ-muht-ē, TREM-uht-ē   'treːməţiˑ, 'treməţiˑ

Trempealeau
   river, county, WI   TREM-puh-LŌ   'trempəˌloː

Trengganu
   river, state, Malaysia   treng-GAHN-ōō   treŋ'ganuː

Key (col. 2):   a: fad   ā: fade   ah: father   ar: Mary   aw: law   e: fed   ē: feed   er: merry   i: hid   ī: hide   ō: coat   ōō: boot
oi: boy   ow: now   u: put   uh: above   uhr: bird   ch: chop   ng: ring   sh: show   th: thick   th: this   zh: measure

Trent
   river, NC, Canada, England; city,   TRENT   'trent
   Italy

Trenton
   city, NJ   TRENT-n   'trentṇ

Tres Equis (XXX)
   Mexican beer   trās Ā-kēs   treːs 'eːkiːs

Treutlen
   county, GA   TR$\overline{OO}$T-luhn   'truːtlən

Trevelyan
   George, British historian; pers.   tri-VIL-yuhn, truh-VEL-yuhn   tri'viljən, trə'veljən
   name

Trèves
   French name for Trier   TREV   trev

Treves
   English name for Trier   TRĒVZ   'triːvz

Trevi, Fontana di
   fountain, Rome, Italy   fōn-TAHN-uh dē TRĀ-vē   foːn'tanə diː 'treːviˑ

Trevino
   Lee, US golfer   truh-VĒ-nō   trə'viːnoː

Trevithick
   Richard, English engineer   TREV-uh-thik   'trevəθik

Trevor
   pers. name   TREV-uhr   'trevə^r

Triangulum
   constellation   trī-ANG-gyuh-luhm   traɪ'æŋgjələm

Triangulum Australe
   constellation   trī-ANG-gyuh-luhm aw-STRĀ-lē,   traɪ'æŋgjələm ɔː'streːliˑ,
                     ahs-TRĀ-lē   ɑs'treːliˑ

Triassic
   geologic period   trī-AS-ik   traɪ'æsik

Tribeca, TriBeCa
   neighborhood, Manhattan, New   trī-BĒ-kuh   traɪ'biːkə
   York City

Triceratops
   dinosaur   trī-SER-uh-TAHPS   traɪ'serə,tɑps

Tricia
   pers. name   TRISH-uh   'triʃə

Tridentine
   pert. to city of Trent; pert. to   trī-DEN-TĪN, -TÊN, -tuhn   traɪ'den,taɪn, -,tiːn, -tən
   Council of Trent

Trier
   city, Germany   TRIR   'triˑ^r

Trieste
   prov & town, Italy   trē-EST, trē-ES-tē   triː'est, triː'estiˑ

Trigère
   Pauline, US fashion designer   tri-ZHER   tri'ʒe^r

Trigonella
   herb   TRIG-uh-NEL-uh   ,trigə'nelə

Trilby
   novel, G. Du Maurier; hat   TRIL-bē   'trilbiˑ

Trillo
   Manny, Venezuelan baseball   TRĒ-(y)ō, TRĒL-yō   'triː(j)oː, 'triːljoː
   player

Foreign Sounds: ue: *Fr.* **rue**, *Ger.* **füllen**   uh(r): *Fr.* **boeuf**, *Ger.* **Höhle**   <u>kh</u>: *Ger.* i**ch**, *Scot.* lo**ch**   ḡ: *Sp.* ami**g**o   <u>v</u>: *Sp.* ha**b**lar
hl: *Welsh* L**l**anelli.   CAPITALS: primary stress.   SMALL CAPS: secondary stress.   Ⓢ: U.S. pron.   Ⓑ: British pron.

Trimurti
  Hindu trinity   tri-MURT-ē   tri'mu^{r}ti·

Trina
  pers. name   TRĒ-nuh   'tri:nə

Trinacria
  ancient name for Sicily   tri-NAK-rē-uh, trī-NAK-rē-uh   tri'nækri:ə, trɑi'nækri:ə

Trincomalee
  city, Sri Lanka   TRING-kō-muh-LĒ   ˌtriŋko:mə'li:

Trinidad and Tobago
  islands, West Indies   TRIN-uh-DAD uhn(d) tuh-BĀ-gō   'trinəˌdæd ən(d) tə'be:go:

Trinidadian
  pert. to Trinidad   TRIN-uh-DĀD-ē-uhn, -DAD-ē-uhn   ˌtrinə'de:di:ən, -'dædi:ən

Trinity
  Christian godhead   TRIN-uht-ē   'trinəʈi·

Triple sec
  liqueur   TRIP-uhl SEK   'tripəl ˌsek

Tripoli
  city, Lebanon; city, Libya; region,   TRIP-uh-lē   'tripəli·
    Africa

Tripolis
  Phoenician colony, Africa   TRIP-uh-luhs   'tripələs

Tripolitania [Tripoli]
  region, Africa   trip-AHL-uh-TĀN-yuh,   trip,ɑlə'te:njə, ˌtripələ'te:njə,
        TRIP-uh-luh-TĀN-yuh, -TĀ-nē-uh   -'te:ni:ə

Triptolemus
  Eleusian hero favored by Demeter   trip-TAHL-uh-muhs   trip'tɑləməs

Tripura
  state, India   TRIP-uh-ruh   'tripərə

Trish
  pers. name   TRISH   'triʃ

Tristán
  pers. name, Spanish   trē-STAHN   tri:'stɑn

Tristan
  1. pers. name   TRIS-tuhn, TRIS-TAHN, TRIS-TAN   'tristən, 'trisˌtɑn, 'trisˌtæn
  2. French   trē-STE^n tri:stẽ
  3. Romanian   trē-STAHN   tri:'stɑn

Tristan da Cunha
  island, Atlantic   TRIS-tuhn duh KOO-nuh   ˌtristən də 'ku:nə

Tristão
  pers. name, Portuguese   trēsh-TOW^n, trēs-   tri:ʃ'tɑũ, tri:s-

Tristram
  pers. name   TRIS-truhm, TRIS-tuhm   'tristrəm, 'tristəm

Triton
  Greek sea god; satellite of   TRĪT-n   'trɑitn̩
    Neptune; College, IL

Trivandrum
  city, India   truh-VAN-druhm   trə'vændrəm

Trixie
  pers. name   TRIK-sē   'triksi·

Trnava
  town, Slovakia   TUHR-nuh-vuh   'tə^{r}nəvə

Troad
  region around ancient Troy   TRŌ-AD   'tro:ˌæd

Troas
  region around ancient Troy   TRo-AS   'tro·ˌæs

Key (col. 2):   a: fad   ā: fade   ah: father   ar: Mary   aw: law   e: fed   ē: feed   er: merry   i: hid   ī: hide   ō: coat   ōō: boot
oi: boy   ow: now   u: put   uh: above   uhr: bird   ch: chop   ng: ring   sh: show   th: thick   <u>th</u>: this   zh: measure

Trobriand
  Islands, *New Guinea*   TRŌ-brē-AND   'troːbriːˌænd

Trobriander
  a person from the Trobriand   TRŌ-brē-AN-duhr   'troːbriːˌændəʳ
    Islands

Trocaire
  College, *NY*   trō-KAR, trō-KER   troːˈkæʳ, troːˈkeʳ

Trochilus
  son of Io   TRŌ-kuh-luhs   'troːkələs

Troezen
  ancient town, Greece   TRĒ-zuhn   'triːzən

Trofim
  pers. name, Russian   TRUHF-YĒM   ˌtrəfˈjiːm

Trogon
  bird   TRŌ-GAHN   'troːˌgɑn

Troilus
  Trojan hero & lover   TROI-luhs   'trɔiləs

Trois Gymnopédie
  piano pieces, E. Satie   T(R)WAH ZHIM-nō-pā-DĒ   ˌt(r)wa ˌʒimnoːpeːˈdiː

Trois-Rivières
  Canada   TRWAH-rēv-YER   ˌtrwɑriːvˈjer

Trojan
  inhabitant of Troy; *tdmk for*   TRŌ-juhn   'troːdʒən
    condoms

Trollope
  Anthony, *British writer*   TRAHL-uhp   'trɑləp

Troms
  county, Norway   TRUM(P)S   'trum(p)s

Tromsø
  seaport, Norway   TRUM-SUH(R), Ⓢ TRAHM-SŌ   'trumˌsœː, Ⓢ 'trɑmˌsoː

Trondheim
  city, Norway   TRUN-HĪM, Ⓢ TRAHN-HĀM   'trunˌhaim, Ⓢ 'trɑnˌheːm

Trophonius
  legendary Greek architect   truh-FŌ-nē-uhs, truh-FŌN-yuhs   trəˈfoːniːəs, trəˈfoːnjəs

Tros
  Trojan hero; father of Ilus   TRŌS   'troːs

Trossachs
  valley, Scotland   TRAHS-uhks, TRAHS-AKS   'trɑsəks, 'trɑsˌæks

Trotsky
  Leon, *Russian revolutionary*   TRAWTS-kyi, Ⓢ TRAHT-skē,   'trɔːtskjij, Ⓢ 'trɑtski',
                                TRAWT-skē   'trɔːtski'

Trotskyite
  pert. to or supporter of Trotsky   TRAHT-skē-ĪT   'trɑtskiːˌait

Troupial
  South American songbird   TR͞OO-pē-uhl   'truːpiːəl

Trousdale
  county, TN   TR͞OOZ-DĀL   'truːzˌdeːl

Trouville
  port, France   tr͞oo-VĒL   truːviːl

Troy
  ancient city, Asia Minor; pl name,   TROI   'trɔi
    US

Troyes
  city, France   TRWAH, Ⓢ truh-WAH   trwɑː, Ⓢ trəˈwɑ

Foreign Sounds: ue: *Fr.* **rue,** *Ger.* **füllen**   uh(r): *Fr.* **boeuf,** *Ger.* **Höhle**   <u>kh</u>: *Ger.* **ich,** *Scot.* **loch**   ḡ: *Sp.* **amigo**   <u>v</u>: *Sp.* **hablar**
hl: *Welsh* **Llanelli.**   CAPITALS: primary stress.   SMALL CAPS: secondary stress.   Ⓢ: U.S. pron.   Ⓛ: British pron.

Trucial Oman
former name of United Arab　　TROO-shuhl ō-MAHN　　　　,truːʃəl ɔːˈmɑn
Emirates

Trucial States
former name of United Arab　　TROO-shuhl STĀTS　　　　　,truːʃəl ˈsteːts
Emirates

Trudeau
Garry, *US cartoonist;* Pierre,　　troo-DŌ　　　　　　　truːˈdoː
Canadian politician

Truett McConnell
College, *GA*　　　　　　　　TRU-uht muh-KAHN-l　　　ˈtruət məˈkɑnl̩

Truffaut
François, *French film director*　　true-FŌ, Ⓢ troo-FŌ　　tryːfoː, Ⓢ truˈfoː

Trujillo
1. *city, Peru; city, state, Venezuela*　troo-KHÊ(L)-yō, Ⓢ troo-HÊ-(y)ō　truːˈçiː(l)joː, Ⓢ truˈhiː(j)oː
2. *see* Ciudad Trujillo

Trujillo Molina
Rafael L., *Dominican political*　troo-KHÊ(L)-yō mō-LÊ-nah,　truˈçiː(l)joː mɔːˈliːna,
leader　　　　　　　　Ⓢ troo-HÊ-(y)ō　　　Ⓢ truˈhiː(j)oː

Truk
Islands, *Pacific*　　　　　TRUHK, TRUK　　　　　ˈtrək, ˈtruk

Trukese
lang., Polynesia　　　　tru-KÊZ, troo-KÊZ, -KÊS　truˈkiːz, truːˈkiːz, -ˈkiːs

Truman
Harry S., *33rd US president; pers.*　TROO-muhn　　　　　ˈtruːmən
name

Trumbull
pers. name　　　　　　TRUHM-buhl　　　　　ˈtrəmbəl

Trümmelbach
waterfall, Switzerland　　TRUEM-uhl-BAH<u>KH</u>　　ˈtryməl,bɑx

Trung-Thu
Vietnamese festival　　TRUNG-TOO　　　　ˈtruŋˈtuː

Truong
pers. name, Vietnamese　　TROO-awng　　　　ˈtruːɔːŋ

Truro
town, Nova Scotia; town, MA;　TRUR-ō　　　　　ˈtruroː
city, England

Truva
city, Turkey [Troy]; *brandy*　TROO-vuh　　　　ˈtruːvə

Tryggve, Trygve
pers. name, Norwegian　　TRUEG-vuh, Ⓢ TRIG-vē　ˈtrygvə, Ⓢ ˈtrigviˑ

Tryon
Thomas, *US author; village, NE*　TRĪ-uhn　　　　ˈtraiən

Tsaiwa
lang., China　　　　CHĪ-WAH　　　　ˈtʃaiˈwɑ

Tsana [Tana]
lake, Ethiopia; river, Kenya　(T)SAHN-uh　　　ˈ(t)sɑnə

Tsao Chun
Chinese festival　　CHOW JOON　　ˈtʃau ˈdʒuːn

Tsavo
river, Africa　　　　(T)SAHV-ō　　　ˈ(t)savoː

Tschaikovsky
see Tchaikovsky

Tsezar
pers. name, Russian　　TSEZ-uhr　　　ˈtsezər

Key (col. 2):　a: fad　ā: fade　ah: father　ar: Mary　aw: law　e: fed　ē: feed　er: merry　i: hid　ī: hide　ˈō: coat　oo: boot
oi: boy　ow: now　u: put　uh: above　uhr: bird　ch: chop　ng: ring　sh: show　th: thick　<u>th</u>: this　zh: measure

Tshiluba		
African trade lang.	chi-L$\overline{OO}$-buh	tʃiˈluːbə
Tshombe		
Moise K., *African political leader*	CHAWM-bā	ˈtʃɔːmbeˑ
Tsimshatsui		
business section, Kowloon, Hong Kong	(T)SIM-SHAHT-S$\overline{OO}$-ē	ˈ(t)simˈʃatˈsuˑiˑ
Tsimshian		
N. American people	CHIM-shē-uhn, TSIM-shē-uhn	ˈtʃimʃiːən, ˈtsimʃiːən
Tsinan		
see Jinan		
Tsing Hai, Ching Hai		
lake, China	CHING HĪ	ˈtʃiŋ ˈhai
Tsinghai		
see Qinghai		
Tsingtao		
see Qingdao		
Tsing Tao, Tsingtao		
Chinese beer	CHING DOW	ˈtʃiŋ ˈdau
Tsinling Shan		
mtn. range, China	CHIN-LING SHAHN	ˈtʃinˈliŋ ˈʃan
Tsitsihar		
see Qiqihar		
Tso-lin		
see Zhang Zuolin		
Tsonga		
lang., Africa	(T)SAWNG-guh	ˈ(t)sɔːŋgə
Tsongas		
Paul, *US politician*	SAWNG-guhs, SAHNG-guhs	ˈsɔːŋgəs, ˈsaŋgəs
Tsugaru		
strait, Japan	(t)su-gahr-$\overline{oo}$	(t)sugɑruː
Tsui Fai		
pers. name, Chinese	(T)SUĒ FĪ	ˈ(t)suiˑ ˈfai
Tsuneo		
pers. name, Japanese	(t)sun-e-ō	(t)suneoː
Tsuruga		
port, Japan	(t)s$\overline{oo}$-r$\overline{oo}$-gah	(t)suːruːgɑ
Tsushima		
island, Japan	(t)s$\overline{oo}$-shē-mah	(t)suːʃiːma
Tsuyoshi		
pers. name, Japanese	(t)su-yō-shē	(t)sujoːʃiː
Tswa		
lang., people, Africa	TSWAH, SWAH, CHWAH, chuh-WAH	ˈtswa, ˈswa, ˈtʃwa, tʃəˈwa
Tswana		
people, lang., Africa	(T)SWAHN-uh, CHWAHN-uh, chuh-WAHN-uh	ˈ(t)swanə, ˈtʃwanə, tʃəˈwanə
Tuamotu		
islands, Pacific; kingfisher	T$\overline{OO}$-uh-MŌ-t$\overline{oo}$	ˌtuːəˈmoːtuː
Tuan Wu		
Chinese festival	TWAHN W$\overline{OO}$	ˈtwan ˈwuː
Tuapse		
port, Russia	tu-AHP-SĀ	tuˌɑpˈseː
Tuareg [Tamashek]		
lang., N Africa	TWAHR-EG	ˈtwarˌeg

Foreign Sounds: **ue**: *Fr.* **rue**, *Ger.* **füllen**   **uh(r)**: *Fr.* **boeuf**, *Ger.* **Höhle**   **kh**: *Ger.* **ich**, *Scot.* **loch**   **g**: *Sp.* **amigo**   **v**: *Sp.* **hablar**
hl: *Welsh* **Llanelli**.   CAPITALS: primary stress.   SMALL CAPS: secondary stress.   Ⓢ: U.S. pron.   Ⓑ: British pron.

Tuatha Dé Danann
  Irish gods   TŌO-uh-huh DĀ DAHN-ahn,   'tuːəhə 'deː 'danan, 'tuːəθə
                 TŌO-uh-thuh

Tübingen
  city, Germany   TUE-bing-uhn, ⑤ T(Y)ŌO-bing-uhn   'tyːbiŋən, ⑤ 't(j)uːbiŋən

Tubruq [Tobruk]
  prov, Libya   tu-BRŌOK   tu'bruːk

Tubulidentata
  aardvarks   T(Y)ŌO-byuh-luh-den-TAHT-uh,   ˌt(j)uːbjələden'taʈə, -'teːʈə
                 -TĀT-uh

Tucana
  constellation   tōo-KĀ-nuh, tu-KAN-uh   tuː'keːnə, tu'kænə

Tucher
  German beer   TŌO-khuhr   'tuːxəʳ

Tuchmann
  Barbara, *US historian, writer*   TUHK-muhn   'təkmən

Tucson
  city, AZ   TŌO-SAHN, tōo-SAHN   'tuːˌsan, tuː'san

Tucumcari
  city, NM   TŌO-kuhm-KAR-ē   'tuːkəmˌkæriˑ

Tudjman
  Franjo, *Croatian politician*   TŌOJ-mahn   'tuːdʒmɑːn

Tudor
  royal family, England, 1485-1603   T(Y)ŌOD-uhr, CHŌOD-uhr   't(j)uːdəʳ, 'tʃuːdəʳ

Tuesday
  day of the week; pers. name   T(Y)ŌOZ-dē, T(Y)ŌOZ-dā   't(j)uːzdiˑ, 't(j)uːzdeː

Tufts
  University, *MA*   TUHF(T)S   'təf(t)s

Tugela
  river, falls, S. Africa   tōo-GĀ-luh   tuː'geːlə

Tuguegarao
  municipality, Philippines   TŌO-gā-guh-ROW   ˌtuːgeːgə'rɑu

Tuileries
  gardens, Paris, France   twēl-RĒ, ⑤ TWĒ-luh-RĒ   tɥiːlriː, ⑤ ˌtwiːlə'riː

Tukulör
  see Toucouleur

Tula
  lang., Nigeria; city, Russia   TŌO-luh   'tuːlə

Tulagi
  island, Solomon Islands   tōo-LAHG-ē   tuː'lagiˑ

Tulalip
  Indian reservation, US   tōo-LAHL-uhp   tuː'laləp

Tulare
  county, CA   tōo-LAR-ē, tōo-LER-ē, tōo-LAR,   tuː'læriˑ, tuː'leriˑ, tuː'læʳ,
               tōo-LER   tuː'leʳ

Tullius
  pers. name, Latin   TUHL-ē-uhs   'təliːəs

Tully
  British name for Roman Cicero;   TUHL-ē   'təliˑ
    pers. name

Tulsa
  city, OK   TUHL-suh   'təlsə

Tulu
  lang., people, India   TŌO-lōo   'tuːluː

Key (col. 2):   a: fad   ā: fade   ah: father   ar: Mary   aw: law   e: fed   ē: feed   er: merry   i: hid   ī: hide   ō: coat   ōo: boot
oi: boy   ow: now   u: put   uh: above   uhr: bird   ch: chop   ng: ring   sh: show   th: thick   th: this   zh: measure

Tumacacori
    National Monument, *AZ*   T͞OO-muh-KAHK-uh-rē   ˌtuːməˈkɑkəriˑ

Tum [Atum]
    Egyptian creator god   TUM   ˈtum

Tumi
    mfrs.   T(Y)͞OO-mē   ˈt(j)uːmiˑ

tungsten
    element   TUHNG-stuhn   ˈtəŋstən

Tung-t'ing Hu
    see Dongting Hu

Tungus
    lang., people, Asia   tung-G͞OOZ, TUHNG-G͞OOZ   tuŋˈguːz, ˌtəŋˈguːz

Tungusic
    lang. family, Manchuria and   tung-GUS-ik, tung-G͞OO-zik   tuŋˈgusik, tuŋˈguːzik
       Siberia

Tunguska
    river, Siberia   tung-G͞OO-skuh, TUHNG-G͞OO-skuh   tuŋˈguːskə, ˌtəŋˈguːskə

Tunica
    county, MS   T(Y)͞OO-ni-kuh   ˈt(j)uːnikə

Tunica-Biloxi
    N. American people   T(Y)͞OO-nuh-kuh-buh-LUHK-sē,   ˈt(j)uːnəkəbəˈləksiˑ,
        -buh-LAHK-sē   -bəˈlɑksiˑ

Tunis
    city, Tunisia   T(Y)͞OO-nis   ˈt(j)uːnis

Tunisia
    country, Africa   t(y)o͞o-NĒ-zh(ē-)uh, -NIZH-(ē-)uh   t(j)uːˈniːʒ(iː)ə, -ˈniʒ(iː)ə

Tunisian
    pert. to Tunisia *or* Tunis   t(y)o͞o-NĒ-zh(ē-)uhn, -NIZH-(ē-)uhn   t(j)uːˈniːʒ(iː)ən, -ˈniʒ(iː)ən

Tunxis
    Community College, *CT*   TUHNG(K)-suhs   ˈtəŋ(k)səs

Tuohey, Tuohy
    family name   T͞OO-ē, T͞OO-hē   ˈtuːiˑ, ˈtuːhiˑ

Tuolumne
    river, mtn., county, CA   to͞o-AHL-uh-mē   tuːˈɑləmiˑ

Tuolumne Rancheria
    Indian reservation, US   to͞o-AHL-uh-mē RAN-chuh-RĒ-uh   tuːˈɑləmiˑ ˌræntʃəˈriːə

Tupamaro
    S. American people   T͞OO-puh-MAHR-ō   ˌtuːpəˈmɑroˑ

Tupelo
    city, MS; tree   T(Y)͞OO-puh-LŌ   ˈt(j)uːpəˌloˑ

Tupí
    lang., people, S America   T͞OO-pē, to͞o-PĒ   ˈtuːpiˑ, tuːˈpiː

Tupí-Guaraní
    S. American people   to͞o-PĒ-GWAH-rah-NĒ   tuːˈpiːˌgwɑrɑˈniː

Tupina
    S. American people   T͞OO-pē-NAH   ˌtuːpiˈnɑ

Tupinambá
    S. American people   T͞OO-pē-NAM-buh, T͞OO-pē-NAM-BAH   ˌtuːpiˈnæmbə,
                                                ˌtuːpiˑˌnæmˈbɑ

Turaco
    African bird   TUR-uh-kō   ˈturəkoˑ

Turandot
    Puccini opera   TUR-uhn-DAHT   ˈturənˌdɑt

Turanian
    Ural-Altaic lang., people   t(y)u-RĀ-nē-uhn, t(y)u-RAHN-ē-uhn   t(j)uˈreːniːən, t(j)uˈrɑniːən

---

Foreign Sounds: **ue**: *Fr.* **r**u**e**, *Ger.* f**ü**llen   **uh(r)**: *Fr.* b**oeu**f, *Ger.* H**öh**le   <u>kh</u>: *Ger.* i**ch**, *Scot.* lo**ch**   g̃: *Sp.* ami**g**o   <u>v</u>: *Sp.* ha**b**lar
hl: *Welsh* **Ll**anelli.   CAPITALS: primary stress.   SMALL CAPS: secondary stress. $: U.S. pron.   Ⓛ: British pron.

Turgenev, Turgeniev
Ivan, *Russian novelist*   tur-GYĀN-yuhf, Ⓢ tur-GĀN-yuhf,   tur'gjeːnjəf, Ⓢ tuʳgeːnjəf,
                                  tur-GEN-yuhf   tuʳgenjəf

Turin
prov & town, Italy   T(Y)UR-uhn, t(y)u-RIN   't(j)urən, t(j)u'rin

Turing
Alan, *English computer theorist* T(Y)UR-ing   't(j)uriŋ

Turkana
lang., people, Sudan, Kenya,   tur-KAHN-uh, tur-KAN-uh   tuʳkanə, tuʳkænə
Ethiopia; lake, Kenya

Turkestan
region, desert, Asia   TUHR-kuh-STAN, -STAHN   ˌtəʳkə'stæn, -'stɑn

Turkey
country, Europe, Asia   TUHR-kē   'təʳkiˑ

Turki
people, lang., Asia   TUHR-kē, TUR-kē   'təʳkiˑ, 'tuʳkiˑ

Turkic
Asian lang. family   TUHR-kik   'təʳkik

Turkish
lang., Turkey, Bulgaria   TUHR-kish   'təʳkiʃ

Turkism, Turcism
customs of the Turks   TUHR-KIZ-uhm   'təʳˌkizəm

Turkmen
lang., people, Asia   TUHRK-muhn   'təʳkmən

Turkmenistan
republic, Asia   tuhrk-MEN-uh-STAN,   təʳk'menəˌstæn,
                                  TUHRK-MEN-uh-STAHN,   ˌtəʳkˌmenə'stɑn,
                                  TUHRK-MEN-uh-STAN   ˌtəʳkˌmenə'stæn

Turkmenskaya
SSR, *Turkmen republic, USSR*   turk-MEN-skuh-yuh   tuʳk'menskəjə

Turkoman
people, Asia   TUHR-kuh-muhn   'təʳkəmən

Turks and Caicos
islands, West Indies   TUHRKS uhn(d) KĀ-kuhs   'təʳks ən(d) 'keːkəs

Turku
port, Finland   TUR-kōō   'tuʳkuː

Turlogh, Turlough
1. *pers. name*   TUHR-lō, TUR-lō   'təʳloː, 'tuʳloː
2. *Irish Gaelic*   THUR-luh(ḡ)   'θurlə(ɣ)

Turmeric
spice   TUHR-muh-rik, T(Y)ŌŌ-muh-rik   'təʳmərik, 't(j)uːmərik

Turner
Kathleen, *US actress; pers. name* TUHR-nuhr   'təʳnəʳ

Turnhout
prov & town, Belgium   TURN-HOWT   'tuʳnˌhɑut

Turnus
king of the Rutuli in the Aeneid, TUHR-nuhs, TUR-nuhs   'təʳnəs, 'tuʳnəs
Virgil

Turnverein
gymnastic club   TURN-fer-ĪN, Ⓢ TUHRN-vuh-RĪN   'tuʳnferˌɑin, Ⓢ 'təʳnvəˌrɑin

Turow
Scott, *US novelist*   T(Y)UR-ō   't(j)uroː

Tuscaloosa
city, county, AL   TUHS-kuh-LŌŌ-suh   ˌtəskə'luːsə

Key (col. 2):   a: fad   ā: fade   ah: father   ar: Mary   aw: law   e: fed   ē: feed   er: merry   i: hid   ī: hide   ō: coat   ōō: boot
oi: boy   ow: now   u: put   uh: above   uhr: bird   ch: chop   ng: ring   sh: show   th: thick   th: this   zh: measure

Tuscan		
pert. to Tuscany	TUHS-kuhn	'təskən
Tuscany		
region, Italy	TUHS-kuh-nē	'təskeniˑ
Tuscarawas		
river, county, OH	TUHS-kuh-RAW-(w)uhs	ˌtəskə'rɔː(w)əs
Tuscarora		
mts., PA, NV; people, lang., N. America	TUHS-kuh-RŌR-uh, -RAWR-uh	ˌtəskə'roːrə, -'rɔːrə
Tuscola		
county, MI	tuhs-KŌ-luh	təs'koːlə
Tusculum		
ancient town, Italy; college, TN	TUHS-k(y)uh-luhm	'təsk(j)ələm
Tuscumbia		
city, AL	tuh-SKUHM-bē-uh	tə'skəmbiːə
Tuskegee		
Institute, *college, AL; N. American people*	TUH-SKĒ-gē	ˌtə'skiːgiˑ
Tussaud		
Marie, *London waxworks founder*	tue-SŌ, [$] TO͞O-sō, tuh-SAWD, tuh-SŌD	tyːsoː, [$] 'tuːsoː, tə'sɔːd, tə'soːd
Tutankhamen		
king of Egypt	TO͞O-TANG-KAHM-uhn, TO͞O-TAHNG-	ˌtuːˌtæŋ'kɑmən, ˌtuːˌtɑŋ-
Tutchone		
N. American people	to͞o-CHŌ-nē	tuː'tʃoːniˑ
Tutelo		
N. American people	to͞o-TĀ-lō	tuː'teːloː
Tutsi [Watusi]		
people, Rwanda, Burundi	TUT-sē, TO͞OT-sē	'tutsiˑ, 'tuːtsiˑ
Tutu		
Desmond, *South African prelate (Nobel 1984)*	TO͞O-TO͞O	'tuːˌtuː
Tutuila		
island, American Samoa	TO͞OT-uh-WĒ-luh	ˌtuːṭə'wiːlə
Tuva [Tuvinian]		
lang., Russia, Mongolian PR	TO͞O-vuh	'tuːvə
Tuvalu		
islands, Pacific	to͞o-VAHL-o͞o, to͞o-VAHR-o͞o	tuː'vɑluː, tuː'vɑruː
Tuvaluan		
pert. to Tuvalu	to͞o-VAHL-o͞o-uhn, to͞o-VAHR-o͞o-uhn	tuː'vɑluːən, tuː'vɑruːən
Tuvinian [Tuva]		
lang., Russia, Mongolian PR	to͞o-VIN-ē-uhn	tuː'viniːən
Twain		
Mark, *pseudonym of* Samuel Clemens, *US writer*	TWĀN	'tweːn
Tweedledee		
character in Through the Looking Glass, *Lewis Carroll*	TWĒD-l-DĒ	ˌtwiːdl̩'diː
Tweedledum		
companion of Tweedledee	TWĒD-l-DUHM	ˌtwiːdl̩'dəm
Tweedsmuir		
provincial park, Canada	TWĒDZ-MYUR	'twiːdzˌmjuʳ
Twi [Akan]		
lang., Ghana, Ivory Coast	TWĒ	'twiː

Foreign Sounds: ue: *Fr.* **rue**, *Ger.* **füllen** uh(r): *Fr.* **boeuf**, *Ger.* **Höhle** kh: *Ger.* **ich**, *Scot.* **loch** g̃: *Sp.* **amigo** v̲: *Sp.* **hablar** hl: *Welsh* **Llanelli**. CAPITALS: primary stress. SMALL CAPS: secondary stress. [$]: U.S. pron. [£]: British pron.

Twickenham
   former borough, England   TWIK-uh-nuhm   'twikənəm

Twining
   Nathan F., US general; tdmk for a   TWĪ-ning   'twaɪnɪŋ
   British tea

Twitty
   Conway, US country singer   TWIT-ē   'twɪt̬i·

Twohy
   family name   TO͞O-ē, TO͞O-hē   'tuːi·, 'tuːhi·

Twomey
   family name   TO͞O-mē   'tuːmi·

Twyla
   pers. name   TWĪ-luh   'twaɪlə

Txukahamei
   S. American people   CHO͞O-kuh-HAHM-ī   ˌtʃuːkə'hamˌaɪ

Ty
   1. pers. name   TĪ   'taɪ
   2. Egyptian queen   TĒ, TĪ   'tiː, 'taɪ

Tybalt
   character in Romeo & Juliet,   TIB-uhlt   'tɪbəlt
   Shakespeare

Tyburn
   execution site, London, England   TĪ-buhrn   'taɪbəʳn

Tyche
   Greek goddess of fortune   TĪ-kē   'taɪki·

Tychius
   shieldmaker for Ajax   TĪ-kē-uhs   'taɪkiːəs

Tycho
   1. crater on Moon   TĪ-kō   'taɪkoː
   2. pers. name, Danish   TUE-kō, ⑤ TĪ-kō, TĒ-kō   'tyːkoː, ⑤ 'taɪkoː, 'tiːkoː
   3. German   TUE-k͟hō   'tyːçoː

Tydeus
   father of Diomedes   TĪD-ē-uhs   'taɪdiːəs

Tyldesley
   town, England   TILZ-lē, TILDZ-lē   'tɪlzli·, 'tɪldzli·

Tylenol
   tdmk for acetaminophen   TĪ-luh-NAWL, TĪ-luh-NAHL   'taɪləˌnɔːl, 'taɪləˌnal

Tyler
   John, 10th US president; pers.   TĪ-luhr   'taɪləʳ
   name

Tyndale
   see Tindale

Tyndale, Tyndall
   pers. name   TIN-dl   'tɪndl̩

Tyndareus
   father of Dioscuri, Helen,   tin-DAR-ē-uhs   tin'dæriːəs
   Clytemnestra

Tyne
   river, England; pers. name   TĪN   'taɪn

Tyne and Wear
   county, England   TĪN uhn(d) WIR   'taɪn ən(d) 'wiʳ

Tynemouth
   port, England   TĪN-MOWTH, TĪN-muhth   'taɪnˌmauθ, 'taɪnməθ

Tyneside
   urban area, England   TĪN-SĪD   'taɪnˌsaɪd

Key (col. 2):   a: fad   ā: fade   ah: father   ar: Mary   aw: law   e: fed   ē: feed   er: merry   i: hid   ī: hide   ō: coat   o͞o: boot
oi: boy   ow: now   u: put   uh: above   uhr: bird   ch: chop   ng: ring   sh: show   th: thick   t͟h: this   zh: measure

Typee		
novel, H. Melville	tī-PĒ	tɑi'pi:
Typhoeus [Typhon]		
monster son of Gaia & Tartarus	tī-FĒ-uhs, tī-FŌ-YO͞OS	tɑi'fi:əs, tɑi'fo:ˌju:s
Typhon		
monster son of Gaia & Tartarus	TĪ-FAHN	'tɑiˌfɑn
Tyr		
Scandinavian battle god	TIR	'tiʳ
Tyrannius		
pers. name, Latin	ti-RAN-ē-uhs	ti'ræni:əs
Tyrannosaurus		
dinosaur	tuh-RAN-uh-SAWR-uhs, TĪ-RAN-uh-SAWR-uhs	təˌrænə'sɔ:rəs, ˌtɑiˌrænə'sɔ:rəs
Tyre		
fishing port, Lebanon; Phoenician capital	TĪR	'tɑiʳ
Tyrell		
pers. name	TIR-uhl	'tirəl
Tyrian		
pert. to ancient Tyre	TIR-ē-uhn	'tiri:ən
Tyro		
mother of Pelias	TĪ-rō	'tɑiro:
Tyrol		
see Tirol		
Tyrolean, Tyrolian		
pert. to the Tirol	tuh-RŌ-lē-uhn, tī-RŌ-lē-uhn	tə'ro:li:ən, tɑi'ro:li:ən
Tyrolese		
pert. to the Tirol	TIR-uh-LĒZ, -LĒS	ˌtirə'li:z, -'li:s
Tyrone		
1. borough, PA	TĪ-RŌN	'tɑiˌro:n
2. former county, N. Ireland	tir-ŌN	tir'o:n
3. pers. name	TĪ-RŌN, ti-RŌN, tir-ŌN	'tɑiˌro:n, ti'ro:n, tir'o:n
Tyrrell		
county, NC	TIR-uhl, TER-uhl	'tirəl, 'terəl
Tyrrhenian		
Sea, *Mediterranean*	tuh-RĒ-nē-uhn	tə'ri:ni:ən
Tyrrhenus		
hero of the Tyrrhenians or Etruscans	tī-RĒ-nuhs	tɑi'ri:nəs
Tyrtaeus		
Spartan poet	TUHR-TĒ-uhs	ˌtəʳ'ti:əs
Tyrwhitt		
Thomas, *English scholar; pers. name*	TIR-uht	'tirət
Tyson		
pers. name	TĪS-n	'tɑisn̩
Tyus		
Wyomia, *sports personality*	TĪ-uhs	'tɑiəs
Tzeltal		
lang., people, Mexico	(t)sel-TAHL	(t)sel'tɑl
Tzigane		
pert. to gypsies or to Romany	(t)sē-GAHN	(t)si:'gɑn
Tzotzil		
lang., people, Mexico	(t)sōt-SĒL	(t)so:t'si:l

Foreign Sounds: ue: *Fr.* **rue**, *Ger.* **füllen** uh(r): *Fr.* **boeuf**, *Ger.* **Höhle** kh: *Ger.* **ich**, *Scot.* **loch** ḡ: *Sp.* amigo v̲: *Sp.* hablar hl: *Welsh* **Llanelli**. CAPITALS: primary stress. SMALL CAPS: secondary stress. [$]: U.S. pron. [£]: British pron.

Tzutuhil
  lang., people, Guatemala   (T)S͞OOT-uh-WĒL   ,(t)suːt̬ə'wiːl

U

U
  Burmese title   O͞O   'uː
U2
  rock group   Y͞OO-T͞OO   'juː'tuː
Ubaid
  Bronze Age culture   o͞o-BĀD, o͞o-BĪD   uː'beːd, uː'baid
Ubaldino
  pers. name, Italian   o͞o-bahl-DĒ-no   ,uːbal'diːnoː
Ubaldo
  pers. name, Italian   o͞o-BAHL-dō   uː'baldoː
Ubangi
  river, Africa   (y)o͞o-BANG-(g)ē   (j)uː'bæŋ(g)iˑ
Ubangi-Shari
  former name of Central African   (y)o͞o-BANG-(g)ē-SHAHR-ē   (j)uː,bæŋ(g)iˑ'ʃariˑ
    Republic
Ubeda
  commune, Spain   O͞O-ya̱-THAH, Ⓢ O͞O-buh-DAH   'uːβeː,ða, Ⓢ 'uːbə,da
Ubertino
  pers. name, Italian   o͞o-ber-TĒ-no   ,uːber'tiːnoː
Uberto
  pers. name, Italian   o͞o-BER-tō   uː'bertoː
Ubykh
  lang., Turkey   O͞O-bik͟h   'uːbix
Ucalegon
  counsellor of Priam   (y)o͞o-KAL-uh-GAHN   (j)uː'kælə,gan
Ucayali
  river, Peru   o͞o-kuh-YAHL-ē   ,uːkə'jaliˑ
Uccello
  Paolo, *Italian painter*   o͞o-CHEL-ō   uː'tʃeloː
UConn
  nickname for U. Connecticut   Y͞OO-KAHN   'juː,kan
Udaipur
  former state, India   o͞o-DĪ-PUR, o͞o-dī-PUR   uː'dai,puʳ, ,uːdai'puʳ
Udall
  Morris K., *US politician*   Y͞OOD-AWL   'juːd,ɔːl
Udmurt [Votyak]
  lang., Russia   ud-MURT   ud'muʳt
U Dub
  nickname for U. Wisconsin,   Y͞OO DUHB   juː 'dəb
    Washington

Key (col. 2): a: fad ā: fade ah: father ar: Mary aw: law e: fed ē: feed er: merry i: hid ī: hide ō: coat o͞o: boot
oi: boy   ow: now   u: put   uh: above   uhr: bird   ch: chop   ng: ring   sh: show   th: thick   t͟h: this   zh: measure

Ueberroth
    Peter, *US businessman*   Y‾O‾O-buh-RAWTH   'juːbə,rɔːθ

Uecker
    Bob, *US entertainer*   Y‾O‾O-kuhr   'juːkəʳ

Uele
    river, Africa   WEL-ē   'weliˑ

Ufa
    river, city, Russia   ‾o‾o-FAH   uːˈfɑ

Uffizi
    gallery, Florence, Italy   ‾o‾o-FIT-sē, ‾o‾o-FĒT-sē   uːˈfitsiˑ, uːˈfiːtsiˑ

UFOlogy
    study of UFO's   y‾o‾o-FAHL-uh-jē   juːˈfɑlədʒiˑ

Uganda
    republic, Africa   (y)‾o‾o-GAN-duh, -GAHN-duh   (j)uːˈgændə, -ˈgɑ·ndə

Ugandan
    pert. to Uganda   (y)‾o‾o-GAN-duhn, -GAHN-duhn   (j)uːˈgændən, -ˈgɑ·ndən

Ugarit [Ras Shamra]
    ancient city, Syria   ‾O‾O-guh-RĒT   ,uːgəˈriːt

Ugaritic
    lang., pert. to Ugarit   (Y)‾O‾O-guh-RIT-ik   ,(j)uːgəˈriṭik

Uggams
    Leslie, *US entertainer*   UHG-uhmz   'əgəmz

Ugni Blanc
    wine   ‾o‾on-yē BLAH[n]   uːnjiː blɑ̃

Ugo
    pers. name, Italian   ‾O‾O-gō   'uːgoː

Ugolino
    pers. name, Italian   ‾O‾O-gō-LĒ-nō   ,uːgoːˈliːnoː

Ugrian
    eastern Finno-Ugric people   (Y)‾O‾O-grē-uhn   '(j)uːgriːən

Ugric
    branch of Uralic langs.   (Y)‾O‾O-grik   '(j)uːgrik

Uhura
    Lt., *character, Star Trek*   u-HUR-uh   uˈhurə

Uighur, Uigur
    lang., people, China, Uzbekistan   wē-GUR, WĒ-guhr   wiːˈguʳ, 'wiːgəʳ

Uillean pipes
    Irish bagpipe   IL-uhn, IL-yuhn   'ilən, 'iljən

Uinta
    river, mts., UT; county, WY   y‾o‾o-INT-uh   juːˈintə

Uintah
    county, UT   y‾o‾o-INT-uh   juːˈintə

Ujiji
    town, Tanzania   ‾o‾o-JĒ-jē   uːˈdʒiːdʒiː

Ujpest
    suburb, Budapest, Hungary   ‾O‾O-ē-PESHT   'uːiː,peʃt

Ukraine
    republic, Europe   y‾o‾o-KRĀN, y‾o‾o-KRĪN, Y‾O‾O-KRĀN   juːˈkreːn, juːˈkrain, 'juː,kreːn

Ukrainian
    lang., pert. to Ukraine   y‾o‾o-KRĀ-nē-uhn, y‾o‾o-KRĀN-yuhn   juːˈkreːniːən, juːˈkreːnjən

Ukrainskaya
    SSR, *Ukrainian republic, USSR*   ‾o‾o-krah-ĒN-skuh-yuh   uːkrɑˈiːnskəjə

Ulaanbaatar
    city, Mongolia   ‾O‾O-LAHN-BAH-TAHR, -TAWR   ,uː,lɑnˈbɑ,tɑʳ, -,tɔːʳ

Foreign Sounds: **ue:** *Fr.* **rue**, *Ger.* **füllen**   **uh(r):** *Fr.* **boeuf**, *Ger.* **Höhle**   <u>kh</u>: *Ger.* i<u>ch</u>, *Scot.* lo<u>ch</u>   ğ: *Sp.* ami<u>g</u>o   <u>v</u>: *Sp.* ha<u>b</u>lar
hl: *Welsh* **Llanelli.**   CAPITALS: primary stress.   SMALL CAPS: secondary stress.   Ⓢ: U.S. pron.   Ⓑ: British pron.

Ulan Bator [Ulaanbaatar]
　city, Mongolia　　　OO̅-LAHN BAH-TAWR　　　　　,uːˌlɑn 'bɑˌtɔːʳ
Ulanov
　see Ulyanov
Ulan-Ude
　city, Russia　　　OO̅-LAHN-u-DA̅　　　　　,uːˌlɑːnu'deː
Ulf
　pers. name, Swedish　　　OO̅LF　　　　　'uːlf
Ulises
　pers. name, Spanish　　　oo̅-LE̅-säs　　　　　uː'liːseːs
Ulisse
　pers. name, Italian　　　oo̅-LE̅S-sä　　　　　uː'liːsseː
Ulithi
　islands, Pacific　　　oo̅-LE̅-the̅　　　　　uː'liːθiˑ
Ull
　Scandinavian hunter god　　　UL　　　　　'ul
Ullman
　Tracy, *English actress*　　　UHL-muhn　　　　　'əlmən
Ullmann
　Liv, *Swedish actress*　　　UL-MAHN　　　　　'ulˌmɑːn
Ulm
　city, Germany　　　ULM　　　　　'ulm
Ulpius
　pers. name, Latin　　　UHL-pe̅-uhs　　　　　'əlpiːəs
Ulrich
　1. pers. name　　　UHL-rik　　　　　'əlrik
　2. French　　　uel-RE̅K　　　　　yːlriːk
　3. German　　　UL-ri<u>kh</u>　　　　　'ulriç
Ulster
　county, NY; prov, Eire　　　UHL-stuhr　　　　　'əlstəʳ
Ultbanerisches
　German beer　　　ult-BAHN-uhr-ISH-uhs　　　　　ult'bɑnərˌiʃəs
Ultima Thule
　the farthest land　　　UHL-tuh-muh TOO̅-le̅, UL-tuh-muh,　　　　　,əltəmə 'tuːliˑ, ,ultəmə,
　　　　　　THOO̅-le̅　　　　　　　　'θuːliˑ
Ult-Münchner
　German beer　　　ult-MUEN<u>KH</u>-nuhr　　　　　ult'mynçnəʳ
Ululu
　Babylonian month　　　OO̅-loo̅-LOO̅, oo̅-LOO̅-LOO̅　　　　　'uːluːˌluː, uː'luːˌluː
Ulyanov, Ulanov
　Vladimir Ilyich, *former name of*　　　oo̅l-YAHN-uhf　　　　　uːl'jɑːnəf
　　Lenin
Ulyanovsk [Simbirsk]
　city, Russia　　　oo̅l-YAHN-uhfsk　　　　　uːl'jɑːnəfsk
Ulysse
　pers. name, French　　　ue-LE̅S　　　　　yːliːs
Ulysses
　1. Latin-derived form of　　　yu-LIS-e̅z　　　　　juˈlisiːz
　　Odysseus; *novel, J. Joyce; pers.*
　　name
　2. German　　　oo̅-LUES-es　　　　　uː'lyses
UMass
　nickname for U. Massachusetts　　　yoo̅-MAS　　　　　juː'mæs

Key (col. 2):　a: fad　ā: fade　ah: father　ar: Mary　aw: law　e: fed　ē: feed　er: merry　i: hid　ī: hide　ō: coat　ō̅o̅: boot
oi: boy　ow: now　u: put　uh: above　uhr: bird　ch: chop　ng: ring　sh: show　th: thick　<u>th</u>: this　zh: measure

Umatilla
   N. American people; river, county,   YO͞O-muh-TIL-uh   ˌjuːməˈtilə
   OR
Umberto
   pers. name, Italian   o͞om-BER-tō   uːmˈbertoː
Umbria
   region, Italy   UHM-brē-uh   ˈəmbriːə
Umbrian
   pert. to Umbria   UHM-brē-uhn   ˈəmbriːən
Umbriel
   satellite of Uranus   UHM-brē-uhl   ˈəmbriːəl
UMIST
   U. Manchester Institute of Science   YO͞O-mist   ˈjuːmist
   and Technology
Umma
   Sumerian city   UHM-uh   ˈəmə
Umm al Qaywayn
   states, United Arab Emirates   O͞OM ahl kī-WĪN   ˈuːm aɪl kaiˈwain
Umpqua
   river, OR   UHM(P)-KWAW   ˈəm(p)ˌkwɔː
Umtata
   river, town, S. Africa   um-TAHT-uh   umˈtɑţə
Una
   pers. name   YO͞O-nuh, O͞O-nuh   ˈjuːnə, ˈuːnə
Unalaska
   Aleutian island, city, bay, AK   UHN-uh-LAS-kuh, UHN-l-AS-kuh   ˌənəˈlæskə, ˌənlˈæskə
Unamuno y Jugo
   Miguel de, *Spanish philosopher*   o͞o-nah-MO͞O-nō ē KHO͞O-gō   uːnɑˈmuːnoː iː ˈxuːgoː
Undarum, Mare
   see Mare Undarum
Undine
   water nymph   UHN-DĒN   ˌənˈdiːn
Undset
   Sigrid, *Norwegian author (Nobel*   UN-SET   ˈunˌset
   1928)
UNESCO
   UN agency   yu-NES-kō   juˈneskoː
Uniat
   member of Eastern church   YO͞O-nē-uht, YO͞O-nē-AT   ˈjuːniːət, ˈjuːniːˌæt
Uniate [Uniat]
   member of Eastern church   YO͞O-nē-uht, YO͞O-nē-ĀT   ˈjuːniːət, ˈjuːniːˌeɪt
Uniatism
   religion   YO͞O-nē-uh-TIZ-uhm   ˈjuːniːəˌtizəm
Unicef, UNICEF
   United Nations International   YO͞O-nuh-SEF   ˈjuːnəˌsef
   Children's Fund
Unicoi
   county, TN   YO͞O-nuh-KOI   ˈjuːnəˌkɔi
Unicorn
   mythical beast; constellation   YO͞O-ni-KAWRN   ˈjuːniˌkɔːʳn
Unilever
   US corp.   YO͞O-nuh-LĒ-vuhr   ˈjuːnəˌliːvəʳ
Uniroyal
   US tire co.   YO͞O-nuh-ROI(-uh)l   ˈjuːnəˌrɔi(ə)l

Unisys
   US computer co.   YOO-nuh-SIS   'juːnə,sis

UNITA
   Angolan political organization   yu-NĒT-uh   ju'niːţə

Unitarian
   religious group   YOO-nuh-TAR-ē-uhn,   juːnə'tæriːən, juːnə'teriːən
                     YOO-nuh-TER-ē-uhn

Unitas
   Johnny, *US football player*   yu-NĪT-uhs   ju'naiţəs

United Arab Emirates
   country, Arabia   EM-uh-ruhts, -RĀTS; i-MIR-uhts   'emərəts, -,reːts; i'mirəts

United States
   republic, N. America   yu-NĪT-uhd STĀTS, *esp. southeastern*   ju,naiţəd 'steːts, *esp.*
               US YOO-NĪT-uhd STĀTS, *in rapid*   *southeastern US*
               speech often yuh-NĪD STĀTS   'juː,naiţəd 'steːts, *in rapid*
                                   speech often jə,naid
                                   'steːts

UNIVAC
   UN agency   YOO-nuh-VAK   'juːnə,væk

Univac
   tdmk for an early computer   YOO-nuh-VAK   'juːnə,væk

UNIX
   computer operating system   YOO-niks   'juːniks

Unocal
   US oil co.   YOO-nuh-KAL   'juːnə,kæl

UNRWA
   United Nations Relief and Works   UHN-ruh   'ənrə
    Agency

Unter den Linden
   main avenue, Berlin, Germany   UN-tuhr den LIN-duhn   ,untəʳ den 'lindən

Unterseeboot
   German for submarine   UN-tuhr-ZĀ-BŌT   'untəʳ,zeː,boːt

Unwin
   pers. name   UHN-wuhn   'ənwən

Upanishads
   basic text of Hinduism   oo-PAHN-i-SHAHDZ,   uː'pani,ʃadz, juː'pænə,ʃædz
                 yoo-PAN-uh-SHADZ

Updike
   John, *US writer; pers. name*   UHP-DĪK   'əp,daik

Upham
   pers. name   UHP-uhm   'əpəm

Upland
   city, CA   UHP-luhnd   'əplənd

Upolu
   island, Samoa   oo-PŌ-loo   uː'poːluː

Upper Volta
   former name of Burkina Faso   UHP-uhr VAHL-tuh, VŌL-, VAWL-   ,əpəʳ 'valtə, 'voːl-, 'vɔːl-

Upper Voltan
   pert. to Upper Volta   UHP-uhr VAHL-tuhn, VŌL-, VAWL-   ,əpəʳ 'valtən, 'voːl-, 'vɔːl-

Uppsala
   county, city, Sweden   UHP-suh-LAH, UHP-SAHL-uh,   'əpsə,la, 'əp,salə, əp'salə
               uhp-SAHL-uh

Upsala
   College, *NJ*   UHP-suh-luh, UHP-suh-LAH,   'əpsələ, 'əpsə,la, əp'salə
               uhp-SAHL-uh

Key (col. 2): a: fad ā: fade ah: father ar: Mary aw: law e: fed ē: feed er: merry i: hid ī: hide ō: coat oo: boot
oi: boy ow: now u: put uh: above uhr: bird ch: chop ng: ring sh: show th: thick <u>th</u>: this zh: measure

Upshaw
    Gene, *US football executive*   UHP-SHAW   'əp,ʃɔː

Upton
    pers. name   UHP-tuhn   'əptən

Ur
    ancient Sumerian city   UHR, UR   'əʳ, 'uʳ

Ural
    river, mtn. range, Russia   YUR-uhl   'jurəl

Ural-Altaic
    pert. to Ural *and* Altai Mts.; *lang.*   YUR-uhl-AL-TĀ-ik   jurəl,æl'teːik
    families

Uralian
    pert. to Ural Mts. *or their*   yu-RĀ-lē-uhn   ju'reːliːən
    inhabitants

Uralic
    pert. to Finno-Ugric *and* Samoyed   yu-RAL-ik   ju'rælik
    langs.

Uralskiy Khrebet
    mtn. range, Russia   yu-RAHL-skyi <u>kh</u>reb-YET   ju'rɑːḷskjij xreb'jet

Urania
    muse of astronomy; street, New   yu-RĀ-nē-uh, yu-RĀN-yuh   ju'reːniːə, ju'reːnjə
    Orleans

uranium
    element   yu-RĀ-nē-uhm   ju'reːniːəm

Uranus
    Greek sky god; planet   YUR-uh-nuhs, yuh-RĀ-nuhs,   'jurənəs, jə'reːnəs, 'urənəs
        UR-uh-nuhs

Urartu
    ancient Assyrian kingdom   ur-AHR-TOO   ur'ɑʳ,tuː

Urban
    pope   UHR-buhn   'əʳbən

Urbana
    city, IL, OH   UHR-BAN-uh   ,əʳ'bænə

Urbano
    pers. name, Italian   oor-BAHN-ō   uːr'bɑnoː

Urdu
    Indic lang.   UR-doo, UHR-doo   'uʳduː, 'əʳduː

Urey
    Harold C., *US physical chemist*   YUR-ē   'juriˑ
    (Nobel 1934)

Urfa
    prov, city, Turkey   ur-FAH   uʳ'fɑ

Urga
    former name for Ulaanbaatar   UR-guh   'uʳgə

Urho
    pers. name, Finnish   UR-haw   'urhɔː

Uri
    1. Swiss commune   UR-ē   'uriˑ
    2. pers. name (U. Geller)   UR-ē, YUR-ē   'uriˑ, 'juriˑ

Uria, Uriah
    Bathsheba's husband; pers. name   yuh-RĪ-uh   jə'rɑiə

Urian
    pers. name   YUR-ē-uhn   'juriːən

Urich
    Robert, *US actor*   YUR-ik   'jurik

Foreign Sounds: ue: *Fr.* **rue**, *Ger.* **füllen** uh(r): *Fr.* **boeuf**, *Ger.* **Höhle** <u>kh</u>: *Ger.* **ich**, *Scot.* **loch** g̃: *Sp.* **amigo** v̱: *Sp.* **hablar**
hl: *Welsh* **Llanelli**. CAPITALS: primary stress. SMALL CAPS: secondary stress. Ⓢ: U.S. pron. Ⓑ: British pron.

Uriel
  pers. name, Portuguese   o͞or-YEL   uːrˈjel

Uris
  Leon, *US author*   YUR-uhs   ˈjurəs

Ur-Marzen
  German beer   UR-MAHRT-suhn   ˈuʳˌmaʳtsən

Urmia
  lake, Iran   UR-mē-uh   ˈuʳmiːə

Ur-Nammu
  king of Ur   UHR-NAHM-o͞o, UR-   ˌəʳˈnɑmˌuː, ˈuʳ-

Urquhart
  family name   UHR-kuhrt, UHR-KAHRT   ˈəʳkəʳt, ˈəʳˌkɑʳt

Ursa Major
  constellation   UHR-suh MĀ-juhr   ˌəʳsə ˈmeːdʒəʳ

Ursa Minor
  constellation   UHR-suh MĪ-nuhr   ˌəʳsə ˈmainəʳ

Ursids
  meteor shower   UHR-sidz   ˈəʳsidz

Ursinus
  antipope; college, PA   UHR-SĪ-nuhs   ˌəʳˈsainəs

Ursprache
  reconstructed parent lang.   UR-SHPRAHKH-uh   ˈuʳˌʃprɑxə

Ursula
  1. Christian saint; pers. name   UHR-s(y)uh-luh   ˈəʳs(j)ələ
  2. Italian   o͞or-SO͞O-lah   uːrˈsuːla

Ursuline
  College, *OH*   UHR-suh-luhn, UHR-suh-LĪN,   ˈəʳsələn, ˈəʳsəˌlain, ˈəʳsəˌliːn
                   UHR-suh-LĒN

Ursulines
  religious order   UHR-s(y)uh-luhnz, -LĪNZ, -LĒNZ   ˈəʳs(j)ələnz, -ˌlainz, -ˌliːnz

Urtyp 1634
  German beer   UR-TUEP TOW-zuhnt SEKHS   ˈur,tyːp ˈtauzənt ˈseçs
                   HUN-duhrt FIR unt DRĪ-sikh   ˈhundəʳt ˈfir unt ˈdraisiç

Uru
  S. American people   O͞O-ro͞o, o͞o-RO͞O   ˈuːruː, uːˈruː

Uruguay
  republic, S. America   (Y)UR-uh-GWĪ, YUR-uh-GWĀ   ˈ(j)urəˌgwai, ˈjurəˌgweː

Uruguayan
  pert. to Uruguay   (Y)UR-uh-GWĪ-uhn,   ˌ(j)urəˈgwaiən, jurəˈgweːən
                   YUR-uh-GWĀ-uhn

Uruk
  Sumerian city   O͞O-RUK   ˈuːˌruk

Urukagina
  Sumerian reformer   O͞O-ruk-AJ-uh-nuh   ˌuːrukˈædʒənə

Ürümqi, Urumchi
  city, China   UE-RUEM-CHĒ, Ⓢ u-RUM-chē   ˈyːˈryːmˈtʃiː, Ⓢ uˈrumtʃiˑ

Urundi
  former name of Burundi   u-RO͞ON-dē   uˈruːndiˑ

Ushant [Ouessant, Ile d']
  island, France   UHSH-uhnt   ˈəʃənt

Ushas
  Vedic dawn goddess   O͞OSH-uhs   ˈuˑʃəs

Ushuaia
  city, Argentina   o͞o-SWĀ-yuh   uːˈsweːjə

Key (col. 2):   a: fad   ā: fade   ah: father   ar: Mary   aw: law   e: fed   ē: feed   er: merry   i: hid   ī: hide   ō: coat   o͞o: boot
oi: boy   ow: now   u: put   uh: above   uhr: bird   ch: chop   ng: ring   sh: show   th: thick   th̲: this   zh: measure

Usk
   river, Wales, England   UHSK   'ǝsk

Uspallata
   mtn. pass, Andes   *in Chile* o͞o-spah-YAHT-ah, *in*   *in Chile* uːspɑ'jɑʈɑ, *in*
                      Argentina o͞o-spah-ZHAHT-ah   *Argentina* uːspɑ'ʒɑʈɑ

Usquaebach
   Scotch whisky   UHS-kwuh-BAH(<u>KH</u>), -BAW(<u>KH</u>)   'ǝskwǝˌbɑ(x), -ˌbɔː(x)

Ussuri
   river, Asia   ˏu-SUR-ē   u'suriˑ

Ustinov
   1. Peter, entertainer   (Y)O͞O-stuh-NAWF, -NAWV   '(j)uːstǝˌnɔːf, -ˌnɔːv
   2. city, Russia   O͞O-sti-NAWF   'uːsʈiˌnɔːf

Utah
   state, US   YO͞O-TAW, YO͞O-TAH   'juːˌtɔː, 'juːˌtɑ

Utahan, Utahn
   pert. to or inhabitant of Utah   YO͞O-TAHN   'juːˌtɑn

Utamaro
   pers. name, Japanese; see   ut-ah-mahr-ō   uʈamaroː
     Kitagawa Utamaro

Ute
   N. American people   YO͞OT   'juːt

Uther Pendragon
   father of King Arthur   (Y)O͞O-thuhr PEN-DRAG-uhn,   '(j)uːθǝʳ 'penˌdrægǝn,
                      pen-DRAG-uhn   pen'drægǝn

Utica
   city, NY; ancient N. African city   YO͞OT-i-kuh   'juːʈikǝ

Utley
   Garrick, *TV personality*   UHT-lē   'ǝtliˑ

Uto-Aztecan
   American lang. family   YO͞OT-ō-AZ-TEK-uhn   juːʈoː'æzˌtekǝn

Utopia
   book, Sir Thomas More; ideal   yu-TŌ-pē-uh   ju'toːpiːǝ
     place

Utrecht
   prov & town, Netherlands   O͞O-TRE<u>KH</u>T, ⑤ YO͞O-TREKT   'uːˌtreçt, ⑤ 'juːˌtrekt

Utrillo
   Maurice, *French painter*   ue-trē-YŌ, ⑤ yo͞o-TRĒ-ō, yo͞o-TRIL-ō   yːtriːjoː, ⑤ juː'triːoː, juː'triloː

Uttar Pradesh
   state, India   UT-uhr pruh-DĀSH, pruh-DESH   ˌuʈǝʳ prǝ'deːʃ, prǝ'deʃ

Utu
   Sumerian sun god   (Y)O͞OT-o͞o   '(j)uːtuː

Uusikaupunki
   port, Finland   O͞O-si-KAH-PUNG-kē   'uːsi'kɑˌpuŋkiˑ

Uvalde
   county, TX   yu-VAL-dē   ju'vældiˑ

Uxbridge
   town, England   UHKS-brij   'ǝksbridʒ

Uxmal
   ancient Mayan city, Mexico   o͞oz-MAHL   uːz'mɑl

Uzbek
   lang., people, Asia   UZ-BEK, UHZ-BEK, uz-BEK   'uzˌbek, 'ǝzˌbek, uz'bek

Uzbekistan
   republic, Asia   uz-BEK-i-STAHN, -STAN;   uzˌbeki'stɑn, -'stæn;
                     uz-BEK-i-STAHN, -STAN   uz'bekiˌstɑn, -ˌstæn

---

Foreign Sounds: ue: *Fr.* **rue**, *Ger.* **füllen**   uh(r): *Fr.* **boeuf**, *Ger.* **Höhle**   <u>kh</u>: *Ger.* **ich**, *Scot.* **loch**   g̃: *Sp.* **amigo**   v̠: *Sp.* **hablar**
hl: *Welsh* **Llanelli**.   CAPITALS: primary stress.   SMALL CAPS: secondary stress.   ⑤: U.S. pron.   ⓣ: British pron.

Uzbekskaya
    SSR, *Uzbek republic, USSR*   ōōz-BEK-skuh-yuh   u·z'bekskəjə
Uzi
    Israeli-designed machine gun   ŌŌ-zē   'u:zi·

V

Vaal
    South African river   VAHL   'vɑl
Vaasa
    prov & town, Finland   VAHS-ah   'vɑsɑ:
Vaccaro
    Brenda, *US actress*   vuh-KAR-ō, vuh-KAHR-ō   və'kæro:, və'kɑro:
Vachel
    pers. name   VĀ-chuhl   've:tʃəl
Václav
    pers. name, Czech   VAHT-SLAHF   'vat,slɑf
Vacuna
    ancient Sabine goddess of leisure   va-K(Y)ŌŌ-nuh   væ'k(j)u:nə
Vadim
    1. Roger, *French director*   vah-DĒM   vɑ:di:m
    2. *pers. name, Russian*   VAHD-yēm   'vɑ:dji:m
Vaduz
    city, Liechtenstein   fah-DŌŌTS   fɑ'du:ts
Vai
    lang., people, Liberia, Sierra Leone   VĪ   'vai
Vaikunth
    Indian festival   V<u>Ī</u>-KUNT   'βai,kunt
Vaishnavism
    worship of Vishnu   VĪSH-nuh-VIZ-uhm   'vaiʃnə,vizəm
Val
    pers. name   VAL   'væl
Valais
    canton, Switzerland   vah-LE, Ⓢ va-LĀ   vɑ:le, Ⓢ væ'le:
Valdai
    hills, Russia   vahl-DĪ   vɑl'dai
Valdemar
    1. *king, Denmark; pers. name, Danish; fictional country, M. Lackey*   VAHL-duh-MAHR   'vɑ:ldə,mɑʳ
    2. *Swedish*   VAHL-duh-MAHR   'vɑ:ldə,mɑ:ʳ
Val-de-Marne
    dept, Ile-de-France   vahl-duh-MAHRN   vɑ:ldəmɑ:rn
Valdepeñas
    commune, Spain   bahl-dā-PĀN-yahs   bɑlde:'pe:njɑs

Key (col. 2):   a: fad   ā: fade   ah: father   ar: **Mary**   aw: **law**   e: fed   ē: feed   er: **merry**   i: hid   ī: hide   ō: coat   ōō: boot
oi: **boy**   ow: **now**   u: **put**   uh: **above**   uhr: **bird**   ch: **chop**   ng: **ring**   sh: **show**   th: **thick**   <u>th</u>: **this**   zh: measure

Valdés
   peninsula, Argentina   vahl-DES   vɑl'des

Valdez
   port, AK   val-DĒZ   væl'diːz

Valdez-Cordova
   division, AK   val-DĒZ-kawr-DŌ-vuh   væl'diːzkɔːʳ'doːvə

Val-d'Oise
   dept, Ile-de-France   vahl-DWAHZ   vɑːldwɑːz

Valdosta
   city, GA   val-DAHS-tuh   væl'dɑstə

Valencia
   1. county, NM   vuh-LEN-ch(ē-)uh,   və'lentʃ(iː)ə, və'len(t)siːə
                        vuh-LEN(T)-sē-uh
   2. region, Spain   vah-LEN-thyah   vɑ'lenθjɑ

Valenciennes
   city, France   vah-lahⁿs-YEN   vɑːlãsjen

Valens
   1. Roman emperor   VĀ-luhnz, VĀ-LENZ, VĀ-luhns   'veːlənz, 'veːˌlenz, 'veːləns
   2. pers. name, German   VAHL-ens   'vɑlens

Valentín
   pers. name, Spanish   bahl-ān-TĒN   bɑleːn'tiːn

Valentin
   1. pers. name, French   vah-lahⁿ-TEⁿ   vɑːlãtẽ
   2. German   VAHL-en-TĒN   'vɑlen,tiːn
   3. Serbo-Croatian   VAHL-en-TĒN   'vɑːlen,tiːn

Valentina
   pers. name, Russian   VUHL-yin-TĒN-uh   ˌvəljin'ťִiːnə

Valentine
   1. saint; sweetheart; pers. name   VAL-uhn-TĪN   'vælən,tɑin
   2. German   VAH-len-TĒ-nuh   ˌvɑlen'tiːnə

Valentinian
   Roman emperor   VAL-uhn-TIN-ē-uhn, -TIN-yuhn   ˌvælən'tiniːən, -'tinjən

Valentinianism
   form of Gnosticism   VAL-uhn-TIN-ē-uh-NIZ-uhm   ˌvælən'tiniːəˌnizəm

Valentino
   1. Rudolph, US actor   VAL-uhn-TĒ-nō   ˌvælən'tiːnoː
   2. pers. name, Italian   VAHL-ān-TĒ-nō   ˌvɑleːn'tiːnoː

Valenzuela
   Fernando, Mexican baseball   VAL-uhnz-WĀ-luh   ˌvælənz'weːlə
     player

Valeri
   pers. name, Russian   VUHL-YER-yi   ˌvəl'jerjij

Valeria
   pers. name   vuh-LIR-ē-uh   və'liriːə

Valerian
   1. Roman emperor   vuh-LIR-ē-uhn   və'liriːən
   2. pers. name, Russian   VUHL-yir-YAHN   ˌvəljir'jɑːn

Valeriano
   pers. name, Spanish   bahl-ār-YAHN-ō   bɑleːr'jɑnoː

Valerianus
   pers. name, Latin   vuh-LIR-ē-Ā-nuhs   vəˌliriː'eːnəs

Valerie
   pers. name   VAL-(uh-)rē   'væl(ə)riˑ

Valérie
   pers. name, French   vah-lā-RĒ   vɑːleːriː

Foreign Sounds: ue: *Fr.* **r**u**e**, *Ger.* f**ü**llen   uh(r): *Fr.* b**oeu**f, *Ger.* H**öh**le   kh: *Ger.* i**ch**, *Scot.* lo**ch**   g̃: *Sp.* ami**g**o   v: *Sp.* ha**b**lar
hl: *Welsh* **Ll**anelli.   CAPITALS: primary stress.   SMALL CAPS: secondary stress.   Ⓢ: U.S. pron.   Ⓔ: British pron.

Valerius		
1. pers. name, German	vah-LĀ-rē-us	vɑ'leːriːus
2. Latin	vuh-LIR-ē-uhs	və'liriːəs
Valéry		
pers. name, French	vah-lā-RĒ	vɑːleːriː
Valga		
town, Estonia	VAL-guh	'vælgə
Valhalla		
hall of the slain in Norse myth	val-HAL-uh, vahl-HAHL-uh	væl'hælə, vɑl'hɑlə
Valium		
tdmk for diazepam	VAL-ē-uhm	'væliːəm
Valjean		
Jean, *hero of* Les Misérables, *V. Hugo*	vahl-ZHAH^{n}	vɑːlʒɑ̃
Valkyrie		
Scandinavian mythical maidens	val-KIR-ē, VAL-kuh-rē	væl'kiriˑ, 'vælkəriˑ
Vallabhbhai		
pers. name, Gujarati	VUHL-luhb-BAH-ē	ˌvəlləb'bɑ-iː
Valladolid		
prov, city, Spain; town, Mexico; city, Philippines	bah(l)-yah-t͟hō-LĒ(T͟H), $ VAL-uh-duh-LID, -LĒD	bɑ(l)jɑðoː'liː(ð), $ ˌvælədə'lid, -'liːd
Vallauris		
commune, France	vah-law-RĒS, vah-lō-RĒS	vɑːlɔːriːs, vɑːloːriːs
Valle Crucis		
abbey, Wales	VAL-ē KRO͞O-suhs	'væliˑ 'kruːsəs
Valle d'Aosta		
region, Italy	VAHL-ā dah-AW-stuh	ˌvɑleː dɑ'ɔːstə
Vallejo		
city, CA	vuh-LĀ-ō	və'leːoː
Valletta		
city, Malta	vuh-LET-uh	və'leţə
Valli		
Frankie, *US singer*	VAL-ē	'væliˑ
Vallombrosa		
resort, Italy	VAL-uhm-BRŌ-suh	ˌvæləm'broːsə
Valmiera		
town, Latvia	VAHL-MYER-uh	'vɑlˌmjerə
Valois		
duchy, France	vahl-WAH	vɑːlwɑː
Valparaíso		
region, city, Chile; city, Mexico	bahl-pah-rah-Ē-sō, $ VAL-puh-RĀ-zō, -RĪ-zō	bɑlpɑrɑ'iːsoː, $ ˌvælpə'reːzoː, -'rɑizoː
Valparaiso		
1. town, FL	VAL-puh-RĪ-zō	ˌvælpə'rɑizoː
2. town, IN	VAL-puh-RĀ-zō	ˌvælpə'reːzoː
Valpolicella		
wine	VAHL-PŌ-luh-CHEL-uh, VAL-	ˌvɑlˌpoːlə'tʃelə, ˌvæl-
Val Verde		
county, TX	val VUHRD-ē	væl 'vəʳdiˑ
Valvoline		
US oil co.	VAL-vuh-LĒN	'vælvəˌliːn
Van		
pers. name	VAN	'væn
vanadium		
element	vuh-NĀD-ē-uhm	və'neːdiːəm

Key (col. 2): a: **fa**d ā: **fa**de ah: **fa**ther ar: **Ma**ry aw: **law** e: **fe**d ē: **fee**d er: **me**rry i: **hi**d ī: **hi**de ō: **coa**t o͞o: **boo**t oi: **boy** ow: **now** u: **pu**t uh: **a**bove uhr: **bir**d ch: **ch**op ng: **ring** sh: **sh**ow th: **th**ick t͟h: **th**is zh: mea**s**ure

Van Allen
    James, *US physicist; radiation*   van AL-uhn   væn ˈælən
    belt above Earth
Van Ark
    Joan, *actress*   van AHRK   væn ˈɑʳk
Van Buren
    Martin, *8th US president;* Abigail,   van BYUR-uhn, vuhn   væn ˈbjurən, vən
    US advice columnist; pers.
    name
Van Cleef
    Lee, *US actor*   van KLĒF   væn ˈkliːf
Vancouver
    city, Canada; city, WA   van-KOO-vuhr   vænˈkuːvəʳ
Vandalia
    city, IL   van-DĀL-yuh   vænˈdeːljə
Vandals
    ancient Germanic people   VAN-duhlz   ˈvændəlz
Van de Graaf
    Robert J., *US physicist*   VAN-duh GRAF, VAN duh GRAF   ˈvændə ˌgræf, ˌvæn də ˈgræf
Vandenberg
    Hoyt S., *US general; US air force*   VAN-duhn-BUHRG, VAN-duhm-BUHRG   ˈvændən,bəʳg,
    base   ˈvændəm,bəʳg
Vanderbilt
    US family name   VAN-duhr-BILT   ˈvændəʳ,bilt
van der Meere
    Simon, *Dutch physicist (Nobel*   VAHN duhr MER   ˌvɑn dəʳ ˈmeʳ
    1984)
van der Waals
    J. D., *Dutch physicist (Nobel*   VAHN DUHR VAHLS, $ VAN duhr   ˌvɑn dəʳ ˈvals, $ ˌvæn dəʳ
    1910)   WAWLZ   ˈwɔːlz
Van Devere
    Trish, *US actress*   VAN duh-VIR   ˌvæn dəˈviʳ
Vandyke, Van Dyke
    pers. name   van DĬK, vuhn DĬK   væn ˈdɑik, vən ˈdɑik
Vane
    Sir John R., *English biochemist*   VĀN   ˈveːn
    (Nobel 1982)
Vanessa
    pers. name   vuh-NES-uh   vəˈnesə
Van Eyck
    Hubert *and* Jan, *Flemish painters*   vahn ĀK, $ van ĪK   vɑn ˈeːk, $ væn ˈɑik
Vanga
    insectivorous bird   VAHNG-guh   ˈvɑŋgə
Van Gogh
    Vincent, *Dutch painter*   vahn ĞAWĞ, $ van GŌ, van GAH<u>KH</u>   vɑn ˈɣɔːɣ, $ væn ˈgoː, væn
     ˈgɑx
Van Heusen
    James, *US composer; brand of*   van HYOO-zuhn   væn ˈhjuːzən
    clothing
Vanier
    city, Canada   vaⁿNYĀ, VAN-YĀ   vãˈnjeː, ˈvænˌjeː
Vanir
    Scandinavian fertility gods   VAHN-IR   ˈvɑn,iʳ
Vanna
    pers. name (V. White)   VAN-uh   ˈvænə

Van Ness
   street, San Francisco, CA; pers.   van-(N)ES   væn'(n)es
   name

Vannevar
   pers. name   vuh-NĒ-VAHR   vəˈniːˌvɑʳ

Van Nuys
   region, Los Angeles, CA   van NĪZ   væn ˈnɑiz

Vanocur
   Sander, *US newsman*   van-Ō-kuhr   væn'oːkəʳ

Van Patten
   Dick, *US actor*   van PAT-n   væn ˈpætn̩

Van Riebeeck Day
   holiday, S. Africa   vahn RĒ-BĀK   vɑn ˈriːˌbeːk

Vantaa
   city, airport, Finland   VAHN-tah   ˈvɑːntɑ

van't Hoff
   Jacobus Hendricus, *Dutch chemist*   vahnt HAWF   vɑnt ˈhɔːf
   (Nobel 1901)

Vanua Levu
   island, Pacific Ocean   vuh-NŌŌ-uh LEV-ōō   vəˈnuːə ˈlevuː

Vanuatu
   islands, Pacific   VAHN-(y)uh-WAH-TŌŌ,   ˌvɑn(j)əˈwɑˌtuː, ˌvænəˈwɑtuː
                    VAN-uh-WAHT-ōō

Vanuatuan
   pert. to Vanuatu   VAHN-(y)uh-WAH-TŌŌ-uhn,   ˌvɑn(j)əˈwɑˌtuːən,
                    VAN-(y)uh-WAHT-uh-wuhn   ˌvæn(j)əˈwɑtəwən

Van Vleck
   John H., *US physicist (Nobel*   van VLEK   væn ˈvlek
   1977)

van Wijk
   pers. name, Dutch   vahn VĀK   vɑn ˈveːk

Van Wyck
   pers. name   van WĪK, van WIK   væn ˈwaik, væn ˈwik

Vanya
   pers. name   VAHN-yuh, VAN-yuh   ˈvɑnjə, ˈvænjə

Van Zandt
   county, TX   van ZANT   væn ˈzænt

Vanzetti
   Bartolomeo, *Italian anarchist*   van-ZET-ē   væn'zeti'
   executed in US

Vaporum, Mare
   see Mare Vaporum

Varanasi [Benares]
   city, India   vuh-RAHN-uh-sē   vəˈrɑnəsi'

Varèse
   Edgard, *US composer*   vuh-RĀZ, vuh-REZ   vəˈreːz, vəˈrez

Varese
   prov, city, Italy   vahr-Ā-sā, ⑧ vuh-RĀ-sē   vɑrˈeːse', ⑧ vəˈreːsi'

Varig
   Brazilian airline   VAHR-ig, VAR-ig   ˈvɑrig, ˈværig

Varius
   pers. name, Latin   VAR-ē-uhs   ˈværiːəs

Varley
   John Herbert, *US author*   VAHR-lē   ˈvɑʳli'

Key (col. 2):   a: **fad** ā: **fade** ah: **father** ar: **Mary** aw: **law** e: **fed** ē: **feed** er: **merry** i: **hid** ī: **hide** ō: **coat** ōō: **boot**
oi: **boy**   ow: **now**   u: **put**   uh: **above**   uhr: **bird**   ch: **chop**   ng: **ring**   sh: **show**   th: **thick**   <u>th</u>: **this**   zh: **measure**

Varmus
Harold E., *US microbiologist*   VAHR-muhs   'vɑʳməs
  (*Nobel 1989*)

Varna
prov, Bulgaria   VAHR-nuh   'vɑʳnə

Varro
Marcus, *Roman scholar*   VAR-ō   'væroː

Varsa
Buddhist penitential period   V̲AHR-shuh   'βɑʳʃə

Vartanantz Day
Armenian commemoration   VAHR-tuh-NAHNTS   'vɑʳtə,nɑnts

Varuna
supreme Vedic god   VUR-un-uh, VAHR-uh-nuh   'vurunə, 'vɑrənə

Vasco
1. *pers. name, Portuguese*   VAHSH-ko͞o, VAHS-ko͞o   'vɑːʃkuː, 'vɑːskuː
2. *Spanish*   BAHS-kō, ⑤ VAS-kō   'bɑskoː, ⑤ 'væskoː

Vasco da Gama
Portuguese navigator   VAHSH-ko͞o thuh G̅AH-muh,   ,vɑːʃkuː ðə 'ɣɑːmə,
     ⑤ VAHS-kō duh GAHM-uh,   ⑤ ,vɑskoː də 'gɑmə,
     GAH-muh; VAS-kō duh GAM-uh   'gɑːmə; ,væskoː də 'gæmə

Vaseline
tdmk for petrolatum   VAS-uh-LĒN, VAS-uh-LĒN   'væsə,liːn, ,væsə'liːn

Vashti
Biblical name   VAHSH-tē, VAHSH-TĪ   'vɑʃtiˈ, 'vɑʃ,tɑi

Vasil
pers. name, Bulgarian   vah-SĒL   vɑːˈsiːl

Vasile
pers. name, Romanian   vah-SĒ-le   vɑˈsiːle

Vasili, -ly
pers. name, Russian   VUHS-YĒL-yi   ,vəsˈjiːljij

Vaslav
pers. name, Russian   VUHT-SLAHF   ,vətˈslɑːf

Vásquez
pers. name, Spanish   BAHS-käs, -käth; ⑤ VAS-K(W)EZ,   'bɑskeːs, -keːθ;
     VAHS-   ⑤ 'væs,k(w)ez, 'vɑs-

Vassar
College, NY   VAS-uhr   'væsəʳ

VAT
value-added tax   VAT, VĒ-Ā-TĒ   'væt, ,viː,eːˈtiː

Vatican
papal state, Rome   VAT-i-kuhn   'væţikən

Vaticanism
doctrine of supremacy of the pope   VAT-i-kuh-NIZ-uhm   'væţikə,nizəm

Vaucluse
dept, France   vō-KLŌOZ   voːkluːz

Vaud
canton, Switzerland   VŌ   voː

Vaughan, Vaughn
pers. name   VAWN, VAHN   'vɔːn, 'vɑn

Vaughan Williams
Ralph, *composer*   RĀF VAWN WIL-yuhmz   'reːf ,vɔːn 'wiljəmz

Vaux
English beer   VAWKS, VAHKS   'vɔːks, 'vɑks

Vauxhall
pers. name   VAHK-SAWL, VAHKS-HAWL   'vɑk,sɔːl, 'vɑks,hɔːl

Foreign Sounds: **ue**: *Fr.* **rue**, *Ger.* f**ü**llen   **uh**(r): *Fr.* b**oeu**f, *Ger.* H**öh**le   **kh**: *Ger.* i**ch**, *Scot.* lo**ch**   **g̅**: *Sp.* ami**g**o   **v**: *Sp.* ha**b**lar
hl: *Welsh* **Ll**anelli.   CAPITALS: primary stress.   SMALL CAPS: secondary stress.   ⑤: U.S. pron.   Ⓛ: British pron.

Vaux's
swift | VAWK-suhz, VAHK-suhz | 'vɔ:ksəz, 'vɑksəz

VAX
tdmk for computer hardware | VAKS | 'væks

Veadar [Adar Sheni]
Jewish month | VĀ-AHD-AHR, VĀ-uh-DAHR, VĒ- | 've:ˌɑdˌɑʳ, 've:ə,dɑʳ, 'vi:-

Veblen
Thorstein B., *US economist* | VEB-luhn | 'veblən

Veda
Hindu sacred writings | VĀD-uh | 've:də

Vedaism
religion | VĀD-uh-ɪZ-uhm | 've:də,izəm

Vedanta
Hindu philosophy | vā-DAHNT-uh, vā-DANT-uh, vuh- | ve:'dɑntə, ve:'dæntə, və-

Vedantism
religion | vā-DAHN-TɪZ-uhm, vuh-DAN- | ve:'dɑn,tizəm, və'dæn-

Vedic
pert. to the Veda | VĀD-ik | 've:dik

Vega
Suzanne, *US singer; star; stringed* | VĒ-guh, VĀ-guh | 'vi:gə, 've:gə
instrument mfrs.

Veii
ancient city, central Italy | VĒ-(Y)Ī, VĀ-(y)ē | 'vi:,(j)ɑi, 've:(j)i:

Vela
constellation | VĒ-luh | 'vi:lə

Velasco
pers. name, Spanish | bā-LAHS-kō, Ⓢ vuh-LAS-kō | be:'lɑsko:, Ⓢ və'læsko:

Velázquez
Diego, *Spanish painter* | bā-LAHTH-kāth, Ⓢ vuh-LAS-kuhs, vuh-LAS-K(W)EZ | be:'lɑθke:θ, Ⓢ və'læskəs, və'læs,k(w)ez

Velcro
tdmk for fasteners | VEL-krō | 'velkro:

Velia
ridge between Palatine and Oppian hills, Rome | VĒ-lē-uh | 'vi:li:ə

Velleius Paterculus
Roman historian | vuh-LĒ-uhs puh-TUHR-kyuh-luhs | və'li:əs pə'təʳkjələs

Vellelus
pers. name, Latin | ve-LĒ-luhs | ve'li:ləs

Velma
pers. name | VEL-muh | 'velmə

Venable
pers. name | VEN-uh-buhl | 'venəbəl

Venables
pers. name | VEN-uh-buhlz | 'venəbəlz

Venancio
pers. name, Spanish | bā-NAHN-syō, -thyō, Ⓢ vā-NAHN-sē-ō | be:'nɑnsjo:, -θjo:, Ⓢ ve:'nɑnsi:,o:

Venango
county, PA | vi-NANG-gō | vi'næŋgo:

Venda
lang., people, Africa; independent homeland, S. Africa | VEN-duh | 'vendə

Vendée
river, dept, France | vahⁿ-DĀ | vãde:

Key (col. 2):   a: fad ā: fade ah: father ar: Mary aw: law e: fed ē: feed er: merry i: hid ī: hide ō: coat ōō: boot
oi: boy ow: now u: put uh: above uhr: bird ch: chop ng: ring sh: show th: thick th: this zh: measure

Vendémiaire		
month, French Revolutionary calendar	vahⁿ-dãm-YER	vãdeːmjer
Venelin		
pers. name, Bulgarian	ve-ne-LĒN	veneˈliːn
Venetia		
region, Italy	vi-NĒ-sh(ē-)uh	viˈniːʃ(iː)ə
Venetian		
pert. to Venice	vuh-NĒ-shuhn	vəˈniːʃən
Venetic		
Indo-European lang., Italy	vuh-NET-ik	vəˈnet̯ik
Veneto		
region, Italy	VĀ-nuh-TŌ, VEN-uh-TŌ	ˈveːnə,toː, ˈvenə,toː
Venezia [Venice]		
city, Italy	vuh-NET-sē-uh	vəˈnetsiːə
Venezuela		
republic, S. America	VEN-uhz(-uh)-WĀ-luh, -WĒ-luh	ˌvenəz(ə)ˈweːlə, -ˈwiːlə
Venezuelan		
pert. to Venezuela	VEN-uhz(-uh)-WĀ-luhn, -WĒ-luhn	ˌvenəz(ə)ˈweːlən, -ˈwiːlən
Venice		
city, Italy; city, CA, FL, IL	VEN-uhs	ˈvenəs
Venite		
liturgical chant	vuh-NĪT-ē, vuh-NĒ-TĀ, VE-	vəˈnaiti̯ˑ, vəˈniː,teː, ve-
Venn		
John, *English logician*	VEN	ˈven
Venta		
river, Latvia, Lithuania	VEN-tuh	ˈventə
Ventnor		
street, Atlantic City, NJ	VENT-nuhr	ˈventnəʳ
Ventôse		
month, French Revolutionary calendar	vahⁿ-TŌZ	vãtoːz
Ventris		
Michael, *British linguist*	VEN-tris, Ⓢ VEN-truhs	ˈventris, Ⓢ ˈventrəs
Ventspils		
port, Latvia	VENT-SPILS	ˈvent,spils
Ventura		
1. city, CA; computer software, US	ven-TYUR-uh, ven-CHUR-uh	venˈtjurə, venˈtʃurə
2. pers. name, Spanish	bān-TŌŌ-rah, Ⓢ ven-TYUR-uh, ven-CHUR-uh	beːnˈtuːra, Ⓢ venˈtjurə, venˈtʃurə
Venturi		
G. B., *Italian physicist;* Ken, *US golfer*	ven-TUR-ē, ven-TYUR-ē, ven-CHUR-ē	venˈturiˑ, venˈtjuriˑ, venˈtʃuriˑ
Venus		
Roman goddess of love; planet	VĒ-nuhs	ˈviːnəs
Venus de Milo		
statue of Aphrodite	VĒ-nuhs duh MĪ-lō	ˌviːnəs də ˈmailoː
Venusian		
pert. to Venus	vuh-NŌŌ-zhuhn, vuhn-YŌŌ-zhuhn	vəˈnuːʒən, vənˈjuːʒən
Venus's-flytrap		
insectivorous plant	VĒ-nuhs(-uhz)-FLĪ-TRAP	ˌviːnəs(əz)ˈflai,træp
Veps		
lang., people, Russia, Europe	VEPS	ˈveps
Vepsian [Veps]		
lang., Russia, Europe	VEP-sē-uhn	ˈvepsiːən

Foreign Sounds: ue: *Fr.* **rue**, *Ger.* f**ü**llen   uh(r): *Fr.* b**oeu**f, *Ger.* H**ö**hle   <u>kh</u>: *Ger.* i**ch**, *Scot.* lo**ch**   g̱: *Sp.* ami**g**o   v̱: *Sp.* ha**b**lar
hl: *Welsh* **Ll**anelli.   CAPITALS: primary stress.   SMALL CAPS: secondary stress.   Ⓢ: U.S. pron.   Ⓔ: British pron.

Vera		
pers. name	VIR-uh, VER-uh	'virə, 'verə
Veracruz		
seaport, state, Mexico	VER-uh-KRO͞OS, VER-uh-KRO͞OZ	ˌverə'kruːs, ˌverə'kruːz
Vercingetorix		
Gallic chieftain	VUHR-suhn-JET-uh-riks	ˌvəʳsən'dʒeţəriks
Verde		
1. river, AZ	VUHRD-ē, VERD-ē	'vəʳdiˑ, 'veʳdiˑ
2. river, Brazil	VERD-uh	'veʳdə
3. cape, Senegal	VUHRD	'vəʳd
Verdelho		
wine	ver-DEL-yo͞o	veʳ'deljuː
Verdi		
Giuseppe, *Italian composer*	VERD-ē	'veʳdiˑ
Verdicchio		
wine	ver-DIK-ē-ō	veʳ'dikiːoː
Verdin		
songbird	VUHRD-n	'vəʳdn̩
Verdun		
city, France; city, Canada	ver-DUH^n, $ vuhr-DUHN	verdœ̃, $ vəʳ'dən
Vereen		
Ben, *US actor, singer, dancer*	vuh-RĒN	və'riːn
Vereeniging		
city, South Africa	fuh-RĒ-ni-KING	fə'riːniˌkiŋ
Verein		
German union association	fer-ĪN	fer'ɑin
Vergil, Virgil		
Roman poet; pers. name	VUHR-juhl	'vəʳdʒəl
Vergilian, Virgilian		
pert. to Vergil	vuhr-JIL-ē-uhn	vəʳ'dʒiliːən
Verlaine		
Paul, *French poet*	ver-LEN, $ vuhr-LĀN	verlen, $ vəʳ'leːn
Vermeer		
Jan, *Dutch painter*	vuhr-MER, vuhr-MIR	vəʳ'meʳ, vəʳ'miʳ
Vermilion		
pl. name, US	vuhr-MIL-yuhn	vəʳ'miljən
Vermont		
state, US	vuhr-MAHNT	vəʳ'mɑnt
Vermonter		
inhabitant of Vermont	vuhr-MAHNT-uhr	vəʳ'mɑntəʳ
Verna		
pers. name	VUHR-nuh	'vəʳnə
Verne		
1. Jules, *French writer*	VERN, $ VUHRN	vern, $ 'vəʳn
2. pers. name	VUHRN	'vəʳn
Verne, La		
see La Verne		
Verner		
1. Karl, *Danish philologist*	VER-nuhr, $ VUHR-nuhr	'veʳnəʳ, $ 'vəʳnəʳ
2. pers. name	VUHR-nuhr	'vəʳnəʳ
3. Swedish	VER-nuhr	'veʳnəʳ
Vernier		
Pierre, *French mathematician; scale*	vern-YĀ, $ VUHR-nē-uhr	vernjeː, $ 'vəʳniːəʳ

Key (col. 2): a: **fad** ā: **fade** ah: **father** ar: **Mary** aw: **law** e: **fed** ē: **feed** er: **merry** i: **hid** ī: **hide** ō: **coat** o͞o: **boot** oi: **boy** ow: **now** u: **put** uh: **above** uhr: **bird** ch: **chop** ng: **ring** sh: **show** th: **thick** t͟h: **this** zh: **measure**

Vernon		
pers. name	VUHRN-uhn	'vəʳnən
Verona		
prov, town, Italy	vuh-RŌ-nuh	və'ro:nə
Veronese		
1. Paolo, *cognomen of* P. Caliari, *Venetian painter*	VĀ-rō-NĀ-zā	ˌve:ro:'ne:ze:
2. pert. to Verona	VER-uh-NĒZ, -NĒS	ˌverə'ni:z, -'ni:s
Veronica		
pers. name	vuh-RAHN-i-kuh	və'ranikə
Verrazano		
Giovanni de, *Italian navigator*	VER-uh-ZAHN-ō, VER-uht-SAHN-ō	ˌverə'zano:, ˌverət'sano:
Verrazano Narrows		
bridge, New York City	VER-uh-ZAHN-ō NAR-ōz	ˌverə'zano: 'næro:z
Verres		
Roman politician	VER-ĒZ	'verˌi:z
Verrius		
pers. name, Latin	VER-ē-uhs	'veri:əs
Versailles		
1. city, France	ver-SAH-yuh, $ vuhr-SĪ, ver-SĪ	versa:j, $ vəʳ'sai, veʳ'sai
2. US pl. name	vuhr-SĀLZ	vəʳ'se:lz
Vertebrata		
subphylum of vertebrates	VUHRT-uh-BRAHT-uh, VUHRT-uh-BRĀT-uh	ˌvəʳţə'braţə, ˌvəʳţə'bre:ţə
Vertumnus		
Etruscan/Roman god of change	vuhr-TUHM-nuhs	vəʳ'təmnəs
Verulam		
Baron, *title of* Francis Bacon	VER-(y)uh-luhm	'ver(j)ələm
Verulamium		
ancient name of St. Albans	VER-(y)uh-LĀ-mē-uhm	ˌver(j)ə'le:mi:əm
Verus		
Lucius, *Roman co-emperor with* M. Aurelius	VIR-uhs, VER-uhs	'virəs, 'verəs
Verwoerd		
Hendrik, *prime minister, S. Africa*	fuhr-VO͞ORT	fəʳ'vu·ʳt
Vesak		
Buddhist holiday	V̲Ā-SHAHK	'βe:ˌʃak
Vesey		
pers. name	VĒ-zē	'vi:zi·
Vespa		
Italian motor scooter co.	VES-puh	'vespə
Vespasian		
Roman emperor; pers. name	ves-PĀ-zh(ē-)uhn	ves'pe:ʒ(i:)ən
Vespucci		
Amerigo, *Italian explorer*	ves-PO͞O-chē	ves'pu:tʃi·
Vesta		
Roman goddess of the hearth; wooden match; pers. name	VES-tuh	'vestə
Vestal Virgins		
Roman virgins in temple of Vesta	VES-tuhl VUHR-juhnz	ˌvestəl 'vəʳdʒənz
Vestmannaeyjar [Westman]		
islands, Iceland	VEST-MAHN-uh-Ā-YAHR	'vestˌmanə'e:ˌjaʳ
Vesuvianite		
mineral	vuh-SO͞O-vē-uh-NĪT	və'su:vi:əˌnait

Vesuvio [Vesuvius]
  volcano, Italy | vä-ZOOV-yō | veːˈzuːvjoː

Vesuvius
  volcano, Italy | vuh-SOO-vē-uhs | vəˈsuːviːəs

Vettisfoss
  waterfall, Norway | VET-uhs-FAWS | ˈvetəsˌfɔːs

Vettius
  Roman name | VET-ē-uhs | ˈveţiːəs

Via Aemilia
  ancient Roman road | VĪ-uh ē-MIL-ē-uh, VĒ-uh | ˌvaiə iːˈmiliːə, ˌviːə

Via Appia
  ancient Roman road | VĪ-uh AP-ē-uh, VĒ-uh | ˌvaiə ˈæpiːə, ˌviːə

Viacom
  US communications co. | VĪ-uh-KAHM | ˈvaiəˌkam

Via Dolorosa
  Christ's route to Golgotha | VĒ-uh DAHL-uh-RŌ-suh, DŌ-luh-RŌ-suh | ˌviːə ˌdaləˈroːsə, ˌdoːləˈroːsə

Via Flamina
  ancient Roman road | VĪ-uh FLAM-uh-nuh, VĒ-uh | ˌvaiə ˈflæmənə, ˌviːə

Via Lata
  ancient Roman road | VĪ-uh LAHT-uh, VĒ-uh | ˌvaiə ˈlaţə, ˌviːə

Via Latina
  ancient Roman road | VĪ-uh luh-TĪ-nuh, VĒ-uh luh-TĒ-nuh | ˌvaiə ləˈtainə, ˌviːə ləˈtiːnə

Via Nova
  ancient Roman road | VĪ-uh NŌ-vuh, VĒ-uh | ˌvaiə ˈnoːvə, ˌviːə

Via Sacra
  ancient Roman road | VĪ-uh SAK-ruh, VĒ-uh, SĀ-kruh | ˌvaiə ˈsækrə, ˌviːə, ˈseːkrə

Via Veneto
  ancient Roman road | VĪ-uh VEN-uht-ō, VĒ-uh | ˌvaiə ˈvenəţoː, ˌviːə

Vibram
  tdmk for shoe soles | VĪ-bruhm | ˈvaibrəm

Viburnum
  plant | vī-BUHR-nuhm | vaiˈbəʳnəm

Vic, Vick
  pers. name | VIK | ˈvik

Vicary
  pers. name | VIK-(uh-)rē | ˈvik(ə)riˑ

Vicente
  pers. name, Spanish | bē-SĀN-tā, bē-THĀN-tā | biːˈseːnteː, biːˈθeːnteː

Vicenzo
  pers. name, Italian | vē-CHENT-sō | viːˈtʃentsoː

Vichy
  1. town, France | vē-SHĒ, Ⓢ VISH-ē, VĒ-shē | viːʃiˑ, Ⓢ ˈviʃiˑ, ˈviːʃiˑ
  2. mineral water | VISH-ē | ˈviʃiˑ

Vichyssoise
  cream of potato soup | VISH-ē-SWAHZ, VĒ-shē-SWAHZ | ˌviʃiːˈswaz, ˌviːʃiːˈswaz

Vicki
  1. pers. name | VIK-ē | ˈvikiˑ
  2. German | VIK-ē | ˈvikiː

Vickie, Vicky
  pers. name | VIK-ē | ˈvikiˑ

Vicksburg
  city, MS | VIKS-BUHRG | ˈviksˌbəʳg

Vico
  Giovanni, *Italian historian* | VĒ-kō | ˈviːkoː

Victoire
> *pers. name, French*   vēk-TWAHR   viːktwɑːr

Victor
> *pers. name, Spanish*   BĔK-tawr   'biːktɔːr

Victor
> *1. pers. name*   VIK-tuhr   'viktəʳ
> *2. Danish*   VĔK-TAWR   'viːk‚tɔːr
> *3. French*   vēk-TAWR   viːktɔːr
> *4. German*   VIK-TAWR   'vik‚tɔːʳ
> *5. Romanian*   vēk-TAWR   viːk'tɔːr

Victoria
> *1. Roman personification of victory; Queen of England; pers. name*   vik-TŌR-ē-uh, vik-TAWR-ē-uh   vik'tɔːriːə, vik'tɔːriːə
> *2. French*   vēk-tawr-YAH   viːktɔːrjɑː
> *3. German*   vik-TŌR-ē-ah   vik'tɔːriːɑ
> *4. Swedish*   vik-TŌO-rē-ah   vik'tuːriːɑː

Victorian
> *pert. to Queen* Victoria *or her reign*   vik-TŌR-ē-uhn, vik-TAWR-ē-uhn   vik'tɔːriːən, vik'tɔːriːən

Victoriana
> *things pert. to Queen* Victoria *or her reign*   vik-TŌR-ē-AN-uh, vik-TAWR-ē-AN-uh, -AHN-uh, -Ā-nuh   vik‚tɔːriː'ænə, vik‚tɔːriː'ænə, -'ɑnə, -'eːnə

Victoriano
> *pers. name, Spanish*   bēk-tōr-YAHN-ō   biːktɔːr'jɑnoː

Victrola
> *tdmk for phonographs*   vik-TRŌ-luh   vik'troːlə

Vida
> *pers. name*   VĒD-uh, VĪD-uh   'viːdə, 'vaidə

Vidal
> Gore, *US writer*   vi-DAHL, vi-DAWL   vi'dɑl, vi'dɔl

Vidalia
> *city, GA; town, LA; onion variety*   vuh-DĂL-yuh, vuh-DĂ-lē-uh, vī-   və'deːljə, və'deːliːə, vai-

Vidal Sassoon
> *haircare products co.*   vi-DAL sa-SŌON, vi-DAHL   vi'dæl sæ'suːn, vi'dɑl

Vidkun
> *pers. name, Norwegian*   VID-kun   'vidkun

Vidmar
> *pers. name*   VID-MAHR   'vid‚mɑʳ

Vieira
> *pers. name, Portuguese*   VYĀ-ruh   'vjeːrə

Viejas
> *Indian reservation, US*   VYĀ-HAHS, vē-Ā-HAHS   'vjeː‚hɑs, viː'eː‚hɑs

Vienna
> *city, Austria*   vē-EN-uh   viːˈenə

Vienne
> *river, dept, France*   VYEN   vjen

Viennese
> *pert. to* Vienna   VĒ-uh-NĒZ, VĒ-uh-NĒS   ‚viːə'niːz, ‚viːə'niːs

Vientiane
> *city, Laos*   vyen-TYAHN   vjen'tjɑn

Vierwaldstätter See [Lucerne]
> *lake, Switzerland*   fir-VAHLT-SHTET-uhr ZĀ   fiʳ'vɑlt‚ʃtetəʳ ‚zeː

Foreign Sounds: **ue:** *Fr.* **rue,** *Ger.* **füllen** **uh(r):** *Fr.* **boeuf,** *Ger.* **Höhle** **kh:** *Ger.* **ich,** *Scot.* **loch** **g̃:** *Sp.* **amigo** **v̧:** *Sp.* **hablar**
hl: *Welsh* **Llanelli.** CAPITALS: primary stress. SMALL CAPS: secondary stress. Ⓢ: U.S. pron. Ⓑ: British pron.

Vietcong
   Communist guerrillas, Vietnam   vē-ET-KAWNG, vyet-KAWNG,   viː‚et'kɔːŋ, vjet'kɔːŋ,
                             VĒ-uht-KAWNG, vēt-KAWNG,   ‚viːət'kɔːŋ, viːt'kɔːŋ, -'kaŋ
                             -KAHNG

Viet Minh
   Vietnamese faction   vē-ET MIN, vyet, VĒ-uht, vēt   viː'et 'min, vjet, ‚viːət, viːt

Vietnam
   country, Asia   vē-ET-NAHM, vyet-, VĒ-uht-, vēt-,   viː'et'nɑm, vjet-, ‚viːət-,
                     -NAM   viːt-, -'næm

Vietnamese
   lang., people, Indochina   VĒ-ET-nuh-MĒZ, VYET-, VĒT-,   ‚viː‚etnə'miːz, ‚vjet-, ‚viːt-,
                        -na-MĒZ, -nah-MĒZ, -MĒS   -næ'miːz, -nɑ'miːz, -'miːs

Vieux Carré
   French Quarter, New Orleans   VYOO KAHR-Ā, VOO   ‚vjuː kɑr'eː, ‚vuː

Vieux Montréal
   College, Canada   vyuh(r) mawⁿ-re-AHL, $ VYUHR   vjœː mõreɑːl, $ ‚vjə^r
                     MAHN-trē-AWL, MUHN-   ‚mɑntriː'ɔːl, ‚mən-

Vigan
   municipality, Philippines   VĒ-GAHN   'viː‚gɑn

Vigdis
   pers. name, Icelandic   VIG-DĒS   'vig‚diːs

Vigilius
   antipope   vuh-JIL-ē-uhs   və'dʒiliːəs

Vigo
   1. prov, Spain   BĒ-ḡō, $ VĒ-gō   'biːɣoː, $ 'viːgoː
   2. county, IN   VĒ-gō, VĪ-gō   'viːgoː, 'vaigoː

Vigoda
   Abe, US actor   vuh-GŌD-uh   və'goːdə

Vijag
   Armenian festival   VĒ-(Y)AHG   'viː‚(j)ɑg

Vijaya
   pers. name, Hindi   vi-JĪ-(y)uh   vi'dʒɑi(j)ə

Vijayawada
   city, India   VIJ-uh-yuh-WAHD-uh   ‚vidʒəjə'wɑdə

Vikenti, -ty
   pers. name, Russian   vēk-YENT-yi   viːk'jentjij

Viking
   Scandinavian pirate   VĪ-king   'vaikiŋ

Vikki
   pers. name   VIK-ē   'vikiˑ

Viktor
   1. pers. name, Czech, German,   VIK-TAWR   'vik‚tɔːr
     Swedish
   2. Russian   VYĒK-tuhr   'vjiːktər

Viktoria
   pers. name, German   vik-TŌR-ē-ah   vik'toːriːɑ

Vila
   seaport, Vanuatu   VĒ-luh   'viːlə

Vila Real
   prov & town, Portugal   VĒ-luh rē-AHL   ‚viːlə riː'ɑl

Vilas
   county, WI   VĪ-luhs   'vailəs

Vilfredo
   pers. name, Italian   vēl-FRĀD-ō   viːl'freːdoː

Key (col. 2):   a: fad   ā: fade   ah: father   ar: Mary   aw: law   e: fed   ē: feed   er: merry   i: hid   ī: hide   ō: coat   o͞o: boot
oi: boy   ow: now   u: put   uh: above   uhr: bird   ch: chop   ng: ring   sh: show   th: thick   th̲: this   zh: measure

Vilhelm
   1. pers. name, Danish, Norwegian   VIL-HELM   'vil,helm
   2. Swedish   VIL-(h)uhlm   'vil(h)əlm

Vilhjálmur
   pers. name, Icelandic   VIL-HYOWL-muhr   'vil,hjɑulmər

Viljandi
   town, Estonia   VIL-YAHN-dē   'vil‚jɑndiˑ

Villa
   Pancho, *Mexican revolutionary &*   VĒ-(y)uh   'viː(j)ə
   outlaw

Villa-Lobos
   Heitor, *Brazilian composer*   vē-lah-LŌ-bush, Ⓢ vē-luh-LŌ-bōs   ‚viːlɑ'loːbuʃ, Ⓢ ‚viːlə'loːboːs

Villanovan
   Iron age culture   VIL-uh-NŌ-vuhn, VĒ-luh-NŌ-vuhn   ‚vilə'noːvən, ‚viːlə'noːvən

Ville de Paris
   dept, France   vēl duh pah-RĒ   viːl də pɑːriː

Villiers
   pers. name   VIL-yuhrz   'viljəʳz

Villius
   pers. name, Latin   VIL-ē-uhs   'viliːəs

Villon
   François, *French writer*   vē-YAWⁿ   viːjõ

Vilmos
   pers. name, Hungarian   VIL-mawsh   'vilmɔːʃ

Vilna [Vilnius]
   city, Lithuania   VIL-nuh   'vilnə

Vilnius
   city, Lithuania   VIL-nē-uhs   'vilniːəs

Viminal
   hill, Rome, Italy   VIM-uhn-l   'vimənl̩

Viña
   pers. name   VĒN-yuh   'viːnjə

Viña del Mar
   town, Chile   VĒN-yuh <u>th</u>el MAHR   'viːnjə ðel 'mɑʳ

Vinayak
   pers. name, Hindi   VIN-ī-(Y)AHK   ‚vinɑi'(j)ɑk

Vincas
   pers. name, Lithuanian   VINT-sahs   'vintsɑs

Vincennes
   1. commune, France   ve ⁿ-SEN   vẽsen
   2. city, IN; US navy warship   vin-SENZ   vin'senz

Vincent
   1. pers. name, English, Norwegian   VIN-suhnt   'vinsənt
   2. Dutch   vin-SENT   vin'sent
   3. French   ve ⁿ-SAH ⁿ   vẽsã

Vincente
   pers. name, Spanish   bēn-THĀN-tä, bēn-SĀN-tä,   biːn'θeːnteː, biːn'seːnteː,
           Ⓢ vin-SEN-tä, vin-SENT-ē   Ⓢ vin'senteː, vin'sentiˑ

Vincentian
   religious order   vin-SENT-ē-uhn, SEN-shuhn   vin'sentiːən, -'senʃən

Vincentius
   pers. name, Latin   vin-SEN-sh(ē-)uhs   vin'senʃ(iː)əs

Vincenzo
   pers. name, Italian   vēn-CHENT-sō   viːn'tʃentsoː

Foreign Sounds: ue: *Fr.* **rue**, *Ger.* **füllen**   uh(r): *Fr.* **boeuf**, *Ger.* **Höhle**   <u>kh</u>: *Ger.* **ich**, *Scot.* **loch**   g̅: *Sp.* **amigo**   v̲: *Sp.* **hablar**
hl: *Welsh* **Llanelli**.   CAPITALS: primary stress.   SMALL CAPS: secondary stress.   Ⓢ: U.S. pron.   Ⓔ: British pron.

Vinci, da
  see Leonardo da Vinci
Vindhya
  mtn. range, India   VIND-yuh, VIN-dē-uh   'vindjə, 'vindiːə
Vingt-et-un
  game   VAN-TĀ-UHN   ˌvæn,teːˈən
Vinho verde
  wine   VĒN-yōō VERD-uh, Ⓢ VĒ-nō VERD-ē   ˌviːnjuː 'veʳdə, Ⓢ ˌviːnoː
                                                                               'veʳdiˑ
Vinland
  region, eastern N. America   VIN-luhnd, VIN-LAND   'vinlənd, 'vinˌlænd
Vinnie
  pers. name   VIN-ē   'viniˑ
Vinson Massif
  mtn. range, Antarctica   VIN-suhn ma-SĒF   'vinsən mæˈsiːf
Vintilă
  pers. name, Romanian   vēn-TĒ-luh   viːnˈtiːlə
Vinton
  Bobby, *US entertainer*   VINT-n   'vintn̩
Viola
  pers. name   vī-Ō-luh, vē-Ō-luh, VĪ-uh-luh,   vaiˈoːlə, viːˈoːlə, 'vaiələ,
                                         VĒ-uh-luh   'viːələ
Violet
  pers. name   VĪ-(uh-)luht   'vai(ə)lət
Vipsania
  pers. name, Latin   vip-SĀ-nē-uh, vip-SĀN-yuh   vipˈseːniːə, vipˈseːnjə
Vipsanius
  pers. name, Latin   vip-SĀ-nē-uhs, vip-SĀN-yuhs   vipˈseːniːəs, vipˈseːnjəs
Virbius
  demon, resurrection of Hippolytus   VUHR-bē-uhs, VIR-bē-uhs   'vəʳbiːəs, 'viʳbiːəs
Vireo
  songbird   VIR-ē-ō   'viriːoː
Virgen del Pilar
  Spanish festival   bir-G̃ĀN ŧhel pē-LAHR   birˈyeːn ðel piːˈlɑr
Virgil
  1. pers. name   VUHR-juhl   'vəʳdʒəl
  2. see Vergil
Virgile
  pers. name, French   vēr-ZHĒL   viːrʒiːl
Virgilian
  see Vergilian
Virginia
  1. state, US; pers. name   vuhr-JIN-yuh, vuhr-JIN-ē-uh   vəʳˈdʒinjə, vəʳˈdʒiniːə
  2. Italian   vēr-JĒN-yah   viːrˈdʒiːnjɑ
Virginie
  pers. name, French   vēr-zhē-NĒ   viːrʒiːniː
Virginius
  pers. name   vuhr-JIN-yuhs, vuhr-JIN-ē-uhs   vəʳˈdʒinjəs, vəʳˈdʒiniːəs
Virgo
  constellation, sign of the zodiac   VUHR-gō, VIR-gō   'vəʳgoː, 'viʳgoː
Virgoan
  person born under sign of Virgo   VUHR-GŌ-uhn, VIR-GŌ-uhn   'vəʳˌgoːən, 'viʳˌgoːən
Virtanen
  Arturi Ilmari, *Finnish biochemist*   VIR-tuh-NEN   'viʳtəˌnen
    (Nobel 1945)

Key (col. 2): a: fad ā: fade ah: father ar: Mary aw: law e: fed ē: feed er: merry i: hid ī: hide ō: coat ōō: boot
oi: boy ow: now u: put uh: above uhr: bird ch: chop ng: ring sh: show th: thick ŧh: this zh: measure

Visa
    tdmk for a credit card   VĒ-zuh, VĒ-suh   'viːzə, 'viːsə

Visalia
    city, CA   vi-SĀL-yuh, vī-SĀL-yuh   vi'seːljə, vai'seːljə

Visayan
    Malay people   vuh-SĪ-uhn   və'saiən

Visby
    city, Sweden   VIZ-bē   'vizbiˑ

Visconti
    Italian family name   vēs-KÔN-tē, Ⓢ vis-KAHNT-ē   viːs'koːntiˑ, Ⓢ vis'kɑntiˑ

Vishnu
    Hindu god, member of the   VISH-noo   'viʃnuː
      supreme triad

Visigoth
    westerly division of the Goths   VIZ-uh-GAHTH   'vizə,gɑθ

Vistula
    river, Poland   VIS-chuh-luh, VIS-tuh-luh   'vistʃələ, 'vistələ

Vital
    pers. name, French   vē-TAHL   viːtɑːl

Vitalian
    pope   vuh-TĀ-lē-uhn, vuh-TĀL-yuhn   və'teːliːən, və'teːljən

Vítézslav
    pers. name, Czech   VĒ-ches-LAHF   'viːtʃes,lɑːf

Vitebsk
    city, Belorussia   VĒ-TEPSK, VĒ-TEBSK, vi-TEPSK   'viː,tepsk, 'viː,tebsk, vi'tepsk

Vitellius
    Roman emperor   vuh-TEL-ē-uhs   və'teliːəs

Viterbo
    1. College, WI   vi-TER-bō, vi-TUHR-bō   vi'teᵊboː, vi'təᵊboː
    2. prov, Italy   vē-TER-bō   viː'teᵊboː

Viti Levu
    island, Fiji   VĒT-ē LEV-oo   ,viːʈiˑ 'levuː

Vitis vinifera
    grape vine   VĪT-uhs vuh-NIF-uh-ruh   'vaiʈəs və'nifərə

Vito
    pers. name, Italian   VĒ-tō, Ⓢ VĒT-ō   'viːtoː, Ⓢ 'viːʈoː

Vitruvius
    Roman architect, author   vuh-TROO-vē-uhs   və'truːviːəs

Vittore
    pers. name, Italian   vēt-TŌ-rā   viːt'toːreː

Vittoria
    pers. name, Italian   vēt-TÔR-yah   viːt'toːrjɑ

Vittorio
    pers. name, Italian   vēt-TÔR-yō   viːt'toːrjoː

Vitus
    1. Christian saint   VĪT-uhs   'vaiʈəs
    2. pers. name, Danish   VĒ-tus   'viːtus

Vivaldi
    Antonio, Italian composer   vi-VAHL-dē, vi-VAWL-dē   vi'valdiˑ, vi'vɔːldiˑ

Vivant
    pers. name, French   vē-VAHⁿ   viːvã

Vivian, Vivien
    pers. name   VIV-ē-uhn, VIV-yuhn   'viviːən, 'vivjən

Foreign Sounds: ue: *Fr.* **rue**, *Ger.* **fü**llen   uh(r): *Fr.* b**oeu**f, *Ger.* H**ö**hle   <u>kh</u>: *Ger.* i**ch**, *Scot.* lo**ch**   ḡ: *Sp.* ami**g**o   <u>v</u>: *Sp.* ha**b**lar
hl: *Welsh* L**l**anelli.   CAPITALS: primary stress.   SMALL CAPS: secondary stress.   Ⓢ: U.S. pron.   Ⓑ: British pron.

Vivienne
  pers. name   VIV-ē-uhn, VIV-ē-EN   'viviːən, ˌviviː'en
Vizcaya
  prov, Spain   bēth-KAH-yah, ⑤ vis-KĪ-(y)uh,   biːθ'kaja, ⑤ vis'kai(j)ə,
         vith-KĪ-(y)uh   viθ'kai(j)ə
Vlaanderen [Flanders]
  region, Belgium   VLAHN-duh-ruh(n)   'vlaːndərə(n)
Vlad
  1. pers. name   VLAD   'vlæd
  2. Romanian   VLAHD   'vlaːd
Vladimir
  pers. name, Czech   VLAH-jim-ĒR   'vlaːdʒim,iːr
Vladimir
  1. pers. name   VLAD-uh-MIR, vluh-DĒ-MIR   'vlædə,mi[r], vlə'diː,mi[r]
  2. Russian   VLUH-DĒM-yir   ˌvlə'ḑiːmjir
  3. Serbo-Croatian   VLAHD-ē-MĒR   'vlaːdiː,miːr
Vladislav
  1. pers. name, Czech   VLAH-jis-LAHF   'vlaːdʒis,laːf
  2. Russian   vluh-di-SLAHF   vləḑi'slaːf
Vladivostok
  city, Russia   VLUHD-yi-vuh-STAWK,   ˌvlədjivə'stɔːk,
         ⑤ VLAD-uh-vuh-STAHK,   ⑤ ˌvlædəvə'stak,
         VLAD-uh-VAHS-TAHK   ˌvlædə'vas,tak
Vlaminck
  Maurice de, French painter   vlah-ME[n]K, ⑤ vluh-MANGK   vlaːmẽk, ⑤ vlə'mæŋk
Vlasic
  US pickle co.   VLAS-ik   'vlæsik
Vlastimil
  pers. name, Czech   VLAHS-chim-IL   'vlaːstʃim,il
Vogul [Mansi]
  lang., people, Russia   VŌ-gul   'voːgul
Voight
  Jon, US actor   VOIT   'vɔit
Voigt
  Cynthia, US author   VOIT   'vɔit
Vojtéch
  pers. name, Czech   VOI-CHEKH   'vɔi,tʃeç
Volans
  constellation   VŌ-luhnz   'voːlənz
Volapuk
  artificial lang.   VŌ-luh-PUK, VAHL-uh-PUK   'voːlə,puk, 'valə,puk
Volcker
  Paul, US economist   VŌ(L)-kuhr   'voː(l)kə[r]
Volga
  river, Russia   VAHL-guh, VAWL-guh, VŌL-guh   'valgə, 'vɔːlgə, 'voːlgə
Volgograd [Stalingrad]
  city, Russia   VUHL-guh-GRAHT,   ˌvəlgə'grat, ⑤ 'valgə,græd,
         ⑤ VAHL-guh-GRAD, VAWL-, VŌL-   'vɔːl-, 'voːl-
Volk
  German for 'people'   FAWLK   'fɔːlk
Volkswagen
  German car   FAWLKS-VAHG-uhn,   'fɔːlks,vagən,
         ⑤ VŌK-SWAG-uhn,   ⑤ 'voːk,swægən,
         VŌKS-VAHG-uhn   'voːks,vagən

Key (col. 2):   a: **fad**   ā: **fade**   ah: **father**   ar: **Mary**   aw: **law**   e: **fed**   ē: **feed**   er: **merry**   i: **hid**   ī: **hide**   ō: **coat**   ōō: **boot**
oi: **boy**   ow: **now**   u: **put**   uh: **above**   uhr: **bird**   ch: **chop**   ng: **ring**   sh: **show**   th: **thick**   <u>th</u>: **this**   zh: **measure**

Volla		
Alessandro, *scientist*	VŌL-lah	'voːllɑ
Volnay		
wine	vawl-NE	vɔːlne
Vologda		
city, region, Russia	VAW-luhg-duh	'vɔːləgdə
Volpone		
play, Jonson	vahl-PŌ-nē	vɑl'poːniˑ
Volsci		
ancient people, Italy	VAHL-SĪ, VAHL-shē	'vɑl,sɑi, 'vɑlʃiˑ
Volscian		
lang., pert. to the Volsci	VAHL-shuhn	'vɑlʃən
Volsunga		
Icelandic saga	VAWL-SUNG-(g)uh	'vɔːl,suŋ(g)ə
Volta		
1. Alessandro, *Italian physicist*	VŌL-tuh, VAHL-tuh, VAWL-tuh	'voːltə, 'vɑltə, 'vɔːltə
2. river, lake, Ghana	VAHL-tuh, VŌL-tuh, VAWL-tuh	'vɑltə, 'voːltə, 'vɔːltə
Voltaire		
François Marie Arouet de, *French philosopher*	vawl-TER, [$] vōl-TAR, vahl-, vawl-, -TER	vɔːlter, [$] voːl'tæʳ, vɑl-, vɔːl-, -'teʳ
Volturno		
river, Italy	vahl-TUR-nō, vōl-, vawl-	vɑl'tuʳnoː, voːl-, vɔːl-
Volturnus		
Roman divinity, father of Juturna	vahl-TUR-nuhs, vōl-, vawl-	vɑl'tuʳnəs, voːl-, vɔːl-
Volusia		
county, FL	vuh-LO͞O-shuh	və'luːʃə
Volvo		
tdmk for a Swedish car	VAHL-vō, VAWL-vō, VŌL-vō	'vɑlvoː, 'vɔːlvoː, 'voːlvoː
Von Bulow		
Claus, *US socialite*	vahn BYO͞O-lō	vɑn 'bjuːloː
Vonnegut		
Kurt, Jr., *US writer*	VAHN-uh-guht	'vɑnəgət
Von Stade		
Frederica, *US mezzo-soprano*	fawn SHTAHD-uh, vahn STAHD-uh	fɔːn 'ʃtɑdə, vɑn 'stɑdə
Von Stroheim		
Erich, *US film director, actor*	fawn SHTRŌ-HĪM, vahn, STRŌ-HĪM	fɔːn 'ʃtroː,hɑim, vɑn, 'stroː,hɑim
Von Sydow		
Max, *Swedish actor*	fawn SUE-DAWF, [$] vahn SĪD-ō	fɔːn 'syː,dɔːf, [$] vɑn 'sɑidoː
Voorhees		
College, *SC*	VUR-HĒZ, VUR-HĒS	'vuʳ,hiːz, 'vuʳ,hiːs
Voronezh		
river, city, region, Russia	vuh-RAW-nish	və'rɔːniʃ
Vosges		
mts., dept, France	VŌZH	voːʒ
Vosne-Romanée		
wine	VŌN-raw-mah-NĀ	voːnrɔːmɑːneː
Vostock		
1. scientific station, Antarctica	VAHS-TAHK	'vɑs,tɑk
2. island, Kiribati	vuh-STAHK	və'stɑk
Vostok 1		
first manned spaceflight, 1961	VAHS-TAHK, VAWS-TAWK	'vɑs,tɑk, 'vɔːs,tɔːk
Votyak [Udmurt]		
lang., Russia	VŌ-TYAHK, VŌT-ē-AK	'voː,tjɑːk, 'voːt̯iː,æk

Vouli		
wine	VŌ-lē, V͞OO-lē	'voːliˑ, 'vuːliˑ
Vouvray		
wine	v͞oov-RE	vuːvre
Voyageurs		
National Park, *Kabetogama, MN*	VWAH-YAH-ZHUHR, VOI-uh-JUHR, VOI-uh-ZHUHR	ˌvwɑˌjɑ'ʒə^{r}, ˌvɔiə'dʒə^{r}, ˌvɔiə'ʒə^{r}
VTOL		
vertical takeoff and landing	VĒ-TAWL, VĒ-TAHL	'viːˌtɔːl, 'viːˌtɑl
Vuelta Abajo		
region, Cuba	BWEL-tah ah-VAH-khō, [$] VWEL-tuh uh-BAH-hō	'bweltɑ ɑ'βɑxoː, [$] 'vweltə ə'bɑhoː
Vuitton		
tdmk for handbags and luggage	vwē-TAW^{n}, [$] vwē-TAHN, vwē-TAWN	vɥiːtɔ̃, [$] vwiː'tɑn, vwiː'tɔːn
Vukovar		
city, Croatia	V͞OO-kuh-VAHR	'vuːkəˌvɑ^{r}
Vulcan		
Roman fire god; alien race, Star Trek	VUHL-kuhn	'vəlkən
Vulgate		
Latin version of the Bible	VUHL-GĀT, VUHL-guht	'vəlˌgeːt, 'vəlgət
Vulpecula		
constellation	VUHL-PEK-yuh-luh	ˌvəl'pekjələ
Vulso		
Manlius, *Roman general*	VUL-sō, VUHL-sō	'vulsoː, 'vəlsoː
Vung Tau		
town, Vietnam	VUNG TOW	'vuŋ 'tɑu
Vyacheslav		
pers. name, Russian	vyi-chis-LAHF	vjitʃis'lɑːf
Vyatka		
river, city, Russia	VYAHT-kuh, vē-AHT-kuh	'vjɑtkə, viː'ɑtkə
Vyazma		
town, Russia	VYAHZ-muh, vē-AHZ-muh	'vjɑzmə, viː'ɑzmə
Vyborg		
port, Russia	VĒ-BAWRG	'viːˌbɔː^{r}g
Vychegda		
river, Russia	VICH-uhg-duh	'vitʃəgdə
Vytautas		
pers. name, Lith.	vē-TOWT-uhs	viː'tauṭəs

Key (col. 2): a: fad ā: fade ah: father ar: Mary aw: law e: fed ē: feed er: merry i: hid ī: hide ō: coat o͞o: boot oi: boy ow: now u: put uh: above uhr: bird ch: chop ng: ring sh: show th: thick th: this zh: measure

W

Waal
  river, Netherlands — VAHL — ˈvɑl

Wabash
  river, US; county, IN, IL; college, — WAW-BASH — ˈwɔːˌbæʃ
  IN

Wabasha
  county, MN — WAW-buh-SHAW — ˈwɔːbə˛ʃɔː

Wabaunsee
  county, KA — wah-BAWN-sē — waˈbɔːnsiˑ

WAC
  Women's Army Corp.,US — WAK — ˈwæk

Wachovia
  region, NC; US bank — wah-CHŌ-vē-uh — waˈtʃoːviːə

Wachusett
  mtn., reservoir, MA — wah-CHOO-suht — waˈtʃuːsət

Wackenhut
  US security services co. — WAK-uhn-HUHT — ˈwækən˛hət

Wacław
  pers. name, Polish — VAHCH-LAHF — ˈvɑːtʃ˛łɑːf

Waco
  city, TX — WĀ-kō — ˈweːkoː

Wadai
  see Ouadai

Waddel, Waddell
  pers. name — wah-DEL — waˈdel

Waddenzee
  inlet, Netherlands — VAHD-n-ZĀ — ˈvɑdn̩˛zeː

Wade
  pers. name — WĀD — ˈweːd

Wade-Giles
  transliteration system for Chinese — WĀD-JĪLZ — ˌweːdˈdʒɑilz

Wade Hampton
  division, AK — WĀD HAM(P)-tuhn — ˌweːd ˈhæm(p)tən

Wadena
  county, MN — waw-DĒ-nuh — wɔːˈdiːnə

Wadham
  college, Oxford Univ. — WAHD-uhm — ˈwadəm

Wadleigh
  pers. name — WAHD-lē — ˈwadliˑ

Wadsworth
  pers. name — WAHDZ-wuhrth — ˈwadzwəʳθ

Wafd
  political party, Egypt — WAHFT — ˈwaft

Foreign Sounds: **ue:** *Fr.* **rue,** *Ger.* **füllen** **uh(r):** *Fr.* **boeuf,** *Ger.* **Höhle** **kh:** *Ger.* **ich,** *Scot.* **loch** **g̃:** *Sp.* **amigo** **v:** *Sp.* **hablar** **hl:** *Welsh* **Llanelli.** CAPITALS: primary stress. SMALL CAPS: secondary stress. Ⓢ: U.S. pron. Ⓛ: British pron.

Wagga Wagga
  city, Australia   WAHG-uh WAHG-uh   ˈwɑgə ˌwɑgə
Wagner
  1. US family name   WAG-nuhr   ˈwægnəʳ
  2. Richard, German composer   VAHG-nuhr   ˈvɑgnəʳ
Wagnerian
  pert. to Richard Wagner   vahg-NIR-ē-uhn, vahg-NER-ē-uhn   vɑgˈniriːən, vɑgˈneriːən
Wagner-Jauregg
  Julius, *Austrian neurologist,*   VAHG-nuhr-YOW-REK   ˈvɑgnəʳˈjau̯ˌrek
  psychiatrist (Nobel 1927)
Wagoner
  Porter, *US country music singer*   WAG-(uh-)nuhr   ˈwæg(ə)nəʳ
Wahconah
  Park, *ballpark, Pittsfield, MA*   wah-KŌ-nuh, wuh-KŌ-nuh   wɑˈkoːnə, wəˈkoːnə
Wahhabi
  Muslim sect   wuh-HAHB-ē, wah-   wəˈhɑbiˈ, wɑ-
Wahhabism
  beliefs of the Wahhabis   wuh-HAHB-IZ-uhm, wah-   wəˈhɑbˌizəm, wɑ-
Wahkiakum
  county, WA   waw-KĪ-uh-kuhm   wɔːˈkaiəkəm
Wahlbündis '90
  political party, Germany   VAHL-BUEN-duhs NOINT-si<u>kh</u>   ˈvalˌbyndəs ˈnɔintsiç
Wahoo
  plant   WAH-HŌŌ, WAW-HŌŌ   ˈwɑˌhuː, ˈwɔːˌhuː
Wahpeton Sioux
  N. American people   WAW-puht-uhn SŌŌ   ˈwɔːpətən ˈsuː
Wahroonga
  town, Australia   wuh-RUNG-guh   wəˈruŋgə
Waialeale
  mtn., HI   wī-AHL-ā-AHL-ā   waiˌaleːˈaleː
Waicuri
  N. American people   wī-KUR-ē   waiˈkuriˈ
Waikiki Beach
  resort, HI   wī-kuh-KĒ BĒCH   ˌwaikəˌkiː ˈbiːtʃ
Waipahu
  city, HI   wī-PAH-hōō   waiˈpɑhuː
Waite
  Ralph, *US actor*   WĀT   ˈweːt
Waits
  Thomas Alan, *US composer,*   WĀTS   ˈweːts
  singer
Wakame
  seaweed   WAHK-uh-mē   ˈwɑkəmiˈ
Wakashan
  N. American lang. family   waw-KASH-uhn, WAW-KASH-uhn   wɔːˈkæʃən, ˈwɔːˌkæʃən
Wakayama
  port, Japan   wah-kah-yahm-ah   wɑkɑjɑmɑ
Waksman
  S. A., *Russian-born US biochemist*   WAHK-smuhn, WAK-smuhn   ˈwɑksmən, ˈwæksmən
  (Nobel 1952)
Wakulla
  county, FL   wah-KUHL-uh   wɑˈkələ
Walachia, Wallachia
  region, Romania   wah-LĀ-kē-uh   wɑˈleːkiːə

Key (col. 2):   a: fad   ā: fade   ah: father   ar: Mary   aw: law   e: fed   ē: feed   er: merry   i: hid   ī: hide   ō: coat   ōō: boot
oi: boy   ow: now   u: put   uh: above   uhr: bird   ch: chop   ng: ring   sh: show   th: thick   <u>th</u>: this   zh: measure

Walcha
  town, Australia   WAHL-kuh, WAWL-kuh   'wɑlkə, 'wɔːlkə

Wald
  George, *US biochemist (Nobel*   WAWLD, WAHLD   'wɔːld, 'wɑld
    1967); Lillian, *US social worker*

Waldbaum
  US grocery store chain   WAWL(D)-BOWM   'wɔːl(d),bɑum

Waldemar
  1. king, Denmark; pers. name,   VAHL-duh-MAHR   'vɑːldə,mɑ^r
    Danish
  2. German   VAHL-duh-MAHR   'vɑldə,mɑ^r
  3. Swedish   VAHL-duh-MAHR   'vɑːldə,mɑː^r

Walden
  town, Ontario, Canada; Pond, *MA*   WAWL-duhn   'wɔːldən

Waldheim
  Kurt, *UN Secy. Genl.*   VAHLT-HĪM, Ⓢ VAWLD-HĪM,   'vɑlt,hɑim, Ⓢ 'vɔːld,hɑim,
         WAWLD-HĪM   'wɔːld,hɑim

Waldmeister
  plant   WAWLD-MĪ-stuhr, VAHLT-MĪ-stuhr   'wɔːld,mɑistə^r, 'vɑlt,mɑistə^r

Waldo
  pers. name   WAWL-dō, WAHL-dō   'wɔːldoː, 'wɑldoː

Waldorf
  hotel, New York City; salad   WAWL-DAWRF   'wɔːl,dɔː^{r}f

Wałęsa
  Lech, *Polish president (Nobel*   vah-LEⁿ-suh, Ⓢ vuh-LEN-suh,   vɑː'lɛ̃sə, Ⓢ və'lensə,
    1983)   vuh-WEN-suh   və'wensə

Wales [Cymru]
  principality, Gt. Britain   WĀLZ   'weːlz

Walgett
  town, Australia   WAHL-guht, WAWL-guht   'wɑlgət, 'wɔːlgət

Walken
  Christopher, *US actor*   WAW(L)-kuhn   'wɔː(l)kən

Walker
  pers. name   WAWK-uhr   'wɔːkə^r

Walkman
  tdmk for a portable cassette player   WAWK-muhn, WAHK-muhn   'wɔːkmən, 'wɑkmən

Walküre, Die
  see Die Walküre

Wallace
  pers. name   WAHL-uhs   'wɑləs

Wallach
  1. Eli, *US actor*   WAHL-uhk   'wɑlək
  2. Otto, *German chemist (Nobel*   VAHL-ahkh, Ⓢ VAHL-uhk, WAHL-uhk   'vɑlɑx, Ⓢ 'vɑlək, 'wɑlək
    1910)

Wallachia
  see Walachia

Walla Walla
  river, city, WA; N. American   WAHL-uh WAHL-uh, WAHL-uh   ,wɑlə 'wɑlə, 'wɑlə ,wɑlə
    people   WAHL-uh

Wallensis
  pers. name   waw-LEN-suhs, wah-   wɔː'lensəs, wɑ-

Waller
  pers. name   WAHL-uhr   'wɑlə^r

Wallerawang
  town, Australia   wuh-LER-uh-WANG   wə'lerə,wæŋ

Foreign Sounds: ue: *Fr.* **rue**, *Ger.* **füllen**   uh(r): *Fr.* **boeuf**, *Ger.* **Höhle**   kh: *Ger.* i**ch**, *Scot.* lo**ch**   g̃: *Sp.* ami**g**o   v: *Sp.* ha**b**lar
hl: *Welsh* **Ll**anelli.   CAPITALS: primary stress.   SMALL CAPS: secondary stress.   Ⓢ: U.S. pron.   Ⓔ: British pron.

Wallis
  pers. name — WAHL-uhs — ˈwɑləs

Wallis and Futuna
  islands, Pacific — WAHL-uhs uhn(d) fōō-TŌŌ-nuh — ˈwɑləs ən(d) fuˈtuːnə

Wallisian
  pert. to Wallis Islands — wahl-ISH-uhn — wɑlˈiʃən

Wallonia
  region, Belgium — wah-LŌ-nē-uh — wɑˈloːniːə

Walloon
  people, Belgium, France; French dialect — wah-LOON, wuh-, waw- — wɑˈluːn, wə-, wɔː-

Wallops
  island, VA — WAHL-uhps — ˈwɑləps

Wallowa
  river, lake, mts., county, OR — wah-LOW-uh — wɑˈlaʊə

Wallo [Welo]
  region, Ethiopia — WAWL-ō — ˈwɔːloː

Wal-Mart
  US retail chain — WAWL-MAHRT — ˈwɔːlˌmɑʳt

Walpole
  city, MA; British family — WAWL-PŌL — ˈwɔːlˌpoːl

Walpurgisnacht
  Walpurgis Night — vahl-PUR-guhs-NAH<u>KH</u>T — vɑlˈpuʳɡəsˌnɑxt

Walpurgis Night
  April 30th holiday, Germany — vahl-PUR-guhs, val-PUHR-juhs — vɑlˈpuʳɡəs, vælˈpəʳdʒəs

Walsh
  family name — WAWLSH — ˈwɔːlʃ

Walsingham
  1. Sir Francis, Elizabethan statesman — WAWL-sing-uhm — ˈwɔːlsiŋəm
  2. town, England — WAWL-zing-uhm — ˈwɔːlziŋəm
  3. cape, Canada — WAWL-sing-HAM — ˈwɔːlsiŋˌhæm

Walston
  Ray, *US actor* — WAWL-stuhn — ˈwɔːlstən

Walt
  pers. name — WAWLT, WAHLT — ˈwɔːlt, ˈwɑlt

Walter
  1. pers. name — WAWL-tuhr — ˈwɔːltəʳ
  2. German — VAHL-tuhr — ˈvɑltəʳ

Waltham
  1. city, MA — WAWL-THAM, *by non-residents often* WAWL-thuhm — ˈwɔːlˌθæm, *by non-residents often* ˈwɔːlθəm
  2. pl. name, England — WAWL-thuhm, WAWL-tuhm — ˈwɔːlθəm, ˈwɔːltəm

Waltham Forest
  borough, England — WAWL-thuhm FAWR-uhst, WAWL-tuhm, FAHR-uhst — ˌwɔːlθəm ˈfɔːrəst, ˌwɔːltəm, ˈfɑrəst

Walther
  1. pers. name, French — vahl-TER — vɑːlter
  2. German — VAHL-tuhr — ˈvɑltəʳ

Walton
  Ernest T., *Irish physicist (Nobel 1951); Izaak, British writer* — WAWLT-n — ˈwɔːltn̩

Walvis
  Bay, *west coast of Africa* — WAWL-vuhs — ˈwɔːlvəs

Key (col. 2): a: fad ā: fade ah: father ar: Mary aw: law e: fed ē: feed er: merry i: hid ī: hide ō: coat ōō: boot
oi: boy ow: now u: put uh: above uhr: bird ch: chop ng: ring sh: show th: thick <u>th</u>: this zh: measure

Wambaugh
Joseph, *US writer* WAHM-BOW 'wɑm,bɑu

Wampanoag
N. American people WAHM-puh-NŌ-AG, WAWM- ,wɑmpə'noː,æg, ,wɔːm-

Wanamaker
John, *US merchant;* Sam, *US* WAHN-uh-MĀ-kuhr 'wɑnə,meːkəʳ
actor, director

Wanda
1. pers. name WAHN-duh 'wɑndə
2. Polish VAHN-dah 'vɑːndɑː

Wanderjahr
a year of travel VAHN-duhr-YAHR 'vɑndəʳjɑʳ

Wandsworth
borough, England WAHN(D)Z-wuhrth 'wɑn(d)zwəʳθ

Wankel
1. Felix, German engineer VAHNG-kuhl 'vɑŋkəl
2. engine WANG-kuhl, VAHNG-kuhl 'wæŋkəl, 'vɑŋkəl

Wanne-Eickel
city, Germany VAHN-uh-Ī-kuhl 'vɑnə'aikəl

Wantage
Community, *religious order* WAHNT-ij, WUHNT-ij 'wɑntidʒ, 'wəntidʒ

Wantagh
town, NY WAHN-TAW 'wɑn,tɔː

Wapakoneta
city, OH WAW-puh-kuh-NET-uh ,wɔːpəkə'neṭə

Wapello
county, IA WAHP-uh-LŌ 'wɑpə,loː

Wapiti
town, WY; elk WAHP-uht-ē 'wɑpəṭiˑ

Wapping
district, England WAHP-ing 'wɑpiŋ

Wappinger
N. American people WAHP-uhn-juhr 'wɑpəndʒəʳ

Wappingers Falls
town, NY WAHP-uhn-juhrz FAWLZ ,wɑpəndʒəʳz 'fɔːlz

Warangal
city, India WAWR-uhng-guhl 'wɔːrəŋgəl

Warburg
Otto H., *German biochemist* VAHR-BURKH, $ WAWR-BUHRG 'vɑʳ,buʳx, $ 'wɔːʳ,bəʳg
(Nobel 1931)

Warcup
pers. name WAWR-kuhp, WAWR-KUHP 'wɔːʳkəp, 'wɔːʳ,kəp

Ward
pers. name WAWRD 'wɔːʳd

Wardell
pers. name wawr-DEL wɔːʳ'del

Wareham
town, England WER-uhm, WAR-uhm 'werəm, 'wærəm

Warhol
Andy, *US artist* WAWR-HAWL, WAWR-HŌL 'wɔːʳ,hɔːl, 'wɔːʳ,hoːl

Waring
tdmk. for small appliances; pers. WAR-ing, WER-ing 'wæriŋ, 'weriŋ
name

Warner
John William, *US politician* WAWR-nuhr 'wɔːʳnəʳ

Warragamba
　river, Australia　　　　　　　WAHR-uh-GAM-buh　　　　　　ˌwɑrəˈgæmbə

Warrawee
　town, Australia　　　　　　　WAHR-uh-wē　　　　　　　　ˈwɑrəwiˑ

Warren
　pers. name　　　　　　　　WAWR-uhn, WAHR-uhn　　　ˈwɔːrən, ˈwɑrən

Warrick
　Ruth, *actress*　　　　　　　WAWR-ik, WAHR-ik　　　　　ˈwɔːrik, ˈwɑrik

Warsaw
　city, prov, Poland; pl. name, US　WAWR-SAW　　　　　　　　ˈwɔːʳˌsɔː

Warsteiner
　German beer　　　　　　　VAHR-SHTĪ-nuhr　　　　　　vɑʳˌʃtainəʳ

Warszawa [Warsaw]
　city, prov, Poland　　　　　vahr-SHAHV-uh　　　　　　vɑːʳˈʃɑːvə

Wartburg
　castle, Germany　　　　　　VAHRT-BURK, ⑤ WAWRT-BUHRG　ˈvɑʳtˌbuʳk, ⑤ ˈwɔːʳtˌbəʳg

Warwick
　1. *pl. name, Australia, Canada,*　WAHR-ik, WAWR-ik　　　ˈwɑrik, ˈwɔːrik
　　England
　2. *city, RI*　　　　　　　　WAWR-wik, WAWR-ik, WAHR-ik　ˈwɔːrwik, ˈwɔːrik, ˈwɑrik
　3. *pers. name*　　　　　　　WAHR-ik, WAWR-ik, WAWR-wik　ˈwɑrik, ˈwɔːrik, ˈwɔːrwik

Warwickshire
　county, England　　　　　　WAHR-ik-shuhr, -SHIR;　　　ˈwɑrikʃəʳ, -ˌʃiʳ;
　　　　　　　　　　　　　　⑤ WAWR-(w)ik-　　　　　⑤ ˈwɔːr(w)ik-

Wasabi
　horseradish　　　　　　　WAHS-uh-bē, wuh-SAHB-ē　ˈwɑsəbiˑ, wəˈsɑbiˑ

Wasatch
　county, UT; mtn. range, US　WAW-SACH　　　　　　　ˈwɔːˌsætʃ

Wasco
　county, OR　　　　　　　WAHS-kō　　　　　　　　ˈwɑskoː

Waseca
　county, MN　　　　　　　wah-SĒ-kuh　　　　　　　wəˈsiːkə

Washakie
　county, WY　　　　　　　WAHSH-uh-kē　　　　　　ˈwɑʃəkiˑ

Washington
　Booker T., *US educator;* George,　WAWSH-ing-tuhn, WAHSH-ing-tuhn,　ˈwɔːʃiŋtən, ˈwɑʃiŋtən, *esp.*
　　1st US president; state, pl.　　*esp. in US Midlands*　　　*in US Midlands*
　　name, US　　　　　　　WAWR-shing-tuhn,　　　　　ˈwɔːrʃiŋtən, ˈwɑrʃiŋtən
　　　　　　　　　　　　　　WAHR-shing-tuhn

Washita
　river, US; county, AR, OK　WAHSH-uh-TAW, WAWSH-uh-TAW　ˈwɑʃəˌtɔː, ˈwɔːʃəˌtɔː

Washoe
　county, NV; N. American people　WAHSH-ō　　　　　　　ˈwɑʃoː

Washtenaw
　county, MI　　　　　　　WAHSH-tuh-NAW　　　　　ˈwɑʃtəˌnɔː

WASP
　white Anglo-Saxon Protestant　WAHSP, WAWSP　　　　　ˈwɑsp, ˈwɔːsp

Wassermann
　diagnostic test for syphilis　WAHS-uhr-muhn　　　　　ˈwɑsəʳmən

Wassily
　pers. name, Russian　　　　VAHS-yil-yi　　　　　　　ˈvɑːsjiljij

Watanabe
　Michio, *Japanese statesman*　wah-tah-nah-bā, ⑤ WAHT-n-AHB-ā,　watanabeˑ, ⑤ ˌwatn̩ˈabeː,
　　　　　　　　　　　　　　WAHT-n-AHB-ē　　　　　　ˌwatn̩ˈabiˑ

Key (col. 2):　a: fad　ā: fade　ah: father　ar: Mary　aw: law　e: fed　ē: feed　er: merry　i: hid　ī: hide　ō: coat　ōō: boot
oi: boy　ow: now　u: put　uh: above　uhr: bird　ch: chop　ng: ring　sh: show　th: thick　th̲: this　zh: measure

Watauga
   river, US; county, NC   wah-TAW-guh   wɑ'tɔːgə

Waterbury
   US pl. name   WAWT-uhr-BER-ē, WAHT-uhr-BER-ē   'wɔːṭəˡˌberiˑ, 'waṭəˡˌberiˑ

Waterford
   county, Ireland; town, CT   WAWT-uhr-fuhrd, WAHT-uhr-fuhrd   'wɔːṭəˡfəˡd, 'waṭəˡfəˡd

Watergate
   hotel, DC; US political scandal   WAWT-uhr-GĀT, WAHT-uhr-GĀT   'wɔːṭəˡˌgeːt, 'waṭəˡˌgeːt

Waterloo
   1. US & Canadian pl. name   WAWT-uhr-L͞OO, WAWT-uhr-L͞OO,   ˌwɔːṭəˡ'luː, 'wɔːṭəˡˌluː,
               WAHT-uhr-L͞OO, WAHT-uhr-L͞OO   ˌwaṭəˡ'luː, 'waṭəˡˌluː
   2. commune, battlesite, Belgium   VAHT-uhr-LŌ, Ⓢ *as above*   'vaṭəˡˌloː, Ⓢ *as above*

Waterston
   Samuel Atkinson, US actor   WAWT-uhr-stuhn, WAHT-uhr-stuhn   'wɔːṭəˡstən, 'waṭəˡstən

Watford
   district, England   WAHT-fuhrd   'watfəˡd

Watkin
   pers. name   WAHT-kuhn   'watkən

Watonwan
   county, MN   WAHT-n-WAHN   'watn̩ˌwan

WATS
   wide-area telephone service   WAHTS   'wats

Watson
   family name   WAHT-suhn   'watsən

Watteau
   Antoine, French painter   vah-TŌ   vɑːtoː

Watusi [Tutsi]
   people, Rwanda, Burundi; dance   wah-T͞OO-sē   wɑ'tuːsiˑ

Watutsi [Tutsi]
   people, Rwanda, Burundi   wah-T͞OOT-sē   wɑ'tuːtsiˑ

Wauchope
   town, Australia   WAW-HŌP   'wɔˌhoːp

Waugh
   Alec, Evelyn, English writers   WAW   'wɔː

Waukegan
   city, IL   waw-KĒ-guhn   wɔː'kiːgən

Waukesha
   city, county, WI   WAW-ki-SHAW   'wɔːkiˌʃɔː

Waupaca
   county, WI   waw-PAK-uh   wɔː'pækə

Wausau
   city, WI   WAW-SAW   'wɔːˌsɔː

Waushara
   county, WI   waw-SHAR-uh, waw-SHER-uh   wɔː'ʃærə, wɔː'ʃerə

Wauwatosa
   city, WI   WAW-wuh-TŌ-suh   ˌwɔːwə'toːsə

Wavell
   Archibald, British militarist   WĀ-vuhl   'weːvəl

Wawrzyniec
   pers. name, Polish   vahv-ZHIN-yets   vɑːv'ʒinjets

Wayne
   pers. name   WĀN   'weːn

Waziristan
   mtn. tract, Pakistan   wuh-ZIR-i-STAN, -STAHN   wəˌziri'stæn, -'stɑn

---

Foreign Sounds: **ue:** *Fr.* **rue**, *Ger.* **füllen**   **uh(r):** *Fr.* **boeuf**, *Ger.* **Höhle**   **kh:** *Ger.* **ich**, *Scot.* **loch**   **g̃:** *Sp.* **amigo**   **v:** *Sp.* **hablar**
hl: *Welsh* **Llanelli.**   CAPITALS: primary stress.   SMALL CAPS: secondary stress.   Ⓢ: U.S. pron.   Ⓑ: British pron.

Weald, The		
wooded district, England	thuh WĒLD	ðə 'wiːld
Weaver		
Sigourney, *entertainer*	WĒ-vuhr	'wiːvəʳ
Webber		
Robert, *US actor*	WEB-uhr	'webəʳ
Weber		
1. *family name, English*	WEB-uhr	'webəʳ
2. *German*	VĀ-buhr	'veːbəʳ
Webster		
Daniel, *US statesman;* Noah, *US lexicographer; pers. name*	WEB-stuhr	'webstəʳ
Wechsler		
David, *US psychologist*	WEK-sluhr	'weksləʳ
Weddell Sea		
arm of Atlantic	wuh-DEL, WED-l	wə'del, 'wedl̩
Wedgeworth		
Ann, *US actress*	WEJ-WUHRTH	'wedʒˌwəʳθ
Wedgwood		
tdmk for ceramic ware	WEJ-WUD	'wedʒˌwud
Wednesday		
day of the week	WENZ-dē, WENZ-dā, Ⓔ *sometimes* WED-nz-dē, WED-nz-dā	'wenzdiˑ, 'wenzdeː, Ⓔ *sometimes* 'wedn̩zdiˑ, 'wedn̩zdeː
Weeghman		
Charles, Park, *former name for* Wrigley Field, *Chicago, IL*	WĒG-muhn, WIG-muhn	'wiːgmən, 'wigmən
Weehawken		
town, NJ	wē-HAW-kuhn	wiː'hɔːkən
Weejuns		
tdmk for shoes	WĒ-juhnz	'wiːdʒənz
Weeks, Weekes		
pers. name	WĒKS	'wiːks
Weelkes		
Thomas, *English composer*	WĒLKS	'wiːlks
Wee Waa		
town, Australia	WĒ WAW	'wiː ˌwɔː
Weicker		
Lowell Palmer, Jr., *US politician*	WĪ-kuhr	'waikəʳ
Weifang		
city, China	WĀ-FAHNG	'weːˈfaŋ
Weigela		
bush	wī-JĒ-luh	wai'dʒiːlə
Weihai		
port, China	WĀ-HĪ	'weːˈhai
Weil		
Simone, *French writer*	VE-yuh, Ⓢ VĀ, VĪL	vej, Ⓢ 'veː, 'vail
Weill		
Kurt, *US composer*	VĪL, WĪL	'vail, 'wail
Weimar		
city, Germany; Republic, *German regime*	VĪ-MAHR, Ⓢ WĪ-MAHR	'vaiˌmaʳ, Ⓢ 'waiˌmaʳ
Weimaraner		
dog breed	vī-muh-RAHN-uhr, wī-; VĪ-muh-RAHN-uhr, WĪ-	ˌvaiməˈranəʳ, ˌwai-; 'vaiməˌranəʳ, 'wai-

Key (col. 2): a: fad ā: fade ah: father ar: Mary aw: law e: fed ē: feed er: merry i: hid ī: hide ō: coat ōō: boot
oi: boy ow: now u: put uh: above uhr: bird ch: chop ng: ring sh: show th: thick th̲: this zh: measure

Weinberg
    Steven, *US physicist (Nobel 1979)*   WĪN-BUHRG   'waɪnˌbəʳg
Weinberger
    Casper Willard, *US government*   WĪN-BUHR-guhr   'waɪnˌbəʳgəʳ
    official
Weiner
    Edmund, *British lexicographer*   VĪ-nuhr   'vaɪnəʳ
Weippe
    prairie, ID   WĒ-ī-pē   'wiːaɪpiˑ
Weiser
    city, ID   WĒ-suhr, WĒ-zuhr   'wiːsəʳ, 'wiːzəʳ
Weiss
    Donald Logan, *US football*   WĪS   'waɪs
    executive
Weissmuller
    Johnny, *US actor*   WĪ-SMUHL-uhr   'waɪˌsmələʳ
Weizenkrone
    German beer   VĪT-suhn-KRŌ-nuh   'vaɪtsənˌkroːnə
Weizmann
    Chaim, *Israeli political leader*   VĪT-smuhn   'vaɪtsmən
Welch
    Raquel, *US actress*   WELCH   'weltʃ
Welega
    mtn. range, Africa   we-LĀ-guh   we'leːgə
Welland
    city, prov, canal, Canada   WEL-uhnd   'welənd
Weller
    T. H., *US physiologist (Nobel*   WEL-uhr   'weləʳ
    1954)
Wellesley
    College, *town, MA*   WELZ-lē   'welzliˑ
Wellington
    pers. name   WEL-ing-tuhn   'welɪŋtən
Welo [Wallo]
    region, Ethiopia   WĀ-lō   'weːloː
Welsh
    lang., people, Wales   WELSH   'welʃ
Weltanschauung
    'world view'   VEL-TAHN-SHOW-uhng,   'velˌtɑnˌʃauəŋ,
                VEL-tuhn-SHOW(-uh)ng   'veltənˌʃau(ə)ŋ
Weltpolitik
    'world politics'   VELT-PAW-luh-tik   'veltˌpɔːlətik
Weltschmerz
    depression; sentimental sorrow   VELT-SHMERTS   'veltˌʃmeʳts
Welty
    Eudora, *US writer*   WEL-tē   'weltiˑ
Welwyn Garden City
    town, England   WEL-uhn   'welən
Wembley
    stadium, London   WEM-blē   'wembliˑ
Wemyss
    region, Scotland   WĒMZ   'wiːmz
Wenatchee
    river, lake, city, WA; N. American   wuh-NACH-ē   wə'nætʃiˑ
    people

Foreign Sounds: **ue**: *Fr.* **rue**, *Ger.* **füllen**   **uh**(r): *Fr.* **boeuf**, *Ger.* **Höhle**   <u>kh</u>: *Ger.* **ich**, *Scot.* **loch**   g̃: *Sp.* **amigo**   <u>v</u>: *Sp.* **hablar**
hl: *Welsh* **Llanelli**.   CAPITALS: primary stress.   SMALL CAPS: secondary stress.   ⓈＳ: U.S. pron.   Ⓛ: British pron.

Wenceslao
　pers. name, Spanish　　　bān-sä-SLAH-ō, wän-, bān-thä-　　beːnseː'slɑ-oː, weːn-, beːnθeː-

Wenceslas
　pers. name　　　WEN-suh-SLAHS, -SLAWS　　'wensə,slɑːs, -,slɔːs

Wenceslaus
　1. pers. name　　　WEN-suh-SLAHS, -SLAWS　　'wensə,slɑːs, -,slɔːs
　2. German　　　VENT-suh-SLOWS　　'ventsə,slɑus

Wen-chou, Wenchow
　see Wenzhou

Wend
　Slavic people of Germany　　　WEND　　'wend

Wendel
　1. pers. name　　　WEN-duhl　　'wendəl
　2. German　　　VEN-duhl　　'vendəl

Wendelin
　pers. name, German　　　VEN-duh-LĒN　　'vendə,liːn

Wendell
　pers. name　　　WEN-duhl　　'wendəl

Wendish [Sorbian]
　lang., Germany　　　WEN-dish　　'wendiʃ

Wendy
　pers. name　　　WEN-dē　　'wendiˑ

Weni
　Egyptian governor　　　WĀ-nē　　'weːniˑ

Wenrohronon
　N. American people　　　WEN-RŌ-RŌ-NAHN　　,wen,roː'roː,nɑn

Wenzel
　pers. name, German　　　VENT-suhl　　'ventsəl

Wenzeslaus
　pers. name, German　　　VENT-suh-SLOWS　　'ventsə,slɑus

Wenzhou, Wen-chou, Wenchow
　port, China　　　WEN-JŌ　　'wen'dʒoː

Werner
　1. Alfred, German-born Swiss　　　VER-nuhr　　'veᵊnəᵊ
　　inorganic chemist (Nobel 1913)
　2. pers. name　　　WUHR-nuhr, VUHR-nuhr　　'wəᵊnəᵊ, 'vəᵊnəᵊ
　3. German　　　VER-nuhr　　'veᵊnəᵊ
　4. Swedish　　　VUHR-nuhr　　'vərnər

Wernher
　pers. name, German　　　VER-nuhr, Ⓢ WUHR-nuhr　　'veᵊnəᵊ, Ⓢ 'wəᵊnəᵊ

Wernicke
　Carl, *German neurologist*　　　VER-nik-uh　　'veᵊnikə

Wernicke's
　area of the human brain　　　VER-ni-kuhz, VER-ni-kēz　　'veᵊnikəz, 'veᵊnikiːz

Weser
　river, Germany　　　VĀ-zuhr, Ⓢ WĒ-zuhr　　'veːzəᵊ, Ⓢ 'wiːzəᵊ

Wesley
　John *and* Charles, *English*　　　WES-lē, WEZ-lē　　'wesliˑ, 'wezliˑ
　　religious leaders; pers. name

Wesleyan
　college & univ. name, US　　　WEZ-lē-uhn　　'wezliːən

Wessex
　medieval British kingdom;　　　WES-iks　　'wesiks
　　fictional county, Hardy

Key (col. 2):　a: fad　ā: fade　ah: father　ar: Mary　aw: law　e: fed　ē: feed　er: merry　i: hid　ī: hide　ō: coat　ōō: boot
oi: boy　ow: now　u: put　uh: above　uhr: bird　ch: chop　ng: ring　sh: show　th: thick　th: this　zh: measure

West Bromwich
  town, England   wes(t) BRUHM-ij, BRUHM-ich   wes(t) 'brəmidʒ, 'brəmitʃ
Westcott
  pers. name   WES(T)-kuht   'wes(t)kət
West Covina
  city, CA   WES(T) kō-VĒ-nuh   ˌwes(t) koː'viːnə
Western Samoa
  independent state, Pacific   WES-tuhrn suh-MŌ-uh   ˌwestəʳn sə'moːə
Western Scheldt
  estuary, Netherlands   WEST-uhrn SKELT   ˌwestəʳn 'skelt
Westerschelde
  estuary, Netherlands   VES-tuhr-SKEL-duh   'vestəʳˌskeldə
Westfalen
  German beer   VEST-FAHL-uhn   'vestˌfɑlən
West Glamorgan
  county, Wales   WES(T) gluh-MAWR-guhn   ˌwes(t) glə'mɔːʳgən
Westley
  pers. name   WES(T)-lē   'wes(t)liˑ
Westman
  Islands, *Iceland*   WES(T)-muhn   'wes(t)mən
West Midlands
  county, England   wes(t) MID-luhn(d)z   wes(t) 'midlən(d)z
Westminster
  city of, borough, England; abbey   WES(T)-MIN(T)-stuhr   'wes(t)ˌmin(t)stəʳ
Westmoreland
  1. William, US general   WES(T)-MŌR-luhnd,   'wes(t)ˌmoːʳlənd,
       WES(T)-MAWR-luhnd,   'wes(t)ˌmɔːʳlənd,
       wes(t)-MŌR-luhnd,   wes(t)'moːʳlənd,
       wes(t)-MAWR-luhnd   wes(t)'mɔːʳlənd
  2. county, PA; city, KS   wes(t)-MŌR-luhnd,   wes(t)'moːʳlənd,
       wes(t)-MAWR-luhnd   wes(t)'mɔːʳlənd
  3. county, VA   WES(T)-mōr-luhn(d),   'wes(t)moːʳlən(d),
       WES(T)-mawr-luhn(d),   'wes(t)mɔːʳlən(d),
       WES(T)-muhr-luhn(d)   'wes(t)məʳlən(d)
Westmorland
  former county, England   WES(T)-muhr-luhnd;   'wes(t)məʳlənd;
       Ⓢ WES(T)-MŌR-luhnd,   Ⓢ 'wes(t)ˌmoːʳlənd,
       -MAWR-luhnd   -ˌmɔːʳlənd
Weston
  Jack, *actor*   WES-tuhn   'westən
Westphalia
  former prov of Prussia   wes(t)-FĀL-yuh, wes(t)-FĀ-lē-uh   wes(t)'feːljə, wes(t)'feːliːə
West Sussex
  county, England   wes(t) SUHS-iks   wes(t) 'səsiks
Westvaco
  US paper and chemical co.   wes(t)-VĀ-kō   wes(t)'veːkoː
West Virginia
  state, US   WES(T) VUHR-JIN-yuh, vuhr-JIN-ē-uh   ˌwes(t) vəʳ'dʒinjə, vəʳ'dʒiniːə
West Yorkshire
  county, England   west YAWRK-shuhr, -SHIR   west 'jɔːʳkʃəʳ, -ˌʃiʳ
Wetherbee
  pers. name   WE<u>TH</u>-uhr-bē   'weðəʳbiˑ
Wetterhorn
  peak, Bernese Alps   VET-uhr-HAWRN   'vetəʳˌhɔːʳn

Foreign Sounds: ue: *Fr.* **rue**, *Ger.* **füllen**   uh(r): *Fr.* **boeuf**, *Ger.* **Höhle**   <u>kh</u>: *Ger.* **ich**, *Scot.* **loch**   ğ: *Sp.* **amigo**   v̲: *Sp.* **hablar**
hl: *Welsh* **Llanelli.**   CAPITALS: primary stress.   SMALL CAPS: secondary stress.   Ⓢ: U.S. pron.   Ⓑ: British pron.

Wey
river, England   WĀ   'weː

Weyerhaeuser
US paper products co.   WER-HOW-zuhr, WĪ(-uh)r-HOW-zuhr   'weʳˌhɑuzəʳ,
                                                                                                                        'wɑi(ə)ʳˌhɑuzəʳ

Weymouth
town, MA; town, England   WĀ-muhth   'weːməθ

Whalen
pers. name   (H)WĀ-luhn   '(h)weːlən

Wharton
Edith, US writer; county, city, TX; (H)WAWRT-n   '(h)wɔːʳtn̩
pers. name

Whatcom
county, town, WA   (H)WAHT-kuhm   '(h)wɑtkəm

Whatmough
family name   (H)WAHT-MŌ   '(h)wɑtˌmoː

Wheaton
pers. name   (H)WĒT-n   '(h)wiːtn̩

Wheelock
pers. name   (H)WĒ-LAHK   '(h)wiːˌlɑk

Whig
US & British political parties   (H)WIG   '(h)wig

Whipple
G. H., US pathologist (Nobel   (H)WIP-uhl   '(h)wipəl
1934)

Whistler
James, US painter   (H)WIS-luhr   '(h)wisləʳ

Whitaker
pers. name   (H)WIT-uh-kuhr   '(h)wit̬əkəʳ

Whitbread
tdmk for a beer   (H)WIT-BRED   '(h)witˌbred

Whitcomb
pers. name   (H)WIT-kuhm   '(h)witkəm

White
family name   (H)WĪT   '(h)wɑit

Whitefield
pers. name   (H)WIT-FĒLD, (H)WĪT-FĒLD   '(h)witˌfiːld, '(h)wɑitˌfiːld

Whitehall
former palace, London; pert. to   (H)WĪT-HAWL   '(h)wɑitˌhɔːl
British government

Whitehead
pers. name   (H)WĪT-HED   '(h)wɑitˌhed

Whitley
pers. name   (H)WIT-lē   '(h)witliˑ

Whitman
pers. name   (H)WIT-muhn   '(h)witmən

Whitmore
James, US actor   WIT-MAWR   'witˌmɔːʳ

Whitney
pers. name   (H)WIT-nē   '(h)witniˑ

Whitsunday
Christian holy day   (H)WIT-SUHN-dē, (H)WIT-suhn-DĀ   ˌ(h)wit'səndiˑ, '(h)witsənˌdeː

Whitsuntide
week beginning 7th Sunday after   (H)WIT-suhn-TĪD   '(h)witsənˌtɑid
Easter

Key (col. 2):   a: **fad** ā: **fade** ah: **father** ar: **Mary** aw: **law** e: **fed** ē: **feed** er: **merry** i: **hid** ī: **hide** ō: **coat** o͞o: **boot**
oi: **boy**   ow: **now**   u: **put** uh: **above** uhr: **bird** ch: **chop** ng: **ring** sh: **show** th: **thick** th̲: **this** zh: **measure**

Whittier
    College, *CA; city, CA; pers. name*   (H)WIT-ē-uhr   '(h)wiţiːəʳ

Whittingham
    pers. name   (H)WIT-ing-uhm, (H)WIT-n-juhm   '(h)wiţiŋəm, '(h)witn̩dʒəm

Whorf
    Benjamin Lee, *US linguist*   (H)WAWRF   '(h)wɔːʳf

Whyalla
    city, Australia   (h)wī-AL-uh   (h)wɑi'ælə

Whydah
    African bird   (H)WID-uh   '(h)widə

Wibaux
    county, MT   WĒ-bō   'wiːboː

Wichita
    river, county, TX; city, county,   WICH-uh-TAW, -TAH   'witʃə,tɔː, -,tɑ
    KS; N. American people

Wickham
    pers. name   WIK-uhm   'wikəm

Wicklow
    county, Eire   WIK-lō   'wikloː

Wicküler
    German beer   VIK-UE-luhr   'vik,yːləʳ

Wicomico
    county, MD   wi-KAHM-i-KŌ   wi'kɑmi,koː

Widener
    univ., PA; library, Harvard Univ.,   WĪD-nuhr   'wɑidnəʳ
    MA; pers. name

Widmark
    Richard, *US actor*   WID-MAHRK   'wid,mɑʳk

Wiedenmeyer
    Park, *former ballpark, Newark, NJ*   WĒD-n-MĪ(-uh)r   'wiːdn̩,mɑi(ə)ʳ

Wieland
    Heinrich, *German organic chemist*   VĒ-LAHNT   'viː,lɑnt
    (Nobel 1927)

Wien
    Wilhelm, *German physicist (Nobel*   VĒN   'viːn
    1911)

Wien/Schwechat
    airport, Vienna   VĒN-SHVĀ-<u>kh</u>aht   'viːn'ʃveːxɑt

Wiener
    1. Norbert, *US founder of*   WĒ-nuhr   'wiːnəʳ
    cybernetics
    2. pers. name   WĒ-nuhr, WĪ-nuhr   'wiːnɑʳ, 'wɑinəʳ

Wiener schnitzel
    veal cutlet   VĒ-nuhr SHNIT-suhl   'viːnəʳ ʃnitsəl

Wien [Vienna]
    city, Austria   VĒN   'viːn

Wiesbaden
    city, Germany   VĒS-BAHD-n, VIS-BAHD-n   'viːs,bɑdn̩, 'vis,bɑdn̩

Wiesel
    1. Elie, *Romanian-born US*   vē-ZEL, VĒ-zuhl, wi-ZEL   viː'zel, 'viːzəl, wi'zel
    author, educator (Nobel 1986)
    2. Torsten N., *Swedish*   VĒ-zuhl   'viːzəl
    neurobiologist (Nobel 1981)

Foreign Sounds: ue: *Fr.* **rue**, *Ger.* **fü**llen   uh(r): *Fr.* b**oeu**f, *Ger.* H**öh**le   <u>kh</u>: *Ger.* i**ch**, *Scot.* lo**ch**   ḡ: *Sp.* ami**g**o   <u>v</u>: *Sp.* ha**b**lar
hl: *Welsh* **Ll**anelli.   CAPITALS: primary stress.   SMALL CAPS: secondary stress.   Ⓢ: U.S. pron.   Ⓑ: British pron.

Wiesenthal

Simon, *Nazi hunter* VĒ-zuhn-TAHL, ⑤ WĒ-zuhn-THAWL, 'viːzən,tɑl, ⑤ 'wiːzən,θɔːl,
-THAHL -,θɑl

Wigan

borough, England WIG-uhn 'wigən

Wigeon

bird WIJ-uhn 'widʒən

Wight, Isle of

island, England; county, VA ĪL uh(v) WĪT ,ail ə(v) 'wait

Wigner

Eugene Paul, *Hungarian-born US* WIG-nuhr 'wignəʳ
physicist (Nobel 1963)

Wilbarger

county, TX WIL-BAHR-guhr 'wil,bɑʳgəʳ

Wilber

pers. name WIL-buhr 'wilbəʳ

Wilberforce

William, *British abolitionist* WIL-buhr-FAWRS 'wilbəʳ,fɔːʳs

Wilbur

pers. name WIL-buhr 'wilbəʳ

Wilcox

county, AL, GA; pers. name WIL-KAHKS 'wil,kɑks

Wilde

Cornel, *US actor;* Oscar, *Irish wit* WĪLD 'waild
& writer

Wilder

pers. name WĪL-duhr 'waildəʳ

Wilds

pers. name WĪL(D)Z 'wail(d)z

Wiles

pers. name WĪLZ 'wailz

Wilfred

pers. name WIL-fruhd 'wilfrəd

Wilfrid Laurier

University, *Canada* WIL-fruhd lawr-YĀ 'wilfrəd lɔːr'jeː

Wilfried

pers. name, German VIL-FRĒT 'vil,friːt

Wilhelm

1. pers. name WIL-HELM 'wil,helm
2. Danish, German, Norwegian VIL-HELM 'vil,helm
3. Swedish VIL-(h)uhlm 'vil(h)əlm

Wilhelmina

1. pers. name WIL-hel-MĒ-nuh ,wilhel'miːnə
2. Dutch VIL-hel-MĒ-nah ,vilhel'miːnɑː
3. German VIL-hel-MĒ-nah ,vilhel'miːnɑ

Wilhelm Meister

novel, Goethe VIL-HELM MĪ-stuhr 'vil,helm 'maistəʳ

Wilhelmshaven

port, Germany VIL-helms-HAHF-uhn ,vilhelms'hafən

Wilhelmstrasse

street, Berlin, Germany VIL-helm-SHTRAHS-uh 'vilhelm,ʃtrasə

Wilhelmus

pers. name, Dutch vil-HEL-mues vil'helmys

Wilibald

pers. name, German VIL-ē-BAHLT 'viliː,balt

Key (col. 2):   a: **fad** ā: **fade** ah: **father** ar: **Mary** aw: **law** e: **fed** ē: **feed** er: **merry** i: **hid** ī: **hide** ō: **coat** ōō: **boot**
oi: **boy** ow: **now** u: **put** uh: **above** uhr: **bird** ch: **chop** ng: **ring** sh: **show** th: **thick** th̠: **this** zh: **measure**

Wilkes-Barre
   city, PA   WILKS-BAR-uh, WILKS-BAR-ē,   'wilks͵bærə, 'wilks͵bæri',
                   WILKS-BAR   'wilks͵bæ^r

Wilkins
   M. H. F., British physicist (Nobel   WIL-kuhnz   'wilkənz
     1962); Roy, *US civil rights*
     leader; pers. name

Wilkinson
   Sir Geoffrey, *English inorganic*   WIL-kuhn-suhn   'wilkənsən
     chemist (Nobel 1973)

Will
   pers. name   WIL   'wil

Willa
   pers. name   WIL-uh   'wilə

Willacy
   county, TX   WIL-uh-sē   'wiləsi'

Willamette
   river, OR   wuh-LAM-uht   wə'læmət

Willard
   pers. name   WIL-uhrd   'wilə^rd

Willem
   pers. name, Dutch   VIL-uhm   'viləm

Willemstad
   port, Curaçao   VIL-uhm-STAHT   'viləm͵stɑt

Willesden
   former borough, England   WILZ-duhn   'wilzdən

Willi
   pers. name, German   VIL-ē   'viliː

William
   pers. name   WIL-yuhm   'wiljəm

Williams
   1. family name   WIL-yuhmz   'wiljəmz
   2. Ralph Vaughan, *see Vaughan*
     Williams

Willibald
   pers. name, German   VIL-ē-BAHLT   'viliː͵bɑlt

Willie
   pers. name   WIL-ē   'wili'

Willis
   Bruce, *US actor; pers. name*   WIL-uhs   'wiləs

Willoughby
   city, OH; pers. name   WIL-uh-bē   'wiləbi'

Willstätter
   Richard, *German organic chemist*   VIL-SHTET-uhr   'vil͵ʃtețə^r
     (Nobel 1915)

Willy
   1. pers. name   WIL-ē   'wili'
   2. German   VIL-ē   'vili'

Wilma
   pers. name   WIL-muh   'wilmə

Wilmer
   pers. name   WIL-muhr   'wilmə^r

Wilmette
   town, IL   wil-MET   wil'met

Foreign Sounds: ue: *Fr.* **rue,** *Ger.* füllen   uh(r): *Fr.* **boeuf,** *Ger.* Höhle   <u>kh</u>: *Ger.* i**ch,** *Scot.* lo**ch**   ğ: *Sp.* ami**g**o   <u>v</u>: *Sp.* ha**b**lar
hl: *Welsh* **Llanelli.**   CAPITALS: primary stress.   SMALL CAPS: secondary stress.   Ⓢ: U.S. pron.   Ⓑ: British pron.

Wilmington		
city, DE, NC	WIL-ming-tuhn	'wilmɪŋtən
Wilmot		
pers. name	WIL-muht	'wilmət
Wilshere		
pers. name	WIL-shuhr, WIL-SHIR	'wilʃəʳ, 'wil‚ʃiʳ
Wilson		
Thomas Woodrow, *28th US*	WIL-suhn	'wilsən
president; family name		
Wilsonian		
pert. to Woodrow Wilson	wil-SŌ-nē-uhn, wil-SŌN-yuhn	wil'soːniːən, wil'soːnjən
Wilton		
pers. name	WILT-n	'wiltn̩
Wiltshire		
county, England	WIL-chuhr, WILT-shuhr, WILT-SHIR	'wil-tʃəʳ, 'wilt-ʃəʳ, 'wilt‚ʃiʳ
Wilts [Wiltshire]		
county, England	WILTS	'wilts
Wima'kwari		
Mexican festival	wĒ-muh-KWAHR-ē	‚wiːmə'kwɑriˑ
Wimbledon		
section of London; tennis	WIM-buhl-duhn	'wimbəldən
tournament, England		
Wiminuche Ute		
N. American people	WIM-uh-N(Y)OO-chā YOOT	‚wimə'n(j)uːtʃeː 'juːt
Wimpole		
street, London	WIM-PŌL	'wim‚poːl
Wincent		
pers. name, Polish	VĒNT-sent	'viːntsent
Wincenty		
pers. name, Polish	vēnt-SEN-ti	viːnt'senti
Winchester		
1. *city , England*	WIN-chuh-stuhr	'wintʃəstəʳ
2. *pl. name, US; pers. name*	WIN-CHES-tuhr, WIN-chuh-stuhr	'win‚tʃestəʳ, 'wintʃəstəʳ
Windaus		
Adolf, *German chemist (Nobel*	VIN-DOWS	'vin‚daus
1928)		
Windermere		
lake, town, England	WIN-duhr-MIR, WIN-duh-MIR	'windəʳ‚miʳ, 'wində‚miʳ
Windham		
county, CT, VT	WIN-duhm	'windəm
Windhoek		
city, Namibia	VINT-HUK	'vint‚huk
Windom		
William, *US actor*	WIN-duhm	'windəm
Windsor		
pl. name; pers. name	WIN-zuhr	'winzəʳ
Windward		
Islands, *Caribbean*	WIN-dwuhrd	'windwəʳd
Winegar		
pers. name	WĪ-nuh-GAHR	'wainə‚gɑʳ
Winfield		
Paul Edward, *US actor;* Dave, *US*	WIN-FĒLD	'win‚fiːld
baseball player; pers. name		
Winfred		
pers. name	WIN-fruhd	'winfrəd

Key (col. 2):   a: fad   ā: fade   ah: father   ar: Mary   aw: law   e: fed   ē: feed   er: merry   i: hid   ī: hide   ō: coat   ōō: boot
oi: boy   ow: now   u: put   uh: above   uhr: bird   ch: chop   ng: ring   sh: show   th: thick   <u>th</u>: this   zh: measure

Winfrey
    Oprah, *US entertainer*   WIN-frē   'winfriˑ
Winifred
    pers. name   WIN-uh-fruhd   'winəfrəd
Winkler
    Henry, *US actor*   WING-kluhr   'wiŋkləʳ
Winnebago
    US pl. name; tdmk for campers;   WIN-uh-BĀ-gō   ˌwinə'beːgoː
    N. American people
Winneshiek
    county, IA   WIN-uh-SHĒK   'winəˌʃiːk
Winnipeg
    river, lake, city, Canada   WIN-uh-PEG   'winəˌpeg
Winnipegosis
    lake, Canada   WIN-uh-puh-GŌ-suhs   ˌwinəpə'goːsəs
Winnipesaukee
    lake, NH   WIN-uh-puh-SAW-kē, -SAHK-ē   ˌwinəpə'sɔːkiˑ, -'sɑkiˑ
Winona
    city, MN   wuh-NŌ-nuh   wə'noːnə
Winooski
    river, city, VT   wuh-NOO-skē   wə'nuːskiˑ
Winslow
    pers. name   WINZ-lō   'winzloː
Winston
    pers. name   WIN-stuhn   'winstən
Winston-Salem
    city, NC   WIN(T)-stuhn-SĀ-luhm   'win(t)stən'seːləm
Winterthur
    1. town, Switzerland   VINT-uhr-TUR   'vintəʳˌtuʳ
    2. museum, DE   WINT-uhr-THUR, WINT-uhr-thuhr   'wintəʳˌθuʳ, 'wintəʳθəʳ
Wintun
    N. American people   win-TOON   win'tuːn
Winwood
    Stephen Lawrence, *British*   WIN-WUD, WIN-wuhd   'winˌwud, 'winwəd
    musician
Wirt
    county, WV; pers. name   WUHRT   'wəʳt
Wisbech
    borough, England   WIZ-BĒCH   'wizˌbiːtʃ
Wisconsin
    state, US   wis-KAHN(T)-suhn   wis'kɑn(t)sən
Wisconsinite
    inhabitant of Wisconsin   wis-KAHN(T)-suh-NĪT   wis'kɑn(t)səˌnɑit
Wisła [Vistula]
    river, Poland   VĒ-slah   'viːsła
Withycombe
    family name   WITH-i-kuhm   'wiðikəm
Witoto
    S. American people   wuh-TŌT-ō   wə'toːʈoː
Witt
    Katarina, *German figure skater*   VIT   'vit
Wittekop
    Belgian beer   VIT-uh-KAWP, -KAHP   'viʈəˌkɔːp, -ˌkɑp

Foreign Sounds: **ue**: *Fr.* **rue**, *Ger.* **füllen** **uh(r)**: *Fr.* **boeuf**, *Ger.* **Höhle** <u>kh</u>: *Ger.* **ich**, *Scot.* **loch** **ğ**: *Sp.* **amigo** <u>v</u>: *Sp.* **hablar**
hl: *Welsh* **Llanelli**. CAPITALS: primary stress. SMALL CAPS: secondary stress. Ⓢ: U.S. pron. Ⓑ: British pron.

Wittenberg

    1. town, Germany   VIT-n-BERK, ⑤ VIT-n-BUHRG,   'vitn̩,beʳk, ⑤ 'vitn̩,bəʳg,
                                  WIT-n-BUHRG   'witn̩,bəʳg

    2. mtn., NY   WIT-n-BUHRG   'witn̩,bəʳg

Wittgenstein

    Ludwig, *Austrian philosopher*   VIT-guhn-SHTĪN, ⑤ -STĪN   'vitgən,ʃtain, ⑤ -,stain

Wittig

    Georg, *German organic chemist* VIT-i<u>kh</u>   'vitiç
    (Nobel 1979)

Witwatersrand

    region, South Africa   WIT-WAWT-uhrz-RAHND, -RAND   'wit,wɔːtəʳz,rɑnd, -,rænd

Wladimir

    pers. name, German   vlah-DĒ-mir   vlɑ'diːmiʳ

Władysław

    pers. name, Polish   vlah-DIS-lahf   vła'disłɑːf

Włodzimierz

    pers. name, Polish   vlaw-JĒM-yesh   vłɔ'dʒiːmjeʃ

Wobegon

    Lake, *fictional place, G. Keillor* WŌ-bi-GAWN, -GAHN   'woːbi,gɔːn, -,gɑn

Woburn

    1. city, MA   W̄OO-buhrn, WŌ-buhrn   'wuːbəʳn, 'woːbəʳn

    2. parish, England   W̄OO-buhrn   'wuːbəʳn

Wodehouse

    P. G., *English author; pers. name* WUD-HOWS   'wud,haus

Woden, Wodan [Odin]

    supreme Scandinavian god   WŌD-n   'woːdn̩

Wojciech

    pers. name, Polish   VOI-che<u>kh</u>   'vɔitʃeç

Wojtyla

    Karol (Pope John Paul II)   voi-TIL-ah   vɔi'tilɑː

Woking

    town, England   WŌ-king   'woːkiŋ

Wokingham

    town, England   WŌ-king-uhm   'woːkiŋəm

Woldemar

    1. pers. name, Finnish   WAWL-de-MAHR   'woːlde,mɑːʳ

    2. German   VAWL-de-MAHR   'vɔːlde,mɑʳ

Wolds Way

    footpath, England   WŌDZ WĀ   ,woːdz 'weː

Wole

    pers. name, West Africa   WŌ-lā, WAW-lā   'woːleː, 'wɔːleː

Wolf

    1. pers. name   WULF   'wulf

    2. German   VAWLF   'vɔːlf

Wölfbräu

    German beer   VUH(R)LF-BROI   'vœlf,brɔi

Wolfe, Wolff

    pers. name   WULF   'wulf

Wolfgang

    pers. name, German   VAWLF-GAHNG   'vɔːlf,gaŋ

Wolfram

    Walt, *US linguist; former name for* WUL-fruhm   'wulfrəm
    tungsten

Wolfram von Eschenbach

    German poet   VAWL-FRAHM fawn ESH-uhn-BAH<u>KH</u>   'vɔːl,fram fɔn 'eʃən,bax

---

Key (col. 2):   a: fad ā: fade ah: father ar: Mary aw: law e: fed ē: feed er: merry i: hid ī: hide ō: coat o͞o: boot
oi: boy ow: now u: put uh: above uhr: bird ch: chop ng: ring sh: show th: thick <u>th</u>: this zh: measure

Wolfsberg
  town, Austria — VAWLFS-BERK, ⑤ WULFS-BUHRG, -BERG — 'vɔːlfs₎beʳk, ⑤ 'wulfs₎bəʳg, -₎beʳg

Wolfsburg
  city, Germany — VAWLFS-BURK, ⑤ WULFS-BUHRG, -BURG — 'vɔːlfs₎buʳk, ⑤ 'wulfs₎bəʳg, -₎buʳg

Wolfson
  college, Oxford Univ., Cambridge Univ. — WULF-suhn — 'wulfsən

Wollaston
  pers. name — WUL-uhs-tuhn — 'wuləstən

Wollongong
  city, Australia — WUL-uhng-GAHNG, -GAWNG — 'wuləŋ₎gɑŋ, -₎gɔːŋ

Wollstonecraft
  pers. name (M. W. Shelley) — WUL-stuhn-KRAFT, -KRAHFT — 'wulstən₎kræft, -₎krɑːft

Wolof
  lang., people, Africa — WŌ-LAHF, WŌ-LAWF — 'woː₎lɑf, 'woː₎lɔːf

Wolters Kluwer
  Dutch publishing co. — VAWL-tuhrs KLŌO-uhr, ⑤ WŌL-tuhrz KLU(-uh)r — ₎vɔːltəʳs 'kluːəʳ, ⑤ ₎woːltəʳz 'klu(ə)ʳ

Wolverhampton
  town, England — WUL-vuhr-HAM(P)-tuhn — 'wulvəʳ₎hæm(p)tən

Wonsan
  port, N. Korea — wuhn-sahn — wənsɑn

Wood
  pers. name — WUD — 'wud

Woodbury
  pers. name — WUD-BER-ē, WUD-buhr-ē, -brē — 'wud₎beriˑ, 'wudbəriˑ, -briˑ

Woodrow
  pers. name — WUD-rō — 'wudroː

Woodruff
  pers. name — WUD-ruhf — 'wudrəf

Woodward
  1. Robert Burns, US chemist (Nobel 1965); Robert, US journalist — WUD-wuhrd — 'wudwəʳd
  2. city, county, OK — WUD-wuhrd, WUD-uhrd — 'wudwəʳd, 'wudəʳd
  3. pers. name — WUD-wuhrd, ⓔ WUD-uhrd — 'wudwəʳd, ⓔ 'wudəʳd

Woody
  pers. name — WUD-ē — 'wudiˑ

Woolf
  Virginia, English writer; pers. name — WULF — 'wulf

Woollcott
  Alexander, US writer — WUL-kuht — 'wulkət

Woolloomooloo
  Australia — WUL-uh-muh-LŌO, WUL-uh-muh-LŌO — ₎wuləmə'luː, 'wuləmə₎luː

Woolsey
  pers. name — WUL-zē — 'wulziˑ

Woolwich
  former borough, England — WUL-ij, WUL-ich — 'wulidʒ, 'wulitʃ

Woomera
  township, Australia — WUM-uh-ruh — 'wumərə

Foreign Sounds: **ue**: *Fr.* **rue**, *Ger.* **füllen**   **uh(r)**: *Fr.* **boeuf**, *Ger.* **Höhle**   k̲h̲: *Ger.* **ich**, *Scot.* **loch**   g̱: *Sp.* amigo   v̱: *Sp.* ha**b**lar
hl: *Welsh* **Ll**anelli.   CAPITALS: primary stress.   SMALL CAPS: secondary stress.   ⑤: U.S. pron.   ⓔ: British pron.

Woonsocket
   city, RI, SD   w͞oon-SAHK-uht, W͞OON-SAHK-uht   wuːn'sɑkət, 'wuːn,sɑkət

Woosnam
   Ian, *Welsh golfer*   W͞OOZ-nuhm   'wuːznəm

Wooster
   city, OH; pers. name   WUS-tuhr   'wustəʳ

Worcester
   city, MA, England; county, MA,   WUS-tuhr   'wustəʳ
     MD; pers. name

Worcestershire
   1. former county, England   WUS-tuhr-SHIR, WUS-tuhr-shuhr   'wustəʳˌʃiʳ, 'wustəʳʃəʳ
   2. sauce   WUS-tuhr-SHIR, WUS-tuhr-shuhr,   'wustəʳˌʃiʳ, 'wustəʳʃəʳ,
       WUS-tuhr *[sic]*   'wustəʳ *[sic]*

Wordsworth
   William, *English poet; pers. name*   WUHRDZ-WUHRTH   'wəʳdzˌwəʳθ

Wordsworthian
   pert. to William Wordsworth   WUHRDZ-WUHR-thē-uhn,   ˌwəʳdz'wəʳθiːən,
       WUHRDZ-WUHR-t̲h̲ē-uhn   ˌwəʳdz'wəʳðiːən

Worms
   port, Germany   VAWRM(P)S, Ⓢ WUHRMZ   'vɔːʳm(p)s, Ⓢ 'wəʳmz

Worthing
   town, England   WUHR-t̲h̲ing   'wəʳðiŋ

Wortley
   pers. name   WUHRT-lē   'wəʳtliˑ

Worzel
   pers. name   WUHRT-suhl   'wəʳtsəl

Wotan [Odin]
   supreme Scandinavian god   VŌ-TAHN   'voːˌtɑn

Wotton-under-Edge
   village, England   WUT-n̩-UHN-drij,   ˌwutn̩'əndridʒ,
       WUT-n̩-UHN-duh-REJ   ˌwutn̩ˌəndə'redʒ

Wouk
   Herman, *US writer*   WŌK, W͞OOK   'woːk, 'wuːk

Wozzeck
   opera, A. Berg   VAWT-SEK   'vɔːtˌsek

Wrangell-Petersburg
   division, AK   RANG-guhl-PĒT-uhrz-BUHRG   'ræŋgəl'piːtəʳzˌbəʳg

Wrangell-St Elias
   National Park and Preserve, AK   RANG-guhl-SĀNT-l-Ī-uhs   'ræŋgəlˌseːntl̩'aiəs

Wrexham
   city, Wales; Welsh beer   REK-suhm   'reksəm

Wreyford
   pers. name   RĀ-fuhrd   'reːfəʳd

Wright
   pers. name   RĪT   'rait

Wrigley
   tdmk for a chewing gum; Field,   RIG-lē   'rigliˑ
     ballpark, Chicago

Wriothesley
   Henry, *Shakespearean patron*   RĪ-uhth-slē, RAHT-(uh-)slē, RITH-lē,   'raiəθsliˑ, 'rɑt(ə)sliˑ, 'riθliˑ,
       RIZ-lē   'rizliˑ

Wrocław [Breslau]
   city, voivodship, Poland   VRAWT-SLAHF   'vrɔːtˌsłɑf

Wrotham
   village, England   R͞OOT-uhm   'ruːt̩əm

Key (col. 2):   a: **fad**   ā: **fade**   ah: **father**   ar: **Mary**   aw: **law**   e: **fed**   ē: **feed**   er: **merry**   i: **hid**   ī: **hide**   ō: **coat**   o͞o: **boot**
oi: **boy**   ow: **now**   u: **put**   uh: **above**   uhr: **bird**   ch: **chop**   ng: **ring**   sh: **show**   th: **thick**   t̲h̲: **this**   zh: **measure**

Wu
  lang.; pers. name, Chinese   WŌO   'wuː

Wuchang, Wuch'ang
  city, China   WŌO-CHAHNG   'wuː'tʃaŋ

Wu Chen
  Chinese year (Dragon)   WŌO CHUHN   'wuː 'tʃən

Wuhan, Wu-han
  port, China   WŌO-HAHN   'wuː'hɑn

Wundt
  Wilhelm, *German physiologist*   VUNT   'vunt

Wuppertal
  city, Germany   VUP-uhr-TAHL, Ⓢ WUP-   'vupəʳ,tal, Ⓢ 'wup-

Wurlitzer
  US jukebox mfr.   WUHR-luht-suhr   'wəʳlətsəʳ

Württemberg
  region, Germany   VURT-uhm-BERK;   'vyʳtəm,beʳk;
           Ⓢ WUHRT-uhm-BUHRG,   Ⓢ 'wəʳtəm,bəʳg,
           VIRT-uhm-BUHRG   'viʳtəm,bəʳg

Würzburg
  city, Germany   VUERTS-BURK, Ⓢ WUHRTS-BUHRG,   'vyːʳts,buʳk, Ⓢ 'wəʳts,bəʳg,
           VIRTS-BURG   'viʳts,buʳg

Würzburger
  German beer   VUERTS-BUR-guhr   'vyːʳts,buʳgəʳ

Wüsthof
  German mfr.   VUEST-HAWF   'vyːst,hɔːf

Wu Yue
  mtns., China   WŌO yoo-Ā   'wuː juː'eː

Wyandotte
  city, MI; county, KS; N. American   WĪ-uhn-DAHT, WĪN-DAHT   'waiən,dɑt, 'wain,dɑt
  people

Wyatt
  pers. name   WĪ-uht   'waiət

Wycliffe
  pers. name   WIK-LIF, WIK-luhf   'wik,lif, 'wikləf

Wye
  river, Wales, England   WĪ   'wai

Wyeth
  family of US painters   WĪ-uhth   'waiəθ

Wyeth-Ayerst
  US pharmaceutical co.   wī-uhth Ā-uhrst, ERST   ,waiəθ 'eːəʳst, 'eʳst

Wykeham
  William of, *founder, Winchester*   WIK-uhm   'wikəm
  College, Oxford

Wykehamist
  student of Winchester College   WIK-uh-muhst   'wikəməst

Wylacki Pomo
  N. American people   wī-LAK-ē PŌ-mō   wai'læki' 'poːmoː

Wyld, Wylde
  family name   WĪLD   'waild

Wylie
  pers. name   WĪ-lē   'waili'

Wyman
  Jane, *US actress*   WĪ-muhn   'waimən

Foreign Sounds: ue: *Fr.* **rue**, *Ger.* **füllen** uh(r): *Fr.* **boeuf**, *Ger.* **Höhle** <u>kh</u>: *Ger.* **ich**, *Scot.* **loch** ğ: *Sp.* **amigo** ν̱: *Sp.* **hablar** hl: *Welsh* **Llanelli**. CAPITALS: primary stress. SMALL CAPS: secondary stress. Ⓢ: U.S. pron. Ⓑ: British pron.

Wymondham
   1. town, Leicestershire, England　WĪ-muhn-duhm　　　　　'wɑiməndəm
   2. town, Norfolk, England　WIN-duhm, WIM-uhn-duhm　'windəm, 'wiməndəm
Wyndham
   pers. name　WIN-duhm　　　　　　　　　'windəm
Wynette
   Tammy, *US singer*　wī-NET　　　　　　wɑi'net
Wynkyn
   pers. name　WING-kuhn　　　　　　'wiŋkən
Wynne
   pers. name　WIN　　　　　　　　　'win
Wynona
   pers. name (W. Judd)　wī-NŌ-nuh　　　wɑi'noːnə
Wynooche
   river, WA　wī-N͞OO-chē　　　　　　wɑi'nuːtʃiˑ
Wynter
   Dana, *British actress*　WINT-uhr　　　'wintə˞
Wynton
   pers. name (W. Marsalis)　WINT-n　　　'wintn̩
Wyomia
   pers. name (W. Tyus)　wī-Ō-mē-uh　　wɑi'oːmiːə
Wyoming
   state, US　wī-Ō-ming　　　　　　wɑi'oːmiŋ
Wyomingite
   inhabitant of Wyoming　wī-Ō-ming-ĪT　wɑi'oːmiŋ‚ɑit
WYSIWYG
   "what you see is what you get"　WIZ-ē-WIG, WIZ-ē-WIG　'wiziˑ‚wig, ‚wiziˑ'wig
Wystan
   pers. name　WIS-tuhn　　　　　　'wistən
Wyszyński
   Stefan, *Polish cardinal*　vish-IN-yuh-skē, Ⓢ vuh-SHIN-skē　viʃ'iŋskiˑ, Ⓢ və'ʃinskiˑ

X

X-acto
   tdmk for a graphics knife　ig-ZAK-tō, ek-SAK-tō　ig'zæktoː, ek'sæktoː
Xanadu
   place in Kubla Khan, *Coleridge;*　ZAN-uh-D(Y)͞OO　'zænə‚d(j)uː
     house in film Citizen Kane
Xanthe
   pers. name　ZAN-thē　　　　　　　'zænθiˑ
Xanthippe, Xantippe
   wife of Socrates　zan-TIP-ē, zan-THIP-ē　zæn'tipiˑ, zæn'θipiˑ
Xanthus
   pers. name　ZAN-thuhs　　　　　　'zænθəs

Key (col. 2):　a: fad　ā: fade　ah: father　ar: Mary　aw: law　e: fed　ē: feed　er: merry　i: hid　ī: hide　ō: coat　o͞o: boot
oi: boy　ow: now　u: put　uh: above　uhr: bird　ch: chop　ng: ring　sh: show　th: thick　th̲: this　zh: measure

Xantus's murrelet
sea bird   ZAN-tuhs-uhz MUHR-luht   'zæntəsəz 'məʳlət

Xau
lake, Botswana   KSAH-o͞o, KSOW   'ksɑuː, 'ksɑu

Xaverian Brothers
Roman Catholic teaching order   zā-VIR-ē-uhn BRUH<u>TH</u>-uhrz   zeː'viriːən ˌbrəðəʳz

Xavier
1. University, OH, LA; Christian   ZĀ-vē-uhr, ig-ZĀ-vē-uhr, -vyuhr   'zeːviːəʳ, igˈzeːviːəʳ, -vjəʳ
    saint; pers. name
2. French   gzahv-YĀ   gzɑːvjeː
3. Portuguese   shuhv-YĀR, shahv-YĀR   ʃəv'jeːr, ʃɑːv'jeːr
4. Spanish   <u>kh</u>ahv-YER   xɑv'jer

Xaviero
pers. name, Italian   ksahv-YER-ō   ksɑv'jeroː

Xenia
city, OH   ZĒN-yuh, ZĒ-nē-uh   'ziːnjə, 'ziːniːə

Xenocrates
Greek philosopher   zuh-NAHK-ruh-TĒZ   zə'nɑkrəˌtiːz

xenon
element   ZĒ-NAHN   'ziːˌnɑn

Xenophanes
Greek philosopher   zi-NAHF-uh-NĒZ   zi'nɑfəˌniːz

Xenophon
Greek historian   ZEN-uh-fuhn   'zenəfən

Xeres
former name of Jerez   SHER-ēz, <u>KH</u>ER-es   'ʃeriːz, 'xeres

Xerox
tdmk for a photocopier; US corp.   ZIR-AHKS, ZĒ-RAHKS   'zirˌɑks, 'ziːˌrɑks

Xerxes [Ahasuerus]
Persian king   ZUHRK-SĒZ   'zəʳkˌsiːz

Xhosa, Xosa
Kaffir people, lang.   HAW-sah, KAW-suh, KŌ-suh   'hɔːsɑː, 'kɔːsə, 'koːsə

Xi, Hsi, Si
river, China   SHĒ   'ʃiː

Xiamen, Hsia-men [Amoy]
city, China   shē-AH-MUHN   ʃiː'a'mən

Xian, Xi'an, Sian [Changan]
city, China   SHĒ-AHN   'ʃiː'ɑn

Xiang
lang., China   shē-AHNG   ʃiː'ɑŋ

Xi Jiang, Hsi Chiang [Xi]
river, China   SHĒ jē-AHNG   'ʃiː dʒiː'ɑŋ

Xingu
river, park, beer, Brazil   shēng-GO͞O, shing-GO͞O   ʃiːŋ'guː, ʃiŋ'guː

Xining, Hsining
city, China   SHĒ-NING   'ʃiː'niŋ

Xinjiang, Sinkiang
region, China   SHIN-jē-AHNG   'ʃindʒiː'ɑŋ

Xinjiang Uygur, Sinkiang Uighur
division, China   SHIN-jē-AHNG WĒ-GUR   'ʃindʒiː'ɑŋ 'wiː'guʳ

Xinxiang, Hsin-hsiang
city, China   SHIN-shē-AHNG   'ʃinʃiː'ɑŋ

Xiquets de Valls
Spanish festival   <u>kh</u>ē-KETS <u>th</u>ā VAHLS   xiː'kets ðeː 'vɑls

---

Foreign Sounds: ue: *Fr.* **rue**, *Ger.* **füllen**   uh(r): *Fr.* **boeuf**, *Ger.* **Höhle**   <u>kh</u>: *Ger.* **ich**, *Scot.* **loch**   ḡ: *Sp.* **amigo**   <u>v</u>: *Sp.* **hablar**
hl: *Welsh* **Llanelli**.   CAPITALS: primary stress.   SMALL CAPS: secondary stress.   Ⓢ: U.S. pron.   Ⓑ: British pron.

Xizang
  region, Tibet   SHĒT-SAHNG   'ʃiːt'saŋ
Xmas
  abbreviation for Christmas   KRIS-muhs, EK-smuhs   'krismǝs, 'eksmǝs
Xochimilco
  lake, city, Mexico   SŌ-chē-MĒL-kō, SŌ-shē-, -MIL-kō   ˌsoːtʃiːˈmiːlkoː, ˌsoːʃiː-,
                                                                          -ˈmilkoː
Xosa
  see Xhosa
X-Pert
  Dutch beer   EK-SPERT, Ⓢ EK-SPUHRT   'ek,spert, Ⓢ 'ek,spǝᴿt
Xu Shiyou
  city, China   SHOO SHUH(R)-YOO   'ʃuː 'ʃǝ(r)'juː
Xystus
  pope   SIS-tuhs, ZIS-tuhs   'sistǝs, 'zistǝs

Y

Yaakov
  see Yakov
Yablonoi
  mts., Russia   YAHB-luh-NOI   jɑːblǝ'nɔi
Yablonovy
  mts., Russia   YAHB-luh-nuh-VĒ   jɑːblǝnǝ'viː
Yachats
  town, river, OR   YAH-hahts   'jɑhɑts
Yadkin
  river, county, NC   YAD-kuhn   'jædkǝn
Yagua
  S. American people   YAHG-wuh, YAHG̃-wuh   'jɑgwǝ, 'jɑɣwǝ
Yahgan
  S. American people   YAHG-uhn   'jɑgǝn
Yahoo
  brutes in Gulliver's Travels, *Swift* YAH-hoo, YĀ-hoo   'jɑhuː, 'jeːhuː
Yahweh, Yahveh, Jahveh
  Hebrew name of God   YAH-WĀ, YAH-VĀ   'jɑ,weː, 'jɑ,veː
Yajur Veda
  Hindu book of hymns   YAHJ-ur VĀD-uh   'jɑdʒuᴿ 'veːdǝ
Yakima
  1. river, city, county, WA   YAK-uh-MAW   'jækǝ,mɔː
  2. N. American people   YAK-uh-MAW, YAK-uh-muh   'jækǝ,mɔː, 'jækǝmǝ
Yakov
  pers. name, Russian   YAH-kuhf   'jɑːkǝf
Yakov, Yaakov
  pers. name, Hebrew   YAHK-awv   'jɑkɔːv

Key (col. 2): a: **fad** ā: **fade** ah: **father** ar: **Mary** aw: **law** e: **fed** ē: **feed** er: **merry** i: **hid** ī: **hide** ō: **coat** o͞o: **boot**
oi: **boy** ow: **now** u: **put** uh: **above** uhr: **bird** ch: **chop** ng: **ring** sh: **show** th: **thick** t̲h̲: **this** zh: **measure**

Yakumo
   pers. name, Japanese   yah-ku-mō   jɑkumoː

Yakut
   Siberian people   yuh-K͞OOT   jə'kuːt

Yakutsk
   town, Russia   yuh-K͞OOTSK   jə'kuːtsk

Yale
   univ., CT; pers. name   YĀL   'jeːl

Yalobusha
   river, county, MS   YAL-uh-BUSH-uh   jælə'buʃə

Yalow
   Rosalyn S., US physiologist (Nobel   YAL-ō   'jæloː
    1977)

Yalta
   town, Ukraine   YAWL-tuh   'jɔːltə

Yalu
   river, China   YAH-L͞OO   'jɑ'luː

Yalung
   river, China   YAH-LUNG   'jɑ'luŋ

Yamaha
   Japanese corp.   YAHM-uh-HAH   'jɑmə,hɑ

Yamaichi
   Japanese financial services co.   yah-mah-ē-chē   jɑmaiːtʃiː

Yamamadi
   S. American people   YAHM-uh-MAHD-ē   jɑmə'mɑdiˑ

Yamani
   Ahmed Zaki, Saudi official   yuh-MAHN-ē, yah-   jə'mɑniˑ, jɑ-

Yamasaki
   Minoru, US architect   YAHM-uh-SAHK-ē   jɑmə'sɑkiˑ

Yamasee
   N. American people   YAHM-uh-sē   'jɑməsiˑ

Yamhill
   county, OR   YAM-HIL   'jæm,hil

Yamuna [Jumna]
   river, India   YAH-muh-nuh   'jɑmənə

Yan'an, Yenan
   town, China   YEN-AHN   'jen'ɑn

Yanco
   town, creek, Australia   YANG-kō   'jæŋkoː

Yáñez
   pers. name, Spanish   YAHN-yās, YAHN-yāth   'jɑnjeːs, 'jɑnjeːθ

Yang Chen Ning
   Chinese-born US physicist (Nobel   YAHNG JUHN NING   'jɑŋ 'dʒən 'niŋ
    1957)

Yangchow
   see Yangzhou

Yangtze [Chang Jiang]
   river, China   YANG-SĒ, YANG(K)T-SĒ   'jæŋ'siː, 'jæŋ(k)t'siː

Yangzhou, Yangchow
   city, China   YAHNG-JŌ   'jɑŋ'dʒoː

Yankton
   N. American people   YANG(K)-tuhn   'jæŋ(k)tən

Yao
   lang., people, Africa; lang., people,   YOW   'jɑu
    SE Asia [Man]

Foreign Sounds: ue: *Fr.* **rue**, *Ger.* **füllen**   uh(r): *Fr.* **boeuf**, *Ger.* **Höhle**   <u>kh</u>: *Ger.* **ich**, *Scot.* **loch**   g̃: *Sp.* ami**g**o   <u>v</u>: *Sp.* ha**b**lar
hl: *Welsh* **Ll**anelli.   CAPITALS: primary stress.   SMALL CAPS: secondary stress. $: U.S. pron.   £: British pron.

Yaoundé
  city, Cameroon   yown-DĀ   jaun'deː

Yap [Caroline Islands]
  federated state, Pacific   YAP, YAHP   'jæp, 'jɑp

Yaphank
  town, NY   YAP-ANGK, YAP-HANGK   'jæp,æŋk, 'jæp,hæŋk

Yaqui
  N. American people   YAHK-ē   'jɑkiˑ

Yarborough
  William, *US stock car racer*   YAHR-BUHR-ō, YAHR-brō   'jɑ^r,bəroː, 'jɑ^rbroː

Yaren
  district, Nauru   YAHR-uhn   'jɑrən

Yarmouth
  city, MA; city, England   YAHR-muhth   'jɑ^rməθ

Yaroslavl
  city, Russia   YAHR-uh-SLAHV-uhl   jɑːrə'slɑːvəl

Yarrawonga
  town, Australia   YAR-uh-WAHNG-guh, -WAWNG-guh   jærə'wɑŋgə, -'wɔːŋgə

Yarrow
  Peter, *US folk singer*   YAR-ō   'jæroː

Yasir
  pers. name, Arabic   YAHS-IR, Ⓢ YAS-uhr   'jɑs,ir, Ⓢ 'jæsə^r

Yasmin
  pers. name   YAS-muhn, YAZ-muhn   'jæsmən, 'jæzmən

Yasuga
  pers. name, Japanese   yah-sug-ah   jɑsugɑ

Yasuhiro
  pers. name, Japanese   yah-su-hē-rō   jɑsuhiːroː

Yasuhito
  pers. name, Japanese   yah-su-hē-tō   jɑsuhiːtoː

Yasukini Matsuri
  Japanese memorial   yah-su-kē-nē maht-sur-ē   jɑsukiːniː mɑtsuriˑ

Yasunari
  pers. name, Japanese   yah-su-nahr-ē   jɑsunɑriː

Yasuo
  pers. name, Japanese   yah-sōō-ō   jɑsuːoː

Yathrib
  former name of Medina   YATH-ruhb   'jæθrəb

Yavapai
  1. county, AZ   YAV-uh-PĪ   'jævə,pai
  2. N. American people   YAHV-uh-PĪ, YAV-uh-PĪ   jɑvə'pai, 'jævə,pai

Yazoo
  river, county, MS   ya-ZOO   jæ'zuː

Ybor
  Vicente Martínez, *cigar*   Ē-bawr   'iːbɔː^r
    manufacturer

Yeadon
  1. town, PA   YĀD-n   'jeːdn̩
  2. town, England   YĒD-n, YĀD-n   'jiːdn̩, 'jeːdn̩
  3. family name   YĒD-n, YĀD-n, YED-n   'jiːdn̩, 'jeːdn̩, 'jedn̩

Yeager
  Chuck, *US air force pilot;* Jeana,   YĀ-guhr   'jeːgə^r
    US pilot

Key (col. 2):   a: fad   ā: fade   ah: father   ar: Mary   aw: law   e: fed   ē: feed   er: merry   i: hid   ī: hide   ō: coat   ōō: boot
oi: boy   ow: now   u: put   uh: above   uhr: bird   ch: chop   ng: ring   sh: show   th: thick   th: this   zh: measure

Yeats		
W. B., *Irish poet, playwright (Nobel 1923)*	YĀTS	ˈjeːts
Yehudi		
pers. name	yuh-HŌŌD-ē	jəˈhuːdiˑ
Ye Jiangying		
Chinese communist leader	YUH jē-AHNG-YING	ˈjə dʒiːˈɑŋˈjiŋ
Yellowknife		
river, town, Canada; N. American people	YEL-uh-NĪF, YEL-ō-NĪF	ˈjeləˌnaif, ˈjeloːˌnaif
Yeltsin		
Boris, *Russian politician*	YELTS-yin, [S] YELT-suhn	ˈjeltsjin, [S] ˈjeltsən
Yemen		
republic, Arabian Peninsula	YEM-uhn, YĀ-muhn	ˈjemən, ˈjeːmən
Yemeni		
pert. to Yemen	YEM-uh-nē, YĀ-muh-nē	ˈjeməniˑ, ˈjeːməniˑ
Yenan		
see Yan'an		
Yenisey, -sei		
river, Russia	YEN-uh-SĀ	ˌjenəˈseː
Yeovil		
town, England	YŌ-VIL	ˈjoːˌvil
Yerba Buena		
city, CA	YUHR-buh BWĀ-nuh	ˌjəʳbə ˈbweːnə
Yerba maté		
plant	YER-buh MAH-TĀ, YUHR-buh	ˌjeʳbə ˈmɑˌteː, ˌjəʳbə
Yerevan		
city, Armenia	YER-uh-VAHN	ˌjerəˈvɑn
Yerkes		
Charles, *US financier;* Robert, *US psychologist*	YUHR-kēz	ˈjəʳkiːz
Yeu, Ile d'		
island, France	ēl DYUH(R)	iːl djœː
Yevgeni		
pers. name, Russian	yiv-GYĀN-yi	jivˈgjeːnjij
Yevtushenko		
Yevgeni, *Russian poet*	YEV-tuh-SHENG-kō	ˌjevtəˈʃeŋkoː
Yggdrasill		
tree in Scandinavian myth	IG-druh-SIL	ˈigdrəˌsil
YHWH [Yahweh]		
a Hebrew name of God	YAH-WĀ, YAH-VĀ	ˈjɑˌweː, ˈjɑˌveː
Yi		
lang., China, Burma, Tibet	YĒ	ˈjiː
Yi Chou		
Chinese year (Ox)	YĒ JŌ	ˈjiː ˈdʒoː
Yiddish		
European Jewish lang.	YID-ish	ˈjidiʃ
Yin Yang		
Taoist symbol	YIN YANG	ˈjin ˈjæŋ
Yitzhak		
pers. name, Hebrew	YITS-<u>kh</u>ahk, [S] YIT-sahk	ˈjitsxɑk, [S] ˈjitsɑk
Yizkor		
Jewish memorial service	YIZ-KAWR	ˈjizˌkɔːʳ
Yma		
pers. name	Ē-muh	ˈiːmə

Foreign Sounds: ue: *Fr.* **rue**, *Ger.* **füllen** uh(r): *Fr.* **boeuf**, *Ger.* **Höhle** <u>kh</u>: *Ger.* **ich**, *Scot.* **loch** g̃: *Sp.* **amigo** <u>v</u>: *Sp.* **hablar** hl: *Welsh* **Llanelli**. CAPITALS: primary stress. SMALL CAPS: secondary stress. [S]: U.S. pron. [£]: British pron.

Ymir
  Norse giant — Ē-MIR — 'iː‚mir

Ynys Môn [Anglesey]
  island, Wales — UHN-is MAWN — ‚ənis 'mɔːn

Yoakam
  Dwight, US country musician — YŌ-kuhm — 'joːkəm

Yogi
  cartoon bear; pers. name (Y. Berra) — YŌ-gē — 'joːgiˑ

Yogism
  Yoga philosophy — YŌ-GIZ-uhm — 'joː‚gizəm

Yoknapatawpha
  fictional MS county, Faulkner — YAHK-nuh-puh-TAW-fuh — jɑknəpə'tɔːfə

Yokohama
  city, Japan — yō-kō-hahm-ah, Ⓢ YŌ-kuh-HAHM-uh — joːkoːhɑmɑ, Ⓢ joːkə'hɑmə

Yokosuka
  port, Japan — yō-kō-suk-ah — joːkoːsukɑ

Yokozuna
  sumo wrestling Grand Champion — yō-kō-zun-ah — joːkoːzunɑ

Yolanda
  pers. name — yō-LAN-duh, yō-LAHN-duh — joː'lændə, joː'lɑndə

Yolande
  pers. name, French — yaw-LAHⁿD — jɔːlɑ̃d

Yomba
  Indian reservation, US — YAWM-buh, YAHM-buh — 'jɔːmbə, 'jɑmbə

Yom Ha' Azma'ut
  Jewish holiday — YAWM HAH AHT-smah-OOT, YŌM, YAHM — jɔːm ha ‚atsmaˈuːt, joːm, jam

Yom Hashoa
  Jewish memorial day — YAWM HAHSH-ō-AH, YŌM, YAHM — jɔːm ‚haʃoːˈa, joːm, jam

Yom Kippur
  Jewish fast day — YAWM KI-PUR, YŌM, YAHM, KIP-uhr, KIP-UR — jɔːm kiˈpur, joːm, jam, 'kipər, 'kip‚ur

Yonge
  street, Toronto, Ontario — YUHNG — 'jəŋ

Yonkers
  town, NY — YAHNG-kuhrz — 'jɑŋkərz

Yoplait
  yogurt brand — yō-PLĀ, YŌ-PLĀ — joː'pleː, 'joː‚pleː

Yorba Linda
  city, CA — YŌR-buh LIN-duh, YAWR-buh — joːrbə 'lində, jɔːrbə

Yorick
  character in Hamlet *and* Tristram Shandy — YAWR-ik, YAHR-ik — 'jɔːrik, 'jɑrik

Yorkshire
  former county, England — YAWRK-shuhr, -SHIR — 'jɔːrkʃər, -‚ʃir

Yorktown
  town, VA — YAWRK-TOWN — 'jɔːrk‚taun

Yoruba
  people, lang., Africa — YAWR-uh-buh — 'jɔːrəbə

Yosemite
  waterfall, valley, National Park, CA — yō-SEM-uht-ē — joː'semətiˑ

Yoshihito
  emperor, Japan — yō-shē-hē-tō — joːʃiːhiːtoː

Key (col. 2): a: fad ā: fade ah: father ar: Mary aw: law e: fed ē: feed er: merry i: hid ī: hide ō: coat ōō: boot oi: boy ow: now u: put uh: above uhr: bird ch: chop ng: ring sh: show th: thick th̲: this zh: measure

Yoshisuke
  pers. name, Japanese   yō-shē-suk-e   joːʃiːsuke

Yosuke
  pers. name, Japanese   yō-suk-e   joːsuke

Yothers
  Tina, *actress*   YUH<u>TH</u>-uhrz   'jəðəʳz

Youghal
  town, Ireland   YAWL   'jɔːl

Ypres [Ieper]
  town, Belgium   ĒPR, Ē-pruh, Ⓔ WĪ-puhrz   iːpr, iːprə, Ⓔ 'waipəʳz

Ypsilanti
  city, MI   IP-suh-LANT-ē   ˌipsə'læntiˑ

Yreka
  town, CA   wī-RĒ-kuh   wai'riːkə

Yrjö
  pers. name, Finnish   O͞OR-yuh(r)   'uːrjœː

Yser
  Belgian river   ē-ZER   iː'zeʳ

Ysleta del Sur Pueblo
  Indian reservation, US   ēz-LĂT-uh <u>th</u>el SUR po͞o-EB-lō, del, PWEB-lō, pyo͞o-EB-lō   iː'zˈleːʈə ðel 'suʳ puː'ebloː, del, 'pwebloː, pjuː'ebloː

ytterbium
  element   i-TUHR-bē-uhm   i'təʳbiːəm

yttrium
  element   I-trē-uhm   'itriːəm

Yuan
  dynasty, China; pers. name   yo͞o-AHN   juː'an

Yuan, Yüan
  see Yuen

Yucatán
  state, Mexico   YO͞O-kuh-TAHN, -TAN   juːkə'tan, -'tæn

Yucatec [Maya]
  lang., people, Guatemala, Mexico, British Honduras   YO͞O-kuh-TEK   'juːkəˌtek

Yucatecan
  pert. to Yucatec *or* Yucatán   YO͞O-kuh-TEK-uhn   juːkə'tekən

Yuchi
  N. American people   YO͞O-chē   'juːtʃiˑ

Yuchuan
  Chinese beer   YO͞O-jo͞o-AHN   'juːdʒuː'an

Yue [Cantonese]
  lang., China   yo͞o-Ā   juː'eː

Yuen, Yüan, Yuan
  river, China   yo͞o-EN, yo͞o-AHN   juː'en, juː'an

Yuga
  Hindu age   YUG-uh, YO͞O-guh   'jugə, 'juːgə

Yugo
  automobile   YO͞O-gō   'juːgoː

Yugoslav, Jugoslav
  pert. to Yugoslavia   YO͞O-gō-SLAHV, -SLAV   juːgoː'slav, -'slæv

Yugoslavia, Jugoslavia
  republic, Europe   YO͞O-gō-SLAHV-ē-uh   juːgoː'slaviːə

Yukaghir
  lang., people, Russia   YO͞O-kuh-GIR   juːkə'giʳ

Foreign Sounds: ue: *Fr.* **rue**, *Ger.* **füllen**   uh(r): *Fr.* **boeuf**, *Ger.* **Höhle**   <u>kh</u>: *Ger.* **ich**, *Scot.* **loch**   ḡ: *Sp.* **amigo**   v̱: *Sp.* **hablar** hl: *Welsh* **Llanelli**.   CAPITALS: primary stress.   SMALL CAPS: secondary stress.   Ⓢ: U.S. pron.   Ⓔ: British pron.

Yukawa
   Hideki, *Japanese physicist (Nobel 1949)*   yōō-kah-wah   juːkɑwɑ

Yuki
   N. American people   YŌŌ-kē   ˈjuːkiˑ

Yukon
   river, N. America; territory, Canada   YŌŌ-KAHN   ˈjuːˌkɑn

Yukon-Koyukuk
   division, AK   YŌŌ-KAHN-KĪ-uh-KUHK   ˈjuːˌkɑnˈkɑiəˌkək

Yul
   pers. name   YŌŌL, YUL   ˈjuːl, ˈjul

Yule
   Christmas season   YŌŌL   ˈjuːl

Yuma
   city, AZ; county, AZ, CO; N. American people   YŌŌ-muh   ˈjuːmə

Yunnan [Kunming]
   prov, city, China   YŌŌ-NAHN   ˈjuːˈnɑn

Yupik
   people, lang., AK   YŌŌ-pik   ˈjuːpik

Yurak [Nenets]
   lang., people, Russia   yuh-RAK   jəˈræk

Yuri
   pers. name, Russian   YŌŌR-yi   ˈjuːrjij

Yurok
   N. American people   YUR-AHK, YUR-uhk   ˈjurˌɑk, ˈjurək

Yussuf
   pers. name   YUS-uf, YUS-uhf   ˈjusuf, ˈjusəf

Yves
   pers. name, French   ĒV   iːv

Yves Saint Laurent
   French fashion designer   ĒV seⁿ law-RAHⁿ   iːv sẽ lɔːrɑ̃

Yvette
   pers. name   ē-VET   iːˈvet

Yvon
   pers. name, French   ē-VAWⁿ   iːvɔ̃

Yvonne
   1. pers. name   i-VAHN, ē-VAHN   iˈvɑn, iːˈvɑn
   2. French   ē-VAWN   iːvɔːn

Yvor
   pers. name   Ē-vuhr, Ī-vuhr, Ī-VAWR   ˈiːvəʳ, ˈɑivəʳ, ˈɑiˌvɔːʳ

Key (col. 2):   a: fad   ā: fade   ah: father   ar: Mary   aw: law   e: fed   ē: feed   er: merry   i: hid   ī: hide   ō: coat   ōō: boot   oi: boy   ow: now   u: put   uh: above   uhr: bird   ch: chop   ng: ring   sh: show   th: thick   th: this   zh: measure

Z

Zabar's
    delicatessen, New York City   ZĀ-BAHRZ   'zeːˌbɑʳz

Zacatecas
    state, city, Mexico   zahk-ah-TĀ-kahs   zɑkɑ'teːkɑs

Zachariah
    pers. name   ZAK-uh-RĪ-uh   ˌzækə'rɑiə

Zacharias
    1. Old Testament book; pope; pers.   ZAK-uh-RĪ-uhs   ˌzækə'rɑiəs
    name
    2. Dutch   ZAH-<u>kh</u>ah-RĒ-ahs   ˌzɑːxɑː'riːɑs
    3. German   TSAH<u>KH</u>-ah-RĒ-ahs   ˌtsɑxɑ'riːɑs

Zacharie
    pers. name, French   zah-kah-RĒ   zɑːkɑːriː

Zachary
    pers. name   ZAK-(uh-)rē   'zæk(ə)riˑ

Zachris
    pers. name, Swedish   SAHK-ris   'sɑːkris

Zack
    pers. name   ZAK   'zæk

Zacynthus
    ancient name of Zante   zuh-SIN(T)-thuhs   zə'sin(t)θəs

Zadora
    Pia, *US actress*   zuh-DŌR-uh, zuh-DAWR-uh   zə'doːrə, zə'dɔːrə

Zagat
    restaurant guidebooks   zuh-GAT   zə'gæt

Zagazig
    city, Egypt   ZAG-uh-ZIG   'zægəˌzig

Zagreb
    city, Croatia   ZAH-GREB   'zɑːˌgreb

Zagreus
    son of Zeus and Persephone   ZAG-rē-uhs, ZAG-ROOS   'zægriːəs, 'zægˌruːs

Zagros
    mtn. range, Iran   ZAG-ruhs   'zægrəs

Zaharias
    Babe Didrikson, *US athlete*   zuh-HAR-ē-uhs   zə'hæriːəs

Zaire
    republic, Africa   zah-IR, ZĪR   zɑ'iʳ, 'zɑiʳ

Zairian, Zairean
    pert. to Zaire   zah-IR-ē-uhn, ZĪR-ē-uhn   zɑ'iriːən, 'zɑiriːən

Zak
    pers. name   ZAK   'zæk

Zaki
    pers. name, Arabic   ZAHK-ē   'zɑkiˑ

Foreign Sounds: ue: *Fr.* **rue**, *Ger.* füllen   uh(r): *Fr.* **boeuf**, *Ger.* Höhle   <u>kh</u>: *Ger.* ich, *Scot.* loch   ğ: *Sp.* amigo   v̶: *Sp.* hablar
hl: *Welsh* Llanelli.   CAPITALS: primary stress.   SMALL CAPS: secondary stress.   Ⓢ: U.S. pron.   Ⓔ: British pron.

Zákinthos [Zante]

island, Greece   ZAHK-ēn-THAWS,   'zɑkiːn,θɔːs, ⑤ zə'kin(t)θəs
     ⑤ zuh-KIN(T)-thuhs

Zama

ancient town, Africa   ZĀ-muh   'zeːmə

Zambezi, Zambesi

river, Africa   zam-BĒ̃-zē   zæm'biːziˑ

Zambézia

prov, Mozambique   zam-BĒ̃-zē-uh   zæm'biːziːə

Zambia

republic, Africa   ZAM-bē-uh   'zæmbiːə

Zambian

pert. to Zambia   ZAM-bē-uhn   'zæmbiːən

Zamboanga

port, Philippines   ZAM-buh-WAHNG-guh   ˌzæmbə'wɑŋgə

Zamfir

Gheorghe, Romanian panpiper   ZAHM-FIR   'zɑm,fiˡ

Zamora

river, town, Ecuador; prov, city,   zuh-MŌR-uh, zuh-MAWR-uh   zə'moːrə, zə'mɔːrə
     Spain

Zamuco

S. American people   zuh-MOO-kō, suh-   zə'muːkoː, sə-

Zan

lang., people, Caucasus   ZAHN   'zɑn

Zande [Azande]

lang., people, Africa   ZAN-dē   'zændiˑ

Zander

pers. name   ZAN-duhr   'zændəˡ

Zandra

pers. name   ZAN-druh   'zændrə

Zane

pers. name   ZĀN   'zeːn

Zangwill

Israel, English writer   ZANG-(G)WIL   'zæŋ,(g)wil

Zante

island, Greece   ZAN-tē   'zæntiː

Zanuck

Darryl F., US film producer   ZAN-uhk   'zænək

Zanzibar

island, Tanzania   ZAN-zuh-BAHR   'zænzə,bɑˡ

Zanzibari

lang., native of Zanzibar   ZAN-zuh-BAHR-ē   ˌzænzə'bariˑ

Zaozhuang

city, China   JOW-zhoo-AHNG   'dʒɑuʒuː'ɑŋ

Zapata

1. Emiliano, Mexican political   sah-PAHT-ah, ⑤ zuh-PAHT-uh   sɑ'pɑt̪ə, ⑤ zə'pɑt̪ə
     leader; swamp, Cuba
2. county, TX   zuh-PAHT-uh   zə'pɑt̪ə

Zaporozhe

city, Ukraine   ZAHP-uh-RAW-zhuh   ˌzɑpə'rɔːʒə

Zapotec

N. American people   ZAHP-uh-TEK, SAHP-uh-TEK   'zɑpə,tek, 'sɑpə,tek

Zara

Italian province   ZAHR-uh   'zɑrə

Key (col. 2):   a: fad   ā: fade   ah: father   ar: Mary   aw: law   e: fed   ē: feed   er: merry   i: hid   ī: hide   ō: coat   ōō: boot
oi: boy   ow: now   u: put   uh: above   uhr: bird   ch: chop   ng: ring   sh: show   th: thick   th: this   zh: measure

Zaragoza [Saragossa]
  prov, city, Spain; city, Mexico — thah-rah-GŌ-thah, sah-rah-GŌ-sah — θɑrɑ'goːθɑ, sɑrɑ'goːsɑ
Zarathustra [Zoroaster]
  Persian religious teacher — ZAR-uh-THŌŌ-struh, ZER- — ˌzærə'θuːstrə, ˌzer-
Zasu
  pers. name (Z. Pitts) — ZAHZ-ōō, ZAZ-ōō — 'zɑzuː, 'zæzuː
Žatec
  town, Czech republic — ZHAH-TETS — 'ʒɑˌtets
Zavala
  county, TX — zuh-VAHL-uh — zə'vɑlə
Zaventem
  Bruxelles National Airport — zah-ven-TEM — zɑːven'tem
Zbigniew
  pers. name, Polish — ZBĒG-nyef, ⑧ ZBIG-nē-ōō — 'zbiːgnjef, ⑧ 'zbigniːˌuː
Zdenék
  pers. name, Czech — ZDEN-yek — 'zdenjek
Zdenko
  pers. name, Czech — ZDENG-kō — 'zdeŋkoː
Zealand [Sjælland]
  island, Denmark — ZĒ-luhnd — 'ziːlənd
Zebedee
  biblical name — ZEB-uhd-ē — 'zebədiˑ
Zebulon
  pers. name — ZEB-yuh-luhn — 'zebjələn
Zechariah
  Old Testament book; pers. name — ZEK-uh-RĪ-uh — ˌzekə'rɑiə
Zedekiah
  king of Judah — ZED-uh-KĪ-uh — ˌzedə'kɑiə
Zeebrugge
  port, Belgium — ZĀ-BRUEKH-uh, ⑧ ZĀ-BRUG-uh — 'zeːˌbryxə, ⑧ 'zeːˌbrugə
Zeeland
  prov, Netherlands — ZĀ-LAHNT, ⑧ ZĒ-luhnd, ZĀ-luhnd — 'zeːˌlɑnt, ⑧ 'ziːlənd, 'zeːlənd
Zeeman
  Pieter, Dutch physicist (Nobel 1902) — ZĀ-MAHN, ZĀ-muhn — 'zeːˌmɑn, 'zeːmən
Zeffirelli
  Franco, Italian film director — ZEF-uh-REL-ē — ˌzefə'reliˑ
Zeigler
  pers. name — ZIG-luhr — 'ziglər
Zeiss
  tdmk for binoculars — TSĪS, ⑧ ZĪS — 'tsɑis, ⑧ 'zɑis
Zeitgeist
  spirit of the time — TSĪT-GĪST, ZĪT-GĪST — 'tsɑitˌgɑist, 'zɑitˌgɑist
Zeitschrift
  German for magazine — TSĪT-SHRIFT — 'tsɑitˌʃrift
Zeitung
  German for newspaper — TSĪ-tung — 'tsɑituŋ
Zelda
  pers. name — ZEL-duh — 'zeldə
Zelle
  pers. name, Dutch — ZEL-uh — 'zelə
Zelus
  personification of zeal — ZĒ-luhs, ZEL-uhs — 'ziːləs, 'zeləs

Zemlya Frantsa-Iosifa [Franz Josef Land]
   archipelago, Arctic   ZYIM-lah FRAHNT-sah-YŌS-yi-fah   ˈzjiml̩ə ˌfrɑntsaˈjoːsjifɑ

Zen
   religion   ZEN   ˈzen

Zena
   pers. name   ZĒ-nuh   ˈziːnə

Zend
   translation of the Avesta   ZEND   ˈzend

Zend-Avesta
   Zoroastrian holy books   ZEN-duh-VES-tuh   ˌzendəˈvestə

Zener diode
   semiconductor diode   ZĒ-nuhr DĪ-ŌD, ZEN-uhr   ˌziːnəʳ ˈdɑiˌoːd, ˌzenəʳ

Zenger
   John Peter, *US printer*   ZENG-(g)uhr   ˈzeŋ(g)əʳ

Zengo
   pers. name, Japanese   zeng-gō   zeŋgoː

Zenith
   US electronics co.   ZĒ-nuhth   ˈziːnəθ

Zeno
   Greek philosopher   ZĒ-nō   ˈziːnoː

Zénobe
   pers. name, French   zā-NAWB   zeːnɔːb

Zenobia
   queen of Palmyra   zuh-NŌ-bē-uh   zəˈnoːbiːə

Zenobio
   pers. name, Italian   dzā-NAWB-yō   dzeːˈnɔːbjoː

Zenobius
   pers. name   zi-NŌ-bē-uhs   ziˈnoːbiːəs

Zenón
   pers. name, Spanish   sā-NAWN, thā-NAWN   seːˈnɔːn, θeːˈnɔːn

Zenon
   1. dance co., MN   ZĒ-NAHN   ˈziːˌnɑn
   2. pers. name, Polish   ZEN-AWN   ˈzenˌɔːn

Zephaniah
   Old Testament book; pers. name   ZEF-uh-NĪ-uh   ˌzefəˈnɑiə

Zephyrinus
   pope   ZEF-uh-RĪ-nuhs   ˌzefəˈrɑinəs

Zephyrus
   personification of west wind   ZEF-uh-ruhs   ˈzefərəs

Zeppelin
   German-designed dirigible   TSEP-uh-LĒN, Ⓢ ZEP-uh-luhn, ZEP-luhn   ˈtsepəˌliːn, Ⓢ ˈzepələn, ˈzeplən

Zerah
   pers. name   ZĒ-ruh   ˈziːrə

Zermatt
   village, Switzerland   (t)ser-MAHT   (t)seʳˈmɑt

Zernike
   Frits, *Dutch physicist (Nobel 1953)*   ZER-ni-kuh, ZUHR-ni-kuh   ˈzeʳnikə, ˈzəʳnikə

Zero
   pers. name (Z. Mostel)   ZĒ-rō, ZIR-ō   ˈziːroː, ˈziroː

Zeus
   supreme Greek god   ZOOS   ˈzuːs

Zeuxippe
   mother of Erechtheus and Butes   zook-SIP-ē   zuˈkˈsipiˈ

Key (col. 2):   a: fad   ā: fade   ah: father   ar: Mary   aw: law   e: fed   ē: feed   er: merry   i: hid   ī: hide   ō: coat   oo: boot   oi: boy   ow: now   u: put   uh: above   uhr: bird   ch: chop   ng: ring   sh: show   th: thick   th: this   zh: measure

Zeuxis		
Greek painter	Z̄OOK-suhs, Z̄OOK-sis	'zuːksəs, 'zuːksis
Zevi		
1. pers. name	ZEV-ē	'zeviˑ
2. Hebrew	TSVĒ	'tsviː
3. Russian	ZYÄ-vyi	'zjeːvji
Zgusta		
Ladislav, *Czech-born lexicographer*	ZUH-GUS-tuh	ˌzə'gustə
Zhang Zuolin, Chang Tso-lin		
Chinese general	JAHNG DZU-LIN	'dʒɑŋ 'dzu'lin
Zhao Ziyang		
premier, China	JOW jē-YAHNG	'dʒau dʒiː'jaŋ
Zhejiang, Chekiang		
prov, China	JUH-jē-AHNG	'dʒədʒiː'aŋ
Zhengzhou, Chengchow		
city, China	JUHNG-JŌ	'dʒəŋ'dʒɔː
Zhenjiang, Chen-chiang		
city, China	JUHN-jē-AHNG	'dʒəndʒiː'aŋ
Zhivago		
see Doctor Zhivago		
Zhivkov		
Todor, *president, Bulgaria*	ZHĒV-KAWF	'ʒiːvˌkɔːf
Zhongshan		
city, China	JUNG-SHAHN	'dʒuŋ'ʃan
Zhou Enlai		
see Chou En-Lai		
Zhukov		
Georgi, *Russian militarist*	ZH̄OO-kuhf, -KAWF, -KAWV	'ʒuːkəf, -ˌkɔːf, -ˌkɔːv
Zia		
N. American people	ZĒ-uh, SĒ-uh	'ziːə, 'siːə
Zia-ul-Haq		
Mohammad, *Pakistani leader*	ZĒ-uh-ul-HAHK	ˌziːuul'hɑk
Zibo		
city, China	JĒ-B̄OO	'dʒiː'buː
Ziebach		
county, SD	ZĒ-BAHK, zē-BAH, zē-BAW	'ziːˌbak, ziː'ba, ziː'bɔː
Ziegfeld		
Florenz, *US theatrical producer*	ZIG-FELD, ZEG-FĒLD	'zig,feld, 'ziːg,fiːld
Ziegler		
Karl, *German chemist (Nobel 1963)*	TSĒ-gluhr, Ⓢ ZĒ-gluhr	'tsiːgləʳ, Ⓢ 'ziːgləʳ
Zillertal Alps		
mtn. range, Italy	TSIL-uhr-TAHL, ZIL-uhr-TAHL	'tsiləʳˌtal, 'ziləʳˌtal
Zilpah		
pers. name	ZIL-puh	'zilpə
Zimba		
lang., Africa	ZIM-buh	'zimbə
Zimbabwe		
republic, Africa	zim-BAHB-wā, -wē	zim'bɑbweː, -wiˑ
Zimbabwean		
pert. to Zimbabwe	zim-BAHB-wā-uhn, -wē-uhn	zim'bɑbweːən, -wiːən
Zimbalist		
Efrem, Jr., *US actor;* Stephanie, *US actress*	ZIM-buh-luhst	'zimbələst

---

Foreign Sounds: ue: *Fr.* **rue**, *Ger.* füllen   uh(r): *Fr.* **boeuf**, *Ger.* Höhle   <u>kh</u>: *Ger.* **ich**, *Scot.* lo<u>ch</u>   ḡ: *Sp.* amigo   <u>v</u>: *Sp.* hablar   hl: *Welsh* **Llanelli**.   CAPITALS: primary stress.   SMALL CAPS: secondary stress.   Ⓢ: U.S. pron.   Ⓔ: British pron.

zinc
  element   ZINGK   'ziŋk
Zinfandel
  wine variety   ZIN-fuhn-DEL   'zinfən,del
Zinka
  pers. name, Russian   ZYING-kuh   'zjiŋkə
Zinman
  David, *US conductor*   ZIN-muhn   'zinmən
Zino
  pers. name   zē-NŌ, ZĒ-nō   ziː'nɔː, 'ziːnɔː
Zinsser
  Hans, *US bacteriologist*   ZIN(T)-suhr   'zin(t)səʳ
Zion
  hill, stronghold, Jerusalem; city, ZĪ-uhn   'zaiən
    IL
Zionism
  Jewish movement   ZĪ-uh-NIZ-uhm   'zaiə,nizəm
Zipporah
  1. wife of Moses   ZIP-(uh-)ruh, zuh-PŌR-uh,   'zip(ə)rə, zə'pɔːrə, zə'pɔːrə
                                        zuh-PAWR-uh
  2. pers. name, Hebrew   tsē-PAWR-ah   tsi'pɔːrɑ
zirconium
  element   ZUHR-KŌ-nē-uhm   ,zəʳ'kɔːniːəm
Zoé
  pers. name, French   zaw-Ā   zɔːeː
Zoë, Zoe
  pers. name   ·   ZŌ-ē   'zoːiˑ
Zofia
  pers. name, Polish   ZAWF-yah   'zɔːfjɑː
Zola
  Emile, *French writer*   zaw-LAH, Ⓢ ZŌ-luh, ZŌ-lah, zō-LAH   zɔːlɑː, Ⓢ 'zoːlə, 'zoːlɑ, zoː'lɑ
Zollverein
  union of German states   TSAWL-fer-ĪN   'tsɔːlfer,ɑin
Zoltán
  pers. name, Hungarian   ZAWL-tahn   'zɔːltɑːn
Zomba
  city, Malawi   ZAHM-buh   'zɑmbə
Zombie, Zombi
  voodoo snake deity; walking dead; ZAHM-bē   'zɑmbiˑ
    religious group
Zombiism
  beliefs of Zombi   ZAHM-bē-IZ-uhm   'zɑmbiː,izəm
Zonta
  international women's   ZAHNT-uh   'zɑntə
    organization
Zontian
  member of Zonta   ZAHNT-ē-uhm   'zɑntiːən
Zoque
  N. American people   SŌ-kā   'soːkeː
Zora, Zorah
  pers. name   ZŌR-uh, ZAWR-uh   'zoːrə, 'zɔːrə
Zorinsky
  Edward, *US politician*   zuh-RIN-skē   zə'rinskiˑ
Zoroaster [Zarathustra]
  Persian religious leader   ZŌR-ō-AS-tuhr, ZAWR-   'zoːroː,æstəʳ, 'zɔːr-

---

Key (col. 2): a: fad ā: fade ah: father ar: Mary aw: law e: fed ē: feed er: merry i: hid ī: hide ō: coat o͞o: boot
oi: boy ow: now u: put uh: above uhr: bird ch: chop ng: ring sh: show th: thick th̲: this zh: measure

Zoroastrianism
  religion   ZŌR-ō-AS-trē-uh-NIZ-uhm, ZAWR-   ˌzoːroːˈæstriːə,nizəm, ˌzɔːr-

Zosimo
  pers. name, Italian   DZAW-zē-mō   ˈdzɔːziːmoː

Zosimus
  pope   ZŌ-suh-muhs, ZAHS-uh-muhs   ˈzoːsəməs, ˈzasəməs

Zouave
  body of infantry, French army   zo͞o-AHV   zuˈɑv

Zsa Zsa
  pers. name, Hungarian (Z. Gabor)   ZHAH ZHAH   ˈʒɑ ˌʒɑ

Zsigmond
  pers. name, Hungarian   ZHIG-mawnd   ˈʒigmɔːnd

Zsigmondy
  Richard, *German chemist (Nobel 1925)*   ZHIG-MAWN-dē   ˈʒig,mɔːndiˑ

Zsolt
  pers. name, Hungarian   ZHAWLT   ˈʒɔːlt

Zubin
  pers. name   ZO͞O-buhn   ˈzuːbən

Zuerich
  airport, Zürich   TSUE-ri<u>kh</u>, Ⓢ ZUR-ik   ˈtsyːriç, Ⓢ ˈzurik

Zug
  canton, Switzerland   TSO͞OK, Ⓢ SO͞OK, ZO͞OG   ˈtsuːk, Ⓢ ˈsuːk, ˈzuːg

Zugspitze
  mtn., Germany   TSO͞OK-SHPIT-suh   ˈtsuːk,ʃpitsə

Zuider Zee
  inlet, Netherlands   ZĪD-uhr ZĀ, Ⓢ ZĪD-uhr ZĒ   ˌzaidəʳ ˈzeː, Ⓢ ˌzaidəʳ ˈziː

Zuid Holland
  province, Netherlands   zoit HAWL-AHNT   zɔit ˈhɔːl,ɑnt

Zukerman
  Pinchas, *Israeli-born US violinist*   ZUK-uhr-muhn, ZO͞O-kuhr-muhn   ˈzukəʳmən, ˈzuːkəʳmən

Zukor
  Adolph, *US movie producer*   ZO͞O-kuhr   ˈzuːkəʳ

Zuleika
  character in Zuleika Dobson, *Beerbohm*   zo͞o-LĒ-kuh, zo͞o-LĀ-kuh, zo͞o-LĪ-kuh   zuˈliːkə, zuˈleːkə, zuˈlaikə

Zuléma
  pers. name, French   zo͞o-lā-MAH   zuːleːmɑː

Zulu
  African people   ZO͞O-lo͞o   ˈzuːluː

Zululand
  territory, Republic of South Africa   ZO͞O-lo͞o-LAND   ˈzuːluˑ,lænd

Zumwalt
  Elmo, III, *US admiral*   ZUM-WAWLT, ZUHM-WAWLT   ˈzum,wɔːlt, ˈzəm,wɔːlt

Zuñi
  N. American people   ZO͞O-nē, ZO͞ON-yē   ˈzuːniˑ, ˈzuːnjiˑ

Zuolin
  see Zhang Zuolin

Zürich, Zurich
  canton, city, Switzerland   TSUE-ri<u>kh</u>, Ⓢ ZUR-ik   ˈtsyːriç, Ⓢ ˈzurik

Zwingli
  Ulrich, *Swiss Protestant reformer*   TSFING-lē, Ⓢ ZWING-(g)lē, SWING-(g)lē   ˈtsfiŋliˑ, Ⓢ ˈzwiŋ(g)liˑ, ˈswiŋ(g)liˑ

Zwinglianism
   beliefs of Zwingli & *his followers*   TSFING-lē-uh-NIZ-uhm,   'tsfiŋliːə‚nizəm, 'zwiŋ(g)liː-,
                                   ZWING-(g)lē-, SWING-lē-   'swiŋliː-

Zwolle
   1. city, Netherlands   SFAWL-uh   'sfɔːlə
   2. town, LA   ZWAHL-ē   'zwɑliˑ

Zworykin
   Vladimir, *Russian-born physicist*   ZVAWR-kyin, Ⓢ ZWAWR-i-kuhn   'zvɔːrkjin, Ⓢ 'zwɔːrikən

Zygmunt
   pers. name, Polish   ZIG-mo͞ont   'zigmuːnt

Zyryan [Komi]
   lang., people, Russia   ZIR-ē-uhn   'ziriːən

Zywiec
   town, Poland; Polish beer   ZHIV-uhts   'ʒivəts

Key (col. 2):   a: fad ā: fade ah: father ar: Mary aw: law e: fed ē: feed er: merry i: hid ī: hide ō: coat o͞o: boot
oi: boy ow: now u: put uh: above uhr: bird ch: chop ng: ring sh: show th: thick th̲: this zh: measure

International Phonetic Alphabet Symbols

IPA Symbol	Example	as in
English Consonants		
b	'bid	**bid**
d	'did	**did**
dʒ	'dʒet	**jet**
ð	'ðis	**this**
f	'fit	**fit**
g	'get	**get**
h	'hed	**head**
hw	'hwet	**whet**
j	'jes	**yes**
k	'keːk	**cake**
l	'leg	**leg**
ļ	'midļ	**middle**
m	'men	**men**
m̦	'oːpm̦	**open** (some pronunciations)
n	'net	**net**
ņ	'kitņ	**kitten**
ŋ	'riŋ, 'riŋk	**ring, rink**
p	'pin	**pin**
r	'red, 'meriˑ	**red, merry**
ʳ (raised r)	'kaʳd (= 'kard, 'kaːd)	**card**
s	'sit	**sit**
ʃ	'ʃoː	**show**
t	'toː, 'toːt	**toe, tote**
ţ	'siţiŋ, 'hiːţəd	**sitting, heated** (most U. S. pronunciations)
tʃ	'tʃip	**chip**
θ	'θiŋk	**think**
v	'vet	**vet**
w	'wet	**wet**
z	'zip	**zip**
ʒ	'viʒən, 'beːʒ	**vision, beige**

IPA Symbol	Example	as in
English Vowels		
ə	bə'nænə, 'bəd	**banana, bud**
əʳ	'bəʳd, 'bəţəʳ	**bird, butter**
æ	'fæd, 'æsk	**fad, ask**
ɑ	'bɑðəʳ, 'kɑt, 'fɑðəʳ	**bother, cot, father**
ɑː	'fɑːðəʳ, 'ɑːsk	**father, ask**
ai	'bai, 'raid	**buy, ride**
au	'bau, 'nau	**bough, now**
e	'fed	**fed**
eː	'feːd	**fade**
i	'bid	**bid**
iː	'biːd	**bead**
oː	'koːt	**coat**
ɔː	'kɔːt, 'lɔː	**caught, law**
ɔi	'bɔi, 'kɔin	**boy, coin**
u	'gud, 'put, puʳ	**good, put, poor**
uː	'muːd, 'mjuːzik	**mood, music**
Non-English Vowels		
œ	'hœlə, bœf	German **Hölle**, French **boeuf**
œː	'hœːlə, fœː	German **Höhle**, French **feu**
y	'fylən	German **füllen**
yː	'fyːlən, ryː	German **fühlen**, French **rue**
Non-English Consonants		
β	aβ'lɑr	Spanish **hablar**
ç	'iç	German **ich**
ɣ	a'miːɣoː	Spanish **amigo**
ł	'tʃeslaːf	Polish **Czesław**
ḷ	ḷa'neliˑ	Welsh **Llanelli**
ɲ	'diːɲ	French **digne**
ŗ	'ŗanðə	Welsh **Rhondda**
x	'lax, 'bax	Scottish **loch**, German **Bach**
ɥ	lɥiː	French **lui**
ɕ	'ɕxũ	**!Kung** (an implosive click)
ʖ	'ʃhɔːsaː	**Xhosa** (an implosive click)

Diacritics used in IPA transcriptions

IPA Symbol	Example	as in	Explanation
'	'æpəl	**apple**	primary stress
ˌ	'æpəlˌsɔːs	**applesauce**	secondary stress
ː	'niːt	**neat**	an augmented vowel
ˑ	'hæpiˑ	**happy**	variation between simple and augmented vowels
~	bɔ̃	French **bon**	nasalization of a vowel
̌	'siţiŋ, 'hiːţəd	**sitting, heated**	voicing of a usually unvoiced consonant
̥	ḷa'neḷiˑ	Welsh **Llanelli**	the voiceless equivalent of a voiced consonant
̦	'kitņ	**kitten**	a syllabic consonant
̡	mə'ţildə	Russian **Mathilde**	a palatalized consonant